Seeking St. Louis

Seeking St. Louis

VOICES FROM A RIVER CITY,
1670–2000

EDITED BY

Lee Ann Sandweiss

CONTRIBUTING EDITORS

Robert Boyd, Jan Garden Castro, Gerald Early,
Wayne Fields, and Karen M. Goering

WITH AN INTRODUCTION BY

Eric Sandweiss

MISSOURI HISTORICAL SOCIETY PRESS
SAINT LOUIS

This publication was made possible through the
generous support of the GenAmerica Financial Corporation
in honor of Richard A. and Joanne Liddy
for their steadfast community service and commitment
to bettering the quality of life in the St. Louis area.

Published in the United States of America
by the Missouri Historical Society Press
P.O. Box 11940, St. Louis, Missouri 63112-0040

5 4 3 2 1 00 01 02 03 04

Library of Congress Cataloging-in-Publication Data

"Seeking St. Louis : voices from a river city, 1670-2000 /
edited by Lee Ann Sandweiss ;
with an introduction by Eric Sandweiss ;
contributing editors, Robert Boyd, Jan Garden Castro,
Gerald Early, Wayne Fields, and Karen M. Goering
p. cm.
Includes bibliographical references.
ISBN 1-883982-11-1 (alk. paper)

1. Saint Louis (Mo.)—History—Sources.
2. Saint Louis (Mo.)—Biography.
3. Saint Louis (Mo.)—Literary collections.
I. Sandweiss, Lee Ann

F474.S2 S38 2000
977.8'66—dc21
00-045591
CIP

Distributed by University of Missouri Press

DESIGN BY KRISTIE LEE

COVER IMAGE
Seventh and Locust. Oil on canvas,
by Frank B. Nuderscher, 1927.
Missouri Historical Society Art Collection.

for Ethan and Noah
and future generations of St. Louisans

CONTENTS

We shall not cease from exploration
And the end of all our exploring
Will be to arrive where we started
And know the place for the first time.

—T. S. Eliot, *Four Quartets*, 1941

FOREWORD

MULTIPLE AND DIVERSE VOICES tell the stories that constitute St. Louis. By listening to them, we begin to know not only this city and its region, but also ourselves and the others with whom we share it.

Narratives gradually weave around events; they allow us to preserve and remember the significant moments in our lives. Stories, fixed to chronological sequence, help us to identify who we are, explaining our lives, and mediating our relations with objects, buildings, and landscapes. As we change, our narratives change. They are fluid works in progress, journals that we revise each day as we confront new experiences and find new meanings.

Yet narratives are more than strictly personal documents. They also attach people to one another in a shared environment—a place with a web of reciprocal concerns and obligations. The web begins with family and extends first to neighbors, and then beyond into the complex of social and cultural conditions that make up our larger community. Without shared narratives there cannot be such a community.

This is indeed what has happened in our contemporary world. Narratives have been lost or truncated, with profound results. With few shared stories to connect us, we care less about each other and less still about our places. Without the stories of those who have gone before us, how could we go about seeking St. Louis?

This book is a product of our conviction that it is important for St. Louisans present and future to hear and preserve those stories. Maintaining the thread of narrative woven around this place may, in its own small way, help us in conquering our tendency to emphasize individual rights instead of mutual obligations, in changing our cavalier treatment of environment and resources, or in mending our class and racial divisions. We need to construct new and modified narratives. Narratives that heal divisions and value community will encourage us to construct neighborhoods that invite us to mingle and preserve places that inculcate a sense of continuity with the past. Narratives that confer particular identities on us and our places will stimulate the development of civic space and those "third places" so essential to fostering community. Such narratives are crucial not only for our own happiness but also for the maintenance of our sense of place. Insensibility to the past will contribute to a disregard for the future and thus further imperil our communities. We have a sacred obligation to those generations not yet born—an obligation to bequeath to them healthy communities in a sustainable environment.

Our vital task is to preserve the connections that remain and to work to rebuild those that are broken or lost. In the process of making this anthology, the Missouri Historical Society attempts to conserve, construct, and make available to St. Louisans, and others interested in this region, stories that form a sense of belonging and attachment to this place, stories that vibrate with a reverence for life and link the living, the dead, and those yet to be born, stories that with us are *Seeking St. Louis*.

—ROBERT R. ARCHIBALD

PREFACE

ALTHOUGH *SEEKING ST. LOUIS* is the companion publication to the Missouri Historical Society's permanent exhibition that shares its name, the book project's launch preceded that of the exhibition by many years. More than a decade ago, MHS President Robert Archibald first envisioned a volume that would draw from many genres of writing to examine the question of what defines St. Louis as place. Soon after I arrived as director of publications, Bob presented me with the opportunity and challenge of making the book reality. During the seven years that followed, the Missouri Historical Society Press published twenty-four titles before *Seeking St. Louis*. At times, progress on the "lit anth," as it was affectionately referred to by MHS staff, was negligible, but at no point was there doubt in Bob's mind that the book would be published. His faith kept mine bolstered.

The project received its next critical push on a hot June day in 1994, when five individuals met with Bob and me and agreed to serve as contributing editors. Without their commitment and expertise, this book would not be. Karen Goering, with her thorough grasp of the region's early history and the Society's collections, selected material for the period extending from pre-colonial settlement to the Civil War. Wayne Fields scouted for significant nonfiction dating between the Civil War and the 1904 World's Fair. Robert Boyd covered the years from 1904 to 1945 but concentrated on creative writing, primarily poetry and drama. Jan Garden Castro brought to the post–World War II period her intimate knowledge of St. Louis's contemporary literary scene. Gerald Early did such an outstanding job of selecting African American writings for this project—from throughout the city's long history—that it spawned a separate volume, *"Ain't But a Place": An Anthology of African American Writings about St. Louis*, published by the Missouri Historical Society Press in 1998. Early also contributed a significant portion of the biographical text that precedes the African American writings within *Seeking St. Louis*.

At that first meeting, we established the editorial guidelines that shaped this volume. The thematic common denominator for all selections would be St. Louis as *place*—physical and conceptual. Striving for the broadest perspective possible, we agreed that the writings should span the period from pre-colonial times to the present. (The new millennium, which came before the book, provided an appropriate ending point.) We would, further, include a multiplicity of genres: travel narrative, autobiography, letters, journalism, poetry, drama, and fiction. Inevitably, these genres proved not to be evenly spread across time; readers will note that pre–Civil War selections, for example, are primarily nonfiction, reflecting the concentration of the kind of writing published about St. Louis during that era. The volume is ordered chronologically by date of composition, with the exception that works of nonfiction (such as memoirs) appear in sequence according to their subject matter. Hence you will find Sally Benson's *Meet Me in St. Louis* placed with other literature from the 1940s, rather than at the time of the 1904 World's Fair; Jessie Benton Fremont's firsthand memories of the Civil War, on the other hand, seemed more appropriate as an artifact of the 1860s than of the late 1880s, when they were actually published. Furthermore, although I would be the last to argue that our staff proofreaders are infallible, I can nevertheless assure readers that inconsistencies of spelling and punctuation are due to our desire to remain true to the original text.

After we had set these basic ground rules and the contributing editors had delivered their recommendations, there was plenty of good material for several volumes. Budget considerations determined that the anthology would be a single volume, so I began the painful task of eliminating pieces that often seemed too good to cut. Selections moved from the "Accept" pile to the "Reject" pile and back again. If several selections covered more or less the same topic, I chose what I considered the most interesting and representative piece for that time period. Similarly, certain periods produced abundant material from the same genres or from the same perspective; again I chose the most representative. One perspective, unfortunately, is noticeably absent—early Native American accounts of the region—primarily because they do not exist, at least to my knowledge. Although literary merit and readability ultimately governed most final choices, some pieces were included because of their historical significance or their importance in contributing to the sense of St. Louis as a place.

Because, unfortunately, anthologies are often defined by what they leave out, a brief word about the glaring omissions is in order. A stroll down the Walk of Fame in the Delmar Loop will reveal that St. Louis was home to a number of well-known writers, such as Zoë Akins and Marianne Moore, who are absent from this volume. Alas, famous as they may be, some of the city's most illustrious writers said little about their hometown. So, just as a writer need not have come from St. Louis to be included in *Seeking St. Louis*, the qualifications of being born—or going to high school—here did not guarantee inclusion. Indeed, some of the authors and works that I once would have thought essential to the book are not found here. In the final analysis, they simply did not contribute to the whole as significantly as did some other—perhaps more obscure—piece. Any good anthology is greater than the sum of its parts, and it has become my aim through this long process to do honor both to the parts and to the collective work that comprises them.

The efforts of many individuals contributed to the development and production of *Seeking St. Louis.* Jennifer Jordan Baker's meticulous research, which resulted in a comprehensive bibliography of St. Louis writings, jump-started the editorial process. Robert Boyd, Jan Garden Castro, Gerald Early, Wayne Fields, and Karen Goering remained steadfastly committed to this project—for years—in spite of the ongoing demands of their professional lives. The staff of the Missouri Historical Society's publications division demonstrated their trademark enthusiasm and energy for the book and graciously endured having their supervisor in an editorial role. I will be forever indebted to the editor's editor Matt Heidenry, production diva Robyn Morgan, permissions sleuth and proofreader *par excellence* Josh Stevens, Katherine Douglass, Jacque McCain, and our intrepid interns Cindy Alexander, Maureen Sullivan, Allecia Vermillion, and Lisa Arnold. Special thanks, too, to Kristie Lee for her beautiful design concept.

Additional thanks go to scholars, librarians, and historians at the Society and around the country who provided invaluable information when a dead end seemed inevitable, especially John Aubrey, Randy Blomquist, Ben Cawthra, Martha Clevenger, Tim Fox, John Goaring, Rockwell Gray, Chuck Hill, Dennis Northcott, Duane Sneddeker, the late Frances Hurd Stadler, Jason Stratman, A.T. Stephens, Kathryn Zabelle Derounian-Stodola, Ellen Thomasson, and Emily Miller Troxell.

Ultimately, my deepest gratitude goes to my husband and colleague, Eric Sandweiss, who, like the seekers of St. Louis in this book, helped me find it for myself.

—LEE ANN SANDWEISS

INTRODUCTION

THE SPIRIT OF THE MATTER: A CITY AND ITS STORIES

WHO, I WONDER, wins the prize for being the first to utter the words, "What's the matter with St. Louis?" It wasn't Denton Snider, who merely cited the "ever-repeated question" in his own insightful account of the city's late-nineteenth-century intellectual currents (an account that is excerpted in this volume). Surely it wasn't even the Progressive Era journalist William Marion Reedy, who in 1899 entitled his memorable political profile of the city (also to be found in these pages) with that very phrase.

No, people have been wondering about the "matter" with St. Louis for longer than that. Perhaps the prize should go to the Spanish official, newly arrived in his dank quarters at the Cabildo in New Orleans, who first cast a suspicious eye on the distant outpost to the north, inquiring of his subordinates why *"Pain Court's"* inhabitants seemed more interested in trading for furs along the Missouri River than they were in staying home and growing wheat for their fellow settlers. For all I know, the honor rightly belongs to one among the band of Missouri Indians who, according to Auguste Chouteau's "Narrative" of the city's founding (likewise reprinted in this anthology), asked for—and were summarily denied—permission to settle alongside the French at their riverside encampment in 1764. (If so, he must have chosen not to do so within earshot of Chouteau, who claimed that the rebuff was met only with cheerful assent.)

Whoever said it first, the "What's the matter?" question has since become the closely guarded prerogative of native St. Louisans—a fact that carpet-bagging journalists and out-of-town transplants learn at their own peril. Yet we know, at some level, that there must be more to this persistent display of apparent masochism than meets the eye. If St. Louisans are so dedicated to the exercise of rubbing salt in a self-inflicted wound, we ask, then why do they even bother to stay? What is it that keeps them coming back to the city from distant points; what that makes them identify themselves as "St. Louisans" after years spent in New York or Tangier? What is it, indeed, that accounts for the historical continuity of this place, for the local quirks that somehow resist the relentless pressure of media-driven homogenization, like so many dandelions popping through the cracks of the city's ubiquitous vacant lots? Why, to borrow from St. Louis–born novelist Fannie Hurst, do locals continue to complain that the city "bores the daylights out of them," only to turn around and "defend her to the death"?

It may be that Denton Snider himself was not far from the mark when he traced St. Louisans' endemic and long-lived self-doubt to an equally strong—and continuously frustrated—strain of grandiosity. The fact is that few St. Louisans, even today, can resist secretly sharing with Logan U. Reavis, Gilded Age America's most bald-faced civic booster (and another presence in this book), some trace of the belief that theirs is "the future great city of the world." That St. Louis has, in its 240 years of existence, somehow failed to measure up to a standard met only fleetingly by Athens, Alexandria, and Rome comes as a colossal disappointment to those of us still burdened by this global delusion of grandeur. What *is* the matter with St. Louis, anyway?

The vexed question of what ever happened to America's "future great city" is not a new one to historians. From the critical accounts of urban growth that accompanied the first city plan of 1907, to the so-called "Belcher thesis" of 1943 (an influential attempt to explain how the city lost the economic race to Chicago in the years before and after the Civil War), through the 1973 RAND Corporation Report—which helped to enshrine St. Louis as the poster child for the national Urban Crisis—each of these attempts has pieced together from economic, political, and demographic evidence a reasonable explanation for what are presumed to be the city's ever-waning fortunes.

Yet the allegedly historical questions at the heart of these and other studies are just as surely emotional questions, and many of the St. Louis historians who posed them have themselves been steeped in the civic myth of conjoined insecurity and grandiosity. For all its utility in helping us to understand St. Louis, traditional historical research cannot fully cover the extent to which "the matter with St. Louis" is a matter of attitude as much as it is one of substance, of perception as much as fact. Indeed, local historians have as often transmitted such attitudes themselves as they have stopped to examine them. It would not be entirely inaccurate—nor derogatory, I believe—to consider that the received history of this place (a history refined and disseminated from, among other places, the Missouri Historical Society) is itself a form of literature, inseparable in many ways from the forms that we recognize more clearly as memoir, fiction, or poetry. That convergence, in turn, brings us to this volume: an anthology of literature published by an institution devoted to historical inquiry.

Seeking St. Louis is unique, in the long and generally well-documented history of this city, as a compilation of written reflections that transcend genre in their effort to focus on a common *topic*. The topic, of course, is the city at the confluence of the Mississippi and Missouri: a place that is, as travelers and residents alike have never ceased to point out, neither North nor South, East nor West. It is a slippery subject, this city of contradictions, one that has always begged unorthodox—and perhaps even contradictory—approaches to understanding. This anthology was born in its editors' belief that only the full range of insights offered by St. Louis's explorers and poets, yarn-spinners, novelists, and journalists could possibly help us even to approximate a sense of why this city is as it is; that only a net cast far more widely than the reach of traditional "history" could begin to bring us closer to answering the deceptively simple question, "What's the matter with St. Louis?"

The city that appears from this collection of observations, fantasies, and recollections is every bit as complex and interesting as the city that has been delineated by historians. It is a place driven by its aspirations, yet haunted by its past. It is peopled by immigrants and the descendants of immigrants who are intensely proud of their own heritage but ever suspicious of their neighbors'. Its power structure is (in the eyes of booster and critic alike) entrenched, closed, and often slow to react to crisis. These are all traits that a St. Louisan intuitively recognizes and will have no trouble deducing from even a quick reading of *Seeking St. Louis.* But only a long, slow savoring of the pages that follow can reveal the sheer delight—dare I say the greatness?—of the place in which this unlikely combination of dubious parts results. Together, the story and drama, memoir and poem, transform—no less than does the best historical literature—a bare itinerary of events and dates into a thrilling journey, filled with unfamiliar faces and unexpected places.

The journey begins, appropriately, on the river—or, at least, on the quasi-miraculous waterway depicted in the seventeenth-century journals of Jacques Marquette. For all of the surreal details that attend his approach to the eventual site of St. Louis—the monumental Piasa bird painted high on the Illinois bluffs, the voracious catfish swimming just beneath the surface of the water, the murderous current of the Pekitanoui (Missouri) River—there is nothing in Marquette's narrative to reveal that a city might rise here a century hence. Instead, St. Louis's precise site is conspicuous in its absence; a vaguely remarked point on a long journey filled with encounters, surprises, and wonders.

The task of turning that point into a *place*—that is, of making it the fixed locus of human interaction—had begun at the hands of various Indian tribes, most notably the Kaskaskias and the Tamaroas who had settled near the mouth of the River des Peres sometime around 1700. But responsibility for actually inscribing the lines of a city into the hillside above the riverbank belonged to the band of rough-edged, mostly Canadian *voyageurs* who accompanied Pierre Laclède and his young charge, Auguste Chouteau, on their explorations north from Fort de Chartres, Illinois, in the winter of 1763-64. Chouteau's posthumously published recollection of the founding of St. Louis (a recollection that is itself plagued, in terms of its historical value, by its uncertain origins and its divergences from previous accounts—including Chouteau's own) has transcended its status as historical document and become something more akin to a creation myth for St. Louis. In it, as you will see, are lodged not just mundane details of topography and land allotment, but prescient auguries of the future city's greatness. Here is justified the merit of France's presumptuous claim to land it had barely explored, let alone settled (and land which had, in any case, already been ceded to Spain by the time of the *voyageurs*' arrival). In the 1830s, St. Louis politician Wilson Primm would expand on the narrative—and take issue with portions of it—but its mythic outlines remained. Laclède and Chouteau's arrival on the bluff above the Mississippi signalled, according to the evolving narrative, the creation of a new nexus for the spread of western civilization for more than a century to come.

It is hard for St. Louisans at the beginning of the twenty-first century (especially those of us raised in the belief that there was something inevitable about the city's rise) to imagine that place in its earliest days—how small, how tentative, how impermanent it must have seemed. We can be grateful, then, for such treasures as Nicolas de Finiels' careful, precise report of 1803 (an account that describes each detail of the town, down to the impassably muddy streets—a motif that would inform travelers' reports for the next hundred years), or, from later years, Anne Lucas Hunt's vivid description of the early town's Creole-style houses "built of logs, vertical, like posts . . . [with] a large room in the center and two or three smaller ones around it." Hunt's memoir, published long after St. Louis had ceased to resemble anything like a frontier village, has the added value of offering not only a factual account of the town in its first years of American rule, but also a compelling profile of one young girl seeking her place within it; a girl through whose wide eyes the corner of Seventh and Market Streets seemed "so far away that the Indians might carry me off."

That St. Louis was, indeed, the last stop on the way to the wilderness is in a way true, but the frontier notion carried forth by Hunt and countless others nevertheless reflected the persistent bias of those who saw "civilization" as something that inexorably followed the woodman's axe and the farmer's plow westward from Europe to North America's coasts, and thence into the interior. The Indian captivity narrative of Hannah Lewis, while but one example of a popular literary genre that transmuted itself into many geographical settings, lent further credence to the notion that there was little separating the early St. Louisans from the terrors of the wilderness.

If that sense of danger was ever widespread among the townspeople themselves, it had certainly dissipated by the 1810s. At least two of the area's best-known early immigrants—the German land promoter Gottfried Duden and French-born Sister Philippine Duchesne—saw fit to remark on the disparity between their wild imaginings of the dangers of frontier life and the actual scarcity of their contacts with Native Americans in St. Louis. Instead, after the commencement of American rule, St. Louisans' primary Indian encounters were likeliest to have occurred in the comfortable downtown offices of William Clark, who served here as federal Indian agent for three decades after returning from his storied voyage to the Pacific.

For Duden, Duchesne, and most other immigrants of the early 1800s, the city was more noteworthy for other reasons: among them, its abundance of natural resources (including both the ore-laden hills of the nearby Ozark and St. François ranges and the rich topsoil of the river valleys) and the remarkably mixed population that was by now making its way to St. Louis from points across the nation and the globe. In addition to commenting on the still-conspicuous place held by descendants of the city's Creole aristocracy (an exotic commodity, for people coming from anywhere other than New Orleans), early St. Louisans were already aware of the unprecedented nature of a city that brought into daily contact New Englanders and Kentuckians, Irish and Germans, free and enslaved Blacks. "One would have been puzzled," wrote Jessie Benton Fremont in a recollection only slightly exaggerated for literary effect, "to say whose country it was."

African-descended families, who in 1820 constituted a full one-quarter of the young city's population, would become an ever-smaller part of this ethnic mix as the century wore on. Yet they played a key role in defining the character of the place. The experience of one portion of this group—those who lived in bondage—was vividly documented in a handful of St. Louis–based slave narratives, two of which are excerpted in these pages. To William Wells Brown we owe one of the most thorough examinations available of the "peculiar institution's" face in this border city, including his admonition that "though slavery is supposed by some to be more mild in Missouri, yet no part of our country is more noted for the barbarity of its inhabitants." Elizabeth Keckley, in her own memoir, described a life similar to the lives of many young women pressed into service in early St. Louis households, with the overriding exception that Keckley's labors were unrewarded by either money or basic freedom. Her decision to "turn her face northward" toward a life of freedom reminds us, as do Brown's words, of the city's strong historical ties to the economy and the culture of the American South—ties that became increasingly hard to trace with the passage of time and with the infusion of capital and people arriving through northern routes.

While the city's slaveholding traditions gained increasing national notoriety with the approach of the Civil War, Northern and foreign criticism of St. Louis's intransigence was tempered by a persistent, sentimental appreciation of its fading French heritage. When Charles Dickens debarked here during his celebrated American tour of 1842, he found the city to be full of "quaint and picturesque" houses with "a kind of French shrug about them." Around the same time, the writer, actor, and all-around character Matthew Field—never slow to seize on an opportunity for high drama—used the pending demolition of the Chouteau house as a chance to decry the commercialization and overcrowding of the city. And so it was that—precisely as the city's Creole character began declining as a meaningful factor in St. Louis's economic and political life—writers, travelers, and observant locals began the process of reincarnating it as an object of fascination, curiosity, and nostalgia.

Not everyone succumbed to the charm of faded Creole ways; Auguste Laugel, himself a Frenchman, remarked less sanguinely in 1864 that "St. Louis already looks like an old city"; that the decline of French influence had left only an "asleep, lazy" town in its wake. While it's true that the city at the time had not yet fully attained its promise as an economic powerhouse, Laugel might have been a bit more sensitive to the wrenching impact of the Civil War, which for four years subjected the city's Union and Confederate supporters alike to the confinement of martial law and the hardships of a depressed economy. From the panicked crossfire that erupted outside Camp Jackson in 1861 (an episode witnessed, and memorably described, by St. Louisan William Tecumseh Sherman) to the eerie quiet of the streets that greeted a young Jessie Benton Fremont on her return from Washington, D.C., the war provided St. Louisans with no shortage of vivid and harsh memories. From a historiographic perspective, it also provided a convenient break by which later chroniclers would forever separate the early, Creole-flavored city (a place that was either impractical or dignified, depending on their point of view) from the later, American city (which might, by the same lights, be counted either industrious or money-grubbing).

With the war, too, went something of the freewheeling character that had typified St. Louis during the years when it served as the inland focus not only of American river commerce, but also of virtually all overland travel to the West. This era was memorialized in the city's literature by the vernacular stylings of men like Matthew Field, or by the theatrical impresario Sol Smith, whose fictional character Noah Ridgely exemplified the cantankerous irony of the genre that would come to be known as "Southwestern humor." Another Missourian—Samuel Clemens—continued to perfect and then transcend the genre under the *nom de plume* of Mark Twain; Twain, of course, depended on his memories of antebellum life in the region for the eccentric characters and absurd episodes that enlivened such later writings as *Life on the Mississippi*.

Somewhat less picturesque but still vital to the city's character, in the minds of most St. Louis observers, was its growing "Dutch" population. While the German traveler Nicolaus Mohr noted with some surprise that "you can not tell whether [St. Louis] has a large, small, or no German population in it," the fact remained that by the 1850s more than one third of the city's population was of German birth or parentage—a proportion exceeded, in American cities, only in Milwaukee. St. Louis's German population enjoyed its own newspapers and schools, its own churches and synagogues, its beer gardens and concert halls—all of which came increasingly to be symbols of the city itself, rather than of one component group. Symbolic of the degree to which the immigrants had prospered and assimilated were such leading lights as brewer Adolphus Busch and editor Carl Schurz, not to mention the countless others who founded successful businesses or built homes alongside their well-born Anglo-Saxon counterparts. More typical, however, were the tens of thousands of German families who peopled the crowding neighborhoods of the north and south sides, finding work as wheelwrights and shopkeepers, bricklayers and tavern owners, and giving to the city's landscape much of the stolid, no-nonsense look that it retains.

The German contribution—to the city's population as to its economy—was one important contributor to the mix of promising portents that fueled Logan Reavis's hyperbolic "Future Great City" campaign in the 1870s. Undeterred by spreading economic depression, and unaware of either the impending general strike or the 1880 census results that would appear to show the city's growth slowing to a crawl (a misimpression only partially excused by the fact that the 1870 results had been cooked to make St. Louis's population seem bigger than it actually was), Reavis seized on a theory of manifest destiny that placed St. Louis directly at the heart of all that was good, true, and profitable. Surely, Reavis pleaded, this was the logical site on which to relocate the capital of the mightiest nation on earth.

But (what *is* the matter with St. Louis, anyway?) it didn't happen. Denton Snider later recalled that the city, "in its humiliated mood, began to look backward" some time in the 1880s. Although, as we have seen, looking backward was not a newly acquired skill for most St. Louisans—even then—the past did acquire a newly central place in the minds of many of the city's artists and writers. The first encyclopedic histories of the city date from this period; so, too, do the sanitized historical reconstructions of artist Clarence Hoblitzelle (images that have come, in most people's minds, to represent the real appearance of colonial St. Louis). Historical fiction, like historical art, seldom produced great work (try out this subtle bit of plot exposition, from Kate Chopin's "Maid of Saint Phillippe": "'I have heard, long ago, that King Louis made a gift of his Louisiana possessions to his cousin of Spain; that they jointly granted the East Illinois to England. So that leaves the West under Spanish dominion, Jacques.'"), although Winston Churchill's *The Crisis*, published in 1901, was an important and widely read reevaluation of the Civil War.

Creative historical reconstruction reached its apogee (in St. Louis and, arguably, in the United States) with the Louisiana Purchase Exposition of 1904. In a seven-month period, twenty million visitors witnessed this 1,272-acre ensemble of architecture, landscaping, and exhibitry—all of it unified under the guiding conceit that the continental expansion of American boundaries, begun a century earlier, represented a signal moment in the steady progress of the nation and the planet (and that St. Louis somehow remained the epicenter of that progress). This historical ambitiousness leveled off only slightly a decade later, when the Pageant and Masque—held, like the fair, in Forest Park—presented characters from the city's past who invited citizens to "Behold your city pass . . . Toward the grave states of peace and brotherhood,/The dawning vision of destiny." Did St. Louisans buy this kind of talk? Yes, and no. Perhaps we had best leave the answer in the words of Marietta Holley's Samantha Smith Allen, who, gazing at the World's Fair, allowed that she "'considered the hull thing highly symbolical and loved to see it.'"

Chances are that most St. Louisans, like Samantha, did indeed love to see it. No latter-day cynic should downplay the genuine, shared sense of excitement that came from living in the nation's fourth-largest city at a time when it garnered so much of the world's attention. Yet a part of the pull of the reconstructed past for early twentieth-century St. Louisans must surely have been the sense of peril that permeated the present. This was, after all, the era of William Reedy's defining "What's the Matter with St. Louis?" essay, an era when Lincoln Steffens and Claude Wetmore exposed before a national reading audience the graft that corrupted city government, and when Henry Adams felt free to disparage the place as a "third-rate town of half-a-million people without history, education, unity or art." At a more intimate level, the unblinking reportage of such first-rate local journalists as Theodore Dreiser, Carlos Hurd, and Orrick Johns all brought to St. Louisans' kitchen tables daily reminders of the unpredictable brutality and danger of life in the big city.

But St. Louis's civic complexion, in the early decades of the 1900s, proved neither exceptionally promising nor exceptionally unhappy. Instead, it resembled the city's infamous air: gray. Its population increasingly Americanized, its polarities of wealth and poverty increasingly softened by the more numerous classes that filled the space in-between, St. Louis settled into a generally prosperous—and generally slow-moving—rhythm. This was the city that Fannie Hurst found "conservative, undemonstrative, [and] unostentatious," and that another hometowner, Fannie Cook, described as "an immense hive of home neighborhoods." While civic leaders already fretted, amongst themselves, about the prospect of a decaying downtown, business and retail tenants remained concentrated east of Twelfth Street. And while the growth of such communities as University City, Webster Groves, and

Maplewood hinted at the lure of suburban homeownership, the city's population continued to grow—albeit more slowly—alongside that of the county.

So what is it about this city, during the middle years of the twentieth century, that inspired such a feeling of melancholy among writers? Perhaps that sense is simply typical of the memoir form that comprised so much of the literature of postwar St. Louis; indeed, the city itself, which has lost more than half its population since 1950, lends itself well to the *memento mori*. Still, a reader is struck by the extent to which writers have made of St. Louis a great tragic character. Why should a walk through the West End—steaming under St. Louis's customary "sodden blanket" of summer heat—provoke in Thomas Wolfe the overwhelming sense of being "lost and sunken in America"? Why did the very thought of the city's ubiquitous deep-red brick remind Harold Brodkey of "loneliness and the queer, self-pitying wonder [of] children whose families are having catastrophes"; why did the view out an apartment window call to Tennessee Williams's mind "the dried-blood horror of lower-middle-class American urban neighborhoods"? It is as though the mute walls of the aging city were pleading for a deeper sympathy than that offered by the urban renewers and civic boosters who were busy putting a shining, new face on the burnished landscape. Through the observations of St. Louis writers, those walls spoke one last time of all that they had seen.

Even the public improvements that came at such a dear price to citizens and civic leaders in the 1950s and 1960s could, in the writer's eye, be recast as evidence of loss. "Where," complained a returning William Burroughs, as he stepped from Union Station onto a recently cleared Market Street, "are the tattoo parlors, novelty stores, hock shops?" The Gateway Arch, standing on a cleared riverfront "like the only landmark to survive a nuclear blast," only sharpened Burroughs's sense of loss. Indeed, more than one observer has since cast this stainless symbol of postwar pride to ironic effect; poet John Knoepfle wrote of "watch[ing] a city dying" under its shiny curves, while the peripatetic British writer Jonathan Raban (never known to harbor excessive fondness for any locale) mused on, among other points, the futility of attempting to commit suicide from the Arch's observation room. To the members of Civic Progress, to the real estate developers and city planners and just-plain optimistic St. Louisans who in the 1960s and '70s sought to jump-start civic morale with a tonic of professional sports, public anniversary celebrations, and new buildings, cultural maven Jay Landesman could offer only a friend's rueful farewell: "'St. Louis is something that happens to you once in a lifetime when you are just right for it and then it never happens again.'"

Perhaps the city has not, indeed, "happened again," in the sense that Logan Reavis and his long line of determined descendants might have wished. But somehow others, in the years that have followed Landesman's epitaph, have continued to find themselves "just right" for St. Louis. The city still yields itself to all manner of discovery and appreciation; it continues to demonstrate that reports of its death—to borrow from our best-known laureate, Mark Twain—are indeed greatly exaggerated. The gifted writers who made late-twentieth-century St. Louis their home have handed us an almost endless array of images and interpretations of the city we know today: from the sense of neighborly comfort that infuses the St. Louis reflections of Stanley Elkin and Howard Nemerov; to the picturesque quirkiness captured in the novels of writers as diverse as Ntozake Shange, Michael Kahn, Glenn Savan, and John Lutz; to the menacing, urban-society-on-the-skids quality that unites Allen Steele's and Jonathan Franzen's otherwise quite different portraits of the city of the near-future. In the hands of these and other contemporary writers, St. Louis still reveals facets of itself that are lost in the sweeping strokes of the historian's narrative; it still vibrates with distinct qualities that lie forgotten beneath the determined agendas of policymakers who bemoan the fact that the city can't be more like Portland, Cleveland, Denver, or any of a hundred other cities that it never was and—fortunately—never could be.

So: "What's the matter with St. Louis?" As the contents of this volume demonstrate, the still-familiar question may be evidence less of the city's problems than of its enduring strength. For all of the doubt and insecurity that it conveys, the query reflects a civic conscience, a sense of shared history, a perception of uniqueness that persists—however painfully—at a time when we, like most cities, risk either losing our remaining historic assets altogether or watching them be incorporated into Potemkin-village images of the urban experience. The stories, poems, and essays that follow are reminders of our continued need to heed the admonition of one of America's greatest urban storytellers, Theodore Dreiser. "I learned in time to like [St. Louis] very much," Dreiser recalled of his years here, "but for the things that set it apart from other cities, not for the things by which it sought to rival them." This book is a tribute to the true Spirit of St. Louis, which as always rests in "the things that set it apart."

—ERIC SANDWEISS

Seeking St. Louis

PÈRE JACQUES MARQUETTE

BORN IN LAON, FRANCE, Jacques Marquette (1637-1675) was ordained a Jesuit priest in 1666 and sailed to Québec, Canada, that same year, intending to do missionary work among the Indians. Having acquired fluency in both the Algonquian and Huron languages, Marquette traveled to what is now the Upper Peninsula of Michigan and established the missions of Sault Sainte Marie and St. Ignatius in 1668 and 1671, respectively.

In 1673, Marquette accompanied Louis Jolliet on an expedition to verify the existence of a great river to the west, the "Mesippi," which was the subject of many Indian accounts. In two canoes, Marquette, Jolliet, and several other Frenchmen left Mackinac in mid-May and entered the Mississippi one month later. Passing the mouth of the Missouri River, which Marquette called "Pekitanoui" (or "muddy water," in Algonquian), the party paddled past the present site of St. Louis—nearly a century before Pierre Laclède and Auguste Chouteau established their trading post on that spot—and ventured as far south as the Arkansas River before, fearing a confrontation with Spaniards or hostile Indians, returning north.

Marquette made a second voyage down the Mississippi in 1675, with the goal of establishing a mission at Kaskaskia. Enduring a severe winter on the shore of Lake Michigan near Chicago, Marquette founded the Kaskaskia mission in the spring of 1676 and preached to large numbers of Indians. Though in failing health, Marquette attempted to return to Mackinac and died en route. His remains were transferred and buried near the mission he founded at St. Ignatius (today St. Ignace, Michigan).

Justly regarded as one of the original explorers of the Mississippi, Marquette kept detailed accounts during his voyages. In the following passages from his journal, Marquette describes the strange wildlife he spotted while on the river, including massive catfish and buffalo, his reception by the Illinois and their customs, and his amazement at viewing the Piasa bird painted on the cliffs near the confluence of the Missouri and Mississippi.

MARQUETTE'S FIRST VOYAGE

SECTION 4TH. OF THE GREAT RIVER CALLED MISSISIPI; ITS MOST NOTABLE FEATURES; OF VARIOUS ANIMALS, AND ESPECIALLY THE PISIKIOUS OR WILD CATTLE, THEIR SHAPE AND NATURE; OF THE FIRST VILLAGES OF THE ILINOIS, WHERE THE FRENCH ARRIVED.

Here we are, then, on this so renowned River, all of whose peculiar features I have endeavored to note carefully. The Missisipi River takes its rise in various lakes in the country of the Northern nations. It is narrow at the place where Miskous empties; its Current, which flows southward, is slow and gentle. To the right is a large Chain of very high Mountains, and to the left are beautiful lands; in various Places, the stream is Divided by Islands. On sounding, we found ten brasses of Water. Its Width is very unequal; sometimes it is three-quarters of a league, and sometimes it narrows to three arpents. We gently followed its Course, which runs toward the south and southeast, as far as the 42nd degree of Latitude. Here we plainly saw that its aspect was completely changed. There are hardly any woods or mountains; The Islands are more beautiful, and are Covered with finer trees. We saw only deer and cattle, bustards, and Swans without wings, because they drop Their plumage in This country. From time to time, we came upon monstrous fish, one of which struck our Canoe with such violence that I Thought that it was a great tree, about to break the Canoe to pieces. On another occasion, we saw on The water a monster with the head of a tiger, a sharp nose Like That of a wildcat, with whiskers and straight, Erect ears; The head was gray and The Neck quite black; but We saw no more creatures of this sort. When we cast our nets into the water we caught Sturgeon, and a very extraordinary Kind of fish. It resembles the trout, with This difference, that its mouth is larger. Near its nose—which is smaller, as are also the eyes—is a large Bone shaped Like a woman's busk, three fingers wide and a Cubit Long, at the end of which is a disk as Wide As one's hand. This frequently causes it to fall backward when it leaps out of the water. When we reached the parallel of 41 degrees 28 minutes, following The same direction, we found that Turkeys had taken the place of game; and the pisikious, or wild cattle, That of the other animals.

We call them "wild cattle," because they are very similar to our domestic cattle. They are not longer, but are nearly as large again, and more

Corpulent. When Our people killed one, three persons had much difficulty in moving it. The head is very large; The forehead is flat, and a foot and a half Wide between the Horns, which are exactly like Those of our oxen, but black and much larger. Under the Neck They have a Sort of large dewlap, which hangs down; and on The back is a rather high hump. The whole of the head, The Neck, and a portion of the Shoulders, are Covered with a thick Mane Like That of horses; It forms a crest a foot long, which makes them hideous, and, falling over their eyes, Prevents them from seeing what is before Them. The remainder of the Body is covered with a heavy coat of curly hair, almost Like That of our sheep, but much stronger and Thicker. It falls off in Summer, and The skin becomes as soft As Velvet. At that season, the savages Use the hides for making fine Robes, which they paint in various Colors. The flesh and the fat of the pisikious are Excellent, and constitute the best dish at feasts. Moreover, they are very fierce; and not a year passes without their killing some savages. When attacked, they catch a man on their Horns, if they can, toss Him in the air, and then throw him on the ground, after which they trample him under foot, and kill him. If a person fire at Them from a distance, with either a bow or a gun, he must, immediately after the Shot, throw himself down and hide in the grass; For if they perceive Him who has fired, they Run at him, and attack him. As their legs are thick and rather Short, they do not run very fast, As a rule, except when angry. They are scattered about the prairie in herds; I have seen one of 400.

We continued to advance, but, As we knew not whither we were going,—for we had proceeded over one Hundred leagues without discovering anything except animals and birds,—we kept well on our guard. On this account, we make only a small fire on land, toward evening, to cook our meals; and, after supper, we remove Ourselves as far from it as possible, and pass the night in our Canoes, which we anchor in the river at some distance from the shore. This does not prevent us from always posting one of the party as a sentinel, for fear of a surprise. Proceeding still in a southerly and south-southwesterly direction, we find ourselves at the parallel of 41 degrees, and as low as 40 degrees and some minutes,—partly southeast and partly southwest,—after having advanced over 60 leagues since We Entered the River, without discovering anything.

Finally, on the 25th of June, we perceived on the water's edge some tracks of men, and a narrow and somewhat beaten path leading to a fine prairie. We stopped to Examine it; and, thinking that it was a road which

Led to some village of savages, We resolved to go and reconnoiter it. We therefore left our two Canoes under the guard of our people, strictly charging Them not to allow themselves to be surprised, after which Monsieur Jollyet and I undertook this investigation—a rather hazardous one for two men who exposed themselves, alone, to the mercy of a barbarous and Unknown people. We silently followed The narrow path, and, after walking About 2 leagues, We discovered a village on the bank of a river, and two others on a Hill distant about half a league from the first. Then we Heartily commended ourselves to God, and, after imploring his aid, we went farther without being perceived, and approached so near that we could even hear the savages talking. We therefore Decided that it was time to reveal ourselves. This We did by Shouting with all Our energy, and stopped, without advancing any farther. On hearing the shout, the savages quickly issued from their Cabins, And having probably recognized us as frenchmen, especially when they saw a black gown,—or, at least, having no cause for distrust, as we were only two men, and had given them notice of our arrival,—they deputed four old men to come and speak to us. Two of these bore tobacco-pipes, finely ornamented and Adorned with various feathers. They walked slowly, and raised their pipes toward the sun, seemingly offering them to it to smoke,—without, however, saying a word. They spent a rather long time in covering the short distance between their village and us. Finally, when they had drawn near, they stopped to Consider us attentively. I was reassured when I observed these Ceremonies, which with them are performed only among friends; and much more so when I saw them Clad in Cloth, for I judged thereby that they were our allies. I therefore spoke to them first, and asked them who they were. They replied that they were Ilinois; and, as a token of peace, they offered us their pipes to smoke. They afterward invited us to enter their Village, where all the people impatiently awaited us. These pipes for smoking tobacco are called in This country Calumets. This word has come so much Into use that, in order to be understood, I shall be obliged to use it, as I shall often have to mention these pipes.

SECTION 5TH. HOW THE ILINOIS RECEIVED THE FATHER IN THEIR VILLAGE.

At the Door of the Cabin in which we were to be received was an old man, who awaited us in a rather surprising attitude, which constitutes a part of the Ceremonial that they observe when they receive Strangers. This man stood erect, and stark naked, with his hands extended and lifted toward the sun, As if he wished to protect himself from its rays, which nevertheless shone upon his face through his fingers. When we came near him, he paid us This Compliment: "How beautiful the sun is, O frenchman, when thou comest to visit us! All our village awaits thee, and thou shalt enter all our Cabins in peace." Having said this, he made us enter his own, in which were a crowd of people; they devoured us with their eyes, but, nevertheless, observed profound silence. We could, however, hear these words, which were addressed to us from time to time in a low voice: "How good it is, My brothers, that You should visit us."

After We had taken our places, the usual Civility of the country was paid to us, which consisted in offering us the Calumet. This must not be refused, unless one wishes to be considered an Enemy, or at least uncivil; it suffices that one make a pretense of smoking. While all the elders smoked after Us, in order to do us honor, we received an invitation on behalf of the great Captain of all the Ilinois to proceed to his Village where he wished to hold a Council with us. We went thither in a large Company, For all these people, who had never seen any frenchmen among Them, could not cease looking at us. They Lay on The grass along the road; they preceded us, and then retraced their steps to come and see us Again. All this was done noiselessly, and with marks of great respect for us.

When we reached the Village of the great Captain, We saw him at the entrance of his Cabin, between two old men,—all three erect and naked, and holding their Calumet turned toward the sun. He harangued us In a few words, congratulating us upon our arrival. He afterward offered us his Calumet, and made us smoke while we entered his Cabin, where we received all their usual kind Attentions.

Seeing all assembled and silent, I spoke to them by four presents that I gave them. By the first, I told them that we were journeying peacefully to visit the nations dwelling on the River as far as the Sea. By the second, I announced to them that God, who had Created them, had pity on Them, inasmuch as, after they had so long been ignorant of him, he wished to make himself Known to all the peoples; that I was Sent by him for that purpose; and that it was for Them to acknowledge and obey him. By the third, I said that the great Captain of the French informed them that he it was who restored peace everywhere; and that he had subdued The Iroquois. Finally, by the fourth, we begged them to give us all The Information that they had about the Sea, and about the Nations through Whom we must pass to reach it.

When I had finished my speech, the Captain arose, and, resting His hand upon the head of a little Slave whom he wished to give us, he spoke thus: "I thank thee, Black Gown, and thee, O frenchman,"—addressing himself to Monsieur Jollyet,—"for having taken so much trouble to come to visit us. Never has the earth been so beautiful, or the sun so Bright, as to-day; Never has our river been so Calm, or so clear of rocks, which your canoes have Removed in passing; never has our tobacco tasted so good, or our corn appeared so fine, as We now see Them. Here is my son, whom I give thee to Show thee my Heart. I beg thee to have pity on me, and on all my Nation. It is thou who Knowest the great Spirit who has made us all. It is thou who speakest to Him, and who hearest his word. Beg Him to give me life and health, and to come and dwell with us, in order to make us Know him." Having said this, he placed the little Slave near us, and gave us a second present, consisting of an altogether mysterious Calumet, upon which they place more value than upon a Slave. By this gift, he expressed to us The esteem that he had for Monsieur Our Governor, from the account which we had given of him; and, by a third, he begged us on behalf of all his Nation not to go farther, on account of the great dangers to which we Exposed ourselves.

I replied that I Feared not death, and that I regarded no happiness as greater than that of losing my life for the glory of Him who has made all. This is what these poor people cannot Understand. . . .

SECTION 6TH. OF THE CHARACTER OF THE ILINOIS; OF THEIR HABITS AND CUSTOMS; AND OF THE ESTEEM THAT THEY HAVE FOR THE CALUMET, OR TOBACCO-PIPE, AND OF THE DANCE THEY PERFORM IN ITS HONOR.

When one speaks the word "Ilinois," it is as if one said in their language, "the men,"—As if the other Savages were looked upon by them merely as animals.

It must also be admitted that they have an air of humanity which we have not observed in the other nations that we have seen upon our route. The shortness Of my stay among Them did not allow me to secure all the Information that I would have desired; among all Their customs, the following is what I have observed.

They are divided into many villages, some of which are quite distant from that of which we speak, which is called peouarea. This causes some difference in their language, which, on the whole, resembles allegonquin, so that we easily understood each other. They are of a gentle and tractable disposition; we Experienced this in the reception which they gave us. They have several wives, of whom they are Extremely jealous; they watch them very closely, and Cut off Their noses or ears when they misbehave. I saw several women who bore the marks of their misconduct. Their Bodies are shapely; they are active and very skillful with bows and arrows. They also use guns, which they buy from our savage allies who Trade with our french. They use them especially to inspire, through their noise and smoke, terror in their Enemies; the latter do not use guns, and have never seen any, since they live too Far toward the West. They are warlike, and make themselves dreaded by the Distant tribes to the south and west, whither they go to procure Slaves; these they barter, selling them at a high price to other Nations, in exchange for other Wares. Those very Distant Savages against whom they war have no Knowledge of Europeans; neither do they know anything of iron, or of Copper, and they have only stone Knives. When the Ilinois depart to go to war, the whole village must be notified by a loud Shout, which is uttered at the doors of their Cabins, the night and The Morning before their departure. The Captains are distinguished from the warriors by wearing red Scarfs. These are made, with considerable Skill, from the Hair of bears and wild cattle. They paint their faces with red ocher, great quantities of which are found at a distance of some days' journey from the village. They live by hunting, game being plentiful in that country, and on indian corn, of which they always have a good crop; consequently, they have never suffered from famine. They also sow beans and melons, which are Excellent, especially those that have red seeds. Their Squashes are not of the best; they dry them in the sun, to eat them during The winter and the spring. Their Cabins are very large, and are Roofed and floored with mats made of Rushes. They make all Their utensils of wood, and Their Ladles out of the heads of cattle, whose Skulls they know so well how to prepare that they use these ladles with ease for eating their sagamité.

They are liberal in cases of illness, and Think that the effect of the medicines administered to them is in proportion to the presents given to the physician. Their garments consist only of skins; the women are always clad very modestly and very becomingly, while the men do not take the trouble to Cover themselves. I know not through what superstition some Ilinois, as well as some Nadouessi, while still young, assume the garb of women, and retain it throughout their lives. There is some mystery in this, For they never marry and glory in demeaning themselves to do everything that the women do. They go to war, however, but can use only clubs, and not bows and arrows, which are the weapons proper to men. They are present at all the juggleries, and at the solemn dances in honor of the Calumet; at these they sing, but must not dance. They are summoned to the Councils, and nothing can be decided without their advice. Finally, through their profession of leading an Extraordinary life, they pass for Manitous,—That is to say, for Spirits,—or persons of Consequence.

There remains no more, except to speak of the Calumet. There is nothing more mysterious or more respected among them. Less honor is paid to the Crowns and scepters of Kings than the Savages bestow upon this. It seems to be the God of peace and of war, the Arbiter of life and of death. It has but to be carried upon one's person, and displayed, to enable one to walk safely through the midst of Enemies—who, in the hottest of the Fight, lay down Their arms when it is shown. For That reason, the Ilinois gave me one, to serve as a safeguard among all the Nations through whom I had to pass during my voyage. There is a Calumet for peace, and one for war, which are distinguished solely by the Color of the feathers with which they are adorned; Red is a sign of war. They also use it to put an end to Their disputes, to strengthen Their alliances, and to speak to Strangers. It is fashioned from a red stone, polished like marble, and bored in such a manner that one end serves as a receptacle for the tobacco, while the other fits into the stem; this is a stick two feet long, as thick as an ordinary cane, and bored through the middle. It is ornamented with the heads and necks of various birds, whose plumage is very beautiful. To these they also add large feathers,—red, green, and other colors,—wherewith the whole is adorned. They have a great regard for it, because they look upon it as the calumet of the Sun; and, in fact, they offer it to the latter to smoke when they wish to obtain a calm, or rain, or fine weather. They scruple to bathe themselves at the beginning of Summer, or to eat fresh fruit, until after they have performed the dance, which they do as follows:

The Calumet dance, which is very famous among these peoples, is performed solely for important reasons; sometimes to strengthen peace, or to unite themselves for some great war; at other times, for public rejoicing. Sometimes they thus do honor to a Nation who are invited to be present; sometimes it is danced at the reception of some important personage, as if they wished to give him the diversion of a Ball or a Comedy. In Winter, the ceremony takes place in a Cabin; in Summer, in the open fields. When the spot is selected, it is completely surrounded by trees, so that all may sit in the shade afforded by their leaves, in order to be protected from the heat of the Sun. A large mat of rushes, painted in various colors, is spread in the middle of the place, and serves as a carpet upon which to place with honor the God of the person who gives the Dance; for each has his own god, which they call their Manitou. This is a serpent, a bird, or other similar thing, of which they have dreamed while sleeping, and in which they place all their confidence for the success of their war, their fishing, and their hunting. Near this Manitou, and at its right, is placed the Calumet in honor of which the feast is given; and all around it a sort of trophy is made, and the weapons used by the warriors of those Nations are spread, namely: clubs, war-hatchets, bows, quivers, and arrows.

Everything being thus arranged, and the hour of the Dance drawing near, those who have been appointed to sing take the most honorable place under the branches; these are the men and women who are gifted with the best voices, and who sing together in perfect harmony. Afterward, all come to take their seats in a circle under the branches; but each one, on arriving, must salute the Manitou. This he does by inhaling the smoke, and blowing it from his mouth upon the Manitou, as if he were offering to it incense. Every one, at the outset, takes the Calumet in a respectful manner, and, supporting it with both hands, causes it to dance in cadence, keeping good time with the air of the songs. He makes it execute many differing figures; sometimes he shows it to the whole assembly, turning himself from one side to the other. After that, he who is to begin the Dance appears in the middle of the assembly, and at once continues this. Sometimes he offers it to the sun, as if he wished the latter to smoke it; sometimes he inclines it toward the earth; again, he makes it spread its wings, as if about to fly; at other times, he puts it near the mouths of those present, that they may smoke. The whole is done in cadence; and this is, as it were, the first Scene of the Ballet.

The second consists of a Combat carried on to the sound of a kind of drum, which succeeds the songs, or even unites with them, harmonizing very well together. The Dancer makes a sign to some warrior to come to take the arms which lie upon the mat, and invites him to fight to the sound of the drums. The latter approaches, takes up the bow and arrows, and the war-hatchet, and begins the duel with the other, whose sole defense is the Calumet. This spectacle is very pleasing, especially as all is done in cadence; for one attacks, the other defends himself; one strikes blows, the other parries them; one takes to flight, the other pursues; and then he who was fleeing faces about, and causes his adversary to flee. This is done so well—with slow and measured steps, and to the rhythmic sound of the voices and drums—that it might pass for a very fine opening of a Ballet in France. The third Scene consists of a lofty Discourse, delivered by him who holds the Calumet; for, when the Combat is ended without bloodshed, he recounts the battles at which he has been present, the victories that he has won, the names of the Nations, the places, and the Captives whom he has made. And, to reward him, he who presides at the Dance makes him a present of a fine robe of Beaver-skins, or some other article. Then, having received it, he hands the Calumet to another, the latter to a third, and so on with all the others, until every one has done his duty; then the President presents the Calumet itself to the Nation that has been invited to the Ceremony, as a token of the everlasting peace that is to exist between the two peoples.

Here is one of the Songs that they are in the habit of singing. They give it a certain turn which cannot be sufficiently expressed by Note, but which nevertheless constitutes all its grace.

Ninahani, ninahani, ninahani, nani ongo.

SECTION 7TH. DEPARTURE OF THE FATHER FROM ILINOIS; OF THE PAINTED MONSTERS WHICH HE SAW UPON THE GREAT RIVER MISSISIPI; OF THE RIVER PEKITANOUÏ. CONTINUATION OF THE VOYAGE.

We take leave of our Ilinois at the end of June, about three o'clock in the afternoon. We embark in the sight of all the people, who admire our little Canoes, for they have never seen any like them.

We descend, following the current of the river called Pekitanoui, which discharges into the Mississipy, flowing from the Northwest. I shall have something important to say about it, when I shall have related all that I observed along this river.

While passing near the rather high rocks that line the river, I noticed a simple which seemed to me very Extraordinary. The root is like small turnips fastened together by little filaments, which taste like carrots. From this root springs a leaf as wide As one's hand, and half a finger thick, with spots. From the middle of this leaf spring other leaves, resembling the sconces used for candles in our halls; and each leaf bears Five or six yellow flowers shaped like little Bells.

We found quantities of mulberries, as large as Those of france; and a small fruit which we at first took for olives, but which tasted like oranges; and another fruit as large As a hen's egg. We cut it in halves, and two divisions appeared, in each of which 8 to 10 fruits were encased; these are shaped like almonds, and are very good when ripe. Nevertheless, The tree that bears them has a very bad odor, and its leaves resemble Those of the walnut-tree. In These prairies there is also a fruit similar to Hazelnuts, but more delicate; The leaves are very large, and grow from a stalk at the end of which is a head similar to That of a sunflower, in which all its Nuts are regularly arranged. These are very good, both Cooked and Raw.

While Skirting some rocks, which by Their height and Length inspired awe, We saw upon one of them two painted monsters which at first made Us afraid, and upon Which the boldest savages dare not Long rest their eyes. They are as large As a calf; they have Horns on their heads Like those of deer, a horrible look, red eyes, a beard Like a tiger's, a face somewhat like a man's, a body Covered with scales, and so Long A tail that it winds all around the Body, passing above the head and going back between the legs, ending in a Fish's tail. Green, red, and black are the three Colors composing the Picture. Moreover, these 2 monsters are so well painted that we cannot believe that any savage is their author; for good painters in france would find it difficult to paint so well,—and, besides, they are so high up on the rock that it is difficult to reach that place Conveniently to paint them. Here is approximately The shape of these monsters, As we have faithfully Copied It.

While conversing about these monsters, sailing quietly in clear and calm Water, we heard the noise of a rapid, into which we were about to run.

I have seen nothing more dreadful. An accumulation of large and entire trees, branches, and floating islands, was issuing from The mouth of The river pekistanouï, with such impetuosity that we could not without great danger risk passing through it. So great was the agitation that the water was very muddy and could not become clear.

Pekitanouï is a river of Considerable size, coming from the Northwest, from a great Distance; and it discharges into the Missisipi. There are many Villages of savages along this river, and I hope by its means to discover the vermillion or California sea.

Judging from The Direction of the course of the Missisipï, if it Continue the same way, we think that it discharges into the mexican gulf. It would be a great advantage to find the river Leading to the southern sea, toward California; and, As I have said, this is what I hope to do by means of the Pekitanouï, according to the reports made to me by the savages. From them I have learned that, by ascending this river for 5 or 6 Days, one reaches a fine prairie, 20 or 30 Leagues Long. This must be crossed in a Northwesterly direction, and it terminates at another small river,—on which one may embark, for it is not very difficult to transport Canoes through so fine a country as that prairie. This 2nd River Flows toward The southwest for 10 or 15 Leagues, after which it enters a Lake, small and deep, which flows toward the West, where it falls into The sea. I have hardly any doubt that it is The vermillion sea, and I do not despair of discovering It some day, if God grant me the grace and The health to do so, in order that I may preach The Gospel to all The peoples of this new world who have so Long Groveled in the darkness of infidelity.

AUGUSTE CHOUTEAU

AUGUSTE CHOUTEAU (1750–1829) was only thirteen years old when he accompanied Pierre Laclède on an expedition up the Mississippi from New Orleans to seek a site to establish a trading post for Maxent, Laclède and Company. In December 1763, Laclède identified a desirable spot south of the confluence of the Missouri and Mississippi Rivers and returned to Fort de Chartres near Ste. Genevieve to store his goods and wait out the winter. In February, following Laclède's directive, Chouteau returned to the site with a party of men and began construction of the outpost, named St. Louis in honor of Louis IX, the patron saint of France's King Louis XV.

All historical accounts comment on Chouteau's maturity and wisdom. He quickly established himself as the village's leading citizen and was a trusted arbiter with the Indians. As Laclède's protégé, Chouteau also became a prosperous fur trader and St. Louis's wealthiest citizen and largest landholder. In 1789, a decade after Laclède's death, Chouteau occupied and renovated his mansion on Main Street, between Market and Walnut—St. Louis's grandest house, which not only served to entertain distinguished visitors to the village, but also occasionally functioned as a public meeting place.

In addition to physically claiming the site that is now St. Louis, Chouteau used his wealth and influence to establish systems necessary for making the village a vital urban center. He presided as justice of the first territorial court (after the 1804 Louisiana transfer), served as colonel in the militia, sat on the city's board of trustees, and founded the Bank of Missouri. When Chouteau died, his obituary in the *Missouri Republican* read: "At the advanced age of eighty years, he closed a life of singular usefulness, possessing, in every vicissitude, the esteem of his fellow citizens."

In 1857, Gabriel Chouteau, Auguste's youngest son, gave the Mercantile Library a handwritten passage that he claimed had come from his father's journal. The bulk of the fragment, translated and reproduced here, is Chouteau's account of the founding of St. Louis. In addition to stating that Laclède had selected the site "which might become, hereafter, one of the finest cities in America," Chouteau describes Laclède's sage, if paternalistic, dealings with the Missouri Indians. With its humble eloquence and liberal use of unverifiable quoted statements, as well as the mythic stature of its author, this document is critical to the development of St. Louis civic lore.

NARRATIVE OF THE SETTLEMENT OF ST. LOUIS

In the year 1762, M. D'Abadie, at that time Director General and Commandant of Louisiana, granted to a company the exclusive trade with the savages of the Missouri and all the nations residing west of the Mississippi, for the term of eight years. This company was formed under the name of M. Laclède Ligueste, Antoine Maxan and Company. Immediately after the terms and conditions were signed with the French Government, they took measures to import from Europe all the merchandise necessary to sustain, on a large scale, their commerce, which they proposed to extend as much as possible. While waiting for the arrival of the goods, which they had ordered in Europe, they formed a considerable armament, at the head of which was placed M. Laclède Ligueste, known as a man of great merit, capable, from his experience of conducting with skill and prudence, the interests of the company. He left New Orleans the 3rd of August, 1763, and arrived in Illinois the 3rd of November following.

Observe, that all the establishments which the French had on the left bank of the Mississippi, were ceded to the English by the treaty of 1762, and that upon the right bank, which remained to the French, there was only the small village of Ste. Genevieve, in which M. de Laclède could not find a house capable of containing one-fourth of his merchandise. M. de Neyon, Commandant of Fort de Chartres, learning the embarrassment of M. de Laclède, sent an officer to him, to tell him that he could offer him a place for his goods, until the English should come to take possession. Necessity made him accept this generous offer of M. de Neyon. He left Ste. Genevieve, and arrived at Fort Chartres on the 3rd of November, 1763, where he disembarked all his goods, and prepared immediately all the supplies for the different nations. After all the business of the trade was done, he occupied himself with the means of forming an establishment suitable for his commerce, Ste. Genevieve not suiting him, because of its distance from the Missouri, and its insalubrious situation. These reasons decided him to seek a more advantageous site. In consequence, he set out from the Fort de Chartres in the month of December, took with him a young man in his confidence, and examined all the ground from the Fort de Chartres to the Missouri. He was delighted to see the situation (where St. Louis at present stands); he did not hesitate a moment to form there the establishment that be proposed. Besides the beauty of the site, he found there all the advantages that one could desire to found a settlement which might become very considerable hereafter. After having examined all thoroughly, he fixed upon the place where he wished to form his settlement, marked with his own hand some trees, and said: "Chouteau, you will come here as soon as navigation opens, and will cause this place to be cleared, in order to form our settlement after the plan that I shall give you." We set out immediately afterwards, to return to Fort de Chartres, where he said, with enthusiasm, to Monsieur de Neyon, and to his officers that he had found a situation where he was going to form a settlement, which might become, hereafter, one of the finest cities of America—so many advantages were embraced in this site, by its locality and its central position, for forming settlements. He was occupied the rest of the winter in procuring all things necessary for the settlement—men, provisions, tools, etc.

Navigation being open in the early part of February, he fitted out a boat, in which he put thirty men,—nearly all mechanics,—and he gave the charge of it to Chouteau, and said to him: "You will land at the place where we marked the trees; you will commence to have the place cleared, and build a large shed to contain the provisions and the tools, and some small cabins, to lodge the men. I give you two men on whom you can depend, who will aid you very much; and I will rejoin you before long." I arrived at the place designated on the 14th of February, and, on the morning of the next day, I put the men to work. They commenced the shed, which was built in a short time, and the little cabins for the men were built in the vicinity. In the early part of April, Laclède arrived among us. He occupied himself with his settlement, fixed the place where he wished to build his house, laid a plan of the village which he wished to found (and he named it Saint Louis, in honor of Louis XV, whose subject he expected to remain, for a long time;—he never imagined he was a subject of the King of Spain); and ordered me to follow the plan exactly, because he could not remain any longer with us.

He was obliged to proceed to Fort de Chartres, to remove the goods that he had in the fort, before the arrival of the English, who were expected every day to take possession of it. I followed, to the best of my ability, his plan, and used the utmost diligence to accelerate the building of the house.

Whilst we were all very much occupied with this work, there arrived among us, in the month of ___ all the tribe of the Missouris,—men, women and children; and although they did not appear to have any evil intentions towards us, they were not the less a heavy charge on us, from their continual demands for provisions, and from their thefts of our tools,—telling us, always, that they wished to form a village around the house we intended building, of which it would be the centre. All this talk disturbed me very much, and made me resolve to send for Monsieur de Laclède,—and what still more strongly determined me to do so, was, that there had come from Caos some people to settle in the new village, but who left it again for fear of the Missouris, who numbered about one hundred and fifty warriors, while we were only thirty or thirty-five. But I should say that this tribe never appeared to have any hostile intentions whatever. Monsieur de Laclède arrived, and immediately the Chief of the Missouris came to see him, in order to hold a council. The result of the council was that they were worthy of pity; that they were like the ducks and the geese, who sought open water in order to rest, and procure an easy subsistence; that they did not find any place more suitable, in their opinion, than the place where they were. Upon that, they said many things, which amounted always to this, that they desired to settle where they were. The council ended, Monsieur de Laclède postponed, until the following day, his reply to them. The council again assembled, and, after much vague preliminary talk, Monsieur de Laclède spoke to them with his usual firmness: "You told me, yesterday, that you were like the ducks and the geese, who traveled until they found a fine country, where there was beautiful, open water, that they might rest there, and obtain an easy living; and that you, the Missouris, who were worthy of pity, resembled them, because you traveled like them to find a place to settle yourselves, and that you did not find any one more suitable than that where you are at present; that you wished to form a village around my house, where we should live together in the greatest friendship. I reply to you in a few words, and I will say, that if you followed the example of the ducks and the geese in settling yourselves, you followed bad guides, who have no foresight; because if they had any, they would not put themselves into open water, so that the eagles and birds of prey could discover them easily, which would never happen to them if they were in a woody place, and covered with brush. You Missouris, you will not be eaten by eagles; but these men who have waged war against you for a long time past, who are in great numbers against you, who are few, will kill your warriors, because they will offer resistance, and will make your women and children slaves. Behold what will happen to you, for wishing to follow, as you say, the course of the ducks and geese, rather than the advice of men of experience. You women, who are here present, and who listen to me, go, tenderly caress your children—give them food in plenty; also, to your aged parents,—press them closely in your arms,—lavish upon them all the evidences of the tenderest affection, until the fatal moment which shall separate you from them—and that moment is not far distant, if your men persist in their intention to settle here. I warn you, as a good Father, that there are six or seven hundred warriors at Fort de Chartres, who are there to make war against the English,—which occupies them fully at this moment, for they turn their attention below Fort Chartres, from whence they expect the English,—but if they learn you are here, beyond the least doubt, they will come to destroy you. See now, warriors, if it be not prudent on your part to leave here at once, rather than to remain to be massacred, your wives and children torn to pieces, and their limbs thrown to dogs and to birds of prey. Recollect, I speak to you as a good Father; reflect well upon what I have just told you, and give me your answer this evening. I cannot give you any longer time, for I must return to Fort de Chartres."

In the evening, the whole nation, men, women and children, came to Monsieur de Laclède, and told him that they had opened their ears wide to his discourse, and that they would follow, in all things, his advice: and they prayed him to have pity upon the women and children, and give them provisions, and a little powder and some balls for the men, that they might hunt while going up the Missouri, and defend themselves, if they were attacked. Monsieur de Laclède told them that he would have pity on them, and detained them till the next day. He could not give them anything that day, for he had not enough corn, which he was obliged to send to Caos for. As soon as he had received it, he gave them a large quantity,—some powder, balls and knives, and some cloth; and the day after, all the Missouris went away, to go up the Missouri and return to their ancient village,—having remained here fifteen days, in the course of which I had the cellar of the house, which we were to build, dug by the women and children. I gave them, in payment, vermillion, awls and verdigris. They dug the largest part of it, and carried the earth in wooden platters and baskets, which they bore upon their beads.

Monsieur de Laclède, after giving the orders which he thought necessary, for the works of a settlement, left, a few days after the savages, for Fort de Chartres. Those persons who had fled to Caos on the coming of the savages, returned as soon as they knew that they had gone away, and commenced building their houses, or, to speak more correctly, their cabins, and entered their lands, agreeable to the lines of the lots which I had drawn, following the plan which Monsieur de Laclède had left with me.

Monsieur de Neyon de Villiers, who governed Upper Lousiana, under the name of Illinois, had orders from the Governor-General of the province, to evacuate the whole left bank of the Mississippi, which had been ceded to the English by the treaty of Versailles. In consequence of these orders, he caused to be withdrawn the garrisons of Fort des Pees, upon the Illinois River, that of Fort Marsiaque, on the Belle Riviere; the post of Vincennes, upon the Wabash, where commanded Monsieur de St. Ange de Bellerive; and, although the Fort des Canses was in Missouri, he brought down the little garrison of this post—and even an officer whom he had sent to build a fort on the Osage River, near a village of the tribe of the same name. As soon as he had collected all the troops at Fort de Chartres, he ordered Monsieur de St. Ange to remain there with forty men, one captain and two lieutenants, to deliver up the fort to the English, who were expected every day, and he himself prepared to go down the river on the 10th of July, 1764, with the remainder of his troops, and all the employees of the government, and a large part of the inhabitants of the villages of Fort de Chartres and Prairie du Rocher, for whom he promised to obtain free grants of land, near New Orleans, for the sacrifices they were making of their property, in order to go and settle in Lower Louisiana, under the French government, rather than to remain under the dominion of the English, who were heretics, etc. But the real motive of Monsieur de Neyon was, to take with him a numerous train, and to descend the Mississippi in triumph, to make the government believe that all these people followed him for the great esteem which they had for his person; thereby to gain the confidence of the authorities, in order to obtain a place that he had in view. But when he learned, on arriving at New Orleans, that the country was ceded to Spain, he determined to return to Europe. He forgot all the promises that he had made to these poor, credulous people, who remained upon the strand without knowing where to lay their heads, and the government troubled themselves but little about them, because they knew that the colony would soon change masters. So that these unfortunate people, who had abandoned the little property which they possessed in Illinois, to go and live under the French government, found themselves completely disappointed in their hopes. Some of them, in order to live, went with their families to Opelousas, others to Atakapas, where, however, they could not carry, on account of the want of facilities for transportation, the materials which they had brought down with them; and they were obliged to give them for almost nothing, in order to procure a little maize and rice. Those who, having some means, returned to Illinois, were very happy to find there Monsieur de Laclède, who aided them in a great many ways, and observed to them, that if they had been willing to follow his advice, as others had done, who had not wished to follow their evil destiny, they would not now be in the unpleasant situation in which they found themselves.

Monsieur de Laclède, penetrating the motives which actuated Monsieur de Neyon, did all in his power to hinder them from going down, which he did without any interested view, but through humanity, telling them that the English government was not so terrible as they wished to make them believe; that, for his part, he had a much more favorable opinion of it. However, if, in consequence of false prejudice, they did not wish to remain under this government, he would recommend them to go up to his new settlement, and he would facilitate for them the means of getting there with their effects; and, as for their animals, it was very easy to conduct them by land, since the journey was only nineteen leagues by a good road. Several families accepted these offers, and obtained immediately the wagons and the necessary harness to proceed to St. Louis, and there he aided them in settling and ordered me to assign them lands, according to the plan that he had made, which I did as exactly as possible. As I have already observed, that immediately upon the departure of the tribe of the Missouris, the inhabitants who had fled to Caos had returned, and, with those of Fort de Chartres, commenced to give some permanence to St. Louis.

FERNANDO DE LEYBA

A NATIVE OF BARCELONA, Spain, Fernando de Leyba (?–1780) became lieutenant governor of Upper Louisiana at St. Louis in June 1778, succeeding the popular Francisco Cruzat. While initially he received a warm welcome from early St. Louisans, de Leyba soon faced problems that were insurmountable, and, during his two-year tenure, became the central figure in one of the fledgling town's darkest hours.

As a Spanish outpost and supplier of provisions to the American army, St. Louis had become a thorn in the side of Great Britain. In 1778, shortly after France declared war on Great Britain, British commanders in Canada hatched a plan to debilitate Spanish fortifications along the Mississippi, thus minimizing the strength of the Spaniards' alliance with France and their support to the Americans. In early May 1780, nearly fifteen hundred Indians from more than a half-dozen tribes, led by the British mercenary Emmanuel Hesse, descended the Mississippi with the intention of attacking St. Louis.

Having received word of the impending raid from a fur trader traveling downriver, Fernando de Leyba worked to fortify the village. However, due to a lack of financial support from the Spanish government and the diminished resources of local inhabitants, de Leyba's plan to build four stone towers to defend St. Louis failed. Only one tower, on the west side of the village—near what is now the corner of Fourth and Walnut Streets—was completed, except for the roof. That tower—Fort San Carlos—lent its name to the battle that ensued.

At approximately 1:00 P.M. on May 26, 1780, de Leyba—who was critically ill at the time of the attack—and his meager troops (mostly civilian volunteers) managed to defend St. Louis and turn back the enemy after the first wave of their assault. However, casualties for the struggling settlement were great: twenty-one people were killed, including several unsuspecting citizens who were picking berries in a nearby field; crops were destroyed; and livestock was slaughtered. An additional twenty-five people were captured by Indians and later put to death.

Although de Leyba's strategy saved St. Louis from falling into the hands of the British, local residents had suffered so greatly that they began circulating rumors asserting that de Leyba had botched the defense and attributing to him the most scurrilous behaviors. The rumors that vilified de Leyba developed into a full-blown oral tradition and eventually became recorded as historical fact. Wilson Primm, in his 1831 "History of St. Louis," wrote, "There can be no doubt that Leyba, like another [Benedict] Arnold, was seduced into defection from his duty, and that it was only the unflinching daring of the people of St. Louis, that saved this infant outpost from utter destruction." Primm's assessment of de Leyba was repeated by many subsequent historians for fifty years, before it was questioned by Sylvester Waterhouse, a contributor to Thomas Scharf's *History of St. Louis City and County* (1883). He argued that "public suspicion seems to be the only ground for many of the charges against de Leyba. But, in the absence of proof, repetitions of tradition cannot invest these apparent fictions with a title to a place in authentic history."

The following excerpt is de Leyba's official report of the attack of May 26, 1780, to his superior officer, Bernardo de Gálvez, governor general of Louisiana. Gravely ill since before the attack, de Leyba dictated his June 8 letter to a secretary and died twenty days later. De Leyba's military superiors and the Spanish crown commended him for his wise and valiant conduct during this crisis and posthumously promoted him to the rank of lieutenant colonel.

ACCOUNT OF THE BATTLE OF FORT SAN CARLOS

ST. LOUIS, JUNE 8, 1780

Mon gouverneur:

A sickness by which I was afflicted for a long time did not permit me to write to you by my own hand and the only soldier who is here and who knows how to write in Spanish is not able to write according to my dictation nor is he able to express my ideas—that is the reason why I am taking advantage of this occasion—by my secretary who is French—in order to write to you concerning the events that have occurred at my post during the past few days.

By my letter of the sixteenth of November, 1778, I had the honor to communicate to you that Fort Charles du Missouri was entirely ruined. A most rigorous winter, the like of which was never before experienced in this country, put this fort beyond repair.

The corporal who was attached to that post has withdrawn to a little cabin which was still standing. He advised me on April sixth, last, that the cannon had been abandoned and that the savage nations, excited by the English, were approaching the post. The artillery numbering five pieces was running the risk of being captured; this fact caused me to make the decision to send the captain of the militia with a detachment in order to bring back the cannon, riggings and apparatus to St. Louis, in order to put them in security and to be of service in case of need.

A few days later I was warned by the *chasseurs* of the Mississippi, who had left their *campements* in order to help me, that an army of Englishmen and savages was approaching St. Louis.

Having foreseen for a long time the embarrassment in which I would find myself in case of an attack by the English and savages, I formed the project to construct four towers or forts of stone at the four corners of this village—one on the north, the second on the south, the third on the east, and the fourth on the west—for the purpose of defending and [for] the security of this post. Consequently I assembled the inhabitants in a meeting that took place at my house. I pointed out to them the evident danger to which we were about to find ourselves exposed, in case of an attack by the English and savages, in a village open on all sides to the enemy and without defense; that the few people that we were would not be sufficient to preserve us from the furor of the barbarians unless we ourselves instituted a prompt remedy by making some fortifications. I put before them my project which they found apropos.

Consequently I invited them to consecrate themselves and their families to this defense by cooperating each one according to his means. They have all devoted themselves to this with joy and good will and after each one had offered according to his means I collected one thousand *piastres*. Of this amount I gave 400 out of my own pocket in order to lighten the burden of these poor people. My own means did not permit me to make a greater effort because I have two daughters. These good people have exhausted themselves and have done the impossible in order to furnish among themselves the remaining 600 *piastres* and in addition about 400 working days.

I commenced by ordering one of the towers to be erected on the west which would dominate the major part of this village. This tower was almost finished and a beginning made upon the second one located on the north.

After having ordered the foundation to be excavated and the first stone placed, I calculated the expense of the first one. I saw, with pain, that all the contribution would at most be sufficient to defray the expenses of only the first tower and that it was impossible to continue the other ones on account of the extreme poverty and misery to which the inhabitants have been reduced. They made their last efforts to furnish the 600 *piastres* by depriving themselves of the necessities of maintaining themselves and feeding their families.

All this expense as well as the transporting of the artillery from St. Charles cost the royal treasury nothing.

If it had been possible to construct the three other towers, as the first one, this post would have found itself in a state of defense against the attack of the enemy. With only a few troops and inhabitants, it would thus be possible to keep it in a state of defense and to oppose the attack of the English and savages. It would even be possible to protect a part of the surrounding country where the inhabitants are sowing and harvesting their wheat. Without these fortifications we would be continually exposed to the raids and massacres of the savages who could, considering their number, even enter the village.

On May ninth of this year, I was accurately informed that the army composed of 300 Englishmen and 900 savages were but eighty leagues from this post. This obliged me to take the measures which follow.

I immediately dispatched an order to Ste. Genevieve to send a detachment of sixty men of the militia together with a boat and a Berge, and to add to it the detachment which formed the garrison; all being commanded by the lieutenant of the militia, Mr. De Cartabona. The detachment made haste and arrived at St. Louis on May thirteenth.

I sent an express with orders to call all the *chasseurs* who were scattered on the rivers in the vicinity of twenty leagues from here, who came in haste. I have forbidden those of this post to leave. Therefore within four or five days I was reinforced by about 150 men, all good shots, whom were lodged and fed at the expense of the inhabitants who did this voluntarily—until the thirty-first of May.

I ordered the captain of the militia to go out with forty men in three pirogues in order to reconnoitre the enemy as far as ten to twelve leagues from St. Louis. At the same time two *canots* with six men in each were dispatched to scout to a distance of about twenty leagues from this post.

I was not able to undertake this expedition without incurring some expense to the royal treasury.

The captain was to remain five days and the two *canots* of the *chasseurs* were to remain until they might see the army of the enemy and bring me certain news. The expenses for all this I ordered charged to the lieutenant of the infantry of the militia, Sieur Benito Basquez.

While awaiting the arrival of the enemy army I speeded up the work on the tower and ordered the floor to be constructed. I ordered the five cannons which had been in Fort Charles to be put in place, and at the same time I ordered two *retranchements* to be dug—at each end of the village—one on the north and the other on the south where the enemy might enter. The one on the north was about twelve arpents in length starting from the Mississippi and following along the side of the tower; the one on the south being about twenty arpents long, following like the first and defended by the tower.

On May twenty-third my reconnoitring expedition arrived reporting that they had seen the enemy at a distance of twenty leagues from my post.

The twenty-sixth of the same month of May our enemies attacked the fortifications on the north. The certainty in which they were of finding the post without any fortification caused them to advance like madmen, with an unbelievable boldness and fury, making terrible cries and a terrible firing. At that moment my guard, who was on the fortification, very alert, gave me warning promptly. Although my orders were given in advance, everyone, without excepting anyone, hastened to the fortifications, half on one side, and half on the other. There was not a single man left in the houses. The women and children retired into the governor's mansion, and I placed Lieutenant Cartabona, with twenty men, to guard it. Although quite ill, I went to the tower with the rest of the garrison and with six *chasseurs* to work the cannon. I directed the artillery, and gave my orders in case of an attack on the fortifications. Although the tower was not at all covered, and the parapet for the cannon was not in position, yet we used them successfully, and very much surprised the savages, who did not expect such a maneuver; and if it had not been for the rapidity with which I acted, together with all the people on the fortifications, it would have been the last day of St. Louis. Our soldiers and inhabitants have shown marvels of bravery while facing the most evident dangers for the defense of the fortifications, and even wished to make a sortie against the enemy, if I hadn't prevented them, because of the fear that they might succumb under the great number of the enemy, who awaited only this moment in order to force open and enter into the village.

What was most disconcerting in the attack, was the confusion and the lamentable cries of the women and children who could be heard from the *azile* [government residence] up to the place where the combatants were fighting and it was only due to heroic courage that the arms did not fall from the hands of the fathers of families, who signalized themselves with all imaginable valor on this occasion, in which one would not have believed that there was any hope of success for repelling the enemy on account of the great number who were opposed to us.

Notwithstanding our vigorous defense we could not avoid suffering great losses.

Seeing that they could not force our *retranchements* on account of our vigorous resistance, our enemies scattered themselves about the country where they discovered a number of inhabitants and slaves who were working, sowing *maiz*. They destroyed the fields, killing and *sauvagaient* all that they found: oxen, cows, horses, pigs, hens, and in general they did the most terrible damage, but what was most pitiable and lamentable, was their massacring several persons, who were working in the fields, and who had not had sufficient time to take refuge in the *retranchements*. The list of these unfortunates who were killed and taken prisoner is herewith enclosed.

Alas! my governor, your paternal heart would have shed tears if you had been able to see with your own eyes a spectacle so emotional.

It was an affliction and general consternation, to see these poor corpses cut into pieces, their entrails *arrachez*, their limbs, heads, arms and legs scattered all over the field. What a horrible spectacle, *mon general*. In detailing this to you, I find myself very deeply grieved with great pain. It is the *Champs de St. Louis* where was exercised, in less than two hours, the most unheard of barbarity. It was carried to excess without our being able to avoid it on account of the few people whom I had at my disposal, which altogether consisted of about three hundred: troops, militia, and inhabitants. Judge, *mon gouverneur*, what kind of a fate was awaiting us, if Divine Providence, bravery and activity had not preserved us from the fury of these barbarians, animated by the English.

After the massacre, our enemies withdrew without being in a great hurry, not having been able to win. Prudence did not allow us to pursue them, on account of the fear of leaving the post unprovided and facing an ambush on the part of our enemies. Having sent out men to reconnoitre, I learned that the army had retired to twenty leagues from this post, ascending the Mississippi to the mouth of a river called the Illinois.

One of our prisoners, having escaped, brought me the news that this army had lost only three savages and two wounded and that the army was commanded by an English captain of *troupes reglées*, named Esse, in which there were several Canadian merchants who likewise brought savages with them. The commandant was expecting in this place the junction of the one called Langlade, Canadian officer; that the latter was to join the commandant with an army of savages in order to pounce upon this post a second time. That is the reason that I did not dismiss any foreign soldier from my post and I ordered everybody, old and young, subject to *monter la garde* day and night in the *retranchement*.

As the unfortunate inhabitants are so poor that they can scarcely subsist (their sowing of *maiz* having been a failure this year and having sustained the soldiers from the thirteenth of May until the thirty-first), I took the decision of contracting with the merchant Cerré, in order to supply to the soldiers *une ration par jour*, as long as they would be on duty—in order to alleviate these unfortunate inhabitants. Herein enclosed, I send you, *mon gouverneur*, the copy of this contract.

All the orders which I gave for the expenses, on the enclosed copy, are signed by me with a trembling hand, but the candor with which I am about to explain to you the motives, and your great generosity, will excuse me.

NICOLAS DE FINIELS

IN SPITE OF THE FACT that he wrote one of the most important studies of colonial Upper Louisiana, little is known about Nicolas de Finiels. According to Carl J. Ekberg and William E. Foley, editors and translators of the 1989 edition of de Finiels's *An Account of Upper Louisiana,* the earliest documentation places him in Philadelphia in 1797. The Spanish government commissioned the expatriate Frenchman and engineer to travel to St. Louis and suggest ways to strengthen the town's fortifications. Spending nearly a year in St. Louis, de Finiels, a meticulous draftsman, completed two of the most accurate maps of the region in existence at that time, of the central Mississippi valley and the upper Missouri country, the latter used by Lewis and Clark on their expedition. Unfortunately, de Finiels's assignment was then canceled, and he left St. Louis for New Orleans, where he remained until 1803.

In 1803, after France had reacquired the Louisiana Territory from Spain, de Finiels accepted a commission from his native country to travel again to St. Louis to produce a detailed account of Upper Louisiana. Drawing on much of the information he gathered during his 1797 visit, he wrote the forty thousand-word account in June 1803, shortly before the United States purchased Louisiana.

In the following excerpt from *An Account of Upper Louisiana*, de Finiels describes St. Louis nearly forty years after its founding and details the settlement's shortcomings, including its terrible streets, muddy water, summer heat, and vain women.

FROM *AN ACCOUNT OF UPPER LOUISIANA*

Houses in St. Louis are generally built of stone or timbers, and the interstices between the posts are filled either with masonry or mud and straw; the roofs are always shingled. Nearly all of the houses have galleries front and back, which is the usual manner of building in the whole colony. At first glance St. Louis appears to be of considerable size, and you are surprised to see the figures, which show that its population is quite small. This is explained by the fact that most of the residential parcels are occupied by only two owners, or sometimes three; others are owned by only one person, and the most densely settled are occupied by four families. This apportioning seems generous compared to New Orleans, where the parcels are usually divided into twelve lots. But in a region where each family must provide everything for itself, instead of relying upon markets and butcher shops, the lots are scarcely sufficient. St. Louis has never had a central market, and each resident must have a substantial garden in order to be able to lay in a supply of vegetables for the winter. He must have a poultry yard, a stable, a barn, and sheds in order to house his animals and to store his fodder and farm equipment. His residence in town is a microcosm of a farm, which either provides him with everything he needs or places him in a position to obtain it.

St. Louis's streets are miserable. The least bit of rain renders them absolutely impassable, and there are no sidewalks. The sandy soil of the plateau is always mixed with rocks and rich clay, making it slippery in many places. Almost all of the cross streets are deeply rutted by the water that flows off the bluff behind town and rushes toward the river. When it rains you must remain at home for days on end or put on Creole clothing in order to face the mud, which covers you from head to toe by the time you return home. A horse is the only option in these circumstances, for carriages are very rare in the Illinois Country. Despite its pretentious title, "Capital," St. Louis is in fact only a medium-sized village, and it never seems more like one than when the heavens unleash their cataracts, which happens only too often.

There are not enough cattle in this part of Louisiana to supply the needs of the area, and it is often difficult to obtain subsistence here. Slaughtering is done only sporadically in the summer and never in the winter. Animals graze far from the villages—on the lowlands that border the Missouri, or on Grande Isle and the Isle à Cabaret, which are located between St. Louis and the mouth of the Missouri. On these low, damp lands the cattle graze on horsetail that grows in the shady woods, and which is their sole source of food during winter. Its hollow stems contain water that slakes their thirst. The cattle are so accustomed to this annual migration that when November arrives they take it upon themselves to leave the St. Louis area and roam as far as ten leagues in search of food. Farmers who do not wish to risk losing precious cattle (some always get lost during that season) preempt this migration. Early on, they round up all of their cattle and lead them toward the Isle à Cabaret or Grande Isle. Then they compel them with great difficulty to cross over to one or the other of these islands. In this way they are more likely to find them all when time comes to lead them back.

Once again, it is sloth that creates this destructive custom, which stifles the growth of the herds and which should be abandoned as soon as possible. With a bit more work and effort, shelters could be built to protect the cattle during the winter; and abundant fodder for this bitter season could be obtained from hay, which is common around St. Louis and often of excellent quality. It grows for the most part on public land, and everyone would have the right to harvest it.

The necessity to ensure future subsistence for St. Louis will surely call for wiser and more rational measures, which would in fact serve the interests of the land owners. This is all the more necessary because other sources of subsistence are very precarious. Fishing is confined to the summer because of ice. Some ponds and marshes, however, could furnish an abundance of fish if someone would devote some attention to it. But it is the hunt that is the real mother of subsistence during winter in the Illinois Country—deer, wild turkeys, ducks, coots, geese, swans, rabbits, raccoons, opossums, squirrels are the prey. Some years, however, the hunt is lean. Indians do most of the hunting, and sometimes they are slow getting started; other times there is virtually no game at all, which was true during the winter that I spent in St. Louis during 1797–1798. In such instances, fasting necessarily becomes the order of the day unless you have a well-stocked chicken yard and a good supply of vegetables. . . .

The only water near St. Louis flows out of the pond and empties into the river. This is used by the laundresses, who set up their washboards on the pond's banks and the shores of the creek. They prefer this to using the Mississippi, whose waters must always be left to settle before being used. The Mississippi carries much more sediment in the St. Louis area than in the lower colony. Water taken close to the right bank and allowed to settle in a glass always leaves from one-fifth to one-fourth of the glass full of sediment; taken from the left bank opposite St. Louis it is much clearer, leaving only a small deposit compared to the first.

This muddy water—whose mere appearance would quench the thirst of a man accustomed to the limpid, pure water of fountains—is nevertheless preferred to clearer waters. These could be taken from the Mississippi above the mouth of the Missouri, or from springs, which in several places flow out of the bluffs or can be tapped from the bowels of the earth with wells. It is eagerly drunk, often even before it has settled. Panting boatmen, dripping with sweat, take it along the bank and eagerly gulp it down, and there is no evidence that it has ever caused any problems. Nature knows how to handle quantities of earth that enter the stomach and intestines, but she has not yet revealed her secret.

St. Louis was given a boost when some Americans settled in the area six years ago. They grasped the advantages that they might derive from the natural indolence of the native *habitants*, and their industry has already opened avenues of business that that indolence had precluded. Sawmills now supply abundant planks at twenty-five sous apiece, whereas they used to be scarce and cost four escalins or even one piastre. Iron is available at a better price; masonry, cabinetry, carpentry, and furniture are less expensive, and the residents can enjoy the fruits of labor that they once hesitated to undertake and only rarely brought to completion. Negligent workers left houses unfinished; you had to wait four to six years for windows, doors, and furniture, which grew old in the workshops before they were completed. Vegetables, eggs, poultry, milk, butter, and grain are more readily available, and thanks to the Americans' industry subsistence is generally more secure than before.

The population of St. Louis is composed of Canadians, Creoles, Americans, and some French who have settled there during the last eight to ten years. Earlier, the only way in which the population of the Illinois Country grew was owing to the journeys that some merchants made to Canada. These merchants always returned with ten or twelve *engagés*, all workmen and artisans who obligated themselves to serve in the Illinois Country for several years at modest wages. This was advantageous for Canadians who could not find such wages at home. These useful men, finding Louisiana's climate agreeable, especially in comparison with theirs, immigrated. They were also attracted by the ease with which they could settle there, which was difficult in Canada even with much labor, and by the higher wages. Some of them became farmers, who were all the more precious for Upper Louisiana. In addition to their labor, they brought gentle and steady dispositions, characteristics that earned them the esteem and friendship of a people who have always valued such qualities. . . .

St. Louis's temperature is generally healthy and agreeable, although there may be frequent fluctuations during the same day—as is true in all regions of America. In summer, the heat is often as intense as at New Orleans. In winter, there is bitter cold, which is healthy, and also good for agriculture because it provides the soil with an opportunity to rejuvenate itself. However, the cold makes a considerable dent in your wallet because of the firewood that is required to defend against it. The land is often covered with snow a foot or two deep, which pleases the residents, especially the youngsters. For them it is one of the virtues of winter and provides them with a sport which they love passionately. Scarcely do they notice the delicate flakes gathering on the prairies and fields than they prepare their sleighs; the horses are shod for ice and their harnesses ornamented with bells. Vying with one another, they leap forward, and in the midst of joyous cries of pleasure they cross the milky plain, carving the surface into a myriad of figures. Sometimes the frail vehicles overturn and bury the youngsters in the snow. These repeated accidents only double the fun, and also prolong it by providing subject matter for storytelling upon the return. The river's waters suspend their swift race; they stop, and on their surface forms a layer of ice, thick and solid enough for wagonloads of wood to cross it without danger. Springtime is always rainy. April, May, and June bring torrents of water that scar the earth and carry to the river the soil for alluvial lands. Following violent claps of thunder, hail often mixes with the rain and damages the crops. Tornadoes sweep across the sky more swiftly than streaks of lightning can dissect the scene; with a frightful din they uproot old trees that have survived many a windstorm; they carve swaths across the thickest forests, stripping them of their finest foliage; the earth, covered with debris, is witness to their trail and to the enormous force with which they blazed it. I was in Prairie du Rocher when one of these impetuous tornadoes, preceded by a hailstorm, compelled me to spend the night there. The following day the road along the bluff tops was littered with trees, which forced me to make frequent detours through the woods. Autumn is the finest season in the Illinois Country. It brings serene and temperate days that bridge the gap between crushing heat and bitter cold; it offers to the residents fruits that assuage tempers aroused by the heat. The prairies lose the tall grasses that make them difficult to cross. It's the season for travel. The sun's burning rays descend only obliquely; marshy lands dry out; rivers flow within their channels; all lines of communication are open and easily used.

Although there is a noticeable difference in the moral character of the residents of St. Louis and those of Ste. Genevieve, you nevertheless still discover in the former the imprint of their native simplicity, and you can still easily detect traces of the good nature that they inherited from their forefathers. More affluent outsiders, more wealth, pretension to fine manners, and social distinctions are already tainting native customs, which are not yet entirely lost but which will certainly disappear. The women have cultivated more elegance than the men. Their finer sensibilities prompt them to adorn themselves, and they are beginning to laugh at the naive beauties of Ste. Genevieve; they do not perceive that they are really losing by the price they pay for acquiring affected appearances. Their dress is already more studied, and soon you will clearly see an artificiality that until now has only just appeared. The young men remain far behind in these developments. Although the Indian breechclout hardly ever appears anymore under their tunics, the woolen capot (a hooded cloak) has not yet vanished; it still appears at the most glittering fetes, where it makes a marked contrast to the finery of the young beauties.

During its more than fifty years [*sic*] of existence, St. Louis has enjoyed a sort of privilege, which might be considered an exemption from one of the general laws of nature; this must be reckoned one of the finest gifts that indulgent Mother Nature has ever bestowed upon an area. During this entire period of time, and without the least suggestion of why, this town has been spared the scourge that is most destructive of beauty; from this cruel illness that can in a brief while utterly efface that beautiful flower, so fresh and delicate, and replace it with deformity; from this illness that ferociously ravages regions with warm climates. On several occasions, Indians covered with this disease's virulent pustules sought refuge in town and spent the entire term of the disease there without communicating it to anyone else. It was well established in public opinion that the residents of St. Louis were immune to smallpox, which on several occasions had visited other settlements in the Illinois Country. Last summer, this illusion (so comforting for vanity) was shattered, and mothers were given one more thing to worry about. The illness finally broke down the barriers that nature had seemingly raised against it, and almost all of the residents were afflicted. Some of them succumbed to this mortal disease, and other young beauties had dashed their hopes of numerous conquests, which had earlier been prophesied in their mirrors.

AMOS STODDARD

BORN IN WOODBURY, CONNECTICUT, Amos Stoddard's (1762–1813) career as captain in the U.S. Army played a pivital role in the history of the Louisiana Territory. After serving in the American Revolution for three years, he was appointed clerk of the Supreme Court of Massachusetts and eventually studied and practiced law. In 1798, Stoddard was appointed captain of artillery in the U.S. Army.

In 1804, Captain Stoddard became the central figure in the transfer of the Upper Louisiana Territory. In a period spanning two days, Stoddard received the territory from Spain in the name of France (a cession that had been agreed upon three years earlier but never formally completed), delivered the territory to the United States from France, and then assumed command as its first Civil Commandant. With the purchase of Upper Louisiana, the United States more than doubled in size. The following states emerged from the acquired land and were admitted to the Union: Arkansas, Colorado, Iowa, Kansas, Louisiana, Minnesota, Missouri, Montana, Nebraska, North and South Dakota, Oklahoma, and Wyoming.

The offered passage, delivered at St. Louis in 1804, is Stoddard's official address to the inhabitants of the Upper Louisiana Territory. In this eloquent and politically astute document, Stoddard welcomes the people of the region as full citizens of the United States, with all of the benefits and responsibilities inherent in that citizenship. Stoddard also assures the inhabitants that their customs will be respected and that the new government will work to resolve fairly the muddled land claims in the territory. Although Stoddard closes his address by underscoring his authority in the region, he does so diplomatically, seeking the trust and patience of the people in the territory, whose "prosperity and happiness" he declares his priority.

ADDRESS TO THE PEOPLE OF UPPER LOUISIANA

ST. LOUIS, MARCH 10, 1804

Louisianians,

The period has now arrived, when, in consequence of amiable negociations, Louisiana is in possession of the United States. The plan of a permanent teritorial Government for you, is already under the consideration of Congress, and will doubtless be compleated as soon as the importance of the measure will admit. But, in the mean time, to secure your rights, and to prevent a delay of justice, His Excellency William C. C. Claiborne, Governor of the Mississippi Territory is invested with those authorities and powers (derived from an act of Congress) usually exercised by the Governor General and Intendant under his Catholic Majesty; and permit me to add, that, by virtue of the authority and power vested in him by the President of the United States, he has been pleased to commission me as first civil Commandant of Upper Louisiana.

Directed to cultivate friendship and harmony among you, and to make known the sentiments of the United States relative to the security and preservation of all your rights, both civil and religious, I know of no mode better calculated to begin the salutary work than a circular address.

It will not be necessary to advert to the various preliminary arrangements, which have conspired to place you in your present political situation; with these it is presumed you are already acquainted. Suffice it to observe that Spain in 1800 and 1801 retroceded the Colony and Province of Louisiana to France; and that France in 1803 conveyed the same territory to the United States, who are now in the peaceable and legal possession of it. These transfers were made with honorable views, and under such forms and sanctions as are usually practised among civilized nations.

Thus you will perceive, that you are divested of the character of Subjects, and clothed with that of citizens—You now form an integral part of a great community; the powers of whose Government are circumscribed and defined by charter, and the liberty of the citizen extended and secured. Between this Government and its citizens, many reciprocal duties exist, and the prompt and regular performance of them is necessary to the safety and well fare of the whole. No one can plead exemption from these duties: They are equally obligatory on the rich and on the poor—on men in power as well as on those not intrusted with it. They are not prescribed as whim and caprice may dictate; on the contrary, they result from the actual or implied compact between society and its members, and are founded not only in the sober lessons of experience but in the immutable nature of things. If therefore the Government be bound to protect its citizens in the enjoyment of their liberty, property, and religion—the citizens are no less bound to obey the laws, and to aid the Magistrate in the execution of them—to repel invasion—and, in periods of public danger, to yield a portion of their time and exertion in defense of public liberty. In Governments differently constituted, where popular Elections are unknown, and where the exercise of power is confided to those of high birth and great wealth, the public defence is committed to men who make the science of war an exclusive trade and profession; but in all free republics, where the citizens are capacitated to Elect, and to be Elected, into offices of emolument and dignity, permanent armies of any considerable extent are justly deemed hostile to liberty; and therefore the Militia is considered as the palladium of their safety. Hence the origin of this maxim, that every soldier is a citizen, and every citizen a soldier.

With these general principles before you, it is confidently expected that you will not be less faithful to the United States, than you have been to his Catholic Majesty.

Your local situation, the varieties in your language and education, have contributed to render your manners, laws, and customs, and even your prejudices, somewhat different from those of your neighbors, but not less favorable to virtue and to good order in society. These deserve something more than mere indulgence; they shall be respected.

If, in the course of former time, the people on different sides of the Mississippi, fostered national prejudices and antipathies against each other, suffer not these cankers of human happiness any longer to disturb your repose, or to awaken your resentments; draw the veil of oblivion over the past, and unite in pleasing anticipations of the future; embrace each other as brethren of the same mighty family, and think not that any member of it can derive happiness from the misery or degradation of another.

Little will the example and authority of the best magistrates avail, when the public mind becomes tainted with perverse sentiments, or languishes under an indifference to its interests. Suffer not the pride of virtue, nor the holy fire of religion, to become extinct—If these be different in their nature, they are necessary supports to each other. Cherish the sentiments of order and tranquility, and frown on the disturbers of the public peace—Avoid as much as possible all legal contests; banish village vexation, and unite in the cultivation of the social and moral affections.

Admitted as you are into the embraces of a wise and magnanimous nation, patriotism will gradually warm your breasts, and stamp its features on your future actions. To be useful, it must be enlightened not the effect of passion, local prejudice or blind impulse. Happy the people, who possess invaluable rights, and know how to exercise them to the best advantage; wretched are those, who dare not think and act freely. It is a sure test of wisdom to honor and support the Government under which you live, and to acquiesce in the decisions of the public will, when they be constitutionally expressed. Confide therefore in the justice and integrity of our federal President; he is the faithful guardian of the laws: He entertains the most beneficent views relative to the glory and happiness of this Territory; and the merit alone derived from the acquisition of Louisiana, without any other, will perpetuate his fame to posterity. Place equal confidence in all the other constituted authorities of the Union: they will protect your rights; and indeed your feelings, and all the tender felicities and sympathies, so dear to rational and intelligent creatures. A very short experience of their equitable and pacific policy, will enable you to view them in their proper light. I flatter myself, that you will give their measures a fair tryal, and not precipitate yourselves into conclusions, which you may afterwards see cause to retract. The first official acts of my present station, expressly permitted by high authority, will confirm these remarks.

The United States, in the acquisition of Louisiana, were actuated by just and liberal views. Hence the admission of an article in the Treaty of cession, the substance of which is, that the inhabitants of the ceeded territory shall be incorporated in the union, and admitted as soon as possible to the enjoyment of all the rights, advantages, and immunities of citizens of the United States; and, in the mean time, be maintained and protected in the free enjoyment of their liberty, property, and religion.

From these cursory hints you will be enabled to comprehend your present political situation, and to anticipate the future destinies of your Country. You may soon expect the establishment of a territorial Government, administered by men of wisdom and integrity, whose salaries will be paid out of the Treasury of the United States. From your present population, and the rapidity of its increase, this territorial establishment must soon be succeeded by your admission as a state into the federal Union. At that period, you will be at liberty to try an experiment in legislation, and to frame such a Government as may best comport with your local interests, manners, and customs: Popular suffrage will be its basis. The enaction of laws, and the appointment of Judges to expound them, are among the first privileges of Organized society. Equal to either of these, indeed, is the inestimable right of tryal by Jury. Inseparable from many other obvious advantages are the forms of judicial processes, and the rules for the admission of testimony in Courts of justice.—It is also of importance, that a distinction be made between the tryals of a capital nature and those of an inferior degree, as also between all criminal and civil contests. In fine, Upper Louisiana, from its climate, population, soil, and productions, and from other natural advantages attached to it, will, in all human probability, soon become a star of no inconsiderable magnitude in the American constellation.

Be assured, that the United States feel all the ardor for your interests, which a warm attachment can inspire. I have reason to suppose that it will be among some of their first objects to ascertain and confirm your land titles. They well know the deranged state of these titles, and of the existence of a multitude of equitable claims under legal surveys, where grants have not been procured. What ultimate measures will be taken on this subject does not become me to conjecture—but thus much I will venture to affirm, that the most ample justice will be done; and that, in the final adjustment of claims, no Settler or Land holder will have just cause to complain. Claimants of this description have hitherto invariably experienced the liberality of Government; and surely it will not be less liberal to the citizens of Upper Louisiana, who form a strong Cordon across an exposed frontier of a vast empire and are entitled by solemn stipulations to all the rights and immunities of free men.

My duty, not more indeed than my inclination urges me to cultivate friendship and harmony among you, and between you and the United States. I suspect my talents to be unequal to the duties which devolve on me in the organization and temporary adminstration of the Government. The want of proper knowledge of your laws and language is among the difficulties I have to encounter. But my ambition and assiduity will be excited in proportion to the honor conferred on me. Inflexible justice and impartiality shall guide me in all my determinations. If, however, in the discharge of a variety of complicated duties, I be led into error, consider it as involuntary, and not as the effect of inattention, or of any exclusive favors or affections.

Destined to be the temporary guardian of the rights and liberties of at least ten thousand people, I may not be able to gratify the just expectations of all—but your prosperity and happiness will claim all my time and talents: and no earthly enjoyment could be more compleat than that derived from your public and individual security—from the increase of your opulence and power.

MERIWETHER LEWIS AND WILLIAM CLARK

IN MID-MAY 1804, on the banks of the Missouri River near St. Charles, William Clark (1770-1838) and Meriwether Lewis (1774-1809) were sent off with "three cheers" from an illustrious crowd that contained such notables as Captain Amos Stoddard, Auguste Chouteau, and Charles Gratiot, starting a perilous two-year journey that would forever change the face of America and link their names in history. Both Virginians by birth with military careers behind them, Lewis and Clark brought to the expedition complementary skills. Lewis, formerly Thomas Jefferson's personal secretary, had the superior education and a keen interest in botany and natural history. Clark, an accomplished frontiersman with experience in river navigation, drew maps and charts for the expedition. During the first leg of the journey, the original party, which consisted of forty-two persons in three boats, advanced as far as what is now Bismarck, North Dakota, before the onset of winter forced them to camp in October 1804. The expedition set out again the following April and faced increasing hardship, particularly the scarcity of food—forcing the party to subsist on horse and dog meat—and treacherous navigation. By November 1805, the party reached its goal at the mouth of the Columbia River and had come a distance of over four thousand miles; it then returned to St. Louis on September 23, 1806, much to the amazement of residents, who had given the travelers up for dead.

In 1807, Meriwether Lewis was appointed governor of the Louisiana Territory. Two years later, en route to Washington, D.C., to settle distressing matters of personal finance, Lewis died, most likely a suicide, in Tennessee. William Clark remained in St. Louis for the rest of his life. In 1813, after having served first as brigadier general of the militia, he was appointed governor of the Missouri Territory by President James Madison and held the office until 1821, when Missouri became a state. Clark also served as superintendent of Indian affairs in the West from shortly after his return to St. Louis until his death in 1838.

Called by *Journals* editor Donald Jackson "the writingest explorers" on record, Lewis and Clark left not only rich information, but also a charmingly written legacy. The Missouri Historical Society is the proud repository of an extensive collection of Lewis and Clark papers, including William Clark's elkskin-bound field journal, in which he recorded daily events from September 11 to December 31, 1805. The following excerpts from the journals, introduced by the notes of Nicholas Biddle, the first historian of the expedition, sketchily chronicle the party's departure from and return to St. Louis.

FROM *THE JOURNALS OF LEWIS AND CLARK*

[Biddle]

On the acquisition of Louisiana, in the year 1803, the attention of the Government of the United States was early directed towards exploring and improving the new territory. Accordingly, in the summer of the same year, an expedition was planned by the President for the purpose of discovering the courses and sources of the Missouri and the most convenient water communication thence to the Pacific ocean. His private secretary, captain Meriwether Lewis, and captain William Clarke, both officers of the army of the United States, were associated in the command of this enterprize. After receiving the requisite instructions, captain Lewis left the seat of government and, being joined by captain Clarke at Louisville, in Kentucky, proceeded to St. Louis, where they arrived in the month of December. Their original intention was to pass the winter at La Charrette, the highest settlement on the Missouri. But the Spanish commandant of the province, not having received an official account of its transfer to the United States, was obliged by the general policy of his government to prevent strangers from passing through the Spanish territory. They therefore encamped at the mouth of Wood River on the eastern side of the Mississippi, out of his jurisdiction, where they passed the winter in disciplining the men and making the necessary preparations for setting out early in the Spring, before which the cession was officially announced.

The party consisted of: nine young men from Kentucky; 14 soldiers of the United States Army, who volunteered their services; two French watermen; and interpreter and hunter; and a black servant belonging to captain Clarke. All these except the last were enlisted to serve as privates during the expedition, and three sergeants appointed from amongst them by the captains. In addition to these were engaged a corporal and six soldiers, and nine watermen, to accompany the expedition as far as the Mandan nation, in order to assist in carrying the stores or repelling an attack, which was most to be apprehended between Wood River and that tribe. The party was to embark on board of three boats; the first was a keelboat fifty-five feet long, drawing three feet of water, carrying one large squaresail and twenty-two oars. A deck of ten feet in the bow and stern formed a forecastle and cabin, while the middle was covered by lockers, which might be raised so as to form a breastwork in case of attack. This was accompanied by two perioques or open boats, one of six and the other of seven oars. Two horses were at the same time to be led along the banks of the river for the purpose of bringing home game or hunting in case of scarcity.

MONDAY MAY 14TH 1804

[Clark]

Rained the fore part of the day I determined to go as far as St. Charles a french Village 7 Leags. up the Missourie, and wait at that place untill Capt. Lewis could finish the business in which he was obliged to attend to at St. Louis and join me by Land from that place 24 miles

I Set out at 4 oClock P.M., in the presence of many of the neighbouring inhabitents, and proceeded on under a jentle brease up the Missouri to the upper Point of the 1st Island 4 Miles and camped on the Island which is Situated Close on the right (or Starboard) Side, and opposit the mouth of a Small Creek called Cold water, a heavy rain this after-noon

MAY 15TH TUESDAY

at 9 oClock Set out and proceeded on 9 miles passed two Islands & incamped on the Starbd. Side at a Mr. Pipers Landing opposet an Island, the Boat run on Logs three times to day, owing her being too heavyly loaded a Sturn, a fair after noon, I saw a number of Goslings to day on the Shore, the water excessively rapid, & Banks falling in.

MAY 16TH WEDNESDAY

pass a remarkable Coal Hill on the Larboard Side, Called by the French Carbonere, this hill appear to Contain great quantity of Coal from this hill the Village of St. Charles may be Seen at 7 miles distance. we arrived at St. Charles at 12 oClock a number Spectators french & Indians flocked to the bank to See the party. This Village is about one mile in length, Situated on the North Side of the Missourie at the foot of a hill from which it takes its name *Peetiete Coete* or the *Little hill* This Village Contns. about 100 houses, the most of them small and indefferent and about 450 inhabitents Chiefly French, those people appear Pore, polite & harmonious.

May 17, Warner and Hall court-martialed and sentenced to 25 lashes for being absent without leave, and Collins to 50 lashes for the same offense aggravated by insubordination. Clark remits sentences of Warner and Hall. Lewis joins the party from St. Louis, May 20.

MAY 21ST 1804 MONDAY

[Clark]

All the forepart of the Day arranging our party and procureing the different articles necessary for them at this place. Set out at half passed three oClock under three Cheers from the gentlemen on the bank and proceeded on to the head of the Island (which is Situated on the Stbd. Side) 3 Miles Soon after we Set out to day a hard Wind from the W.SW accompanied with a hard rain, which lasted with Short intervales all night,

MAY 24TH THURSDAY 1804

passed a verry bad part of the River Called the Deavels race ground, this is where the Current Sets against some projecting rocks for half a Mile on the Labbd. Side, passed between a Isld. and the Lbd. Shore a narrow pass above this Isld. is a verry bad part of the river, We attempted to pass up under the Lbd. Bank which was falling in so fast that the evident danger obliged us to cross betweenn the Starbd Side and a Sand bar in the middle of the river, We *hove* up near the head of the Sand bar, the Same moveing & backing caused us to run on the sand. The Swiftness of the Current Wheeled the boat, Broke our *Toe* rope, and was nearly over Setting the boat, all hands jumped out on the upper Side and bore on that Side untill the Sand washed from under the boat and Wheeled on the next bank by the time She wheeled a 3rd Time got a rope fast to her Stern and by the means of swimmers was Carred to Shore and when her stern was down whilst in the act of Swinging a third time into Deep Water near the Shore, we returned, to the Island where we Set out and assended under the Bank which I have just mentioned, as falling in.

MAY 25TH FRIDAY 1804

Camped at the mouth of a Creek called River a Chouritte, above a Small french Village of 7 houses and as many families, settled at this place to be convt. to hunt, & trade with the Indians, here we met with M. Louisell, imedeately down from the Seeder Isld. Situated in the Country of the Sciox 400 Leagues up he gave us a good Deel of information [and] Some letters he informed us that he Saw no Indians on the river below the *Poncrars*.

TUESDAY 23RD SEPTR. 1806

we rose early took the Chief to the publick store & furnished him with Some clothes &c. took an early breckfast with Colo. Hunt and Set out decended to the Mississippi and down that river to St. Louis at which place we arived about 12 oClock. we Suffered the party to fire off their pieces as a Salute to the Town. we were met by all the village and received a harty welcom from it's inhabitants &c. here I found my old acquaintance Majr. W. Christy who had settled in this town in a public line as a Tavern Keeper. he furnished us with store rooms for our baggage and we accepted of the invitation of Mr. Peter Choteau and took a room in his house. we payed a friendly visit to Mr. August Chotau and some of our old friends this evening. as the post had departed from St. Louis Capt. Lewis wrote a note to Mr. Hay in Kahoka to detain the post at that place untill 12 tomorrow which was reather later than his usial time of leaveing it

WEDNESDAY 24TH OF SEPTEMBER 1806

I sleped but little last night however we rose early and commencd wrighting our letters Capt Lewis wrote one to the presidend and I wrote Govr. Harrison & my friends in Kentucky and Sent of George Drewyer with those letters to Kohoka & delivered them to Mr. Hays &c. we dined with Mr. Chotoux to day, and after dinner went to a store and purchased some clothes, which we gave to a Tayler and derected to be made. Capt. Lewis in opening his trunk found all his papers wet, and some seeds spoiled.

THURSDAY 25TH OF SEPTR. 1806

had all of our skins &c. suned and stored away in a storeroom of Mr. Caddy Choteau. payed some visits of form, to the gentlemen of St. Louis. in the evening a dinner & Ball.

HANNAH LEWIS

HANNAH LEWIS HAS NOT YET been positively traced in the historical records, although she is credited with the authorship of an Indian captivity narrative published by H. Trumbull of Boston in 1817. The title page of Lewis's narrative claims that she and her three children "were taken prisoners by the Indians, near St. Louis on the 25th of May 1815." Lewis's account details both the initial Indian attack on her home, when her husband was killed, and her ensuing abduction and captivity, which lasted more than two years. With the help of her eldest son, who had been adopted by their captors, Lewis eventually escaped and returned to St. Louis.

Indian captivity narratives such as Hannah Lewis's were extremely popular in America during the eighteenth and nineteenth centuries. Literally thousands of narratives were published and many of them were reprinted dozens of times. For scholars, the genre of the Indian captivity narrative is problematic for several reasons, not the least of which is the question of authorship. According to Kathryn Zabelle Derounian-Stodola and James Levernier, in *The Indian Captivity Narrative, 1550–1900*, "Distinguishing historically verifiable first-person accounts from edited or fictionalized ones is often impossible owing to multiple authorial contributions, unclear publishing conditions and copyright, and generic overlap within and between works." Hannah Lewis's narrative is considered by these scholars as typical of those published during the period because of its promotion of anti-Indian stereotyping and its emotional ambivalence toward the captors.

The original copy of Hannah Lewis's narrative is held at the Newberry Library in Chicago, the largest repository of captivity narratives. The following excerpt represents more than half of the text of that document.

FROM *NARRATIVE OF THE CAPTIVITY AND SUFFERINGS OF MRS. HANNAH LEWIS*

My husband, James Lewis, with his family, removed from the State of Georgia, to the neighborhood of St. Louis, in the year 1814. —As we were now in the neighborhood of several tribes of Indians, of whose friendly disposition we had much reason to suspect, my husband, for the first nine months, was induced to reside in the fort of St. Louis, but, the Indians at length feigning themselves more friendly, the habitants imprudently laid by their fears, and thought no more of tomahawks, nor scalping knives. Mr. Lewis now thought it safe to remove, with his family, to a tract of land which he had purchased, situated about six miles from the fort. My husband erected a log hut upon his land, where we peaceably dwelt until the night of the 25th May, 1815, which proved, indeed, a fatal night to us! It was between the hours of twelve and one, when we were all suddenly alarmed by a loud rap at the door. Mr. Lewis hastily slipped on his trowsers and stepped to the door, which he incautiously opened—but by opening the door, he opened a scene, terrible to describe—"Indians!" "Indians!" were the first words I heard him utter, and they were probably the last that he spoke, for in an instant a dozen Tomahawks were hurled at his head, which instantaniously dispatched him. I arose hastily from my bed with an intention of attempting to escape with my helpless infant, but eight months old—but in an instant a crowd of savages, painted and yelling horribly, rushed into my room—I screamed and begged for quarter, but they were deaf to my intreaties—they tore my little infant from my arms, and menacing me with instant death, by their motions, if I attempted resistance, led me out of the house, they next brought out my Son and daughter, the former in the 16th year of his age and the latter in her 10th. —Having pillaged the house of every thing valuable, they set fire to it, and having scalped my unfortunate husband, they threw his lifeless body into the flames!

The savages now hastily bundled up what plunder they could conveniently carry, they gave us a few articles of cloathing, and about 3 o'clock in the morning they set out for their settlement, situated about 120 miles west—Alas! my feelings at this moment cannot be described—my little infant I was compelled to carry in a blanket upon my back—we had neither of us hats nor shoes, nor would they allow my son any other cloathing, but his shirt and trowsers, his hands were tied with a cord, a savage having hold of the end of which, they drove him along like a beast to the slaughter—one savage always marching forward of us, and one in the rear, with their tomahawks uplifted, ready to dispatch us at a single blow, had we attempted an escape.

We, for the first fifteen miles, were compelled to travel upon a trot, the savages being apprehensive that the news of our capture might reach the garrison at St. Louis, in which case a party would probably have been dispatched in pursuit of them. After a tedious travel of nearly twenty miles, the Indians came to a halt—it was in the midst of a dismal swamp—they built a fire and broiled some meat, but of which they gave me, and my poor children, a scanty allowance.—The savages seemed much pleased with their success, conceiving themselves now out of danger, the woods resounded with their savage yells and whoops!—our tarry in this place lasted but about two hours, when the Indians having extinguished their fires, again set forward, and travelling with precipitancy until sunset, when they again halted, and began to prepare a temporary lodging for the night—with nought but the sky for a covering, and the ground for a pillow, the fatigues of the preceeding day obliged me and my poor children to sleep several hours, in spite of the horrors which surrounded us.

In the morning we were roused by sunrise, the Indians struck up a fire and made a little broth for breakfast—after partaking of the meagre fare, we were again compelled to proceed on our journey.

None but mothers can figure to themselves my wretched situation—to travel bareheaded and barefooted with my lovely babe, and my two innocent captive children, through a dismal forest, to unknown regions, was distressing beyond description—the melancholly moans of my little daughter, whom I led by my side, the lementations of my poor unfortunate Son, and the cries of my poor little infant, were such as could not fail to operate upon the feelings of any one but those of an unmerciful cannibal!

On the third day from that of my captivity, my weakness became so great that almost every hour I was compelled to solicit my savage masters the indulgence to permit me to sit down upon a stump or log of a tree for a few moments—the night was a scene of distressing fears to me, as I was almost sure that I should not be enabled to travel the ensuing day, and that the savages would dispatch me with their tomahawks! death, indeed, would have at once put an end to my suffering, but the idea of leaving my helpless babe, and my two other children in the hands of my unfeeling captors, was indeed too distressing to conceive of.—In the morning, half chilled with a cold fog, we were ordered from our place of rest.—I found myself greatly relieved by a tolerable good night's rest, and should have travelled with more ease this day had not my half-starved children and helpless infant, formed a scene, that conveyed severer pangs to the heart, than all the sufferings that I endured myself. We travelled this day about 28 miles, when darkness put an end to our painful day's journey—the night was terrible; the first part was Egyptian darkness, attended with sharp lightning and heavy thunder, while the rain fell in torrents.—I pressed my half perished infant to my breast, but not with the most distant thoughts that I should be enabled to preserve its life till morning.

The morning came, and a bright sun re-animated our drowned spirits—little did I expect that the light of another day would witness the existence of all my children—but the same Providence who had brought us so far, continued our protector—in addition to the famine and fatigue which we had sustained, being deprived of our shoes, the thorns and brambles through which we were compelled to travel, tore our feet to a shocking degree.—Four days had now almost elapsed, since the fatal morn, in which we were taken, and by the blessing of that Providence, whose smiles give life to creation, we were still in existence.—Emaciated by a fit of sickness, and surrounded by my poor distressed and helpless children, despair would have robbed me of life, had I not put my whole confidence in that Being, who alone has power to save.

About sunset we arrived within view of the Indians settlement, for which place we were destined, The number of our captors was eleven, two of whom were dispatched to their village, to announce the glad tidings of our arrival.—The savages now halted to prepare us agreeable to their mode of decorating their captives, previous to their introduction to their village—they daubed us with vermillion mixed with bear's grease—when they had arrived, within hearing of their brethren, the atmosphere soon resounded with whoops, yells, shrieks and screams, frightful beyond description—as soon as we reached the skirts of the village, we were met by a throng of savages, of all ages and sexes, who paraded on the right and left, and formed a lane through which we were to pass! the Indians at this moment seizing each of us by the hand, and ordering us to sing the war song, began their march through the gaunlet—the men, women and children on each side being armed with sticks and bludgeons, we experienced the severest beating from these inhuman monsters as we passed—my poor son was so beat over the head and face, as to have scarcely any remains of life—happy might it have been for us had their cruel usage at this time put an end to our sufferings; but our tormentors took care that none of the blows that they thus inflicted should prove mortal, as they wished to reserve us for more severe inflictions.

After having undergone this introductory discipline, my little babe was tore from me, and given to an aged squaw, who the day before had lost her own—in like manner we were all seperated and conveyed to different wigwams in the village—my little daughter begged that she might be permitted to accompany me, but a frightful looking savage at this instant approached her with an uplifted tomahawk compelled her to leave me.—My house was not the most agreeable, a miserable wigwam without a floor, with a fire in the centre, a few burch bark dishes to eat from, and tools for cookery made clumsily of wood, for furniture—such was my place of residence, which the reader cannot imagine could be very pleasing to one accustomed to civilized life.

My loathsome dwelling was not however what gave me the most uneasiness—to be seperated perhaps, forever, from my poor children, my helpless babe, caused much more painful sensations—surrounded by unmerciful savages, there was none to afford me consolation; whenever so overcome with grief that I could not refrain from weeping, I was sure to be used with much greater severity by my savage master, and his not less unfeeling squaw—if I intreated them to permit me to see my little babe once more, they would exultingly reply that "they had given my papoose to their dogs, reserving only the scalp, which they would procure and hang up in their cabin, where I might view it every day!"—Mothers, who are possessed of children, can only judge what my feelings must be at the recital of such heart piercing tidings.

No pains were spared by the savage monsters to inflict me by every means that their inventive faculties could give birth to—some times they would tell me that my two oldest children were to be burnt the next day, and that I would be compelled to be a spectator to witness the tragic scene—the next day we would accordingly set out (as I supposed) for that purpose, but when they had arrived at a suitable place where the thorns and briars grew most, they would divest me of my moccasins, and compel me to sing and dance barefooted an hour among them!—if the wounds which they inflicted caused me to weep, it would seem to afford them the greater satisfaction—in broken English they would tell me that they were teaching me how to dance round my children while they were burning!

Three long months did I pass with these vile, unmerciful savages, without being permitted once to see either of my poor children, or to know whether they had actually fallen victims to savage barbarity. At the expiration of this time, as I was one day employed in pounding samp, the old squaw, to whose lot my infant had fallen, entered with it wrapped in a wolf's skin—the little sufferer unaccustomed to Indian diet, it appeared, had sickened and was about to escape savage cruelty by returning to the merciful God who gave it—the old squaw alarmed at the prospect of losing her little captive, had been induced to return it to me, in hopes that nourishment from its mother's breast might revive it—three months had elapsed since it was torn from my bosom, yet when it was brought to me, it manifested evident signs that it had not forgotten its mother—when the old squaw attempted to take it from me, it screeched aloud and clung to my breast! my sufferings had deprived me of the power to nurse it, and it was carried away by the old squaw in the same situation that it was brought. I never saw it afterward.

Eleven months now passed since the unfortunate day of my capture, and I yet remained the wretched victim of savage brutality! Were I to record every act of cruelty exercised toward me, by these savage monsters, who claimed me as their property, it would swell a volume to a much larger size. I began to despair of ever again enjoying my liberty, or ever being enabled to hear whether my poor children, like myself, were spinning out their lives in bitter captivity. In one of my most gloomy moments as I was sitting one day meditating upon my most wretched situation, I was suddenly aroused by a tremendious Indian whoop at the door of the wigwam—it proceeded from a class of Indians that had just returned from one of their hunting excursions—my master invited them into his wigwam, where they had stopped for refreshment—as they entered, I sit with my head inclined downward, my eyes fixed stedfast upon the ground, nor did I raise them; till I was suddenly clasped round my neck by some one, exclaiming "my mother!" "my mother!"—it was my son!—"Gracious Heaven!" was all I could utter—I clasped his hand, but mingled emotions of joy and grief, forbid me utterance for a considerable time.—Never could I have imagined that so short a period could have caused such an alteration in the appearance of my dear child—his appearance was truly savage, having been taken into favour by one of the Chiefs, he had been persuaded to adopt their mode of dress, manners, &c.

As he had become a favorite of the Savages and adopted in one of their families as one of their own tribe he was no longer considered as a prisoner but enjoyed his liberty in common with the rest—he was permitted to converse with me, and gave me a minute account of his sufferings, and the cruelty exercised toward him by his savage masters, during the first three months of his captivity—his story was truly affecting, it was this:—that after our separation, he was conveyed by four or five Indians to a neighboring village, at the entering of which, he underwent a beating similar to one which he had before experienced—he was next bound hand and foot to a tree, where he concluded they intended to leave him to perish, as they there suffered him to remain twelve hours without food or drink of any kind—from the tree, half dead, he was conveyed to an old wigwam, and delivered in charge of two young Indians, with whom he was given to understand he must remain until the return of their principal chiefs, (who were then out on an expedition against some of the white settlements,) when his fate would be decided—from these two savages he received the most brutal treatment which they could possibly inflict, without destroying life—his food was the offal of wild animals, as the country abounded with, and even this was denied him until after it had remained in a putrified state for some days!—his bedding was still worse, it was a rotten elk skin, covered with vermin!—when his savage masters left their wigwam, for the purpose of hunting, or fishing, they secured him by binding him with withes to a tree, where he sometimes was obliged to remain for two or three days, without food and exposed to the weather!

At the expiration of three months, the chiefs who were to decide his fate, arrived, bringing with them a number of human scalps, and five white prisoners, four men and one woman—A council was immediately called, by whom it was decided that my son with the white woman should be adopted by one of the chiefs, and admitted into his family—by two young warriors they were accordingly immediately unbound and set at liberty.

But, with regard to the other four unfortunate captives, how different was their fate—four of their party, it appeared had been killed by the whites in the expedition, and their friends demanded that the lives of the four captives should atone for their loss, preparations was immediately made to put them to death according to their savage custom—my son was compelled to witness the tragic scene!—the dreadful sentence was no sooner passed, than the whole village set up the death cry,—the unfortunate captives were stripped, and two posts being fastened with withes to two cross pieces, which extended from one post to the other, one about two feet from the ground, the other about six feet higher:—the prisoners being stripped naked, the savages first daubed their whole bodies with pitch!—they then commenced their barbarities by cutting off their fingers and toes, joint by joint!—the poor victims were now surrounded by almost every man, woman and child of the village, every one of whom had liberty to torture them in whatever manner they pleased, each striving to exceed the other in cruelty!—the savages having sufficiently satisfied themselves with the cruelties which they had inflicted in this way, the almost lifeless bodies of the unfortunate captives were then enclosed with dry bark, to which they set fire, which soon reduced them to ashes!

My more fortunate son, after his fate was determined, was taken by the hand, and led to the cabin of the chief, into whose family he was to be adopted, where he was received with all imaginable marks of kindness. He was treated as a son; and apparently they loved and regarded him as if he had been one of their own children—the eight months he had been with him, he had learned much of their language, and had adopted their mode of dressing and painting himself. He had attended them in many of their hunting excursions, and had become a tolerable marksman with the bow and arrow. Since he had obtained his liberty, he had many times solicited permission of the chief, with whom he resided, to visit the nation who held his mother and sisters in bondage, in search of us, but never had been enabled to gain his consent—happily, he now unexpectedly had the good fortune to meet with me. When I gave him an account of the treatment which I had received from the savages, he wept bitterly, declaring that at the risk of his life, he would soon attempt to effect his own, and my escape, from the hands of such unmerciful barbarians—this he thought he should be enabled to effect, when he should make his next hunting excursion with the Indians, who reposing confidence in him, permitted him to wander any where in the woods, unattended by any one.

The Indian whoop or yell in token of their readiness to depart, was given by the commanding chief, when my dear son was obliged to take his leave of me, with only adding "my dear mother I shall not forget you, hold yourself in readiness, for when you little expect it, I may call for you to accompany me to St. Louis, or some other christian settlement."

The parting with my son was as sorrowful as our meeting had been happy—while he in a great measure enjoyed his liberty, I was still held a miserable captive, subject to the controul of those who were never more pleased than when they saw me most afflicted!—O what a great consolation would it have afforded me, could I have had a similar interview with my two other dear children, and to have learned that they were as well provided for—but with regard to their wellfare, I was yet to remain in awful suspence. . . .

Nearly two years now passed since I was forced from my peaceable habitation, conveyed to a wild wilderness, and retained by an unmerciful race of beings, as their lawful prisoner!—as ten months passed without again seeing my son, I harboured fears that he had either given up the idea of attempting an escape, or that he more probably had been detected in the attempt, and had fallen a victim to savage fury and rage!

While one day busily engaged in meditating on my wretched condition, and that of my still more wretched offspring, an Indian (as I then supposed) frightfully painted, and with a horrid yell, entered my master's wigwam—perceiving me seated at one corner, he approached me, and with all the frightful grimances peculiar to a savage, he brandished his long knife around my head, expressing at the same time to my master, with his permission, a willingness to take my scalp!—for my own part I can truly say, that at this moment, I felt all that horror which a miserable captive must feel, when about to fall a victim to savage barbarity!—but, reader, guess my surprize, when expecting every moment to receive the fatal blow, to feel the lips of one whom I supposed would soon be my executioner, applied to my ear, and with a whisper, utter these words:—"mother be not terrified, it is your William, prepare for your deliverance!"—I started as if an angel spoke—I ventured once more to raise my eyes, to examine more minutely, the terrific visage—a smile was fixed thereupon, and the features no longer rendered unnatural by voluntary distortion, became now familiar to me!—Gracious Heaven! it was—my Son!—an assenting nod was all the reply I dare make.

My son now, in the true character of a savage, gave the Indian farewell whoop and departed. By my master he was recognized to be an adopted white prisoner, pleased with a savage life, but not as my son, who ten months before had visited his wigwam. As the savage dreamed of no design, I was permitted as usual to lie at night at the entrance of the wigwam, unguarded;—about twelve, three heavy blows with a hatchet upon a hallow tree nearby, announced the approach of my son—it was the signal—from the hut I withdrew with cautious steps until I was received in the arms of my deliverer—seizing my hand, he hurried me to a thick swamp, which we penetrated for many miles—by his frequent excursions with the Savages, he had obtained a knowledge of the wilderness, even to the white settlements, which proved of the greatest advantage to us—without meeting with a single Savage to molest us, or any thing to retard our flight, in five days we safely arrived at the fort of St. Louis.

ROSE PHILIPPINE DUCHESNE

BORN IN GRENOBLE, FRANCE, to a wealthy family, Rose Philippine Duchesne (1769–1852) rebelled against her parents' wish that she marry well, instead choosing to lead an activist religious life. In the 1790s, Duchesne worked for the underground Catholic Church, risking her life to minister to imprisoned priests and teach cathecism to children. In 1804, Duchesne joined the fledgling Society of the Sacred Heart, which provided her with the opportunity to do missionary work in the New World.

In 1818, when she was forty-eight years old, Duchesne came to the United States at the invitation of Bishop Louis DuBourg of New Orleans, who sought assistance in revitalizing parishes from New Orleans to St. Louis. In the fall of that year, Duchesne established the first free school west of the Mississippi in St. Charles, Missouri, and a tuition-based girls' academy, among whose students were relatives of St. Louis's social elite. A year later, Duchesne and the nuns were transferred to Florissant, where they built a new school and novitiate. In 1827, Duchesne established the Academy of the Sacred Heart in St. Louis, the city's first orphanage for girls, which merged with Villa Duchesne in 1968. In addition to the schools she started in the St. Louis area, Duchesne founded three schools in New Orleans. Today, there are more than a dozen schools and several colleges in the United States that owe their existence to Duchesne's devotion and tireless efforts.

In the last decade of her life, Duchesne finally had the opportunity to fulfill her lifelong dream and work with Indians. In 1841, she traveled with Jesuit missionary Father Pierre DeSmet to Sugar Creek, Kansas, and lived among the Potowatomi, who called her Quah-kah-ka-num-ad, the *"Woman-Who-Prays-Always."* In 1852, at the age of eighty-two, Duchesne died at the society's house in St. Charles, where she was buried. The Roman Catholic Church canonized Rose Philippine Duchesne in 1988.

Many of the following letters, written by Duchesne while she was in the St. Louis area, were sent to Mother Barat, Mother Superior at the Sacred Heart convent near Grenoble. The letters reflect Duchesne's concern with everyday problems—shortage of food and provisions, climatic hardships, financial constraints, enrollment at the schools, and various social issues.

OCTOBER 8, 1818

[TO MOTHER BARAT]

. . . Divine Providence has brought us to the remotest village in the United States. It is situated on the Missouri, which is frequented only by those trading with the Indians who live not very far away from here, but I have not seen any little Indian girls since we came here. . . . Against this race there is not the same prejudice as there is against *Negroes* and *mulattoes*. Monseigneur Du Bourg has said positively that we may not admit them to either of our schools [boarding or free], and he has appointed one day a week for the instruction of the colored people; otherwise, he says, we should not hold the white children in school. He told us of an experience he had in the college in Baltimore, which shows how difficult it is to overcome race-prejudice in this country. He consulted the Archbishop of Baltimore on the matter and was told that this attitude would have to be maintained as the last safeguard of morality and manners in this country.

. . . A few years ago . . . one might have witnessed conduct comparable to pagan bacchanalia: girls scantily clad, holding a bottle of whisky in one hand and a man with the other, dancing every day of the year and never doing any work. Now there is more exterior decency, but these people are as ignorant of morality as the Indians are. In our free school we now have twenty-two children, and in proportion to the population this equals a school of one hundred in France. These children have never heard of our Lord, of His birth or His death, nor of hell, and they listen open-mouthed to our instructions. I have to say to them continually, "Yes, this is really true." All except two are learning the alphabet. Among the children who pay a little fee there is the same ignorance. When we complain to the Bishop that we have no savages, he replies: "Indeed you have, and your work among these children will be wider and more lasting because of the influence of the rich over the poor."

NOVEMBER 20, 1818

[TO MOTHER BARAT]

. . . Living in this remote corner of the world, cut off by the Mississippi and the Missouri rivers, I do not know whether you have received a single one of the letters we have written, but I have had the inexpressible consolation of receiving several from you. . . .

Among all the things we shall need and those I have already asked for, the essentials are such as may keep us alive. . . . We look on potatoes and cabbage as you in France regard rare delicacies. . . . The gift of a pound of butter and a dozen eggs is like a fortune received. . . . During the hunting season, which we are in now, we can procure venison and ducks, but in the spring and summer one can get only salted fish and meat. Many of the cows are almost dry. . . . If we have to buy milk, it costs twelve cents a bottle, and fifteen cents in winter. And with all the salt diet we lack water. The well in our garden is dry and it costs twelve cents every time we send someone to the Missouri to get us two little buckets of water.

DECEMBER 1818

[TO MOTHER THÉRÈSE MAILLUCHEAU IN FRANCE]

. . . I do not know how to describe the place in which we live. Its population is made up of a mixture of American emigrants from the East, French and Canadian Creoles, German, Irish, and Flemish settlers, along with half-breeds. . . . As for real Indians, we never see them because the Americans from the East are pushing them out and making war with them. They are withdrawing further away. . . . We would attract them more quickly with liquor than with sermons. . . . But in conscience no one should give it to them, seeing what a state it puts them in and how dangerous it makes them. God allows some faint light of religion to shine amongst them and bring about conversions, but these are very rare. . . .

We have had the privilege of doing without bread and water. I had expected the former privation, but I never dreamed that on the banks of the Missouri we should lack water with such an abundant flow of it in sight. . . . The Missouri is almost frozen over, and it is so cold that the water freezes beside the fire. . . . We have logs, but they are too large, and there is no one to chop them for us and no saw with which we might cut them ourselves. Laziness is the vice of this region; it belongs to the way of life. People work only when obliged to do so, and pride keeps many from working for wages. . . . We should also value a case of altar wine and one of olive oil—the only edible oil to be had here is bear grease, which is disgusting. . . . I do not see how we shall survive Lent with only fish cooked without either butter or oil, and not an egg to be had till spring. But we are willing and glad to be in want.

FEBRUARY 15, 1819

[TO MOTHER BARAT]

. . . If our sisters in France imagine us surrounded by savages, they are quite mistaken. I have seen only a few old ones who made their first Communion at fifty or sixty years of age, when temptations to passions had passed. But to compensate for our disappointment we have new employments: we dig in the garden, carry out the manure, water the cow, clean out her little stable. . . . And we do all this with as much joy as we would have if we were teaching Indians, for God wills it this way, and our poverty, along with the false pride of the settlers, prevents us from getting servants.

JANUARY 4, 1823

[TO MOTHER BARAT]

. . . There is no denying the fact that temptations are great in St. Louis, and it adds to our distress to realize what we have to fear for the girls who are still in our school. I consider St. Louis as bad as Malacca in the days of St. Xavier. After a short period of fervor, or rather effervescence, there has followed a time of great indifference as regards religion and of excess in the pursuit of pleasure. Our children are taken to balls, shows, speeches, have bad books in their hands, live in idleness. Already several vocations have been undermined in these surroundings, and I foresee that here, as in the time of Jesus Christ, the poor will be chosen to work for Him in preference to the rich.

DECEMBER 28, 1823

[TO HER SISTER, AMÉLIE DE MAUDUIT]

. . . The village in which we live is five leagues from St. Louis, the principal town in the new state of Missouri, and about the same distance from

St. Charles, our first place of residence, which has been for some time the capital of the State. . . . Our convent is built of brick and joins the newly erected parish church. . . . Monseigneur gave the land for the church and made us a gift of the property we own, consisting of a big meadow, a small woodland along a creek, and a garden with a courtyard and a pasture for our animals. We have about 100 chickens, 7 cows, 1 horse. We do not have to buy feed for the animals—we just open the gate and let them out; in the evening they all return to exactly the same gate without shepherd or shepherdess. I forgot to mention our five lambs and sheep and some very handsome geese. In good weather all the livestock graze in the common fields and woods, and in winter these animals have no shelter except a shed covered with thatch.

JUNE 10, 1824

[TO MOTHER BARAT]

. . . Government aid for the civilization of the savages will be given only after the work has been undertaken. Then the missionaries must follow the plan outlined by the Secretary of War in what regards both the boys and the girls. As the Father Rector cannot take the latter group, we hope to do so, trusting in the help of Divine Providence. Food will cost very little; we have a place to house them; and we shall beg clothing for them. The chief agent of Congress for treating with the tribes in this part of the country approves of this plan. He is going to Washington and will see whether the Secretary of War is willing to appropriate money for the traveling expenses of some more of our religious to help with this work. That would be an unprecedented favor for Indian girls, and the agent has little hope of obtaining it. But we must do everything in our power to further this important work which has been the object of so many prayers, which really brought us here, and which is in itself so interesting and offers us more hope of success than anything else does. . . .

If my skin were worth any money, I should willingly sacrifice it to support our missions.

JULY 25, 1824

[TO MOTHER BARAT]

. . . The five Indian boys the Fathers have give them a great deal of trouble now . . .

I do not know when we shall be able to take the Indian girls. We are all eager to do so, but this has been a year of disasters. The Missouri has flooded to a great width and carried off the farmhouses and cattle of many settlers and ruined the crops. There will be almost no grain or vegetables, and we shall soon have only three or four pupils. . . .

Here at Florissant we are no longer afraid of starving to death, and that is something.

DECEMBER 27, 1825

[TO MOTHER BARAT]

. . . The policy of the United States government is to drive all the Indians out of the settled states. Agents buy their lands and push them into uninhabited regions. The chiefs say: You are stronger; we must give way to you—and they withdraw, but not without great suffering, for they have not enough room for hunting. The Sac tribe has made a treaty with the government and reserved a large area of land . . . outside the present territory of the United States. The head man there would be glad to have a priest in residence, but the people are so poor, they could not assure him a living. . . . The Osage are farther away and much more savage, for they have not been brought into contact with ideas of the true religion as have the tribes near Canada. Take this matter to heart, Reverend Mother, and may all turn out well.

MARCH 1, 1827

[TO MOTHER BARAT]

. . . After making many inquiries, I realized that we should need at least 30,000 francs on hand in order to procure a house in St. Louis as good as this one, that we could not count [on others for help]. . . . So I wrote to Mr. Mullanphy, asking him if he would not give us a house, as he owns a great many, and that on favorable conditions in view of our intention of opening a free school for the children of the poor. He answered by asking in turn how many orphans we would house on the following conditions: 1. that he would give us a brick house built about seven years ago, situated at a distance of a fifteen-minute walk from the Catholic church with 24 arpents of land around it . . . the house having 12 fairly large rooms, but not being as large as our convent here; 2. that he or his heirs would give each orphan at her entrance the sum of 50 francs for her bed, etc., and 25 francs yearly for clothing; and 3. that he would give 5000 francs cash for the initial expenses of the foundation. I replied that we would accept 15 or 20 orphans; he wanted 20, and they were to be presented by himself or his oldest daughters.

I went to inspect the house and found the site somewhat similar to that of Ste. Marie, though less attractive. It is high, solitary, and in a healthful location overlooking the Mississippi and the city, from which it is well removed. It seemed to me we should be going against our own best interests to refuse this offer. True, we are taking on a burden for which we shall be responsible, but think of a debt of 20 or 30 thousand francs, or the necessity of being confined to a village where we are shut in by six feet of water up to our door five or six times a year, and that quite suddenly and with such force as to wash away the bridge leading to our house, to flatten all our fences, to destroy our entire garden, which has produced nothing these last two years, as the vegetables have rotted in the water. Besides that, there is the probability that if we do not take the lead someone else may do so, and we shall be without any means of supporting ourselves. Are not these facts worth taking into consideration?

You counseled me to ask advice, and I did so. At first the Father Rector was opposed to the plan, then he thought better of it, though he was not enthusiastic. . . . I told him that you considered an establishment in St. Louis necessary, that you had told me to make plans for it, and that this should come before any other undertaking. The other Jesuit Father is wholly in favor of the St. Louis foundation. So I accepted, and things are getting under way. . . . It was impossible for me to wait for an answer from you in this matter, as several parties were interested in the property—and how could I say when your answer would reach us, with the dangers and delays of sea travel? I am sorry you are not sending a good superior. . . . The people of St. Louis would certainly appreciate a religious who is American in both language and character. No other nation in the world admires itself as this one does. . . . I cling to the thought that the religious who are coming are younger than I and may be able to learn the language and customs of the country.

I think it best for me to go to St. Louis for the foundation. The position might offer some dangers for others, as it is unwise to be too friendly at first with people, lest one make undesirable intimacies. Then, too, there are many well-educated people in St. Louis, and some of our religious might not make a good impression.

SPRING 1828

[TO WILLIAM CARR LANE, THE MAYOR OF ST. LOUIS]

I have recourse to your authority for the redress of an abuse which I look upon as very much against the welfare of our establishment. You know, Sir, that our young ladies, day schollars, . . . have to pass the creek that runs all around our house. The warm weather invites a number of men and boys to swimming in the creek, and every day our young ladies meet with that disagreeable sight, both coming [to] and leaving the house; and as I understand that some regulation of court forbids swimming in public places, I suppose that it is merely by some negligence of the sheriffs in discharge of their duty that it takes place.

As you are Sir, the father of an amiable family I need not say how much that rudeness is against the delicacy of sentiments we strive to endow our young ladies with, and I am convinced that you will be so good as to use your power to remove that obstacle.

MAY 18, 1830

[TO MOTHER BARAT]

We have had the cross of poverty this year to such an extent as to prohibit us from writing to you, as we had not the money to spare for the postage and were not able to get some mail out of the post office for the same reason. The convents at St. Ferdinand and St. Louis have often been several days without a penny, and we have had to pretend that things were otherwise, so as not to lose credit at the stores. At last, however, Mother Eugenie wrote me to draw on her for the money which you were so good as to instruct her to give us . . . We have such scanty resources—eight boarding pupils, twenty-seven people to feed, nineteen of them to support entirely, and 1250 francs to be paid to the hired man. The eighteen day pupils who pay tuition have kept us alive this winter. Day pupils also support St. Charles, where there is only 1 boarding pupil, along with several orphans who are cared for gratis . . .

We have sixty children in the free school, and within a year that school will have given us four postulants.

APRIL 22, 1852

[TO MOTHER BARAT]

I was astonished and greatly consoled on receiving your letter. Since Easter of last year I have not been expecting to live through another twelve months; especially during last summer there were times when I could not even write my own name. When the weather got cool, that gave me back some strength, but my memory has been failing more and more, and also my eyesight. . . .

The charity of our Mother Superior is a wonderful example for all. She sleeps in the same room with me, and this gives her an opportunity to exercise her charity. She has also had still more opportunities because of the illness and death of one of our Sisters and a pupil. . . .

We have enrolled a good number of new pupils, but we cannot take more than thirty-five without being greatly overcrowded and risking fresh cases of illness. There is real need for an addition to the building; and since I am so useless, I have begged God to take me to Himself, as that would give place for two more people. . . .

My letter is very badly written, but I cannot see to rewrite it. I have strength, however, to kneel in spirit at your feet to receive your blessing with all possible love and respect in the Heart of Jesus.

ANGUS UMPHRAVILLE

ANGUS UMPHRAVILLE claimed to have been born in Philadelphia in 1798. Sketchy historical records indicate that Umphraville spent a portion of his childhood in England and was educated there. At the outbreak of the War of 1812, he declined to join the British Army but was determined to come to America. After surviving a mutinous voyage, he arrived in Baltimore in the winter of 1816–17, penniless and desperate to earn a living. Umphraville began writing for a living and soon was commissioned by local booksellers to write a poem about the British attack on Baltimore, which appeared in 1817 as *The Siege of Baltimore, and Other Original Poems*, Umphraville began making his way west. His surviving publications leave the most reliable trail of his course and indicate that he traveled through Pittsburgh and Corydon, Indiana.

Umphraville most likely arrived in St. Louis in late 1820 or early 1821. *Missourian Lays, and Other Western Ditties* was published in the spring of 1821 by Isaac N. Henry & Co. of St. Louis. This seventy-two-page volume was the first book of original poetry published west of the Mississippi. Umphraville, who was but twenty-three years old at the time of the book's publication, dedicated his work to William Clark, stating, "I have chosen to dedicate to you, the first volume of original poems ever published in Missouri, and which perhaps but for your fostering care had never appeared." Umphraville's name does not appear in John Paxton's 1821 St. Louis city directory, indicating that his stay in the city was most likely brief.

Although the few critics who have commented on Umphraville's poetry have unilaterally criticized it as crude and lacking in artistry, they concur that his verse possesses a guileless awe of the region's natural wonders, as well as an energetic quality that characterizes those drawn to western exploration. The following three poems from *Missourian Lays* appear here through the cooperation of the St. Louis Mercantile Library, which holds one of the few existing copies of Umphraville's book.

LINES WRITTEN ON THE BANK OF THE MISSISSIPPI

Respectfully inscribed as an humble tribute of American respect to the poetical genius of Lord George Byron.

Lo! the great river, "FATHER OF THE FLOODS!"
Its turbid tide through prairies and woods,
Pours onward, swelling, boiling, whirling, strong,
Or deep and rapid, shallow now, and slow,
The muddy waters to the Atlantic flow,
Far from its native lake diffus'd away
In golden Mexico's isle sprinkled Bay.
Th' antartic regions, and the northern pole,
May freeze its waves, its softness may control.
Say, if thou canst, drops from its primal spring,
Ere the first Sabbath blest Creation's King.
Do not now wash the shores of distant Greece,
Mingling with waters where the Golden Fleece
By Jason's art in Argonautic pride
Was borne triumphant, and the waves defy'd?
Say, if thou can'st, they lave not now the shores
Of Italy, which arms and arts deplores,
Where gloomy bigotry enchains the mind,
And petty, haughty tyrants tramp mankind;
Which Freedom fled, when all his troubles past,
The patriot Cato nobly breathed his last?
Say, if thou canst, no Mississippi wave
The Gates of Hercules, or Egypt lave,
Or Ithaca, immortal as the fame
Of heav'nly Homer's, or Ulysses' name?
Say, if thou canst, by water spouts obtain'd
None roll'd in clouds, or on Parnassus rain'd?
That none e'er kiss'd the sainted Emerald Isle,
Fam'd Albin's land, where all the Muses smile;
That none e'er foam'd where snow clift Albion thron'd,
Views with her countless ships the ocean crown'd;

Listens enraptur'd while her Byron sings
To magic music from the silver strings
Of that fam'd harp which Orpheus own'd of yore,
Now wildly trembling to romantic lore?
Father of Floods! another race shall view
A Thebes, a Memphis, by the waters blue.
New Tyres, and Londons on thy banks shall rise,
And o'er their tow'rs the banners of the skies
Wav'd by the breeze shall float in billowy pride
Where plenty, peace, and commerce shall reside.

THE OLD MAID OF ST. LOUIS

A TALE

A tall old maid, who long had tarried,
When wither'd quite, would fain be married;
She dress'd, perfum'd, wore many a jewel,
But all mankind seem'd wondrous cruel.
In vain she smil'd, and talked of rings,
And look'd the smartest am'rous things;
Paraded ev'ry street in vain,
Not one poor suitor could she gain;
Yet oft at eve in female ear,
She whisper'd of a dandy dear
Who swore he lov'd her to excess—
More than one language could express!
And if she would but marry then,
He'd be the happiest of men!
If not, with pistols he'd blow out
His brains, and scatter them about.
To think for her his heart did bleed
She own'd she pitied him indeed!
"But I've so many suitors, bless me!

So many flatterers who caress me!
I fear they'll tease me out of life,
Each wishing me to be his wife."
Mark well! old maids are giv'n to lying,
When for a suitor they are dying;
And will pretend they have a host
Of suitors, when not one they boast;
Those who believe their tales are fools,
For arrant lies are old maids' tools.
Her arts were vain, e'en though the fair
With jetty wig hid her grey hair;
At length she curs'd all males on earth,
And sigh'd t' enjoy the second birth!
Sudden, quite solemn grew her face,
She talk'd of judgment, sin, and grace,
She shriek'd in chapel, sometimes fainted,
Till methodists believ'd her sainted;
She soon began to pray aloud,
While groans respond the list'ning crowd.
She then a certain parson saw,
Who overturn'd the moral law;
Told her that grace might much abound,
She must by sin be compassed round;
If she to carnal crime would bow,
The light of heav'n would brighter glow!
She heard and own'd his doctrine wise,
And soon exposed before him lies,
A pious maid in all her charms!
A pious sister fill'd his arms!
Oft they the rosy bliss renew'd,
Oft pray'd that Satan be subdued.
Now psalms they sung, and now they kiss'd,
Who would not sham the Methodist?

It happen'd on a holy-day,
The pious pair were at their play;
Their rapt'rous couch was 'neath a tree,
Sacred to hypocricy;
When silent marching, free from fears,
Drew nigh a corps of volunteers!
The pseudo-christian and the maid,
Both in unseemly posture laid,
Struck full the laughing soldiers' eyes,
And were beheld with great surprise;
Whilst the two, intent on myst'ry,
Thought themselves safe from every eye.
Hark! heard ye not the musket's roar,
Echo round Mississippi's shore?
O! see you not the pious start
From rapture's couch with beating heart,
And faces red as flames of hell!

What modest muse can dare to sing
Of any base immodest thing?
My muse would blush to sing outright
What struck the laughing soldier's sight;
How look the low detected pair,
The wicked priest, and grey-hair'd fair!

Let not sarcastic bach'lors grin,
For they are all inclin'd to sin;
Of them some tales may I relate,
And at no very distant date.
If, as satiric minstrels tell,
Old maids lead apes in droves round h—ll,
Milk jenny cats with fingers sore,
In h—ll for ever evermore.
Old bachelors, misters! tis no fable,
Are made to clean the devil's stable.

THE AFFAIR OF ST. LOUIS

Perplex'd among beauties, his passions on fire,
His heart in his breast, but his soul in his lyre,
A poet, enchanted, survey'd all the fair
Of St. Louis assembled, and Cupid was there!
Rosy Cupid, little Cupid, sly Cupid was there!
He call'd o'er the names of the charmers aloud,
And each answer'd the call from the beautiful crowd.

I. CUPID'S CATALOGUE

Amelia, beautiful and tender,
Julianne, languishing and slender,
Lucina lovely, little maid,
Whose charms the hearts of all invade;
Pretty Elizabeth, whose look
Many a gazer's heart has took;
Charming Sophronia, Cupid's child;
Phyllis, coquettish, careless, wild,
Constance, lovely as the morn;
Lydia, who auburn curls adorn;
Harriot, lovely as the day,
Blooming as the month of May,
Celia sprightly and sincere;
Ellen, to the Muses dear;
Betsy, whose bright sloe-black eyes,
Rival stars which gem the skies;
Mary, matchless, debonaire,
With rosy lips, and radiant hair;
Nymph of love-inspiring eye,
For whom a thousand lovers sigh!
Cath'rine, of angelic form;
Sophy, who takes all hearts by storm;

Julia, with cheeks of roses' hue,
Sally, with eyes divinely blue;
Elvira, beauty's daughter she
Inspirer of lovers' rivalry:
Emily, bashful, and retir'd,
By all who know her, lov'd, desir'd,
Of angel form, and looks divine,
The darling of the sacred Nine,
Apollo's and Minerva's child,
By charming Poësy beguil'd;
To heav'nly themes who strikes the lyre,
And sets enraptur'd hearts on fire!

Cupid, the god, having call'd o'er his list,
Flew round the parterre, ev'ry fair flow'r kiss'd;
Today, said his godship, we keep fancy's feast
In the Temple of Love, and I am high-priest.
I've aim'd at yon poet full many a dart,
Now, ladies, examine the state of his heart.

From his bosom the heart of the minstrel leap'd out,
And on its inspection, what a titler and rout!
On the altar of love, as it lay pierc'd and bleeding,
For on it, indeed, was a great deal of reading;
All the names of Love's List, by the rosy god's art
Were transcrib'd, word for word, and engrav'd on this heart!
So the belles, quite incens'd, would not grant him one kiss,
But drove him away from the mansion of bliss;
He begg'd for his heart, but they turn'd a deaf ear,
And left him in mis'ry, without a compeer.
    Now, therefore, attend ev'ry girl in the nation,
The Poet, bereft, now makes

II. PROCLAMATION

WHEREAS, the charming ladies gay
Of St. Louis, have stolen away
A minstrel's fort and tender heart,
Pierc'd through and through by Cupid's dart
Notice is hereby given, whoe'er
Among the sweet Missourian fair,
Shall to its lawful lord once more
His bleeding heart again restore,
She shall receive ten thousand kisses,
And be enrich'd by other blisses,
But if she gives her own instead,
To Hymen's altar shall be led
By me, and all the world may know it,
Who signs himself
  THE HEART-ROBB'D POET.

GOTTFRIED DUDEN

GOTTFRIED DUDEN (1785–1855), born to an upper-class Prussian family, received a classical education and turned to a career in the civil service. In 1823, with his native region experiencing severe economic hardship from the Napoleonic Wars, Duden journeyed to America with the hope of locating a desirable site for German emigration. Duden arrived in St. Louis in October 1824 and was enchanted with the region. He purchased more than 270 acres of land in present-day Warren County and made an attempt at farming for several years. In 1829, after returning to Europe, Duden published fifteen hundred copies of *Report on a Journey to the Western States of North America*, in which he praises Missouri as an optimum site for German settlement. According to James W. Goodrich, in his introduction to the 1980 edition of Duden's *Report*, the account "helped appreciably to create a favorable climate of public opinion concerning the interior of America, particularly Missouri."

Unfortunately, German settlers found the conditions in Missouri much harsher than portrayed in Duden's romanticized account. By the early 1830s, Duden found himself the brunt of scathing criticism, with his detractors scornfully referring to Missouri as "Duden's Eden."

After spending several years writing defenses of his work, Duden returned to his law practice and forsook efforts to promote German emigration.

Beautifully written in a personal letter format, Duden's *Report* contains detailed descriptions of the St. Louis area's lush indigenous vegetation, rich soil, mineral deposits, Indian populations, and unique archaeological features. In addition, Duden included an all-important postscript to Germans contemplating emigration, in which he offers practical advice regarding the essentials for newcomers settling in the St. Louis region.

FROM *REPORT ON A JOURNEY TO THE WESTERN UNITED STATES OF NORTH AMERICA*

MAY 1826

Surely you must think it strange that in all my former letters I have devoted scarcely a syllable to the Indians. But who in Germany would believe that one could live for years on the distant Missouri without being visited by Indians a single time? Because of various reports about them, they had been the chief cause of my concern for peace in the countryside. But I must tell you that no Indian has been seen in my neighborhood for perhaps ten years. To be sure, almost every week groups of them come down the Missouri River in order to exchange wares in St. Louis or to collect annuities for relinquished areas and then return by land; but they do not leave the direct route and they are seen only there. I met a number of Sacs in the neighborhood of St. Charles where they had set up their tents. One often sees Indians in St. Louis: sometimes Osage, sometimes Kansas, sometimes members of the Fox tribe, sometimes Sioux, and others. They molest no one in any way, as little as do Negroes and whites. To be sure, there are still many tribes on the east side of the Mississippi of which some, for example, the Choctaws, have adopted the European way of life and customs, even owning Negro slaves and keeping inns; but few live in the state of Missouri (I say state because it is to be distinguished from the immense Missouri territory). About fifteen English miles from here on the south side of the Missouri a Shawnee town of about fifty houses existed. Some time ago they abandoned their settlement and moved about a hundred miles farther west. I do not know of any tribe west of the Mississippi that would be closer to me at present than these Shawnees.

When the English incited the Indians during the war year of 1814, settlers along the Missouri suffered severely. According to an old custom the Indians scalped every human being they could get ahold of. No child in its cradle was spared. Usually individual Indians crept stealthily up to farms at a time when the men were absent. The scenes, which are remembered so vividly here, must have been frightful. The father-in-law of my nearest neighbor, by the name of Ramsay, related again a short time ago how he had found his house after an absence of several hours. Whites and Negroes lay on the ground, murdered and scalped. Only a five-year-old boy (a grandson of Ramsay's) was still breathing. At the sight of his grandfather, he tried to sit up and then said: "Granddaddy, the Indians did scalp me." He died soon afterward.—Rarely does a scalped person survive long. Usually death by bleeding (or apoplexy or inflammation of the brain) follows. However, if the wound heals the scar is protected by an airtight plate. I saw a man who wore such a plate. He also had been stabbed in the abdomen.—Now such occurrences are no longer to be feared. The white population has increased too much. In case of a war a number of small forts, erected earlier on the upper outermost borders of the state, would afford effective protection. If the Indians are not stirred up and given considerable assistance by another power, their great fear of the United States easily keeps them within bounds.

The inhuman behavior of the Indians, moreover, is by no means based on hatred toward the white man. In their feuds they do not treat their red brothers any better. There is nothing more one-sided than the fanatical haranguing against the expansion of Europeans together with sentimental paeans of praise to the Indians. The person who looks for virtue among undeveloped people connects entirely erroneous ideas with this word and introduces vague images of a biased imagination into a field that should be reserved for rational thinking. Among children many evil acts are not committed because temptation is lacking. One can call such a negative state innocence, and to that extent the Indians can undoubtedly be compared with children. But one should bear in mind that the innocence of an adult child (if I may express myself thus) should never be confused with that of a real child. It will be unnecessary to remind you of the impulses common to all adults. When the direction of reason is lacking, adult children, as with real children, are controlled by the impulses of the moment, except that their impulses when combined with physical strength result in urges and actions very different from those of a child. The weaker the influence of basic principles (which are to be expected only as a result of culture) the more uncertain is the moral condition of a society within itself; the more dependent on inner contingencies without any consideration of dangerous outside influences, the lower is its true value. If after such observations, one studies a group of human beings who are incited by a national custom to murder women and children in order to acquire a claim to public praise for the scalps collected, one may dare to make the assumption that this custom did not sprout in the garden of innocence. Similar atrocities can be compared to cancerous evils which develop on an already rotten base. Such phenomena do not occur suddenly. Who does not know how common the practice has always been among Indians to kill their own children? Just as well known here are their atrocious sexual aberrations. Bestiality and lewdness with boys are found among most tribes.

Their preference for the roaming life of a hunter not infrequently results in famine which transforms them completely into monsters. There are instances when fathers and mothers have eaten their own children. Old persons are put to death merely as an act of mercy. After such a famine human nature must remain in a state of tension remembering such incidents, so that a feeling of innocence is forever impossible.

Fantastic representations are read with pleasure. Reports of strange customs, stories of individual characteristics, and naive remarks concerning European prejudices have their value as entertainment. For that purpose the darker side will be omitted. Nothing is more harmful than fanciful illusions when they become opinions that direct one's life.

The remarks by Indians about European follies are often correct. But one must not rate them too highly. The Indians are by no means stupid. Wisdom, however, is as foreign to them as innocence. Their religious legends and tales contain not only beautiful poetic characteristics of a mind sensitive to the glory of God but also repelling traces of brutality and moral distortion.

Instead of limiting oneself to vague ideas in using the word *nationality*, one should consider that essentially human nature in all creatures to which the name *man* is applied must be assumed similar. Therefore, as far as essential characteristics are understood in the above-mentioned word, only the study of human nature can supply the answer, and mere phenomena of an unessential character are exempt from a more profound research.

The ambition of uncultured people is always based on low ideals. Their efforts are directed toward physical superiority and everything that (in their eyes) gives the appearance of greater physical strength. Just as the mental world is important to children only because of its spatial power, and as in their play they love to give themselves the appearance of greater strength, adults of inferior culture also have similar ambitions. Even with regard to mental superiority their ambition is directed solely to the external, to that which produces an outward show. From this source originate those characteristics of the Indian that philanthropic visionaries attribute to a high nobility of soul. Especially attributed to this is the feigned indifference in the presence of objects to be admired and in cases of suffering, which those visionaries confuse with Pyrrhonist stoicism, therefore, finally, the striving for formality in relationships and the ambition to shine through externalities, especially through speeches in which they refrain as little as children from boasting. All barbarous people are and were, in this respect, rather similar to the Indians. Indeed they must be called fortunate where ambition does not lead to worse aberrations—unlike the Indians who methodically murder women and children.

Also, are there not incidents in Europe when the most barbarous criminals endured all degrees of torture and met death with unshakable defiance? Do we not find similar characteristics among beasts of prey? A passion that borders on madness makes man resemble these animals more closely. How may one speak of spiritual fortitude in connection with such paroxysms? To restrain the tendency toward pride, toward vengeance, and toward passionate defiance has always been the primary task of a good education. Among the Indians the opposite is true. They seek to attain their greatness by inflexible nurturing of these tendencies. European youth has the same predisposition toward such Indian greatness, and it certainly would not be difficult to develop it fully. The best travel reports agree on this matter. I recall only John Carver, Volney, Romans, Oldmixon, and La Peyrouse. They declare the Indians to be extremely frivolous, inconsistent, and also arrogant; they say their pride is easily incited to cruelty, making them bloodthirsty and implacable. It is especially worth reading what La Peyrouse in his account of the unfortunate incident near the Friendly Islands writes about the Indians and the enthusiastic bias of one of his companions toward them.

I am not speaking here of the treatment that the Indians suffered from the first conquerors. Such an indictment can be applied in general to all people of this earth who have everywhere and at all times been guilty of atrocities. I am speaking of the manner in which the Indians are being treated by the United States. Slavery is out of the question. On the other hand, if the measuring rod of moral values is applicable also to the Indians then all evils that have resulted from associating with citizens of the United States must seem negligible in comparison with the good. Especially in comparison with the effect of the abhorrence that every European, not excepting the crudest hunters and frontier traders, feels concerning the above-mentioned faults. A collection of individual incidents has little weight for one who knows the exaggerations and distortions and the credulity of fanatic anecdote collectors. It is not difficult in this manner to have every people on this earth appear as offsprings of hell. Careful observation of human nature itself and of the source of information is the primary prerequisite for criticism.

That more could be done to further civilize the Indians does not justify a disregard for what is actually being done. Europeans should not take the trouble to offer advice to the United States concerning the promotion of the welfare of mankind. I should think that a mere glance at the need for it at home would deter the friend of his own country from this.

It has long been the endeavor of the United States to influence the Indians to adopt permanent homes and a steady cultivation of the soil. This is the indispensable condition of culture. Some tribes have already adopted this way of life and now realize what they owe to their white brothers. If the Indians are constantly decreasing in number, the United States has no cause to blame itself. The real reason can be found in their way of life and in their constant feuds. These feuds start mostly over hunting. This is not hard to understand if one considers how easily the pursuit of game in Europe, where in general it is only a sport, leads to border crossings and ensuing violent quarrels. For Indians, hunting is their sustenance since they abhor the breeding of cattle and farming. At most they have their women and children cultivate small gardens. To speak of the rights of a few persons to the exclusive possession of large areas is just as ridiculous as to complain about the increasing numbers of whites. The good sons of the forest would thereby be restricted in their hunting grounds and perhaps even be forced to make use of several of the millions of *Morgen* of fertile soil to raise grain or for pastures in order to escape the pangs of hunger. The reasons that move the United States to buy the land from the Indians have nothing to do with the conviction that the aborigines have a sacred right to it. In immeasurable expanses such acquisitions have not even caused an irksome restriction, not to mention dispossession. The United States acquires only such areas as are used by the Indians solely as hunting grounds. The few tribes that engage in agriculture are spared even the suggestion of selling. In order to protect the Indians from fraudulent greed, private citizens have been denied any direct acquisition of their land. Even the individual states no longer possess this right. The federal government has reserved for itself the exclusive right, and its execution is directed on the basis of principles for which no civilized people on this earth need be ashamed. What the situation is at present concerning the affairs between the state of Georgia and the Creeks I do not know. But one must feel no concern that the national government will ignore those principles in this matter. It is incredible how vehemently some German publications criticize the treaties of the national government with the Indians. As if the moderate procedure of the United States had any similarity with that of our honored ancestors who founded their rise to power upon the downfall of all old nations of southern and middle Europe! . . .

SEPTEMBER 28, 1826

I have not told you anything as yet about the antiquities of these regions, about the remains of the constructions erected by the tribes who lived here in past ages. One cannot think of them as works of art (such as those of Hindustan, Egypt, Persia, Greece, and Rome). The American monuments are of historic interest only. In this respect, of course, they are important enough, but my main purpose demanded so much of my attention that on the whole I had to be satisfied with printed reports. On the trip here I could repress my curiosity all the more easily as I knew that a considerable number of these antiquities were in the neighborhood of St. Louis. . . .

Most striking within the territory of the United States are the fortifications and mounds that spread from the southern shores of the Canadian lakes in a southwesterly direction through the western part of the state of New York and the Mississippi states to Mexico. Closer to the Mississippi these monuments are larger. . . .

The fortifications (square and circular entrenchments), as well as the mounds, are built of earth. Walls are rare, although they do exist. The mounds are found chiefly in fertile regions and along rivers with abundant fish, but also on high, stony hills.

The mounds are generally taken for graves, and investigation of their interior confirms this. They can be compared with those of the old world, especially those of the Germanic tribes (for example, those along the Rhine) and also those in Russia (for example, along the Volga), even in regard to the utensils, pottery, swords, axes, and ornaments that are found along with the skeletons. Their height varies from two to one hundred fifty feet. However the mounds inside the fortifications seem to have been built partly because of the view. Not all are conical; some are hemispherical and others angular like pyramids.

Opposite the city of St. Louis, along the Kahokia River, there are more than a hundred fifty of these graves, divided into two groups. Therefore the fertile valley plain there (called *American bottom*), about nine miles wide and eighty miles long, is considered to be the center of a large vanished population. Everywhere in this region, they say, one finds human bones when turning over the surface soil. Close to St. Louis, on the east bank of the Mississippi less than a mile from the river, is the upper group, which from a distance resembles immense haystacks. They are usually round and some have room for several hundred persons on their high tops. The largest stands close to the bank of the Kahokia, and its construction must have provided work for thousands of people for years. The base is a parallelogram eight hundred yards (2,400 English feet) in circumference. It is ninety feet high. Several years ago, some Trappists settled close to the pyramid and turned part of it into a garden.

There are also burial mounds on the western bank of the Mississippi close to the city of St. Louis, and a structure that is known by the name *Fallen Garden* seems to have served for tribal meetings.

Three (English) miles below St. Charles on the north side of the Missouri, where the Missouri valley unites with the Mississippi valley and the hills bordering the two valleys form an angle, there are also two elevations that are considered to be man-made. The French call them *les mamelles* because of their shape. In spite of the skeletons and utensils that reportedly were found there, I must consider them as products of nature, as layers of earth deposited by the two great rivers in times of floods. I confess that the wonderful view that one enjoys from there diverted me from a closer examination. If one faces the Mississippi, one sees to the right the mouth of the Missouri, to the left that of the Illinois, and straight across (on the east bank of the Mississippi), a row of cliffs near which Portage des Sioux is situated. To be sure, the ground of this large valley plain has long been private property, but hardly any settlements can be seen. The owners are speculators who are waiting for higher prices. I wrote you earlier that the Missouri valley and the bordering hills are everywhere densely forested. Here at the junction with the Mississippi valley, meadows prevail, however only in the plain.

The other monuments west of the Mississippi I have not seen. According to the written reports of Lewis and Clarke, Picke, and Nutall, there are extensive fortifications as well as burial mounds as far west as the Rocky

Mountains. Only recently has the closer attention of scholars been directed toward these objects. Probably the next decades will furnish more information about their origin as well as the origin of the American tribes than is at present available. . . .

A POSTSCRIPT FOR EMIGRATING FARMERS AND FOR THOSE WHO CONTEMPLATE COMMERCIAL UNDERTAKINGS

. . . The territory of the western states is very expansive, and in making specific references to it the next question is natural; which part would be best to recommend to the German? To this I answer first that the emigrant who intends to make use of the soil should not settle in the southern states, not there where there is no winter. With an urban life-style the change of climates is far less noticeable. But the farmer who suddenly changes from the German farm life to the work of tropical plantations without intermediate stages exposes his physical constitution to the most dangerous disturbances. Settlements at the mouth of the Arkansas are perhaps already too far south. On the upper Arkansas the climate is more agreeable, as is that along the entire Ohio and its tributaries, the Missouri, and the Illinois. Later, after he has gotten accustomed to the seasons in these areas, the German may attempt to move farther south. Even on the Ohio and Missouri he will, in spite of the bright sky in the spring, summer, and fall, look longingly toward winter during the first years. . . .

Secondly, one should note that the land is that much more expensive the more one moves from the Mississippi toward the East and toward the old states, for no reason other than the greater population. For in general the fertility decreases with the distance from the Mississippi. The greatest expanses of fertile topsoil are near the biggest rivers. And what areas could be better situated for communication with the world than the banks of the Mississippi? With the constant pressure of the population westward and with the exceedingly easy communication by steamboat, the advantage of Ohio and the state of Kentucky, not to mention others, is not so significant that a newcomer from Europe should overlook the advantages of the countries to the west of the Mississippi, which have only been opened during the last two decades. . . .

Consequently I would recommend to the emigrant the state of

Missouri preferably, and I would advise him to travel directly to St. Louis on the Mississippi. . . .

As soon as the emigrant has arrived in St. Louis, he should obtain charts of the federal lands from the land office and undertake a few excursions. I would advise him to travel up the Missouri and then board in the country with a clean farmer. Everywhere in the country he can find complete board for a weekly amount of one, one and a half, to two dollars, which includes the board for his horse. He will need a horse. He can buy it better from a farmer than in St. Louis. For thirty to forty dollars a very adequate animal can be found. Living among the farmers the newcomer will have plenty of opportunity to prepare himself for his future living conditions; he may buy a ready-made homestead or may want to establish a new one. But he must not hurry too much. He has to learn to judge for himself and has to use the advice of others with caution; in general he should follow the examples of the people living inland more than their words. . . .

Whoever erects a brick building, which also may well cost approximately 500 dollars, at such a place will be able to enjoy all comforts and conveniences of country life. It will be unnecessary to warn the newcomer not to settle too far from a navigable river. That would be inexcusable as long as one is so unlimited in one's choice.

Nothing deserves the attention of the settler more than horse breeding. A few good mares, whose care and keep costs practically nothing, will bring more profit than their whole expense will amount to. There is not a shortage of stallions of the most excellent breed. The English have brought them from the Old World from the very beginning. One should keep this line of profitmaking in mind from the beginning when selecting the choice of one's place. Where, for instance, all property is already in the hands of private persons there are usually so many cattle that the feed in the forest is not sufficient. Grapevines, rape oil, and poppy seed oil have, no matter how much their culture may promise, not found the slightest attention either in the state of Missouri or in the bordering countries. As to wine, grapes have always been imported from warmer regions. Also the descendants of the British do not understand viniculture, and those descended from other people have not learned it from their parents. I should think that grapes from the Rhine would do very well on the Missouri, however not in the midst of thick forests. Not far from St. Charles there are extensive areas that ought to be viniculture. . . .

The German who understands Latin or French can learn the English language quickly. There are many low Saxon words which in their pronunciation sound exactly as one hears them in various areas of Westphalia and Lower Saxony. The Latin language is for an Englishman the real emergency reservoir from which he daily adopts new words.—Some instruction in Germany should precede this process, however. Few people enjoy instruction on the ocean. Naturally, above all, the terms of the most common situations of life are to be memorized. It would suffice for a society of emigrants if a few of them understood English. . . .

. . . Any European who is tolerably informed and who comes to the Ohio, the Mississippi, or to the Missouri not entirely without money and does not disdain a normal occupation will find with some persistence an attractive sphere of activity, and a businessman who does not figure to see his hopes fullfilled in the first year should be advised to remain until he has become more familiar with the new things than is possible on a mere tour. He must have stayed among the Americans for at least six months. He may have reasons that persuade him to return to Europe without having had any commercial profit from his trip. This depends on his particular situation. However, if he attributes the blame to the country he should try to show in his own country through his behavior that it was not he himself who was to be blamed when the new world did not appeal to him.

It is very natural for an emigrant to have an inclination to keep, so to speak, one foot in his home country when he roams through foreign countries. Love for one's country can explain this sufficiently. However, he can afford this only in rare cases without considerable cost. As a rule, the emigrant will do well to renounce his home country for the first ten years and to occupy himself seriously with the thought of making America his home. That will give him that foundation that must be the prerequisite for many advantageous undertakings. Fathers of large families have enough reason in Germany, if only for the one reason of being able to give to their children a secure direction, to invest in the opportunity to look around abroad, and it would certainly be a useful intersession, even without any plans of a future settlement, to influence a member of the family to visit the Mississippi countries and to spend a reasonable time there as a good possibility for the future.

WILSON PRIMM

BORN INTO ONE OF ST. LOUIS'S oldest Creole families, Wilson Primm (1810–1878) received a fine education at the old St. Louis College—a prep school that taught sons with such illustrious names as Benton, Chouteau, McNair, and Soulard—and St. Joseph College at Bardstown, Kentucky.

A brilliant student with a facility for languages, Primm excelled in his chosen field of law and began his career in the practice of Edward Bates, who later became attorney general of the United States. Primm was an active public servant, holding a multitude of offices, including deputy clerk of the County Court of St. Louis, justice of the peace, state representative, alderman, and judge of the St. Louis Criminal Court. In addition, he was one of the founders of the St. Louis public school system and served as its first secretary.

Partly because his own lineage was inextricably tied to early St. Louis history, Primm had a passionate interest in researching, recording, and preserving the history of the region. In fact, as a popular public speaker, Primm gave a talk on the church in early St. Louis to the members of the fledgling Missouri Historical Society, of which he was a founder.

One of Primm's most influential addresses was delivered to the St. Louis Lyceum in 1831. The facts in Primm's lecture, "History of St. Louis," were cobbled together from the memories of "living witnesses" that he interviewed. According to Primm, "The knowledge of these persons was cheerfully imparted to me, and it is from copious notes then taken, from the recollections of those who lived in Spanish times after the permanent establishment of St. Louis, from the notes of the late Auguste Chouteau, from the archives of the French and Spanish governments, and from other reliable sources that I have been enabled to prepare a sketch which if it has no other recommendation, has that of truth."

In actuality, the discrepancies that exist in Primm's pioneering lay history were passed on as fact for decades and have become imbedded in the collective consciousness of St. Louisans, so that they are now woven into the fabric of the city's mythology.

The first excerpt that follows is from the first printed edition of Primm's

"History of St. Louis," published in 1832 and revised and reprinted in pamphlet form in 1847. Of special interest here is Primm's use of the testimony of an aged blind woman to determine that Laclède, not Chouteau, was the actual founder of St. Louis, and his vilification of Commander Fernando de Leyba, the lieutenant governor of St. Louis at the time of the 1780 Battle of Fort San Carlos.

In February 1845, the *St. Louis Reveille* published French and English versions of a song recounting the 1780 British-instigated attack on St. Louis by Sioux, Winnebago, Sauk, and Fox warriors. "Chanson de l'Année du Coup" ("Ballad of the Year of the Surprise") was submitted to the paper by Wilson Primm, who signed his introduction to the piece with the initial "P." The English translation was provided by Joseph M. Field, the *Reveille*'s editor.

When the ballad appeared in the *Reveille*, it represented both the popularization of an important historical account and the continuing efforts of Wilson Primm, a passionate Francophile, to assassinate the character of the Spanish governor Fernando de Leyba.

The ballad, introduced by Primm's letter to the *Reveille*, follows his history of St. Louis.

HISTORY OF ST. LOUIS

In several sketches of the history of St. Louis, which have appeared in the public papers, the honor of having founded it is awarded to Mr. Auguste Chouteau. These statements, uncontroverted as they have been, have caused the belief which generally prevails, that he was the founder. The writer risks something, no doubt, in opposing it, but the task which he has assumed, of presenting not only a history of this town, but a correct one, constrains him to do it. The evidence, at least, which opposes the popular belief, is so strong, as to vindicate the writer from the imputation of wishing to pluck from the brow of merit, the chaplet of honor; and the feelings of delicacy, which, under other circumstances, might be indulged, must now be laid aside.

The writer had frequently heard doubts suggested on this subject, but the question was not then of sufficient interest to him to prompt an inquiry. When he undertook, however, to prepare this paper, it became necessary to arrive, if possible, at the truth. With that view, he had recourse to several of the French inhabitants, in the truth of whose statements, he knew the most implicit confidence could be placed. The persons thus applied to are aged, the most of them having been born within ten or fifteen years after the foundation of the town. They knew nothing *personally*, but all concurred in saying that Mr. Laclede was the founder; that Mr. Chouteau was a boy when the town was founded; that thus they had always heard their fathers say. This tradition, though strong evidence, was still not sufficient. The writer called on a lady, who is said to have been the first woman that came to St. Louis. Mrs. Lecomte, though very aged, blind, and almost deprived of the use of her limbs, still retains the faculties of her mind, strong and unimpaired. Her recollection of the scenes through which she has passed, is perfect; in addition to which she has that happy faculty of manner and language, united with a spirit of politeness, which renders the communication of intelligence both striking and agreeable. The details which she gave, are so clear and connected, that it is impossible to doubt them. She was born in the year 1745; in the year 1763, being eighteen years old, she was married and living in Cahokia, when, in the month of November, as she believes, Mr. Laclede passed through that town, on his way towards the mouth of the Missouri, in search of a situation to form an establishment. In the month of February, in the following year, he again passed through the town, with the men he had brought from New Orleans, with some from Fort de Chartres, and some from Ste. Genevieve; amongst these, was Auguste Chouteau, then a boy of about fifteen years of age. Mr. Laclede induced several persons to go from Cahokia, to his proposed establishment, and amongst others, her husband. She remained in Cahokia until the close of the month of May, when the Mississippi rising, overflowed the town, and inundated the floor of the house in which she lived; a Mr. Trotier, a resident of the town, offered her a refuge in his house, which she refused, on the ground that she was compelled to go to *Pain Court* (the name that St. Louis acquired at that time, from the scarcity of provisions, which were brought from Ste. Genevieve), she might as well do it at once. Accordingly, she and her husband moved to St. Louis in the beginning of June. There were then only two or three houses, or rather huts, in St. Louis, one of which belonged to Mr. Laclede. The men were employed in building for Mr. Laclede the house in which Auguste Chouteau resided before his death; while she, and the greater part of the settlers, lived for a time on scaffolds, elevated six or seven feet above the ground, to protect themselves from the wild beasts which abounded. Mr. Laclede gave lots of ground to the settlers, in admeasurement of which, Auguste Chouteau generally carried the chain for him.

Another lady, Mrs. B[razeau], remarkable for her piety, intelligence, and amiable disposition, states that when about eleven or twelve years old, she came from Kaskaskia, where she then resided, on a visit to St. Louis. When she first knew Mr. Chouteau he was a little boy, some three years older than herself. She was godmother to Mr. Chouteau's wife, and he, on that account, also called her godmother; when she would reprove him for it, on the ground that it made her appear older than himself, he invariably stated the difference between their ages to be three years. Mrs. B. is now seventy-eight years old, which would make Mr. Chouteau, at the foundation of St. Louis, about fourteen years of age.

Two other persons who were among the first settlers have made statements similar to the above. Nor are they unsupported. In the Missouri Republican of the 24th February, 1829, we find an obituary notice of Mr. Auguste Chouteau, sanctioned, it is presumed, by his relatives, in which his age, at the time of his death, is stated to have been eighty years. St. Louis had then been founded sixty-five years; consequently, Auguste Chouteau was fifteen years old at the foundation of the city; a fact which, in our opinion, settles the question.

The spot thus selected, was covered with a growth of timber, which extended north and south along the margin of the Mississippi, and west as far as to the prairie. The selection was certainly a happy one. Immediately below the junction of two mighty rivers, and but little above the mouth of another with a chain of water communication from the Atlantic almost to the Pacific ocean, it seems to have been formed by nature, for the site of a great and populous city, and to have been intended for the *depot* of the greater part of the western country. After its foundation, all that was necessary to bear it along in the career of importance, was enterprise and industry. Fortunately, when the country was transferred to the United States, the commercial advantages of St. Louis, the healthiness of its situation, and the fertility of the soil around and above, attracted to it numbers of energetic men, who have caused it to make rapid strides towards greatness. The immense superiority which its locality gives it, will always ensure it the monopoly of the commerce, and render it the mart of the mineral, agricultural, and fur countries which live above it on both sides of the Mississippi river.

"Seventeen months after the foundation of St. Louis, the Fort de Chartres was evacuated by the French troops." (*Dep. of Aug. Chouteau.*) The ostensible cause was that its situation was low, unhealthy, and subject to inundation. The real cause, no doubt, was that the French, having by the treaty of Paris, ceded the country east of the Mississippi to the English, were obliged to abandon the military posts they possessed in that country. "On the 17th of July, 1765, *M. de St. Ange de belle rive*, the commander of the Fort de Chartres, together with officers and troops, arrived at St. Louis, and assumed the reins of government." (*Dep. of Aug. Chouteau.*) Whether authority was delegated to him by the Director General, or whether it was a mere assumption of power on his part, cannot now be ascertained; certain it is, that his authority was submitted to by the inhabitants, and immediately after his arrival, St. Louis was considered the capital of Upper Louisiana. . . .

Under the administration of St. Ange, St. Louis assumed more definitely the appearance of a town. The soldiers had, by degrees, become amalgamated with the inhabitants; comfortable dwellings were erected; and small fields in the neighborhood, now called *common fields*, had been opened and improved. The government was in a manner patriarchal; the whole community seemed to compose one family, under the guidance of a common father, and enjoying a common patrimony. Perhaps a sense of their weak and somewhat perilous situation, tended to bring into existence and strengthen the bonds of amity and good feeling, and to maintain that order, harmony, and subordination, which it is so difficult to maintain in infant colonies.

On the 11th of August, 1768, three years after St. Ange established himself at St. Louis, Mr. Rious arrived with Spanish troops, and took possession of Upper Louisiana, in the name of his Catholic Majesty; but did not exercise any jurisdiction over the country, as appears from the fact that St. Ange continued to perform official acts until the beginning of 1770. From this it is to be inferred that the powers of Mr. Rious were limited to the bare taking possession of the country, and that no jurisdiction was to be exercised by him, until the dissatisfaction against the transfer had been worn away, and the inhabitants become reconciled to their new master. Their habits, manners, and customs, which they retained under the new government, and long after its extinction, being entirely French, they would naturally be averse to the change; and their remoteness from the source of power, imperatively required delicacy and prudence in such measures as might be adopted towards them.

The arrival of Count O'Reilly at New Orleans, and the revolution that consequently occurred there, caused the evacuation of Upper Louisiana by the Spanish troops, and their departure for New Orleans in July, 1769. The transfer having been completely effected, a new government organized, and a new code of laws established by Count O'Reilly, he directed his attention to the province of Upper Louisiana, of which he appointed Pedro Piernas Lieutenant Governor. This officer, under the Spanish government, was invested with extensive powers: he was military and civil commandant of the whole province over which he was delegated, having authority in whatever concerned the administration of justice, or the defence of the country; he appointed commandants of posts and towns within his jurisdiction, their acts being subject to his approval, and themselves removable at his pleasure; he had the power of making grants of land, which grants, or *concessions*, as they were called, were to be confirmed by the governor general; and with the exception that his acts could be revised and he removed by the power that appointed him, he was invested with despotic sway.

On the 29th of November, 1770, Mr. Piernas arrived at St. Louis, with a body of troops, and took possession of Upper Louisiana again; but he did not begin to exercise his functions as Lieutenant Governor, until the month of February following. The inhabitants soon became reconciled to the new dominion, for Spain adopted the prudent plan of tempering the mandates of government with parental mildness. Such measures, indeed, were necessary towards men who were placed on the verge of civilization, and with whom, harshness would have had no beneficial effect. It resulted in a firm attachment to the government, which displayed itself in their regret and dissatisfaction at the retrocession to France, in 1800. . . .

Mr. Piernas was succeeded by Francisco Cruzat in 1775, and the latter, by Fernando de Leyba, in July, 1778.

Until the present time, although danger had been apprehended from the Indians, yet no injury had been experienced from them. The territory on which St. Louis stood, that on which several other towns had been located, and the surrounding country, were claimed by the Illinois Indians; (*Dep. of A. Chouteau*); but they had acquiesced in the intrusion of the whites, and had never disturbed them in the enjoyment of the land. A rumor, however, was now spread abroad, that an attack would shortly be made upon the town by the Canadians, and such Indians as were friendly to the English. The town was almost destitute of works of defense, but the inhabitants, amounting to little more than a hundred *men*, immediately proceeded to inclose it with a species of wall, formed of the trunks of small trees, planted in the ground, the interstices being filled up with earth. The wall was some five or six feet high. It started from the *half moon*, a kind of fort in that form, situated on the river, near the present *upper ferry landing*, and ran from thence a little above the brow of the hill, in a semicircle, until it reached the Mississippi, somewhat above the bridge .Three gates were formed in it, one near the bridge, and two others on the hill, at the points where the roads from the north-western and south-western parts of the common field came in. At each of these gates was placed a piece of heavy ordnance, kept continually charged, and in good order. Having completed this work, and hearing no more of the Indians, it was supposed that the attack had been abandoned. Winter passed away, and spring came; still nothing was heard of the Indians. The inhabitants were led to believe that their apprehensions were groundless, from the representations of the Commandant Leyba, who did every thing in his power to dissipate their anxiety, assuring them that there was no danger, and that the rumor of the proposed attack was false. The month of May came, the labors of planting were over, and the peaceful and happy villagers gave themselves up to such pursuits and pleasures as suited their taste. An observer of the beautiful and quiet scene which this country then presented would never have dreamed that the angry passions of men were at work to mar it.

A few days before the attack an old man named Kenelle [Quenell], a resident of St. Louis, had gone over to the mouth of Kahokia creek to catch fish. While watching his lines on the south bank of the creek, he heard a slight noise on the opposite side. Looking up, he beheld an acquaintance who had formerly resided in St. Louis, but who had absconded from thence on account of some crime which he had committed. His name was Ducharme, and he was afterwards ascertained to be one of the leaders of the attack upon the town. His strange and sudden appearance, the circumstances under which he had left St. Louis, and the rumor of the meditated attack—all these combined, induced Kenelle to refuse to cross the creek, at the invitation of Ducharme. He was confirmed in his refusal by perceiving, a few moments after, the eyes of several Indians glaring upon him from the bushes in which they were concealed. "Come over," said Ducharme, "I have something very particular to tell you." "No," said Kenelle, "your request is not intended for my benefit, or the gratification of your friendly feelings. Though I am old and bald, yet I value my scalp too highly to trust myself with you." So saying, he embarked in his canoe, and crossing over to St. Louis, informed the commandant of what he had seen. The people became alarmed, but the commandant, calling his informant an old dotard, ordered him to be put in prison. This proceeding had the effect of again calming their minds and banishing apprehension.

In the meantime, numerous bands of the Indians living on the lakes and the Mississippi—the Ojibeways, Menomonies, Winnebagoes, Sioux, Sacs, etc., together with a large number of Canadians, amounting, in all, to upwards of fourteen hundred, had assembled on the eastern shore of the Mississippi, a little above St. Louis, awaiting the 6th of May, the day fixed for the attack. The 5th of May was the feast of *Corpus Christi*, a day highly venerated by the inhabitants, who were all Catholics. Had the assault taken place then, it would have been fatal to them; for, after divine service, all, men, women, and children, had flocked to the prairie to gather strawberries, which were that season very abundant and fine. The town, being left perfectly unguarded, could have been taken with ease, and the unsuspecting inhabitants, who were roaming about in the search of fruit, have been massacred without resistance. Fortunately, however, a few only of the enemy had crossed the river and ambushed themselves in the prairie. The villagers frequently came so near them in the course of the day, that the Indians, from their places of concealment, could have reached them with their hands. But they knew not how many of the whites were still remaining in the town, and in the absence of their coadjutors, feared to attack, lest their pre-concerted plan might be defeated.

On the 6th, the main body of the Indians crossed, and marched directly towards the fields, expecting to find the greater part of the villagers there; but in this they were disappointed, a few only having gone out to view their crops. These perceived the approach of the savage foe, and immediately commenced a retreat towards the town, the most of them taking the road that led to the upper gate, nearly through the mass of Indians, and followed by a shower of bullets. The firing alarmed those who were in town, and the cry "to arms! to arms!" was heard in every direction. They rushed towards the works and threw open the gates to their brethren. The Indians advanced slowly, but steadily, towards the town, and the inhabitants, though almost deprived of hope, by the vast superiority in number of the assailants, determined to defend themselves to the last.

In expectation of an attack, Silvio Francisco Cartabona, a governmental officer, had gone to Ste. Genevieve for a company of militia to aid in defending the town, in case of necessity, and had, at the beginning of the month returned with sixty men, who were quartered on the citizens. As soon as the attack commenced, however, neither Cartabona nor his men could be seen. Either through fear or treachery, they concealed themselves in a garret, and there remained until the Indians had retired. The assailed, being deprived of a considerable force by this shameful defection, were still resolute and determined. About fifteen men were posted at each gate; the rest were scattered along the line of defense, in the most advantageous manner.

When within a proper distance, the Indians began an irregular fire, which was answered with showers of grape shot from the artillery. The firing, for a while, was warm; but the Indians, perceiving that all their efforts would be ineffectual, on account of the intrenchments, and deterred by the cannon, to which they were unaccustomed, from making a nearer approach, suffered their zeal to abate, and deliberately retired. At this stage of affairs the Lieutenant Governor made his appearance. The first intimation that he received of what was going on, was by the discharge of artillery, on the part of the inhabitants. He immediately ordered several pieces of cannon, which were posted in front of the government house, to be spiked and filled with sand, and went, or rather was rolled in a wheelbarrow, to the scene of action. In a very peremptory tone, he commanded the inhabitants to cease firing and return to their houses. Those posted at the lower gate did not receive the order and consequently kept their stations. The commandant perceived this and ordered a cannon to be fired at them. They had barely time to throw themselves on the ground, when the volley passed over them, and struck the wall, tearing a great part of it down. These proceedings, as well as the whole tenor of his conduct, since the first rumor of an attack, gave rise to suspicions very unfavorable to the Lieutenant Governor. It was bruited about, that he was the cause of the attack, that he was connected with the British, and that he had been bribed into a dereliction of duty, which, had not Providence averted, would have doomed them to destruction. Under the pretext of proving to them that there was no danger of an attack, he had, a few days before it occurred, sold to the traders all the ammunition belonging to the government; and they would have been left perfectly destitute and defenseless, had they not found in a private house, eight barrels of powder, belonging to a trader, which they seized in the name of the King, upon the first alarm. General George Rogers Clark, who was at this time in Kaskaskia, with a few men under his command, understanding that an attack was meditated on the town, offered all the assistance in his power, to aid in the defense. This offer was rejected by the Lieutenant Governor. All these circumstances gave birth to a strong aversion to the commandant, which evinces itself, even at this day, in execrations of his character, whenever his name is mentioned to those who have known him. Representations of his conduct, together with a detailed account of the attack, were sent to New Orleans by a special messenger, and the result was, that the Governor General appointed Mr. Francisco Cruzat, to the office of Lieutenant Governor.

As soon as it was ascertained that the Indians had retired from the neighborhood, the inhabitants proceeded to gather the dead, that lay scattered in all parts of the prairie. Seven were at first found, and buried in one grave. Ten or twelve others, in the course of a fortnight, were discovered in the long grass that bordered the marshes. The acts of the Indians were accompanied by their characteristic ferocity. Some of their victims were horribly mangled. With the exception of one individual, the whites who accompanied the Indians did not take part in the butcheries that were committed. A young man named *Calvé*, was found dead, his skull split open, and a tomahawk, on the blade of which was written the word Calvé, sticking in his brain. He was supposed to have fallen by the hand of his uncle. Had those who discovered the Indians in the prairie, fled to the lower gate, they would have escaped; but the greater part of them took the road that led to the upper gate, through the very ranks of the enemy, and were thus exposed to the whole of their fire. About twenty persons, it is computed, met their death in endeavoring to get within the intrenchments. None of those within them were injured, and none of the Indians were killed, at least, none of them were found. Their object was not plunder, for they did not attempt, in their retreat, to take with them any of the cattle or horses that were in the prairie, and that they might have taken; nor did they attack any of the neighboring towns, where danger would have been less, and the prospect of success greater. The only object they had in view, was the destruction of St. Louis; and this would seem to favor the idea that they were instigated by the English, and give good ground, when connected with other circumstances, to believe that Leyba was their aider and abettor. . . .

Thus ended an attack, which, properly conducted, might have been destructive to the infant town, and which, from the number of the enemy and the danger incurred, was calculated to impress itself deeply upon the minds of those who witnessed it. It forms an era in the history of the place; and the year in which it occurred, has ever since been designated by the inhabitants, as the *year of the great blow.* "L'année du grand coup."

CHANSON DE L'ANNÉE DU COUP; OR, BALLAD OF THE YEAR OF THE SURPRISE

OLD TIMES IN ST. LOUIS

Messrs. Editors!—The following specimen of poetic ability in the early days of St. Louis, is nearly forgotten. The fact of its being in the French language will not be an objection to its insertion in your columns, as I know that the language is vernacular to many of your best subscribers. Besides, its insertion may act as a *Reveille* upon the dormant memories of many old citizens, and induce them to furnish for your paper their recollections of *Paincourt*, as our city was once named.

The following are the incidents connected with the versification:

In the month of May, in year 1780, St. Louis was attacked by a large number of Indians and Canadians. Notwithstanding the treachery of Fernando de Leyba, who was then acting as Lieutenant Governor of Upper Louisiana, under the Spanish Government, the attacking party were repulsed—not, however, until after they had killed several of the most valuable inhabitants of the town; amongst others, the first "*American*" who had ever been with them.

After the attack had been repulsed, a courier express was sent by the inhabitants to the Governor General of Louisiana, at New Orleans, with information of the events which had just occurred. The courier was the bearer, likewise, of the piece of versification which I give you below; and tradition says, that the venerable schoolmaster of the village, who composed it, received from the Governor General, in return, a handsome present.

I will merely add, that the verses were set to music, and, for years afterwards, and until the inhabitants, by intermixture with the "Americans," laid aside or forgot their old habits, customs and reminiscences, were sung by all, with the same spirit and zest that a Frenchman sings the Marseillaise.

P.

We give, below, a free translation of this, perhaps, *father* of all Western poems. Shades of "*le grand Leyba*," and "*fameux Cartabona!*" it is not the first time that your rest has been disturbed by the *Reveille.*

BALLAD OF THE YEAR OF THE SURPRISE

GOVERNOR

Courier, say, what is the news
That seems thy fancies to confuse?
What! have we lost the *Illinois*?
The English—do they the land enjoy?
Down hearted, thus! speak, courier, say
What great misfortune has happen'd, I pray?

COURIER

Oh, General, General, all is lost,
If not redeemed with speed and cost;
We've been by savages attacked—
They threaten us, still, by others backed:
Ever so many, alas, were killed—
Unable to aid them—with grief we're filled.

When the enemy first appeared,
To arms we ran, no one afeared;
Townsmen, traders, grave and gay,
Bravely to battle and win the day;
But, by command, we were forbid
To quit the trench where our ranks were hid.

GOVERNOR

What did they in that moment—then?
Lacked they, all, the souls of men!
What! had ye not the great Leyba!
Where was the famous Cartabona!
Your Major! where was he, as well;
The Garrison, too, your force to swell?

Oh, that moment! what did they, then?
Lacked they, all, the souls of men!
Homeward cravens, come ye back;
Long have we feared your course, alack;
Here we've, at least, within our wall,
To watch our standard—prevent its fall,
An officer prudent, bold and wise,
Who'll valiantly guard you against surprise.

Calve, the petty tinkering knave!
Called he himself a warrior brave,
Yet saw his nephew slain, alas,—
Kinsmen and friends on the prairie grass,—
Helpless, abandoned, to meet their fate
From the savages' fierce and furious hate!

Heartless Canadians! 'Twas their deed!
Brothers and sisters, you saw them bleed!
Cut-throats exult in your acts of night,
And, coward-like, safety seek in flight.

MATTHEW C. FIELD

OF IRISH DESCENT and reared in England, Matthew Field (1813-1844) emigrated to the United States, where he first settled in New York City and learned the jewelry trade. Following in the footsteps of his older brother, Joseph Field, Matt sought a career in the theatre. By the early 1830s, he was a popular matinee idol along the Mississippi River. He made his debut in St. Louis in 1835 and regularly performed at the St. Louis Theatre, which was owned and operated by Noah Ludlow. Field eventually married Ludlow's daughter, Cornelia.

A prolific journalist who wrote under the pen name "Phazma" for the *New Orleans Picayune* and other papers, Field also helped his brother Joseph establish the *St. Louis Reveille*. Having suffered from a fragile constitution most of his adult life, Field was advised by a physician that western air would be good for him. In 1839, he joined an expedition to Santa Fe. During the trip, Field kept detailed journals, which served as the basis of his entertaining sketches on western culture that appeared in the *Reveille* and *Picayune*.

The first of the following selections is a passage from Field's diary—housed in the archives of the Missouri Historical Society—that describes his health problems, his residence in St. Louis, and his spiritual anguish. Field had toyed with the idea of studying for the clergy but abandoned the plan in favor of going on the Santa Fe expedition and continuing his acting career.

The second entry, Field's poem, "The Chouteau House," first was published in August 1841 in J. C. Wild's *The Valley of the Mississippi, Illustrated,* a monthly publication that featured "embracing pictures of the principal cities and towns, public buildings, and remarkable picturesque scenery, on the Ohio and Mississippi Rivers."

This poem is a cry of protest against the razing of the Laclède-Chouteau house, St. Louis's first substantial stone structure. Under the direction of Auguste Chouteau, the original building was constructed in 1764 as a warehouse for goods for the trading firm of Maxent, Laclède and Company. According to Chouteau's narrative of St. Louis's founding, the building's cellar was dug by Missouri squaws in exchange for "vermilion, awls and verdigris." Several years after Laclède's death in 1778, Chouteau acquired the structure and added the second story. In addition to being Chouteau's private residence, the building functioned as a public meeting house.

John Darby, recalling his arrival in the town in 1818, remarked in his memoir, "The splendid abode with its surroundings had indeed the appearance of a castle." With St. Louis rapidly growing in the 1840s, there was a great demand for land near the center of town. Consequently, Chouteau's aged widow, Thérèse, sold the house and plot—bounded by Main, Market, Walnut, and Second Streets—to developers. In spite of Field's impassioned plea, the building was destroyed in October 1841, two months after the poem first appeared. Matthew Field died of tuberculosis three years later, at the age of thirty-one.

TUESDAY, APRIL 2, 1839

Arrived in St. Louis. A report had been through the city that I was dead, and my friends were all very glad to see me. Met Irin Thorington who had been sent some twelve months ago to the Rocky mountains, to be out of the way of dissipation—he is quite reformed and looks like another man.

Dined at Mrs. Fleishmans and eat too much—Must break myself of this very bad habit. Agreed to pay Sol. Smith $5 a month for privilege to sleep in my Dressing Room in the theatre. Accordingly had my luggage taken up. The room is in the south corner of the building, on the high Carpenters Gallery, has two windows and a free prospect of half of the city, and a large sweep of the Mississippi. I can see all the boats arriving and departing. The magnificent Catholic Cathedral is directly in front of me as I write. It has a very high steeple with a golded ball and cross from the top of which the lightning rod projects many feet in the air. The steeple has a covering of zinc, and at this moment is shining with dazzling brightness in the light of the setting sun. This steeple is the first object that strikes the traveller in approaching the city, and the next is the Theatre—the high building I am now sitting in. I have shaked hands with probably five hundred people since morning. Signor Blitz the magician exhibits in the Theatre tonight, and the rest of this week. My stomach is very uneasy and I am feeling worse all the time. Called on Dr. McCabe and on telling him my continued bad symptoms he advised me to go to the mountains. Asked So. Smith to release me from my engagement—a company was the very next day starting up the Yellow Stone River—he could not let me go and I must try and fight it out, at least till June.

I am enduring most horrible sensations, called on Mrs. Roper with Mrs. Brown's letter—found Mrs. Roper a very charming lady, and as I talked to her thought she would make a very agreeable wife—an hour afterwards I lay on the bed in torture studying how to convey or rather how I could have conveyed my rags and remnants of chattles to my Mother in case I should die. And thus is my mind fluctuating from day to day constantly between Death and Marriage. Strange union of opposites! Posted 5 Letters to Wing Allen—one to Brother Joe. Must as soon as I can compose my mind and my nerves sit down and write a very serious and interesting letter to Parson Hamilton of Mobile. I owe him much gratitude for his kind advice in recommending to me *Doddridge's rise and progress of Religion in the soul*; a most beautiful and interesting book which has done me more good than any book I ever read in my life. It has made a Christian of me, and if it will please God to restore me to health, my future life shall be spent in goodness and virtue.

THURSDAY, APRIL 4, 1839

Altho I am behind I shall continue to date regular—it will make no material difference. Oh, How I have learned to love life! I bless God for every breath I draw. "Sweet indeed are the uses of adversity!" Had I never known sickness, I should never have known the delight I feel at this moment in breathing the God's blessed atmosphere, and thanking him for it. The beautiful pigeons too are circling about my window and I joy to see them. The bright high spire of the Cathedral is before me. The Broad Mississippi rolls away in the distance. The green shores opposite are verdant in their livery of spring. The white front of the Court House too is in my prospect and I can sit in my window and look upon them all while the cool breeze plays around my loosened breast and on my calm cold brow. There is the Museum. I was in it on Saturday—and spent half an hour contemplating the bones of a Mastadon—May not some of those enormous creatures be living yet? There is a Giraffe now in the city, brought from the wilds of Africa—they were supposed to be extinct, yet they are now discovered to be living in herds as numerous as the Buffaloe upon the mountain prairies. Why may there not be in the yet untraversed wildernesses of the West some of these Mammoth creatures yet living? Is it not quite as likely as that there should be Giraffes.

This Diary never can be of any use for publishing, but should I live and have children it will be a treasure to them. It will show them the history of my turning from folly and will be to them like tablets of gold. Or should it please God to make me die early, and never know the affection of a wife, or the fond delights of parental love, yet I anticipate, as I mean now to conduct myself in life, leaving behind me many dear and valuable friends—not friends of today who would love me only as a companion in vicious pleasures, but friends who shall love me for virtue—who shall honor me while living and cherish my memory when dead. To such friends will I leave my little Diary and they shall find in it interest and pleasure, and they shall yield a tear to my worldly sorrow and a prayer to Heaven for my future happiness.

THE CHOUTEAU HOUSE

Touch not a stone! An early pioneer
Of Christian sway founded his dwelling here,
   Almost alone.
Touch not a stone! Let the Great West command
A hoary relic of the early land;
   That after generations may not say,
   "All went for gold in our forefathers' day,
And of our infancy we nothing own."
   Touch not a stone!

Touch not a stone! Let the old pile decay,
A relic of the time now pass'd away.
   Ye heirs, who own
Lordly endowment of the ancient hall,

Till the last rafter crumbles from the wall,
    And each old tree around the dwelling rots,
    Yield not your heritage for "building lots."
Hold the old ruin for itself alone;
    Touch not a stone!

Built by a foremost Western pioneer,
It stood upon Saint Louis bluff to cheer
    New settlers on.
Now o'er it tow'rs majestic spire and dome,
And lowly seems the forest trader's home;
    All out of fashion, like a time-struck man,
    Last of his age, his kindred and his clan,
Lingering still, a stranger and alone;—
    Touch not a stone!

Spare the old house! The ancient mansion spare,
For ages still to front the market square;—
    That may be shown,
How those old walls of good St. Louis rock,
In native strength, shall bear against the shock
    Of centuries! There shall the curious see,
    When like a fable shall our story be,
How the Star City of the West has grown!
    Touch not a stone!

CHARLES DICKENS

CHARLES DICKENS (1812–1870), of Portsmouth, England, endured a childhood marked by hardships similar to those of his young male protagonists like David Copperfield and Oliver Twist. Out of financial necessity, Dickens took his first job as an office boy, studied shorthand, and began a career as a newspaper reporter. By his early twenties, Dickens's ability to write well and prolifically was evident, and he contributed to a variety of periodicals.

In 1836, Dickens launched his career as a novelist with the publication, in twenty monthly numbers, of *The Posthumous Papers of the Pickwick Club*. The book was published in volume form the following year, when Dickens was just twenty-five years old. After the success of his first novel, Dickens's future looked bright, with the public and publishers clamoring for more.

Dickens and his wife, Catherine Hogarth, took a six-month tour of America in 1842, and his autobiographical account of the trip, *American Notes*, was published later that year. Although the book was eagerly anticipated on both sides of the Atlantic, it garnered a mixed, even controversial, reception. Dickens's impressions of America were favorable overall, yet he still recorded his disillusionments, especially on the institution of slavery, with uncompromising honesty. Refusing to recant his observations, Dickens wrote in his preface to the 1850 edition, "I have nothing to defend or explain away. The truth is the truth; and neither childish absurdities, nor unscrupulous contradicitons, can make it otherwise."

The following excerpt is from Chapter XII of *American Notes*, in which Dickens describes his steamboat voyage to St. Louis, by way of Cincinnati and Louisville. In addition to containing his acerbic remarks about fellow passengers and the climate in the Mississippi Valley, this passage indicates that Dickens had a fairly balanced view of St. Louis, remarking on the splendor of some of the citizenry and architecture, as well as the squalor of tenements in the old French quarter of the city.

FROM *AMERICAN NOTES*

FROM CINCINNATI TO LOUISVILLE IN ANOTHER WESTERN STEAMBOAT; AND FROM LOUISVILLE TO ST. LOUIS IN ANOTHER. ST. LOUIS.

Leaving Cincinnati at eleven o'clock in the forenoon, we embarked for Louisville in the Pike steamboat, which, carrying the mails, was a packet of a much better class than that in which we had come from Pittsburg. As this passage does not occupy more than twelve or thirteen hours, we arranged to go ashore that night: not coveting the distinction of sleeping in a state-room, when it was possible to sleep anywhere else.

There chanced to be on board this boat, in addition to the usual dreary crowd of passengers, one Pitchlynn, a chief of the Choctaw tribe of Indians, who *sent in his card* to me, and with whom I had the pleasure of a long conversation.

He spoke English perfectly well, though he had not begun to learn the language, he told me, until he was a young man grown. He had read many books; and Scott's poetry appeared to have left a strong impression on his mind: especially the opening of The Lady of the Lake, and the great battle scene in Marmion, in which, no doubt from the congeniality of the subjects to his own pursuits and tastes, he had great interest and delight. He appeared to understand correctly all he had read; and whatever fiction had enlisted his sympathy in its belief, had done so keenly and earnestly. I might almost say fiercely. He was dressed in our ordinary every-day costume, which hung about his fine figure loosely, and with indifferent grace. On my telling him that I regretted not to see him in his own attire, he threw up his right arm for a moment, as though he were brandishing some heavy weapon, and answered, as he let it fall again, that his race were losing many things besides their dress, and would soon be seen upon the earth no more: but he wore it at home, he added proudly.

He told me that he had been away from his home, west of the Mississippi, seventeen months: and was now returning. He had been chiefly at Washington on some negotiations pending between his Tribe and the Government: which were not settled yet (he said in a melancholy way), and he feared never would be: for what could a few poor Indians do against such well-skilled men of business as the whites? He had no love for

Washington; tired of towns and cities very soon; and longed for the Forest and the Prairie.

I asked him what he thought of Congress? He answered, with a smile, that it wanted dignity in an Indian's eyes.

He would very much like, he said, to see England before he died; and spoke with much interest about the great things to be seen there. When I told him of that chamber in the British Museum wherein are preserved household memorials of a race that ceased to be, thousands of years ago, he was very attentive, and it was not hard to see that he had a reference in his mind to the gradual fading away of his own people.

This led us to speak of Mr. Catlin's gallery, which he praised highly: observing that his own portrait was among the collection, and that all the likenesses were "elegant." Mr. Cooper, he said, had painted the Red Man well; and so would I, he knew, if I would go home with him and hunt buffaloes, which he was quite anxious I should do. When I told him that, supposing I went, I should not be very likely to damage the buffaloes much, he took it as a great joke and laughed heartily.

He was a remarkably handsome man; some years past forty I should judge; with long black hair, an aquiline nose, broad cheek bones, a sunburnt complexion, and a very bright, keen, dark, and piercing eye. There were but twenty thousand of the Choctaws left, he said, and their number was decreasing every day. A few of his brother chiefs had been obliged to become civilised, and to make themselves acquainted with what the whites knew, for it was their only chance of existence. But they were not many; and the rest were as they always had been. He dwelt on this: and said several times that unless they tried to assimilate themselves to their conquerors, they must be swept away before the strides of civilised society.

When we shook hands at parting, I told him he must come to England, as he longed to see the land so much: that I should hope to see him there one day: and that I could promise him he would be well received and kindly treated. He was evidently pleased by this assurance, though he rejoined, with a good-humoured smile and an arch shake of his head, that the English used to be very fond of the Red Men when they wanted their help, but had not cared much for them since.

He took his leave; as stately and complete a gentleman of Nature's making as ever I beheld; and moved among the people in the boat, another kind of being. He sent me a lithographed portrait of himself soon afterwards; very like, though scarcely handsome enough; which I have carefully preserved in memory of our brief acquaintance.

There was nothing very interesting in the scenery of this day's journey, which brought us at midnight to Louisville. We slept at the Galt House; a splendid hotel; and were as handsomely lodged as though we had been in Paris, rather than hundreds of miles beyond the Alleghanies.

The city presenting no objects of sufficient interest to detain us on our way, we resolved to proceed next day by another steamboat, the Fulton, and to join it, about noon, at a suburb called Portland, where it would be delayed some time in passing through a canal.

The interval, after breakfast, we devoted to riding through the town, which is regular and cheerful: the streets being laid out at right angles, and planted with young trees. The buildings are smoky and blackened, from the use of bituminous coal, but an Englishman is well used to that appearance, and indisposed to quarrel with it. There did not appear to be much business stirring; and some unfinished buildings and improvements seemed to intimate that the city had been over-built in the ardour of "going ahead," and was suffering under the reaction consequent upon such feverish forcing of its powers.

On our way to Portland we passed a "Magistrate's Office," which amused me, as looking far more like a dame school than any police establishment: for this awful Institution was nothing but a little, lazy, good-for-nothing front parlour, open to the street; wherein two or three figures (I presume the magistrate and his myrmidons) were basking in the sunshine, the very effigies of languor and repose. It was a perfect picture of Justice retired from business for want of customers; her sword and scales sold off; napping comfortably with her legs upon the table.

Here, as elsewhere in these parts, the road was perfectly alive with pigs of all ages; lying about in every direction, fast alseep; or grunting along in quest of hidden dainties. I had always a sneaking kindness for these odd animals, and found a constant source of amusement, when all others failed, in watching their proceedings. As we were riding along this morning, I observed a little incident between two youthful pigs, which was so very human as to be inexpressibly comical and grotesque at the time, though, I dare say, in telling, it is tame enough.

One young gentleman (a very delicate porker with several straws sticking about his nose, betokening recent investigations in a dunghill), was walking deliberately on, profoundly thinking, when suddenly his brother, who was lying in a miry hole unseen by him, rose up immediately before his startled eyes, ghostly with damp mud. Never was pig's whole mass of blood so turned. He started back at least three feet, gazed for a moment, and then shot off as hard as he could go: his excessively little tail vibrating with speed and terror like a distracted pendulum. But, before he had gone very far, he began to reason with himself as to the nature of this frightful appearance; and as he reasoned, he relaxed his speed by gradual degrees; until at last he stopped, and faced about. There was his brother, with the mud upon him glazing in the sun, yet staring out of the very same hole, perfectly amazed at his proceedings! He was no sooner assured of this; and he assured himself so carefully that one may almost say he shaded his eyes with his hand to see the better; than he came back at a round trot, pounced upon him, and summarily took off a piece of his tail; as a caution to him to be careful what he was about for the future, and never to play tricks with his family any more.

We found the steamboat in the canal, waiting for the slow process of getting through the lock, and went on board, where we shortly afterwards had a new kind of visitor in the person of a certain Kentucky Giant, whose name is Porter, and who is of the moderate height of seven feet eight inches in his stockings.

There never was a race of people who so completely gave the lie to history as these giants, or whom all the chroniclers have so cruelly libelled. Instead of roaring and ravaging about the world, constantly catering for their cannibal larders, and perpetually going to market in an unlawful manner, they are the meekest people in any man's acquaintance: rather inclining to milk and vegetable diet, and bearing anything for a quiet life. So decidedly are amiability and mildness their characteristics, that I confess I look upon that youth who distinguished himself by the slaughter of these inoffensive persons as a false-hearted brigand, who, pretending to philanthropic motives, was secretly influenced only by the wealth stored up within their castles, and the hope of plunder. And I lean the more to this opinion from finding that even the historian of those exploits, with all his partiality for his hero, is fain to admit that the slaughtered monsters in question were of a very innocent and simple turn; extremely guileless and ready of belief, lending a credulous ear to the most improbable tales; suffering themselves to be easily entrapped into pits; and even (as in the case of the

Welsh Giant), with an excess of the hospitable politeness of a landlord, ripping themselves open, rather than hint at the possibility of their guests being versed in the vagabond arts of sleight-of-hand and hocus-pocus.

The Kentucky Giant was but another illustration of the truth of this position. He had a weakness in the region of the knees, and a trustfulness in his long face, which appealed even to five-feet-nine for encouragement and support. He was only twenty-five years old, he said, and had grown recently, for it had been found necessary to make an addition to the legs of his inexpressibles. At fifteen he was a short boy, and in those days his English father and his Irish mother had rather snubbed him, as being too small of stature to sustain the credit of the family. He added that his health had not been good, though it was better now; but short people are not wanting who whisper that he drinks too hard.

I understand he drives a hackney coach, though how he does it, unless he stands on the foot-board behind, and lies along the roof upon his chest, with his chin in the box, it would be difficult to comprehend. He brought his gun with him, as a curiosity. Christened "The Little Rifle," and displayed outside a shop-window, it would make the fortune of any retail business in Holborn. When he had shown himself and talked a little while, he withdrew with his pocket instrument, and went bobbing down the cabin, among men of six feet high and upwards, like a lighthouse walking among lamp-posts.

Within a few minutes afterwards we were out of the canal, and in the Ohio River again.

The arrangements of the boat were like those of the Messenger, and the passengers were of the same order of people. We fed at the same times, on the same kind of viands, in the same dull manner, and with the same observances. The company appeared to be oppressed by the same tremendous concealments, and had as little capacity of enjoyment or light-heartedness. I never in my life did see such listless heavy dullness as brooded over these meals: the very recollection of it weighs me down, and makes me, for the moment, wretched. Reading and writing on my knee, in our little cabin, I really dreaded the coming of the hour that summoned us to table; and was as glad to escape from it again as if it had been a penance or a punishment. Healthy cheerfulness and good spirits forming a part of the banquet, I could soak my crusts in the fountain with Le Sage's strolling player, and revel in their glad enjoyment: but sitting down with so many fellow-animals to ward off thirst and hunger as a business; to empty each creature his Yahoo's trough as quickly as he can, and then slink sullenly away; to have these social sacraments stripped of everything but the mere greedy satisfaction of the natural cravings; goes so against the grain with me, that I seriously believe the recollection of these funeral feasts will be a waking nightmare to me all my life.

There was some relief in this boat, too, which there had not been in the other, for the captain (a blunt, good-natured fellow) had his handsome wife with him, who was disposed to be lively and agreeable, as were a few other lady passengers who had their seats about us at the same end of the table. But nothing could have made head against the depressing influence of the general body. There was a magnetism of dullness in them which would have beaten down the most facetious companion that the earth ever knew. A jest would have been a crime, and a smile would have faded into a grinning horror. Such deadly leaden people; such systematic, plodding, weary, insupportable heaviness; such a mass of animated indigestion in respect of all that was genial, jovial, frank, social, or hearty; never, sure, was brought together elsewhere since the world began.

Nor was the scenery, as we approached the junction of the Ohio and Mississippi Rivers, at all inspiriting in its influence. The trees were stunted in their growth; the banks were low and flat; the settlements and log-cabins fewer in number: their inhabitants more wan and wretched than any we had encountered yet. No songs of birds were in the air, no pleasant scents, no moving lights and shadows from swift-passing clouds. Hour after hour, the changeless glare of the hot, unwinking sky shone upon the same monotonous objects. Hour after hour, the river rolled along as wearily and slowly as the time itself.

At length, upon the morning of the third day, we arrived at a spot so much more desolate than any we had yet beheld, that the forlornest places we had passed were, in comparison with it, full of interest. At the junction of the two rivers, on ground so flat and low and marshy, that at certain seasons of the year it is inundated to the housetops, lies a breeding-place of fever, ague, and death; vaunted in England as a mine of Golden Hope, and speculated in, on the faith of monstrous representations, to many people's ruin. A dismal swamp, on which the half-built houses rot away: cleared here and there for the space of a few yards; and teeming, then, with rank, unwholesome vegetation, in whose baleful shade the wretched wanderers who are tempted hither droop, and die, and lay their bones; the hateful

Mississippi circling and eddying before it, and turning off upon its southern course, a slimy monster hideous to behold; a hotbed of disease, an ugly sepulchre, a grave uncheered by any gleam of promise: a place without one single quality, in earth or air or water, to commend it: such is this dismal Cairo.

But what words shall describe the Mississippi, great father of rivers, who (praise be to Heaven!) has no young children like him? An enormous ditch, sometimes two or three miles wide, running liquid mud, six miles an hour: its strong and frothy current choked and obstructed everywhere by huge logs and whole forest trees: now twining themselves together in great rafts, from the interstices of which a sedgy, lazy foam works up, to float upon the water's top: now rolling past like monstrous bodies, their tangled roots showing like matted hair; now glancing singly by like giant leeches; and now writhing round and round in the vortex of some small whirlpool like wounded snakes. The banks low, the trees dwarfish, the marshes swarming with frogs, the wretched cabins few and far apart, their inmates hollow-cheeked and pale, the weather very hot, mosquitoes penetrating into every crack and crevice of the boat, mud and slime on everything: nothing pleasant in its aspect, but the harmless lightning which flickers every night upon the dark horizon.

For two days we toiled up this foul stream, striking constantly against the floating timber, or stopping to avoid those more dangerous obstacles, the snags, or sawyers, which are the hidden trunks of trees that have their roots below the tide. When the nights are very dark, the look-out stationed in the head of the boat knows, by the ripple of the water, if any great impediment be near at hand, and rings a bell beside him, which is the signal for the engine to be stopped; but always in the night this bell has work to do, and, after every ring, there comes a blow which renders it no easy matter to remain in bed.

The decline of day here was very gorgeous; tinging the firmament deeply with red and gold, up to the very keystone of the arch above us. As the sun went down behind the bank, the slightest blades of grass upon it seemed to become as distinctly visible as the arteries in the skeleton of a leaf, and when, as it slowly sank, the red and golden bars upon the water grew dimmer, and dimmer yet, as if they were sinking too; and all the glowing colours of departing day paled, inch by inch, before the sombre night; the scene became a thousand times more lonesome and more dreary than before, and all its influences darkened with the sky.

We drank the muddy water of this river while we were upon it. It is considered wholesome by the natives, and is something more opaque than gruel. I have seen water like it at the Filter shops, but nowhere else.

On the fourth night after leaving Louisville we reached St. Louis, and here I witnessed the conclusion of an incident, trifling enough in itself, but very pleasant to see, which had interested me during the whole journey.

There was a little woman on board, with a little baby; and both little woman and little child were cheerful, good-looking, bright-eyed, and fair to see. The little woman had been passing a long time with her sick mother in New York, and had left her home in St. Louis in that condition in which ladies who truly love their lords desire to be. The baby was born in her mother's house; and she had not seen her husband (to whom she was now returning) for twelve months: having left him a month or two after their marriage.

Well, to be sure there never was a little woman so full of hope, and tenderness, and love, and anxiety as this little woman was: and all day long she wondered whether "He" would be at the wharf; and whether "He" had got her letter; and whether, if she sent the baby ashore by somebody else, "He" would know it, meeting it in the street: which, seeing that he had never set eyes upon it in his life, was not very likely in the abstract, but was probable enough to the young mother. She was such an artless little creature; and was in such a sunny, beaming, hopeful state; and let out all this matter, clinging close about her heart, so freely; that all the other lady passengers entered into the spirit of it as much as she; and the captain (who heard all about it from his wife) was wondrous sly, I promise you: inquiring, every time we met at table, as in forgetfulness, whether she expected anybody to meet her at St. Louis, and whether she would want to go ashore the night we reached it (but he supposed she wouldn't), and cutting many other dry jokes of that nature. There was one little, weazen, dried-apple-faced old woman, who took occasion to doubt the constancy of husbands in such circumstances of bereavement; and there was another lady (with a lapdog) old enough to moralise on the lightness of human affections, and yet not so old that she could help nursing the baby now and then, or laughing with the rest when the little woman called it by its father's name, and asked it all manner of fantastic questions concerning him in the joy of her heart.

It was something of a blow to the little woman, that when we were within twenty miles of our destination, it became clearly necessary to put this baby to bed. But she got over it with the same good-humour; tied a handkerchief round her head; and came out into the little gallery with the rest. Then, such an oracle as she became in reference to the localities! and such facetiousness as was displayed by the married ladies! and such sympathy as was shown by the single ones! and such peals of laughter as the little woman herself (who would just as soon have cried) greeted every jest with!

At last there were the lights of St. Louis, and here was the wharf, and those were the steps: and the little woman, covering her face with her hands, and laughing (or seeming to laugh) more than ever, ran into her own cabin, and shut herself up. I have no doubt that, in the charming inconsistency of such excitement, she stopped her ears, lest she should hear "Him" asking for her: but I did not see her do it.

Then, a great crowd of people rushed on board, though the boat was not yet made fast, but was wandering about, among the other boats, to find a landing-place: and everybody looked for the husband: and nobody saw him: when, in the midst of us all—Heaven knows how she ever got there—there was the little woman clinging with both arms tight round the neck of a fine, good-looking, sturdy young fellow! and, in a moment afterwards, there she was again, actually clapping her little hands for joy, as she dragged him through the small door of her small cabin, to look at the baby as he lay asleep!

We went to a large hotel, called the Planter's House: built like an English hospital, with long passages and bare walls, and sky-lights above the room-doors for the free circulation of air. There were a great many boarders in it; and as many lights sparkled and glistened from the windows down into the street below, when we drove up, as if it had been illuminated on some occasion of rejoicing. It is an excellent house, and the proprietors have most bountiful notions of providing the creature comforts. Dining alone with my wife in our own room one day, I counted fourteen dishes on the table at once.

In the old French portion of the town the thoroughfares are narrow and crooked, and some of the houses are very quaint and picturesque: being built of wood, with tumble-down galleries before the windows, approachable by stairs, or rather ladders, from the street. There are queer little barbers' shops, and drinking-houses too, in this quarter; and abundance of crazy old tenements with blinking casements, such as may be seen in Flanders. Some of these ancient habitations, with high garret gable windows perking into the roofs, have a kind of French shrug about them; and, being lop-sided with age, appear to hold their heads askew besides, as if they were grimacing in astonishment at the American Improvements.

It is hardly necessary to say that these consist of wharfs and warehouses, and new buildings in all directions; and of a great many vast plans which are still "progressing." Already, however, some very good houses, broad streets, and marble-fronted shops have gone so far ahead as to be in a state of completion; and the town bids fair, in a few years, to improve considerably: though it is not likely ever to vie, in, point of elegance or beauty, with Cincinnati.

The Roman Catholic religion, introduced here by the early French settlers, prevails extensively. Among the public institutions are a Jesuit College; a convent for "the Ladies of the Sacred Heart;" and a large chapel attached to the college, which was in course of erection at the time of my visit, and was intended to be consecrated on the second of December in the next year. The architect of this building is one of the reverend fathers of the school, and the works proceed under his sole direction. The organ will be sent from Belgium.

In addition to these establishments, there is a Roman Catholic cathedral, dedicated to St. Francis Xavier; and a hospital, founded by the munificence of a deceased resident, who was a member of that church. It also sends missionaries from hence among the Indian tribes.

The Unitarian church is represented, in this remote place, as in most other parts of America, by a gentleman of great worth and excellence. The poor have good reason to remember and bless it; for it befriends them, and aids the cause of rational education, without any sectarian or selfish views. It is liberal in all its actions; of kind construction; and of wide benevolence.

There are three free-schools already erected and in full operation in this city. A fourth is building, and will soon be opened.

No man ever admits the unhealthiness of the place he dwells in (unless he is going away from it), and I shall therefore, I have no doubt, be at issue with the inhabitants of St. Louis in questioning the perfect salubrity of its climate, and in hinting that I think it must rather dispose to fever in the summer and autumnal seasons. Just adding, that it is very hot, lies among great rivers, and has vast tracts of undrained swampy land around it, I leave the reader to form his own opinion.

JOSEPH M. FIELD

JOSEPH FIELD (1810–1856) was two years old when his father emigrated from Dublin, Ireland, to Baltimore and became the publisher of the first Catholic almanac in the United States. Following his father's premature death, Field gravitated to a career in the theatre and became a popular actor, appearing in St. Louis for the first time in July 1835 in the title role of Richard III.

Like his younger brother, Matthew, Joseph Field was multi-talented. In addition to his success on the stage, Field was one of the most popular writers in the country, having become famous for his humorous sketches in the *New Orleans Picayune*, which were published under the *nom de plume* "Straws."

In 1844, Joseph Field, newspaperman Charles Keemle, and Matthew Field combined their talents and energies to start the *St. Louis Reveille.* Located at 22 Olive Street near Main, the *Reveille* was widely popular with St. Louis readers, but publication ceased in May 1849 when the Great Fire destroyed its office and plant.

A jack-of-all-trades journalist, Field was not only a competent translator for the *Reveille*, as evidenced by his translation of the famous "Chanson de L'année du Coup" (1845), but also a masterful storyteller. In 1844, Field wrote and published the "Death of Mike Fink," a fairly straightforward version of the death of the legendary keelboatman, in the *Reveille.* Although so much of the lore about Fink is of dubious veracity, Charles Keemle was present at the site of Fink's death on the Yellowstone River in 1823 and provided Field with the facts he uses in the 1844 account.

After the destruction of the *Reveille*, Field returned to the theatre but his endeavors produced little commercial success. His St. Louis company, "Field's Varieties," opened in 1852, but folded soon after. Field eventually left St. Louis and started another theatre company in Mobile, Alabama, where he died of pneumonia in 1856.

MIKE FINK

ALTHOUGH MIKE FINK (1770-1823) led an extraordinary life, facts about him have been inextricably woven with stories and legends that grew out of his exploits, imbuing Fink with virtually immortal stature. The year and place of Mike Fink's birth are most frequently given as 1770 near Fort Pitt (Pittsburgh, Pennsylvania). Before he entered his teens, Fink established himself as an exceptional marksman, adventurer, and braggart, a characteristic which undoubtedly provided material and momentum for the tales that spun around him.

In his early career, Fink was a market hunter, supplying meat to Pittsburgh merchants. He then became an Indian scout and fighter during the Indian wars in the upper Ohio valley. Like many scouts, Fink changed careers after the Indian wars subsided, opting for adventure on the Mississippi and Ohio Rivers as a boatman.

The last phase of Fink's adventurous life began in St. Louis in 1822, when he responded to an advertisement in St. Louis's *Missouri Republican* calling for "enterprising young men . . . to ascend the Missouri river to its source." Fink and two of his friends, Bill Carpenter and Levi Talbot, joined a Missouri Fur Company expedition at St. Louis and traveled up the Missouri to the mouth of the Yellowstone River, where they camped for the winter. Victims of the hard-drinking, brawling culture they embraced, Fink and his companions increasingly grew contentious, and, in an episode of drunken gunplay, Fink killed—whether accidentally or intentionally is unclear—Bill Carpenter. Shortly thereafter, Levi Talbot shot and killed Fink, who was buried at Fort Henry.

The following excerpt is drawn from Joseph Field's 1844 account, "Death of Mike Fink," published in the *St. Louis Reveille*. In 1847, the *Reveille* published a lengthy serialization of the exploits of Fink, also written by Field. However, the later account omits the intimation of a possible homosexual relationship between Fink and Carpenter that is present in the 1844 version.

DEATH OF MIKE FINK

"The Last of the Boatmen" has not become altogether a *mythic* personage. There be around us those who still remember him as one of flesh and blood, as well of proportions simply human, albeit he lacked not somewhat of the *heroic* in stature, as well as in being a "perfect terror" to people!

As regards Mike, it has not yet become that favorite question of doubt—"Did such a being really live?" Nor have we heard the skeptic inquiry—"Did such a being really die?" But his death in half a dozen different ways and places has been asserted, and this, we take it, is the first gathering of the *mythic* haze—that shadowy and indistinct enlargement of outline, which, deepening through long ages, invests distinguished mortality with the sublimer attributes of the hero and the demi-god. Had Mike lived in "early Greece," his flatboat feats would, doubtless, in poetry, have rivalled those of Jason in his ship; while in Scandinavian legends he would have been a river-god, to a certainty! The Sea-kings would have sacrificed to him every time they "crossed the bar" on their return; and as for Odin himself, he would be duly advised, as far as any interference went, to "lay low and keep dark, or *pre*-haps," &c.

The story of Mike Fink, including a death, has been beautifully told by the late Morgan Neville of Cincinnati, a gentleman of the highest literary taste as well as of the most amiable and polished manners. "The Last of the Boatmen," as his sketch is entitled, is unexceptionable in style, and, we believe, in *fact*, with one exception, and that is, the statement as to the manner and place of Fink's death. He did *not die* on the Arkansas, but at Fort Henry, near the mouth of the Yellow Stone. Our informant is the senior editor of this paper, who held a command in the neighborhood, at the time, and to whom every circumstance connected with the affair is most familiar. We give the story as it is told by himself.

In the year 1822, steamboats having left the "keels" and "broad-horns" entirely "out of sight," and Mike having, in consequence, fallen from his high estate—that of being "a little bit the almightiest man on the river, *any* how"—after a term of idleness, frolic and desperate rowdyism along the different towns, he, at St. Louis, entered the service of the Mountain Fur Company raised by our late fellow-citizen Gen. W. H. Ashley as a trapper and hunter; and in that capacity was he employed by Major Henry, in command of the Fort at the mouth of Yellow Stone river when the occurrence took place of which we write.

Mike, with many generous qualities, was always a reckless daredevil; but at this time, advancing in years and decayed in influence, above all become a victim of whisky, he was morose and desperate in the extreme. There was a government regulation which forbade the free use of alcohol at the trading posts on the Missouri river, and this was a continual source of quarrel between the men and the commandant, Major Henry, on the part of Fink, particularly. One of his freaks was to march with his rifle into the fort and demand a supply of spirits. Argument was fruitless, force not to be thought of, and when, on being positively denied, Mike drew up his rifle and sent a ball through the cask, deliberately walked up and filled his can, while his particular "boys" followed his example, all that could be done was to look upon the matter as one of his "queer ways," and that was the end of it.

This state of things continued for some time; Mike's temper and exactions growing more unbearable every day, until, finally, a "split" took place, not only between himself and the commandant, but many others in the fort, and the unruly boatman swore he would not live among them. Followed only by a youth named Carpenter, whom he had brought up, and for whom he felt a rude but strong attachment, he prepared a sort of cave in the river's bank, furnished it with a supply of whisky, and with his companion *turned in* to pass the winter, which was then closing upon them. In this place he buried himself, sometimes unseen for weeks, his *protege* providing what else was *necessary* beyond the whisky. At length attempts were used, on the part of those in the fort, to withdraw Carpenter from Fink; foul insinuations were made as to the nature of their connection; the youth was twitted with being a mere slave, &c., all which (Fink heard of it in spite of his retirement) served to breed distrust between the two, and though they did not separate, much of their cordiality ceased.

The winter wore away in this sullen state of torpor; spring came with its reviving influences, and to celebrate the season, a supply of alcohol was procured, and a number of his acquaintances from the fort coming to "rouse out" Mike, a desperate "frolic," of course, ensued.

There were river yarns and boatmen songs and "nigger breakdowns," interspersed with wrestling-matches, jumping, laugh, and yell, the can circulating freely, until Mike became somewhat mollified.

"I tell you what it is, boys," he cried, "the fort's a skunk-hole, and I'd rather live with the *bars* than stay in it. Some on ye's bin trying to part me and my boy, that I love like my own cub—but no matter. Maybe he's *pi*soned against me; but, Carpenter (striking the youth heavily on the shoulder), I took you by the hand when it had forgotten the touch of a father's or a mother's—you know me to be a man, and you ain't a going to turn out a dog!"

Whether it was that the youth fancied something insulting in the manner of the appeal, or not, we can't say; but it was not responded to very warmly, and a reproach followed from Mike. However, they drank together, and the frolic went on until Mike, filling his can, walked off some forty yards, placed it upon his head, and called to Carpenter to take his rifle.

This wild feat of shooting cans off each other's head was a favorite one with Mike—himself and "boy" generally winding up a hard frolic with this savage but deeply-meaning proof of continued confidence;—as for risk, their eagle eyes and iron nerves defied the might of whisky. After their recent alienation, a doubly generous impulse, without doubt, had induced Fink to propose and subject himself to the test.

Carpenter had been drinking wildly, and with a boisterous laugh snatched up his rifle. All present had seen the parties "shoot," and this desperate aim, instead of alarming, was merely made a matter of wild jest.

"Your grog is spilt, forever, Mike!"

"Kill the old varmint, young 'un!"

"What'll his skin bring in St. Louis?" &c., &c.

Amid a loud laugh, Carpenter raised his piece—even the jesters remarked that he was unsteady,—"crack!"—the can fell,—a loud shout,—but, instead of a smile of pleasure, a dark frown settled upon the face of Fink! He made no motion except to clutch his rifle as though he would have crushed it, and there he stood, gazing at the youth strangely! Various shades of passion crossed his features—surprise, rage, suspicion—but at length they composed themselves into a sad expression; the ball had grazed the top of his head, cutting the scalp, and the thought of treachery had set his heart on fire.

There was a loud call upon Mike to know what he was waiting for, in which Carpenter joined, pointing to the can upon his head and bidding him fire, if he knew how!

"Carpenter, my son," said the boatman, "I taught you to shoot differently from that *last* shot! You've *missed* once, but you won't again!"

He fired, and his ball, crashing through the forehead of the youth, laid him a corpse amid his, as suddenly hushed, companions!

Time wore on—many at the fort spoke darkly of the deed. Mike Fink had never been known to miss his aim—he had grown afraid of Carpenter—he had murdered him! While this feeling was gathering against him, the unhappy boatman lay in his cave, shunning both sympathy and sustenance. He spoke to none—when he did come forth, 'twas as a spectre, and only to haunt the grave of his "boy," or, if he did break silence, 'twas to burst into a paroxysm of rage against the enemies who had "turned his boy's heart from him!"

At the fort was a man by the name of Talbott, the gunsmith of the station: he was very loud and bitter in his denunciations of the "murderer," as he called Fink, which, finally, reaching the ears of the latter, filled him with the most violent passion, and he swore that he would take the life of his defamer. This threat was almost forgotten, when one day, Talbott, who was at work in his shop, saw Fink enter the fort, his first visit since the death of Carpenter. Fink approached; he was careworn, sick, and wasted; there was no anger in his bearing, but he carried his rifle, (had he ever gone without it!) and the gunsmith was not a coolly brave man; moreover, his life had been threatened.

"Fink," cried he, snatching up a pair of pistols from his bench, "don't approach me—if you do, you're a dead man!"

"Talbott," said the boatman, in a sad voice, "you needn't be afraid;—you've done me wrong—I'm come to talk to you about—Carpenter—my boy!"

He continued to advance, and the gunsmith again called to him:

"Fink! I know you;—if you come three steps nearer, I'll fire, by——!"

Mike carried his rifle across his arm, and made no hostile demonstration, except in gradually getting nearer—*if* hostile his aim was.

"Talbott, you've accused me of murdering—my boy—Carpenter—that I raised from a child—that I loved like a son—that I can't live without! I'm not mad with you *now*, but you must let me show you that I *couldn't* do it—that I'd rather died than done it—that you've wronged me——"

By this time he was within a few steps of the door, and Talbott's agitation became extreme. Both pistols were pointed at Fink's breast, in expectation of a spring from the latter.

"By the Almighty above us, Fink, I'll fire—I don't want to speak to you now—don't put your foot on that step—don't—."

Fink did put his foot on the step, and the same moment fell heavily within it, receiving the contents of both barrels in his breast! His last and only words were,—

"I didn't mean to kill my boy!"

Poor Mike! we are satisfied with our senior's conviction that you did *not* mean to kill him. Suspicion of treachery, doubtless, entered his mind, but cowardice and murder never dwelt there.

A few weeks after this event, Talbott himself perished in an attempt to cross the Missouri river in a skiff.

CHARLES LANMAN

CHARLES LANMAN (1819–1895), of Monroe, Michigan, received his education in New England and returned to his hometown in 1845 to edit the *Monroe Gazette*, thus launching his career in journalism. In 1846, Lanman spent the summer traveling along the Upper Mississippi and recorded his impressions in *A Summer in the Wilderness,* which became a popular book, one of several volumes Lanman wrote on his extensive travels around North America. For more than forty years of his life, Lanman held prominent appointments in Washington, D.C. He served as librarian of the War Department, librarian of copyrights for the State Department, private secretary to Daniel Webster, librarian of the House of Representatives, and librarian of the Washington, D.C., City Library, among other positions. Concurrently, Lanman continued to write numerous articles and books.

The following excerpt is Lanman's account of his visit to St. Louis from *A Summer in the Wilderness.* Although the book was well received by the general public and such notables as Washington Irving, Lanman received harsh criticism from at least one prominent journalist for taking undue "poetical license" with fact. Critics and historians have exonerated Lanman from such charges, maintaining that he, also being a talented painter, told his account from the romantic viewpoint of a young artist, and that the book was meant to entertain readers more than to inform them about conditions in the hinterlands. This assessment seems to hold particularly for this excerpt, in which Lanman refers to St. Louis as the "River Queen" and remarks on its romantic nature. Lanman also goes on at some length about Charles Deas, a St. Louis–based artist whose work he admired. The passage closes with Lanman's description of an especially moving twilight experience in the city's Old Cathedral.

FROM *A SUMMER IN THE WILDERNESS*

SAINT LOUIS, JUNE, 1846

The River Queen, as Saint Louis is sometimes called, is looked upon as the threshold leading to the wild and romantic region of the Upper Mississippi. It was founded in the year seventeen hundred and sixty-four, by two Frenchmen, named Laclede and Chouteau, who were accompanied by about thirty Creoles. The first steamer which landed here came from New Orleans in the year eighteen hundred and nineteen; but the number now belonging here is rated at three hundred, many of which are unsurpassed in speed and splendor of accommodations. The population of this city amounts to forty thousand souls. It is elevated some eighty feet above the low-water mark of the Mississippi, and from the river presents a handsome appearance. The old part of the town is inhabited by a French population, and is in a dilapidated condition; but the more modern portion is distinguished for its handsome streets, and tastefully built mansions and public buildings. Fronting the levee or landing are several blocks of stone stores, which give one an idea of the extensive business transacted here. On one occasion I saw this wharfing ground so completely crowded with merchandise of every possible variety, that travellers were actually compelled to walk from the steamboats to the hotels. This city is the home market for all the natural productions of a wilderness country extending in different directions for thousands of miles, and watered by several of the largest rivers in the world. Its growth, however, has been somewhat retarded by the peculiar character of its original inhabitants. The acknowledged wealth of many of its leading men can only be equalled by their illiberality and want of enterprise. But time is committing sad ravages among these ancient citizens, for they are, from age and infirmities, almost daily dropping into the place of graves. Under the benign influence of true American enterprise, this city is rapidly becoming distinguished for its New England character, in spite of the retarding cause alluded to above, and the baneful institution of Slavery. In fine, it possesses, to an uncommon degree, all the worthy qualities which should belong to an enlightened and eminently prosperous city.

There is one unique feature connected with the River Queen, which gives it, at times, a most romantic appearance. It is the point whence must start all distant expeditions to the North and West, and where the treasures of the wilderness are prepared for re-shipment to the more distant markets of our own and foreign countries. Here, during the spring and summer months may often be seen caravans about to depart for California, Santa Fe, the Rocky Mountains, and Oregon, while the sprightly step and sparkling eye will speak to you of the hopes and anticipations which animate the various adventurers. At one time, perhaps, may be seen a company of toil-worn trappers entering the city, after an absence of months, far away on the head waters of the Mississippi and Missouri rivers, where they have hunted the beaver, the buffalo, the otter, the bear, and the deer; and as they steal away to their several homes, from the door of the Fur Company, where they have just rendered their account, it does the heart good to ponder on the joys which will be brought into existence by the happy return. And the Indians, from different nations, who often visit this place, also add greatly to the picturesque appearance of its streets. Summoned by curiosity, they congregate here in large numbers, and while their gaudy trappings and painted faces remind us of the strange wild life they lead, their prowling propensities and downcast eyes inform us of the melancholy fact, that they are the victims of a most heartless, though lawful oppression. This remark, by the way, reminds me of a living picture which I lately witnessed, and will briefly describe. It was the sunset hour, and I was returning from a ride on the eastern bank of the great river. The western sky was flooded with a saffron glow, in the midst of which floated unnumbered cloud-islands, tinged with deepest gold. Underneath lay the beautiful city, with its church-spires uppointing to the Christian's home; then passed the rushing tide of the Mississippi ploughed by many a proud keel; and in the foreground was a woody bluff, on the brow of which sat a solitary Indian, humming a strangely solemn song, as his white locks and eagle plumes waved in the evening breeze. I asked no question of the sorrowing dreamer, but pursued my way, pondering on the cruel destiny which has power to make man a stranger and an exile, on the very soil from which he sprang, and where repose the ashes of his forgotten kindred.

Lover as I am of genuine art, it will not do for me to leave this city, the sturdy child of a new and great empire, without alluding to its treasures in this particular. The bright particular star, who uses the pencil here, is Charles Deas. He is a young man who left New-York about eight years ago, for the purpose of studying his art in the wilds west of the Mississippi. He makes this city his head-quarters, but annually spends a few months among the Indian tribes, familiarizing himself with their manners and customs, and he is honorably identifying himself with the history and scenery of a most interesting portion of the continent. The great charm of his productions is found in the strongly marked national character which they bear. His collection of sketches is already very valuable. The following are a few of the pictures which I saw in his studio, and which pleased me exceedingly. One, called the Indian Guide, represents an aged Indian riding in the evening twilight on a piebald horse, apparently musing upon the times of old. The sentiment of such a painting is not to be described, and can only be felt by the beholder who has a passion for the wilderness. Another, Long Jake, is the literal portrait of a celebrated character of the Rocky Mountains. He looks like an untamed hawk, figures in a flaming red shirt, and is mounted on a black stallion. He is supposed to be on the ridge of a hill, and as the sky is blue, the figure stands out in the boldest relief. Artistically speaking, this is a most daring effort of the pencil, but the artist has decidedly triumphed. In a picture called Setting out for the Mountains, Mr. Deas has represented a species of American Cockney, who has made up his mind to visit the Rocky Mountains. He is mounted on a bob-tailed, saucy-looking pony, and completely loaded down with clothing, pistols, guns, and ammunition. He is accompanied by a few covered wagons, a jolly servant to be his right-hand man, and two dogs, which are frolicking on the prairie ahead, and while the man directs the attention of his master to some game, the latter shrugs his feeble shoulders, seems to think this mode of travelling exceedingly fatiguing, and personifies the latter end of a misspent life. You imagine that a few months have elapsed, and, turning to another picture, you behold our hero Returning from the Mountains. Exposure and hardships have transformed him into a superb looking fellow, and he is now full of life and buoyancy, and riding with the most perfect elegance and ease a famous steed of the prairies. The wagons, servant and dogs, are now in the rear of our adventurer, who, comically dressed with nothing but a cap, a calico shirt, and pair of buckskin pantaloons, is dashing ahead, fearless of every danger that may happen to cross his path. These pictures completely epitomize a personal revolution which is constantly taking place on the frontiers. One of our artist's more ambitious productions, represents the daring feat of Captain Walker, during a recent memorable battle in Mexico. The story is that the Captain, who happened to be alone on a plain, had his horse killed from under him, and was himself wounded in the leg. Supposing, as was the case, that the Mexican savage would approach to take his scalp, he feigned himself dead, as he lay upon his horse, and as his enemy was about to butcher him, he fired and killed the rascal on the spot, and seizing the reins of his enemy's horse, he mounted him and rode into his own camp. In the picture Walker is in the act of firing. But the picture upon which Mr. Deas's fame will probably rest, contains a large number of figures, and represents the heroism of Captain James Clarke, who, when about to be murdered by a council of Indians at North-Bend, threw the war-belt in the midst of the savages, with a defying shout, and actually overwhelmed them with astonishment, thereby saving his own life and those of his companions. This picture is true to history in every particular, and full of expression.

But enough about these productions of art. I am bound to the fountain head of the Mississippi, and feel impatient to be with nature in the wilderness. Before concluding this chapter, however, I will describe a characteristic incident which I met with in Saint Louis.

I had been taking a lonely walk along the banks of the Mississippi, and, in fancy, revelling amid the charms of this great western world, as it existed centuries ago. My mind was in a dreamy mood, and as I re-entered the city the hum of business fell like discord on my ear. It was the hour of twilight and the last day of the week, and the citizens whom I saw seemed anxious to bring their labors to a close that they might be ready for the Sabbath.

While sauntering leisurely through a retired street, I was startled from a waking dream, by the sound of a deep-toned bell, and, on lifting my eyes, I found that I stood before the Catholic cathedral. I noticed a dim light through one of the windows, and as the gates were open, I remembered that it was the vesper hour, and entered the church. The inner door noiselessly swung to, and I found myself alone, the spectator of a most impressive scene. A single lamp, hanging before the altar, threw out a feeble light, and so feeble was it, that a solemn gloom brooded throughout the temple. While a dark shadow filled the aisles and remote corners, the capitals of the massive pillars on either side were lost in a still deeper shade. From the ceiling hung many a gorgeous chandelier, which were now content to be eclipsed by the humble solitary lamp. Scriptural paintings and pieces of statuary were on every side, but I could discern that Christ was the centre of attraction in all. Over, and around the altar too, were many works of art, together with a multitudinous array of sacred symbols. Just in front of these, and in the centre of the mystic throne, hung the lonely lamp, which seemed to be endowed with a thinking principle, as its feeble rays shot out into the surrounding darkness. That part of the cathedral where towered the stupendous organ, was in deep shadow, but I knew it to be there by the faint glistening of its golden pipes: as to the silence of the place, it was perfectly death-like and holy. I chanced to heave a sigh, and that very sigh was not without an echo. The distant hum of life, alone convinced me that I was in a living world.

But softly! A footstep now breaks upon the silence! A priest in a ghost-like robe, is passing from one chancel door to another. Another footstep! and lo! a woman, clothed in black, with her face completely hidden in a veil, passes up an aisle and falls upon her knees in prayer. She has come here to find consolation in her widowhood. And now, slowly tottering along, comes a white-haired man, and he, too, falls in the attitude of prayer. With the pleasures of this world he is fully satisfied, and his thoughts are now taken up with that strange pilgrimage, whence travellers never return, and upon which he feels he must soon enter.

Other life-sick mortals, have also entered the sanctuary, offered up their evening prayer, and mingled with the tide of life once more. But again the front door slowly opens, and a little negro boy, some seven years of age, is standing by my side. What business has he here,—for surely this offspring of a slave, and a slave himself, cannot be a religious devotee? I take back that thought. I have wronged the child. The Spirit of God must tabernacle in his heart, else he would not approach the altar with such deep reverence. Behold him, like little Samuel of old, calling upon the Invisible in prayer! What a picture! Twilight in a superb cathedral, and the only worshipper a child and a slave!

WILLIAM WELLS BROWN

WILLIAM WELLS BROWN (ca. 1814–1884), born a slave in Lexington, Kentucky, was moved to St. Louis by his master, Dr. Young, in 1827. While in St. Louis, Brown was hired out to multiple businessmen, most notably the famed abolitionist Elijah P. Lovejoy and Mr. Walker, a slave trader.

After several attempts, Brown escaped from slavery to work transporting fugitive slaves across Lake Erie to Canada. In 1847, the Massachusetts Anti-Slavery Society published *The Narrative of William Wells Brown, A Fugitive Slave, Written By Himself.* The society also employed Brown as a circuit lecturer to northern abolitionists.

Brown was second only to Frederick Douglass as the most accomplished African American of letters during the antebellum era, and in some ways he exceeded Douglass because his output was more varied. *Three Years in Europe; or, Places I Have Seen and People I Have Met* (1852), chronicling his sojourn in Europe in the 1850s, was the first travel book (a popular genre of the day) by an African American. *Clotel; or, The President's Daughter: A Narrative of Slave Life in the United States* (1853), long considered the first African American novel, further fueled the long-standing rumor that Thomas Jefferson fathered a child by a slave woman. *The Escape; or, A Leap for Freedom* (1858) was the first published play by an African American.

Brown also wrote several histories, including *The Black Man: His Antecedents, His Genius, His Achievements* (1863) and *The Rising Son; or, The Antecedents and Advancement of the Colored Race* (1874). His final book, an oddly nostalgic look at plantation life—*My Southern Home; or, The South and Its People*—appeared in 1880, the first study by an African American about the South as a distinct region.

This excerpt from the 1847 *Narrative* covers Brown's boyhood and adolescence in St. Louis and his time on the steamboats working in the slave trade as an assistant to the infamous Walker. Here we see in some detail the features of urban slavery; Brown, for instance, had a great deal more freedom of movement than he would have had on a plantation. Also, we come to understand the system of hiring out slaves, a common practice for city slaveholders. The genre of the slave narrative, arguably America's first social protest literature, was very popular during the antebellum era, and such narratives often went through several editions.

FROM *NARRATIVE OF WILLIAM WELLS BROWN*

Soon afterwards, my master removed to the city of St. Louis, and purchased a farm four miles from there, which he placed under the charge of an overseer by the name of Friend Haskell. He was a regular Yankee from New England. The Yankees are noted for making the most cruel overseers.

My mother was hired out in the city, and I was also hired out there to Major Freeland, who kept a public house. He was formerly from Virginia, and was a horse-racer, cock-fighter, gambler, and withal an inveterate drunkard. There were ten or twelve servants in the house, and when he was present, it was cut and slash—knock down and drag out. In his fits of anger, he would take up a chair, and throw it at a servant; and in his more rational moments, when he wished to chastise one, he would tie them up in the smokehouse, and whip them; after which, he would cause a fire to be made of tobacco stems, and smoke them. This he called "*Virginia play*."

I complained to my master of the treatment which I received from Major Freeland; but it made no difference. He cared nothing about it, so long as he received the money for my labor. After living with Major Freeland five or six months, I ran away, and went into the woods back of the city; and when night came on, I made my way to my master's farm, but was afraid to be seen, knowing that if Mr. Haskell, the overseer, should discover me, I should be again carried back to Major Freeland; so I kept in the woods. One day, while in the woods, I heard the barking and howling of dogs, and in a short time they came so near, that I knew them to be the bloodhounds of Major Benjamin O'Fallon. He kept five or six, to hunt runaway slaves with.

As soon as I was convinced that it was them, I knew there was no chance of escape. I took refuge in the top of a tree, and the hounds were soon at its base, and there remained until the hunters came up in a half or three quarters of an hour afterwards. There were two men with the dogs, who, as soon as they came up, ordered me to descend. I came down, was tied, and taken to St. Louis jail. Major Freeland soon made his appearance, and took me out, and ordered me to follow him, which I did. After we returned home, I was tied up in the smokehouse, and was very severely whipped. After the Major had flogged me to his satisfaction, he sent out his son Robert, a young man eighteen or twenty years of age, to see that I was well smoked. He made a fire of tobacco stems, which soon set me to coughing and sneezing. This, Robert told me, was the way his father used to do to his slaves in Virginia. After giving me what they conceived to be a decent smoking, I was untied and again set to work.

Robert Freeland was a "chip off the old block." Though quite young, it was not unfrequently that he came home in a state of intoxication. He is now, I believe, a popular commander of a steamboat on the Mississippi River. Major Freeland soon after failed in business, and I was put on board the steamboat Missouri, which plied between St. Louis and Galena. The commander of the boat was William B. Culver. I remained on her during the sailing season, which was the most pleasant time for me that I had ever experienced. At the close of navigation, I was hired to Mr. John Colburn, keeper of the Missouri Hotel. He was from one of the Free States; but a more inveterate hater of the negro, I do not believe ever walked on God's green earth. This hotel was at that time one of the largest in the city, and there were employed in it twenty or thirty servants, mostly slaves.

Mr. Colburn was very abusive, not only to the servants, but to his wife also, who was an excellent woman, and one from whom I never knew a servant to receive a harsh word; but never did I know a kind one to a servant from her husband. Among the slaves employed in the hotel, was one by the name of Aaron, who belonged to Mr. John F. Darby, a lawyer. Aaron was the knife-cleaner. One day, one of the knives was put on the table, not as clean as it might have been. Mr. Colburn, for this offence, tied Aaron up in the wood-house, and gave him over fifty lashes on the bare back with a cow-hide, after which, he made me wash him down with rum. This seemed to put him into more agony than the whipping. After being untied, he went home to his master, and complained of the treatment which he had received. Mr. Darby would give no heed to anything he had to say, but sent him directly back. Colburn, learning that he had been to his master with complaints, tied him up again, and gave him a more severe whipping than before. The poor fellow's back was literally cut to pieces; so much so, that he was not able to work for ten or twelve days.

There was also, among the servants, a girl whose master resided in the country. Her name was Patsey. Mr. Colburn tied her up one evening, and whipped her until several of the boarders came out and begged him to desist. The reason for whipping her was this. She was engaged to be married to a man belonging to Major William Christy, who resided four or five miles north of the city. Mr. Colburn had forbid her to see John Christy. The reason of this was said to be the regard which he himself had for Patsey. She went to meeting that evening, and John returned home with her. Mr. Colburn had intended to flog John, if he came within the inclosure; but John knew too well the temper of his rival, and kept at a safe distance;—so he took vengeance on the poor girl. If all the slave-drivers had been called together, I do not think a more cruel man than John Colburn,—and he too a northern man,—could have been found among them.

While living at the Missouri Hotel, a circumstance occurred which caused me great unhappiness. My master sold my mother, and all her children, except myself. They were sold to different persons in the city of St. Louis.

I was soon after taken from Mr. Colburn's, and hired to Elijah P. Lovejoy, who was at that time publisher and editor of the "St. Louis Times." My work, while with him, was mainly in the printing office, waiting on the hands, working the press, &c. Mr. Lovejoy was a very good man, and decidedly the best master that I had ever had. I am chiefly indebted to him, and to my employment in the printing office, for what little learning I obtained while in slavery.

Though slavery is thought, by some, to be mild in Missouri, when compared with the cotton, sugar and rice growing States, yet no part of our slaveholding country is more noted for the barbarity of its inhabitants than St. Louis. It was here that Col. Harney, a United States officer, whipped a slave woman to death. It was here that Francis McIntosh, a free colored man from Pittsburgh, was taken from the steamboat Flora and burned at the stake. During a residence of eight years in this city, numerous cases of extreme cruelty came under my own observation; to record them all would occupy more space than could possibly be allowed in this little volume. I shall, therefore, give but a few more in addition to what I have already related.

Capt. J. B. Brunt, who resided near my master, had a slave named John.

He was his body servant, carriage driver, &c. On one occasion, while driving his master through the city—the streets being very muddy, and the horses going at a rapid rate—some mud spattered upon a gentleman by the name of Robert More. More was determined to be revenged. Some three or four months after this occurrence, he purchased John, for the express purpose, as he said, "to tame the d——d nigger." After the purchase he took him to a blacksmith's shop, and had a ball and chain fastened to his leg, and then put him to driving a yoke of oxen, and kept him at hard labor, until the iron around his leg was so worn into the flesh, that it was thought mortification would ensue. In addition to this, John told me that his master whipped him regularly three times a week for the first two months:—and all this to "*tame him.*" A more noble looking man than he was not to be found in all St. Louis, before he fell into the hands of More; and a more degraded and spirit-crushed looking being was never seen on a southern plantation, after he had been subjected to this "*taming*" process for three months. The last time that I saw him, he had nearly lost the entire use of his limbs.

While living with Mr. Lovejoy, I was often sent on errands to the office of the "Missouri Republican," published by Mr. Edward Charles. Once, while returning to the office with type, I was attacked by several large boys, sons of slave-holders, who pelted me with snow-balls. Having the heavy form of type in my hands, I could not make my escape by running; so I laid down the type and gave them battle. They gathered around me, pelting me with stones and sticks, until they overpowered me, and would have captured me, if I had not resorted to my heels. Upon my retreat, they took possession of the type; and what to do to regain it I could not devise. Knowing Mr. Lovejoy to be a very humane man, I went to the office, and laid the case before him. He told me to remain in the office. He took one of the apprentices with him, and went after the type, and soon returned with it; but on his return informed me that Samuel McKinney had told him that he would whip me, because I had hurt his boy. Soon after, McKinney was seen making his way to the office by one of the printers, who informed me of the fact, and I made my escape through the back door.

McKinney not being able to find me on his arrival, left the office in a great rage, swearing that he would whip me to death. A few days after, as I was walking along Main Street, he seized me by the collar, and struck me over the head five or six times with a large cane, which caused the blood to gush from my nose and ears in such a manner that my clothes were completely saturated with blood. After beating me to his satisfaction he let me go, and I returned to the office so weak from the loss of blood, that Mr. Lovejoy sent me home to my master. It was five weeks before I was able to walk again. During this time, it was necessary to have some one to supply my place at the office, and I lost the situation.

After my recovery, I was hired to Capt. Otis Reynolds, as a waiter on board the steamboat Enterprise, owned by Messrs. John and Edward Walsh, commission merchants at St. Louis. This boat was then running on the upper Mississippi. My employment on board was to wait on gentlemen, and the captain being a good man, the situation was a pleasant one to me;—but in passing from place to place, and seeing new faces every day, and knowing that they could go where they pleased, I soon became unhappy, and several times thought of leaving the boat at some landing place, and trying to make my escape to Canada, which I had heard much about as a place where the slave might live, be free, and be protected.

But whenever such thoughts would come into my mind, my resolution would soon be shaken by the remembrance that my dear mother was a slave in St. Louis, and I could not bear the idea of leaving her in that condition. She had often taken me upon her knee, and told me how she had carried me upon her back to the field when I was an infant—how often she had been whipped for leaving her work to nurse me—and how happy I would appear when she would take me into her arms. When these thoughts came over me, I would resolve never to leave the land of slavery without my mother. I thought that to leave her in slavery, after she had undergone and suffered so much for me, would be proving recreant to the duty which I owed to her. Besides this, I had three brothers and a sister there—two of my brothers having died.

My mother, my brothers Joseph and Millford, and my sister Elizabeth, belonged to Mr. Isaac Mansfield, formerly from one of the Free States, (Massachusetts, I believe.) He was a tinner by trade, and carried on a large manufacturing establishment. Of all my relatives, mother was first, and sister next. One evening, while visiting them, I made some allusion to a proposed journey to Canada, and sister took her seat by my side, and taking my hand in hers, said, with tears in her eyes,—

"Brother, you are not going to leave mother and your dear sister here without a friend, are you?"

I looked into her face, as the tears coursed swiftly down her cheeks, and bursting into tears myself, said—

"No, I will never desert you and mother." She clasped my hand in hers, and said—

"Brother, you have often declared that you would not end your days in slavery. I see no possible way in which you can escape with us; and now, brother, you are on a steamboat where there is some chance for you to escape to a land of liberty. I beseech you not to let us hinder you. If we cannot get our liberty, we do not wish to be the means of keeping you from a land of freedom."

I could restrain my feelings no longer, and an outburst of my own feelings caused her to cease speaking upon that subject. In opposition to their wishes, I pledged myself not to leave them in the hand of the oppressor. I took leave of them, and returned to the boat, and laid down in my bunk; but "sleep departed from my eyes, and slumber from my eyelids."

A few weeks after, on our downward passage, the boat took on board, at Hannibal, a drove of slaves, bound for the New Orleans market. They numbered from fifty to sixty, consisting of men and women from eighteen to forty years of age. A drove of slaves on a southern steamboat, bound for the cotton or sugar regions, is an occurrence so common, that no one, not even the passengers, appear to notice it, though they clank their chains at every step. There was, however, one in this gang that attracted the attention of the passengers and crew. It was a beautiful girl, apparently about twenty years of age, perfectly white, with straight light hair and blue eyes. But it was not the whiteness of her skin that created such a sensation among those who gazed upon her—it was her almost unparalleled beauty. She had been on the boat but a short time, before the attention of all the passengers, including the ladies, had been called to her, and the common topic of conversation was about the beautiful slave-girl. She was not in chains. The man who claimed this article of human merchandise was a Mr. Walker—a well known slave-trader, residing in St. Louis. There was a general anxiety among the passengers and crew to learn the history of the girl. Her master kept close by her side, and it would have been considered impudent for any of the passengers to have spoken to her, and the crew were not allowed to have any conversation with them. When we reached St. Louis, the slaves were removed to a boat bound for New Orleans, and the history of the beautiful slave-girl remained a mystery.

I remained on the boat during the season, and it was not an unfrequent occurrence to have on board gangs of slaves on their way to the cotton, sugar and rice plantations of the South.

Toward the latter part of the summer Captain Reynolds left the boat, and I was sent home. I was then placed on the farm under Mr. Haskell, the overseer. As I had been some time out of the field, and not accustomed to work in the burning sun, it was very hard; but I was compelled to keep up with the best of the hands.

I found a great difference between the work in a steamboat cabin and that in a corn-field.

My master, who was then living in the city, soon after removed to the farm, when I was taken out of the field to work in the house as a waiter. Though his wife was very peevish, and hard to please, I much preferred to be under her control than the overseer's. They brought with them Mr. Sloane, a Presbyterian minister; Miss Martha Tulley, a niece of theirs from Kentucky; and their nephew William. The latter had been in the family a number of years, but the others were all newcomers.

Mr. Sloane was a young minister, who had been at the South but a short time, and it seemed as if his whole aim was to please the slaveholders, especially my master and mistress. He was intending to make a visit during the winter, and he not only tried to please them, but I think he succeeded admirably. When they wanted singing, he sung; when they wanted praying, he prayed; when they wanted a story told, he told a story. Instead of his teaching my master theology, my master taught theology to him. While I was with Captain Reynolds my master "got religion," and new laws were made on the plantation. Formerly we had the privilege of hunting, fishing, making splint brooms, baskets, &c., on Sunday; but this was all stopped. Every Sunday we were all compelled to attend meeting. Master was so religious that he induced some others to join him in hiring a preacher to preach to the slaves.

My master had family worship, night and morning. At night the slaves were called in to attend; but in the mornings they had to be at their work, and master did all the praying. My master and mistress were great lovers of mint julep, and every morning, a pitcher-full was made, of which they all partook freely, not excepting little master William. After drinking freely all round, they would have family worship, and then breakfast. I cannot say but I loved the julep as well as any of them, and during prayer was always careful to seat myself close to the table where it stood, so as to help myself when they were all busily engaged in their devotions. By the time prayer was over, I was about as happy as any of them. A sad accident happened one morning. In helping myself, and at the same time keeping an eye on my old mistress, I accidentally let the pitcher fall upon the floor, breaking it in pieces, and spilling the contents. This was a bad affair for me; for as soon as prayer was over, I was taken and severely chastised.

My master's family consisted of himself, his wife, and their nephew, William Moore. He was taken into the family when only a few weeks of age. His name being that of my own, mine was changed for the purpose of giving precedence to his, though I was his senior by ten or twelve years. The plantation being four miles from the city, I had to drive the family to church. I always dreaded the approach of the Sabbath; for, during service, I was obliged to stand by the horses in the hot broiling sun, or in the rain, just as it happened.

One Sabbath, as we were driving past the house of D. D. Page, a gentleman who owned a large banking establishment, as I was sitting upon the box of the carriage, which was very much elevated, I saw Mr. Page pursuing a slave around the yard with a long whip, cutting him at every jump. The man soon escaped from the yard, and was followed by Mr. Page. They came running past us, and the slave, perceiving that he would be overtaken, stopped suddenly, and Page stumbled over him, and falling on the stone pavement, fractured one of his legs, which crippled him for life. The same gentleman, but a short time previous, tied up a woman of his, by the name of Delphia, and whipped her nearly to death; yet he was a deacon in the Baptist church, in good and regular standing. Poor Delphia! I was well acquainted with her, and called to see her while upon her sick bed; and I shall never forget her appearance. She was a member of the same church with her master.

Soon after this, I was hired out to Mr. Walker, the same man whom I have mentioned as having carried a gang of slaves down the river on the steamboat Enterprise. Seeing me in the capacity of steward on the boat, and thinking that I would make a good hand to take care of slaves, he determined to have me for that purpose; and finding that my master would not sell me, he hired me for the term of one year.

When I learned the fact of my having been hired to a negro speculator, or a "soul-driver," as they are generally called among slaves, no one can tell my emotions. Mr. Walker had offered a high price for me, as I afterwards learned, but I suppose my master was restrained from selling me by the fact that I was a near relative of his. On entering the service of Mr. Walker, I found that my opportunity of getting to a land of liberty was gone, at least for the time being. He had a gang of slaves in readiness to start for New Orleans, and in a few days we were on our journey. I am at a loss for language to express my feelings on that occasion. Although my master had told me that he had not sold me, and Mr. Walker had told me that he had not purchased me, I did not believe them; and not until I had been to New Orleans, and was on my return, did I believe that I was not sold.

There was on the boat a large room on the lower deck, in which the slaves were kept, men and women, promiscuously—all chained two and two, and a strict watch kept that they did not get loose; for cases have occurred in which slaves have got off their chains, and made their escape at landing-places, while the boats were taking in wood;—and with all our care, we lost one woman who had been taken from her husband and children, and having no desire to live without them, in the agony of her soul jumped overboard, and drowned herself. She was not chained.

It was almost impossible to keep that part of the boat clean.

On landing at Natchez, the slaves were all carried to the slave-pen, and there kept one week, during which time several of them were sold. Mr. Walker fed his slaves well. We took on board at St. Louis several hundred pounds of bacon (smoked meat) and corn-meal, and his slaves were better fed than slaves generally were in Natchez, so far as my observation extended.

At the end of a week, we left for New Orleans, the place of our final destination, which we reached in two days. Here the slaves were placed in a negro-pen, where those who wished to purchase could call and examine them. The negro-pen is a small yard, surrounded by buildings, from fifteen to twenty feet wide, with the exception of a large gate with iron bars. The slaves are kept in the buildings during the night, and turned out into the yard during the day. After the best of the stock was sold at private sale at the pen, the balance were taken to the Exchange Coffee House Auction Rooms, kept by Isaac L. McCoy, and sold at public auction. After the sale of this lot of slaves, we left New Orleans for St. Louis.

On our arrival at St. Louis I went to Dr. Young, and told him that I did not wish to live with Mr. Walker any longer. I was heart-sick at seeing my fellow-creatures bought and sold. But the Dr. had hired me for the year, and stay I must. Mr. Walker again commenced purchasing another gang of slaves. He bought a man of Colonel John O'Fallon, who resided in the suburbs of the city. This man had a wife and three children. As soon as the purchase was made, he was put in jail for safe keeping, until we should be ready to start for New Orleans. His wife visited him while there, several times, and several times when she went for that purpose was refused admittance.

In the course of eight or nine weeks Mr. Walker had his cargo of human flesh made up. There was in this lot a number of old men and women, some of them with gray locks. We left St. Louis in the steamboat Carlton, Captain Swan, bound for New Orleans. On our way down, and before we reached Rodney, the place where we made our first stop, I had to prepare the old slaves for market. I was ordered to have the old men's whiskers shaved off, and the grey hairs plucked out where they were not too numerous, in which case he had a preparation of blacking to color it, and with a blacking-brush we would put it on. This was new business to me, and was performed in a room where the passengers could not see us. These slaves were also taught how old they were by Mr. Walker, and after going through the blacking process they looked ten or fifteen years younger; and I am sure that some of those who purchased slaves of Mr. Walker were dreadfully cheated, especially in the ages of the slaves which they bought.

We landed at Rodney, and the slaves were driven to the pen in the back part of the village. Several were sold at this place, during our stay of four or five days, when we proceeded to Natchez. There we landed at night, and the gang were put in the warehouse until morning, when they were driven to the pen. As soon as the slaves are put in these pens, swarms of planters may be seen in and about them. They knew when Walker was expected, as he always had the time advertised beforehand when he would be in Rodney, Natchez, and New Orleans. These were the principal places where he offered his slaves for sale.

When at Natchez the second time, I saw a slave very cruelly whipped. He belonged to a Mr. Broadwell, a merchant who kept a store on the wharf. The slave's name was Lewis. I had known him several years, as he was formerly from St. Louis. We were expecting a steamboat down the river, in which we were to take passage for New Orleans. Mr. Walker sent me to the landing to watch for the boat, ordering me to inform him on its arrival. While there, I went into the store to see Lewis. I saw a slave in the store, and asked him where Lewis was. Said he, "They have got Lewis hanging between the heavens and the earth." I asked him what he meant by that. He told me to go into the warehouse and see. I went in, and found Lewis there. He was tied up to a beam, with his toes just touching the floor. As there was no one in the warehouse but himself, I inquired the reason of his being in that situation. He said Mr. Broadwell had sold his wife to a planter six miles from the city, and that he had been to visit her—that he went in the night, expecting to return before daylight, and went without his master's permission. The patrol had taken him up before he reached his wife. He was put in jail, and his master had to pay for his catching and keeping, and that was what he was tied up for.

Just as he finished his story, Mr. Broadwell came in, and inquired what I was doing there. I knew not what to say, and while I was thinking what reply to make, he struck me over the head with the cowhide, the end of which struck me over my right eye, sinking deep into the flesh, leaving a scar which I carry to this day. Before I visited Lewis he had received fifty lashes. Mr. Broadwell gave him fifty more after I came out, as I was afterwards informed by Lewis himself.

The next day we proceeded to New Orleans, and put the gang in the same negro-pen which we occupied before. In a short time the planters came flocking to the pen to purchase slaves. Before the slaves were exhibited for sale, they were dressed and driven out into the yard. Some were set to dancing, some to jumping, some to singing, and some to playing cards. This was done to make them appear cheerful and happy. My business was to see that they were placed in those situations before the arrival of the purchasers, and I have often set them to dancing when their cheeks were wet with tears. As slaves were in good demand at that time, they were all soon disposed of, and we again set out for St. Louis.

On our arrival, Mr. Walker purchased a farm five or six miles from the city. He had no family, but made a housekeeper of one of his female slaves. Poor Cynthia! I knew her well. She was a quadroon, and one of the most beautiful women I ever saw. She was a native of St. Louis, and bore an irreproachable character for virtue and propriety of conduct. Mr. Walker bought her for the New Orleans market, and took her down with him on one of the trips that I made with him. Never shall I forget the circumstances of that voyage! On the first night that we were on board the steamboat, he directed me to put her into a stateroom he had provided for her, apart from the other slaves. I had seen too much of the workings of slavery not to know what this meant. I accordingly watched him into the state-room, and listened to hear what passed between them. I heard him make his base offers, and her reject them. He told her that if she would accept his vile proposals, he would take her back with him to St. Louis, and establish her as his housekeeper at his farm. But if she persisted in rejecting them, he would sell her as a field hand on the worst plantation on the river. Neither threats nor bribes prevailed, however, and he retired, disappointed of his prey.

The next morning poor Cynthia told me what had past, and bewailed her sad fate with floods of tears. I comforted and encouraged her all I could; but I foresaw but too well what the result must be. Without entering into any farther particulars, suffice it to say that Walker performed his part of the contract at that time. He took her back to St. Louis, established her as his mistress and housekeeper at his farm, and before I left, he had two children by her. But, mark the end! Since I have been at the North, I have been credibly informed that Walker has been married, and, as a previous measure, sold poor Cynthia and her four children (she having had two more since I came away) into hopeless bondage!

He soon commenced purchasing to make up the third gang. We took steamboat, and went to Jefferson City, a town on the Missouri river. Here we landed, and took stage for the interior of the State. He bought a number of slaves as he passed the different farms and villages. After getting twenty-two or twenty-three men and women, we arrived at St. Charles, a village on the banks of the Missouri. Here he purchased a woman who had a child in her arms, appearing to be four or five weeks old.

We had been travelling by land for some days, and were in hopes to have found a boat at this place for St. Louis, but were disappointed. As no boat was expected for some days, we started for St. Louis by land. Mr. Walker had purchased two horses. He rode one, and I the other. The slaves were chained together, and we took up our line of march, Mr. Walker taking the lead, and I bringing up the rear. Though the distance was not more than twenty miles, we did not reach it the first day. The road was worse than any that I have ever travelled.

Soon after we left St. Charles the young child grew very cross, and kept up a noise during the greater part of the day. Mr. Walker complained of its crying several times, and told the mother to stop the child's d——d noise, or he would. The woman tried to keep the child from crying, but could not. We put up at night with an acquaintance of Mr. Walker, and in the morning, just as we were about to start, the child again commenced crying. Walker stepped up to her, and told her to give the child to him. The mother tremblingly obeyed. He took the child by one arm, as you would a cat by the leg, walked into the house, and said to the lady,

"Madam, I will make you a present of this little nigger; it keeps such a noise that I can't bear it."

"Thank you, sir," said the lady.

The mother, as soon as she saw that her child was to be left, ran up to Mr. Walker, and falling upon her knees begged him to let her have her child; she clung around his legs, and cried, "Oh, my child! my child! master, do let me have my child! oh, do, do, do! I will stop its crying, if you will only let me have it again." When I saw this woman crying for her child so piteously, a shudder—a feeling akin to horror—shot through my frame. I have often since in imagination heard her crying for her child:—

O, master, let me stay to catch
  My baby's sobbing breath,
His little glassy eye to watch,
  And smooth his limbs in death,

And cover him with grass and leaf,
  Beneath the large oak tree:
It is not sullenness, but grief—
  O, master, pity me!

The morn was chill—I spoke no word,
  But feared my babe might die,
And heard all day, or thought I heard,
  My little baby cry.

At noon, oh, how I ran and took
  My baby to my breast!
I lingered—and the long lash broke
  My sleeping infant's rest.

I worked till night—till darkest night,
  In torture and disgrace;
Went home and watched till morning light,
  To see my baby's face.

Then give me but one little hour—
    O! do not lash me so!
One little hour—one little hour—
    And gratefully I'll go.

Mr. Walker commanded her to return into the ranks with the other slaves. Women who had children were not chained, but those that had none were. As soon as her child was disposed of she was chained in the gang.

The following song I have often heard the slaves sing, when about to be carried to the far south. It is said to have been composed by a slave.

See these poor souls from Africa
Transported to America;
We are stolen, and sold to Georgia—
Will you go along with me?
We are stolen, and sold to Georgia—
Come sound the jubilee!

See wives and husbands sold apart,
Their children's screams will break my heart;—
There's a better day a coming,
Will you go along with me?
There's a better day a coming,
Go sound the jubilee!

O, gracious Lord! when shall it be,
That we poor souls shall all be free;
Lord, break them slavery powers—
Will you go along with me?
Lord break them slavery powers,
Go sound the jubilee!

Dear Lord, dear Lord, when slavery 'll cease,
Then we poor souls will have our peace;—
There's a better day a coming,
Will you go along with me?
There's a better day a coming,
Go sound the jubilee!

We finally arrived at Mr. Walker's farm. He had a house built during our absence to put slaves in. It was a kind of domestic jail. The slaves were put in the jail at night, and worked on the farm during the day. They were kept here until the gang was completed, when we again started for New Orleans, on board the steamboat North America, Capt. Alexander Scott. We had a large number of slaves in this gang. One, by the name of Joe, Mr. Walker was training up to take my place, as my time was nearly out, and glad was I. We made our first stop at Vicksburg, where we remained one week and sold several slaves.

Mr. Walker, though not a good master, had not flogged a slave since I had been with him, though he had threatened me. The slaves were kept in the pen, and he always put up at the best hotel, and kept his wines in his room, for the accommodation of those who called to negotiate with him for the purchase of slaves. One day while we were at Vicksburg, several gentlemen came to see him for this purpose, and as usual the wine was called for. I took the tray and started around with it, and having accidentally filled some of the glasses too full, the gentlemen spilled the wine on their clothes as they went to drink. Mr. Walker apologized to them for my carelessness, but looked at me as though he would see me again on this subject.

After the gentlemen had left the room, he asked me what I meant by my carelessness, and said that he would attend to me. The next morning he gave me a note to carry to the jailer, and a dollar in money to give to him. I suspected that all was not right, so I went down near the landing where I met with a sailor, and walking up to him, asked him if he would be so kind as to read the note for me. He read it over, and then looked at me. I asked him to tell me what was in it. Said he,

"They are going to give you hell."

"Why?" said I.

He said, "This is a note to have you whipped, and says that you have a dollar to pay for it."

He handed me back the note, and off I started. I knew not what to do, but was determined not to be whipped. I went up to the jail—took a look at it, and walked off again. As Mr. Walker was acquainted with the jailer, I feared that I should be found out if I did not go, and be treated in consequence of it still worse.

While I was meditating on the subject, I saw a colored man about my size walk up, and the thought struck me in a moment to send him with my note. I walked up to him, and asked him who he belonged to. He said he was a free man, and had been in the city but a short time. I told him I had a note to go into the jail, and get a trunk to carry to one of the steamboats; but was so busily engaged that I could not do it, although I had a dollar to pay for it. He asked me if I would not give him the job. I handed him the note and the dollar, and off he started for the jail.

I watched to see that he went in, and as soon as I saw the door close behind him, I walked around the corner, and took my station, intending to see how my friend looked when he came out. I had been there but a short time, when a colored man came around the corner, and said to another colored man with whom he was acquainted—

"They are giving a nigger scissors in the jail."

"What for?" said the other. The man continued,

"A nigger came into the jail, and asked for the jailer. The jailer came out, and he handed him a note, and said he wanted to get a trunk. The jailer told him to go with him, and he would give him the trunk. So he took him into the room, and told the nigger to give up the dollar. He said a man had given him the dollar to pay for getting the trunk. But that lie would not answer. So they made him strip himself, and then they tied him down, and are now whipping him."

I stood by all the while listening to their talk, and soon found out that the person alluded to was my customer. I went into the street opposite the jail, and concealed myself in such a manner that I could not be seen by any one coming out. I had been there but a short time, when the young man made his appearance, and looked around for me. I, unobserved, came forth from my hiding-place, behind a pile of brick, and he pretty soon saw me and came up to me complaining bitterly, saying that I had played a trick upon him. I denied any knowledge of what the note contained, and asked him what they had done to him. He told me in substance what I heard the man tell who had come out of the jail.

"Yes," said he, "they whipped me and took my dollar, and gave me this note."

He showed me the note which the jailer had given him, telling him to give it to his master. I told him I would give him fifty cents for it—that being all the money I had. He gave it to me, and took his money. He had received twenty lashes on his bare back, with the negro-whip.

I took the note and started for the hotel where I had left Mr. Walker.

Upon reaching the hotel, I handed it to a stranger whom I had not seen before, and requested him to read it to me. As near as I can recollect, it was as follows:—

> Dear Sir:—By your direction, I have given your boy twenty lashes. He is a very saucy boy, and tried to make me believe that he did not belong to you, and I put it on to him well for lying to me.
>
> I remain,
>
> Your obedient servant

It is true that in most of the slave-holding cities, when a gentleman wishes his servants whipped, he can send him to the jail and have it done. Before I went in where Mr. Walker was, I wet my cheeks a little, as though I had been crying. He looked at me, and inquired what was the matter. I told him that I had never had such a whipping in my life, and handed him the note. He looked at it and laughed;—"And so you told him that you did not belong to me?" "Yes, sir," said I. "I did not know that there was any harm in that." He told me I must behave myself, if I did not want to be whipped again.

This incident shows how it is that slavery makes its victims lying and mean; for which vices it afterwards reproaches them, and uses them as arguments to prove that they deserve no better fate. I have often, since my escape, deeply regretted the deception I practised upon this poor fellow; and I heartily desire that it may be, at some time or other, in my power to make him amends for his vicarious sufferings in my behalf.

In a few days we reached New Orleans, and arriving there in the night, remained on board until morning. While at New Orleans this time, I saw a slave killed; an account of which had been published by Theodore D. Weld, in his book entitled "Slavery as it is." The circumstances were as follows. In the evening, between seven and eight o'clock, a slave came running down the levee, followed by several men and boys. The whites were crying out, "Stop that nigger! stop that nigger!" while the poor panting slave, in almost breathless accents, was repeating, "I did not steal the meat—I did not steal the meat." The poor man at last took refuge in the river. The whites who were in pursuit of him, run on board of one of the boats to see if they could discover him. They finally espied him under the bow of the steamboat

Trenton. They got a pike-pole, and tried to drive him from his hiding place. When they would strike at him he would dive under the water. The water was so cold, that it soon became evident that he must come out or be drowned.

While they were trying to drive him from under the bow of the boat or drown him, he would in broken and imploring accents say, "I did not steal the meat; I did not steal the meat. My master lives up the river. I want to see my master. I did not steal the meat. Do let me go home to master." After punching him, and striking him over the head for some time, he at last sunk in the water, to rise no more alive.

On the end of the pike-pole with which they were striking him was a hook which caught in his clothing, and they hauled him on the bow of the boat. Some said he was dead others said he was *"playing possum,"* while others kicked him to make him get up; but it was of no use—he was dead.

As soon as they became satisfied of this, they commenced leaving, one after another. One of the hands on the boat informed the captain that they had killed the man, and that the dead body was lying on the deck. The captain came on deck, and said to those who were remaining, "You have killed this nigger; now take him off of my boat." The captain's name was Hart. The dead body was dragged on shore and left there. I went on board of the boat where our gang of slaves were, and during the whole night my mind was occupied with what I had seen. Early in the morning I went on shore to see if the dead body remained there. I found it in the same position that it was left the night before. I watched to see what they would do with it. It was left there until between eight and nine o'clock, when a cart, which takes up the trash out of the streets, came along, and the body was thrown in, and in a few minutes more was covered over with dirt which they were removing from the streets. During the whole time, I did not see more than six or seven persons around it, who, from their manner, evidently regarded it as no uncommon occurrence.

During our stay in the city I met with a young white man with whom I was well acquainted in St. Louis. He had been sold into slavery, under the following circumstances. His father was a drunkard, and very poor, with a family of five or six children. The father died, and left the mother to take care of and provide for the children as best she might. The eldest was a boy, named Burrill, about thirteen years of age, who did chores in a store kept by Mr. Riley, to assist his mother in procuring a living for the family. After working with him two years, Mr. Riley took him to New Orleans to wait on him while in that city on a visit, and when he returned to St. Louis, he told the mother of the boy that he had died with the yellow fever. Nothing more was heard from him, no one supposing him to be alive. I was much astonished when Burrill told me his story. Though I sympathized with him I could not assist him. We were both slaves. He was poor, uneducated, and without friends; and if living, is, I presume, still held as a slave.

After selling out this cargo of human flesh, we returned to St. Louis, and my time was up with Mr. Walker. I had served him one year, and it was the longest year I ever lived.

A NIGHT VIEW OF OUR COURT HOUSE

SEVERAL VERSIONS OF THE ST. LOUIS Courthouse stood on the Market and Broadway location before the current structure was completed in 1862. Designed by William Rumbold, the construction began in 1839, and when the main portion was completed in 1845, it functioned as the city's premier public building. The building's 128-ton cast-iron, 198-foot-high dome was the first of its kind in the nation and preceded that of the U.S. Capitol by a year and a half. In 1862, painter Carl Wimar completed all but one of four frescoes in the dome, depicting crucial moments in St. Louis history: De Soto discovering the Mississippi River, the landing of Pierre Laclède, the 1780 Indian attack on St. Louis, and the beginning of transcontinental rail travel. Unfortunately, over the decades, Wimar's magnificent murals were defaced by lesser but well-meaning parties in their attempt to restore them. In 1940, when the Civil Courts Building was finished, the city of St. Louis deeded the land on which the original courthouse sits to the National Park Service. From that point forth, the building at Market and Broadway affectionately has been referred to as the "Old Courthouse."

The following essay paying tribute to this significant St. Louis landmark appeared in the *St. Louis Reveille* on October 15, 1848. Although no author credit was given, it is likely that the essay was written by one of the *Reveille* editors, either Charles Keemle or Joseph Field. In this celebratory and romantic tribute, the author anthropomorphizes the structure, comparing it to a "faded beauty" that looks its best in dim light. He also imagines the noble, powerful voices booming under its dome, the rousing political debates, and the multicultural infusion of energy that was the seedbed of St. Louis's rich character. The author strategically neglects to mention that Dred Scott was denied his freedom in this building the previous year—a landmark decision that moved the nation closer to the Civil War—and that slave auctions were regularly held on the steps of this "temple, dedicated to that true spirit of freedom."

A NIGHT VIEW OF OUR COURT HOUSE

Like a faded beauty, our Court House shows to best advantage amid the glitter and blaze which illuminates its rotunda at night, or, when political torches are reflecting their light along its east front, tipping with lurid glare the cornice edge at the base of its frowning dome. It is in its glory when the air within and without is laden with the enthusiastic shouts of western freemen; when each breeze which floats through one portal is wafted through another, vocal with political contradictions; or, when the mighty shouts of a swelling throng are proclaiming the tottering of foreign thrones, and echoing the roar of distant revolution. On these greater occasions music mingles its swell with the sound of human voices—the bonfire and the torch mingle their flames, and the ruddy light of both baptizes the swaying multitude in a flood of crimson brightness. If the light of these political altar fires were like the consuming element, a *purifier*, how much more important it would become than a mere portion of the empty pageant—patriots might then rest from their "eternal vigilence," for the liberties of the people could be preserved by less brilliant lights.

In all cities and towns, Court Houses are the starting points for new movements, the stamping grounds of established parties, the rallying places for the many-headed million, and to this rule ours is no exception. Here patriots, sympathizers, Whigs, Democrats, Native Americans and Free Soilers, all congregate. Here is heard frothy declamation, bubbling forth from the tongue of ambitious youth; or studied sophistry, dropping in measured terms from the lips of designing age. Hark to Benton, the Ajax of Democracy, how he makes our rotunda reverberate with his stern voice of senatorial command. Listen to Bates! With what polished eloquence he courteously tilts at his adversary. See Bowlin, how, like a second Hector, he throws his shield over the administration, and boldly defies its foes, while Wright daringly hurls his shafts of eloquence in a shower round both. Crockett, in more polished phrase than his brave namesake, is "going ahead" against the *veto*, and Polk, with his thoughtful Wesleyan countenance, is holding the same provision up to the Democracy as the preserving power of the Constitution. Treat, with nervous force and scornful finger, is pointing at the Whigs as the opponents of their country in time of war, and Darby is proclaiming with swelling throat, that he would never aggrandize his great country at the expense of a miserable, degraded and weak race.

Blannerhassett, in full round tone, is defending the party platform against the thunder tones of Eager. Hogan is as zealously filling the political rostrum as he ever filled the pulpit, while Krum, with measured tones and legal method, is shielding himself from the blows of his assailants. McDowell, with shrill voice, Randolph-like, smites even friends, rather than smother his caustic wit, and Mullanphy, the people's *Tribune*, sometimes original and ever odd, is congratulating his party on the fact that the oftener it divides, such is its nature, the tighter it becomes bound together! Garesche is telling the Democracy what he *has* done, and the Vulcan Lawhead is telling the Natives what he *would* do. Young Labeaume is raising his voice against emigration, and for his country, and Bogy is desirous of filling that country with the suffering people of Europe. Blair, more wide in his philanthropy, offers, with the boon of political freedom, a free soil, on which to enjoy the blessing, while Haight, looking to the *magic* changes of the future, ties himself to the car of the great political astrologer, and beneath our Court House roof casts a new political horoscope. Thus is the great "mart" of law, and "exchange" of political thought, made to echo the conflicting sounds of partisans, but, more, it echoes them in foreign as well native accents. Primm has here been heard, exulting in his own language, over the successful revolutionary struggles of old Gaul; Kribben, in massive Slavonic over the awakened might of old Germany; McBride, in Milesian accents, mourning over the wrongs of Ireland, and Carroll, in the bold accents of home, fearfully depicting woes which follow the inundation of an alien throng. The graceful secretaries, Pierce C., John Watson, Esq., and Col. Chambers, have here indited, with clerkly care, the doing of their fellow citizens; and the military-looking civilians, McGunnegle and Grimsley, have here received commissions to marshal the city's throng in showy parade, and imposing pageantry. Whitney, beneath its dome, has unrolled his map of empire, and showed how with iron ribs his country may bind distant possessions to her triumphal car; and even the "Hatless Prophet," Munday, has startled its echoes by revelations of human wickedness, strange medley of incongruous sounds, and how at times they have made the public pulse throb with mingled emotions.

On the topmost floor of the rotunda, overlooking the speaker's rostrum, stands a full length portrait of Governor Clark, the great western pioneer, and his shade appears to look out from the canvas, and curiously listen to the strange sounds which float up from beneath. He hears the Democrat declaim against the Whig, as one who opposes the principles of Washington and Jefferson—who labors to elevate an aristocracy, and at the same time shut out the pioneer from the hard-earned privilege of the preemption right. With indignation the robe which wraps his form seems to tremble, and the old patriot is ready to start from the canvas, that he may confront the degenerate children of the Republic; but a silver voice, clear as the tones of a trumpet, and indignant as offended purity, charges the Democracy with trampling upon the delegated rights of the people—setting aside the Constitution, and concentrating the power of the nation in the hands of an individual. The eyes of the old frontier soldier burn, and he is ready to mount his war horse in defence of that sacred instrument from which sprung his country's greatness. The native American's cry of danger stays him to listen further, and he hears of a "foreign horde" sweeping over the rich valley which his valor had aided to win from the savage. Again he is ready to burst the bars of the spirit world, and stride in rage among the living; but the tones of the "returned volunteer" arrests his ear—he listens, and the voice of France, the language of Germany, and the round accents of Ireland, break in patriotic shouts from the bronzed and war worn throng, and he exultingly feels the assurance that all is safe—that the thronging mass, from all climes, are clustering around the revered flag of his country, the protecting shield, whose bright folds—as those men wished who first flung it to the breeze—stand out a beacon light to the oppressed of every land beneath the sun. The patriot shade retires in peace, smiling at the petty war of faction which evoked him from his rest.

Night now gives place to the brightness of day, and amid its affulgence the world rolls on again to night, and each brings its incidents of life. Contention and strife, like froth, rise to the surface of this bubbling sea, and happy they who in quiet lie within the shelter of some peaceful grot, far beneath the region of its raging storms—"Our Court House," to them, is no frightful beacon, indicating dangerous shoals on which human hopes are wrecked, but a bright cliff, bounding the angry billows of political strife, of private wrong, and ruthless crime—a temple, dedicated to that true spirit of freedom—God-like and immutable Justice.

HENRY BOERNSTEIN

BORN IN HAMBURG, GERMANY, to a Catholic father and a Protestant mother, Heinrich Börnstein (Henry Boernstein) (1805-1892) pursued his theatrical and entrepreneurial dreams throughout Europe, settling in Paris in the 1840s, where his activities—writing, journalism, left-wing politics, and the theatre—were a prelude to his operations in St. Louis.

Boernstein emigrated to the United States in 1849 and settled in St. Louis one year later. He soon became the editor of the *Anzeiger des Westens*, Missouri's premier German-language newspaper, and played an important role in shaping the complex political landscape of St. Louis before and during the Civil War. A friend of such notable Missourians as Thomas Hart Benton and Francis Blair, Jr., he was also a playwright, actor, and director, who eventually led the St. Louis Opera House. He also served as a volunteer colonel with the Union forces in Missouri early in the war and participated in the Camp Jackson raid in 1861.

Boernstein's business affairs eventually collapsed in St. Louis, and he left the city permanently in 1862, serving for several years as a U.S. Consul in Bremen. In addition to contributing articles to German newspapers in America, Boernstein wrote his memoirs, which are considered his finest writing. *Memoirs of a Nobody: The Missouri Years of an Austrian Radical, 1849–1866* (Missouri Historical Society Press, 1997) contains Boernstein's vivid descriptions of his experiences in St. Louis and the cultural and political climate of the city during a particularly turbulent period.

The following excerpt is from Boernstein's novel *Die Geheimnisse von St. Louis (The Mysteries of St. Louis),* the first installment of which appeared in the *Anzeiger* in February 1851. Noted Boernstein scholar and translator Steven Rowan refers to *Mysteries* as a "French popular novel written in German and set in America. . . . It is a pastiche of every imaginable convention of Romance novelistic writing."

FROM *THE MYSTERIES OF ST. LOUIS*

Lord Ponce—Who goes?
Bravo—A friend.
Lord P.—Any one can say that. The sign?
[Old Drama.]

Roughly and wildly roared the wind through the dark night, enveloping the streets of St. Louis in a dismal darkness. The rain poured down in torrents, gushing from the roofs of the houses and the pavements into the streets and forming stray currents in the midst of the streets and alleys; the gas lamps flickering faintly by the feeble glare of the flames, fluttering in the wind, it scarcely could be seen, how dark it was. The dwellings of the inhabitants had already been long closed for the night, and only here and there could a dimly lighted window be perceived, betraying the protracted labors of some diligent man, in his endeavors to extract from his exertions in the night sustenance for his loved but suffering family. Save the howling of dogs in the yards and near the river, or the low puffing of a steamboat in the distance, ascending the river, nothing was heard, and silence reigned supreme.

At this extraordinary hour, in the lower part of Carondelet Avenue, a man was leaning against the wall of an old uninhabited frame house, and notwithstanding its old-fashioned, overhanging eaves, almost totally exposed to the "pitiless pelting" of the furious torrent. He was tall and athletic, with a muscular and bony frame—one of those iron natures so frequently to be found among the trappers and hunters of the West. His black, matted and rugged hair hung down wildly and in disorder, over features tanned by exposure to the sun and weather and heightened by the habitual use of ardent spirits. His eyes, shaded by burly lashes, lay dark and dismal in their deep sockets, and a beard, enwrapping chin and cheeks, enshrouded a finely chiselled mouth which was, however, disfigured by a constant inclination to a sneering laugh. In spite of the cold night air and the piercing wind, the man wore only a hickory shirt and linen pants, both full of holes; a broad leather belt, from which hung a huge bowie knife, held both together, and an old Mexican hat, with a pair of coarse boots, completed his not-very-costly wardrobe.

At this moment a strong gust of wind blew from the east and a torrent of rain poured down from the skies, when the stranger, enveloping himself in a buffalo robe, before drawn only over his shoulders, in his anger and impatience muttered to himself unconnected sentences mingled with curses.

"I will be damned," he grumbled, putting a piece of chewing tobacco into his mouth, to appease his anger. "Damned I'll be, if I wait any longer. Weather for the dogs, this. I was seated so comfortable and snugly by Piaza—but now am driven hither, to be whirled round and about by wind and rain, like a weathercock."

At this instant, the beat of a watchman was heard at the corner of the street, answered by another a little distance off. The stranger, interrupted in his soliloquy, stooped down and, crawling along the wall towards the adjoining yard, clambered upon an old hog pen, noiselessly letting himself fall to the bottom, on the ground.

"Dog of a watchman!" he murmured. "Why did you not stay at home in such weather, and sleep comfortably in your warm bed, instead of going on your beat on such a night as this? Your forty dollars would have been equally secure at the end of the month."

The watchman just then passed the frame house, tramping along in his big boots through the bottomless mud, carelessly singing a lively air and repeating, on the next corner, his beat, which was answered by several others, yet a little further off.

"It is Hans, the Bavarian blockhead," growled the man in the buffalo robe, coming cautiously out of the hog pen. "With this damned dog I have yet to settle an old account. Time and place are favorable just now; but delayed is not forgotten."

The rain now ceased, but the wind blew most piercingly from the Illinois shore, and the clouds flew, as if afraid of its unwelcome pressure.

From the Cathedral, the dim sound of two o'clock was heard in the distance.

"I will be damned if I wait any longer," growled the man impatiently, pressing his old hat upon his head and almost over his eyes.

Suiting the action to the word, he had made a few rapid steps from the spot, when he suddenly heard a noise in the stillness of the night, as if one not far distant was striking for fire on flint and steel. The man listened, as if pinned to the ground, when the noise was repeated again and again, and now the striking was heard for the third time. With one leap, the man in the buffalo robe was again in his old place near the house, and taking from his belt steel and flint, he himself struck three times, each time giving three different strokes.

Noiselessly a shutter in the uninhabited house was half opened, and behind the shutter the shadow of a head was seen. But the total darkness in the house, the shutter, and the night itself prevented garments or features from being recognized.

"From where the wind?" it whispered in the house.

"From the rising sun," answered the man outside. "Do not care—it is myself—the air is clear, but you let me wait a damned long time."

"Why did you not go away, if the time was too long for you?" tittered the voice inside, sneeringly.

"I will be damned," growled the man, "if I was not about to do it."

"You would have returned surely, my boy," was heard with a tittering voice behind the shutter. "But now speak out. Did you do the errands I gave you?"

"All!"

"You have been in the jail?"

"Today I hauled a load of coal there, and took enough time in unloading the wagon to settle the business. William I did not see, but to big Conrad I gave the agreed sign, and tomorrow night he will be free."

"How is it with your gang?"

"I have them together," replied the man, "all of them devils of fellows—none of them but is ripe for the place of honor on Duncan's Island—and all worthy of the love's last service of the county marshal. But what have they to do?"

"You shall hear that, when it is the right time," it whispered through the shutter. "Now to something more weighty. Make out as if you had business on the levee tomorrow; stay about the upper part, near where the New Orleans boats are landing. In the course of the day the *Missouri* will arrive, with a great many German immigrants. Among them you will find a family named Boettcher, husband, wife, two sons and a daughter, together with an aged grandmother and some young children. When the boat arrives, go on board, find them out, and offer to carry their luggage on shore, and thus find out where they take up their lodging, and report to me tomorrow evening. Understood?"

"Yes."

"Well, goodnight then."

The shutter was about to be closed, but the man from the outside held back to re-open it. But in an instant he let it go, hurriedly drawing back his hand, from which large drops of blood plentifully flowed, and muttering in a dull, angry voice.

"What are you now wanting?" the voice inside.

"The devil take you, and your whole brood," roared the wounded man, sucking the blood from the wound. "Are you the hangman, to pierce my hand so for nothing?"

"Why did you take hold of the shutter, then? You know our terms. You serve me, and receive your pay—good pay—but you shall never see me, never know who I am, and especially shall never come nearer than I allow. That mere needle prick will be healed tomorrow; but take care in the future. I have other weapons, especially a very pretty little knife, overlaid with poison. One small scratch on the skin, and you are a dead man in five minutes. Therefore—But what more do you want?"

"I have not a red cent in my pocket," murmured the man in the buffalo robe.

"The same as ever! Well, go away; you will get some on account. Go away!!"

"Without any money?"

"I tell you go away! You shall have some."

The shutter was now noiselessly and quickly closed. A death-like tranquility reigned all around.

The man waited a little while longer, but hearing nothing, he turned about with the words, "Old miser! Always promising, never giving; but me you have seen for the last time!"

At this moment he heard a noise, and from the roof of the house a small white package rolled down into the street at his feet. Quickly he picked it up, opened the paper, and with pleasure let the ten dollars, its contents, run through his fingers.

"Ten dollars!" exclaimed he, joyfully. "Hm! The devil is never so black as he is painted."

The church bell now struck three o'clock. The man passed quickly in the shadow of the house, soon reached the gas works, and made through the slough to Duncan's Island. Here a little roof, poorly constructed from posts and boards, covered a sand pit, into which the man descended. He wrapped himself in his buffalo robe and, stretching himself upon the bed of sand, was quickly in the strong embraces of Morpheus.

O! there is sweetness in the mountain air,
And life, that bloated ease can never hope to share.
[Byron]

Joy! the lost one is restor'd
Sunshine comes to hearth and board.
[Mrs. Hemans]

It was the fifteenth of April, 1849. A clear and cloudless sky welcomed the sun, as it gently ascended from the eastern bank of the Mississippi, gently warming and illuminating with its golden rays the river, which smoked in the morning fog. In grand majesty the father of waters rolled onwards, playing with the gigantic oaks as they floated on his surface, as with stalks of straw; yet, here and there, a single ice cake, retarded in its progress by an indentation on the shore, was drifting along, till melted in the warmer regions of the South.

It was yet very early. On both shores everything was quiet and tranquil, save that here and there the vigorous stroke of the woodcutters was heard, and from time to time an old oak or hickory rustled to the ground, felled by the axe of the settler, crushing in its fall the young trees and the bushes around. Now and then the report of a rifle was heard in echo from the hills and prairies, in answer to which a stately deer was thrown down, or a plump turkey tumbled from a tree, where he had been digesting his last meal, and now to form a welcome repast to the experienced hunter.

But all those single, quickly passing sounds were not to be compared in beauty to the deep, majestic tranquility which was reposing on the bosom of the country around, making thereby nature's grave and earnest festival. He only who travels on the great father of waters in a light skiff, or in the venturesome and romantic trip of four to five weeks in a flatboat, to New Orleans, or the vigorous walker on the Mississippi's banks—such only can behold and appreciate the grand and imposing beauties of the Mississippi and its shores, an enjoyment which is utterly lost to him who makes the trip on board of a noisy, smoking, sickly steamboat, with its stiff and ceremonious cabin passengers, whose company is burdensome tediousness—its load of immigrants, herded together on the lower deck, like so many sheep—its black steward and reddened firemen—its unavoidable bar—its three stiff, stereotyped meals, ushered in by the melancholy bell—and the comforting prospect (like the sword of Damocles, hanging over his neck by a single hair), brooding in the mind of every passenger, of a dance in the air, with the exploding boilers of the boat!

Just at this moment one of those steamboats, the stately *Sarah* under the command of the old but brave Captain Young, in ascending the river turned round the head of a small island to get into the broad channel of the river.

As still and tranquil as was the country around, in like degree was it noisome and boisterous on board the boat. In the saloon, the breakfast bell having just then begun to be rung, everything was in an instant in confusion; the passengers were hurrying to one spot, stateroom doors were dashing together, like so many boards of a fuller's mill, and all were hurrying to the richly served table.

On board steamboats, notwithstanding everyone is idle and there is ample time, yet everything is done in a hurry. But now the gentlemen pause for the ladies, who, their eyes not yet redeemed from the dominion of sleep, but with their color slightly heightened by the bracing air, at length take their places at the upper end of the table, on each side of the captain. And now everyone in the cabin is in a hurry—inexplicable to a newcomer—and pouring down the boiling coffee like the melted lead which the incombustible Spaniard of Asbestine notoriety is said to have devoured. Beef steaks and cutlets make an equally speedy disappearance, and as greedily as if he had never seen meat before. And whilst this hasty mastication (noiseless save in the clattering of the dishes) is going on in the cabin, as if millions depended on their speed, bustle and activity were not less visible among the deck passengers.

The immigrants, chiefly German and Irish, were busy at their toilets. Buckets, to which ropes were attached, were let into the river and again drawn out, with the water to clean the coal and dust from their rough faces—the children, on taking their frugal breakfasts, were being combed—a small hand mirror, the property of a journeyman confectioner from Berlin, being the sole luxurious furniture in the steerage, was sent from person to person. Here and there, too, an inexperienced hand was trying his best at self-shaving, the result of which was, partly through the jolting of the boat, that wry faces and barbarous cuts in chin and upper lip were by no means uncommon. The women opened their large trunks, taking out clean linen and their best garments; everywhere the folds were pressed out, the spots and stains brushed off, and, in short, the whole active population seemed to be preparing for a festival.

And so it was; firstly, it was Sunday, and secondly, the boat was expected to reach St. Louis before evening, being the longed for goal of most of the deck passengers. Two long protracted months had they been incarcerated in the damp, tarry steerage of a merchantship, stowed away like goods, not human beings. In this condition they had crossed the Atlantic Ocean, and after one short day's rest at New Orleans had continued the same disagreeable life on the deck of a Mississippi steamer, a life so full of care and peril, so free of comfort. No wonder, then, if the adventurous immigrants, accustomed to work and activity, to fresh air and motion, at last got heartily tired of the hard crackers and tough salt meat, the smell of coal and tar, the damp airless crowding together in a small space, and before and above all, the mind- and body-debilitating idleness and tediousness of a life on shipboard, and that they longed for their place of destination—for work and activity—for fresh air and elbow room.

On the broad stern of the boat stood a young man, between twenty and thirty years of age, his long hair of light chestnut color falling down his broad full shoulders in natural ringlets, while his clear eye, mild and soft, looked fresh and free into the world. His face, a little browned by the sun and weather, betrayed that he had served a hard apprenticeship in the school of life, and that he had not reposed on a bed of roses; but a good-natured smile playing around his lips showed, at the same time, that the young man, in the storm and battle of life, still possessed a true and faithful heart and a warm and vivid feeling for the beautiful and good. His coat was buttoned, as the wind blew keenly from the east; but his neck was free, and his shirt collar *à la Byron* was entwined by a neckerchief lightly bound round it; and an oilcloth cap, with its small rim close to the forehead, gave the young man a very fine and interesting appearance.

"What are you thinking about now?" said the young man, turning to a boat's hand, who was sitting on a plank and eating a huge piece of cornbread and bacon. "When, do you think, we will get to St. Louis?"

"Hem! Don't know," answered the man, not interrupting his busy mastication. "Don't care about it—is the captain and the pilot's business, this; but they don't know themselves. But yes, I recollect very well the *Liberty*—a fine boat that, which floated down the river as sure and as pretty as any steamer in the United States—I was on her, it was near Bayou Sara—remember it as if it had happened only today. A man from shore calls, 'Ho!

Captain, do you want any wood?' And the captain answers, 'Don't want any—be in New Orleans in three hours.' And at that moment the boilers exploded, throwing all the men into the river! I reckon I did swim like a duck; but the captain was drowned, and never reached New Orleans; and neither did the *Liberty*."

"But, if no accident should happen," smiled the young man, "do you think we shall reach St. Louis today?"

"I expect so," murmured the other. "Have a notion we are already past Chester, and I reckon, if nothing that would trouble the insurance companies should happen, we will be there this afternoon."

A sudden alarm interrupted, at this moment, the parley. Quick steps hastened from all sides to the stern, and the call "A man overboard!" sounded dolefully from the pilothouse.

"Stop!" thundered the captain's voice into the engine room.

The engineer's bell rang, the wheels turned themselves more slowly and slowly, the steam meanwhile escaping from the valve.

"For God's sake! My Fred! My Fred!" lamented now a lady's voice.

"Oh, brother! He will be drowned," cried a deadly pale girl.

"Help! —save him! The yawl! The yawl! A rope! A rope!"

These cries were heard from all sides.

It was a boy who, in the act of drawing up a bucket with water, lost his balance and fell into the river. He struggled manfully awhile, but at length gave up the effort, letting himself drive with the stream, but keeping himself by single movements upon the surface, which showed the natural swimmer. The steamer, the engine having ceased to work, sailed slowly after him, the hurricane deck, the galleries, and stern meanwhile filling with passengers, who eyed, with the most varied feelings, the death struggle of the unfortunate victim, who they expected would soon lose his strength and sink. What we have attempted here to portray, in a few words, was in reality the work of a moment; the plunge, the call, the cry, the stopping of the boat, the running of the passengers—all these happened almost simultaneously, and in the midst of this hurry and excitement, suddenly a clear shrill voice was heard.

"Do not come near to me with the boat, but throw a rope to me! I dare it!"

And at the same moment was heard a heavy plunge into the waves, which elevated themselves, foaming, and soon a head and two strong arms were seen above the water, and the young man whom we watched in his parley at the stern was swimming with mighty strokes after the boy. The latter still floated on the surface, and it could plainly be seen that he, as a swimmer, had spared his strength, and was waiting for help from the boat. The young man was about three hundred yards from him.

The death-pale, fear-enchained girl—whose cry "Oh, brother! He will be drowned" had interested all hearts—took now a position on the edge of the boat.

"And he, too," moaned she, from her surcharged heart. "He, too! He and my brother both lost!"

Thus she soliloquized, while her fair ringlets fluttered in the wind, and turned with a despairing look to where the heads of her loved ones now disappeared, and now were seen above the surface; with throbbing heart and beating pulse, her hands convulsively stretched after her dear ones, who now struggled between life and death. The parents of the boy, while the tears coursed down their furrowed cheeks, and speech was denied them, kneeled down on the side of the boat and close to their sorrowing daughter.

"Hm!" murmured the deck hand, to whom the young man spoke some minutes before. "Was in such a hurry to reach St. Louis, and now I reckon he swims back to New Orleans, and further yet. Calculate nobody can know anything beforehand."

"Take care," called out the captain. "Turn the wheel here and there, otherwise we may descend too quick, and ground."

"Keep the rope ready," commanded the mate.

"Calculate in this world he does not want any more rope," murmured the deck hand, quietly eating his breakfast.

At this moment the girl shrilly screamed out. The head of her brother suddenly went out of sight, and he seemed to be sunk. The young man appeared to think so, too, for he redoubled his strokes with renewed activity. But the boy had not sunk, he had merely taken hold of a floating tree, and could not be seen from the boat.

"I will bet a dollar that he will be saved," said a huge sunburnt Arkansas man in a blue blanket coat, sitting with his long rifle between his knees on the hurricane deck and lustily spitting out the brown tobacco juice on the passengers below.

"I'll bet two dollars against you, that both will be lost," responded a bystander.

"Hm! It seems the boy caught the tree, and may sustain himself until the other comes."

"Expect," rejoined the bystander, "this will be his misfortune. You see yonder large tree coming close to him—it will crush him as if he were a straw."

"I will lay a wager that it will not. Do you take it?" called out the Arkansas man, throwing his dollar on the deck. "He will come out safe."

"Taken," repeated the other, throwing his two dollars on deck. "He will not come out."

Immediately all over the boat a joyful expression was heard, which at last swelled to a general outcry.

"He has reached him! He has got hold of him!"

And so it was, indeed; the young man had reached the boy, and was making with him towards the boat.

"Launch the yawl!" commanded the captain.

Quickly this was done, and swift as an arrow it glided down the stream, avoiding the floating trees, and very soon it had reached the two youths. At length they were lifted into the yawl, and the mate, who steered it, having given a signal with his hat, a thundering hurrah broke out on board the boat, and a scene which our readers may conceive, but which we are unable adequately to describe, immediately took place there.

All embraced with transports the parents of the boy, who were drowned in tears of gratitude and joy, while the pale, flaxen-haired girl, moved by the excitement from hope to fear, from despair to rapt possession, could only exclaim, "Saved! Both are saved!"

We leave it to the imagination of our readers to paint to themselves the joyful countenances of those on board the steamer, as they met the yawl ascending through the strong strokes of the boat hands. Ropes were thrown, and the yawl cautiously drawn against the boat; and when at last both were in safety, the savior and saved were surrounded by the whole ship's company, greeted and embraced. While the parents were attending to the sufferings and wants of their dear boy, taking dry garments from their trunks for his use and ever and anon, in the most affectionate manner, asking him if he felt better and inquiring if he was not hurt, the young man stood on the stern of the boat, pressing the water out of his hair and looking for the coat he had taken off before he plunged into the water.

The pale girl now went up to him and, taking him by the hand, said, with the most affectionate expression of face, "Master Charles, never in life will I forget this! I always thought you a good man, and now I know it to a certainty!"

"Mary," said the young man, "your kindness is a far richer recompense than I merit. It was a happy thing that it was your brother I saved."

"Well, stranger," bawled out the deck hand, "I have a notion, after this cold bath, a drink of whisky would do you no harm. Come, let me treat you!"

"Thank you," indignantly replied Charles, at this interruption.

"Oh! I see it!" answered the tar. "You do not like whisky; it is too common. Well, I do not care about a brandy punch, with sherry; but I must treat you. God damn me, you're a fine fellow."

"Gentleman!" said now the big Arkansas man to Charles. "You let me win two dollars, and it is but right that you take part, if I spend them. Well, then, to the bar, if you please."

Charles' protestations were of no avail. A merry band of fellow customers of the "social hall" took him in their midst, bearing him triumphantly upstairs to the barroom.

Where are those sweet scenes of my youth,
Of virtue, innocence and truth?
Ah! like a dream they've passed away,
As all things must decay!
And meek repose, with pliant face,
To an impulsive age gives place.

The purple sun had set behind the Commons field, gilding with his last rays the cupola of the Courthouse and the many slender church steeples which towered above the smoking myriads of houses of St. Louis, when the Sarah, smoking and furrowing the waves, came near the Arsenal.

All the passengers congregated on the bow of the boat to enjoy the beautiful sight which is here presented to the strangers from the Illinois side, now the steamer neared the southern part of St. Louis—the Arsenal, with park-like groves and its batteries within, just returned from the Mexican campaign; the hills rising behind the Arsenal, covered with lovely cottages and neat outhouses; and all teeming with a busy population. All these presented themselves to the delighted view of the spectators while, between the hills and the river, the unbounded mass of houses stretched itself along, whose end was lost in the pale red evening fog, the chimneys and flagstaffs of more than a hundred steamers seeming to form a smoking forest along the far-stretched-out levee.

On the bow of the steamer, now steering for the Illinois shore to gain near Illinois Town the channel near Bloody Island, we see the family of German immigrants with which we got acquainted this morning. The man (Old Boettcher the others called him) cast the most anxious and piercing looks to the shore, as if he expected there to behold dear relations, who might welcome him. His wife, in plain but neat and clean garments, rests her head on his shoulders, and at her side the saved Fred, a fine boy of thirteen years, is viewing with curiosity and amazement the new scene displayed before his eyes while a little sister, seven years old, not touched by the earnest and sad feelings which seize on all immigrants in view of their new home, with childlike enjoyment beholds the waving of the star-spangled banner on the bow of the boat. Joseph, the oldest son, a stout boy of sixteen years, and Mary, seventeen years old, cowered down near the old grandmother, who is setting on a footstool in the midst of the family group and cannot turn her fixed bewildered look from the shore.

The old lady did not exceed seventy years of age, yet she looked considerably older, grief and care having imprinted deep furrows on her face. Her thin white hair covered sparingly her wrinkled forehead, and her bony, fleshless hands betrayed, through their trembling, the great age and the sorrows of the matron. But her small grey eye is yet clear and vivid, and at this moment the whole strength of her body and mind seems to have concentrated in the nerves of her eyes, which, almost protruding from their deep sockets and glancing with a still and deep-felt joy, sent the greeting of a sad unchanging love to the approaching shore. She had already been seated an hour on the very spot where she had caused herself to be placed when the *Sarah* passed *Vide Poche*, and never had she turned her eyes from the shore, as if she wished to renew old impressions and freshen long sleeping remembrances.

As soon as the first houses of St. Louis were seen, the excitement of the old woman reached the highest point; her heart was beating tremblingly, and she drew her breath audibly and anxiously. But as the steamer came nearer to the city, her features grew more sad and dismal. Anxiety and doubts seemed to be taking the place of joy and hope.

"Grandmother," said Maria, "now here is St. Louis, the city of your youth, where you were born. Oh, what must be your joy to see it again!"

"Do you remember all the localities, Grandmother?" asked Joseph, bending down over the old lady. "A good many things may have been altered."

But the old lady shook her head mournfully and indignantly, and murmured hastily, with anxiety depicted in her countenance, "Many houses! Many houses! Nothing but houses! Oh, God! Where is the *Prairie des Noyers?*"

And when the boat reached the levee, after passing quickly the long line of houses and greeting the well-known port with several discharges of cannon, two large tears rolled down the sorrowful and emaciated cheeks of the old lady as she sighed in a tone of the deepest agony, "No! This is not St. Louis—this is a strange city! Where is the *Rue des Granges* ? Where is the *Prairie des Noyers*? Oh, God!"

It was in vain that Joseph and Maria tried to enliven their old grandmother, in vain that Boettcher and his wife endeavored to console her. She spoke not a word more, but pressed her emaciated hands against her eyes, as if she did not wish to behold the sad reality, but would relapse again into her old cherished dreams. The boat had now reached the upper part of the levee; the port inspector provided for the necessary room, the engine had stopped, and the *Sarah* took her place between the *Missouri*—but one hour in from New Orleans—and some other boat. It was Sunday, when on the levee that noisy and boisterous mirth does not take place which, at other times, makes it so intolerable to all except the merchant and the businessman. The levee was empty, and on the place of landing a few baggage cars of the first hotels were to be seen—some boardinghouse keepers and porters, besides some members of the everywhere-present loafers association, light-footed and light-fingered fellows who delight in the arrival of a boat with greenhorns, through whom they may be enabled to do honestly, or anyhow a smart and profitable business.

The cabin passengers hurried to the shore, some of whom were received by their friends and acquaintances, who were waiting for them to conduct them home; some mounted a cab, or hurried with their carpet bags through the well-known streets; while the immigrants in the steerage, being now at the end of their journey, anxiously stared on the city and, quite puzzled, were tarrying, as if they feared to go on shore.

The clerk of the boat, coming down into steerage, informed those unacquainted with the city that, it being Sunday, they might leave their luggage there all night and lodge themselves on board the boat—and then hurried with quick steps into the city, to enjoy the evening in the circle of old friends and acquaintances.

After a while, some of the immigrants left the boat to see relations and friends; some sought out the boardinghouses, already recommended to them in New Orleans; the rest went to their berths, and after dark, as the gas lamps began to shed their glare along the long lines of the houses at the otherwise so noisy boat, all was otherwise quiet and tranquility.

Father Boettcher, his wife, Joseph and Maria sat on their trunks and packages on the deck, talking about the future, whilst the old grandmother and the children had already been a good while resting on their hard couch.

"Now we are luckily arrived at our new home for you all," said Boettcher, "and I might say new to myself, too, although I am born here. I strain my memory to recall remembrances of the years of my youth, but I cannot see one single object which can bring back old impressions. I was only about three years old when I left this country—about Charlotte's age—but everything seems changed to me, more so indeed than I could have dreamt of—the river itself and its banks, one and all are strange and new to me!"

But surely more beautiful than at that time, dear Anton," replied Boettcher's wife. "Think only, it is forty-seven years since then, and a good many more things have changed!"

"It is the same thing with Grandmother," remarked Joseph. "She complains always, 'This is not St. Louis.'"

"And she lamented most bitterly," said Maria, "and would not take any solace. A few minutes since I was in the steerage, believing Grandmother was asleep; but I heard her weeping in the dark. 'Do you complain of anything, Grandmother?' I asked her. 'No, no,' she answered, 'I wish to sleep now; do not wake me. I will sleep and dream of my good old St. Louis—that St. Louis I saw today I do not know.'"

"It is very singular with Mother," said Boettcher again. "She was mainly the cause of our leaving our old home, and emigrating hither. Since my father died, she has talked of nothing but of St. Louis, where she was born, and where she would wish to die. Her ardent desire grew stronger every day, till at last she became sick, and the doctor declared that we must let her have her own way, and send her to America, or her life could not be saved."

"And we could not let her go alone," added Boettcher's wife.

"Certainly not, Elisa, certainly not," replied Boettcher. "And besides, the times were growing daily worse, and life in the old country more intolerable, and I myself longed to come hither; then we sold our little property and emigrated, like thousands of others."

"And do you recollect, Father," replied Maria, "how Grandmamma, hearing this, recovered directly, rose in a short time from her sickbed, and assisted bravely in packing and the other preparations? It was quite astonishing to see the change."

"Certainly," said the father. "As soon as she was on board the ship she was entirely changed. I was afraid of the old lady, on account of the sea voyage, but she bore her troubles and difficulties better than we did."

"Yes; but why did Grandmother long so much for America?" asked Joseph.

"Well," said Boettcher, "this she never clearly explained; she merely said she was compelled to go; and if we too would go, we would not repent it. But now let us take some rest. Children, tomorrow will be a hard day for us. Therefore now goodnight."

"And dreams full of luck: the dreams of the first night in a new home will be fulfilled," said the mother, smiling.

ADOLPHUS M. HART

ADOLPHUS MORDECAI HART (1814–1879) published a half-dozen books during his lifetime, yet little information exists about his personal life other than the fact that he spent enough time in St. Louis to publish a non-fiction book there and use the city as the setting of a fictional account.

Part storyteller, part lay historian, Hart produced two volumes titled *History of the Valley of the Mississippi*, the first of which he self-published in St. Louis in 1852. In his preface, Hart declared the work to be "an accurate account of the discovery and colonization by the French of the country West of the Alleghenies, up to the passing of the Treaty of Aix la Chapelle in 1748." In 1853, a subsequent edition was published in Cincinnati and received a lukewarm review from the Historical and Philosophical Society of Ohio, which maintained that "the facts which the author . . . presented, may in the main, be relied upon as true."

Hart was in his element when penning light comic adventure works, such as *Life in the Far West; or, The Comical, Quizzical, and Tragical Adventures of a Hoosier*, published in both New York and Cincinnati in the 1850s. In the excerpt from the novelette that follows, Hart not only provides a definition of the frequently misappropriated term, "Hoosier," but also follows his protagonist—an "unsophisticated, unvarnished Indianian"—on his misadventures and *faux pas* in the Mound City.

FROM *LIFE IN THE FAR WEST*

INTRODUCTION

The genus known as the Hoosier is found within a large tract of country. The term is a very comprehensive one. It comprises a numerous class, of the free and enlightened citizens of this republic, whose homes are bounded on the North by Michigan, on the West by Illinois, on the East by Ohio, and on the South by Kentucky. The country contains thirty-six thousand square miles, with nearly a million of inhabitants. Not that I would include amongst that class of the nine hundred and ninety-nine thousand people of Indiana, the inhabitants of its metropolis or flourishing cities, nor would I place in the category all the old men, women and children to be met with in the homes and haunts of the people of that interesting section of country, nor the lawyers, doctors, justices, merchants, and men of general intelligence, who abound in all small villages and country towns. It would, indeed, be a herculean task to attempt to paint, in a single picture, such a variety of the human family. All that I can do, is to choose amongst the thousand, or rather, the nine hundred and ninety-nine thousand, the type of that renowned race of men, who have been dignified by the appellation of Hoosiers, and whose manners, habits, and customs, have been the theme of so many remarks and learned disquisitions, among the *literati* of the neighboring States. In this analytic process, I must spare old age and the fair sex, nor will I tamper with the ingenuousness of youth, nor the aspirations of manhood.

In the category of adults who have embarked on the stream of life, from the age of twenty-five to the prime, which some men fix at fifty, a strict and careful analysis would compel me to omit a large class of persons, who at first sight might be taken for Hoosiers, but who, in reality, *are* not so.

Thus, the inhabitant of the little town of Gosport, who has scraped together a sufficient quantity of the white and yellow metals to enable him to travel beyond the limits of his native town, and who has trodden on the soil of the modern city of Gotham, can no longer be considered as a Hoosier. Indulging in the revelries of a Broadway omnibus, and touching the coats of the dandies of the Opera House, he has brushed away a great many of his primitive characteristics, and native-born provincialisms. It is enough that he should have stood at the corner of Broadway and Walker, with his arms akimbo, and his eyes gaping at the beautiful specimens of the fairest portion of creation, now wandering hither and thither, or that he should have been at Barnum's or Niblo's, to see the fair exotics of Europe flourishing in America, and gaping crowds wondering at the feats that are performed; it is enough that he should see all this, to enable him to rub off the primeval rust which has been corroding the escutcheon of his house and family, and which, in times not long since passed away, would have gained for him the enviable appellation of a native-born Hoosier.

Never mind if he be not a metropolitan, most assuredly he is not a

Hoosier. He cannot be classified amongst that respectable and high-spirited class of the great human family. He belongs to that indescribable, undefinable section of the homogeneous race, which, as yet, has been included within no particular category, nor subjected to no regular analysis. I must also except those "potent, grave and reverend seigniors," who annually visit the capital, and those aspiring members of the "Lower House," who go to the expense of getting their speeches printed, to show their constituents how smart they are. These I would except, not that they are free from all the native-born peculiarities and departmental habits which characterize the people of that interesting section of our country; but in their contact with the high and the low, the rich and the poor, the great and the talented, the tall men and the small men, that are to found at Washington, during the sittings of our national legislature, they, too, rub off that brown dirt which has gathered on their garments from time immemorial, and which has made them occasionally assume the airs and put on the face of the varitable Hoosier.

Thus, public functionaries would I except. These gentlemen feed from the public crib, they belong to no particular section, nor no particular country. Their destiny makes them cosmopolites—if they get nothing in Indiana they will go to Kentucky; if they find no sympathy amongst the Hoosiers, they will readily take up their abode amongst the Corn-crackers. I look upon them as so many Chinese mandarins, that I once saw on an organ, whose tongues were made to roll, and whose limbs were made to move by means of hidden springs, that are usually found at the center. Washington is the axle around which they move, and they are constantly turning on an elliptical orbit. They are either whigs or democrats. These I except from the category.

The "happy" of this world—those who possess elevated rank or considerable fortune are also within the exception.

All these would I except, and yet there would remain the plain, honest farmer—the man who has never wandered beyond the precincts of his own native village—the unsophisticated, unvarnished Indianian—the good, the moral, and industrious Hoosier. Such is the type of that class of men whose habits I would pourtray in this delineation of Western character. I would not take one, who arrives in St. Louis in a stage coach or a steamboat, but who harnesses his team, and comes to see the wonders of the Mound City in a four-wheeled wagon, with a plain leather harness, and who leaves his vehicle at Illinois town, to avoid the expense of a ferry.

The wanderings, therefore, and the doings and short-comings of a

"Hoosier in St. Louis," will form the subject of my physiological argument.

VIEW FROM ILLINOIS-TOWN—THE MOUND CITY FIRST DISCLOSED TO THE VIEW OF THE ASTONISHED STRANGER.

Along the road which leads from the beautiful city of Belleville, in the far-famed region of Suckerdom, after leaving the bluffs, which almost assume the size of mountains, towering over the extensive prairies of that State, there are numerous serpentine paths, which the way-farer has to go through, before he reaches its rival city, on the other side of the Mississippi—occasionally he catches a glimpse of the round cupola on the top of the Court House, and now and then he espies some huge building, with its piles of brick and mortar, giving a faint idea of the grandeur and magnificence of the palaces of their merchant princes, but the traveler must wait until he arrive fairly opposite the city, to contemplate the extent and splendor of St. Louis. It is here that he indulges in a fit of extatic delight, at beholding the wonders which he has heard of in his youth, his mind cannot grapple with the numerous reflections which spring up, as from a fountain, from the very depth of his imagination, nor his sight take in, within the limits of the horizon, all the objects which meet his view, as he stands on the sand shores of our neighboring State, gaping at Saint Louis, in all its magnitude and glory. Consider his posture. There he stands, drawn up to his full height, six feet without stockings, chewing his tobacco, his mind filled with cogitations of the most philosophical character, and, foreseeing, as with the eye of a prophet, all the pleasure which is to attend him in his perambulations and adventures through the Mound City. Nor does he pause for a moment to contemplate the dangers, which await him, in his daily contact with the herd of evil and maliciously disposed persons, who abound in all large cities—these he does not take into account. It is true, they are the excrescences of society, committing their depredations merely to remind us how much society owes to the efficiency of laws and a well organized police in densely crowded communities. Were there no pick pockets or thieves, there would be no necessity for judges, lawyers, and police officers, and were there no Hoosiers to prey upon, life would lose one of its greatest varieties, in reading the morning papers to find the daily calendar omitted, which categorizes the nocturnal peccadilloes of some half-starved wretch or the midnight wanderings of some sweet nymph of the pave.

Well—life runs along, as the Mississippi rolls at the feet of our gaping Hoosier, in one long, continuous, unbroken course, until it mingles with the waters of the ocean, which has been likened to that eternity, to which thieves as well as pickpockets, judges as well as lawyers, and all classes of the people are hurrying along with impetuous fury.

Having unharnessed his team and provided his nags with suitable accommodation, at the rate of thirty cents per diem, higgling with the ostler, and casting a glance at the pretty little help who was sweeping away the dust from the doorstep of the town groggery, the Hoosier quietly wends his way from the precincts of the tavern, to the ferryboat, St. Louis, that was lying at the wharf. His trunk and carpet bag are worthy of being described. It was evident the luxury of a capacious leather portmanteau was unknown to his fellow townsmen. If a profusion of hobs of brass nails did not give evidence of the strength and durability of the Hoosier's valise, it bore testimony to the primeval and almost antediluvian character of his traveling appointments. It was about four feet in length, by two and a half in breadth, and as if it were not capacious enough to hold all our traveler's wardrobe, he must, forsooth, have a carpet-bag, to hold his night shirt, and all the little et ceteras that usually fill up that indispensable adjunct on a voyage from the country to the city.

Well, fairly embarked on board the ferry-boat, the Hoosier stares every one out of countenance, speaks with the fireman, asks what time it will take to reach St. Louis, and in his anxiety to get all the information he can, forgets that his best brown coat is placed in such close proximity to the blazing furnace, that the heat singes and scorches his only garment, and compels him to land in St. Louis with long streaks of a greyish hue, all the way down his back, metamorphosing him from a man into a zebra.

Having reached the landing, what a scene of wild disorder and confusion!—porters hurrying here and there, passengers selecting their baggage, the gangway crowded with persons coming aboard and going ashore, and in the midst of all this turmoil and trouble, the Hoosier finds himself transported on the levee, with his trunk and all its nails glittering in the sunshine, but *minus* his carpet bag, which had either been left on board or thrown into the river, in his contact with the crowd on the densely thronged gangway of the steam ferry-boat St. Louis.

THE CRACK HOTEL OF THE MOUND CITY, ITS GORGEOUSNESS AND SPLENDOR— SURPRISE OF THE HOOSIER.

The greatest imprudence which a traveler can commit is to arrive in a strange city, without knowing where he is to live. He at once becomes the dupe of one of those runners of first class hotels, whose daily occupation it is to beguile the unwary into those nets of dissipation and extravagance which beset him at every turn he takes in the modern Thebes and Cairos of America. The choice of a hotel suitable to the condition and circumstances of a traveler, is very important, and should be made beforehand and after the most careful and diligent inquiry. He may have heard of the thousand and one vague stories of the snares, which are laid by the guilty to entrap the innocent, and to lead them unawares into the great thoroughfares of vice and wickedness. He may have been told of the dangers which await him at every step which he takes in the streets of our large cities, but without he knows where to go to, in what lodging house to abide, his path is indeed beset with perils of no ordinary magnitude.

Such was the case with our traveler when he arrived in the Mound City. He willingly accepted the escort of one of that polite class of persons, whom we have mentioned, and was taken to one of those splendid edifices, of which there are many in that city, designed for the especial accommodation of travelers and wayfarers.

As he ascended the steps which led to the spacious hall, surrounded with columns, whose carved work he stopped for a moment to gaze at, he was struck with the magnificence and splendor of the objects which everywhere met his view. He unconsciously sat down on one of those gorgeously decorated fanteuils, which are to be found in the saloon, whilst the porter was bringing in his trunk and umbrella, and gave himself up to a train of ideas connected with the pleasure he should derive from his visit to the Mound City. Happy it was for the Hoosier, that neither the proprietors nor the attendants made a minute inspection of his garments—or otherwise they would have told him that all the rooms were occupied. His outward appearance would certainly betoken that he did not belong to that class of travelers whose circumstances enabled them to put up at one of these splendid establishments. Still happier was it for him that he went through a hall which was rather dimly lighted, or otherwise his striped coat would have met with the notice of some of the numerous attendants about the hotel. The Hoosier followed the waiter, who ushered him into a drawing-room on the third floor, contiguous to his sleeping apartment, and left him in the midst of his reflections on the wealth and luxury of the Mound City.

Before retiring, the waiter saluted him with profound respect, and said:

"When you want me, sir, please ring the bell, I am the attendant on the inmates of room No. 34, and you will find me in the antechamber. Will you dine in your own room, or at the *table d'hote*. Dinner is served at 3 o'clock, and it is now near one."

The Hoosier went down stairs and emerged from the hotel, through a private doorway, in search of the nearest clothing store, where he might renovate his shattered wardrobe and appear to some advantage before the boarders of the hotel. He was not long in finding out one, and making a selection from the large quantity of wearing apparel, that decorates the shelves and counters of one of the fashionable clothing emporiums. He was suited with a pea-green worsted sack, and a vest and trowsers of nankeen, and thus attired he sallied up Chesnut, until he reached Fourth, the object of the gaze and (as he thought) of the admiration of the wondering crowds assembled at the Post Office door. He reached the hotel, but this time instead of going through the private entrance, he strutted with all the dignity of a peacock up the main doorway, and thought, as he was entering the hall, that all the attendants were admiring the beauty and tastefulness of his costume. Such is the vanity even of a Hoosier! Fresh from the country, with none of the frivolities nor gaities of city life, he at once yields himself up to the allurements of dress, and indulges in ostentation and vain parade.

The dinner bell was rung, and the Hoosier was seated at the table, before he had time to admire the gorgeous appointments of the dining room. When the guests were seated, he looked around and was struck with the splendor of the objects which surrounded him. Above him were suspended from the ceiling, three magnificent chandeliers, to which were affixed innumerable prismatic pendants, which reflected the rays of the sun, in every imaginable color. These added to the wonderment and astonishment of the newly-arrived traveller. This was a sight he had never seen in the tavern at Greensburgh, a few miles from his home, whither he was accustomed to go, on market days, with the produce of his farm. My! how the folks would stare if they saw all those *diamonds* hanging over their heads, whilst they were eating their dinner. And then, the arm-chairs made of solid mahogany, and cut and carved in such fantastic shapes, and the covers of solid! silver and the forks and spoons of the same material. Then the neat little dishes, that are brought on the table, with the devil knows what on them to eat, and the potatoes and carrots, worked up in every style and form. There was quite sufficient to attract the atttention of the Hoosier, and he would have been wrapt in admiration during the whole of dinner time, had not the pangs of hunger (for he had eaten nothing since the morning,) awakened him from his reveries.

"Give me some pork and beans," he cried, with such stentorian lungs, as at once to draw the attention of the waiters, not without exciting the notice of all the guests at the table.

One of the waiters drew near him and whispered into his ear, that there was nothing of that kind on the table, but that there was *potage au riz, dindes aux truffles*, and *omelettes, en gelee*, in abundance. Our traveller turned round toward the waiter, and in perfect bewilderment asked him what he meant, and then becoming tired of his foreign dialect, told him very abruptly, that he wanted something to eat? He partook of the most exquisite meats, he drank of the most generous wine, and after having regaled himself to his heart's content, he retired to his room, and reclining on a sofa covered with satin, with the light shut out by rich silk and muslin curtains, he fell into the arms of Morpheus and slept till long past the supper hour. He awakened only to retire to his bed-room, and after thinking over the events of the day, went to bed and slept soundly until morning.

The first thought on arising, was as to how he should spend the day? After the fumes of the wine had dissipated and he had got over the excitement of the preceding evening, the question naturally presented itself: "All this is very fine, but may it not cost a great deal?" He rang the bell and called for his account, which he found amounted to the very moderate! sum of seven dollars and a half!

Seven dollars and a half! for a dinner and a bed—why, he would be ruined if he stayed there, he would hardly have enough funds after a week's sojourn at those rates, to see him home to Greensburgh again. What would the folks say, if he did not return to see them once more; they would think he was dead, that some accident had happened to him, etc. He made but one resolve, and that was to leave the hotel immediately and seek another lodging.

It is true, he had been treated well, that his bed was soft, the food excellent, (withal not substantial,) and the wine of a good quality,—it is true, that the waiters were very attentive, and had even styled him "Sir," when they addressed him, but the price was exorbitant, it was really excessive, and he could not not remain there.

Attacked, in what was most dear to him, in his finances, he expostulated with, and asked himself why he came there at all? He was not a millionaire, and had no business in such places.

All resistance was perfectly useless—in the large hotels as in the small ones, the bill must be paid; they will not abate one cent—he had nothing else to do than to take out his purse and settle with the waiter, who saluted him as he left the room. The salutation was not very graciously received, whilst the Hoosier was cogitating over the experience he had acquired from living in a first class hotel. The sacrifice being made, and having paid the waiter's and porter's fees, our traveller hastened to leave the gilded saloons of his first domicile in the Mound City, and in a quiet and retired situation, in some suburban portion of St. Louis, to seek out a less expensive hotel, a more homely mansion, where he could enjoy his plain food at the moderate rate of half a dollar a day.

THE NEW BOARDING HOUSE—
PREPARATIONS FOR SIGHT-SEEING IN ST. LOUIS.

At the junction of Third and ——— streets, may be seen two antiquated frame houses, that seem to date their existence from the time when the village of St. Louis was the resort of the voyageurs and Indian traders, who came here to receive their supplies to carry on the fur trade. On the north-east and north-west corners of ——— street these mansions are erected, resembling each other so much in appearance, that to the eye of the beholder, it would seem as if they were built by the same architect, and on the same plan. That on the north-east corner was for many years a boarding house, where travelers, whose means did not permit them to live at more expensive hotels, were in the habit of resorting to receive such accommodations as the place afforded. Hither our traveler went, in the expectation of finding a lodging and he was not disappointed. On inquiry, he ascertained that the usual price was half a dollar a day, candles and fire separate. Taking his trunk up stairs and looking around his new apartments, the Hoosier was struck with the great change that had so suddenly taken place in his circumstances. There was no longer the soft cushioned sofa, nor the embroidered silk and muslin curtains, nor the richly enameled bed-room furniture, nor the mirrors, in which he could stand and admire himself for hours together. No, these articles had all vanished, like so many dreams of the imagination. Instead of these, he found the hard stool, the humble couch and the plain-framed looking glass, inviting him, though not so alluringly, to indulge in the pleasures of shaving, before he should sally forth to see the city.

Whilst he is in the act of removing the superfluous hair from his chin, I may be permitted to peep from behind the curtain, and give the reader a faint idea of the *personnel* of the Hoosier.

I have before observed that he was six feet in height, standing without his stockings, he was thirty-nine years of age, had sandy hair, which was brushed smoothly over his forehead, a light complexion, blue eyes, dazzling at times, out of which he could look straight when he chose, but when he indulged in a leer, they finally settle down into a habit of squinting, particularly when any of the fair sex crossed his path; withal, the Hoosier considered himself irresistible with the weaker portion of creation, and when his dress added to the other allurements of his finely-proportioned person, he could compete, and sometimes successfully, too, with those dandies who thought they had greater pretensions. I had forgotten the nose, the handle or the index, it is said, of a man's face. It was protuberant, as with the generality of mortals, but the Hoosier's nose was the most remarkable type of the race. It was long, sharp, and flat, and were I to judge according to the definitions of Hogarth and Lavater, I would say it expressed great determination, with a steadfastness of purpose rarely, if ever, met with.

Such was the outward appearance of our traveller, but inwardly there were as noble sentiments at work, as noble feelings and impulses as are found in others whose exterior is more prepossessing. Nor was his heart insensible to those tender emotions which frequently lighten up the countenance of the most morose; his was susceptible to a very great degree, but in the warmth of his adoration of the fair sex, he mingled a feeling of fear lest his advances might implicate him in some unforeseen difficulty, and as he was not prepared for matrimony he hesitated in making any professions of love, and as is usual in such cases, his taciturnity was taken for melancholy.

In the boarding-house in which he resided, there lived a young lady whose parents had been dead for many years, and who was looked upon by the hostess in the light of an only child. She had been educated by them, and had ever since lived with them, and of course owed them a debt of gratitude which she never could repay. Born of respectable parents, and allied to some of the principal Creole families in the city, she had shared in the pleasures of a circle of acquaintances, whose names were almost unknown to her more humble benefactors. She went by the name of Clementine, but her sirname did not at first reach the ears of the Hoosier. Before making my readers acquainted with the age of the pretty Creole, (for her father was a Frenchman and her mother an American,) I might say that she was high-spirited to a fault, quick at resenting an affront, noble, bold, and impetuous.

In appearance, she was rather tall and commanding; her complexion, like most Creoles, approached toward the brunette; her eyes were dark, and in the general proportion of her features there was much to admire in the pretty Clementine, as she glided along the halls and corridors of the establishment, or attended to her daily domestic duties in the household of her kind host and hostess. She had just attained the age of nineteen, and was surrounded by a crowd of admirers when the Hoosier first came to take up his abode in such dangerous vicinity.

He had just concluded the difficult process of shaving, when the thought struck him that he could not go out in the streets of St. Louis without a guide.

OF GUIDES AND CICERONES IN GENERAL, AND OF THE HOOSIER'S GUIDE IN PARTICULAR—REFLECTIONS OF A FIRST VISIT TO MOUND CITY.

Our traveller sallied forth to see the city with all its sights—its churches, its mansions and theatres—but the sight of external objects was not alone what brought him from his homely retreat near Greensburgh. He had higher and nobler aims to accomplish. He wished to know the city, inwardly as well as outwardly, to study human nature in all its phases, varieties and aspects. He wished to see how much the moral bearing of the people was above that of his own neighbors—how religious! how honest! how moral! they were; and he should return home to give the benefit of his experience to his own fellow townsmen, and lead them in the same paths that the Missourians were following.

He reached the corner of Spruce and Fourth streets, and taking refuge under an awning to enjoy the shade, he philosophized as follows: "Well, here I am at St. Louis at last, the object which I had in view from my boyhood upwards has at length been attained, and I stand in the Mound City, with all its antiquities and novelties—where once stood the Indian wigwams, look there at the proud edifices which supply their places—where once the tomahawk was raised in deadly warfare to procure the scalp of the white man, see the evidence of the dogged perseverance and indomitable energy of that very white man, and mark, (save the mounds,) there is no monument remaining of their early possession of the soil."

In the midst of this moralizing, he put his hand in the right pocket of his sack and pulled out a letter of introduction. He remembered that he had to deliver it, but before doing so he would call on an old school-fellow, and endeavor to procure his assistance as a guide to show him the wonders of the city. Surely, his old acquaintance would be delighted to see him. He had heard that Jack Mowers had become an eminent merchant, but with his change of position he would not, he *could* not forget his school-boy days, the friends of his early years, the companions of his little truant jaunts in the vicinity of Greensburgh. He ascertained from a neighbor the place of his residence, which he found was in one of those squares of splendid edifices to the west of Eighth, on Olive.

Hither he repaired, intent on procuring the kind offices of his old friend Mowers to escort him round the city. He ascended the beautiful granite door-step, and gave a hearty, though somewhat arrogant pull at the bell. The door was opened by none of your powdered domestics in livery, such as we read of in the annals of monarchial governments, but a dark swarthy son of Africa, the slave of the proud owner of the mansion, ushered the Hoosier in the presence of his old friend and schoolmate.

"Jack, how d'ye do?"

Mr. Mowers looked at the stranger in astonishment. The Hoosier said:

"Do you not remember Jemmy Dudwell, who went to school with you at Greensburgh, who played with you on the lawn, and who was your old friend and companion?"

Mr. Mowers' countenance began to relax in its rigidity, the motion extended to the muscles of his right hand, which he gave to the Hoosier, who seemed to regain, by the act, his wonted composure. The Hoosier proceeded:

"I wish you would show me the lions of the city. It is the first time in my life that I have ever travelled beyond the precincts of Greensburgh, and I am told strangers are lost here if they have no guide to show them the way."

"Mr. Dudwell," replied Mr. Mowers, "my engagements are such that I can hardly afford sufficient time to attend to my own domestic duties, or otherwise I should be glad to escort you through the city and renew the acquaintance of our school-boy days. I am very much engaged, sir—very much indeed. Please call another time," (at the same time beckoning to the slave in attendance,) "I shall have more leisure to converse with you."

Hardly had these words been pronounced, when the slave opened the door which lead into the hall, and our traveller, the friend and schoolmate of Jack Mowers of other days, took his departure, deeply chagrined at the nature of the interview he had just held with the quondam companion of his boyhood, and resolved not to expose himself to such humiliation for the future.

What were the reflections of the Hoosier as the door of the stately mansion closed on his receding footsteps? He thought of the origin of that man, how he had raised himself by his own exertions to the proud position he now occupied, and how pride and arrogance and the worst passions of human nature had taken possession of his heart, how they had kept pace with his onward progress to wealth and affluence! That man had learnt no lesson of humility—his trials might yet come. Jemmy Dudwell, in the goodness of his heart, prayed to God that he might avert them.

On going down Fourth, the Hoosier observed on the door-plate of a house, the name of his father's old friend, to whom he had a letter of introduction. Ought he, after the discomfiture he had lately experienced, to try his luck a second time? To resolve was the work of a moment. He knocked at the door, which was opened by Mr. Harcourt himself, to whom he presented the letter, and by whom he was very graciously received. Mr. Harcourt was about sixty-five years of age, rather decrepit and infirm, and in answer to the question put to him by the Hoosier, as to whether he would accompany him through the city, excused himself on the score of lameness, at the same time pointing to a pair of crutches, that stood behind the door in the Hall.

The misfortunes of our traveller seemed to multiply, notwithstanding his perseverance. Intent on procuring a guide, he directed a searching glance at his father's old friend, and beseechingly implored him to find some person, any one, to show him the lions of the Mound City.

Mr. Harcourt had a son called Edward, one who, notwithstanding the sage counsels of his venerable father to the contrary, had launched forth into all the wildness and extravagance of a life in the city. Edward was to be found at all hours of the day, and even late at night, at the billiard tables, faro games, and nine-pin alleys with which the Mound City abounds. He belonged to that class of fashionable young men who think they are born, *consumere fruges nati*, to live on the patrimony of their ancestors; in plain language, who do nothing to gain a livelihood, but who share their most valuable time between the pleasures of the gambling table and the allurements of the fair sex. Such was Edward Harcourt's character, and such was the cicerone to whom the kind and indulgent father confided his Hoosier friend, to guide him through the labyrinths of the Mound City.

Edward was not then at home, but his father promised that he should meet him the following day, at eight o'clock in the morning. Dudwell was true to the appointment, and at the stated hour was at Mr. Harcourt's residence for the purpose of being introduced to his promising son. After waiting for some time, during which the father descanted on the evils resulting from keeping late hours, comparing the manners and customs of his ancestors with those of the present day, and pointing out a few of the evils that afflicted society, there was heard a few footsteps on the stairs, and the figure of a tall, pale young gentleman was seen standing in the hall, in the act of taking his hat from the stand, and sallying out for the day.

"Edward, Edward!" cried the father, "you are forgetting your appointment. You know you promised to escort Mr. Dudwell through the city, and show him the lions of St. Louis. The day is fine, and he has been waiting an hour for you."

Edward seeming to recall the conversation he had held with his father on the preceding evening, advanced toward Mr. Dudwell, apologized for his forgetfulness, and offered to escort him through the city.

Thus was the Hoosier at last provided with a guide, but other unforeseen difficulties stood in the way, which he had never even thought of.

On going out in the street the sun shone so brightly on the pea-green sack of the Hoosier, that it attracted the attention of his companion, who had not before scrutinized the habiliments of his friend from the country. Edward feigned an excuse for a few moments to return to his father, and express to him his unalterable determination not to promenade through Fourth street with his green-coated friend from Greensburgh, Indiana.

Why, the very dogs barked at him, and they had not even gone half a square. What would his friends say to see him in company with a man whose pea-green coat and yellow trowsers made him an object of ridicule amongst all whom they met? No, no; his mind was made up, and he would not go out with Mr. Dudwell until he provided other garments.

Mr. Harcourt at once saw the dilemma in which he was placed. He directed Edward to call in Mr. Dudwell, to whom he imparted, in the kindest and most conciliatory manner, the nature of his son's objections, adding that Edward had a splendid wardrobe, and as they were somewhat about the same size, he might provide himself with whatever clothes his son would be good enough to give him. Edward directed the Hoosier to follow him up stairs into his bed-room, and taking a few clothes out of his closet, threw them on the chair, and told him to put them on.

Our traveller found that the coat suited him as well as if it came from the hands of his tailor, but the trowsers were about six inches too short. He therefore asked permission of his friend to let him wear his nankins until he could provide himself with more fashionable apparel.

The request was acceded to, not, however, without a sneer on Edward's countenance at the unfashionable color of his companion's nether-garments. We shall leave them in their perambulation whilst we turn our attention to what was going on elsewhere.

HENRY LEWIS

BORN IN NEWPORT, ENGLAND, Henry Lewis (1819–1904) emigrated to America at age ten with his father and settled in Boston, where he received a brief formal education and became a voracious reader. In 1836, Lewis accompanied his father to St. Louis and began to teach himself how to paint landscapes. By the mid-1840s, Lewis was enthralled with the concept of painting a moving panorama of the Mississippi River. In 1849, he toured the United States and presented his panorama to paying viewers with mixed success. A few years later he traveled abroad, hoping that his attraction would be better received by Europeans "in the grip of a fanatical love for the United States" and enthusiastic about emigrating. By 1853, Lewis had moved to Dusseldorf, which he made his permanent home. Due to ongoing financial difficulty, he sold the panorama to a wealthy planter from Java, who left Europe with the work but neglected to pay Lewis in full. Rumors circulated about the fate of Lewis's panorama, including the claim that it had fallen into the hands of royalty in the Far East; however, none of the tales were substantiated, and the piece vanished.

Lewis put the panorama fiasco behind him and turned to compiling an illustrated reader of the Mississippi. The German edition, *Das illustrirte Mississippithal (The Valley of the Mississippi Illustrated)* was published serially between 1854 and 1857 by the renowned lithographic institute of Arnz and Company. As with his previous business ventures, Lewis had difficulty with his publisher, which reneged on publishing a complete English edition.

During Lewis's career as a practicing painter in Dusseldorf, his American reputation was eclipsed by those of two Missouri artists, both of them acquaintances of Lewis's: George Caleb Bingham and Carl Wimar. Although he retained contact with family in St. Louis, Lewis enjoyed his comfortable, culturally stimulating adopted home and had no desire to return to America.

The following excerpt was taken from *The Valley of the Mississippi Illustrated*, the 1967 English translation of Lewis's original 1854 German edition. In spite of his considerable reputation as an artist, Lewis is most remembered for this stunning, ambitious volume. The volume opens with a chapter on St. Louis and its history, in which Lewis predicts that "the city of St. Louis [is] destined in all probability to become the largest inland commercial city in the United States." In the following section, Lewis describes the Great Fire of 1849, a calamitous event that started aboard a steamboat docked at the wharf and spread, destroying fifteen square blocks of the city's central business district.

FROM *THE VALLEY OF THE MISSISSIPPI ILLUSTRATED*

THE GREAT FIRE IN ST. LOUIS

This great fire, one of the most dreadful that ever visited the United States, took place on May 7, 1849, about ten o'clock in the evening, and before the devouring element could be brought under control, more than six hundred buildings and twenty-five steamboats had been destroyed by it. The fire originated on the steamboats, whence it was communicated to the enormous piles of hemp, tobacco, and produce which are heaped up at the shipping place at this season of the year. From there the fire spread to the city. Many fires had broken out on the steamboats before this, and in such cases it is customary to cut the burning boat adrift and give it up to the current of the stream, which then carries it to the middle of the river.

This expedient was also to be used on this occasion, but unfortunately there was a very stiff wind, so that, instead of being carried to the middle of the stream, the burning boat was driven down river and ignited all the boats with which it came in contact. Twenty-seven boats lay below the burning vessel, and of those, only two escaped the menacing danger. This is easily explained by the fact that the boats lie so close together, as is shown on our illustration of the city of St. Louis in an earlier part of this work. We have no docks or wharves at the landings of our Western cities along the Mississippi. The street or "levee" (also loading place), as it is called, along the water is a bank which descends steeply by steps down to the level of the water. When the river rises, the street gradually grows narrower. During the great flood in 1844, we saw the water rise to the second stories of the warehouses. When the fire broke out, the water was quite high and the street was therefore very narrow. This narrow space was, as we remarked earlier, covered with a great mass of wares and produce which had been discharged from the upper river boats and awaited reloading onto those going south, and *vice versa*. Among the wares unloaded the previous day were 2,000 bales of hemp heaped up in a great pile. When they caught fire, the flames ignited the nearest houses. At this moment the wind, which had risen to a great violence, drove the flames from north to northeast and brought to naught all human efforts to check it until fortunately, at four o'clock in the morning, the wind suddenly veered and swept over the burning part of the city. Thereby the southern section was spared, and toward eight o'clock the fire began to respond to human efforts.

But now a dismal sight met the eye: nearly all the most beautiful part of the city lay in ashes, and the loss of property ran to more than $5,000,000. The native energy of the people was not, however, prostrated by this terrible affliction, for even before the stones had grown cold, hundreds had already gone to work to clear away the ruins and make preparations for new buildings. After a year, scarcely a trace of the calamity could be seen. A new and more beautiful city had risen from the ground, and many improvements, such as straight and wide streets, which had been too costly earlier, could now be constructed more easily. Since the fire raged in the more affluent part of the city, the poorer classes were little affected by the calamity. So far as we know, there was no bankruptcy or other business stoppage. And although several thousand dollars were collected in various cities for the relief of the sufferers, no claims were made against the fund, and the entire sum was divided among various charitable institutions.

The following detailed account of this event is taken from a newspaper published in St. Louis; and although this report, written during the event, contained many errors, it should be of interest.

> "About ten o'clock last night fire broke out on the steamer *'White Cloud,'* lying near the head of the levee. At the time, there was a stiff breeze blowing from the northeast, which quickly carried the flames over the 'Edward Bates,' the next boat below, and spread from there to the 'Eudora,' lying above them. In this instant one or two boats were dropped downstream, leaving a space between the burning boats and those uninjured. Thereupon the 'Edward Bates,' being about half burned up, was cast loose and went floating down the levee, setting

fire to two more boats. Thirteen other steamboats, besides a great number of wood boats and other vessels, became victims of the flames, and only nine were saved.

"The heat from this conflagration, which extended from the head of the levee to the head of Duncan's Island, was so great that it set fire to several buildings on the levee and at other points, and many wharves between Locust and Vine streets were destroyed. Entire blocks between various streets and a great number of houses on the west side of Main Street are wrapped in flames, which are spreading with fearful intensity in all directions. It is impossible to foresee the end of this terrible catastrophe, the like of which has never before struck any city west of the Allegheny Mountains.

"Besides the property enumerated, grain in sacks, hemp, bacon, etc. on the levee also caught fire and were dumped into the water. On one pile of such goods, which was covered by a tarpaulin, it is said that four persons were sleeping who were apparently ringed by flames and there met their deaths. We ourselves saw one of the victims. There were also kegs of powder on board several boats, and as soon as the ravaging element reached them, they exploded with terrific crashes, scattering burning fragments. Several people were injured or killed by burning pieces, but it would be difficult to guess how many poor wretches may have been destroyed as they sought to escape from [the flames sweeping from] ship to ship and from house to house.

"Meanwhile, a horrible and grand spectacle was exhibited by the burning boats at Duncan's Island, floating along for three-quarters of a mile, their pillars of flame and clouds of smoke mingling in confusion. On the other hand, long rows of warehouses threw out a fiery rain of red flames; a gruesome picture in deep, dark night, where all souls, in horrible suspense, awaited the worst; where one saw men running around half frantic, dragging out their bit of property in despair, followed by a weeping wife and wailing infant. Then the fire progressed farther from the levee, westward to Second Street, and from Locust southward to Elm Street. This entire space is not totally burned down, but before the fire will have been entirely extinguished, the destruction will be complete.

"Since it is not possible to list all the houses that were burned, we will name only the main buildings. They are: the Telegraph office, the

United States Hotel, the Reveille office, the Republican office, the Organ office, and the New Era office. Thus all the English newspaper presses in the city were destroyed except our own, which is located on the north side of Locust and fortunately escaped the danger. We can make no estimate of the loss caused by this fire, but it will presumably amount to about $5,000,000."

The fire broke out on the shore at the end of Locust Street and the levee, where three houses caught fire at once. The flames then spread along Locust, igniting every house except one, and swept over the houses located across from the levee and Main Street. Then it progressed from Locust Street southward to Chestnut Street, a distance of three squares. At Chestnut Street the fire turned to the nearest southern section where Commercial Alley meets this street, and from the Alley to Main, down toward Market, consuming everything with the exception of two buildings on the corner of Market and Commercial Alley. Where Market adjoins Main Street, the flames took a diagonal direction toward the Markethouse, and followed both sides of Market to Second Street. Then turning across Main, the flames caught every house from Locust to Market, except a row of fireproof warehouses below Locust.

The ravaging element swept over Pine Street, Chestnut Street, and Market, consuming every house in its course, up to half of the section north of Olive. In that part of the city the destruction was stayed. But before the flames could be checked, several houses had to be blown up, whereby three people lost their lives. The remains of one body were found on the opposite side of the street. The thigh bone and the foot of another were found at the entrance of Walnut Street three squares away from the house that was blown up.

Now we turn more toward the south, to the entrance of Elm Street, where the fire had fashioned a new hearth. The flames veered diagonally over the complex, laid hold of Main Street, up to Spence Street, a distance northward and southward of two squares, and devastated everything almost to Third Street, three squares west of its origin.

In Main Street the flames progressed to Elm Street and consumed a fourth of the section north of Elm and west of Main. No house remains standing between Elm and Second streets. Through this sad calamity hundreds of families were made homeless, and wealthy men were plunged into poverty.

The South Market and the City Hall were at one time in great danger but, through the efforts of several persons there, they were saved.

The shock which resulted from blowing up the houses with powder broke almost every windowpane within half a block of the corner of Market and Second streets. Furthermore, about fifty people were jailed for looting during the conflagration. There have also been varying reports as to the loss of life. We mourn the loss of two or three of our old, respected fellow citizens, and beyond doubt no inquiries will be made concerning many of the unfortunate ones who were killed, or the many strangers who were on the boats and in the city.

The destruction caused by the conflagration stretches over an area some two blocks wide and almost a mile long. The streets of our city are covered with wreckage of all kinds. We saw neither New York nor Pittsburgh after their great fires, but it is maintained that after our present calamity nothing exceeds the destruction and ruins of our city. As concerns the proportion of loss, we have as yet no definite data. Meanwhile, we do not recall that the loss suffered in New York or Pittsburgh exceeded $5,000,000. If that is so, then St. Louis lost more than either of those cities.

ELIZABETH HOBBS KECKLEY

BORN A SLAVE IN VIRGINIA, Elizabeth Hobbs Keckley (1818-1907) moved to St. Louis around 1836 and was hired out as a seamstress. With the help of some patrons, Keckley and her son purchased their freedom while living in the city. Keckley eventually moved to Washington, D.C., where she quickly gained a reputation as a seamstress to fashionable Washingtonians.

In 1861, Keckley became the personal dressmaker for Mary Todd Lincoln, wife of President Lincoln. Eventually, she became Mrs. Lincoln's traveling companion and confidante; the First Lady confided her opinions concerning both her personal and public life around her to the former slave. Keckley's book, *Behind the Scenes; or, Thirty Years a Slave and Four in the White House* (1868), describes the Lincolns' intimate life during the Civil War, as well as Mary Lincoln's opinions of prominent leaders surrounding her husband.

Unfortunately, the book destroyed Keckley's relationship with Mary Todd Lincoln, who felt betrayed by its close-up view of life in the White House. Even several prominent African Americans criticized the book's revelatory nature and deplored its publication. As a result of its negative reception, Keckley lost most of her clients and could no longer support herself as a seamstress.

In spite of the restrictions that her race and gender put upon Keckley, she used her intelligence and determination to accomplish much. After leaving the Lincoln White House, she held a teaching position at Wilberforce University in Ohio. Keckley was partially supported in retirement by a government pension she received as the mother of a Union soldier killed in action.

In the following passage from *Behind the Scenes,* Keckley describes her life as a seamstress in St. Louis and her struggle to buy freedom for herself and her son, George, who was sired by one of Keckley's former owners. With the emotional and financial support of some affluent benefactors—and the cooperation of her owners, the Garland family—Keckley and George were deeded emancipation in the St. Louis Circuit Court on November 15, 1855.

FROM *BEHIND THE SCENES*

The years passed and brought many changes to me, but on these I will not dwell, as I wish to hasten to the most interesting part of my story. My troubles in North Carolina were brought to an end by my unexpected return to Virginia, where I lived with Mr. Garland, who had married Miss Ann Burwell, one of my old master's daughters. His life was not a prosperous one, and after struggling with the world for several years he left his native State, a disappointed man. He moved to St. Louis, hoping to improve his fortune in the West; but ill luck followed him there, and he seemed to be unable to escape from the influence of the evil star of his destiny. When his family, myself included, joined him in his new home on the banks of the Mississippi, we found him so poor that he was unable to pay the dues on a letter advertised as in the post-office for him. The necessities of the family were so great, that it was proposed to place my mother out at service. The idea was shocking to me. Every gray hair in her old head was dear to me, and I could not bear the thought of her going to work for strangers. She had been raised in the family, had watched the growth of each child from infancy to maturity; they had been the objects of her kindest care, and she was wound round about them as the vine winds itself about the rugged oak. They had been the central figures in her dream of life—a dream beautiful to her, since she had basked in the sunshine of no other. And now they proposed to destroy each tendril of affection, to cloud the sunshine of her existence when the day was drawing to a close, when the shadows of solemn night were rapidly approaching. My mother, my poor aged mother, go among strangers to toil for a living! No, a thousand times no! I would rather work my fingers to the bone, bend over my sewing till the film of blindness gathered in my eyes; nay, even beg from street to street. I told Mr. Garland so, and he gave me permission to see what I could do. I was fortunate in obtaining work, and in a short time I had acquired something of a reputation as a seamstress and dress-maker. The best ladies in St. Louis were my patrons, and when my reputation was once established I never lacked for orders. With my needle I kept bread in the mouths of seventeen persons for two years and five months. While I was working so hard that others might live in comparative comfort, and move in those circles of society to which their birth gave them entrance, the thought often occurred to me whether I was really worth my salt or not; and then perhaps the lips curled with a bitter sneer. It may seem strange that I should place so much emphasis upon words thoughtlessly, idly spoken; but then we do many strange things in life, and cannot always explain the motives that actuate us. The heavy task was too much for me, and my health began to give way. About this time Mr. Keckley, whom I had met in Virginia, and learned to regard with more than friendship, came to St. Louis. He sought my hand in marriage, and for a long time I refused to consider his proposal; for I could not bear the thought of bringing children into slavery—of adding one single recruit to the millions bound to hopeless servitude, fettered and shackled with chains stronger and heavier than manacles of iron. I made a proposition to buy myself and son; the proposition was bluntly declined, and I was commanded never to broach the subject again. I would not be put off thus, for hope pointed to a freer, brighter life in the future. Why should my son be held in slavery? I often asked myself. He came into the world through no will of mine, and yet, God only knows how I loved him. The Anglo-Saxon blood as well as the African flowed in his veins; the two currents commingled—one singing of freedom, the other silent and sullen with generations of despair. Why should not the Anglo-Saxon triumph—why should it be weighed down with the rich blood typical of the tropics? Must the life-current of one race bind the other race in chains as strong and enduring as if there had been no Anglo-Saxon taint? By the laws of God and nature as interpreted by man, one-half of my boy was free, and why should not this fair birthright of freedom remove the curse from the other half—raise it into the bright, joyous sunshine of liberty? I could not answer these questions of my heart that almost maddened me, and I learned to regard human philosophy with distrust. Much as I respected the authority of my master, I could not remain silent on a subject that so nearly concerned me. One day, when I insisted on knowing whether he would permit me to purchase myself, and what price I must pay for myself, he turned to me in a petulant manner, thrust his hand into his pocket, drew forth a bright silver quarter of a dollar, and proffering it to me, said:

"Lizzie, I have told you often not to trouble me with such a question. If you really wish to leave me, take this: it will pay the passage of yourself and boy on the ferry-boat, and when you are on the other side of the river you will be free. It is the cheapest way that I know of to accomplish what you desire."

I looked at him in astonishment, and earnestly replied: "No, master, I do not wish to be free in such a manner. If such had been my wish, I should never have troubled you about obtaining your consent to my purchasing myself. I can cross the river any day, as you well know, and have frequently done so, but will never leave you in such a manner. By the laws of the land I am your slave—you are my master, and I will only be free by such means as the laws of the country provide." He expected this answer, and I know that he was pleased. Some time afterwards he told me that he had reconsidered the question; that I had served his family faithfully; that I deserved my freedom, and that he would take $1200 for myself and boy.

This was joyful intelligence for me, and the reflection of hope gave a silver lining to the dark cloud of my life—faint, it is true, but still a silver lining.

Taking a prospective glance at liberty, I consented to marry. The wedding was a great event in the family. The ceremony took place in the parlor, in the presence of the family and a number of guests. Mr. Garland gave me away, and the pastor, Bishop Hawks, performed the ceremony, who had solemnized the bridals of Mr. G.'s own children. The day was a happy one, but it faded all too soon. Mr. Keckley—let me speak kindly of his faults—proved dissipated, and a burden instead of a helpmate. More than all, I learned that he was a slave instead of a free man, as he represented himself to be. With the simple explanation that I lived with him eight years, let charity draw around him the mantle of silence.

I went to work in earnest to purchase my freedom, but the years passed, and I was still a slave. Mr. Garland's family claimed so much of my attention—in fact, I supported them—that I was not able to accumulate anything. In the mean time Mr. Garland died, and Mr. Burwell, a Mississippi planter, came to St. Louis to settle up the estate. He was a kind-hearted man, and said I should be free, and would afford me every facility to raise the necessary amount to pay the price of my liberty. Several schemes were urged upon me by my friends. At last I formed a resolution to go to New York, state my case, and appeal to the benevolence of the people. The plan seemed feasible, and I made preparations to carry it out. When I was almost ready to turn my face northward, Mrs. Garland told me that she would require the names of six gentlemen who would vouch for my return, and become responsible for the amount at which I was valued. I had many friends in St. Louis, and as I believed that they had confidence in me, I felt that I could readily obtain the names desired. I started out, stated my case, and obtained five signatures to the paper, and my heart throbbed with pleasure, for I did not believe that the sixth would refuse me. I called, he listened patiently, then remarked:

"Yes, yes, Lizzie; the scheme is a fair one, and you shall have my name. But I shall bid you good-by when you start."

"Good-by for a short time," I ventured to add.

"No, good-by for all time," and he looked at me as if he would read my very soul with his eyes.

I was startled. "What do you mean, Mr. Farrow? Surely you do not think that I do not mean to come back?"

"No."

"No, what then?"

"Simply this: you *mean* to come back, that is, you *mean* so *now*, but you never will. When you reach New York the abolitionists will tell you what savages we are, and they will prevail on you to stay there; and we shall never see you again."

"But I assure you, Mr. Farrow, you are mistaken. I not only *mean* to come back, but *will* come back, and pay every cent of the twelve hundred dollars for myself and child."

I was beginning to feel sick at heart, for I could not accept the signature of this man when he had no faith in my pledges. No; slavery, eternal slavery rather than be regarded with distrust by those whose respect I esteemed.

"But—I am not mistaken," he persisted. "Time will show. When you start for the North I shall bid you good-by."

The heart grew heavy. Every ray of sunshine was eclipsed. With humbled pride, weary step, tearful face, and a dull, aching pain, I left the house. I walked along the street mechanically. The cloud had no silver lining now. The rosebuds of hope had withered and died without lifting up their heads to receive the dew kiss of morning. There was no morning for me—all was night, dark night.

I reached my own home, and weeping threw myself upon the bed. My trunk was packed, my luncheon was prepared by mother, the cars were ready to bear me where I would not hear the clank of chains, where I would breathe the free, invigorating breezes of the glorious North. I had dreamed such a happy dream, in imagination had drunk of the water, the pure, sweet crystal water of life, but now—now—the flowers had withered before my eyes; darkness had settled down upon me like a pall, and I was left alone with cruel mocking shadows.

The first paroxysm of grief was scarcely over, when a carriage stopped in front of the house; Mrs. Le Bourgeois, one of my kind patrons, got out of it and entered the door. She seemed to bring sunshine with her handsome cheery face. She came to where I was, and in her sweet way said:—

"Lizzie, I hear that you are going to New York to beg for money to buy your freedom. I have been thinking over the matter, and told Ma it would be a shame to allow you to go North to *beg* for what we should *give* you. You have many friends in St. Louis, and I am going to raise the twelve hundred dollars required among them. I have two hundred dollars put away for a present; am indebted to you one hundred dollars; mother owes you fifty dollars, and will add another fifty to it; and as I do not want the present, I will make the money a present to you. Don't start for New York now until I see what I can do among your friends."

Like a ray of sunshine she came, and like a ray of sunshine she went away. The flowers no longer were withered, drooping. Again they seemed to bud and grow in fragrance and beauty. Mrs. Le Bourgeois, God bless her dear good heart, was more than successful. The twelve hundred dollars were raised, and at last my son and myself were free. Free, free! what a glorious ring to the word. Free! the bitter heart-struggle was over. Free! the soul could go out to heaven and to God with no chains to clog its flight or pull it down. Free! the earth wore a brighter look, and the very stars seemed to sing with joy. Yes, free! free by the laws of man and the smile of God—and Heaven bless them who made me so!

JAMES THOMAS

JAMES THOMAS (1827–1913) was born in Nashville and was the son of a prominent judge, John Catron, chief justice of the Tennessee Supreme Court, and an African American laundress, Sally, who bought her son's freedom for four hundred dollars in 1834. However, since Thomas did not leave the state, as Tennessee required of free blacks, he legally remained a slave until he was twenty-three, when the state court granted his petition for freedom.

Having worked as a master barber in Nashville, Thomas had many prominent clients and amassed a considerable sum of money. He came to St. Louis in July 1857 and remained there for the rest of his life. In 1858, Thomas worked for Henry Clamorgan, brother of Cyprian Clamorgan, in one of the city's finest barber shops. "He is very genteel in his manners, attentive to business, and is a remarkably fine looking man," wrote Cyprian of James Thomas in his booklet *The Colored Aristocracy of St. Louis* (1858). Clamorgan added that Thomas had a fortune of fifteen thousand dollars, a tremendous sum for anybody in 1858, but astonishing for a former slave.

By 1873, Thomas owned numerous properties around St. Louis, in addition to other real estate in Memphis and Nashville. His fortune, over a half million dollars, made him one of the wealthiest African Americans in Missouri and one of the richest black men in the country. After the Panic of 1893, Thomas lost most of his fortune, and by the time of his death, Thomas's personal property had an assessed value of $1.43. During the last decade of his life, Thomas finished his autobiography, eventually published as *From Tennessee Slave to St. Louis Entrepreneur: The Autobiography of James Thomas* (1984). In the following excerpt from that volume, Thomas describes conditions in St. Louis on the eve of the Civil War.

FROM *THE AUTOBIOGRAPHY OF JAMES THOMAS*

ST. LOUIS ON THE EVE OF WAR

The southern states, clearing the deck for action, commenced an attack on free persons. Louisiana, Ark., Tenn., and Missouri were conspicuous. In Louisiana the creoles were badly scared at the threat of taking their oath. Many creoles in La. owned plantations and slaves. In Tenn., Missouri, and Ark. it amounted to a removal of free col^{d} people from the state (those becoming free) or else compel them to selected a white man to stand their guardian. The property owned by them was to be applied to the education of poor whites. The ablest men in Tenn opposed it bitterly, and in other states equally so. The state of Ark lost no time in passing it. The measure was pending in the other states and would have been passed but for the coming on of the War. It was passed in the Missouri legislature but the govt troops gave them no chance to enforce it. I like the southern people individualy, but collectively and politicaly, "Dam 'em."

St. Louis during the winter of 1860 and 1861 as far as business was concerned was dull. Merchants seemed to have an abundance of leisure. There was a frightful schrinkage in values. There was no buyers for property in the line of Real Estate. I heard one Merchant say he would not give as much for property along fourth st. by the Acre as it had bringing pr. foot. People who had a little money hid it away there to remain indefinitely. Summer came. Many people continued to wear their old thread bare winter clothes.

All the younger people reading or rather studying Hardy^{s} tacktics. Whenever one took a seat, he would reach for his pocket and get out Hardee and try to get into his head how to parry and thrust. Boats were carrying large quantities of freight south such as would be needed in case of trouble. One Gentleman, a Merchant who had just returned from New Orleans, said that the people there had made up their minds and were making every preparation and that they had about Thirty million dollars hoarded up in banks. Many thought the matter would be settled without any serious trouble. Some said, O for a Webster or a Clay to pour oil on the troubled waters. Instead of the Political sky clearing a little it seemed to grow darker. They thought Mr Crittendon of Kentucky might be listened to but no talk from him or anybody made any impression. The masses wanted war talk, something like Mr Wigfall of Texas, such as "unfurl the banner to the breeze and write resistance on every square inch." Forensic efforts were common in Washington and strong language was used. Pryor of Virginia challenged Mr Potter. Potter choose Bowie Knives. Pryor declined the brutal method. Mr. Lander said he would fight Pryor anyway and with any weapon he choose. It looked now as though both sides were in pure earnest.

In 1861 Capt Lyons had home guards and regulars at the Arsenal in St Louis. Being a little crowded he placed them on the commons around the Arsenal grounds. They were regarded as necessary to prevent the Arsenal from seizure. The citizens complained of having the city property used for soldiers to camp on and prevailed on the mayor to request Capt Lyons to take his camp inside the Arsenal grounds. Capt Lyons replied that he would wait for orders from Washington before he would remove the troops.

The time had come when everybody was expected to show his hand. When he didn't do so he was asked how he stood in the matter. In other words what is your politics. Still the cooler heads were hoping that there would be an Amicable adjustment of the differences and that peace and quiet might return. A republican replying to the question, "What is your politics," was almost sure to say, I am a republican but no Abolitionist. There were not many men that had the boldness to admit themselves to be Abolitionist. To make that admission meant a coolness and maybe ostracism from neighbors on account of his (what was termed) fanatical Ideas. But the free soil doctrine had been gaining in St Louis under the leadership of F. P. Blair.

The old and wealthy families of St Louis were all southern in sentiment with few exceptions. A good many northern people and some foreigners joined their ranks to be classed with Aristocrats. When a string of foreigners came into the country, people knew it meant so many votes for the Democracy. The Whigs were the more [prosperous] of the two and controlled the bulk of the wealth. A few foreigners turned Whig, not until they had been in the country several years, made money and began to feel Aristocratic. The Germans North soon advocated and adhered to the free soil move. Then they were early in advocating freedom for the bondsmen. The Irish were Democrats and they wanted "Dooglass" made president because his wife was a Catholic. At all events they were "dimocrats" and ninety nine out of a hundred were southerners in sympathy. In fact, old St Louis, which was closely associated with the south through family relations and business, had a secession feeling. As a general thing they were strong in their utterances. The Irish belonged to the unterified democracy. The churches themselves were accused of being in politics. The old colored Catholics wanted to see Federal bayonets brought in. They had been on the anxious seat long enough.

The Women were if anything busier than the men. It must be remembered that women have ruled and ruined since the world began. I mean in alteration, not all rule nor all ruin, but just enough to add spice to the repast. I will say this, It has been my opinion that Mr. Douglas would have been nominated at the Charleston Convention If some men had not been advised to never allow that Estimable woman Mrs. Douglas to become Mistress of the White house. I have never heard anybody say anything about the matter, but while Miss Harriet Lane and many other ladies were parraded before the public in newspapers, there was a studied silence towards Mrs. Douglas. Availability goes a long ways in Selecting a candidate for so Important a position as president of the United States. All that was necessary was to nominate Stephen A Douglas. They would have had a patriot and a good man at the helm of State, but the women didn't want his wife and the men acted according to Instructions. Which was well, as is well known we got a better man.

The Young and old or middle aged ladies would meet their Gentlemen friends on the street, contrary to their former habits, stop and exchange a few words, sometimes hold a hurried consultation, then pass on. The young ladies, it appeared, were encouraging their big brother and sweetheart to go and share in the glory of putting the Yankees to flight. Some got tired waiting for the return of their choice and married somebody else.

The condition of the social, Financial and Political fabric was undergoing a strain.

Army officers were resigning their positions and going home in the south.

Jews were coming into the country from all parts of the world apparently. One told me what time he left Rio Janeiro. In fact they were about the only contented people or the most contented to be met with. While other people expected to lose, they expected to do some business.

The legislature of Missouri was kept so busy with more serious matters, had not found the time to take up the "free Nigger bill" and before they did reach it and while the free people were uneasy concerning it, The county court rounded up all the free people, ascertained their callings and their standing in the community, gave all permission to remain, which eased their minds. So the free Negroes got permission to remain and before a great while the legislative body had to make a precipitate move which dissolved that body of wise men for good. In rounding up the free people before the court there were many who were Indians, Spaniards, French, whose chocolate colored mothers had lived under the three flags. But they were not called on to prove nothing.

The Southern people used to repeat a small portion of what might be termed history. It seemed their Vocabulary of profanity was inexaustable when a little excited. They would say, Now look, them blue bellied scoundrels went to Africa, stole the niggers, brought them here, sold them to us, then stole them from us, starved them and otherwise mistreated them, now they pretend and do want to tell us what to do with the balance of them.

Those self appointed conservitors of the peace were constantly nosing around to see what the niggers were doing. They never grew tired of lecturing the Niggers. Their lecture consisted of about ten words, which amounted to "You fellows must remember this is a white man's country yet." "I have no objection to a nigger as long as he keeps his place." If anybody ever made a remark in the Negro favor the question was put, do you want a nigger to marry your daughter, sit at your table.

In St Louis there were many quiet men who said but little, was awaiting developments. But many of them secretly thought that just such a man as Genl Andrew Jackson would be the right sort of man for the times.

The Germans were ultra in their political opinions and at heart felt like wiping out the last vestige of the [secessionist] feeling from the city or country. There had been no real cordial feeling between the two factions in St Louis. The Americans had attempted to check their sunday parades. The Germans claimed they had the right to spend the sunday to their own liking and intended to do it.

The home guard used to parade the street in Squads, looking close right and left. Many men stood along the side walk, hands on hip pocket. On two or three occasions a pistol was fired and the guards emptied their guns in the direction of where the shot came from. As to be expected, somebody was hurt. Those parading said it was a pistol. Others said Stick broke. Some of those Germans couldn't speak English but were purely in Earnest and wished for a chance to kill the "Seush", it made no difference whether was governor or United states senator, he ought to be hung for insulting "my country's flag." Many of those Germans knew no English but "Cot fur tam."

All this talk back and forth was from the time of Mr Lincoln^{s} nomination and before. The people all knew Mr Lincolns sentiments. "We dont want to take anybodys property, Slaves or Otherwise. We do oppose an extension of slavery." After the War began, Anything but a destruction of the Union.

After the Election the friends of Mr Lincoln thought it better to get him into Washington without his being generaly recognized. According to reports, they disguised him with a Scotch Cloak or some other. Any how those who opposed him in politics laughed heartily at the Idea. Peoples ideas were formed. When a man said we ought to go slow, Mr Lincoln may make a good president, the ultra element, who could be heard above all others, would cry out, "submissionist," "Abolitionist," and other unpleasant sayings. When an old cry baby would say we ought not to get into trouble among ourselves, "brother against brother," would only give the rabid a fresh start and would say something about such brothers in a severe manner. One man said if that kind went to heaven he didnt want to go there. Yankees.

Those in sympathy with the south were highly pleased when they saw the name of another of the Generals in the army and who had served with distinction handing in their resignations. That continued until a long list of the most familiar names had been marked off as out of the service of the United States. The incoming administration began looking to see what it had. They knew what they ought to have but they wanted to see in what condition it was in, whether it was fit for immediate use. The man that counted the money had the easiest job for there was no money to count, or less than a dollar, so they said. The arms of the government that should have been found in place by all means had been shipped south and placed where the stronger party could take possession when ready to do so, as all the south had been taught that the trouble would result in a walk over when the dogs of war were let loose.

But the dogs of war were let lose in a manner that at first attracted no special attention. Here and there an arsenal was seized all right. The people could say nothing. But there was a goodly supply of United States guns just lately received at St Louis. All or many of the arsenals were taken in South. The people of St Louis would have been not the least surprised and rather expected an attack or an attempt to seize the Arsenal. The seceders would rather have had somebody else than Capt Lyons to deal with and the Union people felt confident in his earnestness to the cause of the Union. Besides

Lyons, Col. Blair had been made Col. of a regiment containing foot and horse, two thousand men. While the southern people were elated with the seizure of United Stats property elsewhere they themselves didn't relish the Idea of trying to seize the St Louis arsenal with Col Blair and Capt Lyons to defend it.

Many of the older men looked haggard and worn under the strain. It was clear that talk would do no good. It seemed clear that the differences must be settled with blood shed after the south had been supplied with United States weapons By Mr Floyd, they said, leaving the United States government nothing to fight with. The leading Military men (officers) gave no money. The government had simple to begin over. All that visiting which occured a year or two before Col. Ben McCullough and other southern men Many of them traveled on the Morrison were then arranging for this thing which was arranged and carried out as they, I supposed, wished.

Now the Germans were highly Elated over the report that Genl Franz Seigal was coming from the "faderland" and such was his knowledge and ability as a commander that scarcely anybody else would be needed In case of War which was certain to unless a back down from some one.

When it became known to the military authorities that some guns were brought to the city and had been received by the commander at what was named Camp Jackson, where there was quite a gathering of what was known (to all who felt inclined to investigate) to be secessionist. Those guns had been carried out to the camp. The people felt satisfied that as soon as the camp felt strong enough they would be hurled against the Arsenal. The commander at the Arsenal, Capt Lyons, sent word to the commander of Camp Jackson that he wanted those guns belonging to the United States. The Commander of the Camp's reply was if he wanted the guns, he had better come and get them. Possibly, he thought they wouldn't come.

The reply of the commander of the Camp (to "come and get them") was of a sort that could not well be ignored. In the afternoon on the 10th May, Capt Lyons & Col. Blair went after those guns. They at the same time took along a few friends. The invitation didnt specify who must or who must not come. The best wines and liquors were plentiful, cigars abundant in the camp. All callers were well received. Visitors used to tell me how well every body was treated and several of the officers had invited me to come and I had promised to go.

On the memorable tenth of May in the afternoon a cloud of dust was seen approaching the camp from two or three different streets. Many in the Camp wondered what that meant but in short time it was made clear. Blair and Lyons had brought friends numbering about nine thousand Dutch and other soldiers. In addition to them there were almost as many more curious people, who knew what was intended, had followed along to see the fun and climbed on the fences and any place to get a good view.

The soldiers under Lyon and Blair surrounded the camp, unlimbered their guns (according to all the accounts I heard given of the affair) and demanded those guns. In addition they demanded an immediate and unconditional surrender of the camp. While those negotiations were going on, the german soldiers fired a volley in the direction of where they thought harm was intended, their bullits ploughing through the ranks of the spectators killing fortunately only a few. One fellow who had climbed the fence to get a good view told me how he and a thousand others, supposing they had been shot, let go the fence and fell to the ground like a thousand of bricks and was afraid to raise their heads up expecting another volley. If there was ever a humiliated and disgusted set of people in the world they could be found among those at Camp Jackson that night. They swore and ripped, "Cussed" the dutch, but they had to take the oath of Allegiance or go to their friends in the south.

The capture of Camp Jackson cast a gloom over the old set. They criticised the dutch harshly. Many of their conversations were in french. I believe the majority of those young men went south and remained there until the close of hostilities.

In the beginning of Mr Lincolns administration there were divers of opinions and sugestions made. Some of the leading men said let them go out of the Union if they want to. They will gladly come back before long. Different mens opinions were given daily, while Mr Lincoln was steadfast for the preservation of the union. No compromising with Lincoln. The union gentleman, the union. The people laughed at "uncle Abes" grammer and the way he said things and used to compare his language with Mr Jeff Davis, who was a finished scollar. Now we only hear what "Abe" said, never hear of Jeff.

The southern people always expected in case of trouble between sections that we would have foreign intervention and that the European powers would not allow all ports blockaded. There were several southern gentlemen in Europe, there for the purpose of teaching the people the justness of their cause and to tell how they had been goaded into doing what they had done.

Training the guns on fort Sumpter stopped all talk of speculative kind. Then the southern people had to hold their sides again when they read that Mr Lincoln had called for seventy five Thousand volunteers. Those of the seventy five thousand that came to St Louis were sent off under Genl Lyons to beat back Genl Ben McColloughs army that was then invading Missouri did not have the time to be Uniformed. Lyons was killed. The seventy five Thousand were enlisted for three months. Their time expired about the time the battle was fought which was the battle of Wilson Creek. The fight was not far from a draw but it was regarded by many southern people as a victory because Genl Lyons was killed. The first I learned of the death of Lyons was from a young southern man who said to me hurry up and let me out of here. I'm told Lyons was killed and I want to get drunk.

People of the East nagged the life out of the gov[t] to hurry up, close the war. After a while, which seemed a long time to those who expected the war to close after one battle, the army went down to Bull Run to clean out the Confederates. The people of St Louis as elsewhere were eager for reports of the fight. Extras were issued often. It was a hot day. Many Congressmen went along to see what battle looked like. A dispatch came stating that the battle was on in earnest. One of the dispatches read that the boys were fighting hard and had removed their shirts. All of those reports only increased the interest. The last read that the Union forces had stopped to give the horses water. Lastly it intimated that the battle would not be resumed that day. The following morning the papers gave a full account of a stampede of the Union Army. Instead of running towards Richmond, they had run every foot of the distance to Washington where they started from. It was highly entertaining to hear the southern people of St Louis talk and laugh over the affair. They were tickled nearly to death. They tried to look serious and sorry for "our" discomfiture before the Union people, but among themselves they laughed until tears came. They were only sorry the Confederates didnt follow up their advantage and seize Washington and then defy them.

WILLIAM TECUMSEH SHERMAN

THE SIXTH OF ELEVEN CHILDREN, William T. Sherman (1820–1891) was born in Lancaster, Ohio. In 1829, young William's father died, and Thomas Ewing, a family friend and future U.S. Senator, stepped in to become his foster father. Ewing arranged for Sherman's entry into West Point, where he proved an outstanding cadet. While at West Point, Sherman met Ulysses S. Grant, who would become his military commander and lifelong friend.

Sherman first came to St. Louis in 1850 and was stationed briefly at Jefferson Barracks. After spending much of the 1850s pursuing a variety of professions (banking, law, school administration) around the country, Sherman returned to St. Louis in 1861 and found a short-lived post as president of the Fifth Street Railroad Company. In October of that year, Sherman rejoined the army and proved a brilliant commanding officer. He was rapidly promoted and led several key campaigns, including the Battle of Bull Run and the famous "March to the Sea" from Atlanta. During the war, Sherman experienced great personal tragedy: the deaths of his two young sons, nine-year-old Willie, and infant Charles, whom he had never seen. Both of the boys were buried in St. Louis's Calvary Cemetery.

When Grant became president in 1869, he appointed Sherman commander-in-chief of the U.S. Army. After his military retirement in 1883, Sherman returned to St. Louis and lived at 912 Garrison Avenue for several years. Although both Sherman and his wife, Ellen, died in New York City, they were buried in St. Louis at Calvary Cemetery next to their sons.

In the following excerpt from his *Memoirs*, Sherman recalls his negotiations with the War Department that led to his receiving a command in the army at the outbreak of the Civil War and his eyewitness account of the struggle for control of the St. Louis Arsenal, often referred to as the Camp Jackson Affair.

FROM *MEMOIRS OF GEN. W. T. SHERMAN*

Mrs. Sherman and I gathered our family and effects together, started for St. Louis March 27th, where we rented of Mr. Lucas the house on Locust Street, between Tenth and Eleventh, and occupied it on the 1st of April. Charles Ewing and John Hunter had formed a law-partnership in St. Louis, and agreed to board with us, taking rooms on the third floor. In the latter part of March, I was duly elected president of the Fifth Street Railroad, and entered on the discharge of my duties April 1, 1861. We had a central office on the corner of Fifth and Locust, and also another up at the stables in Bremen. The road was well stocked and in full operation, and all I had to do was to watch the economical administration of existing affairs, which I endeavored to do with fidelity and zeal. But the whole air was full of wars and rumors of wars. The struggle was going on politically for the border States. Even in Missouri, which was a slave State, it was manifest that the Governor of the State, Claiborne Jackson, and all the leading politicians, were for the South in case of a war. The house on the northwest corner of Fifth and Pine was the rebel headquarters, where the rebel flag was hung publicly, and the crowds about the Planters' House were all more or less rebel. There was also a camp in Lindell's Grove, at the end of Olive Street, under command of General D. M. Frost, a Northern man, a graduate of West Point, in open sympathy with the Southern leaders. This camp was nominally a State camp of instruction, but, beyond doubt, was in the interest of the Southern cause, designed to be used against the national authority in the event of the General Government's attempting to coerce the Southern Confederacy. General William S. Harney was in command of the Department of Missouri, and resided in his own house, on Fourth Street, below Market; and there were five or six companies of United States troops in the arsenal, commanded by Captain N. Lyon; throughout the city, there had been organized, almost exclusively out of the German part of the population, four or five regiments of "Home Guards," with which movement Frank Blair, B. Gratz Brown, John M. Schofield, Clinton B. Fisk, and others, were most active on the part of the national authorities. Frank Blair's brother Montgomery was in the cabinet of Mr. Lincoln at Washington, and to him seemed committed the general management of affairs in Missouri.

The newspapers fanned the public excitement to the highest pitch, and threats of attacking the arsenal on the one hand, and the mob of d——d rebels in Camp Jackson on the other, were bandied about. I tried my best to keep out of the current, and only talked freely with a few men; among them Colonel John O'Fallon, a wealthy gentleman who resided above St. Louis. He daily came down to my office in Bremen, and we walked up and down the pavement by the hour, deploring the sad condition of our country, and the seeming drift toward dissolution and anarchy. I used also to go down to the arsenal occasionally to see Lyon, Totten, and other of my army acquaintance, and was glad to see them making preparations to defend their post, if not to assume the offensive.

The bombardment of Fort Sumter, which was announced by telegraph, began April 12th, and ended on the 14th. We then knew that the war was actually begun, and though the South was openly, manifestly the aggressor, yet her friends and apologists insisted that she was simply acting on a justifiable defensive, and that in the forcible seizure of the public forts within her limits the people were acting with reasonable prudence and foresight. Yet neither party seemed willing to invade, or cross the border. Davis, who ordered the bombardment of Sumter, knew the temper of his people well, and foresaw that it would precipitate the action of the border States; for almost immediately Virginia, North Carolina, Arkansas, and Tennessee, followed the lead of the cotton States, and conventions were deliberating in Kentucky and Missouri.

On the night of Saturday, April 6th, I received the following dispatch:

WASHINGTON, APRIL 6, 1861

Major W. T. SHERMAN:

Will you accept the chief clerkship of the War Department? We will make you assistant Secretary of War when Congress meets.

M. BLAIR, *Postmaster-General*

To which I replied by telegraph, Monday morning, "I cannot accept;" and by mail as follows:

OFFICE ST. LOUIS RAILROAD COMPANY,
MONDAY, APRIL 8, 1861

Hon. M. BLAIR, *Washington, D.C:*

I received, about nine o'clock Saturday night, your telegraph dispatch, which I have this moment answered, "I cannot accept."

> I have quite a large family, and when I resigned my place in Louisiana, on account of secession, I had no time to lose; and, therefore, after my hasty visit to Washington, where I saw no chance of employment, I came to St. Louis, have accepted a place in this company, have rented a house, and incurred other obligations, so that I am not at liberty to change.
>
> I thank you for the compliment contained in your offer, and assure you that I wish the Administration all success in its almost impossible task of governing this distracted and anarchical people.
>
> Yours truly, W. T. SHERMAN

I was afterward told that this letter gave offense, and that some of Mr. Lincoln's cabinet concluded that I too would prove false to the country.

Later in that month, after the capture of Fort Sumter by the Confederate authorities, a Dr. Cornyn came to our house on Locust Street, one night after I had gone to bed, and told me he had been sent by Frank Blair, who was not well, and wanted to see me that night at his house. I dressed and walked over to his house on Washington Avenue, near Fourteenth, and found there, in the front-room, several gentlemen, among whom I recall Henry T. Blow. Blair was in the back-room, closeted with some gentleman, who soon left, and I was called in. He there told me that the Government was mistrustful of General Harney, that a change in the command of the department was to be made; that he held it in his power to appoint a brigadier-general, and put him in command of the department, and he offered me the place. I told him I had once offered my services, and they were declined; that I had made business engagements in St. Louis, which I could not throw off at pleasure; that I had long, deliberated on my course of action, and must decline his offer, however tempting and complimentary. He reasoned with me, but I persisted. He told me, in that event, he should appoint Lyon, and he did so.

Finding that even my best friends were uneasy as to my political status, on the 8th of May I addressed the following official letter to the Secretary of War:

OFFICE OF ST. LOUIS RAILROAD COMPANY,
MAY 8, 1861

Hon. S. CAMERON, *Secretary of War, Washington, D.C.*

Dear Sir: I hold myself now, as always, prepared to serve my country in the capacity for which I was trained. I did not and will not volunteer for *three months*, because I cannot throw my family on the cold charity of the world. But for the *three-years* call, made by the President, an officer can prepare his command and do good service.

I will not volunteer as a soldier, because rightfully or wrongfully I feel unwilling to take a mere private's place, and, having for many years lived in California and Louisiana, the men are not well enough acquainted with me to elect me to my appropriate place.

Should my services be needed, the records of the War Department will enable you to designate the station in which I can render most service.

Yours truly, W. T. SHERMAN

To this I do not think I received a direct answer; but, on the 14th of the same month, I was appointed colonel of the Thirteenth Regular Infantry.

I remember going to the arsenal on the 9th of May, taking my children with me in the street-cars. Within the arsenal wall were drawn up in parallel lines four regiments of the "Home Guards," and I saw men distributing cartridges to the boxes. I also saw General Lyon running about with his hair in the wind, his pockets full of papers, wild and irregular, but I knew him to be a man of vehement purpose and of determined action. I saw of course that it meant business, but whether for defense or offense I did not know. The next morning I went up to the railroad-office in Bremen, as usual, and heard at every corner of the streets that the "Dutch" were moving on Camp Jackson. People were barricading their houses, and men were running in that direction. I hurried through my business as quickly as I could, and got back to my house on Locust Street by twelve o'clock. Charles Ewing and Hunter were there, and insisted on going out to the camp to see "the fun." I tried to dissuade them, saying that in case of conflict the by-standers were more likely to be killed than the men engaged, but they would go. I felt as much interest as anybody else, but staid at home, took my little son Willie, who was about seven years old, and walked up and down the pavement in front of our house, listening for the sound of musketry or cannon in the direction of Camp Jackson. While so engaged Miss Eliza Dean, who lived opposite us, called me across the street, told me that her brother-in-law, Dr. Scott, was a surgeon in Frost's camp, and she was dreadfully afraid he would be killed. I reasoned with her that General Lyon was a regular officer; that if he had gone out, as reported, to Camp Jackson, he would take with him such a force as would make resistance impossible; but she would not be comforted, saying that the camp was made up of the young men from the first and best families of St. Louis, and that they were proud, and would fight. I explained that young men of the best families did not like to be killed better than ordinary people. Edging gradually up the street, I was in Olive Street just about Twelfth, when I saw a man running from the direction of Camp Jackson at full speed, calling, as he went, "They've surrendered, they've surrendered!" So I turned back and rang the bell at Mrs. Dean's. Eliza came to the door, and I explained what I had heard; but she angrily slammed the door in my face! Evidently she was disappointed to find she was mistaken in her estimate of the rash courage of the best families.

I again turned in the direction of Camp Jackson, my boy Willie with me still. At the head of Olive Street, abreast of Lindell's Grove, I found Frank Blair's regiment in the street, with ranks opened, and the Camp Jackson prisoners inside. A crowd of people was gathered around, calling to the prisoners by name, some hurrahing for Jeff Davis, and others encouraging the troops. Men, women, and children, were in the crowd. I passed along till I found myself inside the grove, where I met Charles Ewing and John Hunter, and we stood looking at the troops on the road, heading toward the city. A band of music was playing at the head, and the column made one or two ineffectual starts, but for some reason was halted. The battalion of regulars was abreast of me, of which Major Rufus Saxton was in command, and I gave him an evening paper, which I had bought of the newsboy on my way out. He was reading from it some piece of news, sitting on his horse, when the column again began to move forward, and he resumed his place at the head of his command. At that part of the road, or street, was an embankment about eight feet high, and a drunken fellow tried to pass over it to the people opposite. One of the regular sergeant file-closers ordered him back, but he attempted to pass through the ranks, when the sergeant barred his progress with his musket "a-port." The drunken man seized his musket, when the sergeant threw him off with violence, and he rolled over and over down the bank. By the time this man had picked himself up and got his hat, which had fallen off and had again mounted the embankment, the regulars had passed, and the head of Osterhaus's regiment of Home Guards had come up. The man had in his hand a small pistol, which he fired off, and I heard that the ball had struck the leg of one of Osterhaus's staff; the regiment stopped; there was a moment of confusion, when the soldiers of that regiment began to fire over our heads in the grove. I heard the balls cutting the leaves above our heads, and saw several men and women running in all directions, some of whom were wounded. Of course there was a general stampede. Charles Ewing threw Willie on the ground and covered him with his body. Hunter ran behind the hill, and I also threw myself on the ground. The fire ran back from the head of the regiment toward its rear, and as I saw the men reloading their pieces, I jerked Willie up, ran back with him into a gulley which covered us, lay there until I saw that the fire had ceased, and that the column was again moving on, when I took up Willie and started back for home round by way of Market Street. A woman and child were killed outright; two or three men were also killed, and several others were wounded. The great mass of the people on that occasion were simply curious spectators, though men were sprinkled through the crowd calling out, "Hurrah for Jeff Davis!" and others were particularly abusive of the "damned Dutch." Lyon posted a guard in charge of the vacant camp, and marched his prisoners down to the arsenal; some were paroled, and others held, till afterward they were regularly exchanged.

A very few days after this event, May 14th, I received a dispatch from my brother Charles in Washington, telling me to come on at once; that I had been appointed a colonel of the Thirteenth Regular Infantry, and that I was wanted at Washington immediately.

Of course I could no longer defer action. I saw Mr. Lucas, Major Turner, and other friends and parties connected with the road, who agreed that I should go on. I left my family, because I was under the impression that I would be allowed to enlist my own regiment, which would take some time, and I expected to raise the regiment and organize it at Jefferson Barracks. I repaired to Washington, and there found that the Government was trying to rise to a level with the occasion. Mr. Lincoln had, without the sanction of law, authorized the raising of ten new regiments of regulars, each infantry regiment to be composed of three battalions of eight companies each; and had called for seventy-five thousand State volunteers. Even this call seemed to me utterly inadequate; still it was none of my business. I took the oath of office, and was furnished with a list of officers, appointed to my regiment, which was still incomplete. I reported in person to General Scott, at his office on Seventeenth Street, opposite the War Department, and applied for authority to return West, and raise my regiment at Jefferson Barracks, but the general said my lieutenant-colonel, Burbank, was fully qualified to superintend the enlistment, and that he wanted me there; and he at once dictated an order for me to report to him in person for inspection duty.

Satisfied that I would not be permitted to return to St. Louis, I instructed Mrs. Sherman to pack up, return to Lancaster, and trust to the fate of war.

I also resigned my place as president of the Fifth Street Railroad, to take effect at the end of May, so that in fact I received pay from that road for only two months' service, and then began my new army career.

JESSIE BENTON FREMONT

JESSIE ANN BENTON (1824-1902), daughter of Senator Thomas Hart Benton, spent her childhood divided between Washington, D.C., and St. Louis. Very much her father's daughter, Jessie served as his secretary and eventually became recognized as nearly as formidable, both in opinion and eloquence, as the man called "Old Bullion."

At age seventeen, Jessie eloped with John C. Fremont, an army officer her parents thought beneath her station, and began to apply her literary talents on his behalf. Jessie acquired respect as a writer and editor by transforming Fremont's expedition notes into a book published by the U.S. Senate. Gradually, she became an influential adviser—a peculiar role for a nineteenth-century woman—and a political asset for Fremont, who became the Republican Party's first presidential candidate in 1856.

Although the Fremonts were in Europe when the Civil War erupted, they were in St. Louis during much of the conflict, with John having assumed command of the Department of the West. "General Jessie," as she became known, took an active role in strategic discussions at her husband's headquarters and worked to improve sanitary conditions for wounded soldiers. However, John committed a political blunder that ultimately cost him his post and political future. Without the approval of President Lincoln, John issued a declaration of emancipation for Missouri slaves. Jessie used her influence to attempt to sway President Lincoln on her husband's behalf, but her efforts proved fruitless.

Jessie became the stabilizing force in her family, weathering the ups and downs of her husband's erratic business ventures after the war. When John declared bankruptcy in 1873, Jessie's writing became the family's sole means of support. She was a prolific writer, producing articles about her life, experiences, and acquaintances. These pieces subsequently were collected in a series of volumes, including *Souvenirs of My Time* (1887), from which the following account of her early married life in St. Louis is taken.

FROM *SOUVENIRS OF MY TIME*

Coming back to Saint Louis always in spring-time, even after the mild winters of Washington the contrast was charming. The Potomac was a wide and beautifully blue river, but it did nothing, and was nothing more than a feature in the landscape, while here the tawny swift Mississippi was stirring with busy life, and the little city itself, was animated from its thronged river-bank out through to the Indian camps on the rolling prairie back of the town.

And it was such an embowered fragrant place in that season; the thickets of wild plum and the wild crab-apples which covered the prairie embalmed the air, and everywhere was the honeyscent of the locust. What the elm is to some New England towns the locust was to Saint Louis; the narrow streets were bordered by them and they were repeated everywhere. My father had an affection for this tree and had planted a great many about his house when he first settled there—long before he was married. In my young day these were fine large trees. A line of them made a delicate green screen to the wide galleries which ran the length of the house, on both stories, and their long clusters of vanilla-scented blooms made part of our home-memories. Years after, in California, this delicate intangible link made a curious adventure for me with a person no one ever connected before with any good or gentle idea. It is a severe pull on my natural tendency to digress not to tell it now, but I will "in its place," for it shows how loyally my father was remembered by old Missourians.

Not only did the blossoming town seem *en fête*, but everybody seemed light and gay, and my father, freed from the official and exacting life of Washington, reverted to his cheerful out-door life. The long gallery of the parlor-floor was his place when at home, even if light rains were falling. He never breathed in-door air when he could be, head uncovered, in a bath of sunshine. His "settee" and a table, and "a colony of chairs" for others, made his favorite settlement, where the early light breakfast of coffee and bread and fruit was taken—by any number who might chance to come. I *never* heard the word "*trouble*" applied to household arrangements. For all we knew, everything grew ready to be served.

The day begins early in warm climates, and from early morning on, there was a coming and going of varied but all welcome friends. There came governing citizens to talk of political affairs. Much had to be only personal information in those days before railways and telegraphs, and when the plans of an administration were only talked over confidentially with its friends. The father of Mrs. Grant was one of my father's old friends and political allies of that time. General Grant honored himself by the honor and thoughtful attention he always gave to this venerable man who was a conspicuous figure in the Presidential receptions. After I had made my respects to the President and Mrs. Grant, one or the other would be sure to say, "Now step back here and talk to Mr. Dent"—who always kept me sitting by him on his sofa, talking of my father and telling of the great contests they had gone through together; and when his memory failed calling me only "Mrs. Benton," but always lighting up with pleased remembrances.

There, too, came officers of the army. My father was their comprehending friend. Himself an old officer, and for twenty years Chairman of the Senate Military Committee, he was their sure and intelligent friend. With both knowledge and good will, such a position can be made of the utmost advantage to the service, as well as of personal advantage to officers. The certainty of sympathy and proper official aid never failed those who came to him. He was practically the Secretary of War in all those years, for he was a fixture while a Secretary is only a political accident, and in the War and Navy Departments usually quite ignorant of the personal as well as of the special requirements of service. Through such ignorance much injustice can be done, but in all my long knowledge of Washington, I have known of but one Secretary who found actual pleasure in giving pain to officers and in thwarting all personal feelings, even family feelings.

The French neighbors enjoyed coming for their chat, and invariably brought some fine fruit or flower for Madame, who fully appreciated both the kindly feeling and the fine skilful cultivation.

There too came many priests who were soldiers in their missionary work, and had as stirring adventures to relate as the trappers and hunters who knew they were always welcome to my father.

And often, gliding past into my mother's rooms, would come the good Sister Elizabeth on active duty for her hospital—going away with a basket of useful things and many a solid piece of money from those on the gallery, with a "*permettez ma sœur*" and a warm "*Bon jour, ma sœur*" from every one.

Two friends of my father's were specially interesting to me. One a Spanish officer *and gentleman*, in the fullest meaning, who had served under Wellington in Spain; the other who was already a captain in the French army when Waterloo broke it up. Col. Garnier was much the elder. He had accepted his exile and its resulting poverty and sufferings with silent dignity. My father had a good knowledge of Spanish, but he always tried to add improvement to all his knowledge, and Col. Garnier and himself had a Spanish talking-lesson daily. He taught us our Spanish also. My father thought we ought to know the language of our near neighbor, Mexico, with whom closer relations must come. I was a great favorite with Col. Garnier. Some fancied resemblance to a little sister, won for me his kindest voice and the name of "Rosita." Usually he took the early coffee with my father, and if Judge Lawless (once Capt. Lawless) joined them as he often did, then their talk was sure to fall on the Peninsular war. A sign would send me in for the maps and the box of pins—beeswax heads for the Spanish troops, red wax for the English, and for the French, black.

Never was that discussion ended. Not only day after day, but summer after summer, did those three move those pins that put the troops in differing positions, and proved "what might have been;" but never did either of the three convince the other. For hours they would be at it; generally the heat of discussion would be stopped by my mother's sending out an iced watermelon or a great basket of fruit which was a signal they understood. Her feeling was English—without discussion. My father's mother used to say to us, "Your mother is English; and she has the English genius for home comfort."

This grandmother was one of our returning pleasures in going back to Saint Louis where she had lived chiefly after my father's going there. She was more English than my mother in nearness to the mother-country, but she had a singularly large unprejudiced view of things, and had outlived every personal interest except in my father and a few of her grandchildren. Both her father and husband were English—both scholarly men and misfits in a new country. My Grandfather Benton's library in Greek, Latin, French, Spanish and English had been his joy while he lived and made the atmosphere in which my father grew up—guided by his mother and his father's close friend, a clergy-man, like himself an Oxford man, who put my father at his Greek Testament when he was but eight; at which age my grandfather's death left him the eldest son in a family of seven children.

My father has told me of the awe and singular feeling of loss of youth that fell on him when, after his father's death and a long illness which came on his mother, he was taken in to see her.

She was about thirty; a very tall slender woman with blue eyes that never lost their steady clearness. And, as all the Hart family, she had splendid long, thick, waving, auburn-brown hair. In her six weeks' illness this had changed to a silvery white—which, with her white and thinned face, so alarmed my father that he ran into a grove near by when he came out, and "had to war with himself to accept that shadow as his mother." Nearly all her children died young; of rapid consumption, as their father had died; and the silent grief with which my grandmother bore her eighty-three years of life invested her with a dignity none intruded on. She had her wing in my father's house, and her own old servants who knew her ways. A fall on the ice and a badly-set leg crippled her and caused keen suffering from rheumatisms for the last years of her life, but her powerful clear inquiring mind made books a great solace.

Our Virginia grandmother, with her unbroken domestic life, her active health and child's heart for simple pleasures, was just the opposite to my Grandmother Denton, who could not tolerate our sewing. "It is not good for your chest," she would say; and "you should never waste your time, doing what an uneducated person can do better for you."

One of her few pleasures was to have her hair brushed. This remained thick and long; so long that the thick plait reached nearly to the knee. When coiled around her head it filled the crown of the "mob-cap," as the widow's cap of that day was called, leaving only space for the band of black crape back of the narrow crimped ruffles. It was a pleasure to her and a privilege to me to let down and brush and smooth out this beautiful hair, and to hear her talk. Her extensive reading made all countries familiar to her. She made on me, even as a young child, the effect of being above other people. And though she died when I was but thirteen I have kept the realization of a lofty and great soul. I know that my father and his nearest friends very often referred questions to her and deferred to her calm wisdom and unprejudiced perceptions.

In Washington all our lessons were had at home but my father did the important part of appointing studies and preparing us for our teachers, making broad and lucid what they might have left as "parrot-ing," as he expressed it. Here in Saint Louis we were let to go to school; chiefly for the practice in French among other children.

It makes me smile to look back at that word "school" which had not the first idea of studies, of punctuality, or discipline attached to it as I knew it. The going there each morning was as good as playing truant. *Never* could it happen that children of any position left the house alone, or even together.

We were big girls of eight and ten and every one knew us, and the distance was only a short mile between houses and grounds of friends; but to go without a maid was never dreamed of. We should have greatly preferred our French nurse, Madeleine, but she was not sufficiently important for such duty. Our mother's maid, "aunt" Sara, was. She had been trained from her youth up for her post—as was the Southern custom—and understood "manners." Erect, silent, holding a hand of each, she drilled us in manners as we went along. When we passed the small house of M'âme Desirée where she in *very* negligée loose gown patted her muslins on the sunny gallery, we had to stop if she spoke to us.

M'âme Desirée was the clear-starcher and fine muslin genius of Saint Louis; too fat now, but still a most handsome quadroon who had a gay word for every passer-by. M'âme Saraah was a crony of hers, and when she would give us the good day and praise our neatness and good condition (as all due to M'âme Saraah!) we had to wait and listen politely: "You can't hurry her, because she is a poor working woman and it would hurt her feelings"—aunt Sara had never heard the words, but her conviction was that "Time was made for slaves," and not for little young ladies.

Then the garden doors of many pleasant enclosures would be open and, the various Madame Augustes or Madame Caddys would be out in the fresh of the morning and the ladies themselves—also in most easy negligée—going about their grounds. If they saw us we would be called in and *cette bonne Sara* asked after Madame and praised for her *petites*. And with deliberation (time no object), some pretty fruit would be chosen for us and we would recommence our walk to stop again and again; for, "Madame Auguste is a lady and you can't hurry her"—in fact, there was no hurry anywhere.

When we did reach the school we were consigned to Madame Savary who did not teach, but who looked after us; a small vivacious Swiss-Frenchwoman with a mania for making preserves and doing fine sewing. Monsieur Savary was capable of far more than was required of him. I think he had put away his pride and resigned himself to what he could, not what he would, do. He was a spare tall man with flat black hair and gold spectacles and always wore a short-waisted very long and full-skirted frock coat of gray, with collar and cuffs of black velvet, a sort of uniform for teachers which you often see in old-fashioned French illustrations. He was quiet, gentle and forbearing and had need to be so as there were about thirty girls, from six to sixteen—of course not a fraction of a boy in a French school—

and not one with any intentions of study or habit of discipline; good-natured enough, but trying. They may have learned something. We were there only for easy handling of familiar French; and except some spelling, and reading aloud in Telemachus, I do not recall anything of lessons. But I won honors in whipping ruffles and hemming handkerchiefs for Madame Savary, and what was really important was when we, the younger ones, were permitted to help her make preserves. If a quantity of strawberries or currants were sent to her all hands turned in to prepare them. For the object my father had in view, it was more useful than reading, from a book and vastly better for health than sitting still on a bench; for we adjourned, we young ones I mean, to the inevitable gallery, or the garden which was on the bluff overlooking the river. By one o'clock aunt Sara had come for us to go home and as this was our dinner hour we made no delays.

In French schools Thursday is the holiday. Saturday and Sunday, they think, make too much holiday together. But to us Americans the Sunday was not a holiday in their sense, where after mass all their children were taken around among their elder relations and it was a family fête-day.

We did not go on Saturdays to school. That day our mother had us get our Sunday-school lessons with her—telling us many interesting things and making them, as all our home lessons were, a real pleasure and improvement. Our Sunday dresses were decided on and each thing reviewed and put in order that no delay might come. All our dolls and toys and weekday story-books were put away until Monday; and then we had as wild a play as big grounds and good health and early youth could give. In this our French nurse Madeleine was a great factor; she was so gay and knew such beautiful songs and danced such queer dances in her pretty carved sabots that we doted on her.

Her family had come away from France, from near Bordeaux, because of the cholera. French people do not like to leave their country, the women especially, and these were well-to-do farming people. But the horror of cholera was on them and they came to New Orleans. There they found the climate would not let them work in the fields and they would have to buy slaves. So they came on up the river to the free State of Illinois, and bought a fine farm just across from Saint Louis. There, as the old man said, his own large family, girls and boys—could all work and his and their delight in the rich earth and easy ploughing was great. He had great pride in his vegetables and melons, and my father was capable of doing away with indefinite melons—both the great red watermelons and the delicate little cantelopes which the French cultivate so well. Whenever La Mère had a specially fine melon she brought it to my father; and always we heard over again, and sorrowed with her afresh for the parting from their farm in France. One sister was in service with us, and another, Annette, was nurse in the family of my father's niece. These young ones were satisfied with the change; more than satisfied when they exchanged field and farm labor for the ease of life as nurses and the pleasure of wearing their Sunday clothes every day.

Sometimes, in a summer's day you feel, before you see why, a chill in the air. Something has changed; and though the day looks the same its sweetness is gone. So, in the summer I was about eight, this bright careless Saint Louis life seemed to chill over. At first we were only told we were not to go to school. Then, we were to play only with each other in our own grounds and no more little friends visited us or we them. The friends who came to my father on the long gallery were as many as ever, but they and he himself no longer had any pleasant leisure, but were quick and busy in coming and going, and all looked grave. The tears were all the time on Madeleine's face and constantly she was on her knees telling her beads and praying and sobbing. We saw many, many funerals passing. Our house was on a sloping hill, and we saw to all sides of the square. Then, soon, drays with several coffins piled on jolted fast along the rough street, or a wagon-load of empty coffins would cross another street. Madeleine would run in from the gallery hiding her eyes; "Ah, *Mon Dieu*, it is all funerals on every side—*C'est le cholera*."

It was the cholera; among a people excitable and ignorant of its treatment, who gave up to it as a fatality if they could not fly from it.

In this condition of universal alarm, when nearly all who could, fled from the town, even clergymen deserting their churches, my father thought it right for him to stay and give the encouragement and example of his presence. With his courage and sense of duty this was easy, but it must have been hard to him to risk my mother and all of us children. The Catholic clergy were true to their post; and among the Protestant clergymen who remained was a young man who became loved and honored there, the Rev. Mr. Potts. He became very intimate with my parents during this cholera time, and later, married a niece of my father's.

I was too young to know details, but I know how the Peninsular war was laid aside for good work from both officers among the sufferers. All were busy, and all needed, for a panic had set in and nothing is so cruel as fear.

Our poor gentle Mr. Savary died—alone. Gay M'âme Desirée nursed others like a hero but was herself a victim. Our Madeleine became almost entirely blind—nervous paralysis of the eyelid from the terrified shrinking eye from constant passing coffins. Otherwise the disease did not touch one of our family and spared our nearest friends. Our house was a "diet-kitchen;" good soups, preparations of rice, and well-filtered and purified water, it became the occupation of the house to keep ready.

All the water was brought in large barrels from the river and poured bucket by bucket, into great jars of red earthenware, some of them five feet high. These jars had their own large cool room paved with glazed red brick and level with the street. The jars of drinking water and for cooking were clarified of the mud of the river by alum and blanched almonds, and then filtered. So much was needed now that even we children were useful in this sort of work. In that cool dark room the melons used to be kept, but there were no melons or fruit now—we ate only rice and mutton and such simple things.

The sad summer ended as all things must end, bad or good. *Tout passe.* When all seemed safe, suddenly my mother was taken down with cholera, and the nurse who had become blinded by one shock recovered her sight from this other. It was a bad illness, but with that one brush of the dark angel's wing our home stood as before.

ANTHONY TROLLOPE

ANTHONY TROLLOPE (1815–1882) enjoyed a successful career as a civil servant in the British post office in London—introducing the pillar-mounted mailbox—while simultaneously launching his literary career. A voluminous writer with forty-seven novels, several travel books, and multiple collections of short stories and sketches, Trollope attributed his tremendous output to strict self-discipline, forged by writing while holding down a demanding job. In 1867, Trollope retired from the post office with sufficient means to devote the rest of his life to writing.

Trollope was simply following a family tradition when in the fall of 1861 and spring of 1862 he toured the United States and then returned to England to write about the "cousins." His mother, Frances, had published the best-selling *Domestic Manners of the Americans* in 1832. Mrs. Trollope's book so offended Americans that her name came to stand for all that was smug and supercilious in European visitors to the United States. A decade later, Charles Dickens received similar criticism for his *American Notes*. Anthony Trollope suggested in his autobiography that he found his mother's portrayal "somewhat unjust" and that he had long intended "to follow her footsteps there, to write another book."

The outbreak of the Civil War certainly complicated the younger Trollope's travels, and his pro-Northern stance aggravated many in England, where Southern sympathy was strong. In his study of North America, the author, although often critical and always slightly ill at ease, favorably reviewed his host nation.

In the following excerpt from the "Missouri" chapter of *North America,* Trollope describes St. Louis under martial law and his horrifying visit to the hospital at Benton Barracks. Trollope also relates his visit to nearby Rolla and offers an analysis of the differences in American regional character.

FROM *NORTH AMERICA*

MISSOURI

Missouri is a slave State lying to the west of the Mississippi and to the north of Arkansas. It forms a portion of the territory ceded by France to the United States in 1803. Indeed, it is difficult to say how large a portion of the continent of North America is supposed to be included in that territory. It contains the States of Louisiana, Arkansas, Missouri, and Kansas, as also the present Indian territory; but it also is said to have contained all the land lying back from them to the Rocky Mountains, Utah, Nebraska, and Dacotah, and forms no doubt the widest dominion ever ceded by one nationality to another.

Missouri lies exactly north of the old Missouri compromise line, that is, 36-30 north. When the Missouri compromise was made it was arranged that Missouri should be a slave State, but that no other State north of the 36-30 line should ever become slave soil. Kentucky and Virginia, as also of course Maryland and Delaware, four of the old slave States, were already north of that line; but the compromise was intended to prevent the advance of slavery in the north-west. The compromise has been since annulled, on the ground, I believe, that Congress had not constitutionally the power to declare that any soil should be free, or that any should be slave soil. That is a question to be decided by the States themselves, as each individual State may please. So the compromise was repealed. But slavery has not on that account advanced. The battle has been fought in Kansas, and after a long and terrible struggle, Kansas has come out of the fight as a free State. Kansas is in the same parallel of latitude as Virginia, and stretches west as far as the Rocky Mountains.

When the census of the population of Missouri was taken in 1860, the slaves amounted to 10 per cent of the whole number. In the Gulf States the slave population is about 45 per cent of the whole. In the three border States of Kentucky, Virginia, and Maryland, the slaves amount to 30 per cent of the whole population. From these figures it will be seen that Missouri, which is comparatively a new slave State, has not gone a head with slavery as the old slave States have done, although from its position and climate, lying as far south as Virginia, it might seem to have had the same reasons for doing so. I think there is every reason to believe that slavery will die out in Missouri. The institution is not popular with the people generally; and as white labour becomes abundant,—and before the war it was becoming abundant,—men recognize the fact that the white man's labour is the more profitable. The heat in this State, in midsummer, is very great, especially in the valleys of the rivers. At St. Louis, on the Mississippi, it reaches commonly to 90, and very frequently goes above that. The nights moreover are nearly as hot as the days; but this great heat does not last for any very long period, and it seems that white men are able to work throughout the year. If correspondingly severe weather in winter affords any compensation to the white man for what of heat he endures during the summer, I can testify that such compensation is to be found in Missouri. When I was there we were afflicted with a combination of snow, sleet, frost, and wind, with a mixture of ice and mud, that makes me regard Missouri as the most inclement land into which I ever penetrated.

St. Louis, on the Mississippi, is the great town of Missouri, and is considered by the Missourians to be the star of the West. It is not to be beaten in population, wealth, or natural advantages by any other city so far west; but it has not increased with such rapidity as Chicago, which is considerably to the north of it on Lake Michigan. Of the great western cities I regard Chicago as the most remarkable, seeing that St. Louis was a large town before Chicago had been founded.

The population of St. Louis is 170,000. Of this number only 2000 are slaves. I was told that a large proportion of the slaves of Missouri are employed near the Missouri river in breaking hemp. The growth of hemp is very profitably carried on in that valley, and the labour attached to it is one which white men do not like to encounter. Slaves are not generally employed in St. Louis for domestic service, as is done almost universally in the towns of Kentucky. This work is chiefly in the hands of Irish and Germans. Considerably above one-third of the population of the whole city is made up of these two nationalities. So much is confessed; but if I were to form an opinion from the language I heard in the streets of the town, I should say that nearly every man was either an Irishman or a German.

St. Louis has none of the aspects of a slave city. I cannot say that I found it an attractive place, but then I did not visit it at an attractive time. The war had disturbed everything, given a special colour of its own to men's thoughts and words, and destroyed all interest except that which might proceed from itself. The town is well built, with good shops, straight streets, never-ending rows of excellent houses, and every sign of commercial wealth and domestic comfort,—of commercial wealth and domestic comfort in the past, for there was no present appearance either of comfort or of wealth. The new hotel here was to be bigger than all the hotels of all other towns. It is built, and is an enormous pile, and would be handsome but for a terribly ambitious Grecian doorway. It is built, as far as the walls and roof are concerned, but in all other respects is unfinished. I was told that the shares of the original stockholders were now worth nothing. A shareholder, who so told me, seemed to regard this as the ordinary course of business.

The great glory of the town is the "levée," as it is called, or the long river beach up to which the steamers are brought with their bows to the shore. It is an esplanade looking on to the river, not built with quays or wharves, as would be the case with us, but with a sloping bank running down to the water. In the good days of peace a hundred vessels were to be seen here, each with its double funnels. The line of them seemed to be never ending even when I was there, but then a very large proportion of them were lying idle. They resemble huge wooden houses, apparently of frail architecture, floating upon the water. Each has its double row of balconies running round it, and the lower or ground floor is open throughout. The upper stories are propped and supported on ugly sticks and ricketty-looking beams; so that the first appearance does not convey any great idea of security to a stranger. They are always painted white and the paint is always very dirty. When they begin to move, they moan and groan in melancholy tones which are subversive of all comfort; and as they continue on their courses they puff and bluster, and are for ever threatening to burst and shatter themselves to pieces. There they lie in a continuous line nearly a mile in length along the levee of St. Louis, dirty, dingy, and now, alas, mute. They have ceased to groan and puff, and if this war be continued for six months longer, will become rotten and useless as they lie.

They boast at St. Louis that they command 46,000 miles of navigable river water, counting the great rivers up and down from that place. These rivers are chiefly the Mississippi, the Missouri and Ohio which fall into the Mississippi near St. Louis, the Platte and Kansas rivers—tributaries of the Missouri, the Illinois, and the Wisconsin. All these are open to steamers, and all of them traverse regions rich in corn, in coal, in metals, or in timber. These ready-made highways of the world centre, as it were, at St. Louis, and make it the depot of the carrying trade of all that vast country. Minnesota is 1500 miles above New Orleans, but the wheat of Minnesota can be brought down the whole distance without change of the vessel in which it is first deposited. It would seem to be impossible that a country so blessed should not become rich. It must be remembered that these rivers flow through lands that have never yet been surpassed in natural fertility. Of all countries in the world one would say that the States of America should have been the last to curse themselves with a war; but now the curse has fallen upon them with a double vengeance. It would seem that they could never be great in war: their very institutions forbid it; their enormous distances forbid it; the price of labour forbids it; and it is forbidden also by the career of industry and expansion which has been given to them. But the curse of fighting has come upon them, and they are showing themselves to be as eager in the works of war as they have shown themselves capable in the works of peace. Men and angels must weep as they behold the things that are being done, as they watch the ruin that has come and is still coming, as they look on commerce killed and agriculture suspended. No sight so sad has come upon the earth in our days. They were a great people; feeding the world, adding daily to the mechanical appliances of mankind, increasing in population beyond all measures of such increase hitherto known, and extending education as fast as they extended their numbers. Poverty had as yet found no place among them, and hunger was an evil of which they had read, but were themselves ignorant. Each man among their crowds had a right to be proud of his manhood. To read and write,—I am speaking here of the North,—was as common as to eat and drink. To work was no disgrace, and the wages of work were plentiful. To live without work was the lot of none. What blessing above these blessings was needed to make a people great and happy? And now a stranger visiting them would declare that they are wallowing in a very slough of despond. The only trade open is the trade of war. The axe of the woodsman is at rest; the plough is idle; the artificer has closed his shop. The roar of the foundry is still heard because cannon are needed, and the river of molten iron comes out as an implement of death. The stone-cutter's hammer and the mason's trowel are never heard. The gold of the country is hiding itself as though it had returned to its mother-earth, and the infancy of a paper currency has been commenced. Sick soldiers, who have never seen a battlefield, are dying by hundreds in the squalid dirt of their unaccustomed camps. Men and women talk of war, and of war only. Newspapers full of the war are alone read. A contract for war stores,—too often a dishonest contract,—is the one path open for commercial enterprise. The young man must go to the war or he is disgraced. The war swallows everything, and as yet has failed to produce even such bitter fruits as victory or glory. Must it not be said that a curse has fallen upon the land? . . .

St. Louis, and indeed the whole State of Missouri, was at the time of my visit under martial law. General Halleck was in command, holding his head-quarters at St. Louis, and carrying out, at any rate as far as the city was concerned, what orders he chose to issue. I am disposed to think that, situated as Missouri then was, martial law was the best law. No other law could have had force in a town surrounded by soldiers, and in which half of the inhabitants were loyal to the existing government, and half of them were in favour of rebellion. The necessity for such power is terrible, and the power itself in the hands of one man must be full of danger; but even that is better than anarchy. I will not accuse General Halleck of abusing his power, seeing that it is hard to determine what is the abuse of such power and what its proper use. When we were at St. Louis a tax was being gathered of 100*l*. a head from certain men presumed to be secessionists, and as the money was not of course very readily paid, the furniture of these suspected secessionists was being sold by auction. No doubt such a measure was by them regarded as a great abuse. One gentleman informed me that, in addition to this, certain houses of his had been taken by the government at a fixed rent, and that the payment of the rent was now refused unless he would take the oath of allegiance. He no doubt thought that an abuse of power! But the worst abuse of such power comes not at first, but with long usage.

Up to the time however at which I was at St. Louis, martial law had chiefly been used in closing grog-shops and administering the oath of allegiance to suspected secessionists. Something also had been done in the way of raising money by selling the property of convicted secessionists; and while I was there eight men were condemned to be shot for destroying railway bridges. "But will they be shot?" I asked of one of the officers. "Oh, yes. It will be done quietly, and no one will know anything about it. We shall get used to that kind of thing presently." And the inhabitants of Missouri were becoming used to martial law. It is surprising how quickly a people can reconcile themselves to altered circumstances, when the change comes upon them without the necessity of any expressed opinion on their own part. Personal freedom has been considered as necessary to the American of the States as the air he breathes. Had any suggestion been made to him of a suspension of the privilege of habeas corpus, of a censorship of the press, or of martial law, the American would have declared his willingness to die on the floor of the House of Representatives, and have proclaimed with ten million voices his inability to live under circumstances so subversive of his rights as a man. And he would have thoroughly believed the truth of his own assertions. Had a chance been given of an argument on the matter, of stump speeches, and caucus meetings, these things could never have been done. But as it is, Americans are, I think, rather proud of the suspension of the habeas corpus. They point with gratification to the uniformly loyal tone of the newspapers, remarking that any editor who should dare to give even a secession squeak, would immediately find himself shut up. And now nothing but good is spoken of martial law. I thought it a nuisance when I was prevented by soldiers from trotting my horse down Pennsylvania Avenue in Washington, but I was assured by Americans that such restrictions were very serviceable in a community. At St. Louis martial law was quite popular. Why should not General Halleck be as well able to say what was good for the people as any law or any lawyer? He had no interest in the injury of the State, but every interest in its preservation. "But what," I asked, "would be the effect were he to tell you to put out all your fires at eight o'clock?" "If he were so to order, we should do it; but we know that he will not." But who does know to what General Halleck or other generals may come; or how soon a curfew-bell may be ringing in American towns? The winning of liberty is long and tedious, but the losing it is a downhill easy journey.

It was here, in St. Louis, that General Fremont had held his military court. He was a great man here during those hundred days through which his command lasted. He lived in a great house, had a bodyguard, was inaccessible as a great man should be, and fared sumptuously every day. He fortified the city,—or rather, he began to do so. He constructed barracks here, and instituted military prisons. The fortifications have been discontinued as useless, but the barracks and the prisons remain. In the latter there were 1200 secessionist soldiers who had been taken in the State of Missouri. "Why are they not exchanged?" I asked. "Because they are not exactly soldiers," I was informed. "The secessionists do not acknowledge them." "Then would it not be cheaper to let them go?" "No," said my informant;

"because in that case we should have to catch them again." And so the 1200 remain in their wretched prison,—thinned from week to week and from day to day by prison disease and prison death.

I went out twice to Benton barracks, as the camp of wooden huts was called, which General Fremont had erected near the fair-ground of the city. This fair-ground, I was told, had been a pleasant place. It had been constructed for the recreation of the city, and for the purpose of periodical agricultural exhibitions. There is still in it a pretty ornamented cottage, and in the little garden a solitary Cupid stood dismayed by the dirt and ruin around him. In the fair-green are the round buildings intended for show cattle and agricultural implements, but now given up to cavalry horses and Parrott guns. But Benton barracks are outside the fair-green. Here on an open space, some half-mile in length, two long rows of wooden sheds have been built, opposite to each other, and behind them are other sheds used for stabling and cooking-places. Those in front are divided, not into separate huts, but into chambers capable of containing nearly two hundred men each. They were surrounded on the inside by great wooden trays, in three tiers,—and on each tray four men were supposed to sleep. I went into one or two while the crowd of soldiers was in them, but found it inexpedient to stay there long. The stench of those places was foul beyond description. Never in my life before had I been in a place so horrid to the eyes and nose as Benton barracks. The path along the front outside was deep in mud. The whole space between the two rows of sheds was one field of mud, so slippery that the foot could not stand. Inside and outside every spot was deep in mud. The soldiers were mud-stained from foot to sole. These volunteer soldiers are in their nature dirty, as must be all men brought together in numerous bodies without special appliances for cleanliness, or control and discipline as to their personal habits. But the dirt of the men in the Benton barracks surpassed any dirt that I had hitherto seen. Nor could it have been otherwise with them. They were surrounded by a sea of mud, and the foul hovels in which they were made to sleep and live were fetid with stench and reeking with filth. I had at this time been joined by another Englishman, and we went through this place together. When we inquired as to the health of the men, we heard the saddest tales,—of three hundred men gone out of one regiment, of whole companies that had perished, of hospitals crowded with fevered patients. Measles had been the great scourge of the soldiers here,—as it had also been in the army of the Potomac. I shall not soon forget my visits to Benton barracks. It may be that our own soldiers were as badly treated in the Crimea; or that French soldiers were treated worse on their march into Russia. It may be that dirt, and wretchedness, disease and listless idleness, a descent from manhood to habits lower than those of the beasts, are necessary in warfare. I have sometimes thought that it is so; but I am no military critic and will not say. This I say,—that the degradation of men to the state in which I saw the American soldiers in Benton barracks, is disgraceful to humanity.

General Halleck was at this time commanding in Missouri, and was himself stationed at St. Louis; but his active measures against the rebels were going on to the right and to the left. On the left shore of the Mississippi, at Cairo, in Illinois, a fleet of gun-boats was being prepared to go down the river, and on the right an army was advancing against Springfield, in the south-western district of Missouri, with the object of dislodging Price, the rebel guerilla leader there, and, if possible, of catching him. Price had been the opponent of poor General Lyon who was killed at Wilson's Creek, near Springfield, and of General Fremont, who during his hundred days had failed to drive him out of the State. This duty had now been intrusted to General Curtis, who had for some time been holding his head-quarters at Rolla, halfway between St. Louis and Springfield. Fremont had built a fort at Rolla, and it had become a military station. Over 10,000 men had been there at one time, and now General Curtis was to advance from Rolla against Price with something above that number of men. Many of them, however, had already gone on, and others were daily being sent up from St. Louis. Under these circumstances my friend and I, fortified with a letter of introduction to General Curtis, resolved to go and see the army at Rolla.

It was dark when we got into Rolla. Everything had been covered with snow, and everywhere the snow was frozen. We had heard that there was an hotel, and that possibly we might get a bedroom there. We were first taken to a wooden building, which we were told was the head-quarters of the army, and in one room we found a colonel with a lot of soldiers loafing about, and in another a provost-marshal attended by a newspaper correspondent. We were received with open arms, and a suggestion was at once made that we were no doubt picking up news for European newspapers. "Air you a son of the Mrs. Trollope?" said the correspondent. "Then, sir, you are an accession to Rolla." Upon which I was made to sit down, and invited to "loaf about" at the headquarters as long as I might remain at Rolla. Shortly, however, there came on a violent discussion about waggons. A general had come in and wanted all the colonel's waggons, but the colonel swore that he had none, declared how bitterly he was impeded with sick men, and became indignant and reproachful. It was Brutus and Cassius again; and as we felt ourselves in the way, and anxious moreover to ascertain what might be the nature of the Rolla hotel, we took up our heavy portmanteaux—for they were heavy—and with a guide to show us the way, started off through the dark and over the hill up to our inn. I shall never forget that walk. It was up hill and down hill, with an occasional half-frozen stream across it. My friend was impeded with an enormous cloak lined with fur, which in itself was a burden for a coal-heaver. Our guide, who was a clerk out of the colonel's office, carried an umbrella and a small dressing-bag, but we ourselves manfully shouldered our portmanteaux. Sydney Smith declared that an Englishman only wasted his time in training himself for gymnastic aptitudes, seeing that for a shilling he could always hire a porter. Had Sydney Smith ever been at Rolla he would have written differently. I could tell at great length how I fell on my face in the icy snow, how my friend stuck in the frozen mud when he essayed to jump the stream, and how our guide walked on easily in advance, encouraging us with his voice from a distance. Why is it that a stout Englishman bordering on fifty finds himself in such a predicament as that? No Frenchman, no Italian, no German, would so place himself, unless under the stress of insurmountable circumstances. No American would do so under any circumstances. As I slipped about on the ice and groaned with that terrible fardle on my back, burdened with a dozen shirts, and a suit of dress clothes, and three pair of boots, and four or five thick volumes, and a set of maps, and a box of cigars, and a washing-tub, I confessed to myself that I was a fool. What was I doing in such a galley as that? Why had I bought all that useless lumber down to Rolla? Why had I come to Rolla, with no certain hope even of shelter for a night? But we did reach the hotel; we did get a room between us with two bedsteads. And, pondering over the matter in my mind, since that evening, I have been inclined to think that the stout Englishman is in the right of it. No American of my age and weight will ever go through what I went through then; but I am not sure that he does not in his accustomed career go through worse things even than that. However, if I go to Rolla again during the war, I will at any rate leave the books behind me.

What a night we spent in that inn! They who know America will be aware that in all hotels there is a free admixture of different classes. The traveller in Europe may sit down to dinner with his tailor and shoemaker; but if so, his tailor and shoemaker have dressed themselves as he dresses, and are prepared to carry themselves according to a certain standard, which in exterior does not differ from his own, In the large Eastern cities of the States, such as Boston, New York, and Washington, a similar practice of life is gradually becoming prevalent. There are various hotels for various classes, and the ordinary traveller does not find himself at the same table with a butcher fresh from the shambles. But in the West there are no distinctions whatever. "A man's a man for a' that" in the West, let the "a' that" comprise what it may of coarse attire and unsophisticated manners. One soon gets used to it. In that inn at Rolla was a public room, heated in the middle by a stove, and round that we soon found ourself seated in a company of soldiers, farmers, labourers, and teamsters. But there was among them a general;—not a fighting, or would-be fighting general of the present time, but one of the old-fashioned local generals,—men who held, or had once held, some fabulous generalship in the State militia. There we sat, cheek by jowl with our new friends, till nearly twelve o'clock, talking politics and discussing the war. The General was a stanch Unionist, having, according to his own showing, suffered dreadful things from secessionist persecutors since the rebellion commenced. As a matter of course everybody present was for the Union. In such a place one rarely encounters any difference of opinion. The General was very eager about the war, advocating the immediate abolition of slavery, not as a means of improving the condition of the southern slaves, but on the ground that it would ruin the southern masters. We all sat by, edging in a word now and then, but the General was the talker of the evening. He was very wrathy, and swore at every other word. "It was pretty well time," he said, "to crush out this rebellion, and by —— it must and should be crushed out; General Jim Lane was the man to do it, and by —— General Jim Lane would do it!" and so on. In all such conversations the time for action has always just come, and also the expected man. But the time passes by as other weeks and months have passed before it, and the new General is found to be no more successful than his brethren. Our friend was very angry against England. "When we've polished off these accursed rebels, I guess we'll take a turn at you. You had your turn when you made us give up Mason and Slidell, and we'll have our turn by-and-by." But in spite of his dislike to our nation he invited us warmly to come and see him at his home on the

Missouri river. It was, according to his showing, a new Eden,—a Paradise upon earth. He seemed to think that we might perhaps desire to buy a location, and explained to us how readily we could make our fortunes. But he admitted in the course of his eulogiums that it would be as much as his life was worth for him to ride out five miles from his own house. In the meantime the teamsters greased their boots, the soldiers snored, those who were wet took off their shoes and stockings, hanging them to dry round the stove, and the western farmers chewed tobacco in silence and ruminated. At such a house all the guests go in to their meals together. A gong is sounded on a sudden, close behind your ears; accustomed as you may probably be to the sound you jump up from your chair in the agony of the crash, and by the time that you have collected your thoughts the whole crowd is off in a general stampede into the eating room. You may as well join them; if you hesitate as to feeding with so rough a lot of men, you will have to sit down afterwards with the women and children of the family, and your lot will then be worse. Among such classes in the western States the men are always better than the women. The men are dirty and civil, the women are dirty and uncivil.

On the following day we returned to St. Louis, bringing back with us our friend the German aide-de-camp. I stayed two days longer in that city, and then I thought that I had seen enough of Missouri;—enough of Missouri at any rate under the present circumstances of frost and secession. As regards the people of the West, I must say that they were not such as I expected to find them. With the Northerns we are all more or less intimately acquainted. Those Americans whom we meet in our own country, or on the Continent, are generally from the North, or if not so they have that type of American manners which has become familiar to us. They are talkative, intelligent, inclined to be social, though frequently not sympathetically social with ourselves; somewhat *soi-disant*, but almost invariably companionable. As the traveller goes southward into Maryland and Washington, the type is not altered to any great extent. The hard intelligence of the Yankee gives place gradually to the softer, and perhaps more polished manner of the Southern. But the change thus experienced is not so great as is that between the American of the Western and the American of the Atlantic States. In the West I found the men gloomy and silent,—I might almost say sullen. A dozen of them will sit for hours round a stove, speechless. They chew tobacco and ruminate. They are not offended if you speak to them, but they are not pleased. They answer with monosyllables, or, if it be practicable, with a gesture of the head. They care nothing for the graces,—or shall I say, for the decencies of life? They are essentially a dirty people. Dirt, untidiness, and noise, seem in nowise to afflict them. Things are constantly done before your eyes, which should be done and might be done behind your back. No doubt we daily come into the closest contact with matters which, if we saw all that appertains to them, would cause us to shake and shudder. In other countries we do not see all this, but in the western States we do. I have eaten in Bedouin and have been ministered to by Turks and Arabs. I have sojourned in the hotels of old Spain and of Spanish America. I have lived in Connaught, and have taken up my quarters with monks of different nations. I have, as it were, been educated to dirt, and taken out my degree in outward abominations. But my education had not reached a point which would enable me to live at my ease in the western States. A man or woman who can do that may be said to have graduated in the highest honours, and to have become absolutely invulnerable, either through the sense of touch, or by the eye, or by the nose. Indifference to appearances is there a matter of pride. A foul shirt is a flag of triumph. A craving for soap and water is as the wail of the weak and the confession of cowardice. This indifference is carried into all their affairs, or rather this manifestation of indifference. A few pages back, I spoke of a man whose furniture had been sold to pay a heavy tax raised on him specially as a secessionist; the same man had also been refused the payment of rent due to him by the government, unless he would take a false oath. I may presume that he was ruined in his circumstances by the strong hand of the northern army. But he seemed in nowise to be unhappy about his ruin. He spoke with some scorn of the martial law in Missouri, but I felt that it was esteemed a small matter by him that his furniture was seized and sold. No men love money with more eager love than these western men, but they bear the loss of it as an Indian bears his torture at the stake. They are energetic in trade, speculating deeply whenever speculation is possible; but nevertheless they are slow in motion, loving to loaf about. They are slow in speech, preferring to sit in silence, with the tobacco between their teeth. They drink, but are seldom drunk to the eye; they begin at it early in the morning, and take it in a solemn, sullen, ugly manner, standing always at a bar; swallowing their spirits, and saying nothing as they swallow it. They drink often, and to great excess; but they carry it off without noise, sitting down and ruminating over it with the everlasting cud within their jaws. I believe that a stranger might go into the West, and passing from hotel to hotel through a dozen of them, might sit for hours at each in the large everlasting public hall, and never have a word addressed to him. No stranger should travel in the western States, or indeed in any of the States, without letters of introduction. It is the custom of the country, and they are easily procured. Without them everything is barren; for men do not travel in the States of America as they do in Europe, to see scenery and visit the marvels of old cities which are open to all the world. The social and political life of the Americans must constitute the interest of the traveller, and to these he can hardly make his way without introductions.

I cannot part with the West without saying in its favour that there is a certain manliness about its men, which gives them a dignity of their own. It is shown in that very indifference of which I have spoken. Whatever turns up the man is still there,—still unsophisticated and still unbroken. It has seemed to me that no race of men requires less outward assistance than these pioneers of civilization. They rarely amuse themselves. Food, newspapers, and brandy-smashes suffice for life; and while these last, whatever may occur, the man is still there in his manhood. The fury of the mob does not shake him, nor the stern countenance of his present martial tyrant. Alas! I cannot stick to my text by calling him a just man. Intelligence, energy, and endurance are his virtues. Dirt, dishonesty, and morning drinks are his vices.

All native American women are intelligent. It seems to be their birthright. In the eastern cities they have, in their upper classes, super-added womanly grace to this intelligence, and consequently they are charming as companions. They are beautiful also, and, as I believe, lack nothing that a lover can desire in his love. But I cannot fancy myself much in love with a western lady, or rather with a lady in the West. They are as sharp as nails, but then they are also as hard. They know, doubtless, all that they ought to know, but then they know so much more than they ought to know. They are tyrants to their parents, and never practise the virtue of obedience till they have half-grown-up daughters of their own. They have faith in the destiny of their country, if in nothing else; but they believe that that destiny is to be worked out by the spirit and talent of the young women. I confess that for me Eve would have had no charms had she not recognized Adam as her lord. I can forgive her in that she tempted him to eat the apple. Had she come from the West country she would have ordered him to make his meal, and then I could not have forgiven her.

St. Louis should be, and still will be, a town of great wealth. To no city can have been given more means of riches. I have spoken of the enormous mileage of water-communication of which she is the centre. The country around her produces Indian corn, wheat, grasses, hemp, and tobacco. Coal is dug even within the boundaries of the city, and iron-mines are worked at a distance from it of a hundred miles. The iron is so pure, that it is broken off in solid blocks, almost free from alloy; and as the metal stands up on the earth's surface in the guise almost of a gigantic metal pillar, instead of lying low within its bowels, it is worked at a cheap rate, and with great certainty. Nevertheless, at the present moment, the iron-works of Pilot Knob, as the place is called, do not pay. As far as I could learn, nothing did pay, except government contracts.

ANTOINE AUGUSTE LAUGEL

THOUGH TRAINED AS AN ENGINEER, Antoine Laugel (1830–1914) devoted most of his professional life to studying and writing about political and social situations in Europe and abroad. For more than thirty years, he contributed to two prestigious French newspapers, *Revue des deux mondes* and *Le Temps*, in addition to publishing several significant historical and biographical works, including *Grandes figures historiques* (1857), *Les Etats-Unis pendant la guerre civile 1861–1865* (1866), and *Le Duc d'Aumale* (1897).

Like many other worldly Frenchmen of the nineteenth century, Laugel developed a keen interest in America's economic, political, and cultural development. A desire to study the socio-political climate of the young nation—then in the midst of civil war—drew Laugel to the United States in 1864. During this trip, he visited St. Louis, about which he had written in 1856, "St. Louis is destined, without a doubt, to a future brighter still than Chicago. Just as New York is the capital of the coastal States, there can be little doubt that St. Louis will be, someday, the capital of the mid-continent."

In the following excerpt from *Les Etats-Unis pendant la guerre civile*, Laugel describes the conditions he found in the "border state" of Missouri, particularly in and around St. Louis, during the Civil War. In addition to his insightful, albeit partisan, commentary on the contrasting contributions of French and German settlers in the city, Laugel sketches emotionally evocative scenes inside a military hospital and a refugee camp, all contributing to his depiction of the overwhelming turmoil in the region.

FROM *LES ETATS-UNIS PENDANT LA GUERRE CIVILE 1861–1865*

After crossing the Northern and Western States from the Atlantic coast to the Upper Mississippi, I traveled toward one of the border states where the civil strifes have left deep scars. Time will come when this name "border state," still used quite frequently in America, will have no meaning. Slavery alone had traced, right in the middle of the Union, an ideal border line; war has already erased this border partly, and later the reconstitution of the conquered states will make it disappear completely. . . .

The border state I intended to visit was Missouri. . . . I arrived at night in Quincy, on the Mississippi, and immediately went to the only hotel in town. All day long I had heard rumors of the invasion of Missouri, which the Confederates had entered and where they were perpetrating abuses. As is always the case in similar circumstances, a thousand rumors were heard, and even Quincy was alarmed. Arriving at the hotel I learned that during the evening the gas had suddenly been cut in the city and at the railroad station, by unknown hands. The hotel doorkeeper had patrolled the city with other inhabitants; but as I saw his livid face, it seemed to me that were the Confederates to cross the river and attack Quincy, the city could not count much on this defender. . . .

Located at the limit of the free and slave states, Missouri (where the two largest rivers of the country meet) could not help becoming one of the battle fields of the Civil War—an out-of-the-way battle field—located far from the areas where both parties were to give most of their efforts, and therefore, bound to witness more sorrowful scenes, more exalted passions—more ardent and less tempered by military honor and discipline. . . .

In the drawing room some men, smoking cigars, are gathered around a stove which a Negro fills with coal from time to time. A few wild looking river rogues are gambling; still others are reading the recent Quincy papers; others finally are talking in a low voice, and one hears from time to time the names of Price, Lincoln, and McClellan. There are faces which would not be out of place with the bandits of the Missouri; tangled hair, unshaven, sly eyes, worn-out clothes, hats drawn over their eyes: the whole reminding one of the gangs following Quantrill and Anderson. At the other end of the room are the women, the children, and a few men accompanying them or admitted at their chats. The Missourians aboard the ship are talking about the atrocities of the guerillas. I will only relate one story, since I was able to verify it in Saint Louis.

The second day, the steamship anchored once more to the shore, not very far from the junction with the river Illinois. The next morning, we sighted Alton; the rocky promontory on which this city is built is dominated by a huge penitentiary used as a prison for Confederate soldiers. The bayonets of the guards glistened in the rays of the morning sun, and idle soldiers were pacing the pier. Shortly before our arrival in Alton, a young man who had watched me drawing on the deck, timidly, came to ask me whether I would consent to draw him a sketch of the prison of Alton. Despite his rough reddish beard, his shining eyes, and his messy hair, he looked so naive and candid that I accepted his request. Yet, I inquired why he had selected this point rather than any other. He blushed still more, and told me that many of his hometown friends knew Alton and would be pleased to have such a drawing. A few days later in Saint Louis I found out that the Confederate gangs had planned to attack Alton in order to free the prisoners. The project was not carried out: my drawing, therefore, was of no use, if it ever left the hands of my unknown friend, whom I later suspected of being a member of the rebels' army.

A little below Alton, the Missouri and the Mississippi join their waters; those of the Missouri, muddy, heavy with clay, have the largest volume. So the Mississippi, so far limpid, turns soon to a grey and muddy color which it will keep to its mouth. Finally we saw Saint Louis, the huge factories, the hangars, the stores, the old red houses of the harbor lined up along the pier, crowded with a fleet of white steamers. There was little animation on the harbor. Almost all the lights of the steamships were out, and on the pier one could see only a few bags and barrels. At first glance, the city seemed to me sad and dirty. The brick houses which border the river are all in ruins. Saint Louis already looks like an old city in certain sections, though it is entirely modern. The small post founded by Laclède and Chouteau has become, in twenty years, the trading center of the midcontinent. Today Saint Louis attempts to spread its influence as far as the Pacific Coast; it has its railroad, already finished to Dresden, beyond Jefferson City, the political capital of the State. With its natural advantages (master of the greatest river in North America), Saint Louis could have made faster progress were it not for the enervating influences of slavery. The "Missouri Compromise" opened to the fatal institution a region which should have been preserved from it by its latitude, one which offered to free labor a field of admirable fecundity: it was the first triumph of an unscrupulous policy of invasion. The South then agreed to claim no other territory above the 36 degree latitude for their *favorite institution*. How this promise was kept, what series of humiliations for the North, of victories for the South, led both of them finally to Civil

War, we all know. For Missouri itself, slavery has only been a plague; it has driven away the spirit of enterprise, the emigrants, and industrial genius. Can we compare the forges and factories of Missouri to those of Pennsylvania? Yet Missouri has real iron-ore mountains in the Ozarks; the metallic masses of Iron Mountain and Pilot Knob rival in quality the rich mines of Elba, Sweden, and Norway.

The French population of Saint Louis has always been, and still is, attached to slavery; its fidelity for the ancient colonial traditions is mixed with I don't know what instinctive and distrustful contempt for all that appeals to the invading races which surround her. It is, I must say, a painful spectacle for a Frenchman to see this friendly, rich, esteemed French population almost entirely deprived of influence. While all and everything around her marches forward, this French element remains, and wants to remain, stationary. It never enters into the political arena, and has not yet given a single statesman to the Republic. The Catholic clergy, very rich, and by its virtues worthy of respect, has few interests other than keeping the Catholic children away from the public schools, where the education is free and maintains a lay character. Involuntarily, Saint Louis reminds one of certain provincial French towns, at the same time fluid and fault-finding, asleep, lazy, ruled by people she hardly knows—if at all—unconcerned with or unaware of her municipal and political rights, satisfied with herself without, however, expecting any more from herself. Still more, take away from her the national pride, the echoes of the far away voices of the Capital, the deep and vague sentiment of that powerful solidarity which cements all the souls, the positive hope, finally, of a great future for the Nation: such is the French Saint Louis. Next to this Saint Louis is located the German and American Saint Louis. While not a single French newspaper is published in this city, there appear a great number of German and English news sheets. In fact, it is amidst the German population that one must look for the most exalted defenders of the Union, the staunchest enemies of slavery. Yet, less accustomed than the Anglo-Saxon elements to the habits of public life, the Germans bring to political activities too thoughtless an enthusiasm, a certain naiveté easily satisfied with meaningless sentences, and a stubbornness which disappears in wretched personalities. By flattering their demagogic passions and their vanity, a few leaders opposed to Mr. Lincoln were successful in having them accept the candidacy of General Frémont at the beginning of the presidential campaign of 1864, and when the General withdrew, the

Missouri radicals only gave a lukewarm support to the Republican candidate.

If the radicalism of a segment of the German population of the West caused some embarrassment to the government, it is only fair to admit that the Germans have shown a deep attachment and a great devotion to their new motherland. Understanding, from the very beginning, the character and aim of the Civil War, they embraced the Union cause and the Emancipation program with ardor and passion, the results of which were felt even amidst the Germanic population of Europe. The part they played in the war, the courage they displayed on the battlefields, their opposition to slavery and to the Democratic Party, guarantee them henceforth an important place in the policy of the United States. The Anglo-Saxon mind—exclusive, invading and jealous, one must recognize—accustomed to defeat everything, to absorb all, will have to reckon with this force. In California as in Missouri, the Germans were as American—I would almost say more American—than the *Yankees*; the Civil War signed their final papers (for naturalization). There are, in the German race, qualities and elements destined to rejuvenate the Anglo-Saxon race. The high German culture still has few representatives in the United States, and Germany only sends there the most ignorant and poorest of her children; but they carry in their veins and in their minds the mysterious germs which, in their old fatherland, have already fully bloomed. In the new motherland, these germs will not always remain asleep; something new, more naive and more poetical will be added to the audacity, the tenacity, and the stiffness of the Anglo-Saxons. Even from a purely physical point of view, one should expect some change from the combination; while one race is too nervous and irritable, the other is too rustic and too thick. But their intellectual marriage will no doubt give the most precious products.

The situation of Missouri was far from satisfactory when I was there. Ever since the capture of Vicksburg, the federal gunboats patrolled freely on the Mississippi, but the commercial ties between Saint Louis and New Orleans were almost completely cut. Only the movements of troops gave a little activity to the river; the guerillas still shot frequently at the steamers and made travellers very uncomfortable. The violence of the political parties was extreme. The Democrats blamed Mr. Lincoln for his policy of emancipation, and their candidate for governor was no other than a distant cousin of Sterling Price, who had invaded the province on two occasions.

This cousin, also named Price, had remained faithful to the Union in 1860, and to reward him, as well as to give proof of his conciliatory disposition, Mr. Lincoln had appointed him a brigadier general of the volunteer army. That did not prevent Brigadier-General Price from backing the candidacy of McClellan, in October, 1864, and in a popular assembly he declared that if Mr. Lincoln were reelected, the State of Missouri would have to re-examine the situation and see whether or not it would not be better for the interests of the State to unite its destiny to that of the states of the new Confederation. On the other hand, the Republicans thought they were abandoned, almost betrayed by the government; they reproached Mr. Lincoln for the least concessions to the Democrats; they had obtained, in a convention, a vote for the gradual abolition of slavery, but they feared that the emancipation would remain unapplied if their enemies succeeded in establishing the leading influence in the State. Everywhere the Unionists were exposed to grave dangers; the inertia of the Commandant of the Province had, for the second time, opened the State to hordes of bandits and murderers. On both sides they complained about conscription. Missouri had already given 30,000 men to the Northern army, almost 45,000 had followed the Southern flag, and still they called for a contingent based on the population figure of 1860.

My most interesting visit in Saint Louis was that to the Jefferson Camp, a little distance from the city. I went there by railroad, and noticed on the way one of the eleven forts—today abandoned—erected by order of General Frémont, when he commanded in Saint Louis, and meant more to watch the city than to protect it. The wooden houses of a camp stretch alongside huge parade grounds, next to a park formerly used for agricultural expositions. Amidst the beautiful straight oak trees, one can see a few light buildings converted to hospitals. They have also added many new wooden houses to shelter sick soldiers, colored families, and Southern refugees. The hospital for the latter, which I entered first, was in a very sad condition. Everywhere there were women and children emaciated by long walks, fatigue, hunger, and sickness. They showed me an old woman who, alone, rode on a weak horse from Texas to St. Louis. While I sadly was walking through rows of beds, an old man was agitated by the last convulsions of agony. A putrid smell of cooking and pharmacy made still heavier an atmosphere already heavy from the iron stoves. One could also see, spread on various beds, the rags which the fugitives had brought along. A few bold-looking women were quietly laughing, and their gaiety next to these death-beds was somewhat cynical and sad. Did those who started the Civil War ever see such pathetic sights? And, if they had seen them, how can they prevent their consciences from bothering them?

The military hospital was quite different: the white and clean beds were almost all empty. Paper decorations hung from the ceilings in between the wooden pillars. Above the doors and beds there were hung billboards with lines from the Bible or patriotic sentences written in huge characters. Most of the sick men were colored people. The convalescents were seated in small groups; one had frozen his feet during the siege of Vicksburg; some had their hair braided in small tails standing on their heads; their blue uniforms were shining and very clean.

After the hospitals, I roamed throughout the huts hastily built to shelter the refugees, colored people and poor whites. Small Negro boys seemed to appear from nowhere. Women were cooking. An older lady passed by me carrying *patates*: "Why don't you buy potatoes?" my guide asked her. "They are much cheaper!" "Well," she answered nodding her head and smiling, "do I eat Irish patates?" A bearded white-haired man was enjoying the sun on a stool; he was at least eighty, though he did not know his own age. "Why," he was asked, "did you flee the South?" "To rest—Uncle Sam will no longer make me work!" The houses reserved for the white families were only occupied by women and children; a few men only were around, either too old or too weak to find a job. The members of the same family remained closely gathered. These unfortunate wretches looked at us curiously; the women were more eager to talk; they seemed to ignore the sentiments of embarrassment or of prudishness. A few women, combing their hair, did not even bother to rearrange themselves. My guide, through whose efforts a school had recently been opened for the refugees' children, asked a young woman whose delicate and still childish face revealed she was hardly sixteen, "Did you go to our school yet?" "To school," she answered haughtily and surprised. "I am a married *lady*." All these Southern women are *ladies*, which does not prevent them from smoking earth pipes like soldiers or sailors would. (Footnote of the author: The word *lady* is used abusively in the United States, both North and South. In fact, I was told these words from a sermon: "Who came first at the foot of the Cross? *Ladies!* Who remained longest at the foot of the Cross? *Ladies!*") The young *lady* who had revolted at the thought of going to school was forced to admit, however, that she could not read. She was not the least ashamed of it. The whites, who, in the Southern States, form the intermediary class—between the large landowners and the slaves—live amidst the most complete ignorance. It is within this group—rough, vulgar, half-savage, and long accustomed to a dependent life—that the Southern oligarchy recruited its army. It succeeded in instilling in it horror for all that could regenerate it. These soldiers—whose blood has run on many battlefields—thought they were fighting for independence, while in reality they were fighting to keep their masters. The soldiers of slavery were slaves themselves.

While leaving the camp, I saw a troop of Missourian cavalry coming back from an expedition to Pilot Knob; the squad stopped at the camp door to be assigned quarters. Both men and horses looked equally tired as they had not rested in many days; their blue coats—decorated with yellow hands—their long overcoats, and the black felt hats were covered with dust; their big boots and their Mexican-style stirrups were covered with a thick layer of dried mud. All the men had rifles on their saddles and guns on their belts. They had patrolled the countryside looking for guerillas, though they looked more like guerillas themselves than like regular soldiers. Most of them were so tired that they had fallen asleep on their horses; some seated like amazons, others with their legs crossed on their saddles. There were among them some magnificent military prototypes: I particularly noticed a young captain who had dismounted; with his arm leaning on his saddle, his saber dangling, his martial and smiling face, his teeth shining under a beautiful blond mustache, he looked as gay and rested as if he had just returned from a parade. Seeing the bold faces of these Missourians, one felt that they must fight like demons, but that they prefer adventurous expeditions to life in camps or the long operations of the regular warfare.

The hospitals in Saint Louis and the surroundings were continuously visited by the members of the "Western Sanitary Commission." These commissions, independent from the government, were at work in all the large cities of the Union. They did not hamper the action of the medical corps, nor that of the army officers; they only tried to make their tasks easier. The generosity of the American people furnished them with the means to add, everywhere, a little extra to the necessary, such as fruit, anti-scorbutics, and a few warmer clothes. These same resources helped to found schools for the Negroes and to diminish the sufferings of so many unfortunate people, colored or white, innocent victims of the Civil War. Few sanitary commissions have had as difficult a task as that in the West. The contributions and patriotic gifts, naturally, were mostly directed to the larger commission in Washington and its smaller branches in Boston, Philadelphia, and New York. The Saint Louis and Mississippi Valley Commission had a very modest beginning; after the first battles in Missouri (summer of 1861), nothing was prepared to receive the wounded. They had neither beds nor stoves, neither mattresses nor blankets, neither remedies nor nurses. When I was in Saint Louis, the Commission had already received $275,000, and other contributions for a value of about $1,250,000. The president of the Commission, Mr. James E. Yeatman, had about $2,000 a day to spend. Everywhere new huge hospitals had been erected; the Commission had founded Soldiers' Homes in several towns—establishments where the soldiers bound for the army or their home received free food. The Commission also distributed, through the intermediary of the Army surgeons, blankets, socks, shirts, canned vegetables, wine, fruit, and books to hospitals and camps. All this added to the general well-being of the soldiers. Every day cases arrived from all parts of the Union, filled with the most varied objects; from Maine to Minnesota, from Boston to Saint Louis, there was not a single village which did not send its contribution. The most abundant and most precious gifts came from Massachusetts. Not only did this little state contribute the most important gifts in nature and money; it also gave surgeons, nurses, teachers. The Unitarian minister of San Francisco, Starr King, whose patriotic eloquence perhaps prevented California from leaving the Union, and who obtained as much as $300,000 from this state for the Sanitary Commissions of Washington and Saint Louis, was originally from Boston. Mr. Eliot, Unitarian minister in Saint Louis, who was, with Mr. Yeatman (formerly a slave owner in Tennessee) the soul of the Commission in Saint Louis, also came from New England. I saw one of his nieces, recently arrived in Saint Louis to teach the alphabet to Negro children, spend every day on a bench of a school, though she was only twenty. An angry Democrat one day shouted in front of me: "The present war is the conquest of America by the State of Massachusetts!" He was right, but the conquest was not that of the sword.

When I left Missouri, everything was in confusion; but shortly after my departure General Price was defeated by the strong Kansas militia, with the help of some federal troops and the cavalry of Stoneman. With this first failure, the invading army, demoralized by its own excesses, practically vanished; General Price gathered only a few men and led them into the solitude of the interior of the continent. His second appeal to the population of the State of Missouri had been as useless as the first. He had come, he declared in his address, to free them from the tyranny of Mr. Lincoln and to give them, for the last time, the occasion to arise against the federal government; but he had been able to recruit only bandits and murderers. General Rosecrans, despite the weakness he had shown, still kept his command till the presidential election of November 4; later he was recalled. The State of Missouri gave its vote to Mr. Lincoln; at the same time, the electors selected from the most radical faction of the Republican Party, their governor, the members of the new legislature, and those entrusted with the task of rewriting the Constitution of the State.

The terrible lessons of the war had not been lost on the inhabitants of this unfortunate State, ravaged in all directions and twice condemned to all the horrors of invasion. The new convention began its task immediately and with courage. It refused to let the fatal institution—considered rightly as the cause of the Civil War—last another day, and they erased from the political chart all that could recall it.

FRANCIS GRIERSON

BORN BENJAMIN HENRY JESSE FRANCIS SHEPARD, Francis Grierson (1848-1927)—later taking his mother's maiden name—moved with his parents from England to the United States when he was an infant. The family settled in Sagamon County, Illinois, and moved to Alton a few years later. Early on, it was apparent that Francis had inherited his mother's extraordinary voice, and he began his career of musical performance by singing regularly in an Alton church choir and occasionally at Trinity Episcopal Church in St. Louis. As a boy, Grierson sensed the tensions building in the region during the years leading to the outbreak of the Civil War. For the rest of his life, he recalled hearing the indelible exchange between Abraham Lincoln and Stephen Douglas in their last debate at Alton.

Grierson moved with his family to Niagara Falls in 1863 and, several years later, left for Europe to seek his fortune as a singer and musician. For two years, he toured Paris, London, and Russia, performing private concerts in the salons of royalty and wealthy patrons. A gifted improvisational pianist who had garnered praise in Europe from such luminaries as Stéphane Mallarmé and Alexandre Dumas, Grierson expanded his appreciative following in the United States when he returned in 1874. Although Grierson built an elaborate home in San Diego, he traveled extensively, wrote articles and several books on history and spiritualism, and continued to perform until the moment of his death. Impoverished in his old age, Grierson died while playing the piano at a fund-raising recital given in his honor on May 29, 1927.

Although Grierson was a prolific writer, only one of his works endured. When *The Valley of the Shadows,* a personal narrative recounting the events in Illinois and St. Louis leading up to the Civil War, was originally published in 1909, it received very little attention. Fortunately, Houghton Mifflin rescued the work from obscurity by reprinting it in 1948 and added an in-depth introduction by Theodore Spencer, which sets the book in its proper context. In his preface to the 1948 edition, renowned scholar Bernard DeVoto states, "This is a book . . . which has greatness in it. . . . The hope is that it will now find its audience and that an American classic will be recognized for what it is."

In the following brief chapter from *The Valley of the Shadows*, Grierson describes the ambiance and mystique of one of St. Louis's most legendary buildings and meeting places, the Planters' Hotel, located on Fourth Street between Pine and Chestnut. For more than seventy years, the Planters' House, as it came to be called, hosted virtually every notable that stepped foot in St. Louis—from Daniel Webster and Charles Dickens to P.T. Barnum and Tom Thumb. During the Civil War, the building was one of the only neutral sites that could accommodate both Confederate and Union leaders and was the place where much strategy was devised and debate waged. Old hotel ledgers bear the names William T. Sherman, Jefferson Davis, Abraham Lincoln, Francis Blair, Henry Clay, Nathaniel Lyon, and Sterling Price. Legend has it that not only was the cocktail "Tom and Jerry" invented by a bartender at the Planters' House, but also that the hotel was the first to offer its guests the amenity of placing valuables in a safe. The Planters' House underwent several renovations before a devastating fire forced its closing in 1887. Several years later, a new Planters' Hotel was built on the original site, but it lacked the grandeur and cachet of its predecessor and, by 1922, was converted into an office building.

FROM *THE VALLEY OF THE SHADOWS*

THE PLANTERS' HOUSE

The Planters' House! What did it not represent in the history of the Far West in the early days! To me it was St. Louis itself. This famous hotel typified life on the Mississippi, life on the prairies, life in the cotton-fields, life in the cosmopolitan city. It stood for wealth, fashion, adventure, ease, romance—all the dreams of the new life of the Great West. It was the one fixed point where people met to gossip, discuss politics, and talk business. It was the universal *rendezvous* for the Mississippi Valley. Here the North met the South, the East met the West. It looked like nothing else in the hotel world, but it always seemed to me it was intended more for pilots, river-captains, romantic explorers, far-seeing speculators, and daring gamblers.

It was here the goatee type was seen in all its perfection. On some of the chins the tufts of hard, pointed hair gave a corkscrew look to the dark faces, which somehow harmonised well with the eternal quaffing of mint-juleps, sherry-cobblers, and gin cocktails.

An hour spent in the Planters' House just before the great election was an experience never to be forgotten. All who did not want to shoot or be shot steered a clear course in some other direction, for here, in the bar and lobbies, were the true "fire-eaters" to be met, and while some had already killed their man, others were looking for a man to kill.

The fire-eaters were of two kinds: those who said little, but did much, and those who drank much, talked much, and brandished pistols freely. Besides these there was an independent third party, namely, the listeners. Those were the wise, silent ones. They were, perhaps, the most interesting because they were amusing. The wise, silent listener would be smoking a big El Sol cigar, which gave him something to "chaw" on; and during the fearful oaths and invectives poured forth by the fire-eater the unfortunate victim would find his huge cigar not only smoked but "chawed" down to the very stump. Thus, without knowing it, he would be chewing and smoking at the same time. How innocent and bland he sometimes appeared while in the clutches of a down-river bowie-knife man. The fire-eater could hardly be mistaken for any other type. It was the keen, glossy eye of a snake under strong, dark eyebrows, sometimes thick and shaggy, sometimes thin and arched; and if the latter, the whole aspect of the face was fashioned in harmony with the clear-cut eyebrow, penetrating as a black steel point, above a piercing black eye. A pair of such eyes, once fixed on a lounger, bent on keeping the peace, and his case was settled. But the silent listener at once took refuge behind a vocabulary of stock phrases. After a few drinks the political desperado would feel himself beginning to "b'ile over," and looked about him for someone to blow off steam on. There would be the man of peace who feels that one drink is quite enough and who wishes to take a seat in an arm-chair or lean against the wall of the bar-room, take it easy, and just look and listen; but a fire-eater, just in from the bloody borders of Kansas, has spotted him; he forces him to have another drink, and begins:

"Sorter dull in St. Louis! I reckon things will liven up by election day."

The silent man with a fixed vocabulary answers:

"I reckon they will."

"Looky heah," continues the desperado, placing a hard, lanky hand on the shoulder of his victim, "I've put daylight through more'n one Abolitionist out there in Kansas, an' I'll be hanged if I don't do the same for the fust man here who says he's a-goin' te vote fer that miserable skunk Abe Lincoln."

"Yes, sah."

"I reckon the Planters' House is all sound on the Little Giant, good ole Steve Douglas."

"I reckon she air."

"Now you look like a fair, square, up and down Douglas man, an' solid on the nigger question."

"I reckon I be."

"I kin pick out the skulkin' Yankee cowards in a crowd any day; ye kin tell 'em by their sleek ways an' their innocent looks, eh?"

"I reckon you can, sah."

At this juncture up stalks another fire-eater, eyes glaring, hair long and loose, his big felt hat set back on his head, and, fixing his ferret gaze on the silent man, shouts:

"Hurrah fer Fremont! I fit under John C. Fremont! You're a Fremont man, I know ye air, and we're a-goin' t'elect him. Come on, have a drink with me, gov'nah," and up he drags the wretched victim to the crowded bar, and there, trembling like a canary-bird in a cage between two rattlesnakes, the man of peace and silence has just wit enough left to answer with assumed assurance: "Yes, sah; I reckon ye're right, sah."

But the scene has not ended.

The Kansas fire-eater, who is now fairly on the war-path and itching for a scalp, turns suddenly on the man of peace and shouts:

"Looky heah, stranger, you told me just now you was fer Douglas! What do you mean by harrowin' the feelin's of an honest man? If there's anything I despise worse'n a Yankee it's a turn-coat. Yes, sir-ree, a turn-coat! Set there a-tellin' me how clean broke up ye air on Steve Douglas, and now ye're drinkin' that stranger's whisky an' tellin' him ye're plumb gone on Fremont! Is that there a fair fight?"

By this time the silent man is saying his prayers, also in silence—scared, white in the face, not knowing what to do or what to say, afraid to move, his stock phrases worse than puerile, with just life enough left to hear his heart thumping and not enough strength left in his arm to raise his glass to his lips.

"If I thought you was a turn-coat I tell ye what it is, stranger, I'd let ye have this right through yer gizzard," and out he whips a dirk, pointed and deadly, a fearful gleam whirling in a circle as he brandishes the cold steel over his head with a wicked twist of the shoulder.

But the Fremont man, now beginning to feel the whisky working, stands at the other side of the man of silence. He, too, is armed, but with a revolver.

"See here, pard!" he cries, "suppose we fight it out right now, an' let the gov'nah here hold the stakes, as ye might say."

The gov'nah? Good heavens! He means the wise, silent man, the innocent, neutral lamb, the chewer of peaceful cuds and mumbler of joint-stock phrases.

But listen. You can almost hear what he is thinking. He is saying to himself, "When rogues fall out the honest come by their own"; and at the first sign of hostilities down he dips and, like a yellow dog, wriggles his way through the crowd to the door and "slides out."

The bar-room, corridors, and halls are now filled with excited men under the influence of drink and half wild with suppressed passion. Some, with bloodshot eyes, pass in and out as if seeking someone to devour; the place begins to steam with the heat, and to cool the heated blood more iced mint-juleps are disposed of, and yet more, until heads begin to reel, quarrels arise from mere nothings, and amidst a chorus of howls and imprecations the Yankees, the "Dutch," and sometimes the Irish are denounced as "low white trash," cowards, and traitors.

In such crowds, about that time, might have been seen the auctioneer of human flesh, the professional slave-seller, the boldest, most abandoned of them all, because the law was on his side. Erebus had spewed him up from the nethermost corners—a pollution to the polluted, a creature without wit, humour, or feeling; a menace to civilisation and a curse to patriotism.

The Planters' House was the magnet-stone that attracted not only the country "moss-backs," but the city millionaire, the poor man out of work and the busy man with too much work; and here, with the others, came Captain U. S. Grant, plain, unassuming Mr. Grant, as he was usually called, and if not the plainest man hereabouts, certainly one of the most discouraged and disappointed. He was often to be seen lounging about the public rooms waiting for something to turn up. The future commander-in-chief of the Army belonged to the silent ones, but one whose wits had been sharpened by a vast worldly experience and profound knowledge of human nature, and his silence was not a sign of lethargy and stupidity, but of knowledge and wisdom. I can see him now, sitting in an arm-chair, smoking an El Sol cigar and waiting with an air of extreme patience and resignation. But waiting for what? Did he himself know? Why was he in St. Louis at all? For everything he attempted proved a business failure, from hauling cordwood into town from the log-house he had built for his family out on the Gravois Road and selling it, one load at a time, to the opening of a real estate office for the buying and letting of houses. Everything he now touched failed; and yet, when the critical hour arrived, this plain, silent man, this business failure, would be on hand to offer his services to General Lyon at the United States Arsenal.

My father often talked with Mr. Grant about the price of town lots and the rent of certain houses.

Captain Grant had been all through the Mexican War, and had served nine years in the United States Army, and had seen service in California. He had seen life as few had seen it, yet there he was, one of the most discouraged men to be met with anywhere in the Mississippi Valley.

How different the visits to the Planters' House of Major W. T. Sherman! When this future commander-in-chief came it was not to lounge about, for he was too busy. He too had seen service in California. He declared he had come to settle down in St. Louis as an ordinary business man. Major Sherman lived only four blocks from us, on Locust Street, and Willie Sherman I knew very well.

Whenever I wanted something like an excursion I would take a ride on a Fifth Street car and go for miles in a northerly or southerly direction. Major Sherman, as President of the Fifth Street car line, was often to be seen going to his office in North St. Louis in one of these cars. One day three future generals happened to be riding in the same car together—Grant, the hero of Vicksburg; Sherman, of the great march through Georgia; and Grierson, of the famous raid through Mississippi.

SOLOMON FRANKLIN SMITH

WHILE STILL IN HIS TEENS, Solomon Smith (1801–1869) moved from Norwich, New York, to Louisville, Kentucky. There, he apprenticed himself to a printer and joined a theater company. After casually studying law in Cincinnati, Smith found himself back in the theater—his true calling—and traveled with a company as its principal comedian.

In the mid-1830s, Smith came to St. Louis and introduced the city to its first taste of real theater. On July 3, 1837, Smith and Noah M. Ludlow opened the newly constructed St. Louis Theatre at Third and Olive Streets. It was the first regularly operated theater west of the Mississippi, complete with restrooms, concession stands, and a seating capacity of 1,650 people. Although the venture was financially unstable from the start, the theater did feature such popular actors as Edwin Forrest and Matthew Field. In 1851, Smith and Ludlow sold the theater to the federal government, which razed it to build a new custom house and post office.

Drawing on his experiences as a raconteur, publisher, and theatrical entrepreneur, Smith offered the anecdotes of his remarkable and entertaining career in several collections, including a volume titled *Theatrical Management in the West and South for Thirty Years* (1868). In the following excerpts from that work, Smith recounts several amusing, if not outrageous, events that occurred in St. Louis when he resided in the city.

FROM *THEATRICAL MANAGEMENT IN THE WEST AND SOUTH FOR THIRTY YEARS*

I don't remember much about the season of 1845 in St. Louis, but there was no very favorable change.

This summer (if I remember rightly—I can't find any memoranda to guide me), leaving the theatrical affairs to be mostly conducted, in the details, by my partner, I spent in the *practice of the law,* confining myself, in a great measure, to the Criminal and Recorder's courts. The circuit attorney, Mr. Hall, being called away on business a week or two before the close of the term then being held, I was appointed temporarily to fill his place, which I did to the close of the term. I did some pettifogging too, as practicing before justices of the peace is called. One case before Justice Walsh I must report.

A HUNG JURY

Many of our old citizens will remember Noah Ridgely, as good and true a man as ever acted as clerk of a boat and collected freight-bills. Wherever the steamer Hannibal made a landing (and where is the landing between St. Louis and New Orleans she has not stopped at?), Noah has been seen and known at some time or other; but in St. Louis—well, there's no use writing how well he was known *here*. And, wherever known, Noah was a favorite—I might say a *great* favorite. He had been clerk of the aforesaid Hannibal for I don't know how many years, and during all those years he went round to the consignees at the end of each voyage to collect the freight-bills. So, as I have intimated, everybody knew Noah Ridgely, and liked him.

But to my story. In St. Louis we all know the difficulty of procuring *jurors* to try cases before justices of the peace, it being almost next to an impossibility to get together twelve citizens, "good men and true," who are willing to sit for two or three hours in a justice's office, which is never, by any accident, larger than a moderate-sized bandbox, surrounded by a promiscuous crowd, which always gathers, filling up room, doors, and windows whenever a "jury trial" is to come off, especially if *lawyers* are employed in it.

It so happened, "once upon a time," that two merchants had a little misunderstanding, which resulted in their "going to law" before Justice Walsh. The amount in dispute was a mere trifle, but each was obstinate, and would not give way a jot, so to law they went. To make matters worse, each must have a lawyer to help him on, and one of the lawyers, determined to make as much out of the case as he could, asserted the constitutional right of his client, and *demanded a jury*. A *venire facias* was accordingly issued, and Constable Busby started off to execute his writ.

At the expiration of about an hour, during which the court, attorneys, and spectators waited with exemplary patience, Busby returned, followed by *one solitary individual*, carrying a huge lot of freight-bills in one hand, and a half-smoked cigar in the other. It was Noah.

"Have you summoned the jury, Mr. Constable?" inquired the justice.

"Yes, sir," replied Busby, throwing down upon the table his writ with the names of twelve citizens inscribed thereon; "I have summoned them, but they won't come."

"Won't come? won't come?" remarked the justice. "We'll see about that. Clerk, write out attachments for these gentlemen. How may are there who refuse to obey the order of the Court?"

"Eleven, your honor," answered the sweating constable. "This is the only one of the lot" (pointing to our friend Noah) "I have been able to scare up, and *he* don't seem much disposed to serve; says he intends to *plead his privilege.*"

"What privilege, pray, Mr. Ridgely, have you to plead? What valid reason can you give the Court why you should not serve on this jury?" asked the justice.

"I believe," replied Noah, stretching himself up to his full height, and taking the cigar from his mouth which he had been industriously smoking since he entered the office, "I believe a *fireman* is exempt from jury duty?"

"Certainly, certainly," replied the justice. "But I was not aware you belonged to either of the engine companies. May I ask, Mr. Ridgely, which engine you run with?"

"Which engine? The old St. Louis! You are aware, perhaps, Mr. Justice, that the old steamer St. Louis had *two* engines. One of them constitutes at this time the motive power of the Hannibal, and that is the engine I run with; and when hard pushed for hands, I have, upon occasion, acted as *fireman*, therefore I suppose I'm excused from jury duty."

"Not so fast, my friend," interposed the justice; "this will *not* excuse you—"

"Not!" exclaimed Noah, with apparent surprise. "Then," he continued, taking a seat on the jury-bench, " bring on your case, since I am overruled, and let us get through with it as soon as we can, for I'll be hanged if I stop long."

Busby at this juncture returned from another unsuccessful foray through the neighboring streets and alleys. "Can't scare up a single man," he reported, sitting down and wiping the perspiration from his face with a cotton pocket-handkerchief whcih he carried in his hat.

"What is to be done?" inquired the lawyers.

"I am sure I don't know," answered Justice Walsh, "unless you choose to take Mr. Ridgely here, and let *him* decide your case."

As the laws of Missouri permit parties by mutual consent to take "any number less than twelve" in civil cases before justices of the peace, the lawyers, finding there was no chance of "scaring up" any more jurors, agreed to *take Noah as the jury,* and, after a few modest objections on his part, he was sworn in, and assigned a seat in the centre of the jury-bench.

"Come, now, boys," remarked the solitary juror on taking his seat, "hurry up these cakes; I've got all these freight-bills to collect, and confound me if I can stay here long for *any* body."

The lawyers made short work of the evidence, "not wishing to fatigue the jury," and proposed to submit the case without argument.

The justice thought this was a very good plan—it was near dinner-time—and suggested that perhaps the jury was ready to give a verdict without leaving his seat, when the jury spoke as follows:

"May it please the court, the jury is *not* ready to give a verdict. This is an important matter—a matter involving but a small sum, it is true, but the *principle* to be settled by our decision here to-day is one which interests the whole city, the state, the United States—I may say the whole commercial world! The jury, at great inconvenience, has been dragged here and compelled to sit in judgment. The evidence being through, this jury would like to hear the argument of counsel."

"Very well," answered the counsel for the defense, and immediately poured forth a torrent of eloquence in favor of the side he espoused, which must have had a convincing effect in the right quarter, for when the learned gentleman resumed his seat, the jury expressed himself ready to render a verdict; but the attorney for the plaintiff now insisted upon being heard, and accordingly set forth *his* view of the case in such vivid colors that the jury, before he had finished his hour's speech, had evidently relapsed into a state of doubt and uncertainty.

"If the court pleases," remarked the jury, "before this last speech a verdict might have been given which would have satisfied *one* of the parties at least; *now,* it is impossible; this last speech has turned every thing topsy-turvy. There are some points on which the jury must request the instructions of the court."

The instructions were given, and it was generally supposed that a verdict would be rendered at once, as the dinner-bells were now ringing out in every direction; but not so; *the jury preferred to retire and consider upon its verdict*; and as all parties, *except the jury*, seemed about obeying the summons of the bells, a hint was delicately given that it would be no more than proper, and, indeed, humane, that the jury should be *furnished with refreshments*. The hint was seized upon by the attorneys, and *two* very abundant dinners were in a few minutes passed in through the window from the neighboring Jefferson House, the justice, constables, lawyers, and spectators having left the office in possession of the jury, according to the custom of those times.

After dinner the crowd gradually reassembled in the street, and through the open window the imperturbable jury was seen with one leg cocked over the knee of the other, looking carefully over the "authorities" which had been referred to by the lawyers; then changing his position, and putting the leg which had been under on top, the upper wall of the room was scanned with great earnestness for a few minutes, after which a large volume containing the statutes of Missouri was diligently consulted, and so on. It was evident, from appearances, that the *jury had not yet agreed*.

At six o'clock, under instructions from Justice Walsh, the constable inquired, as is usual in similar cases, "Has the jury agreed?" A solemn "No" was the response and soon after candles were brought and placed upon the table by the constable, who, after lingering a moment in hopes of an intimation that a verdict had been agreed on, was waved out of the room by the jury. From a quarter past 6 until 11 o'clock the jury cogitated without any result. At length Busby was ordered to summon the jury into court, which was done by opening the outer door and admitting the justice and crowd into the presence of the jury.

There sat the jury, as undecided as at dinner-time.

"Gentle*man* of the jury," said the justice, majestically, "have you agreed upon your verdict?"

"May I please the court," answered Noah, with great dignity, "I believe it is customary to *poll the jury* before asking that question."

"Very well," replied the justice, who, it must be confessed, was becoming a little fretful—"poll away."

Busby polled the jury, calling out from his list,

"No-ah Ridgely!"

"Here!" answered the jury.

"All right," reported Busby to the justice.

"*Now*, then—the jury being polled—gentle*man* of the jury," repeated the justice, slowly, "have—you—agreed—upon—your—verdict?"

"May—it—please—the—court—NO!" answered Noah, rising, and shaking his head emphatically.

"Is there any likelihood of the jury being able to agree?" demanded Justice Walsh, desperately.

"Not the least ghost of a chance," replied the person addressed: "THE JURY IS HUNG!"

A dismissal of the jury followed, and a new trial was ordered. The hero of my sketch was ever after, by general consent, considered exempt from jury duty.

A LAPSE OF TWENTY YEARS

The elderly and middle-aged residents of St. Louis all remember the theatre on Second Street, between Olive and Locust Streets, commonly known as the *Salt-house*. The "temple" was somewhat limited in size, of a surety; but it was generally well filled with well-satisfied audiences, and I have always contended that a small theatre FULL was far preferable to a large one half empty. No matter for that; it is all aside from the purpose of my story, which is intended to record one of the most singular coincidences I have ever known.

In the summer of 1827, the company of which I was then a member performed with great success a new drama entitled THE GAMBLER'S FATE, OR A LAPSE OF TWENTY YEARS. It took well with the St. Louisans, and was often repeated.

On one occasion, when this thrilling drama was announced, two young men, just enlisted for a trip to the mountains in the Fur Company's service, attended the theatre to witness the performance. At the end of the first act they got impatient at the length of time the curtain was suffered to remain down, and concluded to go out and *take a drink*. Another drink followed, and then another.

"Come, Jim," said one, "let's return to the theatre; the curtain must be up by this time."

"No," replied the other; "look here—just read that bill, will you?—

Between the 1st and 2d acts twenty years are supposed to elapse."

"Thunder and gunpowder!" exclaimed Joe, the liquor beginning to assert its power, "who's gwine to wait twenty years? Let's go back to the Green Tree tavern and retire to our virtuous beds, for to-morrow we start for the mountains."

"Agreed," says Jim, and off they went. They slept off the effects of the "drink," and next day the party to which they belonged moved westward.

A LAPSE OF TWENTY YEARS

Two middle-aged individuals are seen reading a large poster at the "Green Tree." Rough-looking customers they are, and look toil-worn and browned by the weather, but hardy and honest. They are our old friends who, twenty years ago, went to see THE GAMBLER'S FATE, and retired at the end of the first act. Singularly enough, there is the same play announced, THE GAMBLER'S FATE, OR A LAPSE OF TWENTY YEARS.

Our trappers agree at once to go and *see the rest on't.*

They make their way up Second Street until they come to about the spot where the theatre stood, and then inquire of a passer-by for directions, which are speedily given, and in a few minutes they find themselves in the vestibule of the theatre on Third Street.

"Halloo! old feller," says Joe, addressing the ticket-seller through a hole, "they play THE GAMBLER'S FATE here to-night, don't they?"

"Well, they don't play any thing else," was the polite reply of the gentlemanly treasurer.

"All right, old feller," replied Joe; "I don't want to *see* any thing else, though I believe you advertise a farce with it. Is the first act over?"

"I believe it is," answered the clerk.

"All right again—we only want to see the second act; we saw the other some time ago. What's the price of tickets *now*?"

"The same as a while ago—seventy-five cents."

"What, *now*—and one act over."

"Exactly—one act over."

"But," expostulated Joe, who did all the talking, while Jim stood a little back and chewed tobacco, "we've paid *once before* for seeing this piece, and only staid for the first act."

"Can't help that, my friend," replies the imperturbable ticket-seller; "we have but one price."

"Well, hand out two tickets for up stairs."

The tickets were handed out, the money being first handed *in,* and the two trappers entered the house. In a few minutes the curtain was raised, and the mountaineers finished seeing THE GAMBLER'S FATE, the first act of which they had seen twenty years before in the same city, though not in the same theatre, and with only one person in the cast who had played in it on the previous occasion. In effect, our *voyageurs* witnessed this play with a "real lapse" of twenty years between the acts.

ANNE LUCAS HUNT

ANNE LUCAS HUNT (1796–1879) was born in Pennsylvania to upper-class French émigrés who had come to America believing that the young country held boundless opportunity. In 1805, Thomas Jefferson appointed Anne's father, John Baptiste Charles Lucas, commissioner of land claims and judge of the Louisiana Territorial Court. The Lucases moved to St. Louis, where they quickly established themselves as one of the city's most prominent families.

In 1814, at age eighteen, Anne married Captain Theodore Hunt, a former naval officer who had become a business partner of Manuel Lisa, a leader in St. Louis's lucrative fur trade. Several years later, in 1817, one of the most traumatic events in Anne's life occurred: her brother Charles was killed by Thomas Hart Benton in a duel. After the tragedy, Anne, fearful of meeting Benton on the city streets, moved with her family "out into the country, near Gravois road, and occupied the same house which General Grant now owns"—a site now better known as White Haven.

In 1832, after four years of widowhood, Anne married her late husband's cousin, Wilson P. Hunt, a wealthy St. Louis merchant. Through her parents' vast real estate investments and her own business acumen, Anne compounded the substantial Lucas family fortune, which she managed after her father's and her second husband's death in 1842. At one time, Anne and her brother, James H. Lucas, owned all the land between Market and Olive Streets, west from 12th Street to Jefferson Avenue.

Anne Lucas Hunt became one of St. Louis's earliest and most generous philanthropists. During her lifetime, she gave more than a million dollars to Catholic institutions in and around the city. Near the end of her long and productive life, Anne, who had survived two husbands and five of her eight children, composed a memoir, "Early Recollections," and published it in pamphlet form, "solely for the use of her children and grandchildren." In her narrative, Mrs. Hunt recalls traveling to St. Louis by flatboat at the age of eight and staying at Antoine Soulard's house upon arriving in the city.

The memoir is as charming as it is factual and provides readers with a detailed, firsthand account of life in St. Louis during the city's formative years.

EARLY RECOLLECTIONS

I don't recollect exactly when we reached St. Louis, but it was somewhere in the fore part of September, which would make the entire trip about three months, and that was considered a fast trip in those early days. Such a thing as a hotel or boarding house was of course unknown here; but my father who had been up to St. Louis ahead of us to find out what delayed the keel boat, had requested Mr. [Antoine] Soulard, who resided here, to rent a house for him. When we arrived, Mr. Soulard was absent, but he had left word with a Mr. Mackay to take us to his (Mr. Soulard's) house. We remained at his house until the one which Mr. Soulard had rented for us, from his partner, Mr. [Gabriel] Cerre, was turned over to us, which was in about a week. That house, which was the first we occupied in St. Louis, was on Third Street, about two squares below Market. It was a one-story house, built of logs, vertical, like posts, and had a large room in the center with two or three smaller ones around it. The roof was of shingle, and the shingles were not nailed, but were hung to the rafters with wooden pegs. The chimney was a monstrous affair, and the black walnut mantle piece was so high that none of the children could reach it.

I don't know what the population of St. Louis was then, but it was very small. Most persons had a half square of ground. August Chouteau had a whole square, between Market and Walnut, enclosed with a stone wall. His land faced on La Grande Rue, or Main Street. Second Street was called Rue de L'Eglise, and Third Street, Rue des Granges. Cadet Chouteau's house was some squares higher up than August's. Diagonally opposite August's was Mr. [Bernard] Pratte's place, and above that Mr. [Charles] Gratiot, the father of the late Gen. Charles Gratiot of the army. [Sylvestre] Labadie was the name of one of the old residents, who were nearly all French. Very few of the inhabitants then could speak any English at all.

Wilson P. Hunt (who afterwards became my second husband) had come out from New Jersey and gone into business here before our time, with a man named [John] Hankinson, and I recollect how I and the other children used to admire their gaudily painted sign: "Hunt and Hankinson's New Cash Store." Their store and that of Falconer and Comegys were the only ones that had signs, and we children used to look upon them as great works of art. They were both on Main Street.

Gen. Wilkinson was governor, and lived on Main Street, nearly opposite Cadet Chouteau's. I cannot call to mind the time that the change of flags took place, but I remember my father saying that when it was done, Jefferson and somebody else hugged each other for joy.

We lived in the house on Third Street below Market for a year or two, and then my father bought a house and lot on Second and Cedar. The house had one stone wall on the south, and was built like stockades. My mother died in 1811, and my father then built a house on the corner of what is now Seventh and Market. He had been cultivating ground before that between Seventh and Fourth Streets. Beyond and west of that was his pasture, and right alongside of the pasture he built this house. When we were about to move into it, I remember that people told my father that he was not doing a prudent think in taking me, a fourteen year old girl so far away; that the Indians might carry me off some time when he was down town attending to his business.

My brother Robert, who graduated at West Point in 1806, came to St. Louis about two years after the rest of the family had come. He remained in the army for a short time after graduating, but soon got tired of it and resigned. Subsequently, when the war of 1812 broke out, he received a commission as either captain or major, and served with distinction and credit.

In 1814 I married Captain Theodore Hunt, formerly of the American navy. He resigned in 1811 and came out to Lexington to see a brother of his, and at the same time paid a visit to St. Louis, where he became acquainted with me, proposed and was accepted. He then settled down here, entering into partnership with Manuel Lisa. After our marriage, he bought a place from his partner, on Second Street, where we lived for a good many years. Captain Hunt died in 1832.

My father remained commissioner of land titles as long as the commission existed. On the advice of my mother, who had learned experience from the sale of the Pittsburg lot, he invested his salary in the purchase of land. He bought mostly out lots, facing on what is now Fourth Street, each lot being one arpent wide by forty arpents deep. All this land was used as a common field, each man cultivating what he pleased. There were no fences of any kind on it. By purchasing a lot at a time, he at length came to own all the land from Market Street to St. Charles, and from Fourth Street to Jefferson Avenue. He did not buy it as a speculation, but for what it would produce; it turned out, however, to be an immense speculation, for the whole seven arpents front did not cost him over $700.00, and that property is now worth, I suppose, seventy millions! A hundred dollars was what he usually paid for an arpent in width by forty deep, though sometimes he got it for less. The heirs to this vast estate need not thank my father for it, for he was too much of a politician to think of investing his money in land; it was my mother's fore-sight that suggested the investment which turned out so well. In 1842 my father died, in his eighty-third year in the stone house on the corner of what is now Seventh and Market Streets.

When we first arrived in St. Louis there was only one little church here, and that, of course, was a Catholic one. It was made of wood and stood on Second Street, back of August Chouteau's square—about where the present Cathedral stands.

As I have said, all west of Fourth Street was a common and was called the Common Field. The grass was so high in it that a man riding through it on horse-back could scarcely be seen. There was a pretty fair road from here to St. Charles, but near Cote Brilliante, where the soil is rich, I have seen a team of oxen mired so that they had to be pulled out by horses. That was about where Elleardsville now stands. At Normandy the road branched, one branch going to Florissant and the other to St. Charles. The garrison was then on the Missouri River, four miles above its mouth, at a place called Belle Fontaine. My brother Robert was for a short time in command of it, for I remember his firing off salutes on Fourths of July and other festive occasions. Col. O'Fallon, I recollect, was quite a young man when I was fourteen. After Lewis and Clark's expedition to the Pacific, when they came to St. Louis they were received with great ovation, and took dinner at our house. My mother, I remember, composed a French song in their honor, the first verse of which was:

Le Captaine Louis, pour combler sa glorie
Aux source du Missouri s'en est alle boire,

Du mont ou ce fleuve sort,
Il a pris sa course au nord.

Chorus: Pour faire bonne vie ogue.

The Spanish dollar was the only money here in early days, and in order to make change it was cut into halves, quarters and bits. Some people were so expert at cutting a silver dollar that they could make nine bits out of it without being detected.

The first steamboat that ever came to St. Louis had no paddle-boxes, and the naked wheels looked for all the world like windmills. That was in 1820, when my son Charles was a baby. I took the children for a short excursion on the boat, and although we did not go far, it furnished a topic of discourse for a long time.

It is a great pity that Chouteau's Pond was ever allowed to be drained. It was really a handsome body of water. The "Tumbling Dam," where the water ran over when it got too full, was a very picturesque little waterfall, and the mill creek bridge, which spanned the creek below, was the first ever erected about St. Louis. Many a time have I stood on it and watched the water as it passed underneath; and often have I headed a troop of girls on a fishing expedition to it and beyond. Mr. Chouteau had a very good stone mill at the dam, which he was obliged to keep running for the use of the inhabitants, they giving him the land on which it stood in consideration of the benefits derived from it. Mr. Trudeau also had a mill here, but it was a horse mill. When a child I often used to go to see the horse go around and around, inside the enclosure. Around where the Court House now is, prairie chickens, quails and other game were trapped in abundance. I remember my brother James on one occasion rushing into the house and telling my father that there was a strange animal in one of the traps. They all ran down to see what it was, but very soon came back crestfallen and odoriferous. They had gone too close to the trap and had received a royal salute from a skunk.

We raised most of our wheat on the Commons, but some of it came from Florissant and St. Charles. Fresh meat was hard to get. The man who did the butchering never killed a beef until he had first ascertained who would buy the meat, and as there was no ice put up in those days it had to be eaten pretty quickly in the summer time or it was lost. Of game we always had the greatest plenty.

Up town, about where Gen. [William] Ashley's place was, opposite where Fifth Street runs into Broadway, but down on the river bank, there was a block-house and a fort, built of logs, the upper story being built diagonally with the lower. This was near one of the old Indian mounds, which was turned into part of the fort by being escarped. In the northern part of the city, not far from the river, there was also another fort in the form of a demi-lune.

One of the rarest treats I ever had in my young days was a lot of almonds and raisins, which were given to me by Mr. Wilson P. Hunt, in my ninth year. I married this same Mr. Hunt in 1836, four years after the death of my first husband, whose cousin he was. Mr. Wilson P. Hunt is the gentleman mentioned by Washington Irving in his "Astoria," and was sent by John Jacob Astor on that expedition. It was he who made the trip across the continent, and who contributed most to the success of the undertaking; but, as Mr. Hunt used to say when he read "Astoria," and saw how laudatory it was of Mr. Astor, "It was easy to see who paid the piper." Mr. Astor wanted him to go round the Horn, but he determined to take the land route, and he did so and succeeded, though at one time he was given up as lost. On that expedition he went south of the present Yellowstone Park, down the Snake River to Walla Walla, and down the Columbia River to Astoria.

To show how cheap land was a few years ago, I sold the square between what is now Pine and Olive, and Fifth and Sixth, for $2,000.00, and it was considered a big price. It is worth today, I suppose, four millions. Mr. Von Phul sold half a square, one street farther away, for $1,200.00, and that was looked upon as a first rate sale.

There is one thing that I, perhaps, ought to mention, though the subject is a painful one to me. My brother Charles was killed in a duel by Thomas H. Benton. Benton was an ambitious politician. He had beaten one opponent named David Barton in a political contest, and tried to beat my brother Charles, his other opponent. Something occurred between them which led to a duel. My brother, who was always averse to duelling and who had frequently stated that if he ever was compelled to fight a duel he would not aim at a vital part, struck Benton in the leg. Benton's bullet hit my brother in the jugular vein, and for a long time his life was despaired of. He recovered, however, and soon afterwards he was again challenged by Benton, which led to a second duel in which my brother was killed. I never heard anything of the second duel until the day after it took place. That was in 1817. I was so fearful of meeting Benton after that, that we moved out into the country, near Gravois road, and occupied the same house which General Grant now owns. We sold it early in the spring of 1820 to Mr. Frederick Dent, the father-in-law of General Grant, and in that way it has come into the late President's possession. We then moved to a log cabin which stood on Natural Bridge Plank Road, nine miles north from the Court House, on the site of my present place, the "Shelter." When I first occupied it there was a black jack tree in front of the door, and the place went by the name of The Black Jack, but after awhile we rented it to a man who bored through the black jack tree for the purpose of making a cider press and killed it. Then it was suggested that I should call it "The Lodge," but I never was a great admirer of the Freemasons, so I christened it the "shelter," because I kept it as a shelter in my old age in case I should need it. That and 120 acres are all I have retained out of that particular tract left by my brother Charles.

I have three children living, twenty-one grandchildren and nineteen or twenty great grandchildren, I believe; but they are becoming so numerous that it is almost impossible for me to keep count of them.

JOHN HENTON CARTER

BORN IN MARIETTA, OHIO, John Henton Carter (1832–1910) was a considerable presence in the Mississippi valley in the years following the Civil War. After working as a pastry chef on steamboats (whence his pen name, "Commodore Rollingpin"), Carter moved with his family to St. Louis in 1868, where he began his career as a journalist. Through his work on the *St. Louis Times* and the *St. Louis Post-Dispatch*, he became widely known and acquainted with the city's leading journalists, including Eugene Field and Joseph Pulitzer.

In 1872, Carter added to his popularity as a writer and public speaker by publishing the first edition of *Commodore Rollingpin's Almanac,* an annual of river folklore, humorous sketches, and stories. A reviewer at the time wrote, "It is rich and racy, with a quaint vein of humor, making it interesting from the first to the last page." The *Almanac* soon built a large readership—even Mark Twain refers to it in *Life on the Mississippi*—and provided Carter with the financial security that had eluded him. In 1881, the *Almanac*'s peak year, fifty thousand copies were printed.

Carter left St. Louis for New York in 1883 for a four-year stint as a columnist on the Pulitzer-owned *World*. After returning to St. Louis, he worked as a freelance journalist and writer of poems and stories, and he also published the annual program for the Veiled Prophet Ball.

The following excerpts come from *The Log of Commodore Rollingpin* (1874), the first of Carter's book-length collections of regional wit and wisdom.

FROM *THE LOG OF COMMODORE ROLLINGPIN*

THE BEST MAN IN THE HOUSE

Nearly all Western boatmen used occasionally to go on a spree. They don't do it now, I believe. Their morals, as a class, have greatly improved since a number of us old hands left the river. But the business is not calculated to inspire morality.

After being cooped up on a steamboat for a couple of weeks, and being greatly overworked as well, a fellow feels like having a little fun when he comes into port, and we generally did.

Theatres monopolized the early part of the night. Then we commenced our rounds, and took in the saloons. If we were not on our muscle when we left the boat, we generally got on it by one or two o'clock in the morning, and a fight was pretty sure to result.

On one occasion there were several of us together. We had been running all night, and were about as tight as men can be and keep out of the calaboose. Among the number were Sam Wilks, the boat's barkeeper, and Dick Peebles, a deckhand. Peebles had a grudge against Wilks for refusing him credit on a certain trip at his bar, and had long been watching an opportunity to get even with him.

As time wore on and steam ran higher, Peebles grew more boisterous, and began to boast of his muscular powers in a manner calculated to attract the attention of the neighborhood.

He directed all his conversation to Wilks, whom he seemed determined to draw into a fight, and, to use his own language, "Eat him up without salt." He called him all manner of names; dared him to come outside and fight him like a man, offering him, as a taunt, to tie his right hand behind him, and lick him with his left. But all to no purpose. Wilks wasn't on his muscle. Yet in the wind-work, that was going on, Wilks was fully the equal of his antagonist.

If he wouldn't fight he was not to be bluffed off and was as fertile in resources in successfully sparring off an encounter, as his adversary was in pushing it. In fact, it was known of Wilks, that he was never in his element unless engaged in working up a "muss," which he never failed to turn over to some one else to execute.

But they kept on quarrelling, and Peebles had pushed Wilks back into the corner of the barroom, and was shaking his fist under his nose. Wilks retaliated with words, but wouldn't fight. Peebles was so enraged that he finally slapped Wilks on the face. This touched Wilks' metal. He leaped upon a chair and yelled: "Look here, Sam Peebles, I'm no fighter; I wasn't brought up a fighter; but I don't allow anybody to lick me. You've been blowing around here about licking me for the last three hours; you can't lick nothing; there's a man in this house can eat you up in a minute."

"I am the best man in the house," shouted Peebles, as he staggered up against the counter.

"No you aint," said Wilks; "Rollingpin is the best man in the house. Old Roller's no slouch, as sly as it's kept. If you could only get him started he'd lick anybody. Just feel that muscle" (taking hold of my arm); "and as for that fist, a man had better be kicked by a mule than have that thrown at him."

I had paid little attention to the matter up to this time, further than responding to all invitations to walk up and drink; but I now began to feel terribly strong.

I took handsomely, and Wilks found himself relieved of all further responsibility, and at once became an innocent spectator. I felt the weight of my responsibility, and was determined to acquit myself with honor. I was bound to get away with my man.

I commenced to shed my linen, but two of the boys came up and pushed my coat back onto my shoulders. I next picked up a chair, and threw it across the house with great violence. I looked over in the other corner of the room, and saw Peebles with nothing on but his pants. He was ready for me.

Two of the boys got between us, and moved that, if we must fight, we adjourn to a lumber yard, and fight it out like men. We all took another drink, and started for the scene of the battle. It was now broad daylight, and we went staggering along the street. We passed many boisterous remarks, but no saloons. We took them all in. It was a tedious job, yet we worried through with it.

At about ten o'clock we arrived at the scene of the conflict, and began preparing for the mill. It took seven men to hold us—not from going together, but from going to the ground. We were tired, and wanted to rest.

I have often thought, since that, that would have been one of the hardest-slept fights on record, if we had been permitted to have followed our inclinations. We would have slept it out on that line, if it had taken till the next morning. But the seconds declared everything in readiness, and ordered us to square off and face each other. We did the best we could, and, after sparring a moment, drew nearer, with a determination to force the fighting. I made a few feints, then fell back out of Peebles' reach.

It was a fine move, and well executed, for my seconds found, on bringing me again to the scratch, that I had torn the ground up for about forty feet. Peebles had showed equally good science, for, in his eagerness to escape my great weight,—for I was about to fall over him,—run his head under a pile of lumber.

Finally they got him out, and brought him again to the scratch. We sparred a moment, and then made a lunge for each other (it was accidental, however), and missed. It was the last round. The mill ended. We were both terribly punished.

I have a distinct recollection of rolling down a descent some two hundred feet, and I understand Pebbles canvassed the other side of the same precipice. It was a hard-contested fight, and we were both satisfied to let the matter drop. In settling my little difficulties, however, since that time, I am always particular to ascertain how the ground lies. I prefer to begin at the base and fight up hill. It's slower work, but then it is far more safe.

THE TURKISH BATH

I was walking down the street the other day, when I met Simpson, and he said:

"Come on Rollingpin, let's go and have a Turkish bath, and I'll pay for two."

Said I, "All right, old chum, I never refuse those kind of offers; but I've never taken one."

Said he, "Neither have I; but I want company, so come along."

In a few moments we entered the bath-house. The first thing we did was to register and deposit our valuables and take checks for them. Simpson then handed the man behind the counter a ten-dol-bill, and asked for tickets.

"How many will you have?" said he.

"Give me the worth of that money of them. I want to take these baths regular," replied Simpson.

We were then led into the rear of the building and shown into small stalls, and requested to disrobe. In the meantime we carried on a conversation something after this fashion:

"Hello, Simpson, where are you?"

"Here I am."

"How do you like it?"

"Bully."

"I think it's a good thing; don't you?"

"You bet."

"Cures any disease in the world."

"I should say so."

"Are you ready, gentlemen?" said the attendant, a saddle-colored man, dressed in the style of a Turk.

"All ready," we both answered.

"Then wind the red garment (imported from Turkey) around your loins, and step this way."

We obeyed, and were led into a small room, which resembled a bake oven, in which was placed a row of chairs much the same as are used in barber shops, and upon which we were directed to take our positions. The attendant then wet two large sponges in cold water, and, placing one of them on each of our foreheads, told us to make ourselves comfortable. As he passed out he looked at the thermometer and said it was rather low, only 200 above zero, and he would have to fire it up a little.

We told him to fire away, and give it to us red hot; we wanted the worth of our money.

The attendant said we would have to stay in there half an hour, so we thought we'd pass the time away in discussing the sensation. By this time we were both outsweating a bound boy at a husking, and the water in the sponges on our foreheads had become so hot that the steam was rising off them, until we looked like two high-pressure steamboats blowing off.

"How does she go, Rollingpin?" said Simpson.

"Rich," I answered; "never felt anything like it."

"I wonder who invented this?" said Simpson; "he must have been a smart man—some Turk, I reckon."

"I should say so. No American would ever have thought of it," said I.

"A splendid thing for the women," said Simpson; "cures all kinds of ailments; let's get our wives to try it."

"All right," I replied.

Here the attendant stuck his head in the room and yelled, "Time up, gents; step this way to the scouring ward."

"Aye, aye!" we both answered.

As we stepped on to the floor we found it covered with boiling water six inches deep. The attendant said that was perspiration, and asked us if we felt lighter. We told him that we thought we did, but not until we had lit out of there, for the hot water scalded all our toe nails off. Another attendant was now introduced, and they laid us on two marble slabs and proceeded to scour us. This they called the second course. They rubbed on soap until the lather covered us entirely from view, and we resembled two great bunches of sea foam that had been left by the ebbing tide on the beach. During this process conversation was not in order, all our time being taken up in catching our breath, giggling from being tickled when their hands would come in contact with the soles of our feet and our bodies under our arms. Presently they told us to stand up and take the shower-bath. This they gave us from a boiling-down to an ice-cold temperature, using great precaution all the while to squirt it in our faces, so that we could put in the time in catching our breath and enjoying the thing generally.

After getting us thoroughly rinsed, which must have taken about half the water in the reservoir, they rubbed us down with currycombs, and said we were ready for the plunge.

Simpson said he wouldn't take any plunge in his, and I thought I would follow suit; so we passed the plunge and went into the dry room where, after being mopped off, we were wrapped in sheets and placed in chairs to dry. Here we held another conversation, as follows:

"How do you feel, Rollingpin?"

"Never better, though a little weak."

"A big thing, ain't it?"

"You heard me."

Presently Simpson remarked that we had better dress and go, as the street cars would soon stop running for the night. So we put on our clothes, and were soon ushered into the street. I felt about two ounces lighter than a straw hat, and Simpson remarked that that was about his sensation.

We parted and went home, and went to bed, and I was soon fast asleep. The next day I sent word to the office that I wouldn't be down; and requested the editor to procure some one get up my reports, adding, by way of explanation, "that I was enjoying a Turkish bath, and couldn't tear myself away from its influences."

About a week after I managed, with the assistance of a cane, to reach the office, and reported for duty. Several days later I met Simpson, who was just making his first appearance in the street. His clothes were all too large for him, and hung around his emaciated form in great folds and wrinkles. He resembled a collapsed balloon and seemed to be in search of some one to blow him up to his maximum proportions. I asked him what he thought of the "Turkish" by this time. He put his hand in his pocket and slowly drew forth his pocket-book, and opening it, took out the eight remaining tickets, while his voice betrayed the weak condition of his system, and said:

"I have no enemies that I would wish to afflict with these; perhaps you have; take them, they may prove useful."

"No, I thank you," I replied, "no more 'Turkish' in mine."

ERNST VON HESSE-WARTEGG

OF AUSTRO-GERMAN ARISTOCRACY, Baron Ernst von Hesse-Wartegg (1854–1918) was one of the most ambitious travel writers of the late nineteenth century. In his day, the *New York Times* called Hesse-Wartegg a "traveler of the stamp of Dickens and Mrs. Trollope." Although he had considerable personal wealth to finance his adventures, Hesse-Wartegg supplemented his travel allowance by writing for money and produced more than forty readable and popular travel books and countless articles. Among Hesse-Wartegg's readers was Mark Twain, who quoted from *Mississippi-Fahrten* (1881), the first extensive study of the lower Mississippi, in *Life on the Mississippi,* which appeared a few years later.

According to Hesse-Wartegg's translator, Frederic Trautmann, "During that crucial time between Reconstruction and the rise of the New South, [Hesse-Wartegg] followed the Mississippi from St. Louis to the Gulf and witnessed the agonized transformation of the region." As was common among the upper class, Hesse-Wartegg held paternalistic pro-Confederate sentiments, which some of his writings reflect, and idealized the gentility of antebellum plantation life. In the following excerpt from *Travels on the Lower Mississippi, 1879–1880*, Hesse-Wartegg describes arriving in St. Louis by train and offers his initial impressions of the city, which he calls the "London of the American West."

FROM *TRAVELS ON THE LOWER MISSISSIPPI, 1879–1880*

Day after day we speed from New York straightaway west. Winter submerges the lush gorgeous green of summer's prairie. Deep, steadfast snow levels everything. A million and a half square miles, enough for a nation, yet nothing but snow and ice. We race through a landscape ever the same, blanketed every inch by snow, blinding snow, and its crust of ice. Again and again we stall, stuck in a soft mountain of winter's mire.

Our locomotive frees itself after hours of struggle. Sometimes the sun shines. It beams on thousands and thousands of miles of snow around us. It shimmers and glitters and blinds us hour after hour. Then we again negotiate dense clouds of snow that dim our day to twilight. The moon rises. Its pale light transfigures the night. In roomy Pullman beds we cannot sleep for noonday radiance.

The next day plays yesterday's scenes over again. The hollows are filled, the slopes leveled, the forests covered—as if somebody had spread a great white cloth. Only the cities provide the relief of remote oases in the desert of snow. We pass them with a rush.

Speeding through New York, New Jersey, Pennsylvania, Ohio, Indiana, and Illinois, each in its turn, our express brings us to the Mississippi at last. We cross the "Father of Waters" on a huge, majestic bridge for trains to the capital of the Mississippi valley, St. Louis. The river at our feet does not resemble an ice-covered body of water, but an elongated puddle of frozen mud—an expanse black in some places, dirty-yellow and gray in others, opaque, like dry and frozen land.

In February the metropolis of a million square miles of valley hereabouts has languished under weeks of siege by river ice. The great steamboats of the Anchor and Kountz lines lie at their wharves idle, captains and pilots hibernating. As long as ice grips the Mississippi, the commerce of St. Louis seems to stagnate. The sources might as well fail, the river dry up, and the city of a half-million have its Mississippi no more. The river town, the port city, becomes an inland village, landlocked, communicating with the rest of the world by railway alone.

This year the condition persisted until the beginning of February, when finally the long-desired dispatch from the hinterlands reported break-up. "*The ice-gorge begins to move*" raced along the telegraph lines beside the river, clacking in every station, rousing functionary and river dweller from winter's sleep, warning them to get ready—mobilize! At the waterfront they tie steamboats one to another and the shore with stout chains, irons as thick as the body of a man. Ferries, "*tugs*," and "*towboats*," once frozen somewhere in the river, are moved through the ice and nearer shore. The world awaits the icebergs from the North. During the night the lid blows. Ice no longer covers the river. A rise of muddy, coffee-colored water drifts south. Then we see a parapet of ice blocking the river above the bridge. It creeps closer. Thunder in the approaching mass strikes the ear like the boom of cannon.

Fathom-thick slabs heave and subside, bunch up and dive apart, grind against each other like millstones, and crash and screech. Between steep, high banks the assault advances like a powerful, compact, angry mob. Huge, shifting, convulsive phalanxes reach the St. Louis bridge, rear against the massive stone piles, reshuffle themselves, and pass peaceably beneath the arches.

However colossal the icebergs, they do no harm. Old, rotten with age, they have been on the water since Christmas; they have warmed and been honeycombed and weakened. They do not hurt the steamboats but crumble against the smooth solid hulls. So they clear the harbor here, these old men of ice, and pass Carondelet, and float south in warmer water on an open river. Waves play with them, lap at them, submerge them, and bang them along rocky shores. Such sport diminishes the slabs. They shrink and keep shrinking until—where the first magnolias and oranges greet the river—the mute, resolute, stubborn, dirty-yellow Northside Gang has broken up, melted, and disappeared.

The Mississippi is open. Shipping on the West's main artery begins. Tiny vignettes of steamboats reappear at the head of announcement columns in the big dailies: steamboat X, Y, or Z will depart on such and such a day to Cairo and Cincinnati, to Memphis, Vicksburg and New Orleans—north and south, or east and west—round trips of hundreds of miles. Has color dimmed and verve diminished on the river and in the harbor at this big city since the proud, majestic bridge has been built? The European sees a scene nonetheless new to him, exotic, magnetic: dozens of palatial steamboats painted brilliant white, little tugs, clumsy ferries of a peculiar design. On the other side of the river, grain elevators rise eight to ten stories where dirty black "*wharfboats*" tie up along shores roughly paved in stone; miles of giant warehouses, grim of outline, edge the perimeter of the broad quay opposite. Altogether a singular riverscape with thousands of figures: laborers, freight wagons, spectators, and tourists.

When we look from the cathedral's tall spire, out over urban expanses, a fact strikes us as incredible. Wall after coal-smoke-blackened wall, chimneys beyond number, countless steeples—a sea of buildings, and the fathers of today's residents are supposed to have built them all! This city, one of America's oldest, continued to suffer long after the French founded it. A state of war persisted for years between the Osage Indians and the settlers. A settler could not venture very far outside the city without doing battle.

The savage hordes precluded agriculture. The shortage of grain and other food prompted the French to name their settlement "*Pain Court.*" Accordingly, the city counted barely 1,000 citizens as late as 1788. When it passed to the United States in 1804, the population, largely French, numbered 1,500. Today, scarcely two generations later, 400,000 inhabit the largest, richest, most industrialized city in the million square miles of the Mississippi valley!

The city extends at least twelve miles along heights bounded by the Missouri, the Mississippi, and the Meramec. Many parks and gardens relieve [the expanses of urban architecture]. Thirty railways terminate in grand stations. The port of St. Louis covers more than a mile and a half of waterfront, home to steamboats that traverse a continent on thousands of miles of rivers. The old French city stood where today's business district comprises big hotels, splendid churches, and mammoth buildings of four and six stories. Little remains of the French element. A German presence of at least 150,000 has replaced it. To an extent corresponding to their numbers, they wield influence in commerce, industry, and finance. Probably Germans in no other American city cut the figure they cut here. The St. Louis German is aspiring and robust. His irrepressible conviviality, active societies, thriving clubs, cultivation of art and music, and diligent, able press are to be remarked even by comparison to the Anglo-American life that surrounds his.

Yet St. Louis cannot be called beautiful. Of all cities in my experience, it most resembles London. I mean in situation and appearance, but in other respects too I could not better describe St. Louis than as the London of the American West. Commerce and industry in St. Louis have swelled to incredible size. No fewer than 40,000 passenger trains and 3,000 steamboats arrive each year. Produce of western prairie and output of southern plantation pour in, mounting to some 100 million hundredweights. Bituminous coal comes to about a fifth of it. Every year perhaps thirty million bushels of grain pass through the riverfront elevators, and out of it the mills grind about one and a half million barrels of flour. St. Louis, [as an international port of entry] like Chicago, Memphis, and New Orleans, has authority to collect duties on foreign imports and annually collects two or three million dollars' worth of tariffs. The stockyards get 300,000 to 400,000 cattle a year and a million hogs. Cotton arrives loose and departs for New York in 80,000 to 100,000 bales. Other regions send equal amounts [of their products]. Lumber, having come on rafts from Wisconsin and the rivers of the upper

Mississippi valley, piles up in hundreds of millions of board feet.

St. Louis, not only the commercial but also the industrial hub of this great valley, will become ever more industrialized. Ores occur nearby in unbelievable quantities. Neighboring Illinois and Indiana can match them with soft coal. St. Louis, now spending about $10 million to produce iron and steel, will spend ten times as much in a few years. The increase will not seem fabulous. The future of St. Louis and Missouri can be read in the fact that, despite the interruptions of war, the city nearly quadrupled its industrial output, from $27 million in 1860 to $100 million in 1870. In 1870, St. Louis produced 54,000 tons of iron. Three years later the suburb of Carondelet alone produced three times as much!

Thus the immense new wealth of the people of St. Louis. It shows in homes on the heights outside the city and in public buildings and parks. Horsecars criss-cross the city; they speed us from the grimy smoke-blackened commercial district to fashionable residential ones. There the splendor and elegance of homes—and especially their number—astound us. Street after street of them, on and on, far into the countryside. Along the routes to them, entertainment establishments crowd one another. Theaters. German clubhouses. Beer gardens.

St. Louis also has its seamy side, unfortunately the first the visitor sees. On the street or two along the river, filth flourishes and squalor prevails. Dilapidated buildings provide an apt setting for carousal that runs rampant there. St. Louis is not only the continent's foremost inland port, but also the city nearest the prairies, the Colorado mining districts, and the plains and steppes of New Mexico and Texas. At one time or another, all their riffraff visit St. Louis to spend their hard-earned money, to amuse themselves as they will be amused, and then to resume the rugged life of the frontier. In St. Louis they—together with Mississippi fishermen, mulattoes, sailors and local highwaymen—enjoy a district all their own, of infamous hotels and notorious casinos, saloons and dance halls, and houses of the lowest sort. Between Washington Avenue and Elm Street the situation gets downright horrid unless the police put a stop to dissipation. The fiend of gambling holds sway day and night. Three games of chance of the worst repute—faro, keno, poker—flourished during the slavocracy and retain their luster here and now. Fittingly, many miners, buffalo hunters, adventurers, and river pirates thus spend their time. Leading the exciting and eventful lives of vagabonds, they have long since lost touch with the better elements of the human race.

Time was, the burghers of a city easily got rid of such a district. They set it afire at the corners and burned it and its contents to the ground. Today such absolute methods are passé—unfortunately!

HENRY SHAW

BORN IN SHEFFIELD, ENGLAND, Henry Shaw (1800–1889) traveled to North America with his father, Joseph, in 1818, to elude the elder Shaw's creditors and establish a wholesale cutlery business. The Shaws landed in Quebec, where Joseph remained. Henry journeyed on to New Orleans, where he found business prospects dim. In the summer of 1819, he arrived in St. Louis aboard the *Maid of New Orleans* and began his enterprise. Due to the great demand for his wares and Henry's perfectionist and workaholic nature, the business soon flourished.

Within a few years, Henry was able not only to support his parents and sisters, who had settled in Rochester, New York, but also to expand his entrepreneurial activities to include exporting cotton and tobacco, selling lead and furs, and trading with the Indians and the U.S. Army. Henry wisely invested his profits in real estate. By the late 1830s, he owned a considerable amount of land downtown and southwest of the city limits.

By age forty, Henry Shaw was wealthy enough to retire, and he spent the next decade traveling extensively. Meanwhile, he had two homes built—a country villa, Tower Grove, located several miles from the edge of the city, and a townhouse at Seventh and Locust Streets—both of which were designed by renowned architect George I. Barnett. In 1851, after his visit to the Crystal Palace exhibition in London and the Royal Botanic Gardens at Kew, Shaw returned to St. Louis and resolved to develop a magnificent botanical garden on the property surrounding his country villa.

Sparing no personal expense, Shaw dedicated the next thirty years of his life and entrusted the world's leading botanists and landscapers to realizing his vision. By 1859, the Missouri Botanical Garden was regarded by *The Magazine of Horticulture* as "one of the most magnificent projects in this or any other country, to wit: the establishment and endowment, by private individual munificence, of a Public Garden on a broad and liberal plan. . . ."

Although an Englishman by birth and aesthetics, Shaw was thoroughly American in his work ethic and sense of civic responsibility. Not only did he open his beloved garden to the public, but also he gave 280 acres adjacent to the garden to the city for the development of Tower Grove Park. When he died at age eighty-nine, Shaw had one of the most elaborate funerals

St. Louis had ever seen. His body was interred in the elaborate mausoleum at the center of the Missouri Botanical Garden, still affectionately referred to by contemporary St. Louisans as "Shaw's Garden."

The following excerpt is from one of the first guides to the Missouri Botanical Garden, written by Henry Shaw. The original document, in Shaw's magnificent handwriting, is housed in the garden's archives. In his guide, Shaw presents the garden's intended mission, a brief history of the garden's development, and rules of conduct for visitors.

FROM *A GUIDE TO THE MISSOURI BOTANICAL GARDEN, ST. LOUIS*

Of all public resorts a scientific garden when properly kept, will be found to be, not only one of the most delightful mediums for intellectual gratification and amusement, but, also one of the greatest of temporal blessings that can be enjoyed by a people.

To all classes of society, the old and the young, the infirm invalid, or the robust and the vigorous, the rich and the poor, a garden may be considered, almost alike an object of interest, of instruction, and amusement. It is a field which abounds with objects, that generally make lasting impressions on the mind; and happily there are but few, who, however unacquainted with the principles of botanical science, are not more or less filled with admiration at the endless variety of form, presented by any considerable assemblage of the vegetable kingdom; their grotesque trunks, and tapering stems; their leaves so varied in shape, and so beautiful in structure; their flowers, so curious in their parts, so diversified in colour, and often so exquisitely fragrant; but above all, how admirably adapted is each, in one way or another, for the use and gratification of man.

A Guide that should indicate to strangers the more remarkable features of the Missouri Botanical Gardens of St. Louis, and point out the many interesting plants cultivated there, has long been a desideratum. The very fact of the continual additions to the plants, and their rapid growth, renders it difficult to give a perfect Guide or Handbook, for only reference to the more remarkable objects can be desired; the constantly increasing bulk of the plants, and fresh arrivals of novelties, causes such a guide to become in a measure imperfect soon after its publication. In summer from May to September, most of the plants are placed in the open air; thus individuals that are recorded as occupying any particular plant house, may require shifting the very next day. It must also be obvious to every intelligent observer, that in a comparative limited collection, requiring artificial protection, not botanical arrangement, or class divisions can be expected; in cultivation, the required temperature has to be attended to, any neglect of which would be speedy destruction to tropical plants.

This Guide is historical and descriptive, rather than botanical, a science to which the writer has but small pretensions, and tho' little qualified, knew no other person competent and willing to undertake the task; so it is nothing more in fact, than a compilation of information gathered from various sources. The beauty of these grounds, and the plants they contain, combined with the free admission of the public, attracts, as may be supposed, at certain seasons, a great crowd of visitors, and a few needful regulations here given, are mainly taken from the Guides of the Kew Gardens.

1. Smoking, or eating & drinking or the carrying of provisions of any kind into the Gardens, is strictly forbidden. No dogs can be admitted.

2. No packages or parcels, bags or baskets are allowed to be carried into the grounds. All such must be deposited at the Gate of Entrance, while the owners make the tour of the Gardens.

3. No person attired otherwise than respectably can enter, nor children too young to take care of themselves, unless a parent or suitable person be with them—the police (when there) have orders to remove such, or also persons guilty of any kind of impropriety, and when large schools are admitted they to be accompanied by a requisite number of tutors & in accordance with the rules of the Garden.

4. It is by no means forbidden to walk upon the grass walks; still it is requested that preference be given to the gravel paths & especially that the lawn edges paralel to the walks, be not made a foot way, as nothing renders them more unsightly. It is scarcely needfull to say that all play, leaping over

beds, running on the grass & slopes are prohibited. The Gardens are intended for agreeable recreation and instruction, not for idle sports.

5. It is requested that visitors will refrain from touching the plants, and flowers; a contrary practice can only lead to suspicion, perhaps unfounded, that their object is to abstract a plant or flower, which when detected must be followed by expulsion.

6. In entering the plant houses it is particularly requested that visitors will keep to the right, if they do otherwise they will pass each other which the narrowness of the walks renders difficult, and this must occasion inconvenience to all parties, and often injury to the plants.

BRIEF HISTORIC NOTICE

The public being freely admitted to the Gardens, under a few needful regulations, must naturally want to know something, about improvements, and the intentions of the projector in making these collections of plants & plantations, of trees & shrubs. It is with a view to satisfy such laudable curiosity, and to increase the interest with which the Gardens are visited that this Guide is now compiled.

About the middle of the last century the spot that now forms the Botanical Garden at Tower Grove, was a fertile rolling prairie, & from its productiveness was early selected for cultivation by the inhabitants of the village of St. Louis—it was separated from the Commons by a fence running along what is now call'd Grand Avenue—and concessions or donations of land made by the Spanish Military Commanders to such beads of families as required them, of one or more arpents in width by forty deep running west—& so cultivated in Maize & Wheat, but more frequently left in Natural Grass, to cut for hay—the fence was kept up against animals feeding on Commons, until about 1780. A Gate was kept, near where the East Gate of Tower Grove Park now stands, on Grand Ave., by a concessioner, call'd Louis Denoyer who lived there until the year of the attack by Indians 1780, the place being call'd Barrière à Denoyer, the concessions of land being so designated, as recorded in the old Livre terrien or Land Book.

About the year 1830 Thos Jefferson Payne, becoming the owner of some of the 40 arpent lots, enclosed a portion of the west end & erected a small house in 1840 which Henry Shaw came into possession by purchase & by perfecting the title to the acquisitions of Payne & further purchases from the old French claimants—Payne had built stables for the keeping of blooded horses, and laid off a race tract, the centre of which was the grove, near which in 1849 Shaw (the writer) erected his house, with a tower & called it Tower Grove and from that date to the present time, he has been assiduously occupied in laying off avenues & planting trees. During his travel in Europe from 1840-1850, observing the great attention paid to public Parks & Gardens in England, France & Germany & the high esteem in which these institutions are held by the people of those countries, he conceived the idea of founding a Missouri Botanical Garden—for which, the grounds, ample in extent, & in close vicinity to the future great city of the west were so appropriate, & the quality of the soil being all that could be desired. The plan of the Garden was determined on, drains constructed, & the walls surrounding the same commenced in 1855—a number of Bohemian cultivators were engaged & the soil of the Garden & Fruticetum (16 acres) trenched or turned over two feet deep—the substantial enclosures & entrances being finished, the Museum and Library was built in 1860, the books and herbarium for which were selected by our learned citizen Doct. Geo. Engelmann during his visit to Europe about that time. In 1870 the plants requiring more room than the original houses afforded, the Palm house was erected in a more central part of the Garden, which with the additional wings for mist stove & temperate houses affords accommodation to the accumulative treasures of the vegetable kingdom, for which still further space being required a larger house with double walls & glass was constructed in 1882 and dedicated to Linnaeus by placing his bust on the entrance. That interesting division the Arboretum, was commenced in 1860 & planted from that time to the present—it contains a collection of all such trees as will grow in the open air in the climate of St. Louis—persevering attention has been paid to the pinetum where will be found growing specimen of the Coniferae. The Quercetum includes such Oaks as have been found hardy—when the importance of timber trees is considered and the length of time required for the full growth of the most usefull & desirable kinds these specimens will be most interesting to future planters of timber trees. Medicine, commerce, agriculture, horticulture, & many valuable branches of manufacture, will derive much benefit from the establishment & maintenance of a Botanical Garden at St. Louis—the climate being intermediate more species of plants can be cultivated than either north or south of this latitude—The Garden in its three divisions (comprising from 50 to 60 acres) from the first has been open to the public for daily admittance not only the grounds, but the plant houses, & museum are open to visitors, the number of whom during the past twenty years had been near a million.

LOGAN URIAH REAVIS

L. U. REAVIS (1831–1889) migrated to St. Louis from his native Illinois in 1866. A sometime teacher and newspaperman, Reavis continued his publishing career with *The Daily Press* in his adopted city. When that enterprise failed, he devoted much of his writing and publishing energy to a boosterism campaign designed to move the national capital to the heart of the country—St. Louis.

An outspoken individual with an eccentric manner of dress, Reavis was a colorful figure who cultivated as many detractors as supporters. Late in his life, Reavis married Rebecca Morrow, a much younger poetess who extolled her husband's controversial views in some of her verse.

Reavis's publication *St. Louis, the Future Great City of the World* appeared in a variety of versions, printed, translated, and revised repeatedly in the 1870s and 1880s. In this selection from the 1881 printing, Reavis outlines his argument for the city's destined greatness in the broadest geo-historical terms, romanticizing his subject in the fashion favored by the promoters of the day. But Reavis went one better than his competitors in both the grandiosity of his claims and the flamboyance of his style. Not content with words alone, he also helped organize an 1869 Mercantile Library meeting of delegates from central and midwestern states who planned to lobby Congress to relocate the national capital.

FROM *ST. LOUIS THE FUTURE GREAT CITY OF THE WORLD*

The following six general principles, two of which have ever been all-controlling in the production of great cities, are presented as an impregnable basis on which to found an incontestable argument by which to demonstrate the location of the great city of the future. The third is substantially new and local to America, and must exercise a controlling influence on that continent:

I. It is assumed to be a general truth, founded in nature, that the highest civilization, the greatest concentration of wealth and the growth of the greatest cities, have been attained within an isothermal belt or zodiac of equal temperature, which encircles the earth in the north temperate zone.

II. That all the great cities of the world have grown up near to the line of unobstructed navigation in mid-winter.

III. That human power is developed to its fullest capacity where the productive power of a continent is greatest.

IV. That nearly all the great cities of the world have been built upon rivers.

V. That the arts and sciences do more to increase population and promote the growth of cities in the interior of a country, than upon the seaboards or coast lands.

VI. That to modern civilization, domestic transportation by water and by rail is more valuable to nations of great territorial extent, than ocean navigation.

Assuming that the six fundamental principles just laid down are true, and that by a proper understanding of them it is possible to determine when and where the future great city of the world is destined to grow up on the earth, I shall now make the bold declaration that the great city of the future is to grow up in North America, and that St. Louis is to be that city! The elaboration of our first fundamental proposition demonstrates, beyond question that the center of human power, moving westward in the zodiac of empire, must cross the Atlantic Ocean and make a lodgment in North America, and that where the center of human power is fixed the great city must grow up; there must the center of the commercial, industrial, intellectual, moral and political power of the world's people be.

It must grow up near the axis of that great belt of empire, near the unobstructed line of water navigation in mid-winter; on the great river where climates cannot rudely interpose obstacles to commerce and navigation. This being true, it is a fact of no little importance, that the very axis of the zone of empire—the center of equilibrium between the excess of heat and cold—the January isothermal line of forty-one degrees—passes nearer to the city of St. Louis than to any other considerable city on the continent of America! Close to that same isothermal line lie London, Paris, Rome, Constantinople and Pekin; north of it lie New York, Philadelphia and Chicago, and south of it lies San Francisco. Thus favored in climate, and situated in the very center of that belt of intellectual activity beyond which neither great man nor great city has yet appeared, St. Louis may with reason be expected to attain the highest rank, if other conditions favor.

That St. Louis is not only situated near the axis of the belt of empire, but also near the line of unobstructed navigation in winter, being, in addition, supremely favored as will be shown by the other fundamental principles laid down as the basis of this discussion, is a fact beyond all doubt; and now it only remains to support those principles by local and general facts, to establish the position and certainty of the future great city. Rising from principles to essential necessities for the maintenance of human life, we find that the growth of a city is analogous to the growth of a human being; and that there are certain prime necessities for the maintenance of human life, the abundance of which stimulates health and the rapid increase of population, and consequently stimulates the growth of great cities in proportion to the cheapness and abundance of the supply. The prime necessities are, food, clothing and shelter.

There can be no civilized life without all of these; and as they are the products of labor and skill, where they call be produced cheapest and in the greatest abundance, and used to the greatest advantage, and most extensively, will almost certainly be the place where the center of population will be fixed on this continent, and where the great city will grow up—where our problem will be solved. Added to these prime necessities of man's healthful and civilized growth, should be ample facilities for the intercommunion of the people, one with another, and for the ready exchange of commodities forming foreign and domestic commerce. These may be enumerated as good roads, railways, and navigable waters, with attendant cheap freights.

That St. Louis occupies a geographical position, central to the productive energies of the continent, there can be no question of doubt. In fact no city on the globe is so well favored with the resources necessary, to produce food and the materials out of which clothing and houses are made.

To establish the truth of this statement, we have only to examine, in a cursory manner, the facts—their continental importance, as Providence has bounteously provided them on every hand, throughout the length and breadth of the great valley of the Mississippi. Let us consider them briefly.

Leaving the Atlantic seaboard, and coming west of the Appalachian chain of mountains, we at once enter the domain of the Mississippi Valley, which comprises an area of 2,455,000 square miles, and extends through thirty degrees of longitude and twenty-three degrees of latitude.

The Mississippi Valley embraces, within its vast extent, a variety of climates, an area of rich soil, an extent of river navigation, a supply of mineral wealth, and a configuration of surface, equaled nowhere else on this globe.

Neither Asia, Africa, Europe, nor South America, can boast of a valley so vast in extent, and so bountifully supplied with natural wealth and natural advantages, essential to the industrial and commercial use and progress of man.

To satisfy the reader of the truth of these statements, a few general facts are submitted:

RIVERS OF ASIA

YANGTSEY—Length, 3,200 miles; navigable, 900 to 1,500 miles; area drained, 740,000 square miles.

OBI—Length, 2,530 miles; navigable, 900 miles; area drained, 1,357,000 square miles.

RIVERS OF AFRICA

NILE—Length, 3,600 miles; navigable, unknown; area drained, 520,000 square miles.

NIGER—Length, 2,500 miles; navigable, 700; area drained, unknown.

RIVERS OF EUROPE

VOLGA—Length, 2,150 miles; navigable, 1,800 miles; area drained, 400,000 square miles.

DANUBE—Length, 1,700 miles; navigable, 1,500 miles; area drained, 250,000 square miles.

RIVERS OF SOUTH AMERICA

AMAZON—Length, 4,000 miles; navigable, 3,662 miles; area drained, 2,000,000 square miles.
LA PLATA—Length, 2,550 miles; navigable, 1,250 miles; area drained, 1,250,000 square miles.

RIVERS OF NORTH AMERICA

MISSISSIPPI—Length, 2,616 miles; navigable, 2,200 miles; area drained, 2,455,115 square miles.
MISSOURI—Length, 2,908 miles; navigable, 2,000 miles; area drained, 518,000 square miles.

The above statement of the length, navigable depth and area drained by the ten longest rivers in the world, settles the question of superiority in favor of the great river of North America—the Mississippi—and decides the question of the greatest area of the great basins.

Although geographical science long since established the fact that the Amazon was the king of rivers, modern and minute investigation has proven the basin of the Mississippi, as the above figures show, to surpass in extent any other formation of the kind on the globe. It is true Humboldt estimated the area drained by the Amazon to be 2,800,000 square miles, but it is well known that Humboldt did not make a survey of the Valley of the Amazon, and more recent authorities place the number of square miles waking the area of its basin below that of the Mississippi basin. Not only do the facts demonstrate the Mississippi basin to be larger than that of the Amazon, but the configuration of the two parts of the Western Hemisphere is quite different; that of North America presenting three vast interior plains, comprising more than one-half of its populable area; that of South America presenting a configuration far more mountainous, and devoid of great plains similar to those forming the great basin of the Mississippi.

In the Mississippi Valley which is still new in its development, there are already many large and flourishing cities, each expecting, in the future, to be greater than any one of the others. First among these stand Chicago, Cincinnati, St. Louis, and New Orleans—four cities destined, at no distant day, to surpass in wealth and population the four cities of the Atlantic seaboard—Boston, New York, Philadelphia, and Baltimore. Assuming, then, that the future great city is to be in the Mississippi Valley, we are to ascertain which of the four cities it is to be, or whether some new and more prosperous rival will present itself for that great achievement. As the great city is to be in the future, we must view it as the growth of the well-developed resources of our country; and all things being considered, it is but just to say that, inasmuch as it will be an organism of human power, it will grow up in or near the center of the productive power of the continent. That Chicago, Cincinnati, St. Louis, and New Orleans have each many natural advantages, there can be no question. There is, however, this difference: the area of surrounding country, capable of ministering to the wants of the people and supplying the trade of a city, is broken, in the case of New Orleans, by the Gulf of Mexico, Lake Pontchartrain and by regions of swamps. In the case of Chicago, it is diminished one-third by Lake Michigan; while Cincinnati and St. Louis both have around them unbroken and uninterrupted areas of rich and productive lands, each capable of sustaining a large population. But if it be asked to which of these cities belong the greatest advantages, must we not answer, it is the one nearest the center of the productive power of the continent, and especially to the natural wealth of the Valley of the Mississippi. Most certainly, for there will grow up the human power. And is not this center St. Louis? We have only to appeal to facts to establish the superior natural advantages of St. Louis over any other city on the continent.

To add strength and conclusiveness to the above facts and deductions, do our readers ask for examples? They are at hand. The first city of which we have any record is Nineveh, situated on the Tigris, not less than seven hundred miles front its mouth. Babylon, built not long after, was also situated far in the interior, on the river Euphrates. Most of the great cities of antiquity, some of which were of immense extent, were situated in the interior, and chiefly in the valleys of large rivers meandering through rich alluvial territories. Such were Thebes, Memphis, Ptolemais and Rome.

But when we consider that our position in vindication of the superior growth of interior cities over out-ports is sustained by the civilization of the ancient nations, as found in the examples of their great interior cities, and that, too, when water facilities ruled the commerce of the world, must not all opposing argument in favor of seaboard cities be of naught when we bring to the discussion the power and use of steam, the railway system, and the labor-saving and labor-increasing inventions, which the arts afford? Comprehending this mighty reversal in the order and means of industrial civilization, must we not say with Horace Greeley, that "salt water is about played out"?

Of cities now known as leading centers of commerce, a large majority have been built almost exclusively by domestic trade. What country possesses so many great cities as China—a country, until lately, nearly destitute of foreign commerce?

There are now in the world more than three hundred cities containing a population of fifty thousand and upwards; of these more than two-thirds are interior cities, containing a population vastly greater than belongs to the outport cities. It should, however, be kept in mind that many of the great sea-ports have been built, and are now sustained, mainly by the trade of the nations respectively in which they are situated. Even London, the greatest mart in the world, is believed to derive much the greater part of the support of its vast population from its trade with the United Kingdom. At the present time not one-fifteenth of the business of New York City is based upon foreign commerce, but is sustained by the trade growing out of our home industry.

Though the argument is not exhaustive, it is conclusive. It is founded in the all directing under life-currents of human existence upon this planet, and from those principles there is neither variableness nor shadow of turning away. Man's home is upon the land; he builds his master-works upon its sure foundations. It is upon the land that he invents, contrives, plans and achieves his mightiest deeds. He spreads his sails upon the seas, and battles with the tempest and the storm; and amid the sublimities of the ocean he travels unknown paths in search of fame. The ephemeral waves obliterate the traces of his victories with the passing moments; upon the land, time alone can efface his works.

The organization of society as one whole is yet too imperfect to call for the use of one all-directing head and one central moving heart, and it will only be the ultimate, the final Great City, that will fully unite in itself the functions analogous to those of the human head and heart, in relation to the whole family of man.

The final triumph of the great city will also carry with it a final organization of the world's civilization—a perfect unity of the entire interests of the advanced nations of the earth. The higher functions of intellectual life will be so exerted as to subordinate the passions and sentiments of men to principles of harmonious organization and unity, thus establishing a perfect system of society and government by means of harmony between the active and passive relations—between the individuals and the community.

Assuming these things to be true, the prophecy of the Great City is also a prophecy of the final great center of industrial and commercial life, and the center of this great commercial power will also carry with it the center of the moral and intellectual power. One hundred years, at our previous rate of increase, will give more than four duplications, and more than six hundred millions of people, to the present area of our country. But, allowing twenty-five years for a duplication, and four duplications, we should have six hundred millions, at the close of one hundred years. Of these, not less than four hundred millions will inhabit the interior plain and the region west of it; and not over two hundred millions will inhabit the margin east of the Appalachian chain of mountains. The productions of these four hundred millions, intended for exchange with each other, will meet at the most convenient point central to the place of the growth or manufacture of their products. Where, then, let us inquire again, is most likely to be the center of the most ample and best facilities for the exchange, in the future, of the commodities of that great people? Where will that point be? Which of the four cities we have under consideration is best suited for this purpose? Must it not be St. Louis, commanding, as she will, the greatest railway and river communication? It cannot be Cincinnati, for she is not so well situated in the center of the productive power of the continent. It cannot be New Orleans; higher freights upon the products of the country will be against her. It cannot be New York or San Francisco, for all our six fundamental facts stand against them, and unerringly point to the central plain of the continent, where the six hundred millions of people will prefer to transact business.

The late Dr. Scott of Toledo, by far the most able writer on the cities of this country, under date of February 16, 1873, and singularly in his last letter to me, uses the following significant language, which he desired to be permanently recorded, for future reference:

"I shall not live to see the final triumph of the great city of the future, in our great interior plain, but you may. Please save the opinion I now express, that it will be on a lake border—probably at or near the west end of Lake Erie. I expect the census of 1880 will show the growth of the three cities—Cleveland, Detroit and Toledo—in advance of that of Chicago. Up to this time, Chicago has shot ahead, and is now more populous than the three cities. After 1880, I expect the rivalry will be between the three Lake Erie cities. It is likely that St. Louis will grow faster than you have ventured to foretell—perhaps faster than you have anticipated. But, in my opinion, its location is too far south and west to become the best point for the convergence of commerce, interior and exterior, of our country."

Because of a deep respect for Dr. Scott, his superior abilities, great power of mental forecast, and high moral character, his opinion is cheerfully recorded, with the following remarks:

Dr. Scott's views upon the future of the cities of this country seem, without a question of doubt, to have been shaped by the existing contest between slavery and freedom on this continent, and were not changed after the abolition of slavery.

Previous to the civil war, no man seemed to consider the material progress of this country from any other stand-point than that of the eastward and westward movement of commerce and population. A new lesson is presented for the study of our entire population. The abolition of slavery, and the plain and simple demands of commerce, are now compelling a new—a north and south movement of commerce and population on this continent, which is rapidly superseding and destined to supplant the eastward and westward movement. Dr. Scott did not take into the account of the discussion on the future great city this new movement, and therefore failed to comprehend the new influences destined to be exerted upon the growth of our cities. Assuming it to be true, and no reasonable man can disprove it, that the north and south movement of commerce and population on this continent will supplant, or at least become greater than the movement east and west, it must be conceded that the opinion of Dr. Scott is wrong in every particular; that St. Louis has the vantage ground by her location, and must grow to be the great city of this continent, and "become the best point for the convergence, interior and exterior, of our country."

We have seen that the human race, with all its freight of commerce, its barbarism and civilization, its arms and arts, through pestilence and prosperity, across seas and over continents, like one mighty caravan, has been moving forward since creation's dawn, from the east to the west, with sword and cross, helmet and distaff, to the conquest of the world and, like a mighty army, leaving weakness behind and organizing power in the advance. Hence, we can easily realize that the same inevitable cause that wrested human power from the cities of the ancients and vested it for a time in the city of the Caesars, that moved it hence to the city of London, will, in time, transfer it across the Atlantic Ocean, to grow up on the American continent; and that this power, wealth and wisdom that once ruled Troy, Athens, Carthage and Rome, and is now represented by the city of London—the precursor of the final great city—will, in less than one hundred years, find a resting-place in North America, and culminate in the future great city which is destined to grow up in the central plain of the continent, and upon the great Mississippi river, where the city of St. Louis now stands.

I know there are those who assume that New York is to be the successor of London, and even surpass in population and commercial supremacy that great city of the trans-Atlantic shore, before the position of the final great city is fixed. That is not possible. We have only to comprehend the new character of our national industry, and the diversity of interests which it and our rapidly increasing system of railways are establishing, to know that it is impossible. The city of New York will not, in the future, control the same proportionate share of foreign and domestic commerce of the country that she heretofore has. New Orleans and San Francisco will take some of the present valued trade, and, together with other points which will soon partake of the outport commerce, the trade to and from our country will be so divided as to prevent New York from becoming the rival, much less the superior, of London, as Mr. Scott has so earnestly contended. Then, in the westward movement of human power to the center of the world's commerce, from the city of London to the New World, it is not possible for it to find a complete and final resting place in any city of the Atlantic seaboard, but it will be compelled to move forward, until, in its complete development, it will be organized and represented in the most favored city in the central plain of the continent. Besides the diffusion of our external commerce through so many channels upon our seaboard, so as to prevent its concentration at any one of the seaboard cities, there are elements at work in the interior of the country, which will more surely prevent the city that is to succeed London from growing up on the Atlantic shore of our continent. Every tendency of our national progress is more and more to our continental development—living at home, rather than go abroad to distant markets. There is an inherent principle lurking among all people of great continental nationality and resources, which impresses them stronger with home interests than with external and distant fields of action; and this principle is rapidly infusing itself among the people of these great Valley States; therefore it is needless to look into the future to see our great cities on either seaboard of our continent, for they are not destined to be there. But most certainly will they grow up in the interior, upon the lakes, the rivers and the Gulf, and among these cities of the interior we are to look for the future great city of the world—that which London now heralds, and which the westward tendency of the world's civilization will, in less than one hundred years, build up as the greatest industrial organism of the human race.

Human power is not only moving westward from the old world, but it is also moving from the Atlantic seaboard westward. But a few facts are necessary to demonstrate the truth of this statement: First, in evidence that human power is moving westward from the old world, we have but to refer to the reports of the State Department at Washington upon our foreign commerce, to learn that our imports are greater than our exports, and our internal commerce far greater than our foreign commerce; and by reference to the various reports emigration, we learn that thousands are coming from Western Europe, yearly, to our shores, while but few of our own people are seeking homes on the other side of the Atlantic. Second, in evidence of the westward movement of human power from the Atlantic States, statistical tables show, in the most conclusive manner that human power is moving westward; many thousands of new miles of railway are yearly added to the great system of the Mississippi Valley, and at least three-fifths of the number of miles of railway of the entire country are now in this great Valley.

Nor can these facts, in their magnitude and character, be considered of casual concern to the American citizen, for they are the most important in our national progress. They are the irrefutable evidences of the historic and sublime march of the American people, in the course of the star of empire in its majestic career across the continent.

But granting that human power is moving westward on this continent, a question arises, as to whether, in time, it will be arrested, and make a lodgment somewhere in North America, or whether it will cross the Pacific Ocean to the inferior races of Asia.

To answer this question, we have only to consider the vast material resources of North America, and realize that they are far more inviting to capital and skill than any inducements that Asia can offer. This fact is so palpable that it requires no argument, and therefore must settle the question of the arrest of human power in its westward movement on this continent. Nor will it reach, and make a lodgment on, the Pacific slope.

The vast arid and mountainous regions of the western half of the continent, and the unequaled extent of fertile lands on the eastern half, and adjacent to and on either side of the great river, fixes its location inevitably in the central plain of the continent and in the center of its productive power. And with the development and complete organization of human power in the center of the productive region of the continent, will most certainly grow up the great city of the future—the great material, social, civil and moral heart of the human race. The raw material necessary to the artisan and manufacturer, in the production of whatever ministers to comfort and elegance, are here. The bulkiness of food and raw materials make it to the interest of the artisan and the manufacturer to locate themselves near the place where those materials grow. It is this interest, constantly operating, which peoples our Western towns and cities with emigrants from the Eastern States and Europe. When food and raw materials for manufacture are no longer cheaper in the great Valley than in the States of the Atlantic and the nations of Western Europe, then, and not till then, will it cease to be to the interest of artisans and manufacturers to prefer a location in Western towns and cities. This time will probably be about the period when the Mississippi shall flow toward the Artic regions.

The chief points for the exchange of the varied productions of the Mississippi Valley will necessarily give employment to the great population. Indeed, the locations of our future great cities have been made with reference to their commercial facilities. Commerce has laid the foundation on which manufactures have been, to a great extent, instrumental in rearing the superstructure. Together, these departments of labor are destined to build up in this fertile Valley the greatest cities of the world.

It is something to us Americans that the great city—the great all-directing heart of the race—is to grow up in our land. Even to us of this generation, a conviction of the final growth of the great marvel of future ages is a thought which we can indulge and enjoy with pride in the present and coming conflicts of this progressive life. As we have already seen, St. Louis is substantially central to the Mississippi Valley, and no city on the continent can lay any just claim to become the future great city, or occupy a central position to so many valuable resources, as she does. She is not only substantially in the center of the Mississippi Valley, but, allowing her to be nine hundred miles from New York City, she occupies the center of an area of 2,544,688 square miles, and within a circumference the outer line of which touches Chicago. She occupies the center of an area of country which, in fertility of soil, coal, iron, timber, stone, water, domestic navigation and railways, cannot be equaled on the globe.

Not only so, but when we consider by what general rules the cities have grown and are now growing on this continent, we must conclude that St. Louis still occupies the most favorable position for greatness and power.

The city of St. Louis is situated, geographically, very nearly in the center of the great Valley of the Mississippi, or basin of the continent, on the west bank of the Mississippi river, and about midway between St. Paul and New Orleans, and Pittsburg and Denver City.

The topography of St. Louis County consists of a system of ridges branching from a water-shed between the Missouri, Meramec and Mississippi rivers. This water-shed has a general altitude of two hundred feet above the Mississippi river, and has numerous small ridges or arms branching from it and winding in serpentine courses, and maintaining this general altitude along their summits, and terminating in bluffs or low escarpments and declining grounds towards the Meramec, Missouri and Mississippi rivers.

The city is built geographically on the ends or termination of this ridge system, and extends some fifteen miles up and down the river. The ground rises gently from the river back for one mile to Seventeenth street, which follows in part the apex of the first ridge, and is one hundred and fifty feet above the river. The ground then gently declines, and rises in a second ridge at Twenty-fifth street, or Jefferson avenue, and parts of Grand avenue, and again slopes and rises in a ridge at Cote Brilliante, or Wilson's Hill, four miles west of the river. This point is some two hundred feet above the river and overlooks the city.

Looking at the topography of the site which St. Louis now occupies, the observer will be most intensely impressed with the thought that nature in her immutable decrees had ordained, from the beginning, that here was laid the foundation for a great city—the future imperial city of the world. Nor are the character and superiority of the land circumscribed by the present city limits—not at all. The same beauty in the general formation and adaptability of the ground for building purposes and the consequent expansion of the city, extends back in every way from the river for an indefinite distance, and with still greater advantages for building purposes as we advance into the country.

The geological formation of St. Louis County is limestone, shales, and sandstones of the coal measures, these being covered with alluvial clays from ten to twenty feet deep, making the contour of the ridges wavy and dividing the country into rich rolling prairie, from one to two hundred feet above the rivers, and bordered with belts and groves of black and white oak woods. The country shows many substantial brick mansions, highly cultivated farms, vineyards, orchards, meadows and slopes—forming the most natural grounds for building purposes found in any part of our country. Viewing this rolling prairie, with all its wealth of alluvial soil, its contour of ridge and valley, its springs and meandering streams, it seems as if nature had here amassed her wealth and centralized the material resources to supply the wants of a dense and wealthy population and, not being content with this wealth of soil and art on the surface, had underlaid a large portion of this area with coal veins—St. Louis County containing an undeveloped coal basin of over 10,000 acres.

While New York is limited to a barren, rocky island; Philadelphia to a low ridge between the Delaware and Schuylkill rivers; Washington City to a flat, sterile, uninteresting region; Chicago to land from five to fifteen feet above Lake Michigan, and swampy prairie beyond; Cincinnati to a small circuit surrounded by steep, almost inaccessible hills; St. Louis has the most natural contour of surface for elevation of residence streets deep clay over the limestone for brick, cellars, sewerage and foundations, quarries of building rock in all parts of the city, wells of pure water in the deep clays in many parts of the city, natural sewerage and dome-shaped bills for water-works, and essentially combining all the material resources for a great city. London and Paris are built upon tertiary basins, where the soil is thin and rocks generally too soft for good building material. Grand Avenue is twelve miles long, running parallel with the river, and forming a grand broadway from the north to the south end of the city, and is destined in the future, with its Fair Grounds, its great parks, cathedrals, churches, and private residences, to be the boulevard of the Western continent. And yet, when this has been said, we have but commenced to tell the wonders of a city destined in the future to equal London in its population, Athens in its philosophy, art and culture, Rome in its hotels, cathedrals, churches and grandeur, and to be the central commercial metropolis of a continent.

It may be asked, how shall we have cognizance of the laws to give us faith in this being accomplished? Go, then, in imagination, ninety miles south of the city, over the railroad to the Iron Mountains, where is stored above the level of the valleys, iron ore sufficient to supply the wants of a densely-populated continent. One thousand tons of this ore now comes daily, over a down grade of seven hundred feet, to St. Louis. In another year a double track railroad will be needed. Flanking this iron system are 10,000,000 acres of iron, lead, copper, zinc, antimony, nickel, tin, silver and gold regions; west of this are another 10,000,000 acres, including Southwest Missouri, being fields of similar ores, and part coal. This, you will bear in mind, is south of the city.

Now, let us look east. The four great trunk railroads leading east at ten miles from the city reach the coal measures, run each over two hundred miles of the great Illinois coal basin, where five or six coal veins are piled one vein above the other. To the north this same coal system is found and all the railroads in North Missouri are crossing more or less over coal veins. To the west, the great trunk Pacific railroad, beyond Jefferson City, crosses over vast coal-fields—Kansas City being built centrally in this great field.

Coal and iron are the bones and sinews of the most powerful of modern nations. Lead, zinc and copper add strength. In the future the sections to pay tribute to this center are the vast cotton-fields of the lower Mississippi, the grain-growing regions of the North and West, the argentiferous and argentiferous belts of Colorado and Montana.

St. Louis, like ancient Rome, once with its 10,000,000 population, is destined to be flanked and surrounded with a galaxy or cordon of continental cities. Memphis, Kansas City, St. Joseph, Leavenworth, Dubuque, Keokuk, Davenport, Jacksonville, Springfield, Terre Haute and Indianapolis, are a part of these satellites that in the future are to pay tribute to this center—taking in view the fact of their vast material resources, and these being the center of the great fruit, agricultural and wine belt of the continent.

The people, the Teutonic and Celtic races, are the pioneer people in all the departments of human industry, politics, culture, theology. We apprehend that the most acute vision even were that mind in harmony with the spirit of the times, and enabled through that means to look back through the dim geologic history of the past, when the economic laws were piling the iron, atom by atom, in these iron mountains, growing the dense flora of the coal plants, repleting the veins of lead, zinc, copper, tin, silver and gold: and at the same time comprehend the ridge, valley, spring, prairie, timber and river systems: and was enabled to go back in the ethnography and heraldry of these populations, and could fuse these elements of facts in the future, and at the same time realize the grandeur of the empires of the past—the Persian, under Cyrus; the Macedonian, under Alexander the Great; the Roman, under the Republic and the twelve Caesars—that the truth would be forced upon the mind, that in the future this great Valley of the Mississippi will include the center of an empire, before which, in wealth, power and grandeur, all these shall pale; that St. Louis, sitting like a Queen on the banks of the great Father of Waters, will be the central city of this people, the tidal waves of whose civilization will roll to China and Japan on the west, and to the Bosphorus on the east; and with her continental railroad system, her telegraphs over mountains and under oceans, her vast water communications, will radiate law and order, and become the leading national, mining, and commercial metropolis of the Western hemisphere.

When the site was chosen, and the name St. Louis given to this new offspring of civilization, born to a career of imperial greatness, henceforth it became an object of wonder and admiration. The outpost of a transatlantic government, the child of another nation, fixed in the heart of a continent and upon the bank of the great Mississippi River, and at the confluence of converging navigable rivers, it soon became the center of trade for the savage, the trapper, the hunter and the pioneer. The importance of its locality compelled it to grow more rapidly, and to attain the higher elements of civilization in advance of the people residing throughout the surrounding country. At an early day the name of St. Louis became associated with the great rivers and lakes of the continent, with the Gulf of Mexico and the Rocky Mountains. And soldiers, travelers, explorers and scholars constantly sought it as the place of departure to the wild scenes of the West, to the Federal metropolis, and to the Gulf of Mexico. Through all the years of its growth, St. Louis has been one place of continued attraction, one marvel of civilization, and a commercial emporium of unusual animation, which found the goal of its destiny in prophetic thought.

St. Louis is a well-built city, but its architecture is more substantial than showy. The wide, well-paved streets, the spacious levee and commodious ware houses; the mills, machine shops and manufactories; the fine hotels, churches, and public buildings; the universities, charitable institutions, public schools and libraries, the growing parks, the well-improved and unequaled fair grounds, and Mr. Shaw's jewel of a garden, which is by far the garden of the continent, constitute an array of excellences and of attractions of which any city may justly be proud. The appearance of St. Louis from the eastern bank of the Mississippi is impressive. At East St. Louis the eye sometimes commands a view of one hundred steamboats lying at our levee. A mile and a half of steamboats lying at the wharf of a city 1,000 miles from the ocean, in the heart of a continent, is a spectacle which naturally inspires large views of commercial greatness. The sight of our levee, thronged with busy merchants and covered with the commodities of every clime, from the peltries of the Rocky Mountains to the teas of China, does not tend to lessen the magnitude of the impression.

These thoughts of the growth and commerce of St. Louis could easily be extended to a discussion of the wealth and industry of our continent, but the amplification would be of no avail to a people whose minds, like their eyes, are accustomed to range over large extents, and are not content to sit down after having acquired a little power.

REBECCA MORROW REAVIS

BORN IN COUNTY GALWAY, IRELAND, to a prosperous family, Rebecca Morrow Reavis (1855–1923) exhibited an interest in literature at a very early age and composed her first poetry at age ten. An intelligent and adventurous young woman, she came to the United States in 1876, residing first in Camden, New Jersey, and coming to St. Louis in 1882. The following year, Rebecca married Logan U. Reavis, the well-known St. Louis entrepreneur and booster who launched the campaign to move the U.S. capital to St. Louis. Reavis's theories clearly had a profound impact on his young bride; she gave the following poem the same title as her husband's infamous tract. Also offered here is Rebecca's flowery, pantheistic tribute to James B. Eads, the architect of the first bridge to span the Mississippi at St. Louis, about which poet Walt Whitman wrote, "It is indeed a structure of perfection and beauty unsurpassable, and I never tire of it."

THE FUTURE GREAT CITY OF THE WORLD

ST. LOUIS

Oh! land of the free, and home of the brave,
Oh! land, who to captives their liberty gave,
Revolting 'gainst bondage which crushed the last breath,
With the spirit of men who cried "Freedom or death."
Land, bending the knee to those warriors brave,
And looking away from the blood-watered grave—
Away, away up, where those men long adored
Wave proudly the palm which they gained by the sword.

Oh! land, now enjoying the boon which you bought,
Your freedom, your honor, your skill and your thought,
Subject to no power in heaven or earth,
Than that which had blessed you the hour of your birth.
A literal Canaan in honey and milk,
A rival with China, now gorgeous in silk,
An equal with Athens in art and design,
Minerva exalts you and you are divine.

Fair land, to whom prophets with unerring eye,
Looked through the long vistas of years flitting by;
They found it not difficult looking on thee,
Through thy many advantages, glory to see;
Rejoicing in dawn which had scarcely begun,
Which now in its zenith is bright as the sun,
The ocean they saw waft a kiss on the breeze
From the queen of all lands to the queen of the seas.

A kiss which was freighted with incense of health,
From hills of fertility, valleys of wealth,
And into her lukewarm veins did impart
A trickle of joy from a tropical heart,
And saw, as their lips in identity smacked,
One sovereign supply what the other one lacked—
Like neighbors dividing the bulk of their store;
Thus showing the friendship they each of them bore.

How brightened their eyes as they hailed the glad sight!
They saw thee, America, center of light—
A focus, whose rays to the world were given
As freely received from the sun-god of heaven;
And exultingly now do they look and rejoice,
As developing years speak the truth of their voice;
While they're beating a gem for your majesty's crown,
To which shall its brethren lowly bow down.

Milton, and Cowley, and Sir Thomas Brown,
Two centuries ago their voice handed down
In soft, flowing strains from Poesy's muse,
Inspiring the tongue, while the heart they enthuse;
And since have we others, as Berkeley and Sewall,
Adams, and Shipley, and Governor Pownall;
With Paley, and Burns, and eloquent Sheridan,
Canning, De Tocqueville, Alaman and Cobden.

And others, like them, who the future explored,
Saw thee, fair America, thee they adored
As a beautiful child, who in years would expand
To a type of perfection, a queen in the land;
And now, in the present, we, who have been blest
With the joy of beholding thee, brightest and best—
One thought fills our bosoms, an effort we make
To anticipate the next step you will take.

What step will you take next, fair Queen of the West?
Are you waiting for those who have gone to their rest,
To come from above with a city or town,
All beaten and polished to set in your crown?
Do you think there is nothing now left you to do,
Since you've conquered the old with the sword of the new?
Ah! take care, lest your confidence placed in its hold
Reverse the sharp weapon, like Cassius' of old.

Throughout all the ages in history known,
One gem sparkled brightest, illumined the crown,
Which was placed on the head of the recognized peer,
Who rose in magnificence, trampled on fear.
The ancient days reveled in gems such as these,
Till Britannia arose for her Queen of the Seas,
And won her the honor, a peeress of all,
Through greatness ascending o'er Amsterdam's fall.

Then London, the gem, adorned the crown,
And sparkled on rulers and men of renown;
The world bowed to it, and honor'd its name,
And poets and literature sang of its fame,
Then art, and invention, and grandeur aspired
To outshine in its light, which their spirits inspired,
And commerce enriched it, invading its streets,
With wealth from the holds of its numerous fleets.

And she, like the others, shall waft o'er the sea
Her title of commerce and greatness to thee,
When in the wide future the world shall praise
The Aaronian rod in the height of its days,
For thee, O, America, great in thy strength
Of riches strewn over the breadth and the length.
Of vast tracts devoted to energy's hand,
Shall yet rule the world with a sceptral wand.

Then why not prepare for the crown you shall wear,
The gem which must sparkle the brightest one there?
Already 'tis waiting the artisan's skill
To fashion the model, make it what they will;
For those good men who've gone e'er their vision was blest
With the sight which now greets us, and them in their rest
Are anxiously planning that city's design
Which shall be the great centre, the jewel to shine.

St. Louis! St. Louis! we echo the name,
Repeated by them as the city of fame,
On the banks of that river whose waters embrace
The largest facilities known to the race;
The central point in its beautiful vale,
To which, tip its waters, large traffic must sail
From all the great world beyond the great sea,—
Through the stream unobstructed a gate open free.

And to which throng the people by water and rail;
Who seem in prospective a breath to inhale.
From the future great heart which shall throb in the breast
Of the greatest of nations, the wisest and best;
A heart which shall act as imperial head,
By whose guidance the tide of events shall be led,
Which shall grow and expand like its forces of steam,
Till it rivals with London, now reigning supreme.

Industry and enterprise fast gaining ground,
As numbers and large requisition abound,
Its head lifting high as it daily expands
In its fast-growing buildings, its utilized lands,
But one thing is needed to hasten the time
When shall shine in its splendor this city sublime,
Men need to look on from the present and see
A lesson for them in the wise, working bee;

Add to their industry, intelligence, art,
Invite all the muses to play that great part
Without which no city in eminence grew;
They distinguished the old and must also the new.
Let literature spread her white wings in the air,
And lift from the dungeons of toil and of care
The hearts of the people, who surely should find
The grain, not the husk, to develop the mind.

Like Italy of old, should some Petrarch arise,
Or, Dante, and lift to the vaulted skies,
By some method successful in scholarship's flight,
The tastes of the multitude, then what a light
Would burst on the future great city. For then
The pencil, the brush, the chisel, the pen,
With history, and poetry, and elegance, would glow
As a sunbeam which lights on the beautiful snow.

When this is accomplished, fair Queen of the West,
In the city where commerce and tithe shall invest
So large a production from every land known;
Then, then you'll rejoice, for the gem in your crown.
But patiently wait, while you're working to use
The unparalleled qualities blessing St. Louis,
For cheers shall resound o'er the billowy wave
To the land of the free and the home of the brave.

Oh! beautiful city of futurity!
What a wonderful, wonderful power it must be,
Which can raise thee to glory on pinnacle height,
Where the world's past kingdoms shall pale in the light,
Where Baalbec, and Thebes, and Tyre once shone,
Carthage, Persepolis, each like the sun;
Oh! wonderful city, lift up thy glad voice—
Thy kingdom is coming, thy heart shall rejoice.

ODE TO CAPT. JAMES B. EADS

All hail! Columbia, favored land of Heaven—
    All hail, all hail, resounds from sea to sea;
From pole to pole, by touch electric riven,
    The world salutes this Nation of the free.

What makes it thus in greatness so transcending?
    What lifts its towers and bulwarks up on high?
What architect, with power and genius blending,
    Has fashioned it from models in the sky?

Like that great temple of surpassing splendor,
    While silently arose from stone,
This Nation is the seat of art and grandeur:
    Its architect, its builder—God alone.

Built on a rock, a firm, a sure foundation;
    Built of such stone as braves the wrecks of time;

Built with such zeal as makes it this great Nation;
  Built in men's hearts—a monument sublime.

Columbus, first, by hand of God directed,
  Laid the first stone upon the sacred sod,
Then, on his knees, he humbly dedicated
  The stone and future edifice to God.

Such noble fabric still promotes the building,
  With steel and iron pillars for support,
While Solomon's it does surpass in gilding,
  Of gold and costly gems from port to port.

And now it grows in grandeur, strength and promise;
  A great, colossal statue, spanning o'er
The large expanse of Ocean's ready commerce,
  And stamps its power upon the other shore.

To-day the power of Science is enforcing
  Such laws, commands, as ne'er before were known,
Through active, fiery brains and muscles coursing,
  In form of some great project, leading on.

Those brains through which now flows this subtle current,
  With that impetus which throws head and heart
Before it, with a centrifugal movement,
  Are rather few, and sadly far apart.

Yet 'tis such brains that go to build the structure
  Such heads and hearts are what the Nation needs;
And men to-day are living in the future—
  A future sacred to the name of EADS.

EADS! Captain EADS! The name is grand—ennobling—
  What was to Greece the name Archimedes,
And, what to Germany, was that of Roebling,
  To fair Columbia is that of EADS.

Aye, more, for science in this mighty nation,
  Is great as EADS is peer among his peers.
Like Newton at the foot of Gravitation,
  Does EADS stand at the head of Engineers.

His monuments are those which last forever
That Bridge of wonder—go and mark it well
Go, mark the outlets of that mighty river,
Which to his Genius yield as to a spell.

In coming ages none will question, is he
Whose name is written on it mile by mile,
A greater Hero of the Mississippi,
Than Horatio Nelson, Hero of the Nile.

His iron fleet in '61, is immortal,
Of which Lord Nelson would be justly proud,
And proudly with it entering in the battle
Would gain the day, with power like EADS' endowed.

Now, all his works, with these, a star eclipses—
The Tehuantepec Route, that is the star;
Unlike the river, he would make the Isthmus
A road for ships of peace, instead of war.

Oh, what a mind that opens to each nation
Such golden vistas through that portal wide
Surely the gods will aid the grand creation,
If men be slumbering in Columbia's side.

He would in love for mankind make all countries,
Through dealings with each other, closer friends,
And strew the white crest waves through coming centuries,
With ships well filled with all that Nature sends.

Hark! hear those waves through myriad ages swelling,
In one grand chorus of symphonious song—
The strain caught up on countless harps is telling
The joy of nations to a happy throng.

Among that throng, great hearts are throbbing proudly,
And gazing on the crowning work, rejoice;
I fancy now I see good Abraham Cowley
Smile on the truth of his prophetic voice.

Two centuries since the poet bid the nation
  "To plough the earth, to plough the very main."
No doubt he built upon an EADS foundation
  Who'd "traffic with the universe maintain."

And thus, like him, through time's progressing wonders,
  Shall lie whose works that spirit power proclaim,
Live, after Earth to God His own surrenders—
  On land, and sea, in an immortal name.

For widely o'er creation's vast expanses,
  Where billows roll with God's unfathomed power,
His soul to-day who man's great good advances
  Shall ride triumphant to the eternal shore.

The truth of one whose ashes strewed the river,
  And followed with its windings to the sea,
Now wide as the Atlantic rolling ever,
  Perpetuate the martyr's memory.

So lives the memory of he whose genius
  Now nestles close on the paternal breast,
From which proceed, like placid, shining virtues,
  A progeny unequalled in the West.

With childlike faith within the folds reposing,
  Of shining, wavy coils, there sink to sleep
The little sunbeams, whose bright eyes are closing,
  Weary with many a playful dart and leap.

And when Aurora breathes upon their faces
  Her breath of light, of heat and mother love,
They 'wake, emerge from out the waves' embraces,
  And fly to kiss their father-god above.

And as they go, they touch their golden tresses
  With diamond sparkles from the treasure deep,
More radiant, thus, each little angel blesses
  With double brightness wheresoe'er 'twill peep.

Those diamond sparkles are like dew drops, paling,
Combined with other than effulgent light,
And sheds that light which on the waters sailing;
A beacon is to mariners by night.

It sails away,—*his genius*, whose intention,
Through winding curvatures within the vale,
Leads to the Gulf, by way—his own invention,
Through which the ships of nations now may sail.

'Till in the grand Old Ocean 'tis embosomed,
Where freely now it carries out his plan,
And does to-day as when the May Flower blossomed,
The world enrich with God's great gift to man.

Thus tracing truths as England does her martyr's
We from the River to the Gulf are led,
And from the Gulf to Ocean's boundless waters
Where'er the foot of mankind ever treads.

Perchance there may another brave Columbus,
When this commercial tide is ebbing high,
Break from the line to seek for, not a fabulous,
But actual Cipango, lying nigh.

He'll breathe the tropic fragrance from the garden
It's fruits and vegetation on the breeze;
His heart will swell as nearer draws his Eden,
Which others sought for in enchanted seas.

And sailing up the current of the river,
Which may be Pison, flowing where there's gold,
Praise God who from delusions did deliver,
And lead him to the "Garden of the World."

Or farther down across the Isthmian passage,
Another Raleigh, in the golden land,
Will find the King, to whom he'd bear the message,
Of greater power displayed by greater hand.

He'll tell him that through EADS all nations gather
    Around the cave of Mammon, richer far;
That Oceans crown him, Commerce calls him father;
    He's broken down the one *partition bar.*

That they who had such pangs of hunger suffered,
    Now look and see the maiden at her wheel,
Like Fortunatus, and to them are tendered
    The gold that lasts them through life's woe or weal.

He'll tell him that this noble Hia-watha,
    Lives in no Isle of Brandon, never found,
But close beside the branching water's father,
    Within the glorious "City of the Mound."

That now, no more, men waste their time in seeking
    For Bimini, or other fabled founts
That knowledge, rather is the fount they're reaching
    And drink its waters from our modern Mounts.

EADS' fame's unequalled, while 'tis daily growing
    His power's unlimited in mind and space,
No, *Ne-plus-ultra* of the ancients knowing,
    He builds not their pillars of Hercules.

Nor would they in mythology's tradition
    Cause him, like Hercules, to block the way
Of further claims to progress and ambition,
    In those two Mountain Pillars of to-day.

They would assign to him some brilliant story,
    A birth as wondrous as their Dieties',
And look to him for power, for fame, for glory,
    To aid them in their many victories.

They'd say, perhaps:—"The Standard of his nation
    Had in his talons borne the starry flag,
In moments of ecstatic exultation,
    'Bove pride of place, upon his native crag.

And waved it proudly in the starry world,
With olive branch of peace 'tween man and man,
Displaying thus, as fold by fold unfurled,
A power unequalled since the world began.

The brilliant orbs all claimed the spangled banner;
Each saw its image in the mirror blue,
And asked the bird "to whom belongs the honor?"
He must decide which one to give it to.

The bird reflected, as if undecided,
Whether 'twas best to take it back to earth,
Then thought that "power is strongest undivided:—
Its destiny is equal to its birth."

"'Tis best," he thought, "to leave it to whoever
Is greatest here, than take it back again,
Where wars, the leaves from off the branch might sever,
'Tween hosts of Heaven, and earth's greatest men."

Thus spoke the bird: "Ye shining constellations,
Whiche'er is greatest shall possess the prize;
It symbolizes greatest of Earth's nations,
And must not lose its glory in the skies."

'Twas well, they said, then each its claim submitted.
The bird whose piercing glance discerned far,
Immediately saw which one was best fitted
To hold the flag, then chose his honored star.

"Venus," said he, "the flag to you is presented,
For love is greatest 'mong the powers of Heaven;
As to your form in beauty so transplendent
Upon mount Ida was the apple given."

Then Mars and Jupiter, both pained and jealous,
Said they were greatest and the prize was theirs;
Both warr'd against the noble bird and Venus;
Then Mercury steps in and interferes:

"The flag belongs to Venus—let her have it;
She conquers where subdued are power and wars;
She carried Heaven to its nation's Planet,
And shall to Heaven bear the Nation's Stars."

Then looked the goddess on her treasure, proudly,
And waved it in the ether when she sees
The bird uphold his magic branch and loudly
Proclaim with potent voice, Peace! Peace! Peace!

The bird was free, and now he would return,
And singing deeply, wrapped his pinions round
The sacred flag he had in triumph borne
From off his crag, above the hallowed ground.

She sees the tender pinions wrapped about it,
And Mercury, when both let fall a tear;
"Dear bird, your nation cannot do without it:
Here, take it back, we shall not keep it here."

Thus Venus spoke, in accents low and tender,
While she resigned the honor of her claim,
And then the bird, 'midst lights of golden splendor,
Returned to rest within the land of Fame.

But as once more upon the rocky summit,
With love he plumed his breast in every fold,
He saw two tears made one and falling from it,
Transformed to a star like burnished gold.

Surprised, he watched these curious phenomena:—
The star went sailing o'er the sunny meads
Of Lawrenceburg, in Southern Indiana,
Then heard he angels name it JAMES B. EADS.

Still gazing, saw three Magi kneel before it—
'Twas then a child of Heaven-favored birth,
Their gifts presenting, while all three adored it,
As his attendants on his path through earth.

He grew and flourished in that balmy region,
  With Mercury and Venus at his side,
Led by the Magi whose bright gifts were legion,
  To manhood's stature, into manhood's pride."

Such might have been the Ancient's oft told story;
  And men would build a temple to his name,
But now the temple raised to names of glory,
  Is that erected by the hand of fame.

And so there are such temples scattered over
  The spacious world, in honor of the deeds
Which go to build Columbia's noble structure,
  Whereon's inscribed the living name of EADS.

JOSEPH PULITZER

JOSEPH PULITZER (1847–1911) was born in Hungary to a Jewish father and a Catholic mother. Although he wanted a military career, poor eyesight and a frail constitution kept Pulitzer from being accepted into several armed forces. In 1864, Pulitzer found himself bound for America on a ship carrying illegally recruited soldiers to fight in the country's Civil War. Once Pulitzer discovered this was to be his fate, in a characteristically bold and decisive move, he literally jumped ship and swam to shore in Boston's harbor.

Pulitzer made his way to St. Louis in 1866 and secured his first employment there, tending mules in the stables at Benton Barracks. Within two years, Pulitzer's hard work and innate intelligence had opened doors in the city's thriving German community. In 1868, his career in publishing began when he became a reporter for the *Westliche Post*, the city's leading German-language daily. While covering the state's political scene from Jefferson City, Pulitzer became intrigued by politics and ran for office. As a liberal Republican, he won a legislative seat in Missouri's Fifth District. Holding this office provided Pulitzer with the leverage he needed in what would become a lifelong crusade in social reform.

In 1878, Pulitzer purchased the *Dispatch*, a financially troubled evening paper, for twenty-five hundred dollars. Shortly thereafter, he also purchased the *Post,* a competing but floundering newspaper. On December 12, 1878, Pulitzer combined the two papers, and two weeks later, the paper's name was simplified to the *Post-Dispatch*. While neither the *Post* nor the *Dispatch* had been vocal about political and social issues that impacted St. Louisans, the *Post-Dispatch* plunged into the thick of controversy and reflected Pulitzer's zealous commitment to public service. The paper's first editorial claimed that it "will serve no party but the people . . . will oppose all frauds and shams wherever and whatever they are; will advocate principles and ideas rather than prejudices and partisanship." In its first two years of publication, the *Post-Dispatch* crusaded against such social ills as lottery corruption, transportation monopolies, and labor disputes. The paper's candor at naming the parties involved in nefarious activities frequently alienated—and frightened—the city's power brokers and simultaneously bolstered its national reputation.

In October 1882, a tragic event took place in the editorial offices of the *Post-Dispatch* that precipitated Joseph Pulitzer's move to New York. John A. Cockerill, the *Post-Dispatch*'s managing editor, was confronted by an enraged—and armed—Alonzo Slayback, the law partner of a St. Louis politician who had been the target of a series of Cockerill's scathing editorials. Slayback barged into Cockerill's office and was shot and killed by the editor. Although Cockerill was exonerated and the case dismissed from court as one of self-defense, Pulitzer was shaken by the event and the sensational publicity that followed. In the spring of 1883, Pulitzer moved to New York and expanded his publishing empire by purchasing the *World*, the metropolis's leading liberal paper, thus fulfilling his dream of being able to "speak to a nation." Pulitzer reassured St. Louisans that he would not abandon the *Post-Dispatch* and that the paper would continue to fight for the city's best interests.

The first of the following excerpts is an editorial proposing a fund-raising campaign eventually launched by the *Post-Dispatch* to reduce the dust on St. Louis's streets. The effort ultimately failed, but it is emblematic of Pulitzer's platform of supporting civic improvement causes. The second excerpt is the *Post-Dispatch*'s coverage of the shooting of Alonzo Slayback by the paper's managing editor, John Cockerill.

JOURNALISM FROM THE *ST. LOUIS POST–DISPATCH*

ANTI-DUST

Everybody who has enjoyed the alleged luxury of a drive in the suburbs of St. Louis has felt the full misery of the dust-laden breezes, which put pleasure entirely out of the question, and make the ride a mockery and a sham. There is not a single road leading out of St. Louis, from Bellefontaine on the north to the Stringtown on the south, which is fit for carriage travel. The heavy lime dust lies inches thick on every thoroughfare and is picked up by each breath of air and forced into the lungs of the wayfarer. Where there is no macadam upon the roads the heavy clay has been pulverized even deeper, and it is no exaggeration to say that the hot simoons of dust utterly destroy all the possible enjoyment to be found in the evening drive.

THE WESTERN DRIVE

Despite the unpleasant surroundings Page avenue and the other thoroughfares in the western part of the town are crowded every evening, even now before the season has really opened, and at least a thousand vehicles can be counted every fine afternoon. The Post-Dispatch means to inaugurate an anti-dust mission which will render at least one drive a pleasant one, and which will be so practical and full of good results that the trifling assessment will not be observed by those who are benefited. Out to Grand avenue the streets are kept in a sufficiently clean manner, but beyond that line of demarcation the trouble begins. Along Page avenue, down to Union and along Union to Forest Park, through the park and back to town by Lindell avenue, is a circuit of about five miles. The average distance which would be traveled by those who would use the drive in getting from their houses to Grand avenue would be between two miles and three, thus making

A DRIVE OF EIGHT MILES.

Sprinkling three miles of the route would make the whole a delightful circuit. A mile and a half of Page avenue, half a mile of Union and a mile of Lindell avenue would be all that it would be necessary to water.

It will be seen that if these avenues were dustless a most pleasant drive would be the result; in Forest Park the distance traversed might be extended almost indefinitely, and there is no doubt that travel would increase immensely if the indicated roads were thoroughly and systematically sprinkled.

An effort in this direction was made on Page avenue some years ago, but it fell through, partly because of the scarcity of water, and partly because people did not care to go out and come back on the same road.

The Scheme which the Post-Dispatch has to propose is this, that those gentlemen who use or who would use this drive each contribute a dollar a month for sprinkling. The Post-Dispatch will head the list with $10 a month for the six months of the season, and it calls upon those who want a pleasant roadway to send in their names to this office. Mr. E. C. Simmons and a number of other gentlemen, including Messrs. Gilbert Chapman, Ed. Martin, Samuel Cupples, George D. Cappen, Wm. H. Waters, Charles Greeley, Joseph Garneau, George Goddard, and Lee Wickham, will take charge of the movement and reduce it to practical details. It will cost less than a thousand dollars a month to sprinkle the necessary three miles of the circuit, and the amount ought to be easily raised among the more than a thousand people who use the drive. Gentlemen who are willing to contribute to this scheme will please send their names to the Post-Dispatch office and Mr. Simmons will shortly issue a call for a meeting at which the project may be fully discussed.

Nothing has been said about anything but the pleasure of this scheme. The fact that St. Louis has not had a decent drive to show a stranger has long been a standing reproach for the town, and there is no doubt at all that one class of the community, the livery stable keepers, will reap most substantial benefits from this idea, and should be willing to contribute liberally to its success.

A DOLLAR A MONTH

There is nothing that St. Louis is so deficient in as attractive summer drives. Forest Park has a labyrinth of well-paved, compact-roads, and once there the oppressed victim of summer heat in the city can enjoy the fresh air and the delicious exercise which comes of buggy or carriage riding. But the park is robbed of more than half its beauty by the villainous dust which lies between the city streets and the park gates. To have these stifling, suffocating clouds laid would be a blessing indeed. The city can do nothing in that line, and there are no householders in the belt to sustain the expense.

A number of gentlemen are interesting themselves in a sprinkling boom. They propose to secure for the citizens of St. Louis ten miles of delightful drive by private subscription. By sprinkling Page avenue, Union avenue and Lindell avenue a pleasant circuit can be secured from the sprinkled streets of the city to the cool roads of the Park. One can then drive out Page avenue to Union, down Union to the Park gate, and, after a turn through the park, can return by way of Lindell avenue. It is fair to assume that there are 6,000 people in the city who either own carriages and horses or drive more or less during the summer months. The sprinkling of which we speak can be done for about $1,000 a month—or $6,000 for the season. A small monthly subscription from those who ride and drive would secure this great boon—this splendid luxury. Assuming that all the readers of the Post-Dispatch are fond of riding to and from the park, we will manifest our appreciation of this worthy enterprise by making a monthly subscription of $10 to the cause of anti-dust. We would suggest that all persons who are willing to subscribe to the sprinkling fund send their names to this office. If enough encouragement can be obtained the matter will be placed in the hands of a committee of well-known businessmen, and by the first of May St. Louis will boast of as charming a drive as can be found in the country. Surely one thousand gentlemen can be found willing to contribute a dollar a month toward such a desirable end. Let us hear from the people who ride and drive. Send in your names, gentlemen! One dollar a month will do it.

APRIL 12, 1880

DEPLORABLE TRAGEDY

Late yesterday afternoon the editorial rooms of the Post-Dispatch were the scene of a terrible tragedy, which resulted in the almost instant death of Col. A. W. Slayback, a lawyer well and widely known in this city.

At 5:15 P.M. Slayback walked hurriedly and excitedly into the local rooms of the Post-Dispatch office, followed by W. H. Clopton. As is now well known, Col. Slayback had assailed the Post-Dispatch at a local political meeting held in the Eighteenth Ward on Thursday night. He had called the paper a blackmailing sheet and had bitterly attacked all persons connected with it. He made the statement publicly in his speech that to be connected with the Post-Dispatch and to be a gentleman was an impossible combination. He devoted twenty minutes to a tirade of this nature. As is equally well known, the Post-Dispatch replied to the deliberate attack in the editorial columns yesterday, by simply stating that the man who had made the speech was the same Col. A. W. Slayback about whom John M. Glover had published a card last fall, accusing him of cowardice, and the card was given in full. The publication of this matter brought about Col. Slayback's visit to the office yesterday afternoon. As he entered the local rooms with a rapid step, it was evident that he was in a high state of excitement. The door leading to the private office of John A. Cockerill, the managing editor, opens into the local rooms. It was closed at the time, Mr. Cockerill being in consultation in his office with Mr. John McGuffin, the business manager, and Mr. Victor Cole, the foreman of the composing room, about matters pertaining to advertising. Col. Slayback knew this very well, for he had often been a visitor to the office. He hurriedly opened the door of Mr. Cockerill's office, without knocking or giving any intimation of his presence, and rushed in, followed closely by Clopton. Mr. Henry W. Moore, the city editor, was seated at his desk, in the corner of the local rooms. He turned to look at Col. Slayback as he entered, and Mr. Moore positively states that as Mr. Slayback rushed into Mr. Cockerill's office, he had his right hand under his coat, and to all appearances was grasping a revolver. Mr. Cockerill was seated at his desk. Mr. Slayback rushed towards him and said, according to the statement of eye-witnesses, "Well, here I am!" A few more words were exchanged, the details of which will be found in the statements of eye-witnesses, published below. Col. Slayback drew his revolver, advanced on Mr. Cockerill, and told him to draw. The latter got up from his desk, saying that he did not want any trouble—that he would only defend himself, and warned Col. Slayback to stand back. He repeated the warning several times, having in the meantime taken up his own revolver which was lying on his desk. As Col. Slayback continued to advance, Mr. McGuffin grasped Slayback's pistol. At the same moment Col. Slayback pulled the trigger of the weapon which was still pointed straight at Mr. Cockerill. The hammer descended on Mr. McGuffin's hand, where it left its mark. Slayback and Clopton continued to advance crowding Cockerill into a corner and both being close to him in threatening attitudes, Slayback's pistol still covering him. At this moment a shot was heard, and Col. Slayback fell mortally wounded soon afterwards. The only witnesses were Messrs. McGuffin, Cole and Clopton. The statements given below describe the deplorable tragedy in detail.

After the shot, Clopton continued to struggle with Mr. Cockerill, and was, according to the statements of eye-witnesses, evidently trying to shoot him with his own pistol. Mr. McGuffin, seeing this, presented the revolver, which Col. Slayback in his weakness easily let go, at Mr. Clopton's head, forced him to relinquish his hold upon Cockerill, and to leave the room. Immediately after Col. Slayback was shot he began to show signs of weakness. Several persons among them Mr. Cole, Mr. Cockerill and others took hold of him and laid him on the floor. Blood gushed from his mouth and nose, covering his head and face. Those in attendance wiped the blood from his mouth and lips, but he never spoke and died in less than a minute. Dr. McCarthy, who came as quickly as possible, found him dead when he arrived. The news soon spread, and the friends of the dead man came in, among them his brother, Mr. Charles E. Slayback, President of the Merchants' Exchange. The scene was a most harrowing one as the brother and friends bent over the corpse. Within half an hour the undertaker's wagon came around and the body was taken to Lynch's establishment. Here it was stripped and washed. The bullet was found to have entered the left breast, just over the nipple, and probably passed through the heart. A number of the friends of the deceased gathered at Lynch's, and some of them viewed the body. Later, Mrs. Slayback was driven up and spent some moments in the room with her dead husband. A couple of friends went up to the dead man's residence and procured a suit of clothes. The body was dressed in them and about 8 o'clock it was taken up to the family residence at 2827 Olive street. Here the scene was so sad and heartrending that strong men turned away in tears. The body was placed in a rear room in an ice-box, where it has been lying ever since.

Mr. Cockerill left the office immediately after the unfortunate tragedy in company with Mr. McGuffin. He went up to the Lindell, where he changed his clothes, which were smeared with blood, which covered them while he was helping to place the dying man on the floor. He then went to consult his attorneys, Messrs. Johnson and Lodge, and at a late hour last night gave himself up to the police and was placed in the calaboose at the Four Courts, where he has remained during the day. Nobody deplores the tragedy more than Mr. Cockerill, who expresses the most sincere regret for the unfortunate ending of the affair.

COL. SLAYBACK'S DEATH

In regard to the deplorable tragedy which occurred yesterday evening the Post-Dispatch has nothing to say but words of sorrow for the dead, of sympathy for the bereaved and of simple justice to the gentleman who is one of the most sincere mourners and one of the chief sufferers of this sad affair.

Every person connected with this paper had the kindliest regard for Col. Alonzo W. Slayback, and the proprietor and Col. John A. Cockerill had especially cultivated and maintained the most cordial relations with him.

Nothing personally offensive to him was ever permitted to appear in the columns of this paper, until he had in a public speech on Thursday night, violently denounced, with opprobrious epithets, everybody connected with the Post-Dispatch, and denounced the paper itself as a slanderous and blackmailing sheet. Yesterday there appeared in its columns a brief editorial paragraph repelling this attack in language as mild as the nature of the attack permitted. While the presses were still running off that issue, and while Col. Cockerill was at his desk in the editorial room, talking about a business matter with the foreman and the business manager of the paper, his room was invaded by Col. Slayback and Mr. W. H. Clopton, the former advancing on Col. Cockerill with a pistol. In the ensuing struggle, while Cockerill was crowded against the wall and almost on his knees, regarding himself as assailed with apparently murderous intent by two men, he fired the fatal shot. Fortunately for him, Mr. McGuffin and Mr. Cole were present, and are witnesses of the fact that he fired in necessary self-defense, and that Col. Slayback's pistol was wrenched from his hand by Mr. McGuffin after the shot was fired.

These are the simple facts, and we assure the public that a legal investigation will develop these and other facts proving that this was as clear a case of shooting in self-defense as was ever forced upon any man. Of course all the enmities aroused by the fearless course of this paper are now arrayed against Col. Cockerill, and the *Republican* is pouring out upon him the vials of its long pent-up wrath, villainously and systematically misrepresenting the facts, and doing all that it can to exasperate public feeling against a man who has promptly surrendered himself to the hands of the law and asks nothing but the justice of a fair trial. Leaving the public to characterize as it deserves this cowardly course of the *Republican*, we ask leave to add only that all who know Col. Cockerill know him to be as tender-hearted as a woman, a man of peace, whose whole life has been full of generous and kindly deeds, a man who abhors injustice and is ever ready to repair a wrong.

OCTOBER 14, 1882

MARK TWAIN

MARK TWAIN (1835–1910) was born Samuel Clemens in Florida, Missouri, to parents who embodied the American frontier spirit. His father, a Virginian, settled the family in Hannibal in 1839 and pursued dreams of wealth through land speculation. As a young man, Clemens shared his father's penchant for risk-taking and adventure, restlessly dabbling in a variety of careers before becoming Mark Twain in print and on the lecture circuit. At one time or another, Clemens was a printer, a miner, and a reporter, but no line of work pleased him more than piloting steamboats on the Mississippi, a vocation ended by the Civil War.

Clemens's love for piloting was an extension of his love of the river, a highway that connected his Hannibal childhood to the great world that seemed to radiate from St. Louis, a city which Clemens, as a young pilot, frequently visited. After the Civil War, he briefly lived in St. Louis as the writer Mark Twain, sharing a house with his sister and widowed mother. In 1870, Twain married Olivia Langdon, a genteel easterner, and moved to Connecticut, after which his visits to St. Louis became infrequent. Twain visited St. Louis for the last time in 1902 while traveling to Columbia to receive an honorary degree from the University of Missouri.

Contributing editor Wayne Fields writes, "It is appropriate that our greatest account of the river that flowed through Twain's youth should be 'Old Times on the Mississippi' (subsequently included in *Life on the Mississippi*), surely one of the most beautiful literary accomplishments of his career." Not surprisingly, St. Louis, the city of Twain's boyhood fantasies, provided a regular reference point in his writings. Huck Finn, who drifts past the city in the middle of the night, exclaims, "It was like the whole world lit up." However, in *Life on the Mississippi* (1883), Twain's treatment of St. Louis was not always so complimentary. The following excerpts from that work show the contrast between Twain's youthful yearning for adventure on the river and in "St. Looy," and his middle-age experience, as a famous writer, traveling incognito to the city on a steamboat.

FROM *LIFE ON THE MISSISSIPPI*

THE BOY'S AMBITION

When I was a boy, there was but one permanent ambition among my comrades in our village on the west bank of the Mississippi River. That was, to be a steamboatman. We had transient ambitions of other sorts, but they were only transient. When a circus came and went, it left us all burning to become clowns; the first negro minstrel show that came to our section left us all suffering to try that kind of life; now and then we had a hope that if we lived and were good, God would permit us to be pirates. These ambitions faded out, each in its turn; but the ambition to be a steamboatman always remained.

Once a day a cheap, gaudy packet arrived upward from St. Louis, and another downward from Keokuk. Before these events, the day was glorious with expectancy; after them, the day was a dead and empty thing. Not only the boys, but the whole village, felt this. After all these years I can picture that old time to myself now, just as it was then: the white town drowsing in the sunshine of a summer's morning; the streets empty, or pretty nearly so; one or two clerks sitting in front of the Water Street stores, with their splint-bottomed chairs tilted back against the wall, chins on breasts, hats slouched over their faces, asleep—with shingle-shavings enough around to show what broke them down; a sow and a litter of pigs loafing along the sidewalk, doing a good business in watermelon rinds and seeds; two or three lonely little freight piles scattered about the "levee;" a pile of "skids" on the slope of the stone-paved wharf, and the fragrant town drunkard asleep in the shadow of them; two or three wood flats at the head of the wharf, but nobody to listen to the peaceful lapping of the wavelets against them; the great Mississippi, the majestic, the magnificent Mississippi, rolling its mile-wide tide along, shining in the sun; the dense forest away on the other side; the "point" above the town, and the "point" below, bounding the river-glimpse and turning it into sea, and withal a very still and brilliant and lonely one. Presently a film of dark smoke appears above one of those remote "points;" instantly a negro drayman, famous for his quick eye and prodigious voice, lifts up the cry, "S-t-e-a-m-boat a-comin'!" and the scene changes! The town drunkard stirs, the clerks wake up, a furious clatter of drays follows, every house and store pours out a human contribution, and all in a twinkling the dead town is alive and moving. Drays, carts, men, boys, all go hurrying from many quarters to a common centre, the wharf. Assembled there, the people fasten their eyes upon the coming boat as upon a wonder they are seeing for the first time. And the boat *is* rather a handsome sight too. She is long and sharp and trim and pretty; she has two tall, fancy-topped chimneys, with a gilded device of some kind swung between them, a fanciful pilot-house, all glass and "gingerbread," perched on top of the "texas" deck behind them; the paddle-boxes are gorgeous with a picture or with gilded rays above the boat's name; the boiler deck, the hurricane deck, and the texas deck are fenced and ornamented with clean white railings; there is a flag gallantly flying from the jack-staff; the furnace doors are open and the fire glaring bravely; the upper decks are black with passengers; the captain stands by the big bell, calm, imposing, the envy of all; great volumes of the blackest smoke are rolling and tumbling out of the chimneys—a husbanded grandeur created with a bit of pitch pine just before arriving at a town; the crew are grouped on the forecastle; the broad stage is run far out over the port bow, and an envied deck-hand stands picturesquely on the end of it with a coil of rope in his hand; the pent steam is screaming through the gauge-cocks; the captain lifts his hand, a bell rings, the wheels stop; then they turn back, churning the water to foam, and the steamer is at rest. Then such a scramble as there is to get aboard, and to get ashore, and to take in freight and to discharge freight, all at one and the same time; and such a yelling and cursing as the mates facilitate it all with! Ten minutes later the steamer is under way again, with no flag on the jack-staff and no black smoke issuing from the chimneys. After ten more minutes the town is dead again, and the town drunkard asleep by the skids once more.

My father was a justice of the peace, and I supposed he possessed the power of life and death over all men and could hang anybody that offended him. This was distinction enough for me as a general thing; but the desire to be a steamboatman kept intruding, nevertheless. I first wanted to be a cabin-boy, so that I could come out with a white apron on and shake a table-cloth over the side, where all my old comrades could see me; later I thought I would rather be the deck-hand who stood on the end of the stage-plank with the coil of rope in his hand, because he was particularly conspicuous. But these were only day-dreams,—they were too heavenly to be contemplated as real possibilities. By and by one of our boys went away. He was not heard of for a long time. At last he turned up as apprentice engineer or "striker" on a steamboat. This thing shook the bottom out of all my Sunday-school teachings. That boy had been notoriously worldly and I just the reverse; yet he was exalted to this eminence, and I left in obscurity and misery. There was nothing generous about this fellow in his greatness. He would always manage to have a rusty bolt to scrub while his boat tarried at our town, and he would sit on the inside guard and scrub it, where we could all see him and envy him and loathe him. And whenever his boat was laid up he would come home and swell around the town in his blackest and greasiest clothes, so that nobody could help remembering that he was a steamboatman; and he used all sorts of steamboat technicalities in his talk, as if he were so used to them that he forgot common people could not understand them. He would speak of the "labboard" side of a horse in an easy, natural way that would make one wish he was dead. And he was always talking about "St. Looy" like an old citizen; he would refer casually to occasions when he "was coming down Fourth Street," or when he was "passing by the Planter's House," or when there was a fire and he took a turn on the brakes of "the old Big Missouri;" and then he would go on and lie about how many towns the size of ours were burned down there that day. Two or three of the boys had long been persons of consideration among us because they had been to St. Louis once and had a vague general knowledge of its wonders, but the day of their glory was over now. They lapsed into a humble silence, learned to disappear when the ruthless "cub"-engineer approached. This fellow had money, too, and hair oil. Also an ignorant silver watch and a showy brass watch chain. He wore a leather belt and used no suspenders. If ever a youth was cordially admired and hated by his comrades, this one was. No girl could withstand his charms. He "cut out" every boy in the village. When his boat blew up at last, it diffused a tranquil contentment among us such as we had not known for months. But when he came home the next week, alive, renowned, and appeared in church all battered up and bandaged, a shining hero, stared at and wondered over by everybody, it seemed to us that the partiality of Providence for an undeserving reptile had reached a point where it was open to criticism.

This creature's career could produce but one result, and it speedily followed. Boy after boy managed to get on the river. The minister's son became an engineer. The doctor's and post-master's sons became "mud clerks;" the wholesale liquor dealer's son became a bar-keeper on a boat; four sons of the chief merchant, and two sons of the county judge, became pilots. Pilot was the grandest position of all. The pilot, even in those days of trivial wages, had a princely salary—from a hundred and fifty to two hundred and fifty dollars a month, and no board to pay. Two months of his wages would pay a preacher's salary for a year. Now some of us were left disconsolate. We could not get on the river—at least our parents would not let us.

So by and by I ran away. I said I never would come home again till I was a pilot and could come in glory. But somehow I could not manage it. I went meekly aboard a few of the boats that lay packed together like sardines at the long St. Louis wharf, and very humbly inquired for the pilots, but got only a shoulder and short words from mates and clerks. I had to make the best of this sort of treatment for the time being, but I had comforting day-dreams of a future when I should be a great and honored pilot, with plenty of money, and could kill some of these mates and clerks and pay for them.

I RETURN TO MY MUTTONS

After twenty-one years' absence, I felt a very strong desire to see the river again, and the steamboats, and such of the boys as might be left; so I resolved to go out there. I enlisted a poet for company, and a stenographer to "take him down," and started westward about the middle of April.

As I proposed to make notes, with a view to printing, I took some thought as to methods of procedure. I reflected that if I were recognized, on the river, I should not be as free to go and come, talk, inquire, and spy around, as I should be if unknown; I remembered that it was the custom of steamboatmen in the old times to load up the confiding stranger with the most picturesque and admirable lies, and put the sophisticated friend off with dull and ineffectual facts: so I concluded, that, from a business point of view, it would be an advantage to disguise our party with fictitious names. The idea was certainly good, but it bred infinite bother; for although Smith, Jones, and Johnson are easy names to remember when there is no occasion to remember them, it is next to impossible to recollect them when they are wanted. How do criminals manage to keep a brand-new *alias* in mind? This is a great mystery. I was innocent; and yet was seldom able to lay my hand on my new name when it was needed; and it seemed to me that if I had had a crime on my conscience to further confuse me, I could never have kept the name by me at all.

We left per Pennsylvania Railroad, at 8 A.M. April 18.

> "*Evening.* Speaking of dress. Grace and picturesqueness drop gradually out of it as one travels away from New York."

I find that among my notes. It makes no difference which direction you take, the fact remains the same. Whether you move north, south, east, or west, no matter: you can get up in the morning and guess how far you have come, by noting what degree of grace and picturesqueness is by that time lacking in the costumes of the new passengers;—I do not mean of the women alone, but of both sexes. It may be that *carriage* is at the bottom of this thing; and I think it is; for there are plenty of ladies and gentlemen in the provincial cities whose garments are all made by the best tailors and dressmakers of New York; yet this has no perceptible effect upon the grand fact: the educated eye never mistakes those people for New-Yorkers. No, there is a godless grace, and snap, and style about a born and bred New-Yorker which mere clothing cannot effect.

> "*April 19.* This morning, struck into the region of full goatees—sometimes accompanied by a moustache, but only occasionally."

It was odd to come upon this thick crop of an obsolete and uncomely fashion; it was like running suddenly across a forgotten acquaintance whom you had supposed dead for a generation. The goatee extends over a wide extent of country; and is accompanied by an iron-clad belief in Adam and the biblical history of creation, which has not suffered from the assaults of the scientists.

> "*Afternoon.* At the railway stations the loafers carry both hands in their breeches pockets; it was observable, heretofore, that one hand was sometimes out of doors,—here, never. This is an important fact in geography."

If the loafers determined the character of a country, it would be still more important, of course.

"Heretofore, all along, the station-loafer has been often observed to scratch one shin with the other foot; here, these remains of activity are wanting. This has an ominous look."

By and by, we entered the tobacco-chewing region. Fifty years ago, the tobacco-chewing region covered the Union. It is greatly restricted now.

Next, boots began to appear. Not in strong force, however. Later—away down the Mississippi—they became the rule. They disappeared from other sections of the Union with the mud; no doubt they will disappear from the river villages, also, when proper pavements come in.

We reached St. Louis at ten o'clock at night. At the counter of the hotel I tendered a hurriedly-invented fictitious name, with a miserable attempt at careless ease. The clerk paused, and inspected me in the compassionate way in which one inspects a respectable person who is found in doubtful circumstances; then he said,—

"It's all right; I know what sort of a room you want. Used to clerk at the St. James, in New York."

An unpromising beginning for a fraudulent career. We started to the supper room, and met two other men whom I had known elsewhere. How odd and unfair it is: wicked impostors go around lecturing under my *nom de guerre*, and nobody suspects them; but when an honest man attempts an imposture, he is exposed at once.

One thing seemed plain: we must start down the river the next day, if people who could not be deceived were going to crop up at this rate: an unpalatable disappointment, for we had hoped to have a week in St. Louis. The Southern was a good hotel, and we could have had a comfortable time there. It is large, and well conducted, and its decorations do not make one cry, as do those of the vast Palmer House, in Chicago. True, the billiard-tables were of the Old Silurian Period, and the cues and balls of the Post-Pliocene; but there was refreshment in this, not discomfort; for there is rest and healing in the contemplation of antiquities.

The most notable absence observable in the billiard room, was the absence of the river man. If he was there he had taken in his sign, he was in disguise. I saw there none of the swell airs and graces, and ostentatious displays of money, and pompous squanderings of it, which used to distinguish the steamboat crowd from the dry-land crowd in the bygone days, in the thronged billiard-rooms of St. Louis. In those times, the principal saloons were always populous with river men; given fifty players present, thirty or thirty-five were likely to be from the river. But I suspected that the ranks were thin now, and the steamboatmen no longer an aristocracy. Why, in my time they used to call the "barkeep" Bill, or Joe, or Tom, and slap him on the shoulder; I watched for that. But none of these people did it. Manifestly a glory that once was had dissolved and vanished away in these twenty-one years.

When I went up to my room, I found there the young man called Rogers, crying. Rogers was not his name; neither was Jones, Brown, Dexter, Ferguson, Bascom, nor Thompson; but he answered to either of these that a body found handy in an emergency; or to any other name, in fact, if he perceived that you meant him. He said: —

"What is a person to do here when he wants a drink of water?—drink this slush?"

"Can't you drink it?"

"I could If I had some other water to wash it with."

Here was a thing which had not changed; a score of years had not affected this water's mulatto complexion in the least; a score of centuries would succeed no better, perhaps. It comes out of the turbulent, bank-caving Missouri, and every tumblerful of it holds nearly an acre of land in solution. I got this fact from the bishop of the diocese. If you will let your glass stand half an hour, you can separate the land from the water as easy as Genesis; and then you will find them both good: the one good to eat, the other good to drink. The land is very nourishing, the water is thoroughly wholesome. The one appeases hunger; the other, thirst. But the natives do not take them separately, but together, as nature mixed them. When they find an inch of mud in the bottom of a glass, they stir it up, and then take the draught as they would gruel. It is difficult for a stranger to get used to this batter, but once used to it they will prefer it to water. This is really the case. It is good for steamboating, and good to drink; but it is worthless for all other purposes, except baptizing.

Next morning, we drove around town in the rain. The city seemed but little changed. It *was* greatly changed, but it did not seem so; because in St. Louis, as in London and Pittsburgh, you can't persuade a new thing to look new; the coal smoke turns it into an antiquity the moment you take your hand off it. The place had just about doubled its size, since I was a resident of it, and was now become a city of 400,000 inhabitants; still, in the solid business parts, it looked about as it had looked formerly. Yet I am sure there is not as much smoke in St. Louis now as there used to be. The smoke used to bank itself in a dense billowy black canopy over the town, and hide the sky from view. This shelter is very much thinner now; still, there is a sufficiency of smoke there, I think. I heard no complaint.

However, on the outskirts changes were apparent enough; notably in dwelling-house architecture. The fine new homes are noble and beautiful and modern. They stand by themselves, too, with green lawns around them; whereas the dwellings of a former day are packed together in blocks, and are all of one pattern, with windows all alike, set in an arched frame-work of twisted stone; a sort of house which was handsome enough when it was rarer.

There was another change—the Forest Park. This was new to me. It is beautiful and very extensive, and has the excellent merit of having been made mainly by nature. There are other parks, and fine ones, notably Tower Grove and the Botanical Gardens; for St. Louis interested herself in such improvements at an earlier day than did the most of our cities.

The first time I ever saw St. Louis, I could have bought it for six million dollars, and it was the mistake of my life that I did not do it. It was bitter now to look abroad over this domed and steepled metropolis, this solid expanse of bricks and mortar stretching away on every hand into dim, measure-defying distances, and remember that I had allowed that opportunity to go by. Why I should have allowed it to go by seems, of course, foolish and inexplicable to-day, at a first glance; yet there were reasons at the time to justify this course.

A Scotchman, Hon. Charles Augustus Murray, writing some forty-five or fifty years ago, said: "The streets are narrow, ill paved and ill lighted." Those streets are narrow still, of course; many of them are ill paved yet; but the reproach of ill lighting cannot be repeated, now. The "Catholic New Church" was the only notable building then, and Mr. Murray was confidently called upon to admire it, with its "species of Grecian portico, surmounted by a kind of steeple, much too diminutive in its proportions, and surmounted by sundry ornaments" which the unimaginative Scotchman found himself "quite unable to describe;" and therefore was grateful when a German tourist helped him out with the exclamation: "By—, they look exactly like bed-posts!" St. Louis is well equipped with stately and noble public buildings now, and the little church, which the people used to be so proud of, lost its importance a long time ago. Still, this would not surprise Mr. Murray, if he could come back; for he prophesied the coming greatness of St. Louis with strong confidence.

The further we drove in our inspection-tour, the more sensibly I realized how the city had grown since I had seen it last; changes in detail became steadily more apparent and frequent than at first, too: changes uniformly evidencing progress, energy, prosperity.

But the change of changes was on the "levee." This time, a departure from the rule. Half a dozen sound-asleep steamboats where I used to see a solid mile of wide-awake ones! This was melancholy, this was woful. The absence of the pervading and jocund steamboatman from the billiard-saloon was explained. He was absent because he is no more. His occupation is gone, his power has passed away, he is absorbed into the common herd, he grinds at the mill, a shorn Samson and inconspicuous. Half a dozen lifeless steamboats, a mile of empty wharves, a negro fatigued with whiskey stretched asleep, in a wide and soundless vacancy, where the serried hosts of commerce used to contend! Here was desolation, indeed.

"The old, old sea, as one in tears,
Comes murmuring, with foamy lips,
And knocking at the vacant piers,
Calls for his long-lost multitude of ships."

The towboat and the railroad had done their work, and done it well and completely. The mighty bridge, stretching along over our heads, had done its share in the slaughter and spoliation. Remains of former steamboatmen told me, with wan satisfaction, that the bridge doesn't pay. Still, it can be no sufficient compensation to a corpse, to know that the dynamite that laid him out was not of as good quality as it had been supposed to be.

The pavements along the river front were bad; the sidewalks were rather out of repair; there was a rich abundance of mud. All this was familiar and satisfying; but the ancient armies of drays, and struggling throngs of men, and mountains of freight, were gone; and Sabbath reigned in their stead. The immemorial mile of cheap foul doggeries remained, but business was dull with them; the multitudes of poison-swilling Irishmen had departed, and in their places were a few scattering handfuls of ragged negroes, some drinking, some drunk, some nodding, others asleep. St. Louis is a great and prosperous and advancing city; but the river-edge of it seems dead past resurrection.

Mississippi steamboating was born about 1812; at the end of thirty years, it had grown to mighty proportions; and in less than thirty more, it was dead! A strangely short life for so majestic a creature. Of course it is not absolutely dead; neither is a crippled octogenarian who could once jump twenty-two feet on level ground; but as contrasted with what it was in its prime vigor, Mississippi steamboating may be called dead.

It killed the old-fashioned keel-boating, by reducing the freight-trip to New Orleans to less than a week. The railroads have killed the steamboat passenger traffic by doing in two or three days what the steamboats consumed a week in doing; and the towing-fleets have killed the through-freight traffic by dragging six or seven steamer-loads of stuff down the river at a time, at an expense so trivial that steamboat competition was out of the question.

Freight and passenger way-traffic remains to the steamers. This is in the hands—along the two thousand miles of river between St. Paul and New Orleans—of two or three close corporations well fortified with capital; and by able and thoroughly business-like management and system, these make a sufficiency, of money out of what is left of the once prodigious steamboating industry. I suppose that St. Louis and New Orleans have not suffered materially by the change, but alas for the wood-yard man!

He used to fringe the river all the way; his close-ranked merchandise stretched from the one city to the other, along the banks, and he sold uncountable cords of it every year for cash on the nail; but all the scattering boats that are left burn coal now, and the seldomest spectacle on the Mississippi today is a wood-pile. Where now is the once wood-yard man?

NICOLAUS MOHR

NICOLAUS MOHR (1826–1886) was born in Bremen and studied and taught at the University of Bonn before becoming a journalist in 1853. As editor of *Weser Zeitung*, he became one of Germany's most respected newspapermen and wielded considerable influence among the country's political and business leaders. In 1883, Mohr was one of a large group of prominent Europeans who sailed to the United States as a guest of Henry Villard, president of the Northern Pacific Railroad. Villard had invited political luminaries and investors on a coast-to-coast journey to promote and celebrate the rail linkage of the East Coast and Oregon. While on the three-month journey, Mohr sent dispatches back to his newspaper in Bremen, giving lively descriptive accounts of his impressions of the American cities he visited from a distinctively German vantage point. Mohr published his travel narratives in a single volume, *Ein Streifzug durch den Nordwesten Amerikas* (1884).

In the following passage, which comes from the book's English translation *Excursion through America* (1973), Mohr describes St. Louis in October 1883 during "fair week." Although Mohr visited the city on the return leg of his arduous journey, he was impressed by St. Louis's vitality and the impact of the German population on the city's character and development. Readers may note that Mohr erroneously attributes the design of the Eads Bridge to John A. Roebling.

FROM *EXCURSION THROUGH AMERICA*

ST. LOUIS: THE FIRST DAYS OF OCTOBER, 1883

We left St. Paul, where nightly frosts were already announcing winter, and arrived here in St. Louis to find summer temperatures still prevailing. On the way we passed through Milwaukee, the most German city in the

United States. Unfortunately we rode right through and I only saw the view from the depot. I regard my failure to see Milwaukee as one of the sins committed during my journey through the Northwest. Similarly, we spent only a few hours in Chicago on this return trip. By the second morning we were again riding along the Mississippi and continued close beside it until we reached East St. Louis where we crossed the suspension bridge into the city of St. Louis.

As in New York, it is a suspension bridge designed by Roebling. It is built in three long arches spanning the river and is the only structure of this unusual design. It is stunning in every respect. The bridge has a twofold purpose: on the lower deck it carries trains and on the upper deck provides for pedestrian and wagon traffic. From the bridge we continued to the depot in the middle of the city. The immediate surroundings were ugly and the pavement terrible. St. Louis freely admits that it has never had a reputation for good streets. When it rains, they are covered with mud and during dry spells one can lose his way in the dust.

The city is filled with excitement and festivities. The fair week has just begun and all the hotels are swamped. From far and near the population of Missouri and the neighboring states has flooded into St. Louis. After hard and bitter summer work, everyone is ready for a festival.

We arrived at the risk of not finding overnight accommodations, but my luck held up and in no time I was settled at "Kotter's Hotel," a German inn opposite the famous Southern Hotel. Everything in this hotel is German, but with an American veneer. It is, in fact, astonishing how very little German customs have influenced the exterior form of life in America. Take any American city and you cannot tell whether it has a large, small, or no German settlement in it. Whether it is the style of building, the platting of the streets, the public buildings, the stores, the restaurants, right down to the signs and inscriptions on the business places and in the display windows, every single detail is American, modeled largely after English patterns of living that are strange to us. Likewise the hotels are peculiarly American, even the hotel belonging to Mr. Kotter. Though its owner is a German and its staff as well as customers are all German, nevertheless its style of construction and its furnishings are completely and totally in the American style.

I do not mean to say that the interior arrangements in private dwellings and in hotels are less comfortable than in Germany. The total uniformity of life in the United States has its good side. What develops as a fine practice is immediately recognized and accepted everywhere. Thus the need for certain things is easily satisfied, for it is so universal that it can be accomplished by mass production. On the other hand, in Germany so much consideration is made for individual preferences that too much attention is paid to variations and efforts are scattered. But here I go, digressing into observations which I wanted to save for another time.

Barely had I registered in the hotel when a waiter walked up to announce that for many years he had been a teacher not far from Bremen. Fate had brought him to St. Louis, where he temporarily found a job and lodging in the hotel, but he hoped some day to return to his profession by getting a job in Mexico. At breakfast I bumped into an old schoolmate, who has spent many years here in a small town in Missouri. He operates a fine dry goods business and was in St. Louis both for business and for pleasure. That is, he was making use of the fair week to visit with people and keep up his business contacts while also injecting a little diversion into his routine life.

As you can see, the Germans are not scarce in St. Louis. In fact, to say that a quarter of the population of St. Louis is German is not too high an estimate. In St. Louis the Germans also have political significance. They proudly proclaim that it was their determined stance that broke the wave of rebellion which threatened to erupt in Missouri. They feel St. Louis performed a heroic service in defense of the Union even though this meant going against its own immediate interests, for St. Louis had very close ties with the slave-holding South. If Missouri had seceded from the Union, St. Louis would have found an excellent position within the Confederacy. More important to the citizens of St. Louis, however, was their loyalty to the Union and the preservation of the United States. It was the Germans of St. Louis who made a major contribution to this patriotic outburst of public opinion.

Today, not even two decades have passed since the conclusion of the terrible four-year war. It ended only with the enforced disappearance of a great social evil. Yet how wonderful it is that the deep wounds caused by that conflict seem to be completely healed. Admittedly, there is probably still some silent sympathy for the South among the former soldiers and those who suffered heavy losses, but there is no present threat to the Union of any plots to restore the former status in the South. The black men have become citizens of the Republic, while prejudice has subsided and hate against the black race is no longer expressed in brutal ways.

St. Louis was compelled to make great sacrifices as a result of the war. Through the economic collapse of the plantation owners, the city also suffered. One notices even today that St. Louis was formerly frequented by a rich, aristocratic class of people, although perhaps these reminders derive from a former French influence here.

Nature has not been particularly favorable to St. Louis. One exception of course is the river. Fifteen miles north of St. Louis the waters of the Missouri flow into the Mississippi. From the bridge that rises majestically over the river one has a view over the whole city and its environs.

Seeing the river and its banks inside the city was a great disappointment. I had imagined that the water would be covered with Mississippi steamboats, one next to the other, for miles. So I had read and heard earlier. Such was the picture I had from my earlier reading. But these exciting days have passed and today the river is no longer so important. It is the railroads that count.

Here the banks of the Mississippi are flat. Presently, in the fall of the year before the rainy season, the water is so low that some of the steamboats have stopped running. I was thinking about taking a ride on the river, but I was advised against this because I could be stuck somewhere for days. During November and December the Mississippi usually also has a low flow. In December of 1882, for example, it dropped to a depth of two feet and six inches, while in July it stood at thirty-two feet and five inches.

It was somewhat surprising to learn that for a rather long time in the winter, the river south of St. Louis can become closed by ice. There are, of course, years in which shipping is not stopped for a single day, but in other years the river can remain shut for as much as two and a half months.

St. Louis is among the top commercial cities of the heartland. Thanks to the excellent railroad system, and also to the water route, St. Louis is the focal point for immense masses of products from the interior of the country. From here these items find their way to the sea ports. On the other hand, St. Louis is in an excellent position to be a distributor through which major portions of the neighboring states are supplied with industrial materials from the East and from Europe. In every way it has the characteristics of a large city. According to the census of 1880, St. Louis had a population of 350,000. Today this figure probably stands more nearly at 400,000.

The streets are wide and naturally straight as a bullet. The city layout is just as regular as we have come to expect in every American city. Likewise the building style is not exactly outstanding for its originality, but there are some nice structures. The streets that run down toward the river have been selected by businesses such as banks and insurance companies. Characteristically this is the area of heaviest traffic. The Germans are well represented among the firms in this section as well as in a wide range of positions. On the whole they all do very well. They work much harder here than they did back in Germany. The strong competition demands a larger input of effort and strength. But since people here live decidedly better and become much richer than in our country, even the lower classes are willing to put forth greater effort. The secret of success for the immigrants seems to be this: they have been freed from the former social restraints that hampered their energies and thus feel themselves driven to a more liberated, more energetic use of their strengths and abilities.

A fellow German who was a pleasant and informative traveling companion to all during our trip on the steamer *Elbe* is the owner of a large wholesale hat house in St. Louis and we were pleased to accept his invitation to tour his business. The entire five-floored building was filled from top to bottom with hats, caps, gloves, etc. All the styles of headgear that we have seen during our travels—on the cowboys, the mountaineers, the farmers, and the city folks—could be seen again here. Only here there was not just one of each, but crates of every imaginable kind. On each crate was a model of the contents. In addition to all kinds of hats, there were gloves and mittens for men and women. We saw some built for the cold in certain regions that were so heavy we could only think of Siberia, certainly not of dressy clothes.

Just as large are the wholesale houses for luxury and art items—bronze, chinaware, gold and silver products, as well as wide selections of jewelry, frequently imported from Paris. I would like to pick out one characteristic incident to illustrate how wide the gulf is that separates America from Europe and how difficult it is for ideas and cultural refinement to make their way across the ocean. This remains true despite the fact that every week thirty steamers make their way between the continents. The statue of Hermes of Praxiteles, an incomparable treasure which has become such an everyday item in Germany that no cultured home is without one, is an art object which now is completely unknown in America. I have looked everywhere, in art stores, in plaster reproduction shops, in chinaware stores, but nowhere have I seen a reproduction of this bust. I even checked in different stocks of reproductions retained by antique dealers but Hermes was always missing. Among the most cultured Germans in this country, at least, one finds someone who has a fleeting knowledge that this work of art, one of the finest in the world, exists.

St. Louis is having its fair, what we Europeans call a *Jahrmarkt* or *Kirmes*. To be sure the fair and the *Jahrmarkt* do have certain things in common, but judging by the way they celebrate a fair here, one must admit that it represents a step forward from its sister custom back in the Old World. On the one hand a fair is a folk festival, but it has a serious side to it as well. The St. Louis fair consists primarily of an agricultural exhibit, with displays coming from the entire Mississippi Valley. Simultaneously the fair has the quality of a *Messe* or general market because after being shown, the machinery, cattle, and other products are offered for sale. I must admit I have never seen a finer agricultural display nor a larger accumulation of rural products and animals.

In addition to this business aspect of the fair, there are many other things to be seen: illumination displays, stage performances, military balls, even a festival in the stock exchange.

A theatrical group called the "Veiled Prophets," from Moore's Lalla Rookh, is producing acts for the embellishment of fair week. Accordingly, the veiled prophet, who lives in his water grotto on the river, is honoring the city with his visits. He is surrounded by his fantastic household, including Queen Mab who has been freed from a five-hundred-year captivity and is now introducing her fairies and elves to the New World.

Around this general theme, new and old fairy tales and elf narratives are dramatized and presented to the public from large wagons.

The streets have been wonderfully illuminated. For miles, arches with gas lights have been hung under white or red cupolas all along the route taken by the parade on the first day of the fair. Interspersed with the arches are gas lanterns fastened to poles. These endlessly long streets and avenues so gloriously lighted are really a sight to behold. Admittedly, I missed the first night but the streets have been lit again each evening. They have also made extensive use of electric lighting. Individual business establishments have hung dozens of arc lamps from extensions in their store fronts.

The second major parade was postponed because of rain. It was sponsored and arranged by the merchants and businessmen and was to present some idea about the commerce and trade of the city. All of the significant businesses of St. Louis were represented either realistically or in allegory. A parade was of course nothing new for me after the parades in St. Paul, Minneapolis, and

Portland. But here the exhibitors had more time to prepare, and established traditions probably helped them in certain aspects. Here, as in other parades, it was apparent that Americans have a strong liking for satire and that they can well appreciate a joke. In their wit they display a fresh bold spirit and confidence in the further growth and development of the country. No less interesting than the floats was the accompaniment. There were different military companies which have taken the patterns for their uniforms from the armies of Europe. The fire brigade presented its steam sprayer and entertained our ears with the shrieking sounds from the steam whistles.

To throw light on the individual units, Negroes with torches frequently walked beside the floats. There was a large silk firm which has branches in many cities of the Union, called the Nonotock Silk Company. On its float twenty or more knights in armor held rolls of silk cloth on their lances, with the inscription of the company printed on it. One of the import houses offered a float carrying a little steamship covered with the merchandise which the importer has for sale. The brewers brought out their King Gambrinus on four floats. The Missouri Bicycle Company loaded its float with velocipedes and behind it there rode a troupe of riders using the velocipedes.

Thus followed float after float. Each funny float was received with applause and cheering. For me, the attitudes of the observers were just as interesting as the drama itself. There were perhaps a hundred thousand people lined up along the streets through which the parade moved. The many, many buggies and wagons parked in the side streets brought in curiosity-seekers from the suburbs and surrounding areas. Nowhere did I observe any rough pushing and shoving by young or old as sometimes happens when ruffians take pleasure in making themselves as burdensome and unpleasant as possible to the majority of the audience. And when the performance was over, very few policemen were needed to untangle this crush of buggies and get everybody on the way home. I was amazed at the orderliness and patience of all who took part. It never occurred to anyone to push or rush.

All the taverns and evening spots are crowded during the evenings, and scenes are lively, but nowhere do the police have to be called to restore order. When the festivities are over, everyone leaves peacefully. I do not think we Europeans have any reason to believe that we are superior to the people of the United States. Certainly in times of political turmoil the large masses of people in Europe will not disperse so harmlessly.

St. Louis has its own special place for the fair, called the fairgrounds, which is a park west of the city large enough for cattle and agricultural machinery. The streetcar system in St. Louis is well developed so one can easily get there and at a minimum expense. It is a large area that includes also parks and a zoo. For the different displays, large but simple buildings have been erected. The short time that I had available to spend during the afternoon was entirely insufficient to cover the extraordinarily large fair.

Most intriguing to me was the farm machinery. Here was inventiveness at work trying to solve difficult mechanical problems. The Americans possess a precision of workmanship in carrying through the inventions they have brought to light. A great need for such machines is coupled with the capability to create them. The guiding principle in all of this agricultural machinery is to save on human labor. Indeed, the most diverse branches of technology cooperate to solve the needs of agriculture.

The only thing that could be compared in size to this gigantic display was the wagon and carriage exhibit. There were hundreds of vehicles of every kind. Driving in this country is no luxury; rather it is an everyday necessity. The great distances demand it and, as my fellow Germans who now live here assure me, the climate in America is not suitable for very much walking. After a few years here immigrants break away from their old habits and go to horseback riding or driving a team. Even in those areas of the United States where there are adequate hotels and inns, nobody travels on foot.

The light American carriages with their spider-web frames are extremely practical in their construction. They have all kinds of clever devices to make them open or covered, to turn the seats for ease in getting in and out, etc. Yet I have not come to really fall in love with them. Getting in and out is not very easy. Since the step is between the wheels, I do not see how ladies get in and out without dirtying their dresses. The little, thin wheels are also quite unsteady and when one drives along on those awful streets and roads, he bounces and jumps hither and thither. But the demand for such buggies is enormous.

In the middle of the fairgrounds is an area of animal exhibitions, races, and demonstrations of operational farm machinery. It appears that 10,000 or more people could assemble there. Between the arches that support the grandstand are concessions and restaurants as well as stores and booths, something like the arrangement of our traditional *Jahrmarkt*.

With the beautiful weather which has followed a day of rain, an incredible number of people have crowded into these spaces. It is crowded everywhere, but especially in the restaurants and taverns. Pilsener Beer is presently very popular, but one does not have much trouble getting a glass of good wine in St. Louis either. Just head for the "Bremen Ratskeller." Our offspring in the West is certainly no disgrace to its old namesake. Here too is a cellar with large and mighty arches where the noble liquid is stored in barrels and bottles. And it was a pleasant surprise to find that the Germans on the Mississippi still drink the blessed wines of the Rhine, believing in their hearts that in all the world there is no better wine. It has been great fun during these few days. Drunkenness, loudness, and excesses, if they do occur, are kept quiet and hidden from the light of day. . . .

ORRICK JOHNS

ORRICK JOHNS (1887–1946) was born in St. Louis, the third of four sons, to George Sibley Johns, a prominent editor at the *St. Louis Post-Dispatch,* and Minnehaha McDearmon. At age seven, Johns was hit by a trolley car, which resulted in the amputation of his left leg. While lying immobilized and recuperating in his family's home on Cabanne Place, Johns became a voracious reader and developed a lifelong love of writing and publishing. Johns acquired his education at local public schools—Dozier School, Central High School, and, later, the University of Missouri, which he claimed, "were of a kind in one respect: they were unpretentious, rugged and equalitarian."

Upon graduation from college, Johns worked at a series of uninspiring jobs until William Marion Reedy offered him the position of drama critic at *The Mirror.* Johns enthusiastically accepted Reedy's offer, and his literary career was launched. By 1912, Johns's poetry was attracting attention, and he was developing an interest in leftist politics. As a result, Johns moved to New York City, where he lived and worked intermittently for the next ten years while continuing to write poems and plays. During this period, Johns made regular trips back to St. Louis to visit his father, whom he deeply revered, and wrote some of his best-known works while visiting his native city.

During the 1920s, Johns wrote two volumes of poetry, *Wild Plum* and *Asphalt and Other Poems*, and one extremely successful play, *A Charming Conscience,* which provided him with an income that allowed him to travel extensively in Europe while he indulged in heavy drinking and gambling. Johns returned to the United States in 1929 and settled in Carmel, California, a place known for its hospitality to bohemian culture. While living in California, Johns married his third wife, Caroline Blackman, also a St. Louisan. During this time, Johns became increasingly active in union organizing and began writing for Communist newspapers.

Johns became the supervisor of the WPA Writers' Project in New York City, a position he held for two turbulent years, between 1935 and 1937. During this period, his left-wing politics made him the target of negative media attention and occasional death threats. In 1937, after resigning from the WPA project, Johns published *Time of Our Lives*, which, in addition to being both an autobiography and a biography of his ailing father, paints a detailed portrait of life in St. Louis at the beginning of the twentieth century. In 1938, Johns moved to Connecticut with his fourth wife and continued to make a living writing articles and short stories. He committed suicide on July 8, 1946.

In the following excerpt from *Time of Our Lives*, which covers the years between the mid-1890s to 1911, Johns describes growing up in St. Louis, his college experience at University of Missouri, and his awe of William Reedy, the man who set him on his career path.

FROM *TIME OF OUR LIVES*

We three boys were growing up. The family had moved from the house on Compton avenue, where I was born in 1887, to Cook avenue, much farther west, when I was three or four. The first thing I remember is this house, and the death of my great grandmother, Urilla Orrick. I was by her bedside. Grandma had got up to light the coal fire in the grate, and had lain down again saying she did not feel very well. It was early morning, and my brother George and I, who shared the room with her, had just gone up to the bed in turn, to have her button the backs of our undershirts. She made a joke, at which we were laughing, when I heard a guttural sound. In a moment, mother and father were in the room, half-dressed, and were working over her. She had died instantly of apoplexy.

She must have been very good to us, for my recollection of her is that of a placid old friend, with a serene, not aged or deeply lined, face. The memory is aided perhaps by a portrait of her in youth, which my mother has in her house which was painted before she left Maryland. But the girl of eighteen was still visible in the old lady of eighty.

The houses in our row were all alike, a solid front of gray stone with little stone stoops, scrubbed every day. But it was not a disagreeable neighborhood for kids; we had room and air to play in. Across the vacant lots was the big drum of a gas tank. It seemed huge and high. There were quite jolly times in the house. A young auburn-haired sister of my mother,

Urilla, had just come back from Paris, where she had studied music, and she sang for us in her warm contralto. I remember her odd little jackets with turned up tails, and a hexagonal chatelaine watch she wore, embossed in silver.

There was an uncle Jim that we liked, because he amused us and played practical jokes. Charles Hoyt and Rose Coghlan came there. We had a Negro butler named Lonesome Cloudy Bowers. The day before Thanksgiving he disappeared with the Thanksgiving turkey and father's cigars and liquor. We were sorry about that, because he was a happy companion.

Sometimes steers and pigs were driven through the streets of the city by men on horseback, on their way to the slaughter pens in East St. Louis. On the same street was our first kindergarten, Miss Peters', where all I believe we did was to cut out paper designs. On Finney avenue around the corner was a little notion store that sold candy. We usually bought long licorice shoestrings. Across the street they put up a building taller than the rest called "flats."

After Cook avenue we moved many times. Sometimes we made visits in St. Charles, another time we lived in Kirkwood, a village near St. Louis. Finally we moved far out to the West End of the city, and then we had plenty of fun, jolly companions, open lots, and a delightful school. I was six years old when father bought the house on Cabanne Place in the new western district. It was a town by itself, with new comfortable brick houses and old tree-shaded frame houses, some of which had been farms not long before. There was a creek running under bridges and bordered with trees. Back of the house, on an embankment, ran a little trolley to town, and two blocks beyond the trolley was the Dozier public school.

We entered Dozier school and stayed for the entire eight years' course. The public school system was still in the experimental, growing stage, but I do not suppose there were many public schools like Dozier. It was home, our own backyard, friendly, liberal and encouraging. After my first day—when a bawling, fat boy wetted his clothes and made a puddle on the floor as he stood in line—I cannot recall a self-conscious or awkward moment in it. I think we all felt that way, even the Masonic orphan kids, of whom there were a hundred or more and who were stigmatized by a sort of uniform.

The teachers were women. The principal, an energetic, small, white-haired person, Miss Sally Griffith, was a protegée of Louis Soldan, Superintendent of Schools and a gifted, original educator. She sometimes ruled us with a rod, literally a rattan stick, but it all ended in good humor. The teachers were people of remarkably distinct character, older than the average teacher today.

I suffered humiliating moments at Dozier school, but they were in the playground and were caused by being outjumped or outrun by other boys, or by losing all my flints and chinies to better players. We gambled all the time, with whatever symbols of value boys recognized.

The educational profit of these preparatory years is doubtful in my mind. If knowledge was the aim, half of them were wasted. It seems to me now that we learned very little after the three R's, and we learned one of them, writing, very badly, because the copybook style was changed every few years. On the side of scholarship, we lacked purpose and discipline, and were held back in the elementary things too long. I wish there had been hard, sustained courses in Latin and Greek under real masters. That was certainly the place and the age to learn the fundamentals of those invaluable languages.

On the social and civilizing side, Dozier school was a success. It made for unforced, harmonious, decent rearing of kids, and for real democracy and fair play.

Father had to give up the house in Cabanne Place, and move across the tracks within a year, because of an accident I was in. I was coming home from school one afternoon and was hit by a trolley car, and run over. It seems we were playing tag and I ran back, thinking I could get across. I was brought home and the surgeons took off my left leg on the kitchen table. Father showed his nerve by coming into the operating room and holding my hand. They didn't expect me to live, but the skill of Dr. Tupper and the sharp January cold saved my life.

It affected my mother as badly as it did me. Some lad had rushed home and blurted out the news to her, without any details, while she was in the kitchen getting dinner. She collapsed. She was so ill that my brothers were sent away. They went to stay with the Will Schuylers in the neighborhood, and later to St. Charles for a long visit. I was in bed for six months, with surgeons visiting me twice a week, and my Canadian nurse, Miss Barry, moved in and lived with me. Fortunately for the family, the trolley company defrayed most of these expenses. A suit ran in the courts for years before it resulted in a small sum for damages.

I was seven years old then. As I lay in bed I was acutely sensible of a great loss. It seemed to me that the world and my brothers were growing way beyond me; and that I would never catch up. I recall a pang of envy when they came back in the Spring full of the story of winter sports—how they had ridden bobsled in St. Charles, all the way from Third street, at Grandpa McDearmon's house, to the middle of the frozen Missouri River. That seemed to me a bobsled ride never to be equalled. They had had other novel pleasures, too, and made new friends.

Father, who made hay of everything, used my accident to start a newspaper agitation for the improvement of the trolley system. He forced the companies to install better brakes and put fenders on the cars.

We moved from Cabanne Place to Maple avenue, across the tracks. It was not much of a change. We still had wide fields to play in. The house was bigger and the neighborhood thronged with boys. My brothers were already beginning to show their special characteristics. When George Jr. was nine or ten he had the entire basement of the house on Maple Avenue rigged up with pulleys, lathes and jig-saws run by the basement water tap. He had invented some sort of device by which he used the heat of the furnace draught for power, and he had parchment telephones running to the houses of his friends. My younger brother, Horace, was getting tough and learning wood lore faster than the rest of us, in the woods west of the city. He was the trapper and hunter sort of boy, and hated schooling.

On Maple avenue we began to do a lot of reading: Harry Castlemon, G. A. Henty, Horatio Alger, the Police Gazette, and the paper-back weeklies, Frank Merriwell, Diamond Dick and Nick Carter, which we circulated underground. Father, whether he knew it or not, counteracted a good portion of the effect of these literary aberrations. He read us aloud the whole of the Iliad in the prose translation, *La Morte Arthur*, the Jungle Books of Kipling and a good deal of Stevenson. He had just been relieved of night work as dramatic critic, and spent more evenings at home. The effect of these readings was that we went around talking to each other in a jargon of Homer and Sir Thomas Mallory: "Sir Gawaine hurtled against Sir Lancelot, and brast a spear upon his helm," and "Aurora, rosy-fingered mother of dawn, came from her couch in the wine-dark sea." There was an endless story about a balloon with a De-gravitator, and visits to the moon, which was made up as it went along (or worked over from H. G. Wells). The vogue of adventures based on science was at its height and we never tired of it. Then, of course, we had the *St. Nicholas* magazine, with its more dignified, dressed-up kind of adventure, illustrated by Howard Pyle and Reginald Birch.

When we moved into the house father gave me the job of pasting his name into the books and rearranging them, including some new sets just unpacked. There was a "world classic" series, a "world history" series, from which I learned the names of historians from Herodotus to Parkman, and of philosophers from Plato to Novalis. Other books had more individuality. There were four little antique calf volumes of Horace's Odes and Satires with facing page translations, the big brown Thackerays, the gaudy, ugly covers of Hugo's poems, which had redefined borders on the pages, the large green Whitman, an ugly brown "Poems and Ballads" of Swinburne, with gold edges, the Trilby with attractive illustrations. When they come to mind now I see these old bindings. The two hefty books I first discovered for myself, and read with the greatest excitement were, not surprisingly, "Leaves of grass" and "Poems and Ballads."

William Schuyler came to see us in that house—teacher, musical connoisseur, song collector and novelist. With beetling brow, small goatee, waxed moustaches and beak nose, he made a most quizzical and genial ensemble. Another visitor was the gaunt William Vincent Byars, a prolific and neglected poet. But Byars was other things: one of Pulitzer's ablest editors for a time, a lifelong quixotic (for which he paid with lifelong poverty), and a self-taught scholar in the ancient languages. He had become interested in the versification of the Latin poets; this led him back to the Greek, and at length still further back to the Sanskrit, for the origins of versification and inner rhymes, about which he wrote and published a great deal—and talked more. Byars, one evening when I was eight or nine, recited two lines of the Odyssey to me, and the sound of them has echoed in my mind for many years.

Several events stand out in those middle '90's. One was the Bryan campaign. Father was never a Bryan fanatic and had his doubts about the Silver plank, but we were by tradition on that side. I suppose few presidential campaigns have been so provocative of hate as the first Bryan-McKinley struggle. We hung out a big Bryan poster on the front of the house. The next morning it was torn and spattered with mud balls. We had been fairly popular in the neighborhood, but suddenly we became a small outcast minority. I can still feel the ostracism, the bloody noses, the scorn of those months in the fall of 1896. We had no idea what it was all about; but we had learned by heart the "cross of gold" passage and thought it a holy war. In all other respects, manners, clothes, social standards and material values, the neighborhood was absolutely in agreement.

Another event—which touched us lightly—was the cyclone in the spring of that year. It slashed out a huge path of houses downtown and in the southern part of the city, and killed hundreds of people. We were on the far fringe of the twister, but the curious color and formation of the sky—like a spreading, exploding mass of sickly green puff balls—the ominous atmosphere and the fury of the wind, are still unequalled in my recollection of storms anywhere. We were in a small frame cottage which shook like a cardboard house; we got off with only a fallen chimney and a ripped out cistern. My mother has declared that I read a book throughout the storm.

The most vivid sensation we all had was worry about father. He got home in the early morning in a hack. He had been through the devastated region and helped in the rescue work. For a time, at his office, they had feared that the presses on the third floor would tear loose from their moorings and crash through to the ground floor, where a crowd of people had taken refuge. He told us that he had seen five-foot stone blocks in Eads Bridge that had been lifted and moved around as if a big hand had seized them. The catastrophe left a nervous effect on the whole community. For years after, people talked of cyclone cellars, many built them, and we never saw a cloud without being dragged down into a dark hole.

About this time, also, a street-car strike occurred. Half the ablebodied business men in town were sworn in as deputies and given arms; and we used to see wagons, with boards laid across them, taking men down town with their rifles slung over their shoulders. It brought the feeling of war nearer to us than even the Spanish war pictures in '98.

These were years of adjustment for, me, an effort to achieve hard play in spite of a physical disability. I seem to have done so pretty successfully. My first struggle was with a rickety, noisy, strap-and-hinge contrivance that passed for an artificial leg at that time. I had been led to expect too much from it but I soon hated the sight of mine. It was slow, unstable, squeaking, and broke down faithfully on every excursion away from home, or even at school. I constantly tried to hide it, refused to wear it, and once threw it out of the window. Most of my playing I did on crutches, and attained considerable speed and agility on them. At any rate I was never on the sidelines, but somehow played shinny (lot-hockey with a tin can), rounders-baseball and tennis. I climbed, swam, bicycled and walked on stilts. One year I even skated some, with a spike in the end of a crutch. One develops an extra subtle sense of balance and distance and foresight under a physical handicap. My brothers and companions were all very decent about helping me carry loads on camping trips, and giving me jobs I was best suited to, but I do not think they ever had to cut down their walking pace to suit mine. There were limits, of course: I never could dance, or fight very well, two-fisted.

One panicky experience I recall—walking a long railway trestle in St. Charles. I had started across it without realizing what a dizzying job it is to aim crutches at ties between space. I tried to forget about the train that might be coming, and kept steadily on to the other side; but it was lucky for me one did not come. By degrees I came to use a leg at school; and the legs themselves improved greatly in efficiency.

George Jr., after he had finished Dozier, went to Manual Training School, to develop his mechanical and inventive talents. I went to the Central—and only—High School, and Horace left school entirely for New Mexico. This New Mexican adventure of his grew out of an acquaintance we made, whom I shall have to call by a name that is not his own, "Charley."

Charley was a young man of good birth, education and personality. He had married a girl of social position, the daughter of a prominent citizen, but he had only one interest, and that was in boys. It was not an objectionable interest. We met him first as a Sunday school teacher. We were all Sunday school boys as a matter of form; for a while I sang in the choir and made a dollar a month. At first, Charley helped us organize a club. But soon he was taking four or five youngsters at a time down town. He did this liberally. It began with dinner at some expensive restaurant, with lobster and liqueurs of strange names. He seemed quite disinterested and at dinner quoted Shakespeare and Byron. After dinner he took a closed carriage. He had previously arranged everything with the madame and selected the jolliest girls at some house. For a time it was an institution. Any youth who wanted to be initiated in sex applied to Charley. There was no great harm in it, except to himself.

Then Charley grew more ambitious. One day he appeared with a collection of old stained documents and maps. With these he went to see the parents of several of the more active boys. The documents were clues to the locality of a rich gold mine in New Mexico, discovered by an old prospector but never exploited. The old prospector had died in Charley's arms and given him the secret. Several of the parents believed the story, and they contributed to a fund to finance an expedition. My brother Horace was anxious to go, and father, somewhat sceptically, chipped in with the group. The boys started off, with Charley at their head.

The search for the mine continued for two or three years, when it was discovered to be a hoax of Charley's. He vanished, but some of the boys stayed on. Horace became a forest ranger in the Government service, and remained until he was grown. He returned to St. Louis to go into business and marry, but he was always a rough-edged, backwoods story-teller, with the humor of the trails on his tongue. He had got a better education than the rest of us, I think.

All three of my schools, Dozier, the High School and the University of Missouri, were of a kind in one respect: they were unpretentious, rugged and equalitarian. I met in all of them the same sort of students: ambitious children of the struggling middle class. The idea throughout was to produce this standard Missouri product, inculcated with the well-tried virtues, and satisfied with reasonable hopes of humdrum success. It was not a conscious intention but the schools were the result of the people who needed them, before streamlined luxury had begun to change the appearance of the American world. The sophisticated person was rare, and by his very nature did not belong. At Missouri University there were fraternities, some a little more comfortable than others, but none that would be called smart. The average income in Kappa Sigma, to which I belonged, was less than $25 a month. Now and then some one came from Kansas City or the East, by mistake, and dazzled us, but he could not be popular. We were a horizontal cross-section of the state.

The old Central High School had a similar importance: as the only high school, it brought the whole town of the burgher and professional classes together, and some offspring of workingmen. Four years of it was an education in the social history of the town. We all met there, north, south and west end girls and boys, Germans, French, Jews and the descendants of the old South. What a student learned, or made of his learning, was another matter. The teachers in Central High were all competent, humane and sensible. None was brilliant and none was inspiring, with the exception of Will Schuyler, the assistant principal. You could trust them, and if one of them felt that you responded with particular effort, he might help you advance, but there were no peaks and no depths. The business was to make the average American, Western style, according to a local image long recognizable. There were more exclusive schools in St. Louis than Central High. Smith Academy for boys and Mary Institute for girls were tops. We played our Thanksgiving game with Smith Academy; there was some feeling of snobbishness on both sides, only overcome years later when grown men met in the life of the city without distinction of class. Some well-to-do boys preferred to go to the High School.

I am impressed by one thing as I recall that school. There was no emphasis on religion. I am sure that the majority of the faculty were sceptical, that most of them had gone through the purge of Darwin or Marx or English Materialism, and that Nineteenth Century science had much more weight with them than Fundamentalism. Their names were of German origin, and a few of French, at a time when those racial names stood for purer racial qualities. They had an admirable seriousness. I think that seriousness, as opposed to the waves of American fads and excesses which soon followed, was perhaps a golden period.

THEODORE DRIESER

THEODORE DREISER (1871–1945) was born in Terre Haute, Indiana, to a crippled mill worker and a doting mother, who encouraged him to pursue his studies despite the family's economic hardship. After graduating from high school, Dreiser supported himself by working as a janitor in Chicago. Dreiser's only year of college, at the University of Indiana, was paid for by one of his former high school teachers. Before he launched his career as a novelist, Dreiser was a newspaperman and worked in a number of cities, among them Chicago, St. Louis, Pittsburgh, and New York. During his years as a journalist, Dreiser was encouraged by both his co-workers and his brother Paul to continue to write fiction. Paul, who made a comfortable living as a songwriter, often supplemented his brother's income so that Theodore would have more time to write.

Dreiser was so depressed by the scathing reviews garnered by his first novel, *Sister Carrie* (1900), that he contemplated suicide. Rescued emotionally and financially by his brother, Dreiser persisted in his writing and eventually received critical acclaim in the United States, Western Europe, and Russia, where his anti-bourgeois viewpoint was especially popular. Although Dreiser is not regarded as a master stylist, his best work conveys a pessimistic vision of the futility of the individual's struggle against uncontrollable social and moral forces. Today, *Sister Carrie* and *An American Tragedy* (1925) are regarded as masterpieces of American literary naturalism.

Dreiser became well-acquainted with the harsh realities of the working class while working as a police reporter in St. Louis. From 1892 to 1894, he wrote first for the *St. Louis Globe-Democrat* and later at the *St. Louis Republic*, where he covered a wide range of subjects—from domestic violence to séances. The first passage that follows—from his autobiography, *A Book About Myself* (1922)—describes his impression of St. Louis at the time of his arrival in 1892. Also included are several newspaper stories written by Dreiser—who never was granted his own by-line—while at the *Globe-Democrat* and *Republic*. In these excerpts, Dreiser's gifts for description and dialogue, which are more fully developed in his later fiction, are evident.

FROM *A BOOK ABOUT MYSELF*

The time was November, 1892. St. Louis, as I stopped off the train that Sunday evening, after leaving Chicago in cold dreary state, seemed a warmer clime. The air was soft, almost balmy; but St. Louis could be cold enough too, as I soon discovered. The station, then at Twelfth and Poplar (the new Union Station at Eighteenth and Market was then building), in antiquated affair of brick and stone, with the tracks stretching in rows in front of it and reached by board walks laid at right angles to them, seemed unspeakably shabby and inconvenient to me after the better ones of Chicago. St. Louis, I said to myself, was not as good as Chicago. Chicago was rough, powerful, active; St. Louis was sleepy and slow. This was due, however, to the fact that I entered it of a Sunday evening and all its central portion was still. Contrasted with Chicago it was not a metropolis at all. While rich and successful it was a creature of another mood and of slower growth. I learned in time to like it very much, but for the things that set it apart from other cities, not for the things by which it sought to rival them.

But on that evening how dull and commonplace it seemed—how slow after the wave-like pulsation of energy that appeared to shake the very air of Chicago.

I made my way to a hotel called The Silver Moon, recommended to me by my mentor and sponsor, where one could get a room for a dollar, a meal for twenty-five cents. Outside of Joseph B. McCullagh, editor of the *Globe-Democrat*, and Edmond O'Neill, former editor of the *Republic* to whom I bore a letter, there was no one to whom I might commend myself. I did not care. I was in a strange city at last! I was out in the world now really, away from my family. My great interest was in life as a spectacle, this singing, rhythmic, mystic state in which I found myself. Life, the great sea! Life, the wondrous, colorful riddle!

After eating a bite in the almost darkened restaurant of this hotel I at once went out into Pine Street and stared at the street-cars, yellow, red, orange, green, brown, labeled Choteau Avenue, Tower Grove, Jefferson Avenue, Carondelet. My first business was to find the *Globe-Democrat* building, a prosperous eight-story brownstone and brick affair standing at Sixth and Pine. I stared at this building in the night, looking through the great plate glass windows at an onyx-lined office, and finally went in and bought a Sunday paper.

I went to my room and studied this paper—then slept, thinking of my coming introduction in the morning. I was awakened by the clangor of countless cars. Going to the stationary washstand I was struck at once by the yellowness of the water, a dark yellowish-brown, which deposited a yellow sediment in the glass. Was that the best St. Louis could afford? I asked myself in youthful derision. I drank it just the same, went down to breakfast and then out into the city to see what I should see. I bought a *Globe-Democrat* (a Republican party paper, by the way: all anachronism of age and change of ownership) and a *Republic*, the one morning Democratic paper, and then walked to Sixth and Pine to have another look at the building in which I was to work. I wandered along Broadway and Fourth Street, the street of the old courthouse; sought out the Mississippi River and stared at it, that vast river lying between banks of yellow mud; then I went back to the office of the *Globe-Democrat*, for it was nearing the time when its editor-in-chief might choose to put in an appearance.

Joseph B. McCullagh ("Little Mac" of Eugene Field's verse) was a short, thick, aggressive, rather pugnacious and defensive person of Irish extraction. He was short, sturdy, Napoleonic, ursine rather than leonine. I was instantly drawn and thrown back by his stiff reserve. A negro elevator boy had waved me along a marble hall on the seventh floor to a room at the end, where I was met by an office boy who took in my name and then ushered me into the great man's presence. I found him at a roll-top desk in a minute office, and he was almost buried in discarded newspapers. I learned afterward that he would never allow these to be removed until he was all but crowded out. I was racked with nervousness. Whatever high estimate I had conceived of myself had oozed out by the time I reached his door. I was now surveyed by keen gray Irish eyes under bushy brows.

"Um, yuss! Um, yuss!" was all he deigned to say. "See Mr. Mitchell in the city-room, Mr. Mitchell—um, yuss. Your salary will be—um—um—twenty dollars to begin with" (he was chewing a cigar and mumbled his words), and he turned to his papers.

Not a word, not a sign, that he knew I had ever written a line worth while. I returned to the handsome city-room, and found only empty desks. I sat down and waited fully three-quarters of an hour, examining old papers and staring out of the windows over the roofs until Mr. Mitchell appeared.

Like his employer, he was thick-set, a bigger man physically but less attractive. He had a round, closely-cropped head and a severe and scowling expression. He reminded me of Squeers in *Nicholas Nickleby*. A savage fat man—can anything be worse? He went to his desk with a quick stride when he entered, never noticing me. When I approached and explained who I was and why I was there he scarcely gave me a glance.

"The afternoon assignments won't be ready till twelve-thirty," he commented drily. "Better take a seat in the next room."

It was then only eleven-thirty, and I went into the next room and waited. It was empty but deliciously warm on this chilly day. How different from McEnnis, I thought. Evidently being called to a newspaper by telegram was not to be interpreted as auguring that one was to lie on a bed of roses.

A little bit afraid to leave for this hour, in case he might call, I hung about the two windows of this room staring at the new city. How wonderful it seemed, now this morning, after the quiet of the night before, how strong and forceful in this November air. The streets and sky were full of smoke; there was a clangor of street-car gongs below and the rumble of endless trucks. A block or two away loomed up a tall building of the newer order, twelve stories at least. Most of the buildings were small, old family dwellings turned into stores. I wondered about the life of the city, its charms, its prospects. What did it hold for me? How long would I remain here? Would this paper afford me any real advancement? Could I make a great impression and rise?

As I was thus meditating several newspaper men came in. One was a short bustling fellow with a golden-brown mustache and a shock of curly brown hair, whose name I subsequently learned was Hazard—a fitting name for a newspaper reporter. He wore a fedora hat, a short cream-colored overcoat which had many wrinkles about the skirts in the back, and striped trousers. He came in with a brisk air, slightly skipped his feet as he walked, and took a desk, which was nothing more than a segment of one long desk fastened to the wall and divided by varnished partitions of light oak. As soon as he was seated he opened a drawer and took out a pipe, which he briskly filled and lighted, and then began to examine some papers he had in his pockets. I liked his looks.

There sauntered in next a pale creature in a steel-gray suit of not too new a look, who took a seat directly opposite the first corner. His left hand, in a brown glove, hung at his side; apparently it was of wood or stuffed leather. Later there arrived a negro of very intellectual bearing, who took a seat next the second arrival; then a stout, phlegmatic-looking man with dark eyes, dark hair and skin, which gave me a feeling of something saturnine in his disposition. The next arrival was a small skippity man, bustling about like a little mouse, and having somewhat of a mousy look in his eyes, who seemed to be attached to the main city editorial room in some capacity.

A curious company gradually filed in, fourteen or fifteen all told. I gave up trying to catalogue them and turned to look out the window. The little bustling creature came through the room several times, looked at me without deigning to speak however, and finally put his head in at the door and whispered to the attendant group: "The book's ready." At this there was an immediate stir, nearly all the men got up and one by one they filed into the next room. Assuming that they were going to consult the assignment book, I followed, but my name was not down. In Chicago my city editor usually called each individual to him in person; here each man was supposed to discover his assignment from a written page. I returned to the reporters' room when I found my name was not down, wondering what I should be used for.

The others were not long gone before I was sought by the mouse—Hugh Keller Hartung by name—who whispered: "The city editor wants to see you"; and then for the second time I faced this gloomy man, whom I had already begun not only to dislike but to fear. He was dark and savage, in his mood to me at least, whether unconsciously so or not I do not know. His broad face, set with a straight full nose and a wide thin-lipped mouth, gave him a frozen Cromwellian outline. He seemed a queer, unliterary type to be attached to so remarkable a journalist as McCullagh.

"There's been some trouble down at this number," He said, handing me a slip of paper on which an address was written. "A fight, I think. See if you can find out anything about it."

I hurried out, immensely relieved to get into the fresh air of the city. I finally made my way to the place, only to find a vacant lot. Thinking there might be some mistake, I went to the nearest police station and inquired. Nothing was known. Fearing to fall down on my first assignment, I returned to the lot, but could learn nothing. Gradually it began to dawn upon me that this might be merely a trial assignment, a bright idea of the frowning fat man, a bearings-finder. I had already conceived a vast contempt for him, a stumbling-block in my path, I thought. No wonder he came to hate me, as I learned afterward he did.

I wandered back through the city, looking at the strange little low houses (it was the region between the river and North Broadway, about a mile above the courthouse), and marveling at the darksome character of the stores. Never in my life had I seen such old buildings, all brick and all crowded together, with solid wood or iron shutters, modeled after those of France from whence its original settlers came and having something of the dourness of the poorer quarters of Paris about them, and windows composed of very small panes of glass, evidences of the influence of France, I am sure. Their interiors seemed so dark, so redolent of an old-time life. The streets also appeared old-fashioned with their cobblestones, their twists and turns and the very little space that lay between the curbs. I felt as though the people must be different from those in Chicago, less dynamic, less aggressive.

When I reached the office I found that the city editor, Mr. Mitchell, had gone. The little mousy individual was at one of the parti-divisions of the wall desk, near Mr. Mitchell's big one, diving into a mass of copy the while he scratched his ear or trifled with his pencil or jumped mousily about in his seat.

"Is Mr. Mitchell about?" I inquired.

"No," replied the other briskly; "he never gets in much before four o'clock. Anything you want to know? I'm his assistant."

He did not dare say "assistant city editor"; his superior would not have tolerated one.

"He sent me out to this place, but it's only a vacant lot."

"Did you look all around the neighborhood? Sometimes you can get news of these things in the neighborhood, you know, when you can't get it right at the spot. I often do that."

"Yes," I answered. "I inquired all about there."

"It would be just like Tobe to send you out there, though," he went on feverishly and timidly, "just to break you in. He does things like that. You're the new man from Chicago, aren't you—Dreiser?"

"Yes, but how did you know?"

"He said you were coming," he replied, jerking his left thumb over his shoulder. "My name's Hartung, Hugh Keller Hartung."

He was so respectful, almost fearsome in his references to his superior that I could not help smiling. Now that I had my bearings, I did not feel so keenly about Mr. Mitchell. He seemed dull.

"I suppose you'll find St. Louis a little slower than Chicago," he went on, "but we have some of the biggest newspaper stories here you ever saw. You remember the Preller Trunk Mystery, don't you, and that big Missouri-

Pacific train robbery last year?"

I recalled both distinctly. "Is that so?" I commented, thinking of my career in Chicago and hoping for a duplication of it here.

Heavy steps were heard in the hall just outside, and Mr. Hartung jumped to his work like a frightened mouse; on the instant his head was fairly pulled down between his shoulders and his nose pressed over his work. He seemed to shrivel and shrink, and I wondered why. I went into the next room just as Mr. Tobias Mitchell entered. When I explained that the address he had given me was a vacant lot he merely looked up at me quizzically, suspiciously.

"Couldn't find it, eh? Somebody must have given me the wrong tip. Wait in the next room. I'll call you when I want you."

I returned to that empty room, from which I could hear the industrious pencil of Mr. Hartung and the occasional throat-clearing cough of Mr. Mitchell brooding among his papers.

JOURNALISM FROM THE *ST. LOUIS GLOBE-DEMOCRAT* AND *ST. LOUIS REPUBLIC*

BREAD WAR IN LITTLE RUSSIA

The Russian Jews, who are so thickly settled in the Third Police District, are rapidly falling in the ways of Americans. Carondelet has just recovered from a bread war, and now one that will probably end in trouble is on between Franklin and Cass avenues, west of Broadway. For a long time a few bakeries have controlled the cake and bread trade in Little Russia, and they allowed no one to enter in the field. They manufactured and sold mostly what is known as kosher bread, which is white twists and black or rye bread, prepared in conformity with the religious requirements. These loaves were sold at 5¢ each, or three for 10¢. Those who had a monopoly of the bread trade among these Russians were M. Goldberg, on North Eighth, L. Schneider, on Biddle, and M. Kaiseer, on North Seventh street. A few days ago, so it appears, Jacob Kohn, a baker, opened a shop at 622 Carr street, in opposition to what Kohn called a trust. He was assisted by his beautiful wife, and they soon made friends and began getting the trade. Then the other bakers began cutting prices, selling two loaves for 5¢, to drive Kohn out of the business. Kohn yesterday displayed a painted muslin sign with the picture of a loaf of bread and Jewish lettering to the effect that he also would sell two loaves for 5¢. This sign he tacked over the door, and his rivals at once had similar ones made and placed over their doors. Thus the war went on. Late yesterday afternoon one Abraham Graber who, it seems, is one of Kohn's rivals, rented the store adjoining Kohn's place, and soon had the place stocked up with bread. He had a sign printed in the Jewish language, which was fastened over the door, announcing that he sold three loaves of bread for 5¢, and that he had come to stay. Kohn would not come down in his price last night, but it is expected that he will be compelled to do so to-day.

The police of the Third District are watching the bread war very closely, as they fear trouble before it is ended.

FEBRUARY 10, 1893

THE TROUBLE STILL ON

"No, sir; no siree!" emphatically announced Congressman Charles F. Joy, as he kicked over his legal waste basket in an attempt to "get comfortable," and then deliberately curled his patrician lip as he looked upon a sketch of Colonel Gus V. R. Mechin which a Republic reporter had idly, but injudiciously dashed off, in his presence.

"Gus. V. R. Mechin can't bluff me, even if one or two misguided cranks do call him Colonel."

The exciting remark just quoted took place on the seventh floor of the Bank of Commerce Building in the office of that muscular athlete and all-around Congressman, Charles F. Joy. The cause of his excited exclamation was the statement made by Mr. Mechin that the Owls could wipe the Elks off the face of the earth with one hand in a game of baseball.

"Mechin can talk all he wants to. He can stand out on the corner and sway about with a baseball bat and illustrate how he is going to do us up, but I say he ain't, nor his whole nine ain't; and what I say means business."

At this juncture Mr. Joy slackened up a moment, which gave The Republic representative time to secure a fan. The visit to Mr. Joy's office was made for the purpose of announcing that Sportsman's Park could be secured for Monday, July 17, or some date quite near that, on which day the two clubs may meet and lay the much mooted question as to "which can lick" forever to rest.

The Republic reasoned that if nine strong men, having eaten nine large dinners, and really feeling like nine heavy weight Samsons, felt called upon to go out on the seventeenth day of July and muss, swipe, swab, mop (or any other kind of) up the earth with nine other large and enthusiastic St. Louisans who should come out for the same purpose, why it ought to take advantage of the cyclonic soiree. It felt that it ought to do this, even though there might be "blood and hair and the ground tore up," because of the hundreds and thousands of innocent babies whose lives are endangered by the intense heat of the long summertime and who are pining and dying away for want of fresh air. It feels certain that there are 10,000 people in St. Louis who will go out to Sportsman's Park on July 17 and enjoy the fray and the rolling together of the 18 muscular gentlemen just to aid the babies. So The Republic hurried forward and secured the park for the occasion named. Then Mr. Joy and Mr. Mechin were visited with the intelligence. The information was of all things most soothing to their ferocious desire "for gitten at one another."

Mr. Joy said that he had not kicked in anybody's rib for some time and Mr. Mechin said that the taste of the last car he chewed off had completely faded away, so that both are pining for the enemy and the enemy is equally pining for them. The contest is to be for nine innings only and no gouging. Any kind of bat from a rail to a board fence is permissible, and no one will be permitted to hit the ball twice at the same time. These particulars are the only ones agreed on.

"Mr. Mechin says that you can't play ball," was suggested to Mr. Joy.

"I can't, eh!" answered the Congressman. "Didn't I play right field last year? Didn't I catch the ball in three innings and wasn't I dressed up in a brown and white ball suit. Mechin can talk, but we'll get out and color the mud with his nine. They can't play. A mere lot of scrubs, all of 'em. Wait till you see me," and Mr. Joy leaned back with a vision of himself in a brown and white suit nimbly moving around on the turf and catching the sphere with one hand.

While he was engaged with this ethereal vision the reporter sneaked out and visited Mr. Mechin at his office on Chestnut street.

"Mr. Joy called you and your nine a lot of scrubs," was the opening remark.

"He did, did he?" said Mr. Mechin. "Did Joy call me a scrub? When did he say I was a scrub?"

"He didn't say you were a scrub; he said that you are one."

"I are one," meditated Mr. Mechin.

"That's what he said."

"Well he ought to know. He can't pitch, catch or hit the ball. We'll just wallop him all around and won't half try. Didn't I knock the ball over the fence last year. Didn't I run clean around to third base without stopping. I don't care if they did get me out at first, I ran to third and not one of 'em dared to stay me," and here Mr. Mechin indignantly wiped his perspiring forehead.

"Who will you have in your nine?" was asked.

"Let me see. I've got a list here." A piece of paper was produced and from a scrawled list of characters Mr. Mechin began to read as follows:

"Gus W. Neimann, he's with August Gehner & Co.; Fred Smith, the real estate man; Joe Duffy, in the same business; Otto Stifel, the brewer; Walter Ashton, the engineer; Ed Ambler, the oil dealer; Geo. Mathews, the oil dealer; A. A. Aal of the Parisian Cloak Company and me. I'm with August Gehner."

"Who have the Elks got?"

"Now you're coming to the scrubs," said Mr. Mechin. "He ought to call me a scrub. They've got France Chandler of the Wabash Railroad, Allen McDowell, their grand lecturer, Stanislaus Kehrmann, the florist; John M. Chesbrough, the assistant general passenger agent of the Vandalia; Chalmer D. Colman, George Durant, the telephone man; Al Vallet of the Council and Jimmy Kern, the liquor dealer. Anybody can tell by reading those two lists, who is going to get the worst of it. I tell you right here that we're going to play ball and win, and that we are going to have the honor of netting the Fresh Air Fund a big sum." Mr. Mechin also said that the members of his nine intend to wear each a different costume which shall be representative of the great geniuses of the world. They propose to emulate the various sages in the matter of dress for at least one afternoon. Mr. Mechin poetically remarked, "We're no common baseball skates. We're intellectual St. Louisans and we propose to make a cultured showdown and don't you forget it."

The following telegram was received by Mr. Joy last evening from Chalmer D. Colman, who is at present in Detroit attending the meeting of the Supreme Council of Elks:

> *Mr. Charles F. Joy*, St. Louis, Mo.: The Supreme Council has just decided that if we Elks don't beat the Owls and win the gate receipts

the St. Louis Council will be fired out of the order. I protested, but they would do it.

Colman.

Mr. Joy said that the Supreme Council need not be afraid; that if the local council didn't "wade in and kick up the mud" they ought to be fired out. Mr. Joy afterwards explained that "kicking up mud" was the elite Congressional term for Winning out, which he had picked up in Washington. As The Republic reporter was returning from the office of Mr. Joy he came across Mr. Mechin, armed with a ferocious look and a baseball bat. His progress north on Broadway indicated that he was on his way to Joy's office for the purpose of creating trouble. By rare and most unheard-of strategy Mr. Mechin was inveigled into enjoying a glass of beer. This gave ample opportunity for preserving Mr. Joy, who was notified. The latter gentleman immediately borrowed a silk hat and left for Washington, to stay a week. While this internecine feud is much to be regretted, and while both Mr. Joy and Mr. Mechin are prone to allow their wrath to obtain the "best holt" on them whenever their baseball talents are called into question, yet the object to be attained by having the feud come to a climax and the several gentlemen to bruise one another being so worthy, The Republic is pleased to assuage and condone their conduct as much as possible. Mr. Mechin is now preparing the score cards and training his cohorts for the fray, while Mr. Joy is busily engaged scheming and mapping out various strategic moves whereby he proposes to dump the Owls so prodigiously far and hard that they will not return for a year. Meanwhile the thousands of little infants who are to be taken out into the country by the money so obtained, whose cheeks are to blush redder and whose eyes are to sparkle brighter because of the boon so obtained, are toddling forward to the joyous days "After the Ball" game and stand ever as an indulgence and forgiveness for any and all blood that may be spilled upon the occasion rapidly approaching. The game will be undoubtedly the most entertaining event of the summer, and it is equally without doubt that the affair will be a society event.

JUNE 20, 1893

UNDER THE WHEELS

While Antoinette Edenborn, 15 years old, was riding on her horse on Park avenue, between Iowa and California avenues, yesterday a few minutes after noon, horse and rider were struck by the Lindell red line electric car No. 25 and both were killed.

The girl's mangled remains are at Eberle & Keys' undertaking establishment, where they are being prepared for burial.

James Harrold, the motorman, was taken by an officer to the Fifth District Police Station, where he made a statement of the accident. He was then released without bond. The car was delayed about an hour, and the line was blocked. The cars had not recovered their schedule time and relative distances at a late hour last night.

Another motorman was put in charge of the car, but Charles Sweeney, the conductor, was not taken into custody, and he remained at his post.

Antoinette Edenborn was the daughter of Wm. Edenborn, president of the Consolidated Steel and Wire Co., and resided with her parents at 2017 Park avenue.

Miss Edenborn was fond of horseback riding, and almost every day was seen in the vicinity of her home mounted upon her handsome black horse.

Yesterday, a short time after noon, she rode out to a trysting place where she was to meet some school friends from the female department of Washington University. About 3 o'clock she was upon her way home, going east on Park avenue. Between Iowa and California avenues an electric car came up beside her. The horse was accustomed to cars and trotted along, evidently wishing to keep in the lead of the great red monster.

A piledriver near the middle of the block was puffing and groaning in its laborious task, preparing the foundations of a new building. The horse became frightened and jumped over upon the track in front of the car.

In the next moment of agonizing suspense the doomed girl frantically tugged at the bridle rein, endeavoring to guide her steed from the approaching car, which rolled on with gathered momentum from the descent of the hill. The frightened horse would not obey, and the iron platform struck him with terrific force, despite the motorman's application of the brake. The animal was thrown forward and his mistress was thrown under the wheels.

When the car came to a stop the body of the girl was lying upon the stones of the street, without life, and so mangled as to be all but unrecognizable. The wheels had passed entirely across the body, almost severing it at the waist. She was also badly cut about the head.

A crowd quickly gathered and was not dispersed until the police removed the remains to the undertaking establishment.

Mr. Edenborn was summoned from his place of business to his home. There the fate of his daughter was told him, and his grief was pitiful. When seen, later, he was inclined to be bitter against the street car company and the motorman, but this was more directly the result of his great loss and his grief. He said that he knew little of the manner of his daughter's death, and that little he had learned from a friend, who in turn had his information from eyewitnesses.

Charles Sweeney, conductor upon the fatal car, was still at his post when seen by a reporter. He refused at first to talk of the accident, but finally said:

"The girl was riding along beside the car and a short distance in advance. For some reason her horse got in front of the car and the motorman, James Harrold, stopped it as quickly as I ever knew it to be stopped; but there was too little room, and in a second the whole thing was over. We were going at the usual rate of speed and did not have many passengers.

"Harrold is a careful man, and I think that he did everything he could to avoid the trouble. After it was over he was a very sick man. He sat down on the platform of the car and was too weak to move. I don't believe that he will ever have the nerve to run a car again. I just stayed on the car and have not been molested by the officers, and I don't expect to be."

Motorman Harrold was accompanied by a police officer to the Fifth District Police Station and there made his statement of the tragedy. Upon this statement and the absence of a complaining witness Harrold was allowed to go to his home, which none of the street car officials were able to designate.

The manager of the Lindell Company gave his version of the accident, with little or no variation from the accounts secured elsewhere. He also added that the company stood prepared to give any bond which might be required for the freedom of its two employees whom they regard as entirely free from blame.

The keeper of a livery stable in the block where the girl was killed, and other citizens of Park avenue, assert that the cars upon that thoroughfare are run too fast for the safety of the public and express the hope that the dreadful lesson of yesterday will result in more careful regulations on the part of the street railway company.

JANUARY 6, 1894

KATE CHOPIN

A NATIVE ST. LOUISAN, Kate Chopin (1851–1904) was the daughter of an Irish immigrant, Thomas O'Flaherty, and Eliza Faris, a descendant of old French Creole stock. Her childhood home was a large, Southern-style mansion on Eighth Street, between Gratiot and Chouteau—a fashionable area—and she attended the St. Louis Academy of the Sacred Heart on Fifth Street.

In 1870, Kate moved to Louisiana with her French Creole husband, Oscar Chopin, and bore six children. Although the Deep South—not St. Louis—became the setting of Kate's best-known work, *The Awakening* (1899), her ties to the city remained strong. After her husband's death in 1883, Kate returned to St. Louis, living first on Morgan Street (now Delmar) and then at 4232 McPherson Avenue. From St. Louis, she launched her literary career.

Between 1889 and 1899, Kate was very prolific, becoming a famous—and controversial—author. *The Awakening* shocked reviewers with its frank exploration of an unhappily married woman's emerging sexuality, extramarital affairs, and suicide. Although they had formerly promoted her writing, several St. Louis publications refused to print Kate's work after *The Awakening*, and some local libraries (most notably the Mercantile) pulled the book from their shelves.

Like many St. Louisans in 1904, Kate Chopin made a point of attending the World's Fair. On August 20, one of the hottest days of the summer, Kate spent the day at the fair. That evening she collapsed, apparently having suffered a cerebral hemorrhage, and died two days later. She is buried in St. Louis's Calvary Cemetery alongside all six of her children.

The following three passages are among the only works set in Kate Chopin's native Missouri. The first selection, from her debut novel, *At Fault* (1890), colorfully depicts the Central West End. "The Maid of Saint Phillippe" has a historical setting in an actual but little-known French village on the east side of the Mississippi, ten miles north of Prairie du Rocher, which was deserted by its population in 1765. It first appeared in an early collection of Kate's short stories in 1892. "Elizabeth Stock's One Story," with its bleak urban setting and modern subject—a failed writer—stands in stark contrast to the former. Although written in 1898, the story remained unpublished for sixty-five years. Among the Kate Chopin papers at the Missouri Historical Society, it first appeared in the January 1963 *Missouri Historical Society Bulletin*. The story opens with Elizabeth Stock's death at St. Louis City Hospital, with the main portion of the text presented as the one salvageable story written by the deceased woman.

FROM *AT FAULT*

The wedding was over. Hosmer and Fanny had been married in the small library of their Unitarian minister whom they had found intent upon the shaping of his Sunday sermon.

Out of deference, he had been briefly told the outward circumstances of the case, which he knew already; for these two had been formerly members of his congregation, and gossip had not been reluctant in telling their story. Hosmer, of course, had drifted away from his knowledge, and in late years, he had seen little of Fanny, who when moved to attend church at all usually went to the Redemptorist's Rock Church with her friend Belle Worthington. This lady was a good Catholic to the necessary extent of hearing a mass on Sundays, abstaining from meat on Fridays and Ember days, and making her "Easters." Which concessions were not without their attendant discomforts, counterbalanced, however, by the soothing assurance which they gave her of keeping on the safe side.

The minister had been much impressed with the significance of this re-marriage which he was called upon to perform, and had offered some few and well chosen expressions of salutary advice as to its future guidance. The sexton and housekeeper had been called in as witnesses. Then Hosmer had taken Fanny back home in a cab as she requested, because of her eyes that were red and swollen.

Inside the little hall-way he took her in his arms and kissed her, calling her "my child." He could not have told why, except that it expressed the responsibility he accepted of bearing all things that a father must bear from the child to whom he has given life.

"I should like to go out for an hour, Fanny; but if you would rather not,

I shall stay."

"No, David, I want to be alone," she said, turning into the little parlor, with eyes big and heavy from weariness and inward clashing emotions.

Along the length of Lindell avenue from Grand avenue west to Forest park, reaches for two miles on either side of the wide and well kept gravel drive a smooth stone walk, bordered its full extent with a double row of trees which were young and still uncertain, when Hosmer walked between them.

Had it been Sunday, he would have found himself making one of a fashionable throng of promenaders; it being at that time a fad with society people to walk to Forest park and back of a Sunday afternoon. Driving was then considered a respectable diversion only on the six work days of the week.

But it was not Sunday and this inviting promenade was almost deserted. An occasional laborer would walk clumsily by; apathetic; swinging his tin bucket and bearing some implement of toil with the yellow clay yet clinging to it. Or it might be a brace of strong-minded girls walking with long and springing stride, which was then fashionable; looking not to the right nor left; indulging in no exchange of friendly and girlish chatter, but grimly intent upon the purpose of their walk.

A steady line of vehicles was pushing on towards the park at the moderate speed which the law required. On both sides the wide boulevard tasteful dwellings, many completed, but most of them in course of construction, were in constant view. Hosmer noted every thing, but absently; and yet he was not pre-occupied with thought. He felt himself to be hurrying away from something that was fast overtaking him, and his faculties for the moment were centered in the mere act of motion. It is said that motion is pleasurable to man. No doubt, in connection with a healthy body and free mind, movement brings to the normal human being a certain degree of enjoyment. But where the healthful conditions are only physical, rapid motion changes from a source of pleasure to one of mere expediency.

So long as Hosmer could walk he kept a certain pressing consciousness at bay. He would have liked to run if he had dared. Since he had entered the park there were constant trains of cars speeding somewhere overhead; he could hear them at near intervals clashing over the stone bridge. And there was not a train which passed that he did not long to be at the front of it to measure and let out its speed. What a mad flight he would have given it, to make men hold their breath with terror! How he would have driven it till its end was death and chaos!—so much the better.

There suddenly formed in Hosmer's mind a sentence—sharp and distinct. We are all conscious of such quick mental visions whether of words or pictures, coming sometimes from a hidden and untraceable source, making us quiver with awe at this mysterious power of mind manifesting itself with the vividness of visible matter.

"It was the act of a coward."

Those were the words which checked him, and forbade him to go farther: which compelled him to turn about and face the reality of his convictions.

It is no unusual sight, that of a man lying full length in the soft tender grass of some retired spot of Forest park—with his face hidden in his folded arms. To the few who may see him, if they speculate at all about him he sleeps or he rests his body after a day's fatigue. "Am I never to be the brave man?" thought Hosmer, "always the coward, flying even from my own thoughts?"

How hard to him was this unaccustomed task of dealing with moral difficulties, which all through his life before, however lightly they had come, he had shirked and avoided! He realized now, that there was to be no more of that. If he did not wish his life to end in disgraceful shipwreck, he must take command and direction of it upon himself.

He had felt himself capable of stolid endurance since love had declared itself his guide and helper. But now—only to-day—something beside had crept into his heart. Not something to be endured, but a thing to be strangled and thrust away. It was the demon of hate; so new, so awful, so loathsome, he doubted that he could look it in the face and live.

Here was the problem of his new existence.

The woman who had formerly made his life colorless and empty he had quietly turned his back upon, carrying with him a pity that was not untender. But the woman who had unwittingly robbed him of all possibility of earthly happiness—he hated her. The woman who for the remainder of a life-time was to be in all the world the nearest thing to him, he hated her. He hated this woman of whom he must be careful, to whom he must be tender, and loyal and generous. And to give no sign or word but of kindness; to do no action that was not considerate, was the task which destiny had thrust upon his honor.

He did not ask himself if it were possible of accomplishment. He had flung hesitancy away, to make room for the all-powerful "Must be."

He walked slowly back to his home. There was no need to run now;

nothing pursued him. Should he quicken his pace or drag himself ever so slowly, it could henceforth make no difference. The burden from which he had fled was now banded upon him and not to be loosed, unless he fling himself with it into forgetfulness.

THE MAID OF SAINT PHILLIPPE

Marianne was tall, supple and strong. Dressed in her worn buckskin trappings she looked like a handsome boy rather than like the French girl of seventeen that she was. As she stepped from the woods the glimmer of the setting sun dazzled her. An instant she raised her hand—palm outward—to shield her eyes from the glare, then she continued to descend the gentle slope and make her way toward the little village of Saint Phillippe that lay before her, close by the waters of the Mississippi.

Marianne carried a gun across her shoulder as easily as a soldier might. Her stride was as untrammeled as that of the stag who treads his native hill-side unmolested. There was something stag-like, too, in the poise of her small head as she turned it from side to side, to snuff the subtle perfume of the Indian summer. But against the red western sky curling columns of thin blue smoke began to ascend from chimneys in the village.

This meant that housewives were already busy preparing the evening meal; and the girl quickened her steps, singing softly as she strode along over the tufted meadow where sleek cattle were grazing in numbers.

Less than a score of houses formed the village of Saint Phillippe, and they differed in no wise from one another except in the matter of an additional room when the prosperity of the owner admitted such. All were of upright logs, standing firmly in the ground, or rising from a low foundation of stone, with two or more clustering rooms round a central chimney. Before each was an inviting porch, topped by the projection of the shingled roof.

Gathered upon such a porch, when Marianne walked into the village, were groups of men talking eagerly and excitedly together with much gesture and intensity of utterance.

The place was Sans-Chagrin's tavern; and Marianne stopped beside the fence, seeing that her father, Picoté Laronce, was among the number who crowded the gallery. But it was not he, it was young Jacques Labrie who when he saw her there came down to where she stood.

"Well, what luck, Marianne?" he asked, noting her equipment.

"Oh, not much," she replied, slapping the game-bag that hung rather slack at her side. "Those idle soldiers down at the fort have no better employment than to frighten the game away out of reach. But what does this talk and confusion mean? I thought all the trouble with monsieur le curé was settled. My father stands quiet there in a corner; he seems to be taking no part. What is it all about?"

"The old grievance of a year ago, Marianne. We were content to grumble only so long as the English did not come to claim what is theirs. But we hear to-day they soon will be at Fort Chartres to take possession."

"Never!" she exclaimed. "Have not the Natchez driven them back each time they attempted to ascend the river? And do you think that watchful tribe will permit them now to cross the line?"

"They have not attempted the river this time. They have crossed the great mountains and are coming from the east."

"Ah," muttered the girl with pale exasperation, "that is a monarch to be proud of! Your Louis who sits in his palace at Versailles and gives away his province and his people as if they were baubles! Well, what next?"

"Come, Marianne," said the young man as he joined her outside. "Let me walk to your home with you, I will tell you as we go along. Sans-Chagrin, you know, returned this morning from West Illinois, and he tells astonishing things of the new trading-post over there—Laclede's village."

"The one they call Saint Louis?" she asked half-heartedly, "where old Toussaint of Kaskaskia has taken his family to live?"

"Old Toussaint is far seeing, Marianne, for Sans-Chagrin says the town across the water is growing as if by enchantment. Already it is double the size of Saint Phillippe and Kaskaskia put together. When the English reach Fort Chartres, St. Ange de Bellerive will relinquish the fort to them, and with his men will cross to Laclede's village—all but Captain Vaudry, who has leave to return to France."

"Capt. Alexis Vaudry will return to France!" she echoed in tones that rose and fell like a song of lamentation. "The English are coming from the east! And all this news has come to-day while I hunted in the forest."

"Do you not see what is in the air, Marianne?" he asked, giving her a sideward cautious glance.

They were at her portal now, and as he followed her into the house she half turned to say to him:

"No, Jacques, I can see no way out of it." She sat down languidly at the table, as though heavy fatigue had suddenly weighted her limbs.

"We hate the English," Jacques said emphatically; leaning upon the table as he stood beside her.

"To be sure, we hate the English," she returned, as though the fact were a self-evident one that needed no comment.

"Well, it is only the eastern province of Louisiana that has been granted to England. There is hardly a man in Saint Phillippe who would not rather die than live subject to that country. But there is no reason to do either," he added smiling. "In a week from now, Marianne, Saint Phillippe will be deserted."

"You mean that the people will abandon their homes, and go to the new trading-post?"

"Yes, that is what I mean."

"But I have heard—I am sure I have heard, long ago, that King Louis made a gift of his Louisiana possessions to his cousin of Spain; that they jointly granted the East Illinois to England. So that leaves the West under the Spanish dominion, Jacques."

"But Spain is not England," he explained, a little disconcerted. "No Frenchman who respects himself will live subject to England," he added fiercely. "All are of one mind—to quit Saint Phillippe at once. All save one, Marianne."

"And that one?"

"Your father."

"My father! Ah, I might have known. What does he say?" she questioned eagerly.

"He says he is old; that he has dwelt here many years—"

"That is true," the girl mused. "I was born here in Saint Phillippe; so were you, Jacques."

"He says," continued the young man, "that he could not dispose of his mill and that he would not leave it."

"His mill—his mill! no!" exclaimed Marianne, rising abruptly, "it is not that. Would you know why my father will never leave Saint Phillippe?" approaching as she said this a rear window whose shutters were partly closed, and throwing them wide open. "Come here, Jacques. That is the reason," pointing with her strong shapely arm to where a wooden cross marked the presence of a grave out under the wide-spreading branches of a maple.

They both stood for a while silently gazing across the grassy slope that reflected the last flickering gleams of the setting sun. Then Jacques muttered as if in answer to some unspoken thought:

"Yes, he loved her very dearly. Surely the better part of himself went with her. And you, Marianne?" he questioned gently.

"I, Jacques? Oh, it is only the old whose memories dwell in graves," she replied a little wearily. "My life belongs to my father. I have but to follow his will; whatever that may be."

Then Marianne left Jacques standing by the open window, and went into the adjoining room to divest herself of her hunting raiment. When she returned she was dressed in the garments that had been her mother's once —a short camlet skirt of sober hue; a green laced bodice whose scantiness was redeemed by a muslin kerchief laid in deep folds across the bosom; and upon her head was the white cap of the French working-woman.

Jacques had lighted a fire for her in the big stone chimney, and gone silently away.

It was indeed true. During that autumn of 1765, a handful of English, under command of Captain Sterling of the Highlanders, crossed the Alleghenies and were coming to take peaceful possession of their hitherto inaccessible lands in the Illinois.

To none did this seem a more hated intrusion than to the people of Saint Phillippe. After the excited meeting at Sans-Chagrin's tavern, all went to work with feverish haste to abandon the village which had been the only home that many of them had ever known. Men, women and children seemed suddenly possessed with demoniac strength to demolish. Doors, windows and flooring; everything that could serve in building up the new was rifled from the old. For days there was gathering together and hauling away in rough carts constructed for the sole purpose. Cattle were called from the pasture lands and driven in herds to the northward.

When the last of these rebellious spirits was gone, Saint Phillippe stood like the skeleton of its former self; and Picoté Laronce with his daughter found themselves alone amid the desolate hearthstones.

"It will be a dreary life, my child, for you," said the old man, gathering Marianne in a close embrace.

"It will not be dreary," she assured him, disengaging herself to look into his eyes. "I shall have much work to do. We shall forget—try to forget—that the English are at our door. And some time when we are rich in peltries, we will go to visit our friends in that great town that they talk so much about. Do not think that I am sad, father, because we are alone."

But the silence was very desolate. So was the sight of those abandoned homes, where smiling faces no longer looked from windows, and where music of children's laughter was heard no more.

Marianne worked and hunted and grew stronger and stronger. The old man was more and more like a child to her. When she was not with him, he would sit for hours upon a rude seat under the maple-tree, with a placid look of content in his old, dim eyes.

One day when Captain Vaudry rode up from Fort Chartres, fine as could be in his gay uniform of a French officer, he found Picoté and Marianne sitting in the solitude hand in hand. He had heard how they had remained alone in Saint Phillippe, and he had come to know if it was true, and to persuade them, if he could, to return with him to France—to La Rochelle, where Picoté had formerly lived. But he urged in vain. Picoté knew no home save that in which his wife had dwelt with him, and no resting-place on earth except where she lay. And Marianne said always the same thing—that her father's will was hers.

But when she came in from her hunt one evening and found him stretched in the eternal sleep out under the maple, at once she felt that she was alone, with no will to obey in the world but her own. Then her heart was as strong as oak and her nerves were like iron. Lovingly she carried him into the house. And when she had wept because he was dead, she lit two blessed candles and placed them at his head and she watched with him all through the still night.

At the break of day she barred the doors and windows, and mounting her fleet Indian pony, away she galloped to the fort, five miles below, to seek the aid she needed.

Captain Vaudry, and the others as well, made haste to Saint Phillippe when they learned this sad thing that had befallen Marianne. Word was sent to the good curé of Kaskaskia, and he came too, with prayer and benediction. Jacques was in Kaskaskia when the tidings of Picoté's death reached there, and with all the speed at his command he hurried to Marianne to help her in her need.

So Marianne was not alone. Good and staunch friends were about her.

When Picoté had been laid to rest—under the maple—and the last blessing had been spoken, the good curé turned to Marianne and said:

"My daughter, you will return with me to Kaskaskia. Your father had many friends in that village, and there is not a door but will open to receive you. It would be unseemly, now he is gone, to live alone in Saint Phillippe."

"I thank you, my father," she answered, "but I must pass this night alone, and in thought. If I decide to go to my good friends in Kaskaskia, I shall ride into town early, upon my pony."

Jacques, too, spoke to her, with gentle persuasion: "You know Marianne, what I want to say, and what my heart is full of. It is not I alone but my father and mother as well to whom you are dear, and who long to have you with us—one of us. Over there in the new village of Saint Louis a new life has begun for all of us. Let me beg that you will not refuse to share it till you have at least tried—"

She held up her hand in token that she had heard enough and turned resolutely from him. "Leave me, my friend," she said, "leave me alone. Follow the curé there where he goes. If I so determine, you shall hear from me, if not, then think no longer of Marianne."

So another silent night fell upon Saint Phillippe, with Marianne alone in her home. Not even the dead with her now. She did not know that under the shelter of a neighboring porch Captain Vaudry lay like a sentinel wrapped in his mantle.

Near the outer road, but within the inclosure of Marianne's home, was "the great tree of Saint Phillippe" under which a rude table and benches stood. Here Picoté and his daughter had often taken their humble meals, shared with any passer-by that chose to join them.

Seated there in the early morning was Captain Vaudry when Marianne stepped from her door, in her jerkin of buckskin and her gun across her shoulder.

"What are you doing here, Captain Vaudry?" she asked with startled displeasure when she saw him there.

"I have waited, Marianne. You cannot turn me from you as lightly as you have the others." And then with warm entreaty in his voice he talked to her of France:

"Ah, Marianne, you do not know what life is, here in this wild America. Let the curé of Kaskaskia say the words that will make you my wife, and I will take you to a land, child, where men barter with gold, and not with hides and peltries. Where you shall wear jewels and silks and walk upon soft and velvet carpets. Where life can be a round of pleasure. I do not say these things to tempt you; but to let you know that existence holds joys you do not dream of—that may be yours if you will."

"Enough, Capt. Alexis Vaudry! I have sometimes thought I should like to know what it is that men call luxury; and sometimes have felt that I should like to live in sweet and gentle intercourse with men and women. Yet these have been but fleeting wishes. I have passed the night in meditation and my choice is made."

"I love you, Marianne." He sat with hands clasped upon the table, and his handsome enraptured eyes gazing up into her face, as she stood before him. But she went on unheedingly:

"I could not live here in Saint Phillippe or there in Kaskaskia. The English shall never be masters of Marianne. Over the river it is no better. The Spaniards may any day they choose give a rude awakening to those stolid beings who are living on in half-slumber of content—"

"I love you; oh, I love you, Marianne!"

"Do you not know, Captain Vaudry," she said with savage resistance, "I have breathed the free air of forest and stream, till it is in my blood now. I was not born to be the mother of slaves."

"Oh, how can you think of slaves and motherhood! Look into my eyes, Marianne, and think of love."

"I will not look into your eyes, Captain Vaudry," she murmured, letting the quivering lids fall upon her own, "with your talk and your looks of love—of love! You have looked it before, and you have spoken it before till the strength would go from my limbs and leave me feeble as a little child, till my heart would beat like that of one who has been stricken. Go away, with your velvet and your jewels and your love. Go away to your France and to your treacherous kings; they are not for me."

"What do you mean, Marianne?" demanded the young man, grown pale with apprehension. "You deny allegiance to England and Spain; you spurn France with contempt; what is left for you?"

"Freedom is left for me!" exclaimed the girl, seizing her gun that she lifted upon her shoulder. "Marianne goes to the Cherokees! You cannot stay with me; you need not try to. Hardships may await me, but let it be death rather than bondage."

While Vaudry sat dumb with pain and motionless with astonishment;

while Jacques was hoping for a message; while the good curé was looking eagerly from his door-step for signs of the girl approaching, Marianne turned her back upon all of them.

With gun across her shoulder she walked up the gentle slope; her brave, strong face turned to the rising sun.

ELIZABETH STOCK'S ONE STORY

Elizabeth Stock, an unmarried woman of thirty-eight, died of consumption during the past winter at the St. Louis City Hospital. There were no unusually pathetic features attending her death. The physicians say she showed hope of rallying till placed in the incurable ward, when all courage seemed to leave her, and she relapsed into a silence that remained unbroken till the end.

In Stonelift, the village where Elizabeth Stock was born and raised, and where I happen to be sojourning this summer, they say she was much given over to scribbling. I was permitted to examine her desk, which was quite filled with scraps and bits of writing in bad prose and impossible verse. In the whole conglomerate mass, I discovered but the following pages which bore any semblance to a connected or consecutive narration.

Since I was a girl I always felt as if I would like to write stories. I never had that ambition to shine or make a name; first place because I knew what time and labor it meant to acquire a literary style. Second place, because whenever I wanted to write a story I never could think of a plot. Once I wrote about old Si' Shepard that got lost in the woods and never came back, and when I showed it to Uncle William he said: "Why, Elizabeth, I reckon you better stick to your dress making: this here ain't no story; everybody knows about old Si' Shepard."

No, the trouble was with plots. Whenever I tried to think of one, it always turned out to be something that some one else had thought about before me. But here back awhile, I heard of great inducements offered for an acceptable story, and I said to myself: "Elizabeth Stock, this is your chance. Now or never!" And I laid awake most a whole week; and walked about days in a kind of dream, turning and twisting things in my mind just like I often saw old ladies twisting quilt patches around to compose a design. I tried to think of a railroad story with a wreck, but couldn't. No more could I make a tale out of a murder, or money getting stolen, or even mistaken identity; for the story had to be original, entertaining, full of action and Goodness knows what all. It was no use. I gave it up. But now that I got my pen in my hand and sitting here kind of quiet and peaceful at the south window, and the breeze so soft carrying the autumn leaves along, I feel as I'd like to tell how I lost my position, mostly through my own negligence, I'll admit that.

My name is Elizabeth Stock. I'm thirty-eight years old and unmarried, and not afraid or ashamed to say it. Up to a few months ago I been postmasters of this village of Stonelift for six years, through one administration and a half—up to a few months ago.

Often seems like the village was most too small; so small that people were bound to look into each other's lives, just like you see folks in crowded tenements looking into each other's windows. But I was born here in Stonelift and I got no serious complaints. I been pretty comfortable and contented most of my life. There ain't more than a hundred houses all told, if that, counting stores, churches, postoffice, and even Nathan Brightman's palatial mansion up on the hill. Looks like Stonelift wouldn't be anything without that.

He's away a good part of the time, and his family; but he's done a lot for this community, and they always appreciated it, too.

But I leave it to any one—to any woman especially, if it ain't human nature in a little place where everybody knows every one else, for the postmistress to glance at a postal card once in a while. She could hardly help it. And besides, seems like if a person had anything very particular and private to tell, they'd put it under a sealed envelope.

Anyway, the train was late that day. It was the breaking up of winter, or the beginning of spring; kind of betwixt and between; along in March. It was most night when the mail came in that ought have been along at 5:15. The Brightman girls had been down with their pony-cart, but had got tired waiting and had been gone more than an hour.

It was chill and dismal in the office. I had let the stove go out for fear of fire. I was cold and hungry and anxious to get home to my supper. I gave out everybody's mail that was waiting; and for the thousandth time told Vance Wallace there was nothing for him. He'll come and ask as regular as clockwork. I got that mail assorted and put aside in a hurry. There was no dilly dallying with postal cards, and how I ever come give a second look at Nathan Brightman's postal, Heaven only knows!

It was from St. Louis, written with pencil in large characters and signed, "Collins," nothing else; just "Collins." It read:

"Dear Brightman: Be on hand tomorrow, Tuesday at 10 A.M. promptly. Important meeting of the board. Your own interest demands your presence. Whatever you do, don't fail. In haste, Collins."

I went to the door to see if there was anyone left standing around: but the night was so raw and chill, every last one of the loungers had disappeared. Vance Wallace would of been willing enough to hang about to see me home; but that was a thing I'd broken him of long ago. I locked things up and went on home, just ashivering as I went, it was that black and penetrating—worse than a downright freeze, I thought.

After I had had my supper and got comfortably fixed front of the fire, and glanced over the St. Louis paper and was just starting to read my seaside Library novel, I got thinking, somehow, about that postal card of Nath Brightman's. To a person that knew B. from hill's foot, it was just as plain as day that if that card laid on there in the office, Mr. Brightman would miss that important meeting in St. Louis in the morning. It wasn't anything to me, of course, except it made me uncomfortable and I couldn't rest or get my mind fixed on the story I was reading. Along about nine o'clock, I flung aside the book and says to myself:

"Elizabeth Stock, you a fool, and you know it." There ain't much use telling how I put on my rubbers and waterproof, covered the fire with ashes, took my umbrella and left the house.

I carried along the postoffice key and went on down and got out that postal card—in fact, all of the Brightman's mail—wasn't any use leaving part of it, and started for "the house on the hill" as we mostly call it. I don't believe anything could of induced me to go if I had known before hand what I was undertaking. It was drizzling and the rain kind of turned to ice when it struck the ground. If it hadn't been for the rubbers, I'd of taken more than one fall. As it was, I took one good and hard one on the foot-bridge. The wind was sweeping down so swiftly from the Northwest; looked like it carried me clean off my feet before I could clutch the hand-rail. I found out about that time that the stitches had come out of my old rubbers that I'd sewed about a month before, and letting the water in soaking my feet through and through. But I'd got more than good and started and I wouldn't think of turning around.

Nathan Brightman has got kind of steps cut along the side of the hill, going zig-zag. What you would call a gradual ascent, and making it easy to climb. That is to say, in good weather. But Lands! There wasn't anything easy that night, slipping back one step for every two; clutching at the frozen twigs along the path; and having to use my umbrella half the time for a walking stick; like a regular Alpine climber. And my heart would most stand still at the way the cedar trees moaned and whistled like doleful organ tones; and sometimes sighing deep and soft like dying souls in pain.

Then I was a fool for not putting on something warm underneath that mackintosh. I could of put on my knitted wool jacket just as easy as not. But the day had been so mild, it bamboozled us into thinking spring was here for good; especially when we were all looking and longing for it; and the orchards ready to bud, too.

But I forgot all the worry and unpleasantness of the walk when I saw how Nath Brightman took on over me bringing him that postal card. He made me sit down longside the fire and dry my feet, and kept saying:

"Why, Miss Elizabeth, it was exceedingly obliging of you; on such a night, too. Margaret, my dear"—that was his wife—"mix a good stiff toddy for Miss Elizabeth, and see that she drinks it."

I never could stand the taste or smell of alcohol. Uncle William says if I'd of had any sense and swallowed down that toddy like medicine, it might of saved the day.

Anyhow, Mr. Brightman had the girls scampering around getting his grip packed; one bringing his big top coat, another his muffler and umbrella; and at the same time here they were all three making up a list of a thousand and one things they wanted him to bring down from St. Louis.

Seems like he was ready in a jiffy, and by that time I was feeling sort of thawed out and I went along with him. It was a mighty big comfort to have him, too. He was as polite as could be, and kept saying:

"Mind out, Miss Elizabeth! Be careful here; slow now. My! but it's cold! Goodness knows what damage this won't do to the fruit trees." He walked to my very door with me, helping me along. Then he went on to the station. When the midnight express came tearing around the bend, rumbling like thunder and shaking the very house, I'd got my clothes changed and was drinking a hot cup of tea side the fire I'd started up. There was a lot of comfort knowing that Mr. Brightman had got aboard that train. Well, we all more or less selfish creatures in this world! I don't believe I'd of slept a wink that night if I'd of left that postal card lying in the office.

Uncle William will have it that this heavy cold all came of that walk; though he got to admit with me that this family been noted for weak lungs as far back as I ever heard of.

Anyway, I'd been sick on and off all spring; sometimes hardly able to stand on my feet when I'd drag myself down to that postoffice. When one morning, just like lightning out of a clear sky, here comes an official document from Washington, discharging me from my position as postmistress of Stonelift. I shook all over when I read it, just like I had a chill; and I felt sick at my stomach and my teeth chattered. No one was in the office when I opened that document except Vance Wallace, and I made him read it and I asked him what he made out it meant. Just like when you can't understand a thing because you don't want to. He says:

"You've lost your position, Lizabeth. That what it means; they've passed you up."

I took it away from him kind of dazed, and says:

"We got to see about it. We got to go see Uncle William; see what he says. Maybe it's a mistake."

"Uncle Sam don't make mistakes," said Vance. "We got to get up a petition in this here community; that's what I reckon we better do, and send it to the government."

Well, it don't seem like any use to dwell on this subject. The whole community was indignant, and pronounced it an outrage. They decided, in justice to me, I had to find out what I got that dismissal for. I kind of thought it was for my poor health, for I would of had to send in my resignation sooner or later, with these fevers and cough. But we got information it was for incompetence and negligence in office, through certain accusations of me reading postal cards and permitting people to help themselves to their own mail. Though I don't know as that ever happened except with Nathan Brightman always reaching over and saying:

"Don't disturb yourself, Miss Elizabeth," when I'd be sorting out letters and he could reach his mail in the box just as well as not.

But that's all over and done for. I been out of office two months now, on the 26th. There's a young man named Collins, got the position. He's the son of some wealthy, influential St. Louis man; a kind of delicate, poetical-natured young fellow that can't get along in business, and they used their influence to get him the position when it was vacant. They thinks it's the very place for him. I reckon 'tis. I hope in my soul he'll prosper. He's a quiet, nice-mannered young man. Some of the community thought of boycotting him. It was Vance Wallace started the notion. I told them they must be demented, and I up and told Vance Wallace he was a fool.

"I know I'm a fool, Lizabeth Stock," he said, "I always been a fool for hanging round you for the past twenty years."

The trouble with Vance is, he's got no intellect. I believe in my soul Uncle William's got more. Uncle William advised me to go up to St. Louis and get treated. I been up there. The doctor said, with this cough and short breath, if I know what's good for me I'll spend the winter in the South. But the truth is, I got no more money, or so little it don't count. Putting Danny to school and other things here lately, hasn't left me much to brag of. But I oughtn't be blamed about Danny; he's the only one of sister Martha's boys that seemed to me capable. And full of ambition to study as he was! It would have felt sinful of me, not to. Of course, I've taken him out, now I've lost my position. But I got him in with Filmore Green to learn the grocery trade, and maybe it's all for the best; who knows!

But indeed, indeed, I don't know what to do. Seems like I've come to the end of the rope. O! it's mighty pleasant here at this south window. The breeze is just as soft and warm as May, and the leaves look like birds flying. I'd like to sit right on here and forget every thing and go to sleep and never wake up. Maybe it's sinful to make that wish. After all, what I got to do is leave everything in the hands of Providence, and trust to luck.

WILLIAM MARION REEDY

THE SON OF A POLICEMAN, William Marion Reedy (1862–1920) grew up in St. Louis's Irish Kerry Patch neighborhood. He attended Christian Brothers Academy and then Saint Louis University. After receiving his degree in 1880, Reedy began what would become a long and illustrious publishing career, working first at the *Missouri Republican* and then at the *Globe-Democrat*, where he penned a weekly column called "Sunday in Forest Park."

In 1893, Reedy inherited a failing *St. Louis Mirror*, which he turned into a successful magazine, *The Mirror,* several years later. In addition to covering national and local politics, sports, and other timely events of the day, *The Mirror* became a showcase for new literary talent. Kate Chopin, Edgar Lee Masters, Vachel Lindsay, Fanny Hurst, Orrick Johns, Zoë Akins, and Sara Teasdale are but a few of the well-known authors who first published their work in *The Mirror*.

In addition to discovering up-and-coming writers, *The Mirror*, which was renamed *Reedy's Mirror* in 1913, became a catalyst for social reform in St. Louis at the beginning of the twentieth century.

In 1899, Reedy published a controversial critique of his city's leaders and citizenry titled "What's the Matter with St. Louis?" In this impassioned editorial, Reedy not only chastised St. Louisans for their lack of civic pride and their abundant apathy, but also challenged them to seize opportunity by hosting a World's Fair. As historian Jeffrey E. Smith concisely states, "For Reedy, the World's Fair was more than just an event; it was to be the beginning of a St. Louis Renaissance."

Although a century has passed since Reedy published his essay, many St. Louisans will find its message remarkably relevant in the new millennium; the essay appears here in its entirety.

WHAT'S THE MATTER WITH ST. LOUIS?

AN ATTEMPT AT A DIAGNOSIS OF A GENERALLY OBSERVED AILMENT IN THE FOURTH CITY OF THE UNION.

For using as a heading to this article a paraphrase of Mr. William Allen White's query concerning Kansas there is no other apology necessary than the simple statement that something is the matter with this city.

What is it?

The fourth city of this country, with 700,000 population, is not so well known to the people of the nation as cities far beneath it on the roster of municipalities. It is less familiar in the memories and on the mouths of men and in the papers than a town the size of Cincinnati or Cleveland. Let any citizen of St. Louis leave home for any length of time and read the papers and he will discover how little the city figures in the news of the day. It will not do to apply to the city in this connection the aphorism "happy the people who have no history." St. Louis is the least advertised of any great city in the country. In the most casual enumeration of towns in the usual article in which some such enumeration is necessary you will find this city skipped for lesser towns. There is nothing plainer than that the city is ignored, and when it is mentioned it is too often in some belittling way. The country at large is familiar with men and events in Chicago, Boston, Philadelphia, San Francisco, but St. Louis might as well not be on the map, so far as any evidence of interest in the town upon the part of the nation is concerned. St. Louis is the place that had a cyclone. It is the center of the mule market and the shoe market. It was a great tobacco center. But the city has no well-defined character in the public mind. Mention of its name calls up no mental picture, whatever. There is not even a staple, standing jest about the town.

One reason of this is, that nine travelers out of ten, who touch St. Louis, never see the city. The Union Station prevents that. Close train connections make St. Louis a way station. Everybody, but those who must stay in the city, is shot through it, and through parts of it which are not at all impressive. The great traveling public does not see the city as it sees other cities of less importance. Another reason is that the great source of general information in this country, the Associated Press, disseminates nothing concerning the city except a paragraph, now and then, concerning a murder or a fire, and even a crime in St. Louis is mentioned briefly, whereas a like affair in Chicago is put forth in a fashion which says "this is a horrible thing, but it's big with the bigness of all things about Chicago." The Associated Press is in conspiracy against St. Louis, as those who have endeavored to get that institution to send out matter concerning events in the city, of a quasi public nature, can abundantly testify. We call St. Louis "the convention city," but the news of conventions held here is meager while the reports of matters of like but inferior character, elsewhere, are elaborated upon in every big newspaper in the land. The greater St. Louis newspapers contain comparatively little St. Louis news. Local affairs, generally speaking, are slurred over. In the newspapers of every other city in the country local news comes first in importance and local interests are always furthered enthusiastically. The New York, Boston, Chicago, Cincinnati, Denver, San Francisco and other papers reek with the life and character and interests of the community in which they are published. Here the daily newspaper celebrates anything or anybody but St. Louis and St. Louisans. Journalistic local patriotism is spasmodic and perfunctory. The result is that these newspapers, when read outside the city, convey absolutely no impression of the vast community from which they spring. Another result is that St. Louisans, wrapped in their own affairs, are never reminded of what a really great organization they are a part. A resident of any other city, reading his morning paper at home, reading about the various movements, interests, incidents, personalities of that city says "what a big town this is!"' and feels a certain amount of pride in it. He feels stimulated at the thought of being a part of it all and he goes about boasting somewhat after the old Roman's "Romanus sum."

This brings us to the chief deficiency of St. Louis, which accounts for the poor, almost ridiculous, position of the city in the minds of the country at large. *There is no civic pride in St. Louisans.*

This will be boisterously denied. But it's true. If there were such a thing as civic pride, think you there would be any such holding back, any such bickering, sneering criticism as prevents the speedy completion of the $5,000,000 popular subscription for the World's Fair? Anywhere else all would be for the completion of the subscription, no matter who was at the head of the soliciting organization, no matter what doubt there might have been as to the advisability of the movement at the beginning. The St. Louisan, generally, does not stand up for St. Louis. He is so afraid the man who does "stand up" will make kudos or cash out of his attitude that he manifests a disposition to knock him down, or, at least, to cast aspersions, by innuendo, upon his motives. There is no civic pride, because the people are not led to believe that they live in a city that is worth while. Take the treatment of this World's Fair matter in the St. Louis dailies. Could anything be more dry, tame, flat, colorless, than the accounts of the recent meeting of the general committee having that project in charge? The articles seem to be written by a man whose mouth was filled with sawdust and whose mind was filled with a doubt as to whether he would be paid for writing them. There's not a spark of conviction, not a generous note of enthusiasm, not a gleam of fervent patriotism in them. Is it any wonder the people are cold and unresponsive? Is it any wonder that the greater number of people are inclined to think the project a matter unsettled as yet, instead of feeling that the Fair is a certainty? Is it strange that some of the people in the movement go about furthering its ends after the manner of men who are drafted into a forlorn hope?

See the St. Louisan away from home. Do you ever hear of him standing up for his own town? Not at all, as a rule. You'll find him, probably, spending money like a drunken sailor and proclaiming that it enlarges his alleged soul to get away from a town in which he cannot gratify his aesthetic tastes. You'll find him lavishing money, who, at home, scrimps and scrooges and squeezes and jews down everybody. He and his wife seem to ask everyone if they are not really astonished to find that such fine folk can come from such a god-forsaken, intellectually and artistically desolate spot as St. Louis. He is paying double and treble prices for things he could get here. He "blows himself" in New York, Chicago, London or Paris stores than which there are better establishments in St. Louis. St. Louis is the jumping-off place, to hear him tell it. And he will stand treatment, at the hands of those he deals with, in a servility of spirit in marked contrast with his demand for "the best of it," down to the last copper, in St. Louis. He will pay $3.00 a seat for theater tickets in New York and won't go to a $1.50 show just as good at home. Asked about anyone in St. Louis, this St. Louisan replies in the voice of the "knocker." He will buy daubs abroad at prices that are robbery and he will not look at the work of home artists or pictures in a home gallery. He will give one hundred dollar dinners away from home and never let himself loose, socially, in St. Louis. His pose is that of a rich, rare spirit bound by unkind circumstance to a decadent town. He will come back home and say that such and such a place is the only place to live, but once settled here he proceeds to button up his pocket, put the brakes upon his liberality, give the cold shoulder to society, scoff at all movings of public spirit and begin to salt away more money for another whirl of gluttonous selfishness, when he travels.

St. Louis is belittled by its own people. There is no local evidence of any general love for the city. There is no indication of any feeling working to the end of making this a better place to live in. With a few rare exceptions, St. Louis rich men have never given of their substance for any great public institution or improvement that promised them no immediate cash return. What man has given anything to the city for the use of all the people since Henry Shaw died? You can count on three fingers the men who have made handsome donations to local charity. The men of wealth are afraid to make known their minor charities, lest they be sneered at. There are some wealthy men here who are generous, but the genial currents of their souls are frozen by the terrible, the deadly, mean envy of a lot of snarling rivals in business who foster a public distrust of the successful. It used to be said, twenty years ago, that what St. Louis chiefly needed was "a lot of first-class funerals." Well, we've had the funerals. The wills reveal no bequest to any public benefit or any noble cause. The sons are narrower than the fathers and lacking in their ability. They hold on to the money. They've not got blood enough in them to spend it in picturesque dissipation. In all cities the wealth accumulated by men in those cities is freely given back in donations for public educational or charitable purposes, but not in St. Louis. The men who win out here don't care for the town whose growth has supplemented their qualities in the building of success. The men who win out here do so in the face of a meaner opposition than prevails elsewhere and if one of them does a good deed his rivals find its prompting in some mean motive. Let any man say a good word for a wealthy man in St. Louis and forthwith everyone who has heard it rakes up some discreditable anecdote or reminiscence. So that there is a cause for rich men in St. Louis retiring within their own pockets.

This provincial spirit is instrumental in keeping good men, above corruption, out of our politics. This mean spirit deadens all the inducement to labor for reform. The man who will not crawl on his belly to the lower elements is a dude and a snob. We have an execrably governed city, with public buildings that are disgraceful, with streets that are frightful, with every evidence that there is no strong power working here for the day of better things. The spirit of protest is almost dead. It survives only in a partisanism which aims at the continuance of conditions under the auspices of a different political personnel. A heavy "dope" seems to hold chained and dumb all those elements which, in other cities, keep up a fight, however seemingly ineffectual, for the better ordering of things. Parties here are above any real care for the thought of the better elements. Public spirit in a man is inconceivable. Let him profess it and he is suspect.

Is there any art in St. Louis? The art department at the Exposition will probably be abandoned next year, because painters will not send their pictures where they cannot sell them. Those to whom has been entrusted the fostering of an art feeling here do nothing. They go "touting" for a Zorn from Sweden. They never try to develop an appreciation of good work at home. This paper has often spoken of the miserable showing made by St. Louis in the book trade. The books that sell here are fake subscription books—those editions de luxe manufactured expressly for the newly rich and ignorant. There is nothing in St. Louis that can be called a literary element. Professional men and men of business who exhibit a fondness for books or paintings are thought to be "daffy." A man of any standing in the business or professional world who likes to go to the theater and does go, is thought to be a little light in the upper story. The corporal's guard audiences at the Grau Grand Operas were a disgrace, compared with the audiences in Kansas City. Dramatically, "The Christian" is about our intellectual size. As for music, the Philharmonic has died. The Choral Symphony had hard scratching to raise the $12,000 guarantee, last year. The man who lets his wife stir things up with social entertaining knows that, after each function, the banks are ringing each other up by telephone to find how much paper he may have out at one place or another. Any man in St. Louis who does or tries to do anything for the public or for anyone else is credited with an ulterior selfish design. Ten per cent a month is the only ideal of helping a brother that can get into the heads of most people here. There is no solidarity here of those elements which get together for public good in other cities. Our club life is lugubrious. Clubs might promote friendliness and break down reserve. Therefore, St. Louisans are not clubmen. The Merchants Exchange is not a force, because it is split into cliques, which oppose anything proposed by other cliques, regardless of the general good. There is a painful lack of concerted action for the city's sake, on every hand. There exists a small-souled distrust of anyone who suggests anything "pro bono publico." Members of the Business Men's League or similar organizations know this. "What's in it for him?" is the immediate cry. No one is broad enough to think that even though there be "something in it" for the suggestor that does not necessarily imply that the suggestion may not be good for us all. The World's Fair is a case in point. So-and-so is going to make money out of it. What if he is? Isn't that what we want the Fair for, that as many people as possible may benefit by it, in a commercial or educational way? Everywhere in this town we find this spirit of provincial bigotry and envy. Every man you meet, who does any thinking along higher lines, has nothing to tell concerning the reception of his expressed aspirations for a better and more beautiful and greater St. Louis, but that those who hear him, smile sadly upon him and say he is trying to remove a stone wall by suggestive therapeutics.

St. Louisans are not proud of their city. They are eloquent in denouncing its evils, but you can't get them together for any effort to improve the city and give it a glory, especially if that effort involve going down in their pockets. The dwellers in other cities sing the praises of their cities. They are willing to lose a little money to help the city along. St. Louisans give outsiders the impression that there is nobody in St. Louis who could possibly get away. The nobler St. Louisans, and there are many of them, are without a means of expression. The papers here are gagged by the identification of their owners with the sodden, selfish interests which fear a "renaissance" as something which may bring new men to the front and burst the cinch which those interests have had for years upon everything of material value in the community. There is no outlet for a public opinion which might work a revolution in St. Louis' affairs. Some men who have made their money in St. Louis seem to despise the city. It is a thing to be milked, nothing more. The most sordid elements are in control of everything. They control selfishly, recognizing no duty to do anything for the city as a city.

Each one of the delinquents will read this article and indorse it, saying it means the other fellow.

St. Louis, as a city, has no soul, or, if it has, that soul sings small, under the tyranny of conservatism, satisfied with present profits in cash, or it barely exists in an atmosphere of provincial Philistinism which is favorable only to the flourishing of a dismal respectability, with no aesthetic aspiration above Sunday supplements and no outlook upon the larger life of greater scope than is indicated in the acceptance of an occasional record of dropsical bank clearances as proof that this city is up near the front in the march of progress.

The matter with St. Louis, then, is too much mere matter, too little mind. The people who predominate lack vision. The city is devoid of any community of affectionate desire to make the city great and beautiful as an expression of something besides mere sordid solidity in a financial way. St. Louisans should love St. Louis as Londoners love London, Parisians love Paris, New Yorkers love New York, Chicagoans love Chicago. They should unite in a desire that the world should know their city's merits as a home of people with hearts responsive to beauty and all exalted things.

The World's Fair proposal is one the materialization of which must force us to create something which will be a material expression of a civic idealism, as the White City revealed the soul of Chicago, as the Dewey arch disclosed the idealism of New York. A World's Fair will awaken this city's anaemic soul. It will breathe a soul into beings who now seem not to know what soul means. It will awaken the dormant spirit in many, as the sight of the Acropolis strikes reverence from the silliest "Cookie." We need it that we may not attain a piteous and contemptible distinction as village bloated by sedentary satisfaction into a metropolis of Boeotia. St. Louis needs an awakening, such as described, as much as Havana needed sanitation. Let us work for it.

NOVEMBER 1899

WINSTON CHURCHILL

BORN IN ST. LOUIS to Emma Bell Blaine, a St. Louisan, and Edwin Spaulding Churchill, of Portland, Maine, Winston Churchill (1871-1947) felt torn between St. Louis and New England. After attending Smith Academy in St. Louis, Churchill went to the United States Naval Academy, where he developed a strong interest in American history. Churchill graduated near the top of his class at Annapolis, but he chose a civilian life in publishing over a naval career. He joined the staff of *Cosmopolitan* and wrote fiction, although none of his earliest efforts were published and all have since disappeared.

In 1895, Churchill married Mabel Harlakenden Hall of St. Louis and moved to New Hampshire, where he had purchased a farm. Here, Churchill—a gentleman of fine breeding and independent means—worked diligently to hone his fiction. In 1899, his first historical novel, *Richard Carvel*, was published to an enthusiastic reception. That work and his second novel, *The Crisis* (1901), both were adapted for the stage and enjoyed successful runs. Churchill continued to write and publish novels while cultivating an interest in state politics. He served two terms in the New Hampshire legislature and eventually ran for governor.

The Crisis, passages of which are included here, is set in St. Louis during the Civil War. The novel's dashing protagonist, Stephen Brice, resembles its author not only in his genteel pedigree, but also in his idealism and lofty political aspirations. The excerpt begins with Stephen, a young lawyer returned to St. Louis from the East, summoning the courage to approach the formidable Judge Silas Whipple for a position. While waiting for the judge, Stephen, a staunch abolitionist, witnesses a slave auction in progress near the courthouse and is moved to purchase a woman in order to set her free. These chapters, as well as Churchill's "Afterword" to the novel, reveal the volatile ambiguity peculiar to St. Louis culture and politics during this period of history.

FROM *THE CRISIS*

BLACK CATTLE

Later that evening Stephen Brice was sitting by the open windows in his mother's room, looking silently down on the street-lights below.

"Well my dear," asked the lady at length, "what do you think of it all?"

"They are kind people," he said.

"Yes, they are kind," she assented, with a sigh. "But they are not—they are not from among our friends, Stephen."

"I thought that one of our reasons for coming West, mother," answered Stephen.

His mother looked pained.

"Stephen, how can you! We came West in order that you might have more chance for the career to which you are entitled. Our friends in Boston were more than good."

He left the window and came and stood behind her chair, his hands clasped playfully beneath her chin.

"Have you the exact date about you, mother?"

"What date, Stephen?"

"When I shall leave St. Louis for the United States Senate. And you must not forget that there is a youth limit in our Constitution for senators."

Then the widow smiled,—a little sadly, perhaps. But still a wonderfully sweet smile. And it made her strong face akin to all that was human and helpful.

"I believe that you have the subject of my first speech in that august assembly. And, by the way, what was it?"

"It was on 'The Status of the Emigrant,'" she responded instantly, thereby proving that she was his mother.

"And it touched the Rights of Privacy," he added, laughing, "which do not seem to exist in St. Louis boarding-houses."

"In the eyes of your misguided profession, statesmen and authors and emigrants and other public charges have no Rights of Privacy," said she. "Mr. Longfellow told me once that they were to name a brand of flour for him, and that he had no redress."

"Have you, too, been up before Miss Crane's Commission?" he asked, with amused interest.

His mother laughed.

"Yes," she said quietly.

"They have some expert members," he continued. "This Mrs. Abner Reed could be a shining light in any bar. I overheard a part of her cross-examination. She—she had evidently studied our case—"

"My dear," answered Mrs. Brice, "I suppose they know all about us." She was silent a moment—"I had so hoped that they wouldn't. They lead the same narrow life in this house that they did in their little New England towns. They—they pity us, Stephen."

"Mother!"

"I did not expect to find so many New Englanders here—I wish that Mr. Whipple had directed us elsewhere—"

"He probably thought that we should feel at home among New Englanders. I hope the Southerners will be more considerate. I believe they will," he added.

"They are very proud," said his mother. "A wonderful people,—born aristocrats. You don't remember those Randolphs with whom we travelled through England. They were with us at Hollingdean, Lord Northwell's place. You were too small at the time. There was a young girl, Eleanor Randolph, a beauty. I shall never forget the way she entered those English drawing-rooms. They visited us once in Beacon Street, afterwards. And I have heard that there are a great many good Southern families here in St. Louis."

"You did not glean that from Judge Whipple's letter, mother," said Stephen, mischievously.

"He was very frank in his letter," sighed Mrs. Brice.

"I imagine he is always frank, to put it delicately."

"Your father always spoke in praise of Silas Whipple, my dear. I have heard him call him one of the ablest lawyers in the country. He won a remarkable case for Appleton here, and he once said that the Judge would have sat on the Supreme Bench if he had not been pursued with such relentlessness by rascally politicians."

"The Judge indulges in a little relentlessness now and then, himself. He is not precisely what might be termed a mild man, if what we hear is correct."

Mrs. Brice started.

"What have you heard?" she asked.

"Well, there was a gentleman on the steamboat who said that it took more courage to enter the Judge's private office than to fight a Border Ruffian. And another, a young lawyer, who declared that he would rather face a wild cat than ask Whipple a question on the new code. And yet he said that the Judge knew more law than any man in the West. And lastly, there is a polished gentleman named Hopper here from Massachusetts who enlightened me a little more."

Stephen paused and bit his tongue. He saw that she was distressed by these things. Heaven knows that she had borne enough trouble in the last few months.

"Come, mother," he said gently, "you should know how to take my jokes by this time. I didn't mean it. I am sure the Judge is a good man,—one of those aggressive good men who make enemies. I have but a single piece of guilt to accuse him of."

"And what is that?" asked the widow.

"The cunning forethought which he is showing in wishing to have it said that a certain Senator and Judge Brice was trained in his office."

"Stephen—you goose!" she said.

Her eyes wandered around the room,—Widow Crane's best bedroom. It was dimly lighted by an extremely ugly lamp. The hideous stuffy bed curtains and the more hideous imitation marble mantel were the two objects that held her glance. There was no change in her calm demeanor. But Stephen, who knew his mother, felt that her little elation over her arrival had ebbed. Neither would confess dejection to the other.

"I—even I—" said Stephen, tapping his chest, "have at least made the acquaintance of one prominent citizen, Mr. Eliphalet D. Hopper. According to Mr. Dickens, he is a true American gentleman, for he chews tobacco. He has been in St. Louis five years, is now assistant manager of the largest dry goods house, and still lives in one of Miss Crane's four-dollar rooms. I think we may safely say that he will be a millionaire before I am a senator."

He paused.

"And mother?"

"Yes, dear."

He put his hands in his pockets and walked over to the window.

"I think it would be better if I did the same thing."

"What do you mean, my son—"

"If I went to work,—started sweeping out a store, I mean. See here, mother, you've sacrificed enough for me already. After paying father's debts, we've come out here with only a few thousand dollars, and the nine hundred I saved out of this year's Law School allowance. What shall we do when that is gone? The honorable legal profession, as my friend reminded me to-night, is not the swiftest road to millions."

With a mother's discernment she guessed the agitation he was striving to hide; she knew that he had been gathering courage for this moment for months. And she knew that he was renouncing thus lightly, for her sake, an ambition he had had from his school days.

The widow passed her hand over her brow. It was a space before she answered him.

"My son," she said, "let us never speak of this again. It was your father's dearest wish that you should become a lawyer, and—and his wishes are sacred. God will take care of us."

She rose and kissed him good-night.

"Remember, my dear, when you go to Judge Whipple in the morning, remember his kindness, and—"

"And keep my temper. I shall, mother."

A while later he stole gently back into her room again. She was on her knees by the walnut bedstead.

At nine the next morning Stephen left Miss Crane's, girded for the struggle with the redoubtable Silas Whipple. He was not afraid, but a poor young man as an applicant to a notorious dragon is not likely to be handled with velvet, even though the animal had been a friend of his father. Dragons as a rule have had a hard time in their youths, and believe in others' having a hard time.

To a young man, who as his father's heir in Boston had been the subject of marked consideration by his elders, the situation was keenly distasteful. But it had to be gone through. So presently, after inquiry, he came to the open square where the new Court House stood, the dome of which was indicated by a mass of staging, and one wing still to be completed. Across from the building, on Market Street, and in the middle of the block, what had once been a golden hand pointed up a narrow dusty stairway. Here was a sign, "Law office of Silas Whipple."

Stephen climbed the stairs, and arrived at a ground-glass door, on which the sign was repeated. Behind that door was the future: so he opened it fearfully, with an impulse to throw his arm above his head. But he was struck dumb on beholding, instead of a dragon, a good natured young man who smiled a broad welcome. The reaction was as great as though one entered a dragon's den, armed to the teeth, to find a St. Bernard doing the honors.

Stephen's heart went out to this young man,—after that organ had jumped back into its place. This keeper of the dragon looked the part. Even the long black coat which custom then decreed could not hide the bone and sinew under it. The young man had a broad forehead, placid Dresden-blue eyes, flaxen hair, and the German coloring. Across one of his high cheek-bones was a great jagged scar which seemed to add distinction to his appearance. That caught Stephen's eye, and held it. He wondered whether it were the result of an encounter with the Judge.

"You wish to see Mr. Whipple?" he asked, in the accents of an educated German.

"Yes," said Stephen, "if he isn't busy."

"He is out," said the other, with just a suspicion of a *á* in the word. "You know he is much occupied now, fighting election frauds. You read the papers?"

"I am a stranger here," said Stephen.

"Ach!" exclaimed the German, "now I know you, Mr. Brice. The young one from Boston the judge spoke of. But you did not tell him of your arrival."

"I did not wish to bother him," Stephen replied, smiling.

"My name is Richter—Carl Richter, sir."

The pressure of Mr. Richter's big hands warmed Stephen as nothing else had since he had come West. He was moved to return it with a little more fervor than he usually showed. And he felt whatever the Judge might be, that he had a powerful friend near at hand—Mr. Richter's welcome came near being an embrace.

"Sit down Mr. Brice," he said; "mild weather for November, eh? The Judge will be here in an hour."

Stephen looked around him: at the dusty books on the shelves, and the still dustier books heaped on Mr. Richter's big table; at the cuspidors; at the engravings of Washington and Webster; at the window in the jog which looked out on the court-house square; and finally at another ground-glass door on which was printed:—

SILAS WHIPPLE

PRIVATE

This, then, was the den,—the arena in which was to take place a memorable interview. But the thought of waiting an hour for the dragon to appear was disquieting. Stephen remembered that he had something over nine hundred dollars in his pocket (which he had saved out of his last year's allowance at the Law School). So he asked Mr. Richter, who was dusting off a chair, to direct him to the nearest bank.

"Why, certainly," said he; "Mr. Brinsmade's bank on Chestnut Street." He took Stephen to the window and pointed across the square. "I am sorry I cannot go with you," he added, "but the Judge's negro, Shadrach, is out, and I must stay in the office. I will give you a note to Mr. Brinsmade."

"His negro!" exclaimed Stephen. "Why, I thought that Mr. Whipple was an Abolitionist."

Mr. Richter laughed.

"The man is free," said he. "The Judge pays him wages."

Stephen thanked his new friend for the note to the bank president, and went slowly down the stairs. To be keyed up to a battle-pitch, and then to have the battle deferred, is a trial of flesh and spirit.

As he reached the pavement, he saw people gathering in front of the wide entrance of the Court House opposite, and perched on the copings. He hesitated, curious. Then he walked slowly toward the place, and buttoning his coat, pushed through the loafers and passers-by dallying on the outskirts of the crowd. There, in the bright November sunlight, a sight met his eyes which turned him sick and dizzy.

Against the walls and pillars of the building, already grimy with soot, crouched a score of miserable human beings waiting to be sold at auction. Mr. Lynch's slave pen had been disgorged that morning. Old and young, husband and wife,—the moment was come for all and each. How hard the stones! and what more pitiless than the gaze of their fellow-creatures in the crowd below! O friends, we who live in peace and plenty amongst our families, how little do we realize the terror and the misery and the dumb heart-aches of those days! Stephen thought with agony of seeing his own mother sold before his eyes, and the building in front of him was lifted from its foundation and rocked even as shall the temples on the judgment day.

The oily auctioneer was inviting the people to pinch the wares. Men came forward to feel the creatures and look into their mouths, and one brute, unshaven and with filthy linen, snatched a child from its mother's lap. Stephen shuddered with the sharpest pain he had ever known. An ocean-wide tempest arose in his breast,—a Samson's strength to break the pillars of the temple, to slay these men with his bare hands. Seven generations of stern life and thought had their focus here in him,—from Oliver Cromwell to John Brown.

Stephen was far from prepared for the storm that raged within him. He had not been brought up an Abolitionist,—far from it. Nor had his father's friends,—who were deemed at that time the best people in Boston—been Abolitionists. Only three years before, when Boston had been aflame over the delivery of the fugitive Anthony Burns, Stephen had gone out of curiosity to the mass meeting at Faneuil Hall. How well he remembered his father's indignation when he confessed it, and in his anger Brice had called Phillips and Parker "agitators." But his father, nor his father's friends in Boston, had never been brought face to face with this hideous traffic.

Hark! Was that the sing-song voice of the auctioneer? He was selling the cattle. High and low, caressing and menacing, he teased and exhorted them to buy. They were bidding, yes, for the possession of souls, bidding in the currency of the Great Republic. And between the eager shouts came a moan of sheer despair. What was the attendant doing now? He was tearing two of them from a last embrace.

Three—four were sold while Stephen was in a dream.

Then came a lull, a hitch, and the crowd began to chatter gayly. But the misery in front of him held Stephen in a spell. Figures stood out from the group. A white-haired patriarch, with eyes raised to the sky; a flat-breasted woman whose child was gone, whose weakness made her valueless. Then two girls were pushed forth, one a quadroon of great beauty, to be fingered. Stephen turned his face away,—to behold Mr. Eliphalet Hopper looking calmly on.

"Wal, Mr. Brice, this is an interesting show now, ain't it? Something we don't have. I generally stop here to take a look when I'm passing." And he spat tobacco juice on the coping.

Stephen came to his senses.

"And you are from New England?" he said.

Mr. Hopper laughed.

"Tarnation!" said he, "you get used to it. When I come here, I was a sort of an Abolitionist. But after you've lived here awhile you get to know that niggers ain't fit for freedom."

Silence from Stephen.

"Likely gal, that beauty," Eliphalet continued unrepressed. "There's a well-known New Orleans dealer named Jenkins after her. I callate she'll go down river."

"I reckon you're right, Mistah," a man with a matted beard chimed in, and added with a wink: "She'll find it pleasant enough—fer a while. Some of those other niggers will go too, and they'd ruther go to hell. They do treat 'em nefarious daown thah on the wholesale plantations. Household niggers! there ain't none better off than them. But seven years in a cotton swamp,—seven years it takes; that's all, Mistah."

Stephen moved away. He felt that to stay near the man was to be tempted to murder. He moved away, and just then the auctioneer yelled, "Attention!"

"Gentlemen," he cried, "I have heah two sisters, the prope'ty of the late Mistah Robe't Benbow, of St. Louis, as fine a pair of wenches as was ever offe'd to the public from these heah steps—"

"Speak for the handsome gal," cried a wag.

"Sell off the cart boss fust," said another.

The auctioneer turned to the darker sister.

"Sal ain't much on looks, gentlemen," he said, "but she's the best nigger for *work* Mistah Benbow had." He seized her arm and squeezed it, while the girl flinched and drew back. "She's solid, gentlemen, and sound as a dollar, and she kin sew and cook. Twenty-two years old. What am I bid?"

Much to the auctioneer's disgust, Sal was bought in for four hundred dollars, the interest in the beautiful sister having made the crowd impatient. Stephen, sick at heart, turned to leave. Halfway to the corner he met a little elderly man who was the color of a dried gourd. And just as Stephen passed him, this man was overtaken by an old negress, with tears streaming down her face, who seized the threadbare hem of his coat. Stephen paused involuntarily.

"Well, Nancy," said the little man, "we had marvellous luck. I was able to buy your daughter for you with less than the amount of your savings."

"T'ank you, Mistah Cantah," wailed the poor woman, "t'ank you, suh. Praised be de name ob de Lawd. He gib me Sal again. Oh, Mistah Cantah" (the agony in that cry), "is you gwineter stan' heah an' see her sister Hester sol' to—to—oh, ma little chile! De little chile dat I nussed, dat I raised up in God's 'ligion. Mistah Cantah, save her, suh, f'om dat wicked life o' sin. De Lawd Jesus'll rewa'd you, suh. Dis ole woman'll wuk fo' you twell de flesh drops off'n her fingers, suh."

And had he not held her, she would have gone down on her knees on the stone flagging before him. Her suffering was stamped on the little man's face,—and it seemed to Stephen that this was but one trial more which adversity had brought to Mr. Canter.

"Nancy," he answered (how often, and to how many, must he have had to say the same thing), "I haven't the money, Nancy. Would to God that I had, Nancy!"

She had sunk down on the bricks. But she had not fainted. It was not so merciful as that. It was Stephen who lifted her, and helped her to the coping, where she sat with her head bowed between her knees, the scarlet bandanna awry.

Stephen Brice was not of a descent to do things upon impulse. But the tale was told in after days that one of his first actions in St. Louis was of this nature. The waters stored for ages in the four great lakes, given the opportunity, rush over Niagara Falls into Ontario.

"Take the woman away," said Stephen, in a low voice, "and I will buy the girl,—if I can."

The little man looked up, dazed.

"Give me your card,—your address. I will buy the girl, if I can, and set her free."

He fumbled in his pocket and drew out a dirty piece of pasteboard. It read: "R. Canter, Second Hand Furniture, 20 Second Street." And still he stared at Stephen, as one who gazes upon a mystery. A few curious pedestrians had stopped in front of them.

"Get her away, if you can, for God's sake," said Stephen again. And he strode off toward the people at the auction. He was trembling. In his eagerness to reach a place of vantage before the girl was sold, he pushed roughly into the crowd.

But suddenly he was brought up short by the blocky body of Mr. Hopper, who grunted with the force of the impact.

"Gosh," said that gentleman, "but you are inters'ted. They ain't begun to sell her yet—he's waitin' for somebody. Callatin' to buy her?" asked Mr. Hopper with genial humor.

Stephen took a deep breath. If he knocked Mr. Hopper down, he certainly could not buy her. And it was a relief to know that the sale had not begun.

As for Eliphalet, he was beginning to like young Brice. He approved of any man from Boston who was not too squeamish to take pleasure in a little affair of this kind.

As for Stephen, Mr. Hopper brought him back to earth. He ceased trembling, and began to think.

"Tarnation!" said Eliphalet. "There's my boss. Colonel Carvel, across the street. Guess I'd better move on. But what d'ye think of him for a real Southern gentleman? The young dandy is his nephew, Clarence Colfax. He callates to own this town." Eliphalet was speaking leisurely, as usual, while preparing to move. "That's Virginia Carvel, in red. Any gals down Boston-way to beat her? Guess you won't find many as proud."

He departed. And Stephen glanced absently at the group. They were picking their way over the muddy crossing toward him. Was it possible that these people were coming to a slave auction? Surely not. And yet here they were on the pavement at his very side.

She wore a long Talma of crimson cashmere, and her face was in that most seductive of frames, a scoop bonnet of dark green velvet. For a fleeting second her eyes met his, and then her lashes fell. But he was aware, when he had turned away, that she was looking at him again. He grew uneasy. He wondered whether his appearance betrayed his purpose, or made a question of his sanity.

Sanity! Yes, probably he was insane from her point of view. A sudden anger shook him that she should be there calmly watching such a scene.

Just then there was a hush among the crowd. The beautiful slave-girl was seized roughly by the man in charge and thrust forward, half fainting, into view. Stephen winced. But unconsciously he turned, to see the effect upon Virginia Carvel.

Thank God! There were tears upon her lashes.

Here was the rasp of the auctioneer's voice—:

"Gentlemen, I reckon there ain't *never* been offered to bidders such an opportunity as this heah. Look at her well, gentlemen. I ask you, ain't she a splendid creature?"

Colonel Carvel, in annoyance, started to move on.

"Come Jinny," he said, "I had no business to bring you over."

But Virginia caught his arm. "Pa," she cried, "it's Mr. Benbow's Hester. Don't go, dear. Buy her for me. You know that I always wanted her. Please!"

The Colonel halted, irresolute, and pulled his goatee. Young Colfax stepped in between them.

"I'll buy her for you, Jinny. Mother promised you a present, you know, and you shall have her."

Virginia had calmed.

"Do buy her, one of you," was all she said.

"You may do the bidding, Clarence," said the Colonel, "and we'll settle the ownership afterward." Taking Virginia's arm, he escorted her across the street.

Stephen was left in a quandary. Here was a home for the girl, and a good one. Why should he spend the money which meant so much to him? He saw the man Jenkins elbowing to the front. And yet—suppose Mr. Colfax did not get her? He had promised to buy her if he could, and to set her free.

Stephen had made up his mind. He shouldered his way after Jenkins.

SILAS WHIPPLE

The trouble with many narratives is that they tell too much. Stephen's interview with his mother was a quiet affair, and not historic. Miss Crane's boarding-house is not an interesting place, and the tempest in that teapot is better imagined than described. Out of consideration for Mr. Stephen Brice, we shall skip likewise a most affecting scene at Mr. Canter's second-hand furniture store.

That afternoon Stephen came again to the dirty flight of steps which led to Judge Whipple's office. He paused a moment to gather courage, and then, gripping the rail, he ascended. The ascent required courage now, certainly. He halted again before the door at the top. But even as he stood there came to him, in low, rich tones, the notes of a German song. He entered. And Mr. Richter rose in shirt-sleeves from his desk to greet him, all smiling.

"Ach, my friend!" said he, "but you are late. The Judge has been awaiting you."

"Has he?" inquired Stephen, with ill-concealed anxiety.

The big young German patted him on the shoulder. Suddenly a voice roared from out the open transom of the private office, like a cyclone rushing through a gap.

"Mr. Richter!"

"Sir!"

"Who is that?"

"Mr. Brice, sir."

"Then why in thunder doesn't he come in?"

Mr. Richter opened the private door, and in Stephen walked. The door closed again, and there he was in the dragon's den, face to face with the dragon, who was staring him through and through. The first objects that caught Stephen's attention were the grizzly gray eyebrows, which seemed as so much brush to mark the fire of the deep-set battery of the eyes. And that battery, when in action, must have been truly terrible.

The Judge was shaven, save for a shaggy fringe of gray beard around his chin, and the size of his nose was apparent even in the full face.

Stephen felt that no part of him escaped the search of Mr. Whipple's glance. But it was no code or course of conduct that kept him silent. Nor was it fear—entirely.

"So you are Appleton Brice's son," said the Judge, at last. His tone was not quite so gruff as it might have been.

Yes, sir," said Stephen.

"Humph!" said the Judge, with a look that scarcely expressed approval. "I guess you've been patted on the back too much by your father's friends." He leaned back in his wooden chair. "How I used to detest people who patted boys on the back and said with a smirk, 'I know your father.' I never had a father whom people could say that about. But, sir," cried the Judge, bringing down his fist on the litter of papers that covered his desk, "I made up my mind that one day people should know *me*. *That* was my spur. And you'll start fair here, Mr. Brice. They won't know your father here—"

If Stephen thought the Judge brutal, he did not say so. He glanced around the little room,—at the bed in the corner, in which the Judge slept, and which during the day did not escape the flood of books and papers; at the washstand, with a roll of legal cap beside the pitcher.

"I guess you think this town pretty crude after Boston, Mr. Brice," Mr. Whipple continued. "From time immemorial it has been the pleasant habit of old communities to be shocked at newer settlements, built by their own countrymen. Are you shocked, sir?"

Stephen flushed. Fortunately the Judge did not give him time to answer.

"Why didn't your mother let me know that she was coming?"

"She didn't wish to put you to any trouble, sir."

"Wasn't I a good friend of your father's? Didn't I ask you to come here and go into my office?"

"But there was a chance, Mr. Whipple—"

"A chance of what?"

"That you would not like me. And there is still a chance of it," added Stephen, smiling.

For a second it looked as if the Judge might smile, too. He rubbed his nose with a fearful violence.

"Mr. Richter tells me you were looking for a bank," said he, presently.

Stephen quaked.

"Yes sir, I was, but—"

But Mr. Whipple merely picked up the *Counterfeit Bank Note Detector.*

"Beware of Western State Currency as you would the devil," said he. "That's one thing we don't equal the East in—yet. And so you want to become a lawyer?"

"I intend to become a lawyer, sir."

"And so you shall, sir," cried the Judge, bringing down his yellow fist upon the *Bank Note Detector.* "I'll make you a lawyer, sir. But my methods ain't Harvard methods, sir."

"I am ready to do anything, Mr. Whipple."

The Judge merely grunted. He scratched among his papers, and produced some legal cap and a bunch of notes.

"Go out there," he said, "and take off your coat and copy this brief. Mr. Richter will help you to-day. And tell your mother I shall do myself the honor to call upon her this evening."

Stephen did as he was told, without a word. But Mr. Richter was not in the outer office when he returned to it. He tried to compose himself to write, although the recollection of each act of the morning hung like a cloud over the back of his head. Therefore the first sheet of legal cap was spoiled utterly. But Stephen had a deep sense of failure. He had gone through the ground glass door with the firm intention of making a clean breast of the ownership of Hester. Now, as he sat still, the trouble grew upon him. He started a new sheet, and ruined that. Once he got as far as his feet, and sat down again. But at length he had quieted to the extent of deciphering ten lines of Mr. Whipple's handwriting when the creak of a door shattered his nerves completely.

He glanced up from his work to behold—none other than Colonel Comyn Carvel.

Glancing at Mr. Richter's chair, and seeing it empty, the Colonel's eye roved about the room until it found Stephen. There it remained, and the Colonel remained in the middle of the floor, his soft hat on the back of his head, one hand planted firmly on the gold head of his stick, and the other tugging at his goatee, pulling down his chin to the quizzical angle.

"Whoopee!" he cried.

The effect of this was to make one perspire freely. Stephen perspired. And as there seemed no logical answer, he made none.

Suddenly Mr. Carvel turned, shaking with a laughter he could not control, and strode into the private office. The door slammed behind him. Mr. Brice's impulse was flight. But he controlled himself.

First of all there was an eloquent silence. Then a ripple of guffaws. Then the scratch-scratch of a quill pen, and finally the Judge's voice.

"Carvel, what the devil's the matter with you, sir?"

A squall of guffaws blew through the transom, and the Colonel was heard slapping his knee.

"Judge Whipple," said he, his voice vibrating from suppressed explosions, "I am happy to see that you have overcome some of your ridiculous prejudices, sir."

"What prejudices, sir?" the Judge was heard to shout.

"Toward slavery, Judge," said Mr. Carvel, seeming to recover his gravity. "You are a broader man than I thought, sir."

An unintelligible gurgle came from the Judge. Then he said,—

"Carvel, haven't you and I quarrelled enough on that subject?"

"You didn't happen to attend the nigger auction this morning when you were at the court?" asked the Colonel, blandly.

"Colonel," said the Judge, "I've warned you a hundred times against the stuff you lay out on your counter for customers."

"You weren't at the auction, then," continued the Colonel, undisturbed. "You missed it, sir. You missed seeing this young man you've just employed buy the prettiest quadroon wench I ever set eyes on."

Now indeed was poor Stephen on his feet. But whether to fly in at the one entrance or out at the other, he was undecided.

"Colonel," said Mr. Whipple, "is that true?"

"Sir!"

"MR. BRICE!"

It did not seem to Stephen as if he was walking when he went toward the ground glass door. He opened it. There was Colonel Carvel seated on the bed, his goatee in his hand. And there was the Judge leaning forward from his hips, straight as a ramrod. Fire was darting from beneath his bushy eyebrows. "Mr. Brice," said he, "there is one question I always ask of those whom I employ. I omitted it in your case because I have known your father and your grandfather before you. What is your opinion, sir, on the subject of holding human beings in bondage?"

The answer was immediate,—likewise simple.

"I do not believe in it, Mr. Whipple."

The Judge shot out of his chair like a long jack-in-the box, and towered to his full height.

"Mr. Brice, did you, or did you not, buy a woman at auction to-day?"

"I did, sir."

Mr. Whipple literally staggered. But Stephen caught a glimpse of the Colonel's hand slipping from his chin over his mouth.

"Good God, sir!" cried the Judge, and he sat down heavily. "You say that you are an Abolitionist?"

"No, sir, I do not say that. But it does not need an Abolitionist to condemn what I saw this morning."

"Are you a slave-owner, sir?" said Mr. Whipple.

"Yes, sir."

Then get your coat and hat and leave my office, Mr. Brice."

Stephen's coat was on his arm. He slipped it on, and turned to go. He was, if the truth were told, more amused than angry. It was Colonel Carvel's voice that stopped him.

"Hold on, Judge," he drawled, "I reckon you haven't got all the packing out of that case."

Mr. Whipple looked at him in a sort of stupefaction. Then he glanced at Stephen.

"Come back here, sir," he cried. "I'll give you a hearing. No man shall say that I am not just."

Stephen looked gratefully at the Colonel.

"I did not expect one, sir," he said.

"And you don't deserve one, sir," cried the Judge.

"I think I do," replied Stephen, quietly.

The Judge suppressed something.

"What did you do with this person?" he demanded.

"I took her to Miss Crane's boarding-house," said Stephen.

It was the Colonel's turn to explode. The guffaw which came from him drowned every other sound.

"Good God!" said the Judge, helplessly. Again he looked at the Colonel, and this time something very like mirth shivered his lean frame. "And what do you intend to do with her?" he asked in strange tones.

"To give her freedom, sir, as soon as I can find somebody to go on her bond."

Again silence. Mr. Whipple rubbed his nose with more than customary violence, and looked very hard at Mr. Carvel, whose face was inscrutable. It was a solemn moment.

"Mr. Brice," said the Judge, at length, "take off your coat, sir. I will go her bond."

It was Stephen's turn to be taken aback. He stood regarding the Judge curiously, wondering what manner of man he was. He did not know that this question had puzzled many before him.

"Thank you, sir," he said.

His hand was on the knob of the door, when Mr. Whipple called him back abruptly. His voice had lost some of its gruffness.

"What were your father's ideas about slavery, Mr. Brice?"

The young man thought a moment, as if seeking to be exact.

"I suppose he would have put slavery among the necessary evils, sir," he said, at length. "But he never could bear to have the *Liberator* mentioned in his presence. He was not at all in sympathy with Phillips, or Parker, or Sumner. And such was the general feeling among his friends."

"Then," said the Judge, "contrary to popular opinion in the West and South, Boston is not all Abolition."

Stephen smiled.

"The conservative classes are not at all Abolitionists, sir."

"The conservative classes!" growled the Judge, "the conservative classes! I am tired of hearing about the conservative classes. Why not come out with it, sir, and say the moneyed classes, who would rather see souls held in bondage than risk their worldly goods in an attempt to liberate them?"

Stephen flushed. It was not at all clear to him then how he was to get along with Judge Whipple. But he kept his temper.

"I am sure that you do them an injustice, sir," he said, with more feeling than he had yet shown. "I am not speaking of the rich alone, and I think that if you knew Boston you would not say that the conservative class there is wholly composed of wealthy people. Many of my father's friends were by no means wealthy. And I know that if he had been poor he would have held the same views."

Stephen did not mark the quick look of approval which Colonel Carvel gave him. Judge Whipple merely rubbed his nose.

"Well, sir," he said, "what were his views, then?"

"My father regarded slaves as property, sir. And conservative people" (Stephen stuck to the word) "respect property the world over. My father's argument was this: If men are deprived by violence of one kind of property which they hold under the law, all other kinds of property will be endangered. The result will be anarchy. Furthermore, he recognized that the economic conditions in the South make slavery necessary to prosperity. And he regarded the covenant made between the states of the two sections as sacred."

There was a brief silence, during which the uncompromising expression of the Judge did not change.

"And do you, sir?" he demanded.

"I am not sure, sir, after what I saw yesterday. I—I must have time to see more of it."

"Good Lord," said Colonel Carvel, "if the conservative people of the North act this way when they see a slave sale, what will the Abolitionists do? Whipple," he added slowly, but with conviction, "this means war."

Then the Colonel got to his feet, and bowed to Stephen with ceremony.

"Whatever you believe, sir," he said, "permit me to shake your hand. You are a brave man, sir. And although my own belief is that the black race is held in subjection by a divine decree, I can admire what you have done, Mr. Brice. It was a noble act, sir,—a right noble act. And I have more respect for the people of Boston, now, sir, than I ever had before, sir."

Having delivered himself of this somewhat dubious compliment (which he meant well), the Colonel departed.

Judge Whipple said nothing.

AFTERWORD

The author has chosen St. Louis for the principal scene of this story for many reasons. Grant and Sherman were living there before the Civil War, and Abraham Lincoln was an unknown lawyer in the neighboring state of Illinois. It has been one of the aims of this book to show the remarkable contrasts in the lives of these great men who came out of the West. This old city of St. Louis, which was founded by Laclede in 1765, likewise became the principal meeting-place of two great streams of emigration which had been separated, more or less, since Cromwell's day. To be sure, they were not all Cavaliers who settled in the tidewater Colonies. There were Puritan settlements in both Maryland and Virginia. But the life in the Southern states took on the more liberal tinge which had characterized that of the Royalists, even to the extent of affecting the Scotch Calvinists, while the asceticism of the Roundheads was the keynote of the Puritan character in New England. When this great country of ours began to develop, the streams moved westward; one over what became the plain states of Ohio and Indiana and Illinois, and the other across the Blue Ridge Mountains into Kentucky and Tennessee. They mixed along the line of the Ohio River. They met at St. Louis, and, farther west, in Kansas.

Nor can the German element in St. Louis be ignored. The part played by this people in the Civil War is a matter of history. The scope of this book has not permitted the author to introduce the peasantry and trading classes which formed the mass in this movement. But Richter, the type of the university-bred revolutionist which emigrated after '48, is drawn more or less from life. And the duel described actually took place in Berlin.

St. Louis is the author's birthplace, and his home,—the home of those friends whom he has known from childhood and who have always treated him with unfaltering kindness. He begs that they will believe him when he says that only such characters as he loves are reminiscent of those he has known there. The city has a large population,—large enough to include all the types that are to be found in the middle West.

One word more. This book is written of a time when feeling ran high. It has been necessary to put strong speech into the mouths of the characters. The breach that threatened our country's existence is healed now. There is no side but Abraham Lincoln's side. And this side, with all reverence and patriotism, the author has tried to take.

Abraham Lincoln loved the South as well as the North.

CLAUDE H. WETMORE

AFTER ATTENDING Western Reserve University and the Ecole Polytechnique in Lausanne, Switzerland, Claude Wetmore (1862–1944), an Ohio native, traveled for nearly a decade in Europe and South America. During the 1890s, Wetmore moved to St. Louis, where he became city editor of the *St. Louis Post-Dispatch*. After his tenure at the *Post-Dispatch*, Wetmore embarked on his own publishing ventures and started *Wetmore's Journal of St. Louis* and the Pan-American Press Publishing Company. In addition, Wetmore wrote prolifically—a half-dozen book-length adventures set in South America and *Out of a Fleur-de-Lis: The History, Romance, and Biography of the Louisiana Purchase Exposition* (1903), which was authorized by David R. Francis and other exposition officials. While the latter work is unabashed boosterism, Wetmore also had a reputation for his biting editorials that criticized city government.

In 1902, Wetmore was commissioned by *McClure's Magazine* editor Lincoln Steffens (1866–1936) to write an article on corruption in the power structure of St. Louis. Reluctant to alienate prominent St. Louisans implicated in the scandal, Wetmore drafted an innocuous version of "Tweed Days in St. Louis," which Steffens substantially revised. At Wetmore's request, Steffens listed himself as co-author when the article appeared in the October 1902 issue of *McClure's*. Presented here in an abridged version, the scathing exposé brought corruption in St. Louis government and business affairs to national attention and furthered the illustrious career of Steffens, who went on to uncover similar forms of corruption in other American cities. The central figure of this sensational piece of journalism is St. Louis's Circuit Attorney, Joseph W. Folk, a courageous reformer who prosecuted high-level perpetrators of corruption in the city and who also went on to become governor of Missouri. "Tweed" refers to "Boss" William Tweed of New York City, whose name had become synonymous with corruption and favoritism in city government.

TWEED DAYS IN ST. LOUIS

St. Louis, the fourth city in size in the United States, is making two announcements to the world: one that it is the worst governed city in the land; the other that it wishes all men to come and see it. It isn't our worst governed city; Philadelphia is that. But St. Louis is worth examining while we have it inside out.

There is a man at work there, one man, working all alone, but he is the Circuit (district or state) Attorney, and he is "doing his duty." That is what thousands of district attorneys and other public officials have promised to do and boasted of doing. This man has a literal sort of mind. He is a thin-lipped, firm mouthed, dark little man, who never raises his voice, but goes ahead doing, with a smiling eye and a set jaw, the simple thing he said he would do. The politicians and reputable citizens who asked him to run, urged him when he declined. When he said that if elected he would have to do his duty, they said, "Of course." So he ran, they supported him, and he was elected. Now some of these politicians are sentenced to the penitentiary, some are in Mexico. The Circuit Attorney, finding that his "duty" was to catch and convict criminals, and that the biggest criminals were some of these same politicians and leading citizens, went after them. It is magnificent, but the politicians declare it isn't politics.

The corruption of St. Louis came from the top. The best citizens—the merchants and big financiers—used to rule the town, and they ruled it well. They set out to outstrip Chicago. The commercial and industrial war between these two cities was at one time a picturesque and dramatic spectacle such as is witnessed only in our country. Businessmen were not mere merchants and the politicians were not mere grafters; the two kinds of citizens got together and wielded the power of banks, railroads, factories, the prestige of the city, and the spirit of its citizens to gain business and population. And it was a close race. Chicago, having the start, always led, but St. Louis had pluck, intelligence, and tremendous energy. It pressed Chicago hard. It excelled in a sense of civic beauty and good government; and there are those who think yet it might have won. But a change occurred. Public spirit became private spirit, public enterprise became private greed.

Along about 1890, public franchises and privileges were sought not only for legitimate profit and common convenience, but for loot. Taking but slight and always selfish interest in the public councils, the big men misused politics.

The riff-raff, catching the smell of corruption, rushed into the Municipal Assembly, drove out the remaining respectable men, and sold the city—its streets, its wharves, its markets, and all that it had—to the now greedy business men and bribers. In other words, when the leading men began to devour their own city, the herd rushed into the trough and fed also.

So gradually has this occurred, that these same citizens hardly realize it. Go to St. Louis and you will find the habit of civic pride in them; they still boast. The visitor is told of the wealth of the residents, of the financial strength of the banks, and of the growing importance of the industries, yet he sees poorly paved, refuse-burdened streets, and dusty or mud-covered alleys; he passes a ramshackle fire-trap crowded with the sick, and learns that it is the City Hospital; he enters the "Four Courts," and his nostrils are greeted with the odor of formaldehyde used as a disinfectant, and insect powder spread to destroy vermin; he calls at the new City Hall, and finds half the entrance boarded with pine planks to cover up the unfinished interior. Finally, he turns a tap in the hotel, to see liquid mud flow into wash-basin or bath-tub.

The St. Louis charter vests legislative power of great scope in a Municipal Assembly, which is composed of a Council and a House of Delegates.

From the Assembly, bribery spread into other departments. Men empowered to issue peddler's licenses and permits to citizens who wished to erect awnings or use a portion of the sidewalk for storage purposes charged an amount in excess of the prices stipulated by law, and pocketed the difference. The city's money was loaned at interest, and the interest was converted into private bank accounts. City carriages were used by the wives and children of city officials. Supplies for public institutions found their way to private tables; one itemized account of food furnished the poorhouse included California jellies, imported cheeses, and French wines! A member of the assembly caused the incorporation of a grocery company, with his sons and daughters the ostensible stockholders, and succeeded in having his bid for city supplies accepted although the figures were in excess of his competitors'. In return for the favor thus shown, he indorsed a measure to award the contract for city printing to another member, and these two voted aye on a bill granting to a third the exclusive right to furnish city dispensaries with drugs.

Men ran into debt to the extent of thousands of dollars for the sake of election to either branch of the Assembly. One night, on a street car to the

City Hall, a new member remarked that the nickel he handed the conductor was his last. The next day he deposited $5,000 in a savings bank. A member of the House of Delegates admitted to the February Grand Jury that his dividends from the combine netted $25,000 in one year; a Councilman stated that he was paid $50,000 for his vote on a single measure.

Bribery was a joke. A newspaper man overheard this conversation one evening in the corridor of the City Hall.

"Ah there, my boodler!" said Mr. Delegate.

"Stay there, my grafter!" replied Mr. Councilman. "Can you lend me a hundred for a day or two?"

"Not at present. But I can spare it if the Z— bill goes through to-night. Meet me at F—'s later."

"All right, my jailbird; I'll be there."

The blackest years were 1898, 1899, and 1900. Foreign corporations came into the city to share in its despoilation, and home industries were driven out by blackmail. Franchises worth millions were granted without one cent of cash to the city, and with provision for only the smallest future payment; several companies which refused to pay blackmail had to leave; citizens were robbed more and more boldly; pay-rolls were padded with the names of non-existent persons; work on public improvements was neglected, while money for them went to the boodlers.

Some of the newspapers protested, disinterested citizens were alarmed, and the shrewder men gave warnings, but none dared make an effective stand. Behind the corruptionists were men of wealth and social standing, who, because of special privileges granted them, felt bound to support and defend the looters. Independent victims of the far-reaching conspiracy submitted in silence, through fear of injury to their business. Men whose integrity was never questioned, who held high positions of trust, who were church members and teachers of Bible classes, contributed to the support of the dynasty—became blackmailers, in fact,—and their excuse was that others did the same, and that if they proved the exception it would work their ruin. The system became loose through license and plenty till it was as wild and weak as that of Tweed's in New York.

Then the unexpected happened—an accident. There was no uprising of the people, but they were restive; and the opposition party leaders, thinking to gain some independent votes, decided to raise the cry "reform" and put up a ticket of candidates different enough from the usual offerings of political parties to give color to their platform. These leaders were not in earnest. There was little difference between the two parties in the city; but the Republican rascals had been getting the greater share of the spoils, and the Democrats wanted more than was given to them. "Boodle" was not the issue, no exposures were made or threatened, and the bosses expected to control their men if elected. Simply as part of the game, the Democrats raised the slogan, "reform" and "no more Ziegenheinism."

Mayor Ziegenhein, called "Uncle Henry," was a "good fellow," "one of the boys," and though it was during his administration that the city grew ripe and went to rot, his opponents talked only of incompetence and neglect, and repeated such stories as that of his famous reply to some citizens who complained because certain street lights were put out: "You have the moon yet—ain't it?"

When somebody mentioned Joseph W. Folk for Circuit Attorney the leaders were ready to accept him. They didn't know much about him. He was a young man from Tennessee; had been President of the Jefferson Club, and arbitrated the railroad strike of 1898. But Folk did not want the place. He was a civil lawyer, had had no practice in criminal law, cared little about it, and a lucrative practice as counsel for corporations was interesting him. He rejected the invitation. The committee called again and again, urging his duty to his party, and the city, etc.

"Very well," he said, at last, "I will accept the nomination, but if elected I will do my duty. There must be no attempt to influence my actions when I am called upon to punish lawbreakers."

The committeemen took such statements as the conventional platitudes of candidates. They nominated him, the Democratic ticket was elected, and Folk became Circuit Attorney for the Eighth Missouri District.

Three weeks after taking the oath of office his campaign pledges were put to the test. A number of arrests had been made in connection with the recent election, and charges of illegal registration were preferred against men of both parties. Mr. Folk took them up like routine cases of ordinary crime. Political bosses rushed to the rescue. Mr. Folk was reminded of his duty to his party, and was given to understand that he was expected to construe the law in such a manner that repeaters and other Election Day criminals who had hoisted Democracy's flag and helped elect him might be either discharged or receive the minimum punishment. . . .

The election cases were passed through the courts with astonishing rapidity; no more mercy was shown Democrats than Republicans, and before winter came a number of ward heelers and old-time party workers were behind the bars in Jefferson City. He next turned his attention to grafters and straw bondsmen with whom the courts were infested, and several of these leeches are in the penitentiary to-day, and the system is broken up because of his activity. But this was little more than the beginning.

One afternoon, late in January of this year, a newspaper reporter, known as "Red" Galvin, called Mr. Folk's attention to a ten-line newspaper item to the effect that a large sum of money had been placed in a bank for the purpose of bribing certain Assemblymen to secure the passage of a street railroad ordinance.

No names were mentioned, but Mr. Galvin surmised that the bill referred to was one introduced on behalf of the Suburban Railway Company. An hour later Mr. Folk sent the names of nearly one hundred persons to the sheriff, with instructions to subpoena them before the grand jury at once. The list included Councilmen, members of the House of Delegates, officers and directors of the Suburban Railway, bank presidents and cashiers. In three days the investigation was being pushed with vigor, but St. Louis still was laughing at the "huge joke." Such things had been attempted before. The men who had been ordered to appear before the grand jury jested as they chatted in the anterooms, and newspaper accounts of these preliminary examinations were written in the spirit of burlesque.

It has developed since that Circuit Attorney Folk knew nothing, and was not able to learn much more during the first few days; but he says he saw here and there puffs of smoke and he determined to find the fire. It was not an easy job. The first break into such a system is always difficult. Mr. Folk began with nothing but courage and a strong personal conviction. He caused peremptory summons to be issued, requiring the immediate attendance in the grand jury room of Charles H. Turner, president of the Suburban Railway, and Philip Stocke, a representative of brewers' interests, who he had reason to believe was the legislative agent in this deal.

"Gentlemen," said Mr. Folk, "I have secured sufficient evidence to warrant the return of indictments against you for bribery, and I shall prosecute you to the full extent of the law and send you to the penitentiary unless you tell to this grand jury the complete history of the corruptionist methods employed by you to secure the passage of Ordinance No. 44. I shall give you three days to consider the matter. At the end of that time, if you have not returned here and given us the information demanded, warrants will be issued for your arrest."

They looked at the audacious young prosecutor and left the Four Court's building without uttering a word. He waited. Two days later, Charles P. Johnson, the veteran criminal lawyer, called, and said that his client, Mr. Stocke, was in such poor health that he would be unable to appear before the grand jury.

"I am truly sorry that Mr. Stocke is ill," replied Mr. Folk, "for his presence here is imperative, and if he fails to appear he will be arrested before sundown."

That evening a conference was held in Gov. Johnson's office, and the next day this story was told in the grand jury room by Charles H. Turner, millionaire president of the Suburban Railway, and corroborated by Philip Stocke, man about town and a good fellow:

The Suburban, anxious to sell out at a large profit to its only competitor, the St. Louis Transit Co., caused to be drafted the measure known as House Bill No. 44. So sweeping were grants that Mr. Turner, who planned and executed the document, told the directors in his confidence that its enactment into law would enhance the value of the property from three to six million dollars. The bill introduced, Mr. Turner visited a politician who had long been known as a legislative agent and asked his price for securing the passage of the measure. "One hundred and forty-five thousand dollars will be my fee," was the reply. The railway president demurred. He would think the matter over, he said, and he hired a cheaper man, Mr. Stocke. Stocke conferred with the representative of the combine in the House of Delegates and reported that $75,000 would be necessary in this branch of the Assembly. Mr. Turner presented a note indorsed by two of the directors whom he could trust, and secured a loan from the German American Savings bank.

Bribe funds in pocket, the legislative agent telephoned John Murrell, at that time a representative of the House combine, to meet him in the office of the Lincoln Trust Company. There the two rented a safe-deposit box. Mr. Stocke placed in the drawer the roll of $75,000, and each subscribed to an agreement that the box should not be opened unless both were present. Of course the conditions spread upon the bank's day book made no reference to the purpose for which this fund had been deposited, but an agreement entered into by Messrs. Stocke and Murrell was to the effect that the

$75,000 should be given Mr. Murrell as soon as the bill became an ordinance and by him distributed to the members of the combine. Stocke turned to the Council, and upon his report a further sum of $60,000 was secured. These bills were placed in a safe-deposit box of the Mississippi Valley Trust Co., and the man who held the key as representative of the Council combine was Charles H. Kratz.

All seemed well, but a few weeks after placing these funds in *escrow*, Mr. Stocke reported to his employer that there was an unexpected hitch due to the action of Emil Meysenburg, who, as a member of the Council Committee on Railroads, was holding up the report on the bill. Mr. Stocke said that Mr. Meysenburg held some worthless shares in a defunct corporation and wanted Mr. Stocke to purchase this paper at its par value of $9,000. Mr. Turner gave Mr. Stocke the money with which to buy the shares.

Thus the passage of House Bill 44 promised to cost the Suburban Railway Co. $144,000, only one thousand dollars less than that originally named by the political boss to whom Mr. Turner had first applied. The bill, however, passed both houses of the Assembly. The sworn servants of the city had done their work and held out their hands for the bribe money.

Then came a court mandate which prevented the Suburban Railway Co. reaping the benefit of the vote buying, and Charles H. Turner, angered at the check, issued orders that the money in safe-deposit boxes should not be touched. War was declared between bribe-givers and bribe-takers, and the latter resorted to tactics which they hoped would frighten the Suburban people into submission—such as making enough of the story public to cause rumors of impending prosecution. It was that first item which Mr. Folk saw and acted upon.

When Messrs. Turner and Stocke unfolded in the grand jury room the details of their bribery plot, Circuit Attorney Folk found himself in possession of verbal evidence of a great crime; he needed as material exhibits the two large sums of money in safe-deposit vaults of two of the largest banking institutions of the West. Had this money been withdrawn? Could he get it if it was there? Lockboxes had always been considered sacred and beyond the power of the law to open. "I've always held," said Mr. Folk, "that the fact that a thing never had been done was no reason for thinking it couldn't be done." He decided in this case that the magnitude of the interests involved warranted unusual action, so he selected three of the grand jurors and visited one of the banks. He told the president, a personal friend, the facts that had come into his possession, and asked permission to search for the fund.

"Impossible," was the reply. "Our rules deny any one the right."

"Mr.—," said Mr. Folk, "a crime has been committed, and you hold concealed the principal evidence thereto. In the name of the State of Missouri I demand that you cause the box to be opened. If you refuse, I shall cause a warrant to be issued, charging you as an accessory. "

For five minutes not a word was spoken by any one in the room; then the banker said in almost inaudible tones:

"Give me a little time, gentlemen. I must consult with our legal adviser before taking such a step."

"We will wait ten minutes," said the Circuit Attorney. "By that time we must have access to the vault or a warrant will be applied for."

At the expiration of that time a solemn procession wended its way from the president's office to the vaults in the sub-cellar—the president, the cashier, and the corporation's lawyer, the grand jurors, and the Circuit Attorney. All bent eagerly forward as the key was inserted in the lock. The iron drawer yielded, and a roll of something wrapped in brown paper was brought to light. The Circuit Attorney removed the rubberbands, and national bank notes of $1,000, $500, and $100 denominations spread out flat before them. The money was counted, and the sum was $75,000!

The boodle fund was returned to its repository, officers of the bank were told they would be held responsible for it until the courts could act. The investigators visited the other financial institution. They then met with more resistance there. The threat to procure a warrant had no effect until Mr. Folk left the building and set off in the direction of the Four Courts. Then a messenger called him back, and the second box was opened. In this was found $60,000. The chain of evidence was complete.

From that moment events moved rapidly. Charles Kratz and John K. Murrell, alleged representatives of Council and House combines, were arrested on bench warrants and placed under heavy bonds. Kratz was brought into court from a meeting at which plans were being formed for his election to the National Congress. Murrell was taken from his undertaking establishment. Emil Meysenburg, millionaire broker, was seated in his office when a sheriff's deputy entered and read a document that charged him with bribery. The summons reached Henry Nicolaus while he was seated at his desk, and the wealthy brewer was compelled to send for a bondsman to avoid passing a night in jail. The cable flashed the news to Cairo, Egypt, that Ellis Wainwright, many times a millionaire, proprietor of the St. Louis brewery that bears his name, now a member of a New York broker's firm, had been indicted. Julius Lehmann, one of the members of the House of Delegates, who had joked while waiting in the grand jury's anteroom, had his laughter cut short by the hand of a deputy sheriff on his shoulder and the words, "You are charged with perjury." He was joined at the bar of the criminal court by Harry Faulkner, another mirth-provoking member.

Consternation spread among the boodle gang. Some of the men took night trains for other States and foreign countries; the majority remained and counseled together. Within twenty-four hours after the first indictments were returned, a meeting of bribe-givers and bribe-takers was held in South St. Louis, the total wealth of those in attendance being $30,000,000, and their combined political influence sufficient to carry any municipal election under normal conditions.

This great power was aligned in opposition to one man, who still was alone. It was not until many indictments had been returned that a citizens' committee was formed to furnish funds, and even then most of the contributors concealed their identity. Mr. James L. Blair, the treasurer, testified in court that they were afraid to be known lest "it ruin their business."

At the meeting of corruptionists three courses were decided upon. Political leaders were to work on the Circuit Attorney by promise of future reward, or by threats. Detectives were to ferret out of the young lawyer's past anything that could be used against him. Witnesses would be sent out of town and provided with money to remain away until the adjournment of the grand jury.

Mr. Folk at once felt the pressure, and it was of a character to startle one. Statesmen, lawyers, merchants, clubmen, churchmen—in fact, men prominent in all walks of life visited him at his office and at his home, and urged that he cease such activity against fellow-townspeople. Political preferment was promised if he would yield; a political grave if he persisted. Threatening letters came, warning him of plots to murder, to disfigure, and to blackguard. Word came from Tennessee that detectives were investigating every act of his life. Mr. Folk told the politicians that he was not seeking political favors, and not looking forward to another office; the others he defied. Meantime he probed the deeper into the municipal sore. With his first successes, and aided by the panic among the boodlers, he soon had them suspicious of one another, exchanging charges of betrayal, and ready to "squeal" or run at the slightest sign of danger. One member of the House of Delegates became so frightened while under the inquisitorial cross-fire that he was seized with a nervous chill, and his false teeth fell to the floor. The rattle so increased his alarm that he rushed from the room without stopping to pick up his teeth, and boarded the next train.

It was not long before Mr. Folk had dug up the intimate history of ten years of corruption, especially of the business of the North and South and the Central Traction franchise grants, the last named being even more iniquitous than the Suburban.

Pitiful? Yes, but typical. Other cities are to-day in the same condition as St. Louis before Mr. Folk was invited in to see its rottenness. Chicago is cleaning itself up just now, so is Minneapolis, and Pittsburgh recently had a bribery scandal; New York is contented with a respectable outside, Boston is at peace, Cincinnati and St. Paul are satisfied, while Philadelphia is happy in the worst government in the world. As for the small towns and the villages, many of these are as busy as bees at the loot.

St. Louis, indeed, in its disgrace, has a great advantage. It was exposed late; it has not been reformed and caught again and again, until its citizens are reconciled to corruption. But, best of all, the man who has turned St. Louis inside up, turned it, as it were, upside down, too. In all cities, the better classes—the business men—are the sources of corruption; but they are so rarely pursued and caught that we do not fully realize whence the trouble comes. And so most cities blame the politicians and the ignorant and vicious poor. Mr. Folk has shown St. Louis that its bankers, brokers, corporation officers, its business men are the sources of evil, so that from the start it will know the municipal problem in its true light. With a tradition for public spirit, it may drop Butler and its runaway bankers, brokers, and brewers, and pushing aside the scruples of the hundreds of men down in blue book, and red book, and church register, who are lying hidden behind the statutes of limitations, the city may restore good government. Otherwise the exposures by Mr. Folk will result only in the perfection of the corrupt system. For the corrupt can learn a lesson when the good citizens cannot. The Tweed regime in New York taught Tammany to organize its boodle business; the police exposure taught it to improve its method of collecting blackmail. And both now are almost perfect and safe. The rascals of St. Louis will learn in like manner; they will concentrate the control of their bribery system, excluding from the profit sharing the great mass of weak rascals, and carrying on the business as a business in the interest of a trustworthy few. District Attorney Jerome cannot catch the Tammany men, and Circuit Attorney Folk will not be able another time to break the St. Louis ring. This is St. Louis's one great chance.

But, for the rest of us, it does not matter about St. Louis any more than it matters about Col. Butler et al. The point is, that what went on in St. Louis is going on in most of our cities, towns, and villages. The problem of municipal government in America has not been solved. The people may be tired of it, but they cannot give it up—not yet.

OCTOBER 1902

HENRY ADAMS

A DESCENDANT OF PRESIDENTS and Boston Brahmins, Henry Adams (1838–1918) received the finest education attainable, attending Harvard and doing post-graduate work in Germany. Nevertheless, the unconventional Adams maintained that the traditional course of learning was inadequate for understanding man's relationship to the world, a stance that would shape his most significant writings.

Adams eschewed politics—to which so many of his family had gravitated—and turned to writing and teaching as a career. Early in his professional life, he worked as a correspondent for several newspapers, including the *Boston Daily Advertiser,* the *Boston Courier*, and the *New York Times*. In 1870, Adams accepted a position teaching history at Harvard and simultaneously assumed the editorship of the *North American Review*.

Adams's life was forever changed by the suicide of his wife, Marian, in 1885, after which he began to travel extensively. From his travels, Adams gathered material for the first volume expounding his theory of history, *Mont-Saint-Michel and Chartres* (1904), which contrasted the human in perfect harmony with nature—as represented by the symbol of the Virgin in the thirteenth century—with the human at odds with nature—symbolized by the dynamo he first viewed at the Paris Exposition in 1900.

The Education of Henry Adams (1907), excerpted here, is considered the companion volume to *Mont-Saint-Michel and Chartres*. Not a conventional autobiography, the work is an elaboration of Adams's theory of the acceleration of historical force, wherein he uses himself as "a manikin [sic] on which the toilet of education is to be draped." Henry Adams acquired part of his "education" at the 1904 World's Fair, which he viewed with his customary esoteric mode of criticism.

FROM *THE EDUCATION OF HENRY ADAMS*

St. Gaudens came on to model his head, and Sargent painted his portrait, two steps essential to immortality which he bore with a certain degree of resignation, but he grumbled when the President made him go to St. Louis to address some gathering at the Exposition; and Mrs. Hay bade Adams go with them, for whatever use he could suppose himself to serve. He professed the religion of World's Fairs, without which he held education to be a blind impossibility; and obeyed Mrs. Hay's bidding the more readily because it united his two educations in one; but theory and practice were put to equally severe test at St. Louis. Ten years had passed since he last crossed the Mississippi, and he found everything new. In this great region from Pittsburgh through Ohio and Indiana, agriculture had made way for steam; tall chimneys reeked smoke on every horizon, and dirty suburbs filled with scrap-iron, scrap-paper and cinders, formed the setting of every town. Evidently, cleanliness was not to be the birthmark of the new American, but this matter of discards concerned the measure of force little, while the chimneys and cinders concerned it so much that Adams thought the Secretary of State should have rushed to the platform at every station to ask who were the people; for the American of the prime seemed to be extinct with the Shawnee and the buffalo.

The subject grew quickly delicate. History told little about these millions of Germans and Slavs, or whatever their race-names, who had overflowed these regions as though the Rhine and the Danube had turned their floods into the Ohio. John Hay was as strange to the Mississippi River as though he had not been bred on its shores, and the city of St. Louis had turned its back on the noblest work of nature, leaving it bankrupt between its own banks. The new American showed his parentage proudly; he was the child of steam and the brother of the dynamo, and already, within less than thirty years, this mass of mixed humanities, brought together by steam, was squeezed and welded into approach to shape; a product of so much mechanical power, and bearing no distinctive marks but that of its pressure. The new American, like the new European, was the servant of the powerhouse, as the European of the twelfth century was the servant of the Church, and the features would follow the parentage.

The St. Louis Exposition was its first creation in the twentieth century, and, for that reason, acutely interesting. One saw here a third-rate town of half-a-million people without history, education, unity, or art, and with little capital—without even an element of natural interest except the river which it studiously ignored—but doing what London, Paris, or New York would have shrunk from attempting. This new social conglomerate, with no tie but its steam-power and not much of that, threw away thirty or forty million dollars on a pageant as ephemeral as a stage flat. The world had never witnessed so marvellous a phantasm; by night Arabia's crimson sands had never returned a glow half so astonishing, as one wandered among long lines of white palaces, exquisitely lighted by thousands on thousands of electric candles, soft, rich, shadowy, palpable in their sensuous depths; all in deep silence, profound solitude, listening for a voice or a foot-fall or the plash of an oar, as though the Emir Mirza were displaying the beauties of this City of Brass, which could show nothing half so beautiful as this illumination, with its vast, white, monumental solitude, bathed in the pure light of setting suns. One enjoyed it with iniquitous rapture, not because of exhibits but rather because of their want. Here was a paradox like the stellar universe that fitted one's mental faults. Had there been no exhibits at all, and no visitors, one would have enjoyed it only the more.

Here education found new forage. That the power was wasted, the art indifferent, the economic failure complete, added just so much to the interest. The chaos of education approached a dream. One asked oneself whether this extravagance reflected the past or imaged the future; whether it was a creation of the old American or a promise of the new one. No prophet could be believed, but a pilgrim of power, without constituency to flatter, might allow himself to hope. The prospect from the Exposition was pleasant; one seemed to see almost an adequate motive for power; almost a scheme for progress. In another half-century, the people of the central valleys should have hundreds of millions to throw away more easily than in 1900 they could throw away tens; and by that time they might know what they wanted. Possibly they might even have learned how to reach it.

This was an optimist's hope, shared by few except pilgrims of World's Fairs, and frankly dropped by the multitude, for, east of the Mississippi, the St. Louis Exposition met a deliberate conspiracy of silence, discouraging, beyond measure, to an optimistic dream of future strength in American expression. The party got back to Washington on May 24, and before sailing for Europe, Adams went over, one warm evening, to bid good-bye on the garden-porch of the White House. He found himself the first person who urged Mrs. Roosevelt to visit the Exposition for its beauty, and, as far as he ever knew, the last.

He left St. Louis May 22, 1904, and on Sunday, June 5, found himself again in the town of Coutances, where the people of Normandy had built, towards the year 1250, an Exposition which architects still admired and tourists visited, for it was thought singularly expressive of force as well as of grace in the Virgin. On this Sunday, the Norman world was celebrating a pretty church-feast—the Fête Dieu—and the streets were filled with altars to the Virgin, covered with flowers and foliage; the pavements strewn with paths of leaves and the spring handiwork of nature; the cathedral densely thronged at mass. The scene was graceful. The Virgin did not shut her costly Exposition on Sunday, or any other day, even to American senators who had shut the St. Louis Exposition to her—or for her; and a historical tramp would gladly have offered a candle, or even a candle-stick in her honor, if she would have taught him her relation with the deity of the Senators. The power of the Virgin had been plainly One, embracing all human activity; while the power of the Senate, or its deity, seemed—might one say—to be more or less ashamed of man and his work. The matter had no great interest as far as it concerned the somewhat obscure mental processes of Senators who could probably have given no clearer idea than priests of the deity they supposed themselves to honor—if that was indeed their purpose; but it interested a student of force, curious to measure its manifestations. Apparently the Virgin—or her Son—had no longer the force to build expositions that one cared to visit, but had the force to close them. The force was still real, serious, and, at St. Louis, had been anxiously measured in actual money-value.

That it was actual and serious in France as in the Senate Chamber at Washington, proved itself at once by forcing Adams to buy an automobile, which was a supreme demonstration because this was the form of force which Adams most abominated. He had set aside the summer for study of the Virgin, not as a sentiment but as a motive power, which had left monuments widely scattered and not easily reached. The automobile alone could unite them in any reasonable sequence, and although the force of the automobile, for the purposes of a commercial traveller, seemed to have no relation whatever to the force that inspired a Gothic cathedral, the Virgin in the twelfth century would have guided and controlled both bag-man and architect, as she controlled the seeker of history. In his mind the problem offered itself as to Newton; it was a matter of mutual attraction, and he knew it, in his own case, to be a formula as precise as $S = \frac{gt^2}{2}$, if he could but experimentally prove it. Of the attraction he needed no proof on his own account; the costs of his automobile were more than sufficient: but as teacher he needed to speak for others than himself. For him, the Virgin was an adorable mistress, who led the automobile and its owner where she would, to her wonderful palaces and chateaux, from Chartres to Rouen, and thence to Amiens and Laon, and a score of others, kindly receiving, amusing, charming and dazzling her lover, as though she were Aphrodite herself, worth all else that man ever dreamed. He never doubted her force, since he felt it to the last fibre of his being, and could no more dispute its mastery than he could dispute the force of gravitation of which he knew nothing but the formula. He was only too glad to yield himself entirely, not to her charm or to any sentimentality of religion, but to her mental and physical energy of creation which had built up these World's Fairs of thirteenth-century force that turned Chicago and St. Louis pale.

MARIETTA HOLLEY

BORN IN UPSTATE NEW YORK, Marietta Holley (1836–1926) began her literary career early, first writing poetry under the pen name "Jemyma." After writing magazine articles for many years, Holley published a breakthrough piece, written in dialect, in *Peterson's Magazine*. In 1873, her first full-length novel, *My Opinions and Betsy Bobbet's: by Josiah Allen's Wife,* launched Holley's popular fiction series, which became an international phenomenon for four decades. As a humorist, Holley is often compared with Mark Twain for her droll wit and skill with dialect. But the comparison ends there, for, in her prose, Holley slyly championed women's rights and exposed the inequities thrust upon her gender by society. As some of Holley's novel titles reveal, her most popular character, Samantha Smith Allen—alias "Josiah Allen's wife"—infiltrates and comments on some of the most critical events and issues of the late nineteenth and early twentieth centuries: *Samantha at the Centennial* (1877), *Samantha at Saratoga* (1887), *Samantha on the Race Problem* (1892), *Samantha at the World's Fair* (1893), *Samantha in Europe* (1895), *Samantha at the St. Louis Exposition* (1904), and *Josiah Allen on the Women Question* (1914).

In the following passage, from the fifth chapter of *Samantha at the St. Louis Exposition*, Samantha and her dim-witted husband, Josiah, enter the main gates of the 1904 World's Fair and begin to take in the sights. Ever the reliable narrator, Samantha exclaims, "I hain't goin' to describe what I looked down on, for I can't. No, if I had a big book of synonyms to the words Grand and Glorious and used every one of 'em tryin' to describe that seen I couldn't begin to do justice to it. . . ."

FROM *SAMANTHA AT THE ST. LOUIS EXPOSITION*

Josiah wuz for goin' into the show by the entrance nighest to Miss Huff's, but I said, "No, that may do for other times, but when I first enter this Fair ground as a Observer (for in our visit to the Inside Inn we wuz only weary wayfarers, too tired to observe, and the Sabbath we felt wuz no time to jot down impressions). No, this day I felt wuz in reality our *dayboo*, and I sez impressively, "I will not go sneakin' in by any side door or winder, I'm goin' to enter by the main gateway."

Josiah kinder hummed:

> "Broad is the road that leads to death
> And thousands walk together there."

But when he found we could go in there at the same price he didn't parley further, and Billy took us to the car that would leave us where I wanted to be.

The main entrance is in itself a noble sight worth goin' milds and milds to see, a long handsome buildin' curvin' round gracefully some in shape like a mammoth U only bendin' round more at the ends, and endin' with handsome buildin's, and tall pillars decorate the hull length and flags wave out nobly all along on top.

Mebby it wuz meant for a U and meant Union, a name good enough for entrance into anything or anywhere. And if it wuz I approved on't, and would encouraged 'em by tellin' 'em so if they'd asked me beforehand. Union! a name commandin' world-wide respect, writ in blue and gray on millions of hearts, sealed with precious blood.

The centre of the long buildin' peaks up and arches over you in such a lofty and magnificent way that you feel there some as Miss Sheba must have felt when she went to visit Mr. and Miss Solomon or the Misses Solomon, I spoze I ort to say, he had a variety of wives, though it is nothin' I ever approved on, and would told him so if I'd had the chance.

But good land! Mr. Solomon never had any sights to show Miss Sheba approachin' this Fair, I wouldn't been afraid to take my oath on't.

We riz the flight of steps which hundreds and hundreds could rise similtaneously and abreast, paid our three fares and went in. And when you first stand inside of that gate the beauty jest strikes you in your face some like a great flash of lightnin', only meller and happifyin' instead of blindin'.

And the vastness of it as you look on every side on you impresses you so you feel sunthin' as you would if you wuz sot down on the Desert of Sara, and Sara wuz turned into vistas of bewilderin' beauty towards every pint of her compass.

There wuz broad, smooth paths leadin' out on every side all on 'em full of folks from every country in the world, and clad in every costoom you ever see or ever didn't see before. Folks in plain American dress side by side with dark complected folks wropped up seemin'ly in white sheets, jest their black-bearded faces and flashin' eyes gleamin' at you from the drapery. Then there would be mebby a pretty young girl with a rose-bud face under a lace parasol. Two sweet-faced nuns in sombry black with their pure white night caps on under their clost black bunnets and veils, and follerin' them some fierce lookin' creeters in red baggy trousers embroidered jackets and skull caps with long tossels on 'em; Persians mebby, or Arabs.

As Josiah looked at these last I hearn him murmur as if to himself, "Why under the sun didn't Samantha put in my dressin' gown with tossels, and the smokin' cap Thomas J. gin me, I could showed off some then."

But I pretended not to hear him for my eyes wuz fastened on the passin' pageant. Smart lookin' bizness men with handsome well-dressed wives and children, then a Injun with striped blanket, beaded moccasins and head-dress of high feathers. Then a American widder, mebby a plain one, and mebby grass; then some more wimmen. Then some Chinamen with long dresses and pig-tails follered by some gawky, awkwud country folks; some more smart-lookin' Americans. Some English tourists with field-glasses strapped over one shoulder. Some Fillipinos in yellerish costoom. Then a kodak fiend ready to aim at anything or nothin' and hit it; then some Scotchmen in Tarten dress and follerin' clost some Japans, lots and lots of them scattered along. Then some brown children and their mothers, the children dressed mostly in a sash and some beads, and some more pretty white children dressed elaborate, and some niggers, and some soldiers, and some more wimmen, and more folks, and some more, and some more, in a stiddy and endless stream.

Good land! I couldn't sort out and describe them that passed by in an hour even, no more than I could sort out and describe the slate stuns in Jonesville creek, and you well know that wagon loads could be took out of one little spot.

Josiah said to me, "Why jest to look at this crowd, Samantha, pays anybody for comin' here clear from the Antipathies."

Sez I, "Josiah, you mean the Antipodes."

"I mean what I say!" he snapped out, "and les's be movin' on, no use standin' here all day."

He don't love to be corrected. But truly that immense and strangely assorted crowd constantly comin', constantly goin' and changin' all the time wuz a sight well worth comin' from Jonesville to see, even if we didn't see a thing more. But, oh, what didn't we see! what a glorious sight as our eyes left the crowd and looked 'round us. Why the wonder and beauty on't fairly struck you in the face some like a flash of lightnin' only more meller and happifyin'."

There you are in the beautiful Court of St. Louis. And right in the centre sets Saint Louis himself on a prancin' horse, holdin' up a cross, I wuz glad to see that cross held up as if in benediction over all the immense crowd below, it seemed as if it begun the Fair right, jest as it begins the week right to go to meetin' Sunday.

I always sot store by Saint Louis. Leadin' them Crusades of hisen to protect Christians and free the Holy Land from lawless invaders. How much I thought on him for it. Though I could advised him for his good in lots of things if I'd been 'round.

Now his marryin' a girl twelve years old who ort to been in pantalettes and high aprons, I should tried to break it up, I should told him plain and square that I wouldn't have heard for a minute to his marryin' our Tirzah Ann at that age. She shouldn't married him if he'd been King Louis twenty or thirty instead of nine. But I wuzn't there and he went on and had his way, as men will.

But he acted noble in lots of things, made a wise ruler and a generous one, lived and died like a hero. And I was glad to see him riz up in such a sightly place, holdin' up the cross he wuz willin' to give his life for.

He looked first rate, he wore a sort of a helmet and had a cloak on, shaped some like my long circle cape, only it didn't set so good, and I wuz sorry they didn't have my pattern to cut it by. Hisen kinder curled up at the back, they ort to cut it ketterin'. Two noble statutes stood on each side on him, kinder guardin' him as it were, though he didn't need it as long as he clung to the cross. Scattered all along by the side of the broad paths wuz little green oasises, on which the splendor-tired and people-tired eyes could rest and recooperate a little.

In front of you quite a little ways off on each side stood immense snow-white palaces each one on 'em seemin' more beautiful than the last one you looked at, full of sculptured beauty and with long, long rows of pearl white collumns and ornaments of all kinds. Beyond, but still as it were in the foreground, as it ort to, high up on a lofty pedestal stood the statute of Peace.

My pardner, who for reasons named, wuz inclined to pick flaws in this glorious Exposition, sez to me:

"What's the use of sculpin' Peace up on so high a monument and showin' her off as if she wuz safe and sound, and then histin' cannons up right by her throwin' balls that will travel twenty miles and then knock her sky high."

I sithed, but almost onbeknown to myself looked at the Cross, and hoped that that divine liglit would go ahead through the wilderness of world warfare makin' a safe path, so Peace could git down from her high monument bime-by and walk round some through the world without gittin' her head blowed off.

Smilin' and gleamin' jest beyond wuz the bright sunny waters on which little boats painted in bright colors with gay awnin's wuz glidin' about here and there, and bursts of melodious song come from the gayly attired boatmen anon or oftener. And furder on wuz the Grand Basin, a large beautiful piece of water, and back on't down a green hill seventy feet high leaps and bounds and gurgles and sings three glitterin' cascades, each one seemin' to start out from a splendid buildin' up on the hill.

The ones on the side smaller, but the middle one a grand and stately palace called Festival Hall, and jinin' these three buildin's together are what they call the Collonnade of States. A impressive row of snow-white pillows, and on them pillows, settin' up in the place of honor, are big statutes of female wimmen, fourteen in number, symbolic of the original States of the Louisiana Purchase.

I wanted to go right up to Festival Hall the first minute, it didn't seem fur it wuz through such seens of bewilderin' beauty, but a bystander standin' by said it wuz half a mild.

But Josiah kinder nudged me and said, "Mebby we'd better take the Immoral Railway. With you by my side, Samantha, I feel I can face its dangers."

Sez I, "Where has your principle gone that you had this mornin', Josiah?"

"I have got it, Samantha, jest the same; I hain't used none this time o' day.

But I thought I would kinder love to tell the brethren I'd rid on it." And before I could parley with him he asked that same bystander, a good lookin' iron gray man,

"Where is the Immoral Railway?"

"The Intre Moral Railway starts there," sez he, pintin' to a place quite nigh to us.

"Intre Moral," sez I to myself; "that is a good name." And as we wended our way to it through the crowds of folks of every name and nation I sez to myself, "I'd love to ride on it." For havin' naterally so scientific and deep a mind I love to trace back words like little rivulets, to their source, and see where they spring from. For meandering through the ages they gather lots of foreign stuff and take queer turns.

Intre Moral, I took it that that meant extra moral. I liked the sound on't, and we got on and rode quite a spell, and see everything we could, and when we went clear 'round on that, we got onto a big ortomobile and rid 'round on that so's we could see the hull Fair as it were in one picture, before we examined its glories more minutely one by one.

And I should have took sights of comfort viewin' the magnificent seens spread out and growin' and changin' every minute if I hadn't had to kep' one eye onto Josiah Allen all the time, or as you may say two eyes, one my own gray orb and the other the eye of my specs. The seen wuz so hugely grand, so magnificently stupendous, and the mind that it wuz my duty as first chaperone to guard wuz so small I sez to myself, could it be bombarded by that immense grandeur and not utterly collapse. But Blandina wuz on the other side on him, so I didn't feel as I should had the responsibility devolved on me alone.

But he bore it well. He looked off on the seen grander than anything Fairy Land ever dremp on or ever will, I believe. And then he looked pensively at my silk bag where I'd stored all the cookies and nut-cakes it would hold, to keep up his strength between meals.

And so gradually I dropped my agonizing anxiety and let my eyes drink in the onequalled beauty of the seen as we went by the tall glorious palaces towerin' up in white magnificence. Past sparklin' water spaces filled with gay pleasure craft full of happy white-robed voyagers. Past the spans of arched bridges leadin' from one seen of glory to another, past tall white shafts carryin' up to the listenin' Heavens deeds of glory and valor.

Past white statutes more beautiful than poet's dreams, risin' up from green velvet lawns or marble terraces. Broad highways would dawn on our vision, anon vistas of incomparable beauty way off, way off as fur as we could see would open up other views jest as fair. Anon the columned walls of some nearby palace would seem to close in the view, and then agin the fur vision, and anon the blue waters flowin' on and on. And scattered all over the ground roamed the happy people, men, wimmen and children of every name and nation, clothed in every garb that folks ever wore under the sun, and some, it seemed to me, made up jest for that occasion, as Eve started her new fashion of fall dress, only this wuzn't made of leaves, no indeed! fur from it.

But I believe the foreign costoom we see most of all wuz the Japan. And all through the Fair that nation seemed to show off in the very first rank. Well, I wuz willin', I always kinder liked 'em, they're so polite and courteous to everybody, and as for makin' storks and folks settin' on nothin, and lookin' perfectly comfortable settin' on it, they go fur ahead of anybody else, and they have lots of other noble qualities. In cleanin' house time, now I have fairly begreched the ease and comfort of them Japanese housewives who jest take up their mat and sweep out, move their paper walls a little mebby and there it is done.

No heavy, dirt-laden carpets to clean, no papered walls and ceilings to break their back over, no trumpery brickaty brack to take care of and dust and make life a burden. Kind hearted, reverent to equals and superiors—trained to kindness and courtesy and reverence in childhood when American mothers are ruled and badgered by short skirted and roundabout clad tyrants.

I set store by the Japans and am glad to hear how fast they're pressin' forwards in every path civilization has opened; science, art and the best education. And wuz glad to see so many of 'em here. They could give Uncle Sam a good many lessons if he wuz willin' to take 'em. But good as he is he is a heady old creeter, and won't be driv into anything and has a powerful good opinion of himself.

But to resoom forwards. After we'd gone the complete 'round of the Intre Moral Railway and ortemobile we got out agin on the Plaza, not fur from where we embarked, and at my request we took a boat. Josiah chose one of the handsomest ones with the front end kinder bowin' up and a bright-colored awnin' over it; they called it a gondola.

The gondolier had bold flashin' black eyes and a gay suit that struck

Josiah's fancy, and I knowed by his looks he wuz meditatin' on what Might Have Been. I felt that he wuz in fancy rowin' a boat up our creek in a red coat and green hat with yeller feathers mebby, carryin' sister Submit Tewksbury or sister Gowdey, sailin' towards his own Exposition of St. Josiah. There wuz a sad pensive look on his liniment that belonged to ruined hopes and blighted emotions.

Blandina whispered to me she thought the gondolier a image of beauty and wondered if he had a companion; she said she believed he would be devoted to a wife if he had one that looked up to him.

I answered her like one talkin' onbeknown to herself, two of my eyes and my spectacles furtively watchin' the liniment of my beloved pardner, and my speritual eyes feastin' on the perfect loveliness of the seen. Broad smooth waters how beautiful they were, dotted with craft similar to ourn and freighted with happy voyagers dartin' here and there, and some of the boats wuz the queerest shapes, one on 'em looked jest exactly like a big white swan, and there wuz one, if you'll believe it, that looked like a sea serpent, I wouldn't have rid in it for a dollar bill, though Josiah said he'd love to tell Deacon Henzy that he'd straddled the old sea serpent and rid to shore on it.

But I sez, "Good land, Josiah, you don't ride on the outside on it, there is a place fixed inside somewhere for passengers."

But most of the boats wuz handsome. Anon the water lay smooth and fair about us, and fur off we could see immense fountains risin' right up out of the glassy surface, sprayin' up and glitterin' down floods of rainbow glory.

Agin we landed on terry firmy I a feelin' as if we wuz roamin' through Fancy's fields, for it seemed as if cold Reality never could have planned anything approachin' what wuz all round us. For as you draw nigh the glittering Cascades you fairly stop bewildered by the beauty, and most want to shet your eyes on it, not knowin' what path to choose where all are so bagonin' full of allurements and the hull world seemin' to be allured there by 'em. On one side the glory of the waters dashing, sparkling, bounding along down, with fountains sprayin' up every little while, and white statutes smilin' down on us nigher by. On the other side green verdure and beyond and on every side the glory of the water, and above us the most magnificent buildin' in the world flanked on each side with the long Colonnade of States.

And speakin' of statutes, jest think of the sculptured groups we passed by that eventful day, more'n I could describe in a month of Sundays. Louis and Clark, the very men I'd read about in Gasses Journal, how I wished their eyes could see and their ears hear me. How interested and proud they would have been to hear me tell how even as a child I loved to hear mother Smith read about their journeyin's into the new and onexplored country, findin' swamps and stumps and savages, where now wuz smilin' gardens and palaces. Then there was Robert Livingstone, and Franklin, noble high souled old creeter, I always loved him in a meetin' house sense, drawin' down lightnin' and so forth—he wuz the very Pa of electricity as you may say.

And James Monroe, and Boone, and Settin' Bull, yes there wuz Settin' Bull settin' or ruther standin' right in that great company. And all on 'em mute and onafraid, onmindful of the presence of a Samantha and Josiah, I felt to pity 'em.

But the noblest meanin' statute of all in my eyes wuz right in front of the main Cascade. There stood a immense statute of Liberty, raisin' the veil of Ignorance and protectin' Truth and Justice. Ignorance don't want her eyes oncovered, she'd 'drather keep on blind as a bat. But Liberty hain't goin' to mind her, she wuz bound to git the bandages off; I wanted to encourage her in it and I waved my hand towards her and smiled in lovin' greetin'. Josiah thought I wuz flirtin', and asked me anxiously if I'd got sight of any man from Jonesville. I wouldn't dain to reply to him—at my age! and with my reputation to carry round! The idee!

Well, when we stood on the stun balcony over the spot where the central cascade gushes out, what a seen lay spread out before us. You can look off two milds one way and most a mild another. And wuz there ever in the world milds so crowded full of beauty and each beauty differin' from the other as one star differs from another in glory. Eight magnificent palaces are in full sight, their walls bathed by the blue waters, and beyond 'em, interspersed by green foliage, wuz a perfect wilderness of towers, minarets, domes, banners, battlements.

I hain't goin' to describe what I looked down on, for I can't. No, if I had a big book of synonyms to the words Grand and Glorious and used every one on 'em tryin' to describe that seen I couldn't begin to do justice to it, and so what is the use of tryin' with the Jonesville vocabulary.

And if I can't describe it, don't for pity sake ask Josiah Allen to, for you might know that if I couldn't he wouldn't stand no chance. But I hearn him gin a sort of gaspin' sithe as he looked, and Blandina I believe forgot for a few minutes her passionate though chaste, overrulin' passion.

As magnificent as the hull of St. Louis Exposition is, it naterally has one spot handsomer than the rest, a particular beauty spot as you may say. Why every house has it. The beauty of my parlor kinder branches out, as you may say, from my new rep rocker, a lovely work of art that cost over six dollars. I keep it in the sightliest place, where the eye of man can fall on it at first. And the central beauty spot of the Fair wuz centered in the place I have been talkin' about.

I'd hearn that it wuz some the shape of a fan and we had talked it over between us, whether it would look like my best paper fan I carry to meetin' Sundays, or my big turkey feather fan. But, good land! they dwindled down so in my mind while I stood there that I might be said to never have sot my eyes on a turkey's feather, or a turkey or anything. It is a spectacle that once seen is never forgot.

The central spot, or handle of the fan (in allegory), is occupied by Festival Hall and on either side stretches out the beautiful Collonnade of States with its lovely and heroic female wimmen settin' up there as if sort o' takin' care of the hull concern. I spoke to Blandina about it, how pleased I wuz to see my sect settin' up so high in the place of honor, and she sez:

"Oh, Aunt Samantha, I cannot rejoice with you, it rasps my very soul to see men slighted! What would the world do without men?"

"Well," sez I, wantin' to please her, "men do come handy lots of times. But," sez I reasonably, "the world wouldn't last long if it wuzn't for wimmen." But to resoom.

At each end of the Collonnade, peakin' up a little higher, is a sort of a round shaped buildin', beautiful in structure, where food can be obtained. And knowin' the effect on men of good food I knowed this wuz a sensible idea, for no matter how festivious a man may be, and probably is in Festival Hall, yet his appetite stretches out on both sides on him jest as it wuz depicted here. And female wimmen stand between him and starvation most of the time. I considered the hull thing highly symbolical and loved to see it.

But jest think of a magnificent picture containin' all that is most beautiful in land and water, extendin' in a graceful, curvin' way three thousand feet. Why that's as fur as from our house over the Ebenezer Bobbettses, and I d'no but furder, and every foot and inch of it perfectly beautiful. How much land do you spoze is took up by this central spot of beauty? Now if I should ask sister Sylvester Gowdey, who always thinks she knows everything worth knowin', if I should say, "How much land do you spoze, sister Gowdey, is took up by jest this central beauty spot of the Fair?" I'll bet she'd say, "Mebby half an acre."

But I'd say, "Melissy, it occupies six hundred acres."

I d'no as sister Gowdey would believe me, but it's so, the livin' truth. Why, the three Cascades are three hundred feet long. Beautiful in the daytime as a dream of Paradise! fancy it in the evening when thousands and thousands of colored lights lend their glowin' charm to the seen. Why you almost cover your eyes from the bewilderin' glory on't. And as I said to Josiah, "We shall never see another seen so beautiful till we see Jerusalem the Golden descend before our rapt vision." And he bein' kinder fraxious, sez:

"I hain't seen that yet, nor you nuther."

"By the eye of Faith I have, Josiah."

"Well, tain't no time or place for preachin', we better be gittin' along!"

Right under the main Cascade we went down into a beautiful grotto all lighted up, with one hull side of the room made of fallin' water. I never expected to step into such a place. I have felt perfectly satisfied when I've papered over my dining-room with paper a shillin' a roll, and it did look well. But what wuz it to this? Refreshments are served down there clost to the sparklin' liquid side of the room, and Josiah wantin' to go the hull figure, set down and eat a nut-cake which I gin him.

They say stimulants can be obtained down here. And mebby they can, them that seek can generally find, there wuz a serpent in Paradise; but *I* didn't see any, I spoze the noble look on my face would dant any dealer in such pizen from displayin' it to me. And it ain't likely that Josiah with two chaperones would set eyes on any.

EDWARD GARNER LEWIS

BORN IN CONNECTICUT and hailing from a long line of Episcopalian clergymen on his paternal side, E. G. Lewis (1869-1950) received private schooling, including a stint at a military academy and Trinity College in Hartford, his father's alma mater. While Lewis was a poor student in college, he distinguished himself on campus as a charming, glib salesman—qualities he would capitalize on later in his checkered business career. Lewis embarked on his first sales venture—selling a bogus anti-smoking aid—after dropping out of college, and he later hawked a variety of products, most notoriously a pesticide called "Anti-Skeet," which claimed to repel mosquitoes. Lewis sold "Anti-Skeet" in Tennessee until the authorities began to investigate complaints about its ineffectiveness. According to NiNi Harris, author of *Legacy of Lions* (1981), "The product's greatest value lay in its imaginative name."

In 1894, Lewis and his wife, Mabel, came to St. Louis with a large supply of "Anti-Skeet" in tow, which Lewis claimed to have sold in several weeks, making more than forty thousand dollars. Lewis used the earnings to launch a variety of pyramid-scheme enterprises before embarking on magazine publishing—the venture that would become his legacy and the source of his notoriety in St. Louis. At the height of its circulation, Lewis's *The Woman's Magazine* claimed more than a million subscribers. Although it was modeled on *The Ladies' Home Journal*, Lewis's magazine was essentially a mail-order catalogue that also offered domestic advice and homemaking tips. Lewis used his editorial page to promote his new enterprises—primarily real estate ventures and subscription sales—and to playfully chide his growing band of detractors. As much a visionary and entrepreneur as he was an opportunist and schemer, Lewis began to promote the 1904 World's Fair a year before it opened, championing the splendor of his real estate along Delmar and his plan for temporary accommodations—a tent city—for fairgoers, which he named "Camp Lewis." From the magazine's profits, Lewis purchased a large tract of land north of Delmar outside the city limits. There, in 1902, he built the octagonal "Magazine Building." With huge stone lions guarding its entrance, the building is still a familiar St. Louis landmark and serves as University City's city hall. Simultaneously, Lewis laid out a small university, as well as "University Heights One," a subdivision of diverse architectural styles, adjacent to the building that housed his magazine operations. In 1906, Lewis was elected mayor of his utopian city—a place in which parks, cultural institutions, and Ivy League–named streets all testified to Lewis's social and cultural aspirations.

In 1908, at the height of the progressive reform movement, Lewis's empire began to unravel when he was brought to trial for mail fraud. Although Lewis was acquitted three times, the damage was done. By 1912, his holdings were in receivership and his belongings were auctioned. Lewis left St. Louis for California and founded Atascadero, another community built on his patented dreams and schemes. There, the law finally caught up with him, and in 1928, Lewis began serving a six-year sentence for mail fraud.

In Lewis's defense, his boundless belief in the possibilities of human ingenuity and determination is kindred to that of the city boosters who—against all odds—willed the 1904 World's Fair into being. And while the fair was but an ephemeral moment in the city's history, Lewis's lions still majestically survey the community he planned and built, which remains one of the region's cultural centers and most desirable residential areas. Of Lewis, fellow publisher William M. Reedy wrote in 1906, "In each new undertaking he departed from the beaten track and introduced new features which made his efforts unique in their way, and which invariably brought success."

In the following editorial from the June 1904 issue of *The Woman's Magazine*, Lewis describes his publishing operation in the new Magazine Building and his plans for starting a bank based, as all his endeavors were, on the creative use of the United States Postal Service.

TEN MILLION WOMEN

The great publishing house owned by The Woman's Magazine was built for cash without mortgage or loan, and about it are eighty-five acres of the finest residence property in St. Louis, which we have laid out into a beautiful private residence park, where the officers of the Company are building their own homes and where, in one part, many beautiful little homes will be built by the Company for its employees, to be paid for in small monthly payments, and where a great encampment has been laid out for our readers during the Fair. Two hundred of our readers have already earned free trips to the Fair at our expense, and three hundred poor, patient self-sacrificing little girls will be brought here for a week each at the Fair at our expense, they to be selected by our readers as the "sweetest girls" in their towns.

Taking the Delmar Garden car, the visitor reaches the entrance grounds of the great octagonal building which stands on a high hill overlooking the World's Fair, and which is now a landmark from all parts of the West End. Beautiful walks lead up to a grand entrance, on each side of which stand enormous carved stone lions ten feet in height. The office building proper is octagonal in shape, built of cut stone, terra cotta, brick and steel, 85 feet in diameter by 135 feet in height, and crowned by an immense dome of copper, about which are perched sixteen carved Cupids, each ten feet high and weighing two and one-half tons. The ground floor is open like the interior of a great bank, and, in fact, was designed for a great bank, which is to do business through the mails exclusively with the 2,000,000 families who each month read the magazine; but more of that later. The floor is in mosaics, and about the grand central staircase the bank fixtures, of marble, hard woods and bronze, are grouped. In the center of this floor rises what is probably the most beautiful stair in America, built of white Italian marble and bronze at a cost of $17,000.

On the second floor a balcony surrounds the central stair well, upheld by eight great marble pillars. This balcony is faced to the ceiling with beautiful marbles, while on the ceiling itself are superb mural paintings by one of the foremost artists of America. About this balcony are the editorial and executive offices, finished in hard woods and beautifully decorated. At the head of the stair is the president's office, probably the most beautifully furnished office in the city.

Leaving the editorial floor, one passes up to the third floor, on which are located the composing room, artists' studio, filing-rooms where the millions of letters are all kept carefully filed for instant reference; the mailing-room, where the outgoing correspondence is folded, put in its envelopes and stamped (for even this simple process requires the work of twenty girls), and the barber shop. On the fourth floor is located the great subscription room, where 180 young women care for the vast detail of the subscription list, numbering over 2,000,000 subscribers. Here every subscriber's name is carefully kept in card files, and eight young ladies occupy all their time in making the changes in address made necessary each day by the moving about of the 2,000,000 subscribers. If only one family out of a thousand moves each month, this means two thousand changes to be made each month in the subscription files. The light and ventilation in this room are perfect, and every possible comfort and convenience is provided.

On the fifth floor a grand banquet hall, occupying the entire floor, is being finished off with a domed ceiling thirty feet in height. Passing up onto the observation platform at the top of the great dome, all St. Louis lays below, for it is by far the highest building in the city. Directly to the east the finest residence district of the city reaches almost to the corner of the grounds, while to the south Washington University and the World's Fair grounds seem so close one could almost jump off into them. Taking the elevator to the basement, one passes through a short tunnel into a great palm house and conservatory, 100 feet in width, now being filled with the choicest plants; then down a stair to a grand balcony overlooking the largest and most complete press rooms in the world, 275 feet in length by 100 feet in width.

Here visitors can sit and watch the wonderful process of producing 2,000,000 completely printed and bound copies of the two publications owned by the company, which is done in eight days' time each month. On one side is a row of nine great presses, on the other are eight great folding and binding machines; against the wall, at the west, are the massive cutting machines, which trim the edges, and in the middle seven government mail cars stand in line waiting for the 200 tons of magazines that go out to all quarters of the globe each issue. Not a shaft or belt is in sight. Each machine is run by hidden motors, receiving their power from the great noiseless engines at the far end. Throughout both buildings every convenience and comfort for the employees has been provided, even to the piping of drinking water from a spring half a mile away, which flows out in little marble fountains in each room. . . .

Now, I have the largest and probably the most prosperous publishing business in the world. It is more to me than my own life, for to lose it would be worse than death; my heart is in it. For years I have been studying over another thing, and so firmly convinced am I that I am right in it that I am going to stake on it not only my entire personal fortune but that of some of my friends; and, what is more, the confidence my readers have in me, the loss of which means the death of my publishing business. I do not believe in half-way doing things, and I realize that the five dollars or five hundred dollars of thousands of my readers means quite as much to them as my million-dollar business and my beloved magazine does to me. I do not ask you to join me in this thing, and hold out a safe reserve for myself. I am putting into it ALL, and I shall give to it everything there is in my manhood that is strong and good. My great establishment, which thousands of you will visit this year, is clean and beautiful. I spent a hundred thousand dollars in making its interior the most beautiful in the world, so that those who were employed in it and helped to form the thoughts and character of each issue should have only clean and beautiful surroundings, and each of them shares in its earnings.

THE PEOPLE'S POSTAL BANK

Of all forms of human enterprise there is one that is the safest and most profitable, and which in consequence is entirely monopolized by wealthy men, and that is BANKING. A bank stands for all that is responsible and strong. It, too, must exist through CONFIDENCE. Let the depositors of a bank lose confidence, and the bank must quit business. The merchandise of a bank is money. Those who own its stock are secured by its cash capital of equal amount, and so closely is a bank watched by the government and state that it is the SAFEST form of investment—so much so that the stock of a good bank commands a high premium even though it pays but a small rate of dividend. . . .

I believe that a great bank, a bank of the PEOPLE, owned by the people, paying its earnings to them; standing like a rock of Gibraltar between them and the thousands of unscrupulous stock speculators and swindling schemes holding out hopes of sudden riches; a bank with a hundred thousand families owning its stock, which they purchased at par; a bank with a half million small depositors; a bank which no man or clique of men, no matter what their wealth was, could ever gain control of for their own evil ends; a bank which was so free from the control of any body of wealthy speculators, so fearless and so strong that it could send out a timely warning and would stand as counsellor and advisor for the vast number of people who, now having no such general institution, are taken in and defrauded in a thousand schemes; would soon become the most powerful financial organization in the world. Such a bank to answer such a purpose must be equally accessible to the man or woman a thousand miles away as to the one near by; it must transact its business BY MAIL. . . .

I have written a letter and am sending it to each reader of The Woman's Magazine, telling about the proposed bank. I am pledging my all to you in this proposition, and I am going further than that; if you will join me now, with your dollars instead of your dimes, if you will extend to me your help, I will do more than my share. The labor of sending out these two million letters is great, and the expense is enormous; this labor and expense I must advance myself, for under the banking laws of Missouri the capital stock must be paid in cash, and ours will be paid in full in cash to make it non-assessable. I must pay dollar for dollar in cash for my own stock, the same as you do, and if the capital is one million dollars, one million dollars in cash in full must be on hand the day the charter is granted. If it is five million, then that sum must be in cash. There is no "promoters'" stock in this bank, and no man can purchase over $500 of it. I will organize it, I will hedge it about with every safeguard that human mind can devise, I will place the loaning of its funds in the hands of a board of fifteen of the most experienced bankers of the country. Five of the greatest banks in the United States will be the correspondents of this bank. I will give it all that there is in me of ability, and I will be true to your confidence and trust. I have all that any one man is entitled to in the income from my publishing business, and have many opportunities to make money that you can not have, and I shall so place my own large interests in our bank that every dollar of profit that would come to me from it SHALL, INSTEAD, go to those of the other stock-holders whose opportunities and fortunes are not so good, by adding MY share of the profits to the RESERVE OF THE BANK EACH YEAR, thereby strengthening and increasing the value of your stock year by year. I shall try to make our bank the PEOPLE'S bank, and if I can carry with me, when my turn comes to go, the confidence, the love, the respect and the gratitude of a million families whose fortunes, prosperity and happiness have been enlarged and strengthened through our great bank, the PEOPLE'S bank, I will take with me something that will be of more value THEN than all the millions I leave behind. . . .

My letter and booklet explains the plan fully, and although but a small part of the two million letters have gone out at this date (May 14th), yet over twenty thousand subscriptions to the stock have already been received; already the success of the plan is assured, as no other bank in America ever had such a start at its organization as ours already has. If my letter fails to reach you by June 30th, write me AT ONCE, as the task of sending them out is a great one, and thousands of letters asking questions must be answered each week in addition, and yours may have miscarried in the mail. Do your part, and I will do mine.

E. G. LEWIS,
President, The Lewis Pub. Co.
JUNE 1904

THE POTTER'S WHEEL

EVERY OTHER FRIDAY AFTERNOON, from November 1904 until October 1907, a group of young St. Louis women who shared a passion for the literary and visual arts met at each other's homes, combining their talents to produce an exquisite, hand-made magazine called *The Potter's Wheel.* Led by photographer Williamina Parrish, who informally dubbed the group the "Self and Mutual Admiration Society," the Potters believed in developing and supporting their individual and collective talents. In addition to Parrish and her sister Grace, a photographer as well, the group comprised Caroline Risque, an accomplished sculptor who went on to found the art department at John Burroughs School in 1929, and a number of writers, including Celia Harris, Inez Dutro, Vine Colby, Edna Wahlert, Petronelle Sombart, and Sara Teasdale, who became the group's most famous member.

Each issue of the magazine featured original artwork, poetry, fiction, translations (usually by Teasdale), and photography. Williamina Parrish, the magazine's self-appointed editor-in-chief, imposed deadlines on the group, made sequencing decisions, and physically bound the pages together. The overall visual and tactile effect of the magazine is nothing short of breathtaking. Each cover was an original work of art, often depicting mythological or fantastical scenes, in tones resembling stained glass. Each issue—wrought on richly textured paper in muted shades of brown, tan, and gray—included intricate border designs, illuminations, and watercolors. Although the magazine was produced by women who were St. Louisans, it did not contain much writing that reflected upon local subjects. Rather, the *Wheel* tended to celebrate Greek and Celtic myths and legends, as well as the work of the Pre-Raphaelites and Lewis Carroll. After the production of each issue—and there was only *one* copy—the Potters circulated the magazine among themselves, each writing commentary on that issue in a separate notebook. For the most part, the comments were favorable and any negative criticism was mild, in keeping with the Potters' spirit of mutual support and admiration.

The Potter's Wheel attracted the attention of William Marion Reedy, who was so favorably impressed by the magazine that he commissioned an article on it for a 1905 issue of *The Mirror.* In that article, Frances S. Porcher wrote, "It is rare to find a set of girls so nearly equal in their work or so thoroughly in harmony, and in light of what they have accomplished . . . they have almost reached the parting of the ways where they must be more—or less." Porcher's comment was prophetic; in spite of the perfection of their creation—or because of it—two years later, the Potters gathered for the last time at 5607 Cabanne Avenue, the home of the Parrish sisters. The group drew lots for the few precious issues of their magazine. Teasdale's three copies ended up at Yale University, but the Missouri Historical Society was the fortunate recipient of sixteen issues, including twelve supplemental issues of the group's self-criticism.

The following story, "Her America," by Edna Wahlert, appeared in the May 1906 issue of *The Potter's Wheel*. It is an unusual piece for the magazine for a number of reasons. First, the story is set in St. Louis, rare for works in the *Wheel*, and secondly, it deals with decidedly feminist issues. The protagonist, an innocent young Danish woman named Anna, emigrates to St. Louis hoping to find work and a bright future. Instead, she is wooed by—and subsequently marries—a man who turns out to be a drunken brute with unruly children. In spite of her lack of sophistication and the social conventions of the time, Anna finds the strength and self-respect to rescue herself from her unfortunate domestic circumstances.

HER AMERICA
BY EDNA WAHLERT

She was overly developed with high bust and sinewy arms that could pull oxen along straight lines.

"Good-bye, sis," mumbled a bashful and Danish combination of red and white, as he edged up to kiss her.

"Good-bye," she murmured, as he pecked at her lips. "Tell mother I left all right."

"Yes;" and the boy hurried away, glad to get out of the crowd.

Anna gazed about the deck and slowly gravitated towards a comfortable and stout woman who was beaming complacently at nothing in particular.

"You go to America?" this woman asked Anna in bad Danish.

"Yes—Ja."

"And I go too, there. German am I before I my man took. Then I had been American, I now have visited Denmark and my name is Mrs. Schneck. And you?"

"Anna Deng."

"Anna Deng—why do you to America go. Relatives there?"

"No. I am going to work."

Her eyes were very bright; for it is as natural for a Danish peasant girl to turn her long-striding dreams to America, the land of plenty and no work, as it is for a man to swear occasionally. Anna had caught the journey-fever young; but not until she was sixteen, as there was no perspiring Adonis to tie her affections to her native soil, did her family, wearied, cease from arguments and prohibitions and permit her to set sail. She had not a clear idea of America and its promises, but she *felt* that it would be good to live there. During the voyage, which lasted three weeks, she drank in eagerly every word Mrs. Schneck told her of America. The woman was kind to the girl and taught her a bit of bad English.

"You think to stay in New York?" she asked one day. "My—but do not. It is a place awful—most big and full of people that have no place to breathe unless they go the elevateds. But in Saint Louis—ach, every one speaks the German and the houses are big, and the wages so good that you buy everything you want for. Come to America, Ja, and come to Saint Louis. You have money?"

"Yes I have money."

"Come with me. I will get you a place."

The girl smiled brightly. "Yes, I will go to Saint Louis," she said.

Mrs. Schneck found a situation for the girl as housemaid,—a few days after they arrived in Saint Louis. The wages promised her reached Anna's highest expectations, and her work, although a trifle confining, was, compared with the old sixteen hour days on the farm, child's play. By some streak of fortune her mistress, Mrs. Gray, was a kindly woman, and the children liked to climb on Anna's back to be trotted about, while their brunetteness and American cuteness filled the girl with a delight that cattle and stretches of barley fields had never called forth. America *was* good to live in.

Every afternoon she went to the grocery store, and every afternoon she saw a man lurking at the door of a saloon—a bartender, judging by his apron. He leered at her after seeing her pass for a week or so, because she blushed and looked 'green.' She had never cared about a man, and this Irishman assumed all the virtues and likablenesses of her mind's Sir Galahad after he had spoken to her a few times.

It came about queerly—their acquaintance. After she had begun to notice him, she went to the store as often as possible and took the children with her. Invariably they needed shaking, or patting, or a ribbon tied when they came near the saloon; and the man always grinned at those little scenes.

One day he drawled, "fine day, ain't it?"

She startled. "Ja," she said then quickly, and blushed.

"Want to go to the Fair?" he asked with a look that made her say—"Oh—I don't know—" and hurry away.

The next few days she walked on the opposite side of the street. She did not know *why*; she did it instinctively. But about a week later when she passed, he came out of the saloon with his hat and coat on.

"In a hurry?" he asked as he caught up to her—for she had quickened her steps when she saw him walking after her.

"Nej-no," she said.

"Don't want to go to the Fair with me, do you?"

"I—Ja—I—"

"Oh, you do. When did you come over?"

"From Denmark—" she looked at him and blushed.

Then they made arrangements to go to the Fair together.

After that her plebian sense went swimming and during its absence she married him. Her mistress, Mrs. Gray, was glad for the girl, for Anna had been faithful: she deserved a good home and husband. But Anna's only other friend, Mrs. Schneck, was not so satisfied.

"You don' know vot he's got," she said, when Anna told her of the marriage. "You hardly know his name. How do you know he got a place to put you?"

"Oh, he has," answered the girl, quite happy. "He haf a house. I go there in two days when Mrs. Gray's new help comes. *Jeg er leigkeilig*."

Mrs. Schneck continued her grumbling, which did not, however, dampen Anna's spirits; for the girl was in a bubbling state of not-knowing-why happiness. On the evening that he came to take her 'home,' she was indefinably contented. She had not even asked where he lived. What difference did the *where* make? She was going with him.

They stopped before a long row of flats. He entered a lower one, and Anna found herself in a tiny, dirty room, with two dirty youngsters grinning at her from the room beyond.

"Here she is, kids," called the husband. "Now we'll have some one to cook for us."

Anna blushed. "Who—" she began.

"My kids," he said briefly.

She did not ask questions. She was hardly surprised; at least, she accepted the situation unquestioningly. She felt no objection to the children, and she did not dream that they would object to her presence. The man grinned at the torment they, youngster-like, prepared for her in the most remarkable and modern while-you-wait fashion. But Anna gave no thought to discouragement. She put and kept the three rooms in beautifully clean order, mended and sewed, and was satisfied and completely rewarded by an alcoholic kiss from her spouse. She was glad she had come to America. After two months of wedded bliss, the husband informed her that he had been deprived of his work. Nobly did she dry his eyes, and go out washing by the day. He was proud of her. He believed in a theory that the ideal state of life is attained when everyone does ungrumblingly what he can do *best*. So, as Anna was a far better père de famille than himself, he continued jobless.

Had it not been for the excitement that Mrs. Schneck showed at this turn to Anna's conditions, the girl would never have questioned, even in her mind, her fate. One day Mrs. Schneck saw Anna's husband reeling across the street on the arm of a *bon comarade*. She boiled inwardly at the sight of him and his insolent drunkenness, and then, full of indignation, hurried to Mrs. Gray's home, where Anna was 'helping'. Differently from the majority of women who fell in holy frenzies when conscious of sacrifices, Anna was happy in an unconscious state of martyrdom. She did not mind work. The boys were in school the greater part of the day, thus giving her but little trouble. She had ample time to attend to her home duties, for her husband helped with the meals;—indeed, he often prepared them himself. he was either in a good humor, or asleep when she saw him. Of what should she complain?

Mrs. Schneck did not share this point of view, for, as her own husband had ceased his living existence some fifteen years prior to her acquaintance with Anna, the good woman had rose-colored views of matrimony. *Her* husband had handled her with gloved hands. *Her* husband had given her all his wages to use as she saw fit. *Her* husband had been a steady worker and had died leaving her a house by which by taking roomers, she could easily support himself. While this poor child—

Anna was scrubbing the back porch of the Gray homestead when Mrs. Schneck entered the yard.

"I haf seen your man," announced that woman with arms akimbo.

"Ja?" quoth Anna.

"Yess, Ja. And he vas as drunk as a man can get. He could stand up no more. The uder man was pullink him!"

Anna's face clouded.

"That is no godt for him," she sighed.

"Gut vor *him*. It's sehr gut vor you, ain't it? Awful gut vor you to scrub and vork yourself to skin and rags."

"Me? Ach—I am strong."

"You don' need to tell me dot. But you von't be so for efer, und he von't work no more ven you humor him a few years longer. Und ven die children come—ver will you be?—in a hole."

Anna carefully rinsed out her scrub cloth and threw the water down the sewer.

"He is godt to me," she said, simply.

Then she began to talk Danish words so quickly that Mrs. Schneck could not follow.

So the good woman, having cooled considerably after audibly expressing her feelings, waved her arm. "Vell den, all right," she said. "Are you coming home now? Ve vill valk together."

For some months, matters continued as they had begun. Anna worked and slept; then worked again uncomplainably. One of the favorite adjectives applied to the girl by her step-sons was 'dutchy,' and the word made the girl rankle, while at the same time it made her wake up as to the condition of her personal appearance. She would probably have paid no attention to the word had not her husband always leered at her in a bleary fashion when the boys said it. Her successor at Mrs. Gray's, where she worked two days each week, initiated her into the mysteries of the curling iron. But she wanted a new dress, one that would fit like American clothes; and at this request her husband first grinned, then scoffed, and at length swored. So Anna was silent about the dress for a time.

Mrs. Schneck felt swamped in sorrow at Anna's misfortunes. Almost every evening she called for the girl at the different places where she worked, and walked to the flat with her. Anna would not always permit the woman to speak of family affairs, and Mrs. Schneck did not always feel inclined to do so. Nevertheless although the ungrateful husband question was rarely openly discussed, a mist of meaning enveloped the conversation of the two women when together.

"Anna," said Mrs. Schneck one evening, "I am going to haf a party on Sunday. Vill you and your man come?"

"No," said the girl slowly. "I haf no dress."

Then Mrs. Schneck boiled; and reproaches and denunciations were fired at Anna's ungrateful husband, while the girl herself was condemned as a fool who "would be sorry, yah, someday." Anna did not reply to the outburst; but she felt restless. She entered her home quietly. The man's bulky form, stretched full length across the bed, was the first sight that greeted her eyes, and she was glad that Mrs. Schneck had not come in with her as the good woman often did, for she would have re-opened fire at once—had she seen him.

He was red and made noises as he breathed. Anna began to prepare the evening meal, a discontented, discouraged something clouding her heart.

Soon the boys came in. Anna bade them wash their hands. They fooled around and made faces at her until she shook the smaller one, who began to howl—naturally—and the man awoke, heavy, dull. He swore at the boys and he swore at Anna. During the evening the boys quarreled and threw water at one another. The father cuffed one, and swore at Anna because she, unintentionally, stood between him and the other youngster who thus escaped his blows. Not his words, but his tone, hurt.

Quickly, without one formulated thought, Anna put on her shawl, left the flat and went to Mrs. Schneck's.

"You haf left him?" asked that woman, excited but right well pleased.

"Yes-s."

"Vot vill you do?"

"Vork."

"Und mit the money, vill you go back to Denmark? Or vill you stay with me? You are two gut vor him. Vill you go back to Denmark?"

The girl was silent. A queer, half purrilled-look came into her eyes.

"Denmark—" she repeated slowly. "Back to Denmark?" Then she laughed outright—softly. "Good night," she said, rubbing her shawl lovingly over her cheek, "good-night—I guess I'll go back—home."

ROLLA WELLS

THE NAME OF WELLS had long been associated with progress and change in St. Louis. Erastus Wells, father of Rolla Wells (1856–1944), came to St. Louis in 1843 and started the first streetcar line west of the Mississippi. With his business acumen, the elder Wells commanded the respect not only of the city's civic leaders, but also of the general public, and he served long terms both on the City Council and in the U.S. Congress. Educated at Washington University and Princeton, Rolla Wells started his business career at age twenty-two, when he became manager of the Missouri Railroad Company, one of his father's properties. Like his father, Rolla quickly developed a reputation for having a keen business sense and expanded the family fortune by investing in ranching, gold mining, and most significantly, steel. By 1893, Wells was president of the American Steel Foundry Company, and although he continued to lead its affairs, Wells was, by then, an incredibly wealthy young man who began to turn his attention to local politics.

In 1901, Wells was elected mayor of St. Louis and served two consecutive terms. Having run on the platform "New St. Louis," Wells was committed to rectifying some of the city's largest infrastructure problems, such as water purification, cleaner air, and the need for more public parks and playgrounds. The 1904 Louisiana Purchase Exposition, held during Wells's first term, only put added pressure on his administration to improve the appearance of the city. Although Wells held office at a time when political corruption in St. Louis was attracting national attention, and many of his acquaintances fell under scrutiny, he managed to maintain a relatively pure reputation.

After his tenure as mayor, Wells continued to lead a life of civic service, holding offices in the Federal Reserve Bank, the Businessmen's League, the Democratic National Committee, and the United Railways Company. In 1933, Wells published his memoirs, *Episodes of My Life*, in which he reflects on the half-century of public service he gave St. Louis. In the following excerpt from that volume, Wells describes the 1906 dedication of the statue of St. Louis that still adorns the crest of Art Hill near the entrance to the St. Louis Art Museum.

FROM *EPISODES OF MY LIFE*

THE STATUE OF ST. LOUIS

By proclamation, a half-holiday was declared for the fourth of October, 1906, the occasion being the unveiling of the equestrian statue of Saint Louis, a majestic figure in bronze, on the crest of Art Hill, placed immediately in front of the Art Museum and overlooking what had been the main picture of the World's Fair.

The work was designed by Charles Henry Niehaus. The statue itself is twenty-one feet in height from the base of the bronze plinth to the unlifted hilt of the sword. The sword in the hand of the Crusader is transposed, denoting Peace, the symbol of the Louisiana Purchase Exposition for happiness, prosperity and advancement in the tranquility of peace. The base is nineteen feet, six inches in height. From the ground to the hilt-end of the sword is forty and a half feet.

A grand demonstration was held, and it was said that 200,000, or more, persons were assembled at the ceremony. There was a parade of more than 7,000 men, which was almost two hours in passing the reviewing stand on Art Hill. It was made up of representatives of the post office department, the police department, the fire department and civic organizations, accompanied by brass bands.

Colonel E. J. Spencer was in command, and at the conclusion of the parade it was my privilege to extend to him my congratulations.

The procession was headed by a platoon of seventy-five mounted policemen, followed by six hundred officers on foot. The police division was led by Chief Creecy, who appeared for the first time as commander of the department in a dress parade.

The post office department, led by Postmaster Frank Wyman, contributed 1,500 men. Six hundred mail carriers appeared in the regulation uniforms, while 700 clerks of the various offices were neatly attired in black trousers and soft white shirts.

Mr. William H. Lee was chairman of the ceremonies and Mr. David R. Francis, for the Exposition Company, made the presentation address, a part of which I quote as follows:

"The St. Louis World's Fair marks a new epoch in the history of the city, state and country in which it was held, and a new era in our relations with other countries.

"This reproduction of the equestrian statue of Saint Louis in the massive proportions that delighted the millions of spectators who viewed it in the Plaza, of, St. Louis has been erected to mark the site where were congregated the representatives of the thought and progress of all ages, and where were assembled in friendly rivalry the choicest products of the brain and brawn of man. It is presented to the City of St. Louis in appreciation of the interest manifested and the support rendered by the municipal government and by all the people. This spot was selected for its location and is eminently fit. Here it is in front of the palace where were exhibited so many invaluable works of art, and the only permanent building of the thirteen stately structures which were erected. It overlooks the scene of the incomparable picture whose beauty entranced millions, and which was at once a poem and a song. This noble monument and this magnificent palace of art should form, it would seem, a fitting climax, and a rounding out of the task which has consumed eight years of time filled with increasing and unselfish labors, and has had the good-will and material support of city, state and nation.

"In conclusion, Mr. Mayor, I deliver to you for the City of St. Louis this magnificent monument. The Exposition company is confident that it will be preserved with patriotic care for ages to come. May it quicken the civic pride of our people, and serve as an incentive to greater undertakings and grander achievements.

"You have been chief magistrate of this city since the organization of the Exposition Company. Throughout its vicissitudes and labors you have always extended to the movement your encouragement and all the official assistance permitted by your unselfish devotion to duty or sanctioned by your high standard of public service. The Exposition management makes its acknowledgements to you, and to all the members of your administration and to the municipal assembly.

"Into the keeping of the municipal government of St. Louis, as the property of the people, I confide this superb statue of our patron saint."

The unveiling party consisted of Jane Howard Wells, Isabel Wyman, Mrs. Rolla Wells and Mrs. David R. Francis, who were seated on a stand adjacent to the statue.

At the close of the address of presentation my daughter, Jane Howard Wells, stepped to the front of the platform and drew the cord which caused the great white canvas cover to fall to the ground, unveiling the statue.

The Star Spangled Banner was played and Battery A fired the first of the twenty-one guns, and with uncovered heads a mighty cheer swept over Art Hill.

It was then my privilege, as Mayor, to accept this magnificent monument, with the following address:

"The vigorous and hearty cheers we have indulged in, resulting from the unveiling of the magnificent statue now exposed to our view, are the echo of the sentiment and opinion of every citizen of the City of St. Louis that the Louisiana Purchase Exposition was conceived in wisdom and consummated in success.

"Almost two years have passed since the closing of the Exposition gates, and it is evidenced on every side within the boundaries of the City of St. Louis that it was not held in vain; that the generosity of the people that made it possible was not misplaced; that the management and organization that brought it to such a successful ending were of the highest order.

"Mr. President, this commemoration statue, which you, representing the stockholders of the Louisiana Purchase Exposition, have just presented to the City of St. Louis, will be a monument of remembrance to generations to come of the able and disinterested part that you and your co-workers have taken in the production of an exposition never before equaled.

"It is my grateful privilege, Mr. President, on behalf and in the name of every inhabitant of the City of St. Louis, to accept this token of your public spirit and civic pride, and well may we all, as long as time permits, look upon the statue of Saint Louis as our most cherished work of art."

Who of us who witnessed this remarkable demonstration and heard the mighty roar of exultation in the greeting of the bronze Saint Louis, could help feeling warm tears in his eyes with laughter in his heart? A symbol of peace had been given to our children!

LEO A. LANDAU

ALTHOUGH IN HIS NOVEL, *The Big Cinch,* Leo Landau (1881–1926) rails against affluent business leaders for abusing their influence over public officials for financial gain, Landau himself was the son of a prosperous St. Louis banker and merchant, Maurice Landau. Several scholars, including Scot McConachie and James Neal Primm, credit maverick publisher William Marion Reedy with coining the term "The Big Cinch," in reference to the clique of St. Louis leading citizens and businessmen who controlled the city's infrastructure and economic existence. Among the most prominent members of the "Cinch" were Mayor Rolla Wells and Louisiana Purchase Exposition President David R. Francis. According to Primm, Wells, like other technically honest Cinch members, was guilty of a distorted perspective that enabled him to see himself "not as a member of a privileged 'nobility,' but as a responsible 'leading citizen' rendering unselfish service," though, in reality, his actions and those of his associates served some elements of the community at the expense of others.

Published in 1910, in the wake of Joseph Folk's crusade to reform the city's government, *The Big Cinch* is set in the city of Louisberg, a thinly disguised representation of St. Louis. The novel's tension springs from the efforts of a noble young reporter, Jack McNair of the *Louisberg News-Herald,* to disclose the bribery of elected officials by agents working for Louisberg's railroad owners. For the most part, the novel's *News-Herald* represents the *St. Louis Post-Dispatch,* whose editor, Joseph Pulitzer, had doggedly used his paper to expose graft and, in Primm's words, "harass the ruling class" since the 1880s.

In the novel's opening chapters, which follow, Landau introduces the book's central tension between the honest and the corrupt, the seduction of the easy bribe, and the deals that are made in the smoke-filled, paneled rooms of the city's power brokers.

FROM *THE BIG CINCH*

A SIGNIFICANT GAME OF CARDS

"Sorry I can't agree with you, gentlemen, but I believe that every city and town in the State is perfectly capable of taking care of itself on that proposition."

"But, Governor, don't you think it is treating us a little roughly to permit such fellows as that House of Delegates in Louisberg to decide on what terms we shall abolish our crossings in the city?"

The attitude of Governor Bolt's visitors indicated plainly that the executive's view of the matter was extremely distasteful.

"Oh, I suppose your lawyers will take good care that you don't get *too* much the worst of it," was the Governor's retort.

"Well, we think that's an unfair bill, Governor, and we're going to fight it."

"Why, that's no surprise to me, I expected as much. But the bill is going to receive all the support that this office can possibly give to it and I feel rather certain that it will become a law."

"We'll see about that. So long, Governor."

The Governor's visitors left abruptly.

Governor Bolt reached forward, took a cigar from a mahogany humidor on his desk and after taking a puff or two of a short, thick weed, suddenly started as though a thought struck him and pressed the button to his right.

"Tell Lou to come here a moment."

A tall, smooth shaven man soon walked hurriedly into the Governor's private office.

"Lou, you know Ellis Hobart, don't you?"

"The Toledo Central's man? Sure."

"And George Fulton?"

"Iowa Northern? Sure."

"Those two were in just now and they are offended at my attitude on the Grade Crossing bill and they have assured me that the bill will be killed. You know what I think of those two fellows, Lou, and I want you to sort of take them in hand and if anything 'raw' turns up put me next, you hear?"

"I savy."

"Humph," and Governor Bolt busied himself with a mass of correspondence on the desk before him.

Upon leaving the Capitol Building, Hobart and Fulton, the two railroad attorneys, walked to the Savoy Hotel where most of the legislators stopped.

Heston, the Capital of the State, is generally pretty quiet.

But not when the Legislature is in session. Then the little city is fairly aglow. Hundreds of lobbyists from all over the State, representing everything from large monopolies to "anti-spitting" societies, crowd the place and fill the hotels and resorts of amusement.

The Savoy Hotel, just across from the Governor's mansion, is headquarters for the members of the Legislature and the lobbyists and the lobby of the hotel was crowded as usual, when Fulton and Hobart entered the place.

During a session of the State Legislature the State senators are always the most sought after. Especially are they sought after by those who are *opposed* to some measure, because the State Senate is a much smaller body than the House of Representatives and fifteen to twenty votes in that body of the General Assembly is enough to defeat any legislation.

The two railroad representatives in edging their way through the lobby were careful not to overlook greeting every State Senator they saw.

Whispered conferences between groups of four and five men in almost every corner of the lobby is the sight which the "stranger to politics" beholds at the Savoy, while the State Legislature is in session.

Arguments for this bill or against that bill, four to five hundred men busily engaged in discussing these things, telephone calls for Mr. So and So and Senator So and So—in short, a bustling, busy mass of shrewdness with always a certain evident air of mystery that is enticing; all these things make it well worth while and an education for any one who can spare the time, to spend a day or two at the Capital when the Legislature is in session.

"Just a minute, Senator."

A well dressed man to whom Hobart addressed the words joined him and the two walked into the busy bar adjoining the lobby. Here again in the crowded bar room, one finds the same confidential groups talking things over.

The Senator who accompanied Hobart to the bar was not from "up state" as his attire easily showed. A tailor-made suit and top coat, an immaculate shirt front, from which gleamed a two carat diamond and the peculiar shaped derby hat were immediately noticeable on the person of Senator Dustin of Louisberg.

"Al, can you get Don to come up to the room in about half an hour?" asked Hobart, when the two had ordered drinks.

"I guess so. I haven't seen him around, but I guess I can find him. What's up?"

"Oh, nothing particular. Just want to have a little talk."

"All right, Ellis, I'll be up."

"Say, Al, Senator Downs of Kade County is pretty strong with that country bunch, isn't he?"

"What he says, goes with them, Ellis," was the significant retort.

"Try and get him to come up too, will you?"

"Sure. I guess Don can get him to come."

"See you in half an hour, Al."

"All right."

When Hobart entered the room which the two railroad attorneys occupied, he found Fulton talking to Louisberg on the long distance telephone.

"What do you think of the idea, Colonel?" Fulton was saying over the telephone.

"Say, Colonel," continued Fulton, "we are going to play a little cards this evening." Fulton smiled as he spoke these words.

Hobart also smiled at Fulton when he heard this part of the conversation.

"Oh, that's all right, Colonel, I'll call you again in the morning. Good bye." And Fulton hung up the receiver.

"Say, Al," said Fulton, walking into the bathroom where Hobart was washing, "I wonder if we could 'put over' an amendment making that bill apply everywhere in the state *except* Louisberg?"

"Gee, that would be raw! I don't think you could do it."

"Oh, I don't know. We've got ten thousand dollars to take care of it with."

"But the News-Herald will take a spasm about it."

"The News-Herald be blowed, if we can get it through. They can yell all they want when it's done."

"But will those country fellows vote for the amendment?"

"Why not? It don't affect them any, and say, a hundred dollars or two, looks like a mountain to those jays."

"We'll see what Downs has to say about it. He's a pretty wise duck. Just wait until he wins a few good pots."

"I'll tell you, Al, the Governor is watching this thing pretty close and we want to—"

A knock at the door halted the conversation.

Fifteen minutes later, found State Senators Dustin and Ladely of Louisberg, Senator Downs of Kade County and Messrs. Hobart and Fulton, the two railroad attorneys, engaged in a "friendly" game of poker. At the end of an hour or so, the three senators had won something like two hundred dollars each and were very jubilant. Several bottles of wine had been opened and the air was thick with smoke from large three-for-a-dollar cigars.

Whenever one of the senators would open the pot, either Hobart or Fulton would "raise" him. The senator would "re-raise" and after fifty or sixty one-dollar chips had been thus placed in the pot, the senator was "called" and upon announcing his hand, was always told that it was "good" and either Hobart or Fulton, which ever it happened to be, would throw his cards in the deck, and thus lose the pot.

At about 1 A.M. lunch was served and during the luncheon the conversation turned to Senate Bill 182, "giving to all the cities and towns in the State, the power to compel railroads, passing through the city or town, to build viaducts or tunnels at such crossings, on such terms as shall be designated by the city or town through which such railroad passes," etc.

Fulton argued that the law would be a great hardship upon all the roads entering Louisberg and that the railroads would be at the mercy of the House of Delegates at Louisberg, whose reputation was well known all over the State. Senator Downs was assured that the railroads had no objection to the bill as far as it concerned the smaller towns, but that an exception should be made in the case of Louisberg. Asked whether he thought the country senators would vote for an amendment to the bill, making the city of Louisberg an exception, Senator Downs said he thought he could "convince" them that it was the "fair" thing to do. Senators Dustin and Ladely from Louisberg felt sure that the senators from their city would vote in favor of the amendment. They were sure they could "convince" them, too.

Fulton said he would have the amendment drawn and placed in Senator Downs' hands for introduction. This plan being agreed upon, the game of cards was resumed.

The "limit" was taken off, and at 4 A.M., when the players stopped, Senator Downs of Kade County had "won" about $5,000; Senators Dustin and Ladely of Louisberg had "won" about $2,000 apiece and of the $9,000 "lost," Fulton and Hobart, the two railroad attorneys, had "lost" respectively about $3,000 and $6,000.

"We'll get even with you some other time" was the last word of Hobart as their Legislator friends left the room, $9,000 "winner."

"I guess that was bad, eh?" said Fulton after closing the door.

"Do you think it will all come out all right, Al?"

"*Sure.* They'll put it over so quick, you won't know what happened."

"But can we fool McNair?"

"Ah, the devil with him; we'll try to get him out of the way when it happens."

So the two railroad attorneys retired at 5 A.M. satisfied that they had arranged to turn a trick that would defeat the Governor's purpose, fool the Louisberg News-Herald and save the railroads, which they represented, something like $500,000.

The game of cards was played; $9,000 had been "handed" to three state senators, presumably for "distribution" among as many others as needed.

Nothing crooked about it. Certainly *not. Anybody* is likely to "loose" at poker, isn't it so?

THE AMENDMENT IS ADOPTED

Jack McNair, the political reporter for the Louisberg News-Herald, was the most cordially disliked man in Heston. The News-Herald, the largest and most influential paper in the state, was often caustic in its criticism of certain members of the State Legislature and was not a bit backward about expressing its opinions. McNair had been its political reporter for years, and no man in the entire country was so widely acquainted with politicians or so hard to fool as Jack.

There are always from fifty to a hundred lobbyists at a session of a State Legislature, and Jack knew every one of them like a book. And they knew him, too. Realizing that he represented a newspaper that was entirely independent and without fear or favor, Jack reported things "without gloves" and never cared a rap whether the politicians and lobbyists liked it or not. Therefore, while all of them apparently treated him cordially and with the greatest attention, secretly, they wished that he was ten thousand miles away. But they didn't fool Jack. He realized their inner feelings and took many confidential "tips" that were given him, with many grains of salt.

About the first thing that Fulton did the morning following the card game seance, was to locate Jack McNair. To say that Fulton was pleased to learn Jack had gone to Louisberg for a day, was putting it mildly.

Jack had carefully analyzed the work of the Assembly for the day, and feeling satisfied that nothing very important was likely to occur, had gone back to the city.

As the big bell in the Capitol tower tolled the hour of ten, the president of the state senate brought down his gavel with a bang, and the senate was convened.

Of the two bodies composing a State Legislature, the Senate is quite the more dignified.

There are many things that go to make it naturally so. The state senate has only forty-two members, while the house of representatives has about two hundred. Inasmuch as the senate has to concur in all legislation enacted, every state senator is a factor. He's very much "somebody."

No being on earth realizes so entirely the importance of his position as a politician. Therefore every senator is always mighty dignified or, at least as dignified as he knows how to be.

The furnishings of the senate are very much more elaborate than those of the "house."

The hall in which it meets is almost as large as that of the house, which is just across the hall, but there are only forty-two desks as compared with two hundred, allowing much more room. Then the desks are much larger and finer than those across the hall. Another thing: the presiding officer of the state senate is the Lieutenant Governor of the state, who is usually a very prominent, as well as a very brainy man. He, therefore, lends dignity and precision to the deliberations of the body over which he presides.

On this particular morning there were present thirty-eight out of the forty-two members of the Senate. Some routine business was transacted, such as second reading of bills, their reference to certain committees, etc.

Suddenly at an apparently prearranged point in the proceedings, Senator Dustin of Louisberg arose, was recognized by the president and said, very quickly:

"Mr. President, I move that Senate Bill 182 be amended so as to except the City of Louisberg."

"Second the motion," said Senator Downs of Kade County.

"All those favoring the amendment proposed by the senator from Louisberg, will make known by saying 'aye.'"

"Aye," was the response.

"Those opposed to the amendment?"

Not a voice was heard.

"The amendment prevails."

Shortly after, the senate adjourned for the day.

THE "SPECIAL INTEREST" NEWSPAPERS

There was quite some excitement at the newspaper table when this resolution was introduced and passed so rapidly. The reporters from other parts of the state took, of course, only a passing interest, but the representatives of the Louisberg newspapers realized at once that an action of great news importance to their papers had taken place.

Only the reporters for the Louisberg morning papers were present, McNair of the News-Herald being absent.

"What do you think of it?" said one to the other.

"Holy Moses, that was awful," was the reply.

Both reporters had been reporting political work so long that they had become accustomed to seeing that sort of "business" done. It was nothing new to them. Recognizing that the item would be given much space in their respective papers, each wrote about a column on the story.

Now let's see how this important news item was "published" in the great metropolitan dailies which these two reporters represented.

"Call for Mr. Wenzel."

The page at the Noonday Club in Louisberg called loudly.

A few minutes later Wenzel was talking to Fulton, the railroad attorney, at the state capital.

"We'll arrange *that* all right, Fulton. I want to hear all about it, too. Mrs. Wenzel has made an engagement for tonight, but we'll break it. I'll have Delting and Weltnor there, too. I'll expect you about nine o'clock, eh?"

"Good-bye."

At about 9:30 P.M. a taxicab drove into the carriage entrance of Wenzel's palatial home and five minutes later found Fulton, the railroad attorney, in conference with three members of Louisberg's "Big Cinch."

Edward Wenzel was a multi-millionaire, and a leading, if not *the* leading, citizen of Louisberg. His time was divided about evenly between serving on the directorate of big public service corporations, two or three banks, a trust company and a railroad company; traveling around the country, directing a large real estate concern and politics.

No affair of public importance in Louisberg was complete unless Wenzel was at the speaker's table.

He was also the leading spirit in the city's largest business club, an organization of several hundred members, paying one hundred dollars a year dues each, and whose members had about as much influence in directing the affairs of the club as they had in directing the movement of the planets! Wenzel, Delting, Weltnor and one or two other members "guided" the organization and Delting and Weltnor *always* agreed with Wenzel's ideas.

Delting and Weltnor were millionaires with about the same interests as Wenzel, only not quite so extensive.

These three "leading" citizens of Louisberg and George Fulton sat around a table in the luxurious smoking room at Wenzel's.

Fulton explained how he and Hobart had visited the Governor the day before, how they had "lost" so large an amount of money at cards, how the amendment had been introduced and passed and other less important details of their work at the State Capital.

All agreed that it had been a good day's business and congratulated Fulton on his success.

"Yes," spoke Fulton, "But there's something mighty important for *you* fellows to do now and you had better get busy on it real quick, too."

"Well?" asked Wenzel.

"You know the News-Herald didn't get the story of this amendment, but the two Louisberg morning papers *did*, and if they tell all about the sensational things that happened at Heston, tomorrow morning, the News-Herald will follow it up in the afternoon and people will go bug house and they'll have those country fellows who voted with us crazy, too."

"You say the morning papers have the story?" asked Wenzel.

"Certainly. Both their reporters were there and they have it written it up good and strong, too. You can't fool those fellows, you know."

"What's the difference what the papers say, now that the thing is done?" asked Delting.

"Sure, let them publish it, you can't prevent it anyhow," chimed in Weltnor.

All this time Wenzel was puffing away at his cigar nonchalantly and when Delting and Weltnor looked at him, certain that he would agree with their views, he startled them by saying:

"George is correct! That story, if it gets into the papers, will cause lots of trouble, sure."

"What difference would there be, if it *did*," said Weltnor, "the bill is 'fixed' now, isn't it?"

"Oh," said Wenzel, "the News-Herald would carry on in sensational style about it: how an awful blunder had been made, how the citizens of Louisberg had been deprived of their rights, how the country senators had erred, and all that sort of thing."

"Well, suppose they do *all* that, what effect can it possibly have?" asked Delting.

"I'll tell you what would happen," exclaimed Fulton. "You'd have those fellows *'reconsidering' that amendment!"*

"Do you really think that's possible?"

"It's been done before," coolly spoke Wenzel.

"Mr. Wenzel," said Fulton, "*you* ought to be able to take care of those morning papers. You've done it before."

Wenzel studied for a minute.

"I'll see what I can do. Get Cummings on the phone for me, Fulton."

Cummings was the president of the corporation that published one of the Louisberg morning papers.

Fulton left the room to telephone and in a few moments returned saying that Cummings was not at home.

"They say he'll be home at about eleven o'clock."

"Leave word for him to phone me the minute he gets in. That's time enough."

"How about the Journal?" (The other morning paper.)

"Call up Jennings," said Wenzel.

Jennings was chief owner in the other morning paper.

Fulton left the room and in a few minutes returned again, saying, "He's out, too."

"Certainly," said Wenzel, "He's at the same place where I expected to be tonight. Wait a second. I know where to get him."

In a few minutes Wenzel was talking to Jennings, the principal stockholder in the Louisberg Journal.

Jennings was a millionaire, director in one of the banks with Wenzel and a close acquaintance.

"Hello, Ed," said Jennings, "we looked for you here tonight. Why the deuce didn't you show up?"

"Something turned up to make it impossible for me to get there, Henry."

"That's too bad. Mrs. Jennings wondered why you hadn't come. What's on your mind, Ed?"

"Say, Henry, you know the legislature at Heston has been deliberating on that Grade Crossing Bill."

"Yes."

"Well, there was an amendment passed this morning that makes the city of Louisberg an exception, if the bill passes."

"Get out."

"Yes. And, say, Henry, I don't think there's any occasion for the morning papers to say much about it, do you?"

"Oh, not particularly, if you say so, Ed. You know I'm always ready to please you, old man. But how about the other paper?"

"Well, I've tried to get hold of Cummings, but he's out. I left word to call me up as soon as he comes home."

"Suppose you talk to Surrey, the editor. I think he will understand the situation. He knows your relations with Cummings."

"All right, I'll do that. Thanks for the tip, Henry, and say, can I tell him that you have agreed to give it very small space?"

"Say that we have agreed to leave it out altogether if they will do the same."

"Good! I'll get in touch with him right away."

"Good-bye, Ed."

"So long, Henry."

Wenzel immediately proceeded to get in touch with Surrey, editor of the Leader.

In about the same way as explained to Jennings, Wenzel told Surrey about the amendment to the bill at Heston, explaining that he had tried to reach Cummings and that Jennings had agreed not to publish the item, if the Leader took the same action.

"I'm sorry, to disagree with you and Mr. Jennings, Mr. Wenzel," spoke Surrey, "but I think that article is of the greatest importance to the readers of our paper. That seems to have been a rather high-handed action there at Heston, anyhow. No, I wouldn't think of withholding such a piece of news from publication!"

"But it means a whole lot to many people, among them, Mr. Cummings, if that item goes in," replied Wenzel, "and besides, what can be the difference if the other paper takes the same action?"

"I don't see that that should have any influence with us," answered Surrey.

"Well, I'll see what Cummings thinks about it, Mr. Surrey. You seem to be an awful loyal servant to the people." (This last sentence, sneeringly.)

"We won't argue about the matter, Mr. Wenzel. I have a right to my opinions."

"I think your opinions are damn poor ones, Surrey."

Bang! Went the receiver at Surrey's end of the line.

Wenzel returned where the others were waiting and reported what had taken place.

"I said a few things to that fellow, Surrey," added Wenzel. "I guess we'll have to wait until Cummings gets home."

Wenzel now led the way to a lavishly furnished "lunchery" where refreshments were served.

In about half an hour a servant entered.

"Mr. Cummings is at the phone to speak to you, Mr. Wenzel."

Wenzel hastened to the telephone. Before taking up the receiver he paused, scratched his chin and thought for a few seconds, then, suddenly making up his mind, picked up the receiver.

"Hello."

"Hello, Wenzel?"

"Yes."

"What the devil you want at this hour of night, Ed, need any money?"

Wenzel laughed. Cummings was a large *borrower* in the bank which Wenzel practically *controlled*.

"No. But say, Lou"—and he repeated the story that Surrey had heard, saying that he had requested Surrey to take the same action that the other paper agreed to take, and that Surrey had refused.

"That fellow Surrey makes me tired," he concluded.

"Surrey's a fine fellow, Ed. You got him worked up, that's all," replied Cummings.

"But, say, Ed," Cummings continued, "How the deuce can I take a hand in this, especially now that you have spoken to Surrey and he got so sore about it?"

"Now, Lou," spoke Wenzel, "You know what this thing means to us. It means as much to you as it does to us."

"I know that, Ed, but I haven't taken any interest in the editorial part of the paper in years. If I gave such an order as that, they would think I was crazy."

This angered Wenzel and he began to "show his teeth."

"Now listen here, Lou, you *can* stop the publication of that matter in both the morning newspapers, and that means the afternoon papers, too. I've told you what this means to us, and there isn't a *director in the Commercial Bank* that isn't *interested*, and you ought to take these things into consideration before you stand on so many scruples."

It will be recalled that Cummings was a large borrower in the bank that Wenzel practically controlled and this was the bank to which Wenzel now referred.

A long pause followed this crude but telling remark of Wenzel's, which meant, in so many words, *"If you don't stop the publication of this item, your borrowing account at the bank will be affected!"*

It was simply an instance of what the "Big Cinch" power was, when things *had* to be done.

Finally, Cummings spoke again:

"You're asking a whole lot of me, Ed, but I'll see what can be done. I'll have a talk with Surrey and call you up later. I won't promise what will be done, though."

"That's the way to talk, Lou. You're the *boss* of the paper. I'll wait for you to call up, so I can tell Jennings what you have agreed to do. Good-bye, old man."

"Good-bye."

A few minutes later Cummings had gotten into communication with Surrey, editor of the Louisberg Leader.

"Mr. Surrey, I am informed that the item relative to the action of the legislature this morning on the Grade Crossing Bill, will, if published, cause a great deal of unnecessary sensation. You know our policy is to avoid sensation whenever we can. Don't you think it would be wise, if the Journal will do the same, to omit the article altogether?"

"Hasn't Mr. Wenzel already given you my views on the matter, Mr. Cummings?"

"Yes, he said something to me about it, but I thought I would call you up about it."

"Well, I'm very much opposed to handling this news in any other than the usual way and this is a big item, too."

"Well, I'll tell you, Surrey, I'd really like to cut the thing out. Now, confidentially, *I am under very great obligations to Mr. Wenzel* and others interested in this matter and it would be a great *favor to me* if you would take care of the matter for them. You know it is not my habit to interfere with your running of the paper, but I want you to *understand* the situation and I assure you that your action in assisting me will be duly '*appreciated*.'"

Surrey smiled. He realized that the item would *have* to be cut out anyhow, so long as Mr. Wenzel was so deeply interested, and now he figured that he might just as well handle the thing diplomatically and derive the greatest amount of benefit out of it for *himself*.

Slowly he spoke: "Well, Mr. Cummings, if the matter really interests you so much I suppose it will not make so very much difference and we will arrange to leave it out."

"Surrey," said Cummings, "I appreciate that action on your part and it will not go unrewarded, I assure you. Then I can assure Mr. Wenzel that it will not be published?"

"Certainly."

"Good-night, Surrey. Anything new on the wire?"

"No. Only a boiler explosion at the car sheds."

"Good-night."

"Good-night, Mr. Cummings."

Surrey sent for the political editor.

"John, the Journal is not going to publish any story on that legislature matter and we are going to omit it too."

"What? You don't mean it?"

"Yep."

They looked at each other for a few seconds and then the political editor said very quietly:

"Why, because?"

"Cummings."

"Phew! 'Big Cinch?'"

Surrey nodded. Both smiled knowingly.

Fifteen minutes later Cummings telephoned Wenzel.

Wenzel immediately telephoned Jennings.

Jennings immediately telephoned *his* paper.

And the dear public knew nothing about the amendment to the Grade Crossing Bill, next morning.

SARA TEASDALE

SARA TEASDALE (1884-1933) was the eldest of the triumvirate of great poets who were born in St. Louis in the 1880s, and like T. S. Eliot and Marianne Moore, she left her hometown as soon as circumstances allowed. Teasdale's family lived at 3668 Lindell Boulevard and later at 38 Kingsbury Place. Both homes were designed by Mrs. Teasdale and were appointed with a private suite for her daughter, who had a separate entrance and spent much time alone in her room. Teasdale was educated at Mary Institute—a school founded by Eliot's grandfather—and absorbed the genteel sensibility of that Midwest outpost of New England Unitarianism.

Although she was born into the same sort of wealth and privilege as Eliot, Teasdale never achieved the sense of release from obligation that would have allowed her to follow his experimental course as a poet, and she and her work remained conservative until the end. Teasdale's first book of poetry, *Sonnets to Duse and Other Poems,* was published in 1907 by William Marion Reedy, the well-known editor of *The Mirror*, who had noticed her work in the local literary magazine, *The Potter's Wheel.* The book established her reputation as a major new poet. Teasdale moved freely between St. Louis, New York, and Chicago in the large orbits that wealth allows and eventually settled in Chicago, where she was courted by Vachel Lindsay until finally refusing his proposal. In 1914, Teasdale married Ernest R. Filsinger, a St. Louis businessman, but the relationship, never fulfilling for either party, ended in 1929 with a moderately scandalous Reno divorce.

During the last years of her life, Teasdale lived in New York with a female companion and continued writing poetry while working on a biography of Christina Rossetti that she never completed. Suffering from depression (caused, in part by the irreconcilable conflicts of her desire for love, her bisexuality, and her need to be alone), Teasdale committed suicide in 1933. She is buried in St. Louis's Bellefontaine Cemetery.

Although today many critics consider Teasdale a minor poet, others believe her work is seriously undervalued. While her poems were conventional in structure, Teasdale's voice was unique, and her ideas, frequently feminist, were expressed with subtle grace and force. Although St. Louis, once called a "howling wilderness" by Teasdale, does not figure prominently in her work, the following poems, written between 1907 and 1919, are lyrical reflections on regional subjects.

THE RIVER

I came from the sunny valleys
    And sought for the open sea,
For I thought in its gray expanses
    My peace would come to me.

I came at last to the ocean
    And found it wild and black,
And I cried to the windless valleys,
    "Be kind and take me back!"

But the thirsty tide ran inland,
    And the salt waves drank of me,
And I who was fresh as the rainfall
    Am bitter as the sea.

SUNSET

(ST. LOUIS)

Hushed in the smoky haze of summer sunset,
When I came home again from far-off places,
How many times I saw my western city
    Dream by her river.

Then for an hour the water wore a mantle
Of tawny gold and mauve and misted turquoise
Under the tall and darkened arches bearing
  Gray, high-flung bridges.

Against the sunset, water-towers and steeples
Flickered with fire up the slope to westward,
And old warehouses poured their purple shadows
  Across the levee.

High over them the black train swept with thunder,
Cleaving the city, leaving far beneath it
Wharf-boats moored beside the old side-wheelers
  Resting in twilight.

RED MAPLES

In the last year I have learned
How few men are worth my trust;
I have seen the friend I loved
Struck by death into the dust,
And fears I never knew before
Have knocked and knocked upon my door—
"I shall hope little and ask for less,"
I said, "There is no happiness."

I have grown wise at last—but how
Can I hide the gleam on the willow-bough,
Or keep the fragrance out of the rain
Now that April is here again?
When maples stand in a haze of fire
What can I say to the old desire,
What shall I do with the joy in me
That is born out of agony?

REDBIRDS

Redbirds, redbirds,
   Long and long ago,
What a honey-call you had
   In hills I used to know;

Redbud, buckberry,
   Wild plum-tree
And proud river sweeping
   Southward to the sea,

Brown and gold in the sun
   Sparkling far below,
Trailing stately round her bluffs
   Where the poplars grow—

Redbirds, redbirds,
   Are you singing still
As you sang one May day
   On Saxton's Hill?

EUGENE FIELD

BORN IN ST. LOUIS, Eugene Field (1850–1895) lived with his family at 634 South Broadway, in the house that currently operates as a museum in his honor. His father, Roswell Field, is noted for having defended Dred Scott in the infamous trial that helped to set the course of the Civil War. At age seven, following his mother's death, Field was sent to live with relatives in Amherst, Massachusetts. He began his college education at Williams, but moved in successive years to Knox College and then to the University of Missouri. In May 1873, he began his career as a reporter on the *St. Louis Evening Journal*. Field then took on the city editor position at the *St. Joseph Gazette* before returning to St. Louis, where he served as an editorial writer on the *St. Louis Times Journal*. Field moved to Chicago in 1883 to take a job with the *Chicago Morning News* and wrote a popular column called "Sharps and Flats," in which he made humorous observations on American society.

Although Field has been called, not entirely to his satisfaction, "The Poet Laureate of Childhood," he was much more than a writer of sentimental pleasantries like "Wynken, Blynken, and Nod." Field's satirical and sometimes controversial journalism, as evidenced in "Sharps and Flats," has been cited as a model for the work of contemporary writers such as Mike Royko. As a poet, Field had a remarkable range. His collected poetry includes deft translations of European romantics such as Heine and Hugo, striking local color poems—often in dialect—and sophisticated and ironic poems on themes such as the pleasures of alcohol. In response to the many requests he received for biographical information, Field published a pamphlet (written in his inimitable style and tone) titled "Auto-Analysis" in which he wrote, "I believe that if I live, I shall do my best literary work when I am a grandfather." Unfortunately, Field did not live to see if his prediction would serve true. He died of heart failure at age forty-five.

The following poems, which allude to Field's Missouri roots and appeared in the 1913 edition of his collected poems, are good examples of his witty use of rhyming verse in depicting local color.

A WESTERN BOY'S LAMENT

I wish't I lived away down East, where codfish salt the sea,
And where the folks have pumpkin pie and apple-sass for tea.
Us boys who's livin' here out West don't get more'n half a show;
We don't have nothin' else to do but jest to sort of grow.

Oh, if I was a bird I'd fly a million miles away
To where they feed their boys on pork and beans three times a day;
To where the place they call the Hub gives out its shiny spokes,
And where the folks—so father says—is mostly women-folks.

LITTLE MACK

This talk about the journalists that run the East is bosh,
We've got a Western editor that's little, but, O gosh!
He lives here in Mizzoora where the people are so set
In ante-bellum notions that they vote for Jackson yet;
But the paper he is running makes the rusty fossils swear,—
The smartest, likeliest paper that is printed anywhere!
And, best of all, the paragraphs are pointed as a tack,
  And that's because they emanate
    From little Mack.

In architecture he is what you'd call a chunky man,
As if he'd been constructed on the summer cottage plan;
He has a nose like Bonaparte; and round his mobile mouth
Lies all the sensuous languor of the children of the South;
His dealings with reporters who affect a weekly bust
Have given to his violet eyes a shadow of distrust;
In glorious abandon his brown hair wanders back
  From the grand Websterian forehead
    Of little Mack.

No matter what the item is, if there's an item in it,
You bet your life he's on to it and nips it in a minute!
From multifarious nations, countries, monarchies, and lands,
From Africa's sunny fountains and India's coral strands,
From Greenland's icy mountains and Siloam's shady rills,
He gathers in his telegrams, and Houser pays the bills;
What though there be a dearth of news, he has a happy knack
  Of scraping up a lot of scoops,
    Does little Mack.

And learning? Well he knows the folks of every tribe and age
That ever played a part upon this fleeting human stage;
His intellectual system's so extensive and so greedy
That, when it comes to records, he's a walkin' cyclopedy;
For having studied (and digested) all the books a-goin',
It stands to reason he must know about all's worth a-knowin'!
So when a politician with a record's on the track,
  We're apt to hear some history
    From little Mack.

And when a fellow-journalist is broke and needs a twenty,
Who's allus ready to whack up a portion of his plenty?
Who's allus got a wallet that's as full of sordid gain
As his heart is full of kindness and his head is full of brain?
Whose bowels of compassion will in-va-ri-a-bly move
Their owner to those courtesies which plainly, surely prove
That he's the kind of person that never does go back
  On a fellow that's in trouble?
    Why, little Mack!

I've heard 'em tell of Dana, and of Bonner, and of Reid,
Of Johnnie Cockerill, who, I'll own, is very smart indeed;
Yet I don't care what their renown or influence may be,
One metropolitan exchange is quite enough for me!
So keep your Danas, Bonners, Reids, your Cockerills, and the rest,
The woods is full of better men all through this woolly West;
For all that sleek, pretentious, Eastern editorial pack
  We wouldn't swap the shadow of
    Our little Mack!

PLAINT OF THE MISSOURI 'COON IN THE BERLIN ZOOLOGICAL GARDENS

Friend, by the way you hump yourself you're from the States, I know,
And born in old Mizzoorah, where the 'coons in plenty grow.
I, too, am native of that clime; but harsh, relentless fate
Has doomed me to an exile far from that noble State;
And I, who used to climb around, and swing from tree to tree,
Now lead a life of ignominious ease, as you can see.
Have pity, O compatriot mine! and bide a season near,
While I unfurl a dismal tale to catch your friendly ear.

My pedigree is noble: they used my grandsire's skin
To piece a coat for Patterson to warm himself within,—
Tom Patterson, of Denver; no ermine can compare
With the grizzled robe that Democratic statesman loves to wear.
Of such a grandsire I am come; and in the County Cole
All up an ancient cottonwood our family had its hole.
We envied not the liveried pomp nor proud estate of kings,
As we hustled round from day to day in search of bugs and things.

And when the darkness fell around, a mocking-bird was nigh,
Inviting pleasant, soothing dreams with his sweet lullaby;
And sometimes came the yellow dog to brag around all night
That nary 'coon could wallop him in a stand-up barrel fight.
We simply smiled and let him howl, for all Mizzoorians know
That ary 'coon can best a dog, if the coon gets half a show;
But we'd nestle close and shiver when the mellow moon had ris'n,
And the hungry nigger sought our lair in hopes to make us his'n.

Raised as I was, it's hardly strange I pine for those old days;
I cannot get acclimated, or used to German ways.
The victuals that they give me here may all be very fine
For vulgar, common palates, but they will not do for mine.
The 'coon that's been accustomed to stanch Democratic cheer
Will not put up with onion tarts and sausage steeped in beer!
No; let the rest, for meat and drink, accede to slavish terms,
But send *me* back from whence I came, and let me grub for worms!

They come, these gaping Teutons do, on Sunday afternoons,
And wonder what I am,—alas, there are no German 'coons!
For if there were, I still might swing at home from tree to tree,
The symbol of Democracy, that's woolly, blithe, and free.
And yet for what my captors are I would not change my lot,
For *I* have tasted liberty, these others, *they* have not;
So, even caged, the Democratic 'coon more glory feels
Than the conscript German puppets with their swords about their heels.

Well, give my love to Crittenden, to Clardy, and O'Neill,
To Jasper Burke and Colonel Jones, and tell 'em how I feel;
My compliments to Cockrill, Stephens, Switzler, Francis, Vest,
Bill Nelson, J. West Goodwin, Jedge Broadhead, and the rest.
Bid them be steadfast in the faith, and pay no heed at all
To Joe McCullagh's badinage or Chauncey Filley's gall;
And urge them to retaliate for what I'm suffering here
By cinching all the alien class that wants its Sunday beer.

THOMAS WOODS STEVENS AND PERCY MACKAYE

IN 1913, THOMAS WOODS STEVENS (1880–1942), then director of the school of drama at the Carnegie Institute in Pittsburgh, accepted a commission from the city of St. Louis to write and produce a pageant commemorating the city's sesquicentennial. Led by Charlotte Rumbold, St. Louis's leading activist for public recreation, the St. Louis Pageant Drama Association envisioned a grand public event to be held in the natural amphitheater north of the Art Museum in Forest Park. An established playwright with several civic pageants to his credit, the thirty-four-year-old Stevens teamed up with Harvard-educated Percy MacKaye (1875–1957), also a professional dramatist who specialized in socially conscious theatre, and divided the ambitious project in half. Stevens wrote and produced the Pageant, and MacKaye authored and directed the Masque.

There were intentional and clear distinctions between the content and presentation of the Pageant and Masque. To further emphasize their unique qualities, the events were held at different times, with the Pageant taking place during the day, and the Masque performed in the evening. Stevens's Pageant focused on actual historic events connected to the founding of St. Louis, and its dialogue was literal and naturalistic. In his preface to *St. Louis: A Civic Masque,* MacKaye underscored their differences thus: "In the Pageant are presented as important persons of the white man's civilization at St. Louis such local leaders as Pierre Laclede, Governor Piernas, St. Ange, Auguste Chouteau, Daniel Boone, etc. In the Masque, on the other hand, none of these historical persons appear, but—expressive of their several leaderships, as well as of the racial and human forces of millions of their fellow citizens, during those successive generations—there rises . . . the single symbolic figure of St. Louis." In the highly allegorical Masque, MacKaye pits St. Louis against other large symbolic figures, such as Gold, War, and Poverty. To emphasize the Masque's mission of civic pride and solidarity, the St. Louis figure is heralded by other American cities that were, in some cases, actually portrayed by their current mayors.

Performed between May 28 and June 1, 1914, the St. Louis Pageant and Masque attracted an audience of more than four hundred thousand people and featured more than seven thousand local citizens as "extras" in the extravaganza. According to historian Donald Bright Oster, "Discounting religious revivals, auto races, rock music concerts and civil rights demonstrations, it still has to be regarded as one of the biggest single attractions in the history of any American city." Although production costs exceeded $125,000—an exorbitant figure for the time—the project made a $17,000 profit. Yet, perhaps more important to the civic boosters and visionaries like Charlotte Rumbold, the St. Louis Pageant and Masque proved successful, if only for a fleeting moment in a few "nights of fantasy," in promoting community collaboration and solidarity.

The first of the two excerpts recorded here is taken from *The Pageant of St. Louis*, written by Stevens. It is followed by Part II of *St. Louis: A Civic Masque*, by MacKaye. The differences in the themes and their treatment of St. Louis in the two pieces should be strikingly apparent.

FROM *THE PAGEANT OF ST. LOUIS*

SECOND MOVEMENT

[A boat appears at the right, towed by men with cordelles. Young Auguste Chouteau stands in the prow.]

CHOUTEAU

This is the place, men. Make fast.

[They make fast the ropes.]

A BOATMAN

What place, Monsieur Chouteau?

CHOUTEAU

The place where Monsieur Laclede blazed the trees. Here we are to take the goods ashore.

[The crew at once sets to work to unload the boat, Chouteau directing them. As the packs are landed, the men set up canvas and board shelters over them; this work progresses as the dialogue is spoken.]

TAILLON

[Coming up to Chouteau.]

Monsieur Auguste.

CHOUTEAU

What is it, Taillon?

TAILLON

Monsieur Laclede has sent us here. He has told us to take from you his commands. We do so. You came with him before. We wish to ask what is to be done here. Is it here Monsieur Laclede will have his settlement?

CHOUTEAU

Yes.

TAILLON

And build his house?

CHOUTEAU

Yes.

TAILLON

And why in this place?

CHOUTEAU

He has examined all the land from Fort Chartres to the Missouri. Ste. Genevieve will not do. It is too far from the Missouri, and there is no place to store the goods.

TAILLON

But here is no place to store the goods.

CHOUTEAU

Monsieur Laclede said to me, "Auguste, go to the place where I blazed the trees. Clear the ground. Build a large shed for the goods, and cabins for the voyageurs. I give you two men you can trust, who will help you very much. I will come soon." That is what he told me. Taillon, you are one of those two.

TAILLON

My respects, Monsieur Chouteau. We will do as you command.

[He turns to the work, and they raise the side of a large shed; Chouteau watches them for a moment, looking down stream expectantly.]

CHOUTEAU

Ah, Taillon—Monsieur Laclede comes!

[Taillon joins Chouteau; Laclede appears in a canoe, two voyageurs paddling.]

TAILLON

Monsieur Laclede comes!

[The men crowd back of Chouteau and Taillon as Laclede lands; they doff their hats and bow.]

CHOUTEAU

You are most welcome, sir.

LACLEDE

[Looking at the sheds and work done.]

Well done, my lad. Taillon, the work moves. My friends, in a little while the English will come to take the land across the river. You are all loyal subjects of France. I have chosen this place that you may still be her subjects, in the hope that our village may become considerable hereafter.

[A general murmur of applause from the men.]

You come here willingly, gladly?

[General assent.]

I pledge you what I have, and the good will of our company, for your prosperity. Taillon, Marcheteau, Kierceraux, Deschamps—what will you choose to do in our village?

TAILLON

Monsieur Laclede, they are all for trading with the Indians, and growing rich.

LACLEDE

Some must build the houses, some must plant the corn, and some must run the mills.

TAILLON

So I have said. I am a miller, I, Joseph Taillon. But to grind flour I must have grain. There must be farmers. Look you, Monsieur, this will not be called your settlement, Laclede's town—no. It will be called Paincourt—short of bread.

LACLEDE

No, my friends—we will give it another name. A name deep in the hearts of you Frenchmen who come here.

[He takes out a map and spreads it before him.]

Look you, here is the plan of my city—for this shall come to be a city in good time. Here is the public square, the *Grand Place*. Here is the street of the church, high up, on the hill. Ah, you shall see it, my friends—the houses and the towers, the people going about their business, the boats with their cargoes along the river's edge, the steeples and the bells swinging on the Sabbath day. Our city—and we shall name it Saint Louis!

[The men take up the words in a low shout, "Saint Louis!"]

And now— to your work.

[They return to their building, and he goes over to Chouteau.]

Here you will have them begin my house. I will come back soon.

[He goes back to his canoe.]

Goodbye, Auguste.

CHOUTEAU

Au revoir, father.

[As Laclede disappears, the Indians—Missouris—enter from the left, coming down and surrounding the men eagerly. Some of them start to set up tepees. The Chief, with a group of braves, approaches Chouteau, who is evidently disturbed, but stands his ground.]

MISSOURI CHIEF

You come to live on our lands?

CHOUTEAU

This is Monsieur Laclede's land.

MISSOURI CHIEF

What you give us?

CHOUTEAU

I give you nothing. Monsieur Laclede will deal with you, when he comes.

[As they stand speaking, a brave tries to steal a blanket from the packs; Chouteau sees him, shouts at him, and drives him off; as Chouteau turns back, a group of squaws comes up on the other side, whining and begging.]

CHOUTEAU

If you want anything, you must work, as we do.

[The squaws nod assent, the braves turning indignantly away.]

Here, Taillon, bid them help you in the digging of the cellar; we will give them some vermillion when they have done.

[The squaws begin work carrying earth out of the cellar, as the settlers set up the house; the braves and children are continually trying to steal from the packs, and are continually chased away by the men.

Enter a group of settlers, right; they see the Indians, and draw together closely, calling to Chouteau.]

A SETTLER

Is this Laclede's settlement?

CHOUTEAU

Yes, Monsieur.

[They consult together, gesturing toward the Indian tepees.]

Will you not make camp with us? Monsieur Laclede would welcome you.

SETTLER

We will not come while the Missouris are here. No.

[The settlers go back as they came. The Indians again crowd around Chouteau, begging. He and Taillon are hard put to it to keep them from carrying off the goods. Re-enter Laclede. The Indians fall back as he approaches, and the Chief steps forward.]

MISSOURI CHIEF

Father, will you not sit in council with us, for we wish to make our village here with you.

[Laclede nods, and the Indians sit in council, Laclede and the Chief in the center.]

Father, we are your children. We are your hungry and homeless children. We are worthy of your pity. We are like the wild fowl that seek for open water, where they may rest from the storm. We have wandered in many places, but here is the place we like best. And here we have chosen to make our home, with you.

LACLEDE

My children, when you followed the wild fowl to the open water, you followed bad guides. For in the open the eagles can best find you, and swoop upon you, and devour you.

MISSOURI CHIEF

Our father will protect us from the eagles.

LACLEDE

You Missouris will not be eaten by the eagles. But you must know that at Fort Chartres are seven hundred warriors who are your enemies. They wait to fight the English. But if they learn that you are here, they will come and destroy you. I can not help you. If you would not have your women and children torn to pieces, if you would not be slain, you warriors, you will not follow the wild fowl, but listen to men who are wise. Go back to your old places. I will give you powder and lead that you may hunt on the way. I speak to you as a good father, but I can not save you from your foes.

MISSOURI CHIEF

Father, our ears have been open. Have pity on our women and children, and give them a little corn. We have heard your wisdom and we will go back to our old villages.

FROM *ST. LOUIS: A CIVIC MASQUE*

PART TWO

[The bright-colored crowd now, parting, draw back with startled and pitying gestures, revealing in their midst groups of haggard women and forlorn children, old men bowed over, and young men darkly brooding; among them, a masked female Form in black, a scarlet band about her forehead.

Chanting their dirge, the dun-colored pageant moves haltingly toward the mound.

Last in the pageant walks a tall Figure completely hooded in black featureless mask, and straight-robed in black.

Moving below the mound, the masked Woman's form raises her thin hands toward Saint Louis, as the dirge continues.]

SAINT LOUIS

[Gazing with awe at the hooded Woman below.]
In Christ His name, what are you?

THE WOMAN

Poverty:
These are my children.
[Pointing at the black-hooded Figure.]
Yonder stands their father.

SAINT LOUIS

But they—what are their names?

POVERTY

He christened them: Shame is my eldest: Vice and Plague I bore
Twins, to his power; next Dumbness and Despair,
And here you see their offspring. Yonder—ah,
There stands my brooding son, Rebellion. These,
And many more, their father brands with names;
But I—I call them all my comrades.

SAINT LOUIS

Tell:

What bodes that scarlet band about your brow?

POVERTY

Ask him who tied it there.

[She points again at the hooded Figure.]

SAINT LOUIS

But what is he?

POVERTY

[Shrinking back.]

I dare not name him. He is never named

When I am near.

SAINT LOUIS

Speak, hooded shape: What are you?

[The Figure in black moves silently toward Saint Louis, and begins to ascend the steps of the mound.]

Why do you mount toward *me*?—Stay! Are you dumb?

Your silence cries to God!

[Saint Louis draws back. The Figure approaches him with slow menace and touches his arm.]

Your hand is cold.

Why have you left your place?

THE FIGURE

My place is here.

SAINT LOUIS

Your voice—it chills my heart. What power is yours?

THE FIGURE

[Pointing below.]

My power is placed above the reach of—those.

[He grasps the hilt of Saint Louis' sword.]

SAINT LOUIS

[Wresting it from him.]

Unloose my sword!

[The Figure reaches upward.]

Touch not my star! Dark shape,

I will unmask you.

[Tearing the hood from the face, Saint Louis starts back. Dropping the robe from his shoulders, the Figure steps forth all gleaming, as Saint Louis cries out:]

Gold!

GOLD

We meet once more.

[Wrenching the sword from Saint Louis, Gold strides up the steps to the shrine, and turns, brandishing it.]

Hail me, my Earth Spirits!

[Cry from below.]

VOICES

Gold! Yo, Gold!

[Appearing from behind the mound, the Earth Spirits rush up the slopes and steps.]

THE PIONEERS AND ADVENTURERS

[Shout.]

Saint Louis!

GOLD

[Exultant.]

Wings! Now their *wings* are mine! Surround my temple!

[Gold goes into the shrine, bearing the sword.

The Earth Spirits rush up after him, and stand guard about the closed door with outspread wings.

There they confront Saint Louis, who pauses midway on the steps, clutching the air dazedly for his reft sword.]

THE WOMEN AND CHILDREN

[From below.]

Save us, Saint Louis!

[Saint Louis stands, groping upward. From the sky, a shooting-star starts and falls beyond the temple, as the deep sky voice calls:]

THE SKY VOICE

Saint Louis!

SAINT LOUIS

Hark! the omen!

THE SKY VOICE

Saint Louis, call your brothers!

SAINT LOUIS

Wásapédan.
I hear!

THE SKY VOICE

Alone, you fall. Make league together.
Call on the cities!—League, and conquer Gold!

SAINT LOUIS

Cahokia, your vision falls on me:
Here on your mound, I hark now, and remember!

THE WOMEN

[From below.]

Saint Louis, save us!

SAINT LOUIS

Bear with me, my sisters!
Your sorrow is our nation's. I will call
My brother cities here, and purge our temple.

[To his gesture, four mounted Heralds move forward on the space below. Their horses are plumed with long, slim wings like swallows.]

Ride, Heralds!—Make your trumpets the four winds!

Call to the cities and proclaim our League!

[Spurring their horses to the four corners of the plaza, the Heralds sound their trumpets with loud peals.

From far away, martial replies come back like echoes.

Saint Louis speaks again to the dun-colored figures below.]

Rise up, pale women. Watch beside me here,

For they are coming. Rise now, Poverty,

For you shall find your rest here on my mound,

And sleep with your sad children.

[Beckoning the masked Form, Saint Louis himself goes down and leads her up the mound's level, trailed after by others of the dark pageant.

There for a moment Poverty stands beside him, then sinks down, where he bends over her. The others also sink down, and Saint Louis speaks with gentle gesture.]

Now, sweet dreams!

To-morrow these shall wake with other names!

[The light now fades from the mound, from all except the figure of Saint Louis and above him the shrine, with the Earth Spirits on guard.

Rising, Saint Louis makes signal again to the Heralds, who blow their trumpets, a second time.

The trumpets' echo sounds louder.

A third time they blow.

The peal is replied to from all parts, and now by land and water, to a march music of spirited solemnity, the Pageant of the Cities begins majestically to enter.

In seven major groups come the cities of the Union, representing all the states and the islands, and leading them—the Federal Capital. Accompanying them rides a group of foreign cities, representing countries of South America, Canada, England, and Europe.

The seven groups of the Union are marshalled in this wise:

By water, the cities of the Rivers, led by New Orleans; and of the Lakes, led by Chicago.

By land, those of the Eastern seaboard, led by New York; of the Western coast, by San Francisco; of the Mountains, by Denver; of the Islands—by Honolulu.

Attending the cities are their distinctive industries.

Marshalling them all rides the city Washington.

In his train are groups of the nation's Arts, Sciences, and Professions.

As they approach, the Pioneers and Adventurers move on either side to the middle and background.

Converging like a vast V, whose apex is the foot of the mound, the city groups take their stations on the plaza foreground—Washington and his group at the apex.

There Washington salutes Saint Louis, and speaks.]

WASHINGTON

Saint Louis, to our states and sister lands,
Our coasts, and isles, our mountains, rivers, and lakes
The winds have borne your cry, and we respond.

THE SEVEN GROUPS

[Calling, through their masked spokesmen.]

[I]

I from the eastern sea have come—New York.

[II]

I from the western—San Francisco.

[III]

I speak from the lakes—Chicago.

[IV]

I from the rivers—New Orleans.

[V]

On the mountains—Denver, I.

[VI]

I call from the far islands—Honolulu!

WASHINGTON

[VII]

And I from the Capitol.—We hail you, brother!
What urging cause now calls us to make league?

SAINT LOUIS

Gold has usurped our temple.—In our path
Lo, we have grappled the Elements, Earth, and War

And overcome them. Gold alone has slipped
Our grasp, eluding us in subtle guises.
Here, in his train, behold this pallid troup
Of Poverty, bowed in dark.—Cities, my brothers,
Gold has usurped our temple and our sword:
How shall we cope with Gold?

WASHINGTON

[Turning to his group.]
Imagination,
Reveal, and answer! For if you are blind,
The nations walk in darkness.

[From the group of Arts and Sciences, Imagination stands forth—a noble female Form, masked in serene beauty.]

IMAGINATION

Lords of the earth,
And you, then, stricken so dumb? And are you dazzled
When Gold draws near to God? And do your souls
Cry for a saviour?
Close your eyes, O people!
Gaze there in your own darkness:
What do you behold there?
Follow me: I will show you.

[Through the fallen figures on the steps, she mounts to the mound level, where she stands in the dimness and looks back on the illumined plaza.]

In all this gorgeous pageant of the world
Has none beheld him? Nay, he sits in twilight
And broods by fallen Poverty. Behold him!—

[She points beside the stricken form of Poverty to where a slight, slim Figure sits.]

A child: a child!—And wings he bears—and thorns!
[Reaching her hand.]
Arise, dear Love, and lead me to the temple.

[The child rises from his brooding, and steps into sudden light. Bare-limbed, he wears a dim blue tabard, through which at the shoulders spring iris wings. On his head thorns glitter like a garland.

Taking Imagination's outstretched hand, and passing Saint Louis [who gazes with awe], he leads her up the steps to the shrine and pauses.

Saint Louis follows part way up the steps.

At the approach of the child, the Earth Spirits draw back from the closed door, screening their eyes.

The child draws nearer and—as Imagination stands beside him—knocks.

The door clangs with a deep booming, and swings open.

Slowly Gold comes forth, holding the sword.

Confronting the child, he raises the sword above his head to strike.

The child looks up at him.

Gold pauses, wavering.

The sword falls from his grasp, and he bows down with a deep cry.]

GOLD

Master!

[The child touches his bowed form.

Gold raises his head, reaches for the sword, and holds it up.

Imagination takes the sword and speaks.]

IMAGINATION

Now, Gold, rejoin these Earth Spirits. You
Henceforth are one of them—to serve us.

[Gold draws back and joins the group of Earth Spirits, who bow down with him.]

THE EARTH SPIRITS

Ee-yo!

IMAGINATION

[Gazing below at the stricken forms.]
Now wake, you lonely and despairing ones!
Wake from your dark, and be what you have dreamed!
Saint Louis, guard the sword!—Love holds the temple.

[Standing the sword against the lintel, Imagination and Love go within.

Saint Louis, from midway of the steps, ascends and takes the sword.

Standing before the temple shrine, he turns and looks below.

On the mound level and the lower steps, a dreamy light reveals where

Poverty and the other stricken shapes have risen from their dun garb, now clad in forms of light and graciousness.]

SAINT LOUIS

[Addressing them and the multitude.]
O sisters—brothers—cities leagued by Love!
If we are dreaming, let us scorn to wake;
Or waking, let us shape the sordid world
To likeness of our dreams. For 'tis a little,
When we, too, like Cahokia, shall lie down,
And this our city be a silent mound,
Silent, save over all—the chanting stars!

[Beyond him, from the sky, slowly the Great Bear gleams, while the star-choirs sing, remote:]

CHORUS OF THE STARS

Out of the formless void
Beauty and order are born:
One for the all, all in one,
We wheel in the joy of our dance.

WÁSAPÉDAN

St. Louis.

SAINT LOUIS

Hark—the voice!

WÁSAPÉDAN

Behold the wings!

SAINT LOUIS

What wings, O Wásapédan?

WÁSAPÉDAN

Eagle's wings!

SAINT LOUIS

What eagle flies?

WÁSAPÉDAN

America! Your league

Rides on his wings, and rises toward the stars.

[Wásapédan fades.

Saint Louis, looking toward the southern tower, points there with his sword, and turns toward the great assemblage.]

SAINT LOUIS

Cities! My brothers—sing! Our league is born!

ALL THE ASSEMBLAGE

Saint Louis! The League of Cities!

[Suddenly all start, uplifting their arms, and gazing toward the tower entrance, cry out]:

Wings! the Wings!

[Beyond, from the outside darkness, a great whirring hums; groups of the people start back and forward, leaving a wide pathway, along which—emerging from the dimness—a gigantic Bird sweeps whirring, darts for an instant through bright radiance, then soars into the night, circling upward and scattering wild sparkles of fire in its wake. In configuration and color an eagle, the bird, of course, is an aeroplane, serving thus for the first time the symbolism of dramatic poetry. The sparkles in its wake are vari-colored fireworks, shot off as it soars.

Saint Louis stands, pointing skyward with his sword.

Meantime, from the gazing hosts of the plaza, swaying with rhythmic motion, a mighty chorus rises.]

CHORUS

Out of the formless void
Beauty and order are born:
One for the all, all in one,
We wheel in the joy of our dance.

Brother with brother
Sharing our light,
Build we new worlds
With ancient fire!

[From far above temple and plaza, the colossal Eagle still drops his fiery plumes.]

FINIS.

CARLOS F. HURD

BORN THE SON OF A CONGREGATIONAL MINISTER in Cherokee, Iowa, Carlos Hurd (1877–1950) began working for the *St. Louis Post-Dispatch* after graduating from college. In his early days at the paper, Hurd bicycled around the city in order to make it to the scene of his next story. During his half-century with the *Post-Dispatch*, Hurd developed a reputation as a fine journalist and by the end of his career was revered by his peers. In 1947, when Hurd contributed an essay on St. Louis to Robert S. Allen's volume *Our Fair City,* he was called by Allen "the dean of the contributors."

Hurd was an eyewitness reporter to two of the most sensational and tragic events of the first decades of the twentieth century, one of which occurred at sea and one on the east bank of the Mississippi River. In 1912, Hurd and his wife, Katherine, were passengers on the *S.S. Carpathia*, the ship that rescued victims from the *S.S. Titanic*'s tragic maiden voyage. Hurd's five thousand-word "scoop" of the maritime disaster appeared first in *The Evening World* and was immediately picked up by the Associated Press, which transmitted it to virtually every newspaper in the world. According to Vera and John Gillespie, who shared Hurd's experience with the shipwreck and his subsequent fame for breaking the story to the world in their book *The "Titanic Man,"* Hurd bore that nickname for the remainder of his long, illustrious career.

Just five years after the *Titanic* tragedy, Hurd was witness to another devastating human event, the race riot in East St. Louis on July 2, 1917, often cited by sociologists as one of the worst episodes of racial violence in American history. In the following excerpt from his account of the riot, published in the *Post-Dispatch* on July 3, Hurd abandons any pretense of adopting a dispassionate professional stance and vehemently expresses his disgust and horror at the white mob's viciousness toward innocent, unarmed African American men and women.

ST. LOUIS POST-DISPATCH ACCOUNT OF EAST ST. LOUIS RIOTS

For an hour and a half last evening I saw the massacre of helpless negroes at Broadway and Fourth Street, in downtown East St. Louis, where a black skin was a death warrant.

I have read of St. Bartholomew's night. I have heard stories of the latter-day crimes of the Turks in Armenia, and I have learned to loathe the German army for its barbarity in Belgium. But I do not believe that Moslem fanaticism or Prussian frightfulness could perpetrate murders of more deliberate brutality than those which I saw committed, in daylight, by citizens of the State of Abraham Lincoln.

I saw man after man, with hands raised, pleading for his life, surrounded by groups of men—men who had never seen him before and knew nothing about him except that he was black—and saw them administer the historic sentence of intolerance, death by stoning. I saw one of these men, almost dead from a savage shower of stones, hanged with a clothesline, and when it broke, hanged with a rope which held. Within a few paces of the pole from which he was suspended, four other negroes lay dead or dying, another having been removed, dead, a short time before. I saw the pockets of two of these negroes searched, without the finding of any weapon.

ROCK DROPPED ON NEGRO'S NECK

I saw one of these men, covered with blood and half conscious, raise himself on his elbow, and look feebly about, when a young man, standing directly behind him, lifted a flat stone in both hands and hurled it upon his neck. This young man was much better dressed than most of the others. He walked away unmolested.

I saw a negro woman begging for mercy and pleading that they had harmed no one, set upon by white women of the baser sort, who laughed and answered the coarse sallies of men as they beat the negress's face and breasts with flats, stones and sticks. I saw one of the furies fling herself at a militiaman who was trying to protect a negress, and wrestle with for his bayoneted gun, while other women attacked the refugee.

What I saw, in the 90 minutes between 6:30 P.M. and the lurid coming of darkness, was but one local scene of the drama of death. I am satisfied that, in spirit and method, it typified the whole. And I cannot somehow speak of what I saw as mob violence. It was not my idea of a mob.

CROWD MOSTLY WORKINGMEN

A mob is passionate, a mob follows one man or a few men blindly; a mob sometimes takes chances. The East St. Louis affair, as I saw it, was a man hunt, conducted on a sporting basis, though with anything but the fair play which is the principle of sport. The East St. Louis men took no chances, except the chance from stray shots, which every spectator of their acts took. They went in small groups, there was little leadership, and there was a horribly cool deliberateness and a spirit of fun about. I cannot allow even the doubtful excuse of drink. No man whom I saw showed the effect of liquor.

It was no crowd of hot-headed youths. Young men were in the greater number, but there were the middle-aged, no less active in the task of destroying the life of every discoverable black man. It was a shirt-sleeve gathering, and the men were mostly workingmen, except for some who had the aspect of mere loafers. I have mentioned the peculiarly brutal crime committed by the only man there who had the appearance of being a business or professional man of any standing.

I would be more pessimistic about my fellow-Americans than I am today, if I could not say that there were other workingmen who protested against the senseless slaughter. I would be ashamed of myself if I could not say that I forgot my place as a professional observer and joined in such protests. But I do not think any verbal objection had the slightest effect. Only a volley of lead would have stopped those murderers.

"Get a nigger," was the slogan, and it was varied by the recurrent cry, "Get another!" It was like nothing so much as the holiday crowd, with thumbs turned down, in the Roman Coliseum, except that here the shouters were their own gladiators, and their own wild beasts.

When I got off a State street car on Broadway at 6:30, a fire apparatus was on its way to the blaze in the rear of Fourth street, south from Broadway. A moment's survey showed why this fire had been set, and what it was meant to accomplish.

FIRE DRIVES OUT NEGROES

The sheds in the rear of negroes' houses, which were themselves in the rear of the main buildings on Fourth street, had been ignited to drive out the negro occupants of the houses. And the slayers were waiting for them to come out.

It was stay in and be roasted, or come out and be slaughtered. A moment before I arrived, one negro had taken the desperate chance of coming out, and the rattle of revolver shots, which I heard as I approached the corner, was followed by the cry, "They've got him!"

And they had. He lay on the pavement, a bullet wound in his head and his skull bare in two places. At every movement of pain which showed that life remained, there came a terrific kick in the jaw or the nose, or a crashing stone from some of the men who stood over him.

At the corner a few steps away, were a Sergeant and several guardsmen. The Sergeant approached the ring of men around the prostrate negro.

"This man is done for," he said. "You'd better get him away from here." No one made a move to lift the blood-covered form, and the Sergeant walked away, remarking, when I questioned him about an ambulance, that the ambulances had quit coming. However, an undertaker's ambulance did come 15 minutes later, and took away the lifeless negro, who had in the meantime been further kicked and stoned.

By that time, the fire in the rear of the negro houses had grown hotter, and men were standing in all the narrow spaces through which the negroes might come to the street. There was talk of a negro in one of the houses, who had a Winchester, and the opinion was expressed that he had no ammunition left, but no one went too near, and the fire was depended on to drive him out. The firemen were at work on Broadway, some distance east, but the flames immediately in the rear of the negro houses burned without hindrance.

MILITIAMEN TRY TO CURB MOB

A half-block to the south, there was a hue and cry at a railroad crossing, and a fusillade of shots was heard. More militiamen than I had seen elsewhere, up to that time, were standing on a platform and near a string of freight cars, and trying to keep back men who had started to pursue negroes along the track.

As I turned back toward Broadway, there was a shout at the alley, and a negro ran out, apparently hoping to find protection. He paid no attention to missiles thrown from behind, none of which had hurt him much, but he was stopped, in the middle of the street by a smashing blow in the jaw, struck by a man he had not seen.

"Don't do that," he appealed. "I haven't hurt nobody." The answer was a blow from one side, a piece of curbstone from the other side, and a push which sent him on the brick pavement. He did not rise again, and the battering and kicking of his skull continued until he lay still, his blood flowing half way across the street. Before he had been booted to the opposite curb, another negro appeared, and the same deeds were repeated. I did not see any revolver shots fired at these men. Bullets and ammunition were saved for use at longer range. It was the last negro I have mentioned who was apparently finished by the stone hurled upon his neck by the noticeably well-dressed young man.

The butchering of the fire-trapped negroes went on so rapidly that, when I walked back to the alley a few minutes later, one was lying dead in the alley on the west side of Fourth street and another on the east side.

And now women began to appear. One frightened black girl, probably 20 years old, got so far as Broadway with no worse treatment than jeers and thrusts. At Broadway, in view of militiamen, the white women, several of whom had been watching the massacre of the negro men, pounced on the negress. I do not wish to be understood as saying that these women were representative of the womanhood of East St. Louis. Their faces showed, all too plainly, exactly who and what they were. But they were the heroines of the moment with that gathering of men, and when one man, sick of the brutality he had seen, seized one of the women by the arm to stop an impending blow, he was hustled away, with fists under his nose, and with more show of actual anger than had been bestowed on any of the negroes. He was a stock, nervy chap, and he stood his ground until a diversion elsewhere drew the menacing ring of men away.

"Let the girls have her," was the shout as the women attacked the young negress. The victim's cry, "Please, please, I ain't done nothing," was stopped by a blow in the mouth with a broomstick, which one of the women swung like a baseball bat. Another woman seized the negress' hands, and the blow was repeated as she struggled helplessly. Fingernails clawed her hair, and the sleeves were torn from her waist, when some of the men called, "Now let her see how fast she can run." The women did not readily leave off beating her, but they stopped short of murder, and the crying, hysterical girl ran down the street.

An older negress, a few moments later came with two or three militiamen, and the same women made for her. When one of the soldiers held his gun as a barrier, the woman with the broomstick seized it with both hands, and struggled to wrest it from him, while the others, striking at the negress, in spite of the other militiamen, frightened her thoroughly and hurt her somewhat.

From negress baiting, the well-pleased procession turned to see a lynching. A negro, his head laid open by a great stone-cut, had been dragged to the mouth of the alley on Fourth street and a small rope was being put about his neck. There was joking comment on the weakness of the rope, and everyone was prepared for what happened when it was pulled over a projecting cable box, a short distance up the pole. It broke, letting the negro tumble back to his knees, and causing one of the men who was pulling on it to sprawl on the pavement.

STOUTER ROPE OBTAINED

An old man, with a cap like those worn by street car conductors, but showing no badge of car service, came out of his house to protest. "Don't you hang that man on this street," he shouted. "I dare you to." He was pushed angrily away, and a rope, obviously strong enough for its purpose, was brought.

Right here I saw the most sickening incident of the evening. To put the rope around the negro's neck, one of the lynchers stuck his fingers inside the gaping scalp and lifted the negro's head by it, literally bathing his hand in the man's blood.

"Get hold, and pull for East St. Louis!" called a man with a black coat and a new straw hat, as he seized the other end of the rope. The rope was long, but not too long for the number of hands that grasped it, and this time the negro was lifted to a height of about seven feet from the ground. The body was left hanging there.

While this lynching was in preparation I walked to Broadway, found a

Corporal's guard of militiamen, who had just come from where the firemen were working, and called their attention to what was going on. I do not know that they could have done anything to stop it. I know that they did not try to.

In the first hour that I was there I saw no sufficient body of militiamen anywhere, and no serious effort, on the part of the few who were about, to prevent bloodshed. Most of the men in uniform were frankly fraternizing with the men in the street. But beginning at 7:30, I did see instances of what national guardsmen, in reasonable numbers, and led by worthy officers can do.

RESCUE SOME NEGROES

First, there came a hollow square of soldiers from the fire zone along Broadway. In the front row of the frightened group within the square was a mulatto boy, not more than 6 years old. Further within the group were other children with their mothers. The negro men were marching with their hands raised, and some of the women were also holding up their hands.

The natural point of attack was in the rear, and the soldiers, under sharp commands from an officer, repeatedly turned about and made room with their bayonets. The pitiful procession got safely around the corner and to the police station. Some smaller rescues of a similar kind were carried out in the next few minutes.

Following one of these rescue parties to the police station, I suddenly became aware that a new man, and a new spirit of soldiery, and entered into the situation. A man in a light suit and a straw hat, who had just come into town, was listening to a few details of what had happened in the neighborhood. He gave some quick commands, and in a moment, the first adequate body of guardsmen that I had seen was marching toward Broadway. The solders were from B company and other companies of the Fourth Illinois, and the apparent civilian in command was Col. Stephen O. Tripp of the Adjutant General's office in Springfield.

As they turned into Broadway, double-quick was ordered, and it was none too quick, for another lynching was being prepared. This lynching was apparently to be on Broadway, and a negro, his head cut, but still conscious and struggling, was being dragged along the pavement with a rope around his neck.

"Get those men!" was the command, and a moment later several white men were in line on the south sidewalk, some of them with hands raised, while guardsmen faced them with bayonets. On the opposite sidewalk, the soldiers merely told the men to "move on," and this brought a sharp reprimand from Col. Tripp. "Don't let them get away," he ordered. "Make them prisoners." Most of these men were again lined up, and the two lines of prisoners, 25 or 30 men in all, were then marshaled in the car tracks, and the march to the station began, a guard being left behind to protect the negro, and to keep the street clear. I did not learn what became of this negro.

TEMPER OF CROWD CHANGES

The temper of the men in the street showed a change after the first encounter with Tripp methods. It began to seem that the situation had found its master. But the most efficient Colonel cannot be everywhere at once, and while the uniformed line was busy keeping a crowd from forming about the police station, scattered shooting began in the neighborhood of the recent killings.

One negro ran the gauntlet on Broadway. Several shots were fired at him, in a reckless fashion that explains the number injured by stray bullets earlier in the day. But it appeared that he got away.

It was nearly dark, and the fire on Broadway was becoming more threatening. A half-hour before, some lines of hose, through apparently in insufficient number, had been in use, but now the use of water had ceased, and it was said that the hose had been cut. The fire was nearing the Mollman harness establishment, in which the mayor of East St. Louis is interested, and the big wooden horse on top of the building was silhouetted in the twilight.

As I returned from a look at the fire, I saw an ambulance drive into Fourth street, to get the bodies which had been lying there for nearly an hour. I saw one body placed in the ambulance. I heard it said, as I was leaving town, that the men in the street had prevented the removal of one of the bodies, saying that the negro was not dead, and must lie there until he died. I did not verify this, and I do not state it as a fact. Every thing which I have stated as a fact came under my own observation. And what I saw was, as I have said, but a small part of the whole.

JULY 3, 1917

DENTON SNIDER

DENTON JACQUES SNIDER (1841–1925) was born in Mt. Gilead, Ohio, and attended Oberlin College. In 1864, he accepted a position teaching classics at Christian Brothers College in St. Louis. As a member of several St. Louis literary and philosophical societies, Snider became deeply involved in the city's intellectual life. An extremely prolific writer in multiple genres, Snider produced more than fifty books between 1880 and 1920, most of which were published in St. Louis. Although many of Snider's works are poetry, fiction, and drama, the critical consensus is that Snider was more a scholar than a creative writer. Most of Snider's poetry not only suffers from overbearing classical aspirations and references, but also is stilted and stylistically awkward. According to Elijah Jacobs and Forrest Wolverton, co-authors of *Missouri Writers*, "When one considers Snider's reputation as scholar and teacher, and his copious production of books, one is prepared for higher performance than he finds."

However, as a writer of nonfiction and social commentary, Snider excelled, as the following excerpts from *The St. Louis Movement* (1920), an ambitious work he referred to as his "life's narrative," reveal. In the first excerpt, Snider identifies—in the spirit of a true classicist—four elements that compose the elusive character of St. Louis along the lines of the four humors the Greeks believed determined human nature. In the second excerpt, Snider delivers an insightful critical analysis of St. Louis's character, focusing on its hubristic belief in a predestined greatness.

FROM *THE ST. LOUIS MOVEMENT*

THE FOUR ELEMENTS OF ST. LOUIS

"Tell us without going further," I hear my alert reader demanding, "what, who is this St. Louis of yours? Analyze her a little for us, that we may catch some notion of the original stuff of which she may be composed. As she too must have a soul, which has become so deeply ingrown with yours, can you not draw a slight sketch of her elemental psychology?"

Let it be said at once in reply that I asked a similar question as I took my early surveys of the city, which finally revealed to my prying vision several heterogeneous cleavages or layers in its folk, not simply ethnical but pronouncedly cultural. Various nations were indeed present and active, but more fundamentally various cultures were present and active. Of these I shall first give some reckoning, as I understand them.

My studies of the city taken as a whole soon led me to see in it four distinct strains, not so much national or racial as spiritual, which have held their way alongside of one another, touching on the edges, intermingling at times, but often secretly or openly colliding. To this inner fundamental separation may be in part ascribed that lack of communal unity and enterprise which has been so many times noted by impartial and even friendly observers. St. Louis has seemed cut not merely in two but in four down to its very soul, which deepest scission has been in part the ground-work of its fate.

On a number of sides I began to come upon this ultimate fact in the course of my experience. Still I clung to the city and shared its hope. The St. Louis Movement, being of a cultural character, thus fell athwart other and older cultures already inoculated and bearing fruit. I have often tried to think that this on the whole was the city's advantage, perchance its opportunity. For these four diverse and somewhat antagonistic streams of human spirit were mutually limiting and to a degree mutually neutralizing, so that the field was open for any new doctrine, which a single dominant belief or established creed might persecute or undermine or even openly suppress.

These four cultural elements which I found here distinctly marked off when I arrived, and which remained deeply graven on the communal character for many years, and are still not wholly obliterated, I shall set down as follows: the Roman-Catholics, the New Englanders, the Southerners, the Germans. It will be seen that the division is not strictly racial, not national, not religious, though race and nation and religion played in sometimes with no little intensity. But the profounder and more influential distinction I believe to have been cultural, being based upon the deepest spiritual affiliations of the very conglomerate population. Most of the newcomers would easily fall into one of these four classes. For instance

I, rather a misfit everywhere, was born in Ohio of Southern parentage, but was educated at Oberlin College which was decidedly of the old Puritanic type. Hence, amid these clashing elements I felt myself at first more closely related to New England, and even let people call me a Yankee, when they were curious about my antecedents. Still I felt a certain aloofness from and ignorance of all these forms of St. Louis humanity, yet with an intense desire to know them and even to share in their consciousness.

1. The Roman Catholics I place at the head, since they were the most numerous, diversified, and pervasive element, and at the same time the one with which I experienced my first contact, to my great astonishment. For I did not know that the Christian Brothers were a Catholic Order when I engaged by letter from Cincinnati to teach in their school, and they wrote me never a word about religion. Association with them for over two years in their daily work was a great new experience, producing a decided expansion of my mental horizon. Toward me, though not of their confession, they were tolerant, honest, and appreciative, and I tried to requite their goodness, certainly to my moral betterment and intellectual illumination through life. More intimately than ever before or since I beheld the Catholic world-view at work in the human soul, and some of the characteristic results thereof, perhaps not the deepest. Also I experienced with a thrill the Church's world-organization when some Superior of the Order, a monk from Paris or possibly from Rome, came into my Latin class and examined my pupils and myself with friendly approval in broken English. Such was my Catholic epoch, no negligible part of this earthly apprenticeship of mine. It helped to universalize me.

The mother-church in St. Louis held under her wings many different peoples with their different tongues, histories, prejudices, antagonisms. The old French families of the first settlers were still in evidence, but seemed on the decline. The Irish held ecclesiastical sway from the archbishop down the whole hierarchical line; their zeal and energy won and deserved the prize. German Catholics also were numerous, as well Slavic. All these different and often recalcitrant ethnic elements were fused together by the church in a common faith and in a common education, so that they, in all their diversities, national and otherwise, formed a single cultural element in the city. Outside of this bond, the religious primarily, they were often inclined to fly asunder and showed cleavages, especially political. Thus Catholicism was busied with its peculiar problems in St. Louis. As far as I remember, it never had a pronounced representative in our Philosophical Society, though Dr. Harris himself, in his later years, showed a tendency to Catholize, as some of us thought, through his sympathetic study of Aquinas and the Scholastics, as well as on account of his self-surrendering love of the poet Dante. And perhaps in his universality he could not altogether omit that institution which asserts in its very title the claim to be universal. Here it may be added that two other members of the St. Louis Movement manifested a Catholicizing stage in their evolution, without, however, crossing over and getting inside the Church's boundary.

II. The New England element I may place next both for the sake of contrast and of similarity. It was the least in numbers, yet the most homogeneous; its chief cleavage was probably a religious or rather a theological one, for it had brought along to the West its two sorts of theology, the trinitarian and unitarian, with their accompanying congregations. But its chief cultural power and influence lay in the field of education; to its enthusiasm as well as to its ability must be largely ascribed the city's system of Public Schools for the commonalty, as well as Washington University for the higher disciplines. The majority of the teachers were of the New England mould, though not always of New England birth. Indeed American popular education had its unflagging propagation as well as its origin, in the land of the Puritans.

The Public School was the main though not the only seed-field of the St. Louis Movement. This was doubtless owing to the influence of Superintendent Harris, a born New Englander. Washington University, decidedly New Englandish, however, held aloof; only one of its Professors, George H. Howison, ever became an active member, and he quit us and the city after a few years' domicile.

III. The Southern element was well represented in the city, and put its decided impress upon the same, so that St. Louis might well in one sense be called a Southern city. This element showed itself in a pervasive social character, and still more in a superior political ability. A strain of Southern courtesy made itself pretty generally felt, not without its streak of arrogance perhaps; but the creative greatness of the South before the War was its gift of leadership, especially in politics—a gift which has shown itself emphatically in the history of St. Louis as well as of the United States. The leaders of all parties were for the most part Southerners—of Union and Disunion, of Anti-slavery and Pro-slavery, of the Future and of the Past. Very significant is the fact that the greatest leader the North ever had was a born

Southerner—Abraham Lincoln. So in this city we may cite the instance of Francis P. Blair along with many others.

But in St. Louis the Southern element became hopelessly divided and crippled by the Civil War. Its leaders gradually failed to keep their political hold on affairs. Indeed the South as a whole seems to have lost in the Nation's strife its former preeminent gift of statesmanship, which during the conflict showed itself so strikingly inferior to its soldiership. True political foresight would have kept it out of the war in the first place, and then after the Union victories of Vicksburg and Gettysburg, would by a peace have saved its people from untold loss, suffering, and humiliation. And since the war what shall we say to Southern statesmanship?

IV. And now we come to speak of the strongest, most emphatic element of all, the German, high in the ascendant on account of its numbers, its aggressiveness, its general intelligence, and its unity of spirit. Against the German solidarity, based upon education and military training in the Fatherland, and brought along in its very soul to America, the other elements were weaker and internally divided. When I reached the city in 1864, the great War was drawing to a victorious close, and therewith in proportion the Germans of St. Louis were rising in authority and also in self-assertion. For it was chiefly through their strength and initiative that the first decisive blow for the Union had been struck at Camp Jackson, with a victory which on the whole never stopped its course for four years till it had rolled down the Mississippi, then wheeled eastward to Chattanooga, to Atlanta, to Savannah, then surged northward through the Carolinas toward the border of Virginia for the final struggle, where it was halted by Grant (so he says in his Memoirs). German regiments from St. Louis and from Missouri had been in the thick of the fight all the way, and soon were returning home with a justifiable good opinion of themselves and of their services. Here, accordingly, the Teutonic spirit was mounting upward in lofty self-confidence compared to that of the other elements. . . .

Such were the four cultural elements of St. Louis as I found them existent on my arrival and at work with more or less energy. In a way I was sympathetic with them all. They represented the tradition, religious, social, educational, descending down the ages, and coming from abroad to our city in which they were planted afresh, and throve according to their inner vigor. I could not help noting the gradual retreat, if not defeat of French St. Louis some time before the battle of Sedan, with which it seems to have shown a distant parallelism. The old French Market was no longer French but German. In the country, say at Florissant, it was pointed out to me that the Teutonic farmer was slowly getting possession of the Creole's land. Though some of the wealthiest people of St. Louis still bore French names, the mighty inrushing and still rising popular tide was German.

Strangely, during these same years a similar up-burst of the Teutonic Spirit was taking place on the other side of the earth. I wonder if there might be some connection aerial or subterranean, telephonic or telepathic, between child St. Louis and old Fatherland! Then lay we here, on the banks of the Mississippi, not all by ourselves, self-absorbed in our little local doings, but we were unconscious participators in a globe-encircling world-movement, which revealed itself in our deeds and possibly had begotten the same in some hidden genetic kinship. The year in which I arrived at St. Louis is the date of that peculiar modern start of Prussia toward universal domination which was halted only yesterday, and still lies in the throes of some unfathomable finale. I remember that I felt the first early throb of the awakening Fatherland in the animated conversation of a large German boarding-house on Market street, where I swallowed the talk more eagerly and more easily than the potato salad—a dish then wholly new to my taste and to my imagination.

THE GREAT ST. LOUIS ILLUSION

St. Louis has a soul of her own, and has had from the time when I began to get acquainted with her—a unique civic Psyche, amenable only to the laws of Psychology. Toward me she stands in the relation of a Person who has gone through many changes since I have known her, that is, during more than fifty years. Her life is associated with mine in a greater or less intimacy, and has often determined it to a new turn of its labyrinthine errantry. . . .

So much by way of preface to a cardinal statement: this city-soul, as I may call it, was getting to have one all-dominating psychical trait when I first breathed of its atmosphere, which trait I soon caught, and then it caught me. I quickly found the one faith universal, that St. Louis could not help becoming the largest, richest, most influential city in the land, with all the gain and glory and dominion resulting from such pre-eminence. In religion, politics, and love its multiracial polyglottic people might differ, but in one creed they were united, or rather fused to a kind of fanaticism: the doctrine of the future supremacy of St. Louis.

Of course I soon found myself a convert, and a very zealous one, if not quite purblind, and ready to do battle for my new conviction. Still further, I became warmly attached to the community under whose banner I had enlisted as a fighter, and with whose changes of fortune I rose and fell in my deepest heart-throbs. To this time and its testful experience I attribute my life-long underlying predilection for St. Louis in spite of many hurtful counter-strokes. If she slapped me out of her presence, I would in the course of years sneak back at least for a look. . . .

Looking backward through the long trial of the years we can see that such a prediction or anticipation of her all-overtopping pre-eminence has never been fulfilled, that it was in fact a huge mirage floating before the vision of a great population across the empty desert of the future. So the interesting question in folk-psychology pushes up with no little importunity in the mind: What pre-disposed the St. Louis soul to such a phantasm? . . . For we all lay under that spell of enchantment for years, veritably a kind of civic megalomania, from which the levelest heads were not exempt—not even the solidest mind in the city, and the greatest mechanical genius of the country, if not of the world—I mean the river-spanning bridge-builder James B. Eads. On the opposite side of the mental scale we philosophers, supposed to be addicted to topsy-turvy idealism by nature and by training, and otherwise deemed not well-balanced of brain, took up with the glorious phantasmagory of our town's coming greatness, and philosophized it into a vast city ruled by philosophers, somewhat after the model of that ancient Neo-Platonic polity called Platonopolis. . . . If a doubter from some Eastern State or from Chicago should wag his tongue or even shake his head in question, there would at once burst up a violent eruption which would not only blaze white-hot but smell sulphurous with wrathful energy.

Such was to me the grand psychical phenomenon of St. Louis, pervasive, all-coercing, allowing no interrogation of its validity, certainly not when at its highest overflow. I remember my own discussions of the subject with skeptical outsiders; nothing could make me flare up internally sooner than the scoffing word of the belittler or even the quiet argument of the opposer. I shared completely, I may say devoutly, in this faith of the city's own soul as it went on dreaming of its multifarious grandeurs never to be realized.

Hence with some emphasis I jot down here in my life's narrative *The*

Great St. Louis Illusion, which spell-bound me and the city, as I remember the matter, in a sort of dream-world for a goodly number of years. To be sure on all other affairs we were sane enough, but on the one topic we would fly off into a lying dream. How many years did it last? As I recall the time and its craze of caprices, the Illusion began to show itself shortly after the close of the Civil War, and must have maintained its tyranny for some twelve or fifteen years. Undoubtedly it started to wane after its first full effulgence, but the spell was not completely broken till the census of 1880 smote the somnolescent city with the awakening thunder-words: population of St. Louis 350,000; of Chicago, 503,000.

I can still see the old lady jump up from her sleep at the bodeful figures, and challenge the correctness of the Washington enumeration, with no little wrath, though with an undershiver of anxiety. Not so easily would she renounce her long sweet Illusion; so she resolved to take her own census. The best mathematician of her University was called upon to oversee accurately the arithmetic of the thing, and to insert all the omitted names, of which a number had been dug up in the slums and elsewhere. The result, however, was a practical confirmation of the first dream-destroying figures. Then followed a corresponding overflow of Disillusion and of general dismay, at first running toward despair. The outside world and Chicago especially failed not to enjoy what they regarded as the denoument of a great civic comedy, funning and bemocking the disenchantment of the badly fooled victim at the end of the play. . . .

In its humiliated mood the town began to look and to trace the source of deception. Those tell-tale figures of the census showed that it had been outstripped for years in the grand race for the urban primacy of the West. The confession had to be made: Yes, already in 1870 our rival Chicago must have surpassed us in population, though the census of that year had made St. Louis the larger by some 15,000. But can it be possible? Where is this thing going to end? The newspapers start quickly on the scent with a prodigious outcry all over the country: a national fraud has been committed; the Great St. Louis Illusion has had the power somehow to transform the United States Census Bureau into the image of itself, turning the same to the Great Illusion of a Census, the whole of which begins to look insubstantial. But in 1880 the trick is uncovered, and there follows a long penitential era with heart's sorrow and confession, and with an access of despairful lethargy. One estimate now before me places these illusory inhabitants of St. Louis in 1870 at not less than 100,000, a ghostly multitude who were duly counted for our city but had never lived here or anywhere else. Such we may deem the supreme tricksy act of the Great St. Louis Illusion: it threatens to transform the nation, if not the whole world into a phantasm like unto itself. But mark the fateful consequence! Thus the city is lured to believe its own lie, manufactured by itself and imposed upon itself, and the Great Illusion wins ten years more of life, till the next Census.

Dare we here try to conceive for a moment what might otherwise have happened, in the interest of eternal verity? If our community had only accepted the truth of itself, whose oracle was not hard to find just across the River, and if it had set its house in order and had lived according to its own reality it might have been a different St. Louis with its city-soul still here in full energy at the center of a continent. But can the leopard change his spots? So in a kind of defiant megalomania our urban folk is destined to gorge itself a decade longer upon the very vanity of existence, upon its own self-made Illusion.

CHARLES A. LINDBERGH

THE SON OF C.A. LINDBERGH, SR., a prosperous Detroit attorney who later served in the U.S. Congress, and Evangeline Lodge Land, a schoolteacher, Charles Lindbergh (1902–1974) spent his life in many parts of the country—primarily Minnesota, New Jersey, Missouri, and Michigan. While each state lays claim to him in its own way, Lindbergh transcended the stature of regional hero and became a full-fledged American icon with his historic transatlantic flight in 1927.

A handsome, restless youth who eschewed academic pursuits and gravitated toward daredevil activities and mechanical innovation, Lindbergh initially came to St. Louis in 1923 to attend air races at Lambert Field, while he awaited admission to the Army Air Corps. After graduating first in his class from the Air Corps, Lindbergh returned to St. Louis and became chief pilot of Robertson Aircraft Corporation. While at Robertson, Lindbergh organized and flew successful round-trip St. Louis–Chicago mail runs and began to contemplate more dramatic possibilities for long-distance flight. In less than a year, Lindbergh inspired a small group of powerful St. Louis businessmen to bankroll the construction of a plane that would be capable of flying nonstop from New York to Paris. On May 20, 1927, Lindbergh left Roosevelt Field and arrived in Paris thirty-three hours later to screaming hordes who damaged his plane and stole his meticulous log of the historic flight.

Lindbergh's successful daring mission and his movie star looks catapulted him into a perpetual limelight and permanent celebrity status that was daunting, even by today's standards. After May 1927, every aspect of his life was scrutinized by the media—from his personal life to his politics. In 1932, Charles and Anne Morrow Lindbergh's first-born son, Charles, Jr., was kidnapped and murdered, a tragedy that received ceaseless and sensational international press coverage that showed little respect for the family's grief.

A complex, enigmatic figure, Lindbergh has been the subject of dozens of books. Some of the contradiction and mystery surrounding Charles Lindbergh's aura can be summarized thus: in 1928 he received the Congressional Medal of Honor; ten years later, old friends were calling him a Nazi sympathizer. Whoever the *real* Charles Lindbergh was, St. Louis continues to love and claim him as a native son. Apparently, Lindbergh felt the same way about the city of St. Louis. In the summer of 1927, Lindbergh donated more than fifteen thousand artifacts—personal items and gifts he received after his flight—to the Missouri Historical Society, where they remain the most popular collection in the institution's vast holdings.

Although in his articles on aviation and other shorter works Lindbergh exhibited ability as a writer, the literary world was awed upon publication of his autobiography, *The Spirit of St. Louis,* in 1953. Lindbergh had worked on the book intermittently since 1938 and relied largely on his own memory of the events recounted. In his eloquent preface, Lindbergh writes, "Searching memory might be compared to throwing the beam of a strong light, from your hilltop camp site, back over the road you traveled by day." As one well-acquainted with groping through the darkness to find his destination, Lindbergh again was successful in his mission: *The Spirit of St. Louis* won the Pulitzer Prize for Biography in 1954.

In the following excerpt from that work, Lindbergh describes his efforts to garner the financial support for his transatlantic flight from a small circle of St. Louis businessmen, who believed—as he did—in the future of aviation.

FROM *THE SPIRIT OF ST. LOUIS*

Lambert Field lies in farming country about ten miles northwest of the St. Louis business district. A pilot, flying high above its sodded acres, sees the Missouri River in the distance, bending north and then east to spew its muddy waters into the clearer Mississippi. The city nestles vaguely in its pall of smoke, a different textured patch contrasting with fields and forests. Southward, wooded foothills step up toward the distant Ozark Mountains.

Lambert Field is named after Major Albert Bond Lambert, who commanded a school for balloon pilots during the World War, and who is among the most active leaders in Midwestern aviation. Selected for the site of the National Air Races in 1923, it was enlarged to present size by planking over a little stream which cut through the eastern end. There are no runways, but the clay sod is good surface for any size of aircraft during summer months.

In freezing weather, gusty winds and deepening ruts make operation difficult.

Lambert Field's major commercial activity is carried on by the Robertson Aircraft Corporation, built and managed by the Robertson brothers, Bill, Frank, and Dan. A little, stove-heated office, two frame warehouses for airplane and engine parts, and half of a civilian hangar, house its operations. The Corporation's major income results from the sale of reconditioned Army training planes, engines, and spares—all placed on the market at extraordinarily low prices.

Except on week ends, when the National Guard squadron comes out in force, there are seldom more than a half-dozen pilots on the field, and the chief activity consists of training students. One can always make a few extra dollars and build up flying time by instructing. Besides there is no better way to learn the tricks of air and aircraft.

Those of us who instruct know Lambert Field as a child knows the details of his home and yard. We know the erosions on its shallow slope, the downdraft over Anglum, the depressions where drain tiles have caved in. In every azimuth there's a reminder of some past incident of flight. One pushes his plane out of a hangar that housed the Curtiss Navy racer. (It left its source of sound somewhere in the air behind as it flashed around the pylons.) At this spot, just beyond the line, George Harmon was killed when his pilot stalled on a left chandelle. (I helped cut him out of the wreckage —unconscious but still alive. He died on the road to the hospital.) Against an east wind, one takes off over the cornfield where Captain Bill spun in after his National Guard Jenny's engine failed. (By some miracle he wasn't hurt, and climbed out of the crash before we reached him.) There's where Smith and Swengrosh died when they lost a wing in a loop. There's where Frank Robertson and Pres Sultan clipped the top from a big cottonwood tree, without even cracking a spar. (The trunk was eight inches in diameter where their Jenny snapped it off.) On the side of that ditch is where Bud Gurney broke his arm in a parachute spot-landing contest. The pigpen by the white farmhouse is where O. E. Scott once nosed over.

How Scotty loves to tell that story! His engine cut on take-off. He wasn't high enough to turn. Straight ahead lay the pigpen, and in it he landed. Muck caught his wheels and whipped him upside down. He found himself hanging on the safety belt, his head two or three feet above a stinking wallow, "with all those pigs squealing and nudging in around me, just as though I was one of 'em!"

Scotty is manager of the field, and its oldest and most cautious pilot. He owns an OX-5 Standard with wings that haven't been re-covered for so many years that you can poke your finger through their varnish-stiffened fabric. When weather is good his plane is always on the line, ready to carry any passenger who'll pay five dollars for a ride. Scotty is also pilot of the new Travel Air which was bought last year by Harold Bixby, a St. Louis banker who became interested in aviation. With an OXX-6 engine, deep blue fuselage, and shining, nickel-plated struts, it's the most modern and attractive plane in our hangars.

Scotty has let me fly the Travel Air several times, and introduced me to its owner. To us on the field it's more than a symbol of better aircraft to come. It's a link with the powerful business world. Bixby is one of the men who run the great city of St. Louis, yet he looks on flyers as something more than acrobats and daredevils. Judging from a more stable viewpoint, he too believes that aviation has a future. His Travel Air, resting on the line, is like a signpost assuring us that the road we follow leads toward fertile lands.

Since Bixby bought his plane several of the city's businessmen have started flying. There's Harry Knight the broker, who's taking lessons. And Earl Thompson the insurance executive, with his golden-winged Laird. I've given him a little instruction now and then. Thompson is the kind of man who'll listen to my ideas. I've often talked to him about aviation, and he knows that I can fly. I'll telephone tomorrow for an appointment. Meanwhile, I'll get a pad of paper and outline a plan of action.

ST. LOUIS—NEW YORK—PARIS FLIGHT

ACTION

1. Plan
2. Propaganda
3. Backers
4. Equipment
5. Co-operation of manufacturers
6. Accessory information
7. Point of departure
8. Advertising

ADVANTAGES

1. Revive St. Louis interest in aviation
2. Advertise St. Louis as an aviation city
3. Aid in making America first in the air
4. Promote nation-wide interest in aeronautics
5. Demonstrate perfection of modern equipment

RESULTS

1. Successful completion, winning $25,000 prize to cover expense
2. Complete failure

CO-OPERATION

1. Plane manufacturers
2. Motor manufacturers
3. Weather Department
4. State Department
5. Newspapers
6. Steamships

EQUIPMENT

1. Raft (sail)
2. Rockets
3. Clothing (waterproof)
4. Condensed food
5. Still (water)

MAPS

1. Prevailing winds
2. Coast and interior
3. Islands
4. Steamship travel

LANDMARKS

1. Islands
2. List of coast towns
3. Index to towns
4. Characteristic names
5. Characteristic terrain

That list will do for a start. I'll add to it, improve it, and clarify it as time passes.

I've begun work on my propaganda, too. That shouldn't be difficult, because fact and adventure are both on my side. I feel sure there's a tremendous future for the commerce of the air. I reread the first paragraph I've drafted.

St. Louis is ideally situated to become an aviation city.—We have one of the finest commercial airports in the United States, and we will undoubtedly become a hub of the national airways of the future. Some day airliners on their way from New Orleans to Chicago, and from Los Angeles to New York, will be landing on our airport.—

That should interest people, especially the businessmen. And I've started working on the schedule and cost of an air-mail line to New York by way of Indianapolis, Columbus, and Pittsburgh. Even with DHs we'd be able to make the eastward trip within twelve hours, including time for stops. With a Bellanca—well, that's what this propaganda's for. I must show what can be accomplished with aircraft like the Bellanca.

I push the bell button at No. 1 Hortense Place, and step back on the porch to wait. Earl Thompson said he could see me at once at his office or spend an evening with me at his house the next week. I chose the latter. It seemed less likely that one could sell a flight across the ocean at an office desk. Besides, time builds dignity and thought.

A maid shows me to the living room. Mr. Thompson comes in. We shake hands. He motions me to a chair. I feel uncomfortable in the soft upholstery. I don't seem to fit into a city parlor. It would be easier to talk on the flying field. There, the sound of engines and the contours of wings would surround my arguments with factual elements of flight. When one sees a plane suspended in the sky, it's more difficult to use such words as "impractical" or "can't be done." Now I've got to sit inside a carpeted and curtained room and believe as well as convince another, that an airplane can take me, without landing, between New York and Paris.

"Mr. Thompson," I start out, "I've come to ask your advice about a project I'm considering."

He smiles and nods encouragement.

"You've heard about the Orteig prize of $25,000 for a nonstop flight between New York and Paris," I continue. "I think a modern plane can make that flight. I'd like to try it. It would show people what airplanes can do. It would advance aviation, and it would advertise St. Louis."

I go on to explain that I want to get a group of businessmen behind me to finance the project and give me the prestige I'll need in dealing with aircraft manufacturers.

"I can furnish $2000 myself," I say. "But the right kind of plane will probably cost at least ten thousand."

Mr. Thompson's face becomes serious. "What kind of plane would you get for that flight, Captain?" he asks.

"I think the Wright-Bellanca could probably make it," I tell him.

"But the Wright-Bellanca is a land plane—and it has only one engine, hasn't it?" His voice is as disturbed as his question. "You aren't thinking of flying over the ocean in a single-engined airplane, are you? I think it's a very interesting idea, but I'd want you to have a flying boat, or a plane with enough engines so you wouldn't have to land in the water if one of them stopped. Have you considered using a three-engined Fokker, like Commander Byrd's?"

I was afraid of that. Businessmen are always conservative. But at least he's taking my idea seriously.

"Well," I argue, "a flying boat can't take off with enough fuel, and a tri-motored Fokker would cost a huge amount of money. I don't know what they sell for; but I'm afraid it would be at least $30,000 and it might be considerably more. Besides, I'm not sure three engines would really add much to safety on a flight like that. You see the plane would be overloaded with fuel anyway. There'd be three times the chance of engine failure; and if one of them stopped over the ocean, you probably couldn't get back to land with the other two. A multiengined plane is awfully big and heavy. [This is my trump card.] You know Fonck had three engines, but that didn't help him any when his landing gear gave way. A single-engined plane might even be safer, everything considered."

"Well, you know a lot more about airplanes than I do," Mr. Thompson says. "But I don't like the idea of a single engine out over the ocean. If you really want to make that flight, I think you ought to consider getting a tri-motored plane, like a Fokker."

We spend the entire evening talking about aircraft and the New York–to–Paris flight. Mr. Thompson is definitely interested. He's encouraging, but cautious and greatly concerned about the risks involved. After all, his business is insurance. He has to be conservative. . . .

"Slim, you ought not to be running around worrying about raising money. You've got to put all your attention on that flight if you're going to make it."

I'm talking to Harry Knight in his brokerage office at Fourth and Olive Streets. I've come to ask his advice in regard to other businessmen I might approach with my project, and in the hope that he'll take some part himself. Harry Knight is president of the St. Louis Flying Club. I met him three or four times on the airfield last summer when he was taking flying lessons from Cloyd Clevenger. He's a stocky, abrupt young man in a brown suit, not much older than myself. He doesn't believe in wasting too much time by being tactful. I fully expected to be turned down at once, or put off with one of those evasive, business executives' statements about wanting to think the matter over. But:

"Let me talk to a friend of mine in the bank," he continues. "Maybe we can take care of the financial end for you. How much money is it going to take?"

His words strike like the flash of an airfield's beacon on a stormy night. Then I'm not lost—here's help, someone to share responsibility.

"If we can get the plane and engine manufacturers to stand part of the expense, I think $10,000 would be enough," I tell him. "If we can't get them to take part, it might cost as much as $15,000 to buy the plane and engine, and make the flight."

"You're talking about a single-engine plane. Wouldn't a trimotor be better for that kind of flight?" he asks.

I start in with my old arguments again:

"It would cost $29,000 to get a trimotored plane from Bellanca. The Fokker Company wants $90,000 for one of theirs. And I don't know how long it would take to build one. Multiengined planes are more complicated; there are more things likely to go wrong with them. Besides, the greatest danger lies in weather, and in take-off with a full load—not in engine failure—Whirlwind engines are averaging 9000 hours to a failure. As a matter of fact, I think I'd rather make the flight with one engine than with three, to say nothing of the difference in cost. A big ship is hard to handle in thick weather—"

Knight suddenly swings around in his chair, and picks up the telephone.

"Get me Harold Bixby at the State National Bank," he says—"Bix, how about coming over here for a few minutes?—sure you can—okay—in my office."

"He's only a block up the street," Knight tells me after hanging up, "—Fourth and Locust. You know he's president of the Chamber of Commerce."

Within ten minutes Bixby knocks on the door. He's a man you like right away—smiling and full of humor. But his penetrating brown eyes size you up and warn you that you'd better pass inspection. You know you can depend on Harold Bixby, and that if he can't depend on *you* he won't be around you very long.

Harry Knight outlines my project for flying an airplane from St. Louis to New York to Paris.

"You think a plane with a Whirlwind engine can make a flight like that?" Bixby asks.

"Yes, sir," I answer. "Bellanca says his can make Paris from New York with a good reserve of fuel."

"How much does a Bellanca cost?"

"I don't know," I answer. "But I'm not sure I can buy one." I tell about my trip to New York and my talks with the Wright Corporation and Bellanca.

"You'd have to have a new plane built, then?" Knight asks.

"It might work to put an oversize wing on an existing fuselage," I tell him. "That shouldn't add very much to the cost. Besides, there's not time to do a lot of building. I want to be ready to start as soon as the weather breaks next spring."

"Why wouldn't the Wright Company furnish an engine for the advertising they'd get?"

"They might," I reply, "but I don't think we can count on it. They didn't make any offer in that direction when I was at Paterson. Of course then I wasn't in a very good position to trade. If I can show them we mean business, I think we can at least get a reduction in price."

"You said you already have some money lined up. Who's in this project with you?"

"Yes, sir. I can put in two thousand dollars myself. Major Lambert has promised to put in a thousand. Earl Thompson and Bill Robertson say they'll take part, but I haven't talked to them about amounts."

"Slim, don't you think you ought to have a plane with more than one engine for that kind of flight?" Bixby asks.

Harry Knight laughs. "That's what I asked him, Bix; but he doesn't think it would be much safer."

"Suppose one of the engines cuts out halfway across the ocean," I put in. "I couldn't get to shore with the other two."

"No, but you might be able to stay up long enough to find a ship you could land beside," Bixby argues.

"I can't see myself circling around over the water looking for a boat," I say. "You know, I don't believe a flight to Paris would be any more dangerous than a winter on the mail line. If one of our DH engines cuts on a bad night, it's pretty serious too—and we've only got rebuilt Liberties. None of the lines coming in to Chicago has multiengine planes, you know—except when Ford makes those experimental runs. A pilot can't fly at all without taking some risk. I've weighed my chances pretty carefully—"

Bixby breaks in. "Yes, you've only got a life to lose, Slim. But don't forget, I've got a reputation to lose."

"The Army's 'round-the-world' planes had only single engines," I say, searching desperately for new arguments.

"Yes, but half of them didn't make it," Bixby counters. "And they had the whole government behind them." Then, instead of following through the opening I've given him, he adds, "You let us think about this for a day or two, and talk to some of our friends. If you're going to make the flight, we've got to get started right away. Come down and see me next Wednesday. How about ten A.M., at my office?"

"Any time at all. I'll be there at ten."

I can hardly believe what I'm hearing. I hoped, at most, to get a pledge for another thousand dollars. I never dreamed of finding anyone with sufficient interest to suggest taking over the entire financial burden. . . .

"What would you think of naming it the *Spirit of St. Louis*?"

Bixby's question strikes vaguely through my ears. I'm staring at the shredded and color-stained figures on a slip of paper in my hand—FIFTEEN THOUSAND DOLLARS. This slip can be traded for the Wright-Bellanca, and this slip is mine—"Pay to the order of Charles A. Lindbergh" it says on the back.

The *Spirit of St. Louis*—it's a good name. "All right, let's call it the *Spirit of St. Louis*." My eyes go back to the check. "I didn't know you were going to make this out to me personally," I say.

Bixby laughs. "Well, Slim, Harry and I decided that if we couldn't trust you with a check, we ought not to take part in this project at all."

"When do you plan on starting back to New York?" Knight asks.

"I'll take the train this afternoon," I tell him.

"We'll start setting up a *Spirit of St. Louis* organization while you're away," Bixby says. "Let us know as soon as you can when you'll be here with the plane. How long do you think it will take to put the tanks in?"

"Maybe I can fly back while the tanks are being made," I reply. "They can be installed later on. I'll try to land the Bellanca on Lambert Field within a week."

"Grand. We'll be out to meet you—Good luck!"

T. S. ELIOT

THOMAS STEARNS ELIOT (1888–1965) was born at 2635 Locust Street in St. Louis, in a home owned by his grandfather, William Greenleaf Eliot, who founded Mary Institute and Washington University. Eliot's father, Henry Ware Eliot, was a successful brick manufacturer, and his mother, Charlotte Champe Stearns, a poet and social reformer. The Eliot family later moved to 4446 Westminster Place.

Although Eliot is a favorite son of St. Louis, he left the city in 1905 at age sixteen to attend the Milton Academy and returned infrequently. However, the year before he left St. Louis, Eliot paid multiple visits to the 1904 World's Fair. After graduating from Harvard University, Eliot moved to England and became an adamant expatriate, describing himself as "Anglican in religion and Royalist in politics." While generating poetry, criticism, and drama that would establish him as one of the most influential writers in the English language, Eliot earned a living as a teacher, a banker, and, finally, a publisher. At the time of his death, he was director of Faber and Faber, an English publishing house.

While Eliot produced outstanding works in a variety of genres, he was above all else an innovator as a poet, as influential in the development of modern verse as Walt Whitman. In the longest view, Eliot is remembered for the voice in his "serious" poems: laconic but elegant, ironic but intense, and full of a self-conscious erudition that can seem alternately witty and condescending. His subjects—the disintegration of the personality in the early poems, the disintegration of society in "The Waste Land," and the emergence of the possibility of reintegration and salvation in the later *Four Quartets*—represent a personal and emotional response to the stages of his life's journey rather than a philosophical perspective. In addition to the multitude of awards he received during his lifetime, Eliot received the Order of Merit from King George VI and the Nobel Prize in Literature in 1948.

Although Eliot does not mention St. Louis specifically in any of his major works, he claimed that the area and the Mississippi River had a profound impact on him. In fact, the name of the main character in Eliot's 1917 masterpiece, "The Love Song of J. Alfred Prufrock," comes from the name of a furniture store located at 1104 Olive Street. In the first of the following three selections, a 1923 letter from Eliot to a former school chum, Edna McCourt, Eliot expresses amazement that his work is known in his hometown. In the second piece, a letter from Eliot to the St. Louis *Post-Dispatch* editorial writer Marquis Childs dated 1930, Eliot reminisces about the St. Louis of his childhood. Lastly, "The Dry Salvages" (1941) from the *Four Quartets*, which begins with Eliot's famous metaphor of the river as a "strong brown god," is an apt description of the Mississippi River and goes on to contemplate life as eternal suspension in a continuous current that asks us to "consider the future/And the past with an equal mind."

LETTER TO EDNA MCCOURT

JANUARY 12, 1923

9, Clarence Gate Gardens,
London, N.W.1,

Dear Miss McCourt,

Thank you very much indeed for your kind letter of December 17th. It is rare for me to receive letters of this sort, and this is the first letter I have received from my native city. Indeed, it is the first intimation that I have had that my work is known there, and you must know that in spite of the admonition of the old proverb, or perhaps because of it, a prophet always particularly hankers after honour in his own country. At least, this is true of minor prophets.

It is many years since I have been in St. Louis. Men's memories are short, especially in a growing and changing town, and I doubt if many of those who owe most to the university there even know that it was named after my grandfather (and later changed at his insistence) or have ever noticed his portrait hanging there. But I am very proud of all that he did for the city and for all that he did for the nation at the most critical moment in its existence. And these feelings give me still more pleasure in having this letter from you to which to reply.

LETTER TO *ST. LOUIS POST-DISPATCH*

AUGUST 8, 1930

Marquis W. Childs Esqre.,
Editorial Department
St. Louis Post-Dispatch,
St. Louis, Mo.

Dear Sir,

I have your letter of August [sic] 22nd 1930; and am very happy to comply as well as I can with your request. But it is very puzzling to try to condense a biography, an "attitude", and an estimate of how St. Louis affected me, into a paragraph.

As I spent the first 16 years of my life in St. Louis, with the exception of summer holidays in Maine and Massachusetts, and a visit to Louisiana which I do not remember, it is self-evident that St. Louis affected me more deeply than any other environment has done. These 16 years were spent in a house at 2635 Locust Street, since demolished. This house stood on part of a large piece of land which had belonged to my grandfather, on which there had been negro quarters also in his time; in my childhood my grandmother still lived at a house 2660 Washington Avenue, round the corner. The earliest personal influence I remember besides that of my parents, was an Irish nursemaid named Annie Dunne, to whom I was greatly attached; she used to take me to my first school, a Mrs. Lockwood's which was a little way out beyond Vandeventer Place. The River also made a deep impression on me; and it was a great treat to be taken down to the Eades Bridge in flood time.

Then I was sent naturally to the now defunct Smith Academy, which was then somewhere at the lower end of Washington Avenue; I graduated from there with some distinction, having produced the Class Poem, which even now seems to me not bad. I remember with particular regard Mme. Jouvet-Kaufmann, the French mistress, who gave me my first taste for that language, Mr. Roger Hatch, the English master, who encouraged my first attempts at verse, and Dr. Jackson, the Latin master—the third and last subject in which I attained any proficiency. I left St. Louis in 1905, to go to Milton Academy in Massachusetts; and apart from a few Christmas holidays, I have never seen St. Louis again.

I do not quite know what else to say. But I find that as one gets on in middle life the strength of early associations, and the intensity of early impressions, becomes more evident; and many little things, long forgotten, recur. The occasions on which my nurse took me with her to the little Catholic Church which then stood on the corner of Locust Street and Jefferson Avenue, when she went to make her devotions; spring violets, and the rather mangy buffalo which I photographed in Forest Park; the steamboats blowing in New Year's day; and so on. And I feel that there is something in having passed one's childhood beside the big river, which is incommunicable to those who have not. Of course my people were Northeners and New Englanders, and of course I have spent many years out of America altogether; but Missouri and the Mississippi have made a deeper impression on me than any other part of the world. Besides, my father gave a good part of his life, and my grandfather the greater part, to the service of St. Louis and the State; and my mother took a leading part in Juvenile Court Reform there; and they all lie in Bellefontaine now.

THE DRY SALVAGES

I

I do not know much about gods; but I think that the river
Is a strong brown god—sullen, untamed and intractable,
Patient to some degree, at first recognised as a frontier;
Useful, untrustworthy, as a conveyor of commerce;
Then only a problem confronting the builder of bridges.
The problem once solved, the brown god is almost forgotten
By the dwellers in cities—ever, however, implacable,
Keeping his seasons and rages, destroyer, reminder
Of what men choose to forget. Unhonoured, unpropitiated
By worshippers of the machine, but waiting, watching and waiting.
His rhythm was present in the nursery bedroom,
In the rank ailanthus of the April dooryard,
In the smell of grapes on the autumn table,
And the evening circle in the winter gaslight.

The river is within us, the sea is all about us;
The sea is the land's edge also, the granite
Into which it reaches, the beaches where it tosses
Its hints of earlier and other creation:
The starfish, the horseshoe crab, the whale's backbone;
The pools where it offers to our curiosity
The more delicate algae and the sea anemone.
It tosses up our losses, the torn seine,
The shattered lobsterpot, the broken oar
And the gear of foreign dead men. The sea has many voices,
Many gods and many voices.
                                        The salt is on the briar rose,
The fog is in the fir trees.
                                        The sea howl
And the sea yelp, are different voices
Often together heard: the whine in the rigging,
The menace and caress of wave that breaks on water,
The distant rote in the granite teeth,
And the wailing warning from the approaching headland
Are all sea voices, and the heaving groaner
Rounded homewards, and the seagull:
And under the oppression of the silent fog
The tolling bell
Measures time not our time, rung by the unhurried
Ground swell, a time
Older than the time of chronometers, older
Than time counted by anxious worried women
Lying awake, calculating the future,
Trying to unweave, unwind, unravel
And piece together the past and the future,
Between midnight and dawn, when the past is all deception,
The future futureless, before the morning watch
When time stops and time is never ending;
And the ground swell, that is and was from the beginning.
Clangs
The bell.

II

Where is there an end of it, the soundless wailing,
The silent withering of autumn flowers
Dropping their petals and remaining motionless;
Where is there an end to the drifting wreckage,
The prayer of the bone on the beach, the unprayable
Prayer at the calamitous annunciation?

There is no end, but addition: the trailing
Consequence of further days and hours,
While emotion takes to itself the emotionless
Years of living among the breakage
Of what was believed in as the most reliable—
And therefore the fittest for renunciation.

There is the final addition, the failing
Pride or resentment at failing powers,
The unattached devotion which might pass for devotionless,
In a drifting boat with a slow leakage,
The silent listening to the undeniable
Clamour of the bell of the last annunciation.

Where is the end of them, the fishermen sailing
Into the wind's tail, where the fog cowers?
We cannot think of a time that is oceanless
Or of an ocean not littered with wastage
Or of a future that is not liable
Like the past, to have no destination.

We have to think of them as forever bailing,
Setting and hauling, while the North East lowers
Over shallow banks unchanging and erosionless
Or drawing their money, drying sails at dockage;
Not as making a trip that will be unpayable
For a haul that will not bear examination.

There is no end of it, the voiceless wailing,
No end to the withering of withered flowers,
To the movement of pain that is painless and motionless,

To the drift of the sea and the drifting wreckage,
The bone's prayer to Death its God. Only the hardly, barely prayable
Prayer of the one Annunciation.

It seems, as one becomes older,
That the past has another pattern, and ceases to be a mere sequence—
Or even development: the latter a partial fallacy,
Encouraged by superficial notions of evolution,
Which becomes, in the popular mind, a means of disowning the past.
The moments of happiness—not the sense of well-being,
Fruition, fulfilment, security or affection,
Or even a very good dinner, but the sudden illumination—
We had the experience but missed the meaning,
And approach to the meaning restores the experience
In a different form, beyond any meaning
We can assign to happiness. I have said before
That the past experience revived in the meaning
Is not the experience of one life only
But of many generations—not forgetting
Something that is probably quite ineffable:
The backward look behind the assurance
Of recorded history, the backward half-look
Over the shoulder, towards the primitive terror.
Now, we come to discover that the moments of agony
(Whether, or not, due to misunderstanding,
Having hoped for the wrong things or dreaded the wrong things,
Is not in question) are likewise permanent
With such permanence as time has. We appreciate this better
In the agony of others, nearly experienced,
Involving ourselves, than in our own.
For our own past is covered by the currents of action,
But the torment of others remains an experience
Unqualified, unworn by subsequent attrition.
People change, and smile: but the agony abides.
Time the destroyer is time the preserver,
Like the river with its cargo of dead negroes, cows and chicken coops,
The bitter apple and the bite in the apple.

And the ragged rock in the restless waters,
Waves wash over it, fogs conceal it;
On a halcyon day it is merely a monument,
In navigable weather it is always a seamark
To lay a course by: but in the sombre season
Or the sudden fury, is what it always was.

III

I sometimes wonder if that is what Krishna meant—
Among other things—or one way of putting the same thing:
That the future is a faded song, a Royal Rose or a lavender spray
Of wistful regret for those who are not yet here to regret,
Pressed between yellow leaves of a book that has never been opened.
And the way up is the way down, the way forward is the way back.
You cannot face it steadily, but this thing is sure,
That time is no healer: the patient is no longer here.
When the train starts, and the passengers are settled
To fruit, periodicals and business letters
(And those who saw them off have left the platform)
Their faces relax from grief into relief,
To the sleepy rhythm of a hundred hours.
Fare forward, travellers! not escaping from the past
Into different lives, or into any future;
You are not the same people who left that station
Or who will arrive at any terminus,
While the narrowing rails slide together behind you;
And on the deck of the drumming liner
Watching the furrow that widens behind you,
You shall not think "the past is finished"
Or "the future is before us."
At nightfall, in the rigging and the aerial,
Is a voice descanting (though not to the ear,
The murmuring shell of time, and not in any language)
"Fare forward, you who think that you are voyaging;
You are not those who saw the harbour
Receding, or those who will disembark.
Here between the hither and the farther shore

While time is withdrawn, consider the future
And the past with an equal mind.
At the moment which is not of action or inaction
You can receive this: 'on whatever sphere of being
The mind of a man may be intent
At the time of death'—that is the one action
(And the time of death is every moment)
Which shall fructify in the lives of others:
And do not think of the fruit of action.
Fare forward.
O voyagers, O seamen,
You who come to port, and you whose bodies
Will suffer the trial and judgement of the sea,
Or whatever event, this is your real destination."
So Krishna, as when be admonished Arjuna
On the field of battle.
Not fare well,
But fare forward, voyagers.

IV

Lady, whose shrine stands on the promontory,
Pray for all those who are in ships, those
Whose business has to do with fish, and
Those concerned with every lawful traffic
And those who conduct them.

Repeat a prayer also on behalf of
Women who have seen their sons or husbands
Setting forth, and not returning:
Figlia del tuo figlio,
Queen of Heaven.

Also pray for those who were in ships, and
Ended their voyage on the sand, in the sea's lips
Or in the dark throat which will not reject them
Or wherever cannot reach them the sound of the sea bell's
Perpetual angelus.

V

To communicate with Mars, converse with spirits,
To report the behaviour of the sea monster,
Describe the horoscope, haruspicate or scry,
Observe disease in signatures, evoke
Biography from the wrinkles of the palm
And tragedy from fingers; release omens
By sortilege, or tea leaves, riddle the inevitable
With playing cards, fiddle with pentagrams
Or barbituric acids, or dissect
The recurrent image into pre-conscious terrors—
To explore the womb, or tomb, or dreams; all these are usual
Pastimes and drugs, and features of the press:
And always will be, some of them especially
When there is distress of nations and perplexity
Whether on the shores of Asia, or in the Edgware Road.
Men's curiosity searches past and future
And clings to that dimension. But to apprehend
The point of intersection of the timeless
With time, is an occupation for the saint—
No occupation either, but something given
And taken, in a lifetime's death in love,
Ardour and selflessness and self-surrender.
For most of us, there is only the unattended
Moment, the moment in and out of time,
The distraction fit, lost in a shaft of sunlight,
The wild thyme unseen, or the winter lightning
Or the waterfall, or music heard so deeply
That it is not heard at all, but you are the music
While the music lasts. These are only hints and guesses,
Hints followed by guesses; and the rest
Is prayer, observance, discipline, thought and action.
The hint half guessed, the gift half understood, is Incarnation.
Here the impossible union.
Of spheres of existence is actual,
Here the past and future
Are conquered, and reconciled,

Where action were otherwise movement
Of that which is only moved
And has in it no source of movement—
Driven by daemonic, chthonic
Powers. And right action is freedom
From past and future also.
For most of us, this is the aim
Never here to be realised;
Who are only undefeated
Because we have gone on trying;
We, content at the last
If our temporal reversion nourish
(Not too far from the yew-tree)
The life of significant soil.

W. E. B. DU BOIS

NOVELIST, POET, ESSAYIST, and civil rights pioneer, William Edward Burghardt Du Bois (1868–1963) is arguably the most famous black intellectual and scholar in the history of the Western world. Born of mixed French, Dutch, and African parentage in Barrington, Massachusetts, Du Bois received degrees from Fisk University and Harvard, where he was the first African American to earn a Ph.D.

At the beginning of the twentieth century, Du Bois, a harsh critic of Booker T. Washington's gradualist stance on achieving racial equality, emerged as the country's leading spokesperson in the arena of racial politics. In 1905, he and other black leaders met near Niagara Falls to formulate a plan for equal opportunity and freedom of speech for blacks. "The Niagara Movement" ultimately led to the founding of the NAACP in 1909, and for the next twenty-five years, Du Bois served as director of research for that organization and editor of its magazine, *Crisis*. In July 1917, after the East St. Louis race riot, W. E. B. Du Bois and Martha Gruening, a white colleague, were sent to that city by the NAACP to investigate the incident and report their findings. A portion of their resultant report appears in *"Ain't But a Place": An Anthology of African American Writings about St. Louis*, edited by Gerald Early (Missouri Historical Society Press, 1998).

Although he essentially believed in the power of the social sciences to solve the race problem, Du Bois became increasingly disenchanted with the lack of progress in civil rights in the United States. Through the 1950s, he became an advocate of socialism and active in world peace movements. Two years before his death, Du Bois joined the American Communist Party and emigrated to Ghana; he died a citizen of that country.

In the following essay, Du Bois returns to the topic of East St. Louis, addressing racism and the 1917 riot not only in historical terms, but also with elegant, metaphorical prose that pays homage to apocalyptic prophesy.

OF WORK AND WEALTH

St. Louis sprawls where mighty rivers meet,—as broad as Philadelphia, but three stories high instead of two, with wider streets and dirtier atmosphere, over the dull-brown of wide, calm rivers. The city overflows into the valleys of Illinois and lies there, writhing under its grimy cloud. The other city is dusty and hot beyond all dream,—a feverish Pittsburg in the Mississippi Valley—a great, ruthless, terrible thing! It is the sort that crushes man and invokes some living super-man,—a giant of things done, a clang of awful accomplishment.

Three men came wandering across this place. They were neither kings nor wise men, but they came with every significance—perhaps even greater—than that which the kings bore in the days of old. There was one who came from the North,—brawny and riotous with energy, a man of concentrated power, who held all the thunderbolts of modern capital in his great fists and made flour and meat, iron and steel, cunning chemicals, wood, paint and paper, transforming to endless tools a disemboweled earth. He was one who saw nothing, knew nothing, sought nothing but the making and buying of that which sells; who out from the magic of his hand rolled over miles of iron road, ton upon ton of food and metal and wood, of coal and oil and lumber, until the thronging of knotted ways in East and real St. Louis was like the red, festering ganglia of some mighty heart.

Then from the East and called by the crash of thunderbolts and forked-flame came the Unwise Man,—unwise by the theft of endless ages, but as human as anything God ever made. He was the slave for the miracle maker. It was he that the thunderbolts struck and electrified into gasping energy. The rasp of his hard breathing shook the midnights of all this endless valley and the pulse of his powerful arms set the great nation to trembling.

And then, at last, out of the South, like a still, small voice, came the third man,—black, with great eyes and greater memories; hesitantly eager and yet with the infinite softness and ancient calm which come from that eternal race whose history is not the history of a day, but of endless ages. Here, surely, was fit meeting-place for these curiously intent forces, for these epoch-making and age-twisting forces, for these human feet on their super-human errands.

Yesterday I rode in East St. Louis. It is the kind of place one quickly recognizes,—tireless and with no restful green of verdure; hard and uneven of street; crude, cold, and even hateful of aspect; conventional, of course, in its business quarter, but quickly beyond one sees the ruts and the hollows, the stench of ill-tamed sewerage, unguarded railroad crossings, saloons outnumbering churches and churches catering to saloons; homes impudently strait and new, prostitutes free and happy, gamblers in paradise, the town "wide open," shameless and frank; great factories pouring out stench, filth, and flame—these and all other things so familiar in the world market places, where industry triumphs over thought and products overwhelm men. May I tell, too, how yesterday I rode in this city past flame-swept walls and over gray ashes; in streets almost wet with blood and beside ruins, where the bones of dead men new bleached peered out at me in sullen wonder?

Across the river, in the greater city, where bronze St. Louis,—that just and austere king—looks with angry, fear-swept eyes down from the rolling heights of Forest Park, which knows him not nor heeds him, there is something of the same thing, but this city is larger and older and the forces of evil have had some curbing from those who have seen the vision and panted for life; but eastward from St. Louis there is a land of no taxes for great industries; there is a land where you may buy grafting politicians at far less rate than you would pay for franchises or privileges in a modern town. There, too, you may escape the buying of indulgences from the great terminal fist, which squeezes industry out of St. Louis. In fact, East St. Louis is a paradise for high and frequent dividends and for the piling up of wealth to be spent in St. Louis and Chicago and New York and when the world is sane again, across the seas.

So the Unwise Men pouring out of the East,—falling, scrambling, rushing into America at the rate of a million a year,—ran, walked, and crawled to this maelstrom of the workers. They garnered higher wage than ever they had before, but not all of it came in cash. A part, and an insidious part, was given to them transmuted into whiskey, prostitutes, and games of chance. They laughed and disported themselves. God! Had not their mothers wept enough? It was a good town. There was no veil of hypocrisy here, but a wickedness, frank, ungilded, and open. To be sure, there were things sometimes to reveal the basic savagery and thin veneer. Once, for instance, a man was lynched for brawling on the public square of the county seat; once a mayor who sought to "clean up" was publicly assassinated; always there was theft and rumors of theft, until St. Clair County was a hissing in good men's ears; but always, too, there were good wages and jolly hoodlums and unchecked wassail of Saturday nights. Gamblers, big and little, rioted in East St. Louis. The little gamblers used cards and roulette wheels and filched the weekly wage of the workers. The greater gamblers used meat and iron and undid the foundations of the world. All the gods of chance flaunted their wild raiment here, above the brown flood of the Mississippi.

Then the world changed; then civilization, built for culture, rebuilt itself for wilful murder in Europe, Asia, America, and the Southern Seas. Hands that made food made powder, and iron for railways was iron for guns. The wants of common men were forgotten before the groan of giants. Streams of gold, lost from the world's workers, filtered and trickled into the hands of gamblers and put new power into the thunderbolts of East St. Louis.

Wages had been growing before the World War. Slowly but remorselessly the skilled and intelligent, banding themselves, had threatened the coffers of the mighty, and slowly the mighty had disgorged. Even the common workers, the poor and unlettered, had again and again gripped the sills of the city walls and pulled themselves to their chins; but, alas! there were so many hands and so many mouths and the feet of the Disinherited kept coming across the wet paths of the sea to this old El Dorado.

War brought subtle changes. Wages stood still while prices fattened. It was not that the white American worker was threatened with starvation, but it was what was, after all, a more important question,—whether or not he should lose his frontroom and victrola and even the dream of a Ford car.

There came a whirling and scrambling among the workers,—they fought each other; they climbed on each others' backs. The skilled and intelligent, banding themselves even better than before, bargained with the men of might and held them by bitter threats; the less skilled and more ignorant seethed at the bottom and tried, as of old, to bring it about that the ignorant and unlettered should learn to stand together against both capital and skilled labor.

It was here that there came out of the East a beam of unearthly light,—a triumph of possible good in evil so strange that the workers hardly believed it. Slowly they saw the gates of Ellis Island closing, slowly the footsteps of the yearly million men became fainter and fainter, until the stream of immigrants overseas was stopped by the shadow of death at the very time when new murder opened new markets over all the world to American industry; and the giants with the thunderbolts stamped and raged and peered out across the world and called for men and evermore,—men!

The Unwise Men laughed and squeezed reluctant dollars out of the fists of the mighty and saw in their dream the vision of a day when labor, as they knew it, should come into its own; saw this day and saw it with justice and with right, save for one thing, and that was the sound of the moan of the Disinherited, who still lay without the walls. When they heard this moan and saw that it came not across the seas, they were at first amazed and said it was not true; and then they were mad and said it should not be. Quickly they turned and looked into the red blackness of the South and in their hearts were fear and hate!

What did they see? They saw something at which they had been taught to laugh and make sport; they saw that which the heading of every newspaper column, the lie of every cub reporter, the exaggeration of every press dispatch, and the distortion of every speech and book had taught them was a mass of despicable men, inhuman: at best laughable; at worst, the meat of mobs and fury.

What did they see? They saw nine and one-half millions of human beings. They saw the spawn of slavery, ignorant by law and by deviltry, crushed by insult and debauched by systematic and criminal injustice. They saw a people whose helpless women have been raped by thousands and whose men lynched by hundreds in the face of a sneering world. They saw a people with heads bloody, but unbowed, working faithfully at wages fifty per cent lower than the wages of the nation and under conditions which shame civilization, saving homes, training children, hoping against hope. They saw the greatest industrial miracle of modern days,—slaves transforming themselves to freemen and climbing out of perdition by their own efforts, despite the most contemptible opposition God ever saw,—they saw all this and what they saw the distraught employers of America saw, too.

The North called to the South. A scream of rage went up from the cotton monopolists and industrial barons of the new South. Who was this who dared to "interfere" with their labor? Who sought to own their black slaves but they? Who honored and loved "niggers" as they did?

They mobilized all the machinery of modern oppression: taxes, city ordinances, licenses, state laws, municipal regulations, wholesale police arrests and, of course, the peculiarly Southern method of the mob and the lyncher. They appealed frantically to the United States Government; they groveled on their knees and shed wild tears at the "suffering" of their poor, misguided black friends, and yet, despite this, the Northern employers simply had to offer two and three dollars a day and from one-quarter to one-half a million dark workers arose and poured themselves into the North. They went to the mines of West Virginia, because war needs coal; they went to the industries of New Jersey and Pennsylvania, because war needs ships and iron; they went to the automobiles of Detroit and the loadcarrying of Chicago; and they went to East St. Louis.

Now there came fear in the hearts of the Unwise Men. It was not that their wages were lowered,—they went even higher. They received, not simply a living wage, but a wage that paid for some of the decencies, and, in East St. Louis, many of the indecencies of life. What they feared was not deprivation of the things they were used to and the shadow of poverty, but rather the definite death of their rising dreams. But if fear was newborn in the hearts of the Unwise Men, the black man was born in a house of fear; to him poverty of the ugliest and straitest type was father, mother, and blood-brother. He was slipping stealthily northward to escape hunger and insult, the hand of oppression, and the shadow of death.

Here, then, in the wide valley which Father Marquette saw peaceful and golden, lazy with fruit and river, half-asleep beneath the nod of God,—here, then, was staged every element for human tragedy, every element of the modern economic paradox.

Ah! That hot, wide plain of East St. Louis is a gripping thing. The rivers are dirty with sweat and toil and lip, like lakes, along the low and burdened shores; flatboats ramble and thread among them, and above the streamers bridges swing on great arches of steel, striding with mighty grace from shore to shore. Everywhere are brick kennels,—tall, black and red chimneys, tongues of flame. The ground is littered with cars and iron, tracks and trucks, boxes and crates, metals and coal and rubber. Nature-defying cranes, grim elevators rise above pile on pile of black and grimy lumber. And ever below is the water,—wide and silent, gray-brown and yellow.

This is the stage for the tragedy: the armored might of the modern world urged by the bloody needs of the world wants, fevered today by a fabulous vision of gain and needing only hands, hands, hands! Fear of loss and greed of gain in the hearts of the giants; the clustered cunning of the modern workman, skilled as artificer and skilled in the rhythm of the habit of work, tasting the world's good and panting for more; fear of poverty and hate of "scabs" in the hearts of the workers; the dumb yearning in the hearts of the oppressed; the echo of laughter heard at the foot of the Pyramids; the faithful, plodding slouch of the laborers; fear of the Shadow of Death in the hearts of black men.

We ask, and perhaps there is no answer, how far may the captain of the world's industry do his deeds, despite the grinding tragedy of its doing? How far may men fight for the beginning of comfort, out beyond the horrid shadow of poverty, at the cost of starving other and what the world calls lesser men? How far may those who reach up out of the slime that fills the pits of the world's damned compel men with loaves to divide with men who starve?

The answers to these questions are hard, but yet one answer looms above all,—justice lies with the lowest; the plight of the lowest man,—the plight of the black man—deserves the first answer, and the plight of the giants of industry, the last.

Little cared East St. Louis for all this bandying of human problems, so long as its grocers and saloon-keepers flourished and its industries steamed and screamed and smoked and its bankers grew rich. Stupidity, license, and graft sat enthroned in the City Hall. The new black folk were exploited as cheerfully as white Polacks and Italians; the rent of shacks mounted merrily, the street car lines counted gleeful gains, and the crimes of white men and black men flourished in the dark. The high and skilled and smart climbed on the bent backs of the ignorant; harder the mass of laborers strove to unionize their fellows and to bargain with employers.

Nor were the new blacks fools. They had no love for nothings in labor; they had no wish to make their fellows' wage envelopes smaller, but they were determined to make their own larger. They, too, were willing to join in the new union movement. But the unions did not want them. Just as employers monopolized meat and steel, so they sought to monopolize labor and beat a giant's bargain. In the higher trades they succeeded. The best electrician in the city was refused admittance to the union and driven from the town because he was black. No black builder, printer, or machinist could join a union or work in East St. Louis, no matter what his skill or character. But out of the stink of the stockyards and the dust of the aluminum works and the sweat of the lumber yards the willing blacks could not be kept.

They were invited to join unions of the laborers here and they joined. White workers and black workers struck at the aluminum works in the fall and won higher wages and better hours; then again in the spring they struck to make bargaining compulsory for the employer, but this time they fronted new things. The conflagration of war had spread to America; government and court stepped in and ordered no hesitation, no strikes; the work must go on.

Deeper was the call for workers. Black men poured in and red anger flamed in the hearts of the white workers. The anger was against the wielders of the thunderbolts, but here it was impotent because employers stood with the hand of the government before their faces; it was against entrenched union labor, which had risen on the backs of the unskilled and unintelligent and on the backs of those whom for any reason of race or prejudice or chicane they could beat beyond the bars of competition; and finally the anger of the mass of white workers was turned toward these new black interlopers, who seemed to come to spoil their last dream of a great monopoly of common labor.

These angers flamed and the union leaders, fearing their fury and knowing their own guilt, not only in the larger and subtler matter of bidding their way to power across the weakness of their less fortunate fellows, but also conscious of their part in making East St. Louis a miserable town of liquor and lust, leaped quickly to ward the gathering thunder from their own heads. The thing they wanted was even at their hands: here were black men, guilty not only of bidding for jobs which white men could have held at war prices, even if they could not fill, but also guilty of being black! It was at this blackness that the unions pointed the accusing finger. It was here that they committed the unpardonable crime. It was here that they entered the Shadow of Hell, where suddenly from a fight for wage and protection against industrial oppression East St. Louis became the center of the oldest and nastiest form of human oppression,—race hatred.

The whole situation lent itself to this terrible transformation. Everything in the history of the United States, from slavery to Sunday supplements, from disfranchisement to residence segregation, from "Jim-Crow" cars to a "Jim-Crow" army draft—all this history of discrimination and insult festered to make men think and willing to think that the venting of their unbridled anger against 12,000,000 humble, upstriving workers was a way of settling the industrial tangle of the ages. It was the logic of the broken plate, which, seared of old across its pattern, cracks never again, save along the old destruction.

So hell flamed in East St. Louis! The white men drove even black union men out of their unions and when the black men, beaten by night and assaulted, flew to arms and shot back at the marauders, five thousand rioters arose and surged like a crested storm-wave, from noonday till midnight; they killed and beat and murdered; they dashed out the brains of children and stripped off the clothes of women; they drove victims into the flames and hanged the helpless to the lighting poles. Fathers were killed before the faces of mothers; children were burned; heads were cut off by axes; pregnant women crawled and spawned in dark, wet fields; thieves went through houses and firebrands followed; bodies were thrown from bridges; and rocks and bricks flew through the air.

The Negroes fought. They grappled with the mob like beasts at bay. They drove them back from the thickest cluster of their homes and piled the white dead on the street, but the cunning mob caught the black men between the factories and their homes, where they knew they were armed only with their dinner pails. Firemen, policemen, and militiamen stood with hanging hands or even joined eagerly with the mob.

It was the old world horror come to life again: all that Jews suffered in Spain and Poland; all that peasants suffered in France, and Indians in Calcutta; all that aroused human deviltry had accomplished in ages past they did in East St. Louis, while the rags of six thousand half-naked black men and women fluttered across the bridges of the calm Mississippi.

The white South laughed,—it was infinitely funny—the "niggers" who had gone North to escape slavery and lynching had met the fury of the mob which they had fled. Delegations rushed North from Mississippi and Texas, with suspicious timeliness and with great-hearted offers to take these workers back to a lesser hell. The man from Greensville, Mississippi, who wanted a thousand got six, because, after all, the end was not so simple.

No, the end was not simple. On the contrary, the problem raised by East St. Louis was curiously complex. The ordinary American, tired of the persistence of "the Negro problem," sees only another anti-Negro mob and wonders, not when we shall settle this problem, but when we shall be well rid of it. The student of social things sees another mile-post in the triumphant march of union labor; he is sorry that blood and rapine should mark its march,—but, what will you? War is life!

Despite these smug reasonings the bare facts were these: East St. Louis, a great industrial center, lost 5,000 laborers,—good, honest, hard-working laborers. It was not the criminals, either black or white, who were driven from East St. Louis. They are still there. They will stay there. But half the honest black laborers were gone. The crippled ranks of industrial organization in the mid-Mississippi Valley cannot be recruited from Ellis Island, because in Europe men are dead and maimed, and restoration, when restoration comes, will raise a European demand for labor such as this age has never seen. The vision of industrial supremacy has come to the giants who lead American industry and finance. But it can never be realized unless the laborers are here to do the work,—the skilled laborers, the common laborers, the willing laborers, the well-paid laborers. The present forces, organized however cunningly, are not large enough to do what America wants; but there is another group of laborers, 12,000,000 strong, the natural heirs, by every logic of justice, to the fruits of America's industrial advance. They will be used simply because they must be used,—but their using means East St. Louis!

Eastward from St. Louis lie great centers, like Chicago, Indianapolis, Detroit, Cleveland, Pittsburg, Philadelphia, and New York; in every one of these and in lesser centers there is not only the industrial unrest of war and revolutionized work, but there is the call for workers, the coming of black folk, and the deliberate effort to divert the thoughts of men, and particularly of workingmen, into channels of race hatred against blacks. In every one of these centers what happened in East St. Louis has been attempted, with more or less success. Yet the American Negroes stand today as the greatest strategic group in the world. Their services are indispensable, their temper and character are fine, and their souls have seen a vision more beautiful than any other mass of workers. They may win back culture to the world if their strength can be used with the forces of the world that make for justice and not against the hidden hates that fight for barbarism. For fight they must and fight they will!

Rising on wings we cross again the rivers of St. Louis, winding and threading between the towers of industry that threaten and drown the towers of God. Far, far beyond, we sight the green of fields and hills; but ever below lies the river, blue,—brownish-gray, touched with the hint of hidden gold. Drifting through half-flooded lowlands, with shanties and crops and stunted trees, past struggling corn and straggling village, we rush toward the Battle of the Marne and the West, from this dread Battle of the East. Westward, dear God, the fire of Thy Mad World crimsons our Heaven. Our answering Hell rolls eastward from St. Louis.

A. E. HOTCHNER

AARON EDWARD HOTCHNER (1920–) was born and raised in St. Louis and attended Soldan High School. From an impoverished childhood, Hotchner attended Washington University on a partial scholarship, earning both a bachelor's and a law degree. Hotchner was a young lawyer working in St. Louis at the outbreak of World War II, and he joined the air corps. Although Hotchner had dreams of becoming a war hero, he was assigned to make training films, providing his first experience with making movies. After his military service, Hotchner decided to pursue a literary career. While soliciting stories from well-known writers for a magazine—or, as he remarked in one interview, acting as a "literary bounty hunter"—Hotchner met Ernest Hemingway, with whom he became close friends. *Papa Hemingway* (1966), one of Hotchner's most acclaimed books, is a memoir of their friendship. A prolific writer, Hotchner is also the author of *Blown Away* (1990), an account of the Rolling Stones, as well as novels, screenplays, articles, and television scripts. In 1982, Hotchner formed a partnership with actor Paul Newman and started the "Newman's Own" line of specialty foods, the profits from which go to charity.

Hotchner drew on his St. Louis roots for two novels, *King of the Hill* (1972), an autobiographical story of growing up in the city during the depression, and *Louisiana Purchase* (1996), a fictional account of the city's founding. Filmed in St. Louis, *King of the Hill* was made into a movie directed by Steven Soderbergh in 1992. Interviewed by MHS president Robert Archibald in 1996, Hotchner stated, "There is nothing made up in *King of the Hill*. Everything in *King of the Hill* actually happened." The following excerpt is the novel's first chapter.

FROM *KING OF THE HILL*

Last summer really started May 9th, the day they put the lock on 326. You may think May is too early for summer, but let me tell you, not in St. Louis. In geography we studied about the equator running through Africa and all that, but believe me St. Louis is the equator of the U.S.A. The St. Louis sun passes through about three hundred magnifying glasses. You keep a candle on the bureau, and once that St. Louis sun really gets going the wick is right down tickling the bureau top. And that's what it does to your brain. Melts it down, and if the brain had a wick, by July it'd be tickling your eyeballs. The only good thing about the St. Louis sun is when it really gets going it melts the streets and you can just dig a finger in and scoop out a hunk and chew the black tar same as Wrigley's.

Well, it wasn't all that hot, this May 9, 1933, I'm talking about, but it was already hot enough anyplace else would think it was a heat wave. When you come out of the St. Louis sun into a dark hallway, your eyes see green for a while, which is maybe why I didn't see the lock at first. That and the fact that I was walking with my head down, watching carefully so as not to step on the black tiles which were sudden death. The black tiles were diamond-shaped in the corners of every four white tiles, and if any part of my Keds touched black, I'd be struck down, ke-boom! not even time to scream. Dead in my tracks.

But I returned to the door of 326 after I passed it, and there was the lock. Yale. An old lock, used a lot, you could tell, scratched and turned color, but big and Yale. Just hanging there by its bowlegged top loop, hooked through the bracket that had been freshly screwed into the wood. Hanging there like it was Sandoz himself.

"Sandoz!" I wasn't *calling* him—I knew he couldn't be locked inside—just saying his name out loud when it dawned on me whose room it was. "Oh, no, not Sandoz!"

I raced around the turn in the corridor, second base on my way for a triple, my Keds squeaking real good against the tiles, raced down the corridor to the end, last room, 309, our room, the one with the NRA eagle on the door, and barged in.

"Mom! Listen . . ." But as I got into the room I stopped in my tracks, because there was a most unusual sight, my mother lying on the bed, the one by the window, a wet towel across her face. I had never seen my mother in bed during the day. She was always busy with a thousand things, washing things out in the basin, cooking something on the hot plate, writing things in her Windy City Hosiery book, sewing, always sewing, trying to keep things that were about worn out from giving up the ghost.

But there she was on the bed, her eyes closed, this wet cloth across her face, not moving. I tossed my schoolbooks on the table and went over and looked at her. On the wall above her head was this big blue NRA eagle, a cogged wheel in one claw and three forks of lightning in the other. My father put NRA eagles everywhere.

"Mom! You hurt or something?"

"Just a toothache," she said, keeping her eyes closed and opening her mouth just enough to say it. The whole side of her face was puffed out.

"Criminy, you're swole up—it must hurt a whole lot."

"M-m-m-m."

"Listen, Mom, guess what—there's a lock on Sandoz's door, three-twenty-six!"

She opened her eyes and raised her head a little. "What?" She put her head back. "Oh, God, wait till your father hears. They said it would never happen on the third floor."

To understand about the third floor, you have to understand about the Avalon. According to my parents, it was once, not too long ago, a pretty good hotel. Kingshighway and Delmar, right on the southwest corner. Not the greatest, like the Forest Park or the Jefferson or the Mayfair, but pretty good. A nice little restaurant, three bellhops and a captain, a pitcher of ice water on the bureau in your room when you checked in. My parents and I had stayed there for a few weeks when I was three years old. We had been living in New York City for almost a year, but things didn't go well there so they decided to return to St. Louis. Of course, I don't remember much about it, except one day a Western Union boy riding his bike on the sidewalk knocked into this woman coming out of the hotel and broke her arm. I remember that. Anyway, a year ago, when we returned from the terrible six months we spent with my grandparents in Chicago, we again came back to the Avalon, because my parents had remembered what a good hotel it had been.

But in nine years the same thing had happened to the Avalon that had happened to our family. You could tell the minute you set eyes on it. Half the bulbs were out in the Avalon sign that ran up and down along the corner of the building. The glass canopy over the entrance had several jagged holes in it, and there was a big electric sign alongside the main entrance, "GOOD TIMES DANCE," that had all its bulbs lighted. Below the sign was an arrow of moving lights that pointed to a door that led to the basement. There was one bellhop, no ice water, and no restaurant.

But the rent for a large double room with two full-size beds was only thirty-five dollars a month and that was a blessing, since all we had was the sixty-five dollars we got for selling our bedroom furniture before we left Chicago. The same owner, Mr. Desot, was there, and my father bragged a lot that he had given us a room with double exposure. Double exposure was a big thing with my father. In one wall was this window that looked out on the cinder parking lot in back of the hotel, and the other wall had a small window that opened on a shaftway that separated the hotel from the brick wall of the next building. But my father would say, "If you count opening the transom, it's really a triple exposure." He was very big on exposures. There wasn't enough air came through that shaftway to flicker a candle, but my father could sit in front of it with the sweat running down his temples and talk about how lucky we were that he had such pull with Desot as to get us this palace of a room with double exposure.

My parents originally took the room for a month, while they lined up something, but a year and a half had passed and they still hadn't lined up anything.

But to tell you the truth I liked the Avalon way better than living above Sorkin's delicatessen, or next to the fire station on North Union. And even in a way—but just in *a* way—better than Parker or Lawn or Art Hill. Because those places—even Concordia Lane, which was really nice—I'd come home and the place would be all empty, with my mother at work and my father out with his line, and I'd maybe eat something like a peanut-butter sandwich, and turn on the radio, but it was so *empty*. My mother always straightened up before she left for work, so when I'd come home from school it was so neat with everything put away that I felt like nobody lived there. But the Avalon—sure, everybody had a lot of troubles, but I could ride up and down in the elevator and talk to Arletta, or Danny wanted to hunk around in the turtle room, or Old Lady Heinson wanted to show me some old stuff out of her newspapers. So, even if I sat in our room and did some homework, I knew if I went out and walked down the corridor there'd be a lot of people there if I wanted to see them. Of course, I had to be awful careful not to step on the black tiles or scre-e-e! it would be all over. Sometimes I'd stomp on one on purpose; then, Ai! I'd stiffen up all over and pitch forward falling smash on my face, but I had this way of keeping my hands on my chest so my nose would wind up about an inch from the floor. Falling stiff-dead from black-tile scrunch was one of my best tricks. Sometimes, seeing me do it for the first time, people would scream. Grownups. It gave me a lot of satisfaction. I got this whole thing in me that likes to show off.

Now, about the third floor. That's where all the permanents were. The fourth floor was closed off because there wasn't enough business. Except for the Desots' suite and Danny's turtle room. The second floor was for transients. There had been a lot of lockouts on the second floor. But the third floor were the regular people. Some of them had lived there a long time. Old Lady Heinson, for example. Not only lived there for sixteen years, but hadn't left her room for twelve. Ever since they shut down the kitchen, a waiter from the Woodbine, on the other side of Delmar, brought her her meals on a tray. He'd bring the dinner menu at lunchtime, and the next day's lunch menu at dinner.

Almost everybody on the third floor was behind in rent, but they paid something in every once in a while and all the permanents believed there'd never be a lockout on their floor. But the lock on 326 changed all that. It made the third floor afraid. It caused a different kind of smell on the floor. I really mean it. I can smell when people get afraid. It has a smell to it. It really has. Kind of a putrid musty thing, like something rotting in an old, old library. Whenever I'd get in trouble with some new guy in a neighborhood we were just moving into, some bully, and I got this smell off him, I always knew I could take him easy. I've got a great nose, I really have. I never once got beat up because my nose failed me. If I didn't get the smell off some guy acting tough, I'd just yell a lot and do a little pushing and sort of get in the way of other guys standing around. I didn't get beat up very often. And for a guy who went to eleven different grammar schools, that's a pretty big compliment.

We owed $172, which is pretty good owing considering the rent was only thirty-five, so when my father came in and heard about the lock it really got to him and I could smell the fear rising off him and filling up the room. He had just been to three dentists around the neighborhood, trying to get one to take my mother, but my father owed all of them and they wanted to be paid in advance. I know about how all the dentists operate, because I had this really awful toothache and my father took me to Dr.

Olvera, who had an office on the ground floor of the hotel that you entered through the back of the lobby. He had something in Spanish framed on the wall with a big gold seal and ribbons, so I guess he was an okay dentist in Cuba or Puerto Rico or somewhere.

"This boy has a cavity in his twelve-year-old molar," he said, only I'm not writing it the way he said it in broken-down Spanish-type English.

"Well, then, fix him up," my father said.

"It's a dollar for a silver filling," Dr. Olvera said.

"A dollar!" my father yelled, like Olvera had just stuck an ice pick in his gizzard. "How big can it be, a twelve-year-old boy?"

"It's a big cavity," Dr. Olvera said. "It's a dollar, in advance."

"Here's fifty cents cash," my father said, putting two quarters on the stand under the drill. Dr. Olvera looked at the quarters. My tooth hurt so bad I wanted to throw up.

"For fifty cents the tooth can be pulled," Dr. Olvera said. "Fillings are one dollar."

"Will it stop the pain to pull it?" my father asked.

"Yes."

"Well, then, if it's such a big cavity, we might as well pull it."

"It's the boy's permanent molar," Dr. Olvera said, looking at the quarters again. I was trying to sit quiet and grip the chair arms very hard to hold in the pain, but it was running through my eyes now like a hot needle going up my cheek and right through one eye and across my forehead into the other, and I let out some kind of sound because of the pain. I didn't mean to. It just came out.

Dr. Olvera took the two quarters and put them in his pocket. He opened a drawer and took out a kind of pliers which he wiped off with a towel that was draped over the back of my chair. "If you'll hold his head," Dr. Olvera said to my father. "The roots aren't very deep yet." He stuck the cold pliers in my mouth and my father pressed my forehead against the chair back. The jaws of the pliers clunked onto my poor tooth and Dr. Olvera gave a mighty yank, tearing my head right out of the socket, but the tooth didn't give. It hurt like holy hell. It took about six yanks and Dr. Olvera was sweating and my father kept saying "Now you got it!" which, of course, he hadn't. I bled all over the place. Dr. Olvera gave my father the tooth.

On the way out, my father said to me, "That tooth would have given you a lot of trouble." Even now, every time the tip of my tongue plays around with that hole among my teeth, with the soft skin at the bottom, I can feel Dr. Olvera's grippers yanking me like I still had the twelve-year-old molar in my mouth.

"Did you try Dr. Olvera?" I asked my father.

"He's gone."

"Why, he was there a couple of days ago. I saw him."

"He was arrested."

Probably for pulling twelve-year-old molars.

Then my father said to my mother, "There was a room in the back of his office, where he . . . you know."

"No!" my mother said.

That's another thing about my father, always saying "you know" to my mother and giving her looks and making me feel like I was some kind of German spy. The only time I ever got to hear anything halfway decent was at night when we were all in bed, with the screen between us, and they thought I was asleep. But even then I never heard much because I'm such a quick sleeper.

So there was my poor mother dying from this toothache and my father without five cents to pay a dentist. Also, one look at the breadbox with its lid off, getting sunned, and I knew it was another night of no food. On the days Minnie was going to come through with her fifty cents, she always did it by noon, so my mother could get things. So one look and I could always tell if there was going to be any dinner. The Avalon did not allow cooking in the rooms, so there were no iceboxes or anything. If there was anything to eat, it was right there out in the open. My father had long ago pawned everything pawnable except the radio and Skippy, and frankly I don't think Skippy was pawnable, since Lester says pawnshops won't take anything they have to feed. Skippy was our canary, who was about as old as me. He could both chop and roll, which is pretty special. Your ordinary run-of-the-mill canary only does one or the other, but old Skippy kept throwing in chops right along with his rolls. I used to talk to him a lot, and he'd talk back, sometimes, in chops.

"Aaron, we've got to get your mother some aspirin. Go ask Aunt Minnie if she has any."

I really hated asking anybody for anything. They mostly didn't have it or pretended they didn't have it. Nobody in the Avalon went around asking anybody else in the Avalon for anything. But this was an emergency if my poor mother's tooth felt anything like my twelve-year-old molar before Dr. Olvera slaughtered it. So I went across to Minnie's room, 320, an outside room facing Delmar.

Minnie was Mrs. Minnie Rosenthal, who was rich. She had her own bathroom and she had big rings on her fingers, that had not been pawned, and her rent was paid up. She was the one who gave us the hot plate, and the deal was she could eat with us whenever she wanted by paying fifty cents for her share of the food. What she didn't know was that fifty cents paid for *all* of the food. My mother shopped at the Piggly-Wiggly, which was about four blocks over, at Cabanne and Union. Eggs were about ten cents a dozen, soup meat ten cents a pound, chickens cost a quarter, and you could get two loaves of day-old bread for a nickel. So, you see, you could eat plenty okay, all of us, for fifty cents.

The one day Aunt Minnie *always* ate with us (God, I hated to call her that but she liked it and after all it didn't *kill* me, considering she was our one and only meal ticket) was Friday. Without fail. And also without fail, every Friday after supper I'd go with her to her room and play cards with her for an hour. We played rummy and I discovered the second time we played that she cheated by dropping cards in her lap.

It bothered me that she cheated, but after thinking about it I decided not to say anything, because I figured that it didn't harm anyone since I didn't care if I won or lost. (I always lost, naturally.) Also, at the end of each card game, she would announce happily, "Well, looks like I've had a lucky run tonight," and then she'd fish in her purse and find a quarter, which was for me to go to the movies. She cheated clumsily, and sometimes it was hard for me not to see the cards in her hand being exchanged for the cards in her lap.

Minnie and my father argued a lot. Once they had this big argument, yelling back and forth at each other, over whether butterflies eat anything or whether they just fly around and look beautiful for a while and then drop dead. Don't ask me how they got into that one. You should have heard some of their arguments. Plain goofy.

"Look at moths!" my father yelled. "Tell me they don't eat!"

"Moths aren't butterflies!" Minnie yelled.

"Moths aren't butterflies? What are they?"

"Moths!"

"There isn't anything that don't eat—call the *St. Louis Post-Dispatch*! Find out!" My father was always telling people to call the *Post-Dispatch*.

"I don't have to call anybody! It's been proved! Butterflies don't eat. It's a scientific fact. It's been proved!"

"Just call the *Post-Dispatch*!"

"It's been proved, I tell you, Eric."

And on and on and on and on and on and on, for about six zillion times. That's the time I almost *did* call the *Post-Dispatch*, since I was trying to study for a history test and I wanted them to shut up, but rooms behind in rent had no phone service.

Minnie came to the door and smiled at me. She was pretty ugly when she smiled. She had a big nose that got bigger when she smiled, and she had all these old teeth that were yellow from smoking so much.

"My mother was wondering if she could borrow two aspirin, Aunt Minnie."

Her smile dropped down to her socks. "You tell your mother I never allow an aspirin in my medicine chest. They cause cancer. It's been proved." She was always telling me everything'd been proved. She had this thing about flies, for instance—I mean she was really anti-fly like you can't possibly believe, with maybe forty dozen fly swatters all over the place, and this one time she gave me a big lecture about how flies caused rheumatism. We happened to be studying insects so I asked my teacher, but when I told Minnie my teacher said she was wrong, all Minnie did was get red in the face and tremble a little bit, and stomp around saying it had been proved.

Anyway, I simply told my father Minnie didn't have any aspirin, not mentioning the cancer. He told me to try the McShanes. Criminy, I barely *knew* the McShanes. They were this mother and daughter who lived two doors down in 313. They never seemed to go anywhere. Maggie, the floor maid, said the girl was fourteen but she was a little fourteen, kind of skinny with glasses. And very pale. White. Like she lived in a closet. I really *hated* to go knocking around on people's doors. But I would do anything for my mother.

The daughter answered the door. She didn't have her glasses on and her hair, which usually hung down her face, was pulled back. "Oh, sure, we've got aspirins," she said. "Just a minute." Then she closed the door while I waited in the hall. That's how it was in the Avalon. Nobody hardly ever went into anybody else's room. I guess because with two or three people living in a room it was usually pretty crowded and messed up. Also, if you had anything around that could be eaten, there was always the danger you'd have to share it if someone was sitting there drooling all over himself at the sight of it. What I hated was the way soon as people got together they trotted out all their miseries and talked about them for hours. There I'd be trying to forget I was dying of hunger, and some slob would be sitting there going on and on about not having eaten for about a week and how he tried this and that and the other place and they turned him down, and the hell with the Salvation Army and all that. There was this one friend of my father, Mr. Able, who lived around in 340, who was always coming in and giving a report on his weekly meal with his daughter. They took him out to a restaurant every Thursday, and as far as I could tell Mr. Able filled up his stomach to last the week like his stomach was the hump of a camel. So now every time he came knocking around I left, because when you were hungry and trying to do homework and the last thing you had was a teeny hamburger about a year ago, what you didn't want to hear was how Mr. Able started with chicken soup and worked his way through a hundred courses, even giving you the kind of sauce he had on his ice cream, for crying out loud.

We did have one pretty big get-together in our room when Mr. Roosevelt made his first speech last March. There must have been fifteen people from our floor. They brought chairs and sat around and listened to Mr. Roosevelt promise to do his duty and all that. As for me, I didn't like to listen to politics. Everyone said pretty much what everyone else said, how it was a great old country and things were going to get better, and then dumped everything onto God and asked Him to show us the way and all that. I don't know why everyone just doesn't vote for God and get it over with.

So while they were listening to Mr. Roosevelt, I shot marbles on the rug. That's what I always did when the radio was on. The grownups all sat there staring at that stupid box as if their eyes were glued to their ears. What in Sam Hill was there to look at? Even when the baseball games were on, which were the only things I *really* liked on the radio, and even if I was keeping box score, I shot marbles. They held on the rug pretty good.

But one thing that I really liked about Mr. Roosevelt was his voice. I mean the sound. Not the speeches so much—when he speeched, he put his voice up and got a little faky—but when he sat at his fireside and talked, the sound of his voice was just right. Like the time a couple of months ago when he said he wanted everyone to take all the gold they had and bring it back to the banks. The banks were all out of money and shut down, for Pete's sake, and here he was with this voice of his asking everyone to haul their gold out of their mattresses and stick it in these busted banks.

Well, you know something? The next morning on my way to school, where going along Kingshighway there were four banks, they all had mobs around them, all these people with satchels and packages, bringing their gold back to these busted banks. There was one geezer with a white mustache and a vest sitting there in his Pierce-Arrow while his chauffeur was up in line. I looked in the window and would you believe he had gold bars, really *bars*, stacked up all over the back seat, not wrapped or anything? What a sight that was, all those people shoving each other to give up their gold to those busted banks. I don't know what I'da done if I'd had any gold. Kept it, I think. I really like Mr. Roosevelt, even though so far we're no better off than when he took over, but I don't get along with banks, and any gold I'da had I'da kept in the fingers of my fielder's mitt.

The McShane girl gave me four aspirins, and I thanked her and brought them back to the room and my mother took two. My father was carrying on and on about Sandoz, and how he was going to give Desot a piece of his mind. My father was always giving someone a piece of his mind. There was a note on the table I hadn't seen before, from Lester, telling me to meet him in the Vampire Room at six o'clock. I really felt awful about Sandoz. All his paintings locked in there, and I guess his paints, and all those other things of his from Mexico he used to show me. On top of our dresser was this baby picture of my brother. Sandoz had painted an eggshell around the head, with the top broken, so it looked like my brother had just come into the world out of an egg. That's what Sandoz did for a living. He went around to people's houses and told them he would paint an eggshell around their baby's picture for fifty cents. He was a wonderful painter, but that's what he had to do for a living. But even so, he didn't make a lot, and out of what he made he was always sending something back to Mexico where his family was. He used to tell me about it. I was practically his only friend. He told me a lot about Mexico and about how he once tried to be a bullfighter. Some of his paintings were about bullfighting, but he never painted bulls getting stabbed. His paintings were mostly the colors that bullfighting makes. I guess that's how you'd describe it. He even painted me one day. Or I should say, one week. I came in every day and just leaned against the wall and he painted me like that. I could never understand why, since, believe me, I'm no prize that has to be painted. Just the ordinary kind of skinny kid with a zillion freckles and kind of red hair. My mother calls it auburn, but auburn's for girls. It was me, all right, leaning there against

Sandoz's wall and he wanted to give me the painting, but in that small room of ours if I had had to look at myself hanging on the wall all the time, I'd have puked. I'm pretty homely, actually.

There were two hours to kill before I'd meet Lester and I was already bored of my father's droning on about what was going to be in the piece of mind he was going to give to Mr. Desot, so I got my Feltie and went out. My mother was too sick to ask me where I was going. That's one of the things that gnawed me about my mother. Every time I went out of the door, she asked me where I was going, did I have a handkerchief, and to be careful crossing the street. Criminy, I was going to be graduated from the Admiral Dewey Elementary School in about a month, but you'd have thought I was on my way to kindergarten. Oh, yes, and nine times out of ten she asked me if I had to put that dirty thing on my head. That dirty thing happened to be the best old Feltie in the neighborhood. My father called it a skullcap. I found this really great fedora in a trash can in the park, and cut out the crown and cut designs in it, and I had some really nifty buttons stuck all over it, especially this one of Mr. Herbert Hoover smiling, which, believe me, was some rare button.

I checked to see if Danny Desot was around but he wasn't, so I started down Delmar to look for cigar bands. I hadn't gone more than a block when I found a Petit Bouquet, which was on my most-wanted list. I once spotted a man who was smoking one and followed him for blocks and blocks, but when it went out he just kept chewing on the end and I knew he'd never throw it away. But here it was, right at my feet, on a cigar that was teetering right on the edge of the sewer opening, so I picked it up carefully. It was wet, so I had to go very easy taking it off: "Petit" on top, "Bouquet" on bottom, two gold coins on each side, and some kind of gold medal hanging between the "Petit" and the "Bouquet." In that St. Louis sun, the gold on the band looked real. I took out the two pieces of blotting paper I always carried in my pocket, and laid the band flat between them. It was like when Hoot Gibson or somebody was panhandling out there in the West and suddenly there was this shiny nugget in the pan. That's how it was walking the gutters looking for cigar bands. Sometimes you could walk all day and find nothing but Cremos and Dutch Masters and junk like that, and other days you went out for thirty minutes and struck gold.

MAYA ANGELOU

BORN MARGUERITE ANNIE JOHNSON (1928–) in St. Louis, Maya Angelou is widely recognized as one of the most original women of letters in the second half of the twentieth century. At the time of her birth, Angelou's parents, Bailey and Vivian Baxter Johnson, were living on Hickory Street in St. Louis, but they moved shortly thereafter to Stamps, Arkansas. After the Johnsons' marriage disintegrated, Maya and her brother moved several times, staying with relatives in California, Arkansas, and St. Louis.

An accomplished poet, autobiographer, playwright, performer, educator, and civil rights activist, Angelou is best known for her stunning autobiographical work, *I Know Why the Caged Bird Sings* (1969), which recounts the powerful and often painful events in her formative years. *Caged Bird* has become one of the most popular works by a black woman in American literary history. Angelou's other autobiographical works are *Gather Together in My Name* (1974), *Singin' and Swinging and Getting Merry Like Christmas* (1976), *The Heart of a Woman* (1981), and *All God's Children Need Traveling Shoes* (1986). A natural trailblazer and role model for African American women, Angelou wrote the screenplay to *Georgia, Georgia*, the first script by a black woman to be produced as a feature film. Although she had been a prolific and published poet for many years, Angelou became a household name for mainstream America when she read her poem "On the Pulse of Morning" at President Bill Clinton's inauguration in January 1993. The recipient of numerous awards and honorary degrees, Angelou is currently Reynolds Professor in American Studies at Wake Forest University in Winston-Salem, North Carolina.

In the following excerpt from *I Know Why the Caged Bird Sings,* Angelou describes her life in St. Louis at age eight, after she returned to the city to live with her maternal grandmother.

FROM *I KNOW WHY THE CAGED BIRD SINGS*

Grandmother Baxter was a quadroon or an octoroon, or in any case she was nearly white. She had been raised by a German family in Cairo, Illinois, and had come to St. Louis at the turn of the century to study nursing. While she was working at Homer G. Phillips Hospital she met and married Grandfather Baxter. She was white (having no features that could even loosely be called Negroid) and he was Black. While she spoke with a throaty german accent until her death, he had the choppy spouting speech of the West Indians.

Their marriage was a happy one. Grandfather had a famous saying that caused great pride in his family: "Bah Jesus, I live for my wife, my children and my dog." He took extreme care to prove that statement true by taking the word of his family even in the face of contradictory evidence.

The Negro section of St. Louis in the mid-thirties had all the finesse of a gold-rush town. Prohibition, gambling and their related vocations were so obviously practiced that it was hard for me to believe that they were against the law. Bailey and I, as newcomers, were quickly told by our schoolmates who the men on the street corners were as we passed. I was sure that they had taken their names from Wild West Books (Hard-hitting Jimmy, Two Gun, Sweet Man, Poker Pete), and to prove me right, they hung around in front of saloons like unhorsed cowboys.

We met the numbers runners, gamblers, lottery takers and whiskey salesmen not only in the loud streets but in our orderly living room as well. They were often there when we returned from school, sitting with hats in their hands, as we had done upon our arrival in the big city. They waited silently for Grandmother Baxter.

Her white skin and the pince-nez that she dramatically took from her nose and let hang free on a chain pinned to her dress were factors that brought her a great deal of respect. Moreover, the reputation of her six mean children and the fact that she was a precinct captain compounded her power and gave her the leverage to deal with even the lowest crook without fear. She had pull with the police department, so the men in their flashy suits and fleshy scars sat with churchlike decorum and waited to ask favors from her. If Grandmother raised the heat off their gambling parlors, or said the word that reduced the bail of a friend waiting in jail, they knew what would be expected of them. Come election, they were to bring in the votes from their neighborhood. She most often got them leniency, and they always brought in the vote.

St. Louis also introduced me to thin-sliced ham (I thought it a delicacy), jelly beans and peanuts mixed, lettuce on sandwich bread, Victrolas and family loyalty. In Arkansas, where we cured our own meat, we ate half-inch slabs of ham for breakfast, but in St. Louis we bought the paper-thin slices in a strange-smelling German store and ate them in sandwiches. If Grandmother never lost her German accent, she also never lost her taste for the thick black German *Brot*, which we bought unsliced. In Stamps, lettuce was used only to make a bed for potato salad or slaw, and peanuts were brought in raw from the field and roasted in the bottom of the oven on cold nights. The rich scents used to fill the house and we were always expected to eat too many. But that was a Stamps custom. In St. Louis, peanuts were bought in paper bags and mixed with jelly beans, which meant that we ate the salt and sugar together and I found them a delicious treat. The best thing the big town had to offer.

When we enrolled in Toussaint L'Ouverture Grammar School, we were struck by the ignorance of our schoolmates and the rudeness of our teachers. Only the vastness of the building impressed us; not even the white school in Stamps was as large.

The students, however, were shockingly backward. Bailey and I did arithmetic at a mature level because of our work in the Store, and we read well because in Stamps there wasn't anything else to do. We were moved up a grade because our teachers thought that we country children would make our classmates feel inferior—and we did. Bailey would not refrain from remarking on our classmates' lack of knowledge. At lunchtime in the large gray concrete playground, he would stand in the center of a crowd of big boys and ask, "Who was Napoleon Bonaparte?" "How many feet make a mile?" It was infighting, Bailey style.

Any of the boys might have been able to beat him with their fists, but if they did, they'd just have had to do it again the next day, and Bailey never held a brief for fighting fair. He taught me that once I got into a fight I should "grab for the balls right away." He never answered when I asked, "Suppose I'm fighting a girl?"

We went to school there a full year, but all I remember hearing that I hadn't heard before was, "Making thousands of egg-shaped oughts will improve penmanship."

The teachers were more formal than those we knew in Stamps, and although they didn't whip their students with switches, they gave them licks in the palms of their hands with rulers. In Stamps teachers were much friendlier, but that was because they were imported from the Arkansas Negro colleges, and since we had no hotels or rooming houses in town, they had to live with private families. If a lady teacher took company, or didn't receive any mail or cried alone in her room at night, by the weeks' end even the children discussed her morality, her loneliness and her other failings generally. It would have been near impossible to maintain formality under a small town's invasions of privacy.

St. Louis teachers, on the other hand, tended to act very siditty, and talked down to their students from the lofty heights of education and whitefolks' enunciation. They, women as well as men, all sounded like my father with their *ers* and *errers*. They walked with their knees together and talked through tight lips as if they were as afraid to let the sound out as they were to inhale the dirty air that the listener gave off.

We walked to school around walls of bricks and breathed the coal dust for one discouraging winter. We learned to say "Yes" and "No" rather than "Yes, ma'am," and "No, ma'am."

Occasionally Mother, whom we seldom saw in the house, had us meet her at Louie's. It was a long dark tavern at the end of the bridge near our school, and was owned by two Syrian brothers.

We used to come in the back door, and the saw dust, stale beer, steam and boiling meat made me feel as if I'd been eating mothballs. Mother had cut my hair in a bob like hers and straightened it, so my head felt skinned and the back of my neck so bare that I was ashamed to have anyone walk up behind me. Naturally, this kept me turning quickly as if I expected something to happen.

At Louie's we were greeted by Mother's friends as "Bibbie's darling babies" and were given soft drinks and boiled shrimp. While we sat on the stiff wooden booths, Mother would dance alone in front of us to music from the Seeburg. I loved her most at those times. She was like a pretty kite that floated just above my head. If I liked, I could pull it in to me by saying I had to go to the toilet or by starting a fight with Bailey. I never did either, but the power made me tender to her.

The Syrian brothers vied for her attention as she sang the heavy blues that Bailey and I almost understood. They watched her, even when directing their conversation to other customers, and I knew they too were hypnotized by this beautiful lady who talked with her whole body and snapped her fingers louder than anyone in the whole world. We learned the Time Step at Louie's. It is from this basic step that most American Black dances are born. It is a series of taps, jumps and rests, and demands careful listening, feeling and coordination. We were brought before Mother's friends, there in the heavy saloon air, to show our artistry. Bailey learned easily, and has always been the better dancer. But I learned too. I approached the Time Step with the same determination to win that I had approached the time tables with. There was no Uncle Willie or sizzling pot-bellied stove, but there was Mother and her laughing friends, and they amounted to the same thing. We were applauded and given more soft drinks and more shrimp, but it was to be years later before I found the joy and freedom of dancing well.

Mother's brothers, Uncles Tutti, Tom and lra, were well-known young men about St. Louis. They all had city jobs, which I now understand to have been no mean feat for Negro men. Their jobs and their family set them apart, but they were best known for their unrelenting meanness. Grandfather had told them, "Bah Jesus, if you ever get in jail for stealing or some such foolishness, I'll let you rot. But if you're arrested for fighting, I'll sell the house, lock, stock, and barrel, to get you out!" With that kind of encouragement, backed by explosive tempers, it was no wonder they became fearsome characters, Our youngest uncle, Billy, was not old enough to join in their didoes. One of their more flamboyant escapades has become a proud family legend.

Pat Patterson, a big man, who was himself protected by the shield of a bad reputation, made the mistake of cursing my mother one night when she was out alone. She reported the incident to her brothers. They ordered one of their hangers-on to search the streets for Patterson, and when he was located, to telephone them.

As they waited throughout the afternoon, the living room filled with smoke and the murmurs of plans. From time to time, Grandfather came in from the kitchen and said, "Don't kill him. Mind you, just don't kill him," then went back to his coffee with Grandmother.

The went to the saloon where Patterson sat drinking at a small table. Uncle Tommy stood by the door, Uncle Tutti stationed himself at the toilet door and Uncle Ira, who was the oldest and maybe everyone's ideal, walked over to Patterson. They were all obviously carrying guns.

Uncle Ira said to my mother, "Here, Bibbi. Here's this nigger Patterson. Come over here and beat his ass."

She crashed the man's head with a policeman's billy enough to leave him just this side of death. There was no police investigation nor social reprobation.

After all, didn't Grandfather champion their wild tempers, and wasn't Grandmother a near-white woman with police pull?

I admit that I was thrilled by their meanness. They beat up whites and Blacks with the same abandon, and liked each other so much that they never needed to learn the art of making outside friends. My mother was the only warm, outgoing personality among her siblings. Grandfather became bedridden during our stay there, and his children spent their free time telling him jokes, gossiping with him and showing their love.

Uncle Tommy, who was gruff and chewed his words like Grandfather, was my favorite. He strung ordinary sentences together and they came out sounding either like the most profane curses or like comical poetry. A natural comedian, he never waited for the laugh that he knew must follow his droll statements. He was never cruel. He was mean.

When we played handball on the side of our house, Uncle Tommy would turn the corner, coming from work. He would pretend at first not to see us, but with the deftness of a cat he would catch the ball and say, "Put your minds where your behinds are, and I'll let you on my team." We children would range around him, but it was only when he reached the steps that he'd wind up his arm and throw the ball over the light post and toward the stars.

He told me often, "Ritie, don't worry 'cause you ain't pretty. Plenty pretty women I seen digging ditches or worse. You smart. I swear to God, I rather you have a good mind than a cute behind."

They bragged often about the binding quality of the Baxter blood. Uncle Tommy said that even the children felt it before they were old enough to be taught. They reminisced over Bailey's teaching me to walk when he was less than three. Displeased at my stumbling motions, he was supposed to have said, "This is *my* sister. *I* have to teach her to walk." They also told me how I got the name "My." After Bailey learned definitely that I was his sister, he refused to call me Marguerite, but rather addressed me each time as "Mya Sister," and in later more articulate years, after the need for brevity had shortened the appellation to "My," it was elaborated into "Maya."

We lived in a big house on Caroline Street with our grandparents for half the year before Mother moved us in with her. Moving from the house where the family was centered meant absolutely nothing to me. It was simply a small pattern in the grand design of our lives. If other children didn't move so much, it just went to show that our lives were fated to be different from everyone else's in the world. The new house was no stranger than the other, except that we were with Mother.

Bailey persisted in calling her Mother Dear until the circumstance of proximity softened the phrase's formality to "Muh Dear," and finally to "M'Deah." I could never put my finger on her realness. She was so pretty and so quick that even when she had just awakened, her eyes full of sleep and hair tousled, I thought she looked just like the Virgin Mary. But what mother and daughter understand each other, or even have the sympathy for each other's lack of understanding?

Mother had prepared a place for us, and we went to it gratefully. We each had a room with a two-sheeted bed, plenty to eat and store-bought clothes to wear. And after all, she didn't have to do it. If we got on her nerves or if we were disobedient, she could always send us back to Stamps. The weight of appreciation and the threat, which was never spoken, of a return to Momma were burdens that clogged my childish wits into impassivity. I was called Old Lady and chided for moving and talking like winter's molasses.

Mother's boyfriend, Mr. Freeman, lived with us, or we lived with him (I never quite knew which). He was a Southerner, too, and big. But a little flabby. His breasts used to embarrass me when he walked around in his undershirt. They lay on his chest like flat titties.

Even if Mother hadn't been such a pretty woman, light-skinned with straight hair, he was lucky to get her, and he knew it. She was educated, from a well-known family, and after all, wasn't she born in St. Louis? Then she was gay. She laughed all the time and made jokes. He was grateful. I think he must have been many years older than she, but if not, he had the sluggish inferiority of old men married to younger women. He watched her every move and when she left the room, his eyes allowed her reluctantly to go.

THOMAS WOLFE

THOMAS WOLFE (1900–1938) was born in Asheville, North Carolina, and attended the University of North Carolina and, later, Harvard University, where he began his literary career studying playwriting.

After his brief stint in the theatre failed, Wolfe turned to writing fiction while teaching English at New York University. In 1930, Wolfe received a Guggenheim Fellowship, which enabled him to devote himself to writing and travel. Although Wolfe's lengthy and strongly autobiographical masterpiece, *Look Homeward, Angel* (1929), established his reputation as one of America's finest novelists, some scholars consider Wolfe's true genius exhibited in the shorter novella form. Highly productive in his brief lifetime, Wolfe is acknowledged as a major influence on such prominent Southern writers as James Dickey, Walker Percy, and William Styron. He died in Baltimore at age thirty-eight of tuberculosis of the brain.

In 1937, Wolfe completed a four-part novella titled *The Lost Boy*, in which he continues the saga of the Gant family, first launched eight years earlier in *Look Homeward, Angel*. Wolfe's editor radically reduced the length and content of the work, which was published as a short story in *Redbook Magazine* for fifteen hundred dollars—the largest payment Wolfe had ever received for a story. In *The Lost Boy*, an autobiographical and experimental work, Wolfe tells the heartbreaking story of the death of an adolescent boy, Grover Gant, in St. Louis during the 1904 World's Fair.

Like the narrator in the fourth section of *The Lost Boy*, which follows, Wolfe returned to St. Louis in 1935 to search for the boardinghouse where his family had lived during the tragic summer of 1904, when his older brother, Grover, died of typhoid.

FROM *THE LOST BOY*

. . . . "*This* is King's Highway," a man said.

And then I looked and saw that it was just a street. There were some big new buildings, a big hotel, some restaurants and "bar-grill" places, of the modern kind, the livid monotone of Neon lights, the ceaseless traffic of the motor cars—all this was new, but it was just a street. And I knew that it had always been a street, and nothing more—but somehow—I stood there looking at it, wondering what else I had expected to find.

The man kept looking at me with inquiry, and I asked him if the Fair had not been out this way.

"Sure, the Fair was out beyond here," the man said. "Where the park is now. But this street you're looking for?—Don't you remember the name of the street or nothin'?" the man said.

I said I thought the name of the street was Edgemont Street, but that I was not sure. But that it was something like that. And I said the house was on the corner of this street and of another street. And then the man said, "What street was that?" I said I did not know but that the house was on the corner of the street, and that King's Highway was a block or so away and that an interurban line ran past about half a block or so from where we lived.

"What line was this?" the man said, and stared at me.

"The interurban line," I said.

Then he stared at me again and at the man with him, and finally, "I don't know no interurban line," he said.

I said it was a line that ran behind some houses and that there were board fences there and grass beside the tracks. I said it seemed to go right through somewhere behind some houses. But somehow I could not say that it was summer in those days and that you could smell the ties, a kind of wooden tarry smell, and feel a kind of absence in the afternoon after the car had gone. I only said the interurban line was back behind somewhere between the back yards of some houses and some old board fences, and that King's Highway was a block or two away.

I did not say King's Highway had not been a street in those days but a kind of road that wound from magic out of some dim and haunted land and that along the way it had got mixed in with Tom the Piper's son, with hot cross buns, with all the light that came and went, and with cloud shadows passing on the mountains, with coming down through Indiana in the morning, and the smell of engine smoke, the Union-Station, and most of all with voices lost and far and long ago that said "King's Highway."

I didn't say these things about King's Highway because I looked about me, and I saw what King's Highway was. King's Highway was a street, a broad and busy street with new hotels and hard bright lights, and endless flocks of motors swarming up and down. All I could say was that the street was near King's Highway, and was on the corner, and that the interurban trolley line was close to there. I said it was a stone house, and that there were stone steps before it, and a strip of grass. I said I thought the house had had a turret at one corner, I could not be sure.

The men looked at me again, and one said, "This is King's Highway, but we never heard of any street like that."

I left them then and went on till I found the place. And again, again, I turned into the street, finding the place where the two corners meet, the huddled block, the turret, and the steps, and paused a moment, looking back, as if the street was Time.

So I waited for a moment for a word, and for a door to open, for the child to come. I waited, but no words were spoken; no one came.

Yet all of it was just as it had always been except the steps were lower and the porch less high, the strip of grass less wide than I had thought, but all the rest of it as I had known it would be. A graystone front, three-storied, with a slant slate roof, the side red brick and windowed, still with the old arched entrance in the center for the doctor's use.

There was a tree in front, a lamp post, and behind and to the side more trees than I had known there would be. And all the slatey turret gables, all the slatey window gables going into points, the two arched windows, in strong stone, in the front room. The small stone porch, stone-carved, with its roof of gabled slate beside.

And it was all so strong, so solid and so ugly—and all, save for the steps and grass, so enduring and so good, the way I had remembered it, the way I knew that I would not get fooled, the way I knew it would not lie to me, really just the way that it had always been, except I did not smell the tar, the hot and caulky dryness of the old cracked ties, the boards of backyard fences and the coarse and sultry grass, and absence in the afternoon when the street car had gone, and the twins, sharp-visaged in their sailor suits, pumping with furious shrillness on tricycles up and down before the house, and Simpson coming back from somewhere with his basket, and the feel of the hot afternoon, and that every one was absent at the Fair.

Except for this, it all was just the same, except for this and for King's Highway, which was now a street, except for this, King's Highway, and the child that did not come.

It was a hot day. Darkness had come, the heat rose up and hung and sweltered like a sodden blanket in St. Louis. It was wet heat, and one knew that there would be no relief or coolness in the night, and one knew the heat would stay. And when one tried to think of the time when the heat would go away, one said, "It cannot last. It's bound to go away," as we always say it in America. But one did not believe it when he said it. The heat soaked down and men sweltered in it, the faces of the people were pale and greasy with the heat. And in their faces was a kind of patient wretchedness, and one felt the kind of desolation that one feels at the end of a hot day in a great city in America—when one's home is far away, across the continent, and he thinks of all that distance, all that heat, and feels, "Oh God! but it's a big country!"

The way it made one feel was the way one feels when he is far away and all alone in a big city on a day like this, and hears the sound of trains, of bells, of engine whistles, and of boats out on the river, and when he walks along the street beneath hot clusters of electric light, or seeks the park—the bleached grass, the littered rubbish of soiled newspapers, and people sprawled out on the yellowed grass—or when he sees the kind of bench they put in the parks here in America to make one cheerful at the end of a hot day—a concrete bench, with the hard hot glare of dead electric light upon it, so that people will behave themselves, and with a concrete arm or barrier across the middle, so that people won't lie down.

Or it makes one feel the way one feels in a city like this when he comes out on an open place, a fine square, a civic center, and sees a fine new city hall or community center, all lighted up with searchlights and surrounded by fine new standard lamp posts, each with five hard grapes of dead electric light. He sees men in shirtsleeves and sag faces lounging at the corners, or women sitting on the porches with no stockings on, relapsing limply to the heat with the hard hot white of dead electric light upon them.

And he hears the trains, the engine whistles and the boats out on the river, and thinks of all that distance, all that heat, and not with joy, and not with hope, and not as one who thinks of the Great West and of the rampart of the shining mountains, but as some one drowned and lost and sunken on the sea floors of unending desolation, as of some one swimming in a dream.

He knows that it is endless, he is drowned, that he cannot escape. He knows that he is lost and sunken in America, that it is too big for him, and that he has no home. He knows he cannot grasp and hold it or comprise it, shape it to a flaming word, as once, in the exultant hope and madness of youth and loneliness and night, he *knew* he could. He knows now that he is only a nameless atom lost in vacancy, a brief and dusty cipher, whirled homelessly in unnumbered time, and that all the dreams, the strength, the passion, the belief of youth have gone amort.

And he feels nothing but absence, absence, and the desolation of America, the loneliness and sadness of the high, hot skies, and evening coming on across the Middle West, across the sweltering and heat-sunken land, across all the lonely little towns, the farms, the fields, the oven swelter of Ohio, Kansas, Iowa and Indiana at the close of day, and voices, casual in heat, voices at the little stations, quiet, casual, somehow faded into that enormous vacancy and weariness of heat, of space, and of the immense, the sorrowful and most high and awful skies.

Then he hears the engine and the wheel again, the wailing whistle and the bell, the sound of shifting in the sweltering yard, and walks the street, and walks the street, beneath the clusters of hard lights, and by the people with sagged faces, and is drowned in desolation and in no belief. "Why here? What shall I do now? Where shall I go?"

He feels the way one feels when one comes back, and knows that he should not have come, and when he sees that, after all, King's Highway is—a street; and St. Louis—the enchanted name—a big hot common town upon the river, sweltering in wet dreary heat, and not quite South, and nothing else enough to make it better.

It had not been like this before. I could remember how it would get hot, and how good the heat was, and how I would lie out in the back yard on an airing mattress, and how the mattress would get hot and dry and smell like a hot mattress full of sun, and how the sun would make me want to sleep, and how, sometimes, I would go down into the basement to feel coolness, and how the cellar smelled as cellars always smell—a kind of cool, stale smell, a smell of cobwebs and of grimy bottles. And I would remember, when you opened the door upstairs, and went down to the cellar, the smell of the cellar would come up to you—cool, musty, stale and dank and dark—and how the thought of the dark cellar always filled me with a kind of numb excitement, a kind of visceral expectancy.

I could remember how it got hot in the afternoons, and how I would feel absence in the afternoons, a sense of absence and vague sadness in the afternoons, when every one had gone away. The house would seem so lonely in the afternoons, and sometimes I would sit inside, on the second step of the hall stairs, and listen to the sound of silence and of absence in the afternoon. I could smell the oil upon the floor and on the stairs, and see the sliding doors with their brown varnish and the beady chains across the door, and thrust my hands among the bead chains, and gather them together in my arms, and let them clash, and swish with light beady swishings all round me. I could feel darkness, absence, varnished darkness and stained light, within the house, through the stained glass of the window on the stairs, through the small stained glasses by the door, stained light and absence, silence and the smell of floor oil and vague sadness in the house in a hot mid-afternoon. And all these things themselves would have a kind of life: would seem to wait attentively, to be most living and most still.

I would sit there and listen. I could hear the girl next door practice her piano lessons in the afternoon, and hear the street car coming by between the backyard fences, half a block away, and smell the dry and sultry smell of backyard fences, the smell of coarse hot grasses by the car track in the afternoon, the smell of tar, of dry caulked ties, the smell of bright worn flanges, and feel the loneliness of back yards in the afternoon and the sense of absence, absence, when the car is gone.

Then I would long for evening and return, the slant of light, and feet along the street, the sharp-faced twins in sailor suits upon their tricycles, the smell of supper and the sound of voices in the house again, and Grover coming from the Fair.

. . . . And again, again, I turned into the street, finding the place where the two corners meet, turning at last to see if Time was there. I passed the house, some lights were burning in the house, the door was open and a woman sat upon the porch. And presently I turned and stopped before the house again. The corner light fell blank upon the house. I stood looking at the house a moment, and I put my foot upon the step.

Then I said to the woman who was sitting on the porch: "This house. . . .

excuse me. . . . but could you tell me, please, who lives here in this house."

I knew my words were strange and hollow and I had not said what I wished to say. She stared at me a moment, puzzled.

Then she said, "I live here. Who are you looking for?" she said.

I said, "Why, I am looking for. . . ."

And then I stopped, because I knew I could not tell her what it was that I was looking for. My words were wrenched and foolish now when I felt her looking at me, and I did not know what to say.

"There used to be a house—" I said.

The woman was now staring hard at me. I said—"I think I used to live here"—she said nothing.

In a moment I continued—"I used to live here in this house," I said, "when I was a little boy."

She was silent for a moment, looking at me, then she said, "Oh. Are you sure this was the house? Do you remember the address?"

"I have forgotten the address," I said, "but it was Edgemont Street, and it was on the corner. And I know this is the house."

"This isn't Edgemont Street," the woman said, "the name is Bates."

"Well, then, they changed the name of the street," I said, "but this is the same house. It hasn't changed."

She was silent a moment, then she nodded: "Yes. They did change the name of the street. I remember hearing that it used to have another name. When I was a child they called it something else," she said. "But that was a long time ago. When was it that you lived here?"

"In 1904."

Again she was silent, looking at me for a moment. Then presently: "Oh. . . . That was the year of the Fair. You were here then?"

"Yes," I now spoke rapidly, with more confidence, "my mother had the house, and we were here for seven months. . . . and the house belonged to Dr. Packer,"—I went on—"We rented it from him—"

"Yes," the woman said, and nodded now—"this was Dr. Packer's house. I never knew him. I've only been here a few years, but Dr. Packer owned this house. . . . He's dead now, he's been dead for many years. But this was the Packer house, all right," the woman said.

"That entrance on the side," I said, "where the steps go up, that was for Dr. Packer's patients. That was the entrance to his office. That's the way his patients came and went."

"Oh," the woman said, "I didn't know that. I've often wondered what it was. I didn't know what it was for."

"And this big room in front here," I continued, "that was the doctor's office. And there were sliding doors, and next to it, a kind of alcove for his patients—"

"Yes, the alcove is still there, only all of it has been made into one room now—and I never knew just what the alcove was for."

"—And there were sliding doors on this side too that opened on the hall—and a stairway going up upon this side. And half way up the stairway, at the landing, a little window of colored glass—and across the sliding doors here in the hall, a kind of curtain made of strings of beads."

She nodded, smiling. "Yes, its just the same—we still have the sliding doors and the stained glass window on the stairs. There's no bead curtain any more," she said, "but I remember when people had them. I know what you mean."

"When we were here," I said, "we used the doctor's office for a parlor—except later on—the last month or two—and then we used it for—a bedroom."

"It is a bedroom now," she said. "I run the house—I rent rooms—all of the rooms upstairs are rented—but I have two brothers and they sleep in this front room."

And we were silent for a moment, then I said, "My brother stayed there too."

"In the front room?" the woman said.

I answered "Yes."

She paused a moment, then she said, "Won't you come in? I don't believe it's changed much. Would you like to see?"

I thanked her and I said I would, and I went up the steps. She opened the screen door and I went into the house.

And it was just the same,—the stairs, the hallway, and the sliding doors, the window of stained glass upon the stairs. And all of it was just the same, except for absence, absence, in the afternoon, the stained light of absence in the afternoon, and the child who sat there, waiting on the stairs, and something fading like a dream, something coming like a light, something going, passing, fading, like the shadows of a wood.

It was all the same except that I had sat there feeling things were *Somewhere*—and now I *knew*. I had sat there feeling that a vast and sultry river was somewhere—and now I knew! I had sat there wondering what King's Highway was, where it began, and where it ended—now I knew! I had sat there haunted by the magic word "downtown"—now I knew!—and by the street car, after it had gone—and by all things that came and went and came again, like the cloud shadows passing in a wood, that never could be captured—the memory of another house, and sunlight, April, and the seasons passing, as the shadows pass, a train, a river, morning and the hills of home.

For all would come again, and I would sit there on the stairs, in absence, absence, in the afternoon, and try to get it back again. And it would come and go and come again until I had it back, I had it back, and it was mine and I could remember all that I had seen and been—that yet had all the lights of time on it, the shadowy echoes of a thousand lives, that brief sum of me, the universe of my four years that was so short to measure, so far, so endless to remember.

It would all come back to me like his dark eyes, his quiet face. And I would see my small face pooled in the dark mirror of the hall, my grave eyes, and my quiet self, the lone integrity of Me, and know that I was just a child, yet know all-clearly that a man could ever know, which was, "Here—a child, my core, my kernel—and here House and here House listening—and here absence, absence in the afternoon—oh utter universe, I know you:—here am I!"

And then it would be gone again, fading like cloud shadows in the hills, going like lost faces in a dream, coming like the vast, the drowsy rumors of the distant and enchanted Fair, and coming, going, coming, being found and lost, possessed and held and never captured, like lost voices in the mountains, long ago, like the dark eyes and the quiet face, the dark lost boy, my brother, who himself like shadows, or like absence in the house, would come, would go, and would return again.

SALLY BENSON

BORN SARAH SMITH, Sally Benson (1900–1972) lived at 5135 Kensington Avenue in St. Louis until age ten, when her family moved to New York City. After graduating from Horace Mann School, Sally chose not to attend college and entered the work force instead. At age nineteen, she married Reynolds Benson, an administrator at Columbia University, with whom she had a daughter, Barbara. The Bensons eventually divorced. Sally worked briefly as a journalist before turning to creative writing. A frequent contributor to the *New Yorker*, Benson garnered national recognition when her first collection of short stories, *Junior Miss*, was a Book-of-the-Month Club selection. An energetic writer, Benson simultaneously published mystery stories under the name Esther Evarts.

Benson eternally endeared herself to St. Louisans when a collection of stories about her St. Louis childhood was published as the novel *Meet Me in St. Louis* (1941) and made into a popular film starring Judy Garland. Benson moved to Southern California during the filming of *Meet Me in St. Louis* and became a prominent screenwriter, composing scripts for such films as *National Velvet, Little Women*, and *Anna and the King of Siam*. She triumphantly returned to St. Louis for the film's premier, and again in 1960 for the stage premiere of *Meet Me in St. Louis* at The Muny. A fan of horse racing, Benson said in a *St. Louis Post-Dispatch* interview that she frequently bet on a horse named Odeon, because it reminded her of the old Odeon Theatre in St. Louis. Benson's celebrated childhood home at 5135 Kensington Avenue was demolished in 1994.

The following passage is the last chapter of *Meet Me in St. Louis*. The action centers around the Smith family's much-anticipated visit to the 1904 World's Fair, shortly before their move from St. Louis to New York City. Benson, who was only four at the time of the Fair, portrays herself as the youngest child, Tootie.

FROM *MEET ME IN ST. LOUIS*

The miracle of the World's Fair in St. Louis, rising as it did out of the wilderness, stunned everyone. It seemed impossible that only two years before, Governor Francis of Missouri had driven in the first stake with a silver ax while crowds walking through the briers and coarse grass to witness the ceremony carried heavy sticks to protect themselves from snakes. The enthusiasm of the press was unlimited, and verses appeared daily in the newspapers.

The greatest show that ever showed
Will rise beside the Skinker Road.

The buildings were elegant and formal and were constructed in the approved palatial style. There was no thought of dynamic expression or crude force in back of anything. The force was refined. There were no statues of workmen adorning the buildings, no bits of machinery were glorified in the exhibits. Greek goddesses presided over the domes, classic and beautiful. The savages, the Igorots, the Moros, the Bagobos, and Fiji Islanders, had been brought there to be stared at and not to be educated. And bandstands were everywhere. Bands from Bolivia, Honduras, Colombia, dressed in green, yellow, and scarlet. The Philippine constabulary ranged over the place. There seemed to be millions of them—small brown men in uniform, constantly hurrying. And the grounds were filled with girls—girls in the daytime in linen skirts and bolero jackets, pink, blue, yellow, and lavender, in white embroidered hats and bows to match their suits; girls in the evening in flowered organdies, who danced in the various state buildings with West Point cadets or laughed, looked on, and ate chicken salads at Mrs. Rohrer's. To the people of St. Louis, the Fair was finished, perfect. It was the cream of everything in the world. There was nothing better to come. Only the visitors complained of the mud, and the West Point Year Book ran a verse.

Ach, St. Louis,
Ach, St. Louis,
Your name's mud,
Thick and gooey.

After the opening the cultural excitement died down somewhat and people began to enjoy the Fair. They paid high prices for things and boasted about it, and what they got free they enjoyed and were silent.

A few weeks after the Fair had opened the Smith family sat at the breakfast table. It was Saturday, and they talked excitedly. "Tootie and Agnes can go with Grandpa," Mrs. Smith said. "The girls and Lon can go along with their friends. And Papa and I will get off when we can. I think it's too much to go all together."

"I don't want to go with Tootie," Agnes said. "She hasn't any interest in it, really. She wants to stay on the Pike all the time, or ride on the camels."

"I would just as soon stay home and play," Tootie said mildly. "Helen Ferris and I made a discovery yesterday. We discovered that if we start at the top of Union Hill just when we hear the brewery horses driving through the alley halfway down, we can skate right under their noses when they come out into the street."

Agnes put down her spoon. "You're a horrible girl, Tootie Smith," she said. "You might run right into those horses and hurt them."

Tootie drank her cocoa from a saucer. "We never hit them. We didn't hit them at all," she said.

"You'll go with your grandfather," Mrs. Smith said to Tootie. "I'm not going to have you carried home on a stretcher when there's no one here to take care of you."

"Then I'll go with Corinne," Agnes said. "We've decided that we'll call it the Louisiana Purchase Exposition, which it really is, instead of the World's Fair. We think World's Fair doesn't sound as nice."

"Well, Rose and I are going to see the Princeton track team with Lon," Esther said. "Just think of the bad luck! If Lon weren't a freshman, he'd probably have been running in front of all those people."

"Maybe," Lon said. "By the way, Agnes, Bob Harris was asking for you yesterday."

"Bob Harris!" Agnes gasped. "He never was!"

Rose raised her eyes. "Who on earth is Bob Harris?" she asked.

"He's a member of the Kwakiutl tribe," Agnes answered loftily. "His real name is Klakoglas, and it means 'Man who has copper.' I met him for the first time day before yesterday. He's not as good-looking as Charles James Nowell. He's a member of the tribe, too. But Bob Harris is the friendliest."

"Didn't anybody ask for me?" Tootie said.

Lon frowned and nodded. "I heard Bulon, the Chief of the Bagobos, mentioning your name," he said. "He was sharpening an ugly-looking knife and the rest of the Bagobos were dancing around, swinging their bolos and beating tom-toms. I wouldn't go near him today if I were you. He's getting ugly."

"I didn't do a thing to him," Tootie said. "And he has beautiful hair three feet long."

Mrs. Smith got up from the table. "Well," she said. "Suppose we all meet by the steps at Festival Hall at nine this evening. Then we can see the lights, and then Papa and I, the children and Grandpa can come home. Lon, you see that the girls are all right."

"They'll be all right," Lon said.

"Corinne and I are going to look at the paintings," Agnes said, "and then we're going to spend the rest of our time in the Liberal Arts Building." She got up and left the table, the skirt of her black-and-white plaid jumper dress swishing from side to side.

Rose walked to the window and stood looking out across the side yard. The weeping birch was in full leaf and the snowball bush was in bloom. "A day like today is divine," she said. "I feel absolutely scintillating."

"Well, scintillate yourself upstairs and get ready," Lon said.

Esther stood up and put her arm lightly around Lon's shoulder. "Lon," she said sweetly, "do you mind if Ida Boothby comes along with us? You know how Rose is! She'll be snapped up right off the bat by a crowd of West Pointers, especially Douglas Moore. And they consider us too *young*. So if you'll just stay with us until maybe we meet someone we know, that's all we'll ask."

"Who is Ida Boothby?" Lon asked.

"She's a girl Esther met," Rose said. "She's from Joplin, Missouri. She's a nice little thing. Her folks are down for the fair."

"She's not pretty, exactly," Esther said. "But she's real cute. She's staying with the Dodges, and we can stop by on our way to the trolley and pick her up."

"All right," Lon said. "Hurry up."

He stepped out onto the back porch. The air was soft and the sun was already beating down. There wasn't a cloud in the sky. Lon took his pipe out of his pocket, filled and lit it. The smoke curled around him in the still air and finally disappeared. He thought of the summer that lay ahead, of the long, hot evenings and the thunderstorms that sometimes flashed and cracked for an hour before the hot rain fell, and subsided, leaving the city steaming and torrid. He supposed Rose would be taken up with her new West Point beau and there wouldn't be so many evenings spent around the piano as there had been. Since he had got home he hadn't touched his mandolin once. He turned and went back into the house and into the front hall, where his mandolin case stood in the corner by the piano. He opened the case, took the mandolin out, and picked at the strings. The instrument was out of tune, and he held it near his ear, turning the keys and touching each string with his tortoise-shell pick. Then he put the mandolin back in the case.

It was cool and quiet in the hall. The front door stood open and a yellow butterfly fluttered outside the screen. The leaves of the honeysuckle vine had opened and there were a few flowers on the vine. The sun, striking the wooden steps, was almost blinding. Katie had turned the hose on the porch earlier in the day, but now it was almost dry, and small pools of water stood only where the steps had sagged in the middle. The iceman's wagon had stopped next door and the horse stamped his hoofs on the brick street and twitched his tail, impatient with the flies. Down the block, Lon could hear the sound of roller skates and the strawberry man's voice as he called, "Strawberries, nice strawberries." He listened to the chant of five notes and hummed them to himself. Although it was only May, he thought the street smelled of summer, of fruit, watermelon, and cool cucumbers. It was a smell that made him homesick, even as he stood there. He wondered what they would do at the Fair that day before and after the track meet. All the girls in town would be at the track meet, and their eyes would be worshipping. They worshipped anything, he thought. Rose and her friends considered it a disgrace to be without a West Point escort, although they pretended to be excited over the fact that so many of the boys they had known all winter were working in the concessions at the Fair. He turned away from the door and called up the stairs, "Get a move on!"

Esther and Rose came down the stairs. They were pretty and their clothes were clean and starched. Rose wore a deep-pink linen skirt, a white blouse under her jacket, and a white hat trimmed with a pink bow. Esther wore a white skirt, with a red bow in her hat and a red belt. They smelled of violets.

Lon took his hat from the hatrack and followed his sisters down the porch steps. Walking along the sidewalk with the girls fluttering at his side, he felt dull and apathetic. As they neared the Dodges' house they heard the sound of a piano.

"That's Ida," Esther said. "She plays some. She sings too. She sings very well."

"She doesn't sing anywhere nearly as well as you do, Ess," Rose said. "Her voice isn't as high. She sings a good alto, though."

They stopped in front of the house to listen. The Dodges' porch looked different, somehow, Lon thought. Someone had run a blue ribbon through the back of one of the wicker rockers, and by the side of the rocker there was a guitar tied with a large blue bow.

"Ida!" Esther called. "Sing it!"

"All right!" Ida called back. She began to sing "Nut-Brown Maiden." Her voice was low and true.

As she started to sing the second verse, Lon stepped up to the porch and sang through the screen door a parody of the song:

Nut-brown maiden, I love thy pearly, pearly teeth.
Nut-brown maiden, I love thy pearly teeth.
Thy pearly teeth are false, love,
They rattle when you waltz, love.
Nut-brown maiden, I love thy pearly teeth.

Ida swung around on the piano stool and stared at him through the screen, humming the tune with him. She saw a thin young man with light-brown hair. When the song was finished she came to the screen and opened it. As she stood there with the sun shining on her, Lon thought he had never seen a prettier girl. She was small and brown-skinned and her hair was brown, without a trace of red in it.

"This is my brother, Lon," Esther said. "Lon, I want you to meet my friend, Miss Boothby."

Ida Boothby smiled and nodded her head.

I've never heard *that* version," she said to Lon. "I don't think those are very nice words for such a pretty song." She moved away from the door, and in a few minutes she was back, holding her hat in her hand. She wore a brown linen skirt with no coat, and the hat she carried was made of brown leghorn with brown velvet ribbons. "I'll put it on when I get there," she said. "In Joplin we don't go in for hats much."

They started down the street to the trolley.

Lon walked in front with Rose, and Esther and Ida trailed along behind. "She's a sweet little thing," Rose said.

"She's just a kid," Lon said. "She looks younger than Ess."

"That's just her way," Rose said. "She's no *younger.* As a matter of fact, I think she's older."

On the trolley, Rose sat down near the window and motioned to Esther to sit beside her. As the car started, Ida lurched to the side and Lon caught her by the arm. They laughed and moved to a seat nearer the front. The window was open, and Ida leaned out and let the wind blow through her hair. Her hair was short and curly and was caught into a knot at the top of her head. She wore no pompadour. "I'm disgracefully tanned," she said.

"What of it?" Lon said. "The girls here are scared of a little tan. You look all right tanned. You look like a pecan."

"Esther tells me you are a Princeton man," she said.

Lon blushed. "What's your favorite college?" he asked.

She glanced at him through her lashes. "Princeton," she said.

At the fairgrounds, they made their way through the crowds to the Plaza of St. Louis, where Rose had promised to meet Douglas Moore. Ida walked beside Lon. It was cool at the Plaza and the mist from the fountains blew into her face. She stood back from the Lagoon and looked up at the statue of St. Louis mounted upon a Norman horse. The statue guarded the gates to the great central plaza of the exposition, and St. Louis held high the cross hilt of his sword. Nearby were equestrian statues of Joliet and DeSoto. The four young people breathed in the cool air.

"Here he is," Rose said. "Here's Mr. Moore. He's got somebody with him."

Esther looked at her sister, suspicion in her eyes. "If you—" she began.

"I didn't say a word, I assure you," Rose said.

The two young men were out of breath. "Good morning, Miss Smith," Douglas Moore said to Rose. "I hope we haven't kept you waiting. We've been parading and it held us up. Miss Smith, I'd like you to meet my brother John. He's not a West Pointer now, but he will be in the fall."

John Moore was smaller than his brother and very blond. He glanced admiringly at Rose, but it was plain that his real interest lay in the two younger girls. He looked Ida Boothby over and, seeing that she was standing close to Lon, he discarded her and turned to Esther, pleased and excited. "I hoped you were going to turn out to be the one," he said.

The girls screamed, and Ida Boothby called out "Well, I like that, I must say."

Rose gave a last little laugh and fanned her face with her handkerchief. "Now, suppose we decide what to do," she said.

"Well, if Miss Esther doesn't mind, it's Asia for me," John Moore said.

"Oh, I adore Asia," Esther said. "And I've never ridden on the camels."

"*I* would like to stroll around," Rose said. "And then maybe have some Scotch scones."

"I think it would be nice to see all the state buildings," Ida Boothby said. "I haven't been in one of them."

"All right," Douglas Moore said. "We'll make it this way. I'll stroll with Miss Smith. And John and Esther and Lon and Miss Boothby can do what they want to do. And if we don't meet at the track meet, where can we meet?"

"Well, we promised our family that we would meet them at nine by Festival Hall," Rose said. "Of course, nine is awfully long, and we may get tired of one another."

They laughed hilariously at this and started out across the Plaza.

Tootie skipped by Grandpa Prophater's side. "Let's see the Galveston Flood again, shall we?" she asked. "Let's see it as many times as we can and then go on to the Pike." She shifted a handful of spun sugar from one hand to the other and looked up at him. "We're really right by the Galveston Flood," she said.

Grandpa Prophater looked toward the building, which had "GALVESTON FLOOD" in large letters across the front, and sighed. Then he put his hand in his pocket, rattling his loose change, and walked through the archway, holding Tootie by one sticky hand. They sat down and waited for the theatre to grow dark. Tootie sat forward on her seat, her eyes staring fixedly at the curtain. "How much did it cost to make this?" she asked.

"A lot of money," Grandpa Prophater said. "About fifty or sixty thousand dollars."

"Golly!" Tootie said.

The house grew dark and the curtain rose. At the foreground there were grass, trees, and fences of real material, and in back of these was a canvas painted to represent the city of Galveston and the Galveston beach. The beach had real water washing up on it, and farther out to sea the waves rolled. Boats moved in and out of the harbor. Little streetcars ran along the streets and trains ran across the trestlework spanning Galveston Bay. The day closed with wonderful cloud effects and the sun set a blazing track across the ocean. As the sunlight faded, Tootie gripped her grandfather's arm. "Here it comes now!" she whispered. "Here it comes! Here's where the storm begins." The dark clouds gathered and the gale began. The water rose and the waves increased in size until the water filled the streets. The fury of the storm grew until a mist enveloped the whole city and a dreadful roaring sound filled the air. Suddenly the rain stopped and the waves rolled back. Ships lazy strewn on the beach and the city was shown in ruins. The stage grew dark again, and then the new Galveston was revealed, salvaged and rebuilt from the disaster.

Tootie stood up. "I don't like it when the city gets all fixed again," she said. "I like it when it's flooded and horrible."

"You wouldn't like it if you were there," Grandpa Prophater said. He snorted and looked down at her as she wriggled through the crowds like an eel. "At that," he added, "you might like it. You'd probably live through it, too."

"Now the Pike?" she asked.

He took a worn five-dollar bill from his pocket. "Now the Pike," he said. He spoke with an air of happy anticipation.

Agnes and Corinne stood in front of a painting of Mary Magdalene. "I'm tired," Corinne said. "And I think we should have something to eat."

"Don't bother me when I'm taking notes," Agnes said. "That's the Cross of Jesus." She looked at the lovely arms of Mary Magdalene as she knelt at the foot of the Cross, and at her hands, that caressed the feet of her Saviour.

Corinne stood dumbly in front of the picture, and as Agnes turned away she repeated, "I do think we ought to eat."

"We'll eat as soon as we look at 'Beneath the Beech.' We have to stand in front of it for twenty minutes at least," Agnes said.

"We've stood in front of them all for twenty minutes," Corinne said.

"Do you want to come out of here with nothing?" Agnes asked. "Unless you stand twenty minutes in front of a work of art you come out with nothing."

They moved toward the Belgian section of the Palace of Arts, and Agnes looked around until she found the painting she had been looking for. It showed a flock of sheep feeding in the shade of a huge beech tree. A shepherdess watched over the flock.

"Those don't look like leaves to me," Corinne said. "They look like blots of paint."

"You have to pretend they're leaves," Agnes said. "I can pretend easy. I never saw anyone who could pretend less than you. Even Tootie can see anything she wants to."

They stood in front of the painting for exactly twenty minutes by Agnes's small watch, and then moved on.

It was after nine when Mr. and Mrs. Smith got to Festival Hall. They had decided to stay home after all and had taken the trolley to the fairgrounds in the cool of the evening. It was still twilight and the lights were not turned on. "I hope they get here before the electricity begins," Mrs. Smith said. "It is almost ghostly to see it."

To their right they saw Grandpa Prophater and Tootie. Grandpa was walking slowly, but Tootie danced and skipped at his side. He walked up to his daughter and turned his pockets inside out. "Well, Annie," he said. "She cleaned me."

"Have you had any dinner?" Mrs. Smith asked.

"No," he said. "But we've had everything else. So don't ask me if I'm hungry. I never expect to be hungry again."

"We went in this place, Mamma," Tootie said. "This place on the Pike. There was a girl in there with a spangled dress that came to her knees. She had on a lot of ruffles, too. And she had her face all painted up to look pretty. We stayed and saw her three times."

"Father!" Mrs. Smith said.

Grandpa Prophater shrugged his shoulders. "I didn't want to stay," he said. "She was the one. She knows the whole act and all the words to the song."

"I do. That's right," Tootie said. "It's called 'Teasing.' It goes, 'Teasing, teasing, I was only teasing you.' I'm going to do it all for Lon. He'll like it."

Agnes came running along the cement path toward her mother. "Mamma!" she cried breathless. "Guess what they have. It's the best you ever saw. I mean it's the best of them all. It's a black-and-white chicken and a red barn, and it might just as well be at Grandma's. I liked it much better than the odalisques. And I wrote down a beautiful description of it. It's by a man named Zorn. Just a black-and-white chicken. I suppose it was his favorite and he painted its portrait."

Mrs. Smith drew her arm around Agnes and pulled her close to her skirts. "You're tired," she said. "And where is Corinne?"

"Her!" Agnes exclaimed. "*She* got tired. She doesn't care anything about paintings. All she thinks is eat, eat, eat."

"Didn't you get a bite *anywhere*?" Mrs. Smith asked.

"I ate some ice cream," Agnes said. "I spent the rest of my money on postcards they sell at the Palace of Arts."

In couples, the rest of the family arrived, Lon with Ida, Rose with Douglas Moore, and Esther hanging onto John Moore's arm and laughing foolishly. They stood talking and laughing, waiting for the lights to go on.

Lon hummed "Nut-Brown Maiden" into Ida's ear, and she smiled. "But with the *right* words," she said.

"The right words," he repeated. He never remembered feeling half so happy before in his life. And he wondered that a girl as feminine as Ida would go to the Transportation Palace with him, a building that suggested a magnificent railroad terminal.

"Mamma," Rose said, "Mr. Moore has asked me to West Point next winter. Don't you think I might say yes?"

Mrs. Smith gave a sharp glance toward Mr. Moore. He was a nice-looking boy, she thought. "Ask your father, Rose," she said.

"I think it would be more than all right," John Moore said. "Especially if Miss Esther were allowed to come, too."

"Well—" Mrs. Smith began as tiny sparks of light outlined the Cascades, Festival Hall, and the Colonnade of States. Suddenly the outlines of the columns, the arches, and the great statues were obliterated entirely. The lights glowed in dull redness and expanded into white light. It was as though the picture had been rebuilt in a minute, not of substance but of light. The successive falls of the Cascades shone in the brilliance. The white lights faded out and from bottom to top, from end to end, the Festival Hall, the Colonnade, and the Pavilions stood out in carmine.

Everyone stopped talking, and Rose drew in her breath sharply. "There never has been anything like it in this world," she said. "There never will be."

Mr. Smith put his arm around his wife's waist and Tootie and Agnes clung to Grandpa Prophater. "And just think," Mrs. Smith said, her voice soft and awe-stricken. "It's all right here where we live."

"Right by the old Skinker Road," Mr. Smith said.

"I remember when the road didn't amount to a hill of beans," Grandpa

Prophater said.

"It's where we live," Agnes repeated. "We don't have to visit here. We don't have to come on a train, or stay at a hotel, or anything. They won't ever tear it down, will they?"

"No," Tootie said. "They will never tear it down. It will be like this forever."

"I can't believe it," Agnes said. "Right here where we live. Right here in St. Louis."

MILES DAVIS

UNDOUBTEDLY ONE OF THE MOST INFLUENTIAL musicians of the twentieth century, Miles Davis (1926–1991) was born in Alton, Illinois, but grew up in East St. Louis, where his family moved when he was a year old. The son of a dentist, Davis enjoyed a middle-class upbringing that provided him with fine clothes and music lessons. At age thirteen, Davis began taking lessons from "a great German trumpet teacher named Gustav," who played first chair trumpet with the St. Louis Symphony Orchestra. At age sixteen, Davis began playing trumpet with Eddie Randle and his Blue Devils, a popular band in the St. Louis area, and was fully aware that music was his destiny.

In the fall of 1944, after graduating from Lincoln High School, Davis left East St. Louis for New York City, where he attended the Juilliard School of Music, which he eventually left to play with Charlie Parker. Throughout the 1950s and '60s, Davis worked on developing his unique style and emerged as one of the most innovative figures in jazz. An automobile accident in 1972 briefly halted Davis's career, but he went on to produce six more albums and made his last St. Louis appearance at Kiel Opera House in 1981.

The following excerpt is from the second chapter of his autobiography, *Miles: The Autobiography* (1989, with Quincy Troupe). In this passage, Davis recalls discovering his talent and passion for music and his decision to leave St. Louis.

FROM *MILES: THE AUTOBIOGRAPHY*

By the time I was twelve, music had become the most important thing in my life. I probably didn't realize how important it would become, but looking back, I can see just how important it was. I still played baseball and football, still hung out with my friends like Millard Curtis and Darnell Moore. But

I was seriously taking trumpet lessons and was really into my horn. I remember going to Boy Scout camp near Waterloo, Illinois, when I was about twelve or thirteen. It was Camp Vanderventer, and Mr. Mays, the Head Scoutmaster, knew that I played trumpet. He gave me the job of playing taps and reveille. I remember how proud I was for him to ask me, picking me out from everyone. So I guess by then I was starting to play all right.

But I really started to stretch on out as a player after I left Attucks Junior High and went to Lincoln High School. My first great teacher, Elwood Buchanan, was at Lincoln. Lincoln was both a junior and senior high school; I went there for junior high and stayed all the way to graduation. When I started playing in the band I was younger than everybody else. After my father, Mr. Buchanan was the biggest influence on my life up until then. He was definitely the person who took me all the way into music at that time. I knew I wanted to become a musician. That was all I wanted to be.

Mr. Buchanan was one of my father's patients and drinking buddies. My father told him how interested I was in music and in playing trumpet, specifically. So he said he would give me trumpet lessons and that was that. I was going to Attucks when I first started taking lessons from Mr. Buchanan. Later, after I started going to Lincoln High School, he still sort of looked after me to keep me on the right track.

On my thirteenth birthday, my father bought me a new trumpet. My mother wanted me to have a violin, but my father overruled her. This caused a big argument between them, but she soon got over it. But Mr. Buchanan was the reason I got a new trumpet, because he knew how bad I wanted to play.

It was about that time that I first started having serious disagreements with my mother. Up until then, it had been over small things. But it just kind of went downhill. I don't really know what her problem was. But I think it had something to do with her not talking real straight to me. She was still trying to treat me like I was a little baby, the way she was treating my brother, Vernon. I think this had something to do with him becoming a homosexual. The women—my mother, my sister, and my grandmother—always treated Vernon like a girl. So, I wasn't having none of that shit from them. It was a matter of talking straight to me or not talking to me at all. My father told my mother to leave me alone when we started having problems. And she did most of the time, but we really got into some bad arguments. Despite all that, my mother did buy me two records by Duke Ellington and Art Tatum, though. I used to listen to them all the time and that helped me later in understanding jazz.

Because Mr. Buchanan had already given me trumpet lessons at Attucks before I came to Lincoln, I was advanced on the instrument. I was already playing pretty good. Then in high school I also started studying with a great German trumpet teacher named Gustav who lived over in St. Louis and played first trumpet with the St. Louis Symphony Orchestra. He was a bad motherfucker. He also made great trumpet mouthpieces, and I use one of his design even today.

At Lincoln High, the band under Mr. Buchanan's direction was a motherfucker. We had a hell of a cornet and trumpet section. It was me, Ralaigh McDaniels, Red Bonner, Duck McWaters, and Frank Gully—who played first trumpet and was a bad motherfucker. He was about three years older than I was. Because I was the smallest and youngest person in the band, some of the kids would pick on me. But I was mischievous, too, playing little pranks on people and shit—throwing spitballs and hitting people upside the head when they weren't looking. You know, little kid, teenage shit, wasn't none of it serious.

Everybody always seemed to like my tone, which I kind of got from the way Mr. Buchanan played at the time. This was on cornet. As a matter of fact, Red and Frank and everybody else who was playing cornet or trumpet in the band used to pass around Mr. Buchanan's instrument; I think I was the only one in the cornet section who had his own instrument. But even though they were all older than me and I had a lot to learn, they all encouraged me, liked the way I sounded, the way I approached playing. They always used to tell me I had a lot of imagination on the instrument.

Mr. Buchanan kept us playing strictly marches and shit like that. Overtures, real good background music, John Philip Sousa marches. He didn't let us play no jazz shit while he was around, but when he would leave the band room for a while we would try to get into some jazz. One of the hippest things Mr. Buchanan taught me was not to play with vibrato in my tone. At first, I used to like to play with vibrato because of the way most of the other trumpet players played the instrument. One day while I was playing in that style, with all this vibrato, Mr. Buchanan stopped the band and told me, "Look here, Miles. Don't come around here with that Harry James stuff, playing with all that vibrato. Stop shaking all those notes and trembling them, because you gonna be shaking enough when you get old. Play straight, develop your *own* style, because you can do it. You got enough talent to be your own trumpet man."

Man, I never forgot that. But at the time, he hurt and embarrassed me. I just loved the way Harry James played. But after that I started to forget James and found out that Mr. Buchanan was right. At least, he was right for me.

By the time I was in high school I started getting really serious about my clothes. I started caring about the way I looked, trying to look hip and everything, because about this time girls started paying attention to me—although at age fourteen I wasn't really into them yet. So I started dressing real hip, taking a lot of time about selecting the clothes I bought and wore to school. Me and a couple of my friends—who were also into clothes—started comparing notes on what was hip and what wasn't. I liked the dress style of Fred Astaire and Cary Grant back then, so I created a kind of hip, quasi-black English look: Brooks Brothers suits, butcher boy shoes, high top pants, shirts with high tab collars that were so stiff with starch that I could hardly move my neck.

One of the most important things that happened for me in high school—besides studying under Mr. Buchanan—was when one time the band went to play in Carbondale, Illinois, and I met Clark Terry, the trumpet player. He became my idol on the instrument. He was older than me and was a drinking buddy of Mr. Buchanan. Anyway, we went down there to Carbondale to play and I saw this dude and walked right up to him and asked him if he was a trumpet player. He turned and asked me how I knew he was a trumpet player. I told him I could tell by his embouchure. I had on my school band uniform and Clark had on this hip coat and this bad, beautiful scarf around his neck. He was wearing hip butcher boy shoes and a bad hat cocked ace-deuce. I told him I could also tell he was a trumpet player by the hip shit he was wearing.

He kind of smiled at me and said something that I have forgotten. Then, when I asked him some things about playing trumpet, he sort of shined on me by telling me that he didn't want to "talk about no trumpet with all them pretty girls bouncing around out there." Clark was really into the girls at that time, and I wasn't. So what he said to me really hurt me. The next time we met it was a different story altogether. But I never forgot that first time me and Clark met, how hip he was. I decided then I was going to be that hip, even hipper, when I got my shit together.

I started hanging out with my friend Bobby Danzig. Bobby was about the same age as me and was a hell of a trumpet player. We used to go around listening to music and sitting in wherever we could. We went everywhere together, we were both into clothes, even thought a lot alike. But he was more outspoken than me. He would tell a motherfucker off in a minute. Man, we'd go to a club and listen to a band and if the horn player was standing wrong, or the drummer had his drums set up wrong, Bobby would say, "Let's get out of here, man, because this motherfucker can't play. Look at how the drummer done set up his drums, man; they're wrong. And look at how that trumpet player's standing. His posture's all fucked up. Now, you *know* that motherfucker can't play standing up there on the bandstand like that! So let's get out of here!"

Man, Bobby Danzig was something else. He was a great trumpet player and he was even a greater pickpocket. He'd get on one of them trolleys that was running in St. Louis and by the time it had reached the end of the line, Bobby would have himself $300, or more on a great day. I met Bobby when I was sixteen and I think he was the same age. We joined the union together and we'd go everywhere together. Bobby was my first musical best friend, my running partner. Like I said, it was him who went with me to the Riviera when I went to audition for the Billy Eckstine band, and he could play trumpet like a motherfucker. I later became good friends with Clark Terry, but Clark was about six years older than I was and so we were into different head sets. But Bobby was right there in the things we liked to do together. Except I was never into picking pockets like he was. He was the best at it I have ever seen.

Another great trumpet player was Levi Maddison. My teacher Gustav used to rave about him. Levi was his star pupil, and man, he was a motherfucker. Back in those days, around 1940, St. Louis was a great city for trumpet players and Levi was one of *the* baddest, if not the baddest. But Levi was a crazy motherfucker who went around laughing to himself all the time. And once he started laughing at something he couldn't stop. A lot of people said he was laughing all the time because he was despondent. I don't know *what* Levi was despondent over, but I know he could sure play the trumpet. I used to love to watch him. His trumpet was an extension of him. But all of the trumpet players from St. Louis at that time played like that—Harold "Shorty" Baker, Clark Terry, and myself. We all played like that, had what I used to call "that St. Louis thing."

Levi would always be smiling with that crazy look in his eyes. That distant thing. He was out and he was always being confined in the nuthouse for a few days. He didn't never hurt nobody, he wasn't violent or anything like that. But I guess people back in those days didn't want to take no chances. Later, after I left St. Louis to live in New York, every time I would come back home for a visit I would go and see Levi. Finding him was sometimes difficult. When I found him, though, I would always ask him to put the trumpet to his mouth just because I loved the way he held it. And he would, with a big smile on his face.

Then once when I came back I couldn't find him. They said he started laughing one day and couldn't stop. So they took him to the sanatorium and he never came out again. Or, at least, nobody ever saw him again. But the thing Levi used to do on trumpet was just too bad, man, he was a hell of a musician. When he picked up the horn you would hear all this tone and brilliance, you know? Nobody else had it and I have yet to hear a tone like that. It's almost like mine, but it was rounder—sort of in between Freddie Webster's and mine.

And Levi had that air about him when he picked up his horn that you were going to hear something you'd never heard before in your life. Only a few people had that attitude. Dizzy had it and I think I have it. But Levi was the man. He was a motherfucker. If he hadn't gone crazy and went to the nuthouse, people would have been talking about him today.

Gustav would tell *me* I was the worst trumpet player in the world. But later, when Dizzy had a hole in his lip that wouldn't heal and so he went to see Gustav about changing mouthpieces, he said Gus told him that I was his best pupil. All I know is that Gus never told me that to my face.

Maybe Gus thought that by telling me I was his worst student that I would play harder. Maybe he thought that was the way to get the best out of me. I don't know. But it didn't bother me. As long as he taught me that half an hour for the $2.50 I paid him, he could say anything he wanted. Gus was a technician. He could run chromatic scales about twelve times in one breath. He was something. But by the time I was going to him for lessons I already had some confidence in my playing. I knew I wanted to be a musician and so everything I did was leaning toward that.

While I was in high school I started hanging out with a piano player named Emmanual St. Claire "Duke" Brooks. (His nephew, Richard Brooks, an all-American football player, is now the principal of Miles Davis Elementary School.) He got his nickname "Duke" because he knew and could play all of Duke Ellington's music. He used to play with the bassist

Jimmy Blanton at a place across the street from where I lived then called the Red Inn. Duke Brooks was two or three years older than me, but he had a big influence on me because he was into the new music that was happening at the time.

Duke Brooks was a hell of a piano player. Man, the motherfucker played like Art Tatum. He used to teach me chords and shit. He lived in East St. Louis and had a room by himself in his parents' house, off the porch. I'd go over to his house and listen to him at lunchtime when I was going to Lincoln High School. He lived about two or three blocks from school. He smoked a lot of reefer and I think he was the first person I knew who did that. I never did it with him, though. I never did like reefer too much. But then, at that time, I wasn't doing nothing, not even drinking.

Duke eventually got killed when he was hoboing a ride on a train somewhere in Pennsylvania. He was in one of those cars filled with gravel and sand. I heard the shit fell on him and he suffocated. I think this was in 1945. I still miss him and think about him even up until today. He was a hell of a musician and if he hadn't gotten killed, he would have been a motherfucker on the music scene.

I was starting to play the running trumpet style that I was hearing around St. Louis. Me and Duke and a drummer named Nick Haywood—who had a hump in his back—had a little group together. We used to try to play like the black guys who played in Benny Goodman's band. Benny had a black piano player named Teddy Wilson. But Duke played hipper than Teddy Wilson. Duke played piano then like Nat "King" Cole. He was just that slick, Duke was.

The only new records we had during this time were mostly the records they took out of jukeboxes and sold you for a nickel. And if you didn't have money to buy it then you'd just have to go and cop it by listening to the jukebox. I was playing by ear back then. Anyway, our little group would play tunes like "Airmail Special." We'd play it with those hip accents. Duke was such a motherfucker on the piano that it made me play in the running style he had.

About this time I was starting to have a little reputation around East St. Louis as an up-and-coming trumpet player. People—musicians—thought I could play, but I wasn't vain enough to admit it out loud. But the way I was beginning to think to myself was that I could play as good as any motherfucker walking. I probably thought I could play better. Because when it came to reading music and remembering the parts, I had a photographic memory. I didn't forget anything. I was also improving as a soloist from working with Mr. Buchanan and being around guys like Duke Brooks and Levi Maddison. So, a lot of things were starting to fall into place. Some of the best musicians around East St. Louis wanted me to play with them. I was beginning to think I was the hippest thing around.

Maybe one of the reasons I didn't say it out loud was because Mr. Buchanan was still on my back to get better at Lincoln High. Although he leaned toward me in the band after Frank Gully graduated—I was playing most of the first parts—he still came down on me hard sometimes. He'd say my sound was too small or he'd tell me he couldn't hear me sometimes. But he was always like that—hard on you, especially if he thought you could play. Once when I was younger and everybody was thinking I was going to be a dentist, he had told my father, "Doc, Miles ain't gonna be no dentist. He's gonna be a musician." So he'd already seen something in me even back then. He told me later that it was my curiosity, wanting to know so much about music, that was my edge. That was carrying me forward all the time.

Duke Brooks and Nick Haywood, some other guys, and me used to play at a place called Huff's Beer Garden. Frank Gully used to play there with us sometimes. We'd make some pocket change on Saturdays. But it wasn't nothing to call home about. We'd just make the gigs for the fun of it. We played all kinds of little gigs in East St. Louis: social clubs, church affairs, any place we could play. Sometimes we'd make as much as six dollars a night. We used to practice in my basement too. Man, did we play loud. I remember one time my father came by Huff's to hear us play. When he told me about it the next day, he said all he could hear was the drums. Anyway, we were trying to play all of Harry James's tunes. But after a while, I quit the band, because outside of Duke's playing there wasn't nothing happening for me in it.

Thinking about nothing but music cut me out of the gang wars and shit, and limited the time for playing sports. I was practicing every chance I got—fucking around trying to learn how to play piano, too. I was learning how to improvise and really getting deep into jazz. I wanted to be able to play the things I heard Harry James playing. So I quickly got tired of listening to motherfuckers who couldn't play hip shit. Some of the guys who weren't advanced in music started to laugh at me for trying to play the newer music. But I didn't give a fuck about what they were talking about. I *knew* that I was on the right track.

About the time I was sixteen I had a chance to play some gigs on the road—Belleville, Illinois, places like that. My mother said I could play on weekends. This was with a guy named Pickett. We used to play shit like "Intermezzo," "Honeysuckle Rose," and "Body and Soul." I would just play the melodies because nothing else hip was happening. We were making a little pocket change. But I was learning all the time. Pickett played that roadhouse music, or what some call honky-tonk. You know. That shit that they play in black "bucket of blood" clubs. "Bucket of blood" refers to the fights that were likely to jump off in those clubs. But after a while I got tired of asking when I was going to be able to get off—play the hip shit I was getting into. It wasn't long before I quit Pickett's band.

By the time I was fifteen or sixteen, I had learned how to play chromatic scales, too. When I started playing that shit everybody around Lincoln stopped and asked me what I was doing. They started looking at me differently after that. Also, me and Duke were beginning to catch jam sessions in Brooklyn, Illinois—just up the road from East St. Louis. One of my father's best friends was the mayor of Brooklyn, so he let me play even though I was too young to be going into clubs. A lot of really fine musicians played those riverboats on the Mississippi from New Orleans to St. Louis. They were always sitting in up in those all-night Brooklyn nightspots. Man, them places was always jumping, especially on weekends.

East St. Louis and St. Louis were country towns full of country people. Both towns are real square, especially the white people from around there—*really* country, and racist to the bone. Black people from around East St. Louis and St. Louis were country, too, but kind of hip in their countryness. It was a hip place. A lot of people from that area had a whole lot of style back in those days—still probably do. Black people from that area of the country are kind of different from black people in other places. And I think when I was growing up it was because of the people—especially black musicians—moving back and forth from New Orleans. St. Louis is close to Chicago and Kansas City, as well. So people would bring the different kinds of styles of those places back to East St. Louis.

There was a hipness in the black people then. After St. Louis closed down at night, everybody over there came to Brooklyn to listen to the music and party all night long. People in East St. Louis and St. Louis worked their asses off in them packing and slaughterhouses. So you know they was mad when they took off work. They didn't want to hear no dumb shit off nobody, and would kill a motherfucker quick who brought them some stupid shit. That's why they were serious about their partying and listening to music. That's why I loved playing up in Brooklyn. People were really into listening to what you were playing. If you weren't playing anything, the people in Brooklyn would let you know it quick. I've always liked honesty and can't stand people being any other way.

About this time I was starting to make a little money, not much. My teachers at Lincoln knew that I was serious about being a musician. Some of them heard me up in Brooklyn on weekends or at other jam sessions. But I made it a point to do real good in my studies, because if I didn't, I knew my mother and father weren't going to let me play. So I studied harder.

When I was sixteen, I met Irene Birth, who was going to Lincoln with me. She had real pretty feet. I was always a sucker for pretty little feet. She was about five feet six inches tall and weighed about 103 pounds. A slender woman, but a real nice figure—reminded me of a dancer's body. She was half yellow-looking in color. You know, kind of light-skinned, but half-assed light skin. Outside of her being pretty and hip, with a good body, her feet is what really attracted me. She was a little older than I was—I think she was born May 12, 1923—and a couple of grades ahead of me. But she liked me and I liked her and she was the first real girlfriend that I had. . . .

Irene was the person who, when I was seventeen, dared me to call up Eddie Randle and ask him for a job in his band. Eddie Randle's Blue Devils band was hot, man; them motherfuckers could play their asses off. I was over to her house when she dared me, so I told her to give me the phone, and I called him up. When he answered the phone, I said, "Mr. Randle, I hear you need a trumpet player; my name is Miles Davis."

He said, "Yeah, I need a trumpet player. Come on over and let me hear you."

So I went over to the Elks Club in downtown St. Louis where the Rhumboogie Club was located. It was on the second floor, up a long, narrow flight of stairs, in a building sitting off by itself. It was in the black community, so the place would be packed with black people who really were into music. This was where Eddie Randle played. His band was also billed as the Rhumboogie Orchestra. I auditioned with another trumpet player and got the job.

The Blue Devils played hot dance music so good and there were so many good musicians in that band that everybody used to come hear us play, no matter what kind of music they themselves played. Duke Ellington came through and heard Jimmy Blanton, the great bass player, sitting in with us one night and hired him on the spot.

There was an alto saxophone player in the Blue Devils named Clyde Higgins, who was one of the baddest motherfuckers I ever heard. His wife, Mabel, played piano with the Blue Devils. She was a great musician and a great woman. She was fatter than a motherfucker, though, and Clyde was skinnier than a motherfucker. But she was something else, a beautiful person. I spent a lot of time learning from her. She showed me a lot of shit on piano, which helped me to develop even faster as a musician.

Another dude who played a great alto was Eugene Porter. He was almost as bad. He was younger than Clyde and wasn't in the band, but he sat in a lot. Eddie Randle played a mean trumpet himself. But Clyde Higgins was so bad that when him and Eugene Porter went down to audition for a gig with Jimmie Lunceford's band, Clyde blew them all away. See, Clyde was a tiny, real black man, and he looked like a monkey. Back during those days a lot of bands that played for white people liked to hire light-skinned musicians, and so Clyde was too dark for them. Eugene said when Clyde went for the audition and told Lunceford he was a saxophone player, everybody laughed at him and started calling him "the little monkey." They gave him the toughest music they had in their book to play. Clyde, being the great musician that he was, ran right through it like it wasn't nothing. At least, that's what Eugene said. When Clyde got through playing, all them cats in Lunceford's band had their mouths hanging open. So Lunceford said to them, "Well, how y'all like that?" Nobody said nothing. Clyde didn't get the job, though. Eugene did, because he was better-looking and light-skinned, and a real good alto player. But he wasn't even close to Clyde Higgins. And he told everybody that Clyde should have gotten the job. But that's the way things were back then in those days.

Playing with Eddie Randle had to be one of the most important steps in my career. It was with Eddie Randle's band that I really started opening up with my playing, really got into writing and arranging music. I became the musical director of the band, because most of the other guys in the band were working regular gigs in the daytime, so they didn't have the time to get the music together. I was in charge of setting up rehearsals and rehearsing the band. They had other acts at the Rhumboogie, like dancers and comedians, singers, shit like that. So sometimes the band accompanied another act and I had to get the band ready for that. We traveled some and played all over the St. Louis and East St. Louis areas. I met many other great musicians when they came through. I learned a lot being in Eddie Randle's band, and I made more money than I had ever made, about $75 or $80 a week.

I stayed with Eddie Randle's band for about a year, from 1943 to 1944, I think. I used to call him "Bossman," because that's what he was to me—the boss—and he ran a tight band. I learned a lot from him about how to run a band. We used to do the musical charts and arrangements of Benny Goodman, Lionel Hampton, Duke Ellington, and all them bad cats that were playing back then. There were a lot of great bands around St. Louis, like the Jeter-Pillars Band and George Hudson's band. Man, both of *them* bands was motherfuckers, too. But Ernie Wilkins, who was the arranger for the Blue Devils when I was in that band, and Jimmy Forrest came out of Eddie Randle's band, so I guess I would have to say that he—Eddie Randle—was a leader of great musicians. But George Hudson was a mean trumpet player, too. St. Louis, like New Orleans, is a big trumpet player's town, maybe because of all those marching bands in St. Louis. All I know is that some bad motherfuckers on trumpet came out of there and when I was growing up trumpet players from all over the country used to come through to play in those jam sessions. But I hear it's a lot different today.

I remember when I ran into Clark Terry again at the Rhumboogie; it was a different story from when I had first met him. Now, here he comes into the Rhumboogie to hear *me* play. I said to him when he ran up to me telling me how bad I was, "Yeah, motherfucker, you come up to me now saying that shit, when you wouldn't even talk to me when I first met you over in Carbondale; I'm the little dude you shined on over there." So man, we just laughed, and have been great friends ever since. But him telling me I was bad and could really play at that time did a lot of good. I already had confidence, but Clark telling me this just gave me more. After Clark and I became friends, we hung out all over the St. Louis area, sitting in and going to jam sessions, and when people heard that Clark and I were going to be sitting in on a particular night, the place would fill up quick, be jammed-packed with people. Clark Terry was the one who really opened up the St. Louis jazz scene for me, taking me with him when he would go sit in. I learned a lot from listening to him play the trumpet. He introduced me to the fluegelhorn, too, which I played for a while, calling the one I had "my fat girl," because of the way it was shaped.

But I had an impact on Clark also, because he used to borrow my fluegelhorn and keep it for a couple of days because I preferred playing the trumpet. That's how he started playing fluegelhorn, and he's still playing it today and is one of the best in the world at playing it, if not *the* best. All through this period I loved Clark Terry—still do to this day—and I think he felt the same way about me. Every time I got a new horn back in those days, I would go looking for Clark to fix up my horn, get the valves to working, and he would fix it up like nobody else could. Man, Clark had a way of twisting and lightening the spring action of the pumps of a trumpet, just by adjusting the springs around, that would make your horn sound altogether different. It made your horn sound like magic, man. Clark was a magician with that shit. I used to love for Clark to fix my valves. And he used to always use those Heim mouthpieces of Gustav's design with his instrument, because they were very thin but very deep, and gave a big, round, warm sound. All the St. Louis trumpet players used them. One time I lost mine and Clark got me a new one. After that, every time he would find an extra one he'd get it for me in St. Louis.

While I was with Eddie Randle's band, like I said, a lot of other great musicians used to come and listen to the band—people like Benny Carter and Roy Eldridge, and the trumpet player Kenny Dorham, who came all the way from Austin, Texas, to hear me play. He had heard about me all the way down there. Then there was Alonzo Pettiford, who also played trumpet, and who was the bass player Oscar Pettiford's brother. He was from Oklahoma and was one of the baddest trumpet players around back in those days. Man, could that motherfucker play fast—his fingers were a blur. He played that real fast, hip, slick Oklahoma style. Then there was Charlie Young, who played both saxophone *and* trumpet, and played both of them *real* good. And then I met "the President," Lester Young, when he would come down from Kansas City to play in St. Louis. He'd have Shorty McConnell on trumpet in his band, and sometimes I'd come over with my horn to where they were playing and sit in. Man, playing with Prez was something. I learned a lot from the way he played the saxophone. As a matter of fact, I tried to transpose some of his saxophone licks over to my trumpet.

Then there was "Fats" Navarro, who came through from Florida or New Orleans. Nobody knew who he was, but that motherfucker could play like I had never heard nobody play before. He was young, like me, but he was already advanced in his concept of how to play the instrument. Fats was in a band of Andy Kirk's and Howard McGhee's, who was also a fantastic trumpet player. One night him and me got into a jam session on trumpet that was a motherfucker, turned the whole place out. I think this was sometime in 1944. After I heard that band, Howard became my idol, replacing Clark Terry for a while, until I heard Dizzy.

I also met Sonny Stitt around this time. He was playing in Tiny Bradshaw's band and so in between sets at the club he was playing at he would come over to the Rhumboogie to catch our set. After Sonny Stitt heard the band and my playing, he approached me about going on the road with Tiny Bradshaw's band. Man, talk about excited, I couldn't wait to get home to ask my parents if I could go. Plus, Sonny had told me I looked like Charlie Parker. All the cats in the band had their hair slicked back, was wearing hip shit—tuxedos and white shirts—and acting and talking like they was the baddest motherfuckers in the world. You know what I mean? They impressed the fuck out of me. But when I got home and asked my parents, they said no, because I hadn't finished high school yet. I would have been making only $60, $25 less than I was making with Eddie Randle's Blue Devils. I think it was the idea of traveling on the road with a big time band that impressed me the most. Plus, they seemed so hip and were wearing such hip shit. At least, it seemed that way to me back then. I got other offers from Illinois Jacquet, McKinney's Cotton Pickers, and A. J. Sullivan to travel on the road playing in their bands. I also had to turn them down until I graduated from high school. Man, I wanted to hurry up and graduate so that I could get on with playing music and living my life. I was still quiet. Still didn't talk much. But I was changing on the inside. And I really was into clothes—I was clean as a motherfucker, or like they used to say back in St. Louis, cleaner than a broke-dick dog.

Things were going great for me musically, but things at home were not going so good. My parents were getting along worse than ever and were just about to separate. They did separate around 1944, I forget which year it was. My sister, Dorothy, was starting college at Fisk, and by this time people in East St. Louis felt that Vernon was on his way to being a homosexual. Back in them days that was some other kind of shit.

My father had bought a three-hundred-acre farm in Millstadt, Illinois, before he and my mother separated. But she didn't like being out there with all the horses, cows, and prize-winning pigs my father was raising. My mother wasn't into the country living like my father was. But he started spending a lot of time out on his farm and this probably caused them to break up quicker than they would have. My mother didn't cook or do housework. So we had a cook and a maid. But that still didn't seem to make her happy. I liked it out in Millstadt—riding horses and all. It was peaceful and beautiful. I've always been into shit like that. In fact, it reminded me of my grandfather's place, only it was bigger. The house was white, with colonial-style columns, and had about twelve or thirteen rooms. It was two stories high and had a guesthouse. It was really a beautiful place, with a lot of grounds and trees and flowers. I used to love to go out there.

After my mother and father separated, things got real bad between my mother and me. I stayed with her after they separated, but we didn't seem to agree on anything, and with my father not there to keep her off me, there were a lot of screaming arguments. I was getting independent, but I think that the real cause of the problem with my mother was my relationship with my girlfriend Irene Birth.

My mother liked Irene, but she was pissed off when Irene got pregnant. She had plans for me going to college and this was going to cause a problem. My father, like I said, didn't like Irene, although he warmed up to her later. So when I first heard about Irene being pregnant, I went and told my father and he said, "So? So what? I'll take care of it for you."

So I said, "No, Dad, it don't go like that. I'll take care of it myself. I helped do it and I got to be man enough to take care of it." So he kind of paused for a minute and then he said, "Listen, Miles, the baby might not even be yours, because I know all them other niggers she's been fucking. So don't be walking around thinking you are the only one. There's others, plenty of others." I knew Irene was messing around with another dude named Wesley, I forgot his last name, who was older than me. And I knew she was going with a drummer named James—a little bitty guy—who used to play around East St. Louis; I would see her with him from time to time. But then again, Irene was fine and popular with the men. So my father wasn't telling me nothing I didn't already know. But I was convinced that the baby was mine and that I was doing the right thing by owning up to it. My father was really pissed off with Irene for getting pregnant. I think it was one of the things that stood between them ever really getting tight as they could have been. Anyway, I graduated from Lincoln in January 1944, although I didn't get my degree until that June. We had our first child, a daughter, Cheryl, that year.

Meanwhile, I was making about $85 a week playing in Eddie Randle's band and with other people, and I was buying myself some hip Brooks Brothers suits. I had myself a new horn, so I wasn't doing too bad. But the problems with my mother were getting out of hand, and I knew I had to do something about that and also do something about taking care of my family. I never married Irene legally, but we were still like man and wife. But I started to see some other things about how women were with men. I was also starting to think seriously about leaving the St. Louis area to live in New York. . . .

Once I had graduated from high school I was finally free to do what I wanted to do for at least a year or so. I had decided to try to go to the Juilliard School of Music in New York City. But I couldn't get in until September, and I still would have to pass an audition to be accepted. So I decided to get in as much playing and traveling as I could before I went to Juilliard.

In June 1944, I decided to leave Eddie Randle's band to play with a group out of New Orleans called Adam Lambert's Six Brown Cats. They had a kind of modern swing style, and Joe Williams, the great jazz singer—who was unknown at the time—was singing with them. Their trumpet player, Tom Jefferson, had gotten homesick for New Orleans while the band was playing in Springfield, Illinois, and decided to go home. I was recommended to take his place and they paid me good money. So I went with them to Chicago—the first time I had been to that city.

After a few weeks with the band, I came back home because I didn't like what they were playing. That's when Billy Eckstine's band came to St. Louis and I got that chance to play with them for two weeks. This really made up my mind for me to go to New York and attend Juilliard. My mother wanted me to go to Fisk, where my sister, Dorothy, was. She was telling me about how good Fisk's music department was and about the Fisk Jubilee Singers. But after I had heard and played with Charlie Parker, Dizzy Gillespie, Buddy Anderson (the trumpet player I replaced in the band in St. Louis; he got sick with tuberculosis and went back to Oklahoma and never played again), Art Blakey, Sarah Vaughan, and Mr. B himself, I *knew* I had to be in New York, where the action was. But my father had to settle the argument between my mother and me over my choice of school, and even though Juilliard was a world-famous music school, it still didn't make no difference to my mother. She wanted me to go to Fisk, where my sister could keep an eye on me. But I wasn't having none of that.

East St. Louis and St. Louis were getting so depressing to me around this time that I had to go someplace, even if it was wrong. I especially felt like this after Clark Terry left and joined the Navy. For a while, I was so down, I thought of joining the Navy myself so I could play with the great Navy band they had up there in the Great Lakes. Man, they had Clark, Willie Smith, Robert Russell, Ernie Royal and the Marshall brothers, and a whole lot of other dudes who used to play with Lionel Hampton's band, and Jimmie Lunceford's band. They didn't have to do no drills or duty or nothing; all they had to do was play music. They went to boot camp, but that was it. But finally, you know, I said, fuck it, because Bird and Dizzy weren't there and that's where I wanted to be, around them; that was where it ultimately was at and they were in New York, so that's where I took my ass. But I came real close to joining the Navy in 1944 after I got out of high school. Sometimes I wonder what would have happened if I had done that instead of moving to New York.

I left East St. Louis for New York in early fall 1944. I had to pass my audition to get into Juilliard, and I passed with flying colors. The two weeks I had spent with B's band in St. Louis had been good for me, but I had been a little hurt when B didn't take me with them to play in Chicago's Regal Theatre. B had gotten Marion Hazel to replace me, since Buddy Anderson wasn't coming back. That had hurt my confidence a little. But playing around East St. Louis and St. Louis again before I went up to New York helped me regain my confidence in myself. Plus Dizzy and Bird had told me to look them up if I ever came to the Big Apple. I knew I had learned all I could from playing around St. Louis, knew it was time to move on. So I packed up my stuff in the early fall of 1944 and took a train up to New York City, confident in my heart that I was going to have some shit for them motherfuckers playing up there. I ain't never been scared of doing new things, and I wasn't scared when I got to New York City. But I knew I had to get my shit together if I was going to hang with the big boys. I also knew I *was* going to do just that. I thought I could play the trumpet with anybody.

FANNIE COOK

WRITER AND SOCIAL ACTIVIST Fannie Cook (1893-1949) was born in St. Charles, Missouri, to Julius and Jennie Michael Frank. The family moved to St. Louis when Fannie was very young, and the city played an important role in her life—and she in its—for the rest of her days. After graduating from Soldan High School, Fannie attended the University of Missouri at Columbia, where she earned a degree in English in 1914, and went on to do graduate work at Washington University. Although Fannie soon married Dr. Jerome S. Cook, a prominent St. Louis physician, she continued to teach at the university while starting a family—an unusual course for a married woman at the beginning of the twentieth century.

By 1920, Cook was active in the St. Louis chapter of the League of Women Voters and worked to reform the city's school board election process. Through the mid-1930s, Cook was an influential figure in civil rights and labor struggles in St. Louis but was forced to curtail her social activism after being diagnosed with a serious heart ailment. During her brief retirement, Cook pursued her creative writing, which bore the stamp of her passion for liberal causes, and won several literary awards for her short fiction. By 1939, Cook was back in the public eye, leading a cause to assist displaced sharecroppers in Missouri's bootheel, and her novel, *Boot-heel Doctor* (1941), explores the plight of the people in that region.

The following excerpt from the novel *Mrs. Palmer's Honey* (1946) depicts life inside and outside of the Ville, an African American neighborhood in St. Louis, even as it addresses the persistent issues of racism and segregation.

FROM *MRS. PALMER'S HONEY*

That morning dawn smiled timidly across the vast gray fabric of roofs spread from the river to a distant crescent of hills. The river was the Mississippi, a mile wide and muddy. It held the city within a giant bend ribbed by bridges. Near the crook of the bend were skyscrapers, but mostly the city was an immense hive of home neighborhoods where two-storied school buildings seemed tall.

One of these neighborhoods was the Ville. It lay a little north of the exact center. Once it had been Elleardsville, a suburb, but the metropolis had grown around the region as a tree will in time encompass a foreign body, and now no one living there ever thought of it as anything but the Ville, part of the fabric, part of the city.

Few white people ever thought of it at all. Few knew it was there. Though several miles long and several wide, the Ville remained obscure and lived secretly. Streetcars and busses ran along its boundaries as if afraid or too incurious to enter.

Prospering white people lived miles west, where the fabric began to fray into large estates, small farms, emerald golf courses. Vaguely they believed St. Louis had but one colored district, the be-taverned crisscross of shabby streets near Union Station. Observing that region's slatternly ways, they would at times consider sending their dark-skinned cooks to a clinic for tests and treatment.

Prospering colored people lived in the Ville and let the people from the pretty fringe of the fabric believe what they pleased. It was only among themselves that they called it the Ville, and only to one another that they spoke of its ways. To them the black folks near Union Station were "immigrants," newly come north from Mississippi or Louisiana. A few were Ville folks fallen from grace, but more were sharecroppers with the dust of cabin floors still beneath their toenails, dreams of northern freedom still in their eyes, snuff still in the mouths of the women as well as the men. Their ways slowed the climb for other Negroes. Because of that, the Ville bore them a grudge.

Houses in the Ville were low—cottages with slanted attics. Suburban trees were still to be seen, and suburban fences around the small front lawns. Here and there a door was painted a brilliant blue or a porch of happy yellow was trimmed in scarlet, but by and large the Ville lived sedately in imitation of the white folks' way of living.

Unlike a white folks' neighborhood, however, the Ville did not pivot around a central shopping district. Instead there was a campus worn bare by the great American game of baseball. Flanking the campus were handsome modern brick buildings which the Ville would have regarded with pride had it been able to take pride in a handsome insult.

The buildings were for black folks set aside to live separately. They housed a Negro high school, a Negro grade school, a school for doubly handicapped children—both Negro and blind or deaf or lame—a Negro teachers' college, a Negro city hospital. Indoors were jobs and learning and cures, fine gifts ungraciously given and ungraciously received.

At either end of the campus stood splendid structures erected by a brown woman grown fabulously rich from marketing a fluid which straightened Negroid hair. One was an orphanage; the other a hotel, primly run, a model of Christian respectability.

The Ville was a city within a city.

A vagrant ray from the timid dawn tapped Honey's eyelids. Sleep became a tossing mist. At first she knew only that another day had come, then that the ache along her legs was from all that crazy dancing with Snake. Turning, her brown body relished the smoothness of the new sheets.

The first thing the Hoop girls had done with their defense-factory pay was to fill a chest of drawers with neat stacks of new sheets and pillowslips and towels. Honey had made pink ribbon tie-arounds for them like the Palmer tie-arounds while Eulatha, laughing, tore up the old linens. Eulatha liked to tear up.

Eulatha woke now with the suddenness of a pistol shot. An elbow caught Honey in the ribs. The telephone rang, and Eulatha was after it, a man hunt in her eyes.

"Better you forget that Jo-Jo," Honey mumbled.

Eulatha came back yawning.

"'Mis Palmer for Honey,'" she mimicked, soprano. Then, in a surly contralto, she added, "Tell her you got you a job now—with holidays!"

"Hush your face!" Honey scolded.

At the telephone in the next room her voice was smooth and sweet.

Mrs. Palmer said she was in a terrible fix. Mr. Palmer was to be awarded the First Citizen's medal——

Honey said she felt right proud of that, all the Hoops had, as soon as they read it last night. It was in the Ville newspapers——

—and it was to be given to him, Mrs. Palmer continued, at a ceremony at the Auditorium late this afternoon. Mr. Palmer—"You know how he is, Honey!"—and Mrs. Palmer giggled in fond adoration of all Mr. Palmer's ways—had forgotten about ration points and Honey's not being there any more, not for months now; in short he had invited one after another for dinner just as he always had before the war. This time he had invited those who were going to sit on the platform with him at the services, men Mrs. Palmer didn't know, and their wives, whom she didn't know either. Fortunately the mayor hadn't accepted. Bruce was home on leave with a sweet soldier boy from Maine, and Dorothy Jane had invited one of her beaux and—in a whisper—there'd been no word from Junior in Africa for forty-eight days now, though Mr. Palmer had scarcely mentioned it, and of course, this being his big day, Mrs. Palmer wasn't saying a word, not a word!—and anyhow Mrs. Palmer was at her wit's end and would Honey save her life?

"What time must I save it? I reckon Mr. Junior ain't wrote no letter—like he done us that time at college."

"As fast as you can get out here, Honey. . . . I hope you're right!" There was a whistling sigh.

"I'll make tracks," Honey answered and went back to bed to warm her feet.

"You're a fool!" Eulatha observed. "You done cooked Palmer turkeys for twelve Thanksgivings. Now the war freed you and you're going back to cook more. What-for you earning eighteen hundred a year?"

"What-for Mrs. Palmer lend me money during the depression? What-for Mrs. Palmer help me to keep all you Hoops rolling?"

"Rolling downhill. . . . Ain't she took it off a dollar a week? Poof! Every penny of it!"

Honey studied the ceiling dreamily. "I ain't never minded much about any of the depression, onliest thing I hated so was going on the streetcar with all them runs down my stockings!"

Laughing, Eulatha imitated Honey's voice. "'Someday when I gets me lots of cash money, I'm going to buy me two pairs of silk stockings every Saturday. Two pairs!' Now you got lots of cash money and the white folks' war fixed it so you can't buy no silk stockings a-tall!"

While Honey was putting on her clothes she paused occasionally to button or tie something for one of the little children who came because they found her hands gentler than Big Mama's. Some were her own brothers and sisters; others were the children of sisters who had married disastrously or not at all. Two called Eulatha Mama. All gave Big Mama their first obedience.

Idly Eulatha watched Honey and wondered what her sister thought about her own body. It was the color of bottled bourbon, lean like a young girl's, though Honey was past thirty. The breasts were firm and the waist small. The legs tapered smoothly.

It was a sleek body. Eulatha thought it wasted on Honey, who had sought so little pleasure from it. Last night was the first time in years Honey had danced, the only time she had ever really danced.

Carmen, in the far bed with two of the baby girls, stirred and stretched. Carmen had been created a schoolteacher out of Honey's dimes and dollars fetched from the Palmer kitchen. A Spanish course at the high school had changed her from Carrie to Carmen, a transformation Honey discovered on the night she attended a school play to inspect the costume which cost her a week's wages. She saw on the program it was worn by Carmen Hoop. She saw too that Carrie had a preference for *dicktee* folks, so Honey came home and told Mama to let the kid go to teachers' college. Mama said it would break up the family, but Honey, who had mothered Carrie more than any of Mama's children except Lamb, answered that she'd break up Carrie if it did, break up her head with a chair.

Dressing, Honey became in rapid succession two people. First she was a pretty, demure, big-eyed woman in a maid's uniform. Then she slipped above the uniform a street dress so similar to her own bourbon tones that it seemed to return her to nudity. With quick movements she put on a pair of ivory earrings, a turban to match her dress, crowded her feet into high-heeled slippers, clutched a brown patent-leather purse beneath her elbow, tossed a plaid heather tweed coat over her arm, and in a swirl of graceful motion turned to leave the room, a modishly dressed brown girl, dashing but no longer demure.

Eulatha closed her eyes. Chuckling, she delivered a compliment and a taunt. "Some folks is maids and looks like teachers, and some folks is teachers and looks like maids."

The covers of Carmen's bed heaved. A hard voice answered, "Certainly— Honey is the Hoop beauty. No doubt about that. None whatever."

Briefly the thrust silenced Eulatha. Then she rose angrily on her elbow.

Honey interrupted their talk. "Eulatha, you keep your mouth shut! You got Jo-Jo, and someday Carmen'll get her a *dicktee* man. So hush your fighting. You're going to wake up Lamb. Lamb worked the night shift. He dead asleep down there."

Carmen spoke from the depths of her covers. "Lamb isn't the only one asleep in the basement. Snake is down there too."

Honey came back to the center of the room. "What's that evil doing in our basement again?"

Both beds were silent.

"He's your evil," Eulatha answered at last.

"Talk fast!" Honey commanded. "What's he doing in our basement?"

Eulatha yawned. "Mama, she done it. Told him he could come back."

"Snake?"

"Yes, Snake!"

Carmen sat up. "Ben Boston's worth forty Snakes. Why you don't marry Ben while you have the chance is more than I can understand."

Eulatha laughed. "Teachers, they can't understand lots. That's why-for they're teachers."

Honey wasn't listening to their talk. Thudding sounds came from the stairway. Big Mama was limping a step at a time down from her attic bedroom.

Midway, Big Mama stopped. She saw Honey dressed in her best, looking both pretty and ladylike, more than most white women could do.

"Is you going to church with Ben?"

"Mama, why-for you let Snake sleep with our Lamb?"

Mama resumed the downward thudding, her big knobby hand rubbing the rheumatism in her left thigh. "You ain't answered."

"I'm helping Mrs. Palmer with her Thanksgiving dinner."

When Honey earned extra, Mama got extra. "Honey, you my bestest child. Lawd Gawd, this misery at your poor old ma this morning!"

"Snake, he's evil, Mama. He ain't going to do Lamb no good."

"Snake, he ain't evil. He just down on white folks. Poor fellow, he needs a place to sleep."

"He's been sleeping. You let him go back yonder to sleep where-at he been sleeping ever since we run him out."

They moved into the kitchen. Mama's nightgown showed from beneath a green calico dress. She was a big-boned woman, tall, lilac-black, and nearly toothless. Her crinkled lips had a trick of creasing into a swift and surly grin.

She lighted a fire under a pot and said to Honey, "Eat some grits."

"Mama, you got to answer me about Snake. He don't belong down there with Lamb."

"Snake, he's going to pay right good for that there bed."

"We Hoops got more money now then we ever had! We don't need Snake's money none."

Mama's lips folded upon each other. "That's right. Hoops got war money now. Ain't no sense sleeping crowded up no more. We going to move. Then Lamb, he'll have a room to himself, and Big Mama, she gets Snake's cash money just the same.

Honey saw that Mama was in one of her moods. "Where-to we going to move?"

The big hands fumbled in a pocket. They gave Honey a patch of torn newspaper, marked with a red checkmark from Carmen's pencil. It was an advertisement of a house "to rent for colored."

"You come home early, Honey. We'll look at it, just you and me. You're the onliest one I got to count on."

"Mama, this here ain't in the Ville. Mount Vernon Street's white!"

"It says 'for colored.'"

"It ought to say 'for trouble.' Mama, this ain't got no sense to it. Carmen, she's crazy!"

"What-for we Hoops got war money 'less'n we spend it! Tell me that!" Mama leaned her face toward Honey's angrily. "You come home early like I said."

"Mrs. Palmer's going to need me. Reckon I can't come home early." Honey shook her head. "This here's white, Mama. I know."

"Ain't going to be lily-white no more when the Hoops move in!" Mama, dishing out grits to the grandchildren and children crowding around her, rose to ecstasy. "The Hoops, they been down long enough. The Hoops going to roll to glory. That there house, it's got ten rooms!"

"The Hoops ain't got no call to go to moving out of the Ville. First you take in Snake, then you want more rooms. It don't make sense."

The little children were standing in a row eating from bowls Big Mama placed upon a long board supported at each end by a raw-wood horse. Her own cup of coffee stood untasted. Her grin came and went in sudden clicks. Her eyes were far back in her head like china-doll eyes come loose, about to fall inside.

"Honey sweet," she whimpered, "seems like I been crowded down all my life. They've been times when I never thought about it none, but I was feeling it just the same. Now come this here war. The Hoops got luck for once. Money, money, money, coming in fast. Defense jobs and Lamb not fitten for the Army. So now we on Easy Street. I want to see my children living good—"

"We living all right, Mama."

"You living all right, Honey, 'cause you don't want nothing. You got your pretty face and good clothes and a *dicktee* beau. Ben Boston, he's right nice. You got a chance at Snake too, I reckon, come you want to pleasure yourself with trouble. But Carmen, she ain't got no man. She needs a teacher man or a preacher man or the likes of that—"

"Carmen got to get her a man with her own flesh like everybody else do. Carmen will. Someday Carmen'll get her a good man."

"How she gonna get her a good man with her home overrun with Hoops like as if they was ants?" Mama asked, waving to the row of children.

"You don't see our neighbors carrying on the way the Hoops do! Mostly the Ville's better'n we is. We ain't good enough for the Ville. We got to wait."

"Your papa, he can't stand this crowding up no more. Working like he do out at that there swell country club, he can't come home to this here dicebox and listen to the rattling. He don't hardly come home no more at all. Onliest time he come back is to fetch him clean clothes or the likes of that. He sleeping out there most the time." Big Mama's eyes were glazed with tears.

"Reckon I'll try to come home early, Mama."

"You got to come, Honey! Ain't no other one of my children I can count on."

"Take Carmen with you."

"Carmen ain't proud of her mama no more. 'Sides, Carmen ain't got none of the kind of sense a body can use."

Honey spoke slowly. "Ben, he likely will come around this morning, Mama. Tell him to fetch me at Mrs. Palmer's along about the middle of the afternoon. You be in the back seat, Mama."

Snake, lounging against a tree, saw as soon as the door opened that Honey this morning was not at all Honey last night. Same dress. Same hat. Same earrings. Same head held high. The walk still had panther in it, but the panther drowsed.

He remembered the first time he ever saw Honey. Under his breath he mumbled, "Hot stuff!" A fellow he didn't know laughed at him and said, "She's got a nickname. The men call her the Virgin of the Ville." Snake answered hopefully, "Because she's not?" The other said, "Because she is," and sauntered off, chuckling.

Snake fell in step with her now. "Your panther," he teased, "must have joined the Y.W.C.A."

Her proud head tilted higher. "Snake, I don't want you teaching Lamb no bad."

"Ain't Lamb slave, black, and twenty-one?"

"That's what I mean, Snake. That kind of talk—"

"Talk never hurt nobody."

"Ain't nothing but talk ever did hurt nobody. Bad talk. Then fighting begins."

He took her elbow. "You kind of a mother to Lamb, ain't you, sweet?"

"Lamb's a good boy. Honey's got a lot of faith rolled up in Lamb. You lay off of him!"

"What-for you think I hurt Lamb? Lamb and me are friends. Friends ever since last August. The day I begun to work on the line. The day I met the prettiest girl in the Ville."

"All I know is, Lamb, he's kind of young in the head and you old in the head. You got hate in your heart and Lamb got love. Mama ain't got no call to let you two go to sharing a bed."

"Last night you thought Snake good enough to dance with." He was leaning over, smiling into her eyes, teasing her. "To drink with too."

"I like you, Snake, but you ain't no good."

"Good! Good! Good! What is all this here good? How you know Honey's so damned good?"

"Honey's good," she said quietly.

"How you know?"

"'Cause I don't wish nobody evil and I don't do no evil."

"You don't wish white folks evil?"

"No."

He laughed falsetto. "Me neither. Onliest thing I wish that there Hitler would come right on in this here town, ride right up Olive Street on a white horse and shout that this here war's over and the black man, he's the big winner!"

"This ain't no war between white folks and black folks—"

"That's all you know about it! This here war's to see if Snake Williams got him the right to join a white union. Not the damned auxiliary union where he can't vote. Not the one that makes him work in a separate building because he's not good enough to use a white man's toilet."

"Hush your talk! That ain't this war, and you knows it!"

Again he laughed falsetto. He ran his hand up her arm. He chanted, "Dear little white man fixing for a fall."

"Snake, that's the kind of talk I don't want Lamb to hear none. You got to keep still with such talk." She shook her arm free of his hand.

Snake seized it again and squeezed. He whistled softly into her ear. Briefly his lips brushed the edge. He saw lightning race through Honey's body.

"Please, Snake," she said.

"O.K. I ain't going to teach Lamb nothing he don't already know. That boy black, but he ain't crazy. He sure sees what this war's for. This here's my war. It's a war about me. Wherever I live. Africa. India. Deep South. It's a war to find out whether the ball and chain is going to come off my leg. Snake ain't one to stand by idle, taking no sides."

He whistled a soft dance tune between his teeth. He smiled at Honey. His smile was malefic.

Honey wanted to answer, but she didn't know the answer. There was always so much sense and so much crazy in what Snake said. Those eyes with their long lashes making haloes around them were the devil's eyes.

"You got you a union out at the plant," she said at last.

"Sure, we got us a union! White man's union. Union to keep us out of their toilets. Keep us from voting when anything real come up. One of these fool-yourself unions. I got me a button." He touched it.

He didn't return his hand to Honey's arm or look into her face again. His freckled tan cheeks sagged. His eyebrows scowled low over his eyes. As he walked, he held his elbows rigidly against his body, twisting like a dancer.

"Don't take on so, Snake. Ain't nothing you can do about it. You just make yourself sick."

"Ain't nothing nobody can do about it," he grumbled. His mood changed. He leaned over and looked into her eyes. "You is a good girl, Honey. You ain't got no hate in you. That's right for a woman. I reckon a woman, she ain't got the nature for hate. Only for love. . . . Go dancing tonight with Snake?"

"I got a date."

"I slice that black man's neck! You got a date with Snake. Snake's going to buy Honey an orchid and take her prancing mighty fine, prancing high!"

"I is got a date. Snake . . . I'll go dancing . . . come you promise to move out of our house."

They watched the earth-colored plant bus rock toward the corner. Lamb was across the street, ready to get in, waiting for Snake. He was black and thin of body, but chubby-faced. He looked like a good boy on his way to school.

The bus was filling rapidly. Snake gave Honey's arm a final fond, insinuating squeeze. "Got to hurry." For a moment he looked as he had last night, then as he turned to Honey in farewell, his face wore a scowl. "Could be some of them high-riding white men fixing for a fall!" In another instant he was loping toward the bus, a tall, lean, shambly body with big feet and big, dangling hands on swinging arms.

Honey's heart was pounding. Snake was the only man who had ever made her heart pound like that. If only he were all evil, she thought; but he's good too. He's like a kid who's been hurt and gets mad to keep from crying. Likely if somebody took him in her arms to cry it out, then maybe he'd be good.

Reckon Honey's arms might go to getting her into a heap of trouble.

Honey didn't look to see whether she knew any of the other women on their way to prepare Thanksgiving turkeys for white families. She scorned them for baldly displaying bundles of shoes or uniforms or folded, empty reticules in happy anticipation of gifts or even of gifts self-given. They were older women, the age of Big Mama, and as stiff of joint. They wore their work and their troubles showily, as badges to be seen. In their own homes they were Big Mamas, slapping and loving and ruling. At work they were yes-ma'am women. At church they were ladies and benefactresses. Between places they were strangers to themselves and to one another. Their daughters had become workers in defense plants and this morning were enjoying their holiday in bed, wearing gowns which matched their robes. Some had bed jackets of maribou.

Honey wondered whether all this new and easy money was good for the Ville. Its pulse had quickened. Its heart, like Mama's, throbbed for more. It had a little new furniture and some good clothes and hungered for things not to be bought while guns had to be made. Most important of all, the Ville had taken out its anger, looked at it carefully, and concluded that it was good.

Before the war the Ville's resentment had mated with laughter. Honey could remember parties Mama gave for the neighbors, cocoanut-cake parties where the talk would be of the ways of white folks and the laughter loud and scornful and sure. Most Ville parties had been like that. Someone would tell about going to a white folks' store to buy a dress and how a lady buttoned it up for her, but later when the brown woman wanted to buy a pair of gloves she wasn't allowed to try them on even by herself. Wha-wha-wha-wha-a-a-a-a-a! They would throw back their heads and laugh at the white folks. They would have a good time.

Now people were working too hard for parties. Talking on the busses and streetcars, in church and at the market, they no longer laughed. Boys carried knives. Girls carried sassy tongues and swift elbows.

Honey's heart kept hovering around Snake. Through all his evil, she could see a man she might have loved with her whole heart. He would have stood taller, looked straighter, laughed sweeter. He would not have been a man in love with Honey and with the devil too.

Don't you go to mothering Snake, she admonished herself. You done mothering enough with Mama's babies. Mothering ain't nothing only a sweet feeling made up mostly of hurt and fear and hope and the kind of love what is hurt and fear and hope. You got to learn to let it alone. It's sure your poison. When you pick you a man, Honey Hoop, you pick a man who's going to take care of you!

Then she saw Ben coming toward her and saw that he was such a man and that she didn't want him.

Ben Boston approached bowing and smiling. He was an undertaker and made good money. He was neatly dressed in a dark blue business suit, a brown overcoat, and brown hat set level on his brow. When he removed his hat to greet Honey, his eyeglasses twinkled as if amused by their repetition of the round of his head, of his cheeks, of his mouth, of his nostrils, of his ears.

The eyes back of the glasses were gentle. Ben's skin was black satin, smooth and gleaming.

In a way he loved Honey as unwillingly as she loved Snake, if what she felt was love. Ben Boston knew he ought to marry an educated girl, a girl who talked as up-to-date as Honey looked, a girl light enough to make the ticket seller at the white folks' theaters hesitate. Only such a wife could help him up the ladder his mother had held steady for his climbing all these years.

But his heart clung to Honey. It loved her beauty, her gentle voice, the modest way she was folding one gloved hand upon the other even now. He saw no panther in her walk, only a grace which made him think of nymphs in floating draperies, a biblical urn on the shoulder, flowers in the hair. He admired her chin held high, her head back-tilted and a trifle on the side. He waited for the arch smile which would lift one of those even, widely curving eyebrows in sweet and modest coquetry.

The wide space between Honey's eyes, her drowsy lids gave to the upper half of her face a look of deep serenity. The lower half was handsomely formed and spirited.

"How are you doing?" Ben asked in his good-morning voice.

"Nicely, thank you," Honey replied.

"Miss Carmen said over the phone I'd likely find you along about here. I planned to carry you to work in my car, but a tire wearied out on me just now. If I have your permission, I'll ride with you a ways on the streetcar."

"You're right welcome," Honey answered.

"Your mother told me about the house on Mount Vernon." Ben was tactful. Knowing the whites said "Mount Vernon Avenue" and the Ville "Mount Vernon Street," he said neither.

"I'm not for moving out of the Ville, Ben. Can't figure what's come over Mama. Too much money, I reckon. The Ville's the onliest place to live come you're colored and ain't in search of trouble."

"I've got a sister hasn't ever been out of the Ville," Ben said.

"You mean never?"

"Never. Loraine went clear through grade school, high school, and teachers' college. Finished Sunday school. Had appendicitis the week our hospital moved in."

"Ain't she never been downtown or to Union Station or to the movies or—"

"Only to this little old movie in the Ville."

"Why-for is that, Ben?"

"My mother's been against it. Loraine's her only girl. Seems like she must have had so much trouble bringing up us boys that she got to being afraid of bringing up a girl. Figured she'd be safer staying right in the Ville."

"Maybe she figured Loraine would be happier not going places she wasn't wanted."

Ben thought about this. "My mother isn't one to take much stock in happiness."

"Seems kind of funny teaching her to be smart in school and not letting her find out what she's going to be up against."

Ben laughed. "When Loraine was a little kid she used to hide when she saw the white man who delivered for the dairy. She figured he looked white because he was sick. She still stares too much."

Honey's mind was considering the value of happiness. "Bringing up our babies at home, I always figured, after teaching them to be good, the next thing a body should do was let them be happy. Their noise runs you nearly crazy that way, but always seemed to me that was right."

"You'd be a sweet mother, Honey. Any baby'd be lucky to find himself yours."

Honey laughed softly. "I ain't hankering for babies, Ben. Reckon I had enough with Mama's fifteen and all them others at the house. Reckon that ain't no way to talk except that it's the truth."

Ben was silent. . . . "I reckon you couldn't help loving a baby."

"I loved all Mama's once they was born, but I cried every time I knew another was coming."

"You cried? . . . What made you cry?"

"Mama, she got times when seems like she just gets fed up. Them's the times everything falls right smack in Honey's lap. Reckon I done washed more diapers than most girls ever seen in they whole lives. Washed diapers and babies and looked to Mama's temper besides. Not that Mama ain't good. She's mighty good. Reckon I loves my mama more'n anybody in the world except Lamb. But I loves her like as if she was my sister. Mama was only fifteen when I come. We closer in years than I is to my baby sister."

Ben whistled. "Your mama looks old enough to be your grandmother."

"I ain't had no fifteen children. And I don't seem to be hankering for none, Ben."

To herself Honey commented that she had refused Ben right polite. Just to look at Ben a body could see he was fixing to be a papa in a nice house with a nice automobile and a nice wife, only I ain't going to be that wife. If I going to break down for any man, I going to want to.

She puzzled a little over how she had suddenly made her decision. It was a right funny time to make it just after her and Ben had the only real talk they ever spoke. Most of the time talking to Ben was like playing hopscotch back and forth over the same squares, what he thought about the weather, what his mother thought about it, how pretty Honey looked, how pretty his last funeral was, and how pretty the minister prayed. Honey never seemed to be able to make herself care about any of it.

At the intersection there were a dozen or more fat brown women waiting for the car. Their talk stopped as Honey and Ben approached. A great chocolate bonbon of a woman dried her eyes in deferential memory of other occasions when she had seen Ben Boston. Several greeted him.

One inquired about Honey's mother. She answered softly, "Nicely, thank you." Her manner was polite but cool.

After that everyone stood in silence looking for the streetcar or facing the great scarlet ball which was the sun dulled by the smoke of the city.

As they got into the car, the women held up their passes without glancing at the motorman. They seated themselves in little groups where they could find spaces. Honey and Ben stood. Snatches of the talk floated up to them.

The car was crossing Enright Avenue where the *dicktee* folks lived. Boastfulness came into the colored women's voices. The street was broad and heavily treed. There was little traffic, and the houses stood far back, as if withdrawing from the little there was. These were ample houses with generous porches and side yards of an age less crowded and less hurried.

Ben said, "See the third house, the one with the bay window? I got that house rented out. I bought it two years back, It's where I'm going to live someday. . . . I hope I am."

Honey's forehead pressed against the window. Chills ran in waves down her back as she saw Honey Hoop living in that house. She walked through the first floor, empty of sleeping beds, spread the china-closet shelves with gleaming white paper, edged them with fancy scallops just like Mrs. Palmer's. The doorbell rang. It was *dicktee* folk, friends of Ben's, light-skinned women in furs with rich, dark-skinned husbands. She could hear his mother, who didn't take much stock in happiness, hurrying down the steps. Honey knew she wouldn't like being mistress of that great house.

A second later Lamb-back-yonder-waiting-at-the-corner plunged a dagger through her heart. "Ben," she gasped, "why-for was Lamb waiting for the bus?" Her terrified fingers dug into Ben's arm. "He worked the night shift, Lamb did. Why-for—"

"Honey girl, what's come over you?" Ben whispered. "Maybe Lamb's shift was changed."

Honey breathed in deep, swift snatches. The tune Snake had whistled pounded against her throbbing ears. "White man fixing for a fall. . . ."

"I reckon I ought to see about Lamb. He been acting funny."

Ben laughed a round, carefree laugh. "How old's Lamb?" he teased. Then he whispered a thousand meanings, "Reckon some folks want babies more than they know they do."

She wasn't listening. She was trying to force her memory to toss up what had been said at home about Lamb's working hours.

Their car stood at the transfer point. Nearly everyone was getting off. Ben and Honey got off too. They crossed the street to wait for the car running toward the fine houses near the farm-land fringe. They were now in the white part of town.

Echoing Honey's change of mood, the women stood untalking as if preparing for entry into foreign territory where combat would be solitary. Some heads twisted obsequiously, some defiantly.

They were no longer neighbors to one another, yet Honey, aloof from them in the Ville, now felt herself a daughter of their family.

In the westbound car, sleek with shiny chromium rods to hold to, handsome with fine green plush seats, the sociability did not return. The car was nearly empty. The colored women sat singly, each next to a window.

Ben and Honey sat together. Back of them were a pair of shriveled, elderly women. They too carried folded reticules hopefully; they too were going out to cook turkeys not their own. They stared at the colored women.

One mumbled, "They always sit strung out."

"For meanness," the other answered.

"Yesterday I had to stand all the way out to my job."

"And the seats next to them empty, I bet."

"Ten empty seats, all next to niggers."

"They oughtn't be allowed to string out."

Ben sought his handkerchief and mopped his brow.

Honey spoke in low tones. "Reckon when you gets your tire fixed, Ben, you mightn't mind going around to my house and asking about Lamb. You could phone me. At Palmers'. I'd be mighty obliged."

Ben's black satin checks folded back. "You still worrying about Lamb!" Then the folds became wrinkles. "It's the talk in this car that bothers me."

Honey's hand dropped to his forearm in comfort. She whispered in his ear.

"Hush your nonsense, listening to that, Ben Boston! These folks ain't nothing but what the Palmers call poor white trash." Ben was nice, right nice.

For a moment Ben's feelings snuggled within the comfort of that phrase. Then he shook his head. "It isn't friendly of them."

"Nobody ain't friendly, Ben, only your own. I don't take up none with the girls at the plant, and they is colored girls. I just do my work and speak a polite good evening and go back home."

The car was filling now with white people. Ben noticed that several whose eyes passed Honey by chance returned them to stare at her beauty.

She wasn't talking to Ben any more. He saw that she wasn't going to talk. She had her mind fixed on Lamb.

When Ben got up to leave she said, "It's right nice of you, Ben. I thanks you." Her smile was sweet.

"I'll call for you at Mrs. Palmer's," he answered, smiling back.

PETER TAYLOR

BORN IN TRENTON, TENNESSEE, Peter Hillsman Taylor (1919–1994) attended Vanderbilt University and Kenyon College. As a writer, Taylor is associated with the Southern Renaissance or Agrarian movement in American literature that emerged in the 1920s and 1930s, through the influence of his college mentors Allen Tate and John Crowe Ransom. Although Taylor established himself as a playwright, novelist, and editor, he is most recognized for his accomplishments in the short story genre.

Taylor primarily set his fiction in the mid-South (including St. Louis) between the 1930s and 1950s, a period in which much of the agrarian culture of the region gave way to industrialization and urbanization. The characters in Taylor's stories of the "New South" are usually members of the upper middle class who reflect on the past and their fading culture as they wrestle with contemporary social forces. During his lifetime, Taylor produced seven collections of short stories and won the PEN/Faulkner Award for Fiction for his 1985 collection, *The Old Forest and Other Stories*. Although Taylor has been classified as a regional writer, many critics praise his elegant exploration of themes with universal relevance and appeal. As J. D. McClatchy remarked, "The South is his setting, but Taylor could as well be writing about any society in transition. He has an eye for a slow crack in the social veneer, a new tone in a child's voice."

McClatchy's observation is borne out in the following story, "The Little Cousins," which first appeared in the *New Yorker*, and was later collected in *The Old Forest and Other Stories.* Set in St. Louis, "The Little Cousins" is awash with the conflicting emotions of the young male narrator and his older sister as they eagerly await the annual Veiled Prophet Ball.

THE LITTLE COUSINS

To the annual Veiled Prophet's Ball children were not cordially invited. High up in the balcony, along with servants and poor relations, they were tolerated. Their presence was even sometimes suffered in the lower tiers and, under certain circumstances, even down in the boxes. But, generally speaking, children were expected to enjoy the Prophet's parade the night before and be content to go to bed without complaint on the night of the Ball. This was twenty-five years ago, of course. There is no telling what the practices are out there in St. Louis now. Children have it much better everywhere nowadays. Perhaps they flock to the Veiled Prophet's Ball by the hundred, and even go to the Statler Hotel for breakfast afterward.

But I can't help hoping they don't. I hope they are denied something. Else what do they have that's tangible to hold against the grown-ups? My sister and I were denied *every*thing. She more than I, since a boy naturally didn't want so much—or so much of what it was St. Louis seemed to offer us. Having less to complain of myself, however, I undertook to suffer a good many things for Corinna. And she suffered a few for me. We were motherless, and very close to each other at times.

What I suffered for Corinna I suffered in silence. But the grand thing about Corinna was that she could always find the right words for my feelings as well as her own. The outrage I felt, for example, at our being always taken down to Sportsman's Park to see the Browns play and never the Cardinals left me grimly inarticulate. But Corinna would say for me that it seemed "such an empty glory" to have box seats at the Browns' games. "Any fool had rather sit in the bleachers and watch the Cardinals," she said, "than have the very best box seats to see a Browns' game." She phrased things beautifully. At our house we had always to serve Dr Pep instead of Coca-Cola. Of this Corinna said, "It makes us seem so provincial." But we both knew that with a father like ours we just had to endure these embarrassments. According to Corinna, Daddy was "blind to the disadvantage he put us at"—disadvantage, that is, with our friends at Mary Institute and Country Day. What's more, she had divined at an early age what it was that blinded Daddy: It was always some friend or other of his who owned or manufactured the product imposed on us. We even had Bessie Calhoun because of one of his friends—Bessie, from Selma, Alabama, instead of some stylish, white foreign governess who might be teaching us French or German. "Except for Bessie," Corinna said, "we would be bilingual, like the Altvaders and the Tomlinsons."

The year Corinna and I were finally taken to the Ball, the project was kept a secret from us until the last moment—or practically. I came in from school at five-thirty, and Corinna had got home two hours before that, as usual. At the side door, which Bessie made us use on all days but Sunday in order to save "her floors," Corinna was waiting for me with narrow eyes and pursed lips. "You and I are going to the VP tonight," she said, "but they couldn't permit us the pleasures of anticipation. Isn't that typical?" The news had been broken to her when she came in from school and told Bessie she was going down the block to play. Corinna was already twelve at this time, and though at school she would never deign to associate with girls in the lower grades, out of school she spent most of her time playing with the younger children in our block. The little girls adored her, and I used to watch her sometimes, mothering them and supervising their games. She never seemed happier than then, and she often spoke of the younger children as her "little cousins." This, I suppose, was in fond allusion to all the tales we had listened to from Daddy, and from Bessie, too, about the horde of first, second and third cousins they each had grown up among—Daddy in Kentucky, Bessie in Alabama. At any rate, when Bessie told her she had to stay in and do her homework that afternoon, Corinna wasn't satisfied until she had wrung the reason out of her, and then, of course, she was indignant.

"*Why* didn't you tell me before, Bessie?" she said. "Two other girls in my class were lording it over everybody else today because *they're* going."

"That's it," said Bessie. "I didn't want you lording it over everybody you saw today. That's not the way I'm bringing you up. And I didn't want you being flighty about your lessons."

Corinna knew that Daddy must have told her not to tell us. Or she knew at least that Bessie had got his approval. Yet Bessie always pretended to do everything absolutely on her own authority. And this made life more difficult. This made us forget that she was merely someone hired to take charge of us. It made us try to reason with her about things, made us pretend to be sick sometimes in order to break down her resistance, made us nag at her continually for all kinds of privileges. Bessie's utter disregard for what we considered justice and reason was something else that made us forget who she was, and she never showed any fear of our telling on her or going over her head. Her favorite answer to our "whys" was "Because I said so" or

"Because I said to." And if one of us gobbled up his dessert and begged for a share of the other's, Bessie was as apt as not to make the other one share. She was illogical, and she was inconsistent. When we were disobedient, she would hand out terrible punishments—dessertless days and movieless weekends—but then sometimes she would forget, or weaken of her own accord at the last moment. You could not tell about her.

There was her brutal frankness, too. Though she was as blind as Daddy to any need of ours to have our egos bolstered—such as by serving our friends the right drink—and as blind as he to our deep moral and intellectual failings—failings that we ourselves were aware of and often confessed to each other—still she never failed to notice the least sign of vanity in either of us. Corinna was beginning to worry about her looks, and when she asked Bessie whether she thought she would grow up to be as beautiful as a certain Mary Elizabeth Caswell, Bessie said, "Your legs are too thin. You'll have to do a lot of filling out before you can talk about that." I was proud of my drawing ability, and I tried to get Bessie to say she thought I might grow up to be an artist. "Do you like nature?" she said, and I had to admit what she already knew: Flowers and trees had little attraction for me. Bessie only shook her head and gave me a doubting look.

Yet when I was sick in bed with mumps or measles she would often read my palm, and, among other glories, she saw that I would be a great musician. I objected that the singing teacher at school said I couldn't even carry a tune. "What does *he* know about how you may change if you keep trying? I know how little teachers know." It was when we were sick that we discovered Bessie's real talents and saw how indulgent she could be when she had a mind to. This made us sick a good deal; and pretended illness was one of our moral failings that Bessie was blind to. I never knew her to doubt a headache or a stomachache or even "a funny feeling all over." When we were sick, she played cards with us, told our fortunes, read to us.

She read to us a lot even when we were well. She had taught school in Alabama before she came north and went into service, but it wasn't the kind of stories we were used to in St. Louis schools that she read to us, She read "Unc' Edinburg's Drowndin'" and "No Haid Pawn," and her favorites were the *Post* stories by Octavus Roy Cohen. When she read us those stories, she would sometimes throw back her head and laugh and slap her thigh the way she never did about anything else. We loved hearing her read, but we didn't ourselves think the stories were so funny. "Never mind," said Bessie.

"*You* don't have to think they're funny."

In conversation Bessie had only two real subjects, and one of them was Mary Elizabeth Caswell. Mary Elizabeth was bane of Corinna's existence. Bessie had brought up Mary Elizabeth to the age of thirteen. When our mother died, Mr. Caswell had sent Bessie over to us—supposedly for only a few days. I was five at the time and Corinna was eight. Mr. Caswell came to our house on several occasions during those first days and had long conferences with Bessie; it was finally decided between them that she would stay with us. Probably Mr. Caswell felt that Daddy's need was greater than his own. Though Mary Elizabeth was motherless, too, it was already known that Mr. Caswell was going to marry again within a few months. Besides, not only was Mary Elizabeth a big girl then, but her mother had been of an old family in the city and there was an abundance of aunts and other female relatives to guide her. And so we got Bessie, with the result that Corinna had to "spend her life," as she said, listening to unfavorable comparisons of herself to Mary Elizabeth.

Bessie's other subject was her own family down in Alabama and, more particularly, her half sister, Lilly Belle Patton. Lilly Belle was a saint. Bessie assured us that Lilly Belle was nothing like her, had none of her bad temper and selfish ways, was always doing for others and asked nothing for herself. Lilly Belle was the finest-looking, the smartest, and the best-natured of all Bessie's mama's eleven children. Yet she hadn't insisted on going through high school, the way Bessie had, and she hadn't married. Bessie not only went through school and took to teaching afterward but the money she made teaching she spent foolishly—not on her mama, who was pretty greedy about money anyway, but on first one husband and then another. But Lilly Belle was content to stay at home and help Mama, who was certainly never much help to herself. Lilly Belle took in washing and looked after her little half brothers and sisters, of which Bessie was next to youngest, and even "adopted-like" two orphaned cousins. She was a hard church worker, a beautiful seamstress and laundress, she was the best cook in the whole town of Selma, she kept a garden that was the envy of everyone.

Corinna and I never tired of hearing about Lilly Belle, but for Corinna the most interesting part was always Lilly Belle's courtship. Lilly Belle never felt she could go off and marry while the younger children were still at home to be looked after, and by the time the younger ones were up and gone ("gone to the bad, most of them") Mama was too old to leave at home alone.

But Lilly Belle had a faithful suitor, who had been waiting for her through all the years. He was, in fact, still waiting, and Lilly Belle wasn't even engaged to him. Sometimes Bessie had letters from a neighbor friend telling her she ought to make Lilly Belle have pity on Mr. Barker. It seems that on summer evening he and Lilly Belle kept company sitting together on her front porch. Neighbors would hear Mr. Barker break down and sometimes they would hear their voices over there, and cry as he begged her "at least to get engaged" to him. But Lilly Belle knew what was right; she had taken a vow not even to get *engaged* while Mama lived. Sometimes, too, there would be a letter that Lilly Belle had asked the neighbor friend to write Bessie, warning her that Mama was "low sick." Bessie always "reckoned" Mama was really going this time. And Corinna would be on tenterhooks about it for days. She would try to linger in the mornings till the postman came, and she would run home from school in the afternoon to see if there was any news. "If Mama goes this time," she would ask "will Lilly Belle really get engaged to Mr. Barker?" And Bessie would reply, "Of course she will. She hasn't kept him waiting for nothing."

The unfavorable comparisons that Bessie made between herself and Lilly Belle were much more severe than those she made between Corinna and Mary Elizabeth. Yet, quite naturally, Corinna was able to think of Lilly Belle as a heroine of pure romance, whereas she saw Mary Elizabeth as a "pampered, spoiled, stuck-up thing." The worst of it was, Corinna was subject to wearing hand-me-downs from Mary Elizabeth. There was no need for it, of course, but Mr. Caswell and Daddy were that close. Or perhaps Bessie Calhoun was still *that* close to the Caswell family. The dresses would just appear in Corinna's closet and be allowed to hang there for her to ignore until she could resist them no longer. Once she had taken them down and begun wearing them, they became her favorite dresses. She may have managed to forget who it was they had belonged to. Or, without admitting it to me and perhaps to herself, she may have remembered how lovely Mary Elizabeth had looked in them; because Corinna had never lacked opportunity for observing Mary Elizabeth Caswell firsthand. The older girl and Corinna were in the same school together until Corinna was ten. After that, Mary Elizabeth went off to finishing school for two years, but even so she was home for all the holidays, and she and her father and the stepmother would be at our house for meals or we would be at their house. Daddy, during these two years, had begun going about with a very stylish-looking young widow, who was a close friend of Mr. Caswell's second wife. Corinna and I knew this lady then as Mrs. Richards. It was not to be long before she would become our stepmother—a fact that deserves mention only because it explains why our family and the Caswells were now thrown together still more than formerly.

Bessie Calhoun had a clear recollection of every mark Mary Elizabeth ever received in the lower grades at Mary Institute. "Because of Mary Elizabeth," said Corinna, "I have to live in mortal dread of not making the honor roll." At an early age, Mary Elizabeth could cook and sew in a way that promised to rival the arts of Lilly Belle. This information cost Corinna many precious hours that might have been spent with her "little cousins." And because Mary Elizabeth had had a little pansy garden of her own, Corinna was sent "grubbing in the earth" every spring. On the other hand, Mary Elizabeth was almost certainly not the reader that Corinna was, or not the reader of novels—the old best-sellers on the shelves of what had been our mother's sitting room. One day Corinna inquired after Mary Elizabeth's reading habits. Bessie didn't answer right away—something unusual for her. "At your age that child read the Bible, honey." Corinna opened her mouth in astonishment and then she closed it again without saying anything. This was one time when both she and I doubted Bessie's veracity, but Corinna let it pass. There was a limit to what she would undertake. She never raised the question again.

We knew perfectly well why we were being taken to the Veiled Prophet's Ball. This was the year that Mary Elizabeth Caswell was going to be presented. As a matter of fact, Corinna had nagged Daddy about it one Sunday afternoon in the early fall. Since Mary Elizabeth was to be one of the debutantes this year, didn't he think Bessie might take us to watch from the balcony? ("Mary Elizabeth ought to be good for *something* to us," she had said to me in private beforehand.) But Daddy replied, "Don't be silly. You couldn't either of you stay awake that late. You can come downtown and watch the parade from my office the night before. One school night out will be enough." And, of course, we did go down and watch the parade. In fact, we went downtown for dinner with Daddy and Mrs. Richards, and the Caswells and some other grown-ups joined us at the office afterward. They all had a party, with drinks and hors d'oeuvres, while we tossed confetti out the window and watched the floats go by. I hadn't even realized that Mary Elizabeth wasn't present until Mrs. Caswell came over to the window where we were and said, "Mary Elizabeth's out with some of her own crowd, Corinna. But she told me to give you her love and say she would be thinking about you tomorrow night. She's dying for you to see her dress."

Suddenly Corinna leaned so far out the window that I thought she was sure to fall, and I grabbed hold of her.

"Stop it, stupid," she hissed. "Here comes the Prophet's float. The parade's nearly over."

Just below us was passing the last of the countless tableaux representing life in French colonial times and in the days of the Louisiana Territory. We had seen Lewis and Clark, Marquette and Joliet, Indians, fur traders, French peasant girls, river bullies from the days of the keelboat and the pirogue. The parade had begun, for some reason, with Jean Lafitte in the Old Absinthe House at New Orleans, and the final tableau was of Thomas Jefferson signing the Louisiana Purchase. Beyond Jefferson, in his oversized wig and silk knee breeches, I could see the Prophet's float approaching. But I knew that for me the best part of the parade was already over. After so many Indians and fur traders, after the French explorers, after the pirates, the Prophet, with his veil-hidden face and all his Eastern finery, was bound to seem an anticlimax. I stood beside Corinna, hardly watching the royal float go by. As she continued to lean far out over the window ledge, I quietly took hold of the sash of her dress and, without her knowing it, held on to it tightly as long as we remained at the window.

The night of the Ball, we had an early dinner without Daddy. He came in and went up to dress while we were still at the table. After dinner, he sent for us to come to his room, where he said that he wanted us to behave ourselves that night "as never before." He was going out to dinner with the Caswells and Mrs. Richards and some other friends, but he would send the car and chauffeur to fetch us to the Colosseum. He didn't tell us that Bessie wasn't going to accompany us or that we would be sitting with him in one of the boxes downstairs.

And Bessie herself withheld this information till the very last. When it was finally divulged, we had already been so dazzled by another piece of news that the evening before us and these unexpected arrangements seemed of little consequence. When we were both dressed, we went into the sewing room, where Bessie always sat in the evening, to have her look us over.

"How do I look?" Corinna asked.

"You look fine," said Bessie. Then she saw Corinna eyeing herself in the mirror stand, and she added, "But no better than you should."

Corinna went up on her tiptoes and said, "I ought to have on heels."

"Behave yourself tonight, Corinna," Bessie said. "And see that *he* does." She didn't took at me, even. Then leaning back in her chair she said, "I've got something to tell both of you."

"What?" said Corinna.

"I want you to behave yourself next week, too."

"Oh, I thought it was something," said Corinna.

"It *is* something. They've sent for me down home. I'll be gone on the train before you get home tonight."

Corinna stared at Bessie in the mirror. "It's Mama? she asked, breathless. "*Tell* me, Bessie!"

Bessie nodded. "She's dead. She's been dead for two days. I've just been waiting around here to get tonight over."

Corinna observed a moment of silence. She knew that Mama had been "no pleasure to herself or anybody else" for several years now. Further, she knew that she had never heard Bessie say one good word for her mama, and that no commiseration was expected. But still, the respectful silence would be appreciated and would assure her getting answers to the questions she was bound to ask presently. She sat down on a wooden stool by the mirror and placed her feet, in their patent leather slippers, close together. She sat there smoothing the black velvet skirt over her knees. "Lilly Belle?" she said. "Is she engaged to Mr. Barker yet?"

Bessie nodded again. "She already has Mr. Barker's ring on her finger."

Now it was safe for Corinna to look up. "Will it be a long engagement?" she asked, still restraining herself somewhat.

"I'm going to stay over for the wedding Sunday week."

Corinna sprang to her feet. "Bessie!" she said. "Let me lend you my Brownie so you can bring us some pictures!"

Bessie shook her head. "Never mind about that. Lilly Belle's not going to get herself married to Mr. Barker without some high-type photographer there."

"Bessie, I wish I could go with you! Remember *every*thing."

"When did I forget anything, Corinna? Is there anything I haven't told you about Lilly Belle before this? I'll tell you one thing now. She's going to marry in her mourning, with a black veil to the floor."

Corinna sat down on the stool again, obviously stunned—more by the striking picture in her mind than by the impropriety. But presently she did ask, "Will that be quite proper, though, Bessie?"

"Of course it's proper, if black becomes you like it does Lilly Belle."

Corinna fixed her gaze on the wastebasket in the far corner of the room. "Do you think—" she began, speaking in a tone at once admiring and suspicious, "Do you think maybe she's kept Mr. Barker waiting just so she could marry in black?"

"How can you ask that, Corinna? Do you suppose Lilly Belle's as vain as *you* are?" Then she got up from her chair and said, "It's time for you-all to start downstairs. That car will be here."

It was only after we were out in the upstairs hall that we realized she wasn't going with us. At first, Corinna said she would refuse to go without her. It would be much more fun just to stay at home and talk, she said. "Yes," said Bessie heavily. "I can just see us sending word to your daddy and Mrs. Richards that you've decided to stay home and talk to Bessie."

"Then you'll *have* to come with us," Corinna said. "How can we go by ourselves?"

"Yes, 'have' to come with you," Bessie said. "Can't you just see me in my six-dollar silk sitting down there in the box with you-all and the Caswells." That was the first we knew of where we would be sitting.

We heard Mrs. Richards's voice downstairs; she had convinced Daddy that he couldn't merely have the chauffeur pick us up and have us arrive at the Colosseum by ourselves. And so there Daddy and Mrs. Richards were, waiting for us at the foot of the stairs. As Bessie helped Corinna into her Sunday coat, she said in an undertone, "Behave yourself, Corinna. Don't act silly. Remember this isn't just something gay tonight. I suspect you'll see folks crying. You know, it'll be like a wedding or funeral. There'll be something sad about seeing Mary Elizabeth and all of those other debutantes walking out in their white dresses."

Then we started down, with Bessie still watching from the head of the stairs and Daddy and Mrs. Richards waiting below.

Only a scene as strange and brilliant as that in the Colosseum could have made Corinna forget Lilly Belle altogether. But perhaps the pleasures of anticipation made her begin forgetting in the car. Or it might have been the sight of Mrs. Richards in her furs at the foot of the stairs. I had noticed before that night that with Mrs. Richards Corinna could be counted on to act more grown up than she did with anyone else. As we rode through town to the Colosseum, she and Mrs. Richards conversed, it seemed to me, with wonderful ease. Mrs. Richards had been a Special Maid at the Veiled Prophet's Court when she was a debutante some fifteen years before. She described the excitement of it as though it had been only yesterday—how you waited behind the curtains to hear the herald call out your name, and then how you heard, or imagined you heard, the gasps of surprise from the throngs whose admiring eyes would presently be focused on you as you walked, trembling, the length of the Colosseum, and knelt before the Prophet to be crowned, and then took your place on the dais.

For me, the Colosseum was like the most unreal of dreams. Before that night it had meant to me a wide sawdust arena with metal girders overhead and surrounded by gloomy, often half-empty tiers of seats. It was where I was taken to watch the annual horse show, the radio show, and the Boy Scout Jamboree. Now it had been transformed, by untold yards of bunting and by acres of white canvas on the floor, into a quite cheerful, if rather bathroomy-looking, ballroom. At one end were the thrones of the Prophet and his Queen-to-be, on a raised dais underneath a tasseled canopy, and they were flanked on either side by tiers of folding chairs provided for members of the Court. At the other end were the immense and immaculate white portieres through which the entrances of all persons of the first importance would be made.

After a drill by the Prophet's Guard of Bengal Lancers, the Prophet himself, attired in splendid medieval-Oriental garments and with his face veiled, made his duly ceremonious entrance, I was so bedazzled by the drill of the Prophet's guards and then by the arrival of the pirates and fur traders and Indians I had seen on the floats the night before that I hardly noticed when the Matrons of Honor began filing past our front-row box. These ladies, perhaps forty of them, circled the whole arena and at last took the places reserved for them on the Prophet's left. Even when the debutantes themselves, in white dresses and long white gloves, began to file by, I found it hard not just to sit there peering between them for glimpses of the people in costumes, who now occupied their places in the Court.

It was Corinna who brought me down to earth and reminded me of where my attention ought to be directed. She didn't do it intentionally, with a nudge or a cross whisper, but by her erratic behavior. She was sitting on the edge of her chair and leaning halfway across my lap trying to see the faces of the debutantes, who were now emerging from a small gateway on our side of the arena. I felt that she ought to wait and see them when they passed before our box.

"Stop," I said, trying to push her from in front of me.

"Oh, hush," she said, not budging.

She and I were in the very front row, and I glanced over my shoulder to see if Daddy had noticed her behavior. I discovered that he, along with everybody else in the box, was beaming at her. I was glad they couldn't see her face, or couldn't see it as well as I could, or at any rate didn't know what her narrowed-eyes-and-pursed-lips expression meant. Everything suddenly became clear to me. I knew what all the adults' smiling indulgence meant. Mary Elizabeth Caswell was going to have a place of honor in the Prophet's Court, and they expected Corinna to be thrilled by this. But I knew what tortures Corinna was suffering. Probably she was wishing I had let her fall out of that window last night. For, after this, how could she hope to measure up to Mary Elizabeth? It was hopeless. Now I began watching the faces of the girls as intently as she.

When the last debutante had passed us, Mrs. Richards leaned forward, smiling, and said to Corinna, "I didn't see Mary Elizabeth, did you?" And somehow, probably just because it was Mrs. Richards, Corinna managed to give her a very knowing, grown-up smile. When she turned around and faced the arena, she sat staring straight ahead with a glazed look.

After this came the separate entrances of the four Special Maids, each summoned individually to the Court of Love and Beauty by the Prophet's herald, each making her entrance between the great portieres and walking the length of the arena with measured steps and drawing after her a wide satin train. How I prayed each time that the next would be Mary Elizabeth! But already I knew that Mary Elizabeth would be nothing less than the Queen. Corinna knew it, too. By the time that awful announcement came, Corinna was even able to turn and smile at Mr. and Mrs. Caswell.

"His Mysterious Majesty, the Veiled Prophet, commands me to summon to his Court of Love and Beauty to reign as Queen for one year . . . Miss Mary Elizabeth Caswell." That was all. The Queen's subjects came to their feet. Between the white portieres Mary Elizabeth appeared, arrayed in her white silk coronation gown, its bodice and its wide skirts embroidered all over with pearls and sparkling beads; her slender arms held gracefully, if just a little too stiffly, away from her body and encased in pure white kid so perfectly and smoothly fitted that only the occasional trembling of Mary Elizabeth's hands could suggest there were real hands and arms beneath; and her hair, her head of golden blond hair, fairly shimmering under the brilliant lights that now shone down on her from somewhere up among the panoplied steel girders. The orchestra, perched in a lofty spot directly above the portieres, began to play. To the strains of "Pomp and Circumstance," Mary Elizabeth moved across our vision, with four liveried pages holding up the expanse of her bejeweled train—moved across the white canvas floor of the Colosseum toward her throne.

When the brief coronation ceremony was finished, the Prophet took his Queen's hand and led her out onto the floor for their dance. After only a few measures, the guards broke their formation, each of them going to seek the hand of one of the debutantes as a dancing partner. The Ball had officially commenced.

Very soon, Daddy and Mrs. Richards went out on the floor, with the Caswells, to congratulate the Queen and to join in dancing themselves. Corinna and I were urged to come along, but I rejected the idea even quicker than Corinna did. We would wait in the box and find a chance to congratulate Mary Elizabeth later.

In almost no time, the floor was crowded with dancers. All but those who sat in the balcony were free to participate. Corinna and I sat with our elbows on the rail of the box, staring into the crowd. It was curious to see the Prophet's guards dancing in their heavy shoes, and it was most curious to me to see in how many instances there was a person in costume dancing with someone in ordinary evening clothes. I was seeking among the dancers for Mary Elizabeth and the Prophet.

It was Corinna, of course, who spied Mary Elizabeth first. "There she is," she said in a perfectly flat voice, indicating where with a tilt of her head, being very careful not to point. "She's not dancing with the Prophet anymore."

And then I saw her out there, not twenty feet from us, dancing with a dark-haired young man in white tie and tails. Just as I caught my first glimpse of her, another young man tapped this one on the shoulder, and she changed partners. She was, as Corinna might have phrased it, the cynosure of all eyes.

Corinna was on her feet. She cupped her hands to her mouth and shouted, "Lilly Belle's engaged!"

Mary Elizabeth couldn't hear her above the music.

But she stopped dancing and started toward us, leading her partner by the hand. The other dancers respectfully made way for her. When she had come about half the distance, Corinna called out again, "Lilly Belle's engaged!"

"No!" Mary Elizabeth called back, and her voice and her radiant countenance expressed astonishment and delight. "Is it Mr. Barker?"

"None other!" said Corinna in her most grown-up tone. Mary Elizabeth was hurrying toward us now, and I beheld the spectacle of Corinna and Mary Elizabeth Caswell throwing their arms about each other. In that moment all was forgiven—all those splendid accomplishments, and all those unfavorable comparisons: forgiven forever. That which had separated them for so long had now united them.

"But Bessie didn't tell me!" Mary Elizabeth was saying. "She was by, this very morning, to have a close-up look at my dress."

"It's gorgeous," said Corinna.

"Isn't it!" And now another embrace.

"She told me just before I left the house," said Corinna. (Told *me*, not *us*? Before *I* not *we*, left the house? How selfish that sounded.) "The wedding's Sunday week. And Lilly Belle's going to marry in her mourning veil!"

"Oh no! Stop it!" cried Mary Elizabeth, and she and Corinna shrieked with laughter.

"Bessie's taking the train to Alabama late tonight," Corinna said when she had got her breath again.

"Oh, that wonderful Bessie!" said Mary Elizabeth.

"Isn't she splendid!"

"Have you seen her?"

"Seen her?"

"Up there," said Mary Elizabeth, pointing to the balcony opposite us. "I spotted her a while ago and waved to her."

"Why, she didn't tell me she was coming!" said Corinna. "Isn't that typical?"

The two girls tried to locate Bessie again but soon gave it up. Next, I heard Mary Elizabeth introducing us to her partner, referring to us as her two "little cousins," and realized that Bessie must have talked to her about us. She went on to say how brilliant Corinna was in school and how well

I could draw and what "perfect lambs" we both were.

I didn't stop searching for Bessie when they did, and I didn't hear what they were saying any longer. My eyes traveled up one row of the balcony and down the next, searching for Bessie's green silk dress. The crowd up there was thinning out; the poor relations and the children and the servants were going home. Bessie had likely hurried off to catch her train. Already I felt that I might never see Bessie Calhoun again.

But I kept looking for her until I could bear my lonely thoughts no longer. I put my arms on the railing before me, hid my face in them, and commenced to sob.

Instantly all attention was turned toward me, but I wouldn't look up or answer questions. In a matter of seconds Daddy and Mrs. Richards arrived.

"What is it, honey?" I heard Mrs. Richards say.

"He's just tired," Daddy said. "He's not used to being up so late. This is what it means, bringing children to something like this."

Then I was led to a seat at the rear of the box, where I wouldn't be so conspicuous. The Caswells had returned, too, now. I heard Mrs. Caswell say, "Poor little fellow," and this evoked fresh tears and deeper sobs.

"What is it, Son?" Daddy said. "You must try to tell me."

Finally I knew I had to say something—something that would sound reasonable to him. I swallowed hard and lifted my face and found Daddy. I don't know whether or not I knew what I was going to say before I said it. What I said was "Bessie's mama is dead."

"How did you know that, Son?" Daddy asked.

"She told me just before I was leaving the house tonight," I said. Then I hid my face and tried to begin crying again, but I couldn't.

"How awful of her!" I heard Mrs. Richards say, threateningly. "How really unspeakably awful!"

I sat with my face in my hands. After a moment I felt someone's arm go around my shoulder. I didn't know or care whose it was. Probably it was my father's though it may have been Mrs. Richards's, or even Corinna's. Whosever it was, it didn't have the feel I wanted, and I purposely kept my face hidden until it had been removed.

DICK GREGORY

BORN IN ST. LOUIS, Richard Claxton Gregory (1932–) knew abject poverty as a child, and adverse socio-economic conditions, injustices, and inequalities of all kinds came to shape his life's work. A track star at Sumner High School, Gregory attended Southern Illinois University at Carbondale on an athletic scholarship.

In 1956, Gregory went to Chicago to become a comedian. His big break came in 1961 when he performed at the Playboy Club, substituting for an ill Professor Irwin Corey. Gregory, with his cool, ironic humor, often about racial issues, was a huge success.

By 1962, Gregory was a major star and perhaps the most successful black comedian since Stepin Fetchit, though of a far different nature to be sure. Gregory was an active and prominent participant in the civil rights movement. He became a writer, publishing *From the Back of the Bus* in 1962 and *Nigger: An Autobiography*, with Robert Lipsyte, probably his best-known book, in 1964. Gregory also starred in a 1966 film, *Sweet Love, Bitter*, based loosely on the life of jazz musician Charlie Parker.

As the sixties progressed, Gregory devoted his energies to still more causes, including the anti–Vietnam War movement and militant vegetarianism. Like Gandhi, he fasted for lengthy periods to protest social injustices. Gregory ran for mayor of Chicago in 1967 and for the presidency on the U.S. Peace and Freedom Party ticket in 1968. He virtually abandoned nightclub performing, mainly working the college circuit.

Gregory continued to publish books, most of them outlining his case for the existence of right-wing and government-sponsored political conspiracies. These included *No More Lies: The Myth and Reality of American History* (1971, with James R. McGraw); *Code Name Zorro: The Murder of Martin Luther King, Jr.* (1971, with Mark Lane); and *Dick Gregory's Political Primer* (1972). He published the second installment of his autobiography, *Up From Nigger,* with James R. McGraw, in 1976.

As the 1970s and 1980s progressed, Gregory became more known for his vegetarian diet and radical weight-loss regimens. In 1974, he published *Dick Gregory's Natural Diets for Folks Who Eat, Cookin' with Mother Nature*. In the 1980s, Gregory marketed his Slim-Safe Bahamian Diet, a powdered diet mix.

Gregory can still be found on the front line of political causes. He last returned to St. Louis in the mid-1990s to campaign for human dignity and was an observer and commentator at the O. J. Simpson trial.

In the following excerpt from *Nigger*, Gregory recalls being the victim of racial violence in 1951 and his notoriety as a track star and senior class president at Sumner High School.

FROM *NIGGER: AN AUTOBIOGRAPHY*

That was a long summer, the summer of 1951. I was waiting for the scholastic record book to come out. In the spring I had won the mile in 4 minutes 28 seconds at the Missouri state meet for Negroes, one of the best high school times of the year, and I could hardly wait to see my name in the book when it came out in the fall. It was a long summer, and a hot one. The papers always had pictures of people frying eggs on the sidewalk in front of their houses. The mud on the river banks baked into a powdery dust that blew all over the city. All through June and July, Boo and Presley and I went downtown looking for jobs. Every day. Never got anything. "Sorry, boys, we're not hiring colored today." By August, Boo and Presley gave up. But I couldn't go back to shining shoes and running to the store for the neighbors. My name would be in a book soon. I kept going downtown alone.

It hit 109 degrees one day that August, so hot that skin peeled off my hand when I held a brass door handle too long. I had a nickel in my pocket that day, no job, and I started to walk home. Forty-five blocks, and every time I took a breath, the heat got caught in my throat. I thought I was going to pass out. And then I saw a beautiful sign on a restaurant window—AIR-CONDITIONED—SODA WATER 5¢. It was cool inside, and the soda jerk looked like an angel in his clean, white uniform.

"We don't serve niggers here."

I just stood there, trying to get my mouth wet enough to tell him what I'd gone through that day . . .

"What'sa matter, you deaf, boy?" . . . to tell him how good it felt in here, to tell him I was sorry I was a Negro.

Someone in the corner smashed a pop bottle against the marble counter and came toward me.

He came around in front of me, waving the broken bottle in his hand like Humphrey Bogart would do in the movies. There were others in back of him, grinning. He shoved the broken bottle at me, and I put my hand in front of my face. I didn't feel anything, but they started yelling. The soda jerk came flying over the counter like Alan Ladd, and he and Humphrey Bogart threw me out.

I started walking again, choking on the heat and the dust, watching my blood run down the sidewalk and the insides come out of my hand. It was white. Then I fainted. A wonderful feeling, like falling away from the world.

When I woke up, a white lady was kneeling in the gutter next to me, her arm under my head. Her other hand was stroking the lump on my forehead where it hit the pavement. "Everything will be all right, you're going to be all right, young man."

There was a white policeman standing next to her, and I tried to tell them that I wasn't bothering the lady, that I hadn't touched her. But my mouth was still too dry.

"Leave him alone, lady, I'll take care of this. The ambulance'll be right here."

"Where are you taking him, officer?"

"The nigger hospital."

"I beg your pardon?"

"Homer G. Phillips."

"That's too far. We'll take him to Barnes."

"Barnes ain't for niggers, lady. You'd better mind your business."

"Officer, do you know who I am?"

"Some nigger-lover who . . ."

The lady said her name then and the cop's mouth dropped open and he took a step backward. "I have your badge number and you can consider yourself fired." The cop began to apologize and help me into the ambulance. The lady got into the back with me. "Barnes Hospital, and quickly, please, this young man is seriously injured."

They turned on the siren. For me. Cars got out of the way. When she took me into the lobby of Barnes Hospital, I was a little ashamed of all the blood and dirt on my clothes. I had heard of Barnes, but never expected to be inside. They treated me well. Right upstairs, no waiting, one doctor to clean my hand, another to sew eight stitches and put on a clean white bandage. They all seemed to know the lady, and she stayed with me all the time.

Afterwards, she took me downstairs and called a cab. The driver looked at us strangely, but the lady got right in. She asked me where I lived, and she told the driver. She kept talking to me the whole ride, but I didn't hear a word. I just kept staring at the beautiful white bandage on my hand. Nobody in my neighborhood had ever had such a beautiful white bandage.

"I think I better get off here, ma'am."

"But this isn't North Taylor."

"I know, ma'am, but my Momma would think I did something wrong if she saw me come home with a white lady." That was true, but I couldn't tell her I wanted to slip in the back door and surprise everyone with my bandage.

"Are you sure you'll be all right?"

"Yes, ma'am."

"Are you really sure?"

"Yes, ma'am, and thank you very much. Thank you, too, sir," I told the cab driver. When I got out, the lady waved to me through the back window.

I started to run. I felt so good I ran five blocks, then ten blocks past my house. Finally, hot, my hand throbbing, I went home. I slipped in the back door. "Hey, everybody, come in here, you want to see something, you really want to see something?"

Momma put me to bed and I stayed there for three days. I only got up to put white shoe polish on my bandage when it started to get dirty. Everyone came to see me, and I told them about the white lady and the ambulance and going into Barnes Hospital. I didn't know the lady's name, and I think some people didn't believe my story.

After a week or so, Momma told me to go to the City Hospital to have the stitches removed. I didn't want to go there, but nobody at Barnes had said anything about my coming back. So I took the stitches out myself. One by one, with a needle and scissors. It wasn't that hard.

That September the scholastic record book came out and my name wasn't in it. I went down to the Board of Education and a man told me that records set in all-Negro track meets were never listed. Coach St. James told me the same thing. You have to run with the white boys to get your name in the book.

The next time I went down to the Board of Education I took a couple of thousand friends with me and I got my name on television and in the *St. Louis Post Dispatch.*

What really happened was that the Sumner High PTA organized a march on the Board that September to protest overcrowded conditions. There were a lot of tensions and fears. Pop Beckett stood in front of the school with a baseball bat in his hand and when he saw me he told me not to get involved.

"Got to go, Pop. My Momma doesn't know I was one of the best milers in the country this year."

He just looked at me, amazed.

My job on the march was to run up and down the line, keeping the kids in order and warning them not to steal from fruit stands along the way. The line got longer and longer, as kids from other Negro high schools joined. I never did get a chance to talk to the Mayor about my time for the mile. The newspaper and television reporters along the way thought I was kidding when I said I was protesting because my name wasn't in the scholastic record book. So I told them how there were eighty kids in the English class, and we learned math in the machine shop because there weren't enough rooms in school, and the last ten kids to get to History had to stand up for an hour because there weren't enough seats. They wrote in the papers that I was the leader of the demonstration. It's not as if I really *told* them that.

The police broke up the demonstration at Locust Street, in front of the Board building. They said it was a breach of the peace. And a man came out and told us that if we wanted better schools we should return to them. And another white man said that six adults from the PTA could come into the building and discuss the matter if the rest of us went back to classes. We did. The city was pretty well turned upside down by all this Negro marching and chanting and sign-waving. It wasn't even a matter of wanting to sit down with white kids. It was just a matter of wanting to sit down. Back at school everyone told me I was going to get expelled, and back home Momma was all upset. The white folks had told her that the march was Communist-inspired. I told her I didn't even know how to spell Communist.

Nothing much happened right away, but the next week the high school cross-country program was integrated. I don't know if it had anything to do with the march. It was the first time Negro and white ever competed against each other in the high schools of St. Louis, and things really began to open up for me.

It was wild. There were rumors and excitement and electricity in the air. We didn't know the white boys and they didn't know us. We'd never had a chance to love or hate each other on a man-to-man basis, to watch each other run, to see each other naked. There were Negro rumors that the white boys had special conditioning and food that gave them the strength to beat us in the long distances. There were white rumors that we needed only three runners at a track meet: one would win the 100 and the 220, the second would win both hurdles, and the third would win the half and the mile. Then the three regulars would borrow a Negro water boy and win the relays.

My first integrated meet was a cross-country run over at Wood River. I was so nervous I was shaking when we came to the line. Coach St. James had given us a big buildup for weeks. He had made us learn strategy all over again, made us promise to lay off the grandstanding. No argyle socks, no saluting, no crossing the tape holding your buddy's hand, no waving at your girl friends. This was big time. If we won we'd get our names in the white newspapers the next day—we wouldn't have to wait until the *Argus*, the weekly Negro newspaper, came out on Thursday. And the coach had told me that there was a little white boy in the race who had one of the best scholastic three-mile times in the country, and if I could beat him I could win the race. But we had never run the course before. And we didn't even know which was the white boy to beat.

Bang.

I didn't break out too fast. Let the pack go on ahead, this is a long race. You could see right away how different it was, running against boys who had eaten better and taken better care of their bodies all their lives. They looked smooth, they ran smooth. I moved up into the pack, and then went on ahead. I didn't know any of these white boys, which were the early pace-setters, which were the ones saving themselves for a final sprint. So I decided to stay with the leaders. There was a little white boy way ahead of everyone else, running as easy as flowing water. He took the corners sharply, and never seemed to get scratched by the bushes along the course. I got scratched all the time. I decided he had to be the white boy to beat.

I moved up, past the leaders, and started to dog that white boy. He was running too fast for me, and when I tried to match his pace my breath got short and it felt like somebody was sewing up the left side of my stomach and there was broken glass inside my shoes. He kept running easy. I knew I could never outrun him. Have to trick this race, Greg.

About the two-mile mark, I came up alongside him and slapped him on the butt. "Nice going, baby," I said, and I fell back fast so he wouldn't hear me panting.

A little bit later I came up again and kicked him on the heel of his shoe. Not enough to break his stride or bother him or get myself disqualified. Just enough so I could say, "Excuse me, baby." Again I dropped back fast so he wouldn't hear my breath come out. That upset him, but he didn't break.

Not much time left now. Last chance. I came right up behind him and I held my breath. He felt me running right behind him and he heard my feet, but he never heard me breathe. There was a fire in my chest, and my mind got fuzzy, and when I tried to take a shallow breath my brain kept clicking to shut it off, but he was looking around him now and his eyes were wide and he was so scared he speeded up. I held my breath as long as I could, then I dropped back to where he couldn't hear me and I let it all out and got myself together again. He had speeded up too early, and when he tried to slow down and settle back into his pace his smooth stride was broken, and he was off. He was destroyed. He wasn't running his race any more; he was scared and his mind was all messed up.

I came up again and I knew I could pass him any time I wanted to, now. But I didn't know the course, and I didn't want to take the chance of making a wrong turn and getting disqualified. So I stayed a few yards behind him until the last 200 yards, a straight shot to the tape. I could see the officials and the band and the crowd and the photographers and I passed him going away, and watched my knees all the way down the stretch, higher and higher, right through the tape. And then I got to see how Whitey treats his heroes.

First-class all the way. Had my picture on the front page of the Wood River paper, and on the sports pages of all the white St. Louis papers. Dick Gregory. No. 1. That was the start of a hell of a year, that last year in high school. I won the state cross-country meet at Forest Park, white and Negro. State champion. And then I finished second in a fifteen-mile race, the only high school runner in a field of college boys. People started listening to me that year, taking me to dinners, giving me awards. Outstanding citizen. They always introduced me as Dick Gregory, a boy who was born and raised on relief. Look at him now, they said. As if relief was all in the past, as if Momma wasn't still dragging home from the white folks, as if I wasn't taking five dollars at a time out of her pocketbook. I was too busy being a good example to go out and work, to be much of a son or a brother.

I took the high school cooking course that year because I wanted to learn etiquette. I was getting to be a big man around and I wanted to learn how to hold a knife and fork. I always used to eat one course at a time, clean off the meat, then turn the plate and clean off the potatoes, turn it again and clean off the greens. I had to convince them at Sumner that I was going to be a cook after graduation so they would let me take the home economics course. That meant I had to take sewing, too. But I learned how to eat right. I never told them the real reason I took the course, so they put COOK after my name in the yearbook.

Didn't matter. I was captain of the track team that year, and the cross-country team, and I played the kettledrum in the orchestra and the bass drum in the band, and the bongos for a dance club called the Rockettes. Even started taking girls to the movies. I was so cool I always took them up to the balcony, the sophisticated place in those Negro movie houses in St. Louis. If the picture wasn't so good you could always smoke and hug your girl and make jokes.

The trick there was to go to the movie house before you picked up your girl and slip the usher some money to save you a couple of balcony seats. Then you'd come back with your girl and wink at the usher and say: "Hi, baby," and he'd take you right upstairs. Sometimes, the usher would be out to lunch and all the balcony seats would be filled. That was the worst feeling in the world. But usually you'd get up there, and when the movie was over you'd strut down from the balcony, real slow, so everyone could see how cool you were, how important. You knew somebody, you had connections. You never let anyone know you tipped the usher. In those days, all I really wanted out of life was always to be able to sit in the balcony.

That year, I was in the balcony all right, winning races, playing drums, going out. Everything went my way. Once there was a night track meet, and the lights went out in the middle of the race. I sneaked off across the field, taking a short cut, and fell over a hurdle. I was lying there when the lights went on again. The officials tried to disqualify me. Not a chance. I told them that any fool knows that when the power fails during a night athletic event, the race in progress is automatically canceled and then rerun.

They looked at each other and coughed, and I guess they didn't know their own rules too well. I had just made that up on the spur of the moment. The race was rerun.

And then one day I decided I wanted to be president of my senior class. Only certain people had ever been class president: kids from high-class families who had perfect attendance records, were in the National Honor Society, belonged to the French Club and the Math Club and the service organizations. So I got my own organization. The hoodlums. I went around and talked to all those cats who used to stand outside the proms, all those guys who didn't have anything going for them and I told them I wanted this thing, that I was their representative. They went and they got it for me, they spread the word that if anybody else won the election he might as well quit. I was class president.

That was another turning point for me. A new feeling of responsibility for others. In track, I was running just for myself. But as president of the graduating class at Sumner High School I knew my shirt had to be clean, my shoes had to be polished, I couldn't cut class or come late or sit in the toilet and watch crap games or yell out crazy things in class. There were obligations, meetings to go to, a Senior Day speech to write. I had to talk to the white man who came through selling senior class rings for twenty dollars each. I had to work out how he would take his orders and collect his money and then give out the rings. I wasn't able to afford one myself.

I had never really thought about college until that last semester in high school when scholarship offers began coming in from colleges around the country. Momma had only finished the third grade, and so just finishing high school was a big dream in our family. College was for people with money. After high school you get yourself some kind of a job. There were more than one hundred offers, colleges from California to Massachusetts, but my grades were too low for most of the schools. I was probably the only class president in the country that year who was in the lowest fifth of more than 700 students. I tried to study that year, to read books, but I just didn't know how. At eight o'clock, after track practice, I'd sit down in the kitchen and try to read. God, I'm going to sit here until midnight if I have to, I'm going to read this book, even if it takes an hour to read every page, I'm going to sit here and read, one word at a time. And then the words started getting fuzzy and my mind started drifting, floating off to a million places.

Didn't matter, it was still my year. Coach St. James had gone to Southern Illinois University in Carbondale, and he said he could help me get in. He thought it would be the best school for me, a chance to be a big fish in a little pond. Southern Illinois wanted to give me an entrance exam, but I didn't even show up for it, I was so sure I would flunk. I talked to the coach down there and told him that if he wanted me to run track for him I wouldn't take any tests. He sent me to the dean, who made a deal: I could go to college, on an athletic-work scholarship, without taking the entrance exam. But the first quarter I made bad grades I'd have to take the exam and pass it, or leave school. Ironman Gregory won again.

Didn't have to study, didn't even have to train for my track meets any more. Wrapped my legs in tape and told the coach I hurt too much to practice. I stayed out late, went to dances, took girls up to the balcony, drank beer. Even bought a pack of cigarettes. I started letting the vice-president of the class go to the student government meetings. When the teachers kept asking me if my Senior Class Day speech was ready yet, I told them I was working on it. Tomorrow. It'll be ready tomorrow. I guess I thought I'd just go up there and tell jokes. I really thought I was great stuff, bigger than the Gregory family, bigger than the school, right up there with God. I remember the day we walked out to Forest Park for the final meet of my high school career, and all along the way there were papers on the newsstands with headlines that read: "Dick Gregory Closes Out One of Most Brilliant Careers in History of St. Louis H.S. Track." One headline even read: "Dick Gregory Wins State Meet Second Year in Row." Somebody must have lost his job on that one, because it rained when we got out to Forest Park and the meet was postponed.

All that week there were stories in the newspapers about how Dick Gregory was going to close out his high school career in style, in a blaze of glory. I believed every word. Didn't bother to train, stayed up late, made all the senior parties. Then we went out to Forest Park again and the sun was out and the press was there and the bands and the photographers and crowds were waiting for me to close out this brilliant high school career. It was a hell of a close-out all right. I finished seventeenth.

I couldn't believe it. Neither could anyone else. After the race I just hung around the finish line, waiting for them to disqualify the sixteen runners who finished ahead of me. The coach was mad and the press was disgusted and I was ashamed. The headlines didn't even mention who won the race, just: "Dick Gregory Finishes Disappointing 17th." I went back to school, and they started asking me about my speech again, and I just shrugged and walked away. I had gotten so big in my own mind that when I disappointed myself there was nothing left to fall back on. Too big for Momma, too big for the teachers, too big for God. But I was wrong again. The day before the senior ceremony, one of the English teachers handed me a speech.

I walked up on the stage that day and it seemed as though the whole world was holding its breath. When the principal pinned the school colors on me, his hand was shaking so much he stuck the pin right into my chest. I stepped behind the microphone. Suddenly I had that feeling again, the hot water flowing upward, the monster growing to crush the world, and that teacher's speech felt like it was mine.

"You know, since the beginning of time, man has used symbols . . ."

Suddenly, the whole goddamned auditorium stopped shifting and whispering, everyone froze, spellbound.

". . . the crude stone tablets, unearthed by archeologists, symbolized the feeble attempt of man to record his thoughts and his history . . ."

The teachers lost their terrified expressions, the students' mouths dropped open.

". . . the cross, so familiar in Christian civilization . . . the bald eagle . . . to many a symbol of democratic ideals . . ."

They were leaning toward me now, everybody, as if they wanted to run up and hug me.

". . . a symbol of man's efforts to live harmoniously with his fellow man. Today, we have gathered for a great symbolic experience. Colors Day. The maroon and white of Sumner High School, a symbol that for years has caused a little fire to burn in the hearts of many. Now we have joined this multitude. Needless to say, we will wear the maroon and white, this symbol of the years we have spent in learning and thought and growth, with justifiable pride in the years to come."

I was done and you could hear the breath rush out of hundreds of lungs, and then they started cheering and shouting and the hoodlums nearly tore the auditorium down and the teachers were smiling and shaking each other's hands and I looked down at Momma, and all I could see was tears in her eyes and she was moving her lips and I knew just what she looked like when she was alone and saying, Thank God, oh, thank God.

HAROLD BRODKEY

BORN AARON ROY WEINTRAUB in Alton, Illinois, Harold Brodkey (1930–1996) was adopted at age two by his father's second cousin, Doris Brodkey, and her husband, following his mother's death. A high-strung child who suffered several nervous breakdowns, Brodkey was raised in University City and, in 1947, attended Harvard University. In the early 1950s, Brodkey attracted the attention of William Maxwell, then an editor at the *New Yorker*, and thus began a long association with the magazine.

The 1958 publication of his first collection of short stories, *First Love and Other Sorrows*, catapulted Brodkey to literary fame, and he quickly developed the reputation of *enfant terrible*—gifted, volatile, and under-prolific. Brodkey seemed to avoid publishing his work, bringing out only three short story collections over several decades, while working on and compulsively revising a long novel. Finally, in 1991, the long-awaited novel, *The Runaway Soul,* appeared and received mixed critical reception. Three years later another novel, *Profane Friendship* (1994), which concerns a homosexual affair, appeared, also to mixed reviews. Shortly after this novel's publication, Brodkey announced that he had AIDS. In his posthumously published memoir, *This Wild Darkness* (1996), Brodkey wrote, "It bothers me that I won't live to see the end of the century, because, when I was young, in St. Louis, I remember saying to Marilyn, my sister by adoption, that that was how long I wanted to live: seventy years. And then to see the celebration."

The following story, "The State of Grace," one of the autobiographical works included in *First Love and Other Sorrows*, is set in St. Louis. Once called "the American Proust" by critic Harold Bloom, Brodkey displays in this story his keen sensitivity to the emotional turbulence and powerlessness of childhood.

THE STATE OF GRACE

There is a certain shade of red brick—a dark, almost melodious red, sombre and riddled with blue—that is my childhood in St. Louis. Not the real childhood, but the false one that extends from the dawning of consciousness until the day that one leaves home for college. That one shade of red brick and green foliage is St. Louis in the summer (the winter is just a gray sky and a crowded school bus and the wet footprints on the brown linoleum floor at school), and that brick and a pale sky is spring. It's also loneliness and the queer, self-pitying wonder that children whose families are having catastrophes feel.

I can remember that brick best on the back of our apartment house; it was on all the apartment houses on that block, and also on the apartment house where Edward lived—Edward was a small boy I took care of on the evenings when his parents went out. As I came up the street from school, past the boulevard and its ugliness (the vista of shoe-repair shops, dime stores, hairdressers', pet shops, the Tivoli Theatre, and the closed Piggly Wiggly, about to be converted into a Kroger's), past the place where I could see the Masonic Temple, built in the shape of some Egyptian relic, and the two huge concrete pedestals flanking the boulevard (what they supported I can't remember, but on both of them, in brown paint, was a large heart and the information that someone named Erica loved someone named Peter), past the post office, built in W.P.A. days of yellow brick and chrome, I hurried toward the moment when at last, on the other side, past the driveway of the garage of the Castlereagh Apartments, I would be at the place where the trees began, the apartment houses of dark-red brick, and the empty stillness.

In the middle of that stillness and red brick was my neighborhood, the terribly familiar place where I was more comfortably an exile than anywhere else. There were two locust trees that were beautiful to me—I think because they were small and I could encompass them (not only with my mind and heart but with my hands as well). Then came an apartment house of red brick (but not quite the true shade) where a boy I knew lived, and two amazingly handsome brothers, who were also strong and kind, but much older than I and totally uninterested in me. Then came an alley of black macadam and another vista, which I found shameful but drearily comfortable, of garages and ashpits and telephone poles and the backs of apartment houses—including ours—on one side, the backs of houses on the other. I knew many people in the apartments but none in the houses, and this was the ultimate proof, of course, to me of how miserably degraded I was and how far sunken beneath the surface of the sea. I was on the bottom, looking up through the waters, through the shifting bands of light—through, oh, innumerably more complexities than I could stand—at a sailboat driven by the wind, some boy who had a family and a home like other people.

I was thirteen, and six feet tall, and I weighed a hundred and twenty-five pounds. Though I fretted wildly about my looks (my ears stuck out and my hair was like wire), I also knew I was attractive; girls had smiled at me, but none whom I might love and certainly none of the seven or eight goddesses in the junior high school I attended. Starting in about second grade, I always had the highest grades—higher than anybody who had ever attended the schools I went to—and I terrified my classmates. What terrified them was that so far as they could see, it never took any effort; it was like legerdemain. I was never teased, I was never tormented; I was merely isolated. But I was known as "the walking encyclopedia," and the only way I could deal with this was to withdraw. Looking back, I'm almost certain I could have had friends if I'd made the right overtures, and that it was not my situation but my forbidding pride that kept them off; I'm not sure. I had very few clothes, and all that I had had been passed to me from an elder cousin. I never was able to wear what the other boys wore.

Our apartment was on the third floor. I usually walked up the back stairs, which were mounted outside the building in a steel framework. I preferred the back stairs—it was a form of rubbing at a hurt to make sure it was still there—because they were steep and ugly and had garbage cans on the landings and wash hanging out, while the front door opened off a court where rosebushes grew, and the front stairs were made of some faintly yellow local marble that was cool and pleasant to the touch and to the eye. When I came to our back door, I would open the screen and call out to see if my mother was home. If she was not home, it usually meant that she was visiting my father, who had been dying in the hospital for four years and would linger two more before he would come to terms with death. As far as I know, that was the only sign of character he ever showed in his entire life, and I suppose it was considerable, but I hoped, and even sometimes prayed, that he would die—not only because I wouldn't have to visit the hospital again, where the white-walled rooms were filled with odors and sick old men (and a tangible fear that made me feel a falling away inside, like the plunge into the unconscious when the anesthetic is given), but because my mother might marry again and make us all rich and happy once more. She was still lovely then, still alight with the curious incandescence of physical beauty, and there was a man who had loved her for twenty years and who loved her yet and wanted to marry her. I wished so hard my father would die, but he just wouldn't. If my mother was home, I braced myself for unpleasantness, because she didn't like me to sit and read; she hated me to read. She wanted to drive me outdoors, where I would become an athlete and be like other boys and be popular. It filled her with rage when I ignored her advice and opened a book; once, she rushed up to me, her face suffused with anger, took the book (I think it was *Pride and Prejudice*), and hurled it out the third-story window. At the time, I sat and tried to sneer, thinking she was half mad, with her exaggerated rage, and so foolish not to realize that I could be none of the things she thought I ought to be. But now I think—perhaps wistfully—that she was merely desperate, driven to extremes in her anxiety to save me. She felt—she knew, in fact—that there was going to come a moment when, like an acrobat, I would have to climb on her shoulders and on the shoulders of all the things she had done for me, and leap out into a life she couldn't imagine (and which I am leading now), and if she wanted to send me out wrapped in platitudes, in an athletic body, with a respect for money, it was because she thought that was the warmest covering.

But when I was thirteen, I only wondered how anyone so lovely could be so impossible. She somehow managed it so that I hated her far more than I loved her, even though in the moments before sleep I would think of her face, letting my memory begin with the curving gentleness of her eyelids and circle through all the subtle interplay of shadows and hollows and bones, and the half-remembered warmth of her chest, and it would seem to me that this vision of her, always standing in half light (as probably I had seen her once when I was younger, and sick, perhaps, though I don't really remember), was only as beautiful to me as the pattern in an immeasurably ancient and faded Persian rug. In the vision, as in the rug, I could trace the lines in and out and experience some unnamed pleasure, but it had almost no meaning, numbed as I was by the problems of being her son.

Being Jewish also disturbed me, because it meant I could never be one of the golden people—the blond athletes, with their easy charm. If my family had been well off, I might have felt otherwise, but I doubt it.

My mother had a cousin whom I called Aunt Rachel, and we used to go and see her three or four times a year. I hated it. She lived in what was called the Ghetto, which was a section of old houses in downtown St. Louis with tiny front porches and two doors, one to the upstairs and one to the downstairs. Most people lived in them only until they could move to something better; no one had ever liked living there. And because of that, the neighborhood had the quality of being blurred; the grass was never neat, the window frames were never painted, no one cared about or loved the place. It was where the immigrants lived when they arrived by train from New York and before they could move uptown to the apartments near Delmar Boulevard, and eventually to the suburbs—to Clayton, Laclede, and Ladue. Aunt Rachel lived downstairs. Her living room was very small and had dark-yellow wallpaper, which she never changed. She never cleaned it, either, because once I made a mark on it, to see if she would, and she didn't. The furniture was alive and frightening; it was like that part of the nightmare where it gets so bad that you decide to wake up. I always had to sit on it. It bulged in great curves of horsehair and mohair, and it was dark purple and maroon and dark green, and the room had no light in it anywhere. Somewhere on the other side of the old, threadbare satin draperies that had been bought out of an old house was fresh air and sunshine, but you'd never know it. It was as much like a peasant's hut as Aunt Rachel could manage, buying furniture in cut-rate furniture stores. And always there were the smells—the smell of onion soup and garlic and beets. It was the only place where I was ever rude to my mother in public. It was always full of people whom I hardly ever knew, but who knew me, and I had to perform. My mother would say, "Tell the people what your last report card was," or "Recite them the poem that Miss Huntington liked so well." That was when the feeling of unreality was strongest. Looking back now, I think that what frightened me was their fierce urgency; I was to be rich and famous and make all their tribulations worth while. But I didn't want that responsibility. Anyway, if I were going to be what they wanted me to be, and if I had to be what I was, then it was too much to expect me to take them as they were. I had to go beyond them and despise them, but first I had to be with them—and it wasn't fair.

It was as if my eyelids had been propped open, and I had to see these things I didn't want to see. I felt as if I had taken part in something shameful, and therefore I wasn't a nice person. It was like my first sexual experiences: What if anyone knew? What if everyone found out? . . . How in hell could

I ever be gallant and carefree?

I had read too many books by Englishmen and New Englanders to want to know anything but graceful things and erudite things and the look of white frame houses on green lawns. I could always console myself by thinking my brains would make me famous (brains were good for something, weren't they?), but then my children would have good childhoods—not me. I was irrevocably deprived, and it was the irrevocableness that hurt, that finally drove me away from any sensible adjustment with life to the position that dreams had to come true or there was no point in living at all. If dreams came true, then I would have my childhood in one form or another, someday.

If my mother was home when I came in from school, she might say that Mrs. Leinberg had called and wanted me to baby-sit, and I would be plunged into yet another of the dilemmas of those years. I had to baby-sit to earn money to buy my lunch at school, and there were times, considering the dilemma I faced at the Leinbergs', when I preferred not eating, or eating very little, to baby-sitting. But there wasn't any choice; Mother would have accepted for me, and made Mrs. Leinberg promise not to stay out too late and deprive me of my sleep. She would have a sandwich ready for me to eat, so that I could rush over in time to let Mr. and Mrs. Leinberg go out to dinner. Anyway, I would eat my sandwich reading a book, to get my own back, and then I would set out. As I walked down the back stairs on my way to the Leinbergs', usually swinging on the railings by my arms to build up my muscles, I would think forlornly of what it was to be me, and wish things were otherwise, and I did not understand myself or my loneliness or the cruel deprivation the vista down the alley meant.

There was a short cut across the back yards to the apartment house where the Leinbergs lived, but I always walked by my two locust trees and spent a few moments loving them; so far as I knew, I loved nothing else.

Then I turned right and crossed the street and walked past an apartment house that had been built at right angles to the street, facing a strange declivity that had once been an excavation for still another apartment house, which had never been built, because of the depression. On the other side of the declivity was a block of three apartment houses, and the third was the Leinbergs'. Every apartment in it had at least eight rooms, and the back staircase was enclosed, and the building had its own garages. All this made it special and expensive, and a landmark in the neighborhood.

Mr. Leinberg was a drug manufacturer and very successful. I thought he was a smart man, but I don't remember him at all well (I never looked at men closely in those days but always averted my head in shyness and embarrassment; they might guess how fiercely I wanted to belong to them) and I could have been wrong. Certainly the atmosphere then, during the war years—it was 1943—was that everyone was getting rich; everyone who could work, that is. At any rate, he was getting rich, and it was only a matter of time before the Leinbergs moved from that apartment house to Laclede or Ladue and had a forty-thousand-dollar house with an acre or so of grounds.

Mrs. Leinberg was very pretty; she was dark, like my mother, but not as beautiful. For one thing, she was too small; she was barely five feet tall, and I towered over her. For another, she was not at all regal. But her lipstick was never on her teeth, and her dresses were usually new, and her eyes were kind. (My mother's eyes were incomprehensible; they were dark stages where dimly seen mob scenes were staged and all one ever sensed was tumult and drama, and no matter how long one waited, the lights never went up and the scene never was explained.) Mrs. Leinberg would invite me to help myself in the icebox, and then she would write down the telephone number of the place where she was going to be. "Keep Edward in the back of the apartment, where he won't disturb the baby," she would tell me. "If the baby does wake up, pick her up right away. That's very important. I didn't pick Edward up, and I'll always regret it." She said that every time, even though I could see Edward lurking in the back hallway, waiting for his parents to leave so he could run out and jump on me and our world could come alive again. He would listen, his small face—he was seven—quite blank with hurt and the effort to pierce the hurt with understanding.

Mrs. Leinberg would say, "Call me if she wakes up." And then, placatingly, to her husband, "I'll just come home to put her back to sleep, and then I'll go right back to the party—" Then, to me, "But she almost always sleeps, so don't worry about it."

"Come on, Greta. He knows what to do," Mr. Leinberg would say impatiently.

I always heard contempt in his voice—contempt for his wife, for Edward, and for me. I would be standing by the icebox looking down on the two little married people. Edward's father had a jealous and petulant mouth. "Come on, Greta," it would say impatiently, "We'll be back by eleven," it would say to me.

"Edward goes to bed at nine," Mrs. Leinberg would say, her voice high and birdlike, but tremulous with confusion and vagueness. Then she would be swept out the front door, so much prettily dressed matchwood, in her husband's wake. When the door closed, Edward would come hurtling down the hall and tackle my knees if I was staring after his parents, or, if I was facing him, leap onto my chest and into my arms.

"What shall we play tonight?"

He would ask that and I would have to think. He trembled with excitement, because I could make up games wonderful to him—like his daydreams, in fact. Because he was a child, he trusted me almost totally, and I could do anything with him. I had that power with children until I was in college and began at last to be like other people.

In Edward's bedroom was a large closet; it had a rack for clothes, a washstand, a built-in table, and fifteen or twenty shelves. The table and shelves were crowded with toys and games and sports equipment. I owned a Monopoly board I had inherited from my older sister, an old baseball glove (which was so cheap I never dared use it in front of my classmates, who had real gloves signed by real players), and a collection of postcards. The first time I saw that closet, I practically exploded with pleasure; I took down each of the games and toys and played with them, one after another, with Edward. Edward loved the fact that we never played a game to its conclusion but would leap from game to game after only a few moves, until the leaping became the real game and the atmosphere of laughter the real sport.

It was comfortable for me in the back room, alone in the apartment with Edward, because at last I was chief; and not only that, I was not being seen. There was no one there who could see through me, or think of what I should be or how I should behave; and I have always been terrified of what people thought of me, as if what they thought was a hulking creature that would confront me if I should turn a wrong corner.

There were no corners. Edward and I would take his toy pistols and stalk each other around the bed. Other times, we were on the bed, the front gun turret of a battleship sailing to battle the Japanese fleet in the Indian Ocean. Edward would close his eyes and roll with pleasure when I went "Boom! Boom! BOOOOM!"

"It's sinking! It's sinking, isn't it?"

"No, stupid. We only hit its funnel. We have to shoot again. Boom, Boom—"

Edward's fingers would press his eyelids in a spasm of ecstasy; his delirious, taut, little boy's body would fall backward on the soft pillows and bounce, and his back would curve; the excited breathy laughter would pour out like so many leaves spilling into spring, so many lilacs thrusting into bloom.

Under the bed, in a foxhole (Edward had a Cub Scout hat and I had his plastic soldier helmet), we turned back the yellow hordes from Guadalcanal. Edward dearly loved to be wounded. "I'm hit!" he'd shriek. "I'm hit!" He'd press his hand against his stomach and writhe on the wooden floor. "They shot me in the guts—"

I didn't approve of his getting wounded so soon, because then the scene was over; both his and my sense of verisimilitude didn't allow someone to be wounded and then get up. I remember how pleased he was when I invented the idea that after he got wounded, he could be someone else; so, when we crawled under the bed, we would decide to be eight or twelve or twenty Marines, ten each to get wounded, killed, or maimed as we saw fit, provided enough survived so that when we crawled out from under the bed we could charge the Japanese position under the dining-room table and leave it strewn with corpses.

Edward was particularly good at the detective game, which was a lot more involved and difficult. In that, we would walk into the kitchen, and I would tell him that we had received a call about a murder. Except when we played Tarzan, we never found it necessary to be characters. However, we always had names. In the detective game, we were usually Sam and Fred. We'd get a call telling us who was murdered, and then we'd go back to the bedroom and examine the corpse and question the suspects. I'd fire questions at an empty chair. Sometimes Edward would get tired of being my sidekick and he'd slip into the chair and be the quaking suspect. Other times, he would prowl around the room on his hands and knees with a magnifying glass while I stormed and shouted at the perpetually shifty suspect: "Where were you, Mrs. Eggnogghead [giggles from Edward], at ten o'clock, when Mr. Eggnogghead [laughter, helpless with pleasure, from Edward] was slain with the cake knife?"

"Hey, Fred! *I found bloodstains*." Edward's voice would quiver with a creditable imitation of the excitement of radio detectives.

"Bloodstains! Where, Sam? Where? This may be the clue that breaks the case."

Edward could sustain the *commedia dell' arte* for hours if I wanted him to.

He was a precocious and delicate little boy, quivering with the malaise of being unloved. When we played, his child's heart would come into its own, and the troubled world where his vague hungers went unfed and mothers and fathers were dim and far away—too far away ever to reach in and touch the sore place and make it heal—would disappear, along with the world where I was not sufficiently muscled or sufficiently gallant to earn my own regard. (What ever had induced my mother to marry that silly man, who'd been unable to hang on to his money? I could remember when we'd had a larger house and I'd been happy; why had she let it get away?) It angered me that Edward's mother had so little love for him and so much for her daughter, and that Edward's father should not appreciate the boy's intelligence—he thought Edward was a queer duck, and effeminate. I could have taught Edward the manly postures. But his father didn't think highly of me: I was only a baby-sitter, and a queer duck too. Why, then, should Edward be more highly regarded by his father than I myself was? I wouldn't love him or explain to him.

That, of course, was my terrible dilemma. His apartment house, though larger than mine, was made of the same dark-red brick, and I wouldn't love him. It was shameful for a boy my age to love a child anyway. And who was Edward? He wasn't as smart as I'd been at his age, or as fierce. At his age, I'd already seen the evil in people's eyes, and I'd begun the construction of my defenses even then. But Edward's family was more prosperous, and the cold winds of insecurity (*Where will the money come from?*) hadn't shredded the dreamy chrysalis of his childhood. He was still immersed in the dim, wet wonder of the folded wings that might open if someone loved him; he still hoped, probably, in a butterfly's unthinking way, for spring and warmth. How the wings ache, folded so, waiting; that is, they ache until they atrophy.

So I was thirteen and Edward was seven and he wanted me to love him, but he was not old enough or strong enough to help me. He could not make his parents share their wealth and comfort with me, or force them to give me a place in their home. He was like most of the people I knew—eager and needful of my love; for I was quite remarkable and made incredible games, which were better than movies or than the heart could hope for. I was a dream come true. I was smart and virtuous (no one knew that I occasionally stole from the dime store) and fairly attractive, maybe even very attractive. I was often funny and always interesting. I had read everything and knew everything and got unbelievable grades. Of course I was someone whose love was desired. Mother, my teachers, my sister, girls at school, other boys—they all wanted me to love them.

But I wanted them to love me first.

None of them did. I was fierce and solitary and acrid, marching off the little mile from school, past the post office, all yellow brick and chrome, and my two locust trees (water, water everywhere and not a drop to drink), and there was no one who loved me first. I could see a hundred cravennesses in the people I knew, a thousand flaws, a million weaknesses. If I had to love first, I would love only perfection. Of course, I could help heal the people I knew if I loved them. No, I said to myself, why should I give them everything when they give me nothing?

How many hurts and shynesses and times of walking up the back stairs had made me that way? I don't know. All I know is that Edward needed my love and I wouldn't give it to him. I was only thirteen. There isn't much you can blame a boy of thirteen for, but I'm not thinking of the blame; I'm thinking of all the years that might have been—if I'd only known then what I know now. The waste, the God-awful waste.

Really, that's all there is to this story. The boy I was, the child Edward was. That and the terrible desire to suddenly turn and run shouting back through the corridors of time, screaming at the boy I was, searching him out, and pounding on his chest: Love him, you damn fool, love him.

FANNIE HURST

IN 1889, ROSE KOPPEL HURST and her husband, Sam, were living in St. Louis but returned to her family's home in Hamilton, Ohio for the birth of their daughter, Fannie (1889–1968). After Fannie's arrival, the Hurst family returned to their home at 5641 Cates Avenue. Although Sam Hurst, a moderately successful businessman, could afford to send Fannie to private schools—and she briefly attended Harperly Hall—she graduated from Central High School and went on to Washington University, from which she graduated in 1909. While in college, Fannie published her first story, which was originally written for an English course, in *The Mirror*. Hurst, who had aspirations to be a writer, received strong encouragement from William Reedy to move to New York and pursue her dream. After graduating from college, Hurst did just that and became an internationally celebrated writer, with more than twenty-nine screen adaptations made from her novels and short stories. Among her most popular books are *Back Street* (1931) and *Imitation of Life* (1933).

During her lifetime, Hurst's sense of personal style and panache, as well as her unconventional marriage to Russian musician Jacques Danielson, held the fascination of the public. In addition, Hurst's close friendship with Eleanor Roosevelt drew her into various social and political causes. In 1952, President Truman appointed Hurst as the U.S. delegate to the U.N. World Health Assembly. Although Hurst is usually associated with New York City, she once remarked that her "characters and locale really belonged to St. Louis." Although Hurst did not come from a religiously observant family, she identified closely with her Jewish heritage. After her death in New York City, Hurst's remains were buried in the New Mount Sinai Cemetery in St. Louis.

The first of the following pieces is an article on Hurst's impressions of St. Louis, which first appeared in the *American Mercury* magazine and was reprinted in the *St. Louis Globe-Democrat* in 1955. The second piece, in which this native daughter recalls her school days and literary debut in *The Mirror*, is excerpted from Hurst's autobiography, *Anatomy of Me* (1958).

SAINT LOUIS

St. Louis is my home town. Not quite literally because I saw my first light of day in Hamilton, Ohio. But I was merely taken there for the purpose of being born in the same house in which my mother came into this life, and as soon as possible thereafter, returned to the Missouri metropolis.

So actually, St. Louis is the scene of my earliest recollections.

One of these is walking along a high bluff with my hand in my father's, and pausing with him to look out over the wide Mississippi River as it flowed, slow-moving as molasses, past our city.

"There goes one of the greatest rivers in the world," he said. "Pretty muddy looking, isn't she, to be so important?"

I remember her mud because it made our levees so cozy. On steamboat rides to Keokuk, Cape Girardeau, or Memphis, we churned it up in clouds.

During my childhood, Mississippi mud vitiated our drinking water. Most households used small filters, attachable to the kitchen faucet. I used to beg for the privilege of cleaning ours. The filter stone lifted out of its metal container, covered with a heavy coating of thick yellowish slime which washed off as you held it beneath the faucet and ran thick as gravy into the sink.

It was a thankful job in a way, because then you reinserted a clean filter ready to absorb its next load.

Today, of course, due to modern processes, the great city of 800,000 population, boasts immaculate and sparkling drinking water.

So does it boast all of the accoutrements and glamorous advantages of a progressive metropolis, fit to rank among the leading cities of the nation.

Situated on the west bank of the Mississippi River, on flat far-flung terrain of rich agricultural yield, she not only dominates the State of Missouri, but geographically and dramatically speaking, is the Gateway to the West!

A far cry, this modern imperial city, from that summer back in 1764 when a Frenchman, Pierre Laclede Liguest, set out from New Orleans for Louisiana, there to start a new trading post in the furs which were so fabulously enriching that region.

After adventures inherent in such an enterprise, he explored the Mississippi up as far as the Missouri. Suddenly, spread before him like an answer to his prayer, was the site upon which was to rise the eighth largest city in the nation.

The St. Louis of today, with its accrued wealth of solid industries, gargantuan department stores, factories, major league baseball teams; its avenues, boulevards, residential streets with stone gates that are locked at night; its meatpacking, shoe, fur, chemical and heavy industries; its staggering brewing interests, its mercantile and manufacturing importance, its family mansions; all this staid conservatism of contemporary St. Louis has a background of trappers, of voyageurs, such as the Chouteaus; of Louisiana Purchase pathfinders; of Lewis and Clark, who blazed a trail into the fur monopolies upon which so much St. Louis history rests.

Hurtling the fascinating historical narrative of the Mississippi and the Missouri Rivers; the 1811 appearance of the first Mississippi steamboat; the weaving of the highways, airways, waterways that form spokes into all parts of America, let us now enter St. Louis by way of Union Station.

It is an outmoded Union Station, but in its day, which must be about a half-century back, it was nation-wide, headline news. The last word in tailored railroad terminals.

At that time, you no sooner emerged from the much-touted magnificence of the station, than the eye banged against a slum area of Negro tenements and shacks. These are now cleared. Today a superb Carl Milles fountain, symbolizing the meeting of the Mississippi and Missouri Rivers, dominates the handsome Plaza in front of Union Station. But despite splendid ornamental waters, the taint of slums still vitiates the area.

In many ways, St. Louis has become sort of a last stronghold of a vanishing era. Believe it or not, in this apartment-house-and-family-hotel era, St. Louis is still a town of many, many mansions. Ten, 15 and 20-room ones at that. Apparently that vanishing race, domestic servants, has not altogether disappeared in this handsome, matronly city. Its beautiful tree-lined residential boulevards and landscaped areas abound in Georgian, Norman, Greek, ranch and adobe mansions, surrounded by ornate lawns, lariat driveways, ornamental garages. Radiating toward and from these highly exclusive sections are miles and miles of two and three-story family and apartment structures.

St. Louisans are essentially home folks. Their living rooms are used, their dining-room tables are the expandable sort. St. Louis eats "in" and eats well. A chronic complaint of restaurateurs and theater managers is that St. Louis is too much of a "home city," for their kind of business.

Come evening, St. Louis likes to enjoy its comfortable living rooms or glassed-in porches, its television, cards, or social gatherings. Downtown streets are largely deserted, theaters indifferently attended.

One splendid exception to this general rule is the huge and magnificent outdoor Municipal Theater in Forest Park. World renowned.

But this too is a gathering of the community, sitting out in the open, under starry Middle West skies, to enjoy the best in drama, opera and ballet.

But make no mistake, downtown St. Louis in the last word in modern hotels, department stores, mercantile establishments, clubs. The Kiel Auditorium seats 20,000. The 31-story Telephone Building is a skyscraping achievement.

But apart from its physical splendors there is a subtle "feel" to the city not easily definable. The real "spirit of St. Louis" lurks not in the Lindbergh airplane of that name, which she sent winging on its immortal flight, but in the behavior and the attitudes of the people.

They are conservative, undemonstrative, unostentatious. The New England infiltration of its early history has left a Yankee influence.

The mistresses of many of the magnificent mansions, who are members of the exclusive St. Louis clubs and snobbish social cliques, market their own fowl for dinner and prod chicken flesh for tenderness across the butcher's counter. Their men, who sit on some of the greatest fortunes in the nation but could easily be overlooked in a crowd, usually prefer it that way. Despite sophistication, know-how and progressiveness, thrift runs through their pattern.

When St. Louisans who have struck out to seek, or make, name and fame for themselves in far-flung places, feel the nostalgic pull to return for a visit, they will be assured a quiet but undemonstrative welcome.

During World War II, I found myself one of a coast-to-coast traveling team of authors, including Louis Bromfield, Ogden Nash, Clifton Fadiman and Gen. Carlos Romulo.

When we reached St. Louis, as the home-town girl, I was thrust to the front of our party and placed in the first car. As we left the station with the paraphernalia of motorcar escort, a policeman turned to me and said: "My wife just loves you on the radio, Baby Snooks." "Alas," I explained, "I'm not Fannie Brice. I'm Fannie Hurst."

"Oh," he remarked casually, "then you must know my son. I think he used to be in your class at school."

Then he mentioned his name. His son and my classmate had become a man of international fame.

On that same trip, which was at least 15 years after I had left St. Louis, I met an old school friend who greeted me warmly:

"Why hello, Fannie. How've you been? Haven't seen you for a long time. Been away?"

St. Louisans are like that. And, St. Louis is like this:

You can fry an egg on its August sidewalks. To be sure, so can you in a score of American cities, but like Pittsburgh for its smoke, St. Louis takes the rap for its heat. St. Louis winter dampness is content with nothing short of getting into the marrow of your bones and rattling them.

Even the oldest inhabitants complain that their home town "bores the daylights" out of them, cramps their style, and induces sleeping sickness. But in the same breath they will defend her to the death.

You have to be a St. Louisan to know the taste of her autumns and of her Missouri crab apple jelly and the carnival fun of the Veiled Prophet annual parade and ball.

A one-time eminent president of Washington University, which overlooks the city, remarked to me while I was a student there:

"It's the darndest thing (Yes, the president put it that way!), I'm a New Englander by birth, and by preference. I want to get back there and end my days where I began them. But I just can't want to leave this town enough to do something about it, so I guess I'll have to end my days right here." He did.

Charles Lindbergh, baseball, Anheuser-Busch, and the St. Louis Blues may be her chief claim to popular fame, but as her Chamber of Commerce might proudly put it, St. Louis, metropolis of the Middle West, is an old city with new ideals. And the old wine is in modern new bottles.

Foremost in the Mississippi Valley (and what a valley!), it is a queen of a city, surrounded by the United States and packed with the meaning of America.

The last time I was there, I ran into an old crony of my father's.

"Aren't you about ready to come back and settle down in St. Louis?" he asked. "Most of the things you are traipsing around trying to find in life, you'll find right here, only better."

St. Louisans feel that way!

FROM *ANATOMY OF ME*

In the questionnaire passed around my senior year in Central High I wrote yes after the query: Do you intend to go to college or university? What college or university? Only prestige names occurred to me. I wrote in three: Bryn Mawr, Wellesley, Smith.

Actually, I had not faced the matter, but as graduation approached the hour for decision was imminent.

Mama recoiled. Why college? You have a good education. What do you want to be? An old-maid schoolteacher like Tillie Strauss?

Papa said: Rose, if Fannie wants to continue learning, we should be in favor of it. Knowledge is power.

You'll sing a different tune when you hear what it costs to send a girl to college. And for what? If she wants to learn, she can learn at home.

Perhaps your mother is right. Study in the home.

Oh no, Papa.

That Washington University out there is an old maids' nest.

I want to go away to college.

Leave home?

All the girls do.

What do you think of that, Sam? She not only wants to go away from home, but our own Washington University, one of the finest in the country, isn't good enough.

Hold your horses, Rose. Let's talk this thing out.

My daughter wants to leave home to become another Tillie Strauss, instead of being a comfort to her parents after graduation like other children. I could cry my eyes out.

At long last I compromised on the University of Missouri, noted for its school of journalism. Several weeks before graduation, Mama and I set out for Columbia, Missouri, to register in advance and arrange for living quarters.

Bertha Schaeffer, the daughter of our dentist and a second-year student there, guided us over the campus, assisted in the matter of registration, and, since freshmen could not live on the campus, led us to a quiet home on a side street of modest frame houses. Almost every one of them took student roomers. The double room which Bertha's one-time landlady would only rent to two students was clean but depressing, and to be shared with its present occupant, a young lady from Peoria.

The fact that Bertha had lived there her freshman year was sufficient recommendation for Mama to pay an advance on the room months ahead of my arrival.

I had matriculated at the University of Missouri! I had a room engaged in a college town! Fannie Hurst. University of Missouri.

But Mama was a deterrent to dignity. Bertha, you will watch over my child, won't you? She's never been away from home. Do you think six sheets is enough? See that she sends her things home to be laundered and mended.

But on that walk back to the Columbia depot, not even the embarrassment of Mama's violent maternalism in public mattered. I was about to major in journalism at the University of Missouri.

The reaction began to set in as we rode in a shabby day coach through the thickening twilight of flat Missouri country. Isolated houses along the way began to show their lighted windows, the stretches of open field between darkening into vast loneliness. I could feel my high spirits plummet like lead.

Soon this same lonely kind of twilight would shut me into a strange world of strange people in that gray little house on that gray little street. That shoebox-shaped room with my future roommate's family photographs on her side of the dresser and her toothbrush in its holder on her side of the washstand. Mama?

Seated beside me, she was crying quietly into her handkerchief. As I spoke, she broke: Don't go, Fannie. Don't leave us. You're all we have—stay home, baby—with us. Go to Washington University if you must—do anything you want at home—but don't leave us.

I could scarcely breathe from emotion and relief at this opportunity to withdraw and yet save face.

Mama had saved me from a rapidly mounting impulse to turn to her with something like: I don't want to do this. I love you so. Mama, don't let me leave you.

Don't leave us, Fannie.

I won't, Mama—not for anything, I said with magnanimity.

Now came the suspenseful weeks. Would I be chosen to deliver a paper at commencement?

On the premise that I would, Mama began one shopping onslaught after another, even including fancy accessories for Aunt Jennie and Aunt Bettie to wear at the exercises.

Papa said: Rose, for pity's sake, don't be so ostentatious.

Mama said: You mind your business, Sam, and I'll mind mine, which is to see that my child doesn't graduate like a pauper. Besides, I am spending my own hard-earned savings.

Looking back, it seems incredible that I permitted Mama to overload me with finery so at variance with the remainder of the class. We graduated in dresses with trains. Mine was white net over taffeta, trimmed and trimmed in Valenciennes lace and Valenciennes lace. Weeks before the event, the frock hung from the chandelier in our sewing room, to be inspected and "ohed" over by the neighbors.

The class flower was the carnation, each girl to bring a dollar and a half to school for her bouquet.

Nothing of the sort for Mama. I was to carry a shower of three dozen giant carnations, especially ordered from a florist of her choosing.

Papa said: You'll make us all ridiculous, Rose.

Mama said: You don't deserve to have a daughter on the graduating program.

Mama, I haven't been chosen yet.

Nevertheless, there was open speculation that I would be. I proceeded on that premise, planning and plotting my paper. It was not to be about an event in history or a character analysis of Thomas Jefferson or the story of the Statue of Liberty and our debt to France. I preferred to write a paper about people who were not in history. People. The people in the streets and in little houses who were thick as ants and got stepped on like ants. I captured a wonderful title. "All the Little Human Ants." My fingers itched to begin. . . .

Then one morning I was summoned from the study hall to the office. The students buzzed. I was to be named!

But something told me that all was not well. Miss Hurst, the principal began coolly, we have unearthed a surprising situation. How many compositions have you written for members of English 4 that were handed in by other pupils under their own names?

I was stunned.

For almost the entire semester I had been writing compositions in exchange for ill-gotten help in algebra and chemistry from students facile in those departments.

I stood accused and guilty.

I wrote their compositions, I half explained, because it was difficult for them and easy for me.

Did it occur to you that here we operate under an honor system?

I guess it did. But I liked to write them—and did.

You realize that this is a matter for suspension, even expulsion. Do you expect to be graduated under these circumstances?

I thought of Mama and Papa and the graduation dress hanging from the chandelier. I thought of "All the Little Human Ants!" Except for horror of displaying emotion, I could have wept. I didn't think. I'll do anything if you'll let me graduate. My mother and father . . .

You didn't think. Well, last evening we held a special faculty meeting on the matter, and we did some thinking.

I stood numb.

Last week, Miss Hurst, you were unanimously chosen out of a class of three hundred and ten to deliver an original composition at the graduation exercises. You have forfeited your right to that honor. We will permit you and the recipients of your compositions to graduate, but all of you without distinction.

So it came to pass that a heavy-hearted, overdressed, flower-laden graduate sat in the last row of her class, while a mouse-colored little prodigy in physics, in his first long trousers, droned a thesis on Newton, Father of the Law of Gravity.

So far as I am concerned, time is a swift river, rising at my birth and riding me toward eternity. The years pile up, the arteries narrow, telephone-book print dims. The zenith of life comes, lo the span is more than half spent, the timetable shortens, and more and more of one's contemporaries begin to show up in the daily death notices.

Confusion that had to do with an annuity insurance policy once revealed the fact that the Hamilton, Ohio, birth records show confusion about my age. I am either two years younger or older than I reckoned.

I am pleased to give myself the benefit of the doubt and assume that my arteries are the two years younger. I confess, with embarrassment for my puniness, to answering at the voting polls: Over twenty-one. I omit the date of my birth in *Who's Who*. I even lie to doctors, although when explaining to one that I did not know my exact age, he replied: Never mind, we can tell.

Thus the college years glide timelessly through my memory. They are as remote as Mars, as close as yesterday.

Even with Papa's lip service of acquiescence, I think he secretly depended upon Mama, despite her capitulation, to divert me from my avowed intentions.

This she did as her emotional reactions subsided following our return from Columbia.

So far as she was concerned, I was crossing over, by way of college, into the barren wastelands of the Tillie Strausses, where femininity died on the vine, where no eligible man entered, where parents of erudite unmarried daughters buried their dead hopes.

Only a small percentage of young ladies, principally those with the ultimate purpose of teaching and self-support, were entering institutions of higher learning at that period.

But generally the bridge-of-sighs beyond a girl's graduation from finishing or secondary school was as brief a span as possible. Parents saw to it, to the limit of their financial abilities and often beyond, that daughters were placed promptly on the market.

During the period when my college plans still hung in the balance, Mama attempted to reach me with offers to move into a finer home, even build one, travel, follow the current fashion and take lessons in burnt wood, have a little Model T Ford car of my own, extend my piano education at the finest conservatory in town.

To add degrees to Mama's fever, Irene Wertheim, a featureless girl in my graduation class, became engaged to the son of the president of a mammoth burlap bag concern in East St. Louis. At Mama's urging, Aunt Jennie came to visit us. An obsessive matchmaker and advocate of early marriage, she dared be even more outspoken than Mama.

I am ashamed for the people in Hamilton. I brag about my brilliant niece and, meanwhile, the nieces of most of the women I know marry off, while you are still without even an admirer. Your mother tells me that Milton Jelenko, who is marrying that Wertheim girl, would have been glad to call on you if you had ever given him the opportunity. Your mother is right. Tillie Strauss is written all over you.

Now, *Gensbebla*, you and Rose leave Fannie to work it out her own way. There is no hurry about such things.

Sam doesn't talk that way, Jennie, when we're alone. That child and her father just aren't themselves before one another.

That was the way it went, up to the hour I became a freshman at

Washington University.

Now, for the first time, it seems to me, I become intellectually awake, where before I had only dragged back my eyelids. I select courses close to my interest, based on my need to know, rather than for convenience.

Shades of the halls of learning began to close in my growing self. The university buildings were massive Gothic, the men of the faculty, in my fancy, Olympians who had temporarily descended to the lecture halls.

Interest in the outer world receded. After the day's lectures I lingered on the campus, in the library or on its great stone porch, filling composition books with vaporings. A course in the major Elizabethan poets drenched me in the reflected light of the era. My freshman year I submitted a masque in blank verse to *The Saturday Evening Post*. That same year I offered twice the required number of assigned "themes" to my English professor.

This struggle to capture the winged words that seemed to fly through my mind in flocks was almost as old as I was. It did not matter that once on paper they lost much of their iridescence—there was always the next clean page of the composition book.

As I examine those days under the microscope, I recapture the adult anguishes that went with them. Tormented, violently ambitious, jealous of the achievements of others, I slashed about in all directions at once.

I recall, when I was no more than five, Papa remarking to a business associate who was visiting our house: By the way, my little daughter has written some verse. Would you like to read it? Extracting a bit of paper from his waistcoat pocket, he watched anxiously the guest's face for reaction. So did I. It came promptly, in an m-m-m. Thus Papa's guest handed me my first rejection slip.

At this period of my freshman year, the march of the long envelope containing the returned manuscript with a rejection slip was uninterrupted. For years our faithful Willie had been marching upstairs mornings with the mail: Miss Fannie, here's another story come back, and each time, as every writer must know, that plop down into the bottomless pit.

Now I was also battering against the portals of the college weekly, *Student Life,* meanwhile almost automatically sending stories to *Reedy's Mirror*, an outstanding literary publication of the Middle West, the St. Louis *Post-Dispatch, Saturday Evening Post*, and the Munsey group of magazines.

Word got around during the first half of my second year that Neal Patterson, daughter of a Missouri state senator, a St. Louis girl who in her late twenties had made a name in the literary world, was returning to St. Louis to spend part of the winter with her parents and would attend courses at Washington University.

I had never seen, much less known, a writer. The prospect of encountering her on the campus excited and filled me with a jealous kind of anguish.

In due time Neal arrived, she was interviewed and photographs of her appeared in the newspapers. People said to me: just keep at it and one day you may be a Neal Patterson.

Before her arrival, I wrote with accelerated speed, striving by way of daily themes to hurl myself before the attention of Mr. Starbuck, our young professor in English composition. I did succeed in attracting some notice from him but somewhere, despite my determination for leadership, I missed along the way.

I was not invited to join a sorority and it was many a month before I was to understand why. *The Potter's Wheel*, an exclusive literary college group to which you were eligible only by qualification and invitation, passed me by; and I lost a race, for political reasons to be sure, for vice-presidency of the sophomore class. Probably one of the best-known girls on the campus, if not the best-known, where co-eds were in the enormous minority, I was more conspicuous than distinguished.

Mama continued to complain that I was wasting my time in college with girls who were destined to be old maids.

Papa said: Knowledge is power.

The coming of Neal Patterson began for me in the key of fantasia.

A little streetcar spur operated between the end of the main line, a few blocks from Cates Avenue, and the University, which at the time was about a mile beyond city limits.

One wintry morning, while waiting for the "dinky," a sporty little open roadster driven by a young woman in a long streaming "automobile veil" sped past me, then drew up suddenly and began to back.

Oh, she cried in disappointed inflection as she came closer, I thought for a moment you were my best friend, Ethel Barrymore. She is playing here next week.

I was a thickset sixteen. If she had said: I mistook you for Joan of Arc or Helen of Troy, I could not have been more surprised and, I must say, amused. I had seen so many photographs of the luminous Ethel Barrymore looking like no one in the world but Ethel Barrymore.

I'm Neal Patterson, pursued the girl in the car. Going out to the University? Want a lift?

She talked solo, every inch of the way. Ethel Barrymore was her bosom friend. One of the reasons, in fact, that she had returned to St. Louis earlier than she had planned. She was writing a play for her. Great names of the theater, Nat Goodwin, William Faversham, Marie Doro, Jane Cowl, fell from her lips as easily as loose coins from a purse. Marion Reedy, editor of the St. Louis *Mirror*, was also her "best friend." She was taking a course in Shakespeare and one in advanced French—going to France for the summer—did I know Colette?

I rode beside her in a daze, hating her for all the things she was and I was not, blistering rather than basking in her reflected glory.

I knew in advance the adulation she was certain to receive on the campus from students and faculty alike. Her like was without precedent in our concentrated world. Her very existence was driving me further in my sullen determination to do something also. Be something. A writer—greater than—well, anyway, a writer . . .

And so it happened. Neal took the University by storm. She addressed us in chapel on the American drama and was immediately made honorary member of the Literary Society. Her presence in my English class doused me like a candle flame. Where before I had been the articulate one, most frequently selected to read my work aloud to the class, now I sat rigid and speechless before the worldliness, the flair, the professional status of Neal. A one-act play of hers, "Venus Out of Love," had been published in book form and frequently produced by amateur organizations. We read it aloud in class, the various characters assigned to students. I read my role from the lips out, burning inside because they were not my lines.

Neal for the most part seemed to have forgotten my existence. Then one day I met her downtown in Scrugg's, Vandervoort and Barney's Department Store, and she said: Walk up as far as Grand Avenue with me?

It was a considerable distance and on the way she regaled me with the romantic side of her life, of which I had heard provocative rumors.

More frustration. I tried to ease the impact by assuring myself that she was fabricating. Easy enough to tell us way out in St. Louis about her relationships with the great. But, nevertheless, her words did carry conviction. She showed me a photograph, in a locket, of one of the male idols of the theater. Read me excerpts from a letter from another, but kept the signature out of sight.

You would know him. The whole world knows him.

On Pine Street, where the residences grew finer, she paused before an immense dwelling.

Do you know who lives here? I did not. It's the old Schrank mansion, she pursued, mentioning a name high in the social and industrial annals of St. Louis. Rod Schrank begged me to marry him for two years before he finally settled on the rebound for Marjorie Lippe.

It had to be true. She would not dare use local names that way. What did men see in her? She too was on the bulky side.

A sense of grievance against Mama and Papa rose in me. We did not know anybody who was anybody. We just ate and slept and ate and slept. Went nowhere, had no interesting friends, and all the while books were being written, songs were being sung, and pictures painted. Great people were doing great things. Neal's plays were being performed and she was being loved by men and going places while we "hucked."

Why couldn't my mother and father have been intellectual and out of the rut instead of keeping me down in one with them?

I resented the things they were not, mostly, alas, the things which were secondary and which I had not the wisdom to recognize as such.

Neal commented: What Starbuck needs, referring to our English professor, is a good hot love affair. I give them to him on paper. He blushes when he reads my themes. You write pretty well too, Fannie. But what you also need is more "pash" in your pen. You are about as passionate as a yard of cotton wadding.

"Pash" meant to be like Sappho or Helen and launch a thousand ships. Mama and Papa felt deeply for one another, but in the cotton-wadding way—the way Neal said it was with me.

Other girls seemed to come into their inheritance of boy-meets-girl so easily. If, during my high school or college years, they had practiced premarital irregularities, it was beyond the periphery of my knowledge. There were those who "spooned" or let the boys touch or "fool" around with them. I knew what I knew, and it was plenty, from the unbridled hours of reading and piecing together scraps of sotto voce information from Mama's conversation with the ladies of the *Kaffeeklatsches*. Not infrequently I sat on the stairs eavesdropping . . . she had a miscarriage . . . he gallivants . . . she has it behind her ears . . . doctor says she can't have another . . . she blames him . . . .

If I entered the room conversation halted abruptly.

The business of coming to life was evidently a shameful affair, going on behind the palm of the hand, behind the door of Mama's and Papa's bedroom, or, for all I knew, between the girls and boys at school. What were they experiencing that I was missing? I blamed my weight. I blamed Mama and Papa. Very occasionally I blamed myself, for holding back when I wanted to rush in. . . .

I was far from that day when either as person or writer I was to realize that I would always be more intimate with the anonymous public than with my closest friend—or to fully comprehend what Nietzsche describes as the "pathos of distance" between one individual and another.

Then, too, that freshman year I felt that if only I had it in me to project myself into the attention of instructors and professors I could somehow, some way, gain their interest in the very special being I believed myself to be.

The word "pragmatism" was not yet in my vocabulary; but nevertheless it was being borne in upon me as I scratched away at my little writings that the meaning of life must reside in the soul of the artist as well as in the world about him. It must reside in me, in the faces of our neighbors on Cates Avenue, in the people on the streets, even when they seemed faceless . . . it was for me to take in and give out . . . the vast design of truth. . . .

My instructors wrote notations on the margins of my themes. Fine character delineations. Rings true. Avoid purple patches. Excellent story-telling. You get into the heart.

Mama said: M-m-m-m.

Papa said: Goes to show, perseverance brings success.

Mama said with a straight face: Knowledge is power.

Papa, unplumbed, said: That's right.

Then one day in my junior year the English professor came into class with an air of excitement.

Without preamble he came out with the highest tribute he had to offer: A member of his class, he announced, has written a weekly theme so good I might have written it myself. Faces swung in my direction. Yes, Miss Hurst has not only done it again, this time she has outdone herself.

Later that day I crammed the longhand-written theme into an envelope and raced with it down to the office of *Reedy's Mirror*.

St. Louisans subscribed to this well-known weekly chiefly for its spicy columns and local news outside the pale of the ordinary newspaper. A smaller percentage read it for its literary merit, including Marion Reedy's brilliant editorial forays into diverse areas as farflung, erratic, and erotic as he was. First to publish Edgar Lee Masters' "Spoon River," Sara Teasdale, Zoë Akins, Orrick Johns, he was a sage who lived loosely and unwisely; but his tombstone, if he has one, must have a gleam to it.

The obscure office, high in a downtown office building, was locked the early afternoon I arrived. I dropped the long envelope through a slot in the door and, when I did not hear the inner thud, fell to my knees to peer through the door crack to see if it had landed.

The waiting weeks lengthened. Then one day my stalwart friend Olna flew across the campus toward me, waving *Reedy's Mirror.* Look, she gasped, have you seen this?

There it was, "Ain't Life Wonderful," by Fannie Hurst.

I wanted to run in all directions at once, and so I just stood. I wanted to embrace—everything. And so I just stood. . . .

About this time, epitaphs from *Spoon River Anthology* by an author named Edgar Lee Masters began to appear occasionally in *Reedy's Mirror.*

Of all my undisciplined hodgepodge reading, first, second, and third rate, Edgar Lee Masters' *Spoon River* was to become a major literary experience; and this, mind you, following a period of extracurricular reading which included Hall Caine, Boccaccio's *The Decameron*, Maeterlinck, Smollet, Gertrude Atherton, Gilbert Chesterton, Norman Douglas, D'Annunzio, Upton Sinclair, Mary Wilkins Freeman, Thomas Hardy, Arnold Bennett, Alice Hegan Rice, Olive Schreiner.

Spoon River brought my first intimations of the vineyards in which I, too, must labor. The vineyards of the common people. Masses of them. This was more of a visceral reaction than a conclusion. But indubitably, Masters had given me direction. A light had come out on the flat stretch between Chicago and St. Louis. The light was a stubby Chicago lawyer who, in the midst of law practice, was relating the fearful and wonderful story of the common man in terms of his headstones.

The saga of any man or woman's span of life moved before the reader in about twenty lines, the drama of human existence tamped down tightly into a form no larger than a sonnet or two.

Awe of Edgar Lee Masters' accomplishment has come down the years with me into today, a tour de force contemporaneously equaled only by Thornton Wilder's *Our Town.*

Masters jolted me into new aches and pains. What skills and wisdoms, I told and retold myself, must have stalked that brain of his so that people lived their lifetimes in his few lines. What skills and wisdoms needed to reside in the minds and souls of all good writers.

When we went to Hamilton our train passed through Indianapolis, a city irradiated, in my mind, by the fact that it was Booth Tarkington's home. Once when our train stopped there I wrote him a postcard something to this effect: Dear Booth Tarkington, Indianapolis will always be the most wonderful town in the world to me because you live there and write about people you make so real they live there, too. I think about you a great deal and wonder how you do it. He never replied. A lesson to me who all my subsequent life have answered every communication personally.

Wondering how they do it, I began an onslaught into biography and autobiography. St. Augustine, Cellini, Rousseau, da Vinci, George Moore.

It was difficult to realize that, even as Fannie Hurst on Cates Avenue, these authors were of the stuff that would suffer if you held a lighted cigarette against them. Men and women on their way to possible immortality should, like Olympians, have immunities from the way of all flesh. But their histories revealed that indigestion, jealousy, hunger, toothaches, loneliness plagued them as they plagued the ordinary people of Cates Avenue and those of Edgar Lee Masters' tombstones.

Reading biography was like entering a garden. But wandering deeply enough into the stories of their lives, you were likely to come upon areas as realistic as dumping grounds for old tires, stoves, discarded shoes, tin cans, and the litter of everyday living.

Everyone in Spoon River, from the lowliest to the first citizen, went to molder in his grave, tagged with the author's overall knowledge of their mere mortalness and their sublimity.

I wrote Masters letter after letter; none was ever sent.

Next I yearned to meet Reedy, who, I speculated, must have personal contact with Masters. But the days passed into weeks and still no acknowledgment from the editor who had published my piece in his *Mirror.*

Now, after the excitement of it had subsided somewhat, and the worn-ragged copies of the *Mirror* containing my story, which Mama and Papa had shown about, had gone the final rounds, Mama exploded: Don't magazines pay for what they print? Why doesn't that Reedy pay you?

It is we who should be willing to pay him for the honor he has bestowed on Fannie, said Papa.

He wouldn't print it if it wasn't good. I'm going to send him a bill.

Mama, if you do I'll never show my face in this town again.

Your mother doesn't mean all she says, Fannie.

No one respects what they get for nothing. Don't you ever send him anything again. The nerve!

What Mama and Papa did not know was that, since the publication of my first piece, I had been bombarding the Reedy office with subsequent offerings which were neither acknowledged nor returned.

The idea began to overhang that one of these days, if I could muster courage, it might be well for me to go personally to the Reedy office and collect them. I lived with the thought for weeks, fascinated by the gossip surrounding Reedy and inhibited by my mental picture of the sage, sitting there in his lair, thinking both massive and lascivious thoughts.

Town talk concerning him penetrated the campus and even Cates Avenue. According to legend, naughty ladies and the cup that cheers were his pastimes. Mama said he was a nix-nux. I concluded he must be like François Villon.

Before Neal left our campus, leaving it gray, she had given the class a character sketch of Reedy. Speculation had it that he had fancied Neal herself.

Up there in his office, less than an hour away from where I lived, his mind burning like a live volcano, sat the controversial figure, like Teufelsdröckh in his tower, while I dwelt down among the people who never looked up or smelled the stars.

One day, following an impulse, I polished myself up and boarded a streetcar for *Reedy's Mirror.*

This time he was not only in but the open door revealed him practically reclining in a swivel chair, his feet high on an incredibly littered desk, his vast body seeming to run downhill in an avalanche of fat, mussed shirt crawling up out of his low-waisted trousers, a pair of cracked glasses low on his nose, dark graying hair pushed around on his bead, eyeshade dangling from his neck like a bib.

Books, books, stacked on the floor, on chairs, overflowed the place.

I must have presented something of a spectacle myself, standing rapt in the dirty wintry light and gazing, I am sure beatifically, at the vast troglodyte deep in his cave of confusion. He slid his glasses higher on his nose and regarded me.

I am Fannie Hurst.

The ensuing douse was delivered with a smile.

And what am I supposed to say to that?

I wrote "Ain't Life Wonderful." You printed it.

Say, now, that was a good little piece. Sit down, he directed, sweeping sheaves of paper to the floor. What struck me was your keen observation. That gal in your story was so real you could have pinched her behind, he said, and laughed down the slanting front of him.

I had seldom if ever heard anything so grossly articulated.

Now, you just sit down on that pretty little fanny of your own, Fannie, and tell me about yourself.

It was also the first intimation I had ever had that all was not good in the pure application of my given name. I hesitated to be seated, which would indicate that I knew what he meant.

A wave of resentment toward Mama went over me. Mama and Papa had debated between Fannie and Beulah, and Mama had chosen in favor of the former. At least you did not sit on your beulah.

Reedy talked to me until dusk, without even a telephone call to interrupt. Read me excerpts from a book which lay open before him. Ovid's *The Art of Love*, luminous and lecherous-sounding to my Cates Avenue ears, erotica strangely in keeping with the red-light Olympus district in which dwelt this satirical fat man who laughed with his belly and talked like a cross between a scholar and a bum.

He told me of a talented St. Louis girl who, as he put it, needed to be bombed out of her virginity, of another who should have been sealed into hers.

Sara Teasdale he labeled a middle-western Sappho who bathed under a sheet. Most contemporary American writers, he declared, were wired with suppressed desires, but their sex life took place chiefly between book covers.

You are too young, he added, for me to talk this into you. Some lucky guy will one day kiss it into you and may I add, he continued, that you are exercising admirable restraint with me, or is it admirable?

This sort of talk was one thing on the pages of Flaubert or Lady Duff Gordon. But spoken, the words smoked. What could one say to this kaleidoscopic man who should have outraged you and somehow did not?

What could one retort to a man who said: I think you will write one day, girl, if you let go. The question, as I look at you, is: Have you anything to let go?

I sensed double entendre of some sort and wondered what Neal would have said. Something brilliant and triple or quadruple entendre no doubt.

Well, I managed to retort, my mind doesn't bathe under a sheet. This seemed to amuse him, because he threw back his head and laughed, sobering suddenly.

Where do you live? Parents? Father's occupation? What stock?

Here it came.

Irish? Presbyterian? Catholic?

Since this is a clinical analysis, not a celebration of me, I am obliged to confess that my mind locked against what I knew I should or must reply.

We are American.

He did not pursue the subject. The suspicion flashed miserably over me that now he knew me for the snide person I was. But for the life of me I could not retract or supplement.

Had I known Reedy better I would have realized how transcendent his tolerance and compassion; I would have recognized the strange kind of spirituality that rode him with cloven hoofs, hurdling the untidy mishmash of the visible fat man who sprawled there amid tobacco and alcoholic fumes.

He talked of an H. L. Mencken, of a fellow named Theodore Dreiser, and then of the more familiar Bernard Shaw, Yeats, Hamlin Garland, Jack London, Amy Lowell, finally rising in dismissal.

Go home and write me some more shorts. Sweat for them and you may have something.

I have already sent you three, following the first.

They are not up to the Fannie Hurst first. Go home, you nice big healthy girl, and write like hell.

His parting words doused some of the new fire he had set going in me. Nice big healthy girl! Hunk of a girl. Hunk of a brain. . . .

HERMAN DREER

BORN IN WASHINGTON, D.C., Herman H. Dreer (ca. 1884–1981) was a Phi Beta Kappa graduate of Bowdoin College in Maine. In 1914, he moved to St. Louis to teach English at Sumner High School. After being denied entrance to both Saint Louis University and Washington University because of his race, he eventually earned degrees in English and Sociology from the University of Chicago.

Concerned that St. Louis did not offer college training for its African American students, in 1934 Dreer reopened Douglass University, originally started in 1926 by B. F. Bowles, former principal of Lincoln High School in East St. Louis. Using teachers from the St. Louis public school system, Douglass University taught African American students until 1942. Dreer is also credited with initiating Black History Month, and he served as pastor of King's Way Baptist Church.

A prolific writer and editor, Dreer compiled *American Literature by Negro Authors* (1950) and edited the *St. Louis Tribune*, a weekly newspaper, and the *Masonic Journal of Missouri*, a monthly publication. Dreer also wrote a column titled "Highlights of Negro History" for the *St. Louis Argus* for many years. The following excerpt is from Dreer's novel, *The Tie That Binds: A Novel of a Youth Who Seeks to Understand Life* (1958), which tells the story of an idealistic young St. Louisan's desire to improve racial and social conditions in his hometown. This scene, which culminates at the Veiled Prophet Ball, features two of the women in the hero's life, one representing the elite class from which he hails, and the other representing the down-to-earth common folk he romanticizes.

FROM *THE TIE THAT BINDS*

On the Sunday before the public schools opened in September of 195–, the daily newspapers of St. Louis at the request of the Chamber of Commerce had carried an announcement of the coming of the Veiled Prophet of Khorassan to St. Louis the first Tuesday and Wednesday in October. On Tuesday would occur the Coronation Ball in the Convention Hall of the Kiel Auditorium, and the night following the Veiled Prophet, along with his Queen of Love and Beauty, would in an elaborate parade bestow his blessings upon all the people of St. Louis.

The newspapers stated that the twenty-six floats would portray significant events in the history of St. Louis. The various events were enumerated. The following line of the parade was given: from Ranken and Laclede where the floats were made and stored, it would move west on Laclede Avenue to Grand Avenue, north on Grand to Franklin Avenue, east on Franklin to Leffingwell Avenue, south on Leffingwell to Washington Avenue, east on Washington to Broadway, south on Broadway to Olive Street, west on Olive to Channing Avenue, south on Channing to Laclede, and west on Laclede to the barn at Ranken. It was estimated that the parade would take about three hours to cover the route.

Great publicity as in the past was used for this event. Hundreds of thousands of four-page leaflets giving the history of the celebration, a list of the names of the floats, and the events in the history of St. Louis they were to convey, were distributed to the various schools in and near St. Louis. Teachers placed an announcement of the event on their bulletin boards. Besides, they used the event as a project in social studies.

Later announcements and an outline of the route of the parade followed two weeks, one week, two days, and one day before the parade; and the final announcements occurred on the day of the parade. Besides, the event was often announced by radio and television.

This was just a part of the preparation. The municipal buildings and downtown businesses decorated the outside of their buildings with flags, bunting, and large banners carrying V. P. in the midst of an oriental setting. Shields with a blue background for yellow or gold letters were attached to lamp posts or trolley posts along the line of march.

Streamers announcing the coming of the Veiled Prophet were stretched across streets of the route of the parade. Besides, various stores had within them pictures of the affair. One could not escape knowing that some important event was about to occur.

The men who would attend the Ball had very little to do; for they were to wear full dress suits, which were easily obtained. The elaborate preparation was for the women. They had to do much shopping. Their dresses had to be designed and made according to their specific instructions. Some of these were imported from Paris. The women had to see also that their shoes, gloves, and purses were to match in a color scheme. Consequently, the ladies had to know far in advance that they were to attend this social affair of highest brilliancy.

Aware months ahead that she was going to attend the Veiled Prophet Ball, Alice did not have to rush; her boudoir by the first week in September was complete with all the garments and trinkets she would need for this great social event. Her dress was pink basically with a mixture of silk and gold, ornamented with oriental designs about the top of the blouse, just above the waist and just below the waist, and a three inch border at the bottom of the skirt carrying pagodas before which stood a Chinese priest. The gown was strapless. With a crinoline underskirt, the garment had the fashionable spread. Her diamond rings and ear drops, her golden slippers, and her gloves and purse that matched her dress made her look like a dainty reigning queen of the Orient.

This done, she had time for her other activities: horseback riding, golf, bridge, her sorority, and the rifle club. At the rifle club, she met Margaret Longrove, who had become so expert in trap shooting as to win in the open tournament the first prize.

Angela, on the other hand, had a great task before her. As an artist, she knew exactly what she wanted. As she did most of her shopping at Scruggs, Vandervoort, and Barney, Famous and Barr, and Grand Leader—the largest department stores in St. Louis—she consulted their fashion experts concerning her desires. As soon as she reached a final decision on all matters, she and the designers she chose worked out the patterns.

She decided upon Egyptian cloth of silk interwoven with strands of light blue and gold that produced a glow that lured and fascinated the beholder. She had puffed sleeves with a border that stopped just above the elbow. On this border were ancient Egyptian princesses attended by their maids in a bower of lotus flowers. About her waist was a belt that carried Egyptian scrolls in gold. There was a one-inch gold border about the neck of her blouse that dropped low and a two-inch border of gold at the hem, embossed with Egyptians hunting as they rode in chariots and with Egyptians canoeing on the Nile. She carried a black stole embossed in silver with Egyptian artisans engaged in different kinds of work. Her slippers were covered with the same kind of material used in the skirt. Her gloves matched with the dress, which was bespangled with rhinestones. She carried also an Egyptian fan of ivory and peacock feathers. Her purse matched the rest of the outfit. One week before the event, when she was satisfied with the work of her dressmaker, she put on her outfit and asked her parents how she looked in it.

"Like an angel," her father said, who generally was the first to speak concerning parental and domestic matters. "Like an angel of delight."

"Angy, you look beautiful, beautiful," said the mother. "I know Colonel Haverill is going to be proud of you."

"I did not seek a Parisian designer, because this affair is being given by the St. Louis Chamber of Commerce, and as a St. Louisan, I thought that I should have my dress made by a St. Louis firm. Besides, I think our St. Louis designers are just as artistic as those of Paris," she said with patriotic enthusiasm.

Calvin now called on her once a week and talked with her about various details of the affair. He had arranged with six of his friends to take dances with Angela in exchange for his dancing with their company. He was to have the first two and the last two dances with her. She was well pleased with this arrangement. Of course, he had some dances in between.

After Calvin asked her to be his company at the Veiled Prophet Ball, she began to read carefully the society section of the Globe-Democrat, The Post Dispatch, and The Sentinel, the daily newspapers of St. Louis. Hitherto, she had only glanced casually at those pages; but now she was spending much time upon them, in order that she might be well informed concerning the wealthiest and the most influential at families of St. Louis and St. Louis County. She soon observed that most of these lived on private streets in St. Louis or they lived in St. Louis County.

She was especially interested in the activities of the younger set. She accordingly noticed on several occasions an item concerning a Women's Rifle Club. The names most frequently mentioned as winners of prizes with the pistol or the rifle and in trap shooting were those of Margaret Longrove and Alice Lee. Their names had appeared not only in the Society

Section but in the Sports Section of these dailies.

Finally arrived the night of the Veiled Prophet Ball. Mr. and Mrs. Galasso both left their hotel early, in order to be at home when Angela would leave. Calvin called for her at seven-thirty, because he did not want her to miss any of the ceremony involved in crowning the Queen of Love and Beauty.

Mrs. Galasso met him at the door and ushered him into the living room. "Good evening, Colonel Haverill," she said, bowing very courteously and offering to take his wraps. Mr. Galasso was not far behind.

"See you again, Colonel Haverill," said Galasso. "Hope you have fine evening. Take good care of Angy."

"I certainly will," he smiled. "Never fear."

"Have a seat, Colonel Haverill," Mrs. Galasso, said, "She's ready, and will come right down."

Almost immediately he heard light footsteps on the stairs. She soon stepped into the living room dressed as a paragon of beauty, to be the cynosure of most eyes, gorgeous but not ostentatious, lovable and adorable. The charm of her natural beauty combined with her appealing and winsome personality, magnified by the splendor of her apparel, sank deep into Calvin's heart.

"You certainly deserve your name, Angela; you make me think of heaven," he exclaimed.

"Calvin, oh, Calvin, I thank you!" she sweetly responded. "Get my coat now. It's in the guest closet."

He brought the one of cloth.

"The fur one tonight, Calvin," came from her tenderly.

He put back the first, brought the one of fur, and held it for her. She then placed a silk Egyptian scarf over her head, and said, "Bye, bye, Father. Bye, bye, Mother," and kissed them both. Calvin escorted her to the front seat in his Cadillac. After closing the door on her side with a smile, he opened the other door and took his seat at the wheel beside her. As the car started away, they waved at Mr. and Mrs. Galasso, who were standing in the doorway.

It was not long before they reached the Kiel Municipal Auditorium. After checking their wraps, they entered reserved seats in the west first balcony, just behind the seats reserved for the former queens, who occupied the first two rows of seats in that section. The people came in so rapidly, that by ten minutes to eight, almost all of the ten thousand seats were occupied. In the center of the stage was the dais on which were two throne chairs, which could be reached by the way of seven, wide carpeted steps. On each side of the steps were large Doric columns, between which were reddish maroon draperies that were set with emblems of the reigning monarch. Palms, chrysanthemums, and other flowers were placed around about the throne.

The orchestra, which was composed largely of members of the St. Louis Symphony Orchestra, played the national anthem, "The Star Spangled Banner," with the audience standing. This was the beginning of the affair. First, came in the merry makers: acrobats and mummers, who skillfully and amusingly demonstrated various aspects of their art. When they had completed their acts, there came in Knights Templars on horses in full armor, returning home having taken the Holy Sepulchre. As they rode in, the orchestra played that great march from Richard Wagner's opera *Tannhäuser*, "Once More Dear Home I With Rapture Behold Thee." After saluting the Veiled Prophet, they circled the auditorium and went out. Finally, rode in St. Louis, who was Louis IX of France, in full armor on a white horse. St. Louis, who went to church or chapel, twice a day and who had priests to ride at his side chanting prayers and sermons, was the ideal king of the Middle Ages. He was followed by a float, drawn by horses. This float showed the founding of St. Louis with Pierre Laclede and August Chouteau, his young helper. Laclede held high a cross suggesting that he was establishing St. Louis as a city built upon God and that our city would thrive as it followed the teachings of the Son of God, Jesus Christ. Beside Laclede stood Chouteau holding somewhat lower than the cross the flag of France. Kneeling in a circle about these two were Indians. Each group of actors received much applause. The greatest applause, however, came for St. Louis, Laclede, and Chouteau.

As soon as the float bearing Laclede departed, the floor was rapidly cleaned and waxed. The orchestra, during the cleaning and polishing, played "The Overture to William Tell" and "The Poet and the Peasant." Thus the audience was kept in a happy mood.

At the close of the second selection, the curtain slowly rose in the midst of great applause, showing the Veiled Prophet seated upon his throne and by his side the retiring Queen of Love and Beauty, who would yield her throne to the newly selected Queen.

On each side of the stage in front of the double column stood a page in medieval costume. Beside him stood a herald. Following a blare of the trumpets, a herald announced that His Majesty, the Veiled Prophet of Khorassan, had returned to St. Louis and had selected a new queen who was to reign over the social activities of St. Louis for the ensuing year, and that she would come and take her seat following the gathering of her attending maids of honor.

Upon the completion of this announcement of the Veiled Prophet's Proclamation, the heralds alternated in announcing the maids of honor selected. As each name was called there was great applause. When the applause ceased, the orchestra played strains of the Triumphal March of Verdi's "Aida," which continued until each maid of honor took her place about the seat of the retiring queen. Finally, the chief herald announced the coming of the queen, saying: "The Fairest of the Fair, the Queen of Love and Beauty, who is to reign over the social activities of St. Louis for this year, until the Veiled Prophet returns." There was great silence, because the name of the honored young lady is not revealed until the night of the coronation.

The herald then called: "Come forth, O Queen of Love and Beauty, your subjects welcome you, Miss Cynthia Alethia McAllister, the Queen!" Immediately came an outburst of applause that lasted about three minutes.

The orchestra then resumed its music, to the accompaniment of which Miss McAllister, the eighteen-year-old daughter of the president of the Third National Bank of St. Louis, marched up the white carpeted aisle, with her train held by two eight-year old pages. As she came opposite the balcony where sat former queens, she turned and bowed low. This courteous acknowledgment brought forth another round of applause. Miss McAllister continued her march up to the steps before the throne. Then the retiring Queen vacated her seat to assist the new Queen up the steps. Having reached the top of the platform, Miss McAllister kneeled before His Majesty in obeisance and kept that position, until the retiring Queen obtained the new crown that was held on a cushion by a page and placed it on the head of the kneeling Sovereign. Then the new Queen of Love and Beauty sat beside the Veiled Prophet, and the outgoing Queen sat to the left of one of the maids of honor. Thus ended the pageantry of the evening with the coronation of the new Queen of Love and Beauty.

Immediately began the ball with the Queen and the Veiled Prophet remaining on their thrones. Each maid of honor and the new Queen were escorted on their march to the platform by some outstanding business man of St. Louis, whose name was also called as the escort; but when she reached the steps leading to the throne, the business escort surrendered the honored lady to the young man who was to be her company for the evening. The elderly escort took no place on the stage, but occupied a reserved seat on the floor. The young companions stood on the steps on each side, and formed a part of the pageant.

The orchestra began the Ball with "Dardanella," which was the invitation to the guests in the first floor balconies to leave their seats and begin to dance.

Calvin and Angela left their seats and took advantage of the first selection. When it came to a close, Calvin introduced Angela to several of his acquaintances, and they in turn introduced her to their company. These cordially received her.

They could talk only for a little while, for their conversation was soon interrupted by the strains of that fine classic of Oscar Strauss, "The Blue Danube Waltz." Calvin danced with Angela again. The music was so entrancing and Angela so nimble and graceful, that they seemed to float along; and Calvin thought of Kismet floating on his magic carpet.

While dancing this number, Calvin and Angela passed close by Alice and Mr. Lang. Alice bowed her head and smiled, and Calvin did likewise, just as he had acknowledged other acquaintances.

As they danced, Calvin asked Angela, "Are you enjoying the evening?"

"Yes, Calvin," she replied, full of glee. "I'm supremely happy, happy to be here and happy to be with you."

"I'm happy too, Angela," he remarked. "I believe from the way I've felt tonight that I should go occasionally to social affairs; but I'd want you to be with me."

"Calvin, I'd be delighted; for you are a delightful host, ever attentive to the wishes of your guest," she said with sparkling pleasure.

"Your next three dances, Angela," he reminded her, "are exchanges. My friends, whose names are on your card, are all here, and they will come with their company to us. I will introduce you and turn you over to my friend; he in turn will surrender his lady to me." His plan proceeded just as he had arranged it. First, came Stevely Grandison and Anastasia Comeisky. Grandison was the treasurer of the St. Louis Aluminum Corporation. Next, came Harold Flannigan and his wife, Marcia. The next exchange couple was Hugh Fitzgerald and Barbara St. John. Hugh was the chief accountant for the Supreme Universal Life Insurance Company.

"I'm glad you thought of this exchange plan, Colonel," Fitzgerald said. "It keeps us from being selfish and snobbish."

As Alice came near Calvin, she looked circumspectly at Angela as long as the whirling couples did not obstruct the view, admiring Angela's dress and her entrancing beauty. About the middle of the evening, it was Calvin's time to dance with Alice. Accordingly, Calvin had Angela accompany him to Alice and her escort.

"Miss Lee and Mr. Lang," Calvin said, "meet my friend, Miss Galasso."

"I'm delighted to meet you, Miss Galasso!" exclaimed Alice vivaciously.

"And I too, Miss Galasso," declared Mr. Lang.

"And I'm happy to meet you, Miss Lee, and you too, Mr. Lang," Angela smiled, bubbling over with jollity. Then she asked, "Are you, I wonder, Miss Alice Lee, of whom I've read as a sports champion?"

"I suppose I am," Alice replied modestly. "I've been active in a rifle club and in tennis."

"I've admired you as you've brought honors to our city. Oh, how great it must be to be a sports champion!" exclaimed Angela.

At this point, the orchestra began to play Duke Ellington's "Solitude," arranged as a waltz. Mr. Lang then took Angela by the hand, saying, "Miss Galasso, I believe that this is my time to dance with you."

"Yes, Mr. Lang, it is, according to my card," she replied.

"And according to mine," he said, as he and Angela proceeded through the throng for dancing space.

"Are you enjoying this gay festival?" he asked as a matter of formality.

"Yes, Mr. Lang, every minute of it," she replied as they darted around the floor among the various couples.

"Who decorated the auditorium?" she inquired. "Did you select the artists?"

"As the executive secretary of the Chamber of Commerce, I did have the final word concerning it; but it was done by Bontonelli, O'Hara, and Boisseu, international decorators," he replied.

"I could see at once that the hall had the touch of artists."

"Are you an artist, Miss Galasso?"

"I am a student of art in St. Louis under a French and an Italian artist." So they conversed as they danced along.

When Calvin took Alice for this dance, he said, "Alice, I'm glad this is a waltz."

"So am I," she responded, as he took her in his arms and whirled away.

"A waltz, while it inspires joy, it arouses within one also a sense of the sublime. It stirs our deeper emotions, and takes us out of self," he said.

"It's an appropriate number because of its soft, calm, sweet melody. It's heavy enough to be a classic and light enough to be popular," she uttered as they sailed gracefully over the floor. "Duke Ellington, in composing this selection, I suppose, out of a period of his own solitude, experienced some gladdening success."

"For the selection," Calvin said, "is not at all depressing; it is definitely one of triumphant joy."

"I wish I could be as joyful in my periods of solitude," she wistfully remarked.

"You don't have periods of solitude, do you, Alice?" he zealously inquired. "With your sports and your social life, it seems to me that you'd be so busy, that you'd hardly have a moment of solitude."

"Well, sometimes, I do," she admitted. "Those activities are my means of escape from a vital reality of life. Some days I'm all right; but on other days at times I do have a period of solitude."

"That's strange, Alice."

"It shouldn't even seem so, because one can be lonely in a crowd, Calvin. Haven't you ever had that experience?"

"Yes, Alice, I have. I had it when I returned to the States—from Casablanca. But by becoming active, I slowly overcame it."

"So, I'm trying to overcome mine," she remarked. "These periods of solitude and depression have followed me since you last left Brunswick, Maine." At this point of their conversation the music stopped. "This dance has been delightful, Calvin, reminding me of old times."

"I always enjoy dancing with you, Alice," he admitted.

"This is not our last one tonight, is it? No. We do meet again," was her response. "Calvin," she continued, "you have charming company. Miss Galasso is winsome. You must tell me about her, when we dance again."

By this time Lang and Angela joined them in the midst of applause for an encore. The selection was repeated and the exchange of partners continued to the strains of "Solitude."

During the intermission, Calvin and Angela went to the restaurant for some refreshments. He ordered for himself a banana split and an orange soda. For her, he ordered a strawberry sundae. A few of the others about them ordered soft drinks also; but many of the guests ordered a light wine or a cocktail.

When they finished their snack, they moved among various guests with Calvin introducing Angela to all he met. All received her warmly. Some of the ladies invited her to join their bridge clubs. Angela at each offer said that she would consider it; but she could not join at that time because of the demands made upon her by her teachers of art. As the women talked with each other, they admired her physical beauty and her taste as exhibited by the splendor and artistry of her dress. Several went so far as to ask her, "Who made your dress? Did you have a Parisian designer?"

Her answer always was, "No, as a loyal St. Louisan, my dress is a creation of St. Louis artists."

The women wanted to know more about her; for this was the first time any of them had seen this charming beauty at one of their social affairs. They longed to know more about this unknown young lady who had captured the heart of the popular and brilliant, young attorney, Colonel Haverill.

Meanwhile Calvin had been looking for his parents, to have them meet his company. As soon as he spied them going to the balcony where they had sat during the coronation, he led Angela to them. As he started towards them, he said, "Angela, for some time I've been looking for my parents. They've moved about so much, that I've had difficulty keeping up with them. I want you by all means to meet them."

"Yes, Calvin. I certainly want to. Let's hunt until we find them."

"I see them now. They shall not elude me further," he assured her. Shortly after they sat down, he and Angela reached them. "Father, Mother, you've been hard to catch; but I have you now. Please meet my friend, Miss Angela Galasso."

"I'm glad to meet you, Miss Galasso," said Mrs. Haverill.

"And I too, Miss Galasso," remarked the father.

"You know I'm delighted to meet you both," responded Angela with a gracious bow.

"We've been watching you, as you and our son seemed to flit over the floor, and admired you from afar," the father said.

"I would have felt the evening incomplete," Mrs. Haverill remarked, "if it had closed without our having met you in person."

"I would have felt the same, Mrs. Haverill. Colonel Haverill for some time had been trying to find you," Angela said in her sweet, melodious tones.

"Sit down a while, Miss Galasso, until the music starts again, at least for a while," Mrs. Haverill pleaded.

"Gladly, Mrs. Haverill," she said, as she took a seat beside her. "For some time I had hoped to meet you and Mr. Haverill."

"Calvin should have brought you by," his mother stated, as she adored Angela. "Why didn't you, Calvin?"

"Mother, I preferred to do it this way."

Resuming her effort to become better acquainted with Angela, Mrs. Haverill remarked, "Calvin said that you are a public school teacher."

"I am. I teach elementary school children—the eighth grade. The group I have now is to enter high school in January."

"You're in a very strategic position," interrupted Mr. Haverill.

"A very responsible one," Angela affirmed.

"Calvin said also that you are a demonstration teacher."

"Yes, I am, Mr. Haverill, I have to teach before cadet and in-service teachers."

"Father, I don't know whether I told you of her hobbies."

"What are they, Miss Galasso?" Haverill promptly inquired eagerly.

"Painting, ceramics, and music," she said. "Though I teach painting to pupils of high school age on Tuesdays at the Peoples Art Center, I am also a student of art under a French and an Italian master in St. Louis. I like making articles out of clay, and I like singing."

"We heard you sing 'Cavalleria Rusticana' at the homecoming dinner given by St. Louis for our returning officers."

"You were there?" she modestly asked.

"Yes," replied Mrs. Haverill. "My husband was there too. I thought you were wonderful."

"She was," Calvin interrupted.

"I have thought of getting a leave-of-absence for a year beginning in June, in order that I might take intensive training under several masters in Italy. I'd like to sing someday like Alma Gallicurci or Lily Pons."

"I think it not impossible," responded Mrs. Haverill.

"You recall, Mother, I told you that she is the leading soprano in the Senior Choir of the Second Baptist Church."

Turning to Calvin, she asked, "Is that why you left us and joined there?"

Calvin smiled, "Partly, Mother."

"I think it is wonderful that one as talented as you should not withhold her talent from the church. I've endeavored to guide Calvin in the same direction."

The conversation then was interrupted by fascinating strains of "La Paloma," fascinating because of its beautiful tango rhythm. "Please excuse us now, Mother and Father," Calvin requested.

"All right," the parents said.

"Miss Galasso," Mrs. Haverill continued, "at some early date, we must renew our conversation. I hope Calvin will bring you by."

"I thank you for the invitation. I'll come whenever Colonel Haverill will bring me," Angela smilingly remarked, as she and Calvin returned to the floor to dance.

About one o'clock there was the grand march, for which the orchestra played that classic of Philip Sousa, the march king, "Stars and Stripes Forever." This event gave the spectators an excellent opportunity to view the gala attire of the ladies. It was another thrill for Angela, for when she left the line, she could get a close view of many of the costumes too.

Then came the final dance. It was the "St. Louis Blues." As they danced, Angela said to Calvin, "There's nothing blue about that composition. It's truly a great classic. It never grows old, because it's lively and cheerful. There may be something blue in the words; I don't know the words of that piece; but the music is really fascinating. And since this affair is glorifying St. Louis, this selection is appropriate for the closing."

"I agree with you, Angela," Calvin said, "that number, which is according to tradition, makes us love dear St. Louis more and more."

When "The St. Louis Blues" came to an end, the orchestra played sixteen measures of "Till We Meet Again" as the finale. Thus ended the Veiled Prophet Ball of 195–.

As Calvin and Angela rode away, they were extremely happy: he, because she had lived up to all his expectations; and she, because she had been accepted by the ladies who ranked highest in St. Louis and also because Calvin had thought enough of her to give her this chance to meet the people who were the makers of St. Louis. She made friends quickly, because at all times she had deported herself with dignity, cordiality, and grace.

As the car drove up to her house, Mrs. Galasso opened the door. "You up this late, Mother?"

"Yes, Angy, I couldn't help waiting for you. Your father and I watched the crowning of the Queen, and also the dance. When he saw you, he said,

'Look at Angy. She's right there with 'em.' He looked a while longer and then went to bed. Now that you're home, I can go to bed too. Thank you, Colonel Haverill, for taking such good care of our daughter."

"Mrs. Galasso, I couldn't have done otherwise, because she is very dear to me." Mrs. Galasso then retired at once. Turning to Angela, he said, "You have a very dear and understanding mother."

"Yes, Calvin, I have," she said, "and I appreciate her greatly. I love her dearly." Then extending her hand to him, she jovially concluded, "Thanks, Calvin, for the wonderful evening."

He took her hand in his right and patted it several times with his left hand, and then said, "And I thank you for accepting my invitation. I hope you rest well. I'll see you Sunday evening."

"Calvin, I'll be expecting you."

"Good night, Angela."

"Good night, Calvin."

Soon he had sped away.

When Angela went upstairs, she had planned to talk to her mother; but her parents' bedroom was dark. It was long, however, before she retired; for she was thinking of the joys of the evening: the many outstanding people of St. Louis she had met, and the cordiality of the people, the joyful music, and the grand coronation; but most of all, she was thinking of the attention and devotion of Calvin Haverill.

CHARLES GUENTHER

A ST. LOUIS NATIVE, Charles Guenther (1920–) has been a familiar and active participant in the region's literary scene since the early 1960s. Guenther received degrees from Harris Teachers College and Webster University, in addition to doing doctoral work in languages at Saint Louis University. In 1979, he was awarded an honorary Doctor of Human Letters degree from Southern Illinois University at Edwardsville. During his diverse career, Guenther served as a government translator, historian, librarian, educator, and, since 1953, a regular book reviewer for the *St. Louis Post-Dispatch*.

A prolific author whose work has appeared in numerous journals in the United States and abroad, Guenther has six volumes of poetry and translations to his credit, including *Phrase/Paraphrase* (1970), *Paul Valéry in English* (1970), *Voices in the Dark* (1974), and *The Hippopotamus: Selected Translations* (1986).

Critic Robert L. Kindrick once wrote that Guenther is "one of the St. Louis poets most immediately touched by his environment." Written over several decades, starting in the 1960s with the construction of the Arch, the poems which follow bear out this assessment.

ARCH

Founder of stone open now to all O Pierre O Auguste of Pain Court log cabins Levee men labored on hot summer afternoons and hauled flour and furs over the muddy uncobbled riverbank or in winter cold cut ice from the water as puffing packets whirled soot upward into blue air and trains hooted tooted & went clang!

Gaslit silver & gold chandeliered purple-draped palaces of gray busts & brocades are gone O Eero but your ARCH rose a hero's window on a court of freedom falling or rising Elk-coated Lewis & Clark's little town—

palisaded & river-facing turned around to west meeting mirroring the married streams Jacob's Manuel's (O sage traders) fortunes rocketing Risen out of flames or plague you flourished and grew Bellefontaine & south into Carondelet and west a jewel-park shimmering structures So proudly open your steel gate St. Louis!

THREE SISTERS

I. SARA PONDERING

(on Sara Teasdale and Vachel Lindsay)

Maybe it was some power in him you feared
as he went about trading his rhymes for sustenance,
an unbroken bronco whose exuberance
broke at last when his hope and fortune disappeared,

or maybe it was the fiery evangelist
in him, the visionary hustler of empty schemes,
or the carnival prophet hawking impractical dreams
or the missionary poet, the ragtime rhapsodist?

—all these perhaps.

As we'd mistrust some wild
dark of the woods or an unknown deep of the sea,
your taming spirit couldn't be reconciled

to the eagle in him you admired flying free
into the sun where together alike are lost
your August rain and his November frost.

II. REMEMBERING MARIANNE

(on letters from Marianne Moore, April 1962)

When I asked if the house I'd lived in was your same
childhood home and described it: the long antique
veranda, 1840s, cisterns, frame
now stuccoed yellow and tiled, where a stony little creek

trickled through a wild orchard of red plums
and a field of dewberries—you didn't say.
(Still

our separate worlds were linked by the chromosomes,
as you called them, of each clustered syllable.)

Those years I took circuitous roads to truth,
ignored your hints, suggested even doing a "feature"
on you, but patiently you'd shrug and sluff

it off, saying, "I'm not important enough,"
adding, "Eliot is ideal."

We'll forget the architecture,
but I know I tasted those wild plums of your youth.

UNION STATION

Only the swallows circling these cones of silence
Make this their hostel now. Their invisible track
Circumscribes a valley where ancient springs
Flowed from the western hills before the air
Droned with wheels by the dam and the artificial pool
In the mills that stood near the gorge where Rock Creek ends.

How the face of the valley changes! One thing ends,
Replaced by another with intervals of silence:
Once there was a prairie with scrub oak, an occasional pool

Where buffalo grazed and drank, their rumbling track
Mistaken for thunder shook the morning air.
Flushing out every creature that flies or springs.

Yet who knows how many thousands of springs
The same scenario plays before it ends,
How many upheavals of earth and air
Hold no recollection in postludes of silence;
Only a beetle perhaps, inscribing its track
Patiently, returns to the edge of an obscure pool.

And here the Osage camped where the bed of the pool
Lay, settlers came for the pure springs
And the black earth, mountain men left to track
Deer and beaver from where the Missouri ends
Up to its headwaters in the lands of silence,
And boatmen labored and danced to some old French air.

Under cedars and cottonwoods, ghosts in the moonlit air.
Lovers pressed on the grass by the glassy pool
(Where have they gone? Only a winter silence
Lies with the faded stones by the vanished springs).
The valley reclaimed, the pond was drained to the ends
Of its arms and coves to lay the parallel track,

Nineteen miles of tentacular steel track!
Gray stones and Spanish tiles, spires in the air,
Rose over the roundhouse where the landscape ends,
Apex and terminus once of a human pool
That swarmed to the coupled cars with the well-oiled springs,
Where rolling stock stands here rusting in silence.

In the lace of a trestle and track, a sunken pool,
Honeysuckle hangs in the air: a new life springs
Until everything ends once more in the music of silence.

WILLIAM S. BURROUGHS

WILLIAM S. BURROUGHS (1914–1997) was born in St. Louis, the second son of Mortimer and Laura Lee Burroughs. The family lived at 4664 Pershing Avenue. Named after his paternal grandfather, the inventor of the Burroughs adding machine, William was reared in an upper-class milieu and attended Community School and John Burroughs School—to which there was no familial connection—in Ladue. After finishing prep school in New Mexico, Burroughs attended Harvard University, where in 1936 he received a baccalaureate degree in English.

After graduating from college, Burroughs traveled extensively—a lifelong habit—and returned to the United States before the outbreak of World War II. Although he was drafted into the army, Burroughs was discharged after only three months and moved to Greenwich Village, where he embarked on a life of excess and extreme that he chronicled in much of his writing. While in New York, Burroughs befriended two other young writers, Jack Kerouac and Allen Ginsberg, with whom he would be forever linked as the core of the Beat Generation, a literary movement that disdained the establishment and embraced visionary creativity, which was frequently drug induced.

Burroughs led a life filled with scandal and controversy. A militant homosexual at a time when alternative lifestyles were rarely public, he was also embroiled in two sensational murders. In 1944, Burroughs was caught up in the investigation of the stabbing death in New York of David Kammerer—a John Burroughs alum and Washington University English teacher—by another St. Louis friend, Lucien Carr. Seven years later, Burroughs was acquitted in the accidental shooting death of his second wife, Joan Vollmer, in Mexico City. The accident allegedly occurred when the couple—both in an alcohol- and drug-induced haze—played a "William Tell game" that involved William attempting to shoot a glass of water off of Joan's head. His poor aim not only led to her immediate death, but also to the birth of Burroughs's literary career. He claimed that Joan's tragic death "brought me into contact with the invader, the Ugly Spirit and maneuvered me into a lifelong struggle, in which I have had no choice but to write my way out." A prolific writer, Burroughs wrote dozens of novels and works of nonfiction during his lifetime, most of which contained autobiographical references to a life of addiction. Among the best known are *Junkie* (1953), *Naked Lunch* (1959), *The Soft Machine* (1961), *Exterminator!* (1973), *Cities of the Red Night* (1981), *Queer* (1985), and *Interzone* (1989).

Later in his life, Burroughs expressed himself in a variety of artistic media, including opera, film, and painting. In 1989, he paid his last visit to St. Louis when the Elliot Smith Gallery mounted an exhibition of his "shotgun" paintings, which were created with plywood, silk-screens, and shotgun blasts. The same year, Burroughs briefly appeared as a dissipated, aging junkie in the movie *Drugstore Cowboy.* In 1991, his most famous work, *Naked Lunch*, was released as a feature film by director David Cronenberg.

In the following essay, "St. Louis Return," Burroughs describes his visit back to his hometown in the early 1960s, which included a stay at the Chase Plaza Hotel.

ST. LOUIS RETURN

(ticket to St. Louis and return in a first class room for two people who is the third that walks beside you?) After a parenthesis of more than 40 years I met my old neighbor, Rives Skinker Mathews, in Tangier. I was born 4664 Berlin Avenue changed it to Pershing during the war. The Mathews family lived next door at 4660—red brick three-story houses separated by a gangway large back yard where I could generally see a rat one time or another from my bedroom window on the top floor. Well we get to talking St. Louis and "what happened to so and so" sets in and Rives Mathews really knows what happened to any so and so in St. Louis. His mother had been to dancing school with "Tommy Eliot"—(His socks wouldn't stay up. His hands were clammy. I will show you far in dancing school)—Allow me to open a parenthesis you see Rives Mathews had kept a scrapbook of St. Louis years and his mother left a collection of visiting cards from the capitals of Europe. I was on my way back to St. Louis as I looked through Rives' scrapbook dim flickering pieces of T. S. Eliot rising from the pages—(But what have I my friend to give you put aside on another tray? Those cards were burned in my winter house fire, October 27, 1961—Comte Wladmir Sollohub Rashis Ali Khan Bremond d'ars Marquis de Migre St. John's College 21 Quai Malaquais Principe de la Tour—Gentilhomo di Palazzo—you're a long way from St. Louis and vice versa.)

"I want to reserve a drawing-room for St. Louis."

"A drawing-room? Where have you been?"

"I have been abroad."

"I can give you a bedroom or a roomette as in smaller."

"I will take the bedroom."

6:40 P.M. Loyal Socks Rapids out of New York for St. Louis—Settled in my bedroom surrounded by the luggage of ten years abroad I wondered how small a roomette could be. A space capsule is where you find it. December 23, 1964, enlisting the aid of my porter, a discreet Oriental personage and a far cry indeed from old "Yassah Boss George" of my day, a table was installed in this bedroom where I could set up my Facit portable and type as I looked out the train window. Snapping an occasional picture with my Zeiss Ikon, I could not but lament the old brass spittoons, the smell of worn leather, stale cigar smoke, steam iron and soot. Looking out the train window—click click clack—back back back—Pennsylvania Railroad en route four people in a drawing room::::One leafs through an old joke magazine called *LIFE*:— ("What we want know is who put the sand in the spinach?")—A thin boy in prep school clothes thinks this is funny. Ash gathers on his father's Havana held in a delicate gray cone the way it holds on a really expensive cigar. Father is reading *The Wall Street Journal*. Mother is putting on the old pancake, *The Green Hat* folded on her knee. Brother—"Bu" they call him—is looking out the train window. The time is 3 P.M. The train is one hour out of St. Louis, Missouri. Sad toy train it's a long way to go see on back each time place what I mean dim jerky far away. */Take/* Look out the window of the train. Look. Postulate an observer Mr. B from Pitman's Common Sense Arithmetic at Point X one light hour away from the train. Postulate further that Mr. B. is able to observe and photograph the family with a telescopic camera. Since the family image moving at the speed of light will take an hour to reach Mr. B., when he takes the 3 P.M. set the train is pulling into St. Louis Union Station at 4 P.M. St. Louis time George the porter there waiting for his tip. (Are you a member of the Union? Film Union 4 P.M.?) The family will be met at the station by plain Mr. Jones or Mr. J. if you prefer. (It was called Lost Flight. Newspapers from vacant lots in a back alley print shop lifted bodily out of a movie set the Editor Rives Mathews. Mr. and Mrs. Mortimer Burroughs and their two sons Mortimer Jr. and William Seward Burroughs of 4664 Berlin Avenue changed it to Pershing during the war. I digress I digress.)

Postulate another observer Mr. B-1 at Point X-1 two light hours away. The train in his picture is now two light hours out of St. Louis at 2 P.M. still in the dinner. The train is stopped by a vacant lot distant 1920 wind and dust /*Take*/ remote foreign suburbs—end of a subdivision street—What a spot to land with a crippled ship—sad train whistles cross a distant sky. See on back what I mean each time place dim jerky far away not present except in you watching a 1920 movie out the train window? Returning to 1964 or what's left of it—December 23, 1964, if my memory serves I was thinking about a friend in New York name of Mack Sheldon Thomas not a finer man in Interzone than old S.T. has this loft apartment and every time he leaves the bathroom door open there is a rat gets in the house so looking out the train window I see a sign: Able Pest Control /*Take*/

"I tell you boss when you think something you see it—all Mayan according to the Hindu philosophizers," observed B. J. who fortunately does not take up any space in the bedroom.

"B. J. there is no call to theorize from a single brass spittoon or even a multiple smell of worn leather. You know I dislike theories."

"George! the nudes!"—(He knew of course that the nudes would be waiting for me in front of the Union Station.)

Look out the train window /*Take*/ :acres of rusting car bodies—streams crusted with yesterday's sewage—American flag over an empty field—Wilson Stomps Cars—City of Xenia Disposal—South Hill a vast rubbish heap—Where are the people? What in the name of Christ goes on here? Church of Christ /*Take*/ crooked crosses in winter stubble—The porter knocks discreetly.

"Half an hour out of St. Louis, sir."

Yes the nudes are still there across from the station recollect once returning after a festive evening in East St. Louis hit a parked car 60 MPH thrown out of the car rolled across the pavement and stood up feeling for broken bones right under those monumental bronze nudes by Carl Milles Swedish sculptor depict the meeting of the Missouri and Mississippi river waters. It was a long time ago and my companion of that remote evening is I believe dead. (I digress I digress).

But what has happened to Market Street the skid row of my adolescent years? Where are the tattoo parlors, novelty stores, hock shops—brass knucks in a dusty window—the seedy pitchmen—("This museum shows all kinds social disease and self abuse. Young boys need it special"—Two boys standing there can't make up their mind whether to go in or not—One said later "I wonder what was in that lousy museum?")—Where are the old junkies hawking and spitting on street corners under the gas lights?—distant 1920 wind and dust—box apartments each with its own balcony—Amsterdam—Copenhagen—Frankfurt—London—anyplace.

Arriving at the Chase Plaza Hotel I was shown to a large double room a first class room in fact for two people. Like a good European I spent some time bouncing on the beds, testing the hot water taps, gawking at the towels the soap the free stationery the television set—(And they call *us* hicks).

"This place is a paradise," I told B. J.

And went down to the lobby for the local papers which I check through carefully for items or pictures that intersect amplify or illustrate any of my writings past present or future. Relevant material I cut out and paste in a scrapbook—(some creaking hints—*por eso* I have survived) Relevant material I cut out and paste in a scrapbook—(Hurry up please it's time)—For example, last winter I assembled a page entitled *Afternoon Ticker Tape* which appeared in *My Magazine* published by Jeff Nuttall of London. This page, an experiment in newspaper format, was largely a rearrangement of phrases from the front page of *The New York Times*, September 17, 1899, cast in the form of code messages. Since some readers objected that the meaning was obscure to them I was particularly concerned to find points of intersection, a decoding operation you might say relating the text to external coordinates: (From *Afternoon Ticker Tape:* "Most fruitful achievement of the Amsterdam Conference a drunk policeman"). And just here in the *St. Louis Globe Democrat* for December 23, I read that a policeman has been suspended for drinking on duty slobbed out drunk in his prowl car with an empty brandy bottle—(few more brandies neat)—(From *A.T.T.*: "Have fun in Omaha")—And this item from Vermillion, S.D.: "Omaha Kid sends jail annual note and $10"—Please use for nuts food or smokes for any prisoners stuck with Christmas in your lousy jail" signed "The Omaha Kid"—(From *A.T.T.*: "What sort of eels called Retreat 23?")—*St. Louis Globe Democrat*: "A sixth army spokesman stated two more bodies recovered from the Eel River. Deaths now total 23."—(From *A.T.T.*: "Come on Tom it's your turn now")—*St. Louis Post Dispatch*: "Tom Creek overflows its banks."

Unable to contain himself B. J. rolled on the bed in psychophantic convulsions: "I tell you boss you write it and it happens. Why if you didn't write me I wouldn't be here."

I told him tartly that such seeming coincidence was no doubt frequent enough if people would just keep their eyes and ears open. We descended to The Tenderloin Room for dinner where I was introduced to an American speciality: baked potato served with sour cream. Ausgezeichnet.

"I tell you boss you couldn't touch this food in Paris for anywhere near the price."

The next day very mild and warm I walked around the old neighborhood which is not far to walk now the old Bixby place used to be right where the hotel is now and I passed it every day as a child on my way to Forest Park with brother "Bu" and our English governess who always told me:—"Don't ask questions and don't pass remarks"—. This cryptic injunction I have been forced to disregard for professional reasons, you understand. So prowling about with my camera looking for 1920 scraps—bits of silver paper in the wind—sunlight on vacant lots—The Ambassador—"Home With A Heart"—where an old friend Clark St. lived—4664 still there looking just the same—("Do you mind if I take a few pictures? used to live here you know.")—so few people on the street—Convent Of The Sacred Heart—This message on a stone wall—"Gay—Lost—" the houses all look empty—It was not given to me to find a rat but I did photograph several squirrels (offered us his pictures of a squirrel hunt)—So back to my quiet remote room and my scrapbooks.

"Ash pits—an alley—a rat in the sunlight—It's all here," I tapped my camera, "all the magic of past times like the song says right under your eyes back in your own back yard. Why are people bored? Because they can't see what is right under their eyes right in their own back yard. And why can't they see what is right under their eyes?—(Between the eye and the object falls the shadow)—And that shadow, B. J., is the *pre-recorded word*."

"Oh sir you slobbered a bimfull."

"Like I come out here to see 'a bunch of squares in Hicksville'? Well I will see just that. I come here to see what I see and that's another story. Any number of stories. Walk around the block keeping your eyes open and you can write a novel about what you see—down in the lobby last night—smoky rose sunset across the river."

"The river is in the other direction boss."

"So what? Shift a few props. Now would you believe it people are sitting there with their back to that sunset."

"I don't want to believe it boss."

"B. J., remember the roller coaster at Forest Park Highlands.?"

"I sure do boss. Why one time me and that Mexican girl used to work in the Chink laundry on Olive Street—"

"All right, B. J. cut. From now on we run a clean show. A show you can take your kids and your grandmother to see it. Just good clean magic for all the family. Remember Thurston?"

"I sure do boss. He made a white elephant disappear."

"Exactly—a white elephant—all our gray junk yesterdays—everything sharp and clear like after the rain."

At this point B. J. jumped to his feet, opened an umbrella and bellowed out "April Showers"—(White rain sloshed down—a wall of water you understand.)

"All right, B. J., Cut!"

Sunday December 27 driving around St. Louis with brother "Bu" stopping here and there to take pictures—The Old Courthouse and all the records */Take/* and there by the river across the river depending on which way you come on it is the arch still under construction at that time 600 feet high when they finished it—(Gateway To The West)—has an ominous look like the only landmark to survive an atomic blast or other natural catastrophe */Take/* cobblestone streets along the levee—refuge of river boat days—strata of brick and masonry—geology of a city—MacArthur Bridge */Take/* and just *there* a truck will crash through the guard rail and fall 75 feet killing the driver you can see the dotted line in the *Post Dispatch* picture */Take/* River Queen and the Admiral just like they used to be red plush guilt the lot cruising down the river on a Sunday afternoon.

"Shall we take in the West End?"

Clayton and the West End suburbs now built up beyond recognition after 20 years absence. In the 1920's my family moved out west on the Price Road—(700 S. */Take/* and just down the road is the John Burroughs School and there is the locker room door */Take/* where I stood one afternoon a long time ago and watched the torn sky bend with the wind lightning struck the school just *there /Take/* (Whoever said lightning never strikes twice in the same place was no photographer.)—1929 tornado if my memory serves when all the records went up name and address old arch there by the river with the cold spring news.

"Cruising Down the River on a Sunday Afternoon"—(This music across the water—The Veiled Prophet Ball off stage)—On the scene photographs by William Born Field *St. Louis Magazine* 52, Retarded Children's Project, young St. Louis citizens bicentennial salute: (Happy New Year Comte Hector Perrone de San Martine Mrs. Edge at home last Thursday in May, Fete Dieu, Principe de la Tour, Gentilhomo di Palazzo, you're a long retarded children project veiled way from St. Louis. I, Famous Bar Prophet, had not thought Death Magazine 52 had undone so many for I have known them all: Baron Rashid Pierre de Cobo—Helen Zapiola Theresa Riley—I digress I digress.)

"Now what in Horton Vernet Gen-San Martine Zapiolo The Swan Last Day de Cobo Principe di Castel Hose it Chicale Randy Veiled Miguel Garcia de Rube Gordon Hell does that mean?" interjected B. J.

(A long review—human voices—*They* expected answers?)

Family Reunion at my Aunt K's. B. J. has observed with his usual astuteness in such matters that there is only half a bottle of whiskey on the side board, volunteered for bartender duty surreptitiously serving himself double measure so when another bottle is produced rather sooner than later we both feel a little well you know B. J. is an old Alcohol Anonymous as used to electrify the meetings with his confessions: "Once at the house of a friend" he begins sepulchrally "in the dead of night—I"—he stabs a finger at his chest—"sneaked into the room of my host's adolescent son." He tiptoes across the platform and turns to the audience. "You get the picture?" The audience stirs uneasily. B. J. shifts an imaginary flashlight—"arrowheads—a stone axe—butterfly trays—the cyanide jar—a stuffed owl—Whoo whoo whoo drank the alcohol off the boy's preserved centipede?"—It was emetic in the good sense. (I digress—a drunk policeman—Stein reverts to his magazine.)

I address myself to a cousin who is now account executive for an advertising firm: "What I say is time for the artist and the ad man to get in a symbiotic way and give birth to what we may call 'Creative Advertising' I mean advertisements that tell a story and create character. Like this see? So you handle the Southern Comfort account?"

"Ty Bradly river boat gambler at your service, suh." His blue eyes fixed quizzically on the barmaid's ample bosom, he drawled out "I'll take double Southern Comfort, Ma'am."

"Pardon me are you Colonel Bradly? Colonel Ty Bradly?"

Bradly turned to face the question his eyes unbluffed unreadable two fingers in a vest pocket rested lightly on the cold blue steel of his Remington derringer.

"I am suh."

"Yeah and think what we could do with the Simmons Mattress account," interjected B. J.

(All right, B. J., /*Cut*!/) See what I mean? glamour—romance—Inspector J. Lee of the Nova Police smokes Players—(flashes his dirty rotten hunka tin)—Agent K9 uses a Bradly laser gun—Advertisements should provide the same entertainment value as the content of a magazine. *Your* product deserves the best. Why make up silly jingles? Why not use the good old songs like "Annie Laurie." There's a story goes with that song. Remember a young cop whistling "Annie Laurie" down cobblestone streets? Then he stopped in the corner saloon for a glass of Budweiser which he couldn't have done really being on duty. Yes he would have approved your favorite smoke. Show your cards all Players. And remember a young cop whistling "Annie Laurie" down cobblestone streets twirling his club drew September 17, 1899 over St. Louis.

(The sky goes out against his back.)

Mr. Dickson Terry of the *St. Louis Post Dispatch* interviews your reporter: "As you know in the 1890's St. Louis was famous throughout the world for such restaurants as Tony Faust—But when I was last here 20 years ago there was not a first class eating place to be found in the city—You might say all the uh flavor had been siphoned off into the subdivisions and country clubs of the West End—This process is now being reversed—any number of excellent restaurants—three in fact right here in the Chase Plaza Hotel—a movement *back* to the city—*back* to the 1890's finds expression in Gas Light Square and the refurbished river boats—yes decidedly the reversal of a trend which I for one found deplorable—and that is what I am getting at in this seemingly obscure passage." I taped a text on the table between us, a text using the three column format of a small town newspaper.

THE MOVING TIMES

September 17, 1899 Mr Bradly Mr Martin stood there on dead stars heavy with his dusty answer drew September 17, 1899 over New York that morning giving you my toy soldiers put away in the attic.

Attic of the Eugene Field House you understand never happened. Remember the *Mary Celeste*? ghost ship abandoned back in 1872 all sails set nobody on board fresh southerly winds a long time ago for such a purpose? Now here is the front page of the *Chicago Tribune* Monday January 4, 1965 The American Paper For Americans:

Tempest Hurls 807 On Ship Like Ten-pins—16 Hurt in Nightmare.

The American liner *Independence*—North Atlantic storm—ripped open a weather door on a lower deck smashed a porthole on an upper deck and hurled half a ton of ice water on a couple asleep—(presumably waking them)—Captain Riley of the *Independence* described the storm as the worst he had encountered in more than 40 years at sea. "It was like riding a roller coaster."

("By the way, B. J. what ever happened to Forest Park Highlands?"

"It burned down, boss—hot peep shows in the penny arcade.")

Well now it so happens that I repatriated myself on the *Independence* docked December 8, 1964 if my memory serves I had the pleasure of meeting Captain Riley at the Captain's Cocktail Party where no one seemed to know who anybody else was supposed to be and everybody a bit miffed in consequence. I approached the Captain directly: "Captain, may I ask you a question? a *novelist's* question?" (For I was you understand the distinguished novelist of whom nobody had heard.)

"Why uh yes," he replied guardedly.

"Please tell me Captain quite frankly do you have any theories or guesses in short any shall we say *notions* with regard to the *Mary Celeste*?"

He replied after a short pause that he could think of no explanation that accounted for all the facts.

"Captain," I stated firmly "the plain fact is that there are no facts. I myself—and I may tell you in strictest confidence that I was once a private investigator—have sifted this matter to the bottom most deep and established every reason to doubt that such a ship as the *Mary Celeste* ever existed. The whole thing was a fabrication out of whole cloth or paper more precisely—The Captain's Log Book you understand"—and I gave him a straight look—

"Is this the starboard side?" I asked.

"Why yes it is."

"Ah—just so—you see—"

So with the picture of that old sea dog shifting slightly as the ship rolled ports of the world in his eyes and a picture postcard of the *SS Independence* pasted into my own log of the voyage steaming across a paper sea just as empty as the *Mary Celeste*—paper you understand—not a passenger in sight—well just so—"The American paper for Americans—*Independence* —"

So I make these last entries in the log book of my St. Louis return—luggage stacked in the lobby—back through the ruins of Market Street to the Union Station nudes waiting there in the dry fountain of an empty square—I have returned to pick up a few pieces of sunlight and shadow—silver paper in the wind-frayed sounds of a distant city.

JAY LANDESMAN

JAY LANDESMAN (1919–) was born Irving Ned Landesman in St. Louis, the youngest of Benjamin C. and Beatrice Landesman's three sons. Benjamin had come to St. Louis in 1904 to paint murals for the German Pavilion at the World's Fair and stayed in the city as the proprietor of a successful antique business, Landesman Galleries.

After studying English literature at the University of Missouri–Columbia and Rice University, Jay ran the family antique business and launched a literary career. His first venture was founding and editing the quarterly magazine *Neurotica*, a controversial publication that featured the work of emerging writers such as Allen Ginsberg, Kenneth Patchen, and Marshall McLuhan. Published between 1948 and 1952, *Neurotica* featured poetry and fiction as well as social criticism about the anxieties of life in post–World War II America.

Although Landesman divided his time between New York and St. Louis through the 1950s and 1960s, he and his wife, Fran, made a substantial commitment to St. Louis in 1952 when they opened the Crystal Palace on Olive Street east of Grand. Six years later the successful cabaret moved to its better-known location, on Olive west of Boyle, in the district becoming known as Gaslight Square, which was, in essence, St. Louis's answer to Greenwich Village.

In 1959, the Landesmans presented their musical drama, "The Nervous Set," at the Palace. Considered the first and only Beat musical, the show eventually made it to Broadway, where it received a lukewarm reception and folded after a three-week run. Chandler Brossard, a former Palace bartender who went on to become an editor at *Look* magazine, described Landesman as "very insightful, very ahead of everybody on the culture scene, and very encouraging." Entertainers who performed at the Crystal Palace include Phyllis Diller, the Smothers Brothers, Lenny Bruce, Dick Gregory, Woody Allen, and Barbra Streisand; for some it was their first break into show business. In 1964, the Landesmans closed the Crystal Palace due to financial difficulties, and the couple—a musical playwriting team—moved to England to pursue new artistic ventures.

In addition to being a playwright, Landesman has written novels and two books of memoirs, *Rebel Without Applause* (1987) and *Jaywalking* (1992). In the first volume, from which the following passage is taken, Landesman focuses on his bohemian St. Louis years and running the Crystal Palace.

FROM *REBEL WITHOUT APPLAUSE*

RUNNING DRY/RUNNING OFF

When word got around the Square that I had signed Gypsy Rose Lee for a two week engagement, a roar of disapproval went up among the proprietors. They lived in mortal fear that the strippers would some day invade the Square and it would be all over. That I should be the first to bring them in was, they said, an incredible act of betrayal. Gypsy Rose Lee's image as Queen of the Strippers was still very much alive, in spite of the fact that she had not shed anything more than a glove in twenty years. The hypocrisy of it all concerned our audiences; where once we required coats and ties for admission, in the race for the buck nobody cared what customers took off.

Once again I was needed to prop things up in the Twist Room, which was starting to fade. I tried a number of unique acts, including a young black Yoga disciple who meditated on a bed of nails while another stood on him, chanting. It was impressive, but not a crowd pleaser.

"Can you eat glass?" I asked them in desperation.

What the Palace needed were new friends as well as a new act. A patron's group to help foster new shows and spark local talent was organized. After much publicity and hard work, we found that only a handful of people responded. Then we began to offer the shows free to civic, cultural and educational groups just to cash in on the drinks. One of the programs we offered was *An Evening with Brecht and Weil.*

It was an attempt to recreate the atmosphere of the old Berlin cabaret during the last days of the Weimar Republic; we felt it was an appropriate symbolic gesture commemorating our own dying days. Unfortunately, it was sponsored by the local B'nai Brith. Since the show was sung in the original German, the audience, predominantly Jewish, walked out *en masse*. They were shocked that we would present such a bill of fare while the memory of six million Jews murdered by the Germans was still fresh in their minds. They weren't the only ones who didn't like it. A young critic on the *Post-Dispatch*, eager to establish his reputation, chose the Crystal Palace as his target for abusive reviews. No matter what we did, his bitter attitude turned audiences against us. It was the first sign of the backlash of criticism that Gaslight Square was about to be subjected to.

When a visitor to the Square was mugged in an adjoining area, the newspapers gave it front page space: MUGGING IN GASLIGHT SQUARE. Not only was it inaccurate and unfair, it was signing our death warrant. People had always felt safe on their nights out on the Square. Now, for the first time, they were alerted to be 'on their guard.' After the mugging, there was concern with the rapidly decaying neighborhood that surrounded us. There was no way to stop urban decay and racial tension. Our attempts to have more police patrolling the area only dramatized the situation. It wasn't obvious at first, but we proprietors knew we were under attack. Our organization was helpless in trying to tighten standards.

The new breed of visitors were looking for a different kind of excitement. They were no longer interested in atmosphere. The Youth Culture was emerging. We had become the Establishment. Street action became more colorful than some of the acts presented in the entertainment places. Audience participation was in full swing. Mitch Miller's sing-along influences were to be heard up and down the Square. I'd watch from the door of the Palace the newly-arrived revelers to the Square start to clap and sing to the music of Dixieland jazz from the Golden Eagle fifty yards away. I never realised so many people knew the words to *St. James Infirmary Blues*. The race for the customer's buck was on in earnest now. Jimmy Massucci's prophetic words that "greed was going to be the ruin of the Square" were ringing true. If there had been an audience for an amusing, colorful, tuneful piece of entertainment, Quigley's satirical musical on public relations, *The Raspberry Quee*n, would have run for a year. Unfortunately, it lasted only eight weeks. After it closed, the Crystal Palace went dark for the first time. It would have stayed that way if the Prince of Darkness hadn't called to sell me what he called the "hottest act in showbusiness."

"Bubie, listen. I know how you feel about the Palace. I love what you guys have done out there. It's a class operation, but times are changing. Would I handle anything like belly dancers in the old days?"

I was shocked. The guy was trying to sell me belly dancers? That was the first step to hiring strippers. I would die rather than bring them into the Palace.

"Listen to me, Bubie. Belly dancers are packing them in here in New York. And have I got a class act for you. Believe me, I've never steered you wrong before, have I?"

"I'm listening," I said coldly.

"This one is an artist, I'm telling you. She's the best in the business. Class act. Beautiful. She'll pack the place. You'll love her."

He went on for five minutes about her pelvic charms. I was weakening.

"How much?" I asked. The price he mentioned seemed reasonable, especially since it included her own native musicians. "I'll call you back." My heart was pounding. After all the talk about keeping up the standards of the area, would I be the first to bring in the strippers?

The Prince of Darkness didn't let me down. Habeba and her loud thumping musicians were indeed a class act; ethnic qualities, too. Nothing to be ashamed of, in spite of the disapproving looks of the other proprietors. It was a sensational act. Night after night, I would be out on the sidewalk, hawking Habeba's charms like an old carnival barker.

"Step right in, Ladies and Gentlemen, and see the new sensation of the art of belly dancing. She's Little Egypt, Theda Bara, and Marilyn Monroe rolled up into one package."

After the initial novelty wore off, subsequent belly dancers proved less of an attraction. I couldn't go any lower and bring in the strippers. The Palace went dark for the second time. Then, comedian Irwin Corey dropped by on his way to the West Coast. He had played the Palace before with great success. He couldn't believe what had happened. His pathological compulsion to work would not let him see the Palace dark.

"I'll do a show tonight and split the door with you."

I told him he was mad. "You can't get an audience in fifteen minutes."

"Wanna bet?"

I resisted. I couldn't see the great artist who had played the best (and some of the worst) clubs in America for over thirty years standing outside the door hawking his own appearance, but he didn't give a damn about dignity. I should have known. He had built his whole act around denigrating dignity. It was going to be an interesting experiment. He hurriedly dressed in his baggy pants and long, flowing tail-coat and tennis shoes and battered top hat, the trade mark of his profession, and stood outside the Palace calling the faithful home.

"The world's greatest authority will be performing in fifteen minutes, at reduced prices."

Within half-an-hour, the Professor had enough people in the theatre to give a show. It was one of the best of his career and possibly the longest. I knew it was going to be our last. The Square was still jammed with traffic, but it was over for us. The place that had sparked the whole area into a multi-million-dollar industry was its first casualty.

Never had a bubble glowed with such colors or burst so quickly. Never had a heart broken so completely. There was pressure on me to step down and turn the Palace over to those "who knew how to get the audience back." Negotations began with various groups of people who were sure they had the right formula for success. We finally hammered out a deal to rent out the Palace to one of the other entrepreneurs in the Square. I watched with a certain amount of satisfaction as the new operators brought in acts they thought would revive the place. None of them were successful. They brought in big names of the past, doing shows that went out of style long before I did. I could have told them, but they never asked.

What started out as a party ended up as a tragedy. The Three Fountains went up in flames. Jack O'Neil died waiting for a game at his bridge club. The Palace was dark. Jimmy Massucci went blind. The first murder in Gaslight Square took place in the winter of '64.

After twelve years of producing shows, I was creatively exhausted. Without the Palace, I didn't see any future for us in St. Louis. I couldn't go back to the antique business with Cutie. I didn't want to be trapped in the real world. We began to think of places we could escape to. New York was a possibility; Fran was, by now, a recognized songwriting talent, collaborating with Alec Wilder, one of the most respected composers in the business. There was no doubt that she could promote her career if she lived in Manhattan. But what would I do? There wasn't a big demand for my talents. I revived the idea of us living in Connecticut, in the barn, Fran working at her career, and I would become a country gentlemen with no visible means of support. Fran didn't want to take the chance—her parents were still a hazard. Then I got a fantasy of going someplace exotic, like a Greek Island, leaving the commercial world behind.

"All I want to do is watch the flowers grow."

I tried to make it sound romantic, but the idea of communing with nature gave Fran the horrors. "I don't want to go anyplace where they don't speak English" was the other demand she made.

England seemed to be the perfect answer. The children could go to school there without any problems. There were no medical bills to pay in Great Britain. There was theatre there; perhaps Fran and I could get something going again with our plays. I had finished my play about Stella Brooks; I had a very amusing script of a musical based on *Dracula* by local talent with lyrics by Fran, and there was always the possibility that I could get *A Walk On The Wild Side* produced; even *The Nervous Set* was a possibility. Fran could find another collaborator to write songs with. The music scene was very much alive in England with the arrival of the Beatles. We could live cheaply over there.

Once again, I was breaking with the family that was such an important part of my life. I had only been on my own once before, when I went to New York with *Neurotica*, but then I was single, without family responsibilities. Without the income from the Crystal Palace, it might be tough. I still could get enough to survive on from our partnership, but I felt it unfair to Fred to leave him with everything to take care of and still draw money. Fran's folks, who had never grown accustomed to the idea that we were still married, offered to underwrite our stay in England for a year. As grandparents they were perfect, but Fran and I were still "brats" in their books, which made their support at our time of crisis a complete surprise. I suspected they thought it would do their grandchildren some good to see another part of the world. We took them up on their generous offer.

When the newspapers heard we were going to London, they wrote it up as a news feature: LANDESMANS TO LONDON FOR TALENT TUNE UP. Quigley wrote an article about our leaving that presented a fairly different picture:

> Now Jay and Fran Landesman are leaving town, and their going marks the end of an Era—the Era of The Crystal Palace and High Style. They are leaving with no boo-hoos, no bitterness, but with a little sadness and a touch of puzzlement. They are not leaving for a better offer. They are leaving us to get away from us and take a look

around another town . . . What are they worth to us? What did they cost that we were not willing to pay? All of us, those who love them and those who are saying good riddance—have been enriched by them. We become a little more drab as we wave goodbye.

"St. Louis isn't a place. It isn't a city," wrote Bob Miller to us many years later. "St. Louis is something that happens to you once in a lifetime when you are just right for it and then it never happens again." I knew it was over. I would never return.

When it came to saying goodbye, Alfie dressed the children as if they were going to another party. Fran and I had done nothing about the house, leaving it all in Fred's hands, to dispose of it and the contents any way he saw fit. Saying goodbye to Cutie was going to be the hardest part of leaving.

"Well old girl, you'll be happy to know that the psychiatrists have given us a clean bill of health and we no longer need them."

She looked at me with an expression of old fashioned Jewish contempt.

"So what did you learn from all those fancy doctors?" The corners of her mouth twisted upwards, exposing her two gold incisors.

"They told me that you loved me best of all the children."

Her hand shot out, striking her forehead in the classic gesture of frustration.

"Why didn't you ask me? I could have told you and saved you all that money."

I picked her up and waltzed her around the Galleries for the last time.

"You're right, Cutie, but look at all the fun we would have missed."

JOHN KNOEPFLE

JOHN KNOEPFLE (1923–) was born in Cincinnati and, after serving in the U.S. Navy during World War II, completed two degrees at Xavier University. During the 1950s, Knoepfle taught at a number of colleges and universities in the Midwest before coming to St. Louis in 1961 to teach at Saint Louis University High School. While working on his Ph.D. at Saint Louis University, Knoepfle taught English simultaneously at Maryville College and Washington University.

A prolific and widely anthologized poet, Knoepfle has published nineteen volumes of poetry and received numerous awards, including grants from the Rockefeller Foundation and the National Endowment for the Arts. In addition to his own writing, Knoepfle spearheaded an important oral history project early in his career: interviewing and tape-recording the reminiscences of fifty former rivermen of the Ohio and Mississippi River valleys. In listening to and preserving the colorful tales of a vanishing American culture, Knoepfle found the stories and speech patterns of those he interviewed a rich source of material for his poetry. A complete collection of the inland river recordings is housed at the Cincinnati Public Library and at the University of Illinois at Springfield.

John Knoepfle is professor emeritus of English at the University of Illinois at Springfield (formerly Sangamon State University) and lives in Auburn, Illinois.

LINES FOR MEN OF THE GREATER INTERIOR

The founders did not go away
thinking that everything ended
when they left town,
but they couldn't have known
this year, or the day.

Under the Saarinen Arch
we watch a city dying.

If we have visions,
what will they come to
a century and a half from now?
Men have made nations
ten thousand years.
We live in a valley of many cities.

The hour is immediate,
each moment relevant.
We touch the blind eyes of Osage Sioux,
and they are stones.
We see the delta-shaped wings
that blossom in solar storms
beyond our blue planet,
and they are signed in this city.

We hold a gyroscope on a string.
It has no meaning beyond us.

Under the great arch
they hammered down cellblocks of slaves,
they bulldozed into earth
the jawbones of mound builders.

Hunger and power command the day,
we can't get around that.

Asia is buried in fire.
The slum child does not hear.
Christ is drowsy in his own wounds.

Who will break the bread of sundown
and fill the drinking gourds of dawn?

We shiver in ourselves,
for if a man cannot better the dream of his father,
his sons will judge his loss of courage.

And yet it is good for a man to stand upright.
The man who rises to the sullen day,
trusting his hour,
he is an amnesty for all ages,
cold fire in a darkening sky,
thin word chalked on the blackboard.

RIVERFRONT, ST. LOUIS

On the levee the Saarinen Arch
petitions luck for St. Louis
once and for all.
Cartons of trash
released from the Steamer Admiral
move in file on the Mississippi
with a kind of reverence.
Between cobblestones on the landing,
I discover a Roosevelt dime
blackened by many waters.

ST. LOUIS MIDDAY

Sucking at summer
the black face
floats in the noon
heat. It moves
through hard dust and labor,
not conscious
of its own shadow.
It does not even know
the yellow lizards
crippled in its eyes.

He stacks bricks
in the hot day.
The headache ball
breaks down his home.

ST. LOUIS MIDNIGHT

These pale masks
sound on the wind,
crowding silences
of midtown avenues
until the hour
turns their wandering
where gothic homes
adjust them to
our sleep. Perhaps
they dream
in sober rentals,
white dwarfs
drifting in the universe.

HEMAN AVENUE HOLIDAY

When these georgian apartments are leveled,
bits of plaster clinging to the rooms we knew,
we will crawl naked from the stones of our cellars.
We will crawl up into the light, and among us
there will be pensioners and cooks and musicians,
and we will join together, as in a congregation.
We will not have any names and no identities.
We will have only our sadness for a little while,
the nipples yearning, secret whorls of the hair exposed,
the genitals designed with no further purpose,
the navels mysterious, meaningless, and we will go
and lie down in two long rows on the burnt grass
where the mall was with its cool green sycamores.
We will gather scraps of paper to rest ourselves on,
tissues, the halves of torn letters, school notes,
the waste of our generation on that long mall,
and we will pretend that if someone came with bread
we would not destroy each other for the broken crumbs.
No, we will die together in a greatness of our souls.

EAST ST. LOUIS

Coal sells a bushel a week
at MacArthur Bridge.
Time weighs men by the peck
in the shacks there,
and the January dark
denies a summer delta.
Ice grinds the winter
river, a savage business.

JUNE NIGHT ON THE RIVER

Tonight the river is
calm enough. A string of cars
drums the long Eads Bridge
toward Union Station.
Pullman windows
charge the secret
spans of the bridge and tall
lights travel over the water.
They are hooded monks
gleaming among the piers.

Now I see whole mountains
honeycombed with monks,
and one of these, a boy
from Athos, fills the blue
Aegean with his own
image as he leans
beyond the prow of his skiff
and tries his luck
with a hooked line for his life,
his serious gesture.

The train goes its way,
the long lights
go out. I pour myself
a careful beer, tilting
a cold glass above
the Mississippi. It is
a lost river roiling
underneath the bridge. It came
from a deep cave on this
June night. And still it is
the one river Clemens
gave his own true Huck,
head buried in the black
knees of Jim, and the same
winds howl down streaks
of our summer storms.

HOWARD NEMEROV

HOWARD NEMEROV (1920–1991) was born in New York City to an affluent family. After graduation from Harvard in 1941, Nemerov served as a pilot in the Royal Canadian Air Force and the U.S. Air Force during World War II. In 1946, he returned to the United States with his British-born wife, Margaret, and began a long and illustrious career as a writer and teacher. Before arriving in St. Louis in 1969 to assume a professorship in the English department at Washington University, Nemerov taught at several colleges in the East, including Bennington College in Vermont, where he spent eighteen years. By 1976, Nemerov had published two dozen volumes of poetry, fiction, and criticism, had won numerous prestigious awards, and was appointed the Edward Mallinckrodt Distinguished University Professor at Washington University.

In spite of all the acclaim Nemerov had already achieved by mid-career, his greatest honors were still forthcoming. In 1978, he received both the Pulitzer Prize and the National Book Award for his *Collected Poems*. A decade later, Nemerov was appointed Poet Laureate of the United States, the third person so named. Although Nemerov was an internationally acclaimed man of letters, he was very grounded in St. Louis, walking daily on the tree-lined streets between his home in University City and his campus office, claiming, "Walking is good for poetry—that's why it comes in feet." Nemerov kept in close contact with students and colleagues and was a familiar sight on his legendary strolls, until he lost his prolonged battle with cancer on July 5, 1991.

As a poet, Nemerov worked in traditional forms and valued control and clarity. His range of subjects was wide—from objects in nature to epic historical events to the simplest human ritual. According to critic Julia Randall, "The world, for Nemerov, is a great writing in which we are characters attempting to read our own sentence."

ONE MOMENT IN ETERNITY

Before Our Lady's on Des Peres Boulevard
On a brilliant Sunday morning in December

Is drawn up, idling and breathing smoke,
A sparkling maroon and black Cadillac
Hearse having a heavy silver crucifix
In each side window and in raised relief
The name Boomgartner Funerals scrawled out
In cursive silver script across
The front doors and the back; all this

Inspected by two altar-boys, admiringly:
"Jee*zus*!" says one, and "*Jee*zus!" agrees the other.

Implacably, pretending oblivion,
The liveried black chauffeur stares ahead
Along the hood, sighting between the up-
spreading wings of a silver angel taking off.

WALKING DOWN WESTGATE IN THE FALL

The weather's changes are the private rites
And secret celebrations of the soul
So widely now believed not to exist.
The first clear autumn day, the summer rain,
The sudden fall of winter and the dark
When Daylight Saving goes, the sunny melt
Of several February days, to these
Changes the soul with changes of its own
And overtones responds in resonance.

Down Westgate, in the Fall, the housewives set
Chrysanthemums in bronze or marble bowls
Forth on the stoops, defying ice and snow
With their lion's mane, sun's face ruddy glow of gold.

Things like that marry weather with the soul,
Which would have its seasons if it did exist,
And sing its songs among the falling leaves
Under the autumn rain, and celebrate
Its mass with hymns and litanies of change,
Walking down Westgate past chrysanthemums,
Consenting with the winter soon to come,
Hearing the acorns bang on the roofs of cars
And bounce and roll along the rainy street.

GINKGOES IN FALL

They are the oldest living captive race,
Primitive gymnosperms that in the wild
Are rarely found or never, temple trees
Brought down in line unbroken from the deep
Past where the Yellow Emperor lies tombed.

Their fallen yellow fruit mimics the scent
Of human vomit, the definite statement of
An attitude, and their translucency of leaf,
Filtering a urinary yellow light,
Remarks a delicate wasting of the world,

An innuendo to be clarified
In winter when they defecate their leaves
And bear the burden of their branches up
Alone and bare, dynastic diagrams
Of their distinguished genealogies.

AN ENDING

After the weeks of unrelenting heat
A rainy day brings August to an end
As if in ceremony. The spirit, dry
From too much light too steadily endured,
Delights in the heavy silver water globes
That make change from the sun's imperial gold;
The mind, relieved from being always brilliant,
Goes forth a penitent in a shroud of grey
To walk the sidewalks that reflect the sky,
The line of lights diminishing down the street,
The splashed lights of the traffic going home.

BY AL LEBOWITZ'S POOL

I

Imagine this: three beach balloons of three
Sizes, sometimes spinning and sometimes not,
Float in the transparent water table
Reflecting light blue light up from the floor.
They slightly sink into their own images
Mirrored below themselves as bubbles a bit
Elongate gaining and losing their various colors
According as they move between sun and shade,
Shade of the sailing cloud, shade of the oak
And sycamore and apple standing over
Or bending above, and through the dappled light
Respondingly they drift before light airs,
Sailing in independence that is yet
Relation, unpredictable if not
Quite free, mysteriously going about
Their balancing buoyancies sometimes puffed

On some bits of V-shaped wake; like a mobile
By Calder, only more so—linkages
Invisible, of wind and the watching mind,
Connect and vary their free-hand forms. The world
Is a misery, as it always was; these globes
Of color bob about, a mystery
Of pure relation that looks always right
Whatever it does. A steel-blue-black wasp
Rides on one ball awhile, flies to the next,
Possibly playing, possibly not; by law
Any three things in the wide world
Triangulate: the wasp, and Betelgeuse,
And Our Lady of Liberty in the harbor; if
It's any comfort to us, and it is.

2

Sunshine and rain at once, and the clear pool
At once lights up its light and shadow show,
Doing its free-hand random perfect circles
That on a nucleus of bubble and drop
Grow outward and silently intersect
Without collision or consequence, as if
They lived between the spirit and the world,
And evanescing are replaced by others
In patterns that repeat themselves beneath
In light and shade that seem to ripple away
Between the surface and the floor and dazzle
Again against the sunshine side. Dame Kind
Is doing one of her mighty and meaningless
Experimental demonstrations, but
Of What? Playing, perhaps, with the happiness of
A couple of groups of aperiodic crystals
Like thee and me, who are old enough to know
That if these moments could not pass away
They could not be, all dapple and delight.

3

Two girls in the pool, two old men out of it
Observing with an implicit kind of love
Mildly distinguished from lechery, much from lust,
The slender strong young bodies sudden as fish
To dive and swerve in the dazzled element
And surface (no longer much like fish at all)
Smiling, their long hair asparkle as with stars.
The old men, relaxed into their middle ages
And comfortable in the flesh for yet awhile,
Whom generation has had its will and fill of
And nearly if not quite let go, smile back
Over their drinks and banter with the girls
In a style that allows courtship and courtesy
To show their likenesses and keep their distance,
Just glancingly at risk; and the young women
Kindly respond in kind. No one, praise God,
Is going to get in trouble this time around.
It is late Sunday morning by the pool,
A Sunday morning late in summer time,
A Sunday morning of the middle class,
And no one, praise God, is even like to drown
Before it's time to go indoors for lunch.

4

Likely the last of the summer's storms goes by,
And even the water in the pool looks lank,
With leaves already dead upon its flat
Spinning a while and sinking waterlogged,
A couple of struggling bugs doing the same.
Even the heat begins to ember out,
The year has perceptibly started down again,
And summer's wondering stillness is on the move
Over ourselves as well; a leaf comes down
And alights without a splash; another year
Of the little lot has passed, and what have we

Squirreled away more than this summer's day
With the electric storm hammering down on it
Releasing life? The banked furnace of the sun
With reliquary heat returns in splendor
Diminished some with time, but splendid still.
Beside the pool we drink, talk, and are still,
These times of kindness mortality allows.

5

An afternoon alone beside the pool
Observing, or more like peaceably taking in,
Recording, stillness made of rippling wave
And waving leaf, of shadow and reflected light,
And silence able to draw into its dream
The siren singing on the avenue,
The crying of a child two houses down,
The aircraft laboring through four thousand feet
On the way elsewhere. Stillness and silence still,
Shimmering frequencies of waterlight
Reflected from the planes of leaf above
And from the screening panels of the pool,
So many white oscilloscopes whereon
The brimming water translates into light.

Reflection and reflexion, lovely words
I shall be sorry to let go when I let go:
Reflected light, reflexion of the wave;
For things reflected are more solemn and still
Than in themselves they are, it is the doubling
Perhaps that seems to bring them nearer thought;
Could we reflect, did water not reflect?

Enchanted afternoon, immune from time,
Illusion's privilege gives me the idea that I
Am not so much writing this verse as reading it
Up out of water and light and shadow and leaf
Doing the dance of their various dependencies—
As if I might daydream my way again

Into the world and be at one with it—
While the shadows of harder, more unyielding things
Edge steadily and stealthily around the pool
To translate the revolving of the world
About itself, the spinning ambit of the seasons
In the simple if adamant equation of time
Around the analemma of the sun.

TENNESSEE WILLIAMS

THOMAS LANIER WILLIAMS (1911–1983) was born in Columbus, Mississippi, and moved to St. Louis at age eight, when his father was transferred by his employer, the International Shoe Company. The Williams family first lived at 4633 Westminster Place, and subsequently moved to homes on Pershing Avenue and Arundel Place. Due largely to the alcoholism of Cornelius Williams, Thomas's father, the family's financial situation deteriorated, and they moved to an apartment at 5 South Taylor Avenue. By the time Williams reached adolescence, the family had moved to 6254 Enright Avenue. After graduating from University City High School in 1929, Williams entered the University of Missouri–Columbia and completed three years before financial hardship forced him to withdraw. After working several years for International Shoe, Williams briefly attended Washington University; he eventually received a baccalaureate degree, with a specialization in writing, from the University of Iowa.

Williams took the first name Tennessee partly in homage to his paternal forebears, who were prominent in the politics of that state, and also to distance himself from early writing—mostly mediocre poetry—published under his real name. By 1939, a grant from the Rockefeller Foundation signaled Williams's growing success as a playwright. Williams moved to New York City, where his plays consistently were being produced by small theatre groups in the early 1940s. In 1945, the brilliant success of *The Glass Menagerie* assured Williams financial stability and critical esteem. For fifteen years after the Second World War, he was the most important figure in American theatre. A disciplined individual who wrote a minimum of three hours a day, Williams produced a string of critical and commercial successes, including *A Streetcar Named Desire* (1947), *Camino Real* (1953), *Cat on a Hot Tin Roof* (1955), *Sweet Bird of Youth* (1956), *Suddenly Last Summer* (1959), and *The Night of the Iguana* (1961). He won four New York Drama Critics Circle Awards and two Pulitzers, among other prestigious prizes, and his plays were staged around the world, as well as made into films starring some of Hollywood's biggest stars.

Williams battled severe emotional problems most of his adult life and sought relief in drugs and alcohol. One of Williams's greatest sources of depression was the mental illness and subsequent institutionalization and lobotomization of his beloved sister, Rose, who is the inspiration for some of his fragile heroines. Williams continued to write until the end of his life, although nothing he produced after the 1960s came close to achieving the acclaim of his earlier works. In 1969, Williams suffered a nervous breakdown while in Key West and was flown to St. Louis and admitted to Barnes Hospital by his brother, Dakin. In his *Memoirs* (1975), from which the first of the following excerpts is taken, Williams provides a biting surrealistic passage about his hospitalization in St. Louis, which he refers to as "St. Pollution." Several years later, Williams wrote the little-known two-scene play, *A Lovely Sunday for Creve Coeur* (1978), which is set in St. Louis and, as Williams's biographer Donald Spoto notes, is "spiced with literally two dozen references to his own life in St. Louis in the 1920s and 1930s." An excerpt from Scene One also follows.

In 1983, Williams died in his New York apartment. His body was flown to St. Louis, where his funeral was held at St. Louis Cathedral. Tennessee Williams is buried in Calvary Cemetery next to his mother, Miss Edwina, and sister, Miss Rose.

FROM *MEMOIRS*

In the late summer of 1969, Anne Meacham and Gigi and I returned from our dismal flight to Tokyo and I returned to the little compound in Key West. I was not with it there, I was not at all with it, the collapse had started.

The construction of the big new kitchen had also started, the kitchen which was to cost twice the 1949 purchase price of the entire property. And the erection was to last for nearly four months, which is a much longer-lasting erection than even Casanova might have desired.

The stove had been removed to the patio so I could prepare my morning Silex of coffee. And one nocturnal morning, a few days after the return to Key West, I prepared one Silex of coffee too many. I was, at this time, always falling down, you may recall, and as I removed the boiling coffee from the stove in the patio, I came a cropper on the patio tiles, spilling the boiling coffee over my bare shoulder.

I was so spaced out that I felt no pain and went about my morning's work as usual.

At this point the fog sets in. I remember going to a doctor who bandaged the lobster-red shoulder and then I remember that Dakin was in Key West. Then I remember we were in Key West airport and poor Edie Kidd came by my table and I said to her, "I like your painting, Edie, but have no other interest in you at all."

And then I was in the house on Wydown Boulevard in Clayton, Mom's old Spanish stucco dwelling, and it was morning and I had firmly decided not to enter a hospital.

"Mother, have you ever heard of sibling envy?"

"Oh yes, I think so," said Miss Edwina coldly.

A bit later I said I would go to the hospital provided an ambulance was summoned to take me. Dakin talked me out of that. He got me into his car and drove me to Barnacle Hospital. At first, that first day, I was put in the Queen's Division—and I didn't make up that name, that's just what it's called. It is the rather posh division for the "mildly disturbed." I was placed under the "care" of three neurologists and an internist.

All that I remember of my first day in Queen's Division was lying in bed watching TV. Every program seemed to be directed at me with some thickly disguised hostility, even Shirley Booth's soap opera struck me as a personally menacing thing.

About 6 P.M., in comes Dakin, grinning, with a bunch of yellow flowers and some remarkably talentless crayon drawings that were drawn for my delectation by his two adopted daughters.

Mother marched in, a little Prussian officer in drag.

There was now, quite clearly, something impending of a fearful nature. I sensed this and I scrambled with remarkable agility out of bed and said, "I'm going home right now," and I ran into the closet to get into my clothes.

"Oh no, Son."

"You all will drive me right home or I'll walk."

I got myself dressed with amazing alacrity, all the while shouting abuse at Dakin.

"God damn you and your two adopted children. How dare you give them our family name."

Dakin: "I don't have to sit here and listen to this abuse."

Now fully dressed and totally out of my mind, I charged into the corridor and down to the elevators. I started to enter one, was blocked in this escape effort by a huge young man in hospital uniform. He was blond, I remember, with a beefy, sneering face. I somehow slipped past him into the elevator but he wouldn't let the doors close.

Raging and storming invectives, I rushed back past him to the room where Mother was asking a nurse for smelling salts. Jesus!

Then I lit into her with a vengeance.

"Why do women bring children into the world and then destroy them?"

(I still consider this a rather good question.)

Said Miss Edwina—sincerely?—"I just don't know if we're doing the right thing."

I turned again to the corridor but now the door was obstructed by a wheel-chair with straps and by a goon squad of interns.

Now suddenly I recognized defeat and gave up.

Clutching the flight bag that contained my booze, my pills, my vial of speed, clutching it despairingly and tightly, I was strapped into the chair and rocketed out of Queen's Division to Friggins' Violent Ward—there the flight bag was snatched from me, and at this point I blacked out. . . .

I am in the violent ward of Friggins Division of Barnacle Hospital. I said I had blacked out and so I did—when they snatched my flight bag from me.

Now I am going to tell you as much as I can about my closest brush with death.

After I blacked out, I don't know whether I came to or not.

And I don't know how long the convulsions lasted. I know that there were three of them in one morning and there was the "silent coronary," which is the only thing during the apocalypse that's clear to me, as I felt, through my convulsions, the stabbing pains of it.

I went through a time of total fantasy.

I recall being strapped to a table and wheeled about. But never medicated.

I refuse to ascribe to paranoia my conviction that the resident physician intended to commit legalized murder upon my person and very nearly succeeded.

I had a most extraordinary experience which may or may not have occurred the evening after the convulsions.

I am walking very, very slowly down a corridor toward a lighted room and I am chanting a poem.

The recurrent line of each verse is "Redemption, redemption." And I am performing, as I move slowly down the corridor, a mincing exaggeration of the walk of a drag-queen. What was I chanting about? About the birth of my brother Dakin when I was eight and my first sight of him, suckling the bare breast of my mother in the St. Louis hospital.

Redemption from what? A never-before-spoken sibling rivalry with him, I would suppose. And also a redemption from the "crime" of my love-life with boys and young men. . . .

The truth is that I don't really want to go back over the time in Friggins Division of Barnacle Hospital in the city of St. Pollution. It's all been fairly well taken care of, in a documentary way, in "What's Next on the Agenda, Mr. Williams?"

I shall only recount a few bits omitted from the "poem."

After my convulsions and my indeterminate period of delirium, I woke up in a narrow cubicle in a bed with barred sides like a big baby's crib. And when I say I woke up, I mean my eyes were open and I was experiencing some degree of cogitation but I wasn't really awake for an hour or two, I couldn't have been since I remembered nothing and didn't know where I was.

The realization came upon me like death.

Strange figures passed my open door on a narrow corridor, I couldn't believe they were real. I literally thought I was dreaming.

I don't believe I was visited, perhaps not even brought food, before evening, at least I have no recollection of it.

But in the evening I was outside my cubicle and Dakin was in the "dayroom." He had a sort of triumphant smirk on his face and he bore a copy of *Esquire*, the issue which contained that horror piece of fiction, an article called "A Dream of Tennessee Williams" and his first words to me, beside his grin of greeting and hearty handshake, was the devastating question: "Do you know that you have had a silent coronary? And several convulsions?"

Then he presented me with that issue of *Esquire* and made a grinning departure and I began my desperate effort to hang onto myself in the Violent Ward at Friggins.

In what way was I violent there?

I dutifully came to their atrocious meals and the rest of the time I crouched like a defenseless animal in a corner while the awful pageantry of the days and the nights went on, a continual performance of horror shows, inside and outside my skull.

I intended to survive.

Little mementos of it.

A huge nurse with a great Germanic blond head and a fixed grimace of jubilant authority kept stalking about, arms swinging like a wrestler's before he catches hold of an opponent, oh yes, lovely Miss Rothschild she was, and let me tell you this: I gave that lady no mouth!

Speaking of mouths, there was this fantastically exhibitionist middle-aged queen who paraded about, Miss Rothschild's opposite number, and he was continually arranging his gray hair with his fluttering fingers as he sashayed about and then one day this glowering Irish truck-driver type sprang up and fetched him the most terrible clout in the mouth I've ever witnessed. All of the faggot's front teeth were knocked out as if he'd been struck in the mouth by a sledgehammer. For days, his face was a baboon's ass to look at, the mouth swollen out as far as his nose and its interior a crimson cavern. But this did not diminish his concern with his gray hair, the fingers went on fluttering over the carefully arranged waves.

Then—God help me!—his assailant began to draw a chair up beside mine, in the corner where I crouched, and to stare at me, from time to time, with the same look he had given the Narcissan old queen.

There was the day a young girl with a great head of brilliant red hair was dragged screaming into the ward and thrown into a padded cell and left there screaming all night and when I next saw her, in place of the brilliant and thick head of hair was a mound of bloodstained bandages.

I had begun to ask questions of a young intern who was friendlier than the others and he informed me that the girl had torn all of her hair out while screaming in the padded cell that night, torn it all out by the roots.

I had a few suits in my locker. Dakin had brought them over.

Surreptitiously I searched the pockets and discovered a little cache of "pinkies," about five capsules: I would take one at bedtime to supplement the totally ineffective sleeping medication prescribed by my doctors, who had not yet found time to call on me in the ward.

When these capsules were exhausted I began to spend three and four sleepless nights and days in a row.

Finally there would be a night of such exhaustion that I would sleep an hour.

One night as I was falling asleep—yes, really drifting away—the door flew open upon a young intern who was scarcely describable as friendly.

"My God, what do you want?"

"You didn't turn in your electric shaver at the desk!"

"What of it?"

He snatched the Norelco off the tiny bureau and said, "Patients in this ward are not allowed to keep anything in their rooms that they can hurt themselves with."

I went out into the hall after him and I went up to the night nurse's glassed-in box from which she monitored the inmates.

I pounded on the door. Several nurses and interns gathered and I went into hysteria over the incident just related.

"I was falling asleep, I was really falling asleep after not sleeping four nights and he burst into my room for my electric shaver."

I kept repeating it and I began to sob and the night nurse turned to a woman and she spoke to me gently.

"Go back to your cubicle, your medication may start working again."

It didn't though.

My cubicle was right next to the garbage disposal plant, a huge one, and an hour before first light it would start its grinding thunder and that was the only way I knew when day was approaching, for my watch had also been confiscated since it contained glass and nothing containing glass was permitted to remain in the possession of a patient in that ward.

At first light, a brisk, expressionless nurse with a voice like an automatic drill would charge into the cubicle for an inquisition and the taking of temperature and pulse-rate.

"Bowel-movement yesterday?"

Sometimes I'd give no answers and sometimes I'd groan and cover my face and so my stay in the violent ward was prolonged to a full month—for unco-operative attitudes, I suppose.

In my nature I think that a basic pride of some kind will remain the last thing to go when all else is gone but breath. . . .

The resident physician was very friendly with Dakin and when Dakin came to see me—about once or twice a week—he would chat with him in my presence. He would tell Dakin how I'd had three convulsions in one morning and he told these things with an inflection of pride—as if the convulsions were an accomplishment upon which he congratulated himself.

I had long since read the "Dream of Tennessee Williams" in *Esquire* when one evening a doctor brought me a copy of the issue and said with his evil grin, "I see you've got a very good write-up in here. Want to read it?"

"No, I think not. I've read it."

"Resident physicians are envious of us," said Dr. Levy, "and so they take it out on our patients . . ."

Even in the violent ward, the patients had an hour of occupational therapy in the morning and another in the afternoon.

Each day those whose names had been called as acceptable for O.T. lined up at the elevators. We all had an option of refusal, we could refuse to go down in the elevator for the simplistic occupations that were available to us down there.

Most times I'd decline to go down but then I discovered that I was being monitored badly if I declined. So I started going. I accepted water-colors as the least tedious of the occupations, and for some reason I began to do a water-color of my left hand.

I remember it was just about finished and huge old Dr. Levy came puffing up to me.

"Your little finger isn't that big, Tom."

Did he mean that I still suffered from *folie de grandeur*?

Dr. Levy was the least inhuman of the triumvirate of neurologists and the one who eventually—after I'd survived a month in Violent—transferred me to what is called an "open ward."

What kept me enduring the confinement at Friggins Division were boxes of books sent to me by Andy Brown of the Gotham Book Mart, and the nightly bridge games that occupied the four hours from dinner till lights out, after I'd been transferred to an open ward. There were several excellent female bridge players in the first open ward I went to. I played every night for about four hours. One of the players was a seventy-five-year-old lady who was being put under a relentless series of shock treatments of which she had mortal terror. She would not know until late evening whether or not she was to be subjected again to a shock treatment in the morning. The notice of it would be posted on the door of her cubicle and she would be shattered, trembling and in tears.

After a shock treatment she had difficulty playing bridge. I remember with a warm feeling how we all ignored her memory failures in the card game and how we all comforted her and tried to assuage her panic when she saw that posted notice of a shock treatment scheduled for the next morning.

She had grown sons who dropped in to see her about once a week; why didn't they stop this torture of their old mother? I am just cynical enough to suspect they wanted her "out of the way"—and one of them was a professor at St. Louis University, a Catholic institution.

I am happy to report that some months later in Key West I received a postcard from her that stated that she had been released from Friggins Division and was "back home."

Survival! What an epic capacity of the human heart, young and old!

However dreadful they were at the time of their occurrence, there are incidents and characters whom you recall, at a safe distance, with a shocked amusement. There was, for instance, this great, monolithic black woman who would sit in the center of the dayroom. Whenever I went past her, she would grin at me and say, "You're so sweet, you're a lump of sugar, just a sweet lump of sugar."

Ingenuously, I thought she meant it. And then one day, while delivering this saccharine greeting, she abruptly rose and took a swing at me that would have flattened me on the floor had she not swung off target.

I have incorporated her in my television special *Stopped Rocking*.

Then there were the two very attractive young ladies who had gone on a bad trip on drugs in Istanbul and who could sleep only if they were given, for sleeping medications, the chemical components known to the underworld as a "Mickey Finn." Each night when the sleeping medications were passed out, they would stand up to receive their potions. The moment they had downed them, they would start a mad dash for their cubicles, about twenty-five yards away. And invariably they would collapse to the floor before they reached their doors and would have to be dragged unconscious to bed.

Oh, how I envied those girls! I begged Dr. Levy to let me have the same potion, but he said, "No way."

I was now being permitted to go outside but for at least a month it was only for a walk around the block and I would be followed by a little vehicle from Friggins to make sure that I didn't attempt an escape.

Toward the very end, I was at last allowed to take a cab into downtown Clayton for an hour.

I went straight to a drugstore and bought a nonprescription box of sleeping pills called Nytol.

I found that it blurred my vision so I gave it up.

Then one day, in downtown Clayton, I went into a doctor's office, identified myself as Clemence Otte—the name of a brother of my German grandmother—and said that I was in town for a convention and was unable to sleep and would he please prescribe some Seconal for me.

The doctor insisted upon giving me a physical examination. He noted my cardiac trouble and gave me an EKG. After that he wrote me a prescription for exactly three pinkies . . .

That very same afternoon, when I returned to Friggins, I was summoned to Dr. Levy's office. He announced that I was to be released the next day, after my confinement of three months.

FROM *A LOVELY SUNDAY FOR CREVE COEUR*

SCENE ONE

It is late on a Sunday morning, early June, in St. Louis.

The interior is what was called an efficiency apartment in the period of this play, the middle or late thirties. It is in the West End of St. Louis. Attempts to give the apartment brightness and cheer have gone brilliantly and disastrously wrong, and this wrongness is emphasized by the fiercely yellow glare of light through the oversize windows which look out upon vistas of surrounding apartment buildings, vistas that suggest the paintings of Ben Shahn: the dried-blood horror of lower-middle-class American urban neighborhoods. The second thing which assails our senses is a combination of counting and panting from the bedroom, to the left, where a marginally youthful but attractive woman, Dorothea, is taking "setting-up exercises" with fearful effort.

SOUND: Ninety-one, *ha!*—ninety-two, *ha!*—ninety-three, *ha!*—

ninety-four, *ha!*

This breathless counting continues till one hundred is achieved with a great gasp of deliverance. At some point during the counting, a rather short, plumpish woman, early middle-aged, has entered from the opposite doorway with a copy of the big Sunday St. Louis Post-Dispatch.

The phone rings just as Bodey, who is hard-of-hearing, sits down on a sofa in the middle of the room. Bodey, absorbed in the paper, ignores the ringing phone, but it has caused Dorothea to gasp with emotion so strong that she is physically frozen except for her voice. She catches hold of something for a moment, as if reeling in a storm, then plunges to the bedroom door and rushes out into the living room with a dramatic door-bang.

DOROTHEA: WHY DIDN'T YOU GET THAT PHONE?

BODEY [*rising and going to the kitchenette at the right*]: Where, where, what, what phone?

DOROTHEA: Is there more than one phone here? Are there several other phones I haven't discovered as yet?

BODEY:—Dotty, I think these setting-up exercises get you overexcited, emotional, I mean.

DOROTHEA [*continuing*]: That phone was ringing and I told you when I woke up that I was expecting a phone call from Ralph Ellis who told me he had something very important to tell me and would phone me today before noon.

BODEY: Sure, he had something to tell you but he didn't.

DOROTHEA: Bodey, you are not hearing, or comprehending, what I'm saying at all: Your face is a dead giveaway. I said Ralph Ellis—you've heard me speak of Ralph?

BODEY: Oh, yes, Ralph, you speak continuously of him, that name Ralph Ellis is one I got fixed in my head so I could never forget it.

DOROTHEA: Oh, you mean I'm not permitted to mention the name Ralph Ellis to you?

BODEY [*preparing fried chicken in the kitchenette*]: Dotty, when two girls are sharing a small apartment, naturally each of the girls should feel perfectly free to speak of whatever concerns her. I don't think it's possible for two girls sharing a small apartment *not* to speak of whatever concerns her whenever—whatever—*concerns* her, but, Dotty, I know that I'm not your older sister. However, if I was, I would have a suspicion that you have got a crush on this Ralph Ellis, and as an older sister, I'd feel obliged to advise you to, well, look before you leap in that direction. I mean just don't put all your eggs in one basket till you are one hundred percent convinced that the basket is the right one, that's all I mean. . . . Well, this is a lovely Sunday for a picnic at Creve Coeur. . . . Didn't you notice out at Creve Coeur last Sunday how Buddy's slimmed down round the middle?

DOROTHEA: No, I didn't.

BODEY: Huh?

DOROTHEA: Notice.

BODEY: Well, it was noticeable, Dotty.

DOROTHEA: Bodey, why should I be interested in whatever fractional—fluctuations—occur in your twin brother's waistline—as if it was the Wall Street market and I was a heavy investor?

BODEY: You mean you don't care if Buddy shapes up or not?

DOROTHEA: Shapes up for what?

BODEY: Nacherly for you, Dotty.

DOROTHEA: Does he regard me as an athletic event, the high jump or pole vault? Please, please, Bodey, convince him his shape does not concern me at all.

BODEY: Buddy don't discuss his work with me often, but lately he said his boss at Anheuser-Busch has got an eye on him.

DOROTHEA: How could his boss ignore such a sizeable object?—Bodey, what are you up to in that cute little kitchenette?

BODEY: Honey, I stopped by Piggly-Wiggly's yesterday noon when I got off the streetcar on the way home from the office, and I picked up three beautiful fryers, you know, nice and plump fryers.

DOROTHEA: I'd better remain out here till Ralph calls back, so I can catch it myself. [*She lies on the purple carpet and begins another series of formalized exercises.*]

BODEY: The fryers are sizzling so loud I didn't catch that, Dotty. You know, now that the office lets out at noon Saturday, it's easier to lay in supplies for Sunday. I think that Roosevelt did something for the country when he got us half Saturdays off because it used to be that by the time I got off the streetcar from International Shoe, Piggly-Wiggly's on the corner would be closed, but now it's still wide open. So I went in Piggly-Wiggly's, I went to the meat department and I said to the nice old man, Mr. Butts, the butcher, "Mr. Butts, have you got any real nice fryers?"—"You bet your life!" he said, "I must of been expectin' you to drop in. Feel these nice plump fryers." Mr. Butts always lets me feel his meat. The feel of a piece of meat is the way to test it, but there's very few modern butchers will allow you to feel it. It's the German in me. I got to feel the meat to know it's good. A piece of meat can look good over the counter but to know for sure I always want to feel it. Mr. Butts, being German, he understands that, always says to me, "Feel it, go on, feel it." So I felt the fryers. "Don't they feel good and fresh?" I said, "Yes, Mr. Butts, but will they keep till tomorrow?" "Haven't you got any ice in your icebox?" he asked me. I said to him, "I hope so, but ice goes fast in hot weather. I told the girl that shares my apartment with me to put up the card for a twenty-five pound lump of ice but sometimes she forgets to." Well, thank goodness, this time you didn't forget to. You always got so much on your mind in the morning, civics and—other things at the high school.—What are you laughin' at, Dotty? [*She turns around to glance at Dorothea who is covering her mouth to stifle breathless sounds of laughter.*]

DOROTHEA: Honestly, Bodey, I think you missed your calling. You should be in Congress to deliver a filibuster. I never knew it was possible to talk at such length about ice and a butcher.

BODEY: Well, Dotty, you know we agreed when you moved in here with me that I would take care of the shopping. We've kept good books on expenses. Haven't we kept good books? We've never had any argument over expense or disagreements between us over what I should shop for. —OW!

DOROTHEA: Now what?

BODEY: The skillet spit at me. Some hot grease flew in my face. I'll put bakin' soda on it.

DOROTHEA: So you are really and truly frying chickens in this terrible heat?

BODEY: And boiling eggs, I'm going to make deviled eggs, too. Dotty, what is it? You sound hysterical, Dotty!

DOROTHEA [*half strangled with laughter*]: Which came first, fried chicken or deviled eggs?—I swear to goodness, you do the funniest things. Honestly, Bodey, you are a source of continual astonishment and amusement to me. Now, Bodey, please suspend this culinary frenzy until the phone rings again so you can hear it this time before it stops ringing for me.

BODEY: Dotty, I was right here and that phone was not ringin'. I give you my word that phone was not makin' a sound. It was quiet as a mouse.

DOROTHEA: Why, it was ringing its head off!

BODEY: Dotty, about some things everyone is mistaken, and this is something you are mistaken about. I think your exercises give you a ringing noise in your head. I think they're too strenuous for you, 'specially on Sunday, a day of rest, recreation . . .

DOROTHEA: We are both entitled to separate opinions, Bodey, but I assure you I do not suffer from ringing in my head. That phone was RINGING. And why you did not hear it is simply because you don't have your hearing aid on!

[*The shouting is congruent with the fiercely bright colors of the interior.*]

BODEY: I honestly ain't that deaf. I swear I ain't that deaf, Dotty. The ear specialist says I just got this little calcification, this calcium in my—eardrums. But I do hear a telephone ring, a sharp, loud sound like that, I hear it, I hear it clearly.

DOROTHEA: Well, let's hope Ralph won't imagine I'm out and will call back in a while. But do put your hearing aid in. I don't share your confidence in your hearing a phone ring or a dynamite blast without it, and anyway, Bodey, you must adjust to it, you must get used to it, and after a while, when you're accustomed to it, you won't feel complete without it.

BODEY: —Yes, well—This is the best Sunday yet for a picnic at Creve Coeur . . .

DOROTHEA: That we'll talk about later. Jut put your hearing aid in before I continue with my exercises. Put it in right now so I can see you.

BODEY: You still ain't finished with those exercises?

DOROTHEA: I've done one hundred bends and I did my floor exercises. I just have these bust development exercises and my swivels and—BODEY! PUT YOUR HEARING AID IN!

BODEY: I hear you, honey, I will. I'll put it on right now.

[*She comes into the living room from the kitchenette and picks up the hearing aid and several large artificial flowers from a table. She hastily moves the newspaper from the sofa to a chair behind her, then inserts the device in an ear with an agonized look.*]

DOROTHEA: It can't be that difficult to insert it. Why, from your expression, you could be performing major surgery on yourself!. . . without anesthesia . . .

BODEY: I'm just—not used to it yet. [*She covers the defective ear with an artificial chrysanthemum.*]

DOROTHEA [*in the doorway*]: You keep reminding yourself of it by covering it up with those enormous artificial flowers. Now if you feel you have to do that, why don't you pick out a flower that's suitable to the season? Chrysanthemums are for autumn and this is June.

BODEY: Yes. June. How about this poppy?

DOROTHEA: Well, frankly, dear, that big poppy is tacky.

BODEY:—The tiger lily?

DOROTHEA [*despairing*]: Yes, the tiger lily! Of course, Bodey, the truth of the matter is that your idea of concealing your hearing aid with a big artificial flower is ever so slightly fantastic.

BODEY:—Everybody is sensitive about something . . .

DOROTHEA: But complexes, obsessions must not be cultivated. Well. Back to my exercises. Be sure not to miss the phone.

Ralph is going to call me any minute now. [*She starts to close the bedroom door.*]

BODEY: Dotty?

DOROTHEA: Yes?

BODEY: Dotty, I'm gonna ask Buddy to go to Creve Coeur with us again today for the picnic. That's okay with you, huh?

DOROTHEA [*pausing in the doorway*]: Bodey, Buddy is your brother and I fully understand your attachment to him. He's got many fine things about him. A really solid character and all that. But, Bodey, I think it's unfair to Buddy for you to go on attempting to bring us together because—well, everyone has a type she is attracted to and in the case of Buddy, no matter how much—I appreciate his sterling qualities and all, he simply isn't—[*She has gone into the bedroom and started swiveling her hips.*]

BODEY: Isn't what, Dotty?

DOROTHEA: A type that I can respond to. You know what I mean. In a romantic fashion, honey. And to me—romance is—essential.

BODEY: Oh—but—well, there's other things to consider besides—romance . . .

DOROTHEA [*swiveling her hips as she talks*]: Bodey, can you honestly feel that Buddy and I are exactly right for each other? Somehow I suspect that Buddy would do better looking about for a steady, German-type girl in

South St. Louis—a girl to drink beer with and eat Wiener schnitzel and get fat along with him, not a girl—well, a girl already romantically—pour me a little more coffee?—Thanks.—Why do you keep forgetting the understanding between me and Mr. Ellis? Is that fair to Buddy? To build up his hopes for an inevitable letdown?

[*Dorothea stops her swivels and returns to the living room to get the coffee Bodey has poured for her.*]

BODEY: This Mr. T. Ralph Ellis, well . . .

DOROTHEA: Well, *what*?

BODEY: Nothing except . . .

DOROTHEA: *What*?

BODEY: He might not be as reliable as Buddy—in the long run.

DOROTHEA: What is "the long run," honey?

BODEY: The long run is—*life*.

DOROTHEA: Oh, so that is the long run, the long run is life! With Buddy? Well, then give me the short run, I'm sorry, but I'll take the short run, much less exhausting in the heat of the day and the night!

BODEY: Dotty, I tell you, Dotty, in the long run or the short run I'd place my bet on Buddy, not on a—fly-by-night sort of proposition like this, this—romantic idea you got about a man that mostly you see wrote up in—society pages . . .

DOROTHEA: *That is your misconception!*—Of something about which you are in total ignorance, because I rarely step out of the civics classroom at Blewett without seeing Ralph Ellis a few steps down the corridor, pretending to take a drink at the water cooler on my floor which is two floors up from his office!

BODEY: Not really taking a drink but just pretending? Not a good sign, Dotty—pretending . . .

DOROTHEA: What I mean is—we have to arrange secret little encounters of this sort to avoid gossip at Blewett.

BODEY: —Well—

DOROTHEA: *WHAT*?

BODEY: I never trusted pretending.

DOROTHEA: Then why the paper flowers over the hearing aid, dear?

BODEY: That's—just—a little—sensitivity, there ...

DOROTHEA: Look, you've got to live with it so take off the concealment, the paper tiger lily, and turn the hearing aid up or I will be obliged to finish my hip swivels out here to catch Ralph's telephone call.

BODEY [*as she is turning up the hearing aid, it makes a shrill sound*]: See? See?

DOROTHEA: I think you mean hear, hear! —Turn it down just a bit, find the right level for it!

BODEY: Yes, yes, I—[*She fumbles with the hearing aid, dislodging the paper flower.*]

DOROTHEA: For heaven's sake, let me adjust it for you! [*She rushes over to Bodey and fiddles with the hearing aid.*] Now!—Not shrieking.—But can you hear me? I said can you hear me! At this level!?

BODEY: Yes. Where's my tiger lily?

DOROTHEA: Dropped on the fierce purple carpet. Here. [*She picks it up and hands it to Bodey.*] What's wrong with you?

BODEY: I'm—upset. Over this maybe—dangerous—trust you've got in Ralph Ellis's—intentions . . .

DOROTHEA [*dreamily, eyes going soft*]: I don't like discussing an intimate thing like this but—the last time I went out in Ralph Ellis's Reo, that new sedan he's got called the Flying Cloud . . .

BODEY: Cloud? Flying?

DOROTHEA [*raising her voice to a shout*]: The Reo is advertised as "The Flying Cloud."

BODEY: Oh. Yes. He'd be attracted to that.

DOROTHEA: It was pouring down rain and Art Hill was deserted, no other cars on it but Ralph and I in his Reo. The windows curtained with rain that glistened in the lamplight.

BODEY: Dotty, I hope you're not leading up to something that shouldn't of happened in this Flying Cloud on Art Hill. It really scares me, Dotty . . .

DOROTHEA: Frankly, I was a little frightened myself because we've never had this kind of discussion before, it's rather—difficult for me but you must understand. I've always drawn a strict line with a man till this occasion.

BODEY: Dotty, do you mean—?

DOROTHEA: It was so magical to me, the windows curtained with rain, the soft look in his eyes, the warmth of his breath that's always scented with clove, his fingers touching so gently as he—

BODEY: Dotty, I don't think I want to know any more about this—experience on Art Hill because, because—I got a suspicion, Dotty, that you didn't hold the line with him.

DOROTHEA: The line just—didn't exist when he parked the car and turned and looked at me and I turned and looked at him. Our eyes, our eyes—

BODEY: Your eyes?

DOROTHEA: Burned the line out of existence, like it had never existed!

BODEY: —I'm not gonna tell this to Buddy!

DOROTHEA: You know, I wasn't aware until then that the Reo was equipped with adjustable seats.

BODEY: Seats that—?

DOROTHEA: Adjusted to pressure, yes, reclined beneath me when he pushed a lever.

BODEY [*distracted from the phonebook which she had begun to leaf through*]: —How far did this seat recline beneath you, Dotty?

DOROTHEA: Horizontally, nearly. So gradually though that I didn't know till later, later. Later, not then—the earth was whirling beneath me and the sky was spinning above.

BODEY: Oh-ho, he got you drunk, did he, with a flask of liquor in that Flying Cloud on—

DOROTHEA: Drunk on a single Pink Lady?

BODEY: Pink?

DOROTHEA: Lady. —The mildest sort of cocktail! Made with sloe gin and grenadine.

BODEY: The gin was slow, maybe, but that man is a fast one, seducing a girl with adjustable seats and a flask of liquor in that Flying Cloud on—

DOROTHEA: Not a flask, a cocktail, and not in the Reo but in a small private club called The Onyx, a club so exclusive he had to present an engraved card at the entrance.

BODEY: Oh yes, I know such places!

DOROTHEA: How would you know such places?

BODEY: I seen one at the movies and so did you, at the West End Lyric, the last time you was all broke up from expectin' a call from this Ellis which never came in, so we seen Roy D'Arcy take poor Janet Gaynor to one of them—private clubs to—!

[*Bodey has not found the Blewett number in the phonebook. She dials the operator.*]

Blewett, Blewett, get me the high school named Blewett.

DOROTHEA: Bodey, what are you doing at the phone which I begged you not to use till Ralph has called?

BODEY: Reporting him to Blewett!

DOROTHEA: Bodey, that takes the cake, reporting on the principal of Blewett to Blewett that's closed on Sundays. What a remarkable—

BODEY [*darting about*]: Paper, pen!

DOROTHEA: Now what?

BODEY: A written report to the Board of Education of St. Louis. I tell you, that Board will be interested in all details of how that principal of the school system got you lying down drunk and defenseless in his Flying Cloud in a storm on Art Hill, every advantage taken with Valentino sheik tricks on a innocent teacher of civics just up from Memphis.

DOROTHEA: YOU WILL NOT—

BODEY: DON'T TELL ME NOT!

DOROTHEA: LIBEL THE REPUTATION OF A MAN THAT I LOVE, GAVE MYSELF TO NOT JUST FREELY BUT WITH ABANDON, WITH JOY!

BODEY [*aloud as she writes*]: Board of Education of St. Louis, Missouri. I think you should know that your principal at Blewett used his position to take disgusting advantage of a young teacher employed there by him for that purpose. I know, I got the facts, including the date and—

[*Dorothea snatches up and crumples the letter.*]

My letter, you tore up my—!

DOROTHEA: Bodey, if you had written and mailed that letter, do you know what you'd have obliged me to do? I would be morally obliged to go personally down to the Board of Education and tell them an *opposite* story which happens to be the *true* one: that I *desired* Ralph Ellis, possibly even more than he did me!

[*Bodey buffs and puffs wordlessly till she can speak.*]

BODEY:—Well, God help you, Dotty.—But I give you my word I won't repeat this to Buddy.

DOROTHEA: How does it concern Buddy?

BODEY: It concerns Buddy and me because Buddy's got deep feelings and respect for you, Dotty. He would respect you too much to cross the proper line before you had stood up together in the First Lutheran Church on South Grand.

DOROTHEA: *Now* you *admit* it!

BODEY: It's you that's makin' admissions of a terrible kind that might shock Buddy out of his serious intentions.

DOROTHEA: You are admitting that—

[*As she had threatened, Dorothea has begun doing her hip swivels in the living room, but now she stops and stares indignantly at Bodey.*]

——you've been deliberately planning and plotting to marry me off to your twin brother so that my life would be just one long Creve Coeur picnic, interspersed with knockwurst, sauerkraut—hot potato salad dinners.—Would I be asked to prepare them? Even in summer? I know what you Germans regard as the limits, the boundaries of a woman's life—*Kirche, Küche, und Kinder*—while being asphyxiated gradually by cheap cigars. I'm sorry but the life I design for myself is not along those lines or in those limits. My life must include romance. Without romance in my life, I could no more live than I could without breath. I've got to find a partner in life, or my life will have no meaning. But what I must have and finally do have is an affair of the heart, two hearts, a true consummated romance—yes consummated, I'm not ashamed! [*She gasps and sways.*]

STANLEY ELKIN

THE SON OF A JEWELRY SALESMAN, Stanley Elkin (1930–1995) was born in New York City and raised in Chicago. He began writing fiction while still in elementary school and made this pursuit his life's work. In 1960, after serving in the U.S. Army for two years, Elkin began teaching at Washington University in St. Louis while working on a doctoral dissertation on William Faulkner, which he had started at the University of Illinois before his military stint.

During his thirty-five-year tenure at Washington University, Elkin wrote more than a dozen acclaimed novels and short-story collections, including *Boswell: A Modern Comedy* (1964); *Criers and Kibitzers, Kibitzers and Criers* (1966); *A Bad Man* (1967); *The Dick Gibson Show* (1971); *Searches and Seizures* (1973); *The Franchiser* (1976); *The Living End* (1979); National Book Critics Circle Award–winning *George Mills* (1982); *The Magic Kingdom* (1985); *The MacGuffin* (1991); and *Mrs. Ted Bliss* (1995). Elkin's fiction is known for its biting satire and bleak comic vision, as well as its intricate wordplay and amalgamation of formal and vernacular language. After being diagnosed with multiple sclerosis in 1972, Elkin began to explore the themes of aging, suffering, and illness in his fiction. In a posthumous tribute to Elkin, critic William Grimes remarked, "Although he paid scant attention to plot and incident, his deliberately preposterous fictional situations led him to explore the pain at the heart of the human condition."

In his lifetime, Stanley Elkin was regarded as a lovable curmudgeon by his friends, colleagues, and students. St. Louis loved him and was proud of his achievements, honoring him in 1991 with a star on Delmar Boulevard's Walk of Fame. In the following essay, which first appeared in *Esquire* in 1980, Elkin unabashedly—for Elkin—expresses his appreciation for his adopted city.

WHY I LIVE WHERE I LIVE

Because, to me, it has always looked like what cities are supposed to look like. Like silhouette architecture in funny papers. Moon Mullins's downtown, Krazy Kat's, a warehouse style, a wholesale modality, the furrier's provenance, the jeweler's. Gilt lettering in upper-story windows. And brick from the golden age of brick. Brick so high it could be the dumping ground of brick, stacked as counter on a wondrous roll. And because grand juries seem as if they would meet here, returning true bills, parsing corruption: racketeers whose rackets are old-timey and flagrant and tinged with muscle—teamster stuff, laundry trucks that don't leave the garage, taxis crippled and tampered axles under the trucks that bring the milk, the bread, the paper. Vending-machine brutalities. Soft-drink killings.

And because I'm an American of the vaguely professional class, a tenured academic, the least mobile of men, and you live where they ask you in this business and get maybe two or three solid offers in a working lifetime, and because I've been luckier than most or less brave perhaps and have only received one—two if you count the feeler, pursued half-heartedly on both our parts, from the University of California in Santa Barbara thirteen years ago, and we tried it for a summer and didn't much like it, my wife because it made her nervous to go for bread at eighty miles an hour and me because, as I say, I'm not brave and didn't know if I'd like my friends.

Which is really why I live where I live.

I live in University City, Missouri, a block from the St. Louis city limits. (The city of St. Louis is self-contained as an island, exists in no county, is, in a way, a kind of territory, a sort of D.C., a sort of Canal Zone, gerrymandered as Yugoslavia, its limits fixed years ago, before the fact, staked out, one would guess, by a form of sortilege, a casting, say, of vacant lots, working farms and nineteen miles of the Mississippi River into the equation, the surveyor's sticks and levels and measures doing this tattoo of the possible, of the one-day-could-be, shaping a town like a stomach, stuffing it with ellipses, diagonals, the narrows of neighborhood.) University City is not so much a suburb as St. Louis's logical western addendum. There are over ninety incorporated municipalities surrounding St. Louis, closing it off like manifest destiny, filling it in like some jigsaw of the irrefutable, Mondrian's zones and squares like a budgeted geometry. And I live where I live because of the civilization here.

On the third Tuesday of every month there is a salon at the home of Eli and Lee Robins. The Insight Lady is there (I shall not blow her cover here but can tell you that she is a heroine of song and story, prose and poetry, and, like her husband—you couldn't drag her name from me—the older man and downtown lawyer Albert Lebowitz, a native) putting out her insights like hair or fingernails. Deans are there, chairmen of departments in street clothes. It's all very brilliant.

Eli's spread (both he and his wife are scientists, but the money is Texas) is smaller, I think, than the palace at Versailles but much grander than Madame Récamier's. And because, like me, he is a multiple sclerotic, much of the house is tricked out in the customized hardware of the handicapped, all the expensive gymcrackery of safety: stands of parallel bars like private roads, handles that bloom from the doorways like a steel ivy, cunning chair lifts like an indoor Aspen, Eli's electric cart, Eli's motor pool. We gather on these Third Tuesdays in the smaller of the two living rooms, the library really but with its phones hard by the furniture—I want to sit on the leather chair and call the couch—it could be some plush boiler-room operation. There are discreet files, the latest in dictating equipment, everything state-of-the-art, everything convenient; and for dark reasons I am at home in this house. (I'm crippled too.) And once a month, at the Robinses', I feel free to go public, to clumsy my coffee on the furniture, to crumb the carpet and ash my neighbors as myself. But chiefly to talk. At the top of my voice at the top of my form, vicious, a gossip, clever as a fag, with, to save me, only this: that I am never the hero of my anecdotes but always—I'm crippled too—the fall guy, whiner take all. (On New Year's Eve of 1963, before Eli's disease, before my own, Joan and I were invited to a party at the Robinses'. I had not really known about them, that they lived in a house as big as all outdoors. I had assumed what I assume about everyone I meet, that their backgrounds are the same as mine, that we drive the same cars, get the same mpg, earn the same salaries, and blue is our favorite color. That we're all each other's doppelgängers—how otherwise could we meet in this life?—that we all serve the same conditions, that we share the world like weather. The main party was going on in the larger of the living rooms, a room like a grand salon on an ocean liner, and though there might have been a hundred people in it, I swear to you it looked empty. We left just after midnight, and outside our third-floor walk-up Loop apartment building I kicked dents in the door of our '62 Chevrolet Biscayne. I ripped the ring off the steering wheel. I rent my clothes like an Orthodox. Why not? This was grief, this was grief too. It was years before we went back. When we owned our own home. When disease had collateralized us, when demyelination had doppelgänged us again.)

And this is the point, I think. I live where I live for the odd safety there really is in numbers. Are the crippled as comfortable in Santa Barbara? Could I aspire to Eli Robins's fail-safe gewgaws, his remote-control life, his disease's nifty setup like a model railroader's?

I have been keeping track now since the first Third Tuesday and have never seen the same hors d'oeuvre twice. And that's another thing about St. Louis, about University City. It is the hors d'oeuvre hub and honeypot of the world, its quiche capital. The deli is lousy and the entrees only middling—I mean its steaks and roasts, its chops and chickens—but there are knives, forks, spoons, and stars in its appetizers and something in its soups to float your heart. (It could be the water. Nowhere I have ever been is it softer. In the shower soap comes apart in your hands. It lathers like spindrift, froths and foams like the trick floors of discos. You're clean five to ten minutes sooner than you are in New York or California.)

There is, I think, an appetizer vision, the apéritif heart, something in the soul or character that bumps up hunger without the means or even desire to satisfy it, a teaser temperament—*forshpeiz* forsooth, foreplay forever. All I know is that I love that hour to hour and a half before we go in to dinner (it's no longer Third Tuesday; we're at Martha Rudner's, at the Stangs', the Teitlebaums', the Gasses', the Pepes'), when the patés are passed, the barbecue chicken wings, the plates of pot stickers, the stinging dips and smarting cheeses, all that spicy consubstantiation, the lovely evening's high season of high seasoning, and the talk is general and the gazpacho melts in my mouth. And I live where I live, could be, because I am such a good guest, comfortable in other people's houses as a man in his club and under no obligation to bring wine, flowers, houseplants, the candy gifts and door-prize alms (empty-handed even in a hospital room), taking hospitality for granted as a Greek in an epic, never the first to leave though always the first to leave the dinner table, eschewing tea, coffee, the sugar-silted linen and the sedimental crumbs, no coffee klatcher but the Brandy-and-Soda Kid himself, cordial at cordials and drawn by a drawing room.

Inviting the others, ready to do business, calling "Come here, come here, the fire's still going. Bring your cups. Come where it's comfortable." And I live where I live because they come when I call them—well, what are friends for?—and know things I don't. And because I love to hear Julie Haddad, the Deep Throat of real estate, give the latest market quotation on a neighbor's house, or not *even* a neighbor's, a stranger's, someone the next town over, and Patty Pepe explain the complicated peerage of west-county Jews.

I don't mean gossip in the ordinary sense. There is little hanky-panky where I live. In the twenty years I've lived here only one of my friends has been divorced. No one seems to have affairs. Missouri lust is career-oriented, not sexual. It's one on oneself, not one on one. We want Nobel Prizes, things within Pulitzer's gift, National Book Awards, grants, honors, invitations, hosannas. We talk the ego's bottomless line. Or I do. And I live where I live because there are people who will listen to me speak Self like a challenge dance. Not boasting, understand, not look-Ma-no-hands but something involuntary, reflexive as perspiration, not loose lip, loose *tooth*, worrying away at this sweet-and-sour tooth I have in this city whose specialty is appetizer and whose shape on a map looks like a stomach. I sound awful but it's not what you think.

I haven't seen Bill Gass for a month, say. I bring him out, I draw him forth like a man doing card tricks, I work him close up as a Vegas mechanic, my sleight-of-mouth circumstances and the opening bid of my own poor itinerary in my juggler's distracted jabber. The same with Steve Teitelbaum, John Morris, Howard Nemerov, the same with everybody. (Not boasting, understand. I know where I've been. I need to know where *these* guys are.) All right, it *is* what you think; but win or lose, it clears my air.

And *this* occurs to me. The estimated population of the city of St. Louis on January 1, 1980, was 479,000, that of the metropolitan area, 2,410,628. I've lived here twenty years and have only two friends who work downtown. How many people living in Houston could say the same? Who in greater Omaha could? Who in Chicago? Boston? the Bronx? (Who, for that matter, in St. Louis?) When I moved here in 1960, the city's population was just over 750,000. Urban flight shapes my skyline. It cozies connection and snugs my skyscrapers. It's good, I mean, for the architecture and, the city emptied out, lends a scaled-down look to things. Downtown seems someplace foreign. Or no. *Not* foreign. An American city, but an American city like some Brechtian projection. St. Louis like the City of Mahagonny. And I live where I live because there's nothing beautiful to look at in the store windows.

Because reality looms in them like a loss leader, furniture prole as low company or the circumstances of people on fixed incomes, the fashions dated as nurses' uniforms, a dry-goods sort of town, a hardware one. And I look. I do. Once or twice a month, at night, in the warmer weather, we cruise downtown's empty streets. We park, we window-shop.

Me, most of my friends, we don't dress well. We are barely presentable. And if we're out of the shower ten minutes quicker than New Yorkers, we're out of the bedroom fifteen. We are not laid back. Laid back is studied, sandaled and lightly leathered, capped and cute. It goes with the hairdo. We don't have hairdo. I'm fifty years old and dress like someone on *Bowling for Dollars*, like a guy driving cross-country. Third Tuesdays *and* downtown. The sweet-and-sour heart.

And I live where I live because I am comfortable, because the climate is equable, because the movies come on time but the theater is road show, second company, because the teams are dull but we get all the channels, because there can't be four restaurants in the city that require jackets and ties and there's a $25,000 ceiling on what city employees may earn and I make more than the mayor, the head of the zoo. Because I feel no need to take the paper. Because I feel no need.

And finally because nowhere I have been do so many other people seem to live so well. St. Louis, and University City too, is a city of sealed neighborhoods, gated as railroad crossing, of blocked-off streets and private places, chartered as nation, zoned as meteorological maps, the enclaves and culs-de-sac of stalled weather. Not fortress but subdivision America, everything convenient, stone's-throw as Liechtenstein. My subdivision, Parkview, is separated from Ames Place, the subdivision just west of it, by a walk called the Greenway (I could throw a ball into it, but it's almost a mile by car—the closed-off streets, the wrought-iron gates that are opened on some complicated schedule I have never been able to learn), and, like so many other of the city's private neighborhoods, it is very beautiful. The houses are large. They are brick or stone, two stories or three, with slate roofs, red-tiled, green. Eighty percent of the homes were built between 1906 and 1915 in Gustav Stickley's Craftsman Style. No two are alike, but I have a sense of snowflake disparities, a fraternal-twin aesthetics.

One Third Tuesday a few months back I was telling the Insight Lady's husband that there was nothing I really wanted anymore, that I was just about consumered out. I have a videotape recorder, the TV camera that goes with it, a pool (Parkview looks like something out of *Meet Me in St. Louis*, but we're pooled now as Beverly Hills), quad, the middle-class works. It wasn't time yet to go into the electric golf cart; there was nothing I wanted. Well, maybe *one* thing, but . . . I described plaques I had seen on houses in London where authors had lived. A few weeks later Al brought over a replica of what I'd described. A dark lead slab with raised copper letters:

STANLEY ELKIN
1967–

He drilled holes into the brick for the screws and mounted it on my house.

I'm waiting for Joan. We're going to Bobby's Creole for the barbecue shrimp and then to a movie. I'm sitting on the top stair, next to the railing, at the foot of our walk. Across the street is a triangular park with its honey locusts and tall old pines and oaks. I look toward Pershing at the beautiful homes, seventy-five years old some of them, good as new, better. How lovely, I think. How fortunate we are. Up and down my street, Westgate, the houses make a long gentle convex. Three blocks off, beyond the northern gates, is Delmar Boulevard, a sort of student village, the shops recycled, periodically changed as marquee, head shops where kosher butchers once thrived, the Varsity theater with its 3-D festivals, the Tivoli, which changes its double bill nightly, health food stores and bike shops, record stores, book, boutiques and the co-op grocery, the open-air market, a gallery, Bobby's Creole, where we're going. An odd nostalgia seems to hang over it all, a sawdust chic, grubby and moving. There's a store that sells old movie posters and Blueberry Hill, a pub where the serious dart players go. I lived off Delmar once, as I do now, when it was a ghetto for Orthodox Jews. But one sort of earnestness is not so different from another. Kids', old folks'. I've come a long way from St. Louis. Three or four blocks.

I live where I live. I have a plaque that says so. I wait for my wife and feel fine, within the gates, enjoying for as long as the tenure holds my tucked-in, deck-chair life.

CONSTANCE URDANG

BORN IN NEW YORK CITY, Constance Urdang (1922–1996) published her first poem at age eight in a national children's magazine. Urdang attended the Fieldston School and received a B.A. from Smith College in 1943. During World War II, her work as an army intelligence analyst brought her to Washington, D.C. After the war, Urdang returned to New York to work as an editor with several publishing houses before returning to school and pursuing her own writing on a full-time basis. In 1956, Urdang received her M.F.A. from the University of Iowa Writers' Workshop and married Donald Finkel, another poet included in this volume. The couple moved to St. Louis in 1960, when Finkel took a teaching position at Washington University. The two poets designed the Graduate Writers Program at Washington University, and Urdang served as coordinator for a number of years.

Urdang won many prestigious poetry awards during her lifetime, including the Delmore Schwartz Memorial Poetry Award and a National Endowment for the Arts grant. Also an award-winning fiction writer, Urdang wrote several short novels, the most recent of which was *American Earthquakes* (1988), in which the New Madrid fault plays a significant role. Critics have remarked on Urdang's effective use of a collage technique in her work. In a *St. Louis Post-Dispatch* obituary, Robert W. Duffy wrote, "Urdang found the building stones for her work close at hand. She reported, for example, of an evening at Frank 'n' Helen's restaurant and an arrival at the airport." Elements of the St. Louis landscape are prominent in the following poems.

TO LIVE WITH A LANDSCAPE

1

Take your boulevards, your Locust Street,
Your Chestnut, Pine, your Olive,
Take your Forest Park and Shaw's Garden,
Your avenues that lead past street-corner violence,
Past your West End, past your Limit,
To shabby suburban crime,
Vandalism in the parking-lot,
Abductions from the shopping mall—
Like making the same mistake over and over
On the piano or typewriter keys,
Always hitting the wrong note—
How "very alive, very American"
They are, how chockful of metaphysics,
Hellbent to obliterate the wilderness.

2

Learn to live with sycamores,
Their sad, peeling trunks, scabbed all over
With shabby patches, their enormous leaves
In dingy shades of ochre and dun
Rattling like castanets, their roots
Thick as a man's leg, crawling
Like enormous worms out of the broken pavements,
Continually thrusting themselves up
From pools of shade they make,
Sculpturing the street
With dappled dark and light
As glaucoma, a disease of the eye,
Makes the world more beautiful
With its mysterious rainbows.

3

Already in Iowa the monarchs are emerging,
Signaling with their tawny wings;
In regalia of burnt orange and umber
The spangled imperial procession
Meanders along the democratic roadsides,
Across straight state lines,
Over rivers and artificial lakes
And the loneliness of middle America
On the way to Mexico.
The tiny wind of their passing
Is not even recorded
As a disturbance in the atmosphere.

4

Driving back into the American past,
Homesick for forests, flowers without names, vast savannahs,
Lowlands or mountains teeming with game,
Bluffs crowned with cottonwoods, mudbanks
Where crocodiles might sun themselves;
Finding instead the remains of strange picnics,
Replications of old selves, a cacophony of changes
Like a room crowded with chairs
In which no one can sit, as if history were furniture
Grown splintered and shabby;
Studying a picturesque rustic architecture
To master its splendid abstractions,
Shady verandas and porches,
Or the republican simplicity of a cow.

WAYS OF RETURNING

Returning through the back streets, through alleys so narrow
The walls of the houses part like grass
Leaning backward, their patience demonstrated
By scarred plaster, worm-eaten sills, and,
Thrust through a chalk-blue door,
A clenched brass fist, everything the same
As it was, the sun, boys shooting marbles the same,
The same flies buzzing minarets of garbage, the same fists;
Or skating across the enormous mirrored spaces
Of an airport, in St. Louis or anywhere,
Passing the snack bars, the budget rent-a-car, electronic games,
Seeing the men and women queued up to telephone
To say to someone, to anyone
At the end of the line, Hello, it's me,
I'm back; or, after driving all day long
To come into town at nightfall, the avenues
Festooned with lights, every block so familiar
You catch a glimpse of yourself coming down the street,
Yourself, in a coat you wore then, carrying something
You carried then, or maybe are carrying still.

THE RIVER

Even here we have driven the river underground;
Not because we didn't admire its icy clarity,
Like glass, that scarcely bent the light of the sun;
Or because we didn't want to refresh ourselves
At its bubbling fountain,
Or bathe in it, where it purled over the stones
Singing to itself its endless song;
Not because it didn't water the plain
And carry off our refuse, washing away
The traces of our picnic on the planet;

I have seen it race like a black torrent
Down the steep channel of the street.
I have heard it roaring under the rain,
And searched for it through the dry days, hoping
For a token to show it would return.
But now it is buried under paving stones,
Deep in the rocks from which it sprang.
In the darkness it hisses and mutters, feeling its way
Like a blind man on an unfamiliar street
Tapping his path between strangers.

AT FRANK 'N' HELEN'S

It's Nostalgia Week at Frank 'n' Helen's:
The two cops at the table near the door
Ordering pepperoni pizza have hung up
Their two blue coats, and on their brawny thighs
Their blunt black holsters dream. Under tinsel stars
Left over from Christmas, a party of seven,
Every one a senior citizen,
Is making itself at home. Over baskets
Of steaming fried chicken or shrimp
Carried by waitresses gently perspiring,
Sweethearts and strangers catch one another's eye.

Here, in the odor of down-home hospitality
Dispensed for a price (but reasonable),
America rediscovers itself, all the homely virtues
Displayed in the mirrors behind the booths
Where time has been arrested, and everything
Remains what we recall, as Frank—or Helen—
Dreamed it. Here we are all fed, we can all
Love one another. Let the scarlet hearts
Festoon the ceiling, let the walls leaf out
With mammoth cardboard shamrocks, greener far
Than anything in nature, under the dreaming stars.

JONATHAN RABAN

THE SON OF AN ANGLICAN CLERGYMAN, Jonathan Raban (1942–) was born in Fakenham, Norfolk, England. After receiving his B.A. at the University of Hull in 1963, Raban lectured at several universities in Great Britain and was a visiting lecturer at Smith College in 1972. A prolific journalist and literary critic, Raban had several books to his credit when *Old Glory: An American Voyage* was published in 1981. In this nonfiction memoir, Raban, a lifelong admirer of Mark Twain's *Huckleberry Finn*, chronicles his four-month adventure as an urban Englishman navigating the Mississippi River in a sixteen-foot craft. *Old Glory* garnered several prestigious prizes, including the Thomas Cook Award and the Heinemann Award from the Royal Society of Literature. Raban subsequently published several acclaimed books on travel, including *Coasting: A Private Voyage* (1986); *For Love and Money: A Writing Life, 1969–1989* (1989); *Bad Land: An American Romance* (1996), for which he received the National Book Critics Circle award for nonfiction; and *Passage to Juneau: A Sea and Its Meanings* (1999).

In the following excerpt from *Old Glory*, Raban finds himself in St. Louis's "gaunt" downtown, where he stumbles into a bar and picks up a glamorous woman named Sally, who introduces him to life in Clayton and West St. Louis County.

FROM *OLD GLORY*

MARRIAGE À LA MODE

He had just called his wife long-distance. He had listened to the phone pealing in the empty apartment, counted twelve trills, and hung up. For several minutes he had stayed indecisively in the booth, his head full of numbers. He thought about calling her mother. Then he thought of calling

Jake and Debbie, but he knew that his voice would betray his unreasonable panic. He collected the little pile of quarters which he'd put beside the phone, bought last week's *New Yorker* at the newsstand, and went through to the scaffolded green coffeeshop-cum-bar, where the air was mushy with taped music and there were a dozen or so men looking exactly like himself: all alone, all in business suits that had been worn a day or two too long, all nipping at cocktails which they purchased by showing the number on their room key and signing a card that was beginning to read like the index to a bartender's handbook. 1 *Whiskey Sour.* 1 *Manhattan.* 1 *Vodka Martini.* 1 *Highball* . . . All these men were pretending to read. Some were studying the minutes of meetings whose proceedings they already knew by heart. Others were looking at *Newsweek*, turning its pages backward. Every few moments, someone would glance up, without hope, on the crazy off chance he'd spot a girl in the lobby whom he'd known at college. . . . *Hey, excuse me, but aren't you Cathy Silver?* In these quick, sly twists of the head there were dreams of rescue, of not dining alone, of a miraculous flood of unbuttoned talk in a strange city, and perhaps . . . but then the eyes of the men would drop to their watches. It was already eight-thirty. In ten minutes they would go separately and alone to the restaurant, where each would build a little theater around himself. He would engage the waiter as his audience and do his third-rate vaudeville turn as a regular guy having a darn good time on his ownio.

The man with *The New Yorker* sat at a table a little away from the bar. He had stirred his highball with his purple plastic cocktail stick. He had looked at his watch three times in a quarter of an hour. He had cast the obligatory number of glances at the door. He had turned the pages of his magazine. Considering how things were, he was doing fine.

He thought: If I'd been here a few years back, I would have hunted out a jazz club, a singles bar—anywhere I might have drifted into conversation with a stranger. Now, though, he felt too old for that sort of adventuring. He would be a marked man among the men and women in their twenties, busy with still being young. If they noticed him at all, they would see him as a wrinklie, wearing his pathos on his sleeve. Just that morning he had found himself inspecting his own excrement for traces of blood. No special reason; he had simply come to a point at which it would not have surprised him greatly to learn that he was dying, and his first terminal symptom would be something that he'd notice, more or less idly, one of these days, with a kind of dull recognition, like spotting an unpleasant old acquaintance on the street.

He supposed that if he were someone else, it would be in a mood like this that he would visit a call girl. He had never met a call girl. He believed that the proper thing to do was consult a hotel desk clerk or a cabdriver. After that, he assumed, things sort of took care of themselves. The idea was laughable, though. One, he counted himself as a male fellow traveler with the Women's Movement. Two, he expected that only humiliation could come from such a loveless gymnastic coupling. Three, he was a good deal more terrified of talking to either the desk clerk or the cabdriver than he was of the call girl herself. Four, he had spent the last forty-eight hours in the same pairs of socks and shorts. Q.E.D. Call-girl option closed.

He could try phoning his wife again. On the other hand, he couldn't stand the thought of listening to those long electronic trills, paranoia's own authentic sound; the sound of infidelity and wrecked cars on rainy highways. He looked again at what he had been reading. He had covered the listings of every theater on Broadway. He'd taken in the names of the stars and the belittled, silly plots of all the plays. He never went to New York, and the last time he had been inside a theater was in the 1960s. *Jesus*, he thought; *Jesus*! There must be some part of his mind from which he could take an ironical view of his own self-pity; but he felt that his solitude had paralyzed him as effectively as if he'd had a stroke.

He and I were kinfolks. At least, the copy of *The New Yorker* had been bought by me, and I had been sitting at his table in the coffeeshop bar. The hotel must have held a good three hundred of us, and we were all loosely in the same bag. We were attending a convention, trying to make a sale or just *in transit*, keeping in pointless motion through the hotel's flesh-colored interior, afloat between floors in the glass-walled elevators, checking with the desk for messages that hadn't come through. On these elevator rides we would make a nervous show of conversation.

"You with A.R.T.M.S.?"

"No, I'm on my own."

"I'm with Harmless Radium Testers. Fred Spacks. From Baton Rouge."

"How do you find St. Louis?"

"St. Louis?" Fred Spacks from Baton Rouge looked surprised by the question. He'd quite forgotten that we were actually supposed to be in

St. Louis. "Oh, it's a dump." The words came out in a musical phrase a long semibreve followed by a careless triolet of descending quavers. The phrasing said everything. St. Louis was a place about which one was expected to have no opinion at all; it was just a conveniently central site for everybody's convention. Sure, it was a dump—but it had an airport, hotels, a conference center. So what else do you want? The Taj Mahal, for godsake? The Latin Quarter? Wake up, man: this is *St. Louis*.

I had spent a miserable Sunday. The only people on the streets had been conventioneers, recognizable by the way in which they wandered uncuriously, like well-dressed mental patients on the grounds of a hospital. I had stared at the blank wall of the Tums factory, at the deserted football stadium, at the Old Courthouse. Obediently, as if I had swallowed my dose of Lithium and were following the instructions of the head nurse, I had ridden to the top of the Arch.

The giant feet of the Westward Expansion Memorial Arch stood on a stretch of ground so absurdly desolate that it did induce a momentary glow of good humor. It had been "landscaped." A few million tons of Mississippi mud had been molded into the shape of a rolling hill and valley. Some of this area was covered with flapping sheets of polyurethane. Most of the mud, though, had been coated with some kind of bilious green slime. Its texture was thickly fungoid, its purpose quite inscrutable. A gardener might well have recognized it as the best and latest form of soil nutrient. My own guess was that the city of St. Louis had run out of funds, was unable to plant grass on its artificial hill, and had decided that the only affordable solution was to spray the whole thing with the cheapest and nastiest green paint it could find. The coating might at least deceive a few inattentive passengers in high-altitude jets. At ground level, it gave the impression that the very earth on which St. Louis had been built was grotesquely diseased.

We were cranked up to the top of the Arch in a train of tiny vandalized cars. I was squashed opposite a woman from Sacramento. Since the size of the car forced us to interlock our legs, it seemed natural enough to talk on the bumpy journey up through the dark.

She said: "The Arch is supposed to be to St. Louis what the Eiffel Tower is to Paris." She sounded like a tour guide. We gained another stair in the blackness with a terrific rattle and clank.

"Say that again?"

"The Arch is supposed to be to St. Louis . . ." her voice faltered. "The

Arch is . . ." There was a sniff, and she started again. "The Arch is supposed to be to St. Louis what the Eiffel . . ." But she couldn't manage it. She was helpless with giggles. I tried to say it, and nearly reached the word "Paris" before something broke in my solar plexus. There were five people in the car. By the time we were three-quarters of the way up, we were all trying to get the sentence out and falling, helpless with laughter, into one another's laps. We tried to say it in chorus. I suggested that it might be easier if we sang it. When we reached the top, we were gurgling like maniacs. On the viewing platform, people shrank from contact with anyone from our car, and we in our turn shrank from each other. When I tried to grin at the woman who had started this riot of happy hysteria, she refused to catch my eye.

There was certainly something deeply sobering about the view from the top of the Arch. One had to peer out through tiny windows the size of building blocks. Had they been bigger, the Arch might have turned into the suicide Mecca of the Midwest; but as it was, one would have had difficulty in squeezing a newborn baby through one of these foggy little apertures. Pushing one's face against the glass, one could see all that any human being could reasonably bear of St. Louis: mile after mile of biscuit-colored housing projects, torn-up streets, blackened Victorian factories and the purplish urban scar tissue of vacant lots and pits in the ground. It was The Waste Land. The city succeeded triumphantly in doing what Our Lady of Rivers had totally failed at: it made the Mississippi look puny, an open drain which had taken on the St. Louis colors of rust, soot and rotting brick.

Beside me, the conventioneers were identifying another city altogether. They were pointing out the fine new home stadium of the Cardinals, Stouffers Riverside Towers, the tall glass office buildings. To me, though, the isolated sprouts of life in the surrounding blight were just objects of pathos: a few wan geraniums planted on a garbage dump don't make a garden.

The Arch that we were standing in was quite the weirdest of these forlorn gestures of renewal. Eero Saarinen's huge glittering loop might justifiably have been raised as the crowning splendor of some modernist utopia. Set over St. Louis, linking nothing with nothing, rooted in its own bizarre wilderness of green mud, it looked to me like an expensive practical joke.

Down on the ground again, I watched the flag on the courthouse dome flying in reflection on the cold green mirror slab of the Equitable Life building. Life didn't feel equitable at all, and the Old Glory seemed to have a sarcastic emphasis built into the word *old*. The flag, magnified by the glass, snapped and juddered on its pole. Many stories below, the image of a slack-faced man stared back at me. He carried a *New Yorker*.

"Sir? Mister? Please excuse me. . . ."

The man in the glass turned. He had been joined by a portly Indian who looked as displaced as he felt himself. The Indian had a checked woolen scarf wound around his throat and wore an old, heavy camel overcoat. Since the actual temperature was close to sixty degrees, the weather for which the Indian had dressed himself was the special, metaphysical iciness of the city. It had made me shiver too, and I thought how sensible the man had been to wrap himself up against it.

"Please—I am looking for *downtown*."

"So was I. I'm afraid that this is it."

"*This* is downtown?"

"It seems like it."

"Good gracious," he said, with admirable mildness. We held a one minute silence of appalled wonder at this fact.

"I am looking for Chinese restaurant."

So gaunt was St. Louis that I did remember exactly where I had seen a grubby chop suey joint earlier that afternoon. It was three blocks away, and I said I would take him to it. His loneliness broke like a bubble in a sudden cascade of words. Had I seen Richard Nixon interviewed by David Frost on the TV? Frost came from England, yes? Very good man. Very good. He himself had visited London. Very good city. Did I know the Balls Pond Road? I did? What an amazing coincidence! He had spent one month in the Balls Pond Road. Most convenient for the buses. He had a cousin in Ealing. He was an electrical engineer. No, not the cousin; he . . . *himself*—and the Indian touched his throat as if he half-expected to find that St. Louis had rendered him an immaterial ghost.

I had assumed that he must have arranged to meet someone at the Chinese restaurant, but it turned out that he was going to eat alone. He had fixed on the notion of a Chinese restaurant—any Chinese restaurant—quite arbitrarily. He simply needed a destination, however contrived, to keep what was left of his identity intact. He pressed me to stay with him. I invented an appointment elsewhere. I thought that we might all too easily drive each other to tears.

Once in every half dozen carefully rationed visits, I would find a message for me at the hotel desk. They all seemed to be in code. They said things like TUESDAY 8:15 FXTN . . . KFUO . . . WPTZ . . . KHRB . . . The unpronounceable clusters of initials sounded like business conventions, but if one applied the right sort of acid to them, or held them in front of a fire, they revealed themselves as local radio stations where I was supposed to go and talk to disc jockeys in two-minute intervals between pop records, Lutheran hymns and ads for laxatives and pre-owned autos. As hungry for talk as the Indian, I treasured these abbreviated opportunities for conversation. I hogged the microphone. In crappy single rooms over the tops of Laundromats, in wooden huts on the outskirts of junior-college campuses, in dark closets at the back of churches, I set off on a gibbering trail of free association. I liked the cab rides down long wet boulevards that took me to these assignations; I liked talking to the receptionists at the studios. When I had no radio station to go to, I had no society; and between trips I sat blankly in the coffee shop, an unperson, turning pages backward and sneaking glances at the door. Then another strange conjunction of consonants would turn up and I'd come temporarily to life again.

In one dawn raid on a gospel station, the black cabdriver said, "So, how do you like this city, man?"

"Not very much, I'm afraid; at least, not yet, anyway."

"Not much, huh? Well, I'm telling you: don't you ever go over the river to *East* St. Louis. St. Louis is bad, but East St. Louis . . . they ain't people over there; they is *animals*."

When I had hailed him on the street, he was deep in a newspaper. He passed it over to me. The *Evening Whirl.*

"You can scare the shit out of yourself with that *Whirl.* What they print in that paper is the truth. That's the one paper in this city where they don't tell no lies."

It was smudgily printed on the cheapest sort of paper. Its headline read: HOMICIDE DECLARES WAR ON KILLERS AND ARRESTS 9 IN 3 DAYS. Beneath it was a row of mug shots of local murderers, all of them black. The news stories were written up in hot boogie-woogie prose:

> This is strong and wrong, this act of brutality and mortality. Bloodthirsty Catullus Eugene Blackwater, 28, carried out his plan to murder his friend Larry Brown, 23, of 9375 Wells, in his rave and crave to see human blood flow . . .

> Sex fiends and fools are on the rampant cornering, grabbing and ravishing women nightly . . .

> Hugh Saustell, 25, tried to escape from City Hospital No. 1, but a federal agent saw him, leveled a gun on his head and said, "Ho! Lo! Quit it!" as Hugh was running. He yielded to avoid gunsmoke that would have filled his body with lead.

The inside pages were full of advertisements for clairvoyants and wizards. HAS SOMEONE PUT A HEX, A SPELL, A VOODOO ON YOU? CONSULT: THE MAN WHO KNOWS.

We were deep in the South Side of the city, at the heart of *Whirl* country. Looking out at this battlefield of garbage, ruined streets and housing projects, I was tempted to believe that the awfulness of the place could be accounted for only in terms of hexes and spells.

"You ever hear of Pruitt Igoe?" the cabdriver asked. "That was right there. It got so bad, that place, they had to dynamite it out. Bang!" clapped his hands happily over the top of the steering wheel. "That was something else."

> WHY did Vitalis Pitts Brown, 27, of 6024 W.N. Market, deem it absolutely essential, entirely necessary and a duty to shoot down Cleophus Threlkeld, 41, of 512 E. Linton? He did it.

> WHY does Lafayette Williams, 28, of 4317 N. Market, deal in so much stolen property and loot? Police will get you yet, boy. Beware.

> WHY did Cassius Parker, 33, of 4916 Arlington, shoot at Larry Manning, 26, so many times in an effort to kill him at 6953 Plymouth? All of your bullets went astray. Don't be surprised if Larry kills you Nov. 4, 1979.

> WHY is Ella Sullivan, 45, making things so good to Mr. Horace Jones in her Brown Skinned Beauty Salon at 7423 N. Grand that police had to arrest him for getting so excited and crying like a baby wolf?

Twenty minutes later I had an answer, of a kind, to all these questions. We had left the city behind and arrived at the wooded campus of a religious college with its own radio station on the grounds. The receptionist was knitting at her desk, a stout woman in her fifties with frizzy hair and bifocals. She immediately started to talk about murder. Two women students had been killed on the campus. One had been out jogging, one returning from the college Laundromat. Both had been raped, then knifed.

"I walk in fear of my own shadow," the receptionist said. "One in every four women is a target for rape. You don't have to be young or pretty."

She feared downtown St. Louis even more than she feared the campus. She hadn't been into the city in two years. It was now just a place that she read about in the newspapers, a lurid theater of slayings, stabbings, holdups and rapes.

"You know why we got all this now?"

It was the question on which whole conventions of sociologists and criminologists get wrecked, but the receptionist had the light of salvation dancing behind her glasses.

"It's nutrition. I'm a believer in the nutrition theory. It's fast food. The junk they raise kids up on now, it's doing things to their brains. It's changing the molecular structure of the human brain! I've been reading up on the evidence. They got me convinced, those scientists. You look at the statistics. Did they have crime like this before dogs and burgers and French-fries and high cholesterol? They've done analysis on what rapists *eat*. Junk food! They got these concentrations of it in the *body*. I mean to tell you, it's like passing gas into the head. They go crazy on it, and then they go out and do these terrible things. . . ."

My face must have given me away.

"That's a scientific theory. That's not what I say, that's what scientists all over America are saying: it's in the *diet*."

I saw Cassius Parker, 33, with his .357 Magnum, his stomach distended with a mess of chewed burger, frozen pizza, tacos, ketchup, mustard, French-fries, buns and relishes.

REV. MOTHER TAYLOR
Guarantees Help in 6 Hours

> Got bad luck, voodoo? Do you have a hex on you? Do you have a pain in your body and the doctors say there is nothing wrong with you? Do you want your loved one or sweetheart back? Do you suffer from lack

of money? Do you want to win in everything that you do? Do you have drinking problems? Did your husband or wife leave you and you did not know why? One letter will convince you that Mother Taylor can help you.

The studio receptionist and the witches who advertised in the *Whirl* were on exactly the same path. They lived in a society so baffling and so bad that only magic could explain it. Mother Taylor sold bottles of "blessed oil" to cure the ills of St. Louis. The receptionist had bought her "nutrition theory," complete with its okay status words like *evidence, statistics, analysis, molecular.* What kind of city was this, where people had been reduced to the practice of helpless witchcraft?

Having no one else to call up on the phone, the man dialed Room Service. Asked to identify himself, at first he couldn't remember who he was, then saw that his number was on his telephone. He read it off into the mouthpiece. It was way up in the 1800s; probably the date of some battle in the Crimean War. At least it gave him what the hotel no doubt regarded as a privileged view. From his window he could see six clogged freeways, a line of giant electricity pylons, and the bald, oily levee at the edge of the river. The blue-brick factories below had names in scabbed lettering which meant nothing to him: CRUNDEN MARTIN, NOOTER BOILERMAKERS, CORNELL SEED COMPANY, PEABODY COAL. On the flight that had brought him here, the words of an old Judy Garland song had been going around in his head like a repeating loop of tape. They contained more or less all he had ever known of the city.

Meet me in St. Louis, Louie,
Meet me at the Fair.
Don't tell me the lights are shining
Anyplace but there.

Yet in St. Louis itself, even its own song didn't work. Everyone called it *Lewis*, not *Louie*, and the grinding off-rhyme had been annoying the man since his arrival. He'd searched his head for a better-sounding alternative, but all he'd come up with so far was *Meet me in St. Louis, do, Miss*, which made the words read as if they were addressed to the call girl whom he didn't dare call. He sat aggrievedly by the phone, staring at his fingernails and waiting for the daiquiri that he didn't want. What the hell. *Suez? Who is? Where the zoo is?*

He was, perhaps mercifully, ignorant of one important fact. In this city of desperate magical remedies, he had himself been set up as one of the saviors of St. Louis. He and all the other solitary men in their hotel rooms were supposed to be revitalizing downtown. Almost all native St. Louisans who could afford to had left the city long ago, moving west to Forest Park, Clayton, Ladue and the other suburbs out "in the county" where the tax base was rich, schools were good and trees grew thickly on every street. The city, stripped of all but its very poorest residents, was trying to bring itself back to life with passing tourists, conventioneers, the Saturday ball-game trade, visiting electricians from India, and me.

The city had "rehabilitated" La Clede's Landing for us, installing fake gas lamps on the cobbled streets of wine bars, gift shops and novelty restaurants where we could do inspiriting things like "eat in the authentic atmosphere of an old-time political convention"—rooting for Calvin Coolidge over our Delmonico steaks and swinging to Herbert Hoover with our ice cream. It had built the giant ribbed shell of the Busch Stadium and the great Convention Center on the corner of Seventh and Martin Luther King. The hotels in which we were adrift were part of the plan, and so was the Gateway Arch.

The plan, so far as I could perceive it, struck me as crazy. It seemed on much the same level as Nutrition Theory and Mother Taylor's Blessed Oil. Our gang of well-heeled transients was likely to bring only more miseries to the city. Temporarily uprooted, unfamilied, not even knowing each other, we were hopeless material for citizenship. We didn't know which streets were safe and which weren't. With time and money heavy on our hands, we were natural bait for every crook in town. The only industries that really flourished on our presence were crime and prostitution.

I could see no sense in it at all. Baffled, I went to police headquarters and talked to a captain there.

"It's just like chickens and chicken hawks," he said. "How can you tell a guy who comes to a convention with his wife that if he goes north of the Convention Center he's taking his life in his hands?"

"How far north does he have to go?"

"One block. Then you're in the rat run. It belongs to the hoods. You can't police it. The guys can disappear into any door. They just have to say the cops are on their tail, and the door will open for them and it's 'Here, hide under the bed.' They got it made."

The conventions provided a game reserve which the natives treated as a free larder. We made easy pickings. Better still, we didn't stay in town to give evidence against our attackers on the rare occasions when they were caught. The year before, a dancer in the Bolshoi Ballet had been raped.

"We got the guy. We got a signed confession out of him. And he's walking free out there right now. Where was the girl when his case came up and we needed her to give evidence?"

"Moscow?"

"Well the one place she wasn't was St. Louis. It's the same all over. Guy has his wallet snatched, gets beat over the head, lands in City Hospital, and goes home to Washington State or someplace. We catch the thief. But by the time the case comes up, the guy's saying to himself, 'Hell, what was a hundred dollars and a headache?' He's not going to come back to St. Louis to testify. This is the last goddamn city in the world that he wants to make another visit to."

The captain's reasonable pessimism was lightened by one fact. Around Lafayette Square, on the South Side of the city, there was a cluster of airy brick Victorian houses. Many were in ruins, without windows and roofs; cheap to buy, expensive to knock into any sort of livable shape. Since the gasoline crisis, a lot of young couples moved in from the county to the Lafayette Square district. While they were rebuilding their wrecked houses, they had had to mount twenty-four-hour guards on them. What was restored one day tended to be stolen or desecrated the next night.

"You need a lot of courage to move into Lafayette Square," the captain said. "It could be a nightmare if you've got kids to worry about, but these folks are mostly too young for that. I admire their guts and I kind of feel relieved that nobody in my family's tried it.

These middle-class pioneers had not, at first, been much helped by the police.

"Again and again I was hearing the same line. My cops had been out on an attack or a burglary around Lafayette Square; all they'd said was 'This wouldn't happen to you if you lived out in the county.' I told them, that's the dumbest thing they can say. We need people to stay in the city. We need them to make the tax base bigger. Then we can have more cops, better schools, everything. I tell my guys, 'It's that tax base that's paying your salary, so *listen* to these people. Keep them in the city. If they want protection, give them protection. If they want foot patrols or canine, give 'em foot patrols, give 'em canine.'"

"So if this goes on, how long d'you think it'll take to make the city habitable again?"

"Well . . . if they raised the price of gas to ten dollars a gallon . . . if they gave me another thousand men . . . if . . ." He laughed. "I don't know. Ten years. Maybe. With a big thick lucky streak thrown in."

"Or magic. . . ." I told him about the other potions and theories that were being peddled around his city.

"Yeah. I reckon we ought to send out for a case of that Mother What's'ername's Oil. You know something? Next year, we got a national police convention coming up in St. Louis. I got to do a lot of the organization on that. You know what kind of convention brings more hookers into town than any other? Police conventions. That's the kind of cleft stick I have to live in here in this office."

Or Magic.

MADAM LORAINE
Frank Johnson Speaks

I had bad luck. Everything I did went wrong for me. I felt I had a curse or a spell on me from my enemies because they wanted me to suffer or keep me down. They wanted to put me in an insane asylum or have me go on the operating table. The devil's powers really had me. I went to Madam Loraine. She destroyed the evil curse forever. Now I am successful. I have good luck. She took me out of darkness and brought me to the road of happiness and prosperity in life. Bless God for Madam Loraine. I feel like shouting it to the world.

Do not lose hope. Madam Loraine guarantees to make you well and happy again. Come to Madam Loraine and she will remove the hex or curse from you. She will use her God gifted psychic power to find your lost articles. What you see with your eyes, your heart will believe. Madam Loraine is St. Louis' greatest. 7208 Chippewa - 555-9717

I escaped a consultation with Madam Loraine by a hair's breadth. Somewhere in the deranged alphabet of local radio stations I met a woman who asked me what I was doing for dinner that evening.

Her first word when she arrived was "Plus—" Sally lived in the middle of sentences to which she was making constant additions. She began with afterthoughts.

"Plus I had to stop for gas, which is why I'm late. Plus, I was late anyway."

Her long fur coat looked as if she made a habit of going swimming in it. Her pale hair was making a successful jailbreak from the pins that she had jammed into it. She hadn't yet removed the price tag from the neck of her scarlet cocktail dress.

"Plus . . . I don't know. Oh, hell, just give me what you're drinking, huh? What *are* you drinking?"

"Martini."

"*I hate* Martinis. Yeah. Okay. No, that's what I want. I'd like a Martini."

She brought with her a buzz of static electricity. Tense, slender, she was all sparks and crackling filaments. Thinking, she scrunched her narrow face as thoughts escaped from her in dozens like her unruly hair. Most of what I got was just the spin-offs and industrial waste of this complicated process. Scrunching, she said, "God! . . . like . . . because . . ." and her hand slapped at the air as if she'd seen a blowfly overhead. ". . . kind of . . . well, *you* know . . . right?" Somewhere in the dots between the words lay a whole succession of rejected ideas. It was hard to tell whether they were of the order of grocery lists or of Einstein's relativity theory.

We ate at Anthony's. The big, half-empty restaurant was unnaturally dark; its napery, by fitful candlelight, was unnaturally white. The waiter, insofar as I could clearly see his face, was Henry Kissinger.

"You're not into *cars*—" Sally said, turning on me in a sudden bristle of angry boredom.

"No, not at all." I felt stung.

"God."

"Why?"

"What? Oh . . . I dunno. Yeah. I remembered. Sorry. No, the last guy I dated here, he was into cars. You know what the conversation was? He was going on about *car washes*. I was pretty well switched off, not listening; then he leans over the table and says in this, like, *intimate* voice, 'Which part do you like best? The washing or the waxing?' That was our conversation, for godsake. I went into hiding in the powder room. God, he was a drag."

"Which part *do* you like best—the washing or the waxing?"

"Have you seen my car? I don't wash it. I hate car washes, period." She gave a dismissive, ponylike shake of her head. Pins tinkled on the plates below.

Sally's voice had kept the dry, sandy tone of the Midwest, but it was a voice that had been places. She'd gone to college first in Philadelphia, then on the West Coast. She spent weekends in New York. Her $220-a-week job in her hometown was a stopover between planes, and she was fizzing with impatience at St. Louis. Technically speaking, she was twenty-seven, but she managed to slip, at almost every sentence end, from being seventeen to thirty-four and back again. She liked to keep things fluid. The rush and scatter of her talk left me limping behind, feeling elderly and slow.

"*God*, no—that wasn't on the kib*butz*; this was in the Chinese restaurant in San Fran*cisco* . . ."

In leaps and swoops, we covered the world. I learned how she'd broken with her last "guy" six months before, how she'd rowed with her Catholic boss that morning, how she'd backpacked through France and Italy, how she hated going into bars alone, how she got "dizzy" on wine, how her mother was having difficulty selling luncheon tickets for the forthcoming visit of Isaac Bashevis Singer to the local Hadassah. Just occasionally, I found a couple of bits of the scrambled jigsaw that did fit together.

When I lit her cigarette for her over the cheese board, she cupped her hand around mine to steady the flame. Two days later, following the tracks of several hundred thousand St. Louisans before me, I moved west; into Sally's apartment in Clayton.

It was a magical transformation. Seen from this new angle, from out "in the county," St. Louis was changed as effectively as if a wand had been waved over it. I, too. Repatriated to domestic life, I took to it with the gratitude of a shipwrecked man rescued from a desert island.

In Clayton, estates of half-timbered Tudor houses, gloomy with conifers, stood behind tall wrought-iron gates. As streets in Clayton went, our own street was mean and ordinary; a long avenue of rippling leaves and gabled villas. Women in our neighborhood went shopping in little British sports cars. The neighborhood laundry sold spray cans of Mace for blinding rapists and muggers—the one reminder that another, nastier world lay just a few miles off beyond the trees, that our own safe green exile might come under attack one day. Our country lanes, broad lawns and leaded windows had the special preciousness of things we'd won against the odds from the ugly city at the wrong end of the highway.

Sally's three-room apartment was a little out of phase with Clayton. It didn't feel precious. It had the temporary air of a motel cabin from which she was about to move out at any moment. Nothing in the place looked as if she had deliberately chosen it. Her possessions seemed to have happened to her by accident. There were a foot-high replica of Rodin's *Thinker*, a Buddha, an African girl in fake ebony, a mildly repulsive wall clock made of petrified wood from Arizona, some tired potted plants with candy-striped bows tied around their necks, a glass cylinder of heart-shaped candies. She had papered the walls of kitchen with a design, terrifying in the early mornings, of black on a blood-colored ground. She said that she'd thought "it looked kind of cute," but the emphasis was on the past tense. I wondered whether she had been given the other objects in her life, or whether, like wallpaper, they were all the results of some long-ago passing impulse, tolerated now because Sally had ceased to notice them. I wondered, with a premonitory spasm of disquiet, where I fitted in. Was I kin to the Buddha, the wall clock and the potted plants? I half-suspected so, and rather warmed to them.

The bookshelf in her living room didn't give much away, either. *The Amy Vanderbilt Complete Book of Etiquette* stood at one end; Joseph Heller's *Good as Gold* at the other. In the middle, *The World According to Garp* had *The Shikse's Guide to Jewish Men* as its next-door neighbor.

"You want to put a record on?"

I went through the rack. Most of the records there had been put back in the wrong sleeves. Dave Brubeck had landed inside Folk Songs from Israel, Miles Davis inside Dave Brubeck. No detective searching her apartment could have fingered Sally on this sort of evidence. She had contrived to keep herself to herself and all her options open.

Sally had embraced the adventitious as a sort of moral good, and it enabled us to improvise an instant common life. Within twenty-four hours, we fell into a routine that felt as set as if we'd been following it for years.

Each morning, the alarm went off at some dreadful time in the dark. Sally, trailing around the apartment in blouse and panty hose, would lose things—keys, bras, tape cassettes, skirts—and I would retrieve them for her. I burned the coffee and listened to the tinny squawking of the radio. At 6 A.M., the announcer sounded quite mad, his tidbits of news like the delusions of a fever victim.

"Scientists at New Mexico State University have recovered twenty-nine particles of antimatter from the upper atmosphere. Balloons were used for the ascent, and the particles were found at a height of 120,000 feet. This proves . . ."

"What the hell is a particle of antimatter?"

"I dunno. You seen my other shoe anyplace? I guess it's kind of like . . . Oh, God . . . my goddamn shoe."

At six thirty, we joined the slow shunt of suburban traffic down Route 40 in Sally's blue Volkswagen, our headlights slowly paling in the grubby half-light. On the final, looping stretch of elevated section, we'd see the Arch, an ellipse of tarnished silver framed between factory walls.

"You know," Sally said, "I *like* it. It gives me a kick to see it's still there every morning."

I was taken aback to realize that, as a resident of Clayton, looking in on the city from my fastness in the suburbs, I liked the Arch too.

Sally worked in a shiny black skyscraper. Outside it, we kissed decorously, I moved into the driver's seat, Sally was lost behind the uniformed doorman, and I joined all the other wives and homemakers who made up the convoy of cars returning to Clayton, Ladue, University City, Westwood, Richmond Heights and Frontenac.

I liked being a housewife. I didn't want my consciousness raised. I was sluttish over the morning's *Post-Dispatch*. I scribbled letters to friends on Sally's monogrammed notepaper. I dusted the Buddha, watered the potted plants and made a show of pushing the vacuum cleaner around the carpets. At ten, Sally would telephone from her office, and I'd hang on the details of her working day. She had an interview to do, a script to write, a tape to edit, a press conference to attend. I was appalled that anyone should have been able to buy Sally's electric busyness for $220 a week; I could hear her over the phone, being four people at once and trying to be a fifth to me.

I drove to our local supermarket, and came back with groceries in brown paper bags. I pored over Sally's only cookbook, a mint copy of *The Jewish Gourmet,* I worried a lot about how to make soufflés rise. In the cupboard under the sink I found a hoard of strange machinery. There were electric mixers, whisks, choppers, slicers, graters, mincers, dicers—all still in the plastic cases in which they'd been packed at the factory. I fitted a plug to one of these objects, and succeeded in turning half a dozen egg whites into snow.

"God," said Sally. "What's *that*?"

"White of egg. Where did you get all this stuff? Don't you ever use it?"

"Oh . . . they were gifts."

"They must have cost a fortune."

"I hate to cook. Like, I can boil eggs, you know—"

By afternoon, I would sometimes remember why I was supposed to be in St. Louis. I went to the Museum of Art, where there were river paintings by George Caleb Bingham: *Jolly Flatboatmen in Port, Raftsmen Playing Cards* and *The Wood Boat*. I stood, rapt and critical in front of the pictures. Once I had used Bingham as raw material for a dream of the Mississippi. Now I was able to match his river against mine on something close to equal terms. He had exactly caught the way the current twitched and folded over on itself, the leaden sheen of the water and the ruffled lights of the wind on it. I could steer a safe course through his paintings, watching where the river quickened over a submerged sandbar and made a swirling eddy in the crook of a bend. I had seen the faces of the men, too. They were still on the river, in a change of costume. The only picture that struck a really discordant note was *Jolly Flatboatmen in Port*. The surface of its paint was more chipped and cracked than that of the others, as if it had had to make more of a struggle to survive intact. In it, a barge was moored off-channel, by the warehouses of La Clede's Landing; and the St. Louis waterfront was dense with steamboats, skiffs and rafts. I could redraw the whole thing, square inch for square inch. It would show fungoid green mud, broken cobbles and a convention of undertakers discussing (as I had found out) the problems of transportation involved after the mass suicide in Jonestown, Guyana.

When Sally finished work, I collected her from the lobby of her skyscraper looking drained and wan, the exhausted breadwinner. Our route home took us past the front of my old hotel. Who, I wondered, was up in the 1800s now? I guessed he had a copy of *Playboy* instead of *The New Yorker* . . . bourbon on the rocks from Room Service . . . Nooter Boilermakers and Crunden Martin out the window . . . six-o'clock panic with an empty evening ahead . . . my almost-double, the poor guy.

For me, Sally's office was a running soap opera in which I lived vicariously. For the ten miles along the darkening highway, I pestered her for the gossip of the day. I learned the names of her colleagues. Mildred and Bob and Harry and Jean became brilliant two-dimensional characters, with the exaggerated reality of people in *As the World Turns*. Life at the top of the black skyscraper was exciting stuff, with smoldering enmities, clandestine affairs, intrigues, conspiracies and sudden bolts from the blue. I lapped it up.

"So," Sally said, beginning the sad question that all working husbands have to ask all stay-at-home wives, "what did you do, hon?"

"I went to the art museum." I told her about the Binghams. As material for anecdote they were, if anything, a little flatter than my morning journey around the supermarket. In any case, Sally's interest in paintings was scant. Had she ever been made to confront the hoary question of grandmother versus Rembrandt in burning house, she wouldn't have hesitated for a second in putting her foot through the Rembrandt on the way to rescuing the grandmother. There was a framed print of Grant Wood's *American Gothic* propped against the wall by her dressing table, and a meaningless geometric abstract over her bed; and between them they made up as much art as Sally cared to handle in her life. She now lay stretched out in the passenger seat, blowing smoke rings at the sun visor.

"God, I ought to take you around to these friends of my family's. They got this art collection . . . Like, I mean to say, they've got sort of ten Picassos in every bathroom, you know?"

"What happens when the steam gets to them?"

"I dunno. What d'you reckon? Wilt. I guess."

At home, I mixed the drinks. I brought her little bowls of peanuts and raisins. Sally's face was scrunched in thought. Finally she said, "Plus: . . . oh, I dunno."

For days the fall wind, hot and wet, blew down our street like a monsoon. It came in gusts of fifty and sixty miles an hour, shredding the last leaves from the cherries, sycamores and maples. It croaked and chirruped in the metal fronds of the air conditioner. It made stoplights toss on their overhead wires; street signs shuddered on their poles; the knee-high swirl of leaves on every road gave Clayton the appearance of a lake city on stilts. One early morning, I made a detour around Wharf Street to inspect the river. It looked like an enormous fleece, with a single towboat struggling upstream in a caul of spray. If things went on like this, my own boat, locked away, off the river, wouldn't be launched again until the spring. Even without the wind, one could feel the press of coming winter. For the last week, the television ads for snowblowers had been falling thicker and faster between programs. On the day that I had collected my new set of charts for the Lower Mississippi from the Corps of Engineers, I had bought myself an Eskimo's quilted parka. I hid both it and the charts in my suitcase and said nothing of them to Sally.

Our weekends were snug and sociable. It occurred to me that my charts might turn out to be like Ed's old railway timetable in Muscatine; out of date, good for nothing except grist for some fleeting annual fantasy.

Sally took me to the house where Picassos were rumored to be languishing on the bathroom walls. It was near Washington University, a pretty cottage in the St. Louis–Tudor style. From the outside, it looked like the sort of residence a woodcutter in Sussex in the 1540s might have been proud of; inside, it was more suggestive of the private quarters of a Medici prince. The owners were away in Europe, collecting more treasure, but Sally and I were let in by the light-skinned maid.

A Monet, vast and blue, was hung over the chintz sofa in the sitting room; and the walls were checkerboarded with masterpieces. I couldn't take them in. Instead, I found myself looking at the leftover clutter of family life; the open books on tables, overshoes, half-emptied bottles, ashtrays, papers, coats and hats. Beside these ordinary things, the Picassos, Braques, Matisses, Courbets, Duchamps had the alienated splendor of exiled royalty in a seaside boardinghouse.

Embarrassed at finding my eye so numbed, I asked the maid which picture she liked best. She pointed at a big angular Picasso from the 1920s.

"That's my favorite. I like all the straight lines. I ain't so keen on his figures." Like me, she found the paintings themselves difficult to come to terms with. Her face lit with real enthusiasm only when she explained how the house had been wired against burglars. "You know, you only have to touch a window, just light, like that, and the alarm goes off down in the police station? It's *wonderful*!"

In the study, I tried to concentrate on a lovely Courbet sketch.

Sally said: "What's all this worth? A million? Millions?"

"Tens of millions. Hundreds, probably. I don't know. Billions. Trillions. Squillions."

"God," said Sally, "I'm so innocent about that kind of thing," and suddenly hugged me. With my arms around her, I could feel her pulsing and sparking;

it was like embracing a human-sized microchip with all its circuits on Overload. Next to us stood a skeletal Giacometti on a low side table. Its head was on a level with ours. Sally twisted her face around, stared at the sculpture, and looked back at me.

"Hey—do you think I'm too sort of, well, like, *skinny*?"

We went out into the garden. The swimming pool, drained for winter, was soddenly carpeted by dead leaves. Its marble rim was lined with reclining figures: fat ones by Henry Moore, thin ones by Giacometti and Arp. Together they suggested a group of badly out-of-condition old folks at some Californian hydrotherapy clinic. One expected nurses to come from out of the trees and ease them, one by one, into the pool.

That evening we met Sally's father at the St. Louis Club for dinner. Like just about everything else in the city, the club had moved west; it now occupied the fifteenth floor of an office building on a hill in Clayton, where its fumed oak, sporting prints and civic portraits were surreally suspended in their frame of concrete, glass and steel. From the club dining room, the hideous buildings of the central city looked innocuous and pretty. By night, at this height and distance, they looked like a fleet of lighted ships riding at anchor. We were a long, long way away from the St. Louis of gunmen, black magicians and wretched conventioneers.

Sally's father greeted his daughter with a look of deep mock melancholy. He raised his right hand and slowly clenched and unclenched it three times.

"The market's fallen?" Sally said.

"Fifteen points," her father said. "Tomorrow, know what I'm going to do? I'm going to buy some clothes." He encircled her with his arm. "There's a recession on: let's go shopping."

He was a big man with a frost of white hair over a pouchy, humorous face; a wise and wary ironist. I was frightened of his reputation. I'd heard of him before I met Sally, and he'd been described as "the one man in St. Louis who makes Wall Street listen when he talks." He was "sharp as a pistol." In the business aristocracy of the Midwest, Sally's father was a self-made duke. He handled the marriages and divorces of great companies. He was a conjuror with money. He could, so I was told, pull a handful of the stuff through a napkin ring and make it billow out into a fortune.

As he walked through the dining room, his importance was as manifest as the glow of light around a medieval saint. People stopped talking at their tables and nodded gravely to him as he passed. Waiters flew on wings ahead of him. When Sally announced that she was going to the ladies' room, I panicked at the prospect of being left alone with him.

"That one . . ." he said, half-lowering his large eyelids in the direction of Sally's back, "she's bright." It wasn't a father's fond indulgence so much as a neutral, financier's assessment of a stock.

"Yes," I said. "Isn't she. Very bright. Indeed."

I felt that my own rating on this particular question was already beginning to drop through the bottom of the market. I had only one idea I thought might arouse a glimmer of interest in him, and that was borrowed; from Edmund Wilson's *To the Finland Station*. Wilson had described Karl Marx as a man who had made a kind of poetry out of money and its movements. He had been able to apprehend currency as a sensuous object. He might have been a brilliant capitalist had he not felt revulsion for the financial system which, in his writing, he compulsively caressed, half in tenderness, half in hate.

I put the Wilson argument to Sally's father. Yes, he said; that sounded right. Money was something for which it was possible to have an artist's feeling for his medium. There was still for him as much creative excitement in the making of a deal now as he'd had in his twenties. He loved the sense of "swinging from the rafters." He stopped speaking. Something was nagging at him.

"Look," he said. "You take a book, like the one by this Wilson guy. How many copies would they have to print of that, to make a profit? Five thousand? Ten?"

I told him what little I knew of the commercial side of the book trade, fascinated by the way his eyes followed what I was saying. They were Trappist's eyes: serious, peaceful and contemplative.

"This must all seem terribly small beer to you."

"Small? A dollar interests me. Especially if it's a dollar profit."

Sally came back. Her father, swinging from the rafters between dour puritanism and gross excess, made niggardly sips at a glass of Coca-Cola while he lit each new cigarette from the butt of his last.

All through the meal he was courted by young men. They stood deferentially by the table in hound's-tooth jackets, striped ties and tortoiseshell glasses. Sometime . . . if he could spare a moment . . . perhaps . . . they'd appreciate it. One was thinking of buying a television station in Illinois; another had seen that a baseball team in Florida was up for sale.

"*His* family," said Sally of one of these young men, "they've got quite a bit of money, haven't they?" The question struck me as a shade redundant.

Her father sipped, smoked, smiled. "I haven't counted it," he said.

"Do you ever find yourself taking real pratfalls?" I asked.

"Unh-hunh. Something I learned right back at the beginning. You can make any mistake you like; it doesn't matter. Only never make the same mistake twice."

I talked of what seemed to me to be the cruel division between the deep woodiness of the western suburbs and the bald brick of the city ghettoes. I told Sally's father how my first view of St. Louis had been based on the newspaper story about the rapists who had been caught because their victim had seen a tree through a window. He considered the situation from all sides.

"Now, if they'd had the sense to cut that tree down, those guys'd be running free." He laughed. "Next time, I guess they'll pack an axe."

He left on the dot of ten o'clock. He was always in bed by ten thirty: a rule, he said, that he'd never allowed any boom or crash to interfere with.

"You stay on. Sign for all you want."

"Please," I said, "if I may, I'd like to—"

"No," said Sally. "Daddy *loves* to pay."

We went in for Sunday treats: bagels, fresh-squeezed orange juice, the multistoried edifice of the Sunday *New York Times*, its sections scattered around every room. We squabbled over who got to read the Book Review first. We annoyed each other by reading paragraphs of news out loud. Former President Gerald Ford announced that he was definitely not available for the Republican nomination.

"That means he *must* be running," Sally said.

The Shah of Iran arrived in New York from Mexico for a cancer operation.

"Why can't they take his gallbladder out in Mexico, for godsake?"

"You know why the Mexican put his wife on the railroad tracks?"

"Why?"

"Tequila."

"Huh?"

"That's the funniest joke anyone's ever heard in Buffalo, Iowa."

"It doesn't sound funny to me. Is that some kind of hoosier place?"

We visited with Sally's friends, driving downtown to Lafayette Square. It was exactly as the broad Georgian squares of north London must have looked after the Blitz. There were bright little shops on the corners selling hand-sewn quilts and antique bric-a-brac, and London-like wine bars with gardens; but their gaiety was forced and defiant. For every smart "rehab" there was a blind ruin, its oxidized brickwork falling out, and weeds growing through the trash on its floors. In the sacked Victorian streets around the square one could sense the waiting shadows of Catullus Eugene Blackwater, 28, Hugh Saustell, 25, and all the other thugs who hadn't yet been honored by a mention in the *Whirl*.

Yet sprawled, talking, among colored scatter cushions on a floor of varnished pine, slopping wine from a flagon of Gallo into a tumbler, I felt uncannily at home. It wasn't just the bookish run of the conversation; it was St. Louis itself. The city was supposed to belong to the West. The full title of Saarinen's monumental loop was The Westward Expansion Memorial Arch, and the museum below it commemorated the great nineteenth-century drive west beyond the Mississippi; but St. Louis was the least obviously "Western" town I had been in since I'd started my journey. Its architecture had none of the happy eccentricity of places like Muscatine. It didn't go in for fake steamboats and boondocks-Greek. What St. Louis liked was solid Georgian, Queen Anne, Palladian and half-timbered Tudor. It wanted things to be in prim good taste. It would have got on very nicely over the teacups with my Wiltshire aunts.

Old, genteel St. Louis—T. S. Eliot's city—thought of itself as a slice of cultivated Europe. It seemed mystified as to how it had landed here, stranded on the wrong side of the big American river. Sally and I had spent an afternoon in the Forest Park section, drinking draft Bass in the Welsh pub off Kingshighway and rummaging in the bookstores along Euclid Avenue. *Kingshighway. Euclid Avenue*. Between them, the names defined the wistful snobbery of a city that was soft on royalty on the one hand and on the most severe of classical geometers on the other.

"Really . . ." I heard someone say; ". . . *really*," and the voice had more of the throaty Anglophilia of Beacon Hill, Boston, than of the lolloping drawl of the Midwest. The woman next to me mentioned the word "Missour*a*." It was a pronunciation that had often puzzled me. Some people said "Missouri," others "Missoura." I had asked why before. I'd been told that the *a* was a south-of-state ending, that it was a west-of-state ending, that it was rural usage as against the urban *i*. No one really seemed to know. I said this to the woman.

"Oh, no," she said. "It's perfectly simple. New Money says 'Missouri'; Old Money says 'Missoura.'"

Somewhere in our garden there was a snake, but neither Sally nor I heard its giveaway rattle. The gales had died down; the temperature had settled. The carpet in the apartment was left unswept one morning while I laid out my river charts on the floor and plotted mileages. I didn't pack the charts away, and that evening Sally turned over their big pages until she reached a nowhere down in Arkansas. Not speaking, she put *Miles Davis in Concert* on the turntable and sat listening to it through stereo headphones.

"Martini?"

"Uh-uh." Her face made a quick, negative squirm.

In the Jewish country club in Westwood, where all the crockery was heraldically imprinted with a tennis racket crossed with a niblick or a mashie, we eked out a moody supper, overlit by crystal chandeliers. Passing friends of Sally's parents would save us from each other for five minutes at a time; we'd brighten for them, then fall back to listening to the noise of each other's knives and forks. Gloomily, I remembered that I'd been here before, and at the back of my mind I could see the oily gleam of the river opening out.

Next day the phone rang at ten. I picked it up. "Hi!" said a warm, kittenly voice.

"Sally!" I said. A new leaf. "I'm sorry—"

"This is a recorded message from several chiropractors in your neighborhood. . . ."

I slammed the phone back into its cradle. Sally didn't call.

For dinner we drove to the most expensive restaurant in Clayton, hoping that its showy glamour would restore a little of our own lost shine. We were met by a whole ship's crew of waiters in dress uniform: captains, lieutenants, quartermasters, stewards. It took half a dozen senior officers to escort us to a table for two, but when a pop singer came in, the entire company marched and piped him to his seat. Sally took in his black hat with a Mexican brim, his permed, shoulder-length hair, his beads, boots and caftan.

"That's what I *hate* to see—" But I knew that the singer, in his arrogant duds, was just a convenient stand-in for the man at Sally's own table.

We made a solemn, engrossed play of snapping the shells open around the rubbery bodies of our langoustes. *Rubber*, I thought . . . *bumper*; and tried to talk in our old, light way about the bumper stickers that had kept me half alarmed, half entertained on my rides around the freeways of St. Louis.

GOD, GUNS & GUTS MADE AMERICA GREAT.

DON'T GIVE GOD A VACATION:
TAKE HIM WITH YOU WHEN YOU GO.

"I think the best one I ever saw was around Boston in 1973, just after Nixon had dumped Cox as Watergate Special Prosecutor. Practically every car in Cambridge had one. It said, 'Sack the Cox-Sacker.'"

"That's . . . obscene," Sally said, pronging a soggy tomato.

"You're being stupid and prudish."

"Plus, it's not even funny."

"I saw the weather forecast. It's okay. I'll get moving again tomorrow."

"You know? Something I didn't kind of see you as? You're a coward."

Dinner was our Reno. Before the check came, we'd had our divorce.

NTOZAKE SHANGE

BORN PAULETTE WILLIAMS in Trenton, New Jersey, the acclaimed playwright, poet, and novelist Ntozake Shange (1948–) lived from ages eight to thirteen in north St. Louis's Ville neighborhood. Shange's parents were both medical professionals—her father a surgeon at Homer G. Phillips Hospital and her mother a psychiatric social worker. During her formative years in St. Louis, Shange benefitted from growing up in a home that contained an abundance of books and music, and hosted a number of accomplished artists; among her parents' friends were Miles Davis and Charlie Parker, while Chuck Berry was a next-door neighbor. In a 1996 interview in *Gateway Heritage*, Shange called her St. Louis years "a radically defining time in my life."

Shange attended Barnard College and the University of Southern California, where she earned her B.A. and M.A., respectively. She took the Zulu name Ntozake Shange in 1971; the name means "she who comes with her own things, she who walks with lions." She was married to jazz saxophonist David Murray, and jazz has been a constant influence in her works.

Among her numerous works in poetry, fiction, and drama, the best-known are the Broadway hit musical *For Colored Girls Who Have Considered Suicide/When the Rainbow is Enuf* (1976) and the autobiographical novel *Betsey Brown* (1985), which focuses on the St. Louis black community in 1959 and the upheaval caused by court-ordered integration.

In the following excerpt, which is the first chapter of *Betsey Brown*, Shange depicts life in Betsey's home in St. Louis on a typical weekday morning.

FROM *BETSEY BROWN*

The sun hovered behind a pink haze that engulfed all of St. Louis that Indian summer of 1959. The sun was a singular preoccupation with Betsey. She rose with it at least once a week. She'd shake Sharon or Margot outta they beds and run to the back porch on the second floor to watch the horizon set a soft blaze to the city. Their house allowed for innumerable perspectives of the sun. From the terrace off Betsey's room, where she was not 'sposed to stand, she could see the sun catty-cornered over the Victorian houses that dotted the street behind maples and oaks grown way over the roofs of the sleeping families. On her street you could name the families without children in one breath. Why, one reason to live there was cause there were so many children. Only the Blackmans directly cross from Betsey with their pillars and potted dwarf plants didn't like children, which must be why they didn't have any. In the wintertime Mrs. Blackman would come running out in her furs, shouting for everybody to get off her lawn, even though it was the best one for sledding cause there were two slopes. Whatta shame she couldn't understand that. Yet seen from the terrace, when the dawn came in the winter, Mrs. Blackman's dwarfed plants wrapped in shields of ice glistened like rainbows. Betsey never told Mrs. Blackman that. She didn't mention the shadows of the nuns dressing in the convents, either. There was a preciousness to St. Louis at dawn or dusk that was settling to the child in the midst of a city that rankled with poverty, meanness, and shootings Betsey was only vaguely aware of.

The sun and the stairways protected her, gave her a freedom that was short-lived but never failing. Her house sat on a small hill and there were stairs that went to the front door, but you could use the same stairs to go anywhere around the house cause the stairs also led to a porch that went all the way round the side of the house. That's how come nobody could ever tell exactly where Grandma was. She could be anywhere on that porch just watching you do wrong. Then there were the back stairs, only three of them: one, two, three wooden ones, all creaky and needing paint. Underneath those stairs Betsey helped a stray cat have babies. She lined up worms and rocks. She lay flat on her back sometimes, being quiet and unseen, while everybody went looking for her or while everybody was coming up the steps. She heard a lot of secrets lying under the back stairs. Heard a lot of kissing. Now, kissing is hard to hear, but Charlie kissed back there sometimes. Jane and Greer were always kissing. The stairs to the basement were magnificently narrow, like a dungeon the basement was. In the summer it was ever so cool and in the winter it was warm. Betsey didn't know why more of the family didn't covet the basement. Maybe it was on account of the dark and the smell. It smelled funny down there. Jane said that white folks usedta make the colored help sleep down there. Now that Jane would never do, put a Negro in the basement.

But the best stairs were the back stairs that went all the way to the third floor. These stairs turned this way and then that. Why, a body would hide in a cranny on those stairs and never be found. They were dark, too, a blackish wood gainst blackish walls like servants should never see the light of day. Betsey loved the back stairs that led to the littlest porch on the third floor, which Jane never warned her about, cause Jane'd never seen it, Betsey 'sposed. From there, on fall mornings, in her pajamas and overcoat, Betsey watched the dawn come up over the steeple of the church way down Union Boulevard, past Soldan and the YMHA. The bells would cling a holy cling that no one in the house could hear. They used alarm clocks.

So Betsey had fashioned parameters of her own for the house she shared with everyone else. The only real problem was doors. Every room was connected to another room by a door and Jane forbade anyone to lock the doors. The second floor was a pathway of bedrooms with a hallway right next to it. Only Charlie's room wasn't connected to anything and that was because he was in high school. Betsey didn't see what kinda reason that was to have a room that wasn't connected to everybody else's. That's why Betsey liked to be up before everyone else, out on one of her porches, taking in the world all on her own. There she made up stories or just stayed out of the fracas Sharon, Margot, and Allard would be making all the time. Sound traveled uncannily in this house and everybody was always yelling to everybody else. Arguing all the time. Howdy-Doody or American Bandstand, Little Rock or Amos and Andy.

Alone on her balcony, Betsey luxuriated in the quietness, letting her thoughts ramble.

"Speak up Ike, an' 'spress yo'sef," Betsey murmured, remembering yesterday afternoon on Union Boulevard when Willetta and Susan Ann had ripped into each other over that basketball champ with the good hair, Benny. Betsey kept trying to remember how Willetta's bra looked and how Susan Ann had scratched Willetta's face with the longest red nails. She was certain that the black-laced bra and the red nails had something to do with the way Mr. Paul Laurence Dunbar wanted her to say, "Speak up Ike, an' 'spress yo'self." Some sultry willing-to-fight-over-you-if-you-give-me-a-chance way of saying the line. Today Mrs. Mitchell was having the elocution contest for Class 7B, Betsey's class, with the kids from cross the tracks and the kids from the right side of em too. Willetta and Susan Ann had gathered such a crowd round em, tearing at each other that way. And Benny, he just went on to the game gainst Sumner, like he didn't know nothin bout all this blood and swearing and cussing going on in his name. It was evil and wicked to fight, but Betsey wanted the grown woman bit of it to rub off on her today when she said, "Speak up Ike, an' 'spress yo'self."

"I told you, you had to be out of the bathroom in five minutes! What do you think I'm gonna do? Go to school stink on accounta you take so long, Margot," Sharon was screaming round the corner from Betsey's room. How could she become a great anything with all this foolishness going on around her?

"Listen here, heifer. I'm gonna be in that bathroom in three minutes or you never gonna play with my jacks and I'ma tell Jeannie not to speak to you ever again. Do you hear me? Do you *hear* me?"

Sharon was kicking the bathroom door with her saddles making black streaks long the side board when Jane rolled over in her bed to touch Greer, just once more before her hellish day began. Where was Betsey with her coffee? Why was Sharon shouting the devil out in the hall? How could all this be happening to her?

"Sharon, I am going to whip you good, if I hear you call your sister or anybody else a heifer. Do you hear me? Just wait your turn. The boys are finished and you'll have plenty of time." Jane managed to raise her voice, if not her body. Something had to be done with all these children. "Greer, please, let's not have any more children. But can we make a little bitty bit of love?" Jane was tustled in a mass of auburn hair. Somehow her lavender nightgown was entwined in her arms beneath the pillows. She rolled toward her husband, who, as always when in a good mood, grabbed her reddish ringlets and pulled her mouth to his. The answer was yes, a long and sweet yes.

"Betsey, Betsey, where's my coffee?" Jane breathed deep longing for more of her Greer and that caffeine. She could smell the coffee perking downstairs which meant that Mama was up and about, making lunches for all the children. "Betsey, where is my coffee?" Greer nuzzled a little closer and Jane simmered down and was all purr and open. She forgot about coffee.

Betsey wasn't even dressed, and she hadn't gotten her mama's coffee or her lines right yet. She ran like the Holy Ghost down the back stairs to set up Jane's cup and saucer before Grandma had to do it and broke something. "Speak up Ike, an' 'spress yo'self" rambling through her mind, her little girl hips twitched the way she imagined Susan Ann's had after she left Willetta in the street with nothing but her panties on. Not even a ponytail clasp was on that child once Susan Ann was done. Grandma sure enough had the coffee done.

"Seems to me a child could make an effort to take her hardworking mother a teeny ol' cup of coffee," Grandma murmured in her Carolinian drawl. There was a way about Vida that was so lilting yet direct that Betsey sometimes thought her grandma had a bloodline connection to Scarlett O'Hara.

"I'm sorry, Grandma, but I was practicing my elocution."

"You should have practiced your elocution last evening, instead of jumping all that colored double roping with those trashy gals from round the way."

Grandma poured her daughter's coffee, knowing full well what was goin on upstairs. Her daughter didn't have no common sense, that was the problem. Awready there was a house fulla chirren and she wouldn't stop messin' with that Greer. Jane was lucky, Grandma thought. None of the chirren looked like him, all dark and kinky-headed. Now it was true that Betsey had a full mouth. Margot was chocolate brown. Sharon had a head fulla nappy hair. Allard was on the flat-nosed side. But in Grandma's mind Jane had been blessed, cause each of the chirren was sprightly and handsome on a Geechee scale, not them island ones but the Charlestonians who'd been light or white since slavery. But Grandma didn't like to think bout slavery. She was most white. Slaves and alla that had nothing to do with her family, until Jane insisted on bringing this Greer into the family and he kept making family. Lord knows who could help her.

"Here, Betsey, you carry this on up to your mama, and tell her I said that Allard needs to be looked at for the ringworm and Charlie needs a whipping for calling Sharon out of her name and all the lunches are packed, but I do feel a mite weak and need to rest my bones. I do wish she would quit that old job social-workering and mind you chirren more. I surely do."

Betsey took the coffee from Grandma ever so carefully. She was running late. Her teeth weren't even brushed yet and Charlie was in the bathroom for the second time. Mama still didn't have her coffee, and wouldn't have it when she imagined, cause Betsey drank the whole cup by the time she reached the top of the back stairs that twisted this way and that, leaving a girl time to dream of things to come and womanish ways.

When Betsey reached the top of the winding stairs with the empty cup, she quickly swallowed the little bit that had dropped into the saucer and with military precision made an about face, balancing her mother's wedding china in one hand, feigning a fan in the other, whispering, "Speak up Ike, 'spress yo'self." She could hear Charlie and Sharon arguing about how long was the circumference of the world. Margot adding, "As big as your head." Betsey almost dropped the delicate flowered cup rimmed with gold, seemingly atop a throne of its own. Jane was strolling down the hall, shouting the other way, "Betsey, where's my coffee?"

Sharon was trying to comb Margot's head a hair with a brush that looked like it was only big enough for Betsy Wetsy. "I can't help it. It's the only one I could find." Margot was tying Allard's shoes as he looked around the ceilings for shadows where the spooks that swept down on him in his dreams must live. "I know they're up there, Sharon. Let's getta broom and beat em to the death. Okay?" Sharon had Margot making faces verging on distortion; that hair, that hair had to be combed or Mama was gonna have a fit. "Well, we could tie it with a shoestring in a ponytail," Sharon conceded. Margot smiled so much she cried one big tear. Allard kept trying to get their attention: "Listen, if you all don't help me beat out them spooks, I'm gonna burn em up."

Together Sharon and Margot shouted, "Allard, keep your hands off them matches, do you hear?" Jane heard. Greer was apparently downstairs, already strains of Charlie Parker wafted through the house. Jane was powdering herself by her vanity in a gleam of nostalgia by her wedding photo. Oh that day had been so perfect, so soft and white. Whatta night they had at the Savoy. Why, she danced until she most fainted. Jane giggled and then regained her more official "mother's" stance as Betsey entered the room.

"Well, Betsey, I thought you must have gone all the way to Guatemala to get my coffee."

"No, Mommy, I just was practicing my elocution, when the kids were making all this noise and you wanted your coffee and Grandma insisted on telling me how lucky we look the way we look because of Daddy. There was an awful lot goin on, Mama, honest."

Jane smiled at her miracle child. The baby she thought she couldn't have. What an error of judgment that had been. Still and all, Betsey was her first baby and close to her heart in a peculiar way, as if some real part of her walked out the door every time Betsey went down the front stairs or leaned gossiping, girl-like, over the back porch. Jane pulled Betsey to her, then took a few sips of coffee made exactly how she liked, milk in first, two sugars. And plenty of coffee. Jane still insisted on having her good china and cloth napkins for her coffee upstairs. "There's no reason to give up everything gracious on account of a few moments of hardship" was what she always said if Betsey brought a paper napkin or a mug to her room.

"Mama, you wanna listen to a little bit of my elocution preparation? I'm doing Mr. Paul Laurence Dunbar."

Jane thought, taking her time mischievously, and then shook her head yes.

"Betsey, of course I want to hear your interpretation of Dunbar, but hurry. You know your daddy's getting the morning quiz ready."

Betsey ran to her mama's closet and grabbed the first red womany thing she saw, a scarlet slip she draped round her hips. Jane's eyebrows rose, but she contained herself. After all, elocution was close to theater. Betsey stationed herself by her mother in front of the vanity, wanting to watch her every gesture and facial expression. Mama knew this poem awready, so she had to be good, or at least that's what she thought.

Jane thought anything her little girl did was just fine, but it pleased her that Betsey wanted to impress her.

> "Who dat knockin' at de do'?
> Why, Ike Johnson, yes, fu' sho!
> Come in, Ike. I's mighty glad
> You come down. I t'ought you's
>   mad
> At me 'bout de othah night,
> An was stayin' way fu' spite.
> Say, now, was you mad fu' true
> W'en I kin' o' laughed at you?
>   Speak up, Ike, an 'spress yo'se'f.

Betsey sashayed and threw her teeny hips, glinted her eyes, and coyly demonstrated her newly learned skills as coquette, much to her mother's delight. Jane hugged her girl and was about to offer some dramatic advice, when the morning rituals, authorized and unauthorized, overshadowed them and interrupted that very special moment they'd shared.

"Who's got my geography book?"

"Come on, tie my shoes."

"That dress is not yours. Give it here."

"Lord, Lord, please help me with these chirren."

"I'ma tell Daddy you took my books."

"I bet you won't have no backside side, if he gets holdt to ya."

"Come tie my shoes, please."

"For God's sake, somebody tie Allard's shoes."

"Margot, you better do something with that mess you call hair."

"You said you would comb it for me."

"She sure 'nough did."

"Where's my geography book?"

"Somebody tie Allard's shoes, fore he trips over himself."

"I'ma tell Daddy." The refrain arose from everyone's lips.

No one could find Allard to tie his shoes. Meanwhile Greer had strapped his conga drum round his shoulder. It was the one he'd brought from Cuba where Sharon was conceived under a sky of shooting stars, or so the story went. As if he were a southern Mongo Santamaria, Greer mamboed up the back stairs, through the halls, and down the front steps, gathering the mass of family he called his own, chanting all the while.

"The Negro race is a mighty one
The work of the Negro is never done
Muscle, brains, and courage galore
Negroes in this house
Meet me at the back door
Oh! the Negro race is a mighty one
Each and every one of you is an example of one
Oh! the Negro race is a mighty one
We goin to show the world
What can be done
Cause the Negro race is a mighty one."

Jane was not crazy about her children screaming at each other or about her husband's idea of reveille. Cuba, yes. St. Louis, no. St. Louis was still an old-fashioned place. With "Yes, M'ams" and "No, Sirs" grating Jane's ears every time she heard one of her children say sucha thing, but Greer swore it wouldn't hurt them and Greer knew a lot about the worlds Jane had never considered. Matisse, Gauguin, Pippin, Bearden, and Modigliani. Whenever Dizzy Gillespie came to town, there they were, justa waiting. If Chuck Berry was in a scrap with the law, there they were: Greer operating and Jane taking pictures. Sometimes she couldn't believe what she did for this man. Love and buckshot, music and street diagnoses, late-night feuds bout the future of the Negro race, whether DuBois or Walter White hadda place and where. That time DuBois had carried Betsey to bed was history. Everybody knew what a crotchety ol' figure of a man he was, but couldn't nobody but W. E. B. himself get that child to sleep. Was like the night Betsey'd hid in the back seat of the car to see Tina Turner, as if nobody would want to collect a ticket from her or see some I.D. from an eleven-year-old at the bawdiest night spot on the wrong side of the tracks. Saying "I wanna be an Ikette" didn't do it. Greer had to hightail it back to the house with his girl, trying to explain that Tina Turner didn't accept applications from young women under the age of eighteen. From that second, Betsey decided she would do everything just like Tina Turner do. Greer knew that and that worried him, and then again, he was assured Betsey'd be good at whatever she put her mind on.

Why couldn't Greer see what kind of an influence he was having on the children, Jane worried. Her sister would never have let Charlie stay with them if she'd known all this was going on.

Betsey'd run off behind her father to get ready for the morning quiz. Up and down and round about the house they went with Greer chanting, the children dancing.

They all marched into the kitchen where Grandma sat in a corner by the window that opened on an oak tree frequented by bluejays she fed whenever something was simply beyond her. She hummed, "I been 'buked, & I been scorned." Her daughter had married a mad man, bringing all this Africa mess into her house. Low-down music and prize-fighters at his heels soon as he stepped through the door. Nothing but the lowest of the low appealed to him, cept for her daughter, Jane. How could this be going on in her family? What would her father have thought in his starched trolley-driving uniform? What would her poor early-passt-on mother have made of a household run in such a brazen manner?

Greer paraded the children in file past Grandma to get their lunches and the 35¢ he left in stacks for each of them. Then he began.

"Betsey, what's the most standard of blues forms?"

"Twelve-bar blues, Daddy."

"Charlie, who invented the banjo?"

"Africans who called it a banjar, Uncle Greer."

"Sharon, what is the name of the President of Ghana?"

"Um . . . Nkrumah, I think."

"Thinking's not good enough, a Negro has got to know. Besides, it's Kwame Nkrumah. Margot, where is Trinidad?"

"Off the coast of Venezuela, but it's English-speaking."

"Allard."

Everybody turned around, realizing that Allard was nowhere to be seen. Grandma tutted to herself in the corner. At least one of the chirren wasn't taken in by this mess. Yet if Allard was missing, he was up to something terrible. That boy just loved fires.

"Allard!" Greer shouted out to the back porch, "Allard, come in this minute and put those matches down."

Allard let loose of the rags he'd been piling up and ran back to the house just before his father's hand would have laid a whap, lickety-split.

"Allard, you and I are going to have a talk this evening, but right now I want to know what discipline is?"

Discipline? All the children looked at each other askance. Daddy never asked questions like that. He asked fun questions about the Negroes, or music, or foreign places where colored people ran countries all their own and on their own. "What is discipline?" Now, that wasn't Daddy's kinda question at all.

Allard looked up ingenuously at his father with his shoes still untied, making little lakes around his legs, and answered: "Discipline is the hallmark of a mighty people." Then he sat down to try to tie his shoes again.

When Jane entered the kitchen, the line of children melted into hugs and kisses good-bye to Grandma and thanks to Daddy for the extra nickel for correctly answered questions at morning drill. No one bothered to figure where Allard got his answer from, but it must have been right cause Greer gave him five copper pennies. Jane had found time to do her nails, her hair and face, so she looked more like she was going shopping at Saks than to the segregated colored hospital to work with the crazy ones, the mad niggahs couldn't nobody else talk to. Betsey's word had been "psychopath" one time and she answered, "Mama's patients, niggahs what aint got no sense," for which she'd been sent to her room. Jane was furious. Of all of her children, Betsey should have understood it wasn't that folks didn't have any sense, it was that they were in pain and had so little, so very little to look forward to. Jane loved to miss the morning drill, and show up just in time for a grin from each urchin, a tidying of heads and belts, a moment to take pride in her womb's work. Every time she turned around she was poking out again. Jane loved being pregnant and she loved her children. She loved Greer, motioning for her to get a move on.

"Betsey, good luck today. Allard and Charlie, don't play too rough. Sharon, I bet you get at least a ninety on your geography test. Margot, those are lovely ponytails you've made for yourself. Mama, see you later. Enjoy the TV and let me know what is going on on 'Edge of Night,' you hear."

Greer chimed in, "That's right, Mama, take it easy and I'll bring you something nice. You mustn't strain yourself on accounta your heart. Take a stroll before the heat's too much. I'm gonna bring you something nice."

Jane and Greer sauntered to the car like young lovers. The children raced out the screen door, slammin it each time. "See ya, Grandma," "Bye-bye," "Back after basketball," "Love you, Grandma."

Only Betsey lingered on the porch next to the forsythia and azalea that Grandma loved so much. "Speak up, Ike, an' 'spress yo'se'f." The gentle old lady moved from her bluejays and robins toward her sweet child saying, "It's a matter of faith, Betsey, alla matter of faith." Betsey looked up at her grandma and took a deep breath, those southern eyes were sure of her. Her grandma's silken hands twisted her bangs a bit to the left.

"Betsey, if your grandpa could see you today I swear he'd be so proud. One of his own reciting from the great Mr. Dunbar. Yes, my Frank would certainly have loved to hear your very own rendition in that dialect of our times. I wisht you coulda seen him. I'ma pray for you, ya hear."

With that, Grandma grabbed up her apron and sat upon the porch glider to let the morning sun in her soul as she watched Betsey meander down the driveway with a sullen grace and a child's pace. Then Betsey stood absolutely still, shouting at the top of her lungs "SPEAK UP, IKE, I'S MIGHTY GLAD TO SEE YOU," and off she ran.

From the back porch Grandma could see only the carefully tended beds of tulips and the lengths of coral roses that Mr. Jeff looked after for the family. The small play yard that this ragamuffin loafer had erected for the children when they were little was now the gathering place for Betsey's imaginary friends, her digs to China, and the ripest honeysuckle vines to be found north of Charleston, or so it seemed to Vida. The quiet of the breeze and the smells of roses, honey, and her fresh cornbread eased her soul. Whenever she thought on Jane and that Greer her heart would getta fluttering and she'd verge on shortness of breath. Caint live nobody's life for em, but sometimes Vida wisht to the Heavens she could get inside her daughter's skin and find out how she got in this predicament. The stories were gonna come on and she was gonna remember to tell Jane bout "Edge of Life," or was it "Edge of Night"? Her memory wasn't what it usedta be, couldn't even crochet anymore cause she'd forget what she was making and for who. But it didn't cause anybody any fretting, Grandma was the gem of the household, fulla more stories than a bunch of Will Rogers could ever have told.

Mostly she talked on Frank, her long-passt-on husband, the Valentino of Allendale and the hills there'bout. He was sucha gentle man and couldn't nobody tell he was a Negro, not even when he opened his mouth. Fine diction, mighty fine articulation, Vida'd recall. His dark hair hangin like a drop of black honey cross his eye; that part as straight as a Cherokee's aim. Yes, her Frank was a truly fine man. Not on the order of the modern men of color she'd come across in her daughter's life. No, there was a gentleness bout Frank that they'd lost. Maybe it was the war. No, it couldn't be, Frank had served in '17 in Germany.

"Take it easy and I'll bring you something nice," that's what that Greer had said, as if presents could make up for how black and kinky-headed he was. Oh no, she mustn't think like that. After all he'd done for Jane. What all he'd done to Jane. That was the plus and minus of it. He took Jane outta the Bronx and to this fine old house in St. Louis, but he'd filled her svelte body with more chirren than a she-heifer in heat should ever know. He kept her in nice clothes, took her to Paris and Savannah, no, Havana, that was it. Havana. And he was a hard-working soul, the Lord could attest to that. Why, he worked day and night just to keep all those chirren looking right, and Jane in those hats she loved so much, with veils and feathers and sequins.

Vida turned to go indoors, but the breeze tickled her ankles a wee bit, reminding her: once she was courted and treated real sweet. Once she was courted and swept off her feet in a dingy ol' roadhouse out on the islands where her folks woulda died had they known she was parading in hose and satin where throats got cut and women were easily had. Yes, Greer would bring her something nice and she could fan herself on the front porch recollecting the magnolia and the spanish moss where Frank would hide her in the night for one small kiss. In those times a kiss was very personal. Very committin, like a ring, or a first waltz.

Vida lilted through the house to the front porch like she was waltzing in Frank's very arms, and saw Betsey running down the street to the school.

Was good the school was right cross the street, that way Vida could keep her eyes on every one of her younguns.

The Judge was backing out his driveway, the chauffeur was opening the door for the museum man to go see over all them crypts from Egypt and the busts from Greece, the rich lady was taking her rich white little girl to the rich little school for the likes of tow-headed smart-alecks. Betsey'd picked up more than a few bad ways from that gal. Betsey didn't know yet that white folks could get away with things a Negro'd be killed for. That's what was wrong with this integration talk, it made the children believe in things that just weren't possible. It was best to be the best in the colored world, and leave the white folks to their wanton ways.

Vida hummed to herself, "Lord, I wanna be a Christian in my soul," and sat rocking on the pillared front porch. Miss Pittypat couldn't of done better. Jane had never had to say "I'll never be hungry again," cause Vida'd seen to it that every one of her chirren ate. Every single one of em. All seven. Huhuh-uhmm, maybe wasn't Jane's fault she was so fulla blossom chirren, maybe she took after her mother. Still, that first picture she saw of Greer was most like a monkey-man she'd ever seen. Greer, jet black in his little monkey hat, talking bout bebop or bopbe, some music that a man he callt Bird jingled outta a saxophone. A monkey man in a monkey hat done run off with her daughter and that was that. Four chirren and God only knew how many more. Please, Lord, no more. Thy Bounty Is Mightily Received. Vida swayed in the wicker chair like the lily of a woman she was, amber-ivory skinned, elegance in the morning.

The street grew still, cept for the slurring oaks and jays in the winds. Everybody who had somewhere to go had gone. Brick houses, ranging from sun-yellow to night maroon, etched the walks and the maids swept the stairs as if dirt were a sin. Soon the housewives would saunter back and forth cross fences, sharing gossip and recipes or the plain old doldrums of living in the roses as they did. Haitians, East Indians, Ricans, and prize-fighters' wives went on bout their business: being beautiful and fertile. Weren't many places the likes of them could live in St. Louis and know the nooks and covies of fifteen- and twenty-room houses. Weren't many places the likes of them could be themselves and raise their children to own the world, which was the plan never spoken.

GLENN SAVAN

ST. LOUIS NATIVE GLENN SAVAN (1953–) was raised in University City. After graduating from Parkway Central High School, he attended the University of Iowa and received a B.A. in English and an M.F.A. from the Iowa Writers' Workshop. In 1987, Savan's first novel, *White Palace*, was published. Referred to by one critic as "a contemporary love story with a Pygmalion theme," the novel centers around the unlikely love affair between a young widowed West County advertising executive, Max, and a middle-aged waitress, Nora, who lives in Dogtown. The book takes its title from the name of the greasy burger joint where Nora works. Praised for its gripping narrative and engaging plot, *White Palace* was a tremendous success. Translated into more than fifteen languages, the novel was released as a motion picture in 1990. The movie, which was partially shot in St. Louis, features many local residents, including Savan himself as a disgruntled White Palace customer. The green-shingled, three-room house that served as Nora's residence in the film stood at 1521 West Billon Avenue until 1992, when it was demolished. Savan published his second novel, *Goldman's Anatomy*, in 1993.

In the following excerpt from *White Palace*, Max and his friends are attending a bachelor party at the Cheshire Inn. When the revelers realize that they were shortchanged a number of hamburgers, Max sets out for the restaurant to rectify the situation and meets Nora for the first time.

FROM *WHITE PALACE*

Horowitz, who had taken it upon himself to plan his own bachelor party, had booked a room at the Cheshire Inn—which was where, some fifteen years before, in a much larger room, his bar mitzvah party had been held. He did this, he told Max, partly for the sake of poetic symmetry, but also to prove to the frightened and unhappy thirteen-year-old boy inside himself that even fat ugly men could wind up getting what they wanted. Horowitz had remained a virgin until the scandalous age of twenty-four, and in marrying Rachel Fine, he was finally saying I-told-you-so to all the kids on the old block, starting with himself, who had doubted his manhood.

Max had grown up on that block—three doors down from Horowitz on seedy Raymond Street in University City—and he had been at that bar mitzvah party. As he crossed through the lobby of the Cheshire Inn, with its suit of armor and its tapestry of a unicorn hunt, Max remembered certain things so vividly, they might have happened an hour ago: how the feast had consisted of the unkosher combination of hamburgers and milk shakes; how he had found Horowitz cowering in the men's room and feigning diarrhea because he did not want to be forced to dance with anyone; and how he had stolen away at one point with Janey Roth, who wore a yellow ribbon in her hair, and coaxed her into a janitor's closet somewhere in this hotel, and how, when she finally consented to kiss him, her breath had been redolent of potato chips. That had been an important moment. He had never fully realized before that girls were just as human as boys—that if they put something into their mouths, and you kissed them soon afterward, they would taste of it. Now, riding up the elevator, Max felt the thirteen-year-old boy awaken inside of him; the boy was staring with incredulity through all the intervening years at his rigid, mournful, twenty-seven-year-old self, who was no longer the sort of guy to exuberantly cajole a girl into a closet, and it didn't like what it saw. He was not supposed to have ended up like this.

Max walked down the hallway, watching for Horowitz's room number, and tried to shake his gloom. He was happy for Horowitz—never mind that he himself didn't feel happy—and did not want to do anything to sour the party. He experimented with putting a jaunty bounce into his step, but the pathetic insufficiency of this only depressed him further. He found the room and knocked. Horowitz yelled out to come in.

Max stepped into a bad smell. It was a stale, meaty stink, as if several couples had spent several days in this room engaged in a strenuous orgy without ever opening a window or breaking to bathe. The source of it stood in the middle of the room, in the middle of a card table: three fat white sacks surrounded by a litter of the small white cardboard boxes in which White Palace hamburgers were served.

The three tuxedoed young men avidly feeding there—Larry Klugman,

Marv Miller and Horowitz—comprised, along with Max, the old first string of the high school debate team which had made it to the Missouri State Semi-Finals on the strength of their handling of the topic *Resolved: That the Federal Government Should Continue to Provide Tax Incentives to Corporations.* They were the best team University City High had seen in years, and it was generally agreed that they would have gone all the way had Larry Klugman not lost his mind at a critical moment. Max had witnessed few things as painful to watch as Klugman simply standing there with his hands in the pockets of his checked sport jacket, his eyes glazed over and his mouth hanging open as if he were in silent communion with his ancestors, for the entire minute and a half of his final rebuttal. It was still, after all these years, the one thing you did not kid Klugman about. While Max had gone on to become first an English teacher and then an advertising man, and Horowitz had turned his hobby of photography into a lucrative profession (his specialty was gorgeous commercial photographs of food), Klugman and Miller had remained true to their original vision, fulfilled their early promise, and both became tax attorneys. For four men as young as they were, there was plenty of money in this room.

Horowitz wiped his mouth, rose from his chair, and came over to Max, his enormous landslide of a body straining at the confines of his tuxedo. The two of them embraced, and Max was lost in a wall of fat. Since Horowitz's engagement to Rachel and the dinners at her apartment every evening, he had grown more obese than ever. Max, on the other hand, had been slowly and steadily losing weight. It had been their odd sizes—Horowitz a hulking grizzly bear, Max a tiny doll—which had first drawn them together as children. Nobody ever wanted them on their teams.

Max told Horowitz how happy he was for him. Horowitz grinned and shrugged.

"Are you nervous at all?" Max asked him.

"I'm kind of sad, if you want to know the truth. I'm not sure I want to say good-bye to the rest of my life leading up to this—as rotten as it was. I'm having a heavy attack of nostalgia. Are you hungry?"

Max glanced at the carnage on the card table.

"I don't think so," he said, and went over to greet Klugman and Miller. He shook their hands, asked how they were doing, and then asked after their families. Miller—the brilliant captain of their debate team, who had studied law at Stanford—already had two small boys and a prematurely middle-aged wife. He nodded his head emphatically in response to Max's questions; his mouth was too full for talking. Klugman showed Max a slow-spreading smirk, which was his favorite facial expression, and said, "Sherri's on a sexual strike again."

"How come?"

"Probably because she's figured out how much I like it."

There could have been more than a grain of truth in this. How Klugman had ended up with Sherri, who was not educated, not pretty, and not in any way likable, was one of the great mysteries. She was a tall, morose, evasive woman with liver-colored scoops under her eyes. Talking to her was like yanking teeth, and when she did come out with something, it was almost always negative. Max felt badly for Klugman, not simply because he was married to Sherri, but because he was so obviously and painfully in love with her. When they were out together, Klugman treated her with such anxious attention, you would have thought they were on their first date.

"That's a nicely understated tuxedo you've got on," Max told him.

"Why, thank you," Klugman said, and took a drink of what looked like scotch and water from a plastic tumbler. His tuxedo was shocking pink, with glittery silver lapels. "I thought I'd go for something muted."

Horowitz was back at the table, stuffing a White Palace into his mouth. "Sit down," he said to Max. "Eat."

Max took the chair between Klugman and Miller, tugged straight the creases in his loose pant-legs, then removed a White Palace hamburger from its box and inspected it. The bun was very soft, and when he pulled it away, bits of bread stuck to the meat, which was a flat dead-looking gray, scored with holes and sprinkled with translucent onions. The stale sex-smell was too much for him, and he held it away at arm's length. "Anybody want this?"

Miller snatched it away from him. Miller was an owlish, bony, largely humorless young man whose air of constant aggravation Max attributed to the fact that Miller already had everything that he could possibly want for the rest of his life except for more money which would come along anyway if he simply sat still. He had two supernaturally well-behaved boys, aged two and three, a wife who was as dependable as Gibraltar, a house in Creve Coeur, a restored Bentley in his garage, and a junior partnership in one of St. Louis's most prestigious law firms. Yet Miller walked, and even sat, with a pronounced stoop, as if all of this early good fortune were nothing but an unfair burden, and the Rolex around his wrist merely an upscale manacle.

He blinked at Max through his thick horn-rimmed glasses. "You don't want any?" he asked.

"No."

"Now, wait a minute," Horowitz said. "I paid twenty-four cents apiece for these things. It'd be a sin to let them go to waste. You should think about all the children in Ethiopia going to bed tonight without their White Palaces."

Max laughed. "Horowitz, I'm sorry—but I just don't have the digestion of a twelve-year-old anymore. How can you guys consciously put those things into your mouths?"

"It's interesting," Klugman said, staring at his half-eaten White Palace. "Why *do* we eat these things? You know they're garbage, you know they're going to end up giving you the shits—and then they *do* give you the shits, and then the next thing you know, you've got a bag full of belly-bombers on the seat of your car, and you're stuffing your face with them again. Why? Could it be their very awfulness that makes them so attractive? They taste like sin would taste, if you could eat it—don't you think?"

"It sounds like you're talking about a certain kind of woman," Max said.

Klugman thought about this. "I'm probably talking about Sherri," he said, and finished off the rest of his hamburger.

"Well, anyway," Horowitz said. "Rachel hates these things. If I come home smelling like White Palaces after we're married, she'll probably file for divorce. So this could very well be my last hurrah." He took two White Palace boxes from a sack and lobbed one in front of Max. "Come on, Max—don't you remember going to White Palaces at three in the morning back in the good old days? Just eat one for the sake of nostalgia."

"If I do, I'll be feeling nostalgic about it for the next two days."

"Then have some cheese fries."

"No thanks."

"I hate to say this, Max—but you're really turning into a prig."

This cut. It was the truth.

"Will you at least have a drink with me?" Horowitz said.

"Sure," Max told him.

He followed Horowitz's lumbering body over to the wet bar. Here stood a half-gallon of Chivas Regal, a water pitcher, an ice bucket, two stacks of plastic tumblers, and nothing else. Max asked him if he had any club soda.

"You mean to mix with your scotch?"

"I mean to drink by itself."

"Oh no you don't," Horowitz said, and picked up the bottle. "This is my bachelor party and you're drinking with me tonight—and I don't want to hear any crap about the evils of alcohol or the dangers of drunk driving."

The problem was, Max was wary of what alcohol did to him. He had not gotten completely drunk since the night of Janey's accident. Horowitz had been the first person he had called after the police had called him—he couldn't have dealt with his mother at that point—and once his ordeal with the police, with Horowitz there the whole time at his side, was over, Horowitz had run out for a bottle of Wild Turkey, plucked the phone from its plug, and forced Max to drink until he passed out. Since then, after more than two drinks, panic had set in. But it had been months since Max had taken more than two drinks, and it was entirely possible that he'd gotten over that period of his mourning. Besides, he owed it to Horowitz to give himself over tonight, as far as he could, to celebration.

"All right," Max said, putting his hand on Horowitz's shoulder. "Pour me a drink."

"Now you're talking."

"But make it light."

"Fuck you," Horowitz told him, and poured out two or three fingers worth into a tumbler. He added water and handed it to Max. It was the color of honey.

"I'm making a toast," Max announced.

Klugman and Miller picked up their drinks.

Horowitz ducked his head slightly and plucked at his drooping cossack moustache.

Max had no idea what he meant to say. But having been a teacher for three years, he knew that the only way to start was by opening his mouth.

"To Horowitz," he said, "who I love—well, who I love better than any person I know." Love did not enter into his feelings for his mother. That was purely a matter of duty, pity, and guilt. Now he drew a blank. Beside him, Horowitz rearranged something in the pit of his throat, and Max simply started all over again. "To Horowitz," he said, "the world's slowest bloomer. It took him twenty-four years to get laid, and twenty-eight years to get married, and now I'll just bet that his happiness lasts for the rest of the years of his life. He certainly has it coming to him. *L'chayam*."

Miller applauded, Klugman whistled, and everyone drank. The whiskey jolted Max.

Horowitz guided him back to the table with his big arm draped around his shoulders, then took a seat, reached into a sack, withdrew a box, and stared into it. "Well, how do you like this," he said. "It's empty."

"How could it be empty?" Miller asked him.

"Take a look for yourself," Horowitz said, and tossed the box over to him.

Miller handled it as if it were a piece of state's evidence. "You'd better look at the rest of them," he advised Horowitz.

Horowitz shook out the sack and five empty boxes dropped soundlessly onto the table. "What the hell," he said. "I'm still hungry."

The sight of those empty boxes touched a sore spot inside of Max. He hated to see mistakes made, things overlooked. It was carelessness, after all, that had killed Janey, and it was going to be a moment of pure dumb, unthinking carelessness, he was sure, that would finally trip the switch on Armageddon and blow down the whole house of cards. He took another taste of his scotch. "You've been cheated," he told Horowitz.

"I know," Horowitz said sadly, and went on staring at the boxes.

"Well, what are you going to do about it?"

"What do you mean?"

"Aren't you going to go back there and get it straightened out?"

"Max, I'm having a party for chrissakes. I'm not going to suddenly get into my car and—"

"But you've been cheated, Horowitz."

"It's six lousy White Palaces. Cool down."

But Max was hot. "Do you know what this is? It's the typical passive St. Louis attitude. Why do you think nobody in this town uses their horns?"

"What?"

"You've driven in other cities. People use their goddamned horns in other cities. But not in St. Louis. You could run a red light and mow down an old lady and I guarantee you wouldn't hear a single horn. It's the same damned thing in movie theaters—nobody ever turns around to tell loudmouths to shut up. They just sit there and suffer through it like it's their civic duty to be timid. And how about when that thirteen-year-old girl was raped in the fountain at Forest Park with a whole crowd of rubbernecks just standing there gawking?"

"Max, what the hell are you talking about?"

"I'm talking about how nobody in this city has the imagination to even know when they're getting crapped on."

" Look—I just got crapped on to the tune of a dollar and a half, and I don't care. All right? And if that's a typical St. Louis attitude, then I'm a typical St. Louisan. Now, will you please just drop the whole thing? We're trying to have a party here."

Maybe he was overreacting. But maybe he wasn't. Big things were built out of small things; and it was always in the small things first that principles were compromised away until they were compromised away entirely.

"Doesn't anybody here give a damn about principle?"

"Are you kidding?" Klugman said. "I'm a lawyer."

Miller, who did not laugh easily, hooted at this.

"Which White Palace was this?" Max asked Horowitz.

"I'm not telling you."

"Fine."

Max searched the three sacks until he came up with the receipt. It was the White Palace at Grand and Gravois—right in the heart of redneck South St. Louis. He put the six empty boxes along with the receipt into one of the sacks and stood up.

"I'll be back as soon as I can," Max told Horowitz.

"Max, what the hell do you think you're doing?"

"What the rest of you are obviously too complacent to do," he said, and walked out of the hotel room.

Max punched his tape deck and Bach came on—the fourth Brandenburg Concerto. The serene interplay of the notes was as rational and soothing as the conversation of angels, and Max wondered why they didn't play such music, to the exclusion of everything else, in shopping malls, supermarkets, dentists' offices, elevators. It might have tamed the world.

Or maybe not. He was headed, after all, into the heart of darkness (it didn't matter that this South St. Louis neighborhood was mostly white), where the young men looked like roadies for heavy-metal bands, and the young women, already dragging one or two dirty toddlers behind them, were pregnant again, and where the drivers along Grand Avenue were even more savagely ignorant than usual. They waited to make their turns by jutting out halfway into intersections; when they weren't doubleparking they were lurching out of spaces along the congested street; they wove over the lines as if they were drunk, which they most likely were. Why couldn't people understand that they were sitting inside of deadly weapons? Max's own profession, advertising, was partly at fault; cars were fun, cars were excitement, cars were penises, cars were expressions of your life-style and weltanshauung, cars were everything, in fact, except what they were: huge hunks of metal hurtling through space with no regard for human life, usually commandeered by mental deficients.

Max crept along. He wondered why South St. Louisans were so much uglier than people, say, in Clayton or Ladue. It wasn't simply a matter of bad childhood nutrition; there were the barbaric beards and shaggy hair, the Budweiser T-shirts, the cheap rubber sandals from Woolworth's, the tattoos, the glum faces, the general uncleanliness to account for. Max, too, had grown up poor, if poor meant simply not having enough money. His father, a faceless peddler of women's clothing (his mother kept no pictures of him), had deserted them when Max was an infant, never to be heard from again, and his mother made so little at her cashier's job at Rexall that there was seldom a period in Max's childhood when he wasn't delivering newspapers, collecting bottles and cans, mowing lawns, shoveling snow, or selling subscriptions to *Grit* to help out. But that had been one kind of poor, and down here, south of Highway 44, was another—Max had never been deprived of the benefits of civilization. His gut reaction to what St. Louisans (not to be confused with people from Indiana) labeled as "hoosiers," poor white trash, made him wonder what caliber of mind he really had. He didn't like these surly downtrodden sons and daughters of laid-off brewery workers and transplanted farmers from the Ozarks; they made him uncomfortable; he had a hard time thinking of them as full-fledged human beings. Part of this was due to his Jewish upbringing—Jews were generally democratic only at a distance. But such a prejudice, he knew, wasn't worthy of a tolerant and compassionate soul, not to mention someone of Max's leftist political sympathies. In conversation he was always ready to champion the wretched of the earth, but in reality he did not like to be in their vicinity—especially on a September evening as hot as this one. Heat, for some reason, seemed to be the natural element of hoosiers. It brought them out of doors, sat them down on stoops, increased their intake of Busch beer, melted what was left of their mentalities, and made them still more dangerous behind the wheels of their jacked-up, rusted-out Oldsmobiles and Impalas.

Max suddenly braked for a long-haired young man crossing the street without looking at the traffic—as if this stupidity were some kind of proof of his manhood—and honked his horn at him. Then he nosed forward again with his jaws clenched.

The White Palace came into view. It was indeed a palace, replete with battlements and turrets, which looked to have been built of enormous bathroom tiles. The parking lot was sprawling and chaotic. Max remembered, with a pang, the last time he had been here.

It was another night of celebration. Janey, after six restless years, had finally graduated from the University of Missouri at St. Louis with a degree in general studies, and they had gone to have dinner at Tony's, St. Louis's only five-star restaurant. It was a Saturday night, and the wait for a table was long. Janey, who wore a navy blue dress and the string of real pearls that her parents had given her (along with a brand-new Datsun) as a graduation present, was in an expansive mood, and each time the bartender checked in on them, she ordered another whiskey sour. Max remembered basking in the radiance of her smile and drunken eyes, and feeding on a happiness stirred up by thoughts of yet more happiness to come. They had been married for almost two years, and this was the first time, now that Janey's education was behind her, that they had talked seriously about having children. An hour and a half went by, and still the maître d' hadn't summoned them to a table. Janey leaned against him. "I'm smashed," she said. "If we don't get something to eat pretty soon, I think I'm going to pass out in front of all these beautiful people." Then she sat up, taking her pearls between her fingers, and laughed. "Hey—I've got a great idea. Screw all this high-rolling bullshit. Why don't we go to a White Palace?" And so, dressed to the nines, they had waited for the parking lot attendant to pull their car around, then drove into South St. Louis and gorged themselves at this very same White Palace restaurant, perched here on the corner of Grand and Gravois. Of course they were as sick the next morning as a pair of debauched sailors. But it made a good story, this cheerful descent from top to bottom, from glitter to gutter, and it showed Janey off in her best light: funny, unaffected, surprising. For the four remaining months in which she had left to live, Max told it often.

Now he turned off his tape deck, undid his seat belt, and got out of his Volvo. The heavy damp blanket of heat, after the air-conditioning, nearly knocked him over. He straightened the carnation in his lapel and went into the White Palace, carrying his sack full of evidence.

The smell was fierce. Except for that, and except for the crowd of unhealthy, badly dressed, poorly washed hoosiers all around him, this place could have been a morgue: the walls were of white linoleum tiles, there were gleaming aluminum railings and counters everywhere, and the bitter antiseptic light that was pouring down from the ceiling would go on pouring all night long. These places, like morgues, never closed. Max got into line. In front of him was a stooped old woman with a goiter on her neck the size of a tangerine and he lifted his gaze, instead, to the menu above his head. You could eat here for less than a dollar—how many indigent people on the verge of starvation had White Palaces kept alive over the years? Max, who paid attention to slogans, noticed that the one under the White Palace logo was new, and he had to admit that it was a pretty good one: *White Palace—One Taste and You're Hooked.* He wondered who did their advertising.

"Take your order?"

The woman was not young, and she wore a peaked blue cap; beneath it the bun of her black hair had come partly undone, and two strands of it licked at her neck like tendrils. She looked tired and impatient. Max remembered that he was wearing a tuxedo and saw himself through her exhausted dark blue eyes—another smirky West County slicko down in these parts on a slumming expedition. He sat the sack on the gleaming metal counter between them, which was probably intended to come up to most people's chests, but reached only the middle of Max's neck.

"Hello," Max said. "I have a complaint."

The woman waited.

"Would you please take a look inside this sack?"

The woman's blue-painted eyelids came down a notch; she wasn't in the mood for this. She took a grudging look inside the sack. "Well, Katy-bar-the-door," she said without the slightest intonation of surprise. "Six empty boxes."

Max showed her the receipt. "I paid for thirty White Palaces," he said. "And you gave me only twenty-four."

"Is that right?"

"Yes. And I'd like my money back."

Now the woman showed him a crooked half-smile. "Honey, how do I know you didn't just go and eat those six White Palaces you say we didn't give you?"

Max did not like to have his honesty doubted, even by people who didn't know him. "You're just going to have to take my word for it," he said.

"Now, why should I do that?"

"Because I'm telling you the truth."

"And what if *I* told you I was Marilyn Monroe?"

"If I worked in this restaurant and you were one of my customers," Max said through his teeth, "I'd ask you to give my regards to Joe DiMaggio. Now, I'd like my money back, if you don't mind."

The woman looked at him with what seemed to Max an inappropriate curiosity. One of her hands had gone to her ear to toy with the tiny earring there.

"Look," Max said. "If you won't take my word for it, why don't you just smell one of these boxes? If there was ever a White Palace inside of them, they'd stink of it, wouldn't they?"

"Honey, my nose is so full of White Palaces, I couldn't smell one if you pushed one in my face."

Max's patience had run out.

"I'd like to see your manager," he said. "What's your name, by the way?" He'd noticed that this woman, unlike the other women engaged in their furious dance behind the counter, wasn't wearing a name tag.

"Why would you want to know?"

"Because once I get my money back, I'm going to complain to your manager. You've been extremely rude to me."

The woman's wide mouth settled into a straight line.

Then she punched the register, a bell rang, and she handed him the money. "Here's your refund, sir," she said with a heavy emphasis on the sir. "I'm sorry if we caused you any inconvenience."

"How much were the six White Palaces?"

"A dollar forty-four, plus tax."

"You gave me a dollar seventy-five."

"Go buy some lifts for your shoes with it," she told him, then turned to the restless crowd behind him. "Next!" she called out.

MICHAEL CASTRO

POET AND LITERARY ACTIVIST Michael Castro (1945–) was enamored with creative writing in elementary school in New York, but he did not officially start writing poetry until he moved to St. Louis, at age twenty-two, to do graduate work at Washington University. Although he holds a Ph.D. in English, Castro has always been militantly anti-academic in his approach to literary endeavors. In 1975, he co-founded the nonprofit literary arts organization, River Styx, which also published a magazine by that name. Produced by dedicated volunteers on a shoestring budget, *River Styx* has from its inception published work by internationally known writers—including Allen Ginsberg, Gary Snyder, Derek Walcott, Margaret Atwood, Amiri Baraka, and Grace Paley—as well as work by talented newcomers.

A prolific poet, Castro has published several volumes of verse, the most recent of which is *US* (1991). Also an expert on Native American writing and culture, he is the author of *Interpreting the Indian: Twentieth-Century Poets and the Native American* (1983). A performance artist who draws inspiration from the Beat poets and jazz musicians, Castro is a pioneer in utilizing the airways to deliver poetry to a wider audience and has hosted poetry shows on public radio since the early 1970s. Because of the passion Castro and his poet compadres have poured into *River Styx*, the magazine celebrated a quarter-century of independent, multicultural publishing in 2000. In the following essay, "The Origins of River Styx," which appeared in the magazine's twelve-year retrospective issue, Castro provides a succinct and inspired history of an organization that has become both a catalyst and mainstay of St. Louis's literary culture.

THE ORIGINS OF RIVER STYX

River Styx began when, around 1969, young poets in St. Louis began to get together at impromptu parties to read poems to one another. Fueled by the countercultural spirit that was in the air, by fast food & circulating six-packs, by jugs & joints, we'd get together to get high on poetry. There was a ritualistic quality to these events. Something about sitting in a circle in a smoky room. Something about communing on the turn of words. We'd go round & round, reading what we'd brought to read—our own fledgling poems, found poems, & works by poets who turned us on—into the wee hours. Lots of reading aloud. Very little analytical discussion. In this respect it was nothing like a poetry workshop. We weren't there to analyze poetry. We weren't New Critics. We were there to *sound* the poetry, to *breathe* it, to become *energized* by it. To learn about it that way.

Up to that point in St. Louis, poetry always came with academic trappings. That is, readings were always held on college campuses & tended to be formal, staid, up-tight affairs held by & for members of English departments. Workshops, whether they were attached to the campus or not, inevitably had the atmosphere of an oppressive classroom as poems' blood was drained in the dissection process. The poets & poems that tended to be smiled on in these settings were rarely ones that spoke to us in ways we could hear, or so it seemed. Our collective impulse was that poetry needed a nurturing, non-authoritarian environment to flourish, that it need not be dull, elitist, removed from a larger community & its intensely human & political concerns the way we'd experienced it at universities. No doubt, part of our anti-academicism (ironic, since many of us had ties to the university) was an acting out of the generation gap, the distrust of authority, institutions, & "anyone over thirty" that us now middle-aged baby-boomers had back then. But there was more to it than that. Our literary curriculum at these poetry parties was different than the English departments'. We preferred Williams over Eliot, Blake over Beowulf, Beat poets, Black Mountain poets, deep image poets, ethnic poets; all spoke to us in ways typically frowned on in the classroom. In graduate school, I couldn't talk with my modern poetry professor about Ginsberg, Creeley, Jones-Baraka, Snyder, Bly, Wakoski, Olson, Lamantia, Duncan, Sanders—virtually anyone on the long list of poets that seemed to matter to me. Their work was either unknown, or viewed as somehow suspect. It was these uncanonized poets, not our professors, who guided us to the vital bodies of Asian, African, Latino & Native American poetries that didn't make it into Poetry 101. Tuned to the oral/aural vibrations of poetry, as we permitted ourselves to be, we searched for voices, including our own, that could speak of, to, & through our turbulent times. Sometimes we found them. But even when we didn't, we unwittingly affirmed poetry's most ancient function, using it to find community in each other.

Dan Spell's apartment at 6010 Pershing near the Washington University campus, was the scene of many of these poetry orgies. Spell was working in the university bookstore at the time, presiding over the poetry & music sections (he'd prepared for this by serving as a quartermaster in the Navy), & was constantly pulling our coat-tails to new texts & sources. Michael Corr was another regular at these get-togethers. He worked for the ecologist Barry Commoner's Center for the Biology of Natural Systems at Washington University & had spent several years in Japan studying woodblock printing & Zen Buddhism, befriending in the process the poets Cid Corman & Gary Snyder. Ajule Rutlin often showed up. He was an accomplished percussionist & performance poet, an arts activist & founder of the Black Artists Group (BAG), which had nurtured the talents of numerous poets, painters, musicians, & dancers, among them Oliver Lake, Julius Hemphill, Shirley LeFlore, & Oliver Jackson. Another regular was Howard Schwartz, a fanatic on the subjects of C. G. Jung, Bob Dylan, & ancient Jewish literatures. These four are cited somewhat arbitrarily here to suggest the wide range of perspectives & inputs at these events, which were as richly educational in their informal chaotic way as any coursework I've ever done. Schwartz & Spell were both aficionados of folkdance, capable of breaking into steps without much prodding; visual artists & musicians were often present, & these early get-togethers tended to have the multi-ethnic, multi-media flavor to them that set the tone for the more formalized *River Styx* magazines & readings and series that followed.

By early 1970, Spell, Jan Garden (to whom I was soon to be married), the Native American poet Carter Revard, fiction writer Marvin Hohman, & I were organizing a monthly two hour radio program on KDNA, St. Louis's listener access station. This was the *River Styx Poets* show, a kind of radio version of the parties. It included live readings, interviews, music, storytelling, listener call-ins. The name River Styx was, of course, derived from the mythic river on which one journeys to the Underworld. We wanted, with it, to suggest, poetically, several things at once: our own "underground" status in the poetic pecking order, our geographic location at the confluence of great & ancient rivers, & the "underworld" of the subconscious streaming into the poetic act. While the parties (which continued during the years of the radio program) provided us with rich learning experiences about poetry & a testing ground for own writing, *River Styx Poets* suddenly gave us the opportunity to test the assumptions most of us shared—that an audience for poetry existed beyond the college campuses, & that poetry had a role to play in the consciousness raising that was taking place in the turmoil of the larger culture. Poetry had become for us a means of forming community, & experiencing communion—often crossing barriers of nation, ideology, & ethnicity in the process—& it was this sense of its core humanity that we sought to get across to our listeners. And, to a large extent, experience proved our assumptions correct. We did find an audience, or they found us, & they obviously cared a great deal about poetry for they offered us profuse feedback—both praise & blame—in numbers unequalled by any of KDNA's other programs.

The show went on until 1973, when KDNA was sold & replaced by a commercial station. Suddenly our heady media experience was at an end. We decided to continue our joint efforts, as we called them, this time by moving into the more traditional media of print. We thought, in rather grandiose fashion, we'd form a press. Our plan was to acquire an offset press, make it pay for itself by doing commercial printing, & use the monies we earned to publish our own magazine, newspaper, & books. Unfortunately, none of us knew anything about printing & we were collectively broke. In fact, we were so marginal economically, not one of us had a viable enough credit rating to borrow money for the project. Nevertheless, we developed what in retrospect seems like a harebrained scheme to embark on a series of poetry readings to raise money for River Styx Press.

Our first reading, counter to our anti-academic ravings, was held at Webster University, & attended by maybe fifty people. One of them was a young man named Bernie Rosen, who, amazingly, came up to us afterwards & offered us an offset press he owned & his services as a printer. Suddenly our pipe-dream was smoking. We had a printer & a press. We found an appropriately underground home for our press in the basement of a friendly lawyer's storefront office, & set out to execute our plan with visions of an imminent publishing empire dancing in our heads. We each chose one of the press's proposed activities to focus on. Danny would be the business manager. Bernie would be the head printer & train others. I was to oversee the magazine. Marvin would do the newspaper. Others would become involved as we needed them. In a rush of enthusiasm tinged with bewilderment over the positions we found ourselves in, we each set to work organizing our departments.

All of our literarily inclined publishing activities were put on a back-burner, however, when we landed our first commercial job. Through some intricate networking & outrageous low-bidding, we landed an assignment from an ecological group to print a thousand copies of a 200 page book that was to be presented at a conference in Sweden several months later. This was a larger project than we had dreamed of for starts, & it promised, if & when we completed it, to provide us with a solid financial base to apply to our literary publishing interests. Naturally it put our technical & organizational ability to a severe test. Anyone with even a peripheral connection to *River Styx Poets* was impressed into service either as a volunteer or minimum wage worker, doing the folding, collating, cutting & pasting that our non-automated shop required. At first the enthusiasm of having gotten as far as we had as fast as we had was intoxicating, but soon the strains of the large job for which we were laying out money we didn't have, our inexperience, a high pressure deadline, & last minute changes in the actual copy we were printing, began to take its toll. We miraculously completed the project successfully, shipped the last carton of books off just in time for the conference, but by that time our business manager & printer were not speaking to one another, & everyone else was mad at one or both of them, or at each other. Ultimately, we were never paid for the job—we were simply stiffed by our supposed countercultural allies—& we were too stunned & disheartened to do much more than moan about it. Without the medicine of the anticipated big payoff to sweeten it, the sour taste this experience left us with went from bad to worse. We found ourselves saddled with bad debts & bad feelings, and our poets' leap into the entrepreneurial world of big business & big bucks which had begun with such a big bang, ended with a little whimper. The press disbanded shortly thereafter.

Still, I'd been collecting material for a magazine, & we all liked what had accumulated. In addition to writings by River Styx radio regulars, we'd also been given poems by David Meltzer & Jerome Rothenberg, two poets of international stature whose work was fueling the literary multi-culturalism that interested us. We'd collected some striking graphics as well—a red & black cover of "River Styx Wasego Fish" by Michael Corr; some of Corr's glyphs; funny, cosmic cartoons by Alan Suits; & photographs by Douglas Gaubatz & Jennifer. We had the magazine. All we needed was the means to produce it. After a wound-licking period, we decided we'd find a way to "do" the magazine. Once again the strategy amounted to little more than blind faith in the adage "seek & ye shall find." Money was, as usual, the sticking point. After our recent experience, we were inclined more toward love, & concentrated our efforts on finding a sympathetic printer who hadn't been burned as Bernie had by our poets' ineptitude or bad karma in the world of business. We sought a person who had the abilities, consciousness, & access to a functional press that we needed. Danny Spell, the quarter-master, always our resource man for better or for worse, came up with just such a soul—*River Styx*'s angel of offset, Steve "Huckleberry" Harris. Huck worked at St. Louis University's printshop as a journeyman printer, & loved the magazine project for its own sake & for the opportunity it afforded him for artistic expression. He worked out an arrangement permitting him to print in his off hours, agreed to work for whatever we could scrounge together at the end to pay him, & dug into the job with enthusiasm & relish. Huck would do the printing & the poets would volunteer labor for any support tasks that came up. *River Styx* 1 & 2 were produced in this fashion. Two years after the rise & fall of River Styx Press, we stapled by hand Michael Corr's covers onto the 350 now rare copies of *River Styx* 1 at a big party, & a new magazine was born.

When *River Styx* 1 appeared, we were uncertain if we'd ever do another issue. After the press had folded, completing the magazine project became a matter of salvaging something positive from an otherwise unhappy experience, & also of documenting something of the special community of feeling we'd experienced at the poetry parties & radio station. But the response to *River Styx* 1, particularly from the poets around the country that we admired & sent copies to, was so overwhelmingly positive & encouraging that we were motivated to keep going. The prospect of communicating with an even wider national network of poets & kindred souls was too enticing to quit.

By that time we had organized a monthly poetry reading series at Duff's restaurant at the invitation of its owners, Karen & Dan Duffy. This enabled us once again to present poetry in its oral/aural dimension as a performance & ritual art. It also gave us a place to hawk the magazines, & a live media through which to build a poetry audience. Our support group widened. The creative & pedestrian labors of many people in our emerging community or artists & friends went into the development of the poetry series & the completion of issues 2 & 3. All of these projects were accomplished on shoestring or non-existent budgets, through human networking, hard work, good will & persistence. A lot of luck & a lot of love went into them. But when our printer decided to change professions, we realized we couldn't keep going on a wish & a prayer. Fortunately, by that time we had a track record. We also needed money. Both of these facts dictated that we incorporate as a not-for-profit organization (not for profit, but for prophets), & apply for arts council monies to support the magazines &, eventually, the reading series.

Twelve years after *River Styx* 1 appeared in 1975, we're still at it. Under the editorship of Jan Garden Castro, joined by Quincy Troupe in recent years, & supported by a hard-working staff & board that currently includes William Gass, Carter Revard, Alice Brand, Eugene Redmond, Carol Pierman & others, *River Styx* has become more national & international in flavor, & gained stature & recognition as one of America's excellent literary publications. Despite the wider cast of our nets, despite the fact we've gotten a little slicker, the feeling of a magazine housing a closely knit, multi-cultural community of artists has been miraculously retained over the years, a quality that remains an important part of *River Styx*'s strength. We're pleased with what's been achieved & look forward to more & better works to come. As an indication of "what goes around comes around," we find our future plans including a new radio program & a River Styx Press.

If any lessons have been learned over close to twenty years of "adventures in poetry," they have to do with the value of doggedness, taking chances, sharing—& pursuing, like the Fool in the Tarot deck, the bright butterfly of poetry, even when the effort leads you in your dazzled blindness to the edge of a sheer cliff. Follow that flitting poetic impulse, o bardic blunderers. Keep on stepping. The Tarot's fool is not designated by the number infinity for nothing.

JONATHAN FRANZEN

ST. LOUIS NATIVE Jonathan Franzen (1959–) grew up in Webster Groves, Missouri. After graduating from Webster Groves High School, he attended Swarthmore College and majored in German. Following college graduation in 1981, Franzen lived in Berlin for a year on a Fulbright fellowship and began work seriously on his fiction writing. He worked for a number of years on his first novel, *The Twenty-Seventh City*, which was published in 1988 by Farrar Straus Giroux. The book's title refers to St. Louis's rank in national population surveys in the 1980s, in contrast to its position as the nation's fourth largest city a century earlier. The novel, which received positive critical reception at the time of its publication, is, in the author's words, a "straightforward story of moral corruption."

Set in St. Louis, the story concerns the manipulations of the city's ambitious police chief—a "female of Indian extraction named S. Jammu"—to gain control of the city and, ultimately, to reunite St. Louis city and county, which have been separated from one another since 1875. Laden with references to real places and to recognizable and powerful St. Louisans, Franzen's book understandably piqued the interest—and, in some instances, the ire—of local readers at the time of its release. Franzen told a *St. Louis Post-Dispatch* interviewer in 1988, "Perhaps my ideal reader *is* someone in St. Louis who has a combination of affection and distance for the place." A prolific writer whose work appears frequently in national publications, Franzen is the author of another novel, *Strong Motion* (1992), which deals with a major earthquake and is set in Boston.

The following excerpt from *The Twenty-Seventh City* shows St. Louis, primarily through the eyes of the national media, on the eve of an election that will decide whether or not the city and county remain separated or are reunited.

FROM *THE TWENTY-SEVENTH CITY*

The national press arrived in a stream that widened from a trickle on Thursday to a flood on Saturday, in numbers hitherto seen only in Octobers when the Cards had reached the World Series. CBS, NBC, ABC, CNN and NPR had sent big names. All the nation's major papers found reporters to spare for St. Louis that weekend, and many minor papers did, too. The Wichita *Eagle-Beacon* and the Toledo *Blade*, the Little Rock *Gazette* and the Youngstown *Vindicator*. Internationally, the Toronto *Star* and *L'Express* of Paris had correspondents on hand, and a German crew from Norddeutscher Rundfunk stopped in long enough to be counted and, laughing, to unpack a video camera at one of the baggage-claim carrousels in Lambert Airport.

The network crews were hosted and herded by their local affiliates. The men and women from the large-circulation dailies, all of whom had covered events in St. Louis before, claimed the interviews they'd reserved in advance and set about writing stories from premeditated angles.

The lesser newspeople weren't sure what to do. They'd been assigned to cover the goings-on in St. Louis. But what was going on? All anyone could say for sure was that the police chief was a female of Indian extraction named S. Jammu.

Cradling this knowledge and hoping for a chance to talk to her, small units of reporters began to appear in the dim cubical vestibule of police headquarters, where the guard, austerely denying them entry to the elevator, directed them to the information officer down the dim hall to their right. After the first twenty inquiries, it dawned on this officer that special circumstances were the order of the weekend; he phoned upstairs and received instructions to send the visitors across the street to the PR director's office at City Hall. There they helped themselves to stacks of press releases and three-color brochures on glossy paper, free coffee and doughnuts, a twenty-minute documentary film on the reorganization and current practices of the St. Louis Police Department, unlimited access to Jammu's right-hand officer Rollie Smith, and lottery blanks for the drawing to be held on Sunday morning to determine which thirty-six reporters, in groups of twelve, would be granted twenty-minute interviews on Monday morning with the great lady herself.

As a consolation prize the others would get passes to the press conference she was holding on Monday evening.

The PR director, noting what a marvelously vital and multifaceted place St. Louis had become, urged the out-of-towners to wander about, acquaint themselves with the city's layout, and sample such pleasures and edifications as appealed to them. Interested parties were told which bars and restaurants the local press corps frequented. To the younger female reporters the word was dropped that senior *Post-Dispatch* editor Joe Feig was throwing a Tex-Mex fiesta on Saturday night in his Webster Groves home, nothing formal, come as you are, byob, strictly private, but feel free to crash.

The real newshounds could refer to a three-page list of special events scheduled for the upcoming days and plan to cover whatever they considered most newsworthy. The list included the grand opening of a string of boutiques and bistros in the exciting Laclede's Landing area; a nonstop Lasarium program at the Planetarium entitled "The City and the Stars"; a pops concert in the fine all-purpose Stadium featuring music by Missouri composers; the maiden voyage on Sunday of the completely rebuilt *Admiral*, St. Louis's unique and enormous aluminum-plated Mississippi-cruising pleasure palace; the third and final referendum debate between Mayor Peter D. Wesley and Citizen John Holmes; the opening at 3:00 P.M. Tuesday of an Election Information Center at Kiel Auditorium, free admission to all holders of press cards; and, finally, St. Louis Night.

St. Louis Night was a gala extravaganza to be held from 6:00 until midnight on Tuesday. All of downtown St. Louis would be lit up in celebration of itself. Three soundstages would provide continuous live music and laughter, including appearances by Bob Hope, Dionne Warwick, and the pop group Crosby, Stills & Nash. A dixieland band and an oompah band would rove the streets, spreading good cheer. Favorite sports personalities from the Cardinals, Blues and Big Red would hold autograph sessions. Fifteen of the city's top restaurants would open sidewalk cafés and also booths at which their wares could be sampled by the spoon or by the cup. At midnight a Grucci family fireworks display would cap the festivities. St. Louis Night would unfold regardless of the outcome of the special election. In the event of rain, tents would be erected on the Mall.

Highlights, tabulations and analyses of the special election would become available in printed form at the Election Information Center at 10:00 A.M. on Wednesday.

Insiders could hardly fail to see the thinking behind all these activities.

Tuesday's election promised to be a laugher. The most conservative local pollsters projected that the merger would pass in the city by a four-to-one margin, and in the county by three to one or better, depending on which way the many undecideds went. At this stage of the game, only a public-relations catastrophe of the first order could alter the outcome.

Yet an idle brain is the Devil's workshop. Within hours of arriving, every reporter had fired off to his or her editors a story about the St. Louis equivalent of Amsterdam's brothels or Berlin's Wall. *Chief Jammu is a woman driven* and *Chief Jammu is a woman with a vision* were the two most common lead-paragraph disclosures greeting readers the next day, and as substantiation the reporter would offer his or her top choices from the sayings and confessions of Jammu collected in Handout #24 at City Hall. But after they'd cashed in this journalistic blue chip, the more bored reporters might have sent out feelers of their own, might have spoken with disgruntled cubs and searched back issues of the local papers for dissenting voices. Naturally, if the man from the Fresno *Bee* were to find anything, the news wouldn't reach many ears. But if Erik Tannenberg of *The New York Times*, for example, began turning over large stones and discovered something ugly or even simply peculiar underneath one of them, the consequences for Jammu, the pro-merger campaign, and the city as a whole could be most painful.

There was the little matter of the nine black families illegally occupying a pair of four-bedroom homes in Chesterfield. A removal agency in the employ of Urban Hope had displaced the families from their North Side homes without finesse or compassion. As restless and downtrodden Americans have been doing for two centuries, the families headed west. Construction on the Chesterfield homes had proceeded to the point of drywalling before the builder went bankrupt. Ownership had passed, by default, into the hands of a bank of which Chuck Meisner was director. Happily, the homes were situated in a remote corner of West County accessible only by way of Fern Hill Drive, the new street. Since no one yet lived on Fern Hill Drive, and since Meisner had financed the hasty installation of an eight-foot fence around the entire construction area, the families' presence had not become public knowledge. They'd boarded up the windows and barricaded the doors. They appeared to have enough water to hold out for several weeks. They had plenty of food as well, in the form of the sacks of flour and rice which the Allied Food Corporation had quietly been selling in East St. Louis at a large discount because of unacceptable levels of ethylene dibromide. Armed with shotguns, carbines and a small cannon, the squatters were being held under discreet siege by Missouri state troopers and St. Louis city police, the involvement of the latter rendered legal by direct orders from Missouri's governor. Negotiations had proved fruitless. The families were offered first-class housing in a public project, immunity from prosecution, and a sizable cash damages award. Incredibly, they declined. Their leader turned out to be Benjamin Brown, perennial 21st Ward aldermanic candidate on the Socialist Workers Party ticket. Brown refused to resume negotiations until he'd been given a chance to speak to the media. The siege force requested time to mull this over. It appeared likely that no decision would be reached before Wednesday. Meisner spent the weekend arranging new conduits for the inconveniently large campaign donations his banks wished to make to fund the last-minute pro-merger television blitz.

There was also the little matter of East St. Louis, Illinois. The crime situation on that side of the river had gotten out of hand. It was, to be sure, common knowledge that under Jammu's administration the city of St. Louis had grown markedly less hospitable to bookies, pimps, narcotics dealers and their victims, and that some of these individuals had moved east. The *Globe-Democrat* had printed an editorial lamenting the deterioration of law and order in East St. Louis (not that law and order had ever been that municipality's long suit) and expressing the hope that those people might at last find the courage to face up to their very real problems. But no *Globe* reporter had actually seen the situation firsthand. Nor had any other reporters. People who went to East St. Louis often got shot, and this was a risk that members of the Missouri journalistic community were in no special hurry to take. Illinois was a totally different state, after all. An investigation could wait until after the election on the western side of the river had been covered and analyzed.

There were other matters. Acting on a tip from a Washington University professor of law, a researcher at KSLX-TV had turned up a slight constitutional hitch in the real-estate transactions tax approved by city voters in November. The law apparently could, if challenged, be struck down by an unsympathetic court—for instance, by the conservative Missouri State Supreme Court. But no KSLX reporters were willing to write the information into a story. And when the researcher thereupon wrote it up herself, station executives close to general manager James Hutchinson delayed its airing for more than a week, penciling it in for broadcast on

Tuesday, after the polls closed.

Rumor also had it that a private detective agency was compiling a massive dossier on Chief Jammu and her allies, with evidence suggesting that the Chief's rise to power owed less to her popularity and more to crass horse-trading than was generally supposed.

Barroom cynics maintained that the incorruptible Martin Probst had switched sides on the referendum solely in exchange for sexual favors from a certain somebody in whose cruiser he had been seen to ride.

And then there were the Osage Warriors, those local terrorists who had made the national news repeatedly in the fall and winter. Now their attacks had simply ceased, and investigations by the police and the FBI had turned up no substantial leads. If their sudden appearance had been surprising, their disappearance was even more so. What had it all meant? County conservatives were beginning to wonder why an armed revolutionary group should have tailored its battle plan to suit so neatly the political needs of Jammu and the pro-merger forces.

But the fourth estate heard none of this. It was Saturday, March 31, and the only sounds in the city were the applause and calliopes of special events and the clamor of the fetes to which the major media representatives had been treated.

Late Saturday afternoon a hostage situation developed at a Pizza Hut in Dallas. Many of the reporters decamped for Texas. But many remained. There was nothing to do but see the sights and praise them. On the streets, in the seductive spring twilight, phrases whispered provocatively. *The new spirit of St. Louis . . . Farewell to the blues . . . Arch-rivals no more . . . A great Indian chief . . . A classic example of wise urban planning . . . The cardinal virtues . . . Delightful mix of old and new . . . First truly modern city in the Midwest . . .* And then from a hundred hotel rooms, later in the evening, came the impassioned sounds of typing. A new city, a new national image, was being conceived in the night.

Why us?

Those who might once have asked the question, in the rubble of their late great city, now saw the prospect of a more satisfactory fate, the elimination of the political split which for over a century had halted St. Louis's progress towards greatness. St. Louis had stepped into the limelight. It had cured its ills. Against the odds and contrary to expectations, it was making something of itself.

The local prophets were in twenty-seventh heaven.

But the city? Its self-pitying, self-exalting essence? That part of the place which would not forget and which had asked, Why us?

It was dead. Prosperity, Jammu, and national attention had killed it. St. Louis was just another success story now, happy in the one-dimensional way that all thriving cities are. If it had ever had anything extraordinary to tell the country, anything admonishing or inspiring, it would say it no more.

Oh, St. Louis. Did you ever really believe that Memphis had no history? That citizens of Omaha considered themselves unexceptional? Were you ever really so vain that you hoped New York might one day concede that, for all its splendor, it could never match your tragic glory?

How could you have thought the world might care what became of you?

JOHN LUTZ

BORN IN DALLAS, JOHN LUTZ (1939–) moved to St. Louis with his family at age four. During the mid-1960s, Lutz worked at a variety of jobs—construction worker, truck driver, stock boy—but none provided him with as much gritty experience and detail as his stint as a switchboard operator for the St. Louis Police Department. In his spare time, Lutz voraciously read the work of other mystery writers and eventually decided to try writing himself. Undeterred by the dozens of rejection slips he received, Lutz persisted. His first published story, "Thieves' Honor," was accepted for publication in 1966 in *Alfred Hitchcock's Mystery Magazine*, in which most of his short fiction eventually appeared. An extremely prolific writer, Lutz had published dozens of stories before being laid off from his full-time job in 1973, when he decided to try to make a career as a writer. Since then, Lutz has been extremely successful, with more than thirty novels and two hundred stories to his credit. In 1992, his thriller *SWF Seeks Same* was made into a popular motion picture, *Single White Female*, starring Bridget Fonda and Jennifer Jason Leigh. Lutz has lived in Webster Groves for more than twenty years.

Lutz has created a number of memorable detective characters who work in various American cities, including St. Louis. He introduced one of his most popular characters, hapless St. Louis detective Alo Nudger, in *Buyer Beware* (1976). According to Francis Nevins, Jr., in his introduction to a collection of Lutz's short fiction, *Better Mousetraps* (1988), Nudger's "symbiotic relationship with his city [is] almost as strong as Spenser's with Boston or Philip Marlowe's with L.A." The following excerpt is from one of the Alo Nudger novels, *Dancer's Debt* (1988). In this passage, Nudger trails Jake Dancer, a down-on-his-luck Vietnam veteran with big problems and ill-mannered associates.

FROM *DANCER'S DEBT*

That evening at six-thirty, Nudger sat crammed in his parked Volkswagen on Osage Avenue in South St. Louis. In the outside rearview mirror he could see the entrance of the brick apartment building where Jake Dancer lived with Helen Crane.

It was an old, flat-roofed building with green trim that needed paint. Over the front door was a large stained-glass window that looked as if it belonged in a church. The small front yard had a grassless path worn across it diagonally, and a kid's balloon-tired bike leaned into the shrubs near the entrance so that its handlebars were invisible. Osage was a long street with good and bad blocks. The apartment building wasn't a bad place for this part of town, and Nudger figured the rent wasn't much.

Helen had told Nudger that Dancer would sleep most of the day, then leave in the evening without telling her where he was going. He'd been doing that for the past week, she'd said. She'd tried following him once herself, but he'd seen her and there'd been an argument. Then Dancer had invited her to go drinking with him and she'd refused. Sounded like an up-and-down relationship to Nudger. Yo-yo love. He knew it well.

It was hot in the Volkswagen. He wished, not for the first time, that the little mechanized Beetle had an air conditioner. But not many twelve-year-old Volkswagens came so equipped. There were other things about the car he didn't like. Oh, the dents and the faded red paint didn't bother him. And he liked to think the lack of an adequate heater in the winter had made him hardier. But St. Louis was subject to at least one brutal heat wave every summer, and it was then that Nudger seemed to find himself in the sort of cases that required long hours sitting in the sun-heated, cramped little car and feeling like some sort of casserole.

Then there were the times when the Volkswagen refused to start and merely sputtered at him, as if it were cursing him in German. Nudger didn't like that. Once it had almost cost him his life. "*Götterdämmerung*," the VW seemed to have said. Nudger suspected it of war crimes.

Danny knew of a woman out in the country who'd bought a new car and was going to sell her nine-year-old Ford Granada. It was a bigger car; it was air-conditioned. Danny said it had enjoyed loving care and was in fine shape for its age. Nobody had ever said that about Nudger. He figured he might drive out and take a look at the Granada.

On the other hand, the car's owner was one of Danny's rare regular customers at the doughnut shop. Would a woman on a steady diet of Danny's Dunker Delites treat her car better than her own anatomy?

Nudger squirmed around on the hard vinyl upholstery, checking the street behind him in the mirror and trying to get more comfortable. He could feel his shirt peeling away from where it was plastered with perspiration to the seat back. If he'd been smart, he would have brought a thermos bottle full of something cold to drink. The inside of his mouth felt as if he'd been snacking on chalk.

He peered up at the top floor, west unit—Helen Crane's apartment—and saw that, though the end window was open, the drapes were still closed, swaying in the faint summer breeze. The windows that probably looked out from the living room were shut, and their venetian blind slats were angled for privacy. An air conditioner jutted from the center window and was still running; Nudger could see condensation dripping steadily from it onto the bricks below. It was probably cool in the front room of the old apartment.

Just as Nudger was about to rationalize the idea of hurriedly put-putting to Grand Avenue and getting a Diet Pepsi from one of the drive-through franchises, then quickly returning, a man fitting Dancer's description emerged from the apartment building.

He sat straighter to improve his angle of vision in the mirror. The man reached the sidewalk, hitched up his pants, flipped away a cigarette, then lowered himself into a rusty blue Datsun—Helen Crane's car.

As soon as he saw the tiny Datsun pull away from the curb, Nudger tried to start the Volkswagen. The miniature engine seemed to chuckle at him, as if it enjoyed keeping him in suspense as to whether it would turn over. The starter ground out messages of Teutonic disdain.

Then the engine rattled to life as if to say it was all a joke, and it clattered enthusiastically as Nudger made a nifty U-turn and dropped into traffic behind the Datsun. Old allies, a German car following a Japanese car driven by a veteran of a later war. The patchwork of history. At least Dancer was driving a car that might not be able to outrun the Volkswagen; they could have a low-speed chase not dangerous enough to require seatbelts.

Dancer drove to Grand Avenue and turned north, then aimed the little Datsun up the ramp to Highway 44 and drove east toward downtown. Nudger stayed well back in the outside lane, keeping the Datsun in sight and enjoying the air rushing through the Volkswagen's rolled-down windows and beating a drumlike rhythm in the closed back of the car.

Dancer got off the highway on Memorial Drive, then took Market west and wound north on side streets until he found a parking space near the Old Post Office.

He climbed out of the Datsun and casually slammed the door behind him as he set off walking along the sidewalk. He was dressed in gray slacks and a blue sport coat, no tie. A nice-looking guy, even from a distance.

Nudger drove past him and glanced over for a closer look. Dancer took long strides and swung his arms loosely, moving as if he'd never known worry. His wavy black hair was especially thick above his collar, giving the impression his head was tilted back so he could breathe in something sweet, though actually he was looking straight ahead. Nudger couldn't make out Dancer's expression, but he seemed reasonably alert, not as if he'd been drinking before leaving home. And he was treading a more or less straight line.

After finding a place to park the Volkswagen, Nudger cut back to the corner and fell into step about half a block behind Dancer. They walked at the same casual pace.

There were quite a few people on the downtown streets tonight. The Cardinals were in town, and a game with the Cubs was due to start in half an hour in nearby Busch Stadium. When that happened, the streets would be considerably emptier.

After about five minutes, Dancer adjusted his collar, buttoned his sport coat, and entered the Marriott Hotel. Nudger followed him into the plush lobby and watched him head for the lounge. The place was still full of Cubs fans wearing blue caps and jackets and behaving with jovial hostility as only Cubs fans behaved. One of them had what appeared to be a stuffed cardinal—the bird—dangling from a piece of string as if it had been throttled. The guy was dragging the thing across the floor so it bumped up and down while his buddies laughed. Sports in America.

Dancer would spend time and money in the teeming lounge, Nudger was sure. But he didn't see any point in going in himself and drinking beer he didn't want and listening to baseball arguments no one could win.

He sat in the lobby for a while, watching the blue-adorned fans from Chicago make fools of themselves, then he wandered back outside and up the street about half a block where he could stand and admire the night. To his right glowed the lights of the stadium. Ahead of him and to the left soared the graceful curve of the Arch, catching the rising moonlight on one gleaming side and looking like an ethereal silver ribbon hurled skyward in exuberance. Beyond the Arch, stars were beginning to glitter over East St. Louis, as if to cheer that depressed area with a free show of grandeur. There were times when Nudger wouldn't trade this city, his city, for any other. There were other times he'd trade it for Detroit.

The game had begun. A distant rushing sound reached Nudger: the stadium crowd roaring over hometown heroics. Instant reward for a job well done. Baseball was nothing like life.

Voices from the direction of the Marriott broke into Nudger's early-inning musings.

Dancer was standing on the sidewalk flanked by two men. One of the men was tall, the other was about Dancer's height, which looked to be about five feet ten. They were both beefy beneath lightweight gray suits. Neither of them wore ties, but the tall guy had a tight vest buttoned all the way up to where his white shirt was unbuttoned to reveal a gold chain. The Marriott doorman glanced at them, saw that Dancer was drunk and being supported by the other two men, then looked away; he had the familiar situation pegged and it didn't require further attention.

The two men began walking Dancer in Nudger's direction, each of them holding Dancer by an upper arm. Dancer was laughing and talking, but Nudger couldn't make out what he was saying. The other two men laughed now and then, too, but not as if they thought whatever Dancer was ranting about was all that funny, or even slightly amusing. They seemed instead to be laughing at a private, subtle joke of their own. The bigger one had a shrill horse-laugh that cut through the warm night like sharp ice and touched a nerve in Nudger.

He moved ahead of them for about a hundred feet, then crossed the street so he wouldn't attract their suspicion.

As Dancer and his two companions passed a pool of illumination from a streetlight, there was a shadowy flurry of motion, a change in the timbre of their voices.

It took Nudger a few seconds to realize the two men had turned on Dancer and were beating him. Leather soles made scuffling noises on concrete. Bodies jockeyed for leverage, arms rising and dropping with force.

"Hey!" Nudger yelled. He swallowed hard and started across the street. The curb was higher than he'd thought and he almost twisted an ankle. "Leave him alone!" *And leave me alone!*

A horn blared and it occurred to Nudger he was in the middle of a busy street; the yellow center line was beneath his feet.

He paused to let a huge gleaming shape flash past him, hearing the driver curse. Nudger leaned into the passing vehicle's rush of air, then he looked both ways and ran on toward the struggle on the opposite sidewalk. He was aware of a knot of people outside the Marriott, huddled together silently and staring at what was happening, as if they were actors in this scene but without lines or action. Bystanders only. Couldn't do a thing to help.

As Nudger closed in on the fray, he saw for the first time the glint of metal. The big man in the vest had drawn a knife.

Nudger hesitated, experiencing one of those wrenching moments when he questioned his decision not to carry a gun. Then he swallowed the coppery taste of fear and ran on. He wondered for an instant what he was doing here, why he did what he did for a living. Why wasn't he selling appliances?

"A cop!" somebody down the street finally shouted. "Christ, get a cop!"

The two men stopped beating Dancer when they noticed Nudger's approach. He felt a brief satisfaction. He was galloping to the rescue, spooking the bad guys. Any second they'd turn and run. Bullies were cowards.

The big one stepped forward, raising the knife and holding it delicately out in front of him in the manner of an experienced knife-fighter. "C'mon, fucker!" he yelled. He was up for this, and not running away; he wanted blood. He waggled the long blade. "This is all for you, Mr. Macho. Hoo-eee! C'mon, you Rambo cocksucker!"

Nudger decided that one wasn't spooked; he involuntarily slowed his pace but kept closing distance anyway.

Then the smaller assailant grabbed the big man's arm. Somewhere a woman yelled something about the police.

The big man shifted the knife in his grip so it rested flat against his palm, then whirled with surprising grace and slapped Dancer across the face with it. Dancer, who'd been doubled over between the two men, slumped all the way to the pavement and lay curled on his side.

The smaller man kicked him in the back, then both of Dancer's attackers turned and ran down the street. They were pumping elbows and knees hard, gray coattails flying. As they rounded the corner, two teenage boys pretended they were going to give chase, but they wisely turned back. Maybe they'd glimpsed the knife. Maybe they'd simply gotten smart young.

Nudger helped Dancer to his feet, getting his toes stomped for the effort. That irritated him; sometimes he developed ingrown toenails when his feet were stepped on.

Dancer groaned. "Ah, shit, man, didn't they do a job on me?" Alcohol fumes rose from him. And something else; he'd vomited onto his shirt. Drinker's vomit. Nasty.

"Can you stand by yourself?"

"Oh, sure." But he slumped against Nudger.

"Hurt bad?"

"No," Dancer said. He actually managed a crooked grin. "They were only trying to make an impression on me, you might say." There was a thin cut along his left cheek, where he'd been slapped with the flat of the knife blade, like a shaving cut from a straight razor. Not serious, but it would be painful when Dancer sobered up.

Some impression, Nudger thought. Dancer almost lost his balance, did a precarious little shuffle, said, "Wheee!"

People were starting to gather. Nudger knew the police would be along soon to ask questions, possibly of him. Explanations would be demanded. Facts would be made known. Among them that Nudger was following Dancer, working for Helen Crane. Dancer would find out about the arrangement. A no-no.

"Come on," Nudger said, and began walking Dancer north on Broadway, toward where the Volkswagen was parked. People stared after them, then gradually lost interest.

Dancer had to stop and vomit twice on the way to the car. There was no blood in what he was retching onto the sidewalk; Nudger wasn't sure if Dancer was sick because of the beating or because he'd drunk past his limit.

"Where we goin'?" he asked, as Nudger dumped and shoved him into the passenger seat of the Volkswagen. Dancer seemed to have grown extra arms and legs without joints.

"Someplace where you can sleep off your drunk." Nudger pushed on the door until it latched, as if he were closing an overstuffed trunk. There—Dancer was in!

Nudger walked around the front of the car and got in behind the steering wheel. He got the balky little engine going and jerked the VW away from the curb abruptly enough to snap his and Dancer's heads back. Minor whiplash.

"Car's little," Dancer remarked. "Reminds me of a coffin."

"Me, too, sometimes," Nudger said.

"Get in an accident, they just weld six handles on it and bury you, huh?"

"I don't like to think about that," Nudger said.

"Can you get the ballgame on the radio? I got a bet on the Cards."

Nudger tuned to the KMOX broadcast of the game. The score was already five to nothing, favor of the Cubs. "Shit!" Dancer said.

"It's not over yet," Nudger told him.

"It's never over till the final out," the play-by-play man said over the radio. "We just gotta keep our heads high and hang in there and wait for a break." Just then one of the Cubs hit a home run. That made it six to nothing.

"Turn off the radio, will you?" Dancer said.

Nudger did. Then he got his roll of antacid tablets from his shirt pocket and thumbed two of the chalky white disks into his mouth. Dancer was smelling up the car; it'd be a long time before the odor went away, Nudger realized glumly. He chewed rhythmically, letting the bouncing motion of the Volkswagen aid the action.

By the time he turned the car onto the highway, Dancer was asleep, and most of the knots in Nudger's stomach had finally come untied.

"Can't pay . . ." Dancer moaned, as the Volkswagen picked up speed and the wind buffeted his perspiring face. "Ain't no way. . . ." He opened his eyes momentarily and glanced over at Nudger. Headlight beams from cars passing in the opposite direction flashed across his features, as if lending him vitality and animation and then instantly snatching it away. "You got a hit, pal? Or maybe some money to lend me?"

"I got nothing but hope," Nudger told him.

He'd have had less of that if he'd noticed the black Chrysler convertible that followed them from downtown.

KATHLEEN FINNERAN

KATHLEEN FINNERAN (1957–) was born in St. Louis and grew up in Florissant, Missouri, where she graduated from McCluer North High School. She attended Florissant Valley Community College and Washington University. In 1990, Kathleen was the recipient of a Missouri Arts Council Writers' Biennial Award for her essay, "New Houses," which is reprinted in this volume. Finneran has also been a resident at the MacDowell Colony for the Arts and at the Cottages at Hedgebrook, a writers' colony for women. Her first book, *The Tender Land: A Family Love Story*, was published by Houghton Mifflin in June 2000. Having resided in New York City for nearly a decade, Finneran plans to return to St. Louis to be closer to her family and devote more time to her writing.

NEW HOUSES

1987

This summer, if the spring is not unseasonably severe and construction stays on schedule, my sister and her husband will be moving with their three children into a new house in one of the newest subdivisions in the northern suburbs of St. Louis. Last Sunday they drove out to their lot to look at the excavation that by this week will be their basement. Next Sunday they will tell themselves they'll stay home. There is no need to drive out. There is no point. There is nothing to see. But by three o'clock they will take the baby from her nap, put the kids in the car, and head for the site. Their curiosity about the hole will not subside. It is their home. It is their substructure. They will walk around it and stop. They will survey it from each side. Their son will throw a clod of dirt down onto the cement floor. Their daughter will do the same, and then she will tell on both of them, saying she did it because he did it and that she wouldn't have done it if he hadn't done it at all. Her brother will say, uh-uh, and will want to push her. Their father, knowing this, will say if they're going to fight around the hole, he'll have to take them all home. And their mother, my sister, bouncing the baby in her arms and standing on what might become a flower bed or a back walk, will tell my niece and nephew if that's how they're going to treat their new house they might as well not go to the trouble of having it built; they can just stay in their old house until they learn to behave. Or, more likely, she will simply say "Stop it, you two." Either way they will have had something happen around their hole. Each Sunday they will have had something happen around their hole so that by summer, with two handfuls of dirt in the basement (or not), they will move into their new house with their newly-seeded lawn and not need to remember that sixteen or so Sundays ago they stood around a barren basement—Sarah told on Jesse; Allison could not yet talk—and became familiar with their house from the ground up.

Sarah is six. Jesse is four. Allison just had a birthday, but in the weeks since, she has forgotten her age, or perhaps holding up a single finger is a trick she has grown tired of. Allison, small as she is, is the cause of the new construction. All two feet and twenty pounds of her have put a cramp on the quarters. My brother-in-law was the first to realize it. To say he realized it, though, is to sell him short. He preconceived it. He said one day, around the fourth or fifth month of my sister's pregnancy—it must have been a holiday or an occasion; we were all at their house; we were all there to hear it—he said, "What with the baby coming, this house won't be big enough anymore."

My sister was slower to see it. She re-painted, re-papered, and re-curtained, and just before the baby was born she bought bunk beds. Jesse was assigned the bottom bunk, Sarah the top, and, in the next room, Allison came along for the crib.

Allison was born tiny and has remained tiny. On her regular visits to the doctor, she always comes up short on the scale. It is probable that through most of her pediatric life she will be under par on the proverbial charts. She will never take up much space. She is, as Sarah might say, "small for her size."

Yet it is Allison, little undersized Allison, who has caused my sister (after two months of settling arguments about who gets to sleep on the top bunk) to start thinking about a house with four bedrooms, two baths and a half. "After all," she says, "this house isn't going to get any bigger and with Allison here there's that much less room."

The house Allison has overcrowded sits on the last lot of St. Eugene

Street in the city of Florissant, a suburb of St. Louis. St. Eugene runs between St. Edward and St. Catherine, crossing St. Anthony before branching onto St. Benedict. St. Anthony, it seems, is the patron saint of through traffic, the sacred artery for such side streets as Sts. Edith and Patrice (which turns into St. Maurice); Sts. Bernadette, Brendan, and Bernard; Sts. Richard, Ronald, and Rose; Sts. Nicholas and Malachy. To the north, St. Anthony is graced by Sts. Christina and Regina, Augusta, Baptista, and Diana, and to the south by Sts. Florent and Madeleine. It was to this saintly scheme, to No. 200 St. Patrick Lane—a street that intersects St. Anthony on one end and parallels it on the other—it was to this canonized enclave that my parents came from the city to the suburbs. It is from these streets that my sister, thirty-two years later, will move with her husband and her children—second generation suburbanites—further into the suburbs, into the secular world of the subdivision of Willow Creek.

When my parents moved to the suburbs, North County was more parochial than it is today. I don't mean this in a strictly religious sense, though it was densely Catholic in 1955—as evidenced by the fact that in our neighborhood each street had its own saint and probably has less of a Catholic populace in 1987. When I say that North County was more parochial in 1955, I mean that it had provincial qualities. It was a settlement, not merely a spillover of the metropolis. It was rural. Backyards bordered on farmlands. To live in North County thirty-two years ago, twenty years ago, fifteen years ago, was to live within the discoverable distance of land that was cultivated, not developed. Suburbanism was not yet all sprawl.

That has changed. The house my sister will move into is being built on land that, until last year, was among the numbered acres of open land left in Florissant. Where an uninhabited farmhouse stood, there are now four new model homes—the display line of Willow Creek, a Jones Company community. (There is a creek; I have not yet seen a willow.) A few miles away, the fields of the Jesuit Seminary of St. Stanislaus, a mysterious locale in our childhood lore, are now the site of McBride and Son's homes marketed as River Wood Estates. (Another well-selling name, though not completely untrue. There is a river in the vicinity, and a small stretch of trees have been left undisturbed.)

The names of these new subdivisions offer this allure: the suburbs as serenity, as an environment of fashionable rusticity, charm, and distinction. In truth, the creek behind my sister's new house is known to nearly everyone in Florissant as Coldwater Creek, but The Homes at Coldwater Creek is a name that does not have much chance of escaping the connotation of coldwater flats. The name Willow Creek, on the other hand, conveys a wispy, graceful, and leisurely image, rather than one of old linoleum and a limited supply of hot running water.

Not far from my sister's prospective new home, another subdivision is being christened Cobblestone Creek. I'm not sure if the creek that runs through it is Coldwater Creek or a branch of it that, until now, has been called by another name, but to make the creek's new name appear authentic, the developers have literally cobbled the creek. Its dirt banks have been covered with cobblestones.

In the naming of new subdivisions, creeks and crossings seem to carry cache in the current market. Other subdivisions vying for buyers this year are Deer Creek and Walnut Creek, Quail Creek, Pebble Creek, and Plum Creek. New homes can be bought at Carriage Crossing and Cambridge Crossing, at Drovers Crossing, Hunters Crossing, and Kehrs Mill Crossing, at Victoria Crossing and Woodlyn Crossing. Farms are also popular. New to the suburbs of St. Louis are The Estates at Lexington Farms, Wellington Farm, Coventry Farm, Peachtree Farms, and Pegasus Farms. Trees and horses round out the allusions to affluence—Remington Oaks and Waterford Oaks, Polo Parc and Polo Run.

If I sound skeptical about this stage of suburban development, it is not a skepticism towards suburbia or new houses. It is a judgment about what I think of as a corporate aesthetic, a theme notion of building. I grew up in the suburbs when there was a moment of unpretentiousness about them, when there was no hard sell, when streets could be named after saints without a second thought that it would mean early martyrdom on the market.

Some will argue that I am overlooking the streets in River Wood named for the Jesuit Seminary, and all of the streets—and especially the entrance—of Sacre Coeur Estates. The streets at River Wood—Seminary Court, Benedictine Court, St. Stanislaus Court, Mission Walk Court, and Grotto Court—are, I admit, not the names one would pick for a secular sales pitch, but they are strategic nonetheless. Consider the McBride Company's news release printed in a recent Sunday *Homes* section of the *St. Louis Post-Dispatch:*

> The development is built on 212 acres that once were vineyards and farmlands of the historic St. Stanislaus Seminary. The tradition of the

vineyards and the old Jesuit winery, which made wine in the 19th and early 20th centuries, sets the refined mood and theme for River Wood Estates.

Considerable attention was devoted to the maintenance and enhancement of the natural beauty of the land, and many of the original landmarks have been carefully preserved. The one-time prayer grotto used by the Jesuit brothers was rebuilt and now houses a Madonna, imported from Spain, to commemorate and maintain the traditional character of the grotto. The main avenue of the development closely traces the original pathway once followed by the Jesuits through expansive vineyards.

By retaining ties to the seminary, perhaps McBride and Son's sought historic absolution. But it should be noted that the streets of River Wood named for the seminary are surrounded by streets with more palatable names—Chardonnay, Beaujolais, Chianti—names that can be made to serve as reminders of local vineyard history as well as to suggest wealth and worldliness.

The entrance to Sacre Coeur Estates is undeniably Catholic. Embedded in the low brick walls that announce the subdivision are medallions of Christ with his heart exposed—the Sacred Heart. Once past the entrance, however, decisions were made more ecumenically, with streets named Salvation Road and Justice Road, Goodness Drive, Mercy Drive, Patience Drive, and Chaste Street. Courts were called Christus Court, Joyful Court, Goodness Court, and Advocate Court. In naming the streets of Sacre Coeur, the Christian moral majority was in session in the suburbs.

My sister and her husband see beyond this superficiality that dismays me. They are in most ways more tolerant than I. They will move from their rather anonymous-looking ranch house on St. Eugene into a house being built especially for them. For my brother-in-law, this will be a new experience; he has always lived in second-hand houses. For my sister, it will be exciting but not extraordinary. As children, we never lived in a house that had been previously owned or occupied. No one ever drove by our house, slowed down, and pointed out to someone that there was where they once had lived. No one else had grown up in our house before us or had memories of it as it had originally been, before one thing was added or another thing changed. No one else's treasures—or pets—

had been buried in the backyard.

To be born into a house is to accept its existence almost as it accepts your own. The house my sister Mary and I were born into, the one my brother Michael had moved into as a small boy, was on a street where all the houses were the same size and the same shape, all built at the same time by the same man with the same set of plans. All the trees, having been planted in the same year, were relatively the same height, and all the grass was started from the same seed. Later, all the men would decide to switch to zoysia in the same summer, so that even with changes things stayed the same. Inside the houses, the rooms were such that given conventional fixtures and pieces of furniture, there were not many options for placement, and so the living room in one house was set up pretty much the same as the living room in another—likewise the dining room, the kitchen, the bedrooms, the bath. On that street, we all watched TV facing the same direction, ate facing the same wall, slept under the same window, got up at night and stumbled through the same darkness down the same hall. In everyone's home we were always at home. Life on St. Patrick was for the most part predictable.

In 1960, my father tells me, people put in patios. In 1962, central air. In 1963, one family after another knocked out the wall between the dining room and the basement steps and replaced it with a wrought iron rail that was painted in one color and streaked with another, a finish commonly called "antiqued." In 1964, basements were finished off. This meant putting up paneling, laying down tile, dropping the ceiling, building a bar. All the men on the block helped on one basement and then they helped on another. It was in or around 1964 that life in the suburbs became subterranean.

Parties were held in the basement. First Communion parties. Confirmation parties. Christening parties. Had we not moved from our house on St. Patrick, I suspect the basement would have shaped our memories of graduation parties, wedding showers, fiftieth birthdays, funerals. But instead those times would have as their setting our new house, with its large living room, dining room, family room, and landscaped back lawn. No more the early memories of the finished basement, the hi-fi in the corner, the swaglight and day-bed decor, the sight of a tall uncle ducking on the last step under the low-ceiling, or of my father playing the part of bartender behind the brick bar he built, a shy, self-conscious man trying to look smooth.

These are the memories of the first house, the one I was born into, a small house much like the house my sister will soon move out of, one whose space was filled up by the birth of my brother Sean who—just as my niece Allison had done at my sister's house—caused my parents, in 1967, to start thinking about a bigger house, one with two stories, four bedrooms, two baths and a half.

I don't know if my sister would consider her life as parallel to my parents' as I make it seem. Certainly there are differences; yet the structure she has set up for her three children is much the same as the structure our parents set up for the three of us, then for the four of us—finally there would be five of us—and unique within that structure was the experience of watching our own house being built.

The house my parents built was on the last remaining lot of a subdivision that had been finished eight years earlier. My father hired a contractor whose specialty it was to build on these "last lots." In a small way, our contractor, and other contractors like him, diversified suburbia by going in years after a subdivision had been settled and erecting houses independently designed and privately commissioned. My father called these men "bungalow boys." I don't know if "bungalow boys" is an actual term used within the construction industry; my father likes to call people as he sees fit. But wherever there is a two-story house looming over a street of single stories, or a split-level house on a street where houses are straightforwardly one level or another; wherever the grandiloquence of a brick house makes so many frame houses look informal; where one house looks indigenous and another does not, or something sticks out, stands out, and is stylistically, unavoidably, downright different, it might be a good bet that a bungalow boy had been by.

I could not say with certainty that all families who bought houses built by bungalow boys were welcomed into their neighborhoods with a slight resentment and the rumor of being more affluent than they actually were or ever would be. But I could assume it from experience. The resentment rises because these last lots, vacant for years, come to be thought of as common ground. The man across the street brings his leaves over and burns them. No harm. The boys around the block make a moto-cross course, a dirt bike dream. No more harm. The lady next door puts in a few extra rows of tomatoes by planting over the property line. No harm at all. But then the lot is bought and bulldozed. On the one hand, the people in the neighborhood see the construction as a good thing. The lot was an eyesore. Still, like any takeover—corporate or common ground—there is resentment. The man across the street will have to bag his leaves. When the lot was a lot he could burn them and be happy. Likewise for the boys around the block—no more dirt bike danger, no more dust. And the lady next door, so many tomatoes short, will have to thin out the spaghetti sauce or use store-bought—the choice between rationing or Ragu. That is the resentment. And then the house is built. It is bigger than the others on the block. It is that many years more modern. There is speculation about the people who could afford such a house.

A salesman for Alton Brick, my father was the first white collar worker in his family. But white collar work has a whim all its own. Within a few years after moving into our new house, the brick business bottomed out and my father went back to laying bricks in the coke ovens of the Granite City Steel Mill—the job he had as a young man, the one, in fact, that had caused my mother and father to move to the northern suburbs of St. Louis in the first place. In short, we lived where we lived because my mother refused to reside in a town built around a smelt, Granite City, where my father was born and lived as a boy. No matter; my mother simply said no. New and nearby, North County was as close as my mother would get to Granite City.

Our first house, then, the one I was born into, was chosen because of its convenience to the place where my father apprenticed, learning the trade that had been the livelihood of his family for generations before him. The second house, the one we watched being built, ostensibly because of a new baby, was chosen to symbolize a second career and would outlast the short success that it stood for, reminding us, sadly sometimes, that my father did not get out of life what he hoped for, did not break out of the brick trade and into the brick business.

Our second house was built in a subdivision called Stonehaven, about five miles east of St. Patrick and the other saint streets, but joined to them by the long arm of St. Catherine. The name of our new street was Brookstone, which came off of Creststone, ran into Millstone, and backed up to Bradstone. Our zip code changed a digit; our telephone stayed the same. We moved from the parish of North American Martyrs to that of St. Thomas Apostle and from the jurisdiction of the A&P to that of the IGA.

The house took the best part of a year to build, a year of Sundays driving out to the site. On the day we drove out to see the basement, there was a boy walking on the wall of cement, putting one foot frighteningly in front of the other, arms out for balance. A blond-haired boy of nine or ten, he was wearing blue jeans and a black sweatshirt with gold letters across the chest that spelled ATONEMENT. The sweatshirt was big on the boy; it hung on him like a banner. With his arms outstretched, ATONEMENT was pulled straight across his chest, and his concentration and slow-footedness made it seem as if he were in a parade or a church procession, walking in a rehearsed way and bearing the message of reconciliation.

When we got out of the car, my brother, whose habit it was to read out loud every sign he saw, said "Atonement," and then he yelled to the boy "You go to Atonement?" and the boy, not looking up from his feet, nodded slightly and turned the corner of the wall. Two smaller lines of letters ran across his back. "Lutheran School," my brother read out loud. Just before my father was about to yell at the boy, he jumped off the wall and went home. "Don't you kids get it in your heads to try that," he said to us instead, and my mother, bouncing the baby in her arms and standing on what would become a flower bed or a front walk said, "They ought to put a sign up or something." (This is the kind of thing my mother says, and she means it. Yet if a sign said "Keep Back," she would be the first person to move closer. She touches things where signs say Do Not Touch. She picks flowers in public places and doesn't even hide them in her purse or in her pocket. She has, at times, passed off coupons for products that weren't in her cart. To the matter at hand: if my father had not been with us she would have let us walk that wall—with the caution, of course, to be careful.)

From Sunday to Sunday, the house took shape, changing from a skeletal framework to an enclosed space. Until there were stairs, however, we could not explore what we most wanted to explore—the depths and heights of our house. To us, as children, the stairs were the most crucial part of the construction, and it seemed as if we waited for them forever. Finally, one Sunday, they were there. We rushed to the second story to stake out our territory, to stand in the rooms my parents had pointed out to us on the blueprint, Michael's room, Mary's room and mine, the smallest room belonging to the baby, to Sean, for whom the house had been built.

When we had satisfied ourselves with the second story, we headed for the basement. Only with the promise that we would not step off the stairs would my father allow us to go down. It was dark, he said, and dangerous, with construction materials—nails mostly—lying all over the floor. So, staying on the steps, Michael, Mary, and I descended into the darkness.

I don't know, for sure, if they saw what I saw, but it seemed to me—from the sudden silence—that it was a shared vision. I was nine—Michael and Mary two and four years older—and I had never seen the words, had only heard them once when a boy down the street had shouted them at another boy as their fathers pulled them away from a fight. Fuck you, someone had written, with mud, on our basement wall. When we came back upstairs, none of us said anything about it and later, my father, having seen them himself, went back down and scraped the words off the wall.

In an odd way, it was those words that made me first think of our house as a home. The steps that took us down into the darkness delivered us into the world as we had never experienced it, a profane world, a world that turned on the unexpected, one of which we were undeniably a part. In truth, I was both thrilled and disturbed by those words. I was disturbed that our house had been defaced but, secretly, I was thrilled that someone had dared to do it, had behaved boldly, in a manner I would never have been able to behave myself, timid person that I was and always would be. I was confused by these feelings, and slightly ashamed, but ascending the stairs with Michael and Mary, I felt suddenly safe, as if I realized, for the first time, that a home was a place large enough to house such contradictions.

Since that Sunday, much has happened in our house. A year after we moved in, my sister Kelly was born and rooms were rearranged to accommodate her arrival. Years later, my younger brother Sean, whose birth provided my parents with a reason to build a bigger house, would die suddenly at the age of fifteen. My father would carry him, near death, downstairs from the room he had come to share with Michael on the second story. Fuck you, I wanted to scream at someone—God? I wasn't sure who—when we lost him. Fuck you, I wanted to write on someone else's walls. Our house, now, is emptier without him.

One of these Sundays, before the spring has ended, we will all go with my sister and her family to see the house she and her husband are having built, not far from where we all grew up. Other families will be out surveying their sites, and seeing them there, children in tow, babies in arm, will make all of my reservations about this latest stage of suburban development seem insignificant. By whatever name—Willow Creek, Polo Parc—the suburbs remain places where houses are built and lives are begun. On the Sunday we go out to the site to see it, my sister's house is still roofless and without walls, but despite what is missing, we can make out what is there. Hers is a new house on its way to becoming a home.

EUGENE B. REDMOND

POET, PLAYWRIGHT, AND LITERARY EDITOR Eugene Redmond (1937–) was born in St. Louis but moved with his family to East St. Louis when he was an infant, attended public school there, and considers that city his home. After serving with the U.S. Marine Corps, Redmond came home and earned degrees in English at Southern Illinois University and Washington University in St. Louis. In 1967, Redmond co-founded Black River Writers Press. Since 1968, he has been literary executor of the Henry Dumas Estate, collaborating with Toni Morrison and others in bringing out seven collections of Dumas's poetry and prose.

In 1976, the same year Doubleday published his *Drumvoices: The Mission of Afro-American Poetry: A Critical History*, East St. Louis named Eugene Redmond its Poet Laureate. Another public honor came a decade later, in 1986, when a group of East St. Louis authors formed the Eugene B. Redmond Writers Club in recognition of Redmond's passionate advocacy of African American writing and mentorship of young black writers. Redmond also has poured his creative energy into launching literary magazines such as *Drumvoices Revue, Literati Internazionali*, and *The Original Chicago Blues Annual,* all of which showcase the work of emerging multicultural writers.

Redmond is the author of six volumes of poetry, including *The Eye in the Ceiling: Poems* (1991), which was awarded an American Book Award from the Before Columbus Foundation for Excellence in Multicultural Literature in 1993. Currently, Eugene Redmond is professor of English at Southern Illinois University at Edwardsville.

With the exception of "Honoring the Female Olympian of the Century," the poems that follow are from *The Eye in the Ceiling*.

HONORING THE FEMALE OLYMPIAN OF THE CENTURY

Like batons, history's hand-me-down dreams
pass from brain to limb to breath
& suddenly she becomes songified wings
souloing in air & speed & memory,

introspective as a Miles-muted trumpet

sung by starting blocks, stopwatches, cameras,
measuring tapes & an earthly-astral choir

even as she zings across asphalt,
sand, cement, grass, wood, time zone,
basketball court & water

hurdling injury, setback, rope, tragedy,
bar, stereotype, handicap, statistic & doubt

hurling javelins of hope as she
pushes the cordial dust of defeat
into faces of competitors

tracking and fielding in/her/i/(s)tance:
ancestrails of Jesse Owens,
Spike Perkins & Wilma Rudolph

o aerial Tigerette of Piggott Street,
alumnus of Lincoln Park's Mary Brown Center
& Dunham Technique, of Lincoln High
& high hurdles

raised on rituals of prep, the gospel
according to Motown, & prayer:
orbiting/orbiting Cahokia Mounds
& landing in East St. Louis
aboard a gold & bronze mothership
minted in Franklin School bop,
hip/hopscotch, UCLA, NCAA,
a quartet of Olympics—the fulcrums of

Atlanta, Moscow, New York,
Los Angeles & Goodwill Games

displaying her lavish lust
for the needs of children,
the sung, the unsung, the wannabe
& yet-to-be sung

high-fivin hand-me-down dreams
& premiering yestermorrow's victories
in cinder-quick limb/o of breath,
songified in air & speed & memory

when Jackie is sung she sings for us all

WEDGE WALL, HUGE HAND

(LEFFINGWELL & FRANKLIN AVENUES, ST. LOUIS, MO.)

For Luther Mitchell, the Rev. Charles Koen, Sam Petty and Percy Green.

I

Walls usually obstruct, disrupt
Or hold things up—
Rarely are they pathways to pride and power
Like St. Louis' WALL OF RESPECT,
Black/Built so Blacks can see their (Blackness) tower.

The WALL is a huge hand out-stretched
Or
Turned
On
Its
Edge
Toward the caged overcast;
A hard hand whose horoscopes
Criss-cross
Or

Run parallel in time
3000-years-backwards-in-the-mind;

A hallowed hand
Blood-stained in BLACK BRICK,
Etchings
Of
Unearned
Agony.

II

See: Black people passing by;
Younger girls stop and sigh;
Brick-by brick the faces rise;
Stare, stunned, the stolen eyes.

Ending its day-long glance,
The swollen sun splurges a final stare—
Its stilletto eye having backed bone-hard
The painted faces in the
Skillfully-sculpted hand.

Mounting ladders and platforms
Black artists,
Their solemn sacred tools singing in silence,
Applied pride/pain.

From the valley of asphalt and garbage cans
An uneven line of eyes,
Some leaning against iron knees,
Watched artists moving like
Ancient Egyptian laborers paralyzing sand into
Magnificent faces of Egyptian pyramids.

III

The WALL?
Curiosity turned to reverence!
The ungraspable
Grasped;
Towering untouchability
Over timid stares of the "enemy."

Eye-for-an-eye
For each passerby,
Wooer of wine-washed sidewalks,
The WALL is the people
Is the WALL is
A Whale WALL.

Strikingly still at a vigorous pace;
A haggard beard or a violent face;
Cold, angered stares or a bonnet with lace;
Or Garvey's warm urge: "Up You Mighty Race!"

WALL belongs to the peopleBLACK,
Who come to it,
Like Moslems to Mecca—
Wrested, finally, by truth from colder walls
That dope their minds and give
Them a white Jesus to die for.

The WALL winds miles miles miles miles . . .
And the steel-knuckled fists jut
Like street lamps along the way.

CARRYOVER

(Thinking about Jimmy Dixon, Clarence Nelson and Darnell Sullivan)

I have been tattooed for life:
A thought called EAST SAINT LOUIS
Is etched on each Island of my Brain.
EAST SAINT LOUIS will rise!
Will rise from the muddy gutty Mississippi.
Will rise disguised as AFRICA.
WILL RISE!
WILL RISE THROUGH MIND-EYES OF

hustler & hairdresser
teacher & astronaut

athlete and anchorman
mathematician and mime

waiter & dishwasher
elk & mason

cabdriver and architect
hodcarrier and cartoonist

maid & mechanic
doctor & undertaker

journalist and judge
bluesician and be-bopper

preacher & plumber
gardener & garbage collector

violinist and veterinarian
griot and gutbucketeer

EAST SAINT ain't dead yet!
I've got the scars and tattoos to prove it!
Can't you feel the yeast in the air!

RIVER OF BONES AND FLESH AND BLOOD

(MISSISSIPPI)
For Doris Cason

River of time:
Vibrant vein,
Bent, crooked,
Older than the Red Men
Who named you;
Ancient as the winds
That break on your
Serene and shining face;
One time western boundary of America
From whose center
Your broad shoulders now reach
To touch sisters
On the flanks

River of truth: Mornings
You leap, yawn 2000 miles,
And shed a giant joyous tear
Over sprouting, straggling
Hives of humanity;
Nights you weep
As the moon, tiptoeing
Across your silent silky
Face, hears you praying
Over the broken backs
Of black slaves who rode,
Crouched and huddled,
At your heart in the bellies
Of steamships.

River of Memory:
Laboratory for Civil War
Boat builders
Who left huge eyes of steel

Staring from your sullen depths;
Reluctant partner to crimes
Of Ku Klux Klansmen;
River moved to waves
Of ecstasy
By the venerable trumpet
Of Louis Armstrong.

River of Bones:
River of bones and flesh—
Bones and flesh and blood;
The nation's largest
Intestine
And longest conveyor belt;

River MISSISSIPPI:
River of little rivers;
River of rises,
Sometimes subdued
By a roof of ice, descending finally
On your Southward course
To spit
Into the Gulf
And join the wrath
Of larger bodies.

MONA VAN DUYN

BORN AND RAISED IN IOWA, Mona Van Duyn (1921–) received her bachelor's degree from the University of Northern Iowa (formerly Iowa State Teachers College), her M.A. from the University of Iowa, and honorary doctorates from six universities. During the late 1940s, Van Duyn and her husband, Jarvis Thurston, taught at several universities in the Midwest and the South before coming to Washington University in 1950. While a lecturer at Washington University College, Van Duyn's stature as a poet rapidly ascended, and she garnered numerous prestigious awards before receiving the National Book Award in 1971 for *To See, To Take.* In 1990, Van Duyn's volume, *Near Changes*, received the Pulitzer Prize, and two years later, she was appointed Poet Laureate of the United States, succeeding her University City neighbor, friend, and fellow poet, Howard Nemerov.

In her fifty years as a major American poet, Van Duyn has sustained an aesthetic belief in the power of art to resurrect and redeem the human spirit. She often takes the commonplace occurrences in domestic life as her metaphors for poetry and finds in them emotion and human experience on an epic scale. Of Van Duyn, critic Jane Augustine wrote, "She can be philosophical, ironic, elegiac, penetratingly personal. She lives in and looks at domestic life in suburbia, where she finds that experience is as murderous as on battlefields, highways, and ghetto streets. . . ."

THE BLOCK

Childless, we bought the big brick house on the block,
just in case. We walked the dog. Mornings the women
looked up from their clipping and pruning and weeding
to greet us, at dusk the men stopped their mowing to chat.
The children were newly married or off to college,
and dogs they had left behind them barked from backyards

at our dog, first in warning, later in greeting.
On other blocks we walked in the zany blare
of adolescent records and stepped around skates
and tricycles left on the sidewalk, but our middle-aged block,
busy and quiet, settled us into its solace.

The years bloomed by. The old dogs were put to sleep.
We bought a scoop to walk our new pup on his leash
as the block turned newly cranky about its curbs.
A lucky few dragged a staggering grandchild on visit
up and down, shyly accepting praise.
The wife on the corner shovelled their snow. "They say
it's what kills the men. I won't take a chance with my husband."
Then bad news began to come, hushed voices passed it
across back fences, the job of collecting for plants
found its permanent volunteer on the block. Later
more flowers, and one left alone in some of the houses.
Salads and cakes and roasts criss-crossed the street.

Then the long, warm, secret descent began
and we slid along with it. "We need a last dog," I said,
"but I can't face it." My husband became the husband
of the widows on either side in his husbandly tasks
of lifting and drilling for pictures and fixing faucets,
and a kindly old handyman took over, house by house,
the outdoor chores of mowing and small repairs.
"What would we do without Andrew?" everyone said.
The graying children came oftener, checking on things.
One widower wanted to marry the widow next door,
but "I'm through with *that* business!" she told him. The lone lesbian
kept up her house, but nearly wrinkled away.
I turned my flower borders to beds of groundcover.

The end came before we knew it. All in one year
my husband retired and half of the houses emptied.
Cancer ate four, heart attacks toppled some others,
a nursinghome closed over one, the rest caned off
to apartments with elevators. For Sale signs loomed
like paper tombstones on the weedy lawns.

The gentle years turned vicious all of a sudden.
"I can't believe it," we said. "The block's gone.
No one buys houses now." Those of us left
drew close, exchanged keys "in case something happens."
The wealthy patriarch sat all day on his porch
across the street and watched the distant disaster.
"He's way in his nineties," our busybody reported.
"His day and night nurses keep leaving, he's so awful.
And he won't take his pills. He just says, 'What does it matter?'"

We left on a long vacation. Home to the block,
we saw For Sale signs gone, heard new dog voices.
Bedding plants sucked up color from the old soil.
"The block is filled with young families. Everything's changed,"
we heard right away. A flyer stuck in the door:
"Block Party Sunday. Street Blocked Off All Day.
Bring Something To Share. All Bikes and Trikes Are Welcome."
"Oh Lord, do we have to go to all that bedlam?"
my husband said. "Oh God, I think they eat
hot dogs or something like that," I said. Too late,
Time, in its merciless blindness, gave us children.

ADDENDUM TO "THE BLOCK"

"Three new babies are due all at once on the block,"
our soft-hearted widow tells us, walking her fat,
puffing poodle with a new pink bow on her ear.
"Two on the other side of the street, one here."

Within a week three front-step railings blossom
with pink or blue balloons and bold-faced signs
(commercial aids to displaying the shy new joy)
announcing that IT'S A GIRL or IT'S A BOY.

When one celebration comes down, it reveals a mourner.
A small, black dog runs up "to *everyone*,

all day," says the neighbor, and pleads for babying.
"Her nose is out of joint, poor little thing."

Soon, up and down both sidewalks, three black nannies
(two fat, one thin), each pushing a pristine carriage,
acquaint themselves with each other, paint high-pitched rainbows
of giggles and gossip over the street's doze.

The few old-timers, out for their therapeutic
heart-walks, glare or coo into a carriage
as suits their hearts: "More noise, clutter, *coping*,"
or "More life to wrap one's self in, breath, *hoping*."

Before we know it, dangling by his wrist
from the hand of a leaning mother, one infant lurches
as far as our drive, legs testing this strange notion,
toes touching or missing the ground, eyes wild with promotion.

Much later a crowd chooses our street to parade
"ABORTION KILLS BABIES," their frozen faces
grim, their kids in strollers grim, as if we,
the human block, were beneath reality.

Raked leaves in heaps lie at the curb for pickup.
Soon the cold will keep secret behind each door
pain, pleasure, vital or lifeless conceptions,
boundless scopes or chilling circumscriptions.

This morning, though, the sun sends a wordless, warm
hug to us all—children, parents, barren
couples, frail graybeards, gays—"hello? good-bye?"
reaching out of the newborn blue of the sky.

"WE ARE IN YOUR AREA"

At every hour of morning to night my telephone
brings me the news that they are in our area
(or will be in our area by the next afternoon),
Veterans of every war, in every condition
("Judith, you've *got* to get off that phone a half hour,"
a friend told her teenage daughter. "I'm expecting a call
from Disabled American Veterans!") vying to pick up
kindly old clothes that have learned our old bodies,
old dear castiron skillets, the old chairs
we sit on, re- and re-covered since the fifties,
all Lighthouses for the Blind, all Handicapped Workers
who truck in more, still more, Everlasting Light Bulbs,
brooms and mops for our bulging shelves and closets,
Spreaders of Cement Patios who would disembarrass
our yard of its big warm brick one, Tuckpointers, Roofers,
Venders of the Latest Storm Window, Landscapers, Sweeps,
Construction and Remodelling groups in their urgent dozens
who would rip away our downstairs sideporch library
(where books of our friends nap in grownup silence
till we wake them up for a lively romp with our minds)
and nail on a family room for our long-lost children,
Cleaners of Carpets with Three-room, Ten-room Specials,
who disdain my expertise at pushing battered
sudsers and steamers rented from supermarkets,
Basement Waterproofers for our high, dry basement,
Driveway Glazers and Blacktoppers, Plasterers,
College Student Painting Services, pleading
to repaint the paint just spread by other such Students,
Tree Removers who would rid the birds and squirrels
of fruit and bloom I carefully planted and nurtured,
Lawn Care Specialists, scornful of amateur tending,
who poison, spray, feed and aerate on schedule.
While my husband cleans the gutters of the next-door widow
I am on the phone being wooed by yearning guttermen.
There is such a jam in our area of ghostly vans,

pickups and flatbeds there's nowhere to park our car,
such milling crowds of phantom workmen in frontyards
and backyards one hardly dares to go out the door
and enjoy the garden or feed the birds, such parades
of strange, invisible machines being brought to the houses
one can scarcely walk the dog, one fears for the mailman.
Neighbors' houses are shielded away from a visit
by unseen flying buttresses of ladders.
And, in such a silent bedlam of roaring, smashing,
hacking, pounding, jackhammering, sawing, hissing,
in our area one can hardly hear one'sself think.

II

But why aren't they in our area, why won't they come
when the furnace thermostat dies on the coldest weekend
of the whole winter, when a pipe rusts through and water
is pouring out of the ceiling, when treeroots squeeze
through the sewer pipe and grow into tangled clogs,
when all the lights in the neighborhood go out?
Without even a casual "See ya. ." they have slipped away
to another area where they are all booked up.
And why have they left our area, those tender young boys
with the proud, serious faces of first-time earners,
who will mow the lawn, wash cars, try to do anything?
They have moved far away to full-blown adolescence,
to driving and dates, they will not come back any more.
And why have they left, the long-time friends and neighbors
who moved many miles to country retirement homes
or to condos in far mushroom-bulging developments
which are hard to locate even with good directions?

And why, why, taking so much of ours with them,
have they left, those who always supplied us so freely
with our heat and light, those who drove clear off the maps
and left no directions? Soon we must set off to find
their precious, populous place, to be in their area.

DONALD FINKEL

DONALD FINKEL (1929–) was born in New York City and received his baccalaureate degree in philosophy and master's degree in literature from Columbia University. Finkel taught at several colleges and universities before moving to St. Louis to become Poet-in-Residence at Washington University in 1960. Critics have heralded Finkel's work as highly original and inimitable—an energized pastiche of techniques, infused with wit and daring. In several of his most acclaimed volumes of poetry, Finkel focuses on a central metaphor and employs a variety of forms—narrative, direct quotation, "found" writing—to create a sweeping panorama of his subject.

The works that follow come from Finkel's 1994 volume, *Beyond Despair*. The title pays homage to a local nickname for the River des Peres that runs through St. Louis. The volume's introduction, *Headwaters*, precedes the poetry. As in several of Finkel's earlier works, the poems here incorporate historical documentation into original contemporary verse.

HEADWATERS

The River des Peres winds eastward through the City of St. Louis to empty, near its southern limit, into the Father of Rivers. It is believed that, not quite two hundred years ago, a pair of Jesuit fathers established there at its mouth the first white settlement west of the Mississippi.

Moses Austin (father of Stephen Austin, Father of Texas) mentions in his journal pausing at the mouth of the River of Fathers almost one hundred years later, on his way through the wilderness from his quickly dwindling lead mines in Virginia to inspect the prodigious lead deposits of Missouri. During the next two decades Austin amassed a fortune, founding one day's ride south of the des Peres both a town and an industry. Then Austin's luck went sour once more, and once more he began to cast a speculative eye on the wilderness, this time even farther south. Stephen assures us: "The idea of settling North Americans in Texas originated with my father."

During the first half of this century, in the interest of flood control, almost the entire length of the des Peres was straightened, widened, buried or paved. It runs underground for several miles today, beneath Forest Park. In May of 1988, the River des Peres Sewerage and Drainage Works was designated a National Historic Civil Engineering Landmark.

WHAT'S IN A NAME

Des Peres, the map reads—River of the Fathers—
sidling eastward under a scrim of slate-grey ice
past pennants of saffron plastic clattering in the bracken,
past urine-yellow tabloids, a frozen squirrel
temporizing belly-up, clutching in its mummy paws
one last inedible morsel.

Despair—that's what the locals call her—
a moniker, like Old Trollop, or Granny Goat,
but who knows what names the Father of Rivers
mutters each morning as she ambles to greet him
in her slush peignoir, slovenly, pensive, wanton,
cleansed of hope?

AN ENTIRELY NEW IDEA

In 1915 a stray Gulf Coast hurricane visited St. Louis and gave an entirely new idea of what flood flows in this little creek might amount to.

—W. W. Horner, City Beautiful

And the waters prevailed
11 BODIES FOUND
in a little one-room
David Bowman, a Negro

his wife, Adeline
their grandniece Bessie

Raging down Manchester Avenue
a seven-foot river clawed up paving stones.
Pools of Despair filled the bear pits,
eight inches in the birdcage at the zoo.

the search continues
Annie Wagoner, 80
under her bed, which
by the swirling waters

Near Ferguson, on a flood-stalled train,
a news butcher doubled the tariff on his basket
of elderly sandwiches. Provident roofers
stacked their wagons and readied their ladders.

And the windows of heaven
on Hermitage Avenue
and Noah only remained
and they that were with him

Still no voice from a cloud, nor a bow anywhere,
and the earth, behold, was tainted as ever.

Brooding on rain-grey Market Street,
the Inspector of Sewers drafted a letter.

Gentlemen: The danger
a menace to the health
if for no other reason
must be restrained and civilized

So they ran her down where she strayed through the park,
elm twigs and condoms in her hair,
and straightened her kinks and paved her banks
till she strolled the fairgrounds like a proper lady.

transforming the River
as a sewer, it is probably
the World's Most Gigantic
the biggest and best

For into their hands was every beast delivered,
and every fugitive stream, clean or unclean,
buried or burnt, seedtime or harvest, floodtime or dry—
though now and again she climbed from her bed,
ran barefoot through the August grass,
leaving a trail of baleful lakes—
till they set out to bury her, mile by mile.

FOR WHOSE USE

I have made these few observations of my journey to the Mississippi for the Use of my son, should he live to my Age.

—Moses Austin, *A Memorandum*

For whose use this brave alluvium,
this spindly rivulet, this river of fathers,
slinking through the leavings past a silted log
and trusty trike, past a black plastic
garbage bag thrust though the ice
like a pyramid tent at the bottom of winter?

For whose use, this country overspread
with slag-heaps, tailings, smoldering lakes,
this archive of wreckage, this museum of debris?

ALLEN STEELE

ALLEN STEELE (1958–) was born in Nashville, Tennessee, and attended New England College in Henniker, New Hampshire, where he received a B.A. in communications in 1982. After receiving his M.A. in journalism from the University of Missouri–Columbia, Steele worked as a staff writer for several daily and weekly newspapers, freelanced for business and general-interest magazines, and spent a short tenure as a Washington correspondent, covering politics on Capitol Hill. He became a full-time science fiction writer in 1988, following the publication of his first short story, "Live from the Mars Hotel." Since then, Steele has authored a number of novels, short stories, and essays, with his work published in Great Britain, Russia, Poland, and Japan, among other countries.

Steele has won or been nominated for numerous science fiction awards, including the 1990 Locus Award for Best First Novel for *Orbital Decay*, and the 1996 Hugo Award for Best Novella for *The Death of Captain Future*. Steele now lives in western Massachusetts with his wife and three dogs.

The following excerpt is from Steele's novel *The Jericho Iteration*, which takes place in the year 2012, after a devastating earthquake has struck St. Louis.

FROM *THE JERICHO ITERATION*

Let's talk about Jericho.

According to the Book of Joshua, the Canaanite city of Jericho was destroyed after Joshua marched his army around the city's walls for six days. On the seventh day, upon his command, the Israelites blew their ram's horns and began to shout. The walls collapsed, thus allowing Joshua and his followers to overrun the Canaanites and claim the city as their own.

That's how the legend goes, at any rate. About twenty years ago, archaeologists studying the ruins of Jericho in Israel, just outside Jerusalem, arrived at a different conclusion. They uncovered evidence suggesting that

Jericho had been destroyed not by ram's horns but by a major earthquake caused by a geological fault line running through the Jordan Valley. Furthermore, the city was destroyed at least a hundred and fifty years before the reported date of the Battle of Jericho. Hence, the Talmudic account differs considerably from modern interpretations of the same evidence: in short, people took credit for something nature had already done.

And now it's Friday, April 19, 11:32 P.M. About three and a half millennia since the fall of Jericho, give or take a few hundred years, but who's counting? It doesn't make much difference in the long run. The more things change, the more they remain the same.

I'm sitting cross-legged on the living room floor of an abandoned, half-collapsed house in south St. Louis. It's the middle of the night, and I'm dictating these notes into my pocket computer. Joker's nicad is still fully charged, but I'm nonetheless keeping an eye on the battery LED. If it runs low . . .

Well, I'm sure I can find another. They're not as hard to find on this side of town as, say, an unclaimed can of Vienna sausage. On my way here I passed a scavenged 7-Eleven about four blocks away; southside looters normally don't go after batteries, although you never know.

I heard recently about a teenager who was killed scrounging through a video rental shop; seems he had been trying to make out with an armload of movies when a street gang that had claimed the store as their turf caught him. The story that made its way to the *Big Muddy Inquirer* was that they had strung him up from a telephone pole; when he was found the next morning, he had a copy of *Hang 'Em High* wrapped around his purpled neck. A touch of irony, if you like that sort of thing, although I doubt the guys who murdered him would know irony if it shot 'em in the ass with a Smith & Wesson.

Of course, this could be only another rumor. We've heard a hundred of them since the quake, and since it was never substantiated, we never ran it in the paper. Nonetheless, I think I'll keep talking only until the low-battery light begins to blink. Bopping on down to the 7-Eleven ain't what it used to be.

When the family who once lived here moved out of the city, as have so many others since New Madrid, they took with them whatever they could salvage. What little furniture they left behind is mostly buried beneath the rubble of what used to be their bedrooms; there's also a bad stink from that part of the house. I hope it's only a cat. Dead cats don't bother me, but dead children do.

The former residents left behind the refrigerator and the stove, but since there is no electricity in this neighborhood, they don't work. Union Electric must have determined that this is a vacant block, because even the streetlights are inoperative. There's also a filthy couch infested with insects, a mildewed Mickey Mouse shower curtain, which is the sole clue that there were once kids living here—like I said, I hope it's only a dead cat I smell—and, on the top shelf of the kitchen pantry, a half-empty box of Little Friskies.

Got to be a dead cat.

I'll have to ask the dog if he knows.

The dog who discovered me in the house was glad to have the Little Friskies. I found a forgotten spare key tucked beneath the back-door welcome mat—whoever once lived here didn't have much sense of originality when it came to hiding places, but then again, St. Louis used to be a much safer place—and had invited myself in when I heard something panting behind me. I turned around to find, in the last weak light of day, a full-grown golden retriever who had followed me into the backyard. His big red tongue was hanging out of his mouth, his fur was as wet as my leather jacket, but unlike so many other strays I've seen recently he didn't appear to be feral. Just a big old chow dog, living by his means in what used to be a middle-class neighborhood.

He sniffed me and wagged his tail, and didn't mind when I patted him on the head, so I let him into the house with me. What the hell; we both needed company. As luck would have it—for the dog, at least—there was the box of cat food. He didn't seem to mind the moldy taste. I only wish I could have eaten so well.

Friendly pooch. He decided to stay the night. I warned him that he was accompanying a federal fugitive and was thereby subject to prosecution to the full extent of the law, but the mutt didn't give a shit. I had given him a bite to eat, so I was square in his book, and he paid me back by warning me about the helicopter.

Several hours later: the sun was down, I was exhausted from running. Lying on the couch, idly scratching at the fleas that had come crawling out of the upholstery, listening to the cold, hard rain that pattered on the roof and dribbled through the cracks in the ceiling. Eyes beginning to close. It had been a hell of a day.

The dog was curled up on the bare floor next to the couch, dead to the world, when he abruptly leaped to his feet and began to bark. I opened my eyes, glanced at him, saw that he was looking out the wide picture window on the other side of the room.

I couldn't see anything through the darkness, but I could hear a low drone from somewhere outside the house. . . .

Chopper.

I rolled off the couch and fell to the floor, then scurried across the living room and through the kitchen door, out of sight from the window. By now the sound of rotor blades was very loud.

While I cowered in the kitchen, hugging the wall and sweating rain, the dog fearlessly advanced to the window and stood there, barking in defiance as the clatter grew louder. Then the helicopter was above the front lawn, invisible except for its running lights.

Captured by the Apaches.

One, at least: an AH-64 gunship, twenty-one thousand pounds of sudden death. Maybe it was an antique, but I remembered when I was a kid back in '89 and saw the TV news footage of those things circling the skies above Panama City, hunting for PDF holdouts and some pimple-faced cokehead named Noriega. Now one of them was hunting for a journalist named Gerry Rosen.

By the way, did I mention my name?

For several long minutes the Apache hovered outside the window. I could imagine its front-mounted TADS infrared turret peering into the house, the copilot in the chopper's back seat trying to get a clear fix through the downpour. The helicopter was close enough for me to make out the shadowed forms of the pilot and copilot within its narrow cockpit. The picture window shuddered in its tortured frame from the propwash.

It occurred to me that, if the 30-mm chain gun beneath the forward fuselage were to let go, the plaster wall in front of me wouldn't protect me more than would a sheet of Kleenex . . . and if I ran for the back door, the IR sensors would lock onto me before I could make it through the backyard. Anyone seen on the streets by ERA patrols after the nine o'clock curfew was assumed to be a looter, and in this side of town they didn't bother to make arrests anymore. In fact, they didn't even give you the dignity of slinging an old Clint Eastwood flick around your neck.

I clenched Joker against my chest and waited for the bullets to come through the window. They had found my best friend, they had found the poor bastards from the Tiptree Corporation, and now they had found me. . . .

And yet, despite all the noise, locked in the center of a crosshairs, the dog stood his ground. With his paws jammed against the windowsill, his lips pulled back from decayed brown teeth, his tail down but not tucked between his rear legs, this scrawny, matted stray dog angrily snarled and snapped and barked ferociously at the flying machine on the other side of the window, and in a brief, sudden, very clear moment of understanding, I knew what he was saying—

Get out of here, get out of here, this is my house, my house, MY HOUSE, GET THE FUCK OUT OF HERE THIS IS MY HOUSE!

—and then, in that moment between life and death, the copilot studied the image on his night-vision screen and reached a decision.

Ain't nothing here except a damn dog.

The ERA chopper rose upward, then angled away into the wet night, its lights following the ghostly strip of the ruined street until it vanished from sight.

The dog got some more Little Friskies for his smooth move, and I haven't slept since then.

Perhaps you may feel secure, hiding behind whatever walls you've erected around yourself, but I tell you now, as solid fact, that what happened to me and my city is not far removed from you. None of us is safe, and any sense of security you may have now is a lie.

My name is Gerry Rosen. I'm a reporter, and this is what happened to me during two days and three nights in Jericho, now better known as St. Louis, Missouri.

From The Associated Press (on-line edition): May 17, 2012

ST. LOUIS (AP)—A major earthquake, registering 7.5 on the Richter scale, struck St. Louis today, devastating large areas of the city and surrounding area and killing hundreds of people.

The quake, which began at 1:55 P.M. and lasted approximately 45 seconds, was epicentered in the town of New Madrid, about 130 miles southeast of the city. The quake caused high-rise buildings in the downtown area to sway, destroyed scores of smaller buildings and countless homes across the county, and led to the collapse of a light-rail bridge spanning the Mississippi River.

The exact number of people in St. Louis killed or injured by the quake is not known at this time. However, local police and fire officials say that at least two hundred fatalities have been reported so far and city hospitals are overwhelmed by people seeking medical assistance.

Particularly hard hit by the quake was the downtown business district, where many older buildings suffered extensive damage. Although no high-rise buildings collapsed during the quake, many interior walls fell. Dozens of smaller buildings were completely demolished, burying their occupants under tons of rubble. This included City Hall, where at least 10 office workers are reported missing.

Two local schools were also leveled during the quake.

One city fire official said that there were "hardly any survivors" among the elementary schoolchildren who were attending classes at one of them, a Catholic private school in the city's prosperous west side.

Many streets in the downtown area have been ripped up by the collapse of underground caverns beneath the city, causing dozens of vehicles to fall into the gaping crevasses. Underground sewage pipes and electrical conduits were torn apart by the quake, causing the downtown area to be flooded with raw sewage. At least one chemical storage tank has been ruptured, and hazardous toxins are reported to be flowing through storm drains into the Mississippi.

Electrical power has been lost to most of the city, along with telephone lines and cable communications systems. Scattered fires in various neighborhoods have been reported by utility officials, largely caused by severed gas lines. Efforts to control the fires have been hindered by breakage of municipal water lines to much of the city and the loss of firehouses in at least three wards.

The James Eads Bridge, a major conduit for the city's light-rail system, collapsed into the Mississippi River, and eyewitnesses say that a westbound commuter train was crossing the bridge from East St. Louis, Ill., at the time of the quake. No official statement has yet been issued regarding the number of casualties, but officials at the scene say that dozens of people who were riding the MetroLink train may have fallen to their deaths.

The Gateway Arch, the national landmark on the west bank of the Mississippi that is the city's symbol, survived the quake intact, although roof sections of the underground visitors' center beneath the

Arch fell during the quake, killing at least five people and injuring dozens of others. Witnesses report that the Arch itself swayed during the tremors.

Missouri Gov. Andre Tyrell, who was attending the National Governors Convention in Las Vegas at the time of the disaster, has phoned the President to ask for federal assistance, says spokesman Clyde Thomson at the state capital in Jefferson City, itself rocked by the quake. Thomson said that Tyrell is flying back to the state, although commercial air traffic in and out of St. Louis International Airport has been suspended by the Federal Aviation Administration because of hazardous runway conditions.

Although the local Emergency Broadcast System was crippled by the loss of the KMOX-AM radio tower, St. Louis Mayor Elizabeth Boucher went on the air from radio station KZAK-AM at 2:30 P.M. to plead for calm and cooperation from the city's residents. "Please help our police and firemen do their jobs," she said, "and assist your neighbors in whatever way you can."

"May God help us in this time of crisis," Boucher said, her voice shaking.

Several small towns in eastern Missouri and southwestern Illinois were also devastated by the earthquake, the force of which has been estimated to be equivalent to the detonation of 900,000 tons of TNT, or a nine-kiloton nuclear explosion. Significant damage was also reported in Evansville, Ill., and Memphis, Tenn., and tremors were felt as far west as Kansas City, where a church bell was reported to have rung twelve times during the quake.

Hundreds of National Guard troops from across the midwestern region are being sent to Missouri to aid local relief efforts. Spokesmen at the Washington, D.C., headquarters of the Emergency Relief Agency say that ERA troops are being mobilized at this time . . .

(WEDNESDAY, 9:36 P.M.)

Tell me about freedom. I'm willing to listen. Hell, I'll listen to anything, so long as you'll pardon me if I nod off in the middle of the lecture.

Wet, cold, muddy, and confused, I began the long hike out of the park, following the sidewalk down the hill toward the Forest Park Boulevard entrance. Although a couple of Piranhas and Hummers passed me on the road, their crews were too busy to stop and harass a lone individual on foot. Nonetheless, I crossed the golf course at the bottom of Art Hill to avoid a roadblock at the Lindell Boulevard entrance; two Hummers were parked in front of the gate, and I didn't care to explain myself to the soldiers manning the barricade. Sure, I had my press card and I could point out that I was a working reporter on assignment, but these days that sort of argument would just as likely earn me a trip down to Busch Stadium, and not for a baseball game either. The ERA grunts didn't spot me, though, and I managed to leave the park unmolested.

Grabbing a ride on the MetroLink was another problem. After I trudged the rest of the way through the park, I passed through the main gate at Forest Park Boulevard. The MetroLink platform was at the bottom of a narrow railway trench a block away; it was almost completely vacant, but an ERA trooper was standing guard at the top of the stairs leading down to the tracks, a riot baton cradled in his arms.

I glanced at my watch. It was already a quarter to ten. No choice but to tough it out; I was in no shape to slog all the way back to my digs. Trying not to look like I had just mud-wrestled a gorilla, I strode toward the turnstile, reaching into my pants pocket to fish out my fare card.

The trooper studied me as I walked under the light. I gave him a quick nod of my head and started to pass my card in front of the scanner when he took a step forward and barred my way with his stick.

"Excuse me, sir," he said, "but do you know what time it is?"

In the old days, I might have just looked at my watch, said "Yes," and walked on, but these guys were notorious for having no sense of humor. My mind flipped through a half-dozen preconcocted ploys, ranging from pretending to be drunk to simply acting stupid, and realized that none of them would adequately explain why I looked as disheveled as I did. Telling the truth was out of the question; the average ERA trooper had less respect for a reporter than he would for a suspected looter, and screw the First Amendment.

"Is it after nine already?" I feigned embarrassed surprise, then pulled back my sleeve and glanced at my watch. "Oh, shit, I'm sorry. I didn't realize it was so—"

"May I see some ID, please?" Below us, several people sitting on plastic benches beneath the platform awning watched with quiet curiosity. No doubt they had been forced to go through the same ordeal.

"Hmm? Sure, sure . . ." I pulled my wallet out of my back pocket, found my driver's license, and passed it to him. The trooper's nameplate read B. DOUGLAS; he passed my license under a handscanner, then flipped down a monocle from his helmet and waited for the computers at the city's records department to download my file.

It gave me a chance to size him up as well. What I saw was scary: a kid young enough to be my little brother—twenty-one at most—wearing khaki combat fatigues, leather lace-up boots, and riot helmet, with the sword-and-tornado insignia of the Emergency Relief Agency sewn on the left shoulder of his flak jacket. An assault rifle hung from a strap over his right shoulder, a full brace of Mace and tear gas canisters suspended from his belt. He had the hard-eyed, all-too-serious look of a young man who had been given too much authority much too soon, who believed that the artillery he carried gave him the right to kick butt whenever he wished. In another age he might have been a member of Hitler Youth looking for Jews to beat up or a Young Republican wandering a college campus in search of a liberal professor to harass. Now he was an ERA trooper, and by God this was *his* light-rail station.

"Are you aware that you're in a curfew zone, Mr. Rosen?" He pulled my driver's license out from under his scanner but didn't pass it back to me.

I pretended to be appalled. "I am? This is University City, isn't it? There isn't a curfew here."

He stared back at me. "No, sir, you're downtown now. Curfew starts here at nine o'clock sharp."

I shrugged off-handedly. "I'm sorry. I didn't realize that was the situation." I tried an apologetic smile. "I'll keep that in mind next time I'm down here."

"You look awful muddy, old-timer," he said condescendingly. "Fall down someplace?"

Old-timer, indeed. I was thirty-three and Lord of the Turnstiles knew it. If there were the first few gray streaks in my hair, it was because of what I had seen in the past eleven months. I wanted to tell him that I was old enough to remember when the Bill of Rights still meant something, but I kept my sarcasm in check. Li'l Himmler here was just looking for an excuse to place me under arrest for curfew violation. My police record was clean, and he didn't have anything on me, but my occupation was listed as "journalist." I could see it in his face: reporters for the *Big Muddy Inquirer* didn't get cut much slack on his beat.

"Sort of," I said noncommittally, careful to keep my voice even. B. Douglas didn't reply; he was waiting for elaboration. "I tried to jump over a storm drain a few blocks away," I added. "Didn't quite make it." I shrugged and managed to assay a dopey gee-shucks grin. "Accidents happen, y'know."

"Uh-huh." He continued to study me, his monocle glinting in the streetlight. "Where did you say you were?"

"U-City," I said. "Visiting some friends. We were having a little get-together and . . . y'know, kinda got sidetracked."

It was a good alibi. The U-City neighborhood was only a few blocks west of the station; that's where all us liberal types hung out, listening to old Pearl Jam CDs while smoking pot and fondly reminiscing about Bill Clinton. It fit. Maybe he'd pass me off as a stoned rock critic who had fallen in a ditch after going into conniptions upon seeing an American flag.

Off in the distance I could hear the first rumble of the approaching train, the last Red Liner to stop tonight at Forest Park Station. If Oberleutnant Douglas was going to find a good reason for busting me, it was now or never. After all, he would have to file a report later.

The kid knew it, too. He flipped my license between his fingertips, once, twice, then slowly extended to me as if he was granting a great favor. "Have a good evening, Mr. Rosen," he said stiffly. "Stay out of trouble."

I resisted the mighty impulse to salute and click my heels. "Thank you," I murmured. He nodded his helmeted head and stood aside. The train's headlights were flashing across the rails as I swept my fare card in front of the scanner, then pushed through the turnstile and trotted down the cement stairs to the platform.

The train braked in front of the station, bright sparks of electricity zapping from its overhead powerlines. A couple of my fellow riders looked askance at me as they stood up. One of them was an old black lady, wearing a soaked cloth coat, carrying a frayed plastic Dillards shopping bag stuffed with her belongings.

"What did he stop you for?" she asked as the train doors slid apart and we moved to step aboard.

I thought about it for a moment. "Because of the way I look," I replied.

It was an honest answer. She slowly nodded her head. "Same here," she murmured. "Now you know what it's like."

And then we found our seats and waited for the train to leave the station.

I rode the Red Line as it headed east into the city. Quite a few people got on or off the train at Central West End, most of them patients or visitors at Barnes Hospital, but my car only remained half-full. Most of the passengers were soaking wet. The train was filled with the sound of sneezing and coughing fits, making the train's computerized voice hard to hear as it announced each stop. The Red Line sounded like a rolling flu ward; despite the fact we had just stopped at a hospital, somehow all those free vaccinations we were supposed to receive courtesy of ERA seemed to have missed everyone on this train. On the other hand, this wasn't unusual; most of the people in the city had somehow missed receiving a lot of the federal aid that had been promised to us.

Through the windows, I could see dark vacant lots filled with dense rubble where buildings made of unreinforced brick and mortar had once stood; streets blocked by sawhorses because ancient sewer tunnels and long-extinct clay mines beneath them had caved in; shanties made of scraps of corrugated steel and broken plywood. Armored cars were the only vehicles on the streets, but here and there I spotted figures lurking in the doorways of condemned buildings. Night brought out the scavengers, the teenagers with tire-irons who prowled through destroyed warehouses and demolished storefronts in search of anything to be sold on the black market.

The train left the midtown combat zone and rumbled toward the downtown area. It stopped briefly beneath Union Station, but it passed Auditorium because the platform there no longer existed. Kiel Auditorium itself had survived, but where the old City Hall building and the city jail once stood were now vast lots filled with crumbled masonry, broken cinderblock, bent copper pipes, and shattered glass. Giant piles, which had once been buildings, waiting to be hauled away.

By now the downtown skyscrapers were clearly visible, their windows shining with light; the Gateway Arch, seen above the spired dome of the old state courthouse, reflected the city lights like a nocturnal rainbow. For a minute or two there was no wreckage to be seen. It seemed as if the city had never suffered a quake, that all was sane and safe.

Then the train hurtled toward Busch Stadium, and the illusion was destroyed. Silence descended as everyone turned to gaze out the left-side windows at the stadium. Busch Stadium still stood erect; bright spotlights gleamed from within its bowl, and one could almost have sworn that a baseball game was in progress, but as the train slowed to pull into Stadium Station, the barbed-wire fences and rows of concrete barriers blocking the ground-level entrances told a different story.

A group of ERA soldiers were sitting on benches at the subsurface train platform; a couple of them glanced up as the train came to a halt, and everyone in the train quickly looked away. The doors opened, but no one got on, and nobody dared to get off. There was dead quiet within the train until the doors automatically closed once again. The train moved on, and not until it went into a tunnel and the station vanished from sight did everyone relax.

Busch Stadium wasn't a nice place to visit anymore. Oh, people still did at times, but seldom voluntarily. There were whispered rumors that people who went to the stadium often didn't come out again.

But, of course, that was only hearsay.

A few minutes later the train rolled into 8th and Pine, the underground hub station for the MetroLink. I got off here and took an escalator from the Red Line platform down to the Yellow Line platform. The station was cold, with a breeze that seeped through the plastic tarps covering a gaping hole in the ceiling where the roof had partially collapsed during the quake. A couple of ERA troopers lounged against a construction scaffold, smoking cigarettes as they watched everyone who passed by. I was careful to avoid making eye contact with them, but they were bored tonight, contenting themselves with ousting the occasional vagrant who tried to grab a few winks in one of the cement benches.

I managed to grab the Yellow Line train just before it left the station. It was the last southbound train to run tonight and if I had missed it, I would have had to dodge downtown curfew patrols while I trudged home through the rain. At times like this I wished I still had my own car, but Marianne had taken the family wheels when we had separated. Along with the house, the savings account, and not an inconsiderable part of my dignity.

Not surprisingly, the train was almost vacant. Most of the South-side neighborhoods were under nine-to-six curfew, so anyone with any sense was already at home . . . if they still had a home, that is. Across the aisle, a teenage girl in a worn-out Screamin' Magpies tour jacket was slumped over in her seat, clutching her knees between her arms, she seemed to be talking to herself, but I couldn't hear what she was saying. At the front of the car a skinny black guy with a woolen rasta cap pulled down over his ears was dozing, his head against the front window, rocking back and forth in time with the movement of the train; every so often his eyes slitted open, scanned the train, then closed again. A bearded redneck sat reading a battered paperback thriller, his lips moving slightly as he studied the sentences. An emaciated old codger stared at me constantly until I looked away. A fat lady with a cheap silver crucifix around her neck and an eerie smile. Pretty much your standard bunch of late-night riders.

I had the seat to myself. The train came out of the tunnel; once again I could see the city. For an instant, though, as I stared out the rain-slicked windows at the lights passing by, I felt a presence next to me.

I didn't dare to look around, afraid to see what could not be reflected in the glass: a small boy, wearing a red nylon Cardinals jacket, dutifully marking up his scorecard while mustering the courage to ask me if he could enter a Little League season he would never live to see . . .

Can I play Little League next year?

Goddamn this train.

"Not now, Jamie," I whispered to the window. "Please, not right now. Daddy's tired."

The ghost vanished as if he had never been there in the first place, leaving me only with memories of the happy days before May 17, 2012.

Let's talk about Jericho again.

There had been plenty of advance warning that a major quake might one day rock the Midwest. Geologists had been warning everyone for years that the New Madrid fault as not a myth, that it was a loaded gun with its hammer cocked back, and their grim predictions were supported by history. In 1811, a superquake estimated at 8.2 on the then-nonexistent Richter scale had devastated the Mississippi River Valley, destroying pioneer settlements from Illinois to Kansas; legend told of the Mississippi River itself flowing backward during the quake, and simultaneous tremors were reported as far away as New York and Philadelphia while church bells rang in Charleston, South Carolina.

And there were other historical harbingers of disaster, major and minor quakes ranging between 5.0 and 6.2 on the Richter scale during the years between 1838 and 1976, all caused by a 130-mile seismic rift between Arkansas and Missouri, centered near the little Missouri town of New Madrid. Sometimes the quakes occurred away from the Missouri bootheel, such as the 1909 quake on the Wabash River between Illinois and Indiana, but most of the temblors happened in the region near the confluence of the Mississippi and Ohio rivers, and during even the most minor quakes chimneys crumbled, roofs collapsed, and people occasionally died.

Despite geologic and historical evidence that the city was living on borrowed time, though, most people in St. Louis managed to forget that they lived just north of a bull's-eye.

In August 1990 a New Mexico pseudoscientist named Iben Browning caused a panic by predicting that there was a fifty-fifty chance that a major earthquake would occur between the first and fifth days of December of that year. His prediction, based upon flimsy conjecture involving sunspots and lunar motion, was made during a speech to a group of St. Louis businessmen, and the sensation-hungry local media blared it to the public. By coincidence, Browning's prediction was followed in late September by a minor 4.6 quake epicentered near Cape Giradeau. The quake did little damage, but the general public, already unnerved by war in the Middle East and a shaky national economy, went apeshit.

During a three-month silly season, St. Louis prepared itself for imminent disaster, climaxing on a Wednesday when the city's public schools were shut down, its fire departments mobilized, and scores of citizens left town for vacation. When the prediction proved to be false—as was bound to happen, since earthquake prediction ranks with Rhine card ESP tests for unreliability—St. Louis ruefully laughed at itself and promptly began to forget everything it had learned about earthquake preparedness.

Iben Browning died a short time afterward without ever having made public comment about his apocalyptic predictions. In doing so, he gave the city renewed overconfidence. Earthquake drills were canceled as the 1990 scare settled into the back of everyone's mind, and the people of St. Louis once more settled into the safe, conservative mind-set that Nothing Ever Changes In Our Town. Even the 1994 Los Angeles earthquake did little to shake the city's complacent sense of false security.

And so it went for the next two decades. Our local pundits have often observed, sometimes with barely concealed pride, that St. Louis consistently remains about five years behind the times. Nonetheless, the city was dragged kicking and screaming into the twenty-first century. New buildings were erected, old ones were torn down, and the downtown skyline began to rival Chicago for brightness. The city's building codes were revised to imitate the earthquake-preparedness standards institutionalized in California, but they didn't affect thousands of older buildings or private residences. Electric cars replaced the old gashogs on the highways as new federal laws phased out the use of internal combustion engines in automobiles. A new light-rail system was erected, effectively replacing the old bus lines. The local aerospace industry gradually regeared itself from making warplanes to building spacecraft components. Hemlines rose, fell, and briefly became nonexistent with the short-lived barebuns look of 2000, which contributed to yet another moral revival that lasted until most women decided they really didn't want to wear neck-to-toe chastity gowns in 100-degree summer weather. Extrophy, smart drugs, isometrics, minimalistic education, and at least a half-dozen sociopolitical theories came and went as fads. Two economic recessions were suffered and were survived, the last one finally forcing the county and city governments to merge after more than a century of squabbling; their uneasy shotgun-marriage formed Metro St. Louis, the seventh largest city in the United States.

And there were two or three minor quakes, the largest one being a 5.2 temblor in 2006 that enabled the city to save a few dollars from having to tear down some condemned buildings in the central west end. Nothing serious. But the gun was still cocked and one day in early summer, when no one was paying attention, the hammer finally came down.

That was the day my son was taken from me. . . .

(FRIDAY, 12:01 A.M.)

It was a short, bumpy ride from Soulard to Busch Stadium, little more than a sprint down Broadway, but the LAV's driver seemed hell-bent on finding every pothole in the tortured asphalt and driving through it at top speed. My new pals Bob and Bob got a kick out of watching me try to remain seated with my hands cuffed behind my back. I rocked back and forth, my shoulder muscles aching a little with each unanticipated turn and jar the Piranha took; they thought it was pretty funny.

It's amazing how little it takes to amuse some people. I suppose they had already chewed up their rubber balls and tug-toys.

The bells in the Old Cathedral down by the riverside were tolling twelve times when the armored car slowed down. Its wheels bumped again, this time as if the Piranha was crawling over a curb, then the vehicle ground to a halt. There was a double-rap against the wall in front of the driver's compartment. Mullens stood up, grasped one of my arms, and pulled me out of my seat.

"End of the line, buddy," he said as Hefler unlatched the rear hatches and pushed them open. "Time for you to go see the colonel."

"Yeah," said Hefler as he stepped out of the vehicle. "And when he's through, maybe you can go for another ride with us. Would you like that, huh?"

I kept silent as Mullens hauled me out of the LAV. The vehicle had come to a stop in the middle of the wide plaza in front of the stadium's Walnut Street entrance. Concrete barricades topped with coiled razor wire had been erected around the elm-lined plaza, surrounding the Piranhas parked in front of the closed-down ticket booths and dismantled turnstiles. ERA troopers were goldbricking against the statue of Stan Musial, stubbing out their cigarette butts against his bronze feet. Stan the Man was probably rolling in his grave.

The walkways winding around the curved outside walls of the stadium were vacant of baseball fans; the World Series pennants suspended from the ceiling of the ground-floor concourse hung limp and ignored, relics of a more innocent age. It had been a long time since anyone in this place had heard the crack of a bat or smelled a jumbo hot dog. That was one thing we had learned from all those two-bit dictatorships in Latin America: how to turn a good sports arena into a hellhole.

Bob and Bob escorted me across the plaza to a pair of boarded-up double doors beneath a tattered blue canvas awning. The doors led into a narrow lobby where two more soldiers were standing guard duty in front of a pair of elevator doors. One of the grunts reached out to press the Up button on the wall beneath a black plaque reading MEMBERS ONLY.

"Hey, wait a minute, guys," I said as the left elevator opened. "We can't go up there . . . we're not members."

Hefler actually seemed to hesitate for a moment, confirming my suspicion that he was too stupid even to have held down a job as a busboy when the club had been open. "Shut up, asshole," Mullens growled as he shoved me into the elevator.

I stifled a grin. Some people have no sense of humor.

We rode the elevator up to the loge level and the Stadium Club. I had been here a couple of times before with Uncle Arnie, who was well heeled enough to afford a gold membership card. In its time, the Stadium Club had been one of the ritzier places in the city: good food, good drink, a great view of the diamond from an enclosed eyrie overlooking left field.

When the elevator doors opened again, my first impression was that the place hadn't changed since I had last seen it. The oak reception desk was still there, facing a wall lined with photos of players and pennant teams. The barroom still looked much the same; the Budweiser and Michelob beer taps were still in place behind the horseshoe-shaped bar, as was the enormous framed photo of Ozzie Smith, the legendary shortstop's arms raised in victory as he walked toward the dugout during the final game of the '82 Series.

Then Bob and Bob led me farther into the long, concave room, and I came to see that the club wasn't what it used to be. The round tables and leather chairs were now stacked on top of each other at the far ends of the room; the buffet tables had been brought down to the club's lower deck so that they were now pushed up against the tall glass windows overlooking the field, and instead of rich, happy baseball fans there were now uniformed men and women seated before the windows, their faces illuminated by the blue glow of computer terminals and TV monitors. The voices of KMOX baseball announcers giving play-by-play coverage didn't come from the ceiling speakers; all that could be heard in the darkened room was the low monologue of flight controllers, droning a police-state jargon of ten-codes into their headset mikes.

The Stadium Club had always been a bit snobbish for my taste, but given a choice between a maître d' refusing to seat me for wearing blue jeans and watching a bunch of ERA androids manning a communications center, I would have taken a pompous headwaiter anytime. Still, the real obscenity wasn't here but beyond the windows, out on the playing field beyond the deserted seat rows.

The diamond was gone, its canvas bases long since removed, even the pitcher's mound taken away to another place. Beneath the harsh glare of the stadium lights, a dozen or more helicopters were parked on the field, their rotors and fuselages held down by guy lines while ground crews tinkered beneath their engine cowlings or dragged fat cables to their fuel ports. The giant electronic screens above the center field bleachers, which had once displayed the game score, player stats, and instant replays, were now showing cryptic alphanumeric codes designating flight assignments and mission departure times.

An Apache was lifting off from the first-base zone, rising straight up until it cleared the high walls of the stadium. A couple of jumpsuited pilots were emerging from the home-team dugout behind home plate. Several ground crewmen were sitting on top of the dugout, swilling soft drinks as they rested their butts on the red-painted pennants from World Series games. In the days before ERA had taken over the city, it was unspoken heresy even to step on top of any of those emblems, and only the gods themselves were permitted in the Cardinals' locker room.

Now anyone could get an invitation to the dugouts. Closer to the Stadium Club windows, an Osprey's twin rotors were still in motion as a small group of handcuffed civilian prisoners were led down its ramp by gun-toting guards and marched single file toward the visiting team dugout and whatever brand of hell awaited them in the holding pens beneath the stadium.

Blasphemy.

Busch Stadium had always been the pride of St. Louis, one of the city's sacred places. Generations of baseball fans had watched the Cards win and lose in this ballpark, and even when the team had disastrous seasons, there had always been a certain sense of camaraderie. Now the stadium had been desecrated; even if ERA vacated the place tomorrow, its innocence would be forever lost.

The look on my face must have been obvious. Mullens, the funnyman of the Bob and Bob team, began to sing just above his breath as he stood behind me: "Let's go out to the ball game . . . buy me hot dogs and beer . . . we'll go up to the bleachers . . . get drunk as shit and beat up some queers . . ."

"Wrong town, jerkwad," I murmured. "You must be thinking about New York."

WILLIAM H. GASS

Born in North Dakota, William Gass (1924–) grew up in Ohio and attended Kenyon College, although service in the U.S. Navy during World War II delayed his receiving an undergraduate degree for several years. Gass subsequently did graduate work at Cornell University and held two teaching jobs—at the College of Wooster and Purdue—before coming to Washington University in 1969. At the time of his arrival in St. Louis, Gass was already recognized as one of America's most unconventional prose stylists, whose work revels in wordplay and blurring traditional genres. Prolific in fiction, essays, and literary criticism, Gass has authored numerous acclaimed volumes, including *Omensetter's Luck* (1966), *In the Heart of the Heart of the Country* (1968), *Fictions and the Figures of Life* (1970), *On Being Blue* (1976), and *The World Within the Word* (1978). In 1995, Gass published his long-awaited novel, *The Tunnel*, a linguistically complex, semi-autobiographical work that generated considerable controversy among critics. His latest book, *Reading Rilke,* appeared in 1999. Gass is the recipient of numerous awards, including a Lannan Lifetime Achievement Award and the first PEN/Nabokov Award.

In 1990, Gass, who is the David May Distinguished University Professor Emeritus in the Humanities, started the International Writers Center at Washington University. Since its founding, the center has facilitated conversations among the world's most prominent writers by holding conferences on varied topics—politics, religion, art, etc.—and publishing the proceedings. The center also serves the local literary community by offering readings and publishing a monthly calendar of literary events. In 2000, the center's most recent book, *Literary St. Louis: A Guide*, was published by the Missouri Historical Society Press.

The following essay, in which Gass ponders the unfathomable Mississippi River, first appeared in the *Yale Review* in 1995.

MISSISSIPPI

To live by a river is to live by an image of Time. That has often been remarked. However, unlike Time, which we can no longer think of as the slow unfolding of some divine plan, a river has a culmination; and, unlike music or a movie, whose life is a constantly changing present, a river exists throughout its length as an active thing, not just here and now, while passing our gaze, or here and then, as we are moved to reminisce, but now and next, repeatedly bringing itself into being, and doing itself incessantly in. Oceans, however wildly their waters toss, stand still as stone bowls; whereas the river's streaming waters *are* the river, since it is the flow that's mostly meant when we speak of rivering. A river is nothing but unintended destination. A river serves many ends, none of which is its own. It points, but to no purpose. It goes and goes without a goal, always in action, even when nearly dry and blocked by mud or boulders. Motion is its mission, yet it moves as indifferently as the arrow flies its bow, unconcerned about who aimed it, or any purpose its flight might serve. When we compare Time to a river, it is because we wish both were moving elsewhere than fatally to a Gulf.

Mountains, oceans, deserts, plains: they must wait their winds, invite their changes. They symbolize the passive, the enduring. But the river is inexorable, an image of energy, carving a channel, carrying away earth and habitation, so that, as Heraclitus said, you can't revisit "it": you can stand by its mudflats, on its weedy banks, observe once more its placid widths and overbearing cliffs, its narrow islands and its eddies, its accumulations of debris, but you'll never see "it"—the selfsame river—again, since "it" is always other than "it" was.

We call large lakes and oceans "bodies of water." A river has no body, only a length, a course. It shares a "bed" with the sea, a "bottom" with the ocean; swamps, sandbars, points, and islands with both; yet nearly every one of its features is represented by a word of impediment or motion, direction or shape. It has banks instead of shores, rapids instead of reefs; sawyers, snags, aits, bends, and alluvial fans instead of continental shelves; falls, forks, cataracts, tributaries, streams, feeders, channels, deltas and distributaries, branches and bridges and dams and mouths, but no bays, bites, lagoons, or abysmal deeps.

Although mankind finds in rivers a means of transportation, a source of fresh water and food, and enjoys their accompanying fertility, so that human settlements seem to have had their start at some river's side, it is oceans which are origins, where life not only lives but forms, and where the waves repeat themselves, withdrawing and returning, rising and falling, with immortal monotony.

However, the principal difference between seas and rivers is not salt; it is silence. Except at a rapids or a falls, which represent obstacles inside itself, like indigestion or qualms of conscience, or unless a dam bursts like a broken heart, the river rises above its banks without a sound, and seeps through levees and wells up in low ground, overrunning meadows and filling towns no more noisily than fog. To be afloat on a river is to be held in a huge hush like a comforting hug. Bridging the hush, a bird's call comes, while through the sky run rivers of wind with the sound of urgent whispers.

The movement of unruffled water is not discernible. What we see moving are the branches and the leaves of trees, spring pollen, fall seeds, oil slicks, barge debris, coasting boats; or we see the water when it roils around bridge stanchions, when it laps at jetties, when it eddies about bars, protesting anything it encounters that it cannot carry away, anything which "stands its ground."

The line of the river, as we know, is not idly drawn, but geographically pure and driven. It describes a line of descent more unbroken than a hereditary monarch's, and it always looks, on the map, especially when it is a river as spread-out and far-reaching as the Mississippi, as if it rose from the blue of the ocean, inscribing itself in the continent like the fossil of some prehistoric plant. But, persuasive or no, that is not how the river was formed. The two great movements of life, first that of the plant, stretching out toward the light, leaving the earth for the air, and second that of rain and the river, slowly collecting and gradually gathering together, and returning to their central sea: the pattern for each is like a great liquid tree with fluid leaves and silt-lined roots.

Naturally enough, the northern Mississippi belongs to the cold sky, while the southern Mississippi is allied with the warm, dark earth. In the old days, it made sense to expect that the river, below its juncture with the Missouri, would be dark and muddy, sliding between thickets thick with cane, carving fresh channels, slopping over fields and forming swamps, creating bayous, every day downstream becoming increasingly vaginal as it shaped its delta out of its own details; nevertheless, one wonders if it was only the singular fate of the Deep South which allowed the northern

Mississippi to remain Indian in feature, myth, and meaning, while the southern stretch ran black, as if it bore the blood of that race, flowing into the Mississippi of our musical history—the river of gamblers and cotton, slaves and plantations, gunboats and battles, heat and toil, poverty and pain.

All great rivers lend themselves to the cyclical view of history, surging and waning with the seasons, but above all passing their waters along to the oceans where the sun's rays raise the moisture up to collect like sheep in woolly clouds which the winds then drive inland toward mountains whose peaks promptly pierce them (a pattern of repeated transformations which *Finnegans Wake* insistently sings about), so the skyborne waters fall as rain till rivulets run into rivers again, and we see old Thames, sweet Afton, Joyce's Liffey, just like new, sliding under another bridge.

On the river one is usually at work and at risk, whether gliding downstream or laboring up it, but it is also true that out on the water the world lets go its grip, as if one's scruples had been left in some shabby rucksack back on shore. The boat's continued shift of point of view makes disconnection a kind of permanent condition, with all ties loosed like the ladies loose their stays to offer accommodation, so that for passengers, at least, the normal load of life is lightened, and amorous games of chance enlist their hands and occupy their heads.

The river thinks about itself in threes—its two banks, its single stream—but the river's confining shores face each other across the import of its flowing, and for each of them the scene is as settled as a town: it's always the same lazy crawl of water against the dim backdrop of a far bank. Beyond the barrier it was born to be, behind that curtain of limestone cliffs and stubborn heading of bald bluffs, lies an unattainable paradise, with all the values of the wistfully imagined; whereas the land immediately alongside the river—both up and down—remains, to the banks which know it, the buggy slough, the painful thicket and blunt crop of rock it has always been. In this way, by halves of hope and disappointment, the Mississippi claims the center of its continent, and gives to the Midwest its real definition as the compass of the country—with the edges of the river system, like a funnel, dividing East from West, and with the wide clear portion of the river coming from the North, while the dark deep segment drains into Dixie.

Like most things, the river has private parts as well as public charms: a bottom elusive even to fish, a channel which twists, in the Mississippi's case, as snakily as its sinuous and sibilantly shaped name; it has submerged wing dams which the Army Corps of Engineers has built out into the river at right angles to its banks in order to move water more forcibly into the main channel; there are sandbars, shoals, snags, rocks; it has its rich plant, clam, and fish life, its mordant secrets. The body of a young woman who was raped and compelled to leap from the Chain of Rocks Bridge during one dreadful early morning hour was eventually recovered two hundred miles downstream. Others aren't swept so far, but disappear beneath a jam of brush or logs somewhere, or become lodged in a mire of mud. Both results are not uncommon, and contribute to the modern myth of the river as the dispassionate—indeed pitiless—movement of the earth's unconscious: a will without reason or rhyme.

Some of us live alongside the Mississippi, or we cross it by bridge, or we sail on its surface, but we cannot live in it, not only because we lack gills, but because we couldn't endure such incontinent and palpable darkness. What could be down there? the erased shades of fish perhaps, albino as creatures caught in caves, stygians of long standing? Yet miraculously out of it, as from a deep well, anglers hook game fish of all kinds: black and white bass, bluegill, walleye, channel cat, crappie, and sauger. There are buffalo, ugly as their circumstances, blue and flathead catfish as well, freshwater drum, and numerous others. Largemouth bass lurk beside the abundant piles of fallen brush which are often found in the sloughs marooned behind islands, while the smallmouth favor rip-rapped banks and wing dams near washouts where clouds of food stream through in the current. Autumn is the preferred season, when the river lowers its sights, and the tops of the wing dams can nearly be felt beneath the disturbances they design. Walleye can be taken through the ice in midwinter, and catfish caught from boats or banks or from dams, or by leaning out from tree limbs or overhangs—fish of great size, great age, slyness, or ferocity—although the prevarications of the angler are as wide and incessant as the river, equally faithless and deceptive, and almost as old as its history.

Although the claim is disputed, Mississippi fish are frequently felt to be unsafe to eat now because the tone of the river is monobrown throughout its length, even in the snowmelt sections, and its flow looks ditchborn and sewerish to every approach of the eye. Light cannot penetrate the water to any depth, and like a spritzer then enliven it. There is no surface sparkle either—it shows neither happy dapple nor a deep gleam the way coffee can glow before the cream goes in—as a result, the river's countenance strikes almost everyone as sullen and morose, what might be expected from an unwillingly molten and moving slag of earth. The color of the scud churned up by the paddlewheels of excursion boats is beige, like the foam on dark beer, and an occasional waterskier who has just been pulled upright in the wake of his powerboat will immediately hang on with one hand in order to wipe his mouth with the other, so unclean does the river seem even to one ready to be immersed in it.

So this river is nobody's mirror. You will never see your face. When poured into it, the stars go flat as opened soda, and boat light bounces from the water like a basketball from city asphalt. In the rain, its customary brief pocks pass the hull as firmly fixed in place as those little brown bubbles on the crust of something baked. The quality of the water is the river's greatest handicap, and dulls its otherwise ample attractions; but there can be no doubt that the Mississippi was never meant to be mooned over like some twilit lake, or merely wondered at as we do when we drop our jaws before the grandness of a canyon, or admired the way we applaud certain geysers which periodically burst from the earth like the sneezes of a Polyphemus. The river does not encourage nostalgia because it is impossible, looking at its relentless and opaque passage, to envision a purer time. And how clean could the future be, besmirched by the flood of muck that's coming?

All the more reason to understand the life in its depths, the life it brings to its length, its history, its strength. I would like to see a river museum built at some appropriate point along its journey. I do not mean another quaint collection of old boats and coiled rope; I mean a place whose exhibits would explain the river's formation, course, and flooding—its sandbanks, mudflats, rocky bluffs, and malarial swamps—and would show how its water's color is created; would display the fish and crustaceans which live in it, the plants which weed its banks, the birds which use it as a flyway, the animals which occupy its margins; and, of course, say something of its history, the literature it has inspired, the music, the culture of the ancient Indians, the black laborers, the salesmen, gamblers, untidy ladies who made it lively, the cities which grew up beside it, and in particular the great earth beneath, waiting to wake and once more roll its shoulders.

Many rivers are too narrow, too shallow, too remote, too rocky and rapid to support industry or facilitate labor. Coal companies and gasworks do not site themselves beside them, or crude towns cluster at their mouths or at other moments of confluence and meeting. Certainly much of the Mississippi, especially in its twiggier tributaries, is like that. Such streams, if they don't become industrial dumps, can entertain float trips and look cute. Not for them the burden of gravel, grain, timber, salt, and ore. But the central set of rivers (the Wisconsin, the Illinois, the Missouri, the Ohio, the Arkansas—each important enough to have given its name to a state) once constituted our greatest highway, and long broad gangs of barges travel them still, thanks to the Army Corps of Engineers, which has overcome controversy and struggled for many years to reform the river Mother Nature knew to be inconstant in all its ways because it used to change its course and width and strength of flow upon the orders of the seasons, freezing and flooding, abandoning its banks, even quaking in the New Madrid region, shaking its bottom like a vulgar dancer. Now it mostly exhibits the whimsies of a puppy dog. Normally it pees only in its pan or on paper, nips at nobody, makes scarcely a sound, and sheds no more hair than absolutely necessary for health and good looks. That is, engineers have tried to turn this once powerful river into a pet called a canal: a set of carefully controlled stages through which, as though on a ceremonial stair, most of the nation's inland waters would be collected to descend past formidable flood walls and earthen levees through sluices which deepened, as dredges did, the channel, to refill pools and lakes the locks made until their dams spilled the river onward as its masters chose, snagboats clearing the way, buoys marking its proper course, high banks giving it force, and in that fashion ushering the river down its long flight to a foyer where it would then greet, with appropriate ceremony, the Gulf and other representatives of overseas trade.

It is no longer towns, or the presence of bridges, which make the greatest mark on the river, but the twenty-seven locks and dams which equalize its depths and keep it smoothly flowing. The land around the locks has grown parklike, towns ease gratefully up to the military's tidy trees, and people come to watch the water spill down the middle of the river, or the boats sneak through on its sides. For anyone traveling on the river itself, these locks are like the numbered hours of a watch, and measure the trip, now conceived in linear segments like a length of knotted string. Wildlife refuges have been established, ironically revealing the extent of human domination. Like vegetables in brine, the wilderness is preserved in parks and zoos, in museums and aquariums. The glass of the cases, the bars of the cages, the posted lands protect us from the denizens, and the denizens from us.

Mark Twain chronicled the river's steamboat life, and foresaw its fall at the tug of the lowly tow, which usurped the authority of the river pilot and demeaned his crown.

> First, the new railroad, stretching up through Mississippi, Tennessee, and Kentucky, to Northern railway centers, began to divert the passenger travel from the steamboats; next the war came and almost entirely annihilated the steamboating industry during several years, leaving most of the pilots idle and the cost of living advancing all the time; then the treasurer of the St. Louis association [of river pilots] put his hand into the till and walked off with every dollar of the ample fund; and finally, the railroads intruding everywhere, there was little for steamers to do, when the war was over, but carry freights; so straightway some genius from the Atlantic coast introduced the plan of towing a dozen steamer cargoes down to New Orleans at the tail of a vulgar little tug-boat; and behold, in the twinkling of an eye, as it were, the association and the noble science of piloting were things of the dead and pathetic past!

These vulgar tugs push monstrous tows upriver now, nine barges wide sometimes, and eight containers long, the proverbial size of a football field, and limited only by the capacity of the locks, which lift great weights like this with the ease of a god, elevating the contents of an entire company of silos a speedy fifteen feet, the salt of several mines in minutes, a forest of logs without a sound, enough gravel to bedrock a building, while the captain of the tow and the lockmaster chat of water traffic and river girls, in their familiarly amiable way.

Boats can still run aground, although most often it is barges which break loose and float away to carom from bridge abutments; but there are no more catastrophic boiler explosions, or vessels sawyered by concealed trees, or set afire by sparks from their own stacks; there are no more flatboats to be run down because of a thick fog or a moonless night, no barges to be squeezed in two by ice, keelboats to capsize in hurricanes, or rafts to come apart like sodden paper. Money and engineering have not entirely secured us from damaging floods, and now and then the river rises up like an engorged god and creates a lake around Chicago or overruns levees south of Memphis to swallow already impoverished towns; yet highwaters are no longer as certain and as seasonal as they once were, and often do nothing beyond wetting, like a dipstick, the river's gauges to the height of an astonished "Wow!" The New Madrid fault—alone unmanaged, unengineered—awaits its time when a hundred miles of river may fall through the earth and assume another identity in the realm of shades.

Gambling is back, so is booze, but taverns no longer resound; there are no wharf-boats to rock in tune to a passing wake; knife fights have ceased to enliven the docks; harbors cannot support whores anymore and the gambling that goes on is as tame as life in theme parks; so that when those gray-haired retirees, whom the river cities unconscionably prey upon, realize they've been rouletted out of their pensions and everything their past amounted to, they will not draw derringers from beaded bags to shoot greedy politicians in the knees, or slip stilettos from sheaths concealed beneath those colorful shirts which advertise Dubuque to pierce the money-blooded heart of some crafty Las Vegas entrepreneur, and thereby, like former floods and fires and fights and wrecks upon the river, make the papers, managing in this violent way to remain in someone's memory, and eventually return in myth to enrich the river like another species of bird or fish; no . . . they will merely whimper a while in their motel rooms, sit silent and not sing on the bus ride home, eat rice and beans on weekends, and, by canceling cable or cutting down on macaroons, hope to set a little aside to risk next time on a luckier boat; because there is no reverberation from the river, there's no news now that such monkey business has returned; the Army Corps of Engineers keeps its mouth closed tighter than its locks; and neither the noise of winning nor the smell of losing, certainly not theft or rape when it occurs, escapes a casino, not where it lies at anchor on the Mississippi, cushioned by water, space, and the criminal's concerns; nothing which might tell us what's really cooking will be allowed to leak out and threaten business with the truth; the river has been stripped of its lore by our care, our connivance, and our neglect; it is merely muddy and worldly-wide now, lying like an old road that's been remaindered due to the ruthless rip of an Interstate—empty and endangered by the encroachments of disuse.

As Mark Twain explains, you could not navigate the river in the old days without a memory for its banks and bars, its fickle channel, its sudden storms; you had to know how to read ripples, and diagnose water color; you were an accomplished perceiver, ready when the river rose to rearrange your recollection of some snag so as not to mistake its position; you remembered where silt customarily slipped to, where rocks lurked and currents could double-cross the boat's bow; you listened to the hush caused by heavy clouds as well as to the rhythms of the engine or the sidewheel's thrash through the muddy water; because (living on a stream of change as you did, directing your vessel in rain, fog, wind, and darkness, alert to other ships as well as those submerged trees, called "planters" and "sawyers," which waited to open the bottom of your boat like a letter) you were required to be alive to life, in harmony with nature, humble before its awesome power, cautious as a cat who knows it never had nine lives, and so is in no hurry to spend its only one on the purchase of a speedy passage.

Locks, wing dams, dredges, buoys, and markers reduce the need for watchfulness and memory; the river is an abstraction of its former self; it is the river any ordinary eye might see; the engineers have fixed its flight path finally, so that every trip may be exactly like the last, yet each will feel to the tourists as fresh as the makeup on a madam's working face, since all of the previous passages will have been forgotten.

Initially, the land invited the river, and then the river shaped the land: reamed and rearranged it, eroded and enlarged it, drowned its shrubs and stone. Although, in time, the river would become a canal, it had always been an alley, a gutter of goods and evil. One or another of a steamboat's passengers might be played for a fool in some gambling hell, trinket trap, or whore's store, at a stop along the journey (Natchez Under-the-Hill, for instance, was notorious); but, like the river, none of them stayed. Cargoes were as transient as the waters which bore them, so that soon (the way motels and gas stations would later collect in cloverleafs), at every point where town and barge might meet, sat a saloon, a cheap hotel, a bawdy house; suppliers and repairers set up shops, storage depots were erected, and hauling companies placed their stables and their drays on sloping dockside streets. The workers were a tough lot—brawlers or slaves. The Indians had been driven away, the nice folks, too, and the towns turned their backs—genteelly—on the river, inched their asses up to the water's edge the better to shit without soiling anything of substance, and let the things which went on there go on out of sight of their better life.

Work was seasonal, mostly hot and hard, requiring small use of brains or education. Adventurers are always drawn to places where there's little law, and the river was precisely not land: everything the water touched was loosened in its moral fiber; waterfronts grew riffraff as naturally as frogs and rib grass. There was a lot of mud and trash and steaming dung; stevedores who swore

Keeping to the center of the channel is always a good idea, but you cannot determine the center by simply eyeing the sides, and the same is true of the course which any account may take, for it, like the river, may assume a broad and lakelike aspect, allowing, as it seems, all sorts of latitude and whimsical steerage, when, in point of fact, there is but one right path which will direct you safely along, while the others will surely lure you aground, just as an extended metaphor may, because each image which arrives has so many interesting elements that the mind may wander, amazed, among them, lingering ardently like a lover, but losing sight of the whole sublime design; however, the prose that has perfection will return you always to your center, that of the human soul, to put the grandest gloss upon it, so that as the sentence, like a stream, flows on and on, serenely sometimes, or stormily as it may turn out, the soul of the reader also goes, sharing sense and sentiment like a bit of ritual cake; hence every reader, though built a bit differently, and put into the water at a different place, is carried in the secure hold of the words (though they have come from their own far corner, and regardless of their race, the historic moment, or their temper of mind and taste) toward the same final effect, and thus will come away with a common sense of the journey, even though each passenger may have stood at a slightly different place on the boat, and leaned over his or her own personal run of the rail.

He was a middle-aged long, slim, bony smooth-shaven horse-faced ignorant, stingy, malicious, snarling fault-finding mote-magnifying tyrant

I like to think of this river, in its original reality, as a perfect line of prose, pushing forward forcefully, yet changing its course with a curse, or a cry of surprise; fed by the meanings it attracts merely by moving near them, branching at every opportunity, even slowing some of itself to form bayous and sloughs; still pressing on, nevertheless, deepening its reach with every added letter, as if its secret destination were straight down, as if its theme were so compelling it seemed to bear its words like boats above the main body of its increasing momentum, so that they sometimes assumed the shape of river traffic, like this characterization by Mark Twain of a Mississippi pilot named Brown, which takes on the guise of an extended tow, guiding its description downstream between the high banks of Sam's animosity, the nearby barges carrying a neutral observer's cargo (*long, slim, bony*), the faraway ones a load of prejudicial judgment (*stingy, malicious, snarling*), all of them tied to tyrant, finally, like one long Germanically compounded noun; though this is just one of the forms the words on their float-trip take, since, on other occasions, the language will seem to be more than sounds on a stream of air, but appear to extend itself to include the whole wide watercourse itself—its sodden sides, its rotting trees and too-green weeds, both bluffs and clouds. Then it is a prose made up, in equal parts, of desire's urgency (which drives it on), perception's precision and particularity (which makes its scene), passion's confidence and uninhibited commitment (which allows it to respond to its own depiction), the fairness and detachment of thought (which gives it depth), and imagination's leaps and bounds (which let it illuminate other realms with its own light).

their loads from wharf to wagon; wastrels who had never had a dowry to squander, but spilled their time in team with their urine against the walls of warehouses and the footings of piers. A satisfactory society needs a sane and useful social mix, and this was gradually lost, until amenities were not deemed necessary by anybody. The poor, like flies and skeeters, were hatched in such stagnancies; outcasts and ruffians—rats of all kinds—thrived; every crime and connivance—whatever neglect needed in order to flourish —was present in plenty; and the myths born in such circumstances were almost exclusively about legendary tough guys like Mike Fink, a bruiser who broke noses for a living.

So not even the bluffs were far enough away for the good folk, who withdrew from the region altogether, letting the docks remain as tough as they are in any seaport, out of bounds to the God-fearing, to the temperate and polite, the wealthy and well-born.

> The pavements along the river-front were bad; the sidewalks were rather out of repair; there was a rich abundance of mud. All this was familiar and satisfying; but the ancient armies of drays, and struggling throngs of men, and mountains of freight, were gone; and Sabbath reigned in their stead. The immemorial mile of cheap, foul doggeries remained, but business was dull with them; the multitudes of poison-swilling Irishmen had departed, and in their places were a few scattering handfuls of ragged Negroes, some drinking, some drunk, some nodding, others asleep. St. Louis is a great and prosperous and advancing city; but the river-edge of it seems dead past resurrection.

Before long, tracks took up a position beside the river's banks and ran south with the water. Gradually, trains assumed the practice and the profession of the boats. To get to the river, you had to cross their path. The railroads created their own cuts and haunted any crack in the land which water had once sought, because they loved the downhill and the level too. But if the steamboats had once tied up three deep in front of the docks in St. Louis, it would scarcely be any time before sixty trains a day would be arriving and departing from its huge Union Station, where the railroad ran its own river at right angles to the Mississippi, and ripped west through the landscape with increasing cruelty.

Nothing is more fickle than invention—not the fate of ball teams, not fashion, not winter winds. Nothing is more constant than human greed, human inattention. In no time, by river measure, trains were replaced by trucks. In addition, persons perched in every sort of social position drove their own automobiles, since power had finally been given to the people. Roads, like kudzu, went everywhere, covering the ground, killing the soil. Highway engineers began to eat up hunks of geography, destroying fruitful countryside, giving it over to developers like cadavers to the flies, dictating setbacks and street size, creating irremovable eyesores, bringing city litter to lake and meadow, the passivities of pollution and the excitement of high-speed crashes to every segment of the community. In the cloverleafs (and what a name for such wounds to the world's body!) nothing lived but a few imprisoned bushes and punished trees. Out of these obscenely entangled ovals, smaller roads fed the passing traffic to fast-food outlets, rest-roomed gas stations, and one-nite motels. Union Station was soon down to two trains a day, then to none a month; its grand public rooms lay empty, and nothing moved in the rail shed but pigeons, clearly among God's favored creatures because they could shit freely on the world.

So roads were quickly built alongside both rail and river, though a little higher up on the sides of the valley, a little farther away from flood; and if your vantage point is the water, you can see the same handy containers the barges carry go by on flatcars, or sometimes on trailers. In order to reach the river now, you first have to cross the narrow local road which provides access to the few modest houses lodged on the hills, and then you encounter the wide and deadly Interstate, a swath which countenances no obstacle, cycloning through cities as it does in St. Louis, dividing the downtown from the river with a moat of its own. Next, the deathstrip overcome, there are still the train tracks, slight in size, tame, and mostly silent compared to the hurtle of the highway. Finally, down a muddy, weed-dotted incline, you reach the water's edge, a good way yet from the channel where the river really is—an edge where the flow is a bit sluggish, the water a tad oily, hazed by industrial scum.

If the steamboat made it easy for us to move up and down (though we still had to go where the river went), the train let us cross the country nearly where we willed, and later the automobile ran headlong up hills, putting the power of horse and boat and railroad engine in our personal and private hands. We compressed time, we overcame geography, we circumvented most of the inconveniences of the weather, and we abandoned boat and buggy, train and wagon, the way we left the land and former modes of life when we went west, ashamed to look back. The river was on the wrong side of the tracks.

Now the airplane lets us leave the earth altogether, but airports are great wounds too, and no one wants to live near their nearly incessant howls of pain. One day they will also be abandoned, perhaps for a foldup launching pad or home-based rocket chimney. And their acres of concrete will expand and contract while weeds widen the resulting cracks and turn nice fall colors in their presence. Perhaps kids, covering their fright at life with boyish braggadocio, will kill themselves speeding over the empty tarmacs, playing Chicken late at night or intentionally skidding on no longer treated ice.

It is unlikely that we'll return to them as tourists—these winded fields—or restore the shopping malls as shopping malls or put up historical markers in subdivisions, so full of the city's cravens, because they are either featureless or their features are all the same—even if that's the way we customarily complete the cycle of use/abuse/abandon/reuse for our old Christmas cards, former valentines, broken rockers, dewickered chairs, tin spoons, pie plates, cracked crocks. Decorative whiskey bottles undergo transvaluation and emerge as sweet antiques after their requisite period of neglect and banishment to attic, barn, or basement. Firehouses, churches, rail yards, storage depots, schools are rehabilitated and returned to the community, usually with different identities; worn-out parts of town are patched, deposed presidents regain public favor, discarded mistresses stay on as maiden aunts; railroad rights of way are bike-and-hike trails now; St. Louis's Union Station is a commercial circus; riverfronts, baysides, ocean views are shopping-malled or pocket-parked and covered with charm and other coats of cute—cobblestones are disclosed, bricks are washed, beams are revealed, wrought iron repaired, johns replumbed, and parking put discreetly underground or behind the church, the area zoned so we'll all have access to the handicapped, while the entire project is kept spotless by means of oil drums dressed like clowns or animals with open mouths, and brightly lit by brand-new one-hundred-year-old electrified gas lamps.

All along the river, the indifferent are returning, but it's not out of love, sudden enlightenment, or fresh respect, but once again for profit. We'll fix up the harbor, the locals say; we'll run a highway down there for easy access, make up a museum out of old cloth, crocks, and fambly pitchurs; we'll wrap some ropes and drape some chains about in a nautical way, anchor an old scow to a mud bank, plant lamps and a few harmless trees; we'll lay down a stretch of sod like a rug in front of a picnic table; we'll label the lot. Well, it will be an improvement, and here and there, in some shallow shopworn secondhand store, the visitor will find a treasure to be sure. In that sense, it will be worth it. How long can a hick be expected to gawk at the Arch? Yup, the folks who bus in briefly to lose their change, or conventioneers on vacation from their spouses, will appreciate the touches; and one can sympathize with the needs, the fears, which motivate such unlikely revivals: these are worrisome, out-of-joint times indeed, certainly along the river, particularly for those towns whose industries have shut down, whose "business districts" have decayed, who have been bypassed by circumstances and suffered the river's loss of freights, the weakening of its commercial pull, the increase of its pollution, its disappearance from collective memory.

Big or middle-sized city fathers are not the only profiteers who have eyes for this prize. We should remind ourselves of all those little towns which have sat so long beside the river, their gaze averted, as the urban gaze has been, and whose once proud Main Streets stumble over a pair of tracks and slide like slag down the river's bank toward the water—a water so little regarded it sports shacks, a rotting dock, one or two dead boats, a flurry of carrion birds, and maybe a pair of fuel pumps, rusted the color of the river—and of those citizens who exploited the Mississippi in the old days, a few so successfully they could afford a Queen Anne house on a pretty hillside away from business, and whose business is a little bait-and-tackle shop now, citizens who sell secondhand goods from leftover lives, or the souvenirs of someone else's memories. I think they feel the river's morose indifference, its continued contempt for their own lack of love; because those who take an environment for granted, and who dwell in a place principally for profit, who don't need to learn its nature as the river pilots learned the meaning of the river's every change of feature, but who turn away from their reason for being, like kids embarrassed by the funny foreign habits of their parents, to take up newfangled implements and finer ways, will end, as if in a morality tale, alone, marooned, with their front stoops facing a barren street.

The river won't mind if little bits of its bank receive cosmetic treatment, because it is far too long, too wide and strong, too temperamental; it is still alive and flooding, eating its way south. Furthermore, there is a fundamental difference between the river as simply a neglected and bygone instrument of our needs and ease, and those worn-out tools and rundown towns we've seen iced and cut into museum pieces. The river is not a firm road or a fast track over which horse and car can gallop. It is primeval energy itself. It does the going. Sometimes, with our diesel engines laboring, we valiantly oppose its flow. Nevertheless, the river goes. When we walled and banked and dredged and tanked it, so that the mighty Mississippi might be of some honest use, and when, later, like another Erie Canal, we abandoned it, the river went right on, because it was never a Tinkertoy waterway or drayman's back road or happy family theme park. Even now, as pleasure boats multiply and their motors rattle the aspens worse than wind, and marinas begin to huddle in the vicinity of each river city; as vacation cottages accumulate, especially in the northern sections, and boaters picnic on sandspits or pretend the brown beach is lapped by the transparent and inviting blue water of a movie lagoon; as clammers delve and barges slide quietly along, or an occasional ski-chuter rides up into the air behind an overpowered boat; the river turns its wide brown shoulder, shrugs off such shenanigans, and continues what it's always done.

Because the Mississippi knows its business is to wax and wane as much and often as the moon does. However well-laid our plans, however decently mannered and obedient we believe we've made this river, snow may pile up in Minnesota and Montana and thickly cover the Great Plains, only to thaw with the suddenness of ice dumped into a sink. At the same time it may rain unreasonably, biblically, long past its expected season, and persistent gray skies hinder evaporation, so that eventually the earth is asog, every creek swollen, every tributary running swiftly, and rising rapidly, too, wherever they are compressed by levees, until both sewers and streams begin to back up, the flow of some small rivers is reversed, and the system, so controlled, so safe, so much at peace, begins to leak, the very measures taken to tame it now increasing the danger, for finally all that water will burst out like rage long suppressed, and take back the lowlands beside it, undermine steel and concrete floodwalls, eat away the earthen ones, locate with the skill of Satan himself every weakness, including the flaws in those who are fighting it, tempting a few of them to breach some levees upriver in order to save a few farms farther down. Bridges will be marooned when the river widens beyond their intended spans; islands will disappear from view; lakes will take shape, some shallow as a shoe, one seemingly as large as Erie, yet ponds will drown, too, no less permanently than pastures; waters will run into one another and new tributaries form; channels will be deepened by the weight and force and persistence of the flow. Once out of its banks, blobby and aimless, the river is no longer a river. It has obtained its missing body. It is cloud come down. It is earth alive with sky.

The security of canalside life, which brought people to the riverbanks in search of cheap land with rich soil, will be lost beneath another week of rain, a month of downpour; and houses will fill until water spews out of every shattered window; farmland—crops of corn, soybeans, mustard, sorghum, rye: thousands of acres—will be covered as if with liquid earth and heavily trampled by the remaining rain; animals will drown by the hundreds, rabbits, racoons, and deer invading upland communities where hunters will pursue them; roads will act like aqueducts, carrying water over valleys the river will later remember to fill; and in many places the presence of man will largely be swept away: houses, cribs, silos, barns, tractors, cars, furniture, clothes, hopes, the results of years of labor. Fish, frogs, snakes will suddenly find themselves in strange surroundings: the hallway of a house, the cab of a submerged truck. The world that walked now wades.

All this water will finally subside and leave layers of southborne silt, sand in some places twelve feet deep, muck mixed with rotted wheat, mildew, debris, displaced birds and beasts, waterlogged barns, uprooted trees, sinkholes the size of suburban lots, bags of burlap which held the river back a while, tons of trash in former wallows, new bogs, refreshed wetlands, born-again swamps, and fields which once more invite farmers to till the blue muck the river's recession has abandoned, now that it has returned much of what was for a brief time the Mississippi's lightless bottom to swarms of ill-natured mosquitoes, to the creep of moss up drowned trunks, the reassurance of cattails and the flash of tiger lilies, the restorative growth of grasses, vines, and weeds, and, on puddles and ponds, its leave to float the oil drum's iridescent scum again.

When I watch the Mississippi, or have the opportunity to travel on it a little while, I am impressed by this aspect of its nature. In this mode—with the indifference of divinity—it is silent, even when lapping at the side of a docked boat; in this mode it has all its many properties, but these do not add up to anything other than it is; in this mode there is no hope of meaning; the river refuses iconography; it will not serve as symbol; it disdains interpretation; it merely goes: subsides, widens, rises, flows. In this mode it does not answer our questioning gaze, not even to say "nuffin." Every name, including the word *river* is inadequate. What does it know of "misses" and "sippis"? It goes: subsides, rises, widens, flows. It does not emit a sound or utter a letter, so I must speak for it: go, it says, you have a destination. Go, it says, echoing the poet, for "staying is nowhere." Then to boat on it, to sit beside it, to look down on it from a vast bridge, is much like living, like loving, like reading, since it goes along like a great line of prose, inexorably, every link linked, concerned solely with its own sweet self, its own sufficient sense, and the end which it has already reached, and the beginning it has already begun.

MICHAEL A. KAHN

A ST. LOUIS NATIVE and graduate of University City High School, Michael Kahn (1952–) attended Amherst College, from which he received a B.A. *magna cum laude* in 1974. The following year he earned an M.A. at Northwestern University. After a two-year stint teaching in the Chicago public schools, he was accepted into Harvard Law School, where he received his J.D. with honors in 1979. While earning a living as a trial attorney, Kahn embarked on a literary career on a dare from his wife, Margi, who got tired of hearing him announce each time he finished a paperback thriller, "I could write a better book than this." In response to Margi's challenge to write or stop complaining, Kahn wrote his first novel, *Grave Designs* (1988) in hotels and airplanes while working on an out-of-town lawsuit. Kahn subsequently published four other suspense novels, *Death Benefits* (1992), *Firm Ambitions* (1994), *Due Diligence* (1995), and *Sheer Gall* (1996), all featuring a savvy St. Louis trial lawyer named Rachel Gold. *Publisher's Weekly* has praised Kahn's novels for their "intelligent, breezy dialogue and clever plotting."

In addition to practicing law with Stinson, Mag & Fizzell, a leading midwestern law firm, Kahn is an adjunct professor of media law at Webster University. Kahn, his wife, and their five children live in St. Louis. The following chapter from *Due Diligence*, in which Rachel Gold and her associates search for evidence to solve a case, is set in the caves that lie under portions of south St. Louis.

FROM *DUE DILIGENCE*

St. Louis sits atop a thick bedrock of limestone. For hundreds of millions of years, surface water percolated through fissures in that bedrock and created a vast latticework of streams within the limestone, like arteries within a body. During the wetter millennia, the added water pressure drilled larger and ever larger tunnels through the rock. Gradually, those trickling streams became mighty underground rivers.

Then came the drier millennia. The water table dropped, the surface waters receded to the current channel of the Mississippi River, and the landscape became familiar. By the time New Orleans merchant Pierre Laclede and his fourteen-year-old stepson, Auguste Chouteau, clambered up the west bank of the Mississippi in 1764 to admire the fertile landscape spread before them, the underground rivers had long since run dry. On Valentine's Day, 1764, Pierre Laclede announced that he would erect a settlement on this good land—little realizing that this good land rested, like a massive green carpet, over an extraordinary network of cool limestone caves.

The caves of St. Louis were a provincial curiosity until Gottfried Duden arrived in St. Louis in 1822. Duden was, quite literally, an industrial scout, sent to America by various brewing and manufacturing concerns in the Rhineland who were looking for business opportunities in the New World. Back in the days before electric refrigeration, every brewer the world over dreamed of access to vast natural cooling cellars where the climate remained a dry, constant fifty-two degrees year-round—the perfect temperature for storing and fermenting beer. Accordingly, when Duden discovered what was spread out beneath the streets of that booming town along the Mississippi River, he immediately understood the opportunities it held for his German clients. I have found your Garden of Eden in the New World, he eagerly reported.

Within twenty years, St. Louis had become the largest beer-brewing center in North America. By 1860, there were more than forty breweries in St. Louis, most owned by German immigrants, each operating directly over a limestone cave. There was the Gast Brewery Cave and the Winkelmeyer Brewery Cave and the Clausman Brewery Cave and the Minnehaha Brewery Cave and the Cherokee Brewery Cave.

And then there were the celebrity caves.

There was the Bavarian Brewery Cave, which sat directly below Joseph Schneider's Bavarian Brewery on Pestalozzi Street. When the Bavarian Brewery went bankrupt in 1859, one of its major creditors, Eberhard Anheuser, bought the brewery and changed the company name to his name. A few years later, another German immigrant married Eberhard's beautiful daughter, Lilly. When old man Anheuser died, his son-in-law, Adolphus

Busch, assumed control of the brewery and made one final addition to the company name.

And there was English Cave, nestled beneath Benton Park in south St. Louis. Used as a malt liquor brewery from 1826 to 1847, it was better known for the legend of the beautiful Indian maiden and her lover, who fled from the lecherous tribal chief and hid out in English Cave. The jealous chief posted a guard at the entrance to the cave to make sure she didn't escape. She didn't. The lovers died of starvation, and their skeletons were found wrapped in each other's arms. Or so went the legend.

And there was Uhrig's Cave, an underground saloon and nightclub near the corner of Washington and Jefferson, connected to Joseph and Ignatz Uhrig's brewery by a one-half-mile tunnel in which the brothers had installed a narrow-gauge railroad for movement of beer between the two locations. The brothers held concerts and plays in their converted cave and sold rides on the underground railroad. By the turn of the century, Uhrig's Cave was a prominent national entertainment spot and the site of the North American premieres of *The Mikado* and *Cavalleria Rusticana.*

But of all the caves of St. Louis, none approaches the fabulous story of Gutmann Caverns. In 1846, a German immigrant named Gregor Gutmann purchased a cave near Gravois south of Chippewa. It was an ideal brewery cave. Fifty feet below ground with a constant temperature of fifty-two degrees, the caverns included an enormous main chamber with tunnels at either end, one of which connected to another large chamber that could serve as additional storage space for the enormous casks in which the Gutmann Special Lager would age.

Aboveground, Gutmann built his brewery at one end of the cave. As business expanded and his fortunes grew, he erected a huge family mansion above another portion of the cave. By the turn of the century, Gregor Gutmann's wealthy descendants had bricked and smoothed more than two hundred yards of the family portion of the cave and had installed a variety of opulent underground additions, including, among other things, a full ballroom, a swimming pool, a gymnasium, a miniature railroad, and a theater.

Alas, poor management and constant shareholder battles among the grandchildren mortally weakened the company during the early years of the twentieth century, and Prohibition sounded the death knell. The Gutmann Brewery ended in a liquidating receivership. The last St. Louis remnants of the Gutmann family were evicted from the mansion in 1932, and the structure was condemned two years later. All that remains of the three-story Gutmann Mansion are a series of stunning black-and-white photographs that hang in the main gallery of the Missouri Historical Society. The abandoned brewery building lingered on as a vacant eyesore until the city fathers, spurred into action by a newspaper campaign against urban blight, razed the structure in 1947 and converted part of the property, including the former mansion grounds, into a small city park named after Gregor Gutmann.

The old entrance to the brewery portion of the cave, which was just east of Gutmann Park, was used primarily as a neighborhood garbage dump until 1958. That's when a colorful local entrepreneur and history buff by the name of Mordecai Jacobs entered the picture. He purchased a parcel of property east of the park that included what the neighbors then called the Gutmann Dump.

Jacobs brought in a crew of men to clean out the rubbish and excavate the clay and gook that clogged the first fifty feet into the cave. To his delight, he discovered that the old storage channel was actually the front end of yet another large cave that meandered north and featured a dazzling variety of rooms of many sizes, each festooned with stalactites, stalagmites, and other formations. Even more incredible, two of the workmen exploring some of the smaller branches of the cave stumbled into a room that contained what appeared to be the bones of a large mammal. Jacobs was able to convince the Field Museum of Natural History in Chicago to send down a paleontological crew, which identified the find as a large saber-toothed cat. The crew spent six heavily publicized months in the cave and exhumed more than two thousand bones of prehistoric animals, including three full skeletons of an immense, long-extinct species of saber-toothed cat. As part of his deal with the Field Museum, Jacobs selected one of the skeletons and the museum reconstructed it in a ferocious attack position. Using the lighting director of the St. Louis Muny Opera, Jacobs dramatically spot-lighted the skeleton in the original excavation chamber, which he renamed Saber Tooth Cemetery.

Jacobs had the soul of a carnival barker. He installed electric lights and advertised heavily, not only on local radio and television, but on billboards on every major highway within a 300-mile radius of St. Louis: COME SEE GUTMANN'S CAVERNS—THE EIGHTH WONDER OF THE WORLD! He lured them in from all over the country. During its brief but brilliant heyday, Gutmann Caverns was in the top ten of St. Louis tourist attractions, right up there with the zoo and the riverfront. A visit to Gutmann Caverns included guided tours of all the natural formations (with Satan's Waterfall as the highlight), the family portion of the cave, the beer storage process used by brewery, and, of course, the Saber Tooth Cemetery.

Unfortunately, the reborn Gutmann Caverns lasted less than a decade. In 1965, the Highway Department purchased the aboveground portion as part of the parcel needed to construct a section of I-55. Gutmann Caverns closed on December 1, 1965, and highway construction began the following spring.

One normally would have assumed that the entrance had long since been sealed off, and perhaps it was. But given the recollections of Clara Jacobs' housekeeper and the fact that I had absolutely no other leads on any relevant Beth Shalom or Labadie Gardens medical records, it was definitely worth a trip down to south St. Louis to search for a way into the cave.

We dressed optimistically, i.e., for cave exploration. I wore my running shoes and my jogging sweats—the closest I could come to appropriate attire given the grabbag of outfits Benny had selected for me. Flo put on jeans, a Kansas City Monarchs sweatshirt, and hiking boots. Benny had arrived wearing a Chicago Bulls T-shirt, baggy khakis, and high-top Converse All-Stars. Although the T-shirt wasn't warm enough for cave temperatures, he had a windbreaker in the trunk of his car.

On the drive toward south St. Louis, we stopped at a hardware store for a high-powered flashlight, plenty of fresh batteries, and the sorts of odds and ends that three rookie spelunkers thought might come in handy in a cave, including metal cutters, twenty-five feet of rope, several rolls of film for Flo's 35-millimeter camera, and a backpack in which to carry it all.

Flo drove while Benny and I tried to navigate from the backseat. I had a St. Louis street map open on my lap and Benny had the old cave map on his. We got onto Gravois and stayed with it past the Cherokee intersection. We went several more blocks, turned left at the light and weaved our way through several more intersections as the neighborhood changed from purely residential to a shabbier mix of bungalows, two-flats, and an occasional warehouse or storefront.

Flo slowed the car. "Here we are," she said.

There was a city park up ahead on the right. I looked down at the map for a moment and then back up. "You're right. Gutmann Park."

We peered at it through the windshield.

"Drive around it once," Benny said.

Gutmann Park was, by any standard, entirely unexceptional. It was a rectangle three blocks long and two blocks wide. There were two ball fields, each with a rusting backstop, and a half-court basketball blacktop with several bent and netless hoops. The picnic area consisted of three picnic tables, two metal grills, and a small shelter with restrooms in back. There was a playground with a set of clunky, old-fashioned equipment: swings, slides, jungle gym, merry-go-round. Unfortunately, the one thing we didn't see was a huge flashing red arrow with the message, "This Way to Cave Entrance."

The three of us got out of the car and walked the length and width of the park while Benny and I tried to coordinate the surface with the cave map. Although it was hard to be certain, since the map predated the park by at least a decade, it appeared that the cave ran directly beneath the middle of the park. We hadn't expected to stumble across an actual entrance, of course. Nevertheless, given that the Gutmann Mansion had stood roughly between the two ball fields, I had hoped to find some evidence, although faint, of what had once been. We moved carefully through the entire outfield, but found no sign of the mansion or the cave below. Just the patchy grass and weeds of a poorly maintained field. We even checked out both restrooms, but found nothing to suggest any subterranean access.

"Where was the other cave entrance?" Flo asked. "The one the brewery used?"

I checked the map, got my bearings, and pointed east. "A few blocks over."

Across the street from the park was a row of rundown bungalows. Visible beyond the bungalows were several warehouses and, rising above the warehouses to the right, the long, looping exit ramp off the highway.

We got back in the car. This time I sat in the passenger seat up front. As we drove toward the warehouses, I tried to trace our path on the cave map.

"Stop here," I said.

We were midway down a narrow street. There was a warehouse to our left and another to our right. Visible in the distance and slightly to the right was the descending curve of the exit ramp. The highway itself was beyond and above the tops of the warehouses. You could hear the sounds of cars and trucks rumbling along.

I got out of the car with both maps in my hands. I handed the cave map to Benny. Flo came around to study them with us.

"Nu?" Benny said, studying the street map.

I compared locations on Benny's map and mine. "Come on, guys." I walked toward the end of the block.

"Where are we?" Flo asked.

"Here," I said, pausing to point to the spot on the street map Benny was holding. "The tourist entrance was off Grolier Avenue." We were almost at the end of the block. I checked the cave map again, then the street map. "That means the entrance would have been—let's see—about a block further east."

We both looked up slowly.

"Shit," Benny groaned.

Exactly one block further east was the descending curve of the exit ramp. The ground beneath the entire length of the exit ramp was paved with broad concrete slabs. There wasn't even a hint of what had once been there. It was all covered by cold gray cement.

"Rats," I said in frustration. "It's gone."

"Not gone," Flo said. "Just covered."

"Great." I gave her a look. "Unless you have access to a twenty-man jackhammer crew, it's as good as gone."

We stared in silence.

"Come on," I finally said with a weary sigh. "Back to the drawing board."

The three of us walked slowly toward the car.

Benny paused as he opened the car door and looked around. "This area is the pits," he said. "Talk about urban decay."

I looked up at the warehouse across the street. It clearly was long abandoned: half of the windows were broken, and the rest were filthy. It looked like a rundown building out of a horror film. The sign above the door was battered and grimy. I squinted, trying to read it.

"What do you know," I said with surprise. I could barely make out the legend:

M. JACOBS & COMPANY, INC.

Flo turned to look at the sign. "How about that? Old Mordecai must have owned it."

We got in the car to leave, but as Flo started the engine I grabbed her arm. "Wait."

She gave me a curious look and turned off the engine.

I pointed to the exit ramp in the distance. "If that's over the cave, then so is this warehouse."

"So?" Benny said.

I looked at him impatiently. "Think about it, Benny. If Mordecai Jacobs was storing business records in the cave even after the Highway Department sealed off the tourist entrance to Gutmann Caverns, then he had to have another access to the cave. Maybe that access was through his warehouse."

Flo looked at the warehouse and then back at me. "Let me see that cave map."

I handed it to her.

Benny leaned over to look, too. After a moment, he grumbled, "How do you read this goddam thing?"

"Here." I pointed to the area that appeared to be located below the exit ramp. "You see, the cave splits down there. One branch runs due north, the other runs northwest. Look at the position of the warehouse. It's due north."

They frowned at the map, and then Flo turned to stare up at the warehouse.

"You're not serious, are you?" Benny asked incredulously.

"It's worth a shot," I said.

Flo turned back and winked. "It sure is."

"Hold it," Benny said. "Are you saying you actually intend to go in there?"

I looked at Flo. She smiled at me and nodded. I turned to Benny. "Come on, stud. Let's do it."

"Jesus H. Christ, Rachel," he growled at me under his breath as we got out of the car, "and you actually have the nerve to wonder why I prefer the company of bimbos."

JOHN KEENE

BORN IN ST. LOUIS, John Keene (1965–) graduated from Harvard University in 1987. A member of the Dark Room Collective, a group of African American writers, Keene is a former lecturer at the University of Virginia as well as the managing editor of *Callaloo*, a prominent black literary journal. Considered a rising literary talent, Keene also had the distinction of being New York Times Fellow at New York University. His unusual autobiographical novel, *Annotations*, was named one of the twenty-five best books of fiction in 1995 by *Publisher's Weekly*, which deemed it "an experimental work that pinpoints a new direction for literary fiction in the 21st century." A meditation on growing up in St. Louis, *Annotations* contains a great deal of historical specificity at times, and every chapter in the novel is exactly the same length.

In the following excerpts—which are taken from the beginning, middle, and end of *Annotations*—Keene places his personal experiences in the larger historical context of the middle-class African American experience in St. Louis.

FROM *ANNOTATIONS*

NOTES, INSCRIBED INITIALLY IN THE NARROW, RUNNING MARGIN

Such as it began in the Jewish Hospital of St. Louis, on Fathers' Day, you not some babbling prophet but another Negro child, whose parents' random choices of signs would disorient you for years. It was a summer of Malcolms and Seans, as Blacks were transforming the small nation of Watts into a graveyard of smoldering metal. A crueler darkening, as against the assured arrival of dusk. Selma-to-Montgomery. Old folks liked to say he favored the uncle who died young, an artist. In that way, a sense of tradition was upheld, one's place in the reference-chain secured. Digression. Brick houses uniform as Monopoly props lined the lacework of street for miles. Before there was Arlington, there was Palm, indeed a dimmer entity which burns in one's memory like iodine. "Baltimore Law." They eventually settled on a single-family detached, in the Walnut Park section of the city, after months of wrangling with the agent, as it was quite naturally assumed that they, like others who worked for a living, would eventually own their own property. The red cement porch, which Daddy painted at least one time, beneath the gray-greenish, slate-shingled eaves. The draperies had not yet begun to rot, nor had the ottoman relinquished a leg to leaning. Some of them were working at the post office then, though many were unionized auto-plant or factory workers. Cleverness in conformity often goes unnoticed. The block opened out onto the immense Calvary Cemetery that we had heard to be the haunt of vampire mummies, who would lie in wait beneath the headstones for children who failed to say their prayers. In the mirror, an admirer. You dreamed of romping there when older with the tougher boys, smoking cigarettes, copping feels, jumping out from behind trees, playing like an agent from "Dragnet." Crossing the street was considerably more forbidding. Four, in hand. A home in which to watch the seasons pass, to grow old within a chosen "community." Now names of most neighbors have shifted past his consciousness like afternoon shadows across the living room floor. Everyone, except the neighbors, marveled at the size of the basement. Then no one used heroin because they lacked for "family values," even though they spoke so blithely of our "ghetto." Pruitt-Igoe. Words, wildly uttered, acts unmitigated, emergence of their search for validation. Many backyards wore a chain-link garter that stretched out to the alleyway, and so whenever the rudipoots shattered their wine or soda bottles into smithereens of glass, it always fell to us to sweep them up. Now-or-Laters. Snoopy, the second in a cavalcade of pets, would parade regally about the screened-in back porch. Daddy soaked then bathed him in a pan of gasoline to strip his coat of mange, so that when we spoke of him at all, it was as "under quarantine." Children often see with a clarity that adults ignore. Around the corner, down the hill, three blocks or so, until the fields of St. Catherine Labouré unreeled before us, as in the scenes in that movie usually broadcast during the "sweeps" preceding Christmas, the projector that lighted up the cinema of our childhood dreams. Desire is, among other things, a function of repetition, or so the very patterns of your life have led you to believe. No better place existed to fly kites or box-crates, except Penrose Park, where, one supposed, the nuns never chanced to set habit. You assembled the frame and tail according to the package's confusing directions, which required more than the recommended ten minutes. Junie aided him in getting his aloft, before it tangled and then plummeted with the others. The genius lies in the execution. The Ville, whose village. Shivering, you stood on the sunlight's skirt, yet they laughed as they looked right through you. Shrieks of all sizes and colors would distort the evening air, rendering it opaque and virtually unreadable. Who would not beg to stay out past curfew, when the excitement usually began. "Catch the ball, boy, catch the ball!" as it rearranged the contours of our face. "Tag" became the game of choice, though we occasionally improvised with "Batman" or with "Jonny Quest." Against form. Before the final closing of eyes and the "good night's sleep," the irrepressible march of twilight.

TEXTS, CONTEXT, A FEAR OF CONTAMINATION

Education, they counseled us, is the one, true key, yet the school was known less for its floors of tidy classrooms than for its gym with collapsible bleachers and that polished, hardwood floor. Promise-harness. The committee, comprising the clergy and the most prominent lay members, rechristened the complex after the first Black Catholic bishop, which provided even the most taciturn with an engaging topic of discussion. Simply naming, while powerful, never proves enough. He was usually charily chosen for the kickball teams, or last for any sport requiring aggression. A palpable terror, a shortness of breath. Consolation lay in the reading contests and the sketching assignments, when we could excel far beyond the expectations of both teachers and friends. My teeth cast a gleaming net for you, a white and wordless reply. Cardinal Ritter. "Poetry" served then as the recitative of bible-men and the pimp who stayed on the corner, or the huckster who with brio sold them a faulty vacuum cleaner. In those days we could recall the names and life stories of the major Black inventors almost as readily as our multiplication tables, though in truth a disjuncture persisted between their paradigms and how we perceived them, which neither teachers nor other adults sought to bridge. No one really slept at naptime. After the wedding, marked by a holy sacrament which he believed he understood, he and the other children brought Mrs. Orange her namesake fruit. In fourth grade, following a premise that defied "equality," the classes cleaved into two distinct and ability-based homerooms, which garnered for the smaller, brighter class a rancor it little deserved. "Freedom School." Thus that year proceeded by way of experimental groupings and methods, which sound nothing short of radical in the context of education today. Many the nuns who scored the names of saintly men in their heads until each was resurrected by reflex, and who, in daily sweeps past their desks, left a near-visible trail of camphor. With your hair cut so short, the older boys renamed you "Shine," rubbing your head as though it were their own personal talisman. "Sensitive." Yet who did not desire to follow their model, for they were more real than his idols. What little boys do. Behavior enough to gain us mention in the newspaper, where he spoke of his desire to be popular, or in the parlance of those days, the "Caped Crusader." Ivanhoe, Pip, and Peter Pan led the list of childhood favorites, though it was hard to identify with that bespectacled, British "John." His father would not hesitate to mine him for that single ore of truth, since this, he had convinced himself, was a father's chief occupation. If you therefore were one who regularly lied, then your recollections might consist of the sum total of your childhood fictions. He waited but the invitations never materialized, so he learned to create small diversions for himself. A cleansing thus ensued, an art of remembering developed, a renewal undeniably the result. "Straight-A, Straight-A, nothing but a sissyboy who's scared to play," they screamed burning tracks across the playground, their faces brown, blazing globes of glee, as he crumpled near the swingset like a raveling, forgotten husk-doll. Repression's effects assume manifold forms. One option proposed seriously was that of skipping a grade, though they feared that might warp her emotional development. In other words, neither parent had expected such a fragile character, though they bore the verdict better once they had bought it. Some children are badly suited to this world, though their elders rarely gather this fact until the dawn of the teen years, when the complement of options has shrunk to zero. Baldwins reclined between a Jong, several Cozzenses, and two Morrisons, but Michener's opera had long held sway of the bookshelf. Neither Bolivia nor Paraguay has an ocean port, you learned from encyclopedias at the great-aunt's house. A few of them so old that they crumbled between the fingers, others crinkled with that odor of never having been fully opened. The genius lay in the execution, or at least in how she kept the deception from becoming apparent. Ebony and Black Enterprise graced the marble coffee table, though Jet garnered everyone's initial review. Our generation possesses only a cursory sense of the world that our ancestors braved, though the burdens of history bear unmovably upon us. Homer G. Phillips. Rollerskating in the summer around Steinberg Rink, or else in one of many indoor halls. And when he was old enough to wield a racket, tennis in O'Fallon Park. Sugarloaf Mound. One assessment: the chill cast the courts in a crepuscular light. Stan, who coached the older, lither players, sported a thick, beguiling mustache, while coiled hairs spilled from the V-neck of his jersey, leaving us with a sensation that we were yet unable to name. Ruby, my dear. "Swing, baby, lemme hear that ball sing and dance, serve, but not so much racket string, you got it, now, whoa, don't fling it." By perfecting a strategy, we learned gradually, we could organize and master almost any game, a lesson as applicable and valuable outside the court as on it.

MULTEITIES, DISJUNCTIONS, INTENSE POLYSEMIC PLEASURES

By the autumn of his childhood they had abandoned their prefab in the ghetto for a ranch house in a suburb whose property values and lack of crime could boast of national renown. No one, you understand, carped at the size of the required down payment, since it was assumed that they would eventually own their own property. Ignorance is incapable of concealing itself. Out there many of the Blacks were descended from the slaves or servants who had once managed those estates, so tensions were bound to abound when the educational system finally integrated. Douglass School. Few Negro families had settled land as far out as Red Bud, though even Franklin and Jefferson Counties had shown a minimal Black presence since well before the Civil War. This unconcern with the questions of whether a "there" was there, or of what this "there" consisted, remained unnamed until a later encounter with what they were denouncing as "pragmatism." History has been kindest to the charming old German quarter, where the wealthier or more committed ones had hidden in their rathskellers those dark fugitives headed north for freedom. Information, he first noticed, in a series of notes that someone had inscribed in the narrow, running margin.

"Missouri Compromise." Out there then one never needed to lock one's doors or speak to one's neighbors for weeks. Once a week a man, bearing more than a minor resemblance to the president whose name became a curseword, delivered orange juice and grape drink and lemonade just as they had observed in the movies. My address, Madras. Hush Puppies, bell-bottom denims, a Bengal-striped shirt, though you refused to be photographed in platforms. A fulvous swatch of velour that tired the eyes, your sweater was the only one lighter than your skin. "Dibs on your Tootsie-Roll" was all they had to say to quash any attempts to deny them, so you broke it into morsels as had been demonstrated on TV, and went home without anticipating a "Thank you." Boys should not flap their arms when they run down stairs, or cover their mouths when they laugh, proscriptions made less to correct a child's deportment choices than to allay a parent's useless fears. "Though the crust may be brown the bread is still white." Lacking any real conception of evil, a child is prone to explore the limits of her will. He fought back but they laughed at him, so that he discovered his skill as jokester, but he kept in mind the example of Richard Pryor. Mode for Joe. The father eventually began to dwell on the numerous half-veiled jealousies this move and its aftermath induced. Often, he would speak of Captain Wendell O. Pruitt, and the other Tuskegee flyers, who had never been properly honored. Just remembering the treatment of all those distinguished Black airmen filled his eyes with tears of awe and bitterness. Benign neglect. Who stood and saluted when the flag flapped high, who sang the anthem without anger. Time is no equalizer. As you will recall she was a blond divorcée with two attractive kids, whom she appeared to love more dearly than she did the thought of them. Although working-class and Irish, they quickly ignited a friendship, which differed from what we had encountered in the city. Civility offers an acceptable way to evade the issues at hand. Name us anonymous. "Grumio erat coquus," he yelled out in earnest, to the consternation of a number of his classmates and the instructor. Chalk hurled at the head was the usual punishment, though kneeling while hoisting a dictionary was not unknown. My mind is the sandbox that my thoughts play in, or the court in which they exercise their claims to reason. Nine, the magic number. Quietly they strode through the grounds of the Eden Seminary, the thrill of actually being there far more compelling than anything they encountered therein. Reinhold Niebuhr. Accordingly, along with the doctrinal classes the Opus-Dei brothers offered scale-model construction; however, journalism more thoroughly captured his mood. By then it was the Bicentennial, and you were playing "John Henry" in the program at the Loretto-Hilton, which entailed memorizing a medley of songs, and learning how to swing an invisible hammer. Hurry up this way again. More the name of the Algonquin Golf Club where one caddied than any other identifiable aspect, and the waiting buckets of crawdads which made the traipse across the greens go more quickly. Of course, the city's importance had diminished progressively since the days when it had served as the gateway to the West, though one's perspective on this fact waxes as one gains distance from it. DeSoto. Having abandoned it for the far more sterile suburbs, they were drawn back to that laboratory of human interaction. Against closure. As a result those endlessly engaged in the quest for happiness usually constitute the unhappiest lot. Anthropology offers us among its many conclusions that boys throw a certain way, girls another.

INQUIRY AS THE ACT OF LIVING, VITAL IMPROVISATION

Missouri, being an amalgam of nearly every American region, presents the poet with a particularly useful analogue for an articulation of the "American," though close inspection shows a sum less metaphorically potent than its metonymically dissoluble parts. Show me. Having seen over four hundred skirmishes during the Civil War, the state ranked second only to Virginia in battle quantity, yet this factlet often receives scant mention in the most authoritative studies of that conflict. Yet with her Confederate government-in-exile and Republicanism on the wax, it was hard to keep up interest in the failing Southern cause. When later we spent a few days in Columbia, in Kansas City, in Jefferson City and the Ozark region, the breadth and diversity of the region's people and landscapes impressed themselves on us such that we vowed never again to reduce them to an anecdote. Shepherd of the Hills. And so, despite his urgings and the many texts they were poring through, they never discussed the implications of Duden's Report, the failed revolution of 1848, or the impact of the free blacks and their relationship with the Union Army in any class or forum, believing such trifles of the past at most a burden, and at the very least distasteful. A thirst for the trueness of lives and language, he anguishes ever. "Old Mazoo." More amusing always to prattle about the flailing baseball Cardinals, who, with the acquisition of

Ozzie and Dale and Willie, and the stewardship of Whitey and Red, would reprise their winning ways within a year. To wit, intuit. "Salus populi suprema lex esto," uttered as much to contradict reality as to invoke it. In bygone years a community led by cooks and chauffeurs, carpenters, day laborers, and bootblacks, governed by ministers and Pullman porters, with that rare doctor or lawyer occupying the social summit. Knobnoster. By the time of the Miami riots they had selected new names and identities, thereby casting off another aspect of their oppressive heritage. The legacy as your grandfather and father had bequeathed it, which you rejected in favor of more compelling fantasy. Assembling all these puzzling pieces really requires the skills of a geographer-historian, which put his meager training and interests in some stead. Credit history for its luminous legerdemain, its adroit, unseen revisions, what the first six years write the next six erase, what one century pens with the most illuminative articulation, the consequent one hundred years transform into an entirely new text, unrecognizable at first glance. There but for the great hoax go our eyes. Having outgrown their former diversions, such as bike riding, crawfishing, and skateboarding, they locked themselves up in their rooms where they drew the shades before listening to records alone, or when not on the phone arranging dates and rendezvous, prowled the streets in someone's mother's car. Others might elect drugs as their chief form of recreation, though liquor was certifiably more common. This entails a decentered notion of the "subject." Reefer, rifer. The parents misread the signals or misconstrued each scene as they doggedly followed the trail of assignations. Please wait for dial tone before inserting quarter. The maliciousness of the storeclerks and the indifference of the teachers was later demonstrated to be part of a greater structural problem. Few, however, admit a predilection for improper relations of power, so as to present a front of probity, propriety. In the absence of a system of pure and unmediated signs, he nearly gave up on living altogether. Our recollective faculties extensively employ this function, dredging doggedly through the muck in search of that vital image. Free rides on the roller coaster and ridiculing the tourists from Iowa were the chief benefits of working at Six Flags, yet others who had traveled told of far more gravity-defying attractions and far more gullible targets elsewhere. The genius lies, in the execution. Bidding their co-workers adieu, he drove her home, where she begged him to come in, blow off a few hours, yet he declined, afraid she might be seeking more, for he had been warned innumerable times about their motives. Most lives are held together by this unspoken chain of commitments which we honor or break as the moment demands. "Now look here, baby, don't be wasting my time," as if one's presence alone were insufficient. Your spirit, a small fluorescent candle, never cedes to any circumstance its gleaming. Festival of Lights. Throughout he could recollect no negative references to Jews, though not because his parents rarely encountered them. Your recourse to a chain of corrections thereby functioned as a method of establishing certainty.

DAVID CARKEET

DAVID CARKEET (1946–) was born in Sonora, California, to Ross Albert, a judge, and Mary Carkeet. After receiving his bachelor's degree in English at the University of California–Davis, Carkeet attended the University of Wisconsin–Madison and Indiana University, where he earned his Ph.D. in 1973. The University of Missouri–St. Louis hired Carkeet as an assistant professor of linguistics in the same year. Carkeet quickly distinguished himself as a writer of humorous fiction with his first novel, *Double Negative* (1980), in which he introduces his character Jeremy Cook, a linguist who solves murder mysteries. Cook reappears in Carkeet's *The Full Catastrophe* (1990), this time as a marriage counselor who studies the defective communication between an estranged couple. A versatile writer, Carkeet has also won acclaim for his baseball novel, *The Greatest Slump of All Time* (1984) as well as for *I Been There Before* (1985)—a historical fantasy that features Mark Twain—and several novels for young adults. His most recent novel is *The Error of Our Ways* (1997). Currently a professor of English at the University of Missouri–St. Louis, Carkeet lives with his wife, Barbara, and their three daughters in Olivette, Missouri.

The following essay, in which Carkeet celebrates a popular recreational activity in St. Louis, originally appeared in the Spring 1996 issue of *St. Louis* magazine.

SUNDAY MORNING BALL AT THE J

When I was a boy, I played ball for the 49ers, a Little League team in Sonora, California. I labored under the patient tutelage of my Methodist Sunday-school teacher, who always whistled soft tunes to himself and let our catcher, his son, drive the pickup around in the outfield after practice. Our uniforms were made of wool. We'd swim all day at the Sonora Pool, then, eyes blurry with chlorine, we'd sweat and scratch our way through the game. Then it was off to the brand-new A&W Root Beer stand, which seemed to have plunked into our little town directly from paradise, as a sample.

I read somewhere that everyone has one sharp memory from childhood of a brilliant moment in sports. My moment, which is really only half-brilliant, happened at one of those summer-evening games. I patrolled at shortstop. The batter was a quick grower with a big head, and big teeth, too: Mike Recek. He was from an even smaller town higher up in the Sierras, and he was known to us from days of yore for single-handedly conquering our elementary school in every sport there was. Recek. We called him "Reject" and "Paycheck" because we were hilarious.

Naturally, Recek hit the ball to me. I'd fervently wished that he not do so, and such a wish is a magnet to the ball. It was a mean one-hopper, and somehow it ended up wedged between my forearms. The amazed ump said under his breath, "Nice stop!" (Our trucker-catcher told me this later.) I gunned the ball to first—or rather, toward first, or rather, more toward first than any other base, though not by much. After all, it was Mike Recek, Foothill Olympian, and who was I to throw him out? Some fundamental failure of self-esteem prevented me from completing the play successfully. Recek's big head ended up at second, where it dwarfed me. But I thought then, and later that day, and later still—in fact, just last night in the shower—*Damn, that was a nice stop.*

I left California to see the world but got only as far as Bloomington, Indiana, where I took up the game again. The I.U. English Department fielded an intramural team initially named the Wily Porkers after William Riley Parker, who was department chair when the team was first organized. Like literary criticism itself, the team name grew more obscure in the years I played on it: the Wily Swine, the Gray Swine, and, in our championship season, Naked Came the Swine.

I got traded to St. Louis and ended up playing ball in the JCCA Sunday-morning men's softball league. I walked onto the field for the first time nearly twenty years ago, a tentative gentile, quiet but willing to let his bat do the schmoozing. Now, on the second Sunday in April, it gives me seasonal comfort to pull into the rear lot at the J and hike down the grassy hill to the four-diamond field. I scout for familiar faces. Yes, there's the guy who ran into me at second last year. There's the guy with the annoying chatter. There's the guy who always gets a double out of what would be a single for anyone else—*always*.

I know them as one knows specialized friends. I know mostly first names, not last. I know where each one hits the ball and how fast he runs—and therefore how much time I'll have to make the throw to first. I know who gets mad on the field and who makes a mockery of anger. I know who praises and who carps.

I know them by occupation from overheard dugout chat: lawyers, dentists, accountants (their hitting improves after April 15), retailers, a pawnbroker, a social worker (after failed at-bats, he hurls his bat in anger at the backstop), a high-school math teacher (he likes to call out to opposing pitchers who have given up a run without making an out, "You have an incalculable E.R.A."), and a veterinarian, who prompted the oddest line I've ever heard on the field, called to him between pitches by a fellow outfielder: "Just how *do* you fix a broken nose on a dog?"

Many of them are closely linked by blood, by marriage, by year-round friendship, or by active participation in the J. Others are outsiders like me, but none *quite* like me. I'm the only one who showed up on an obscure Jewish holiday, puzzled by the empty field. And when a teammate once described an opposing player as "meshugah," he felt obliged to ask if I knew what that meant. Though it was intended as a courtesy, I felt singled out.

But I *am* an outsider. So I observe. I hear things and wonder about them. A small, peculiar jogging track lies below the ballfield, where our foul balls and overthrows sometimes end up. "An Israeli track," someone once called it. Why? What does that mean? When a player's wife was due to deliver a child in a few weeks, on the last day of the season a teammate wished him "lots of mazels." Did he make that up or is it common? I wondered, and I still wonder. And when they look at me, do they ever think *non-Jew*? I hope they don't, but they must.

Sonora, home of the 49ers, was not blessed with ethnic richness. Its population broke down as follows:

Hispanic	80
Jewish	8
African-American	1
Asian	0
Other	0
People Like Me	2,911
TOTAL	**3,000**

If Clinton's cabinet looks like America, Ike's looked like Sonora. The one black man in town was blessed daily with the dubious praise, "Why, I don't even think of him as a Negro." The two Jewish families escaped comment, at least within my hearing. I entered college in giddy ignorance of other peoples. Trying to impress a freshman girl I had just met, I made a guess at her religion. "'Catholic?" I said. The fact that her name was Leah Silberstein had been left out of my calculation.

Some years later and little less ignorant, I married into the tribe, which in turn brought me to the J. Coming out of a yoga class there, my wife saw a poster for the men's softball league. She knew I pined for a return to the diamond. She knew of my longing for another chance to throw out Mike Recek, whose name I mutter in fitful sleep. She signed me up.

It's turned out to be a perfect league for me. The quality of play is good, but it's frequently bad enough to give one comfort in one's own naked shame. The intensity is high but not fanatical. There are arguments, occasionally loud ones, but nothing worse. At the end of one testy game, a dentist began to menace the opposing captain, who stopped him with the words, "I'm a lawyer—touch me and I'll sue your ass." That was the closest thing to a fight that I've ever seen.

As ballplayers, they *care*. They want to be good, much better than they are. When they pop up, they cry out in anguish. An infield bobble can become a crisis of introspection. Most of them are Cardinals-raised, and they know the lingo. They call the ump "Blue" without self-consciousness. They know a skillful play from a lucky one; "look what I found!" is the standard jeer for the latter. "Pick me up" is the way they own up to an error. "Shake it off" signals their forgiveness of yours.

There are, of course, days when the league is less than idyllic. The fields are pebbly and erratically graded, and fielding a ball can be punim-threatening. Diamond four lacks a water fountain, and, as Casey Stengel said of Busch Stadium, "It holds the heat well." Sometimes the jokes are tiresome, especially the ones about aging ("You would have beaten that throw last year!"). Jokes about aging are never funny, especially to one who, to avoid being felled by the rifle shot of a pulled hamstring, must arrive early every Sunday for extra stretching.

Over the years, players perhaps wiser than I have retired, and I miss many of them. What happened to Handelman? Where is the third Brodsky brother? Where is Ronnie? Where is pesky Harold? Fleet-footed Rick? Witty

Shawn? I have come close to hanging up my rubber cleats. I know that I could get hurt. I know I need to grow up and stop throwing out Mike Recek. Summer commitments have taken me away for a year here and there. A new baby made me shelve my glove for three years. Each time I quit, I thought it would be for good. But such an ache! It sent me back, nervous at first, but then I was immediately heartened by the welcome, the warmth, the foolish communal joy.

I see things simply now. To quit this league is to die. To quit playing ball is to accept the end. So I will keep showing up on Sunday morning until they carry me off. When this happens, when the ballplayers watch me being borne up the grassy hill on a stretcher, I hope at least one of them turns to another and says, "Was he Jewish?"

EDDY L. HARRIS

BORN IN ST. LOUIS and a graduate of Stanford University, Eddy Harris (1955–) received national recognition for his first book, *Mississippi Solo* (1989), a personal account of canoeing the entire length (2,350 miles) of the Mississippi River. After his solo adventure on the Big Muddy, Harris traveled widely—from Africa, to the Deep South, to Harlem—and wrote about his experiences in three critically acclaimed memoirs. In *Native Stranger: A Black Man's Journey into the Heart of Africa* (1992), Harris speaks to the familiarity and estrangement he felt as an African American in Africa. *South of Haunted Dreams: A Ride through Slavery's Backyard* (1993) recounts Harris's remarkable—and occasionally harrowing—adventures while he traveled through the Deep South on a motorcycle. In *Still Life in Harlem* (1996), Harris describes his two years spent living in a neighborhood that has spawned some of the greatest achievements in African American art and culture yet has become a symbol of urban despair.

Eddy Harris lives in St. Louis and, when he is not traveling, teaches at Washington University. In the following excerpt from *Still Life in Harlem*, Harris recollects how a disconcerting visit to his father's old neighborhood in St. Louis fueled his resolve to move to Harlem.

FROM *STILL LIFE IN HARLEM*

The past is a dangerous place to visit. It offers itself as a safety zone. At the same time it is a place as treacherous as hell. It is beauty. It is also burden. It is where we go, many of us, to remind ourselves who we are, and even sometimes to find it out. It is where we go often when what is here and now begins to overwhelm us, when the present begins to tarnish, when it refuses to sparkle and glow. But if we are not careful there in the past, its hypnotic swirls can suck us into a vortex of irreality and disillusion.

I had been to the past many times before. My father used to take me there when I was a boy. He was looking, I think, for a world that no longer was the past, *his* past, his former world that had in fact vanished a long time ago, a world that in his memory at least was somehow more everything: more fun, more difficult, harsher, softer, simpler, in a way more alive. Together we would search the scenes of his younger days, the places where he had played and gone to school, fought with the boys and toyed with the girls.

But the scenery by the time I got to it had all turned to ashes and ruin. Nothing was as it had once been, of course; nothing ever is. All had crumbled away. You could see the changes washing across my father's face as we drove around the old neighborhood. The laughter from a long time ago that had been ringing in his ears began to fade. The smile he carried at the anticipation of going home again flattened out across his features into an expression bordering on sadness. His eyes had been sparkling like a child's. Now they dimmed a little. The wonder that had been in them was squeezed away in a wince of melancholic pain. The memories were within him still, but none of the people he knew were still living there. No one there knew him. There was no physical proof left that he had ever been there, or that he had quite simply ever been.

He looked at me as if I were his proof. He stared at me much too long with an expression like that of a deranged man or a demon. I have never liked that look. I knew what it meant.

He bit his lip. He shook his head. He asked me to pull up at the corner so he could step into the liquor store. In a little while he would be nearly drunk.

No! Nothing was the same, not on this trip into his past, not on the last one; nor would it be on the next one. Everything had changed, even the response to my father's particular brand of lunacy.

My father is a maniac. Not long ago this crazy man and I took a drive down to visit his sister Leola. She lives still in St. Louis, not very far in fact from the neighborhood where she and my father had been children. She has a nice house, kept up after all these years in a neighborhood that has deteriorated in time around her, and in her backyard there are fruit trees and a vegetable garden. She grows peaches and tomatoes that, while I'm upstairs visiting, my father likes to steal.

When we left my aunt's house we took a drive, as I knew we would, through the old neighborhood. This time, on the way out the smell of barbecue caught us in its grip and lured us with its enchantment. It defined our mission for the rest of the hour.

"Somewhere around here," my father said, "somebody's making our lunch. I think, I think, I think." He put his head out the window and started sniffing.

His smile was coming back.

We drove around awhile. Finally, on the corner of St. Louis Avenue and Newstead, in the derelict parking lot of a discount food store that had notices all over the windows shouting that food stamps were accepted, we found three women sitting in the shade of a makeshift canopy. They were bathing in the cloud of smoke that came from the huge metal barrel behind them that they had turned into the barbecue pit, and were fanning themselves.

As we drove past, my father eyed them carefully. Without turning toward me he said, "What do you think? Do you think it's all right?" Sometimes he can be quite squeamish about what he eats. Sometimes it seems he'll eat almost anything.

"It'll be all right," I said. "I'm hungry."

We parked the car up the street and walked back to the corner. I walked not quite at his side, but a step or two behind him. I was the sidekick. I have always been the sidekick.

I have been this man's sidekick, in fact, since I was four years old and couldn't walk. I was born with a leg and foot deformity, and when I was four it was thought that surgery might correct the problem. During the long convalescence my father would throw me onto his shoulders and carry me wherever he went. We spent many hours together in Gracie's Tavern, on a corner not far from where we lived in those days.

It was a dimly lit place, if I remember correctly. In a corner there was a machine that was like a little bowling alley. My father would stand me up there and let me hurl the balls at those pretend bowling pins, which would retract violently when the ball hit the right spots on the table. Bells would ring, lights would flash, my father laughed. Then we would sit at the bar.

My father drank beer. I drank soda. I would sit on a stool next to him while he flirted with the barmaids or joked with the men. Every once in a while someone would say something to me. I was happy being my father's sidekick.

Since then we have traveled much together, this old man and I, though not as much as I would have liked. But then, he is not my friend the way he is friends with my brother Tommy. We don't share the same interests the way they do, don't talk about the same things. We are not alike at all, it seems, but more alike I suppose than I would ever have guessed. In fact one of the reasons I travel the way and as much as I do is that I learned it from my father. I am far better at it now than he ever was. I have shown him more in places he had been to without me than he ever saw on his own. In many ways he should be the sidekick, but he's not. He is still *the Man.*

He is now an eighty-year-old-plus man. He is to me still and has always been the embodiment of black manhood.

No, that's not quite right. He is the embodiment to me of manhood. When I grow up, I would like to be very much like him, although it can be argued that in a sense he has yet to grow up himself.

We sauntered to the corner, father and son, like two desperadoes in a Western. I stopped at the barbecue stand. My father didn't. He rounded the corner and looked over the scenery.

Many of the houses in the neighborhood looked as if they had been burned out and were boarded up. Most of them were empty. In the space between those houses, the yards were overgrown with weeds and debris. Where people still lived, the houses, the doors and windows, were protected with bars. Looking at this scene, I found it hard to tell if the bars were to keep people in or to keep people out, and just who, in fact, was the prisoner here. My father bit his lip and put on a face half sad, half sickened at the sight.

In the derelict parking lot, three men doing nothing leaned against the wall of the grocery shop. My father went to say something to them, probably about the demise of the old neighborhood, maybe to tell them how grand it once was here or to ask if anybody knew whatever happened to old Cootie Johnson who used to live on this corner, or what became of the tavern that used to be across the street. In a few minutes he had them all laughing. When he came back to where I stood trying to decide what to eat, he was wearing his big grin.

He said to the ladies sitting there, "All right now, baby. Give it up or show me where it is."

Nobody moved a muscle. Nobody knew what he was talking about. Knowing him as I do, I thought he was making some crude sexual innuendo—but again, knowing him as I do, he could have been speaking the language of a holdup man demanding the money or the safe where they hid it. Whatever he was saying, I laughed and he laughed. These three ladies were not in the least bit intimidated or amused, but clearly they didn't know what to make of this old man.

I didn't know what to make of him myself. I'm not sure I have ever known. But I watched with tremendous admiration as he glided into this world with the ease of a native well versed in its ways. The trouble was: these ladies didn't seem to be a part of the world he knew.

The world he knew was not an easy one, certainly. It was riddled with strife and with the struggle for justice and for fair treatment. In creating the world we now know, the larger society put restrictions on fairness, but none on hostility and resentfulness. My father has never been an idealist; he could never afford that comfort. Neither could he allow himself to surrender to the lure or to the luxury of defeat. He filled his world instead with the kind of laughter that made the bitterness bearable. A good time, he used to tell me, was always just a smile or a joke away.

"The white folks," he said, "have such petty concerns. We get the monumental ones. That's why we laugh louder and party harder."

He speaks of a sense of unity that once existed, a sense of common struggle. Now, he says, it's every man for himself.

"It's always been like that," he tells me. "Every man for himself. Every *black* man for himself. Now there's something different about it. We used to like ourselves more. We used to like each other better. We used to have a certain lightness about us, and with all the evil shit going on around us, we knew how to enjoy who we were and what we had."

I watch my father, and he moves as if there is still that unity in blackness, still that enjoyment.

I looked around and I saw that the world my father knew was no more. Not that it mattered to him whether that world was gone or whether these women were a part of it; he carried that world with him always. He was who he was, and he was not going to try to be anything else.

It might have mattered to the women, though. They looked at him as if he were crazy.

When they had served us what we wanted, my father took his lunch away and went to talk to the men leaning against the wall by the grocery store. I watched him walk away. He is indeed an old man now, but he looks twenty years younger. And he acts it.

I spoke to the women.

"Don't mind him," I said. "He just remembers a time when being black was fun—a lot of fun."

I look at this old man who is my father and watch him negotiate his way into this world that I am no longer familiar with. I don't know how familiar with it he still is, since all of the world he knew has changed, but he glides effortlessly here. He seems to know these people, he speaks their language, and they seem to know him as one of their own. He talked to the men in the parking lot for over half an hour.

How much am I merely my father's son, and how much again am I actually my father? When these people see me, do they see the father in the son, do they see the father's world and his experience in my face, in my being and in my bearing? Or am I just the pussycat to the panther, related but not at all a part of this world, not at all belonging to it? Do they look at me and see something familiar, look at me and say, as they say in the South, "I know your people"? Do they see one of their own in me? And am I still in fact, after all this time away, one of their own, and can I make it here?

I get a headache when I try to sort it all out, but these are the questions that drove me to want to live in Harlem—to find out not so much who I am, for I think I know the answer to that one, but where exactly, if anywhere, I might fit in. Who are my people, and about whom should I care the most?

And is in fact any of this really mine?

LAURELL K. HAMILTON

LAURELL HAMILTON (1963–) was born in Hebrew Springs, Arkansas. After a "brief fling with wanting to be Jane Goodall" and earning a biology degree from Marion College, Hamilton also earned an English degree and began to pursue her dream of writing. To date, Hamilton has penned several fantasy novels and nine horror novels in the popular "Anita Blake Vampire Hunter" series.

Interested in vampires since her days watching the Creature Feature movies on television as a child, Hamilton deliberately made Anita Blake a tough, gun-toting heroine, because she felt that women protagonists in the mysteries she had read were too "ladylike." Feisty and fearless, Anita Blake is called the "Executioner" by the vampire population. Hamilton's work has been compared with that of Anne Rice and, like Rice, she has developed a large cult following, with several websites devoted to Anita Blake and her exploits. Currently, Hamilton lives in the St. Louis area with her husband, Gary, and daughter, Trinity.

The following excerpt is from Hamilton's fourth Anita Blake novel, *The Lunatic Cafe* (1996). In this chapter, Anita and her boyfriend, Richard—who happens to be a werewolf—attend a performance of *Guys and Dolls* at the Fox Theatre in midtown St. Louis.

FROM *THE LUNATIC CAFE*

The 1978 Nova that I'd been driving had died a sad and tragic death. I was now driving a Jeep Cherokee Country. It was a deep, deep green that looked black at night. But it had four-wheel drive for winter and enough room to carry goats in the back. Chickens were what I used for zombie raising most of the time, but occasionally you needed something bigger. Carrying goats in the Nova had been a bitch.

I pulled the Cherokee into the last parking space in the lot on Grand. My long, black winter coat billowed around me because I had only buttoned the bottom two buttons. If I buttoned all the buttons I couldn't get to my gun.

My hands were shoved into the coat pockets, arms huddling the cloth around me. I didn't wear gloves. I've never been comfortable shooting with gloves on. The gun is a part of my hand. Cloth shouldn't interfere.

I ran across the street in my high-heeled pumps, careful on the frosty pavement. The sidewalk was cracked, with huge sections broken out of it, as if someone had taken a sledgehammer to it. The boarded-up buildings were as dilapidated as the sidewalk. I'd missed the crowd, being nearly late, so I had the shattered street to myself. It was a short but lonely walk on a December night. Broken glass littered the ground and in heels I had to be very careful where I stepped. An alley cut the buildings. It looked like the natural habitat of *Muggerus americanus*. I watched the darkness carefully. Nothing moved. With the Browning I wasn't too worried, but still . . . You didn't have to be a genius to shoot someone in the back.

The wind gusted cold enough to take my breath away as I neared the corner and relative safety. I wore a lot of sweaters in the winter, but tonight I'd wanted something dressier, and I was freezing my patooties off, but I was hoping that Richard would like the red blouse.

At the corner there were lights, cars, and a policeman directing traffic in the middle of the street. You never saw this many police in this section of St. Louis unless the Fox was on. A lot of wealthy people came down here in their furs, diamonds, Rolex watches. Wouldn't do for a friend of the city council to get mugged. When Topol came to reprise his role in *Fiddler on the Roof,* the audience was very crème de la crème and the place crawled with cops. Tonight there was just the usual. Mostly in front of the theater, mostly doing the seedy backs of buildings in case someone with money wandered away from the light.

I went through the glass doors into the long, narrow entryway. It was brightly lit, shiny somehow. There's a little room to the right where you can pick up your tickets. People streamed out of it, hurrying to the inner glass doors. I wasn't as late as I thought if there were this many people still getting tickets. Or maybe everyone else was as late as I was.

I caught a glimpse of Richard standing in the far right corner. At six foot one he is easier to spot across a crowded room than I am, at my own five foot three. He stood quietly, following the crowd's movement. He didn't seem bored or impatient. He seemed to be having a good time watching the people.

His eyes followed an elderly couple as they walked through the glass doors. The woman used a cane. Their progress was painfully slow. His head turned slowly with them. I scanned the crowd. Everyone else was younger, moving with confident or hurried stride. Was Richard looking for victims? Prey? He was, after all, a werewolf. He'd gotten a bad batch of lycanthropy vaccine. One of the reasons I never get the shots. If my flu shot accidentally backfires, that's one thing, but being furry once a month . . . No, thanks.

Did he realize he was standing there searching the crowd like a lion staring at a bunch of gazelles? Or maybe the elderly couple had reminded him of his grandparents. Hell, maybe I was giving him motives that were only in my suspicious little brain. I hoped so.

His hair was brown. In sunlight it gleamed with strands of gold, hints of copper. I knew the hair was shoulder length, nearly my length, but he'd done something to it, pulled it back somehow so it gave the illusion of being very short and close to his head. Not easy with hair as wavy as his.

His suit was some rich shade of green. Most men would have looked like Peter Pan in a green suit, but on him it looked just right. As I walked closer, I could see his shirt was a pale almost gold, tie a darker green than the suit, with tiny Christmas trees done in red. I would have made a smart remark about the tie, but dressed in red and green with a Christmas angel on my lapel, who was I to complain?

He saw me and smiled. The smile was very bright against his permanently tanned skin. His last name, Zeeman, is Dutch, but somewhere back in his ancestry was something not European. Not blond, not fair, not cold. His eyes were a perfect, chocolate brown.

He reached out and took my hands, gently, drawing me to him. His lips were soft against my mouth, a brief, nearly chaste kiss.

I stepped back, taking a breath. He kept hold of my hand, and I let him. His skin was very warm against my cold hand. I thought about asking him if he'd been thinking about eating that elderly couple, but didn't. Accusing him of murderous intent might spoil the evening. Besides, most lycanthropes weren't aware of doing nonhuman things. When you pointed it out, it always seemed to hurt their feelings. I didn't want to hurt Richard's feelings.

As we went through the inner doors into the crowded lobby, I asked, "Where's your coat?"

"In the car. Didn't want to carry it, so I made a dash for it."

I nodded. It was typical Richard. Or maybe lycanthropes didn't get cold.

From the back I could see he'd braided his hair tight to his scalp. The tip of the braid trailed over his collar. I couldn't even figure out how he'd done it. My idea of fixing my hair is to wash, smear a little hair goop through it, then let it dry. I was not into high-tech hair design. Though it might be fun to figure out the knots in a leisurely fashion after the show. I was always willing to learn a new skill.

The main lobby of the Fox is a cross between a really nice Chinese restaurant and a Hindu temple, with a little Art Deco thrown in for flavor. The colors are so dazzling, it looks like the painter ground up stained glass with bits of light trapped in them. Pit bull–size Chinese lions with glowing red eyes guard a sweep of stairs that lead up to the Fox Club balcony, where for fifteen thousand dollars a year you can eat wonderful meals and have a private box. The rest of us peons mingled nearly shoulder to shoulder in the carpeted lobby, with offerings of popcorn, pretzels, Pepsi, and on some nights, hot dogs. A far cry from chicken cordon bleu or whatever they were serving up above.

The Fox treads that wonderfully thin line between gaudiness and the fantastic. I've loved the building since I first saw it. Every time I come, there is some new wonder. Some color, or carving, or statue that I didn't notice before. When you realize that it was originally built to be a movie theater, you realize how much things have changed. Movie theaters now have the souls of unwashed socks. The Fox is alive as only the best buildings are alive.

I had to let go of Richard's hand to unbutton my coat the rest of the way, but hey, we weren't attached at the hip. I stood close to him in the crowd without touching, but I could feel him, like a line of warmth against my body.

"We're going to look like the Bobsey twins when I take my coat off," I said.

He raised his eyebrows.

I spread the coat like a flasher, and he laughed. It was a good laugh, warm and thick like Christmas pudding.

" 'Tis the season," he said. He gave me a one-armed hug, quick like you'd give a friend, but his arm stayed over my shoulders. It was still early enough in our dating that touching each other was new, unexpected, exhilarating. We kept looking for excuses to touch each other. Trying to be nonchalant about it. Not fooling each other. Not sure we cared. I slipped my arm around his waist and leaned just a bit. It was my right arm. If we were attacked now, I'd never draw my gun in time. I stayed there for a minute thinking it just might be worth it. I moved around him, offering my left hand to him.

I don't know if he caught a glimpse of the gun or just figured it out, but his eyes widened. He leaned close to me, whispering against my hair. "A gun here, at the Fox? You think the ushers will let you in?"

"They did last time."

He got a strange look on his face. "You always go armed?"

I shrugged. "After dark, yes."

His eyes were puzzled, but he let it go. Before this year I'd sometimes gone out after dark unarmed but it had been a rough year. A lot of different people had tried to kill me. I was small even for a woman. I jogged, lifted weights, had a black belt in judo, but I was still outclassed by most professional bad guys. They tended to also lift weights, know martial arts, and outweigh me by a hundred pounds or more. I couldn't arm-wrestle them, but I could shoot them.

Also a lot of this year I'd been up against vampires, and other preternatural creepie-crawlies. They could lift large trucks with a single hand or worse. Silver bullets might not kill a vampire, but it certainly slowed them down. Enough for me to run like hell. To get away. To survive.

Richard knew what I did for a living. He'd even seen some of the messy parts. But I still expected him to blow it. To start playing the male protector and bitch about the gun or something. It was almost a permanent tightness in my gut, waiting for this man to say something awful. Something that would ruin it, destroy it, hurt.

So far, so good.

The crowd started flowing towards the stairs, parting on either side to the corridors leading into the main theater. We shuffle-stepped with the crowd, holding hands to keep from being separated. Sure.

Once free of the lobby, the crowd flowed towards the different aisles like water searching for the quickest route downstream. The quickest route was still pretty slow. I dug the tickets out of the pocket of my suit jacket. I didn't have a purse. There was a small brush, a lipstick, lipliner, eye shadow, ID, and my car keys stuffed in my coat pockets. My beeper was tucked in the front of my skirt, discreetly to one side. When not dressed up, I wore a fanny pack.

The usher, an older woman with glasses, shone a tiny flashlight on our tickets. She took us to our seats, motioned us in, and went back up to assist the next group of helpless people. The seats were good, near the middle, sort of close to the stage. Close enough.

Richard had scooted in to sit on my left without being asked. He's a quick study. It's one of the reasons we're still going out. That and the fact that I lust after his body something terrible.

I spread my coat over the seat, spreading it out so it wouldn't be bulky. His arm snaked across my chair, fingers touching my shoulder. I fought the urge to lay my head on his shoulder. Too hokey, then thought, what the hell. I snuggled into the bend of his neck, just breathing in the scent of his skin. His aftershave was clean and sweet, but underneath was the smell of his skin, his flesh. It made it so the aftershave would never smell the same on anyone else. Frankly, without a drop of aftershave I loved the smell of Richard's neck.

I straightened up, pulling just a little away from him. He looked at me questioningly. "Something wrong?"

"Nice aftershave," I said. No need to confess that I'd had an almost irresistible urge to nibble his neck. It was too embarrassing.

The lights dimmed and the music began. I'd never actually seen *Guys and Dolls* except in the movies. The one with Marlon Brando and Jean Simmons. Richard's idea of a date was caving, hiking, things that required your oldest clothes and a pair of good walking shoes. Nothing wrong with that. I like the outdoors, but I wanted to try a dress-up date. I wanted to see Richard in a suit and let him see me in something frillier than jeans. I was after all a girl, whether I liked to admit it or not.

But having proposed the date, I didn't want to do the usual dipsy-duo of dinner and a movie. So I'd called up the Fox to see what was playing and asked Richard if he liked musicals. He did. Another point in his favor. Since it was my idea, I bought the tickets. Richard had not argued, not even to pay half. After all, I hadn't offered to pay for our last dinner. It hadn't occurred to me. I was betting paying for the tickets occurred to Richard, but he'd let it go. Good man.

The curtain came up and the opening street scene paraded before us, bright colors, stylized, perfect and cheerful, and just what I needed. "The Fugue for Tinhorns" filled the bright stage and flowed out into the happy dark. Good music, humor, soon to be dancers, Richard's body next to mine, a gun under my arm. What more could a girl ask for?

GERALD EARLY

BORN AND RAISED IN PHILADELPHIA, Gerald Early (1952–) developed a love of literature at an early age. Among the literary heroes of his youth were William Shakespeare, Richard Wright, James Joyce, H. L. Mencken, Thomas Wolfe, George Orwell, and, above all, James Baldwin.

Early moved to St. Louis in 1982 to teach at Washington University, where he is now, with Wayne Fields, co-chair of American Culture Studies. Although he has received numerous offers to teach at universities around the United States, Early has chosen to remain in St. Louis, saying in a 1997 *Gateway Heritage* interview, "I've learned a lot about myself from living in this city, and come to a certain level of maturity here. I very much appreciate this city, and I'm thankful. But I also feel in a lot of ways that this city needs me. . . . St. Louis needs that visible demonstration of a certain kind of intellect emanating from a black person."

A highly prolific author of books, essays, reviews, and criticism, Early won critical acclaim for his first book, *Tuxedo Junction: Essays on American Culture,* published in 1990. Since then, Early has also received numerous awards, including the National Book Critics Circle Award for Criticism in 1995 for *The Culture of Bruising: Essays on Prizefighting*. Early's range of interests and literary topics is vast—ranging from sports, to jazz, to parenthood, to the African American experience in St. Louis. In 1998, he edited *"Ain't But a Place": An Anthology of African American Writings about St. Louis*, which was published by the Missouri Historical Society Press. This volume consists of a fuller selection of the material that Early selected while serving as a contributing editor for *Seeking St. Louis*.

Gerald Early is currently Washington University's Merle Kling Professor of Modern Letters. He lives in St. Louis with his wife, Ida, and they are the parents of two daughters. The following essay is taken from the collection *The Place Within: Portraits of the American Landscape by Twenty Contemporary Writers,* edited by Jodi Daynard (1997). Of this piece, Daynard wrote, "Early's essay captures the 'odd angle of Being' for the city's black inhabitants, who have never quite known, despite their long history here, whether this place is truly 'home.'"

ST. LOUIS: THE MIDWESTERN LONG GOOD-BYE

PART ONE: EMBARRASSED SPLENDOR

It is a curious, if not altogether unusual, fact about St. Louis that there is a tendency for at least a certain class of its citizens to apologize for having what appears to them the bland misfortune of living here. This is almost exclusively true of people who are not natives, that is, were not born in St. Louis, especially those born in other major American cities, although I do hear it from time to time from a few who have spent their entire lives here. This singular feeling of inadequacy does not arise from the fact that St. Louis, in spying its downtown skyline, does not seem as relentlessly modernist, as extravagantly Art Deco, as some other cities. It is not a place of many imposing skyscrapers or an overly done up downtown that is like a movie set through which tourists can move with a supremely untroubled sense of distraction (although our waterfront district, Laclede's Landing, has all the Yuppie, faked "authenticity" of Memphis's Beale Street, the contrived spectacle of nineteenth-century gentility without the slave pens and the wharves and the rats and the life-threatening dives, in short, without the stuff that made nineteenth-century St. Louis, for better and for worse, a real place).

St. Louis has a certain modesty in its outline that belies a true richness in its architecture and a kind of subtle beauty in its westward sprawl from the Mississippi. True, on its most ordinary days, the river seems little more than a toxic waste dump. "What's so great about this river?" my oldest daughter said just a year ago as we were standing at a pier on an afternoon, waiting for my mother, who was buying souvenirs in one of the shops. "It looks horrible and it smells bad." I don't recall ever going to the Mississippi simply to see the river because there is, normally, nothing to see, although to take visiting friends and relatives on the River Road to Pere Marquette is scenic enough, indeed, a strikingly lyrical ride. But when the river floods, as it has done twice in the last five years, it seems a muddy magnificence, as mythic and merciless, as grandiose in its apostrophized fury and holy indifference, as Twain's river in *Huckleberry Finn,* as Faulkner's river in "Old Man," as Wright's river in "Down by the Riverside." During the last flood, I was flying back from New York and as the plane circled St. Louis, the river seemed everywhere, certainly everywhere in Illinois and upstate, everything overturned, unmoored, submerged, and uprooted, as if, were God to grant a new heaven and a new earth, then this might be it; a sight of both dread and absurdity, of tragedy and resignation, of suffering and renewal. Not the end of everything is it, but surely the end of some things. And I felt especially as if I were being reminded that, after all, nature is nature and we are, well, what we are, both a part of nature and apart from it. Nothing reminds one of this so well as the flooding Mississippi.

St. Louis possesses a set of charms that make it a city far more worthwhile to see than, say, Kansas City or Milwaukee or Cincinnati. The most compelling man-made landmark in the United States is the St. Louis Gateway Arch, a startling engineering feat, finished in 1965 after seven years of construction. It stands at 632 feet from base to apex. It is, perhaps, as a spectacle the great American rune, an ineffable symbol of the enigma of the great American adventure, the linchpin of East and West that defines what the Middle West is. "That's my middle west," writes Fitzgerald in *The Great Gatsby*, "not the wheat or the prairies or the lost Swede towns, but the thrilling returning trains of my youth. . . ." And my Middle West is that inverted tuning fork pointed straight in the St. Louis sky, humming with a strange running current of subterranean energy, the hieroglyphic of eminence of the Middle West's youthfulness. To go up in the Arch—a crazy elevator ride where one goes both up and sideways and once reaching the top, tries to see St. Louis from a set of small windows that on crowded days are impossible to get to, and at less frequented times seem a bit of a disappointment—this excursion is pointless. For the splendor of the Arch, the silver metal looking almost liquidly transparent in the sun, opaque as an ancient ruin in the rain, the experience of this technical marvel, is standing outside and looking up at it. It was once claimed that only Lenin's Tomb and the two Disney theme parks drew more tourists than the Arch. Still, some of us in St. Louis demur.

I remember once talking to a colleague of mine who works at a prestigious school on the East Coast. "So, you're still out there, heh?" he said, with a shake of the head as if I might feel better to know that he was pitying rather than patronizing me. And I found myself being apologetic: "Well, you know, St. Louis is not such a bad place." I am not sure if this apology, abject and unseemly as it was, resulted from a natural timidity to contradict the stupid and the arrogant, or was the cowering acknowledgment of a paralyzing sense of civic inferiority. I was born and reared in Philadelphia, so perhaps my life here since 1982 has been a long period of cultural slumming, so to speak, in the great American outback. Admittedly, when I first came to St. Louis, I thought it to be a barbaric place for two reasons principally: first, it had no public transportation worthy of the name; and second, it was a town that was impossible to walk in. For the first few years here, I felt imprisoned by my need for a car, which, frankly, I considered to be unnatural and a cause of considerable anxiety. But I have learned since my earliest days here that certain stretches of neighborhood are quite walkable, even if the city as a whole is not.

The Hill, for instance, reminds me of the Little Italy of my native South Philadelphia, and when I lived in an apartment in University City, I used to walk around the area quite often. Indeed, I used to frequently walk to work as the university was close by. Later, when I moved to Olivette, a community just west of University City, I used to walk and run in the park there all the time. Getting a dog after moving to Webster Groves has forced me to walk over a good portion of this town, past Webster University, Eden Seminary, the shops of Old Webster, the Hawken House, the YMCA, much to my pleasure, perhaps the sole pleasure I have discovered in owning a dog. Also, because its public transportation, despite the recent opening of the Metro Link—an elevated train which my very eastern mother refers to as "one-half of one line of a decent train system"—is still not very well developed, the city has taken on, for me, a certain quaint stillness or still quaintness that seems a positive relief whenever I return here from a sojourn in the East, where people seem utterly murderous in their attempt to get somewhere.

It is almost a pleasure to drive in St. Louis, probably in no small measure because there is a strong possibility that one will be able to park one's car upon arriving somewhere. I certainly never felt that way back east. I no longer feel I have lost anything or sacrificed anything to live here. There is no need for me to feel that way, since others have decided to feel that way for me. I have, regrettably and regularly, encountered from people from either coast the sense that it must be a great grief, a wide, wild sorrow to have to live in the Middle West, and even greater the tragedy not to live in Chicago, apparently the sole midwestern location that people on either coast take seriously.

For people in St. Louis, a city once described by former Missouri senator

Thomas Eagleton,[1] who, at the time, was heading an effort to get us a new professional football team, as "a raucous Des Moines," their apologies take many forms. The progressives, leftists, radicals, and liberal elements always talk about how "conservative" the city is, as if to imply that their great self-righteous efforts to make us all better human beings would not be like so many seeds scattered on barren soil if they lived where the population was not so backward and "rich, white men did not run everything." This apology is of course the progressive's own confession that he or she is nothing more than a second-rate leftist; otherwise he or she wouldn't be stuck in this political roadshow called St. Louis where the local wrangling seems downright genteel compared to Chicago or any major East Coast city; where they can scarcely mount a good street demonstration; and where the police do not have nearly the reputation for beating the crap out of people that they do in other places. (Indeed, when I first moved to St. Louis, I thought the police here needed lessons from the cops in Philadelphia in how to intimidate and brutalize citizens in a fruitless effort to control crime, although I am sure there are many who can testify to the fact, as we have no shortage of police brutality claims and accusations, that the police in St. Louis are no kindness, or as Raymond Chandler so aptly put it, "[no] way has yet been invented to say good-bye to them.")

Now, the rich, white men who run St. Louis are collectively called Civic Progress, and progress civically we surely do under the guidance of these wonderful and wise patricians of our order. Most of them are either the leading CEOs—St. Louis has an extraordinary number of corporate headquarters here, including McDonnell-Douglas, TWA, Anheuser-Busch, Ralston-Purina, and Monsanto—or the old St. Louis money families, or

1 Senator Eagleton is a fine man and was a capable, skilled politician during his days in public office. However, to the world outside Missouri he will simply be remembered as the "nutcase" that George McGovern selected as his running mate in the 1972 presidential election. Eagleton was kicked in unceremonious and cowardly fashion from the ticket after an outcry about his having been given electro-shock treatment many years earlier, and replaced by Sargent Shriver. McGovern went down in ignominious and deserved defeat at the hands of Richard M. Nixon.

both.[2] As a ruling class goes, it is no better or worse than the ruling classes of rich, white men who run everything that is worth running in the United States, despite the strenuous efforts of our most committed leftists and multiculturalists at least to give us, if not a ruling class at all, a ruling class "that looks like America." Some of the blacks who live here will also complain about the "conservatism," compared to those bastions of African American political disruption on the East and West Coasts. This too merely reflects that they feel themselves second-raters. Otherwise, they would be where the action supposedly is. The leftists and the African Americans felt a great deal better about themselves when finally, in 1993, a black, Freeman Bosley, Jr.—a man for whom politics is something like the family business, and who combines all the inevitability of a political hack with all the public expectancy of something approaching leadership—was elected mayor of

2 St. Louis lost its professional football team, the Cardinals, because its owner, Bill Bidwell, was not permitted to join Civic Progress. Indeed, he was snubbed by the ruling class here. The poor man actually saw his team as a business, not a hobby, and needed his income from it. In any case, in 1988, Bidwell moved his team to Phoenix, where, presumably, the local ruling class will not snub him. In 1995, St. Louis acquired a new professional team, the former Los Angeles Rams. Presumably, too, its owner, Georgia Frontiere, the hotsy-totsy sixty-something-year-old blonde who grew up here, although she never gave the town a passing thought for nearly her entire adult life until we prostrated ourselves in front of her like a cash cow begging to be bilked, will not be snubbed by our ruling class—saviour that she is by being willing to come here to grow richer instead of some other sexier place, and thus save our civic pride. (Professional sports team owners resemble no one so much in our cultural history as southern plantation owners.) We have built an indoor stadium, the TWA Dome, another civic tribute to business mismanagement as TWA is virtually bankrupt, to the tune of nearly $300 million in her honor and to serve as a better romper room for her football players. When the ruins of this are uncovered five thousand years from now, it may be thought by the inhabitants then that we, in simpler times, prayed to decidedly lesser gods. I am sure our new football owner will be a part of the Veiled Prophets' Ball, some odd, slightly Masonic, faintly racist (although black people now attend in fairly representative numbers and surely some black girl will one day soon be named Veiled Prophet Queen), decidedly atavistic, social register event of the ruling class, where it seems to take both itself and its amusements seriously.

the city. It was embarrassing for them to have a city that is over 40 percent black and not have a black mayor. To have that symbol of progressive change pass us by for so many years *really* made the place seem like a backwater. "We're so conservative, we can't even elect a black mayor," they said. Indeed, the major political offices of the city—the mayor, the police chief, and the city comptroller—are all in the hands of blacks. It is nice for the progressives and the blacks to know that mediocre black leadership can have equal access to the paltry patronage that's left, and that mediocre white leadership controlled for so long.

I must explain a small but important feature of St. Louis's political geography before I go on. The city of St. Louis, with its huge black population (mostly located in North St. Louis, which I will discuss a bit more momentarily), its overwhelmingly black public schools (wretched places, naturally), its high crime ("I try to avoid the city at night except if I'm going to a concert or a ball game," say your average suburban residents), and its eroding tax base (middle-class whites and blacks are fleeing with abandon), is a distinct entity from St. Louis County, although residents here will often refer to the entire region as "St. Louis" in a generic way. As most people who live here have intercourse with and carry on their lives almost daily traveling between both the city and the county, both constitute the identity of the place called St. Louis. The county cannot be seen simply as the suburbs or mere bedroom communities. It consists of independent municipalities, with their own mayors, police forces, fire departments, schools, and the like. Some of them, like Ladue (where some of our richest and most famous citizens live), Clayton (which has our best, our richest public school system), and Frontenac (where our local Neiman-Marcus and Saks Fifth Avenue are located) are lily-white and very exclusive.

Some, like Webster Groves, where I live, boast a considerable history and families who go back many generations. Some, like Kinloch and Wellston, are all-black, very crime-ridden, and very poor, which is, of course, no news as this seems the chronic condition of a significant number of blacks in America. University City prides itself on its diversity—the most rabbinical schools and Afrocentric bookstores—and the fact that it has the closest thing to Harvard Square in an area called the Loop, a mere few blocks from Washington University, the most renowned school in Missouri. Richmond Heights can claim the area's busiest and biggest mall, the Galleria, and one of the principal seminaries. (Webster Groves has the other.) Crève Coeur has the craziest zoning and Kirkwood the best comic book store. Chesterfield may have the hottest real estate development, while Town and Country may have the cleanest streets. The vast majority of people who make up the region known as St. Louis live in the county, over two million. (Considerably less than a million live in the city of St. Louis.) If there is one side of America's political reality in Civic Progress and the existence of an upper-crust ruling class, this bewildering array of townships, this multiplicity of municipal identities is another side of that same reality, the contending, contentious middle-level groups.

People who live in the city assert this with a certain pride as if they, at least, are not abandoning *their* civic duty by running off and leaving the poor behind like the modern-day lepers everybody knows the poor really are.[3] The great advantage that those who live in the city have are these: they live in the area of the most compelling and original architecture, and of all the cultural institutions. All professional baseball, football, and hockey are played downtown. The symphony performs there, as do two of our three major theater companies. Most major concerts are held there, and virtually any jazz worthy of the name can only be heard there. The zoo, the art museum, the history museum, and our outdoor musical theater—the Muny—are all located in Forest Park, which is in the city. Indeed, Forest Park, dedicated in 1876, is one of our major parks. The other major park, Tower Grove Park, was donated to the city by Henry Shaw, the founder of the Botanical Gardens. And the Botanical Gardens, among the most beautiful

3 I am told by several friends and acquaintances, both black and white, that as a middle-class black and, of course, a role model (apparently a professional activity, although I do not know it), I ought to be living in the city instead of the golden triangle of Webster Groves. To those blacks who feel that way, I say that I owe it to the memory of Martin Luther King, Jr., and the continued success of Affirmative Action to integrate wherever and whenever I can. To those whites who feel that way, I say that I have had, after all, the experience of living with and among black folk for many years, having in the process learned their cultural ways and habits to such a degree that I might be said to have some ethnographic expertise about them. "I think you should try living among them now," I say, "as I am sure you will find it as enriching and valuable as I did. There are a good many vacant places going begging in North St. Louis." Nothing follows this but silence.

places to visit in St. Louis, and the one of the finest gardens of their type anywhere in the world, are also in the city. In short, the residents of the county need the city if they want the standard cultural amenities that make suburban living bearable, in fact, that make suburban living possible.

This brings up another way that people apologize for St. Louis: conjuring up this cultural life. All cities and towns do this sort of boosterism, naturally, but there is a certain pitch of desperation in St. Louis's push for cultural relevance. In the Loop area of University City is the St. Louis Walk of Fame, where there is concerted effort to memorialize in concrete every famous, noteworthy person who seemingly ever so much as ate a meal in the environs of St. Louis. I say environs because in our lust for an impressive roster of cultural figures, people who are actually connected to East St. Louis (which is across the river in Illinois and totally unconnected to St. Louis), like dancer Katherine Dunham, track star Jackie Joyner Kersee, and trumpeter Miles Davis, are included. I am not sure if singer Leon Thomas, also of East St. Louis, is included. If not, he will be eventually.

These people played in clubs in St. Louis or competed in St. Louis, so they are connected to the city in some way, I suppose. As with any big city, a fair share of significant people have come from here: Chuck Berry, Tennessee Williams, T. S. Eliot, Dick Gregory, Kate Chopin, Michael and Leon Spinks,[4] John Goodman. Scott Joplin lived here for a brief spell, and Stan Musial came, never to leave. Howard Nemerov and Stanley Elkin died here. Charles Lindbergh's backers were St. Louisans and the plane that

---

4 The emergence of the Spinks brothers as a result of the 1976 Olympics proved a bit of an embarrassment to St. Louis as they both grew up in the Pruitt-Igoe housing project, a disastrously failed experiment in public housing. Pruitt-Igoe consisted of thirty-three eleven-story buildings with a combined capacity for three thousand families. The first units opened in 1954 and 1955. It was one of the largest public housing projects of its kind and was meant to solve the problem of low-cost housing for the poor. By 1965, the projects were unlivable, plagued by crime and vandalism; there was little public transportation, no recreational space, no shopping, and no health services. By 1971, only seventeen of the thirty-three buildings were occupied. By 1975, the entire project was dynamited (shown repeatedly on national television during the Spinks brothers' rise to boxing glory). As historian James Neal Primm put it: ". . . the empty and sterile seventy acres became a stark reminder of good intentions gone wrong."

crossed the Atlantic was called the *Spirit of St. Louis*. But it was certainly not their St. Louis connection that made these people noteworthy. Indeed, St. Louis played very little role in their fame and some might say that, in certain cases, St. Louis was nearly an inimical force. What drove them to be what they became, in many instances, was their sheer hatred of the place. This is not unusual in the case of a great many famous people no matter where they are from, but I believe we in St. Louis feel a bit sheepish about providing such a negative impetus for so many. This might be particularly true for the noteworthy blacks who have come from here. Few ever liked the place, feeling stifled by the powerful tentacles of both black and white provincialism.[5] Hardly any returned to live here once they achieved fame.

PART TWO: THE ODD ANGLE OF BEING

My wife was just elected president of the St. Louis Chapter of the Junior League. She had been a member since 1988. This is historic because my wife is the first black woman ever to be president of this chapter. The first blacks ever to do anything in white America are always historic, although I doubt that it should be so, and one might expect, as integration is still a relatively new mode of social interaction (or engineering, depending on how one sees it) among us, that we will have our share of Jackie Robinsons for some many years yet. I wish my wife well as she embarks on this two-year enterprise. (As many black women in the area have decided to place the entire burden of the success of integration in the Junior League on my wife's shoulders, I am sure that the symbolic weight of all this is something she'd prefer not to have in addition to doing everything else all the white

5 Of course, the whites who write and promote the city's black heritage can find much white provincialism but no black provincialism for as far as the eye can see. All they see with blacks are "forms of resistance" and "courageous building of cultural institutions." These whites project their own fantasies of escaping their own white provincialism through the cultural hardiness and charisma of blacks. They do not have black skins and have never known black experience from the inside out. I have. And there is more soul-killing black provincialism than one can possibly imagine.

past presidents have normally had to do.) Indeed, as I am fond of several of the women in the Junior League, I wish the entire organization well. It is an exciting time for all of them.

The irony is that the headquarters of the Junior League is located in Frontenac where, a few years ago, I had my infamous run-in with local law enforcement and racist presumption while attending a Junior League Christmas Bazaar. A jewelry store owner in the mall where the bazaar took place saw me, the only black man, walking around among a number of white men and women who were also roaming about, and decided I was going to rob his store and rape his clerk. This might have been droll had it not been a dramatization of something very painful in American life for both blacks and whites. I provide a full account of that incident in a book I wrote called *Daughters: On Family and Fatherhood*. What is striking about the incident is that it seems to have a life of its own in St. Louis, where it became a major story at the time, November 1991. As recently as the latest Martin Luther King, Jr., holiday (January 15, 1996), I was interviewed about it. I was more than a little nonplussed as I could not possibly imagine that St. Louis has had no such incidents occur in the last five years. This must be a provincial place if such a relatively minor incident (I was not arrested or beaten by the police or even treated discourteously by them) is still news. "You make a wonderful story because you are the big-shot black professor at the big-shot university. There was no ambiguity in this case. You weren't some sixteen-year-old black kid with a couple of arrests wrongly accused of stealing a shirt from Sears," my wife said. "I just wish the news people would stop mentioning the Earlys with the incident in Frontenac. I'm not in a permanent state of protest against the town of Frontenac. We've been out there many times since the incident and nothing has happened."

I wonder how often the story of the Earlys' attempt to get an apology from Frontenac will come up during my wife's tenure as president of Junior League. It will doubtless be a period of adjustment for the Junior League itself as it discovers that wonderful note of complexity that the presence of Negroes adds to virtually every aspect of American life, for we blacks wind up relating to things in slightly odd angles, a bit in the manner that Thelonious Monk struck chords on the piano. I must admit that going to Frontenac, especially at night, as a black man, fills me with an intense degree of foreboding. The husbands of the other Junior League women, I am sure, never think about this. Oddly, I have experienced far less racism in St. Louis than in any other place I have ever lived.

When we first came to St. Louis, my wife decided, in order to get to know some people, to become very active in the local chapter of her college sorority, Alpha Kappa Alpha. This gave her an automatic entree to black St. Louis that I certainly never had and about which I was a bit envious. She became well acquainted with North St. Louis, and with black St. Louis life by slow stages (she was an outsider and so did not easily penetrate social circles long established by high school and church ties), particularly an area called the Ville where many of her sorority sisters lived. This was a remarkable neighborhood, run-down, defeated, a ghetto, but with the imprint of cultural self-sufficiency and pride. I was not necessarily impressed to learn that blacks like Dick Gregory and Chuck Berry came from this neighborhood. But I was overwhelmed by the number of institutions, functioning and defunct, that the neighborhood contained: all manner of businesses, from funeral homes to insurance companies, from groceries to barbershops, from real estate developers to newspaper offices.

Sumner High School, located in this area, was the first black high school west of the Mississippi. Most people acquainted with black American cultural history have heard of Madame C. J. Walker and her hair-products empire, but Annie Malone of St. Louis amassed a fortune nearly as great selling much the same stuff. She also started the Poro Beauty College in this area, an institution that did far more than merely train beauticians. A children's home in the area now bears the name of this industrious "race" woman. North St. Louis came to my consciousness as a political entity shortly after my arrival because of the huge fight over the fate of the Homer G. Phillips Hospital, which eventually closed in 1984. Blacks began to push for a full-service health facility as early as 1915, according to historian George Lipsitz. Black lawyer and northside leader Homer G. Phillips led the fight for the hospital. One year after his death (which seemed suspiciously like murder) in 1931, construction began on the "colored" hospital that bore his name, after years of agitation, broken promises, and not-so-benign neglect.

The protests to keep the hospital open were not so much for practical reasons as for emotional ones. The hospital was part of the identity of black St. Louis, a symbol of its struggle for recognition and fair treatment (despite the fact that the hospital was always a second-rate, underfunded facility where newborn babies, for instance, were kept in something resembling chicken coops, a clear intention of the policy of segregation whereby whites made sure that blacks never enjoyed the "normal" amenities of any aspect of American life). I understood as soon as I arrived in St. Louis that black people stood at a rather odd angle to the history of the place, as they do to virtually any place. If they were provincial, they were no more so than any other black folk I had ever met or lived with. For I was both moved and frightened by the Ville, a place that was at once so enormously and courageously self-supporting and so terribly self-contained and removed. The worst sort of social cliques are those of the oppressed ethnics, the worst sort of old-boy network is that of the oppressed elite. Always with such groups, merit doesn't count as much as who you're related to, who you know, or, in the case of black folk, how light your skin is.

The ethnics are always mightily aggrandized by ludicrous claims to petty power. The worst ruling class is the one with no real power or authority to rule. It's just like the Little Italy of my boyhood, I thought, which had seemed to me such a remarkable place. The only thing a sensible Italian American could want to do is to get out of this, I thought as a young man. This neighborhood is like being embalmed by your own terrors of what lies beyond it. It is everything as a black person you wish to embrace and escape simultaneously in a contradictory madness that almost always seems as if it will rip you in two. This has often made me wonder what blacks think of the ordinary symbols of our culture, of our American endeavor, in which they share. One day, while standing at the Arch with my youngest daughter (we had just left a Cardinal baseball game at Busch Memorial Stadium, a few blocks away, the place I remember as a boy watching on television a handsome, grim-faced black man named Bob Gibson mow down Red Sox and

---

6 When Bob Gibson mowed down Yankee batters in the 1964 World Series, the Cardinals were still playing at the old ball field, Sportsman's Park. The Cardinals moved into Busch Memorial Stadium, a kind of all-purpose park meant to accommodate both baseball and football with its shape and artificial playing surface, in 1965. It is a decent place to see a ball game but lacks personality. Its inability to accommodate the capacity necessary for professional football led to the departure of the football Cardinals. At the 1966 All-Star game, played at Busch, New York Mets manager Casey Stengel remarked on how well the playing surface held the heat. My youngest daughter, who played in a high school marching band competition at the stadium on a very warm day last fall, agreed with that assessment.

Tiger batters in the 1967 and 1968 World Series),[6] I asked her what she thought of it. "Well, it's the Gateway to the West, right?" she said. "I just can't figure out if it means you're supposed to stop here or go on. I can't figure out if it's saying hello to you or good-bye." Perhaps that is the mystery for blacks in St. Louis as well as they look at what life has meant to them in this city through its greatest symbol: Is it saying hello to me or good-bye?

DAVID HAYNES

BORN IN ST. LOUIS, David Haynes (1955–) had what he describes as a typical American childhood. His father repaired the bodywork of automobiles while his mother prepared "a wholesome selection of recipes from the *Betty Crocker Cookbook.*"

Haynes attended "large overcrowded schools where I didn't pay much attention" and, after graduation from Macalester College in St. Paul, Minnesota, spent twenty years in similar classrooms as a junior high school teacher. He now works for the National Board for Professional Teaching Standards in Washington, D.C., although he lives in St. Paul. The author of six novels, Haynes was named a "best young American novelist" by *Granta* magazine in 1996.

In the following excerpt from Haynes's novel *All American Dream Dolls* (1997), the main character, a stressed-out professional African American woman named Deneen Wilkerson, returns to her hometown of St. Louis and attempts to comes to terms with her mother and twelve-year-old sister, who has started to compete in beauty pageants.

FROM *ALL AMERICAN DREAM DOLLS*

"Can I get you anything?" Megan (or was it Susie) asked me, but before I could answer she was looking over at the man next to me.

The flight attendants in my section of the plane—Megan and Susie—were barely civil to the women and ever so deferential to the men. They were white girls of the kind that seem to grow on trees up here in Minnesota—blue-eyed blondes with the sort of hair you always imagined the Breck girl had, impermeable to the elements, soft-looking, but to the touch would feel like the head of one of those dolls with painted-on hair.

I told her I'd like a sparkling water with no ice, and could I please have the whole can. I was thirsty from the car trip and from the huge serving of peanuts the other Megan or Susie had passed out twenty minutes earlier. Megan or Susie poured the guy a coke and asked, "What did you want again, ma'am?" I thought of saying, "Bitch, look at me when I'm speaking to you." I didn't. I asked again for my sparkling water. She was so busy making party eyes at my seatmate that she allowed the fizz to spill over the top onto her hands. In my condition I saw this as a highly charged erotic symbol. I turned and looked at my neighbor. He was clean and scrubbed in that sales-executive sort of way, with sandy hair and tortoiseshell glasses. He was looking through those glasses at Megan or Susie with the kind of discount lust men of his station reserve for such moments. I suddenly found him breathtakingly appealing. I wondered if that same sandy hair covered his chest. I wondered if, like the other white men I had known, his penis was red all the time, as if it were embarrassed. I even looked at his crotch, but he didn't notice. He was locked on Megan or Susie, and I thought about the fact that he hadn't noticed me at all. Was it because I was a little older, or because I was black? Was it because a man like him could not appreciate a woman who was padded for extra comfort? To hell with him. Let him satisfy himself with one of these scrawny pink peanut servers. Megan or Susie herself was still making a big production out of pouring a few ounces of pop over some ice. I reached up and took the cup from her. Wouldn't you know it: Pepsi. I sipped my drink and tried to figure out how I was going to explain this impulsive visit to my mother.

The thing is, I never went home. Since I graduated from college at the end of the seventies, I had spent maybe a total of a dozen days in St. Louis.

When I was a high school senior at Villa Duchesne, I sat around with my friends, weighing this college against that one, talking with the guidance counselor to come up with our criteria for choosing: the number of students, religious affiliation, departmental strengths, cost. My main criteria: the school had to be at least a full day's drive from my mother.

I loved my mother back then, as much as any seventeen-year-old girl could say she loves her mother, but at the time she was in a serious, serious *bourgeois* phase—black bourgeois, and if you don't know what that's about, try to get a picture in your mind of a cross between Louise Jefferson, Joan Collins, and drag artist RuPaul. Imagine that the main things in your life were shopping, keeping up with the (other) Joneses, and running your daughter's life.

Reina Wilkerson Jones, those are my mother's names. Reina. Means queen, and my mother was the queen of a whole crew of women just like her; school principals, which she is, or teachers or social workers or bureaucrats. They had a club. Sometimes they'd be over at my mother's house, and when I came downstairs, they would be all over me, these enormous, overly made-up, overly dressed, loud, loud women, hugging and kissing on me, fussing with my hair and just generally getting in my face.

Which might have been okay, had it not been for the fact that at the time I was well into what you might call an anachronistic hippie phase, anachronistic because it was 1975, well past the hippie heyday, and also because, as far as I could discover, there hadn't ever been any hippies in St. Louis anyway. I would come home from school and shed my uniform and put on my scoop-neck knit blouse or my tie-dyed T-shirt, my bell-bottoms, my headband, and then lie on my bed and listen to Jimi Hendrix. (Jimi. Part of the problem in my life is that I have searched high and low and cannot discover for the life of me where it is they are keeping the brothers like Jimi—mysterious, soulful, guitar-playing brothers, with big Afros and groovy clothes.) Occasionally, me and a few of the other self-styled hippie girls I knew would go down to the Delmar Loop and hang out at the Tivoli Theater or at the record store or the head shop. Once in a while we would meet some heavy dudes from Wash U and go over to their pad and smoke a joint or whatever. This is, of course, how we talked back then, us pseudo hippie chicks. Reina, as you might imagine, threw fits.

"Mother," I'd say. "Why do we always have to have such a heavy scene? Could you just mellow out, for once."

When I chose the perfect little liberal arts college in Minnesota, I believe that deep down inside my mother was as relieved to be rid of me as I was to be going. I knew what she thought of me. I'd heard her and the women discussing the daughters of other women they knew. Chippies. Tramps. Trash. These were the sorts of names that they used, but it wasn't quite that simple. Their condemnation of these girls wasn't about chastity at all. There wasn't a one of these women who had lived a blameless life, and they didn't care who knew about it, either. They wore their old marriages like merit badges, hinted at all kinds of affairs with one another's husbands and any number of other men as well. The mistake these girls had made—these tramps and strumpets—was being "womanish." "Womanish" meant not only that you knew too much, but also that you flaunted it. That you had the nerve to parade your worldliness up and down the street like it was something to be proud of. A woman earned this kind of pride with age, and "chippies" and other such wanton wayward upstarts had a long way to go. For my mother, then, it wasn't so much the thought that her baby was out participating in a brand of wild living that she condemned. (Even if she had condemned the way I lived, she would have never let on.) For her it was the highly unlikely happenstance that one of her friends might see me living this way, the possibility that somewhere in the St. Louis area in another room full of women just like her so-called friends, my name might come up with the appropriate disparaging moniker attached. Macalester College had a good enough reputation to facilitate her name-dropping, and for me, there were enough burned-out old hippies around to make me feel right at home. Getting me out of town was as much a blessing to her as my leaving was for me.

As luck would have it, I fell in with the wrong crowd. Well, that's how my old hippie friends would have described them. Here I was, suddenly, with these relatively clean-cut, prodigiously hardworking, intelligent young people, and I turned into a model student. My grades soared, my complexion cleared up, and my wardrobe improved, if only marginally.

I would fly home at Christmas in a sharp sweater and a reasonably clean pair of jeans. I had changed (or changed back) into the ideal child I had been in grade school, and my mother began treating me as if I were some fragile porcelain doll, as if I were something precious to be kept in her curio cabinet for display. While she would parade me out for her bourgie friends and brag about me until I could feel my ears burning, at the same time, when we were alone in the house, when it was just her and my stepfather and me, she would handle me with kid gloves. I had no curfews, there were no lectures, I could do whatever I wanted. I stayed overnight one time, at the home of a girl who lived in my dorm. When I came in the next morning she asked me, "Have a good time?" As bright and as cheerful as if I'd just gotten off the roller coaster at Six Flags. I hadn't even told her where I was going the night before. Around then I recognized that, as far as she was concerned, her job had been completed. I think she was afraid that if she said anything to me or did anything at all, that that other girl—the one with the incense and the black rings drawn around her eyes—would come back. Whatever I was up to at the moment must have felt like a better risk.

It's odd: I think we have this picture of mothers steadfastly guiding their daughters to womanhood. Or maybe I've watched too many douche spray commercials where the mama and her grown baby girl are out walking in a field. The mother ever so casually asks the daughter has she ever had that . . . you know, less than fresh feeling. Reina and I seemed to have missed the "less than fresh" phase in our relationship. I think back and try to remember a time when she and I had one of those cozy mother and daughter chats— about anything. They never happened. Maybe those scenes are totally the creation of the ad mongers, of folks like me—hey, maybe I'd swallowed my own bait.

My father was—is?—something of a dog. (Hard to get the tense correct: haven't seen him in twenty years, and it's hard to verify.) He walked out on us when I was twelve, but he had been walking for years before that. The five years before he left, mother spent trying to hold on; the five years after, casting about for his replacement. I remember a rough period in there when the mention of any man would make her rattle like a lidded pot on the boil. This during the time I was just getting ready to figure out the boy thing for myself.

I remember once she was dropping me off at a friend's place in North St. Louis. I was in this phase where I was testing the waters, making a lot of obnoxious statements to a lot of different folks. (I had recently announced to one of the nuns at Villa that I was considering joining a free-love commune. Not that I had any idea what such things were. But I had seen the movie *Woodstock*. Three times! The nun had cast her eyes to the ceiling, not in supplication, but more as if to say, "Yeah, right, Deneen. You in a commune. We'd all like to see that.")

In the car on the way to the city I had turned to my mother and speculated how I might like to get married right out of high school.

Mother had snickered and then mumbled, almost under her breath, "Better just get yourself a nice hot water bottle."

"What?" I'd prodded, but she didn't reply.

So, I knew she was a little bitter. But, at the same time I also knew that she hadn't quite given up on the world of romance. I knew that her eyes had been open, that her circle of women were looking for a man for her, too. For women like these, it just didn't do to be alone too long.

Mother reeled in a keeper just about the time I was on the way out the door, headed to Minnesota for my freshman year in college. My stepfather, I guess he was. He was an alright kind of guy. At least for all I know he was. A bland sort of a man, I recall Mr. Jones was. He seemed to worship her, and she never said anything bad about him. I think they were happy enough. In many ways they had the blandest and most ordinary of marriages.

It's a shame he died, if you want to know the truth.

Still, I think about this and I just get sad. All of that man-work took a lot of energy, I know. I mean, I know it now, at this point in my life. And, having a man meant a lot more to her than it has ever meant to me. As for me on that plane trip, I did not want to be thinking about the time I had wasted chasing one man or another. Or the time I'd spent on any of the other dead ends in my life, for that matter. Bad jobs. Faithless friends. Get-rich-quick schemes. I did not want to think about anything at all.

After college I stayed in Minnesota and began my career as an advertising maven. Which is how I am referred to by Mr. Waltershied. I would visit St. Louis for a day or two now and then and join the new family my mother had created. As the eighties began, she entered a new phase: from queen of the class wars to queen of the homemakers, from Alexis Carrington to Harriet Nelson.

I would arrive at her house—her new husband had moved her from Spanish Lake to Kirkwood (too much riffraff in North County)—and I would think I had walked into the Christmas display at Famous Barr. Every surface was wrapped or tinseled or garlanded or crèched. She kept pots of cinnamon and vanilla bean simmering on the stove in the kitchen, cedar logs burning in the fireplace. How cozy, you might think, and the whole display was certainly eye-catching and inviting. Still, her adornments left me after a while cold and rather bored. The treatment was the same as what you could see on a soap opera or in the aforementioned department store window—magnificent, but what did it have to do with our lives? There wasn't a single thing in the house with any sense of history, not one bauble that meant a thing to me.

One year—I think it was '83—I came in, and she chirped, "Look, we're having an old-fashioned Christmas this year, just like in the old days." Her theme that year was drummer boys and nutcrackers, and I thought, old days? I don't remember any such old days. I remember that my daddy would show up sometimes when I was little, and he and mama would make a pretense of opening gifts. I remember that we went to Jamaica for the holidays a few times when I was in high school. That was about it. Mama's old days must have been in some life other than the one I had lived.

About twelve years ago I stopped going home for good.

Home. I don't even call it that anymore. I had no friends back there. My girls from high school—hippie and otherwise—had moved on after college, just as I had. I'd hear from them, on the East Coast or out in California. I got tired of spending my money to fly down to St. Louis and sit on my mother's sofas.

So, I called, once a month or so. I talked to my mother and my baby sister.

Baby sister. That was another thing I couldn't get past. Forty-seven years old, with a grown daughter—me—and the woman goes and has another baby. That was the other reason I stopped visiting her.

I begged her not to have that child. I said every hateful thing I could think of. I told her she would die in childbirth, or that the baby would be a mongoloid retard. I told her she had better arrange to have the child put in a home right away, cause I wasn't raising it. Mother hung up on me. Over and over again.

She had the baby. Ciara. (Chee-AH-rah.) They were both fine. I really didn't know the child, but she had always sounded like a sweet thing on the phone.

My stepfather died five years ago. So now it is mama and Ciara, and I could never imagine what it was they did with themselves down there, this slightly past-middle-age woman and her child, their dream house in the suburbs. I received snapshots in the mail of Ciara posed in front of a well-known monument, and of mother and Ciara posed together in front of another one. They looked rather innocent and mannered.

Let me tell you: I had no idea. None.

I get dumped on a trip to Door County. At the *beginning* of the trip. (That's my favorite detail.) I have my boyfriend, Calvin, the chump, drop me off at the airport and I get on a plane to St. Louis to visit a family I have avoided for years. I would trace the logic of that, but, as I am trying to explain, I was in a happy land beyond reason.

Yet, there I was, flying back toward my so-called roots. I guess it was sort of a cyclical thing: You drive east on a dream vacation to Door County. You spend a week. You turn around, you come home. Or:

You go away to college.

You make a life for yourself.

Twenty years later you fall apart.

You come home.

I was acting—insofar as I was doing anything conscious at all—in a script that seemed already to have been written. And as I casually drank my Pepsi and munched on yet another linebacker-sized serving of peanuts I had filched from Megan and Susie's trays while they struggled past me with the drink cart, I felt no anxiety at all. The most rational awareness I had was knowing I was going to have to come up with a plausible excuse as to why I, who hadn't set foot in St. Louis since disco was king, would be making an unannounced visit to my mother's house.

I considered the alternatives.

1. I would claim that it was my mother who had invited me in the first place, that she had insisted I come. I would remind her of a nonexistent telephone conversation we had had in which she made the invitation and I accepted. I would offer other examples of her senility that might explain how she could have forgotten such a call.

2a. I would tell her that I had ratted on my boyfriend, Vinnie, and his mob brothers. I needed a place to hide out until I was placed in the Federal Witness Protection Program.

2b. Or that I was the one on the lam, that Vinnie and I had pulled off a heist at the Commercial State Bank, and that I was lying low until the heat was off.

3. I was job hunting. Things at Waltershied, Williams and Caruthers had gotten ugly. I was checking out the game in St. Louis.

4. I would just show up, as if it were nothing out of the ordinary. No explanations, no story, no nothing.

Can you guess which I chose? Have you picked up the pattern yet? Good for you. Yes, it is door number 4.

At the airport, I chose a taxi and gave him my mother's address. Thirty minutes later he pulled up in front of her house in Kirkwood and set my bags on the porch. I rang the bell.

Ciara answered the door. "Who are you?"

"I'm your sister. Deneen."

"Mother!" she called out.

I heard familiar footsteps coming from back where her kitchen was.

"Mother! This . . . person says . . ."

"Oh, hi, Deneen." My mother waved at me cheerily, pointed to the portable phone in her hand, and went back to the sentence she had been in the middle of.

Ciara stood in my way giving me the kind of look that makes your teeth itch.

CARTER REVARD

ONE OF SEVEN mixed-blood children, Carter Revard (1931–) was born in Pawhuska, Oklahoma, an Osage Indian Agency town. Although his Osage forebears had prospered from the discovery of oil on their reservation, the fortune had dwindled by the time Revard was a child, and he grew up in poverty, attending a one-room school through the eighth grade. While attending Bartlesville College High School, Revard won a College Bowl quiz show, which ensured him a college education at the University of Tulsa. Always a superior student, Revard was awarded a Rhodes Scholarship to Oxford University, where he studied with C. S. Lewis and J. R. R. Tolkien and received a B.A. in 1952. That same year, Revard received what he still considers his highest honor: his tribe held an Osage Naming Ceremony, where he was given the name Nom-pe-wa-theh, which means "Thunder Person" and carries ancient associations to the Osage creation story. In 1959, Revard received his Ph.D. in Medieval English literature at Yale University and taught briefly at Amherst College.

In 1961, Revard began teaching literature at Washington University and simultaneously pursued his poetry writing. In addition to being active in St. Louis's literary scene, he has been integrally connected to the area's Indian community. In 1973, Revard helped found the American Indian Center of Mid-America, an organization that helps promote Indian cultural traditions and serves forty-one tribes represented in the St. Louis region.

Widely published as a scholar and a poet, Revard is the author of four volumes of poetry, including *Ponca War Dancers* (1980), *Cowboys and Indians, Christmas Shopping* (1992), and *An Eagle Nation* (1993), from which the following poem is taken. The essay that follows it is a chapter from his book, *Family Matters, Tribal Affairs* (1998). Revard's latest book, *Winning the Dust Bowl*, is forthcoming in late 2000.

DRAGON-WATCHING IN ST. LOUIS

for Stephen, Geoffrey, Vanessa, Lawrence

It would have been a dragon, this monstrous jet,
two hundred years ago, to father and little boy
come out for a stroll, had they seen it go screeching down
into the sunset with sweptback wings downglinting
as their words rose like drowned twigs from a stream,
the little boy exclaiming, the father agreeing.
They would have fled in terror what we take in stride
since we live near an airport and have rendezvoused
with sun and horizon here too often to fear
that this great beast might shatter, his smoky fires dim
the park, touched by the sun's last shining, we've come to see.

By the dark-mortared wall, whose chalk-white stones protect
this place from the fuming roaring freeway just beneath us,
we can look far over the asphalt and across suburban roofs
and see how the jetplane now small and tranquil is sinking,
winking the ruby of its landing light, in the last
seconds before it touches the earth beneath our horizon—
and we listen until it's come safely down like the sun,
till silence tells us it's landed, as darkness tells
that the trillion hydrogen bombs of our sun eyeballing space
to light and warm us this day have held their peace,
as firmness tells feet that the earth whose sensitive crust's
light quiver would bury us in our buildings, now smoothly
turns on appointed rounds as it brings this smoky city
gliding through sunset into starlit night as that dazzle of
cars weaving through traffic snarls, homing on supper smells,
tells us it's time to be strolling back home on the safe
sidewalks of this suburb

where bears and panthers, flood
and fire and that fearful monster the Wild Osage, whose blood
runs in our veins, ranged through these savage woodlands hundreds
of years ago, before the walks were made safe for us to enjoy
this zoo of smoky dragons now swarming from our best brains.

FROM *FAMILY MATTERS, TRIBAL AFFAIRS*

FAMILY REUNION

Hadn't seen my youngest brother and his kids for quite some time. You know how it is here in America, we try to get as far as possible from each other. I mean, the main theory of *family* in psychology seems to be that families which stay together are abnormal—if you try to live near your parents you are abused, and plan to murder them. Why else was Oedipus the model for psychoanalysts to explain the Modern Family's usual condition? Besides, the real reason for coming to America, according to the theory of the Melting Pot, is to *forget* who you were in Europe, or Asia, or even Mexico. (The Africans had *their* old selves dissolved away, of course, on the slave boats.) Once you get here, the idea is to be *only* yourself. Naturally this means you have to disperse: if you belong to some ethnic group you had better move away from them and be really American like the rest of us, or them. It's hard for New Yorkers to do this but even they *can* go to California or Florida to lose their old names, classes, histories. There you can start over, and nobody can hold your past against you, you can invent one if needed. You can make your fortune, and if you want to send a little back to your unmelted kin, your *lumpkins*, the thing for them to do with it is move to Florida, where there are no seasons, just as in Los Angeles the leaves never fall, same as in Eden. Well, I'm probably way out of date with that picture, the place to go now may be San Diego or Vermont, or San Antonio or Santa Fe or some other place properly sainted or desert-like.

Which applies sort of to us here in St. Louis, right in the Middle, where the Mississippi and the Missouri get together not far from the Ohio, where things float by from the Rockies and Great Lakes and Appalachians, down to this center of America where a lot of people for a long time have been gathering and passing on to somewhere else—future, past, whatever the visas allow. And our family, as I say, have pretty well followed the American pattern. I mean we're mixed. I'm Irish, Scotch-Irish, French, Osage Indian, though when I publish as poet I can be only ONE of the Above. My half brother Addison, who's half Osage and half Scotch-Irish and Irish I guess, works for the Defense Department and lives near King George, Virginia, but he married a Lakota woman and their two kids are, well, all those things together. So Addison and I were born in the Osage Agency town of

Pawhuska (which means White Hair, a name gained by an eighteenth-century chief who took a white wig from a British officer in lieu of a scalp) in Oklahoma (which means Land of the Red Man, a name given to indicate that it was forever Indian Territory), and four of our brothers and sisters still live back in Oklahoma, but here I am in St. Louis, and there Addison is in Virginia, and we have cousins out in California, and others of Ponca and Irish etcetera over in White Eagle and Red Rock and Stillwater and all those Oklahoma places, and God knows where the rest of the Scotch-Irish and French-Osage branches have got to by now, which rivers flow beside whatever harps they hang on the willow trees thereby. And with Addison working now for the Defense Department in Virginia, and finishing his Ph.D. in mathematics, we rarely get to see him.

So I was happy one summer when he and the kids could get by here for a visit, on the way back from their brief time with Oklahoma folks. I wanted them to come down and meet some friends at the American Indian Center of Mid-America, where I serve on the Board. And they wanted to see the stainless steel Arch here in St. Louis, and ride up the elevator to its six-hundred-thirty-foot observation windows over the Mississippi, and I wanted to take them over the river to Cahokia Mounds, where the largest town north of Mexico had flourished some hundreds of years before Columbus hit this hemisphere.

We almost forgot to look for the eclipse promised for that day—but coming out of the American Indian Center of Mid-America, my Osage nephew Aaron, or his sister Kimberly—well, their Lakota mom Grace will give me hell unless I say they are Osage *and Lakota* (and for that matter their Irish and Scotch-Irish grandma is up there reminding me of the Camp and Kelley share in all this, all those gatherings from the Fanad Peninsula just west of Londonderry, and from the Black Hills, and the Big Spring on Current River in the Ozarks, and the sandy windings of Bird Creek and Buck Creek among the Osage encampments, and all the way from Mont Revard in the Savoy Alps)—ah, anyhow either Kim or Aaron said, just as we were about to climb into my little blue Japanese Mazda there on our Center's asphalt parking lot, "Hey, Dad! we forgot the eclipse today!"

"Oh yeah," Addison said, "it must have happened already." He looked sideways at me and said, "While you were introducing us in there to the Seneca Receptionist and the Meti Custodian and the Cherokee Employment Specialist and the Anglo Outreach Worker, and finding out that your Comanche Executive Director had been called out to help a Dogrib lady settle a little matter of a brick through a windshield and a bullet through the hip."

"Well," I said, "we have to make sure these members of the Indian Diaspora get together now and then. Never a dull moment around our Indian Center, unless you're waiting for an eclipse. You think it's over?"

"No, Dad," Kim said, "look how the sunlight is, kind of strange—maybe it's still going on."

"Sure," I said, "the paper claimed it would be visible from after one till three o'clock. It's only two-fifteen. You're right, Kim, the light *is* weird, even with that high haze of clouds and this St. Louis steam-bath humidity."

"I see it!" Aaron said. "Part of the lower edge is dark, see?"

"Don't blind yourself, you guys," Addison said.

"One way we worked it, last time an eclipse came here," I said, "was looking down at the leaf-shadows on the sidewalk. The leaves block most of the light, but where the sun comes through them it's like a point source of light, a pinhole in a *camera obscura,* except it's not just one, it's a whole lot of little glowing spots with one part dark."

Kim and Aaron led the charge, across the lot into the shade of a big sycamore. We looked down at the sidewalk there, but saw only blurry shadows. The leaves were too high, too few. They let too much light through, no pinhole sources.

"We could try my glasses maybe," I said. I took them off and held them so the focal points were on the sidewalk, but all they made was dazzling spots that couldn't quite be seen as showing any dark edge. My brother took his off and tried. They were a little better, not much.

Aaron straightened suddenly and bolted toward the Mazda. "Binoculars!" he yelled back. He had brought them from Virginia, used them on the long drive to Oklahoma and then to St. Louis, spotting the license plates on cars ahead of them, staring at hawks on telephone poles or soaring high over a rest-stop—all the ordinary unsuspecting creatures and things that get interesting if you can bring them close, but not so close they might grab or sting or look back at you.

Aaron grabbed the binoculars, slammed the Mazda's door and came trotting back. I had to say, "Don't try and look at the sun through those, Aaron!"

"Oh no—I'll let the sun come through them to the asphalt and see if that will show the blacked-out part." His father pulled a white handkerchief out and spread it on the sidewalk.

"Great, Dad!" Aaron said.

And there it was: the round unbearably bright spot with a black curving bite missing at the lower left. Not as clear as I remembered the many glowing disks beneath our sweetgum tree, the time of our last eclipse, but we all saw it. Just a little—you had to know what you were looking for, but there it was.

How old Kim and Aaron will be, or whether their dad and I will still be around to try looking at the next eclipse, who knows?

So as the light sharpened again, and the steamy St. Louis heat bore down even harder, we buzzed away from the Indian Center and onto the interstate, along that to the Poplar Street Bridge across the Mississippi. I wanted to make sure my niece and nephew looked back in time at what we were passing high above.

"We're just downstream from where the Missouri joins the Mississippi," I told them. "That's where the Great Sioux Crossing was, where our great-great-great-grandparents got together to trade. Indian peoples would come down from way up in the Dakotas or Montana along the Missouri, and down from Minnesota or Canada on the Mississippi. They could come down the Illinois River that joins the Mississippi just north of where the Missouri goes in. And they maybe came up from where the Ohio joins the Mississippi not far south of here, and the Ohio comes down from Pennsylvania and West Virginia. So you had people bringing things down here from the Rockies, and the Great Lakes, and the Alleghenies, and for that matter up the Mississippi from Louisiana and the Gulf of Mexico. There was a big Mound Builder civilization centered here, and a string of towns up and down the Mississippi and Ohio and as far west as Oklahoma. Archaeologists dig up things that came north from Mexico, south from Canada, east from Wyoming and Montana and maybe the Pacific, west from the Appalachians and all."

"It doesn't really look too wide here, where we're crossing," Kim said.

"That's true, where we are the Mississippi is hardly wider than the Thames in London, at least when the tide is in," I said. "It's a lot wider just upstream because there are a lot of locks and dams and it looks more impressive, and the bald eagles hang out there in winter because they can catch fish in the open water below the locks and things. Every January there's an Eagles Day and not long ago Lawrence and I drove up there and counted twenty-nine eagles near Clarksville, mostly sitting around in the trees but some of them skimming down and catching fish."

Across in Illinois, we headed east and north on I-55, toward Cahokia Mounds where the great urban center had flourished for many hundred years and died out mysteriously just before Columbus. We followed the Great River Road signs among reedy swales and sloughs with cattails bending where the redwing blackbirds were perching and spreading their wings and fluting. We saw a line of white cattle egrets winging slowly past.

"See those white birds?" I said, not missing a chance to educate the next generation. "All the way from Africa. They flew the Atlantic. Got here on the trade winds like Columbus."

"The whole Atlantic?" Aaron said.

"The whole way. Not so long ago either that they first got to America. They're spreading west and north. They got across the Southeast from Florida, up into Arkansas. Back in the sixties I first saw some in Oklahoma, over by Grand Lake. They stand around and catch insects in the fields around the cattle, that's why they call them cattle egrets I think."

"I wonder how they navigate," Addison said.

"Me too, I even wonder what they have in mind when they take off from Africa, just fly up from some marshy place by the ocean I guess. I can't imagine what they thought they were doing, the ones that first got up into the wind and went out to sea. What in the world would a bird have in mind to just keep going west, with nothing but ocean underneath it? They used to say cattle egrets got over here by perching on ships or something. Anyhow they got here. Even then, why would they keep on moving from Florida to Alabama and Mississippi and up the Mississippi to here? Scientists even yet can't say how homing pigeons find their way back to a place, I guess it's too much to ask them to look into the neural pathways that kept these big old birds sailing westward like Daniel Boone to settle in these parts."

"I see the mounds, Uncle," Kim said.

"That's them," I said. "I used to drive by here and never notice. Now they have signs to tell us how to get off and see them. See over to the left, that's a wood-henge they've reconstructed, those cedar poles set in a big circle there?"

"Was that what the Indian people here made?"

"That's it. The poles are set just where anybody standing at the center can know where to expect the sun, or moon or stars or whatever, at just the right time of the year. That way they knew the right time to start their ceremonies up on the temple mounds or wherever."

"Yeah, Dad," Aaron said. "These were like computers they were using. They'd probably have made you one of their wise old priests."

"I guess you're right," my brother said. "They probably developed math enough."

"I bet they did," I said. "These guys were in close touch with the Aztecs and Mayans. Those Mayans introduced the zero well before Europeans borrowed it from Arabs. Your daddy has probably told you long ago that the word zero is from the Arabic language. Arabic numbers, Arabic zero. These Mound people probably borrowed numbers from the Mayans the same way. They seem to have sacrificed human beings here sometimes. Not too different from when you Computer People in the Defense Department there in Virginia made flowcharts that direct a Tomahawk Missile the safest way to Baghdad."

"I suppose that's true," my brother said. "They probably were just as proud when the eclipses came on time as we all were when the TV people said the missiles we had programmed did exactly what they were supposed to do."

I didn't want to get much further into all that. I work for a university that depends on defense spending for fighter planes and such. So we zipped on over to the Visitors' Center and made a beeline to the cafeteria and had some Cokes and hotdogs, not to mention bratwursts.

"Oh man!" Kim said, "These eclipses really make you dry!"

"Not to mention your Uncle Professor's explanations," my brother said.

So then we walked around the terrific exhibits where caring and clever and careful people have brought alive that old City of the Flood Plain here. Down in the sawdust and woodchip pits the lifelike dummies of men, women, children stand or squat, gazing just to your left whenever you think to look them in the eye. Makes you want to wake them up. There are their houses, here are their beautifully crafted pots and weapons and toys. We went in to the movie's darkness and heard a voice from some famous white person apparently now dead or maybe not—who can say with a voice, nowadays?—that told us how these Unknown People had done their things and passed away. Then we went into the Museum Shop and got some things, and I gave Addison a book for his fiftieth birthday, a book called *Indian Givers* by Jack Weatherford.

I sneaked a look into Weatherford's book before I gave it to him though, while Kim and Aaron were reading some booklets and Addison was looking through the postcards. It starts with the Silver Mountain high in the Andes at Potosi and how its mines and those of Mexico were dug by Indian slaves for the Spanish and financed the beginnings of European capitalism, and then how the beginnings of corporation structure came from the Canadian and the Virginia settling and trading companies, so Indian capital and the innovations that came in as a result of figuring how to set up colonies created the modern corporate and state structures and of course all this paid not only for the enslavement of Indian peoples but also for much of the Great Art of the Renaissance as well as European wars in the next few centuries.

I even started to read about the way the Inca potatoes changed Ireland and Russia (vodka's made from potatoes, it seems) and Poland and Germany and all, and tomatoes in Italian cuisine that came from Peru and so forth, but Addison came over to see what I was up to and I just went ahead and handed him the book and said here, I thought you ought to get educated now that you're a mature individual, and he said well he expected the professor would give him something educational, but thanks anyway it was the thought that counted. I did say it was a fascinating book and he would want to read it right away and all. He was polite about it and properly grateful. It was not till later that month that I got my own copy of Weatherford's book and finally got into the whole business about curare and quinine and all the things we gave to feed and heal people who would do their best before long to starve and poison Indians in the name of Aristotle and Jesus, according to the famous debates between Sepulveda and De Las Casas around 1550 when De Las Casas argued that it was monstrous to do such things, that the Indians might really be human beings. . . .

We climbed the steps (old railway ties?) up to the top of the highest mound at Cahokia. It's called Monk's Mound, after some Trappist Monks who set their retreat up on its top for a while, maybe to exorcise old demons of the New World. Now the monks are gone, and so are the orchards they put there, but the mounds are still solid. From that highest one you can look westward across the Mississippi and see the great stainless steel Gateway Arch, designed by Eero Saarinen and built by a lot of men who never get mentioned, including some of the "Mohawks of High Steel"—Don White, for instance, a big husky Seneca steelworker and crafts trader I see at our powwows and elections, and Mike Brooks, an even bigger guy (Seneca too, I think). The Arch looks like part of a Titan's handcuff sticking up where it locks the city into the dream called Forever Westward. It has neat little elevators inside its hollow legs and they go ratcheting up with four or five passengers in molded plastic seats, and when we were sightseeing there we all started to cram into one but just as the door started to close my brother Addison suddenly lunged and scrambled out and turned and said, "You guys go on up, I'll meet you back here when you come down." I hadn't known he was claustrophobic; me, I am more afraid of heights than of closed places.

But we had no trouble whatever hiking up the steep timbered steps of Monk's Mound, and once we were on top and rubbernecking there, an intermittent stream of tourists and hikers, some looking to be retirement age, flowed up and around and past us there, some talking, some quiet, all friendly, giving off happiness. And there were short brunettes in shorts, and tall tanned racers in running shoes panting up the long flights of steps, turning round and stilting down again. And butterflies, drifting in the constant gusting winds up there—three tiger swallowtails, some sulfurs, painted ladies, a fritillary. And when we went down, toward the asphalt parking lot, we took a shortcut over rough greensward, beneath black cherry trees with their tall scaly-barked trunks. There were bittersweet cherries dangling from their stems down to our fingers, or underfoot and squashing in the sweat-lodge heat. Smog blurred the St. Louis buildings across the Mississippi, smeared gray haze in front and around its dark-glassed *Terminator* buildings.

"See over there, there used to be a lot of mounds someplace over where St. Louis is," I said, "someplace under those buildings, but the mounds got leveled, all their bones and pots and things dispersed somewhere. Maybe some of the mounds were where Forest Park is. That big Louisiana Centennial World's Fair was headquartered in the park and where Washington University is now. They had Geronimo here as a prisoner of war, they posed him in a 1904 opentop car, in a top hat holding the steering wheel."

"Man, how'd you like to be a traffic cop that pulled *him* over?" my brother said.

"They had a lot of people here, Filipinos of some kind I think. Old Teddy Roosevelt came and talked, so I've heard or read, about how America was now getting the right control of the Pacific and giving freedom to the Philippines from the corrupt and decadent Europeans or maybe just the corrupt and decadent Spanish, Cuba and all that, bringing oppressed people under the American imperium or whatever. Not even the Pacific Ocean could stop our westward expansion. Columbus would have felt vindicated—right on to China and India, Teddy!"

"You think the Indian mounds were over by the university?"

"Some not far from where my classrooms are. I might be teaching where they had their signal fires or sacrificial smokes. You could probably see any of that from right here on this big mound. I don't know whether mounds across the river were rivals of this place or settlements and outposts."

"They might have just been friends and allies," Aaron said. "But where did they all go? What happened, did they just die out or move away or what?"

"Nobody seems to know," I said. "I don't care what they say, though, my view is that things fell apart for them just about when the Siouan peoples were passing westward and southward through here and splitting up. I mean the bunch that turned into our five peoples, the Dhegiha Siouan people that got to be the Ponca and Omaha that went up the Missouri to Nebraska and Dakota, and the Osage and Kaw that were in Missouri and Kansas, and the Quapaw that went down toward Arkansas."

"What's the evidence, though?" Addison asked. "I mean do you just think that because you'd like to believe it, or what?"

"Well, I've actually seen a passage in one of the Osage ceremonies that La Flesche recorded which to me seems to show contact between Osages and these Cahokia Mound people. The ceremony says, *then we joined the people of death and moved to another country.* We may have got some of our astronomical clan-orderings and ceremonial patterns from these Mound People right here where the three greatest rivers of this continent come together."

"You know," Kim said, "I can see the Arch from here and some of those St. Louis buildings, but I never saw this mound when we were up in the Arch. I wonder if you really could see us standing here, if you tried."

"Maybe," I said. "I think the Arch was made as a kind of gunsight that you look through towards the west, though."

"Maybe it's a one-way mirror," Aaron said.

"That's weird," Kim said.

"Got to get back, kids," I said. We crammed back into the car and maneuvered out again onto the freeway and drove back past the sloughs full of ducks and redwing blackbirds and cattails nodding. We drove smoothly on high-banked asphalt roads which twine and wrestle like cobras and spit their traffic into St. Louis. We drove past great waste-mounds and raw landfills out of which the stainless Gateway Arch was Frankenstein-stitched together, through the fragrance of ruined steel mills, of plastic plants, refineries for gasoline and herbicides. The bobsled-run of concrete highways ricocheted us into and through East St. Louis. My brother, looking out his window, said, "Did you see that TV documentary on this place? Is it as bad as the documentary said?"

"Yes and no," I said. "They showed all the buildings falling apart, they let people see a little of how our racist history set up this site to dump stockyard waste and industrial waste, and supply servants for rich St. Louis suburbs and all that. What they missed was the music and poetry, the people, everything that's maybe starting to happen now. They saw the corruption but had no idea of what hope is here if you look and listen. There's poets here, the salt has not lost its savor. You know how bad it was when you and I and all of our dysfunctional family were growing up in Oklahoma, you know the well-off people living around us could have written a documentary on how bad things were for us and how the statistics showed we would be nothing but a burden on society and anybody associated with us. Yet what are we doing now? Here you are, a Naval Defense mathematician and computer expert, here I am a college teacher. We paid a price, we'll go on paying it, but by God our family did not go down, not quite, not all of us all the time. There's strong people doing good things here in East St. Louis right while the media are showing the rest of it. People go around eating apples off the same tree they say has rotten limbs. You should have heard the people reading poems last May at the East St. Louis Community College. People don't stop breathing because the media say they died."

"Yeah, but crime doesn't go away just because a bunch of people are writing poems and reading them to each other. Washington D.C.'s a mess," my brother said.

"Name me a city anywhere that is *not* a mess. London's a mess. What I saw of Naples didn't look too good. All the rivers in the world are dirty with what comes from the cities that saddle the rivers. People have got to clean the rivers so they can wash themselves clean, so they can drink the water again. They may want to think the bad stuff is all on one side of the river but hell it's on both sides and in the river too. Look at that water down there!"

"Wow, look at how it roils around," Kim said. "I'd hate to try swimming in those eddies."

"It looks like it's pumping iron," Aaron said.

"It does, it really does!" Kim said. "That floating driftwood's like tattoos on the Mississippi's chest."

So we drove on over the elevated road and safely back into our suburb's green cooler shade, but I kept seeing in the rear-view mirror the Arch's steely shimmer. And that night going to bed it occurred to me to think again about how from Cahokia Mound we saw St. Louis, far off but clear, those sleek glass towers and the arch—but from the Arch itself we could not see Cahokia's mounds, let alone people standing on top of them. The Arch is a lot higher, six hundred and thirty feet, whereas the highest mound is not much over a hundred, and yet when we had gone up in the Arch and looked east from its windows, out over the Mississippi waters that come here from as far away as winds and seeds and people travel, we could not see the mounds or any people over there. As Indians, we saw St. Louis. As whites, we didn't see Cahokia. They had their ceremonies, those Indian people, their circles, they invited the sun and moon to come and look into the future for them. They surely couldn't have seen us in the future, the way we see them in the past. We had looked earlier this day into a dazzling eclipse, where the moon's shadow bit out a crumb of fire and made the world wear a strange light, showed us how frail the sun is, handled our personal star like an Oreo cookie, dark chocolate and sweet white. Chocolate, I was thinking, an Aztec word, they used it as royal drink—part of the sacred ball game, was it? Probably why pharmacologists named its alkaloid stimulant *theobromine*, food for the gods, because Mayans and Aztecs once handed it around on temple mounds in Mexico? We hand it around the household as a nightcap now, here where the great rivers meet, where their waters reflect on a shimmering steel Arch that will slowly, slowly fall into ruins, where this day we got together and watched a partial eclipse. Depends where you look from, a narrow stripe of chocolate shadow zipping across the earth, people outside it untouched by any difference in the light, but all the people it darkens made momentarily aware of being in the same weird place. Just for the moment they look into the passing stream and see all their faces together there, and then it fades.

CARL PHILLIPS

CARL PHILLIPS (1959–) was born in Washington State and lived on various army bases before his family settled in Massachusetts when Phillips was in his early teens. After receiving a bachelor's degree from Harvard University in 1981, Phillips went on to receive a Master of Arts in Teaching from the University of Massachusetts–Amherst and an M.A. from Boston University.

Phillips has received many awards for his poetry, including a Guggenheim Fellowship and grants from the Massachusetts Artists Foundation and the Academy of American Poets. His first book, *In the Blood* (1992), won the Morse Poetry Prize and his second, *Cortège* (1995), was a finalist for both the National Book Critics Circle Award and the Lambda Literary Award. In 1998, his third volume, *From the Devotions*, was a National Book Award finalist. Critics have praised Phillips's work for its intelligence and sensitivity, as well as its graceful syntax and carefully wrought imagery. Early in 2000, Graywolf Press published Phillips's most recent book, *Pastoral*. Phillips is associate professor of English at Washington University in St. Louis, where he also directs the creative writing program.

The following poems appeared in Phillips's third volume of poetry, *From the Devotions* (1998).

THE FLUME

The idea is to pretend
that it is real,
the hollowed log we

step into, and
not plastic;
that its passage

is random, to do with
current and wind only,
we are to forget

what we know or have
heard of motors
distantly, invisibly

handled, let go all
suspicion of planned
slants and turns to this

channel, narrow,
fiberglass, sectioned,
painted green to seem

verdant, and indeed
as we approximate
swiftness, the effect

is almost banks
overgrown. We are
perhaps meant

to recall Cooper's
slayer of deer, or to
think Lewis and Clark

could, in fact, be
the two men in the log
just before ours

—and they can be,
if we ignore that
the one man does not

merely look as if he
is dying: he really is;
and however often

some may look then
look away from
the other man straddling

the crossbar behind,
his knees half-framing,
half-bracing the man

in front, the two men
are lovers and like us,
in coming here, mean

too, if only briefly,
to come away
from something else.

And briefly,
it is easy, as we are
carried—jostling,

not jostling—to parts
especially protected
by trees, the sun

rare as light
in those paintings
depicting America as lush,

virgin, generally
benighted except at
the one corner

where two men—
are they settlers,
explorers?—stand

dwarfed but not daunted
by the wild around them:
they have found

or they have been found by
the one pocket of light,
so impossible that

Surely, they believe,
It is God and it is
Eden—

for a moment,
it is like that:
leaves, leaves,

the birds are made again
stupid and do not think
to regard us. Then

what has passed for
some time as the land
opens up, and we are

borne severally,
unnaturally, via pulley,
up in preparation to

descend the flume proper,
this ride that, as
it turns out, is no

different in purpose
from the others:
to risk almost-death,

to die nearly—
yes, terror, yes
resistance,

but as well an emptying
of laughter as of
stones from the body and,

never far, the knowing
that it will end
soon, we can somewhere

find food, another ride,
any other and next
thing. For who can

not want to? Who among us
is not now suddenly,
and beautifully,

ravenous?—even,
perhaps especially
the man who, we have

almost forgotten,
is dying but now,
remembering, we want and

don't want to say is
as we are, not any less
long for this world.

MEDITATION: THE RIVER ROAD*

That certain birds—
the eagle, in whom come together in
something like marriage rapaciousness, grace;
or, rapacious too and stuffed with grace,
all manner of falcon, also of hawk each
kind—suggested the archangels:
this makes sense.

And the sky meaning,
more nakedly than usual, only the usual
(try, you will never match it, this blue),
the river widening to reflect so much more
of the same—and weren't you hungry,
besides?—how difficult was it, just
then, to see God?

* *From* Meditation, *a poem in six parts.*

But that stretch of
flat barges on hold, each awaiting the one
sign: *Come, the water lies clear*; how, bored,
you turned away toward the chalk, no, chalk-
colored bluffs that all day had been there
but now, regarded, looked
athletic, fallen—

Confess,
it has surprised you, thus to understand the soul.

WAYNE FIELDS

WAYNE FIELDS (1942–) was born on his grandparents' farm near Wyaconda, Missouri. After graduating from Augustana College in Rock Island, Illinois in 1964, Fields went to the University of Chicago, where he received both his Master's degree and a Ph.D. In 1968, Fields began his academic career at Washington University in St. Louis as an instructor in the English department. Three decades later, having served the university in many administrative roles in addition to his teaching, Fields became the director of the American Culture Studies program. The recipient of numerous teaching awards and academic honors, Fields is also the author of many articles and four books, including *What the River Knows: An Angler in Mid-Stream* (1990), *The Past Leads a Life of Its Own* (1992), and *Union of Words: A History of Presidential Eloquence* (1996). Wayne Fields currently holds the Lynne Cooper Harvey Distinguished Chair in English and Arts & Sciences at Washington University.

As a contributing editor to this volume, Wayne Fields selected much of the prose from the Civil War period to the early twentieth century. In the following essay, Fields reflects on his experience of working on this volume and what he discovered about St. Louisans' attitudes toward their shared history. The essay originally appeared in Fields's column, "Close to Home," in *St. Louis* magazine in June 1998.

OUR CRUEL, TANGLED PAST

For the past several months, more months than I was supposed to take, I have been reading prose, written by St. Louisans about St. Louis and published between the Civil War and 1920. The project is part of an effort by the Missouri Historical Society to assemble a book on the city's literature, and I was invited to participate despite the fact that, apart from the typical English teacher's knowledge of Mark Twain and Kate Chopin, I brought to the assignment a mind as empty as it was open. Consequently I had no real notion of what I was getting into, except that it was history, done with, safe.

I agreed to my small part of the Historical Society project, blithely convinced that the job could not be too demanding—a matter of a few trips to the library to locate a handful of appropriate stories and perhaps one or two essays from the 60 years of my editorial responsibility. But most of the fiction produced by St. Louisans during that period has been neglected for very good reasons, and I found myself desperately looking to other prose for my selections, especially to memoirs, a genre that blossomed after 1860. Ministers, businessmen, politicians, famous wives of famous men all wrote volumes trying to explain themselves and their community, accounting for their lives and actions, describing a time and world that even to them had become, over the years, remote as well as familiar. They are a varied lot, probably not a group that would have gotten together on their own. Frontier impresario Sol Smith looked back on a theatrical career played before backwoods audiences throughout the South and Midwest with such productions as the melodrama *Pizarro*, for which, on one occasion, he hired local Creek Indians to play the Peruvian army, extras so taken with the work that they returned the next night demanding parts in *Macbeth*. Circuit preacher John Mason Peck recalled a St. Louis where the respectable classes (lawyers, he suggested, more than most) killed each other in duels and "one-half, at least, of the Anglo-American population" could—in his pastoral view—be judged "infidels of a low and indecent grade, and utterly worthless for any useful purposes of society." Another minister, Galusha Anderson, remembering his Civil War pastorate in St. Louis, described the terrible irony of how, standing in his pulpit, he faced "a hideous slave-pen" and from his sanctuary watched "men and women, handcuffed and chained together, in a long two-by-two column, driven . . . under the crack of the driver's whip, as though they were so many colts and calves." Worse, he wrote, than even this travesty was the pen at Fifth and Myrtle, where children were kept. "The traffic in children," he wryly noted, "seemed to be specially brisk and profitable."

The past is not an easy place to visit. That is one of the reasons we usually avoid taking the trip, why mostly we prefer to keep our distance, avoiding the disorienting complexities that we would discover there and, instead, amuse ourselves with the sort of postcard accounts we get in popular culture and superficial political discourse. The difficulty results not simply, or even primarily, because there is so much there that we are likely to find offensive but because it is all so complicated. Regardless of our political affiliations or our ideological leanings, we would like it all to be simple, to be able to confidently separate the good guys from the bad, to elect our ancestors from the righteous who deserve unqualified praise. That is why we are warmed by the feel-good accounts our national leaders favor when describing an invariably heroic past, why we take our children to the Disneyfied substitutions for history offered at Frontierland; Main Street, U.S.A.; and the hall of robotic presidents. That is also why, when we acknowledge any evil in our heritage, we rush to hyperbole, singling out those on whose backs we can lay old wrongs in order to isolate it, to say he or these are responsible so that we may keep our personal favorites unbesmirched.

All of this seems pertinent as St. Louis prepares to celebrate the year 2004. It says a great deal about us, as about local history, that the city's benchmark of choice is the anniversary of a fair, an exposition that was itself supposed to be a commemoration of the 1803 Louisiana Purchase, delayed a year by the scale of the project and disagreements in the planning. That we now date ourselves in terms of a previous anniversary rather than the original event suggests both the thinness and the peculiar nature of our historical sense. This is not to trivialize the Louisiana Exposition; it did, after all, in its staging cost as least as much as the original purchase. Rather, my point is how typical that we find it easier to wax nostalgic over a party than over the "birth" that party was thrown to celebrate. In the fair we could reinvent ourselves as a city and a people, could reproduce the national past in pavilions and re-enactments, relate our national history through the shorthand of symbolism with special exhibits such as the Liberty Bell and reproductions of such sacred sites as Jefferson's Monticello and Jackson's Hermitage. It was history made easy just as it was a nation simplified, a proud declaration of our singleness of mind and purpose and accomplishment before the world we invited to attend our celebration.

By contrast, Louisiana itself, as New England congressmen loudly and repeatedly emphasized in their opposition to its purchase, was complicated. It was not one thing or even one place. Its boundaries were, to understate the case, uncertain; its inhabitants, many of them unknown to their new landlord, of many nations and many languages. Americans worried about how large a republic could grow without losing its republican nature and were especially startled at the idea of this one doubling in area with the stroke of a quill. The challenge of such large-scale expansion dominated 19th-century politics, intensifying old antagonisms and generating wholly new ones. The slave states saw the need to claim their own portion of these new lands to protect the interests of their "peculiar institution"; conflicts over monetary policies and federal influence intensified as the stakes got higher; and relations with neighboring nations became increasingly volatile as our mutual borders changed. To further complicate things, much of the newly acquired land was unlike the country we already owned, prairies unyielding before old farming methods and equipment, mountains more rugged than any we had claimed before 1803.

But in 1904 St. Louis and America could suggest before the world it had assembled in Forest Park that all this was resolved, behind us. After all, we were, as one ex-president who lent his presence and voice to the proceedings declared, "a people favored of God." And though I think that a true enough assertion, it is also the case that—as John Mason Peck demonstrated—we have surely proved to be frustrating stuff even for God to whip into shape. In accounts as diverse as those of John Darby, mayor in the 1830s and '40s, and Jessie Benton Fremont, daughter of a senator and wife of the famous "Pathfinder"—the closest thing to royalty this country could produce—we discover a community divided by class and income, as well as by race and ethnicity. We see a city capable in times of crisis of humane and heroic acts but also, in its everyday affairs, often guilty of breathtaking selfishness and perversity. In short, what we find looking back is that the past is very much like the present, our ancestors remarkably like us. The Rev. Anderson summed up this place in his day by saying, "the inhabitants of the city were a conglomerate," and not just in their collective diversity but individually, just as we are, a mixture of motives and minds, capable of pettiness and nobility, of sin as well as virtue.

In 1902, even while civic leaders were putting on their best face for the approaching fair, a St. Louis writer described his hometown in *McClure's Magazine* as a place where "the leading men" have begun "to devour their own city," and among those he implicated were some of the prominent citizens hard at work on the exposition. Eight years later a novel, titled *The Big Cinch* after the local St. Louis leadership, claimed to portray how "a handful of the 'leading' citizens, assisted by the ladies in the family, run things to suit themselves, throttle competition, destroy virtue and place a premium on dishonesty." The differing representations of St. Louis could not be more antithetical or more righteously insistent on the truth of their particular view. That is why looking back is demanding work. There is much to see, much that is conflicted and disturbing.

There have been, in recent years, heated debates about how we should represent our past in everything from museum exhibits to history texts. Western politicians were enraged by what they saw as an overemphasis on exploitation in "The West as America" exhibit sponsored by the National Museum of American Art, and congressional reaction to the National Air and Space Museum's original plans for displaying the Enola Gay was sufficiently fierce to force major revision before the show was allowed to go on.

Such disagreements in themselves argue for the complex nature of the past and, when they don't finally result in a trivializing and antiseptic version of history, can be healthy. But we have to resist our desire to make it all easy, to fill up the past either with blame or nostalgic adoration; to do so is to misrepresent us as well as those we succeed, our own time as well as theirs.

Another writer from the period I have been assigned is Mark Twain, and, in one of his greatest works, *Old Times on the Mississippi*, he described the enormous task an apprentice steamboat pilot took on when he began to "learn" the river. What had at first seemed a simple matter of staying between the banks and enjoying the pleasure of the excursion proved to be the overwhelming challenge of reading a river that is constantly changing, reading it forward and backward in all seasons and all hours, discerning the forces at work below the surface, living with its endless complications. Only when these skills were mastered, Twain insisted, could one presume to navigate the incredible current flowing through the heart of America. History—that of St. Louis or the United States or of each of us individually—is no less demanding or less wondrous than Twain's Mississippi. It is a terrible mistake to assume otherwise. What is past is never over; who we once were is never wholly missing in what we have become; and even we latecomers who have no personal or familial connection to a particular community, simply by finding ourselves in a place, take on a part of its old burdens even as we benefit from its accumulated assets.

BRIAN TAYLOR

Born in England, Brian Taylor (1936–) has lived in St. Louis since 1968. A graduate of Cambridge University, he taught English at Mary Institute and St. Louis Country Day School. Taylor's poetry has been published on both sides of the Atlantic in many periodicals, including *London Magazine*, *Stand*, *The Listener*, *Paris Review*, and *River Styx*. In 1985, the same year that his collection *Transit* was published, Taylor received the Cholmondeley Award for Poets from the British Society of Authors. In 1994, he also received the Wildwood Award in Poetry. A two-time winner of the St. Louis Wednesday Club's Poetry Award, Taylor has subsequently served as a judge for that competition. In addition to writing, he teaches part-time at Washington University, Maryville University, and St. Louis Community College.

AT THE MARJEANETTE APARTMENTS

Skinny-legged girl in droopy socks
and loose underpants—curling-rags
screwing her red hair in knots—Amelia-Anne
stands tiptoe on a stool to reach

the doll's house on the top shelf of the closet.
Pounding with a hammer too heavy
for her brittle wrists,

she is nailing the house door shut.
After a day of dodging the rain
between soured park-shelters,
I returned to my apartment. The key

jammed in the lock. I tried
the other door; easily it swung
open on the livingroom, where old ladies

sagged on the grey sofas, the white
haloes of their hair blued
by the flickering television screen.
"I've come for my things," I said.

Their ivory knuckles tightened on their canes.
I had been there only that morning,
yet long before their time

and their urinous stink of tea-leaves.
One creaked from her seat
and shuffled to the bedroom door.
"In here," she said. And I eased myself in

between the crowded, dark and oily furniture—
yellowed lace on the tables,
bleached wax fruit in smoky bowls,

a wasp's nest disintegrating on the pillow.
Things were not as I had recalled.
On my wardrobe door hung my uniform—
the buttons crusted with verdigris, the crimson

lapels opening to a fog of moths.
In the mirror my face was a milky smear.
When I turn to help the little girl—

her eyes the color of cornflowers—
by lifting the heavy doll's house down,
its frail walls collapse. Its rooms
are clogged with loam.

ROUTE 64

While driving long distance, the game is to find
two things: the most delightful,
the most strange. We stare and think of anything,
everything else as Illinois slides by.

A man's life is like that: over the long ponds
a perturbation—overturned john boats,
tall grass leaning away from the wind, milkweed,
barbed wire, bauchy clay, a barn,
a pair of hogs rootling—over all this, because
this is all, ten thousand days rise
and float and fall like ten thousand starlings
all of one mind. It is like that.

They do not touch. Are not one thing. At best
each day feels the dark breath
of another's wing. Until the swarm breaks up
like pond-fog. It is like that, too.

For hours we have looked for neither delight
nor strangeness. Then you say
you saw two gravestones, side by side, out
in the stubble. Farmer and wife
stand and watch as we commute into our west.

MR. HENRY SHAW COMES TO REST

I. SAINT LOUIS

He never said, "I'll not go back." Being there merely
ceased to be waiting. And the Yorkshire millstone grit—

another place—simply became another time.
There still were drizzly days, with sky the color of stone,

when green hills once again shadowless seemed to hang
in the arms of sweetgum, dogwood, redbud and Ozark pine

that hid from his dreamy gaze thousands of miles of grass.
And also there were nights when one stair in a creaking flight,

where darkies strained on hawsers or slack-handed loped
between the sheds, seemed to be Pennine rock where sheep

jostled against the wall and grouse whirred from the tufts
of wiry grass; nights when one board of a gangway, where

the Mississippi raked and curled out underfoot,
seemed a stepping-stone in an English river where swans

and swans' reflections glimmered on the brown water.
But he was a man who moved, a man whose sudden glimpses

of walks and arbors among crates on crowded wharves
gave but a momentary pang. His boot swung sure

to the next safe step, and almost never now he thought
"There is still time to fetch the bride who waits for me."

II. COMMITMENT

"Thou hast a
lap full of
seed/and this
is a fine

country" All
his letters
to her are
reported

lost. He went
to the slave
girls with their
curious

cheek-scars, no
doubt, or to
French housewives,
peddling his

knives and forks,
accepting
graciously
a glass of

mint tea and
charming them
with his broad
flat Sheffield

vowels. But
most of his
nights he spent—
after the

ledgers had
been filled and
dusted dry—
with the old

man at chess,
from whom he
could learn more
of markets.

A mile from
home, she stopped
the gig at
a place where

the lane dipped
into shade
and the beck
slithered down

between rocks
and leaning
trunks. Against
a bank lay

deep water,
where sunlight
lay sprinkled
like fallen

leaves on the
pebbles of
the pool's bed.
"Why dost thou

not cast thy
seed?" The shafts
of light thrust
up golden

and searing
from the depths
at her feet,
and clutching

her sides she
felt, beneath
whalebone and
linen, loss.

Unmoving,
there lay in
her womb a
planted stone.

III. THE BOTANICAL LEGACY

He paid his former slaves an equitable wage.
With profits from trading cutlery he served his town,

sponsoring opera, purchasing acreage, transplanting trees.
Was never married. With dour companions traveled to Greece.

Kept a journal: amber-skinned children at the water trough.
Now steps he through the bluebells to his tomb. The bulbs—

sent on from England last July and set in beds
of leafmold, river sand, and cowdung mulch—produce

Endymion nonscriptum. Yes, the New World's first!
And so, the fever notwithstanding, he now treads

with care. Outside the stained-glass-windowed mausoleum
the eight-foot doors of massive bronze, yet to be hung,

stand propped against one wall. The dusty mason kneels
beside the marble catafalque. His trowel slips

mortar between the pillow and the trader's effigy
on whose necrotic cheek a fly stands poised for flight.

SPRING

The motor mower is at it again, shaping a text-wrap
path in the wet grass. Just thrust your hand into the hot

entrails of a pile of clippings—all that caloric force
devoted to the serious business of rot. When the Ferris

wheel (two-hundred-forty-feet tall) was wrecked after
the World's Fair, its axle was buried and lost somewhere

under the west end of Forest Park, under the golf course,
maybe, so many tons of steel—that carried a hundred people

towards the clouds and back—decomposing into a slush
of rust like some bog-swallowed Excalibur sheathed in its

own sloughed flakes. When the elements desert the body,
it is air leaves first. Then fire—ash or dirt choking the embers.

Then go all the humors: the slime on the log, the fog that sweats
from cold stone, the comforting slick of the tongue and

the slither of sex. Come this season, the bones of my hand,
cold and dry, retain some life by a ritual of mowing.

QUINCY TROUPE

ST. LOUIS NATIVE QUINCY TROUPE (1943–) was born at Homer G. Phillips Hospital and attended Beaumont High School. The son of Negro Leagues baseball great Quincy Trouppe, young Quincy lived with his mother and brother on Delmar Boulevard and, later, Ashland Avenue, while his father traveled extensively playing baseball. Himself a gifted athlete, Troupe toured Europe on an All-Army basketball team. While sidelined with an injury, he began to write poetry after receiving encouragement from Jean-Paul Sartre. A prolific and energetic man of letters, Troupe is the author of numerous books in multiple genres, including two American Book Award winners: a volume of poetry, *Snake-Back Solos* (1979), and *Miles: The Autobiography* (1990), which he co-authored with Miles Davis. Troupe also received a Peabody Award for *The Miles Davis Radio Project*, which he wrote and co-produced. In 2000, Troupe's most recent work, *Miles and Me: A Memoir of Miles Davis*, was published.

A literary activist, editor, and author, Troupe has called himself a "cultural worker" who is committed to bringing literature to the broadest possible audience. Troupe, whose annual St. Louis readings are packed, has bittersweet feelings for his hometown. In a 1996 *Gateway Heritage* interview, he remarked, "I'm always ambivalent about St. Louis because I think St. Louis has always had great promise and great people and lost opportunities." At present, Troupe is finishing a novel, *The Footman Chronicles*, and is writing a memoir of his own life titled *The Accordion Years: 1965 to 1998*. A professor of creative writing and American and Caribbean literature at the University of California–San Diego, Troupe lives with his wife, Margaret, and their son, Porter, in La Jolla, California.

In the following chapter from *Miles and Me*, Troupe recalls his serendipitous introduction to Davis's music as a high school student in 1953.

LISTENING TO MILES

"DONNA" ON THE JUKEBOX

I entered the world of jazz through a Miles Davis record I heard back in 1955 when I was fifteen years old. I had gone into a fish joint—on Fair Avenue in my hometown, St. Louis, Missouri—to get a jack-salmon fish sandwich (actually a kind of whiting that St. Louis Blacks called "jack-salmon"). It could have been a summer weekday or a Saturday during the school year. I don't remember. All I recall now of walking into that small, nondescript place, since destroyed by so-called urban renewal, is that it was daytime and the sun was shining.

The joint had a yellow linoleum floor and the prefabricated look of vinyl and plastic that later became so popular at McDonalds, Jack 'n the Box, and all the other banal fast-food restaurants that swept over America and inundate our culture today. Back then, this fish joint was cutting edge, even though the black people in the neighborhood hated the way it looked. We called its sterile style "clean looking," to distinguish it from the usual "greasy spoon" style that most local black eateries wore back then. As we liked to say, this joint was "trying to look white." But we loved the great food that was served up there, and we came back time and again despite our reservations about their "fried hair" and "white look."

Once inside, I immediately noticed a booth filled with four black, hip-looking older guys wearing the latest "in" clothes. Smoking cigarettes and wearing shades, their wide-brimmed hats hung majestically on the prongs of two steel poles, which seemed to grow beside their booth like facing trees.

The men were sitting there talking and eating deep-fried "jack-salmon" sandwiches doused with hot sauce, with sides of potato salad and cole slaw. They were also listening to the jukebox that was jamming sounds I had either never heard before or never paid attention to. Whatever it was, it was new to me, and at that moment, I was drawn to it like the rabbit to the tarbaby.

I remember being struck by the music easing out of the brightly colored jukebox, which seemed to match the cool style of the four men sitting there nodding their heads in time with the rhythm. In unison. Although I had intended to buy a takeout sandwich, I decided instead to sit down in a booth to eat and listen to those men talk, and to drink in the music they were nodding their heads to.

They talked about the sounds they were hearing on the box. One man said the trumpet was played by a "homeboy" from across the river, someone named Miles Davis. Another said the tune was called "Donna." I also recall one of them saying that "the young alto player sounds almost like Bird. Man, he's something else." Well, I didn't know who "Bird" was or the young alto player who sounded like him, either, but I found the conversation fascinating and I listened intently while they played the record over and over again. Jazz music made sense to me that day for the first time in my life.

Until then, my choice in music had always been black rhythm and blues; music I could move my body to. Though I suspected that I could also move my body to "Donna," the same way those hip guys were dancing on their hind parts in that booth, nodding their "processed" heads. At that time, I liked the Platters, the Dells, the Cadillacs, Sam Cooke, Johnny Ace, Clyde McPhatter, Jackie Wilson, and the alleged wild man of music who was then living right down the street from me, Chuck Berry. But this music was totally different. It had no words, no voices, no vocal dancing to slide words around, over, ahead, behind, and still land right back on the beat.

It was a completely different kind of music and, after the four men left, I found myself getting up, reaching into my pocket for a nickel, and walking up to the jukebox. I found "Donna," dropped my coin in, turned around and eased my way back to my booth as the music poured out of the box. As I polished off my second fish sandwich, I kept nodding my head to the tune's insinuating rhythms and moving my hind parts in time to the beat.

BECOMING HIP

When I left that joint that afternoon, I felt as though I had undergone a secret initiation, a rite of passage, one that would separate me forever from the rest of the students who attended Beaumont High School, to which I had just transferred. The school was overwhelmingly white and the students there were "square" to the bone. To my way of thinking, hardly anyone there had any sense of style at all.

During the summer of 1954 my mother had moved us from our old black neighborhood. She had wanted us to be the first black family on the block, but actually we were the second. We were a family of six: my grandmother,

Leona Smith; my mother, Dorothy Smith Troupe Brown; my stepfather, China Brown, blues bass player, leader of his own band, and clothes presser at a large cleaning plant; my uncle Allen, unemployed wino, a gentle, harmless man; and my younger brother, Timothy. Our white neighbors hated all of us immediately.

We lived next door to the first black people on the block: a couple, Thomas and Margaret O' Guin. He was a doorman at a local hotel and she was a homemaker. They were older, more conservative than we were, and had no children, which probably explains why they had never had a problem living on Ashland Street before we arrived. Our family brought not only children but young black men into the neighborhood. After we arrived, the whites on the block began leaving faster than people in a movie house when someone's yelled "fire." Our white next-door neighbors never spoke to us, not once.

In this hostile racist environment, I was fast learning to hate myself just for being black. Earlier in my life, living in a black neighborhood, I had never felt any self-hatred. In fact, it was the other way around; I was proud of who my father was, and of what our family name meant in the black community. My father, Quincy Troupe, was a great star in the old Negro baseball league, and his older brother, James ("Pal"), was a leading black political and labor leader around St. Louis, who had also made a ton of money from real estate and "other" investments. A distant cousin, Ernest Troupe, was a lieutenant on the police force. So, within the St. Louis black community, our name was well-known and well-respected. But, of course, none of the white people in the new neighborhood knew any of this. To them, we were just a bunch of "niggers."

Naturally, I hated the new block and would walk back to my old neighborhood every chance I could get (a distance of about four miles). When I asked my mother why she had moved us, she simply said it had been in our "best interests." *She*, however, travelled outside the neighborhood to work as a telephone operator every day, just as my stepfather, China, and my grandmother did. But my brother Timmy and I had to go to school with the racist neighborhood kids every day, and they were like a pack of howling, rabid dogs.

During my first two years in my new home, the white kids (mostly boys) called me every vile name they knew. They called me "nigger," "coon," "monkey," "gorilla," "jiggaboo," "shinola," and "boy," to name just a few. We fought on many occasions. With the exception of one Italian kid, Tom Palazolla, who invited me to his home, they hardly ever spoke to me or even looked my way during my years at Beaumont, except when it came to sports (which is how most whites prefer dealing with black men even today). The entire experience seemed designed to drain me of my racial identity and pride.

That's why Miles Davis and his music came to mean so much to me. The white kids at Beaumont High were into Bill Haley and the Comets and Elvis Presley. But what they really loved was Pat Boone's rendition of "Ain't That a Shame." I hated Boone's version of that song, because I had heard the "real thing" by Fats Domino, and I knew that Pat Boone had "borrowed" it from him and become famous singing it because he was a white man. Boone made a career of such "borrowings." He also made a "mint" with his cover of Little Richard's "Tutti Fruity." But my white schoolmates didn't know or care about any of this. They didn't give a flying fuck if Boone was getting over because he was covering black songs. It certainly didn't matter to them that Elvis Presley was doing the same thing. Chuck Berry lived in the neighborhood, but the white kids didn't even know his name, not to mention what a great contribution he was making to American music.

But I knew. I knew the "real deal" and it bothered the hell out of me that these white teenagers didn't even care that they didn't know shit; that they could think of black people as stupid and uncreative while all the while their musical heroes were stealing our songs, music, and language and calling them their own.

When I discovered Miles Davis, I knew I had found something these white squares didn't and couldn't know. I was hip. I wanted to be seen as someone completely different from the squares. And, "quiet as it's kept," I really saw myself apart from *all* my high school classmates, the black students as well the whites. I had no respect for my black classmates because they had bought into the idea of their own inferiority. They believed that their culture, language, and music were beneath those of their white counterparts. So they tried their best to be as white as they could in their speech, dress, and manners. It sickened me to see my old friends change that way. I refused to change, and I guess that sickened both my black and white classmates because we all quickly drew apart.

What happened to us was sad. But at the time I had no language to explain myself to them, nor they to me. We were mute in our separation and pain. We couldn't explain why we were drifting apart. We only knew that we were and that we were powerless to stop it. But I had Miles Davis in my life, and they didn't, and that's what saved me: his music and his living example of what a black man could be: someone completely independent, amazingly creative, fiercely proud.

As a teenager in the late 1950s, I had few fiercely proud black role models and heroes: Miles Davis, Chuck Berry, Paul Robeson, and my father's older brother, Albert, were at the top of my list. Of these men my Uncle Albert was the only one with whom I had a real personal experience—though Chuck Berry lived three blocks down the street from me and I would see and speak to him on occasion. Uncle Albert taught me firsthand what it meant to be what I later came to know as an "unreconstructed black man." This was a dangerous, lonely, and unrewarding position in which to place oneself. Uncle Albert didn't take anything off anyone—black or white—and the reason my father's family had to leave Dublin, Georgia, during the late 1920s was because Uncle Albert, as a teenager, threatened to kill a white man who had called him a "boy" and a "nigger." He refused to be disrespected, whether by a boss, his friends, or anyone else. As a consequence he kept his self-respect but had a hard time keeping employment and making a living. And although they managed to make a much better living than did Uncle Albert, Chuck Berry, Paul Robeson, and Miles Davis were like that, too.

I began to look for more records by Miles. I found out who "Bird" was by finding Miles Davis' name on some of Charlie Parker's records. In the same way I also found out that the "young alto player" who sounded just like "Bird" was Jackie McLean. I wanted to learn everything I could about Miles Davis. So I started asking some of the older guys about him, which led me to my cousin, Marvin, a very good drummer and everyday criminal and junkie. (He was a junkie so obsessed with getting money to support his large habit that he later broke into his own father's house, my Uncle, James "Pal" Troupe, and stole everything that wasn't tied down. It was the talk of the family for years.) Marvin—dead now—always liked me. He was always telling me I had "potential." Somewhere around 1955 he turned me on to the album *Bags' Groove,* which completely blew my mind because it was so different from "Donna" and all the other music by Miles I had heard until then.

ACKNOWLEDGMENTS

Adams, Henry. Excerpt from *The Education of Henry Adams* by Henry Adams. New York: 1918.

Angelou, Maya. Excerpt from *I Know Why the Caged Bird Sings* by Maya Angelou. Copyright © 1969 by Maya Angelou and renewed 1987 by Maya Angelou. Reprinted by permission of Random House, Inc.

Anonymous. "A Night View of Our Courthouse." Reprinted from *Glimpses of the Past* 1, no. 8 (July 1934): 60–63.

Benson, Sally. Excerpt from *Meet Me in St. Louis* by Sally Benson. Copyright © 1941 by the Sally Benson Estate. Reprinted by permission of the Motion Picture and Television Fund.

Boernstein, Henry. Excerpt from *The Mysteries of St. Louis* by Henry Boernstein. Copyright © 1990 by and reprinted by permission of Charles Kerr Publishing Company.

Brodkey, Harold. "The State of Grace" from *First Love and Other Sorrows* by Harold Brodkey. Copyright © 1988 by Harold Brodkey. Reprinted by permission of International Creative Management, Inc.

Brown, William Wells. Excerpt from *Narrative of William Wells Brown, A Fugitive Slave, Written by Himself* by William Wells Brown. Boston: 1847.

Burroughs, William S. "St. Louis Return" from *The Burroughs File* by William S. Burroughs. Copyright © 1984 by William S. Burroughs.

Carkeet, David. "Sunday Morning Ball at the J" by David Carkeet. Copyright © 1996 by David Carkeet. Reprinted by permission of author. This essay first appeared in *St. Louis* magazine (March/April 1996).

Carter, John Henton. Excerpt from *The Log of Commodore Rollingpin: His Adventures Afloat and Ashore* by John H. Carter. New York: 1874.

Castro, Michael. "The Origins of River Styx" by Michael Castro. Copyright © 1987 by Michael Castro. Reprinted by permission of the author. This essay first appeared in *River Styx* 24.

Chopin, Kate. "The Maid of St. Phillippe" by Kate Chopin, from the *Missouri Historical Society Bulletin* 19, no. 2 (January 1963): 92–98.

———. "Elizabeth Stock's One Story" by Kate Chopin, from the *Missouri Historical Society Bulletin* 19, no. 2 (January 1963): 104–9.

———. "A Self-Assumed Burden" from *At Fault* by Kate Chopin. St. Louis: 1890.

Chouteau, Auguste. "Narrative of the Settlement of St. Louis" by Auguste Chouteau from *Missouri Historical Society Collections* 3, no. 4 (1911): 47–59.

Churchill, Winston. Excerpt from *The Crisis* by Winston Churchill. New York: 1901.

Clark, William and Meriwether Lewis. Excerpt from *The Journals of Lewis and Clark*, edited by Bernard DeVoto. Copyright © 1953 by Avis DeVoto. Reprinted by permission of Houghton Mifflin Company.

Cook, Fannie. Excerpt from *Mrs. Palmer's Honey* by Fannie Cook. Copyright © 1946 by Fannie Cook.

Davis, Miles. Excerpt from *Miles: The Autobiography* by Miles Davis, with Quincy Troupe. Copyright © 1989 by Miles Davis. Reprinted by permission of Simon and Schuster, Inc.

De Finiels, Nicolas. Excerpt from *An Account of Upper Louisiana* by Nicolas de Finiels from reprint edited by Carl Ekberg and William E. Foley. Reprinted by permission of the University of Missouri Press. Copyright ©1989 by the Curators of the University of Missouri.

De Leyba, Fernando. Letter from Captain Fernando de Leyba to Louisiana Governor-General Bernardo de Gálvez, 8 June 1780, from *New Spain and the Anglo-American West* by Herbert Eugene Bolton. Los Angeles: 1932.

Dickens, Charles. Excerpt from *American Notes* by Charles Dickens. Great Britain: 1842.

Dreer, Herman. Excerpt from *The Tie That Binds: A Novel of a Youth Who Seeks to Understand Life* by Herman Dreer. Copyright © 1958 by Herman Dreer. Reprinted by permission of Vivian Dreer.

Dreiser, Theodore. Excerpt from *A Book About Myself* by Theodore Dreiser. New York: 1922.

———. "Under the Wheels" by Theodore Dreiser from the *St. Louis Republic*, 6 January 1894.

———. "The Trouble Still On" by Theodore Dreiser from the *St. Louis Republic*, 20 June 1893.

———. "Bread War in Little Russia" by Theodore Dreiser from the *St. Louis Globe-Democrat*, 10 February 1893.

Du Bois, W. E. B. "Of Work and Wealth" by W. E. B. Du Bois from *The Seventh Son: The Thought and Writings of W. E. B. Du Bois*, edited by Julius Lester. Copyright © 1967 by W. E. B. Du Bois.

Duchesne, Rose Philippine. Letters by Philippine Duchesne reprinted from *Hardship and Hope: Missouri Women Writing about Their Lives, 1820–1920*, edited by Carla Waal and Barbara Oliver Korner, by permission of the University of Missouri Press. Copyright © 1997 by the Curators of the University of Missouri.

Duden, Gottfried. Letters by Gottfried Duden reprinted from *Report on a Journey to the Western States of North America and a Stay of Several Years Along the Missouri (During the Years 1824, '25, '26, 1827)* by Gottfried Duden, by permission of the University of Missouri Press. Copyright © 1990 by the Curators of the University of Missouri.

Early, Gerald. "St. Louis: The Midwestern Long Good-bye" from *The Place Within: Portraits of the American Landscape* edited by Jodi Daynard. Copyright © 1997 by Gerald Early. Reprinted by permission of the author.

Eliot, Thomas Stearns. "The Dry Salvages" from *Four Quartets* by T. S. Eliot. Copyright © 1941 by T. S. Eliot. Reprinted by permission of Harcourt.

———. Letter by T. S. Eliot to *St. Louis Post-Dispatch*, 8 August 1930. Reprinted from the Missouri Historical Society Collections.

———. Letter by T. S. Eliot to Edna McCourt, 12 January 1923. Reprinted from the Missouri Historical Society Collections.

Elkin, Stanley. "Why I Live Where I Live" by Stanley Elkin. Copyright © 1983 by Stanley Elkin. Reprinted by permission of Georges Borchardt, Inc.

Field, Eugene. "Little Mack" from *The Poems of Eugene Field*. New York: 1913.

———. "Plaint of the Missouri 'Coon in the Berlin Zoological Gardens" from *The Poems of Eugene Field*. New York: 1913.

———. "A Western Boy's Lament" from *The Poems of Eugene Field*. New York: 1913.

Field, Joseph M. "Ballad of the Year of the Surprise" by Joseph M. Field. Reprinted from *St. Louis Reveille*, 17 February 1845.

———. "Death of Mike Fink" by Joseph M. Field. Reprinted from *St. Louis Reveille*, 21 October 1844.

Field, Matthew C. Excerpt from the 1839 journals of Matthew Field. Reprinted from Missouri Historical Sociey Archives.

———. "The Chouteau House" by Matthew Field. Reprinted from Missouri Historical Society Archives.

Fields, Wayne. "Our Cruel, Tangled Past" by Wayne Fields. Copyright © 1999 by Wayne Fields. Reprinted by permission of the author. This essay first appeared in *St. Louis* magazine (June 1998).

Finkel, Donald. "An Entirely New Idea" from *Beyond Despair* by Donald Finkel. Copyright © 1994 by Donald Finkel. Reprinted by permission of the author.

———. "For Whose Use" from *Beyond Despair* by Donald Finkel. Copyright © 1994 by Donald Finkel. Reprinted by permission of the author.

Hotchner, A. E. Excerpt from *King of the Hill* by A. E. Hotchner. Copyright ©1972 by A. E. Hotchner. Reprinted by permission of William Morris Agency, Inc.

Hunt, Anne Lucas. "Early Recollections" by Anne L. Hunt from *Glimpses of the Past* 1, no. 6 (May 1934): 41-51.

Hurd, Carlos. "Post Dispatch Man, an Eye-Witness, Describes Massacre of Negroes: Victims Driven from Home by Fire, Stoned, Beaten and Hanged When Dying—Women Fight Militiamen and Assist in Work" by Carlos Hurd from the *St. Louis Post-Dispatch*, 3 July 1917.

Hurst, Fannie. Excerpt from *Anatomy of Me* by Fannie Hurst. Copyright © 1958 by Fannie Hurst.

———. "Saint Louis" by Fannie Hurst from the *St. Louis Globe-Democrat*, 6 November 1955.

Johns, Orrick. Excerpt from *Time of Our Lives: The Story of My Father and Myself* by Orrick Johns. Copyright © 1937 by Orrick Johns.

Kahn, Michael A. Excerpt from *Due Diligence* by Michael A. Kahn. Copyright © 1995 by Michael A. Kahn. Reprinted by permission of the author.

Keckley, Elizabeth. Excerpt from *Behind the Scenes; or, Thirty Years a Slave, and Four Years in the White House* by Elizabeth Keckley. New York: 1868.

Keene, John. Excerpt from *Annotations* by John Keene. Copyright © 1995 by John Keene. Reprinted by permission of New Directions Publishing Corp.

Knoepfle, John. "East St. Louis" from *Rivers into Islands* by John Knoepfle. Copyright © 1965 by John Knoepfle. Reprinted by permission of the author.

———. "Heman Avenue holiday" from *Rivers into Islands* by John Knoepfle. Copyright © 1965 by John Knoepfle. Reprinted by permission of the author.

———. "June night on the river" from *Rivers into Islands* by John Knoepfle. Copyright © 1965 by John Knoepfle. Reprinted by permission of the author.

———. "Lines for Men of the Greater Interior" by John Knoepfle. Copyright © 1965 by John Knoepfle. Reprinted by permission of the author.

Knoepfle, John. "Riverfront, St. Louis" from *Rivers into Islands* by John Knoepfle. Copyright © 1965 by John Knoepfle. Reprinted by permission of the author.

———. "St. Louis midday" from *Rivers into Islands* by John Knoepfle. Copyright © 1965 by John Knoepfle. Reprinted by permission of the author.

Knoepfle, John. "St. Louis midnight" from *Rivers into Islands* by John Knoepfle. Copyright © 1965 by John Knoepfle. Reprinted by permission of the author.

Landau, Leo A. Excerpt from *The Big Cinch* by Leo A. Landau. St. Louis: 1910.

Landesman, Jay. "Running Dry/Running Off" from *Rebel Without Applause* by Jay Landesman. Copyright © 1987 by Jay Landesman. Reprinted by permission of the author.

Lanman, Charles. Excerpt from *A Summer in the Wilderness; Embracing a Canoe Voyage up the Mississippi and around Lake Superior* by Charles Lanman. New York: 1847.

Laugel, Auguste. Excerpt from *Les Etats-Unis Pendant la Guerre Civile, 1861–1865*. Paris: 1866. Reprinted from "Auguste Laugel Visits St. Louis, 1864" by Georges J. Joyaux from the *Missouri Historical Society Bulletin* 14, no. 1 (October 1957): 37-45.

Lewis, Edward Garner. "Ten Million Women" by Edward Garner Lewis from *The Woman's Magazine* (June 1904): 10-11.

Lewis, Hannah. Excerpt from *Narrative of the Captivity and Sufferings of Mrs. Hannah Lewis, and Her Three Children, Who Were Taken Prisoner by Indians* by Hannah Lewis. Boston: 1817.

Lewis, Henry. "The Great Fire in St. Louis" from *The Valley of the Mississippi Illustrated* by Henry Lewis. Copyright © 1967 and reprinted by permission of the Minnesota Historical Society Press.

Lindbergh, Charles A. Excerpt from *The Spirit of St. Louis* by Charles A. Lindbergh. Copyright © 1953 by Charles Scribner's Sons; copyright renewed by Anne Morrow Lindbergh. Reprinted by permission of Simon and Schuster, Inc.

Lutz, John. Excerpt from *Dancer's Debt* by John Lutz. Copyright © 1988 by John Lutz. Reprinted by permission of the author.

MacKaye, Percy. Excerpt from *St. Louis: A Civic Masque* by Percy MacKaye. St. Louis: 1914.

Marquette, Père Jacques. Excerpt from the journal of Père Jacques Marquette, from the original manuscript in the archives of St. Mary's College, Montreal, 1677.

Mohr, Nicolaus. Excerpt from *Excursion Through America* by Nicolaus Mohr, and translated by LaVern J. Rippley. Copyright © 1973 by R. R. Donnelly & Sons Co.

Nemerov, Howard. "By Al Lebowitz's Pool" from *Sentences* by Howard Nemerov. Copyright © 1980 by Howard Nemerov. Reprinted by permission of Margaret Nemerov.

Nemerov, Howard. "An Ending" from *The Collected Poems of Howard Nemerov* by Howard Nemerov. Copyright © 1977 by Howard Nemerov. Reprinted by permission of Margaret Nemerov.

———. "Ginkgoes in Fall" from *The Collected Poems of Howard Nemerov* by Howard Nemerov. Copyright © 1977 by Howard Nemerov. Reprinted by permission of Margaret Nemerov.

———. "One Moment in Eternity" from *The Collected Poems of Howard Nemerov* by Howard Nemerov. Copyright © 1977 by Howard Nemerov. Reprinted by permission of Margaret Nemerov.

———. "Walking Down Westgate in the Fall" from *The Collected Poems of Howard Nemerov* by Howard Nemerov. Copyright © 1977 by Howard Nemerov. Reprinted by permission of Margaret Nemerov.

Phillips, Carl. "The Flume" from *From the Devotions* by Carl Phillips. Copyright © 1998 by Carl Phillips. Reprinted by permission of Graywolf Press.

———. "Meditation: The River Road" from *From the Devotions* by Carl Phillips. Copyright © 1998 by Carl Phillips. Reprinted by permission of Graywolf Press.

Primm, Wilson. "History of St. Louis" by Wilson Primm. Reprinted from *Missouri Historical Society Collections* 4 (1913): 163–69, 174–87.

Pulitzer, Joseph. "Deplorable Tragedy. Alonzo W. Slayback Shot and Killed Yesterday Afternoon" by Joseph Pulitzer from the *St. Louis Post-Dispatch*, 14 October 1882.

———. "Anti-Dust. A Scheme to Give St. Louis One Pleasant Drive" by Joseph Pulitzer from the *St. Louis Post-Dispatch*, 12 April 1880.

Raban, Jonathan. "Marriage à la Mode" from *Old Glory: An American Voyage* by Jonathan Raban. Copyright ©1981 by Jonathan Raban. Reprinted by permission of the author.

Reavis, Logan Uriah. Excerpt from *St. Louis the Future Great City of the World: and Its Impending Triumph* by L. U. Reavis. St. Louis: 1881.

Reavis, Rebecca Morrow. "The Future Great City of the World" from *Consider the Lilies* by Rebecca Morrow Reavis. St. Louis: 1883.

———. "Ode to Captain James B. Eads" from *Consider the Lilies* by Rebecca Morrow Reavis. St. Louis: 1883.

Redmond, Eugene B. "Honoring the Female Olympian of the Century" by Eugene B. Redmond. Copyright © 2000 by Eugene B. Redmond. Reprinted by permission of the author.

———. "Carryover" by Eugene B. Redmond. Copyright © 1992 by Eugene B. Redmond. Reprinted by permission of the author.

Redmond, Eugene B. "River of Bones and Flesh and Blood" by Eugene B. Redmond. Copyright © 1991 by Eugene B. Redmond. Reprinted by permission of the author.

———. "Wedge Wall, Huge Hand" by Eugene B. Redmond. Copyright © 1991 by Eugene B. Redmond. Reprinted by permission of the author.

Reedy, William Marion. "What's the Matter with St. Louis?" by William Marion Reedy from *St. Louis Mirror*, November 2, 1899.

Revard, Carter. "Dragon-watching in St. Louis" from *Winning the Dust Bowl* by Carter Revard. Copyright © 2000 by Carter Revard. Reprinted by permission of the author.

———. "Family Reunion" from *Family Matters, Tribal Affairs*. Copyright © 1998 by Carter Revard. Reprinted by permission of the University of Arizona Press.

Savan, Glenn. Excerpt from *White Palace* by Glenn Savan. Copyright © 1987 by Glenn Savan. Reprinted by permission of the author.

Shange, Ntozake. Excerpt from *Betsey Brown* by Ntozake Shange. Copyright © 1985 by Ntozake Shange. Reprinted by permission of St. Martin's Press, LLC.

Shaw, Henry. "A Guide to the Missouri Botanical Garden, St. Louis" by Henry Shaw. Copyright © 1943 by the Missouri Botanical Garden. Reprinted by permission of the Missouri Botanical Garden. This essay first appeared in *Missouri Botanical Garden Bulletin* 31, no. 7 (September 1943): 136–45.

Sherman, William T. Excerpt from *Memoirs of General W. T. Sherman, Written by Himself* by William T. Sherman. New York: 1892.

Smith, Solomon. Excerpt from *Theatrical Management in the West and South for Thirty Years* by Solomon Smith. New York: 1868.

Snider, Denton. Excerpt from *The St. Louis Movement in Philosophy, Literature, Education, Psychology* by Denton Snider. New York: 1920.

Steele, Allen. Excerpt from *The Jericho Iteration* by Allen Steele. Copyright © 1994 by Allen Steele. Reprinted by permission of the author.

Stevens, Thomas Woods. Excerpt from *The Pageant of St. Louis* by Thomas Woods Stevens. St. Louis: 1914.

Stoddard, Amos. "Captain Stoddard's Address to the People of Upper Louisiana, 10 March 1804" by Amos Stoddard. Reprinted from *Glimpses of the Past* 2, no. 6–10 (May–September 1935): 87–91.

Taylor, Brian. "At the Marjeanette Apartments" from *Transit* by Brian Taylor. Copyright © 1985 by Brian Taylor. Reprinted by permission of the author.

———. "Mr. Henry Shaw Comes to Rest" by Brian Taylor. Copyright © 1985 by Brian Taylor. Reprinted by permission of the author.

Taylor, Brian. "Route 64" by Brian Taylor. Copyright © 1985 by Brian Taylor. Reprinted by permission of the author.

———. "Spring" by Brian Taylor. Copyright © 1985 by Brian Taylor. Reprinted by permission of the author.

Taylor, Peter. "The Little Cousins" from *The Old Forest and Other Stories* by Peter Taylor. Copyright © 1959 by Peter Taylor. Reprinted by permission of Doubleday, a division of Random House, Inc.

Teasdale, Sara. "Red Birds" from *Flame and Shadow* by Sara Teasdale. New York: 1920.

———. "Red Maples" from *Flame and Shadow* by Sara Teasdale. New York: 1920.

———. "Sunset, St. Louis" from *Flame and Shadow* by Sara Teasdale. New York: 1920.

———. "The River" from *Love Songs* by Sara Teasdale. New York: 1917.

Thomas, James. "St. Louis on the Eve of War" from *From Tennessee Slave to St. Louis Entrepreneur: The Autobiography of James Thomas* by James Thomas. Copyright © 1984 by the Moorland-Springarn Research Center.

Trollope, Anthony. "Missouri" from *North America* by Anthony Trollope. New York: 1862.

Troupe, Quincy. "Listening to Miles" from *Miles and Me* by Quincy Troupe. Copyright © 2000 by Quincy Troupe. Reprinted by permission of the author and University of California Press.

Twain, Mark. Excerpt from *Life on the Mississippi* by Mark Twain. Boston: 1883.

Umphraville, Angus. "The Affair of St. Louis" from *Missourian Lays, and Other Western Ditties* by Angus Umphraville. St. Louis: 1821.

———. "Lines Written on the Bank of the Mississippi" from *Missourian Lays, and Other Western Ditties* by Angus Umphraville. St. Louis: 1821.

———. "The Old Maid of St. Louis" from *Missourian Lays, and Other Western Ditties* by Angus Umphraville. St. Louis: 1821.

Urdang, Constance. "At Frank 'n' Helen's" from *Alternate Lives* by Constance Urdang. Copyright © 1990 by Constance Urdang. Reprinted by permission of Donald Finkel for Constance Urdang.

———. "The River" from *Alternate Lives* by Constance Urdang. Copyright © 1990 by Constance Urdang. Reprinted by permission of Donald Finkel for Constance Urdang.

———. "Ways of Returning" from *Only the World* by Constance Urdang. Copyright © 1983 by Constance Urdang. Reprinted by permission of Donald Finkel for Constance Urdang.

Urdang, Constance. "To Live with a Landscape" from *The Lone Woman and Others* by Constance Urdang. Copyright © 1980 by Constance Urdang. Reprinted by permission of Donald Finkel for Constance Urdang.

Van Duyn, Mona. "Addendum to 'The Block'" from *Firefall* by Mona Van Duyn. Copyright © 1993 by Mona Van Duyn. Reprinted by permission of the author.

———. "'We Are in Your Area'" from *Firefall* by Mona Van Duyn. Copyright © 1993 by Mona Van Duyn. Reprinted by permission of the author.

———. "The Block" from *Near Changes* by Mona Van Duyn. Copyright © 1990 by Mona Van Duyn. Reprinted by permission of the author.

Von Hesse-Wartegg, Ernst. Excerpt from *Travels on the Lower Mississippi, 1879–1880* by Ernst von Hesse-Wartegg, edited and translated by Frederic Trautmann. Reprinted by permission of the University of Missouri Press. Copyright © 1990 by the Curators of the University of Missouri.

Wahlert, Edna. "Her America" by Edna Wahlert, from *The Potter's Wheel* 2, no. 7 (May 1906).

Wells, Rolla. "The Statue of St. Louis" from *Episodes of My Life* by Rolla Wells. Copyright © 1933 by Rolla Wells. St. Louis: 1933.

Wetmore, Claude H. and Lincoln Steffens. "Tweed Days in St. Louis: Joseph W. Folk's Single-Handed Exposure of Corruption, High and Low" by Claude H. Wetmore and Lincoln Steffens from *McClure's* (October 1902): 577-86.

Williams, Tennessee. Excerpt from *A Lovely Sunday for Creve Coeur* by Tennessee Williams. Copyright © 1978, 1980 by The University of the South. Reprinted by permission of New Directions Publishing Corp.

———. Excerpt from *Memoirs* by Tennessee Williams. Copyright © 1975 by Tennessee Williams. Reprinted by permission of Doubleday, a division of Random House, Inc.

Wolfe, Thomas. Excerpt from *The Lost Boy* by Thomas Wolfe. Copyright © 1937 by Thomas Wolfe. Reprinted by permission of Macintosh and Otis, Inc.